# THE QUR'ĀN

بسم الله الرحمن الرحيم

# THE QUR'ĀN

*With a Phrase-by-Phrase*
*English Translation*

*Translated by*
'Alī Qulī Qarā'ī

ICAS Press

British Library Cataloguing-in-Publication Data
A catalogue record for this book is available from the British Library

ISBN 1 904063 17 9

*Published by*
Islamic College for Advanced Studies Press (ICAS)
133 High Road, Willesden, London NW10 2SW

# Contents

## The Qur'ān

## Contents

## Appendices

## Publisher's Note

إِنَّ هَٰذَا ٱلْقُرْءَانَ يَهْدِى لِلَّتِى هِىَ أَقْوَمُ

وَيُبَشِّرُ ٱلْمُؤْمِنِينَ ٱلَّذِينَ يَعْمَلُونَ ٱلصَّٰلِحَٰتِ أَنَّ لَهُمْ أَجْرًا كَبِيرًا

Since the first translation of the Holy Qur'ān into English in 1648, there have appeared more than 60 other English translations by Muslim and non-Muslim translators. Why, then, should the Islamic College for Advanced Studies venture to publish a new translation? Moreover, does not the very number of these translations confirm the traditional belief that the Qur'ān is untranslatable?

It is true that no literary masterpiece is ever fully translatable into another language, let alone the Qur'ān. The Holy Qur'ān, according to Pikthall, is a scripture "the very sounds of which move men to tears and ecstasy." How could a text which, in the memorable words of A. J. Arberry, is "neither prose nor poetry, but a unique fusion of both," ever surrender its mysteries to a rendering in another language? The Qur'ān, of course, is a book of innumerable merits, but many of them can, to various degrees, be transposed into other languages to inform and enlighten peoples of different cultures. The most important feature of the Qur'ān, aside from its literary excellence, is its divine guidance, as it is a scripture meant for human enlightenment—enlightenment concerning the most urgent and vital questions of deep concern to every human being. It answers such questions as lie beyond the purview of mere human finding: Where do we come from? Where do we stand? Where do we go from here? Hence it describes itself as a scripture meant for reflection (12:2; 38:29). It is, in its own words, a Book for reflective minds (*ulu al-albāb*), for those who value knowledge (*'ālimūn*), for those who exercise their rational faculties (*qawmin ya'qilūn*), and for those who possess reason and perceptive minds (*ulu al-nuhā* and *mutawassimūn*).

Every translation of the Qur'ān has its merits and shortcomings. The publication of this translation does not by any means imply that other translations have been efforts of no value. However, some novel merits in this new translation make it unique among the existing ones.

The translator, Sayyid 'Alī Qulī Qarā'ī, is a scholar who has dedicated his efforts to translation of the classics of Islamic literature into English, which makes him the most reliable authority for such an undertaking. Furthermore, for such a rendering he has consulted major classical commentaries of the Qur'ān, by both Sunnī and Shī'ī commentators, which offer the reader a broader understanding of some controversial verses in the Qur'ān. Moreover, his innovative approach in translating Arabic idioms, as explained in his introduction, allows a smoother reading of the text.

However, the most outstanding feature of this translation is its new "phrasal approach," which is most useful for those who are eager to collate the Arabic text with the English translation. With the painstaking efforts of the translator and a group of international experts on Qur'ānic sciences the reader would find each phrase of the translation exactly opposite the corresponding Arabic phrase, an arrangement of the source text and its translation that makes possible direct access to the Arabic verses.

The Islamic College for Advanced Studies is honoured to publish this translation of the Holy Book. We pray to God Almighty to give us the insight and inner purity for understanding His message.

**ICAS Press**

January 2004

## Translator's Preface

The Qur'ān as such does not need an introduction. Rather it is *we*, human beings, who need the Qur'ān to be introduced to ourselves, to be provided with an initial knowledge of as to *who* we are, *what* we are, *whence* we come, *where* we stand, and *whither* we are bound. Without such a knowledge, we are lost, living as losers regardless of whatever we may imagine to be our achievements. The Qur'ān is, in its own words, "light,"[1] which means that it is self-manifesting, with no need of an external agent to be made manifest; other things need light to become visible and manifest. *With it Allah guides those who pursue His pleasure to the ways of peace, and brings them out from darkness into light by His will, and guides them to a straight path* (5:16). In this respect it is like its Author and Speaker, who is the *Light of the heavens and the earth* (24:35). Existence being light, all contingent existents stand in need of the Source of Being for their existence, whereas the Source itself is self-subsisting and self-manifesting. All existents exist through Allah and are known through Him, not that He is known through them.

Also, like the Qur'ān and its Author, its communicator, the Seal of the Prophets (ṣ), is a source of light,[2] who brings people out of the darkness of ignorance and ingratitude, unfaith and unreason into the blessed light of knowledge, faith, gratitude and intellect: *[This is] a Book We have sent down to you that you may bring mankind out from darkness into light, by the will of their Lord, to the path of the All-mighty, the All-laudable* (14:1).

Of course, the Qur'ān is not an exception among revealed scriptures in that it is a source of light and guidance. So were the Torah and the Gospel, scriptures that were given to Moses[3] and Jesus.[4] All scriptures of Divine origin that were brought by various prophets were a source of light and guidance.[5] Nor is the Prophet of Islam (ṣ) an exception among God-sent emissaries.[6] He (ṣ) is the ultimate link in a long chain of prophetic missions whose history began with Adam himself. Nevertheless, the Qur'ān is a unique document, not only in the realm of religious literature but also in the domain of language. It is unique

---

[1] The Qur'ān, 4:174; 5:15; 7:157; 42:52; 64:8.

[2] *O Prophet! Indeed We have sent you as a witness, as a bearer of good news and as a warner and as a summoner to Allah by His permission, and as a radiant lamp.* (33:45-46)

[3] 5:44; 6:91; 14:5.

[4] 5:46; 57:27.

[5] 7:184; 35:25.

[6] *Say, 'I am not a novelty among the apostles. . . .'* (46:9)

among revealed scriptures not only because it is the latest and the last, and, therefore, the most up-to-date of them, but also because it is the only one which has been preserved in the original form that it was revealed to its prophet. Therefore, it serves as the ultimate criterion and standard against which the contents of all other religious literature, irrespective of their origin, are to be evaluated and judged. It is a work of inimitable literary beauty and excellence. But unlike other literary works produced by inspired human genius, such as the literary masterpieces in prose and poetry in various languages of the world whose charm and appeal are limited to particular cultures and periods beyond which they have little general relevance or appeal, the language and discourse of the Qur'ān and their relevance are universal and everlasting.

This is not meant to belittle human genius and achievement. After all, the human being is himself one of the greatest masterpieces of Divine creativity, and, at his best, "God's vicegerent on the earth," and his capacities are literally boundless. The Prophet (ṣ) himself was the most eloquent of speakers, whose eloquence has never been equalled by any poet or sage. *An Apostle sent to the unlettered to recite to them His signs, to purify them, and to teach them the Book and wisdom,* even the most learned confess to be "unlettered" before him. The Prophet (ṣ) surpassed all Arabs in eloquence. Yet the beauty and splendour of the Qur'ān far exceeds even the best specimens of the sayings of the Seal of the Prophets (ṣ). The stupendous miracle of the Qur'ān has to be *experienced* in order to be acknowledged as such. The sun, so it is said, is its own evidence. Of course, this applies only to those who can see.

Human speech is a human creation, whereas, the Qur'ān is literally a Divine discourse. No wonder that it is inimitable, for even the humblest of living beings in the realm of Divine creation surpasses human contrivance: *O mankind! Listen to a parable that is being drawn: indeed those whom you invoke besides Allah will never create even a fly, even if they all rallied for it!* (22:73). No wonder, then, that the Qur'ān should be such as described by its own words: *Say, 'Should all humans and jinn rally to bring the like of this Qur'ān, they will not bring the like of it, even if they assisted one another* (17:88).

Every moment of our life, day and night, we are immersed in God's bounteous gifts: *If you enumerate Allah's blessings, you will not be able to count them* (14:34). Yet the Qur'ān is one of the greatest of all gifts to humanity. It is the living Book of life, which addresses itself to "the living": *This is just a reminder and a manifest Qur'ān, so that anyone who is alive may be warned* (36:69-70). Those who are alive to the summons of their being are also alive to its call, receptive to its good news and warnings, a summons that is perpetual, answering which brings further life, a life on the top of life: *O you who have faith! Answer Allah and the Apostle when he summons you to that which will give you life* (6:24). *Whoever acts righteously, [whether] male or female, should he be faithful, We shall revive him with a good life and pay them their reward by the best of what they used to do* (16:97). This promise of a new life is, of course, fulfilled in this very life for those who answer its summons, but there is also the promise of a greater and more splendid life in the Hereafter, in comparison with which the life of this world is no more than diversion and play: *The life of this world is nothing but diversion and play, while the abode of the Hereafter is indeed Life, had they known!* (29:64). There is no death for the pupils of the Qur'ān; for them every 'death' is a birth into a higher realm of existence and entry into a world more vast and expansive than the earlier one: *Take the lead towards forgiveness from your Lord and a paradise as vast as the heavens and the earth, prepared for those who have faith in Allah and His apostles. That is Allah's grace, which He grants to whomever He wishes, and Allah is dispenser of a great grace* (57:21).

This call to a higher life is a summons to a higher knowledge and a higher effort: *Allah will raise those of you who have faith and those who have been given knowledge in rank, and Allah is well aware of what you do* (58:11). *Say, 'Are those who know equal to those who do not know?'* (39:11). It preaches that one's higher efforts and endeavours are the ultimate fruits of one's life: *Nothing belongs to man except what he strives for* (53:39). The life of the Hereafter is only a 'celestial' counterpart of the terrestrial life we live here.

Nothing is more important for man than the knowledge of the very Source of reality. Any knowledge that is not informed with this awareness is just a kind of ignorance. All effort and endeavour that does not derive from this knowledge is ultimately fruitless and fated to end in failure.[1] The Qur'ān is the most reliable source of this knowledge and the best guide for human effort and endeavour. It teaches that the Source of being is also the Source of guidance.

To a humanity wailing under the burden of injustice, the Qur'ān offers a creed of deliverance: *Certainly We sent Our apostles with manifest signs, and We sent down with them the Book and the Balance, so that mankind may maintain justice; and We sent down iron, in which there is a great might and uses for mankind, and so that Allah may know those who help Him and His apostles in [their] absence* (57:25).

To human beings lacking a sense of divinely ordained purpose and direction in life, like seafarers on an uncharted sea without compass or guidance, the Qur'ān offers a delivering vision of life and human destiny, helping them rediscover their destiny and dignity as human beings and recover their true orientation as wayfarers on the Godward path of infinite perfection: *Certainly We have honoured the Children of Adam, and carried them over land and sea, and provided them with all the good things, and given them advantage over many of those We have created with a complete preference* (17:70).

From the viewpoint of the Qur'ān, establishment and maintenance of justice is one of the chief purposes of all religion and revealed scriptures. This is a mission that has always been neglected by mankind, a neglect that has allowed injustice to assume almost cosmic proportions in the present-day world. Being

---

[1] *Say, 'Shall we inform you about the biggest losers in regard to works? Those whose endeavour goes awry in the life of the world, while they suppose they are doing good.' They are the ones who deny the signs of their Lord and the encounter with Him. So their works have failed. On the Day of Resurrection We will not set for them any weight.* (18:103-105)

the last of God-sent scriptures, there is no wonder then that it should lay so much stress upon justice, an emphasis unequalled by any other book, sacred or secular. The Qur'ān preaches an order based on justice. There is no injustice in the realm of creation; it is man who engenders injustice by his wrongdoing, by yielding to misdirected motives in violation of the Divine norms: *Indeed Allah does not wrong people in the least; rather it is people who wrong themselves* (10:44). However, justice remains merely a mirage in a world where inner purity is neglected and where inner spiritual disorder rules unheeded. The call of the Qur'ān is one of constant struggle, purification and *jihād*, inward and outward, against the inner satanic forces of disoriented desires and their external manifestations in the form of the social and political agents and institutions of corruption. It views human history as a continuous struggle against unfaith and untruth, injustice and corruption, and holds out the promise of the ultimate victory of righteousness: *'Indeed My righteous servants shall inherit the earth'* (21:105).

If worldly life is short and its enjoyments and sufferings transitory for all mortals, what is a better life than a life spent for the purpose approved by the very Source of life? If death is inevitable for every mortal, tyrant or victim, faithful or faithless, well-provided or deprived, powerful or powerless, what is a better 'death' than one which is the threshold of an everlasting life of fulfillment? All religions have a high regard for martyrdom, but no scripture describes so vividly the higher life attained by the martyrs, thus giving martyrdom its true appeal: *Do not suppose those who were slain in the way of Allah to be dead; rather they are living and provided for near their Lord, exulting in what Allah has given them out of His grace, and rejoicing for those who have not yet joined them from [those left] behind them that they will have no fear, nor will they grieve. They rejoice in Allah's blessing and grace, and that Allah does not waste the reward of the faithful* (3:169-171).

To a youth languishing on the plane of animal existence, captive of materialistic values and rendered spiritually impotent by sensual pursuits and indifferent to struggle against oppression and injustice, the Qur'ān suggests a spiritual diet and a programme of spiritual rehabilitation, self-purification, and *jihād*. To a world bewildered by the din of the communication media orchestrated by Satanic forces bent on the deception of thinking minds, the Qur'ān gives *a light to walk by*, enabling the faithful human being to see facts through the apparently impenetrable curtains of deceit and disinformation: *O you who have faith! Be wary of Allah and have faith in His Apostle. He will grant you a double share of His mercy and give you a light to walk by, and forgive you* (57:28).

For communities which have lost their moral and spiritual bearings, the Qur'ān holds out the great promise of restoration of their spiritual and moral equilibrium through its high spirituality and ethics.

*About this Translation:*

The Qur'ān is, paradoxically, both untranslatable and 'translation-friendly.' It is a celestial symphony with splendid rhythms and rhymes whose melodious grandeur is rarely captured fully even by the best of the grand masters of *qirā'ah*, the art of Qur'ānic recitation. As such and as a text of matchless literary elegance and eloquence, no translation can ever hope to capture even fleeting flashes of its splendour. At the same time, despite its wonderful aesthetic complexities, the Qur'ānic text is astonishingly clear, simple and straightforward in its style. The simplicity comes firstly from the economy and simplicity of Qur'ānic vocabulary and diction.[1] A second factor is its strikingly uniform phraseology. A third factor is its characteristic syntactical structure made up either of short sentences, as in the brief Makkan *sūrah*s placed at the end of the Book, or of longer sentences wherein clauses and phrases are arranged in a serial logical sequential order. Were it not for this last characteristic of the Qur'ānic text, the approach adopted in the present translation would not have been possible.

The translation of a literary text is expected to meet the following four requirements: it should (1) be able to convey the meanings of the source text in an intelligible manner; (2) have a natural and easy form of expression; (3) convey the spirit and the manner of the original; (4) produce a similar response in the reader. While a translation of the Qur'ān can be expected to succeed in meeting the first two of these requirements in varying degrees, depending on the translator's competence, there appear to be insurmountable barriers in the way of meeting, even partially, the last two requirements.

First, there are visible limits to the extent the translator can convey fully the meanings of the source text. Here the primary problem encountered by the translator is absence in the English language of semantically equivalent terms for certain Arabic words, some of which play a key role in the Qur'ānic message, such as *taqwā, kufr, īmān, shirk, ḥaqq, bāṭil, ma'rūf, munkar, fitnah, ghayb, sunnah, tawbah, walī,* and *ẓulm.* In such cases, the translator has to suffice with approximations which fall short of conveying the full semantic scope and richness of the original terms, giving a truncated or lopsided sense to the message communicated.[2]

As to the second requirement, that the translation have an easy and natural

---

[1] A comparison between the diction of the Arabic poetry of the period and that of the Qur'ān will make this fact evident.

[2] There are other terms which pose problems in varying degrees, such as *amr, āyah, 'aẓm, baghī, barā'ah, ba's, birr, ḍalālah, dhanb, dhikr, faḍl, faḥshā', fasād, fisq, fujūr, ghāwī, ḥanīf, ḥaraj, ḥasanah, ḥarām, hawā, ḥayā', hidāyah, ḥijab, ḥikmah, ḥisāb, ḥukm, iḥsān, islām, ikhlāṣ, 'iṣyān, istikbār, isrāf, 'izzah, jahl, jannah, karīm, khabīth, khashyah, mala', mann, mujrim, munīb, muṭaffif, nabī, nifāq, ni'mah, qiyām, raḥmah, rijs, rushd, ṣalāḥ, sayyi'ah, takdhīb, taskhīr, ṭayyib, ṭughyān, ummah, wakīl, ẓaygh.* Their exact and complete meanings should be sought and elicited from the contexts in which they are employed in the Arabic text. Moreover, there are some common words, such as *abb* (father), *akhkh* (brother), and *ukht* (sister), which have a semantic field different from that of the corresponding terms in English. *Abb* may refer to an uncle (as with reference to Ishmael in 2:133, and also in 6:74, 9:114; 19:42-44, 26:69 with reference to Āzar) or an ancestor, *akhkh* may at times mean a compatriot (as in 7:67, 7:73, 7:85 with reference to the prophets Hūd, Ṣāliḥ and Shu'ayb), and *ukht* may refer to a woman's clan or lineage (as in 19:28 with reference to Mary). In these and similar cases, I have retained the Qur'ānic diction, leaving determination of the meaning to the commentaries.

form of expression, that depends mainly on the translator's understanding of the nature, meaning and purpose of translation and his approach.

Translations in general have been divided into two broad categories, (1) translations which aim at formal equivalence, and the so-called (2) dynamic (or functional) equivalence translations. Formal equivalence translations attempt to reproduce the formal elements of the source text including grammatical units, seek consistency of word usage, and reproduce meanings in terms of the source context. That is, they do not normally attempt to make adjustments in idiom, but rather try to reproduce such expressions more or less literally, so that the reader may be able to perceive something of the way in which the original document employed local cultural elements to convey meanings. A dynamic-equivalence translation has been defined as "the closest natural equivalent to the source language message."[1]

The second approach has an obvious advantage over the first one in that it is better suited to meet the very goal of discourse, which is communication. But it assumes that the translator can fully comprehend and fathom the intents and meanings of the original source text and that the only task that remains for him to accomplish is to find and produce the closest natural equivalent to the source language message. Such an assumption is not always warranted and it takes a simplistic view of the nature and character of discourse and meaning. There are often cases where, firstly, the *real* intent and meaning of the source text may be either indeterminate or it may elude the translator, and, secondly, at times there may be simply no easy and natural equivalent in the target language. However, in many cases the requirement of an easy and natural form of expression obliges the translator to make adjustments of various kinds to produce a stylistically satisfactory equivalent.

The aware reader of translated literary texts is conscious of the approximations or rather the inherent inadequacies involved in the process of translation. This inadequacy is quite evident in the case of Qur'ān translations. The best purpose a translation may serve is as a means of access to the Arabic Qur'ān itself.

Interlinear translations abound in Persian and Urdu. In fact, the interlinear approach has been the dominant practice in translations of the Qur'ān published in these languages during the last two hundred years. Recent translations in Persian show a trend away from this practice, while it is still dominant in Urdu. As these languages are written from right to left like Arabic, the interlinear format—with the Arabic text and its translation appearing in alternating lines—has been a convenient and popular way of presenting the meanings of the Qur'ānic text. This format has been very helpful for readers who do not read the Arabic Qur'ān merely for the sake of the *thawāb* of reciting its text, but are also eager to obtain the additional and higher benefit of understanding its meanings and reflecting upon its verses. There are many Persian- and Urdu-

---

[1] Nida, Eugene A., *Toward a Science of Translating*, pp. 165, 166.

speaking Muslims who have quite an impressive working grasp of the meanings of the Qur'ān without having undergone any formal training in Arabic grammar and without possessing any extensive vocabulary.

Some of these interlinear translations, especially the older versions, are word-for-word renderings. They are in fact dictionaries of the Qur'ān in that they mention the meaning of each Arabic word and phrase in the line below. Although useful as dictionaries, they often fail to make the meanings of the Qur'ānic text intelligible, as the prose of the translated text turns out to be awkward, unnatural and at times inscrutable.

An interlinear English translation of the Qur'ān, similar to those in Urdu and Persian, is obviously of little benefit, as the two languages are written in opposite directions. The phrase-for-phrase approach adopted in this translation is intended to bring some of the advantage of the interlinear translations to English-speaking readers of the Holy Qur'ān. "Mirror-paraphrasing" is a new approach to translation of sacred Islamic texts, mainly the Qur'ān and *ḥadīth*. In this approach, the translation of the source text develops phrase by phrase, with the translation appearing opposite the corresponding phrase in Arabic. Each phrase in the target or receptor language *mirrors* the semantic import of the phrase in the source text.

At first when such an approach was suggested to my mind, it was not at all clear whether it would be feasible. It seemed that it would result in an unnatural and warped style. But as I worked through the translation, it was a surprise to find that it did seem to work (with few exceptions, such as in verse 2:105, where the verb *yawaddu* comes at the beginning of the sentence). In any case, the results were not as dismal as might be expected. However, one had to deal with two constant constraints, firstly, of having to cover the complete meaning of each phrase of the source text in a corresponding phrase of the target text, and, secondly, of connecting the successive phrases in such a manner as to generate, so far as possible, a fluent, clear, intelligible, natural and stylistically acceptable prose.

The utility of such an approach will be evident to the reader who wants to understand the Arabic text by referring to the translation of each phrase and verse. All that he needs for following the meaning of the Arabic text of the Qur'ān is an elementary knowledge of Arabic, which means an elemental knowledge of Arabic vocabulary and morphology. However, a reader who already possesses such an elementary knowledge of Arabic will not find much difficulty in following the Arabic text with the help of the translation provided here. After several readings, it is hoped, the reader will be able to follow the Arabic without needing to refer to the translation.

The main features of the method and approach followed in this translation may be described as follows:

1. As my principal aim was to provide a translation affording direct access to the Arabic Qur'ān, I have tried, so far as possible, to maintain a formal

equivalence between the phrases and clauses of the source and the target text, but I have not hesitated to make adjustments when required by the need for intelligibility, clarity and naturalness of expression, so far as permitted by the constraint imposed by the method of "mirror-paraphrasing." These adjustments are of various kinds and it is not possible to describe all of them here. They involve: making grammatical changes, such as those of tense, aspect, voice, person and number; substitution of nouns by verbs and vice versa;[1] making obligatory omissions[2] and additions; and making explicit what is implicit in the source text.[3] At times they involve adjustments of idiom and syntactical changes. The reader should be aware about the presence of these changes when collating the Arabic text with the translation.

2. Translation has been carried out according to what appeared to be the most probable among the interpretations mentioned by the commentators. Occasionally I have mentioned alternate interpretations in the footnotes when they appeared to be significant. Throughout the course of this translation extensive reference was made to various classical commentaries of the Qur'ān, such as those of Ṭabarī, Rāzī, Zamakhsharī, and Suyūṭī among Sunnī works, and Ṭabāṭabā'ī's *al-Mīzān*, Ṭabrisī's *Majma' al-Bayān*, and Bahrānī's *Tafsīr al-Burhān* among Shī'ī works. Some of the other works consulted are mentioned in the bibliography given at the end of this preface. Exegetical traditions of the Imams of the Prophet's family have been given special attention due to their unparalleled importance for Qur'ānic hermeneutics. Their importance and weight will be evident to anyone who undertakes an unbiased study of their traditions and teachings. In fact, a large part of the early Sunnī hermeneutic tradition, as represented by Ibn 'Abbās, his pupils and the succeeding generations of commentators, also derives from Imam 'Alī b. Abī Ṭālib, with whom Ibn 'Abbās was closely associated and from whom he had acquired his Qur'ānic learning, being a boy in his early teens at the time of the Prophet's demise.

3. The treatment of Qur'ānic idioms is an important part of the policy followed in translation. Broadly speaking, they fall into three categories. There are some Arabic idioms which though unfamiliar to the English-speaking audience are not difficult to understand when translated literally. These have been rendered literally. Examples are:

نَبَذَ فَرِيقٌ مِّنَ ٱلَّذِينَ أُوتُواْ ٱلْكِتَـٰبَ كِتَـٰبَ ٱللَّهِ وَرَآءَ ظُهُورِهِمْ

*a part of those who were given the Book cast the Book of Allah behind their backs.*[4] (2:101);

أَلَآ إِنَّهُمْ يَثْنُونَ صُدُورَهُمْ لِيَسْتَخْفُواْ مِنْهُ

---

[1] E.g. *We delivered those who had faith and were Godwary.* (27:53)

[2] E.g., *whether you advise us or not.* (26:136)

[3] E.g. *Everyone* of them *will return to Us.* (21:93)

[4] The same idiom occurs several times in the Bible (1Kings 14:9, Isaiah 38:17, Ezekiel 23:35, and Nehemiah 9:26).

*They fold up their breasts to hide [their secret feelings] from him*[1] (11:5);

ٱشْدُدْ بِهِۦ أَزْرِى

*Strengthen my back through him* [2] (20: 31);

وَلَا تُصَعِّرْ خَدَّكَ لِلنَّاسِ

*Do not turn your cheek disdainfully from the people* (31:18);

تَتَجَافَىٰ جُنُوبُهُمْ عَنِ ٱلْمَضَاجِعِ

*their sides vacate their beds* (32:16);

حَتَّىٰ تَضَعَ ٱلْحَرْبُ أَوْزَارَهَا

*till the war lays down its burdens* (47:4).

Some idioms are unintelligible when translated literally. These have to be paraphrased appropriately in order to be understood. Examples are:

وَتَوَدُّونَ أَنَّ غَيْرَ ذَاتِ ٱلشَّوْكَةِ تَكُونُ لَكُمْ

*you were eager that it should be the one that was an easy target* [3] (8:7);

فَرَدُّوٓاْ أَيْدِيَهُمْ فِىٓ أَفْوَٰهِهِمْ

*but they did not respond to them,*[4] (14:9);

فَضَرَبْنَا عَلَىٰٓ ءَاذَانِهِمْ فِى ٱلْكَهْفِ سِنِينَ عَدَدًا

*so We put them to sleep* [5] *in the Cave for several years* (18:11);

وَنَحْشُرُ ٱلْمُجْرِمِينَ يَوْمَئِذٍ زُرْقًا

*on that day We shall muster the guilty with blind eyes* [6] (20:102);

قُرَّتُ عَيْنٍ لِّى وَلَكَ

*a [source of] comfort to me and you* [7] (28:9);

وَمَن يُسْلِمْ وَجْهَهُۥٓ إِلَى ٱللَّهِ

*Whoever surrenders his heart to Allah* [8] (31:22);

---

[1] That is, to conceal one's spite within one's heart.

[2] That is, reinforce my strength through him.

[3] Lit., 'one that was free of thorns.' That is, one which was unarmed and, therefore, easy to defeat.

[4] Lit., 'they thrust their hands into their mouths.'

[5] Lit., 'We struck on their ears.' The idiom is probably drawn from the practice of mothers of
putting children to sleep by patting the head with the palm of the hand placed on the ear.

[6] Lit., 'with blued eyes.'

[7] Lit., 'a refreshment of the eye to me and you.'

[8] Lit., 'submits his face toward Allah.'

وَتُقَطِّعُوٓاْ أَرْحَامَكُمْ

*and ill-treat your blood relations*[1] (47:22);

وَلَا يَأْتِينَ بِبُهْتَنٍ يَفْتَرِينَهُۥ بَيْنَ أَيْدِيهِنَّ وَأَرْجُلِهِنَّ

*nor utter any slander that they may have intentionally fabricated* [2] (60:12);

يَوْمَ يُكْشَفُ عَن سَاقٍ

*—the day when the catastrophe occurs*[3] (68:42).

In certain cases it may be possible to substitute an English idiom, as in the following:

فَإِنَّ ذَٰلِكَ مِنْ عَزْمِ ٱلْأُمُورِ

*that is indeed the steadiest of courses* [4] (3:186);

نُوَلِّهِۦ مَا تَوَلَّىٰ

*We shall abandon him to his devices* [5] (4:115);

إِنَّ قَوْمِى ٱتَّخَذُواْ هَٰذَا ٱلْقُرْءَانَ مَهْجُورًا

*Indeed my people consigned this Qur'ān to oblivion* [6] (25:30);

فَأَبَىٰ أَكْثَرُ ٱلنَّاسِ إِلَّا كُفُورًا

*But most people are only intent on ingratitude* [7] (25:50);

فَسَوْفَ يَكُونُ لِزَامًا

*so that will continue to haunt you* [8] (25:77);

قَبْلَ أَن يَرْتَدَّ إِلَيْكَ طَرْفُكَ

*in the twinkling of an eye* [9] (27:40);

فَلَا تَذْهَبْ نَفْسُكَ عَلَيْهِمْ حَسَرَٰتٍ

*so do not fret yourself to death regretting for them* [10] (35:8).

---

[1] Lit., 'sever your wombs (or ties of kinship).'

[2] Lit., 'nor bring any slander which they had forged themselves between their hands and their feet.'

[3] Lit., 'the day that the shin shall be laid bare,' or 'the day the shank shall be uncovered.'

[4] Mir Ahmed Ali: 'that is a result of firm determination of affairs.'

[5] Lit., 'We will turn him to that to which he has himself turned.'

[6] Lit., 'my people have taken this Qur'ān as a forsaken thing.'

[7] Pickthall: 'but most of mankind begrudge aught save ingratitude.'

[8] Lit., 'so it will be inseparable (or ineluctable).'

[9] Pickthall: 'before thy gaze returneth unto thee.'

[10] Mir Ahmed Ali: 'so let not thy self go (in vain) in grief for them.'

كُلُواْ وَٱشۡرَبُواْ هَنِيٓـًٔا

*enjoy your food and drink*[1] (52:19);

4. The translation is based on Ḥafṣ' version of the reading of 'Āṣim, which is the most popular of the readings of the Holy Qur'ān throughout the Muslim world. Some of the alternate readings, where they appeared significant to this translator, have been noted in the footnotes with their translation.

5. Instances of ellipses in the Qur'ān—which in the context of English means "omission of a word or phrase necessary for a complete syntactical construction but not necessary for understanding"—often go beyond such a description and are not always so evident. These have been indicated in the footnotes.

6. Cross references have been mentioned under verses in some cases, but a relatively extensive index of subjects, names and terms has been placed in the appendix. Entries which are not mentioned expressly in the text but involve an implicit reference, as mentioned in commentaries and exegetical traditions, are marked with an asterisk. As the works consulted for preparing the index[2] had made use of copies of the Qur'ān with different systems of numbering the verses, there might be a discrepancy of one or two between the number of a verse as given in the index and its corresponding number in the Arabic text. The verses are numbered in accordance with the now most prevalent system followed by the so-called Madinah codex, despite its serious defect of excluding from the count the *Basmalah*, which is the first verse of every *sūrah* excepting Sūrat al-Tawbah, the ninth *sūrah*. The *Basmalah* at the head of the 113 *sūrah*s is regarded as part of the Qur'ān by many Sunnī authorities and unanimously so by the Shī'ah.

I am grateful to the Centre for Translation of the Holy Qur'ān for entrusting me with the task of working on the English translation of the Qur'ān, in particular to its Director, Ḥujjatulislām Muḥammad Naqdī, for his unflagging support and assistance. During the course of my work I have benefited greatly from the generous encouragement and assistance provided by Dr Muḥammad Legenhausen, who patiently read the entire manuscript and suggested useful changes and corrections. His suggestions have been very helpful in formulating the policy to be followed in this translation. My thanks are also due to Brother Shujā' 'Alī Mīrzā, who has read the entire manuscript and with his suggestions and corrections contributed to the soundness of the final manuscript. However,

---

[1] Pickthall: 'Eat and drink in health (as reward) for what ye used to do.'

[2] These are: (1) K. Fani and B. Khorramshahi, *Farhang-e Mawḍūʿī-ye Qurʾān-e Majīd* (A Subject Index to the Qur'ān), Tehran: Intishārāt-e al-Hudā, 1369 H. Sh., 2nd impression; (2) Muḥammad Fāris Barakāt, *al-Jāmiʿ li Mawāḍiʿ Āyāt al-Qurʾān al-Karīm*, Qum: Dār al-Hijrah, 1404 H.; (3) al-Sayyid Sharaf al-Dīn 'Alī al-Ḥusaynī al-Astarābādī al-Gharawī, *Taʾwīl al-Āyāt al-Ẓāhirah fī Faḍāʾil al-ʿItrat al-Ṭāhirah*, Qum: Mu'assasat al-Nashr al-Islāmī al-Tābiʿah li Jamāʿat al-Mudarrisīn, 3rd impression, 1421 H. Sh.

the responsibility is entirely mine for any lapses and errors that may have remained, and I humbly request the honoured readers to convey their remarks
and suggestions by corresponding on the postal and e-mail addresses provided
herein.

I am most grateful to my friend Muḥammad Riḍā Parvez for procuring for
the Centre the needed software for generating the Arabic text. My thanks are
also due to brothers Mahdī Ṣayf and Mahdī Allāhyārī of the Centre for their
assistance in type work and providing the graphics, and to my sons, Sayyid
Muḥammad Riḍā and Sayyid Ḥasan Riḍā, for their assistance in preparing the
subject index. I am also grateful to Sayyid Muḥammad Riḍā for making a thorough check of the Arabic text in the final print of the manuscript.

It has been my prayer to Allah to divest my motives of all traces of the desire for worldly gain, and to make His good pleasure the sole goal of my intentions and efforts. With the hope that this effort has been made for the sake of
His pleasure—a hope that is not altogether free from trepidation—I dedicate
the reward for it to the noble spirit of my late eldest sister, Martyr Sayyidah
Mahliqā Qarā'ī, and to the spirits of more than 290 innocent souls aboard the
Iranian passenger Airbus plane (Iran Air Flight 655), shot down in Iranian waters in the Persian Gulf on July 3, 1988 by the U.S warship, the Vincennes, in a
flagrant act of state-directed terrorism.

Sayyid ʿAlī Qulī Qarā'ī
*Rabīʿ al-Thānī, 1424*
*July, 2002*

# Bibliography

Aḥmad Mukhtār 'Umar and 'Abd al-'Āl Sālim Mukarram, *Mu'jam al-Qirā'āt al-Qur'āniyyah*, Qum: Intishārāt-e Usweh, 1412/1991.

Ahmed Ali, S. V. Mir, *The Holy Qur'an*, Elmhurst: Tahrike Tarsile Qur'an, 1988.

Arberry, Arthur J., *The Koran Interpreted*, London: Oxford University Press, 1964.

Al-'Askarī, al-Imām Abū Muḥammad al-Ḥasan b. 'Alī, *al-Tafsīr al-Mansūb ilā al-Imām Abī Muḥammad al-Ḥasan b. 'Alī al-'Askarī ('a)*, Qum: Mu'assasat al-Imām al-Mahdī, 1409 H., 1st edition.

Al-Astarābādī, al-Sayyid Sharaf al-Dīn 'Alī al-Ḥusaynī al-Gharawī, *Ta'wīl al-Āyāt al-Ẓāhirah fī Faḍā'il al-'Itrat al-Ṭāhirah*, Qum: Mu'assisat al-Nashr al-Islāmī al-Tābi'ah li Jamā'at al-Mudarrisīn, 1421 H. Sh., 3rd ed.

Al-'Ayyāshī, Abū Naṣr Muḥammad b. Mas'ūd b. 'Ayyāsh al-Salamī al-Samarqandī, *Kitāb al-Tafsīr*, ed. Sayyid Hāshim al-Rasūlī al-Maḥallātī, Tehran: al-Maktabat al-'Ilmiyyah al-Islāmiyyah, n.d.

Al-Baḥrānī, al-Sayyid Hāshim al-Ḥusaynī, *al-Burhān fī Tafsīr al-Qur'ān*, Tehran: Bunyād-e Bi'that, 1415 H., 1st edition.

Bargnaysī, Kāẓim, "Reflections on a Qur'ānic Metaphor: The Meaning of '*khatf al-ṭayr*' in Verse 31 of Sūrat al-Ḥajj," translated from the Persian by A. Q. Qarā'ī, *al-Tawḥīd*, vol. 13, no. 4, pp. 5-35.

Barakāt, Muḥammad Fāris, *al-Jāmi' li Mawāḍi' Āyāt al-Qur'ān al-Karīm*, Qum: Dār al-Ḥijrah, 1404 H.

Bayḍāwī, Nāṣir al-Dīn Abū Sa'īd 'Abd Allāh b. 'Umar b. Muḥammad al-Shīrāzī, *Tafsīr al-Bayḍāwī*, Beirut: Mu'assasat al-A'lamī lil-Maṭbū'āt, 1410/1990, 1st. edition.

Fani, K., and B. Khorramshahi, *Farhang-e Mawḍū'ī-ye Qur'ān-e Majīd* (A Subject Index to the Qur'ān), Tehran: Intishārāt-e al-Hudā, 1369 H. Sh., 2nd ed.

Al-Fayḍ al-Kāshānī, al-Mawlā Muḥsin, *Tafsīr al-Ṣāfī (al-Ṣāfī fī Tafsīr Kalām Allāh)*, Mashhad: Dār al-Murtaḍā lil-Nashr, 1402/1982, 2nd impression.

Furāt al-Kūfī, Abū al-Qāsim Furāt b. Ibrāhīm b. Furāt, *Tafsīr Furāt al-Kūfī*, ed. Muḥammad al-Kāẓim, Tehran: Mu'assasat al-Ṭab' wal-Nashr al-Tābi'ah li Wizārat al-Thaqāfah wal-Irshād al-Islāmī, 1st impression, 1410/1990.

Al-Ḥaskānī, Al-Ḥākim 'Ubayd Allah b. 'Abd Allāh b. Aḥmad, *Shawāhid al-Tanzīl*, ed. al-Shaykh Muḥammad Bāqir al-Maḥmūdī, Tehran: Mu'assasat al-Ṭab' wal-Nashr al-Tābi'ah li Wizārat al-Thaqāfat wal-Irshād al-Islāmī, 1411/ 1990.

Al-Ḥuwayzī, al-Shaykh 'Abd 'Alī b. Jumu'ah al-'Arūsī, *Tafsīr Nūr al-Thaqalayn*, Qum: al-Maṭba'ah al-'Ilmiyyah, n.d., 2nd impression.

Ibn Kathīr, Abū al-Fidā' Ismā'īl al-Qurashī al-Dimashqī, *Tafsīr al-Qur'ān al-'Aẓīm*, Beirut: Dār al-Ma'rifah, 1308/1988, 2nd ed.

Izutsu, Toshihiko, *Ethico-Religious Concepts in the Qur'ān*, Montreal: McGill University Press, 1966.

Jeffery, Arthur, *The Foreign Vocabulary of the Qur'ān*, Baroda: Oriental Institute, 1938.

Al-Kulaynī, *Uṣūl al-Kāfī*, Beirut: Dār al-Aḍwā' lil-Ṭabā'ah wal-Nashr wal-Tawzī', ed. by al-Shaykh Muḥammad Jawād al-Faqīh, 1413 H./1992.

Al-Majlisī, al-Shaykh Muḥammad Bāqir, *Biḥār al-Anwār al-Jāmi'ah li-Durar Akbār al-A'immat al-Aṭhār*, Beirut: Dār Iḥyā' al-Turāth al-'Arabī, 1402/1983, 3rd impression.

Marzūq, 'Abd al-Ṣabūr, *Mu'jam al-A'lām wa al-Mawḍū'āt fī al-Qur'ān al-Karīm*, Cairo: Dār al-Shurūq, 1415/1995, 1st edition.

Al-Mashhadī, al-Shaykh Muḥammad b. Muḥammad Riḍā al-Qummī, *Tafsīr Kanz al-Daqā'iq wa Baḥr al-Gharā'ib*, Tehran: Mu'assasat al-Ṭab' wal-Nashr al-Tābi'ah li Wizārat al-Thaqāfah wal-Irshād al-Islāmī, 1st impression, 1366 H. Sh., 1st impression.

Mujtabawī, Sayyid Jalāl al-Dīn, *al-Qur'ān al-Ḥakīm* (Persian Translation), Tehran: Intishārāt-e Ḥikmat, 1313/1371 H. Sh. 1st edition.

Nida, Eugene A., *Toward a Science of Translating, with Special reference to Principles and Procedures Involved in Bible Translation*, Leiden: E. J. Brill, 1964.

—, and Charles R. Taber, *The Theory and Practice of Translation*, Leiden: E. J. Brill, 1984.

Pickthall, Marmaduke, *The Glorious Qur'an*, New York: Mustazafin Foundation of New York, 1987, 3rd impression.

Qarā'ī, Sayyid 'Alī Qulī, "Dilhā-ye Nāpāk: Taḥqīqī dar bāreh-ye 'Ibārat-e *qulūbunā ghulf*," *Tarjumān-e Waḥy*, vol. 5, no. 1, pp. 4-31, vol. 5, no. 2, pp. 4-25.

Al-Qummī, Abū al-Ḥasan 'Alī b. Ibrāhīm, *Tafsīr al-Qummī*, ed. al-Sayyid al-Ṭayyib al-Mūsawī al-Jazā'irī, Qum: Mu'assasah Dār al-Kitāb lil-Ṭabā'ah wal-Nashr, 1404, 3rd ed..

Qumsheh'ī, Mahdī Ilāhī, *Qur'ān-e Karīm* (Persian Translation), Tehran: Bunyād-e Nashr-e Qur'ān, 1367 H. Sh., 1st ed.

Al-Rāzī, Abū al-Futūḥ Ḥusayn b. 'Alī b. Muḥammad al-Khuzā'ī al-Nayshābūrī, *Rawḍ al-Jinān wa Rawḥ al-Janān*, Bunyād-e Pazhohishhā-ye Islāmī-ye Āstān-e Quds-e Raḍawī, 1374/1366 H. Sh.

Al-Rāzī, al-Fakhr, *al-Tafsīr al-Kabīr*, Beirut: Dār Iḥyā' al-Turāth al-'Arabī, 1415/1995, 1st impression,.

Al-Ṣadūq, al-Shaykh Abū Ja'far Muḥammad b. 'Alī b. al-Ḥusayn b. Bābwayh al-Qummī, *Ma'ānī al-Akhbār*, ed. 'Alī Akbar al-Ghaffārī, Tehran: Maktabat al-Ṣadūq, 1379 H./1338 H. Sh.

—, *'Uyūn Akhbār al-Riḍā ('a)*, ed. al-Sayyid Mahdī al-Ḥusaynī al-Lajīwardī, Tehran: Intishārāt-e Jahān, n.d.

Sha'rānī, Ḥājj Mīrzā Abū al-Ḥasan, *al-Qur'ān al-Karīm* (Persian Translation), Tehran: Kitābfurūshī-ye Islāmiyyah, 1374 H. Sh., 2nd edition.

Shīrāzī, Āyatullāh Nāṣir Makārim, *Qur'ān-e Majīd* (Persian Translation), Qum: Dār al-Qur'ān al-Karīm, 1373 H. Sh., 1st impression.

Al-Suyūṭī, Jalāl al-Dīn 'Abd al-Raḥmān, *Durr al-Manthūr fī al-Tafsīr bil-Ma'thūr*, Qum: Manshūrāt Maktabah Āyatullāh Mar'ashī, 1404.

Al-Ṭabarī, Abū Jaʿfar Muḥammad b. Jarīr, *Jāmiʿ al-Bayān ʿan Taʾwīl Āy al-Qurʾān*, ed. Ṣidqī Jamīl al-ʿAṭṭār, Beirut: Dār al-Fikr, 1415/1995.

—, *Taʾrīkh al-Ṭabarī*, ed. Muḥammad Abū al-Faḍl Ibrāhīm, Cairo: Dār al-Maʿārif, n.d. 6ᵗʰ edition.

Al-Ṭabāṭabāʾī, al-Sayyid Muḥammad Ḥusayn, *al-Mīzān fī Tafsīr al-Qurʾān*, Tehran: Dār al-Kutub al-Islāmiyyah, 1397 H., 3ʳᵈ impression.

Al-Ṭabrisī, Amīn al-Dīn Abū ʿAlī al-Faḍl b. al-Ḥasan al-Ṭūsī, *Majmaʿ al-Bayān fī Tafsīr al-Qurʾān*, Beirut: Dār Iḥyāʾ al-Turāth al-ʿArabī, 1379 H.

Walī Allāh Dehlawī, Shāh, *al-Qurʾān al-Ḥakīm* (Persian Translation), Peshawar: Nūrānī Kutub-khānah, n.d.

Al-Ṭūsī, Abū Jaʿfar Muḥammad b. al-Ḥasan, *al-Tibyān fī Tafsīr al-Qurʾān*, ed. Aḥmad Ḥabīb al-Qaṣīr al-ʿĀmilī, Qum: Maktab al-Iʿlām al-Islāmī, 1409 H.

Yusuf Ali, Abdullah, *The Meaning of the Holy Qurʾān*, Brentwood: Amana Corporation, 1995.

Al-Zamakhsharī, Jār Allāh Maḥmūd b. ʿUmar, *al-Kashshāf ʿan Ḥaqāʾiq Ghawāmiḍ al-Tanzīl wa ʿUyūn al-Aqāwīl fī Wujūh al-Taʾwīl*, Nashr Adab al-Ḥawzah, n.d.

# *Transliteration of Arabic Words*

The following table shows the system followed in transliterating letters of the Arabic alphabet:

| | | | | | | |
|---|---|---|---|---|---|---|
| ا | *alif* | a | | ط | *ṭā* | ṭ |
| | | ā (long vowel) | | ظ | *ẓā* | ẓ |
| ب | *bā* | b | | ع | *'ayn* | ' |
| ت | *tā* | t | | غ | *ghayn* | gh |
| ث | *thā* | th | | ف | *fā* | f |
| ج | *jīm* | j | | ق | *qāf* | q |
| ح | *ḥā* | ḥ | | ك | *kāf* | k |
| خ | *khā* | kh | | ل | *lām* | l |
| د | *dāl* | d | | م | *mīm* | m |
| ذ | *dhāl* | dh | | ن | *nūn* | n |
| ر | *rā* | r | | ه | *hā* | h |
| ز | *zāy* | z | | و | *wāw* | w (consonantal) |
| س | *sīn* | s | | | | ū ( long vowel) |
| ش | *shīn* | sh | | ي | *yā* | y (consonantal) |
| ص | *ṣād* | ṣ | | | | ī (long vowel) |
| ض | *ḍād* | ḍ | | ء | *hamzah* | ' |

| Short vowels | | | | |
|---|---|---|---|---|
| ́ | (*fatḥah*) | = | a |
| ̱ | (*kasrah*) | = | i |
| ̮ | (*ḍammah*) | = | u |

## A Supplication for Recitation on
## Commencing a Reading of the Qur'ān

اللَّهُمَّ رَبَّنَا،    O Allah! Our Lord!

لَكَ الْحَمْدُ.    To You belongs all praise.

أَنْتَ الْمُتَوَحِّدُ بِالْقُدْرَةِ    You alone possess all power

وَ السُّلْطَانِ الْمَتِينِ،    and the firmest authority,

وَ لَكَ الْحَمْدُ.    and to You belongs all praise.

أَنْتَ الْمُتَعَالِي بِالْعِزِّ وَ الْكِبْرِيَاءِ    You are exalted in Your might and supremacy

وَ فَوْقَ السَّمَاوَاتِ وَ الْعَرْشِ الْعَظِيمِ.    and above the heavens and the Great Throne.

رَبَّنَا وَ لَكَ الْحَمْدُ،    Our Lord, to You belongs all praise!

أَنْتَ الْمُكْتَفِي بِعِلْمِكَ    You are self-sufficient in Your knowledge,

وَ الْمُحْتَاجُ إِلَيْكَ كُلُّ ذِي عِلْمٍ.    and every possessor of knowledge stands in need of You.

رَبَّنَا وَ لَكَ الْحَمْدُ،    Our Lord, to You belongs all praise,

يَا مُنْزِلَ الْآيَاتِ وَ الذِّكْرِ الْعَظِيمِ،    O sender of the signs and the Great Reminder!

رَبَّنَا فَلَكَ الْحَمْدُ    Our Lord, to You belongs all praise

بِمَا عَلَّمْتَنَا مِنَ الْحِكْمَةِ    for what You have taught us of wisdom

وَ الْقُرْآنِ الْعَظِيمِ الْمُبِينِ.    and the great manifest Qur'ān.

اللَّهُمَّ    O Allah!

أَنْتَ عَلَّمْتَنَاهُ    You taught it to us

قَبْلَ رَغْبَتِنَا فِي تَعَلُّمِهِ.    before we could be eager to learn it,

وَ اخْتَصَصْتَنَا بِهِ    and singled us out for it

قَبْلَ رَغْبَتِنَا بِنَفْعِهِ.    before we could desire its benefit.

اللَّهُمَّ    O Allah!

فَإِذَا كَانَ ذَلِكَ مِنَّا مِنْكَ،    As such has been Your favour toward us,

| | |
|---|---|
| وَ فَضْلاً وَ جُوداً وَ لُطْفاً بِنَا، | and Your grace, generosity, and kindness to us |
| وَ رَحْمَةً لَنَا وَ امْتِنَاناً عَلَيْنَا، | and Your mercy and Your favour toward us |
| مِنْ غَيْرِ حَوْلِنَا، | —not because of any power that we possessed, |
| وَ لاَ حِيلَتِنَا، | nor because of any devising on our part, |
| وَ لاَ قُوَّتِنَا، | nor because of any strength that we had— |
| اللَّهُمَّ | O Allah, |
| فَحَبِّبْ إِلَيْنَا | give us passion |
| حُسْنَ تِلاَوَتِهِ، | for the charm of its recitation, |
| وَ حِفْظَ آيَاتِهِ، | and memorization of its verses, |
| وَ إِيمَاناً بِمُتَشَابِهِهِ، | faith in its metaphorical parts, |
| وَ عَمَلاً بِمُحْكَمِهِ، | practice of its univocal parts, |
| وَ سَبَباً فِي تَأْوِيلِهِ، | the means to its fulfillment, |
| وَ هُدًى فِي تَدْبِيرِهِ، | guidance in its contemplation, |
| وَ بَصِيرَةً بِنُورِهِ. | and insight through its light. |
| | |
| اللَّهُمَّ | O Allah, |
| وَ كَمَا أَنْزَلْتَهُ | even as You have sent it down |
| شِفَاءً لِأَوْلِيَائِكَ، | as a healing for Your friends, |
| وَ شَقَاءً عَلَى أَعْدَائِكَ، | a wretchedness for Your enemies, |
| وَ عَمًى عَلَى أَهْلِ مَعْصِيَتِكَ، | a blindness for the disobedient, |
| وَ نُوراً لِأَهْلِ طَاعَتِكَ، | and an illumination for the obedient, |
| اللَّهُمَّ فَاجْعَلْهُ لَنَا | so also, O Allah, make it for us |
| حِصْناً مِنْ عَذَابِكَ، | a fortress against Your punishment, |
| وَ حِرْزاً مِنْ غَضَبِكَ، | a bulwark against Your wrath, |
| وَ حَاجِزاً عَنْ مَعْصِيَتِكَ، | a safeguard against Your disobedience, |
| وَ عِصْمَةً مِنْ سَخَطِكَ، | a protection from Your displeasure, |
| وَ دَلِيلاً عَلَى طَاعَتِكَ، | a guide to Your obedience, |
| وَ نُوراً يَوْمَ نَلْقَاكَ، | and, on the day we shall encounter You, a light |
| نَسْتَضِيءُ بِهِ فِي خَلْقِكَ، | whereby we may walk amid Your creatures, |
| وَ نَجُوزُ بِهِ عَلَى صِرَاطِكَ، | cross Your bridge [over hell], |

وَ نَهْتَدِي بِهِ إِلَى جَنَّتِكَ.  and be led by into Your paradise.

اللَّهُمَّ  O Allah!

إِنَّا نَعُوذُ بِكَ  We seek Your protection

مِنَ الشَّقْوَةِ فِي حَمْلِهِ،  from wretchedness in bearing it,

وَ الْعَمَى عَنْ عَمَلِهِ،  from blindness in practising it,

وَ الْجَوْرِ عَنْ حُكْمِهِ،  from deviating from its precepts,

وَ الْعُلُوِّ عَنْ قَصْدِهِ،  from departing from its middle path,

وَ التَّقْصِيرِ دُونَ حَقِّهِ.  and disregarding of its rights.

اللَّهُمَّ  O Allah!

احْمِلْ عَنَّا ثِقْلَهُ،  Lighten for us its burden,

وَ أَوْجِبْ لَنَا أَجْرَهُ،  appoint for us its reward,

وَ أَوْزِعْنَا شُكْرَهُ،  inspire us to give thanks for it,

وَ اجْعَلْنَا نُرَاعِيهِ وَ نَحْفَظُهُ.  and enable us to observe it and commit it to memory.

اللَّهُمَّ  O Allah!

اجْعَلْنَا نَتَّبِعُ حَلَالَهُ،  Enable us to pursue what it declares as lawful,

وَ نَجْتَنِبُ حَرَامَهُ،  to avoid what it declares as unlawful,

وَ نُقِيمُ حُدُودَهُ،  to observe its bounds,

وَ نُؤَدِّي فَرَائِضَهُ.  and to fulfill its obligations.

اللَّهُمَّ  O Allah!

ارْزُقْنَا حَلَاوَةً فِي تِلَاوَتِهِ،  Grant us sweetness in its recitation,

وَ نَشَاطاً فِي قِيَامِهِ،  animation in its performance,

وَ وَجَلاً فِي تَرْتِيلِهِ،  awe in its recitals,

وَ قُوَّةً فِي اسْتِعْمَالِهِ  and strength in putting it into action

فِي آنَاءِ اللَّيْلِ وَ أَطْرَافِ النَّهَارِ.  in the watches of the night and the ends of the day.

اللَّهُمَّ O Allah!

وَ اشْفِنَا مِنَ النَّوْمِ بِالْيَسِيرِ، Refresh us with a little amount of sleep

وَ أَيْقِظْنَا فِي سَاعَةِ اللَّيْلِ، and awaken us in the hour of the night

مِنْ رُقَادِ الرَّاقِدِينَ، from the slumber of the asleep,

وَ نَبِّهْنَا عِنْدَ الْآحَايِينَ، and arouse us at the moments

الَّتِي يُسْتَجَابُ فِيهَا الدُّعَاءُ، wherein supplications are granted

مِنْ سِنَةِ الْوَسْنَانِينَ. from the drowsiness of the drowsy.

اللَّهُمَّ O Allah!

اجْعَلْ لِقُلُوبِنَا Make our hearts

ذَكَاءً عِنْدَ عَجَائِبِهِ perceptive to its wonders

الَّتِي لَا تَنْقَضِي، which are never exhausted,

وَ لَذَاذَةً عِنْدَ تَرْدِيدِهِ، relish the murmuring of it in soft tones,

وَ عِبْرَةً عِنْدَ تَرْجِيعِهِ، take lesson from it when consulting it,

وَ نَفْعاً بَيِّناً and benefit visibly

عِنْدَ اسْتِفْهَامِهِ. when seeking from it an answer to our questions.

اللَّهُمَّ O Allah!

إِنَّا نَعُوذُ بِكَ We seek Your protection

مِنْ تَخَلُّفِهِ فِي قُلُوبِنَا، from its languishing in our hearts,

وَ تَوَسُّدِهِ عِنْدَ رُقَادِنَا، from our turning it into a soporific,

وَ نَبْذِهِ وَرَاءَ ظُهُورِنَا، and from casting it behind our backs.

وَ نَعُوذُ بِكَ We seek Your protection

مِنْ قَسَاوَةِ قُلُوبِنَا from the hardening of our hearts

لِمَا بِهِ وَعَظْتَنَا. to what You have advised us.

اللَّهُمَّ O Allah!

انْفَعْنَا Give us the benefit

بِمَا صَرَفْتَ فِيهِ مِنَ الْآيَاتِ، of the signs You have variegated in it,

وَ ذَكِّرْنَا بِمَا ضَرَبْتَ فِيهِ مِنَ الْمَثُلَاتِ، admonish us by the parables You have drawn in it,

وَكَفِّرْ عَنَّا بِتَأْوِيلِهِ السَّيِّئَاتِ،    absolve us of misdeeds through its fulfillment,

وَضَاعِفْ لَنَا بِهِ جَزَاءً فِي الْحَسَنَاتِ،    double through it our reward of good deeds,

وَارْفَعْنَا بِهِ ثَوَاباً فِي الدَّرَجَاتِ،    elevate us in rank through it as a reward,

وَلَقِّنَا بِهِ الْبُشْرَى بَعْدَ الْمَمَاتِ.    and give us good news through it after death!

اللَّهُمَّ    O Allah!

اجْعَلْهُ لَنَا    Make it for us

زَاداً تُقَوِّينَا بِهِ    a provision with which You may fortify us

فِي الْمَوْقِفِ بَيْنَ يَدَيْكَ،    in the halt before You,

وَطَرِيقاً وَاضِحاً نَسْلُكُ بِهِ إِلَيْكَ،    a clear path by which we may travel towards You,

وَعِلْماً نَافِعاً    a beneficial knowledge

نَشْكُرُ بِهِ نَعْمَاءَكَ،    by which we may thank You for Your blessings,

وَتَخَشُّعاً صَادِقاً    a true veneration

نُسَبِّحُ بِهِ أَسْمَاءَكَ،    with which we may glorify Your Names,

فَإِنَّكَ اتَّخَذْتَ بِهِ عَلَيْنَا حُجَّةً،    for You have made it an argument against us

قَطَعْتَ بِهِ عُذْرَنَا،    whereby You have cut off our excuses,

وَاصْطَنَعْتَ بِهِ عِنْدَنَا نِعْمَةً    and granted thereby a blessing

قَصَرَ عَنْهَا شُكْرُنَا.    for which we can never thank You enough!

اللَّهُمَّ اجْعَلْهُ لَنَا    O Allah! Make it for us

وَلِيّاً يُثَبِّتُنَا مِنَ الزَّلَلِ،    a guardian that saves us from stumblings

وَدَلِيلاً يَهْدِينَا لِصَالِحِ الْعَمَلِ،    a guide that directs us to righteous conduct,

وَعَوْناً هَادِياً يُقَوِّمُنَا مِنَ الْمَيْلِ،    a guiding helper that saves us from deviation,

وَعَوْناً يُقَوِّينَا مِنَ الْمَلَلِ،    a helper that gives us vigour in weariness,

حَتَّى يَبْلُغَ بِنَا أَفْضَلَ الْآمَلِ.    thus enabling us to realize our best aspirations.

اللَّهُمَّ    O Allah! Make it for us

اجْعَلْهُ لَنَا شَافِعاً يَوْمَ اللِّقَاءِ،    an intercessor on the day of encounter,

وَسِلاَحاً يَوْمَ الِارْتِقَاءِ،    an implement for the day of soaring,

وَحَجِيجاً يَوْمَ الْقَضَاءِ،    a pleader on the day of judgement,

وَ نُوراً يَوْمَ الظَّلْمَاءِ،  a light on the day of darkness

يَوْمَ لاَ أَرْضَ وَ لاَ سَمَاءَ،  —a day when there will be neither earth nor heaven,

يَوْمَ يُجْزَى كُلُّ سَاعٍ  a day when every striver will be rewarded

بِمَا سَعَى.  for his endeavour.

اللَّهُمَّ اجْعَلْهُ لَنَا  O Allah! Make it for us

رَيّاً يَوْمَ الظَّمَإِ،  a means of slaking our thirst on a day of thirst,

وَ فَوْزاً يَوْمَ الْجَزَاءِ  a means of deliverance on the day of retribution

مِنْ نَارٍ حَامِيَةٍ  from the scorching Fire

قَلِيلَةِ الْبُقْيَا عَلَى مَنْ بِهَا اصْطَلَى  unsparing to anyone who catches it

وَ بِحَرِّهَا تَلَظَّى.  and is inflamed by its heat.

اللَّهُمَّ اجْعَلْهُ لَنَا  O Allah! Make it for us

بُرْهَاناً عَلَى رُءُوسِ الْمَلَإِ،  an evidence before the assembly of the Elite,

يَوْمَ يُجْمَعُ فِيهِ  on the day wherein are gathered

أَهْلُ الأَرْضِ وَ أَهْلُ السَّمَاءِ.  the inhabitants of the earth and the heaven.

اللَّهُمَّ ارْزُقْنَا  O Allah! Grant us

مَنَازِلَ الشُّهَدَاءِ،  the stations of the martyrs,

وَ عَيْشَ السُّعَدَاءِ،  the life of the felicitous

وَ مُرَافَقَةَ الأَنْبِيَاءِ،  and the company of the prophets.

إِنَّكَ سَمِيعُ الدُّعَاءِ.  Indeed You hear all supplications![1]

---

[1] Al-Kulaynī, *Uṣūl al-Kāfī*, (Beirut: Dār al-Aḍwā' lil-Ṭabā'ah wal-Nashr wal-Tawzī', 1413/1992) Kitāb al-Du'ā', bāb al-du'ā' 'inda qirā'at al-Qur'ān, vol. 2, pp. 550-552, narrated from al-Imām al-Ṣādiq ('a).

# 1. SŪRAT AL-FĀTIḤAH[1]

سُورَةُ الفَاتِحَة

1 بِسْمِ ٱللَّهِ    In the Name of Allah,

ٱلرَّحْمَٰنِ ٱلرَّحِيمِ ۝    the All-beneficent, the All-merciful.

2 ٱلْحَمْدُ لِلَّهِ    All praise belongs to Allah,[2]

رَبِّ ٱلْعَٰلَمِينَ ۝    Lord of all the worlds,

3 ٱلرَّحْمَٰنِ ٱلرَّحِيمِ ۝    the All-beneficent, the All-merciful,

4 مَٰلِكِ يَوْمِ ٱلدِّينِ ۝    Master[3] of the Day of Retribution.

5 إِيَّاكَ نَعْبُدُ    You [alone] do we worship,

وَإِيَّاكَ نَسْتَعِينُ ۝    and to You [alone] do we turn for help.

6 ٱهْدِنَا ٱلصِّرَٰطَ ٱلْمُسْتَقِيمَ ۝    Guide us on the straight path,

7 صِرَٰطَ ٱلَّذِينَ أَنْعَمْتَ عَلَيْهِمْ    the path of those whom You have blessed[4]

غَيْرِ ٱلْمَغْضُوبِ عَلَيْهِمْ    —such as[5] have not incurred Your wrath,[6]

وَلَا ٱلضَّآلِّينَ ۝    nor are astray.[7]

---

[1] That is, 'the opening' *sūrah*. Another common name of the *sūrah* is 'Sūrat al-Ḥamd,' that is, the *sūrah* of the [Lord's] praise.

[2] In Muslim parlance the phrase *al-ḥamdu lillāh* also signifies 'thanks to Allah.'

[3] This is in accordance with the reading *mālik yawm al-dīn*, adopted by 'Āṣim, al-Kisā'ī, Ya'qūb al-Ḥaḍramī, and Khalaf. Other authorities of *qirā'ah* (the art of recitation of the Qur'ān) have read '*malik yawm al-dīn*,' meaning 'Sovereign of the Day of Retribution' (see *Mu'jam al-Qirā'āt al-Qur'āniyyah*). Traditions ascribe both readings to Imam Ja'far al-Ṣādiq ( 'a). See al-Qummī, al-'Ayyāshī, Tafsīr al-Imām al-'Askarī.

[4] For further Qur'ānic references to 'those whom Allah has blessed,' see 4:69 and 19:58; see also 5:22, 110; 12:6; 27:19; 28:17; 43:59; 48:2.

[5] This is in accordance with the *qirā'ah* of 'Āṣim, *ghayril-maghḍūbi,* which appears in the Arabic text above. However, in accordance with an alternative, and perhaps preferable, reading *ghayral-maghḍūbi* attributed to Imam 'Alī b. Abī Ṭālib ( 'a) as well as to Ibn Mas'ūd and Ubayy b. Ka'b among the Companions, and to Ibn Kathīr al-Makkī, among the seven authorities of *qirā'ah*, the translation will be: 'not those who have incurred Your wrath, nor those who are astray.' (see *Mu'jam al-Qirā'āt al-Qur'āniyyah*)

[6] For further references to 'those who incur Allah's wrath,' see 4:93; 5:60; 7:71, 152; 8:16; 16:106; 20:81; 42:16; 48:6; 58:14; 60:13.

[7] For further references to 'those who are astray,' see 2:108, 175; 3:90; 4:116, 136, 167; 5:12, 60, 77; 6:74, 77, 125, 140; 7:30, 179; 14:3, 18, 27; 15:56; 17:72, 97; 19:38; 22:4, 12; 23:106; 25:44; 28:50; 31:11; 33:36, 67; 34:8; 36:47; 38:26; 39:22; 40: 34; 41:52; 42:18; 45:23; 46:5, 32; 60:1.

# 2. SŪRAT AL-BAQARAH[1]

سُورَةُ البَقَرَةِ

بِسْمِ اللَّهِ
الرَّحْمَٰنِ الرَّحِيمِ

**In the Name of Allah,
the All-beneficent, the All-merciful.**

الٓمٓ ۝ 1 *Alif, Lām, Mīm.*

ذَٰلِكَ ٱلْكِتَٰبُ لَا رَيْبَ ۛ فِيهِ 2 This is the Book,[2] there is no doubt in it,

هُدًى لِّلْمُتَّقِينَ ۝ a guidance to the Godwary,[3]

ٱلَّذِينَ يُؤْمِنُونَ بِٱلْغَيْبِ 3 who believe in the Unseen,

وَيُقِيمُونَ ٱلصَّلَوٰةَ and maintain the prayer,

وَمِمَّا رَزَقْنَٰهُمْ يُنفِقُونَ ۝ and spend[4] out of what We have provided them with;

وَٱلَّذِينَ يُؤْمِنُونَ بِمَآ أُنزِلَ إِلَيْكَ 4 and who believe in what has been sent down to *you*[5]

وَمَآ أُنزِلَ مِن قَبْلِكَ and what was sent down before *you*,

وَبِٱلْءَاخِرَةِ هُمْ يُوقِنُونَ ۝ and are certain of the Hereafter.

أُو۟لَٰٓئِكَ عَلَىٰ هُدًى مِّن رَّبِّهِمْ 5 Those follow their Lord's guidance,

وَأُو۟لَٰٓئِكَ هُمُ ٱلْمُفْلِحُونَ ۝ and it is they who are the felicitous.

إِنَّ ٱلَّذِينَ كَفَرُوا۟ سَوَآءٌ عَلَيْهِمْ 6 As for the faithless, it is the same to them

ءَأَنذَرْتَهُمْ أَمْ لَمْ تُنذِرْهُمْ whether *you* warn them or do not warn them,

لَا يُؤْمِنُونَ ۝ they will not have faith.

خَتَمَ ٱللَّهُ عَلَىٰ قُلُوبِهِمْ 7 Allah has set a seal on their hearts

---

[1] The *sūrah* takes its name from the story of the cow (*baqarah*) mentioned in verses 67-73.

[2] The term 'the Book' in the Qur'ān, in such contexts, means a Divine scripture.

[3] Or 'This Book, in which there is no doubt, is guidance to the Godwary.' Or 'This Book is no doubt a guidance to the Godwary.'

[4] The expression 'to spend' is used in the Qur'ān elliptically to mean spending in the way of Allah and for the sake of His pleasure. Cf. 2:195, 261-262, 272; 8:60; 9:33; 47:38; 57:16.

[5] That is, the Prophet, may Allah bless him and his Household. Throughout this translation whenever the pronoun 'you' refers to the second person singular in the Arabic and is meant as an address to the Prophet, it has been italicized (for similar reasons, also the related verbs) in order to distinguish it from cases where it stands for the second person plural. This is to avoid the use of 'thee' and 'thou,' which are, unfortunately, archaic in contemporary English.

وَعَلَىٰ سَمْعِهِمْ    and their hearing,

وَعَلَىٰٓ أَبۡصَـٰرِهِمۡ غِشَـٰوَةٌ    and there is a blindfold on their sight,[1]

وَلَهُمۡ عَذَابٌ عَظِيمٌ ۝    and there is a great punishment for them.


وَمِنَ ٱلنَّاسِ مَن يَقُولُ    8 And among the people are those who say,

ءَامَنَّا بِٱللَّهِ وَبِٱلۡيَوۡمِ ٱلۡأٓخِرِ    'We have faith in Allah and the Last Day,'

وَمَا هُم بِمُؤۡمِنِينَ ۝    but they have no faith.

يُخَـٰدِعُونَ ٱللَّهَ    9 They seek to deceive Allah

وَٱلَّذِينَ ءَامَنُواْ    and those who have faith,

وَمَا يَخۡدَعُونَ إِلَّآ أَنفُسَهُمۡ    yet they deceive no one but themselves,

وَمَا يَشۡعُرُونَ ۝    but they are not aware.

فِى قُلُوبِهِم مَّرَضٌ    10 There is a sickness in their hearts;

فَزَادَهُمُ ٱللَّهُ مَرَضًا    then Allah increased their sickness,

وَلَهُمۡ عَذَابٌ أَلِيمٌۢ    and there is a painful punishment for them

بِمَا كَانُواْ يَكۡذِبُونَ ۝    because of the lies they used to tell.

وَإِذَا قِيلَ لَهُمۡ    11 When they are told,

لَا تُفۡسِدُواْ فِى ٱلۡأَرۡضِ    'Do not cause corruption on the earth,'

قَالُوٓاْ إِنَّمَا نَحۡنُ مُصۡلِحُونَ ۝    they say, 'We are only reformers!'

أَلَآ إِنَّهُمۡ هُمُ ٱلۡمُفۡسِدُونَ    12 Look! They are themselves the agents of corruption,

وَلَـٰكِن لَّا يَشۡعُرُونَ ۝    but they are not aware.

وَإِذَا قِيلَ لَهُمۡ    13 And when they are told,

ءَامِنُواْ كَمَآ ءَامَنَ ٱلنَّاسُ    'Believe like the people who have believed,'

قَالُوٓاْ أَنُؤۡمِنُ    they say, 'Shall we believe

كَمَآ ءَامَنَ ٱلسُّفَهَآءُ    like the fools who have belicved?'

أَلَآ إِنَّهُمۡ هُمُ ٱلسُّفَهَآءُ    Look! They are themselves the fools,

وَلَـٰكِن لَّا يَعۡلَمُونَ ۝    but they do not know.

---

[1] The hearing and sight, often mentioned in the Qurʾān, refer to the inner spiritual hearing and vision by the means of which someone possessing faith apprehends the reality lying beyond the physical realm. Cf. 2:17, 20; 3:13; 6:46, 50, 104, 110; 7:179, 197; 10:43; 11:20, 24; 13:16; 16:78, 108; 19:38; 22:46; 23:78; 24:44; 32:12; 35:19; 36:66; 40:58; 45:23; 46:26; 47:23; 50:22; 59:2; 67:23; 75:14; 76:2.

وَإِذَا لَقُوا۟ ٱلَّذِينَ ءَامَنُوا۟ 14 When they meet the faithful,

قَالُوٓا۟ ءَامَنَّا     they say, 'We believe,'

وَإِذَا خَلَوْا۟ إِلَىٰ شَيَٰطِينِهِمْ     but when they are alone with their devils,

قَالُوٓا۟ إِنَّا مَعَكُمْ     they say, 'We are with you;

إِنَّمَا نَحْنُ مُسْتَهْزِءُونَ ۞     we were only deriding [them].'

ٱللَّهُ يَسْتَهْزِئُ بِهِمْ 15 It is Allah who derides them,[1]

وَيَمُدُّهُمْ فِى طُغْيَٰنِهِمْ يَعْمَهُونَ ۞     and leaves them bewildered in their rebellion.

أُو۟لَٰٓئِكَ ٱلَّذِينَ ٱشْتَرَوُا۟ ٱلضَّلَٰلَةَ 16 They are the ones who bought error

بِٱلْهُدَىٰ     for guidance,

فَمَا رَبِحَت تِّجَٰرَتُهُمْ     so their trade did not profit them,

وَمَا كَانُوا۟ مُهْتَدِينَ ۞     nor were they guided.

مَثَلُهُمْ 17 Their parable

كَمَثَلِ ٱلَّذِى ٱسْتَوْقَدَ نَارًا     is that of one who lighted a torch,

فَلَمَّآ أَضَآءَتْ مَا حَوْلَهُۥ     and when it had lit up all around him,

ذَهَبَ ٱللَّهُ بِنُورِهِمْ     Allah took away their light,

وَتَرَكَهُمْ فِى ظُلُمَٰتٍ لَّا يُبْصِرُونَ ۞     and left them sightless in a manifold darkness.[2]

صُمٌّ بُكْمٌ عُمْىٌ 18 Deaf, dumb, and blind,

فَهُمْ لَا يَرْجِعُونَ ۞     they will not come back.

أَوْ كَصَيِّبٍ مِّنَ ٱلسَّمَآءِ 19 Or that of a rainstorm from the sky,

فِيهِ ظُلُمَٰتٌ وَرَعْدٌ وَبَرْقٌ     wherein is darkness, thunder, and lightning:

يَجْعَلُونَ أَصَٰبِعَهُمْ فِىٓ ءَاذَانِهِم     they put their fingers in their ears

مِّنَ ٱلصَّوَٰعِقِ حَذَرَ ٱلْمَوْتِ     due to the thunderclaps, apprehensive of death;

وَٱللَّهُ مُحِيطٌ بِٱلْكَٰفِرِينَ ۞     and Allah besieges the faithless.[3]

يَكَادُ ٱلْبَرْقُ يَخْطَفُ أَبْصَٰرَهُمْ 20 The lightning almost snatches away their sight:

---

[1] That is, by letting them imagine that they are mocking the faithful.

[2] The one who lights the torch in the parable is the Prophet [ṣ], who illuminated the spiritual horizons of the Arabia of those days with the message of Islam. But the hypocrites, with their inward blindness, did not benefit from its light and continued to remain in the darkness of their faithlessness.

[3] This is another parable for the condition of the hypocrites. In it the Prophet's mission, with its downpour of Divine knowledge, the accompanying light of guidance, along with the hardships of struggle against polytheism and injustice, is likened to a rainstorm.

كُلَّمَآ أَضَآءَ لَهُم مَّشَوْاْ فِيهِ    whenever it shines for them, they walk in it,

وَإِذَآ أَظْلَمَ عَلَيْهِمْ قَامُواْ    and when the darkness falls over them, they stand.

وَلَوْ شَآءَ ٱللَّهُ    Had Allah willed,

لَذَهَبَ بِسَمْعِهِمْ    He would have taken away their hearing

وَأَبْصَٰرِهِمْ    and their sight.

إِنَّ ٱللَّهَ عَلَىٰ كُلِّ شَىْءٍ قَدِيرٌ ۝    Indeed Allah has power over all things.

يَٰٓأَيُّهَا ٱلنَّاسُ ٱعْبُدُواْ رَبَّكُمُ    21 O mankind! Worship your Lord,

ٱلَّذِى خَلَقَكُمْ    who created you

وَٱلَّذِينَ مِن قَبْلِكُمْ    and those who were before you,

لَعَلَّكُمْ تَتَّقُونَ ۝    so that you may be Godwary.

ٱلَّذِى جَعَلَ لَكُمُ ٱلْأَرْضَ فِرَٰشًا    22 He who made the earth a place of repose for you,

وَٱلسَّمَآءَ بِنَآءً    and the sky a canopy,

وَأَنزَلَ مِنَ ٱلسَّمَآءِ مَآءً    and He sends down water from the sky,

فَأَخْرَجَ بِهِۦ مِنَ ٱلثَّمَرَٰتِ    and with it He brings forth crops

رِزْقًا لَّكُمْ    for your sustenance.

فَلَا تَجْعَلُواْ لِلَّهِ أَندَادًا    So do not set up equals to Allah,

وَأَنتُمْ تَعْلَمُونَ ۝    while you know.

وَإِن كُنتُمْ فِى رَيْبٍ    23 And if you are in doubt

مِّمَّا نَزَّلْنَا    concerning what We have sent down

عَلَىٰ عَبْدِنَا    to Our servant,

فَأْتُواْ بِسُورَةٍ مِّن مِّثْلِهِۦ    then bring a *sūrah* like it,

وَٱدْعُواْ شُهَدَآءَكُم مِّن دُونِ ٱللَّهِ    and invoke your helpers besides Allah,

إِن كُنتُمْ صَٰدِقِينَ ۝    should you be truthful.

فَإِن لَّمْ تَفْعَلُواْ وَلَن تَفْعَلُواْ    24 And if you do not—and you will not—

فَٱتَّقُواْ ٱلنَّارَ ٱلَّتِى وَقُودُهَا ٱلنَّاسُ    then fear the Fire whose fuel will be humans

وَٱلْحِجَارَةُ    and stones,

أُعِدَّتْ لِلْكَٰفِرِينَ ۝    prepared for the faithless.

وَبَشِّرِ ٱلَّذِينَ ءَامَنُواْ    25 and *give* good news to those who have faith

وَعَمِلُواْ ٱلصَّٰلِحَٰتِ    and do righteous deeds,

أَنَّ لَهُمْ جَنَّـٰتٍ    that for them shall be gardens

تَجْرِى مِن تَحْتِهَا ٱلْأَنْهَـٰرُ    with streams running in them:

كُلَّمَا رُزِقُوا مِنْهَا مِن ثَمَرَةٍ    whenever they are provided with its fruit

رِّزْقًا    for nourishment,

قَالُوا    they will say,

هَـٰذَا ٱلَّذِى رُزِقْنَا مِن قَبْلُ    'This is what we were provided before,'

وَأُتُوا بِهِۦ مُتَشَـٰبِهًا    and they were given something resembling it.

وَلَهُمْ فِيهَآ أَزْوَٰجٌ مُّطَهَّرَةٌ    In it there will be chaste mates for them,

وَهُمْ فِيهَا خَـٰلِدُونَ ۝    and they will remain in it [forever].

إِنَّ ٱللَّهَ لَا يَسْتَحْىِۦٓ أَن يَضْرِبَ مَثَلًا    26 Indeed Allah is not ashamed to draw a parable

مَّا بَعُوضَةً فَمَا فَوْقَهَا    whether it is that of a gnat or something above it.

فَأَمَّا ٱلَّذِينَ ءَامَنُوا    As for those who have faith,

فَيَعْلَمُونَ أَنَّهُ ٱلْحَقُّ مِن رَّبِّهِمْ    they know it is the truth from their Lord;

وَأَمَّا ٱلَّذِينَ كَفَرُوا فَيَقُولُونَ    and as for the faithless, they say,

مَاذَآ أَرَادَ ٱللَّهُ بِهَـٰذَا مَثَلًا    'What did Allah mean by this parable?'

يُضِلُّ بِهِۦ كَثِيرًا    Thereby He leads many astray,

وَيَهْدِى بِهِۦ كَثِيرًا    and thereby He guides many;

وَمَا يُضِلُّ بِهِۦٓ    and He leads no one astray thereby

إِلَّا ٱلْفَـٰسِقِينَ ۝    except the transgressors

ٱلَّذِينَ يَنقُضُونَ عَهْدَ ٱللَّهِ    27 —those who break the covenant made with Allah

مِنۢ بَعْدِ مِيثَـٰقِهِۦ    after having pledged it solemnly,

وَيَقْطَعُونَ    and sever

مَآ أَمَرَ ٱللَّهُ بِهِۦٓ أَن يُوصَلَ    what Allah has commanded to be joined,

وَيُفْسِدُونَ فِى ٱلْأَرْضِ    and cause corruption on the earth—

أُوْلَـٰٓئِكَ هُمُ ٱلْخَـٰسِرُونَ ۝    it is they who are the losers.

كَيْفَ تَكْفُرُونَ بِٱللَّهِ    28 How can you be unfaithful to Allah,

وَكُنتُمْ أَمْوَٰتًا    [seeing that] you were lifeless

فَأَحْيَـٰكُمْ    and He gave you life,

ثُمَّ يُمِيتُكُمْ    then He will make you die,

ثُمَّ يُحْيِيكُمْ    and then He shall bring you to life,

ثُمَّ إِلَيْهِ تُرْجَعُونَ ۝    and then you will be brought back to Him?

هُوَ ٱلَّذِى خَلَقَ لَكُم 29    It is He who created for you

مَّا فِى ٱلْأَرْضِ جَمِيعًا    all that is in the earth,

ثُمَّ ٱسْتَوَىٰ إِلَى ٱلسَّمَاءِ    then He turned to the heaven,

فَسَوَّىٰهُنَّ سَبْعَ سَمَٰوَٰتٍ    and fashioned it into seven heavens,

وَهُوَ بِكُلِّ شَىْءٍ عَلِيمٌ ۝    and He has knowledge of all things.

وَإِذْ قَالَ رَبُّكَ لِلْمَلَٰئِكَةِ 30    When *your* Lord said to the angels,

إِنِّى جَاعِلٌ فِى ٱلْأَرْضِ خَلِيفَةً    'Indeed I am going to set a viceroy on the earth,'

قَالُوٓا۟ أَتَجْعَلُ فِيهَا    they said, 'Will You set in it

مَن يُفْسِدُ فِيهَا    someone who will cause corruption in it,

وَيَسْفِكُ ٱلدِّمَاءَ    and shed blood,

وَنَحْنُ نُسَبِّحُ بِحَمْدِكَ    while we celebrate Your praise

وَنُقَدِّسُ لَكَ    and proclaim Your sanctity?'

قَالَ إِنِّىٓ أَعْلَمُ مَا لَا تَعْلَمُونَ ۝    He said, 'Indeed I know what you do not know.'

وَعَلَّمَ ءَادَمَ ٱلْأَسْمَاءَ كُلَّهَا 31    And He taught Adam the Names, all of them;[1]

ثُمَّ عَرَضَهُمْ عَلَى ٱلْمَلَٰئِكَةِ    then presented them[2] to the angels

فَقَالَ أَنۢبِئُونِى بِأَسْمَاءِ هَٰٓؤُلَاءِ    and said, 'Tell me the names of these,

إِن كُنتُمْ صَٰدِقِينَ ۝    if you are truthful.'

قَالُوا۟ سُبْحَٰنَكَ 32    They said, 'Immaculate are You!

لَا عِلْمَ لَنَآ    We have no knowledge

إِلَّا مَا عَلَّمْتَنَآ    except what You have taught us.

إِنَّكَ أَنتَ ٱلْعَلِيمُ ٱلْحَكِيمُ ۝    Indeed You are the All-knowing, the All-wise.'

قَالَ يَٰٓـَٔادَمُ 33    He said, 'O Adam,

أَنۢبِئْهُم بِأَسْمَآئِهِمْ    inform them[3] of their names,'

فَلَمَّآ أَنۢبَأَهُم بِأَسْمَآئِهِمْ    and when he had informed them of their names,

---

[1] It is to be noted that the pronoun in 'all of them' [*kullahā*] is feminine.

[2] The pronoun in the phrase 'He presented them' [*'araḍahum*] is masculine, indicating that it does not refer to the 'Names' but to their referents.

[3] That is, the angels, about the names of those referents.

7

قَالَ أَلَمْ أَقُل لَّكُمْ

He said, 'Did I not tell you

إِنِّي أَعْلَمُ غَيْبَ ٱلسَّمَٰوَٰتِ

that I indeed know the Unseen in the heavens

وَٱلْأَرْضِ

and the earth,

وَأَعْلَمُ مَا تُبْدُونَ

and that I know whatever you disclose

وَمَا كُنتُمْ تَكْتُمُونَ ۝

and whatever you were concealing?'

وَإِذْ قُلْنَا لِلْمَلَٰٓئِكَةِ 34 And when We said to the angels,

ٱسْجُدُوا۟ لِءَادَمَ

'Prostrate before Adam,'

فَسَجَدُوٓا۟ إِلَّآ إِبْلِيسَ

they prostrated, except Iblis:

أَبَىٰ وَٱسْتَكْبَرَ

he refused and acted arrogantly,

وَكَانَ مِنَ ٱلْكَٰفِرِينَ ۝

and he was one of the faithless.

وَقُلْنَا يَٰٓـَٔادَمُ 35 We said, 'O Adam,

ٱسْكُنْ أَنتَ وَزَوْجُكَ ٱلْجَنَّةَ

dwell with your mate in paradise,

وَكُلَا مِنْهَا رَغَدًا حَيْثُ شِئْتُمَا

and eat thereof freely whencesoever you wish;

وَلَا تَقْرَبَا هَٰذِهِ ٱلشَّجَرَةَ

but do not approach this tree,

فَتَكُونَا مِنَ ٱلظَّٰلِمِينَ ۝

lest you should be among the wrongdoers.'

فَأَزَلَّهُمَا ٱلشَّيْطَٰنُ عَنْهَا 36 Then Satan caused them to stumble from it,

فَأَخْرَجَهُمَا مِمَّا كَانَا فِيهِ

and he dislodged them from what they were in;

وَقُلْنَا ٱهْبِطُوا۟

and We said, 'Get down,

بَعْضُكُمْ لِبَعْضٍ عَدُوٌّ

being enemies of one another!

وَلَكُمْ فِى ٱلْأَرْضِ مُسْتَقَرٌّ

On the earth shall be your abode

وَمَتَٰعٌ إِلَىٰ حِينٍ ۝

and sustenance for a time.'

فَتَلَقَّىٰٓ ءَادَمُ مِن رَّبِّهِۦ كَلِمَٰتٍ 37 Then Adam received certain words from his Lord,

فَتَابَ عَلَيْهِ

and He turned to him clemently.

إِنَّهُۥ هُوَ ٱلتَّوَّابُ ٱلرَّحِيمُ ۝

Indeed He is the All-clement, the All-merciful.

قُلْنَا ٱهْبِطُوا۟ مِنْهَا جَمِيعًا 38 We said, 'Get down from it, all together!

فَإِمَّا يَأْتِيَنَّكُم مِّنِّى هُدًى

Yet, should any guidance come to you from Me,

فَمَن تَبِعَ هُدَاىَ

those who follow My guidance

فَلَا خَوْفٌ عَلَيْهِمْ

shall have no fear,

وَلَا هُمْ يَحْزَنُونَ ۝

nor shall they grieve.

وَٱلَّذِينَ كَفَرُوا۟ وَكَذَّبُوا۟ بِـَٔايَٰتِنَآ 39 But those who are faithless and deny Our signs,

أُوْلَٰٓئِكَ أَصْحَٰبُ ٱلنَّارِ — they shall be the inmates of the Fire

هُمْ فِيهَا خَٰلِدُونَ ۝ — and they shall remain in it [forever].

يَٰبَنِىٓ إِسْرَٰٓءِيلَ 40 O Children of Israel,

ٱذْكُرُوا۟ نِعْمَتِىَ ٱلَّتِىٓ — remember My blessing which

أَنْعَمْتُ عَلَيْكُمْ — I bestowed upon you,

وَأَوْفُوا۟ بِعَهْدِىٓ — and fulfill My covenant

أُوفِ بِعَهْدِكُمْ — that I may fulfill your covenant,

وَإِيَّٰىَ فَٱرْهَبُونِ ۝ — and be in awe of Me [alone].

وَءَامِنُوا۟ بِمَآ أَنزَلْتُ 41 And believe in that which I have sent down

مُصَدِّقًا لِّمَا مَعَكُمْ — confirming that which is with you,

وَلَا تَكُونُوٓا۟ أَوَّلَ كَافِرٍۭ بِهِۦ — and do not be the first ones to defy it,

وَلَا تَشْتَرُوا۟ بِـَٔايَٰتِى ثَمَنًا قَلِيلًا — and do not sell My signs for a paltry gain,

وَإِيَّٰىَ فَٱتَّقُونِ ۝ — and be wary of Me [alone].

وَلَا تَلْبِسُوا۟ ٱلْحَقَّ بِٱلْبَٰطِلِ 42 And do not mix the truth with falsehood,

وَتَكْتُمُوا۟ ٱلْحَقَّ — nor conceal the truth

وَأَنتُمْ تَعْلَمُونَ ۝ — while you know.

وَأَقِيمُوا۟ ٱلصَّلَوٰةَ وَءَاتُوا۟ ٱلزَّكَوٰةَ 43 And maintain the prayer, and give the *zakāt*,

وَٱرْكَعُوا۟ مَعَ ٱلرَّٰكِعِينَ ۝ ✦ — and bow along with those who bow [in prayer].

أَتَأْمُرُونَ ٱلنَّاسَ بِٱلْبِرِّ 44 Will you bid others to piety

وَتَنسَوْنَ أَنفُسَكُمْ — and forget yourselves,

وَأَنتُمْ تَتْلُونَ ٱلْكِتَٰبَ — while you recite the Book?

أَفَلَا تَعْقِلُونَ ۝ — Do you not apply reason?

وَٱسْتَعِينُوا۟ بِٱلصَّبْرِ 45 And take recourse in patience

وَٱلصَّلَوٰةِ — and prayer,

وَإِنَّهَا لَكَبِيرَةٌ — and it[1] is indeed hard

إِلَّا عَلَى ٱلْخَٰشِعِينَ ۝ — except for the humble

ٱلَّذِينَ يَظُنُّونَ 46 —those who are certain

---

[1] The pronoun, being feminine, refers to prayer, rather than to patience or to the seeking of recourse.

أَنَّهُم مُّلَـٰقُواْ رَبِّهِمۡ   that they will encounter their Lord,

وَأَنَّهُمۡ إِلَيۡهِ رَٰجِعُونَ ۝   and that they will return to Him.

يَـٰبَنِىٓ إِسۡرَٰٓءِيلَ   47 O Children of Israel,

ٱذۡكُرُواْ نِعۡمَتِىَ ٱلَّتِىٓ أَنۡعَمۡتُ عَلَيۡكُمۡ   remember My blessing which I bestowed upon you,

وَأَنِّى فَضَّلۡتُكُمۡ عَلَى ٱلۡعَٰلَمِينَ ۝   and that I gave you an advantage over all the nations.

وَٱتَّقُواْ يَوۡمًا   48 Beware of the day

لَّا تَجۡزِى نَفۡسٌ عَن نَّفۡسٍ شَيۡـًٔا   when no soul shall compensate for another,

وَلَا يُقۡبَلُ مِنۡهَا شَفَـٰعَةٌ   neither any intercession shall be accepted from it,

وَلَا يُؤۡخَذُ مِنۡهَا عَدۡلٌ   nor any ransom shall be received from it,

وَلَا هُمۡ يُنصَرُونَ ۝   nor will they be helped.

وَإِذۡ نَجَّيۡنَـٰكُم مِّنۡ ءَالِ فِرۡعَوۡنَ   49 And when We delivered you from Pharaoh's clan

يَسُومُونَكُمۡ سُوٓءَ ٱلۡعَذَابِ   who inflicted a terrible torment on you,

يُذَبِّحُونَ أَبۡنَآءَكُمۡ   and slaughtered your sons

وَيَسۡتَحۡيُونَ نِسَآءَكُمۡ   and spared your women,

وَفِى ذَٰلِكُم   and in that there was

بَلَآءٌ مِّن رَّبِّكُمۡ عَظِيمٌ ۝   a great test from your Lord.

وَإِذۡ فَرَقۡنَا بِكُمُ ٱلۡبَحۡرَ   50 And when We parted the sea with you,[1]

فَأَنجَيۡنَـٰكُمۡ   and We delivered you

وَأَغۡرَقۡنَآ ءَالَ فِرۡعَوۡنَ   and drowned Pharaoh's clan

وَأَنتُمۡ تَنظُرُونَ ۝   as you looked on.

وَإِذۡ وَٰعَدۡنَا مُوسَىٰٓ   51 And when We made an appointment with Moses

أَرۡبَعِينَ لَيۡلَةً   for forty nights,

ثُمَّ ٱتَّخَذۡتُمُ ٱلۡعِجۡلَ   you took up the Calf [for worship]

مِنۢ بَعۡدِهِۦ   in his absence,

وَأَنتُمۡ ظَٰلِمُونَ ۝   and you were wrongdoers.

ثُمَّ عَفَوۡنَا عَنكُم مِّنۢ بَعۡدِ ذَٰلِكَ   52 Then We excused you after that

لَعَلَّكُمۡ تَشۡكُرُونَ ۝   so that you might give thanks.

وَإِذۡ ءَاتَيۡنَا مُوسَى ٱلۡكِتَٰبَ   53 And when We gave Moses the Book

---

[1] That is, through your entering it.

وَٱلْفُرْقَانَ · and the Criterion[1]

لَعَلَّكُمْ تَهْتَدُونَ ۝ · so that you might be guided.

وَإِذْ قَالَ مُوسَىٰ لِقَوْمِهِ 54 · And [recall] when Moses said to his people,

يَـٰقَوْمِ · 'O my people!

إِنَّكُمْ ظَلَمْتُمْ أَنفُسَكُم · You have indeed wronged yourselves

بِٱتِّخَاذِكُمُ ٱلْعِجْلَ · by taking up the Calf [for worship].

فَتُوبُوٓا۟ إِلَىٰ بَارِئِكُمْ · Now turn penitently to your Maker,

فَٱقْتُلُوٓا۟ أَنفُسَكُمْ · and slay [the guilty among] your folks.

ذَٰلِكُمْ خَيْرٌ لَّكُمْ عِندَ بَارِئِكُمْ · That will be better for you with your Maker.'

فَتَابَ عَلَيْكُمْ · Then He turned to you clemently.

إِنَّهُۥ هُوَ ٱلتَّوَّابُ ٱلرَّحِيمُ ۝ · Indeed He is the All-clement, the All-merciful.

وَإِذْ قُلْتُمْ يَـٰمُوسَىٰ 55 · And when you said, 'O Moses,

لَن نُّؤْمِنَ لَكَ · we will not believe you

حَتَّىٰ نَرَى ٱللَّهَ جَهْرَةً · until we see Allah visibly.'

فَأَخَذَتْكُمُ ٱلصَّـٰعِقَةُ · Thereupon a thunderbolt seized you

وَأَنتُمْ تَنظُرُونَ ۝ · as you looked on.

ثُمَّ بَعَثْنَـٰكُم مِّنۢ بَعْدِ مَوْتِكُمْ 56 · Then We raised you up after your death

لَعَلَّكُمْ تَشْكُرُونَ ۝ · so that you might give thanks.

وَظَلَّلْنَا عَلَيْكُمُ ٱلْغَمَامَ 57 · And We shaded you with clouds,

وَأَنزَلْنَا عَلَيْكُمُ ٱلْمَنَّ وَٱلسَّلْوَىٰ · and We sent down to you manna and quails:

كُلُوا۟ مِن طَيِّبَـٰتِ مَا رَزَقْنَـٰكُمْ · 'Eat of the good things We have provided for you.'

وَمَا ظَلَمُونَا · And they did not wrong Us,

وَلَـٰكِن كَانُوٓا۟ أَنفُسَهُمْ يَظْلِمُونَ ۝ · but they used to wrong [only] themselves.

وَإِذْ قُلْنَا ٱدْخُلُوا۟ هَـٰذِهِ ٱلْقَرْيَةَ 58 · And when We said, 'Enter this town,[2]

---

[1] That is, that by means of which truth and falsehood are distinguished from each other (cf. 21:48). Elsewhere (3:4; 25:1) the Qur'ān is also called al-Furqān.

[2] This city, according to tradition (see Tafsīr al-Imām al-'Askarī), was Arīḥā' or Jericho (or Jerusalem, according to some commentators), an ancient city of Palestine near the northwest shore of the Dead Sea. A stronghold commanding the valley of the lower Jordan River, it was captured and destroyed by Joshua forty years later.

11

فَكُلُواْ مِنْهَا حَيْثُ شِئْتُمْ رَغَدًا
and eat thereof freely whencesoever you wish,

وَٱدْخُلُواْ ٱلْبَابَ سُجَّدًا
and enter prostrating at the gate,

وَقُولُواْ حِطَّةٌ
and say, "Relieve [us of the burden of our sins],"[1]

نَّغْفِرْ لَكُمْ خَطَٰيَٰكُمْ
that We may forgive your iniquities,

وَسَنَزِيدُ ٱلْمُحْسِنِينَ ۝
and soon We will enhance the virtuous.'

فَبَدَّلَ ٱلَّذِينَ ظَلَمُواْ قَوْلًا
59 But the wrongdoers changed the saying

غَيْرَ ٱلَّذِى قِيلَ لَهُمْ
with other than what they were told.

فَأَنزَلْنَا عَلَى ٱلَّذِينَ ظَلَمُواْ
So We sent down on those who were wrongdoers

رِجْزًا مِّنَ ٱلسَّمَآءِ
a plague from the sky

بِمَا كَانُواْ يَفْسُقُونَ ۝
because of the transgressions they used to commit.

وَإِذِ ٱسْتَسْقَىٰ مُوسَىٰ لِقَوْمِهِۦ
60 And when Moses prayed for water for his people,

فَقُلْنَا ٱضْرِب بِّعَصَاكَ ٱلْحَجَرَ
We said, 'Strike the rock with your staff.'

فَٱنفَجَرَتْ مِنْهُ ٱثْنَتَا عَشْرَةَ عَيْنًا
Thereat twelve fountains gushed forth from it;

قَدْ عَلِمَ كُلُّ أُنَاسٍ مَّشْرَبَهُمْ
every tribe came to know its drinking-place.

كُلُواْ وَٱشْرَبُواْ مِن رِّزْقِ ٱللَّهِ
'Eat and drink of Allah's provision,

وَلَا تَعْثَوْاْ فِى ٱلْأَرْضِ
and do not act wickedly on the earth,

مُفْسِدِينَ ۝
causing corruption.'

وَإِذْ قُلْتُمْ يَٰمُوسَىٰ
61 And when you said, 'O Moses,

لَن نَّصْبِرَ عَلَىٰ طَعَامٍ وَٰحِدٍ
'We will not put up with one kind of food.

فَٱدْعُ لَنَا رَبَّكَ
So invoke your Lord for us,

يُخْرِجْ لَنَا
that He may bring forth for us

مِمَّا تُنۢبِتُ ٱلْأَرْضُ
of that which the earth grows

مِنۢ بَقْلِهَا وَقِثَّآئِهَا
—its greens and its cucumbers,

وَفُومِهَا وَعَدَسِهَا وَبَصَلِهَا
its garlic, its lentils, and its onions.'

قَالَ أَتَسْتَبْدِلُونَ
He said, 'Do you seek to replace

ٱلَّذِى هُوَ أَدْنَىٰ بِٱلَّذِى هُوَ خَيْرٌ
what is superior with that which is inferior?

ٱهْبِطُواْ مِصْرًا
Go down to any town

فَإِنَّ لَكُم مَّا سَأَلْتُمْ
and you will indeed get what you ask for!'

وَضُرِبَتْ عَلَيْهِمُ ٱلذِّلَّةُ وَٱلْمَسْكَنَةُ
So they were struck with abasement and poverty,

---

[1] Or '[We beseech] forgiveness [for our sins].'

وَبَآءُو بِغَضَبٍ مِّنَ ٱللَّهِ    and they earned Allah's wrath.

ذَٰلِكَ بِأَنَّهُمْ كَانُوا۟ يَكْفُرُونَ    That, because they would defy

بِـَٔايَٰتِ ٱللَّهِ      the signs of Allah

وَيَقْتُلُونَ ٱلنَّبِيِّـۧنَ بِغَيْرِ ٱلْحَقِّ    and kill the prophets unjustly.

ذَٰلِكَ بِمَا عَصَوا۟    That, because they would disobey

وَّكَانُوا۟ يَعْتَدُونَ ۝    and used to commit transgression.

إِنَّ ٱلَّذِينَ ءَامَنُوا۟ وَٱلَّذِينَ هَادُوا۟    62 Indeed the faithful, the Jews,

وَٱلنَّصَٰرَىٰ وَٱلصَّٰبِـِٔينَ      the Christians, and the Sabaeans

مَنْ ءَامَنَ بِٱللَّهِ      —those of them who have faith in Allah

وَٱلْيَوْمِ ٱلْءَاخِرِ      and the Last Day

وَعَمِلَ صَٰلِحًا      and act righteously—

فَلَهُمْ أَجْرُهُمْ عِندَ رَبِّهِمْ    they shall have their reward near their Lord,

وَلَا خَوْفٌ عَلَيْهِمْ    and they will have no fear,

وَلَا هُمْ يَحْزَنُونَ ۝    nor will they grieve.

وَإِذْ أَخَذْنَا مِيثَٰقَكُمْ    63 And when We took a pledge from you,

وَرَفَعْنَا فَوْقَكُمُ ٱلطُّورَ    and raised the Mount above you [declaring],

خُذُوا۟ مَآ ءَاتَيْنَٰكُم بِقُوَّةٍ    'Hold on with power to what We have given you,

وَٱذْكُرُوا۟ مَا فِيهِ    and remember that which is in it,

لَعَلَّكُمْ تَتَّقُونَ ۝    so that you may be Godwary.'

ثُمَّ تَوَلَّيْتُم مِّنۢ بَعْدِ ذَٰلِكَ    64 Then after that you turned away;

فَلَوْلَا فَضْلُ ٱللَّهِ عَلَيْكُمْ    and were it not for Allah's grace on you

وَرَحْمَتُهُ      and His mercy,

لَكُنتُم مِّنَ ٱلْخَٰسِرِينَ ۝    you would surely have been among the losers.

وَلَقَدْ عَلِمْتُمُ    65 And certainly you know

ٱلَّذِينَ ٱعْتَدَوْا۟ مِنكُمْ فِى ٱلسَّبْتِ    those of you who violated the Sabbath,

فَقُلْنَا لَهُمْ    whereupon We said to them,

كُونُوا۟ قِرَدَةً خَٰسِـِٔينَ ۝    'Be you spurned apes.'

فَجَعَلْنَٰهَا نَكَٰلًا    66 So We made it an exemplary punishment

لِّمَا بَيْنَ يَدَيْهَا وَمَا خَلْفَهَا

for the present and the succeeding [generations],

وَمَوْعِظَةً لِّلْمُتَّقِينَ ۝

and an advice to the Godwary.

وَإِذْ قَالَ مُوسَىٰ لِقَوْمِهِ

67 And when Moses said to his people,

إِنَّ ٱللَّهَ يَأْمُرُكُمْ أَن تَذْبَحُواْ بَقَرَةً

'Indeed Allah commands you to slaughter a cow,'

قَالُوٓاْ أَتَتَّخِذُنَا هُزُوًا

they said, 'Do you take us in derision?'

قَالَ أَعُوذُ بِٱللَّهِ

He said, 'I seek Allah's protection

أَنْ أَكُونَ مِنَ ٱلْجَٰهِلِينَ ۝

lest I should be one of the senseless!'

قَالُواْ ٱدْعُ لَنَا رَبَّكَ

68 They said, 'Invoke your Lord for us,

يُبَيِّن لَّنَا مَا هِىَ

that He may clarify for us what she may be.'

قَالَ إِنَّهُ يَقُولُ إِنَّهَا بَقَرَةٌ

He said, 'He says, She is a cow,

لَّا فَارِضٌ وَلَا بِكْرٌ

neither old nor young,

عَوَانٌ بَيْنَ ذَٰلِكَ

of a middle age.

فَٱفْعَلُواْ مَا تُؤْمَرُونَ ۝

Now do what you are commanded.'

قَالُواْ ٱدْعُ لَنَا رَبَّكَ

69 They said, 'Invoke your Lord for us,

يُبَيِّن لَّنَا مَا لَوْنُهَا

that He may clarify for us what her colour may be.'

قَالَ إِنَّهُ يَقُولُ إِنَّهَا بَقَرَةٌ صَفْرَآءُ

He said, 'He says, She is a cow that is yellow,

فَاقِعٌ لَّوْنُهَا تَسُرُّ ٱلنَّٰظِرِينَ ۝

of a bright hue, pleasing to the onlookers.'

قَالُواْ ٱدْعُ لَنَا رَبَّكَ

70 They said, 'Invoke your Lord for us,

يُبَيِّن لَّنَا مَا هِىَ

that He may clarify for us what she may be.

إِنَّ ٱلْبَقَرَ تَشَٰبَهَ عَلَيْنَا

Indeed all cows are much alike to us,

وَإِنَّآ إِن شَآءَ ٱللَّهُ لَمُهْتَدُونَ ۝

and, if Allah wishes, we will surely be guided.'

قَالَ إِنَّهُ يَقُولُ إِنَّهَا بَقَرَةٌ

71 He said, 'He says, She is a cow

لَّا ذَلُولٌ تُثِيرُ ٱلْأَرْضَ

not broken to till the earth

وَلَا تَسْقِى ٱلْحَرْثَ

or to water the tillage,

مُسَلَّمَةٌ لَّا شِيَةَ فِيهَا

sound and without blemish.'

قَالُواْ ٱلْـَٰٔنَ جِئْتَ بِٱلْحَقِّ

They said, 'Now have you come up with the truth!'

فَذَبَحُوهَا

And they slaughtered it,

وَمَا كَادُواْ يَفْعَلُونَ ۝

though they were about not to do it.

وَإِذْ قَتَلْتُمْ نَفْسًا

72 And when you killed a soul,

| | |
|---|---|
| فَٱدَّٰرَٰءْتُمْ فِيهَا | and accused one another about it |
| وَٱللَّهُ مُخْرِجٌ | —and Allah was to expose |
| مَّا كُنتُمْ تَكْتُمُونَ ۞ | whatever you were concealing— |
| فَقُلْنَا ٱضْرِبُوهُ بِبَعْضِهَا | 73 We said, 'Strike him with a piece of it:' |
| كَذَٰلِكَ يُحْىِ ٱللَّهُ ٱلْمَوْتَىٰ | thus does Allah revive the dead, |
| وَيُرِيكُمْ ءَايَٰتِهِۦ | and He shows you His signs |
| لَعَلَّكُمْ تَعْقِلُونَ ۞ | so that you may apply reason. |
| ثُمَّ قَسَتْ قُلُوبُكُم مِّنۢ بَعْدِ ذَٰلِكَ | 74 Then your hearts hardened after that; |
| فَهِىَ كَٱلْحِجَارَةِ أَوْ أَشَدُّ قَسْوَةً | so they are like stones, or even harder. |
| وَإِنَّ مِنَ ٱلْحِجَارَةِ | For indeed there are some stones |
| لَمَا يَتَفَجَّرُ مِنْهُ ٱلْأَنْهَٰرُ | from which streams gush forth, |
| وَإِنَّ مِنْهَا لَمَا يَشَّقَّقُ | and indeed there are some of them that split, |
| فَيَخْرُجُ مِنْهُ ٱلْمَآءُ | and water issues from them, |
| وَإِنَّ مِنْهَا لَمَا يَهْبِطُ | and indeed there are some of them that fall |
| مِنْ خَشْيَةِ ٱللَّهِ | for the fear of Allah. |
| وَمَا ٱللَّهُ بِغَٰفِلٍ عَمَّا تَعْمَلُونَ ۞ ❖ | And Allah is not oblivious of what you do. |
| أَفَتَطْمَعُونَ | 75 Are you then eager |
| أَن يُؤْمِنُوا۟ لَكُمْ | that they should believe you,[1] |
| وَقَدْ كَانَ فَرِيقٌ مِّنْهُمْ | though a part of them |
| يَسْمَعُونَ كَلَٰمَ ٱللَّهِ | would hear the word of Allah |
| ثُمَّ يُحَرِّفُونَهُۥ | and then they would distort it[2] |
| مِنۢ بَعْدِ مَا عَقَلُوهُ | after they had understood it, |
| وَهُمْ يَعْلَمُونَ ۞ | and they knew [what they were doing]? |
| وَإِذَا لَقُوا۟ ٱلَّذِينَ ءَامَنُوا۟ | 76 When they meet the faithful, |
| قَالُوٓا۟ ءَامَنَّا | they say, 'We believe,' |
| وَإِذَا خَلَا بَعْضُهُمْ إِلَىٰ بَعْضٍ | and when they are alone with one another, |

---

[1] This is an address to the Muslims who were eager that the Jews should embrace Islam and follow the Prophet's teachings.

[2] Cf. 4:46; 5:13, 41, for this characteristic of the Jews.

قَالُوٓاْ أَتُحَدِّثُونَهُم    they say, 'Do you recount to them

بِمَا فَتَحَ ٱللَّهُ عَلَيۡكُمۡ    what Allah has revealed to you,

لِيُحَآجُّوكُم بِهِۦ    so that they may argue with you therewith

عِندَ رَبِّكُمۡ    before your Lord?

أَفَلَا تَعۡقِلُونَ ۝    Do you not apply reason?'

أَوَلَا يَعۡلَمُونَ أَنَّ ٱللَّهَ يَعۡلَمُ    77 Do they not know that Allah knows

مَا يُسِرُّونَ    whatever they hide

وَمَا يُعۡلِنُونَ ۝    and whatever they disclose?

وَمِنۡهُمۡ أُمِّيُّونَ    78 And among them are the illiterate

لَا يَعۡلَمُونَ ٱلۡكِتَٰبَ    who know nothing of the Book

إِلَّآ أَمَانِيَّ    except hearsay,[1]

وَإِنۡ هُمۡ إِلَّا يَظُنُّونَ ۝    and they only make conjectures.

فَوَيۡلٌ لِّلَّذِينَ يَكۡتُبُونَ ٱلۡكِتَٰبَ    79 So woe to those who write the Book

بِأَيۡدِيهِمۡ    with their hands

ثُمَّ يَقُولُونَ هَٰذَا مِنۡ عِندِ ٱللَّهِ    and then say, 'This is from Allah,'

لِيَشۡتَرُواْ بِهِۦ ثَمَنًا قَلِيلًا    that they may sell it for a paltry gain.

فَوَيۡلٌ لَّهُم مِّمَّا كَتَبَتۡ أَيۡدِيهِمۡ    So woe to them for what their hands have written,

وَوَيۡلٌ لَّهُم مِّمَّا يَكۡسِبُونَ ۝    and woe to them for what they earn!

وَقَالُواْ لَن تَمَسَّنَا ٱلنَّارُ    80 And they say, 'The Fire shall not touch us

إِلَّآ أَيَّامًا مَّعۡدُودَةً    except for a number of days.'

قُلۡ أَتَّخَذۡتُمۡ عِندَ ٱللَّهِ عَهۡدًا    *Say,* 'Have you taken a promise from Allah?

فَلَن يُخۡلِفَ ٱللَّهُ عَهۡدَهُۥ    If so, Allah shall never break His promise.

أَمۡ تَقُولُونَ عَلَى ٱللَّهِ    Or do you ascribe to Allah

مَا لَا تَعۡلَمُونَ ۝    what you do not know?'

بَلَىٰ مَن كَسَبَ سَيِّئَةً    81 Certainly whoever commits misdeeds

وَأَحَٰطَتۡ بِهِۦ خَطِيٓـَٔتُهُۥ    and is besieged by his iniquity

فَأُوْلَٰٓئِكَ أَصۡحَٰبُ ٱلنَّارِ    —such shall be the inmates of the Fire,

هُمۡ فِيهَا خَٰلِدُونَ ۝    and they shall remain in it [forever].

---

[1] That is, what they learnt through word of mouth from their scribes and priests, rather than from a direct knowledge of the scriptures. Or 'hopes,' or 'lies.'

وَٱلَّذِينَ ءَامَنُوا̇ 82 And those who have faith

وَعَمِلُوا̇ ٱلصَّٰلِحَٰتِ and do righteous deeds,

أُو۟لَٰٓئِكَ أَصْحَٰبُ ٱلْجَنَّةِ —they shall be the inhabitants of paradise;

هُمْ فِيهَا خَٰلِدُونَ ﴿٨٢﴾ they shall remain in it [forever].

وَإِذْ أَخَذْنَا مِيثَٰقَ 83 And when We took a pledge

بَنِىٓ إِسْرَٰٓءِيلَ from the Children of Israel:

لَا تَعْبُدُونَ إِلَّا ٱللَّهَ 'Worship no one but Allah,

وَبِٱلْوَٰلِدَيْنِ إِحْسَانًا do good to the parents,

وَذِى ٱلْقُرْبَىٰ وَٱلْيَتَٰمَىٰ the relatives, the orphans,

وَٱلْمَسَٰكِينِ and the needy,

وَقُولُوا̇ لِلنَّاسِ حُسْنًا and speak kindly to people,

وَأَقِيمُوا̇ ٱلصَّلَوٰةَ وَءَاتُوا̇ ٱلزَّكَوٰةَ and maintain the prayer, and give the *zakāt*,'

ثُمَّ تَوَلَّيْتُمْ إِلَّا قَلِيلًا مِّنكُمْ you turned away, except a few of you,

وَأَنتُم مُّعْرِضُونَ ﴿٨٣﴾ and you were disregardful.

وَإِذْ أَخَذْنَا مِيثَٰقَكُمْ 84 And when We took a pledge from you:

لَا تَسْفِكُونَ دِمَآءَكُمْ 'You shall not shed your [own people's] blood,

وَلَا تُخْرِجُونَ أَنفُسَكُم مِّن دِيَٰرِكُمْ and you shall not expel your folks from your homes,'

ثُمَّ أَقْرَرْتُمْ you pledged,

وَأَنتُمْ تَشْهَدُونَ ﴿٨٤﴾ and you testify[1] [to this pledge of your ancestors].

ثُمَّ أَنتُمْ هَٰٓؤُلَآءِ تَقْتُلُونَ أَنفُسَكُمْ 85 Then there you were, killing your folks

وَتُخْرِجُونَ فَرِيقًا مِّنكُم and expelling a part of your folks

مِّن دِيَٰرِهِمْ from their homes,

تَظَٰهَرُونَ عَلَيْهِم backing one another against them

بِٱلْإِثْمِ وَٱلْعُدْوَٰنِ in sin and aggression!

وَإِن يَأْتُوكُمْ أُسَٰرَىٰ And if they came to you as captives,

تُفَٰدُوهُمْ you would ransom them,

وَهُوَ مُحَرَّمٌ عَلَيْكُمْ إِخْرَاجُهُمْ though their expulsion itself was forbidden you.

أَفَتُؤْمِنُونَ بِبَعْضِ ٱلْكِتَٰبِ What! Do you believe in part of the Book

---

[1] Or 'and you testified.'

وَتَكْفُرُونَ بِبَعْضٍ    and defy another part?

فَمَا جَزَاءُ مَن يَفْعَلُ ذَٰلِكَ مِنكُمْ    So what is the requital of those of you who do that

إِلَّا خِزْيٌ فِي ٱلْحَيَوٰةِ ٱلدُّنْيَا    except disgrace in the life of this world?

وَيَوْمَ ٱلْقِيَٰمَةِ    And on the Day of Resurrection,

يُرَدُّونَ إِلَىٰ أَشَدِّ ٱلْعَذَابِ    they shall be consigned to a severer punishment.

وَمَا ٱللَّهُ بِغَٰفِلٍ عَمَّا تَعْمَلُونَ ۝    And Allah is not oblivious of what you do.

أُوْلَٰئِكَ ٱلَّذِينَ ٱشْتَرَوُا۟ ٱلْحَيَوٰةَ ٱلدُّنْيَا    86 They are the ones who bought the life of this world

بِٱلْأَخِرَةِ    for the Hereafter;

فَلَا يُخَفَّفُ عَنْهُمُ ٱلْعَذَابُ    so their punishment shall not be lightened,

وَلَا هُمْ يُنصَرُونَ ۝    nor will they be helped.

وَلَقَدْ ءَاتَيْنَا مُوسَى ٱلْكِتَٰبَ    87 Certainly We gave Moses the Book,

وَقَفَّيْنَا مِنۢ بَعْدِهِۦ بِٱلرُّسُلِ    and followed him with the apostles,

وَءَاتَيْنَا عِيسَى ٱبْنَ مَرْيَمَ    and We gave Jesus, the son of Mary,

ٱلْبَيِّنَٰتِ    manifest proofs,

وَأَيَّدْنَٰهُ بِرُوحِ ٱلْقُدُسِ    and confirmed him with the Holy Spirit.

أَفَكُلَّمَا جَآءَكُمْ رَسُولٌۢ    Is it not that whenever an apostle brought you[1]

بِمَا لَا تَهْوَىٰ أَنفُسُكُمُ    that which was not to your liking,

ٱسْتَكْبَرْتُمْ    you would act arrogantly;

فَفَرِيقًا كَذَّبْتُمْ    so you would impugn a part [of them],

وَفَرِيقًا تَقْتُلُونَ ۝    and slay a[nother] part?

وَقَالُوا۟    88 And they say,

قُلُوبُنَا غُلْفٌۢ    'Our hearts are uncircumcised.'[2]

بَل لَّعَنَهُمُ ٱللَّهُ بِكُفْرِهِمْ    Rather Allah has cursed them for their unfaith,

---

[1] That is, the Jews.

[2] Uncircumcised: unconverted, heathen, faithless; cf. 4:155. In Leviticus 26.41, it is said of the Israelites, '. . . then when their uncircumcised hearts are humbled and they pay for their sin, I will remember my covenant with Jacob. . . ,' and in Jeremiah 9.26: '. . . even the whole house of Israel is uncircumcised in heart . . .' There are other similar expressions and phrases in the Bible: "uncircumcised lips" (Exodus 6.12 and 6.30); "their ear is uncircumcised and they cannot hearken" (Jeremiah 6.10); "uncircumcised in heart, and uncircumcised in flesh" (Ezekiel 44.7, 9); "uncircumcised in heart and ears" (Acts 7.51), "putting off the body of the sins of the flesh by the circumcision of Christ" (Colossians 2.11).

فَقَلِيلًا مَّا يُؤْمِنُونَ ۝

so few of them have faith.

وَلَمَّا جَاءَهُمْ كِتَبٌ مِّنْ عِندِ ٱللَّهِ

89 And when there came to them a Book from Allah,

مُصَدِّقٌ لِّمَا مَعَهُمْ

confirming that which is with them

وَكَانُوا مِن قَبْلُ يَسْتَفْتِحُونَ

—and earlier they would pray for victory

عَلَى ٱلَّذِينَ كَفَرُوا

over the pagans—

فَلَمَّا جَاءَهُم مَّا عَرَفُوا

so when there came to them what they recognized,

كَفَرُوا بِهِۦ

they defied it.

فَلَعْنَةُ ٱللَّهِ عَلَى ٱلْكَفِرِينَ ۝

So may the curse of Allah be on the faithless!

بِئْسَمَا ٱشْتَرَوْا بِهِۦ أَنفُسَهُمْ

90 Evil is that for which they have sold their souls,

أَن يَكْفُرُوا بِمَا أَنزَلَ ٱللَّهُ

by defying what Allah has sent down,

بَغْيًا

out of envy,

أَن يُنَزِّلَ ٱللَّهُ مِن فَضْلِهِۦ

that Allah should bestow His grace

عَلَىٰ مَن يَشَاءُ مِنْ عِبَادِهِۦ

on any of His servants whom He wishes.

فَبَآءُو بِغَضَبٍ عَلَىٰ غَضَبٍ

Thus they earned wrath upon wrath,

وَلِلْكَفِرِينَ عَذَابٌ مُّهِينٌ ۝

and there is a humiliating punishment for the faithless.

وَإِذَا قِيلَ لَهُمْ

91 And when they are told,

ءَامِنُوا بِمَا أَنزَلَ ٱللَّهُ

'Believe in what Allah has sent down,'

قَالُوا

they say,

نُؤْمِنُ بِمَا أُنزِلَ عَلَيْنَا

'We believe in what was sent down to us,'

وَيَكْفُرُونَ بِمَا وَرَآءَهُۥ

and they disbelieve what is besides it,

وَهُوَ ٱلْحَقُّ

though it is the truth

مُصَدِّقًا لِّمَا مَعَهُمْ

confirming what is with them.

قُلْ فَلِمَ تَقْتُلُونَ

Say, 'Then why would you kill

أَنۢبِيَآءَ ٱللَّهِ مِن قَبْلُ

the prophets of Allah formerly,

إِن كُنتُم مُّؤْمِنِينَ ۝ ❀

should you be faithful?'

وَلَقَدْ جَاءَكُم مُّوسَىٰ بِٱلْبَيِّنَتِ

92 Certainly Moses brought you manifest proofs,

ثُمَّ ٱتَّخَذْتُمُ ٱلْعِجْلَ مِنۢ بَعْدِهِۦ

but then you took up the Calf in his absence,

وَأَنتُمْ ظَلِمُونَ ۝

and you were wrongdoers.

وَإِذْ أَخَذْنَا مِيثَقَكُمْ

93 And when We took covenant with you

وَرَفَعْنَا فَوْقَكُمُ ٱلطُّورَ

and raised the Mount above you [declaring],

19

خُذُواْ مَا ءَاتَيْنَـٰكُم بِقُوَّةٍ 'Hold on with power to what We have given you,

وَٱسْمَعُواْ and listen!'

قَالُواْ سَمِعْنَا وَعَصَيْنَا They said, 'We hear, and disobey,'

وَأُشْرِبُواْ فِى قُلُوبِهِمُ and their hearts had been imbued

ٱلْعِجْلَ with [the love of] the Calf,

بِكُفْرِهِمْ due to their faithlessness.

قُلْ بِئْسَمَا يَأْمُرُكُم بِهِۦٓ إِيمَـٰنُكُمْ *Say*, 'Evil is that to which your faith prompts you,

إِن كُنتُم مُّؤْمِنِينَ should you be faithful!'

قُلْ إِن كَانَتْ لَكُمُ ٱلدَّارُ ٱلْأَخِرَةُ 94 *Say*, 'If the abode of the Hereafter

عِندَ ٱللَّهِ خَالِصَةً with Allah were exclusively for you,

مِّن دُونِ ٱلنَّاسِ and not for other people,

فَتَمَنَّوُاْ ٱلْمَوْتَ then long for death,

إِن كُنتُمْ صَـٰدِقِينَ should you be truthful.'

وَلَن يَتَمَنَّوْهُ أَبَدًۢا 95 But they will not long for it ever

بِمَا قَدَّمَتْ أَيْدِيهِمْ because of what their hands have sent ahead,[1]

وَٱللَّهُ عَلِيمٌۢ بِٱلظَّـٰلِمِينَ and Allah knows best the wrongdoers.

وَلَتَجِدَنَّهُمْ 96 Surely, *you* will find them

أَحْرَصَ ٱلنَّاسِ عَلَىٰ حَيَوٰةٍ the greediest for life, of all people

وَمِنَ ٱلَّذِينَ أَشْرَكُواْ —even the idolaters.

يَوَدُّ أَحَدُهُمْ لَوْ يُعَمَّرُ أَلْفَ سَنَةٍ Each of them is eager to live a thousand years,

وَمَا هُوَ بِمُزَحْزِحِهِ though it would not deliver him

مِنَ ٱلْعَذَابِ from the punishment,

أَن يُعَمَّرَ were he to live [that long].

وَٱللَّهُ بَصِيرٌۢ بِمَا يَعْمَلُونَ And Allah sees best what they do.

قُلْ 97 *Say*,

مَن كَانَ عَدُوًّا لِّجِبْرِيلَ 'Whoever is an enemy of Gabriel [should know that]

فَإِنَّهُۥ نَزَّلَهُۥ عَلَىٰ قَلْبِكَ it is he who has brought it down on *your* heart

بِإِذْنِ ٱللَّهِ with the will of Allah,

---

[1] That is, to the scene of judgement and retribution on the Day of Resurrection. Or 'prepared,' 'made ready,' or 'committed,' 'perpetrated.'

مُصَدِّقًا لِّمَا بَيْنَ يَدَيْهِ

confirming what has been [revealed] before it,

وَهُدًى وَبُشْرَىٰ لِلْمُؤْمِنِينَ ۝

and as a guidance and good news to the faithful.'

98 مَن كَانَ عَدُوًّا لِلَّهِ

[Say,] 'Whoever is an enemy of Allah,

وَمَلَٰٓئِكَتِهِۦ وَرُسُلِهِۦ

His angels and His apostles,

وَجِبْرِيلَ وَمِيكَىٰلَ

and Gabriel and Michael, [let him know that]

فَإِنَّ ٱللَّهَ عَدُوٌّ لِّلْكَٰفِرِينَ ۝

Allah is indeed the enemy of the faithless.'

وَلَقَدْ أَنزَلْنَآ إِلَيْكَ ءَايَٰتٍۭ بَيِّنَٰتٍ

99 We have certainly sent down manifest signs to *you*,

وَمَا يَكْفُرُ بِهَآ إِلَّا ٱلْفَٰسِقُونَ ۝

and no one defies them except transgressors.

أَوَكُلَّمَا عَٰهَدُوا۟ عَهْدًا

100 Is it not that whenever they made a covenant,

نَّبَذَهُۥ فَرِيقٌ مِّنْهُم

a part of them would cast it away?

بَلْ أَكْثَرُهُمْ لَا يُؤْمِنُونَ ۝

Rather the majority of them do not have faith.

وَلَمَّا جَآءَهُمْ

101 And when there came to them

رَسُولٌ مِّنْ عِندِ ٱللَّهِ

an apostle from Allah,

مُصَدِّقٌ لِّمَا مَعَهُمْ

confirming that which is with them,

نَبَذَ فَرِيقٌ مِّنَ ٱلَّذِينَ أُوتُوا۟ ٱلْكِتَٰبَ

a part of those who were given the Book cast

كِتَٰبَ ٱللَّهِ وَرَآءَ ظُهُورِهِمْ

the Book of Allah behind their back,

كَأَنَّهُمْ لَا يَعْلَمُونَ ۝

as if they did not know [that it is Allah's Book].

102 وَٱتَّبَعُوا۟ مَا تَتْلُوا۟ ٱلشَّيَٰطِينُ

And they followed what the devils pursued

عَلَىٰ مُلْكِ سُلَيْمَٰنَ

during Solomon's reign[1]

وَمَا كَفَرَ سُلَيْمَٰنُ

—and Solomon did not turn faithless,

وَلَٰكِنَّ ٱلشَّيَٰطِينَ كَفَرُوا۟

but it were the devils who were faithless—

يُعَلِّمُونَ ٱلنَّاسَ ٱلسِّحْرَ

teaching the people magic,

وَمَآ أُنزِلَ عَلَى ٱلْمَلَكَيْنِ

and what was sent down to the two angels

بِبَابِلَ

at Babylon,

هَٰرُوتَ وَمَٰرُوتَ

Hārūt and Mārūt,

وَمَا يُعَلِّمَانِ مِنْ أَحَدٍ

and they would not teach anyone

---

[1] Or 'they followed what the devils recited during Solomon's reign.' Or 'they followed the lies the devils uttered against Solomon's reign.'

حَتَّىٰ يَقُولَا    without telling [him],

إِنَّمَا نَحْنُ فِتْنَةٌ فَلَا تَكْفُرْ    'We are only a test,[1] so do not be faithless.'

فَيَتَعَلَّمُونَ مِنْهُمَا    But they would learn from those two

مَا يُفَرِّقُونَ بِهِۦ    that with which they would cause a split

بَيْنَ ٱلْمَرْءِ وَزَوْجِهِۦ    between man and his wife

وَمَا هُم بِضَآرِّينَ بِهِۦ مِنْ أَحَدٍ    —though they could not harm anyone with it

إِلَّا بِإِذْنِ ٱللَّهِ    except with Allah's leave.

وَيَتَعَلَّمُونَ مَا يَضُرُّهُمْ    And they would learn that which would harm them

وَلَا يَنفَعُهُمْ    and bring them no benefit;

وَلَقَدْ عَلِمُوا۟ لَمَنِ ٱشْتَرَىٰهُ    though they certainly knew that anyone who buys it

مَا لَهُۥ فِى ٱلْآخِرَةِ مِنْ خَلَٰقٍ    has no share in the Hereafter.

وَلَبِئْسَ مَا شَرَوْا۟ بِهِۦٓ أَنفُسَهُمْ    Surely, evil is that for which they sold their souls;

لَوْ كَانُوا۟ يَعْلَمُونَ ۝    had they known!

وَلَوْ أَنَّهُمْ ءَامَنُوا۟ وَٱتَّقَوْا۟    103 Had they been faithful and Godwary,

لَمَثُوبَةٌ مِّنْ عِندِ ٱللَّهِ خَيْرٌ    the reward from Allah would have been better;

لَّوْ كَانُوا۟ يَعْلَمُونَ ۝    had they known!

يَٰٓأَيُّهَا ٱلَّذِينَ ءَامَنُوا۟    104 O you who have faith!

لَا تَقُولُوا۟ رَٰعِنَا وَقُولُوا۟ ٱنظُرْنَا    Do not say *Rā'inā*, but say *Unẓurnā*,

وَٱسْمَعُوا۟    and listen![2]

وَلِلْكَٰفِرِينَ عَذَابٌ أَلِيمٌ ۝    And there is a painful punishment for the faithless.

مَّا يَوَدُّ ٱلَّذِينَ كَفَرُوا۟    105 Neither the faithless

مِنْ أَهْلِ ٱلْكِتَٰبِ    from among the People of the Book,

وَلَا ٱلْمُشْرِكِينَ    nor the idolaters,

أَن يُنَزَّلَ عَلَيْكُم مِّنْ خَيْرٍ    like that any good be showered on you

---

[1] Or 'temptation.'

[2] The Jews in ridiculing the Prophet would say *rā'inā* [meaning, 'have regard for us'] with a change of accent turning it into another word which made it a term of reproach. The Muslims are told to say *unẓurnā* [meaning, 'give us a little respite'] instead while addressing the Prophet [ṣ], as there is no room in this term for such a distortion.

مِن رَّبِّكُمْ
from your Lord;

وَٱللَّهُ يَخْتَصُّ بِرَحْمَتِهِ
but Allah singles out for His mercy

مَن يَشَآءُ
whomever He wishes,

وَٱللَّهُ ذُو ٱلْفَضْلِ ٱلْعَظِيمِ ۝
and Allah is dispenser of a mighty grace.

مَا نَنسَخْ مِنْ ءَايَةٍ 106
For any verse that We abrogate

أَوْ نُنسِهَا
or remove from memories,

نَأْتِ بِخَيْرٍ مِّنْهَآ
We bring another which is better than it,

أَوْ مِثْلِهَآ
or similar to it.

أَلَمْ تَعْلَمْ أَنَّ ٱللَّهَ
Do you not know that Allah

عَلَىٰ كُلِّ شَىْءٍ قَدِيرٌ ۝
has power over all things?

أَلَمْ تَعْلَمْ أَنَّ ٱللَّهَ لَهُ 107
Do you not know that to Allah belongs

مُلْكُ ٱلسَّمَٰوَٰتِ وَٱلْأَرْضِ
the kingdom of the heavens and the earth?

وَمَا لَكُم مِّن دُونِ ٱللَّهِ
And besides Allah you do not have

مِن وَلِيٍّ وَلَا نَصِيرٍ ۝
any guardian or any helper.

أَمْ تُرِيدُونَ أَن تَسْـَٔلُوا۟ رَسُولَكُمْ 108
Would you question your Apostle

كَمَا سُئِلَ مُوسَىٰ مِن قَبْلُ
as Moses was questioned formerly?

وَمَن يَتَبَدَّلِ ٱلْكُفْرَ بِٱلْإِيمَٰنِ
Whoever changes faith for unfaith

فَقَدْ ضَلَّ سَوَآءَ ٱلسَّبِيلِ ۝
certainly strays from the right way.

وَدَّ كَثِيرٌ مِّنْ أَهْلِ ٱلْكِتَٰبِ 109
Many of the People of the Book are eager

لَوْ يَرُدُّونَكُم مِّنۢ بَعْدِ إِيمَٰنِكُمْ كُفَّارًا
to turn you into unbelievers after your faith,

حَسَدًا مِّنْ عِندِ أَنفُسِهِم
out of their inner envy,

مِّنۢ بَعْدِ مَا تَبَيَّنَ لَهُمُ ٱلْحَقُّ
[and] after the truth had become manifest to them.

فَٱعْفُوا۟ وَٱصْفَحُوا۟
Yet excuse [them] and forbear

حَتَّىٰ يَأْتِىَ ٱللَّهُ بِأَمْرِهِ
until Allah issues His edict.

إِنَّ ٱللَّهَ عَلَىٰ كُلِّ شَىْءٍ قَدِيرٌ ۝
Indeed Allah has power over all things.

وَأَقِيمُوا۟ ٱلصَّلَوٰةَ وَءَاتُوا۟ ٱلزَّكَوٰةَ 110
And maintain the prayer and give the *zakāt*.

وَمَا تُقَدِّمُوا۟ لِأَنفُسِكُم مِّنْ خَيْرٍ
Any good that you send ahead for your souls,

23

تَجِدُوهُ عِندَ ٱللَّهِ

you shall find it with Allah.

إِنَّ ٱللَّهَ بِمَا تَعْمَلُونَ بَصِيرٌ ۝

Indeed Allah sees best what you do.

وَقَالُواْ لَن يَدْخُلَ ٱلْجَنَّةَ

111 And they say, 'No one shall enter paradise

إِلَّا مَن كَانَ هُودًا أَوْ نَصَرَىٰ

except one who is a Jew or a Christian.'

تِلْكَ أَمَانِيُّهُمْ

Those are their [false] hopes!

قُلْ هَاتُواْ بُرْهَٰنَكُمْ

Say, 'Produce your evidence,

إِن كُنتُمْ صَٰدِقِينَ ۝

should you be truthful.'

بَلَىٰ مَنْ أَسْلَمَ وَجْهَهُ لِلَّهِ
وَهُوَ مُحْسِنٌ

112 Certainly whoever submits his will to Allah
and is virtuous,

فَلَهُۥٓ أَجْرُهُۥ عِندَ رَبِّهِۦ

he shall have his reward near his Lord,

وَلَا خَوْفٌ عَلَيْهِمْ

and they shall have no fear,

وَلَا هُمْ يَحْزَنُونَ ۝

nor shall they grieve.

وَقَالَتِ ٱلْيَهُودُ

113 The Jews say,

لَيْسَتِ ٱلنَّصَرَىٰ عَلَىٰ شَىْءٍ

'The Christians stand on nothing,'

وَقَالَتِ ٱلنَّصَرَىٰ

and the Christians say,

لَيْسَتِ ٱلْيَهُودُ عَلَىٰ شَىْءٍ

'The Jews stand on nothing,'

وَهُمْ يَتْلُونَ ٱلْكِتَٰبَ

though they follow the [same] Book.

كَذَٰلِكَ قَالَ ٱلَّذِينَ لَا يَعْلَمُونَ

So said those who had no knowledge,

مِثْلَ قَوْلِهِمْ

[words] similar to what they say.

فَٱللَّهُ يَحْكُمُ بَيْنَهُمْ

Allah will judge between them

يَوْمَ ٱلْقِيَٰمَةِ

on the Day of Resurrection

فِيمَا كَانُواْ فِيهِ يَخْتَلِفُونَ ۝

concerning that about which they used to differ.

وَمَنْ أَظْلَمُ مِمَّن

114 Who is a greater wrongdoer than him who

مَّنَعَ مَسَٰجِدَ ٱللَّهِ

denies access to the mosques of Allah

أَن يُذْكَرَ فِيهَا ٱسْمُهُ

lest His Name be celebrated therein,

وَسَعَىٰ فِى خَرَابِهَآ

and tries to ruin them?

أُوْلَٰٓئِكَ مَا كَانَ لَهُمْ أَن يَدْخُلُوهَآ

Such ones may not enter them,

24

| | |
|---|---|
| إِلَّا خَآئِفِينَ | except in fear. |
| لَهُمْ فِى ٱلدُّنْيَا خِزْىٌ | There is disgrace for them in this world, |
| وَلَهُمْ | and there is for them |
| فِى ٱلْأَخِرَةِ عَذَابٌ عَظِيمٌ | a great punishment in the Hereafter. |

| | | |
|---|---|---|
| وَلِلَّهِ ٱلْمَشْرِقُ وَٱلْمَغْرِبُ | 115 | To Allah belong the east and the west: |
| فَأَيْنَمَا تُوَلُّواْ | | so whichever way you turn, |
| فَثَمَّ وَجْهُ ٱللَّهِ | | there is the face of Allah! |
| إِنَّ ٱللَّهَ وَٰسِعٌ عَلِيمٌ | | Allah is indeed all-bounteous, all-knowing. |
| وَقَالُواْ ٱتَّخَذَ ٱللَّهُ وَلَدًا | 116 | And they say, 'Allah has taken a son.' |
| سُبْحَٰنَهُ | | Immaculate is He! |
| بَل لَّهُ مَا فِى ٱلسَّمَٰوَٰتِ | | Rather to Him belongs whatever is in the heavens |
| وَٱلْأَرْضِ | | and the earth. |
| كُلٌّ لَّهُ قَٰنِتُونَ | | All are obedient to Him, |
| بَدِيعُ ٱلسَّمَٰوَٰتِ وَٱلْأَرْضِ | 117 | the Originator of the heavens and the earth; |
| وَإِذَا قَضَىٰ أَمْرًا | | and when He decides on a matter, |
| فَإِنَّمَا يَقُولُ لَهُ كُن فَيَكُونُ | | He just says to it, 'Be!' and it is. |
| وَقَالَ ٱلَّذِينَ لَا يَعْلَمُونَ | 118 | Those who have no knowledge say, |
| لَوْلَا يُكَلِّمُنَا ٱللَّهُ | | 'Why does not Allah speak to us, |
| أَوْ تَأْتِينَآ ءَايَةٌ | | or come to us a sign?' |
| كَذَٰلِكَ قَالَ ٱلَّذِينَ مِن قَبْلِهِم | | So said those who were before them, |
| مِّثْلَ قَوْلِهِمْ | | [words] similar to what they say. |
| تَشَٰبَهَتْ قُلُوبُهُمْ | | Alike are their hearts. |
| قَدْ بَيَّنَّا ٱلْأَيَٰتِ | | We have certainly made the signs clear |
| لِقَوْمٍ يُوقِنُونَ | | for a people who have certainty. |

| | | |
|---|---|---|
| إِنَّآ أَرْسَلْنَٰكَ بِٱلْحَقِّ | 119 | Indeed We have sent you with the truth, |
| بَشِيرًا وَنَذِيرًا | | as a bearer of good news and as a warner, |
| وَلَا تُسْـَٔلُ | | and you will not be questioned |
| عَنْ أَصْحَٰبِ ٱلْجَحِيمِ | | concerning the inmates of hell. |

وَلَن تَرْضَىٰ عَنكَ ٱلْيَهُودُ    120 Never will the Jews be pleased with *you*,

وَلَا ٱلنَّصَرَىٰ    nor the Christians,

حَتَّىٰ تَتَّبِعَ مِلَّتَهُمْ    unless *you* followed their creed.

قُلْ إِنَّ هُدَى ٱللَّهِ    *Say*, 'Indeed it is the guidance of Allah

هُوَ ٱلْهُدَىٰ    which is the [true] guidance.'

وَلَئِنِ ٱتَّبَعْتَ أَهْوَآءَهُم    And should *you* follow their desires

بَعْدَ ٱلَّذِى جَآءَكَ مِنَ ٱلْعِلْمِ    after the knowledge that has come to *you*,

مَا لَكَ مِنَ ٱللَّهِ    *you* will not have against Allah

مِن وَلِيٍّ وَلَا نَصِيرٍ ۝    any guardian nor any helper.

ٱلَّذِينَ ءَاتَيْنَٰهُمُ ٱلْكِتَٰبَ    121 Those to whom We have given the Book

يَتْلُونَهُ حَقَّ تِلَاوَتِهِ    follow it as it ought to be followed:

أُوْلَٰئِكَ يُؤْمِنُونَ بِهِ    they have faith in it.

وَمَن يَكْفُرْ بِهِ    As for those who defy it

فَأُوْلَٰئِكَ هُمُ ٱلْخَٰسِرُونَ ۝    —it is they who are the losers.

يَٰبَنِىٓ إِسْرَٰٓءِيلَ    122 O Children of Israel,

ٱذْكُرُواْ نِعْمَتِىَ ٱلَّتِىٓ أَنْعَمْتُ عَلَيْكُمْ    remember My blessing which I bestowed upon you,

وَأَنِّى فَضَّلْتُكُمْ عَلَى ٱلْعَٰلَمِينَ ۝    and that I gave you an advantage over all the nations.

وَٱتَّقُواْ يَوْمًا    123 And beware of the Day

لَّا تَجْزِى نَفْسٌ عَن نَّفْسٍ شَيْئًا    when no soul shall compensate for another,

وَلَا يُقْبَلُ مِنْهَا عَدْلٌ    neither shall any ransom be accepted from it,

وَلَا تَنفَعُهَا شَفَٰعَةٌ    nor shall any intercession benefit it,

وَلَا هُمْ يُنصَرُونَ ۝ ✳    nor will they be helped.

وَإِذِ ٱبْتَلَىٰٓ إِبْرَٰهِـۧمَ رَبُّهُۥ    124 And when his Lord tested Abraham

بِكَلِمَٰتٍ    with certain words,

فَأَتَمَّهُنَّ    and he fulfilled them,

قَالَ إِنِّى جَاعِلُكَ لِلنَّاسِ إِمَامًا    He said, 'I am making you the *Imam*[1] of mankind.'

---

[1] That is, the spiritual and temporal guide and leader of mankind. For other Qur'ānic occurrences of this term, see 17:71; 25:74; 28:5; 32:24; 36:12.

قَالَ وَمِن ذُرِّيَّتِى      Said he, 'And from among my descendants?'

قَالَ لَا يَنَالُ عَهْدِى ٱلظَّـٰلِمِينَ ۞      He said, 'My pledge does not extend to the unjust.'

وَإِذْ جَعَلْنَا ٱلْبَيْتَ      125 And [remember] when We made the House

مَثَابَةً لِّلنَّاسِ      a place of reward[1] for mankind

وَأَمْنًا      and a sanctuary, [declaring],

وَٱتَّخِذُواْ مِن مَّقَامِ إِبْرَٰهِـۧمَ مُصَلًّى      'Take the venue of prayer from Abraham's Station.'[2]

وَعَهِدْنَآ إِلَىٰٓ إِبْرَٰهِـۧمَ وَإِسْمَـٰعِيلَ      We charged Abraham and Ishmael

أَن طَهِّرَا بَيْتِىَ      [with its upkeep, saying], 'Purify My House

لِلطَّآئِفِينَ      for those who go around it,

وَٱلْعَـٰكِفِينَ      for those who make it a retreat

وَٱلرُّكَّعِ ٱلسُّجُودِ ۞      and for those who bow and prostrate.

وَإِذْ قَالَ إِبْرَٰهِـۧمُ      126 And when Abraham said,

رَبِّ ٱجْعَلْ هَـٰذَا بَلَدًا ءَامِنًا      'My Lord, make this a secure town,

وَٱرْزُقْ أَهْلَهُ مِنَ ٱلثَّمَرَٰتِ      and provide its people with fruits

مَنْ ءَامَنَ مِنْهُم بِٱللَّهِ      —such of them as have faith in Allah

وَٱلْيَوْمِ ٱلْأَخِرِ      and the Last Day,'

قَالَ وَمَن كَفَرَ      He said, 'As for him who is faithless,

فَأُمَتِّعُهُ قَلِيلًا      I will provide for him [too] for a short time,

ثُمَّ أَضْطَرُّهُ      then I will shove him

إِلَىٰ عَذَابِ ٱلنَّارِ      toward the punishment of the Fire,

وَبِئْسَ ٱلْمَصِيرُ ۞      and it is an evil destination.'

وَإِذْ يَرْفَعُ إِبْرَٰهِـۧمُ ٱلْقَوَاعِدَ مِنَ ٱلْبَيْتِ      127 As Abraham raised the foundations of the House

وَإِسْمَـٰعِيلُ      with Ishmael, [they prayed]:

رَبَّنَا تَقَبَّلْ مِنَّآ      'Our Lord, accept it from us!

إِنَّكَ أَنتَ ٱلسَّمِيعُ ٱلْعَلِيمُ ۞      Indeed You are the All-hearing, the All-knowing.

رَبَّنَا وَٱجْعَلْنَا مُسْلِمَيْنِ لَكَ      128 'Our Lord, make us submissive to You,

---

[1] Or 'confluence,' or 'resort,' depending on whether the term *mathābah* is taken to mean a place of spiritual reward, a place of gathering, or a place to which one frequently returns.

[2] Abraham's Station (*maqām Ibrāhīm*) is a spot at a few meters' distance from the Ka'bah where a stone relic is kept that bears the footprint of Abraham, behind which the pilgrims offer the prayer of the *ṭawāf*.

وَمِن ذُرِّيَّتِنَآ     and [raise] from our progeny

أُمَّةً مُّسْلِمَةً لَّكَ     a nation submissive to You,

وَأَرِنَا مَنَاسِكَنَا     and show us our rites [of worship],

وَتُبْ عَلَيْنَآ     and turn to us clemently.

إِنَّكَ أَنتَ ٱلتَّوَّابُ ٱلرَّحِيمُ ١٢٨     Indeed You are the All-clement, the All-merciful.

رَبَّنَا وَٱبْعَثْ فِيهِمْ     129 'Our Lord, raise amongst them

رَسُولاً مِّنْهُمْ     an apostle from among them,

يَتْلُوا عَلَيْهِمْ ءَايَٰتِكَ     who should recite to them Your signs,

وَيُعَلِّمُهُمُ ٱلْكِتَٰبَ وَٱلْحِكْمَةَ     and teach them the Book and wisdom,

وَيُزَكِّيهِمْ     and purify them.

إِنَّكَ أَنتَ ٱلْعَزِيزُ ٱلْحَكِيمُ ١٢٩     Indeed You are the All-mighty, the All-wise.'

وَمَن يَرْغَبُ عَن مِّلَّةِ إِبْرَٰهِـۧمَ     130 And who will [ever] renounce Abraham's creed

إِلَّا مَن سَفِهَ نَفْسَهُۥ     except one who fools himself?

وَلَقَدِ ٱصْطَفَيْنَٰهُ فِى ٱلدُّنْيَا     We certainly chose him in the [present] world,

وَإِنَّهُۥ فِى ٱلْءَاخِرَةِ     and in the Hereafter he will indeed be

لَمِنَ ٱلصَّٰلِحِينَ ١٣٠     among the Righteous.[1]

إِذْ قَالَ لَهُۥ رَبُّهُۥٓ أَسْلِمْ     131 When his Lord said to him, 'Submit,'

قَالَ أَسْلَمْتُ لِرَبِّ ٱلْعَٰلَمِينَ ١٣١     he said, 'I submit to the Lord of all the worlds.'

وَوَصَّىٰ بِهَآ إِبْرَٰهِـۧمُ بَنِيهِ     132 Abraham enjoined this [creed] upon his children,

وَيَعْقُوبُ     and [so did] Jacob, [saying],

يَٰبَنِىَّ     'My children!

إِنَّ ٱللَّهَ ٱصْطَفَىٰ لَكُمُ ٱلدِّينَ     Allah has indeed chosen this religion for you;

فَلَا تَمُوتُنَّ إِلَّا وَأَنتُم مُّسْلِمُونَ ١٣٢     so never die except as *muslims*.'

أَمْ كُنتُمْ شُهَدَآءَ     133 Were you witnesses

إِذْ حَضَرَ يَعْقُوبَ ٱلْمَوْتُ     when death approached Jacob,

إِذْ قَالَ لِبَنِيهِ     when he said to his children,

مَا تَعْبُدُونَ مِنْ بَعْدِى     'What will you worship after me?'

---

[1] The station of 'the Righteous' referred to in this verse is one which even Abraham will attain in the Hereafter. Cf. 16:122. Otherwise all prophets are, of course, righteous; see 3:39, 46; 6:85; 21:75, 84; 37:112.

قَالُوا۟ نَعْبُدُ إِلَـٰهَكَ They said, 'We will worship your God,

وَإِلَـٰهَ ءَابَآئِكَ and the God of your fathers,

إِبْرَٰهِـۧمَ وَإِسْمَـٰعِيلَ وَإِسْحَـٰقَ Abraham, Ishmael, and Isaac,

إِلَـٰهًا وَٰحِدًا وَنَحْنُ لَهُۥ مُسْلِمُونَ ۞ the One God, and to Him do we submit.'

تِلْكَ أُمَّةٌ قَدْ خَلَتْ 134 That was a nation that has passed:

لَهَا مَا كَسَبَتْ for it there will be what it has earned,

وَلَكُم مَّا كَسَبْتُمْ and for you there will be what you have earned,

وَلَا تُسْـَٔلُونَ and you will not be questioned

عَمَّا كَانُوا۟ يَعْمَلُونَ ۞ about what they used to do.

وَقَالُوا۟ كُونُوا۟ هُودًا أَوْ نَصَـٰرَىٰ 135 And they say, 'Be either Jews or Christians,

تَهْتَدُوا۟ that you may be [rightly] guided.'

قُلْ بَلْ مِلَّةَ إِبْرَٰهِـۧمَ Say, 'Rather [we will follow] the creed of Abraham,

حَنِيفًا a *hanīf*,

وَمَا كَانَ مِنَ ٱلْمُشْرِكِينَ ۞ and he was not one of the polytheists.'

قُولُوٓا۟ ءَامَنَّا بِٱللَّهِ 136 Say, 'We have faith in Allah,

وَمَآ أُنزِلَ إِلَيْنَا and that which has been sent down to us,

وَمَآ أُنزِلَ إِلَىٰٓ إِبْرَٰهِـۧمَ and that which was sent down to Abraham,

وَإِسْمَـٰعِيلَ وَإِسْحَـٰقَ وَيَعْقُوبَ Ishmael, Isaac, Jacob

وَٱلْأَسْبَاطِ and the Tribes,[1]

وَمَآ أُوتِىَ مُوسَىٰ وَعِيسَىٰ and that which Moses and Jesus were given,

وَمَآ أُوتِىَ ٱلنَّبِيُّونَ and that which the prophets were given

مِن رَّبِّهِمْ from their Lord;

لَا نُفَرِّقُ بَيْنَ أَحَدٍ مِّنْهُمْ we make no distinction between any of them,

وَنَحْنُ لَهُۥ مُسْلِمُونَ ۞ and to Him do we submit.'

فَإِنْ ءَامَنُوا۟ بِمِثْلِ مَآ ءَامَنتُم بِهِۦ 137 So if they believe in the like of what you believe in,

فَقَدِ ٱهْتَدَوا۟ then they are certainly guided;

---

[1] That is, the twelve tribes of the Israelites, who received the revelations through the prophets that were sent to them. Cf. 2:140; 3:84; 4:163; 7:160.

29

وَّإِن تَوَلَّوْاْ    and if they turn away,

فَإِنَّمَا هُمْ فِى شِقَاقٍ    then they are only [steeped] in defiance.

فَسَيَكْفِيكَهُمُ ٱللَّهُ    Allah shall suffice *you* against them,

وَهُوَ ٱلسَّمِيعُ ٱلْعَلِيمُ ۝    and He is the All-hearing, the All-knowing.

صِبْغَةَ ٱللَّهِ    138    The baptism of Allah,

وَمَنْ أَحْسَنُ مِنَ ٱللَّهِ صِبْغَةً    and who baptizes better than Allah?

وَنَحْنُ لَهُۥ عَٰبِدُونَ ۝    And Him do we worship.'

قُلْ أَتُحَآجُّونَنَا فِى ٱللَّهِ    139    *Say,* 'Will you argue with us concerning Allah,

وَهُوَ رَبُّنَا وَرَبُّكُمْ    while He is our Lord and your Lord,

وَلَنَآ أَعْمَٰلُنَا    and our deeds belong to us,

وَلَكُمْ أَعْمَٰلُكُمْ    and your deeds belong to you,

وَنَحْنُ لَهُۥ مُخْلِصُونَ ۝    and we worship Him dedicatedly?'

أَمْ تَقُولُونَ إِنَّ إِبْرَٰهِـۧمَ    140    Do you say that Abraham,

وَإِسْمَٰعِيلَ وَإِسْحَٰقَ وَيَعْقُوبَ    Ishmael, Isaac, Jacob,

وَٱلْأَسْبَاطَ    and the Tribes

كَانُواْ هُودًا أَوْ نَصَٰرَىٰ    were Jews or Christians?

قُلْ ءَأَنتُمْ أَعْلَمُ أَمِ ٱللَّهُ    *Say,* 'Is it you who know better, or Allah?'

وَمَنْ أَظْلَمُ مِمَّن    And who is a greater wrongdoer than him who

كَتَمَ شَهَٰدَةً    conceals a testimony

عِندَهُۥ مِنَ ٱللَّهِ    that is with him from Allah?

وَمَا ٱللَّهُ بِغَٰفِلٍ عَمَّا تَعْمَلُونَ ۝    And Allah is not oblivious of what you do.

تِلْكَ أُمَّةٌ قَدْ خَلَتْ    141    That was a nation that has passed:

لَهَا مَا كَسَبَتْ    for it there will be what it has earned,

وَلَكُم مَّا كَسَبْتُمْ    and for you there will be what you have earned,

وَلَا تُسْـَٔلُونَ    and you will not be questioned

عَمَّا كَانُواْ يَعْمَلُونَ ۝ ۞    about what they used to do.

[PART 2]

سَيَقُولُ ٱلسُّفَهَآءُ مِنَ ٱلنَّاسِ    142    The foolish among the people[1] will say,

---

[1] That is, the Jews or the hypocrites amongst Muslims, or both.

مَا وَلَّىٰهُمْ  'What has turned them away

عَن قِبْلَتِهِمُ ٱلَّتِى كَانُوا۟ عَلَيْهَا  from the *qiblah* they were following?' [1]

قُل لِّلَّهِ ٱلْمَشْرِقُ وَٱلْمَغْرِبُ  *Say,* 'To Allah belong the east and the west.

يَهْدِى مَن يَشَآءُ  He guides whomever He wishes

إِلَىٰ صِرَٰطٍ مُّسْتَقِيمٍ ۩  to a straight path.'

وَكَذَٰلِكَ جَعَلْنَٰكُمْ أُمَّةً وَسَطًا  143 Thus We have made you a middle nation

لِّتَكُونُوا۟ شُهَدَآءَ عَلَى ٱلنَّاسِ  that you may be witnesses to the people,

وَيَكُونَ ٱلرَّسُولُ عَلَيْكُمْ شَهِيدًا  and that the Apostle may be a witness to you.

وَمَا جَعَلْنَا ٱلْقِبْلَةَ ٱلَّتِى كُنتَ عَلَيْهَآ  And We did not appoint the *qiblah you* were following

إِلَّا لِنَعْلَمَ  but that We may ascertain

مَن يَتَّبِعُ ٱلرَّسُولَ  those who follow the Apostle

مِمَّن يَنقَلِبُ عَلَىٰ عَقِبَيْهِ  from those who turn back on their heels.

وَإِن كَانَتْ لَكَبِيرَةً  It was indeed a hard thing

إِلَّا عَلَى ٱلَّذِينَ هَدَى ٱللَّهُ  except for those whom Allah has guided.

وَمَا كَانَ ٱللَّهُ لِيُضِيعَ إِيمَٰنَكُمْ  And Allah would not let your prayers go to waste. [2]

إِنَّ ٱللَّهَ بِٱلنَّاسِ لَرَءُوفٌ رَّحِيمٌ ۩  Indeed Allah is most kind and merciful to mankind.

قَدْ نَرَىٰ تَقَلُّبَ وَجْهِكَ  144 We certainly see *you* turning *your* face about

فِى ٱلسَّمَآءِ  in the sky.

فَلَنُوَلِّيَنَّكَ قِبْلَةً تَرْضَىٰهَا  We will surely turn *you* to a *qiblah* of *your* liking:

فَوَلِّ وَجْهَكَ شَطْرَ ٱلْمَسْجِدِ ٱلْحَرَامِ  so turn *your* face towards the Holy Mosque,

وَحَيْثُ مَا كُنتُمْ  and wherever you may be,

فَوَلُّوا۟ وُجُوهَكُمْ شَطْرَهُ  turn your faces towards it!

وَإِنَّ ٱلَّذِينَ أُوتُوا۟ ٱلْكِتَٰبَ  Indeed those who were given the Book

لَيَعْلَمُونَ أَنَّهُ ٱلْحَقُّ مِن رَّبِّهِمْ  surely know that it is the truth from their Lord.

---

[1] The Muslims first used to pray facing in the direction of Bayt al-Maqdis. This and the verses that follow pertain to the change of the *qiblah*, or the direction faced during prayer, from Quds to the Ka'bah, in Makkah.

[2] '*Īmān*' here means prayers. Allah reassures the faithful that the prayers they have offered earlier facing towards Quds will not be wasted by the change of *qiblah*.

وَمَا ٱللَّهُ بِغَـٰفِلٍ عَمَّا يَعْمَلُونَ ۝    And Allah is not oblivious of what you do.

وَلَئِنْ أَتَيْتَ ٱلَّذِينَ أُوتُوا۟ ٱلْكِتَـٰبَ    145 Even if *you* bring those who were given the Book

بِكُلِّ ءَايَةٍ    every [kind of] sign,[1]

مَّا تَبِعُوا۟ قِبْلَتَكَ    they will not follow *your qiblah*.

وَمَآ أَنتَ بِتَابِعٍ قِبْلَتَهُمْ    Nor shall *you* follow their *qiblah*,

وَمَا بَعْضُهُم بِتَابِعٍ قِبْلَةَ بَعْضٍ    nor will any of them follow the *qiblah* of the other.

وَلَئِنِ ٱتَّبَعْتَ أَهْوَآءَهُم    And if *you* follow their desires,

مِّنۢ بَعْدِ مَا جَآءَكَ مِنَ ٱلْعِلْمِ    after the knowledge that has come to *you*,

إِنَّكَ إِذًا لَّمِنَ ٱلظَّـٰلِمِينَ ۝    *you* will indeed be one of the wrongdoers.

ٱلَّذِينَ ءَاتَيْنَـٰهُمُ ٱلْكِتَـٰبَ    146 Those whom We have given the Book

يَعْرِفُونَهُۥ كَمَا يَعْرِفُونَ أَبْنَآءَهُمْ    recognize *him* just as they recognize their sons,[2]

وَإِنَّ فَرِيقًا مِّنْهُمْ لَيَكْتُمُونَ ٱلْحَقَّ    but a part of them indeed conceal the truth

وَهُمْ يَعْلَمُونَ ۝    while they know.

ٱلْحَقُّ مِن رَّبِّكَ    147 This is the truth from *your* Lord;

فَلَا تَكُونَنَّ مِنَ ٱلْمُمْتَرِينَ ۝    so *do not be* among the skeptics.

وَلِكُلٍّ وِجْهَةٌ هُوَ مُوَلِّيهَا    148 Everyone has a cynosure to which he turns;

فَٱسْتَبِقُوا۟ ٱلْخَيْرَٰتِ    so take the lead in all good works.

أَيْنَ مَا تَكُونُوا۟    Wherever you may be,

يَأْتِ بِكُمُ ٱللَّهُ جَمِيعًا    Allah will bring you all together.

إِنَّ ٱللَّهَ عَلَىٰ كُلِّ شَىْءٍ قَدِيرٌ ۝    Indeed Allah has power over all things.

وَمِنْ حَيْثُ خَرَجْتَ    149 Whencesoever *you* may go out,

فَوَلِّ وَجْهَكَ شَطْرَ ٱلْمَسْجِدِ ٱلْحَرَامِ    turn *your* face towards the Holy Mosque.

وَإِنَّهُۥ لَلْحَقُّ مِن رَّبِّكَ    Indeed it is the truth from *your* Lord,

وَمَا ٱللَّهُ بِغَـٰفِلٍ عَمَّا تَعْمَلُونَ ۝    and Allah is not oblivious of what you do.

وَمِنْ حَيْثُ خَرَجْتَ    150 And whencesoever *you* may go out,

فَوَلِّ وَجْهَكَ شَطْرَ ٱلْمَسْجِدِ ٱلْحَرَامِ    turn *your* face towards the Holy Mosque,

وَحَيْثُ مَا كُنتُمْ    and wherever you may be,

فَوَلُّوا۟ وُجُوهَكُمْ شَطْرَهُۥ    turn your faces towards it,

---

[1] That is, every kind of miracle.
[2] Cf. 6:20.

لِعَلَّا يَكُونَ لِلنَّاسِ عَلَيْكُمْ حُجَّةٌ

so that the people may have no argument against you,

إِلَّا ٱلَّذِينَ ظَلَمُواْ مِنْهُمْ

neither those of them who are wrongdoers.[1]

فَلَا تَخْشَوْهُمْ وَٱخْشَوْنِي

So do not fear them, but fear Me,

وَلِأُتِمَّ نِعْمَتِي عَلَيْكُمْ

that I may complete My blessing on you

وَلَعَلَّكُمْ تَهْتَدُونَ ۝

and so that you may be guided.

كَمَآ أَرْسَلْنَا فِيكُمْ رَسُولًا   151 As We sent to you an Apostle

مِّنكُمْ

from among yourselves,

يَتْلُواْ عَلَيْكُمْ ءَايَٰتِنَا

who recites to you Our signs,

وَيُزَكِّيكُمْ

and purifies you,

وَيُعَلِّمُكُمُ ٱلْكِتَٰبَ وَٱلْحِكْمَةَ

and teaches you the Book and wisdom,

وَيُعَلِّمُكُم مَّا لَمْ تَكُونُواْ تَعْلَمُونَ ۝

and teaches you what you did not know.

فَٱذْكُرُونِي أَذْكُرْكُمْ   152 Remember Me, and I will remember you,

وَٱشْكُرُواْ لِي وَلَا تَكْفُرُونِ ۝

and thank Me, and do not be ungrateful to Me.

يَٰٓأَيُّهَا ٱلَّذِينَ ءَامَنُواْ   153 O you who have faith!

ٱسْتَعِينُواْ بِٱلصَّبْرِ وَٱلصَّلَوٰةِ

Take recourse in patience and prayer;

إِنَّ ٱللَّهَ مَعَ ٱلصَّٰبِرِينَ ۝

indeed Allah is with the patient.

وَلَا تَقُولُواْ لِمَن يُقْتَلُ   154 And do not call those who were slain

فِى سَبِيلِ ٱللَّهِ

in Allah's way

أَمْوَٰتٌ

'dead.'

بَلْ أَحْيَآءٌ

Rather they are living,

وَلَٰكِن لَّا تَشْعُرُونَ ۝

but you are not aware.

وَلَنَبْلُوَنَّكُم   155 We will surely test you

بِشَىْءٍ مِّنَ ٱلْخَوْفِ وَٱلْجُوعِ

with a measure of fear and hunger

وَنَقْصٍ مِّنَ ٱلْأَمْوَٰلِ وَٱلْأَنفُسِ

and a loss of wealth, lives,

وَٱلثَّمَرَٰتِ

and fruits;

وَبَشِّرِ ٱلصَّٰبِرِينَ ۝

and *give good news* to the patient

ٱلَّذِينَ إِذَآ أَصَٰبَتْهُم مُّصِيبَةٌ   156 —those who, when an affliction visits them,

قَالُوٓاْ إِنَّا لِلَّهِ

say, 'Indeed we belong to Allah,

---

[1] As suggested by the *Tafsīr al-Qummī*, *illā* here stands for *wa lā*, and does not imply exclusion.

وَإِنَّا إِلَيْهِ رَٰجِعُونَ ۝　and to Him do we indeed return.'

أُوْلَـٰٓئِكَ عَلَيْهِمْ صَلَوَٰتٌ مِّن رَّبِّهِمْ　157 It is they who receive the blessings of their Lord

وَرَحْمَةٌ　and [His] mercy,

وَأُوْلَـٰٓئِكَ هُمُ ٱلْمُهْتَدُونَ ۝ ❖　and it.is they who are the [rightly] guided.

إِنَّ ٱلصَّفَا وَٱلْمَرْوَةَ　158 Indeed Safa and Marwah

مِن شَعَآئِرِ ٱللَّهِ　are among Allah's sacraments.

فَمَنْ حَجَّ ٱلْبَيْتَ　So whoever makes *hajj* to the House,

أَوِ ٱعْتَمَرَ　or performs the 'umrah,

فَلَا جُنَاحَ عَلَيْهِ أَن يَطَّوَّفَ بِهِمَا　there is no sin upon him to circuits between them.

وَمَن تَطَوَّعَ خَيْرًا　Should anyone do good of his own accord,

فَإِنَّ ٱللَّهَ شَاكِرٌ عَلِيمٌ ۝　then Allah is indeed appreciative, all-knowing.

إِنَّ ٱلَّذِينَ يَكْتُمُونَ مَآ أَنزَلْنَا　159 Indeed those who conceal what We have sent down

مِنَ ٱلْبَيِّنَٰتِ وَٱلْهُدَىٰ　of manifest proofs and guidance,

مِنۢ بَعْدِ مَا بَيَّنَّٰهُ لِلنَّاسِ فِى ٱلْكِتَٰبِ　after We have clarified it in the Book for mankind,

أُوْلَـٰٓئِكَ يَلْعَنُهُمُ ٱللَّهُ　—they shall be cursed by Allah

وَيَلْعَنُهُمُ ٱللَّـٰعِنُونَ ۝　and cursed by the cursers,

إِلَّا ٱلَّذِينَ تَابُوا۟　160 except such as repent,

وَأَصْلَحُوا۟ وَبَيَّنُوا۟　make amends, and clarify,

فَأُوْلَـٰٓئِكَ أَتُوبُ عَلَيْهِمْ　—those I shall pardon,

وَأَنَا ٱلتَّوَّابُ ٱلرَّحِيمُ ۝　and I am the All-clement, the All-merciful.

إِنَّ ٱلَّذِينَ كَفَرُوا۟　161 Indeed those who turn faithless

وَمَاتُوا۟ وَهُمْ كُفَّارٌ　and die while they are faithless,

أُوْلَـٰٓئِكَ عَلَيْهِمْ لَعْنَةُ ٱللَّهِ　—it is they on whom shall be the curse of Allah,

وَٱلْمَلَـٰٓئِكَةِ وَٱلنَّاسِ أَجْمَعِينَ ۝　the angels and all mankind.

خَٰلِدِينَ فِيهَا　162 They will remain in it [forever],

لَا يُخَفَّفُ عَنْهُمُ ٱلْعَذَابُ　and their punishment shall not be lightened,

وَلَا هُمْ يُنظَرُونَ ۝　nor will they be granted any respite.

وَإِلَـٰهُكُمْ إِلَـٰهٌ وَٰحِدٌ　163 Your god is the One God,

لَّآ إِلَـٰهَ إِلَّا هُوَ　there is no god except Him,

ٱلرَّحۡمَٰنُ ٱلرَّحِيمُ ۝

the All-beneficent, the All-merciful.

إِنَّ فِى خَلۡقِ ٱلسَّمَٰوَٰتِ وَٱلۡأَرۡضِ

164 Indeed in the creation of the heavens and the earth,

وَٱخۡتِلَٰفِ ٱلَّيۡلِ وَٱلنَّهَارِ

and the alternation of night and day,

وَٱلۡفُلۡكِ ٱلَّتِى تَجۡرِى فِى ٱلۡبَحۡرِ

and the ships that sail at sea

بِمَا يَنفَعُ ٱلنَّاسَ

with profit to men,

وَمَآ أَنزَلَ ٱللَّهُ مِنَ ٱلسَّمَآءِ مِن مَّآءٍ

and the water that Allah sends down from the sky

فَأَحۡيَا بِهِ ٱلۡأَرۡضَ بَعۡدَ مَوۡتِهَا

—with which He revives the earth after its death,

وَبَثَّ فِيهَا مِن كُلِّ دَآبَّةٍ

and scatters therein every kind of animal—

وَتَصۡرِيفِ ٱلرِّيَٰحِ

and the changing of the winds,

وَٱلسَّحَابِ ٱلۡمُسَخَّرِ بَيۡنَ ٱلسَّمَآءِ

and the clouds disposed between the sky

وَٱلۡأَرۡضِ

and the earth,

لَأَيَٰتٍ لِّقَوۡمٍ يَعۡقِلُونَ ۝

are surely signs for a people who apply reason.

وَمِنَ ٱلنَّاسِ

165 Among the people are those

مَن يَتَّخِذُ مِن دُونِ ٱللَّهِ أَندَادًا

who set up compeers besides Allah,

يُحِبُّونَهُمۡ كَحُبِّ ٱللَّهِ

loving them as if loving Allah

وَٱلَّذِينَ ءَامَنُوٓاْ أَشَدُّ حُبًّا

—but the faithful have a more ardent love

لِّلَّهِ

for Allah—

وَلَوۡ يَرَى ٱلَّذِينَ ظَلَمُوٓاْ

though the wrongdoers will see,

إِذۡ يَرَوۡنَ ٱلۡعَذَابَ

when they sight the punishment,

أَنَّ ٱلۡقُوَّةَ لِلَّهِ جَمِيعًا

that power, altogether, belongs to Allah,

وَأَنَّ ٱللَّهَ شَدِيدُ ٱلۡعَذَابِ ۝

and that Allah is severe in punishment.

إِذۡ تَبَرَّأَ ٱلَّذِينَ ٱتُّبِعُواْ

166 When those who were followed will disown

مِنَ ٱلَّذِينَ ٱتَّبَعُواْ

the followers,

وَرَأَوُاْ ٱلۡعَذَابَ

and they will sight the punishment

وَتَقَطَّعَتۡ بِهِمُ ٱلۡأَسۡبَابُ ۝

while all their means of recourse will be cut off,

وَقَالَ ٱلَّذِينَ ٱتَّبَعُواْ

167 and when the followers will say,

لَوۡ أَنَّ لَنَا كَرَّةً

'Had there been another turn for us,

فَنَتَبَرَّأَ مِنۡهُمۡ

we would disown them

كَمَا تَبَرَّءُواْ مِنَّا

as they disown us [now]!'

كَذَٰلِكَ يُرِيهِمُ ٱللَّهُ أَعۡمَٰلَهُمۡ

Thus shall Allah show them their deeds

حَسَرَتٍ عَلَيْهِمْ    as regrets for themselves,

وَمَا هُم بِخَرِجِينَ مِنَ ٱلنَّارِ ۝    and they shall not leave the Fire.

يَـٰٓأَيُّهَا ٱلنَّاسُ    168 O mankind!

كُلُوا۟ مِمَّا فِى ٱلْأَرْضِ حَلَـٰلًا طَيِّبًا    Eat of what is lawful and pure in the earth,

وَلَا تَتَّبِعُوا۟ خُطُوَٰتِ ٱلشَّيْطَـٰنِ    and do not follow in Satan's steps.

إِنَّهُ لَكُمْ عَدُوٌّ مُّبِينٌ ۝    Indeed he is your manifest enemy.

إِنَّمَا يَأْمُرُكُم بِٱلسُّوٓءِ    169 He only prompts you to [commit] evil

وَٱلْفَحْشَآءِ    and indecent acts,

وَأَن تَقُولُوا۟ عَلَى ٱللَّهِ    and that you attribute to Allah

مَا لَا تَعْلَمُونَ ۝    what you do not know.

وَإِذَا قِيلَ لَهُمُ    170 When they are told,

ٱتَّبِعُوا۟ مَآ أَنزَلَ ٱللَّهُ    'Follow what Allah has sent down,'

قَالُوا۟ بَلْ نَتَّبِعُ    they say, 'We will rather follow

مَآ أَلْفَيْنَا عَلَيْهِ ءَابَآءَنَآ    what we have found our fathers following.'

أَوَلَوْ كَانَ ءَابَآؤُهُمْ    What, even if their fathers

لَا يَعْقِلُونَ شَيْـًٔا    neither applied any reason

وَلَا يَهْتَدُونَ ۝    nor were guided?!

وَمَثَلُ ٱلَّذِينَ كَفَرُوا۟    171 The parable of the faithless

كَمَثَلِ ٱلَّذِى يَنْعِقُ بِمَا    is that of someone who shouts after that

لَا يَسْمَعُ    which does not hear [anything]

إِلَّا دُعَآءً وَنِدَآءً    except a call and cry:

صُمٌّ بُكْمٌ عُمْىٌ    deaf, dumb, and blind,

فَهُمْ لَا يَعْقِلُونَ ۝    they do not apply reason.

يَـٰٓأَيُّهَا ٱلَّذِينَ ءَامَنُوا۟    172 O you who have faith!

كُلُوا۟ مِن طَيِّبَـٰتِ مَا رَزَقْنَـٰكُمْ    Eat of the good things We have provided you,

وَٱشْكُرُوا۟ لِلَّهِ    and thank Allah,

إِن كُنتُمْ إِيَّاهُ تَعْبُدُونَ ۝    if it is Him that you worship.

إِنَّمَا حَرَّمَ عَلَيْكُمُ ٱلْمَيْتَةَ    173 He has forbidden you only carrion,

وَٱلدَّمَ وَلَحْمَ ٱلْخِنزِيرِ    blood, the flesh of the swine,

وَمَآ أُهِلَّ بِهِۦ لِغَيۡرِ ٱللَّهِ    and that which has been offered to other than Allah.

فَمَنِ ٱضۡطُرَّ    But should someone be compelled,

غَيۡرَ بَاغٍ وَلَا عَادٍ    without being rebellious or aggressive,[1]

فَلَآ إِثۡمَ عَلَيۡهِ    there shall be no sin upon him.

إِنَّ ٱللَّهَ غَفُورٌ رَّحِيمٌ ۝    Indeed Allah is all-forgiving, all-merciful.

إِنَّ ٱلَّذِينَ يَكۡتُمُونَ    174 Indeed those who conceal

مَآ أَنزَلَ ٱللَّهُ مِنَ ٱلۡكِتَٰبِ    what Allah has sent down of the Book

وَيَشۡتَرُونَ بِهِۦ ثَمَنًا قَلِيلًا    and sell it for a paltry gain

أُوْلَٰٓئِكَ مَا يَأۡكُلُونَ فِى بُطُونِهِمۡ    —they do not take in, into their bellies,

إِلَّا ٱلنَّارَ    [anything] except fire,

وَلَا يُكَلِّمُهُمُ ٱللَّهُ    and Allah shall not speak to them

يَوۡمَ ٱلۡقِيَٰمَةِ    on the Day of Resurrection,

وَلَا يُزَكِّيهِمۡ    nor shall He purify them,

وَلَهُمۡ عَذَابٌ أَلِيمٌ ۝    and there is a painful punishment for them.

أُوْلَٰٓئِكَ ٱلَّذِينَ ٱشۡتَرَوُاْ ٱلضَّلَٰلَةَ    175 They are the ones who bought error

بِٱلۡهُدَىٰ    for guidance,

وَٱلۡعَذَابَ بِٱلۡمَغۡفِرَةِ    and punishment for pardon:

فَمَآ أَصۡبَرَهُمۡ عَلَى ٱلنَّارِ ۝    how patient of them to face the Fire![2]

ذَٰلِكَ بِأَنَّ ٱللَّهَ نَزَّلَ ٱلۡكِتَٰبَ    176 That is so because Allah has sent down the Book

بِٱلۡحَقِّ    with the truth,

وَإِنَّ ٱلَّذِينَ ٱخۡتَلَفُواْ فِى ٱلۡكِتَٰبِ    and those who differ about the Book

لَفِى شِقَاقٍ بَعِيدٍ ۝ ❈    are surely in extreme defiance.

لَّيۡسَ ٱلۡبِرَّ أَن تُوَلُّواْ وُجُوهَكُمۡ    177 Piety is not to turn your faces

قِبَلَ ٱلۡمَشۡرِقِ وَٱلۡمَغۡرِبِ    to the east or the west;

وَلَٰكِنَّ ٱلۡبِرَّ مَنۡ ءَامَنَ    rather, piety is [personified by] those who have faith

بِٱللَّهِ وَٱلۡيَوۡمِ ٱلۡءَاخِرِ    in Allah and the Last Day,

---

[1] According to some exegetical traditions, *bāghī* refers to one who rebels against a just ruler (according to another interpretation, to a hunter), and *'ādī* refers to a thief or highwayman (see Ṭabarī, Rāzī, al-Tafsīr al-Burhān). Cf. 6:145; 16:115.

[2] Or 'what has made them tolerant of the Fire?'

وَالْمَلَـٰٓئِكَةِ وَالْكِتَـٰبِ   the angels, the Book,

وَالنَّبِيِّـۧنَ   and the prophets,

وَءَاتَى الْمَالَ عَلَىٰ حُبِّهِۦ   and who give their wealth, for the love of Him,[1]

ذَوِى الْقُرْبَىٰ وَالْيَتَـٰمَىٰ   to the relatives, the orphan,

وَالْمَسَـٰكِينَ وَابْنَ السَّبِيلِ   and the needy, the traveller

وَالسَّآئِلِينَ وَفِى الرِّقَابِ   and the beggar, and for [the freeing of] the slaves,

وَأَقَامَ الصَّلَوٰةَ وَءَاتَى الزَّكَوٰةَ   and maintain the prayer and give the *zakāt*,

وَالْمُوفُونَ بِعَهْدِهِمْ   and those who fulfill their covenants,

إِذَا عَـٰهَدُواْ   when they pledge themselves,

وَالصَّـٰبِرِينَ فِى الْبَأْسَآءِ وَالضَّرَّآءِ   and those who are patient in stress and distress,[2]

وَحِينَ الْبَأْسِ   and in the heat of battle.

أُوْلَـٰٓئِكَ الَّذِينَ صَدَقُواْ   They are the ones who are true [to their covenant],

وَأُوْلَـٰٓئِكَ هُمُ الْمُتَّقُونَ ۝   and it is they who are the Godwary.

يَـٰٓأَيُّهَا الَّذِينَ ءَامَنُواْ   178 O you who have faith!

كُتِبَ عَلَيْكُمُ الْقِصَاصُ فِى الْقَتْلَى   Retribution is prescribed for you regarding the slain:

الْحُرُّ بِالْحُرِّ وَالْعَبْدُ بِالْعَبْدِ   freeman for freeman, slave for slave,

وَالْأُنثَىٰ بِالْأُنثَىٰ   and female for female.

فَمَنْ عُفِىَ لَهُۥ مِنْ أَخِيهِ شَىْءٌ   But if one is granted any extenuation by his brother,[3]

فَاتِّبَاعٌۢ بِالْمَعْرُوفِ   let the follow up [for the blood-money] be honourable,

وَأَدَآءٌ إِلَيْهِ بِإِحْسَـٰنٍ   and let the payment to him be with kindness.

ذَٰلِكَ تَخْفِيفٌ مِّن رَّبِّكُمْ وَرَحْمَةٌ   That is a remission from your Lord and a mercy;

فَمَنِ اعْتَدَىٰ بَعْدَ ذَٰلِكَ   and should anyone transgress after that,

فَلَهُۥ عَذَابٌ أَلِيمٌ ۝   there shall be a painful punishment for him.

وَلَكُمْ فِى الْقِصَاصِ حَيَوٰةٌ   179 There is life for you in retribution,

يَـٰٓأُوْلِى الْأَلْبَـٰبِ   O you who possess intellects!

لَعَلَّكُمْ تَتَّقُونَ ۝   Maybe you will be Godwary!

---

[1] Or 'despite their love of it.'

[2] That is, in poverty and sickness.

[3] That is, by the heir of the victim.

كُتِبَ عَلَيْكُمْ 180 Prescribed for you,

إِذَا حَضَرَ أَحَدَكُمُ ٱلْمَوْتُ    when death approaches any of you

إِن تَرَكَ خَيْرًا    and he leaves behind any property,

ٱلْوَصِيَّةُ لِلْوَٰلِدَيْنِ وَٱلْأَقْرَبِينَ    is that he make a bequest for his parents and relatives,

بِٱلْمَعْرُوفِ    in an honourable manner,

حَقًّا عَلَى ٱلْمُتَّقِينَ ۝    —an obligation on the Godwary.

فَمَنۢ بَدَّلَهُۥ بَعْدَمَا سَمِعَهُۥ 181 And should anyone alter it after hearing it,

فَإِنَّمَآ إِثْمُهُۥ عَلَى ٱلَّذِينَ يُبَدِّلُونَهُۥٓ    its sin shall indeed lie on those who alter it.

إِنَّ ٱللَّهَ سَمِيعٌ عَلِيمٌ ۝    Indeed Allah is all-hearing, all-knowing

فَمَنْ 182 But should someone,

خَافَ مِن مُّوصٍ جَنَفًا أَوْ إِثْمًا    fearing deviance or sin on the testator's behalf,

فَأَصْلَحَ بَيْنَهُمْ    set things right between them,

فَلَآ إِثْمَ عَلَيْهِ    there is no sin upon him.

إِنَّ ٱللَّهَ غَفُورٌ رَّحِيمٌ ۝    Indeed Allah is all-forgiving, all-merciful.

يَٰٓأَيُّهَا ٱلَّذِينَ ءَامَنُواْ 183 O you who have faith!

كُتِبَ عَلَيْكُمُ ٱلصِّيَامُ    Prescribed for you is fasting

كَمَا كُتِبَ    as it was prescribed

عَلَى ٱلَّذِينَ مِن قَبْلِكُمْ    for those who were before you,

لَعَلَّكُمْ تَتَّقُونَ ۝    so that you may be Godwary.

أَيَّامًا مَّعْدُودَٰتٍ 184 That for known days.

فَمَن كَانَ مِنكُم مَّرِيضًا    But should any of you be sick

أَوْ عَلَىٰ سَفَرٍ    or on a journey,

فَعِدَّةٌ مِّنْ أَيَّامٍ أُخَرَ    let it be a [similar] number of other days.

وَعَلَى ٱلَّذِينَ يُطِيقُونَهُۥ Those who find it straining shall be liable

فِدْيَةٌ طَعَامُ مِسْكِينٍ    to atonement by feeding a needy person.

فَمَن تَطَوَّعَ خَيْرًا    Should anyone do good of his own accord,

فَهُوَ خَيْرٌ لَّهُۥ    that is better for him,

وَأَن تَصُومُواْ خَيْرٌ لَّكُمْ    and to fast is better for you,

إِن كُنتُمْ تَعْلَمُونَ ۝    should you know.

شَهْرُ رَمَضَانَ 185 The month of Ramaḍān

ٱلَّذِىٓ أُنزِلَ فِيهِ ٱلْقُرْءَانُ    is one in which the Qur'ān was sent down

هُدًى لِّلنَّاسِ    as guidance to mankind,

وَبَيِّنَٰتٍ مِّنَ ٱلْهُدَىٰ    with manifest proofs of guidance

وَٱلْفُرْقَانِ    and the Distinguisher.[1]

فَمَن شَهِدَ مِنكُمُ ٱلشَّهْرَ فَلْيَصُمْهُ    So let those of you who witness it fast [in] it,

وَمَن كَانَ مَرِيضًا أَوْ عَلَىٰ سَفَرٍ    and as for anyone who is sick or on a journey,

فَعِدَّةٌ مِّنْ أَيَّامٍ أُخَرَ    let it be a [similar] number of other days.

يُرِيدُ ٱللَّهُ بِكُمُ ٱلْيُسْرَ    Allah desires ease for you,

وَلَا يُرِيدُ بِكُمُ ٱلْعُسْرَ    and He does not desire hardship for you,

وَلِتُكْمِلُواْ ٱلْعِدَّةَ    and so that you may complete the number,

وَلِتُكَبِّرُواْ ٱللَّهَ عَلَىٰ مَا هَدَىٰكُمْ    and magnify Allah for guiding you,

وَلَعَلَّكُمْ تَشْكُرُونَ ۝    and that you may give thanks.

وَإِذَا سَأَلَكَ عِبَادِى عَنِّى 186 When My servants ask *you* about Me,

فَإِنِّى قَرِيبٌ    [tell them that] I am indeed nearmost.

أُجِيبُ دَعْوَةَ ٱلدَّاعِ إِذَا دَعَانِ    I answer the supplicant's call when he calls Me.

فَلْيَسْتَجِيبُواْ لِى    So let them respond to Me,

وَلْيُؤْمِنُواْ بِى    and let them have faith in Me,

لَعَلَّهُمْ يَرْشُدُونَ ۝    so that they may fare rightly.

أُحِلَّ لَكُمْ لَيْلَةَ ٱلصِّيَامِ 187 You are permitted, on the night of the fast,

ٱلرَّفَثُ إِلَىٰ نِسَآئِكُمْ    to go into your wives:

هُنَّ لِبَاسٌ لَّكُمْ    they are a garment for you,

وَأَنتُمْ لِبَاسٌ لَّهُنَّ    and you are a garment for them.

عَلِمَ ٱللَّهُ    Allah knew

أَنَّكُمْ كُنتُمْ تَخْتَانُونَ أَنفُسَكُمْ    that you used to betray yourselves,

فَتَابَ عَلَيْكُمْ وَعَفَا عَنكُمْ    so He pardoned you and excused you.

فَٱلْـَٰٔنَ بَٰشِرُوهُنَّ    So now consort with them,

وَٱبْتَغُواْ مَا كَتَبَ ٱللَّهُ لَكُمْ    and seek what Allah has ordained for you,

وَكُلُواْ وَٱشْرَبُواْ    and eat and drink

---

[1] See footnote at 2:53.

حَتَّىٰ يَتَبَيَّنَ لَكُمُ ٱلْخَيْطُ ٱلْأَبْيَضُ

until the white streak becomes manifest to you

مِنَ ٱلْخَيْطِ ٱلْأَسْوَدِ مِنَ ٱلْفَجْرِ

from the dark streak at the crack of dawn.[1]

ثُمَّ أَتِمُّوا۟ ٱلصِّيَامَ إِلَى ٱلَّيْلِ

Then complete the fast until nightfall,

وَلَا تُبَٰشِرُوهُنَّ

and do not consort with them

وَأَنتُمْ عَٰكِفُونَ

while you dwell in confinement

فِى ٱلْمَسَٰجِدِ

in the mosques.

تِلْكَ حُدُودُ ٱللَّهِ فَلَا تَقْرَبُوهَا

These are Allah's bounds, so do not approach them.

كَذَٰلِكَ يُبَيِّنُ ٱللَّهُ ءَايَٰتِهِ لِلنَّاسِ

Thus does Allah clarify His signs for mankind

لَعَلَّهُمْ يَتَّقُونَ ۝

so that they may be Godwary.

وَلَا تَأْكُلُوٓا۟ أَمْوَٰلَكُم

188 Do not eat up your wealth

بَيْنَكُم بِٱلْبَٰطِلِ

among yourselves wrongfully,

وَتُدْلُوا۟ بِهَآ إِلَى ٱلْحُكَّامِ

nor proffer it to the judges

لِتَأْكُلُوا۟ فَرِيقًا

in order to eat up a part

مِّنْ أَمْوَٰلِ ٱلنَّاسِ بِٱلْإِثْمِ

of the people's wealth sinfully,

وَأَنتُمْ تَعْلَمُونَ ۝ ۞

while you know [that it is immoral to do so].

يَسْـَٔلُونَكَ عَنِ ٱلْأَهِلَّةِ

189 They question *you* concerning the new moons.

قُلْ هِىَ مَوَٰقِيتُ لِلنَّاسِ

*Say,* 'They are timekeeping signs for the people

وَٱلْحَجِّ

and [for the sake of] *hajj.*'

وَلَيْسَ ٱلْبِرُّ بِأَن تَأْتُوا۟ ٱلْبُيُوتَ

It is not piety that you come into houses

مِن ظُهُورِهَا

from their rear;

وَلَٰكِنَّ ٱلْبِرَّ مَنِ ٱتَّقَىٰ

rather piety is [personified by] one who is Godwary,

وَأْتُوا۟ ٱلْبُيُوتَ مِنْ أَبْوَٰبِهَا

and come into houses from their doors,

وَٱتَّقُوا۟ ٱللَّهَ لَعَلَّكُمْ تُفْلِحُونَ ۝

and be wary of Allah, so that you may be felicitous.

وَقَٰتِلُوا۟ فِى سَبِيلِ ٱللَّهِ

190 Fight in the way of Allah

ٱلَّذِينَ يُقَٰتِلُونَكُمْ

those who fight you,

وَلَا تَعْتَدُوٓا۟

but do not transgress.

إِنَّ ٱللَّهَ لَا يُحِبُّ ٱلْمُعْتَدِينَ ۝

Indeed Allah does not like transgressors.

وَٱقْتُلُوهُمْ حَيْثُ ثَقِفْتُمُوهُمْ

191 And kill them wherever you confront them,

---

[1] That is, until the appearance of the dawn.

وَأَخْرِجُوهُم مِّنْ حَيْثُ أَخْرَجُوكُمْ
and expel them from where they expelled you,

وَٱلْفِتْنَةُ أَشَدُّ مِنَ ٱلْقَتْلِ
for faithlessness[1] is graver than killing.

وَلَا تُقَٰتِلُوهُمْ عِندَ ٱلْمَسْجِدِ ٱلْحَرَامِ
But do not fight them near the Holy Mosque

حَتَّىٰ يُقَٰتِلُوكُمْ فِيهِ
unless they fight you therein;

فَإِن قَٰتَلُوكُمْ فَٱقْتُلُوهُمْ
but if they fight you, kill them;

كَذَٰلِكَ جَزَآءُ ٱلْكَٰفِرِينَ ۝
such is the requital of the faithless.

فَإِنِ ٱنتَهَوْا۟
192 But if they relinquish,[2]

فَإِنَّ ٱللَّهَ غَفُورٌ رَّحِيمٌ ۝
then Allah is indeed all-forgiving, all-merciful.

وَقَٰتِلُوهُمْ حَتَّىٰ لَا تَكُونَ فِتْنَةٌ
193 Fight them until faithlessness[3] is no more,

وَيَكُونَ ٱلدِّينُ لِلَّهِ
and religion becomes [exclusively] for Allah.

فَإِنِ ٱنتَهَوْا۟ فَلَا عُدْوَٰنَ
Then if they relinquish, there shall be no reprisal

إِلَّا عَلَى ٱلظَّٰلِمِينَ ۝
except against the wrongdoers.

ٱلشَّهْرُ ٱلْحَرَامُ بِٱلشَّهْرِ ٱلْحَرَامِ
194 A sacred month for a sacred month,

وَٱلْحُرُمَٰتُ قِصَاصٌ
and all sanctities require retribution.

فَمَنِ ٱعْتَدَىٰ عَلَيْكُمْ
So should anyone aggress against you,

فَٱعْتَدُوا۟ عَلَيْهِ
assail him

بِمِثْلِ مَا ٱعْتَدَىٰ عَلَيْكُمْ
in the manner he assailed you,[4]

وَٱتَّقُوا۟ ٱللَّهَ
and be wary of Allah,

وَٱعْلَمُوٓا۟ أَنَّ ٱللَّهَ مَعَ ٱلْمُتَّقِينَ ۝
and know that Allah is with the Godwary.

وَأَنفِقُوا۟ فِى سَبِيلِ ٱللَّهِ
195 Spend in the way of Allah,

وَلَا تُلْقُوا۟ بِأَيْدِيكُمْ
and do not cast yourselves with your own hands

إِلَى ٱلتَّهْلُكَةِ
into destruction;

وَأَحْسِنُوٓا۟
and be virtuous.

إِنَّ ٱللَّهَ يُحِبُّ ٱلْمُحْسِنِينَ ۝
Indeed Allah loves the virtuous.

---

[1] Or 'polytheism.'

[2] That is, if they give up idolatry.

[3] Or 'polytheism,' as narrated fom Imam Muḥammad al-Bāqir (Ṭabrisī), Mujāhid, Qatādah, Rabiʿ, and Ḍaḥḥāk (Ṭabarī).

[4] Cf. 16:126.

وَأَتِمُّوا۟ ٱلْحَجَّ وَٱلْعُمْرَةَ لِلَّهِ    196 Complete the *hajj* and the *'umrah* for Allah's sake,

فَإِنْ أُحْصِرْتُمْ    and if you are prevented,

فَمَا ٱسْتَيْسَرَ مِنَ ٱلْهَدْىِ    then [make] such [sacrificial] offering as is feasible.

وَلَا تَحْلِقُوا۟ رُءُوسَكُمْ    And do not shave your heads

حَتَّىٰ يَبْلُغَ ٱلْهَدْىُ مَحِلَّهُۥ    until the offering reaches its [assigned] place.

فَمَن كَانَ مِنكُم مَّرِيضًا    But should any of you be sick,

أَوْ بِهِۦٓ أَذًى مِّن رَّأْسِهِۦ    or have a hurt in his head,[1]

فَفِدْيَةٌ مِّن صِيَامٍ    let the atonement be by fasting,

أَوْ صَدَقَةٍ أَوْ نُسُكٍ    or charity, or sacrifice.

فَإِذَآ أَمِنتُمْ    And when you have security

فَمَن تَمَتَّعَ    —for those who enjoy [release from the restrictions]

بِٱلْعُمْرَةِ إِلَى ٱلْحَجِّ    by virtue of the *'umrah* until the *hajj*—

فَمَا ٱسْتَيْسَرَ مِنَ ٱلْهَدْىِ    let the offering be such as is feasible.

فَمَن لَّمْ يَجِدْ    As for someone who cannot afford [the offering],

فَصِيَامُ ثَلَٰثَةِ أَيَّامٍ فِى ٱلْحَجِّ    let him fast three days during the *hajj*

وَسَبْعَةٍ إِذَا رَجَعْتُمْ    and seven when you return;

تِلْكَ عَشَرَةٌ كَامِلَةٌ    that is [a period of] complete ten [days].

ذَٰلِكَ لِمَن لَّمْ يَكُنْ أَهْلُهُۥ    That is for someone whose family does not

حَاضِرِى ٱلْمَسْجِدِ ٱلْحَرَامِ    dwell by the Holy Mosque.

وَٱتَّقُوا۟ ٱللَّهَ    And be wary of Allah,

وَٱعْلَمُوٓا۟ أَنَّ ٱللَّهَ شَدِيدُ ٱلْعِقَابِ ۝    and know that Allah is severe in retribution.

ٱلْحَجُّ أَشْهُرٌ مَّعْلُومَٰتٌ    197 The *hajj* [season] is in months well-known;

فَمَن فَرَضَ فِيهِنَّ ٱلْحَجَّ    so whoever decides on *hajj* [pilgrimage] therein,

فَلَا رَفَثَ    [should know that] there is to be no sexual contact,

وَلَا فُسُوقَ وَلَا جِدَالَ فِى ٱلْحَجِّ    vicious talk, or disputing during the *hajj*.

وَمَا تَفْعَلُوا۟ مِنْ خَيْرٍ يَعْلَمْهُ ٱللَّهُ    And whatever good you do, Allah knows it.

وَتَزَوَّدُوا۟    And take provision,

فَإِنَّ خَيْرَ ٱلزَّادِ ٱلتَّقْوَىٰ    for indeed the best provision is Godwariness.

وَٱتَّقُونِ يَٰٓأُو۟لِى ٱلْأَلْبَٰبِ ۝    So be wary of Me, O you who possess intellects!

---

[1] Such as a wound on the scalp.

لَيْسَ عَلَيْكُمْ جُنَاحٌ 198 There is no sin upon you

أَن تَبْتَغُواْ فَضْلاً مِّن رَّبِّكُمْ   in seeking your Lord's grace [during the *hajj* season].

فَإِذَآ أَفَضْتُم مِّنْ عَرَفَٰتٍ   Then when you stream out of 'Arafāt

فَاذْكُرُواْ ٱللَّهَ عِندَ ٱلْمَشْعَرِ ٱلْحَرَامِ   remember Allah at the Holy Mash'ar,

وَٱذْكُرُوهُ كَمَا هَدَىٰكُمْ   and remember Him as He has guided you,

وَإِن كُنتُم مِّن قَبْلِهِ لَمِنَ ٱلضَّآلِّينَ ۝   and earlier you were indeed among the astray.

ثُمَّ أَفِيضُواْ مِنْ حَيْثُ أَفَاضَ ٱلنَّاسُ 199 Then stream out from where the people stream out,

وَٱسْتَغْفِرُواْ ٱللَّهَ   and plead Allah for forgiveness;

إِنَّ ٱللَّهَ غَفُورٌ رَّحِيمٌ ۝   indeed Allah is all-forgiving, all-merciful.

فَإِذَا قَضَيْتُم مَّنَٰسِكَكُمْ 200 And when you finish your rites,

فَٱذْكُرُواْ ٱللَّهَ   then remember Allah

كَذِكْرِكُمْ ءَابَآءَكُمْ   as you would remember your fathers,

أَوْ أَشَدَّ ذِكْرًا   or with a more ardent remembrance.

فَمِنَ ٱلنَّاسِ مَن يَقُولُ   Among the people there are those who say,

رَبَّنَآ ءَاتِنَا فِى ٱلدُّنْيَا   'Our Lord, give us in this world,'

وَمَا لَهُ فِى ٱلْآخِرَةِ مِنْ خَلَٰقٍ ۝   but for such there is no share in the Hereafter.

وَمِنْهُم مَّن يَقُولُ 201 And among them there are those who say,

رَبَّنَآ ءَاتِنَا فِى ٱلدُّنْيَا حَسَنَةً   'Our Lord, give us good in this world

وَفِى ٱلْآخِرَةِ حَسَنَةً   and good in the Hereafter,

وَقِنَا عَذَابَ ٱلنَّارِ ۝   and save us from the punishment of the Fire.'

أُوْلَٰئِكَ لَهُمْ نَصِيبٌ مِّمَّا كَسَبُواْ 202 Such shall partake of what they have earned,

وَٱللَّهُ سَرِيعُ ٱلْحِسَابِ ۝ ۞   and Allah is swift at reckoning.

وَٱذْكُرُواْ ٱللَّهَ فِى أَيَّامٍ مَّعْدُودَٰتٍ 203 Remember Allah in the appointed days.

فَمَن تَعَجَّلَ فِى يَوْمَيْنِ   Then whoever hastens off in a couple of days,

فَلَآ إِثْمَ عَلَيْهِ   there is no sin upon him,

وَمَن تَأَخَّرَ   and whoever delays,

فَلَآ إِثْمَ عَلَيْهِ   there is no sin upon him

لِمَنِ ٱتَّقَىٰ   —that for one who has been Godwary—

وَٱتَّقُوا۟ ٱللَّهَ and be wary of Allah,

وَٱعۡلَمُوٓا۟ أَنَّكُمۡ إِلَيۡهِ تُحۡشَرُونَ ۝ and know that toward Him you will be mustered.

وَمِنَ ٱلنَّاسِ 204 Among the people

مَن يُعۡجِبُكَ قَوۡلُهُۥ فِى ٱلۡحَيَوٰةِ ٱلدُّنۡيَا is he whose talk about worldly life impresses you,

وَيُشۡهِدُ ٱللَّهَ عَلَىٰ مَا فِى قَلۡبِهِۦ and he holds Allah witness to what is in his heart,

وَهُوَ أَلَدُّ ٱلۡخِصَامِ ۝ though he is the staunchest of enemies.

وَإِذَا تَوَلَّىٰ 205 And if he were to wield authority,

سَعَىٰ فِى ٱلۡأَرۡضِ لِيُفۡسِدَ فِيهَا he would try to cause corruption in the land,

وَيُهۡلِكَ ٱلۡحَرۡثَ وَٱلنَّسۡلَ and to ruin the crop and the stock,

وَٱللَّهُ لَا يُحِبُّ ٱلۡفَسَادَ ۝ and Allah does not like corruption.

وَإِذَا قِيلَ لَهُ ٱتَّقِ ٱللَّهَ 206 And when he is told, 'Be wary of Allah,'

أَخَذَتۡهُ ٱلۡعِزَّةُ بِٱلۡإِثۡمِ conceit seizes him sinfully;

فَحَسۡبُهُۥ جَهَنَّمُ so let hell suffice him,

وَلَبِئۡسَ ٱلۡمِهَادُ ۝ and it is surely an evil resting place!

وَمِنَ ٱلنَّاسِ مَن يَشۡرِى نَفۡسَهُ 207 And among the people is he who sells his soul[1]

ٱبۡتِغَآءَ مَرۡضَاتِ ٱللَّهِ seeking the pleasure of Allah,

وَٱللَّهُ رَءُوفُۢ بِٱلۡعِبَادِ ۝ and Allah is most kind to [His] servants.

يَٰٓأَيُّهَا ٱلَّذِينَ ءَامَنُوا۟ 208 O you who have faith!

ٱدۡخُلُوا۟ فِى ٱلسِّلۡمِ كَآفَّةً Enter into submission, all together,

وَلَا تَتَّبِعُوا۟ خُطُوَٰتِ ٱلشَّيۡطَٰنِ and do not follow in Satan's steps;

إِنَّهُۥ لَكُمۡ عَدُوٌّ مُّبِينٌ ۝ he is indeed your manifest enemy.

فَإِن زَلَلۡتُم 209 And should you stumble

مِّنۢ بَعۡدِ مَا جَآءَتۡكُمُ ٱلۡبَيِّنَٰتُ after the manifest proofs that have come to you,

فَٱعۡلَمُوٓا۟ أَنَّ ٱللَّهَ عَزِيزٌ حَكِيمٌ ۝ know that Allah is all-mighty, all-wise.

هَلۡ يَنظُرُونَ إِلَّآ 210 Do they await anything but

أَن يَأۡتِيَهُمُ ٱللَّهُ that Allah['s command] should come to them

فِى ظُلَلٍ مِّنَ ٱلۡغَمَامِ وَٱلۡمَلَٰٓئِكَةُ in the shades of the clouds, with the angles,

وَقُضِىَ ٱلۡأَمۡرُ and the matter be decided [once for all].

وَإِلَى ٱللَّهِ تُرۡجَعُ ٱلۡأُمُورُ ۝ And to Allah all matters are returned.

---

[1] Or 'his life.'

سَلْ بَنِى إِسْرَٰٓءِيلَ 211 Ask the Children of Israel

كَمْ ءَاتَيْنَٰهُم مِّنْ ءَايَةٍ بَيِّنَةٍ    how many a manifest sign We had given them.

وَمَن يُبَدِّلْ نِعْمَةَ ٱللَّهِ    And whoever changes Allah's blessing

مِنۢ بَعْدِ مَا جَآءَتْهُ    after it has come to him,

فَإِنَّ ٱللَّهَ شَدِيدُ ٱلْعِقَابِ ﴿٢١١﴾    indeed Allah is severe in retribution.

زُيِّنَ لِلَّذِينَ كَفَرُواْ ٱلْحَيَوٰةُ ٱلدُّنْيَا 212 Worldly life has been glamorized for the faithless,

وَيَسْخَرُونَ مِنَ ٱلَّذِينَ ءَامَنُواْ    and they ridicule the faithful.

وَٱلَّذِينَ ٱتَّقَوْاْ    But those who are Godwary

فَوْقَهُمْ يَوْمَ ٱلْقِيَٰمَةِ    shall be above them on the Day of Resurrection,

وَٱللَّهُ يَرْزُقُ مَن يَشَآءُ    and Allah provides for whomever He wishes

بِغَيْرِ حِسَابٍ ﴿٢١٢﴾    without any reckoning.

كَانَ ٱلنَّاسُ أُمَّةً وَٰحِدَةً 213 Mankind were a single community;

فَبَعَثَ ٱللَّهُ ٱلنَّبِيِّـۧنَ    then Allah sent the prophets

مُبَشِّرِينَ وَمُنذِرِينَ    as bearers of good news and as warners,

وَأَنزَلَ مَعَهُمُ ٱلْكِتَٰبَ بِٱلْحَقِّ and He sent down with them the Book with the truth,

لِيَحْكُمَ بَيْنَ ٱلنَّاسِ    that it[1] may judge between the people

فِيمَا ٱخْتَلَفُواْ فِيهِ    concerning that about which they differed,

وَمَا ٱخْتَلَفَ فِيهِ    and none differed in it

إِلَّا ٱلَّذِينَ أُوتُوهُ    except those who had been given it,

مِنۢ بَعْدِ مَا جَآءَتْهُمُ ٱلْبَيِّنَٰتُ    after the manifest proofs had come to them,

بَغْيَۢا بَيْنَهُمْ    out of envy among themselves.

فَهَدَى ٱللَّهُ ٱلَّذِينَ ءَامَنُواْ Then Allah guided those who had faith

لِمَا ٱخْتَلَفُواْ فِيهِ مِنَ ٱلْحَقِّ بِإِذْنِهِۦ    to the truth of what they differed in, by His will,

وَٱللَّهُ يَهْدِى مَن يَشَآءُ    and Allah guides whomever He wishes

إِلَىٰ صِرَٰطٍ مُّسْتَقِيمٍ ﴿٢١٣﴾    to a straight path.

أَمْ حَسِبْتُمْ أَن تَدْخُلُواْ ٱلْجَنَّةَ 214 Do you suppose that you shall enter paradise

وَلَمَّا يَأْتِكُم    though there has not yet come to you

مَّثَلُ ٱلَّذِينَ خَلَوْاْ مِن قَبْلِكُم    the like of [what befell] those who went before you?

---

[1] That is the Book.

مَّسَّتْهُمُ ٱلْبَأْسَآءُ وَٱلضَّرَّآءُ

Stress and distress befell them

وَزُلْزِلُواْ حَتَّىٰ

and they were convulsed until

يَقُولَ ٱلرَّسُولُ وَٱلَّذِينَ ءَامَنُواْ مَعَهُ

the apostle and the faithful who were with him said,

مَتَىٰ نَصْرُ ٱللَّهِ

'When will Allah's help [come]?'

أَلَآ إِنَّ نَصْرَ ٱللَّهِ قَرِيبٌ ﴿٢١٤﴾

Look! Allah's help is indeed near!

يَسْـَٔلُونَكَ مَاذَا يُنفِقُونَ

215 They ask *you* as to what they should spend.

قُلْ مَآ أَنفَقْتُم مِّنْ خَيْرٍ

*Say*, 'Whatever wealth you spend,

فَلِلْوَٰلِدَيْنِ وَٱلْأَقْرَبِينَ وَٱلْيَتَـٰمَىٰ

let it be for parents, relatives, orphans,

وَٱلْمَسَـٰكِينِ وَٱبْنِ ٱلسَّبِيلِ

the needy, and the traveller.'

وَمَا تَفْعَلُواْ مِنْ خَيْرٍ

And whatever good that you may do,

فَإِنَّ ٱللَّهَ بِهِۦ عَلِيمٌ ﴿٢١٥﴾

Allah indeed knows it.

كُتِبَ عَلَيْكُمُ ٱلْقِتَالُ

216 Warfare has been prescribed for you,

وَهُوَ كُرْهٌ لَّكُمْ

though it is repulsive to you.

وَعَسَىٰ أَن تَكْرَهُواْ شَيْـًٔا

Yet it may be that you dislike something

وَهُوَ خَيْرٌ لَّكُمْ

while it is good for you,

وَعَسَىٰ أَن تُحِبُّواْ شَيْـًٔا

and it may be that you love something

وَهُوَ شَرٌّ لَّكُمْ

while it is bad for you,

وَٱللَّهُ يَعْلَمُ وَأَنتُمْ لَا تَعْلَمُونَ ﴿٢١٦﴾

and Allah knows and you do not know.

يَسْـَٔلُونَكَ

217 They ask *you*

عَنِ ٱلشَّهْرِ ٱلْحَرَامِ قِتَالٍ فِيهِ

concerning warfare in the holy month.

قُلْ قِتَالٌ فِيهِ كَبِيرٌ

*Say*, 'It is an outrageous thing to fight in it,

وَصَدٌّ عَن سَبِيلِ ٱللَّهِ

but to keep [people] from Allah's way,

وَكُفْرٌ بِهِۦ

and to be unfaithful to Him,

وَٱلْمَسْجِدِ ٱلْحَرَامِ

and [to keep people from] the Holy Mosque,

وَإِخْرَاجُ أَهْلِهِۦ مِنْهُ

and to expel its people from it

أَكْبَرُ عِندَ ٱللَّهِ

are more outrageous with Allah.

وَٱلْفِتْنَةُ أَكْبَرُ مِنَ ٱلْقَتْلِ

And faithlessness is graver than killing.

وَلَا يَزَالُونَ يُقَـٰتِلُونَكُمْ

And they will not cease fighting you

حَتَّىٰ يَرُدُّوكُمْ عَن دِينِكُمْ

until they turn you away from your religion,

إِنِ ٱسۡتَطَٰعُوٓاْ if they can.

وَمَن يَرۡتَدِدۡ مِنكُمۡ عَن دِينِهِۦ And whoever of you turns away from his religion

فَيَمُتۡ وَهُوَ كَافِرٞ and dies faithless

فَأُوْلَٰٓئِكَ حَبِطَتۡ أَعۡمَٰلُهُمۡ —they are the ones whose works have failed

فِى ٱلدُّنۡيَا وَٱلۡأٓخِرَةِ in this world and the Hereafter.

وَأُوْلَٰٓئِكَ أَصۡحَٰبُ ٱلنَّارِ They shall be the inmates of the Fire,

هُمۡ فِيهَا خَٰلِدُونَ ٢١٧ and they shall remain in it [forever].

إِنَّ ٱلَّذِينَ ءَامَنُواْ 218 Indeed those who have become faithful

وَٱلَّذِينَ هَاجَرُواْ and those who have migrated

وَجَٰهَدُواْ فِى سَبِيلِ ٱللَّهِ and waged *jihād* in the way of Allah

أُوْلَٰٓئِكَ يَرۡجُونَ رَحۡمَتَ ٱللَّهِ —it is they who expect Allah's mercy,

وَٱللَّهُ غَفُورٞ رَّحِيمٞ ٢١٨ and Allah is all-forgiving, all-merciful.

يَسۡـَٔلُونَكَ عَنِ ٱلۡخَمۡرِ وَٱلۡمَيۡسِرِ 219 They ask *you* concerning wine and gambling.

قُلۡ فِيهِمَآ إِثۡمٞ كَبِيرٞ *Say,* 'There is a great sin in both of them,

وَمَنَٰفِعُ لِلنَّاسِ and some profits for the people,

وَإِثۡمُهُمَآ أَكۡبَرُ مِن نَّفۡعِهِمَا but their sinfulness outweighs their profit.'

وَيَسۡـَٔلُونَكَ مَاذَا يُنفِقُونَ And they ask *you* as to what they should spend.

قُلِ ٱلۡعَفۡوَ *Say,* 'All that is surplus.'

كَذَٰلِكَ يُبَيِّنُ ٱللَّهُ لَكُمُ ٱلۡأٓيَٰتِ Thus does Allah clarify His signs for you

لَعَلَّكُمۡ تَتَفَكَّرُونَ ٢١٩ so that you may reflect

فِى ٱلدُّنۡيَا وَٱلۡأٓخِرَةِ 220 about the world and the Hereafter.

وَيَسۡـَٔلُونَكَ عَنِ ٱلۡيَتَٰمَىٰ And they ask *you* concerning the orphans.

قُلۡ إِصۡلَاحٞ لَّهُمۡ خَيۡرٞ *Say,* 'It is better to set right their affairs,[1]

وَإِن تُخَالِطُوهُمۡ and if you intermingle with them,

فَإِخۡوَٰنُكُمۡ then they are your brothers:

وَٱللَّهُ يَعۡلَمُ ٱلۡمُفۡسِدَ Allah knows the one who causes corruption

مِنَ ٱلۡمُصۡلِحِ from the one who brings about reform,

---

[1] That is, it is better to manage their affairs than to stand aloof due to the fear of mishandling them. Cf. 4:2.

وَلَوْ شَآءَ ٱللَّهُ  
لَأَعْنَتَكُمْ  
إِنَّ ٱللَّهَ عَزِيزٌ حَكِيمٌ ۝

221 وَلَا تَنكِحُوا۟ ٱلْمُشْرِكَٰتِ حَتَّىٰ يُؤْمِنَّ  
وَلَأَمَةٌ مُّؤْمِنَةٌ خَيْرٌ مِّن مُّشْرِكَةٍ  
وَلَوْ أَعْجَبَتْكُمْ  
وَلَا تُنكِحُوا۟ ٱلْمُشْرِكِينَ  
حَتَّىٰ يُؤْمِنُوا۟  
وَلَعَبْدٌ مُّؤْمِنٌ خَيْرٌ مِّن مُّشْرِكٍ  
وَلَوْ أَعْجَبَكُمْ  
أُو۟لَٰٓئِكَ يَدْعُونَ إِلَى ٱلنَّارِ  
وَٱللَّهُ يَدْعُوٓا۟ إِلَى ٱلْجَنَّةِ وَٱلْمَغْفِرَةِ  
بِإِذْنِهِۦ  
وَيُبَيِّنُ ءَايَٰتِهِۦ لِلنَّاسِ  
لَعَلَّهُمْ يَتَذَكَّرُونَ ۝

222 وَيَسْـَٔلُونَكَ عَنِ ٱلْمَحِيضِ  
قُلْ هُوَ أَذًى  
فَٱعْتَزِلُوا۟ ٱلنِّسَآءَ فِى ٱلْمَحِيضِ  
وَلَا تَقْرَبُوهُنَّ حَتَّىٰ يَطْهُرْنَ  
فَإِذَا تَطَهَّرْنَ  
فَأْتُوهُنَّ مِنْ حَيْثُ أَمَرَكُمُ ٱللَّهُ  
إِنَّ ٱللَّهَ يُحِبُّ ٱلتَّوَّٰبِينَ  
وَيُحِبُّ ٱلْمُتَطَهِّرِينَ ۝

223 نِسَآؤُكُمْ حَرْثٌ لَّكُمْ  
فَأْتُوا۟ حَرْثَكُمْ أَنَّىٰ شِئْتُمْ  
وَقَدِّمُوا۟ لِأَنفُسِكُمْ ۚ وَٱتَّقُوا۟ ٱللَّهَ  
وَٱعْلَمُوٓا۟ أَنَّكُم مُّلَٰقُوهُ  
وَبَشِّرِ ٱلْمُؤْمِنِينَ ۝

and had Allah wished  
    He would have put you to hardship.'  
Indeed Allah is all-mighty, all-wise.

221 Do not marry idolatresses until they embrace faith.  
    A faithful slave girl is better than an idolatress,  
       though she should impress you.  
And do not marry [your daughters] to idolaters  
    until they embrace faith.  
A faithful slave is better than an idolater,  
    though he should impress you.  
Those invite [others] to the Fire,  
    but Allah invites to paradise and pardon,  
       by His will,  
and He clarifies His signs for the people  
    so that they may take admonition.

222 They ask you concerning [intercourse during] menses.  
    *Say,* 'It is hurtful.'[1]  
So keep away from wives during the menses,[2]  
    and do not approach them till they are clean.  
And when they become clean,  
    go into them as Allah has commanded you.  
Indeed Allah loves the penitent  
    and He loves those who keep clean.

223 Your women are a tillage for you,  
    so come to your tillage whenever you like,  
and send ahead for your souls, and be Godwary,  
and know that you will encounter Him;  
    and *give* good news to the faithful.

---

[1] Or 'offensive.'

[2] That is, 'refrain from sexual intercourse.'

وَلَا تَجْعَلُوا اللَّهَ عُرْضَةً لِّأَيْمَـٰنِكُمْ 224 Do not make Allah an obstacle, through your oaths,

أَن تَبَرُّوا وَتَتَّقُوا to being pious and Godwary,

وَتُصْلِحُوا بَيْنَ النَّاسِ and to bringing about concord between people.

وَاللَّهُ سَمِيعٌ عَلِيمٌ ۝ And Allah is all-hearing, all-knowing.

لَّا يُؤَاخِذُكُمُ اللَّهُ 225 Allah shall not take you to task

بِاللَّغْوِ فِىٓ أَيْمَـٰنِكُمْ for what is unconsidered in your oaths,

وَلَـٰكِن يُؤَاخِذُكُم but He shall take you to task

بِمَا كَسَبَتْ قُلُوبُكُمْ for what your hearts have incurred,

وَاللَّهُ غَفُورٌ حَلِيمٌ ۝ and Allah is all-forgiving, all-forbearing.

لِّلَّذِينَ يُؤْلُونَ مِن نِّسَآئِهِمْ 226 For those who forswear their wives[1]

تَرَبُّصُ أَرْبَعَةِ أَشْهُرٍ shall be a waiting for four months.

فَإِن فَآءُو And if they recant,

فَإِنَّ اللَّهَ غَفُورٌ رَّحِيمٌ ۝ Allah is indeed all-forgiving, all-merciful.

وَإِنْ عَزَمُوا الطَّلَـٰقَ 227 But if they resolve on divorce,

فَإِنَّ اللَّهَ سَمِيعٌ عَلِيمٌ ۝ Allah is indeed all-hearing, all-knowing.

وَالْمُطَلَّقَـٰتُ يَتَرَبَّصْنَ بِأَنفُسِهِنَّ 228 Divorced women shall wait by themselves

ثَلَـٰثَةَ قُرُوٓءٍ for three periods of purity [after menses],

وَلَا يَحِلُّ لَهُنَّ أَن يَكْتُمْنَ and it is not lawful for them to conceal

مَا خَلَقَ اللَّهُ فِىٓ أَرْحَامِهِنَّ what Allah has created in their wombs

إِن كُنَّ يُؤْمِنَّ بِاللَّهِ وَالْيَوْمِ الْأَخِرِ if they have faith in Allah and the Last Day;

وَبُعُولَتُهُنَّ أَحَقُّ بِرَدِّهِنَّ and their husbands have a greater right to restore them

فِى ذَٰلِكَ during this [duration],

إِنْ أَرَادُوٓا إِصْلَـٰحًا if they desire reconcilement.

وَلَهُنَّ The wives have rights

مِثْلُ الَّذِى عَلَيْهِنَّ similar to the obligations upon them,

بِالْمَعْرُوفِ in accordance with honourable norms;

وَلِلرِّجَالِ عَلَيْهِنَّ دَرَجَةٌ and men have a degree above them,

---

[1] That is, by pronouncing *īlā,* a pre-Islamic practice which allowed the husband to take an oath to refrain from sexual relations with his wife, which left the wife in a state of uncertainty for an indefinite period. According to this verse, the husband must decide within four months either to restore the marriage or to divorce her.

وَٱللَّهُ عَزِيزٌ حَكِيمٌ ۝

and Allah is all-mighty and all-wise.

ٱلطَّلَٰقُ مَرَّتَانِ ٢٢٩

229 [Revocable] divorce may be only twice;

فَإِمْسَاكٌ بِمَعْرُوفٍ

then [let there be] either an honourable retention,

أَوْ تَسْرِيحٌ بِإِحْسَٰنٍ

or a kindly release.

وَلَا يَحِلُّ لَكُمْ أَن تَأْخُذُوا

And it is not lawful for you to take back anything

مِمَّآ ءَاتَيْتُمُوهُنَّ شَيْـًٔا

from what you have given them,[1]

إِلَّآ أَن يَخَافَآ أَلَّا يُقِيمَا

unless the couple fear that they may not maintain

حُدُودَ ٱللَّهِ

Allah's bounds.

فَإِنْ خِفْتُمْ أَلَّا يُقِيمَا حُدُودَ ٱللَّهِ

So if you fear they would not maintain Allah's bounds,

فَلَا جُنَاحَ عَلَيْهِمَا

there is no sin upon them[2]

فِيمَا ٱفْتَدَتْ بِهِۦ

in what she may give to secure her release.

تِلْكَ حُدُودُ ٱللَّهِ فَلَا تَعْتَدُوهَا

These are Allah's bounds, so do not transgress them,

وَمَن يَتَعَدَّ حُدُودَ ٱللَّهِ

and whoever transgresses the bounds of Allah

فَأُو۟لَٰٓئِكَ هُمُ ٱلظَّٰلِمُونَ ۝

—it is they who are the wrongdoers.

فَإِن طَلَّقَهَا ٢٣٠

230 And if he divorces her,

فَلَا تَحِلُّ لَهُۥ مِنۢ بَعْدُ حَتَّىٰ تَنكِحَ

she will not be lawful for him until she marries

زَوْجًا غَيْرَهُۥ

a husband other than him,

فَإِن طَلَّقَهَا

and if he divorces her,[3]

فَلَا جُنَاحَ عَلَيْهِمَآ أَن يَتَرَاجَعَآ

there is no sin upon them to remarry

إِن ظَنَّآ أَن يُقِيمَا حُدُودَ ٱللَّهِ

if they think that they can maintain Allah's bounds.

وَتِلْكَ حُدُودُ ٱللَّهِ يُبَيِّنُهَا

These are Allah's bounds, which He clarifies

لِقَوْمٍ يَعْلَمُونَ ۝

for a people who have knowledge.

وَإِذَا طَلَّقْتُمُ ٱلنِّسَآءَ ٢٣١

231 When you divorce women

فَبَلَغْنَ أَجَلَهُنَّ

and they complete their term,

فَأَمْسِكُوهُنَّ بِمَعْرُوفٍ

then either retain them honourably

أَوْ سَرِّحُوهُنَّ بِمَعْرُوفٍ

or release them honourably,

وَلَا تُمْسِكُوهُنَّ ضِرَارًا

and do not retain them maliciously

---

[1] That is, to the wives.

[2] That is, the husband and wife.

[3] That is, after she has been divorced by the second husband, the two of them may remarry if they think they can maintain a healthy marital relationship.

51

| | |
|---:|:---|
| لِتَعۡتَدُوا۟ | in order that you may transgress; |
| وَمَن يَفۡعَلۡ ذَٰلِكَ فَقَدۡ ظَلَمَ نَفۡسَهُۥ | and whoever does that certainly wrongs himself. |
| وَلَا تَتَّخِذُوٓا۟ ءَايَـٰتِ ٱللَّهِ هُزُوًا۟ | Do not take the signs of Allah in derision, |
| وَٱذۡكُرُوا۟ نِعۡمَتَ ٱللَّهِ عَلَيۡكُمۡ | and remember Allah's blessing upon you, |
| وَمَآ أَنزَلَ عَلَيۡكُم | and what He has sent down to you |
| مِّنَ ٱلۡكِتَـٰبِ وَٱلۡحِكۡمَةِ | of the Book and wisdom, |
| يَعِظُكُم بِهِۦ | to advise you therewith. |
| وَٱتَّقُوا۟ ٱللَّهَ | Be wary of Allah, |
| وَٱعۡلَمُوٓا۟ أَنَّ ٱللَّهَ بِكُلِّ شَىۡءٍ عَلِيمٌ ۝ | and know that Allah has knowledge of all things. |
| وَإِذَا طَلَّقۡتُمُ ٱلنِّسَآءَ | 232 When you divorce women |
| فَبَلَغۡنَ أَجَلَهُنَّ | and they complete their term, |
| فَلَا تَعۡضُلُوهُنَّ | do not thwart them |
| أَن يَنكِحۡنَ أَزۡوَٰجَهُنَّ | lest they should [re]marry their husbands, |
| إِذَا تَرَٰضَوۡا۟ بَيۡنَهُم بِٱلۡمَعۡرُوفِ | when they honourably reach mutual consent. |
| ذَٰلِكَ يُوعَظُ بِهِۦ | Herewith are advised |
| مَن كَانَ مِنكُمۡ يُؤۡمِنُ بِٱللَّهِ | those of you who believe in Allah |
| وَٱلۡيَوۡمِ ٱلۡءَاخِرِ | and the Last Day. |
| ذَٰلِكُمۡ أَزۡكَىٰ لَكُمۡ وَأَطۡهَرُ | That will be more decent and purer for you, |
| وَٱللَّهُ يَعۡلَمُ وَأَنتُمۡ لَا تَعۡلَمُونَ ۝ ❊ | and Allah knows and you do not know. |
| وَٱلۡوَٰلِدَٰتُ يُرۡضِعۡنَ أَوۡلَـٰدَهُنَّ | 233 Mothers shall suckle their children |
| حَوۡلَيۡنِ كَامِلَيۡنِ | for two full years, |
| لِمَنۡ أَرَادَ أَن يُتِمَّ ٱلرَّضَاعَةَ | —that for such as desire to complete the suckling— |
| وَعَلَى ٱلۡمَوۡلُودِ لَهُۥ | and on the father shall be |
| رِزۡقُهُنَّ وَكِسۡوَتُهُنَّ | their maintenance and clothing, |
| بِٱلۡمَعۡرُوفِ | in accordance with honourable norms. |
| لَا تُكَلَّفُ نَفۡسٌ إِلَّا وُسۡعَهَا | No soul is to be tasked except according to its capacity: |
| لَا تُضَآرَّ وَٰلِدَةٌۢ | neither the mother shall be made to suffer harm |
| بِوَلَدِهَا | on her child's account, |
| وَلَا مَوۡلُودٌ لَّهُۥ بِوَلَدِهِۦ | nor the father on account of his child, |
| وَعَلَى ٱلۡوَارِثِ | and on the [father's] heir devolve [duties and rights] |

مِّثۡلُ ذَٰلِكَ ۗ    similar to that.

فَإِنۡ أَرَادَا فِصَالاً    And if the couple desire to wean,

عَن تَرَاضٍ مِّنۡهُمَا وَتَشَاوُرٍ    with mutual consent and consultation,

فَلَا جُنَاحَ عَلَيۡهِمَا ۗ    there will be no sin upon them.

وَإِنۡ أَرَدتُّمۡ أَن تَسۡتَرۡضِعُوٓاْ أَوۡلَٰدَكُمۡ    And if you want to have your children wet-nursed,

فَلَا جُنَاحَ عَلَيۡكُمۡ    there will be no sin upon you

إِذَا سَلَّمۡتُم مَّآ ءَاتَيۡتُم    so long as you pay what you give

بِٱلۡمَعۡرُوفِ ۗ    in accordance with honourable norms,

وَٱتَّقُواْ ٱللَّهَ    and be wary of Allah,

وَٱعۡلَمُوٓاْ أَنَّ ٱللَّهَ بِمَا تَعۡمَلُونَ بَصِيرٌ ۝    and know that Allah sees best what you do.

وَٱلَّذِينَ يُتَوَفَّوۡنَ مِنكُمۡ    234 As for those of you who die

وَيَذَرُونَ أَزۡوَٰجًا    leaving wives,

يَتَرَبَّصۡنَ بِأَنفُسِهِنَّ أَرۡبَعَةَ أَشۡهُرٍ    they shall wait by themselves four months

وَعَشۡرًا ۖ    and ten days,

فَإِذَا بَلَغۡنَ أَجَلَهُنَّ    and when they complete their term,

فَلَا جُنَاحَ عَلَيۡكُمۡ    there will be no sin upon you

فِيمَا فَعَلۡنَ فِيٓ أَنفُسِهِنَّ    in respect of what they may do with themselves

بِٱلۡمَعۡرُوفِ ۗ    in accordance with honourable norms.

وَٱللَّهُ بِمَا تَعۡمَلُونَ خَبِيرٌ ۝    And Allah is well aware of what you do.

وَلَا جُنَاحَ عَلَيۡكُمۡ فِيمَا عَرَّضۡتُم بِهِۦ    235 There is no sin upon you in what you may hint

مِنۡ خِطۡبَةِ ٱلنِّسَآءِ    in proposing to [recently widowed] women,

أَوۡ أَكۡنَنتُمۡ فِيٓ أَنفُسِكُمۡ ۚ    or what you may secretly cherish within your hearts.

عَلِمَ ٱللَّهُ أَنَّكُمۡ سَتَذۡكُرُونَهُنَّ    Allah knows that you will be thinking of them,

وَلَٰكِن لَّا تُوَاعِدُوهُنَّ سِرًّا    but do not make troth with them secretly,

إِلَّآ أَن تَقُولُواْ قَوۡلاً مَّعۡرُوفًا ۚ    unless you say honourable words,

وَلَا تَعۡزِمُواْ عُقۡدَةَ ٱلنِّكَاحِ    and do not resolve on a marriage tie

حَتَّىٰ يَبۡلُغَ ٱلۡكِتَٰبُ أَجَلَهُ ۚ    until the prescribed term is complete.[1]

وَٱعۡلَمُوٓاْ أَنَّ ٱللَّهَ يَعۡلَمُ مَا فِيٓ أَنفُسِكُمۡ    Know that Allah knows what is in your hearts,

---

[1] That is, until the waiting period of four months and ten days prescribed for the widows is completed.

فَٱحْذَرُوهُ     so beware of Him;

وَٱعْلَمُوٓا۟ أَنَّ ٱللَّهَ غَفُورٌ حَلِيمٌ ۝     and know that Allah is all-forgiving, all-forbearing.

لَّا جُنَاحَ عَلَيْكُمْ إِن طَلَّقْتُمُ ٱلنِّسَآءَ     236 There is no sin upon you if you divorce women

مَا لَمْ تَمَسُّوهُنَّ     while you have not yet touched them

أَوْ تَفْرِضُوا۟ لَهُنَّ فَرِيضَةً ۚ     or settled a dowry for them.

وَمَتِّعُوهُنَّ     Yet provide for them

عَلَى ٱلْمُوسِعِ قَدَرُهُ     —the well-off according to his capacity,

وَعَلَى ٱلْمُقْتِرِ قَدَرُهُ ۚ     and the poorly-off according to his capacity—

مَتَٰعًۢا بِٱلْمَعْرُوفِ ۖ     with a sustenance that is honourable,

حَقًّا عَلَى ٱلْمُحْسِنِينَ ۝     an obligation on the virtuous.

وَإِن طَلَّقْتُمُوهُنَّ مِن قَبْلِ أَن تَمَسُّوهُنَّ     237 And if you divorce them before you touch them,

وَقَدْ فَرَضْتُمْ لَهُنَّ فَرِيضَةً     and you have already settled a dowry for them,

فَنِصْفُ مَا فَرَضْتُمْ     then [pay them] half of what you have settled,

إِلَّآ أَن يَعْفُونَ     unless they forgo it,

أَوْ يَعْفُوَا۟ ٱلَّذِى بِيَدِهِۦ عُقْدَةُ ٱلنِّكَاحِ ۚ     or someone in whose hand is the marriage tie forgoes it.[1]

وَأَن تَعْفُوٓا۟ أَقْرَبُ لِلتَّقْوَىٰ ۚ     And to forgo is nearer to Godwariness;

وَلَا تَنسَوُا۟ ٱلْفَضْلَ بَيْنَكُمْ ۚ     so do not forget graciousness among yourselves.

إِنَّ ٱللَّهَ بِمَا تَعْمَلُونَ بَصِيرٌ ۝     Indeed Allah sees best what you do.

حَٰفِظُوا۟ عَلَى ٱلصَّلَوَٰتِ     238 Be watchful of your prayers,

وَٱلصَّلَوٰةِ ٱلْوُسْطَىٰ     and [especially] the middle prayer,[2]

وَقُومُوا۟ لِلَّهِ قَٰنِتِينَ ۝     and stand in obedience[3] to Allah;

فَإِنْ خِفْتُمْ     239 and should you fear [a danger],

فَرِجَالًا أَوْ رُكْبَانًا ۖ     then [pray] on foot or mounted,

فَإِذَآ أَمِنتُمْ     and when you are safe,

---

[1] That is, the wife's guardian or the husband. The bride's guardian may forgo the half of the dowry which is her right to receive, or the husband may refrain from demanding half of the dowry he has already paid.

[2] That is, the *ẓuhr* (noon) prayer, according to several traditions narrated from the Imams of the Prophet's Household, as well as many traditions narrated in the Sunnī sources (see *al-Tafsīr al-Burhān*, al-Ṭabarī's *Jāmi' al-Bayān*). According to other interpretations, the phrase 'the middle prayer' refers to the *'aṣr* (afternoon), *maghrib* (sunset) or *fajr* (dawn) prayer.

[3] Or 'stand humbly' (or 'prayerfully,' 'devoutly') before Allah.

فَاذْكُرُوا اللَّهَ
remember Allah,

كَمَا عَلَّمَكُم
as He taught you

مَّا لَمْ تَكُونُوا تَعْلَمُونَ ۞
what you did not know.

وَالَّذِينَ يُتَوَفَّوْنَ مِنكُمْ
240 Those of you who die

وَيَذَرُونَ أَزْوَٰجًا
leaving wives

وَصِيَّةً لِّأَزْوَٰجِهِم
shall bequeath for their wives

مَّتَٰعًا إِلَى الْحَوْلِ
providing for a year,

غَيْرَ إِخْرَاجٍ
without turning them out;

فَإِنْ خَرَجْنَ فَلَا جُنَاحَ عَلَيْكُمْ
but if they leave, there is no sin upon you

فِى مَا فَعَلْنَ فِىٓ أَنفُسِهِنَّ
in respect of what they may do with themselves

مِن مَّعْرُوفٍ
observing honourable norms.

وَاللَّهُ عَزِيزٌ حَكِيمٌ ۞
And Allah is all-mighty, all-wise.

وَلِلْمُطَلَّقَٰتِ مَتَٰعٌۢ
241 For the divorced women there shall be a provision,

بِالْمَعْرُوفِ
in accordance with honourable norms

حَقًّا عَلَى الْمُتَّقِينَ ۞
—an obligation on the Godwary.

كَذَٰلِكَ يُبَيِّنُ اللَّهُ لَكُمْ ءَايَٰتِهِۦ
242 Thus does Allah clarify His signs to you

لَعَلَّكُمْ تَعْقِلُونَ ۞ ❊
so that you may apply reason.

أَلَمْ تَرَ إِلَى الَّذِينَ خَرَجُوا۟ مِن دِيَٰرِهِمْ
243 Have *you* not regarded those who left their homes

وَهُمْ أُلُوفٌ حَذَرَ الْمَوْتِ
in thousands, apprehensive of death,

فَقَالَ لَهُمُ اللَّهُ مُوتُوا۟
whereupon Allah said to them, 'Die,'

ثُمَّ أَحْيَٰهُمْ
then He revived them?

إِنَّ اللَّهَ لَذُو فَضْلٍ عَلَى النَّاسِ
Indeed Allah is gracious to mankind,

وَلَٰكِنَّ أَكْثَرَ النَّاسِ لَا يَشْكُرُونَ ۞
but most people do not give thanks.

وَقَٰتِلُوا۟ فِى سَبِيلِ اللَّهِ
244 Fight in the way of Allah,

وَاعْلَمُوٓا۟ أَنَّ اللَّهَ سَمِيعٌ عَلِيمٌ ۞
and know that Allah is all-hearing, all-knowing.

مَّن ذَا الَّذِى يُقْرِضُ اللَّهَ قَرْضًا حَسَنًا
245 Who is it that will lend Allah a good loan

فَيُضَٰعِفَهُۥ لَهُۥٓ أَضْعَافًا كَثِيرَةً
that He may multiply it for him severalfold?

55

وَٱللَّهُ يَقْبِضُ وَيَبْصُطُ

And Allah tightens and expands [the means of life],

وَإِلَيْهِ تُرْجَعُونَ ۝

and to Him you shall be brought back.

أَلَمْ تَرَ إِلَى ٱلْمَلَإِ مِنْ بَنِى إِسْرَآءِيلَ

246 Have *you* not regarded the elite of the Israelites

مِنْ بَعْدِ مُوسَىٰٓ

after Moses,

إِذْ قَالُوا لِنَبِيٍّ لَّهُمُ

when they said to their prophet,

ٱبْعَثْ لَنَا مَلِكًا

'Appoint for us a king,

نُّقَٰتِلْ فِى سَبِيلِ ٱللَّهِ

that we may fight in the way of Allah.'

قَالَ هَلْ عَسَيْتُمْ

He said, 'May it not be that

إِن كُتِبَ عَلَيْكُمُ ٱلْقِتَالُ أَلَّا تُقَٰتِلُوا

you will not fight if fighting were prescribed for you?'

قَالُوا

They said,

وَمَا لَنَآ أَلَّا نُقَٰتِلَ فِى سَبِيلِ ٱللَّهِ

'Why should we not fight in the way of Allah,

وَقَدْ أُخْرِجْنَا مِن دِيَٰرِنَا

when we have been expelled from our homes

وَأَبْنَآئِنَا

and [separated from] our children?'

فَلَمَّا كُتِبَ عَلَيْهِمُ ٱلْقِتَالُ

So when fighting was prescribed for them,

تَوَلَّوْا إِلَّا قَلِيلًا مِّنْهُمْ

they turned back except a few of them,

وَٱللَّهُ عَلِيمٌۢ بِٱلظَّٰلِمِينَ ۝

and Allah knows best the wrongdoers.

وَقَالَ لَهُمْ نَبِيُّهُمْ

247 Their prophet said to them,

إِنَّ ٱللَّهَ قَدْ بَعَثَ لَكُمْ طَالُوتَ مَلِكًا

'Allah has appointed Saul as king for you.'

قَالُوٓا أَنَّىٰ يَكُونُ لَهُ ٱلْمُلْكُ عَلَيْنَا

They said, 'How can he have kingship over us,

وَنَحْنُ أَحَقُّ بِٱلْمُلْكِ مِنْهُ

when we have a greater right to kingship than him,

وَلَمْ يُؤْتَ سَعَةً مِّنَ ٱلْمَالِ

as he has not been given ample wealth?'

قَالَ إِنَّ ٱللَّهَ ٱصْطَفَىٰهُ عَلَيْكُمْ

He said, 'Indeed Allah has chosen him over you,

وَزَادَهُۥ بَسْطَةً

and enhanced him vastly

فِى ٱلْعِلْمِ وَٱلْجِسْمِ

in knowledge and physique,

وَٱللَّهُ يُؤْتِى مُلْكَهُۥ

and Allah gives His kingdom

مَن يَشَآءُ

to whomever He wishes,

وَٱللَّهُ وَٰسِعٌ عَلِيمٌ ۝

and Allah is all-bounteous, all-knowing.'

وَقَالَ لَهُمْ نَبِيُّهُمْ

248 Their prophet said to them,

إِنَّ ءَايَةَ مُلْكِهِۦٓ

'Indeed the sign of his kingship shall be

أَن يَأْتِيَكُمُ ٱلتَّابُوتُ

that the Ark will come to you,

فِيهِ سَكِينَةٌ مِّن رَّبِّكُمْ

bearing tranquillity from your Lord

وَبَقِيَّةٌ مِّمَّا تَرَكَ ءَالُ مُوسَىٰ

and the relics left behind by the House of Moses

وَءَالُ هَٰرُونَ

and the House of Aaron,

تَحْمِلُهُ ٱلْمَلَٰئِكَةُ ۚ

borne by the angels.

إِنَّ فِى ذَٰلِكَ لَءَايَةً لَّكُمْ

There is indeed a sign in that for you,

إِن كُنتُم مُّؤْمِنِينَ ۝

should you be faithful.'

فَلَمَّا فَصَلَ طَالُوتُ بِٱلْجُنُودِ

249 As Saul set out with the troops,

قَالَ إِنَّ ٱللَّهَ مُبْتَلِيكُم بِنَهَرٍ

he said, 'Allah will test you with a stream:

فَمَن شَرِبَ مِنْهُ فَلَيْسَ مِنِّى

anyone who drinks from it will not belong to me,

وَمَن لَّمْ يَطْعَمْهُ فَإِنَّهُ مِنِّى

but those who do not drink from it will belong to me,

إِلَّا مَنِ ٱغْتَرَفَ غُرْفَةً بِيَدِهِ ۚ

barring someone who draws a scoop with his hand.

فَشَرِبُوا۟ مِنْهُ إِلَّا قَلِيلًا مِّنْهُمْ ۚ

But they drank from it, [all] except a few of them.

فَلَمَّا جَاوَزَهُ

So when he crossed it

هُوَ وَٱلَّذِينَ ءَامَنُوا۟ مَعَهُ

along with the faithful who were with him,

قَالُوا۟ لَا طَاقَةَ لَنَا ٱلْيَوْمَ

they said, 'We have no strength today

بِجَالُوتَ وَجُنُودِهِ ۚ

against Goliath and his troops.'

قَالَ ٱلَّذِينَ يَظُنُّونَ أَنَّهُم مُّلَٰقُوا۟ ٱللَّهِ

Those who were certain they will encounter Allah said,

كَم مِّن فِئَةٍ قَلِيلَةٍ

'How many a small party

غَلَبَتْ فِئَةً كَثِيرَةً

has overcome a larger party

بِإِذْنِ ٱللَّهِ ۗ

by Allah's will!

وَٱللَّهُ مَعَ ٱلصَّٰبِرِينَ ۝

And Allah is with the patient.'

وَلَمَّا بَرَزُوا۟

250 So when they marched out

لِجَالُوتَ وَجُنُودِهِ

for [encounter with] Goliath and his troops,

قَالُوا۟ رَبَّنَآ أَفْرِغْ عَلَيْنَا صَبْرًا

they said, 'Our Lord, pour patience upon us,

وَثَبِّتْ أَقْدَامَنَا

make our feet steady,

وَٱنصُرْنَا عَلَى ٱلْقَوْمِ ٱلْكَٰفِرِينَ ۝

and assist us against the faithless lot.'

فَهَزَمُوهُم بِإِذْنِ ٱللَّهِ

251 Thus they routed them with Allah's will,

وَقَتَلَ دَاوُۥدُ جَالُوتَ

and David killed Goliath,

وَءَاتَىٰهُ ٱللَّهُ ٱلْمُلْكَ وَٱلْحِكْمَةَ

and Allah gave him the kingdom and wisdom,

وَعَلَّمَهُ مِمَّا يَشَاءُ and taught him whatever He liked.

وَلَوْلَا دَفْعُ ٱللَّهِ ٱلنَّاسَ Were it not for Allah's repelling the people

بَعْضَهُم بِبَعْضٍ by means of one another,

لَّفَسَدَتِ ٱلْأَرْضُ the earth would surely have been corrupted;

وَلَكِنَّ ٱللَّهَ ذُو فَضْلٍ عَلَى ٱلْعَلَمِينَ but Allah is gracious to the world's creatures.

تِلْكَ ءَايَتُ ٱللَّهِ 252 These are the signs of Allah

نَتْلُوهَا عَلَيْكَ بِٱلْحَقِّ which We recite for *you* in truth,

وَإِنَّكَ لَمِنَ ٱلْمُرْسَلِينَ and *you* are indeed one of the apostles.

[PART 3]

تِلْكَ ٱلرُّسُلُ 253 These are the apostles,

فَضَّلْنَا بَعْضَهُمْ عَلَى بَعْضٍ some of whom We gave an advantage over others:

مِّنْهُم مَّن كَلَّمَ ٱللَّهُ of them are those to whom Allah spoke,

وَرَفَعَ بَعْضَهُمْ دَرَجَتٍ and some of them He raised in rank,

وَءَاتَيْنَا عِيسَى ٱبْنَ مَرْيَمَ ٱلْبَيِّنَتِ and We gave Jesus, son of Mary, manifest proofs

وَأَيَّدْنَهُ بِرُوحِ ٱلْقُدُسِ and strengthened him with the Holy Spirit.

وَلَوْ شَاءَ ٱللَّهُ Had Allah wished,

مَا ٱقْتَتَلَ ٱلَّذِينَ مِنْ بَعْدِهِم those who succeeded them would not have fought each othe

مِنْ بَعْدِ مَا جَاءَتْهُمُ ٱلْبَيِّنَتُ after the manifest proofs had come to them.

وَلَكِنِ ٱخْتَلَفُوا But they differed.

فَمِنْهُم مَّنْ ءَامَنَ So there were among them those who had faith

وَمِنْهُم مَّن كَفَرَ and there were among them those who were faithless,

وَلَوْ شَاءَ ٱللَّهُ and had Allah wished,

مَا ٱقْتَتَلُوا they would not have fought one another;

وَلَكِنَّ ٱللَّهَ يَفْعَلُ مَا يُرِيدُ but Allah does whatever He desires.

يَأَيُّهَا ٱلَّذِينَ ءَامَنُوا 254 O you who have faith!

أَنفِقُوا مِمَّا رَزَقْنَكُم Spend out of what We have provided you

مِن قَبْلِ أَن يَأْتِيَ يَوْمٌ before there comes a day

لَّا بَيْعٌ فِيهِ on which there will be no bargaining,

وَلَا خُلَّةٌ وَلَا شَفَعَةٌ neither friendship, nor intercession.

وَٱلْكَفِرُونَ هُمُ ٱلظَّلِمُونَ ۝ And the faithless—they are the wrongdoers.

ٱللَّهُ لَآ إِلَهَ إِلَّا هُوَ 255 Allah—there is no god except Him—

ٱلْحَىُّ ٱلْقَيُّومُ is the Living One, the All-sustainer.

لَا تَأْخُذُهُ سِنَةٌ وَلَا نَوْمٌ Neither drowsiness befalls Him nor sleep.

لَّهُۥ مَا فِى ٱلسَّمَوَتِ To Him belongs whatever is in the heavens

وَمَا فِى ٱلْأَرْضِ and whatever is on the earth.

مَن ذَا ٱلَّذِى يَشْفَعُ عِندَهُۥٓ Who is it that may intercede with Him

إِلَّا بِإِذْنِهِۦ except with His permission?

يَعْلَمُ مَا بَيْنَ أَيْدِيهِمْ He knows that which is before them

وَمَا خَلْفَهُمْ and that which is behind them,

وَلَا يُحِيطُونَ and they do not comprehend

بِشَىْءٍ مِّنْ عِلْمِهِۦٓ anything of His knowledge

إِلَّا بِمَا شَآءَ except what He wishes.

وَسِعَ كُرْسِيُّهُ ٱلسَّمَوَتِ وَٱلْأَرْضَ His seat embraces the heavens and the earth,

وَلَا يَـُٔودُهُۥ حِفْظُهُمَا and He is not wearied by their preservation,

وَهُوَ ٱلْعَلِىُّ ٱلْعَظِيمُ ۝ and He is the All-exalted, the All-supreme.

لَآ إِكْرَاهَ فِى ٱلدِّينِ 256 There is no compulsion in religion:

قَد تَّبَيَّنَ ٱلرُّشْدُ مِنَ ٱلْغَىِّ rectitude has become distinct from error.

فَمَن يَكْفُرْ بِٱلطَّغُوتِ So one who disavows the Rebels[1]

وَيُؤْمِنۢ بِٱللَّهِ and has faith in Allah

فَقَدِ ٱسْتَمْسَكَ بِٱلْعُرْوَةِ ٱلْوُثْقَىٰ has held fast to the firmest handle

لَا ٱنفِصَامَ لَهَا for which there is no breaking;

وَٱللَّهُ سَمِيعٌ عَلِيمٌ ۝ and Allah is all-hearing, all-knowing.

ٱللَّهُ وَلِىُّ ٱلَّذِينَ ءَامَنُوا 257 Allah is the Master of the faithful:

يُخْرِجُهُم مِّنَ ٱلظُّلُمَتِ إِلَى ٱلنُّورِ He brings them out of darkness into light.

وَٱلَّذِينَ كَفَرُوٓا أَوْلِيَآؤُهُمُ ٱلطَّغُوتُ As for the faithless, their patrons are the Rebels,

يُخْرِجُونَهُم مِّنَ ٱلنُّورِ إِلَى ٱلظُّلُمَتِ who drive them out of light into darkness.

---

[1] The word *ṭāghūt* has also been said to imply Satan (also called 'rebel angel' and 'rebel against God'), idol, soothsayer, magician, rebellious humans and jinn, and the carnal soul. Cf. 4:51 60, 76; 5:60; 16:36.

أُوْلَـٰٓئِكَ أَصْحَـٰبُ ٱلنَّارِ
They shall be the inmates of the Fire,

هُمْ فِيهَا خَـٰلِدُونَ ۝
and they shall remain in it [forever].

أَلَمْ تَرَ إِلَى ٱلَّذِى
258 Have *you* not regarded him[1]

حَآجَّ إِبْرَٰهِـۧمَ
who argued with Abraham

فِى رَبِّهِۦٓ
about his Lord,

أَنْ ءَاتَىٰهُ ٱللَّهُ ٱلْمُلْكَ
because Allah had given him kingdom?

إِذْ قَالَ إِبْرَٰهِـۧمُ
When Abraham said,

رَبِّىَ ٱلَّذِى يُحْىِۦ وَيُمِيتُ
'My Lord is He who gives life and brings death,'

قَالَ أَنَا۠ أُحْىِۦ وَأُمِيتُ
he replied, 'I [too] give life and bring death.'

قَالَ إِبْرَٰهِـۧمُ
Abraham said,

فَإِنَّ ٱللَّهَ يَأْتِى بِٱلشَّمْسِ مِنَ ٱلْمَشْرِقِ
'Indeed Allah brings the sun from the east;

فَأْتِ بِهَا مِنَ ٱلْمَغْرِبِ
now you bring it from the west.'

فَبُهِتَ ٱلَّذِى كَفَرَ
Thereat the faithless one was dumbfounded.

وَٱللَّهُ لَا يَهْدِى ٱلْقَوْمَ ٱلظَّـٰلِمِينَ ۝
And Allah does not guide the wrongdoing lot.

أَوْ كَٱلَّذِى مَرَّ عَلَىٰ قَرْيَةٍ
259 Or him[2] who came upon a township

وَهِىَ خَاوِيَةٌ عَلَىٰ عُرُوشِهَا
as it lay fallen on its trellises.

قَالَ أَنَّىٰ يُحْىِۦ هَـٰذِهِ ٱللَّهُ بَعْدَ مَوْتِهَا
He said, 'How will Allah revive this after its death?!'

فَأَمَاتَهُ ٱللَّهُ مِائَةَ عَامٍ
So Allah made him die for a hundred years,

ثُمَّ بَعَثَهُۥ
then He resurrected him.

قَالَ كَمْ لَبِثْتَ
He said, 'How long have you remained?'

قَالَ لَبِثْتُ يَوْمًا أَوْ بَعْضَ يَوْمٍ
Said he, 'I have remained a day or part of a day.'

قَالَ بَل لَّبِثْتَ مِائَةَ عَامٍ
He said, 'Rather you have remained a hundred years.

فَٱنظُرْ إِلَىٰ طَعَامِكَ وَشَرَابِكَ
Now look at your food and drink

لَمْ يَتَسَنَّهْ
which have not rotted!

وَٱنظُرْ إِلَىٰ حِمَارِكَ
Then look at your ass!

وَلِنَجْعَلَكَ ءَايَةً
[This was done] that We may make you a sign

لِّلنَّاسِ
for mankind.

---

[1] That is, Nimrod.

[2] That is, Ezra ('Uzayr).

وَٱنظُرْ إِلَى ٱلْعِظَامِ كَيْفَ نُنشِزُهَا    And look at the bones, how We arrange them

ثُمَّ نَكْسُوهَا لَحْمًا    and then clothe them with flesh!'

فَلَمَّا تَبَيَّنَ لَهُ قَالَ    When it became evident to him, he said,

أَعْلَمُ أَنَّ ٱللَّهَ عَلَى كُلِّ شَيْءٍ قَدِيرٌ ۝    'I know that Allah has power over all things.'

وَإِذْ قَالَ إِبْرَٰهِـمُ رَبِّ    260 And when Abraham said, 'My Lord!

أَرِنِى كَيْفَ تُحْيِ ٱلْمَوْتَىٰ    Show me how You revive the dead,'

قَالَ أَوَلَمْ تُؤْمِن    He said, 'Do you not believe?'

قَالَ بَلَىٰ    He said, 'Yes indeed,

وَلَـٰكِن لِّيَطْمَئِنَّ قَلْبِى    but in order that my heart may be at rest.'

قَالَ فَخُذْ أَرْبَعَةً مِّنَ ٱلطَّيْرِ    He said, 'Take four of the birds.

فَصُرْهُنَّ إِلَيْكَ    Then cut them into pieces,

ثُمَّ ٱجْعَلْ عَلَىٰ كُلِّ جَبَلٍ مِّنْهُنَّ جُزْءًا    and place a part of them on every mountain,

ثُمَّ ٱدْعُهُنَّ    then call them;

يَأْتِينَكَ سَعْيًا    they will come to you hastening.

وَٱعْلَمْ أَنَّ ٱللَّهَ عَزِيزٌ حَكِيمٌ ۝    And know that Allah is all-mighty and all-wise.'

مَّثَلُ ٱلَّذِينَ يُنفِقُونَ أَمْوَٰلَهُمْ    261 The parable of those who spend their wealth

فِى سَبِيلِ ٱللَّهِ    in the way of Allah

كَمَثَلِ حَبَّةٍ أَنۢبَتَتْ سَبْعَ سَنَابِلَ    is that of a grain which grows seven ears,

فِى كُلِّ سُنۢبُلَةٍ مِّائَةُ حَبَّةٍ    in every ear a hundred grains.

وَٱللَّهُ يُضَٰعِفُ لِمَن يَشَآءُ    Allah enhances severalfold whomever He wishes,

وَٱللَّهُ وَٰسِعٌ عَلِيمٌ ۝    and Allah is all-bounteous, all-knowing.

ٱلَّذِينَ يُنفِقُونَ أَمْوَٰلَهُمْ فِى سَبِيلِ ٱللَّهِ    262 Those who spend their wealth in the way of Allah

ثُمَّ لَا يُتْبِعُونَ مَآ أَنفَقُوا    and then do not follow up what they have spent

مَنًّا وَلَآ أَذًى    with reproaches[1] and affronts,

لَّهُمْ أَجْرُهُمْ عِندَ رَبِّهِمْ    they shall have their reward near their Lord,

وَلَا خَوْفٌ عَلَيْهِمْ    and they will have no fear,

وَلَا هُمْ يَحْزَنُونَ ۝    nor will they grieve.

---

[1] More exactly, with reproachful reminders of favours done. Cf. 2:264 below.

قَوْلٌ مَّعْرُوفٌ وَمَغْفِرَةٌ

263 An honourable word with pardon

خَيْرٌ مِّن صَدَقَةٍ يَتْبَعُهَا أَذًى

is better than a charity followed by affront.

وَٱللَّهُ غَنِىٌّ حَلِيمٌ ۝

Allah is all-sufficient, most forbearing.

يَـٰٓأَيُّهَا ٱلَّذِينَ ءَامَنُوا۟

264 O you who have faith!

لَا تُبْطِلُوا۟ صَدَقَـٰتِكُم

Do not render your charities void

بِٱلْمَنِّ وَٱلْأَذَىٰ

by reproaches and affronts,

كَٱلَّذِى يُنفِقُ مَالَهُۥ

like those who spend their wealth

رِئَآءَ ٱلنَّاسِ

to be seen by people

وَلَا يُؤْمِنُ بِٱللَّهِ وَٱلْيَوْمِ ٱلْءَاخِرِ

and have no faith in Allah and the Last Day.

فَمَثَلُهُۥ كَمَثَلِ صَفْوَانٍ عَلَيْهِ تُرَابٌ

Their parable[1] is that of a rock covered with soil:

فَأَصَابَهُۥ وَابِلٌ فَتَرَكَهُۥ صَلْدًا

a downpour strikes it, leaving it bare.

لَّا يَقْدِرُونَ

They have no power

عَلَىٰ شَىْءٍ مِّمَّا كَسَبُوا۟

over anything of what they have earned,

وَٱللَّهُ لَا يَهْدِى ٱلْقَوْمَ ٱلْكَـٰفِرِينَ ۝

and Allah does not guide the faithless lot.

وَمَثَلُ ٱلَّذِينَ يُنفِقُونَ أَمْوَٰلَهُمُ

265 The parable of those who spend their wealth

ٱبْتِغَآءَ مَرْضَاتِ ٱللَّهِ

seeking Allah's pleasure

وَتَثْبِيتًا مِّنْ أَنفُسِهِمْ

and to confirm themselves,

كَمَثَلِ جَنَّةٍ بِرَبْوَةٍ

is that of a garden on a hillside:

أَصَابَهَا وَابِلٌ

the downpour strikes it,

فَـَٔاتَتْ أُكُلَهَا ضِعْفَيْنِ

whereupon it brings forth its fruit twofold;

فَإِن لَّمْ يُصِبْهَا وَابِلٌ

and if it is not a downpour that strikes it,

فَطَلٌّ

then a shower,

وَٱللَّهُ بِمَا تَعْمَلُونَ بَصِيرٌ ۝

and Allah sees best what you do.

أَيَوَدُّ أَحَدُكُمْ أَن تَكُونَ لَهُۥ

266 Would any of you like to have

جَنَّةٌ مِّن نَّخِيلٍ وَأَعْنَابٍ

a garden of palm trees and vines,

تَجْرِى مِن تَحْتِهَا ٱلْأَنْهَـٰرُ

with streams running in it,

لَهُۥ فِيهَا مِن كُلِّ ٱلثَّمَرَٰتِ

with all kinds of fruit for him therein,

وَأَصَابَهُ ٱلْكِبَرُ

and old age were to strike him

وَلَهُۥ ذُرِّيَّةٌ ضُعَفَآءُ

while he has weakly offspring;

---

[1] Or 'example.'

| | |
|---|---|
| فَأَصَابَهَآ إِعْصَارٌ فِيهِ نَارٌ | whereupon a fiery hurricane were to hit it, |
| فَٱحْتَرَقَتْ | whereat it lies burnt? |
| كَذَٰلِكَ يُبَيِّنُ ٱللَّهُ لَكُمُ ٱلْءَايَٰتِ | Thus does Allah clarify His signs for you |
| لَعَلَّكُمْ تَتَفَكَّرُونَ ۝ | so that you may reflect. |
| يَٰٓأَيُّهَا ٱلَّذِينَ ءَامَنُوٓا۟ | 267 O you who have faith! |
| أَنفِقُوا۟ مِن طَيِّبَٰتِ مَا كَسَبْتُمْ | Spend of the good things you have earned, |
| وَمِمَّآ أَخْرَجْنَا لَكُم | and of what We bring forth for you |
| مِّنَ ٱلْأَرْضِ | from the earth, |
| وَلَا تَيَمَّمُوا۟ ٱلْخَبِيثَ مِنْهُ تُنفِقُونَ | and do not be of the mind to give the bad part of it, |
| وَلَسْتُم بِـَٔاخِذِيهِ | for you yourselves would not take it, |
| إِلَّآ أَن تُغْمِضُوا۟ فِيهِ | unless you overlook it. |
| وَٱعْلَمُوٓا۟ أَنَّ ٱللَّهَ غَنِىٌّ حَمِيدٌ ۝ | And know that Allah is all-sufficient, all-laudable. |
| ٱلشَّيْطَٰنُ يَعِدُكُمُ ٱلْفَقْرَ | 268 Satan frightens you of poverty |
| وَيَأْمُرُكُم بِٱلْفَحْشَآءِ | and prompts you to [commit] indecent acts. |
| وَٱللَّهُ يَعِدُكُم مَّغْفِرَةً مِّنْهُ وَفَضْلًا | But Allah promises you His forgiveness and grace, |
| وَٱللَّهُ وَٰسِعٌ عَلِيمٌ ۝ | and Allah is all-bounteous, all-knowing. |
| يُؤْتِى ٱلْحِكْمَةَ مَن يَشَآءُ | 269 He gives wisdom to whomever He wishes, |
| وَمَن يُؤْتَ ٱلْحِكْمَةَ | and he who is given wisdom, |
| فَقَدْ أُوتِىَ خَيْرًا كَثِيرًا | is certainly given an abundant good. |
| وَمَا يَذَّكَّرُ | But none takes admonition |
| إِلَّآ أُو۟لُوا۟ ٱلْأَلْبَٰبِ ۝ | except those who possess intellect. |
| وَمَآ أَنفَقْتُم مِّن نَّفَقَةٍ | 270 Whatever charity you may give, |
| أَوْ نَذَرْتُم مِّن نَّذْرٍ | or vows that you may vow, |
| فَإِنَّ ٱللَّهَ يَعْلَمُهُ | Allah indeed knows it, |
| وَمَا لِلظَّٰلِمِينَ مِنْ أَنصَارٍ ۝ | and the wrongdoers have no helpers. |
| إِن تُبْدُوا۟ ٱلصَّدَقَٰتِ فَنِعِمَّا هِىَ | 271 If you disclose your charities, that is well, |
| وَإِن تُخْفُوهَا وَتُؤْتُوهَا ٱلْفُقَرَآءَ | but if you hide them and give them to the poor, |
| فَهُوَ خَيْرٌ لَّكُمْ | that is better for you, |
| وَيُكَفِّرُ عَنكُم مِّن سَيِّـَٔاتِكُمْ | and it will atone for some of your misdeeds, |
| وَٱللَّهُ بِمَا تَعْمَلُونَ خَبِيرٌ ۝ | and Allah is well aware of what you do. |

لَّيْسَ عَلَيْكَ هُدَىٰهُمْ 272 It is not up to *you* to guide them;

وَلَٰكِنَّ ٱللَّهَ يَهْدِى مَن يَشَآءُ rather it is Allah who guides whomever He wishes.

وَمَا تُنفِقُواْ مِنْ خَيْرٍ And whatever wealth you spend,

فَلِأَنفُسِكُمْ it is for your own benefit,

وَمَا تُنفِقُونَ إِلَّا ٱبْتِغَآءَ وَجْهِ ٱللَّهِ as you do not spend but to seek Allah's pleasure,

وَمَا تُنفِقُواْ مِنْ خَيْرٍ and whatever wealth you spend

يُوَفَّ إِلَيْكُمْ will be repaid to you in full,

وَأَنتُمْ لَا تُظْلَمُونَ ۝ and you will not be wronged.

لِلْفُقَرَآءِ ٱلَّذِينَ أُحْصِرُواْ 273 [The charities are] for the poor who are straitened

فِى سَبِيلِ ٱللَّهِ in the way of Allah,[1]

لَا يَسْتَطِيعُونَ ضَرْبًا فِى ٱلْأَرْضِ not capable of moving about in the land [for trade].

يَحْسَبُهُمُ ٱلْجَاهِلُ أَغْنِيَآءَ The unaware suppose them to be well-off

مِنَ ٱلتَّعَفُّفِ because of their reserve.

تَعْرِفُهُم بِسِيمَٰهُمْ *You* recognize them by their mark;

لَا يَسْـَٔلُونَ ٱلنَّاسَ إِلْحَافًا they do not ask the people importunately.

وَمَا تُنفِقُواْ مِنْ خَيْرٍ And whatever wealth you may spend,

فَإِنَّ ٱللَّهَ بِهِۦ عَلِيمٌ ۝ Allah indeed knows it.

ٱلَّذِينَ يُنفِقُونَ أَمْوَٰلَهُم 274 Those who give their wealth

بِٱلَّيْلِ وَٱلنَّهَارِ by night and day,

سِرًّا وَعَلَانِيَةً secretly and openly,

فَلَهُمْ أَجْرُهُمْ عِندَ رَبِّهِمْ they shall have their reward near their Lord,

وَلَا خَوْفٌ عَلَيْهِمْ and they will have no fear,

وَلَا هُمْ يَحْزَنُونَ ۝ nor will they grieve.

ٱلَّذِينَ يَأْكُلُونَ ٱلرِّبَوٰاْ لَا يَقُومُونَ 275 Those who exact usury will not stand

إِلَّا كَمَا يَقُومُ but like one

ٱلَّذِى يَتَخَبَّطُهُ ٱلشَّيْطَٰنُ مِنَ ٱلْمَسِّ deranged by the Devil's touch.

ذَٰلِكَ بِأَنَّهُمْ قَالُوٓاْ That is because they say,

إِنَّمَا ٱلْبَيْعُ مِثْلُ ٱلرِّبَوٰاْ 'Trade is just like usury.'

---

[1] That is, due to their engagement in *jihād*, or in learning and teaching Islamic sciences or martial arts, or due to the rigours of spiritual wayfaring.

وَأَحَلَّ ٱللَّهُ ٱلْبَيْعَ وَحَرَّمَ ٱلرِّبَوٰاْ    While Allah has allowed trade and forbidden usury.

فَمَن جَآءَهُ مَوْعِظَةٌ مِّن رَّبِّهِۦ    Whoever, on receiving advice from his Lord,

فَٱنتَهَىٰ    relinquishes [usury],

فَلَهُۥ مَا سَلَفَ    shall keep [the gains of] what is past,

وَأَمْرُهُۥٓ إِلَى ٱللَّهِ    and his matter shall rest with Allah.

وَمَنْ عَادَ    As for those who resume,

فَأُوْلَٰٓئِكَ أَصْحَٰبُ ٱلنَّارِ    they shall be the inmates of the Fire

هُمْ فِيهَا خَٰلِدُونَ ۝    and they shall remain in it [forever].

يَمْحَقُ ٱللَّهُ ٱلرِّبَوٰاْ    276 Allah brings usury to naught,

وَيُرْبِى ٱلصَّدَقَٰتِ    but He makes charities flourish.

وَٱللَّهُ لَا يُحِبُّ كُلَّ كَفَّارٍ أَثِيمٍ ۝    Allah does not like any sinful ingrate.

إِنَّ ٱلَّذِينَ ءَامَنُواْ    277 Indeed those who have faith,

وَعَمِلُواْ ٱلصَّٰلِحَٰتِ    do righteous deeds,

وَأَقَامُواْ ٱلصَّلَوٰةَ وَءَاتَوُاْ ٱلزَّكَوٰةَ    maintain the prayer and give the *zakat*,

لَهُمْ أَجْرُهُمْ عِندَ رَبِّهِمْ    they shall have their reward near their Lord,

وَلَا خَوْفٌ عَلَيْهِمْ    and they will have no fear,

وَلَا هُمْ يَحْزَنُونَ ۝    nor will they grieve.

يَٰٓأَيُّهَا ٱلَّذِينَ ءَامَنُواْ    278 O you who have faith!

ٱتَّقُواْ ٱللَّهَ    Be wary of Allah,

وَذَرُواْ مَا بَقِىَ مِنَ ٱلرِّبَوٰاْ    and abandon [all claims to] what remains of usury,

إِن كُنتُم مُّؤْمِنِينَ ۝    should you be faithful.

فَإِن لَّمْ تَفْعَلُواْ فَأْذَنُواْ بِحَرْبٍ    279 And if you do not, then be informed of a war

مِّنَ ٱللَّهِ وَرَسُولِهِۦ    from Allah and His apostle.

وَإِن تُبْتُمْ    And if you repent,

فَلَكُمْ رُءُوسُ أَمْوَٰلِكُمْ    then you will have your principal,

لَا تَظْلِمُونَ وَلَا تُظْلَمُونَ ۝    neither harming others, nor suffering harm.

وَإِن كَانَ ذُو عُسْرَةٍ    280 And if [the debtor] is in straits,

فَنَظِرَةٌ إِلَىٰ مَيْسَرَةٍ    let there be a respite until the time of ease;

وَأَن تَصَدَّقُواْ    and if you remit [the debt] as charity,

خَيْرٌ لَّكُمْ    it will be better for you,

إِن كُنتُمۡ تَعۡلَمُونَ ۩    should you know.

وَٱتَّقُواْ يَوۡمًا    281 And beware of a day

تُرۡجَعُونَ فِيهِ إِلَى ٱللَّهِ    in which you will be brought back to Allah.

ثُمَّ تُوَفَّىٰ كُلُّ نَفۡسٍ    Then every soul shall be recompensed fully

مَّا كَسَبَتۡ    for what it has earned,

وَهُمۡ لَا يُظۡلَمُونَ ۩    and they will not be wronged.

يَٰٓأَيُّهَا ٱلَّذِينَ ءَامَنُوٓاْ    282 O you who have faith!

إِذَا تَدَايَنتُم بِدَيۡنٍ إِلَىٰٓ أَجَلٍ مُّسَمًّى    When you contract a loan for a specified term,

فَٱكۡتُبُوهُ    write it down.

وَلۡيَكۡتُب بَّيۡنَكُمۡ كَاتِبُۢ بِٱلۡعَدۡلِ    Let a writer write between you with honesty,

وَلَا يَأۡبَ كَاتِبٌ أَن يَكۡتُبَ    and let not the writer refuse to write

كَمَا عَلَّمَهُ ٱللَّهُ    as Allah has taught him.

فَلۡيَكۡتُبۡ    So let him write,

وَلۡيُمۡلِلِ ٱلَّذِى عَلَيۡهِ ٱلۡحَقُّ    and let the one who incurs the debt dictate,

وَلۡيَتَّقِ ٱللَّهَ رَبَّهُۥ    and let him be wary of Allah, his Lord,

وَلَا يَبۡخَسۡ مِنۡهُ شَيۡـًٔا    and not diminish anything from it.

فَإِن كَانَ ٱلَّذِى عَلَيۡهِ ٱلۡحَقُّ سَفِيهًا    But if the debtor be feeble-minded,

أَوۡ ضَعِيفًا    or weak,

أَوۡ لَا يَسۡتَطِيعُ أَن يُمِلَّ هُوَ    or incapable of dictating himself,

فَلۡيُمۡلِلۡ وَلِيُّهُۥ بِٱلۡعَدۡلِ    then let his guardian dictate with honesty,

وَٱسۡتَشۡهِدُواْ شَهِيدَيۡنِ مِن رِّجَالِكُمۡ    and take as witness two witnesses from your men,

فَإِن لَّمۡ يَكُونَا رَجُلَيۡنِ    and if there are not two men,

فَرَجُلٌ وَٱمۡرَأَتَانِ    then a man and two women

مِمَّن تَرۡضَوۡنَ مِنَ ٱلشُّهَدَآءِ    —from those whom you approve as witnesses—

أَن تَضِلَّ إِحۡدَىٰهُمَا    so that if one of the two defaults

فَتُذَكِّرَ إِحۡدَىٰهُمَا ٱلۡأُخۡرَىٰ    the other will remind her.

وَلَا يَأۡبَ ٱلشُّهَدَآءُ إِذَا مَا دُعُواْ    The witnesses must not refuse when they are called,

وَلَا تَسۡـَٔمُوٓاْ أَن تَكۡتُبُوهُ    and do not consider it wearisome to write it down,

صَغِيرًا أَوۡ كَبِيرًا    whether it be a big or a small sum,

إِلَىٰٓ أَجَلِهِۦ    [as being lent] until its term.

ذَٰلِكُمْ أَقْسَطُ عِندَ ٱللَّهِ

That is more just with Allah

وَأَقْوَمُ لِلشَّهَٰدَةِ

and more upright in respect to testimony,

وَأَدْنَىٰٓ أَلَّا تَرْتَابُوٓا۟

and the likeliest way to avoid doubt,

إِلَّآ أَن تَكُونَ تِجَٰرَةً حَاضِرَةً

unless it is an on the spot deal

تُدِيرُونَهَا بَيْنَكُمْ

you transact between yourselves,

فَلَيْسَ عَلَيْكُمْ جُنَاحٌ

in which case there is no sin upon you

أَلَّا تَكْتُبُوهَا

not to write it.

وَأَشْهِدُوٓا۟ إِذَا تَبَايَعْتُمْ

Take witnesses when you make a deal,

وَلَا يُضَآرَّ كَاتِبٌ وَلَا شَهِيدٌ

and let no harm be done to writer or witness,

وَإِن تَفْعَلُوا۟ فَإِنَّهُۥ فُسُوقٌۢ بِكُمْ

and if you did that, it would be sinful of you.

وَٱتَّقُوا۟ ٱللَّهَ وَيُعَلِّمُكُمُ ٱللَّهُ

Be wary of Allah and Allah shall teach you,

وَٱللَّهُ بِكُلِّ شَىْءٍ عَلِيمٌ

and Allah has knowledge of all things.

٢٨٣ وَإِن كُنتُمْ عَلَىٰ سَفَرٍ

283 If you are on a journey

وَلَمْ تَجِدُوا۟ كَاتِبًا

and cannot find a writer,

فَرِهَٰنٌ مَّقْبُوضَةٌ

then a retained pledge [shall suffice].

فَإِنْ أَمِنَ بَعْضُكُم بَعْضًا

And if one of you entrusts to another,

فَلْيُؤَدِّ ٱلَّذِى ٱؤْتُمِنَ أَمَٰنَتَهُۥ

let him who is trusted deliver his trust,

وَلْيَتَّقِ ٱللَّهَ رَبَّهُۥ

and let him be wary of Allah, his Lord.

وَلَا تَكْتُمُوا۟ ٱلشَّهَٰدَةَ

And do not conceal testimony;

وَمَن يَكْتُمْهَا

anyone who conceals it,

فَإِنَّهُۥٓ ءَاثِمٌ قَلْبُهُۥ

his heart will indeed be sinful.

وَٱللَّهُ بِمَا تَعْمَلُونَ عَلِيمٌ

And Allah knows best what you do.

٢٨٤ لِّلَّهِ مَا فِى ٱلسَّمَٰوَٰتِ

284 To Allah belongs whatever is in the heavens

وَمَا فِى ٱلْأَرْضِ

and whatever is in the earth;

وَإِن تُبْدُوا۟ مَا فِىٓ أَنفُسِكُمْ

and whether you disclose what is in your hearts

أَوْ تُخْفُوهُ

or hide it,

يُحَاسِبْكُم بِهِ ٱللَّهُ

Allah will bring you to account for it.

فَيَغْفِرُ لِمَن يَشَآءُ

Then He will forgive whomever He wishes

وَيُعَذِّبُ مَن يَشَآءُ

and punish whomever He wishes,

وَٱللَّهُ عَلَىٰ كُلِّ شَىْءٍ قَدِيرٌ

and Allah has power over all things.

ءَامَنَ ٱلرَّسُولُ 285 The Apostle has faith

بِمَآ أُنزِلَ إِلَيْهِ مِن رَّبِّهِۦ in what has been sent down to him from his Lord,

وَٱلْمُؤْمِنُونَ and all the faithful.

كُلٌّ ءَامَنَ بِٱللَّهِ Each [of them] has faith in Allah,

وَمَلَـٰٓئِكَتِهِۦ وَكُتُبِهِۦ وَرُسُلِهِۦ His angels, His scriptures and His apostles.

لَا نُفَرِّقُ [They declare,] 'We make no distinction

بَيْنَ أَحَدٍ مِّن رُّسُلِهِۦ between any of His apostles.'

وَقَالُوا۟ سَمِعْنَا وَأَطَعْنَا And they say, 'We hear and obey.

غُفْرَانَكَ رَبَّنَا Our Lord, forgive us,

وَإِلَيْكَ ٱلْمَصِيرُ ۝ and toward You is the return.'

لَا يُكَلِّفُ ٱللَّهُ نَفْسًا إِلَّا وُسْعَهَا 286 Allah does not task any soul beyond its capacity.

لَهَا مَا كَسَبَتْ Whatever [good] it earns is to its benefit,

وَعَلَيْهَا مَا ٱكْتَسَبَتْ and whatever [evil] it incurs is to its harm.

رَبَّنَا 'Our Lord!

لَا تُؤَاخِذْنَآ إِن نَّسِينَآ Take us not to task if we forget

أَوْ أَخْطَأْنَا or make mistakes!

رَبَّنَا Our Lord!

وَلَا تَحْمِلْ عَلَيْنَآ إِصْرًا Place not upon us a burden

كَمَا حَمَلْتَهُۥ عَلَى ٱلَّذِينَ مِن قَبْلِنَا as You placed on those who were before us!

رَبَّنَا Our Lord!

وَلَا تُحَمِّلْنَا مَا لَا طَاقَةَ لَنَا بِهِۦ Lay not upon us what we have no strength to bear!

وَٱعْفُ عَنَّا وَٱغْفِرْ لَنَا Excuse us and forgive us,

وَٱرْحَمْنَآ and be merciful to us!

أَنتَ مَوْلَىٰنَا You are our Master,

فَٱنصُرْنَا عَلَى ٱلْقَوْمِ ٱلْكَـٰفِرِينَ ۝ so help us against the faithless lot!'

# سُورَةُ الْعِمْرَانَ     3. SŪRAT ĀL-I 'IMRĀN[1]

بِسْمِ اللَّهِ
الرَّحْمَنِ الرَّحِيمِ

In the Name of Allah,
the All-beneficent, the All-merciful.

الٓمٓ ١   1 *Alif, Lām, Mīm.*

اللَّهُ لَآ إِلَٰهَ إِلَّا هُوَ   2 Allah—there is no god except Him—

الْحَيُّ الْقَيُّومُ ٢   is the Living One, the All-sustainer.

نَزَّلَ عَلَيْكَ الْكِتَٰبَ بِالْحَقِّ   3 He has sent down to *you* the Book with the truth

مُصَدِّقًا لِّمَا بَيْنَ يَدَيْهِ   confirming what was [revealed] before it,

وَأَنزَلَ التَّوْرَىٰةَ وَالْإِنجِيلَ ٣   and He had sent down the Torah and the Evangel

مِن قَبْلُ ٤   before

هُدًى لِّلنَّاسِ   as guidance for mankind,

وَأَنزَلَ الْفُرْقَانَ   and He has sent down the Criterion.[2]

إِنَّ الَّذِينَ كَفَرُوا بِآيَٰتِ اللَّهِ   Indeed those who defy the signs of Allah,

لَهُمْ عَذَابٌ شَدِيدٌ   there is a severe punishment for them;

وَاللَّهُ عَزِيزٌ ذُو انتِقَامٍ ٤   and Allah is all-mighty, avenger.

إِنَّ اللَّهَ لَا يَخْفَىٰ عَلَيْهِ شَيْءٌ   5 Nothing is indeed hidden from Allah

فِى الْأَرْضِ وَلَا فِى السَّمَاءِ ٥   in the earth or in the sky.

هُوَ الَّذِى يُصَوِّرُكُمْ فِى الْأَرْحَامِ   6 It is He who forms you in the wombs

كَيْفَ يَشَاءُ   however He wishes.

لَآ إِلَٰهَ إِلَّا هُوَ   There is no god except Him,

الْعَزِيزُ الْحَكِيمُ ٦   the All-mighty, the All-wise.

هُوَ الَّذِى أَنزَلَ عَلَيْكَ الْكِتَٰبَ   7 It is He who has sent down to *you* the Book.

مِنْهُ ءَايَٰتٌ مُّحْكَمَٰتٌ   Parts of it are definitive verses,

---

[1] The *sūrah* takes its name from the expression 'the house of 'Imrān' (*āl-i 'Imrān*) mentioned in verse 33.

[2] Cf. 2:53.

هُنَّ أُمُّ ٱلْكِتَبِ
which are the mother of the Book,

وَأُخَرُ مُتَشَبِهَتٌ
while others are metaphorical.[1]

فَأَمَّا ٱلَّذِينَ فِى قُلُوبِهِمْ زَيْغٌ
As for those in whose hearts is deviance,

فَيَتَّبِعُونَ مَا تَشَبَهَ مِنْهُ
they pursue what is metaphorical in it,

ٱبْتِغَآءَ ٱلْفِتْنَةِ وَٱبْتِغَآءَ تَأْوِيلِهِۦ
courting temptation and courting its interpretation.

وَمَا يَعْلَمُ تَأْوِيلَهُۥٓ إِلَّا ٱللَّهُ
But no one knows its interpretation except Allah

وَٱلرَّسِخُونَ فِى ٱلْعِلْمِ
and those firmly grounded in knowledge;

يَقُولُونَ ءَامَنَّا بِهِۦ
they say, 'We believe in it;

كُلٌّ مِّنْ عِندِ رَبِّنَا
all of it is from our Lord.'

وَمَا يَذَّكَّرُ
And none takes admonition

إِلَّآ أُوْلُوا ٱلْأَلْبَبِ ۝
except those who possess intellect.

رَبَّنَا لَا تُزِغْ قُلُوبَنَا
8 [They say,] 'Our Lord! Do not make our hearts swerve

بَعْدَ إِذْ هَدَيْتَنَا
after You have guided us,

وَهَبْ لَنَا مِن لَّدُنكَ رَحْمَةً
and bestow Your mercy on us.

إِنَّكَ أَنتَ ٱلْوَهَّابُ ۝
Indeed You are the All-munificent.

رَبَّنَآ إِنَّكَ جَامِعُ ٱلنَّاسِ
9 Our Lord! You will indeed gather mankind

لِيَوْمٍ لَّا رَيْبَ فِيهِ
on a day in which there is no doubt.

إِنَّ ٱللَّهَ لَا يُخْلِفُ ٱلْمِيعَادَ ۝
Indeed Allah does not break His promise.'

إِنَّ ٱلَّذِينَ كَفَرُواْ
10 As for the faithless,

لَن تُغْنِىَ عَنْهُمْ أَمْوَٰلُهُمْ وَلَآ أَوْلَٰدُهُم مِّنَ ٱللَّهِ شَيْئًا
neither their wealth nor their children shall avail them anything against Allah;

وَأُوْلَٰٓئِكَ هُمْ وَقُودُ ٱلنَّارِ ۝
it is they who will be fuel for the Fire;

كَدَأْبِ ءَالِ فِرْعَوْنَ
11 as in the case of Pharaoh's clan

وَٱلَّذِينَ مِن قَبْلِهِمْ
and those who were before them,

كَذَّبُواْ بِـَٔايَٰتِنَا
who denied Our signs.

فَأَخَذَهُمُ ٱللَّهُ بِذُنُوبِهِمْ
So Allah seized them for their sins,

وَٱللَّهُ شَدِيدُ ٱلْعِقَابِ ۝
and Allah is severe in retribution.

قُل لِّلَّذِينَ كَفَرُواْ
12 *Say* to the faithless,

---

[1] Or 'ambiguous.'

سَيُغْلَبُونَ وَتُحْشَرُونَ إِلَى جَهَنَّمَ
وَبِئْسَ ٱلْمِهَادُ ۝

'You shall be overcome and mustered toward hell,

and it is an evil resting place.'

قَدْ كَانَ لَكُمْ ءَايَةٌ
فِى فِئَتَيْنِ ٱلْتَقَتَا

13 There was certainly a sign for you

in the two hosts that met:

فِئَةٌ تُقَاتِلُ فِى سَبِيلِ ٱللَّهِ
وَأُخْرَىٰ كَافِرَةٌ

one host fighting in the way of Allah

and the other faithless,

يَرَوْنَهُم مِّثْلَيْهِمْ رَأْىَ ٱلْعَيْنِ

who saw them visibly twice as many.[1]

وَٱللَّهُ يُؤَيِّدُ بِنَصْرِهِۦ
مَن يَشَآءُ

Allah strengthens with His help

whomever He wishes.

إِنَّ فِى ذَٰلِكَ لَعِبْرَةً
لِّأُوْلِى ٱلْأَبْصَٰرِ ۝

There is indeed a moral in that

for those who have insight.

زُيِّنَ لِلنَّاسِ

14 To mankind has been made to seem decorous

حُبُّ ٱلشَّهَوَٰتِ

the love of [worldly] desires,

مِنَ ٱلنِّسَآءِ وَٱلْبَنِينَ

including women and children,

وَٱلْقَنَٰطِيرِ ٱلْمُقَنطَرَةِ

accumulated piles

مِنَ ٱلذَّهَبِ وَٱلْفِضَّةِ

of gold and silver,

وَٱلْخَيْلِ ٱلْمُسَوَّمَةِ وَٱلْأَنْعَٰمِ وَٱلْحَرْثِ

horses of mark, livestock, and farms.

ذَٰلِكَ مَتَٰعُ ٱلْحَيَوٰةِ ٱلدُّنْيَا

Those are the wares of the life of this world;

وَٱللَّهُ عِندَهُۥ حُسْنُ ٱلْمَـَٔابِ ۝

but Allah—with Him is a good destination.

قُلْ

15 Say,

أَؤُنَبِّئُكُم بِخَيْرٍ مِّن ذَٰلِكُمْ

'Shall I inform you of something better than that?

لِلَّذِينَ ٱتَّقَوْا۟

For those who are Godwary

عِندَ رَبِّهِمْ جَنَّٰتٌ تَجْرِى

there will be gardens near their Lord,

مِن تَحْتِهَا ٱلْأَنْهَٰرُ

with streams running in them,

خَٰلِدِينَ فِيهَا

to remain in them [forever],

وَأَزْوَٰجٌ مُّطَهَّرَةٌ

and chaste mates,

وَرِضْوَٰنٌ مِّنَ ٱللَّهِ

and Allah's pleasure.'

وَٱللَّهُ بَصِيرٌۢ بِٱلْعِبَادِ ۝

And Allah sees best the servants.

---

[1] Or 'whom they [i.e. the faithful] saw visibly twice as many.'

ٱلَّذِينَ يَقُولُونَ رَبَّنَآ    16 Those who say, 'Our Lord!

إِنَّنَآ ءَامَنَّا      Indeed we have faith.

فَٱغْفِرْ لَنَا ذُنُوبَنَا      So forgive us our sins,

وَقِنَا عَذَابَ ٱلنَّارِ ۝      and save us from the punishment of the Fire.'

ٱلصَّٰبِرِينَ وَٱلصَّٰدِقِينَ    17 Patient and truthful,

وَٱلْقَٰنِتِينَ وَٱلْمُنفِقِينَ      obedient and charitable,

وَٱلْمُسْتَغْفِرِينَ بِٱلْأَسْحَارِ ۝      and pleading [Allah's] forgiveness at dawns.

شَهِدَ ٱللَّهُ أَنَّهُۥ لَآ إِلَٰهَ إِلَّا هُوَ    18 Allah bears witness that there is no god except Him

وَٱلْمَلَٰٓئِكَةُ      —and [so do] the angels

وَأُو۟لُوا۟ ٱلْعِلْمِ      and those who possess knowledge—

قَآئِمًۢا بِٱلْقِسْطِ      maintainer of justice,

لَآ إِلَٰهَ إِلَّا هُوَ      there is no god but Him,

ٱلْعَزِيزُ ٱلْحَكِيمُ ۝      the Almighty, the All-wise.

إِنَّ ٱلدِّينَ عِندَ ٱللَّهِ ٱلْإِسْلَٰمُ    19 Indeed, with Allah religion is *Islām*,[1]

وَمَا ٱخْتَلَفَ ٱلَّذِينَ أُوتُوا۟ ٱلْكِتَٰبَ      and those who were given the Book did not differ

إِلَّا مِنۢ بَعْدِ مَا جَآءَهُمُ ٱلْعِلْمُ      except after knowledge had come to them,

بَغْيًۢا بَيْنَهُمْ      out of envy among themselves.

وَمَن يَكْفُرْ بِـَٔايَٰتِ ٱللَّهِ      And whoever defies Allah's signs

فَإِنَّ ٱللَّهَ سَرِيعُ ٱلْحِسَابِ ۝      [should know that] Allah is swift at reckoning.

فَإِنْ حَآجُّوكَ    20 So if they argue with *you*,

فَقُلْ أَسْلَمْتُ وَجْهِىَ لِلَّهِ      *say*, 'I have submitted my will to Allah,

وَمَنِ ٱتَّبَعَنِ      and [so has] he who follow me.'

وَقُل لِّلَّذِينَ أُوتُوا۟ ٱلْكِتَٰبَ      And *say* to those who were given the Book

وَٱلْأُمِّيِّـۧنَ      and the uninstructed ones,[2]

ءَأَسْلَمْتُمْ      'Do you submit?'

فَإِنْ أَسْلَمُوا۟ فَقَدِ ٱهْتَدَوا۟      If they submit, they will certainly be guided;

---

[1] Or 'religion is submission [to Allah].'

[2] That is, the Arabs, who unlike the Jews and the Christians did not possess any scripture and had not received any scriptural instruction.

وَإِن تَوَلَّوْاْ
but if they turn away,

فَإِنَّمَا عَلَيْكَ ٱلْبَلَٰغُ
then *your* duty is only to communicate;

وَٱللَّهُ بَصِيرٌۢ بِٱلْعِبَادِ ۝
and Allah sees best the servants.

إِنَّ ٱلَّذِينَ يَكْفُرُونَ بِـَٔايَٰتِ ٱللَّهِ
21 Those who defy Allah's signs

وَيَقْتُلُونَ ٱلنَّبِيِّـۧنَ بِغَيْرِ حَقٍّ
and kill the prophets unjustly,[1]

وَيَقْتُلُونَ ٱلَّذِينَ يَأْمُرُونَ بِٱلْقِسْطِ
and kill those who call for justice

مِنَ ٱلنَّاسِ
from among the people,

فَبَشِّرْهُم بِعَذَابٍ أَلِيمٍ ۝
*inform* them of a painful punishment.

أُوْلَٰٓئِكَ ٱلَّذِينَ حَبِطَتْ أَعْمَٰلُهُمْ
22 They are the ones whose works have failed

فِى ٱلدُّنْيَا وَٱلْءَاخِرَةِ
in this world and the Hereafter,

وَمَا لَهُم مِّن نَّٰصِرِينَ ۝
and they will have no helpers.

أَلَمْ تَرَ إِلَى ٱلَّذِينَ
23 Have *you* not regarded those

أُوتُواْ نَصِيبًا مِّنَ ٱلْكِتَٰبِ
who were given a share of the Book,

يُدْعَوْنَ إِلَىٰ كِتَٰبِ ٱللَّهِ
who are summoned to the Book of Allah

لِيَحْكُمَ بَيْنَهُمْ
in order that it may judge between them,

ثُمَّ يَتَوَلَّىٰ فَرِيقٌ مِّنْهُمْ
whereat a part of them refuse to comply

وَهُم مُّعْرِضُونَ ۝
and they are disregardful.

ذَٰلِكَ بِأَنَّهُمْ قَالُواْ
24 That is because they say,

لَن تَمَسَّنَا ٱلنَّارُ
'The Fire shall not touch us

إِلَّآ أَيَّامًا مَّعْدُودَٰتٍ
except for a number of days,'

وَغَرَّهُمْ فِى دِينِهِم
and they have been misled in their religion

مَّا كَانُواْ يَفْتَرُونَ ۝
by what they used to fabricate.

فَكَيْفَ
25 But how will it be [with them]

إِذَا جَمَعْنَٰهُمْ
when We gather them

لِيَوْمٍ لَّا رَيْبَ فِيهِ
on a day in which there is no doubt,

وَوُفِّيَتْ كُلُّ نَفْسٍ
and every soul shall be recompensed fully

مَّا كَسَبَتْ
for what it has earned,

وَهُمْ لَا يُظْلَمُونَ ۝
and they will not be wronged?

قُلِ ٱللَّهُمَّ مَٰلِكَ ٱلْمُلْكِ
26 *Say,* 'O Allah, Master of all sovereignty!

---

[1] That is, the Jews. Verses 21-25 relate to them.

تُؤْتِى ٱلْمُلْكَ مَن تَشَآءُ    You give sovereignty to whomever You wish,

وَتَنزِعُ ٱلْمُلْكَ مِمَّن تَشَآءُ    and strip of sovereignty whomever You wish;

وَتُعِزُّ مَن تَشَآءُ    You make mighty whomever You wish,

وَتُذِلُّ مَن تَشَآءُ    and You abase whomever You wish;

بِيَدِكَ ٱلْخَيْرُ    all good is in Your hand.

إِنَّكَ عَلَىٰ كُلِّ شَىْءٍ قَدِيرٌ ۝    Indeed You have power over all things.

27 تُولِجُ ٱلَّيْلَ فِى ٱلنَّهَارِ    You make the night pass into the day

وَتُولِجُ ٱلنَّهَارَ فِى ٱلَّيْلِ    and You make the day pass into the night.

وَتُخْرِجُ ٱلْحَىَّ مِنَ ٱلْمَيِّتِ    You bring forth the living from the dead

وَتُخْرِجُ ٱلْمَيِّتَ مِنَ ٱلْحَىِّ    and You bring forth the dead from the living,

وَتَرْزُقُ مَن تَشَآءُ    and You provide whomever You wish

بِغَيْرِ حِسَابٍ ۝    without any reckoning.'

28 لَّا يَتَّخِذِ ٱلْمُؤْمِنُونَ ٱلْكَٰفِرِينَ أَوْلِيَآءَ    The faithful should not take the faithless for allies

مِن دُونِ ٱلْمُؤْمِنِينَ    instead of the faithful,

وَمَن يَفْعَلْ ذَٰلِكَ    and whoever does that

فَلَيْسَ مِنَ ٱللَّهِ فِى شَىْءٍ    Allah will have nothing to do with him,

إِلَّآ أَن تَتَّقُواْ مِنْهُمْ تُقَىٰةً    except when you are wary of them out of caution.

وَيُحَذِّرُكُمُ ٱللَّهُ نَفْسَهُۥ    Allah warns you to beware of [disobeying] Him,

وَإِلَى ٱللَّهِ ٱلْمَصِيرُ ۝    and toward Allah is the return.

29 قُلْ إِن تُخْفُواْ مَا فِى صُدُورِكُمْ    *Say*, 'Whether you hide what is in your hearts,

أَوْ تُبْدُوهُ    or disclose it,

يَعْلَمْهُ ٱللَّهُ    Allah knows it,

وَيَعْلَمُ مَا فِى ٱلسَّمَٰوَٰتِ    and He knows whatever there is in the heavens

وَمَا فِى ٱلْأَرْضِ    and whatever there is in the earth;

وَٱللَّهُ عَلَىٰ كُلِّ شَىْءٍ قَدِيرٌ ۝    and Allah has power over all things.'

30 يَوْمَ تَجِدُ كُلُّ نَفْسٍ    The day when every soul will find

مَّا عَمِلَتْ مِنْ خَيْرٍ مُّحْضَرًا    present whatever good it has done;

وَمَا عَمِلَتْ مِن سُوٓءٍ    and as to whatever evil it has done

تَوَدُّ    it will wish

لَوۡ أَنَّ بَيۡنَهَا وَبَيۡنَهُۥٓ أَمَدَۢا بَعِيدَاۗ    there were a far distance between it and itself.

وَيُحَذِّرُكُمُ ٱللَّهُ نَفۡسَهُۥۗ    Allah warns you to beware of [disobeying] Him,

وَٱللَّهُ رَءُوفُۢ بِٱلۡعِبَادِ ۩    and Allah is most kind to [His] servants.

قُلۡ إِن كُنتُمۡ تُحِبُّونَ ٱللَّهَ فَٱتَّبِعُونِى    31 *Say,* 'If you love Allah, then follow me;

يُحۡبِبۡكُمُ ٱللَّهُ وَيَغۡفِرۡ لَكُمۡ ذُنُوبَكُمۡۚ    Allah will love you and forgive you your sins,

وَٱللَّهُ غَفُورٌ رَّحِيمٌ ۩    and Allah is all-forgiving, all-merciful.'

قُلۡ أَطِيعُوا۟ ٱللَّهَ وَٱلرَّسُولَۖ    32 *Say,* 'Obey Allah and the Apostle.'

فَإِن تَوَلَّوۡا۟    But if they turn away,

فَإِنَّ ٱللَّهَ لَا يُحِبُّ ٱلۡكَٰفِرِينَ ۩ ❋    indeed Allah does not like the faithless.

إِنَّ ٱللَّهَ ٱصۡطَفَىٰٓ ءَادَمَ وَنُوحًا    33 Indeed Allah chose Adam and Noah,

وَءَالَ إِبۡرَٰهِيمَ    and the progeny of Abraham

وَءَالَ عِمۡرَٰنَ    and the progeny of Imran

عَلَى ٱلۡعَٰلَمِينَ ۩    above all the nations;

ذُرِّيَّةَۢ بَعۡضُهَا مِنۢ بَعۡضٍۗ    34 some of them are descendents of the others,

وَٱللَّهُ سَمِيعٌ عَلِيمٌ ۩    and Allah is all-hearing, all-knowing.

إِذۡ قَالَتِ ٱمۡرَأَتُ عِمۡرَٰنَ    35 When the wife of Imran said,

رَبِّ    'My Lord,

إِنِّى نَذَرۡتُ لَكَ مَا فِى بَطۡنِى    I dedicate to You what is in my belly,

مُحَرَّرًا    in consecration.

فَتَقَبَّلۡ مِنِّىٓۖ    Accept it from me;

إِنَّكَ أَنتَ ٱلسَّمِيعُ ٱلۡعَلِيمُ ۩    indeed You are the All-hearing, the All-knowing.'

فَلَمَّا وَضَعَتۡهَا قَالَتۡ    36 And when she bore her,[1] she said,

رَبِّ إِنِّى وَضَعۡتُهَآ أُنثَىٰ    'My Lord, I have borne a female [child]'

وَٱللَّهُ أَعۡلَمُ بِمَا وَضَعَتۡ    —and Allah knew better what she had borne—

وَلَيۡسَ ٱلذَّكَرُ كَٱلۡأُنثَىٰۖ    'and the female is not like the male.

وَإِنِّى سَمَّيۡتُهَا مَرۡيَمَ    I have named her Mary,

وَإِنِّىٓ أُعِيذُهَا بِكَ وَذُرِّيَّتَهَا    and I commend her and her offspring to Your care

---

[1] That is, Mary (ʿa).

against [the evil of] the outcast Satan.'

فَتَقَبَّلَهَا رَبُّهَا    37 Thereupon her Lord accepted her

بِقَبُولٍ حَسَنٍ    with a gracious acceptance,

وَأَنْبَتَهَا نَبَاتًا حَسَنًا    and made her grow up in a worthy fashion,

وَكَفَّلَهَا زَكَرِيَّا    and He charged Zechariah with her care.

كُلَّمَا دَخَلَ عَلَيْهَا زَكَرِيَّا ٱلْمِحْرَابَ    Whenever Zechariah visited her in the sanctuary,

وَجَدَ عِنْدَهَا رِزْقًا    he would find provisions with her.

قَالَ يَٰمَرْيَمُ    He said, 'O Mary,

أَنَّىٰ لَكِ هَٰذَا    from where does this come for you?'

قَالَتْ هُوَ مِنْ عِنْدِ ٱللَّهِ    She said, 'It comes from Allah.

إِنَّ ٱللَّهَ يَرْزُقُ مَن يَشَآءُ    Allah provides whomever He wishes

بِغَيْرِ حِسَابٍ ۩    without any reckoning.'

هُنَالِكَ دَعَا زَكَرِيَّا رَبَّهُۥ    38 Thereat Zechariah supplicated his Lord.

قَالَ رَبِّ    He said, 'My Lord!

هَبْ لِى مِن لَّدُنكَ ذُرِّيَّةً طَيِّبَةً    Grant me a good offspring from You!

إِنَّكَ سَمِيعُ ٱلدُّعَآءِ ۩    Indeed You hear all supplications.'

فَنَادَتْهُ ٱلْمَلَٰئِكَةُ    39 Then the angels called out to him,

وَهُوَ قَآئِمٌ يُصَلِّى فِى ٱلْمِحْرَابِ    as he stood praying in the sanctuary:

أَنَّ ٱللَّهَ يُبَشِّرُكَ بِيَحْيَىٰ    'Allah gives you the good news of John,

مُصَدِّقًا بِكَلِمَةٍ مِّنَ ٱللَّهِ    as a confirmer of a Word of Allah,[1]

وَسَيِّدًا وَحَصُورًا    eminent and chaste,

وَنَبِيًّا مِّنَ ٱلصَّٰلِحِينَ ۩    a prophet, among the righteous.'

قَالَ رَبِّ أَنَّىٰ يَكُونُ لِى غُلَٰمٌ    40 He said, 'My Lord, how shall I have a son

وَقَدْ بَلَغَنِىَ ٱلْكِبَرُ    while old age has overtaken me

وَٱمْرَأَتِى عَاقِرٌ    and my wife is barren?'

قَالَ كَذَٰلِكَ ٱللَّهُ    He said, 'So it is that Allah

يَفْعَلُ مَا يَشَآءُ ۩    does whatever He wishes.'

قَالَ رَبِّ ٱجْعَل لِّىٓ ءَايَةً    41 He said, 'My Lord, grant me a sign.'

قَالَ ءَايَتُكَ    He said, 'Your sign

---

[1] That is, Jesus ('a).

أَلَّا تُكَلِّمَ ٱلنَّاسَ ثَلَٰثَةَ أَيَّامٍ
is that you will not speak to people for three days

إِلَّا رَمْزًا
except in gestures.

وَٱذْكُر رَّبَّكَ كَثِيرًا
And remember Your Lord greatly,

وَسَبِّحْ بِٱلْعَشِيِّ وَٱلْإِبْكَٰرِ ۞
and glorify Him morning and evening.'

وَإِذْ قَالَتِ ٱلْمَلَٰئِكَةُ
42 And when the angels said,

يَٰمَرْيَمُ إِنَّ ٱللَّهَ ٱصْطَفَٰكِ وَطَهَّرَكِ
'O Mary, Allah has chosen you and purified you,

وَٱصْطَفَٰكِ عَلَىٰ نِسَآءِ ٱلْعَٰلَمِينَ ۞
and He has chosen you above the world's women.

يَٰمَرْيَمُ ٱقْنُتِى لِرَبِّكِ
43 O Mary, be obedient to your Lord,

وَٱسْجُدِى وَٱرْكَعِى
and prostrate and bow down

مَعَ ٱلرَّٰكِعِينَ ۞
with those who bow [in worship].'

ذَٰلِكَ مِنْ أَنۢبَآءِ ٱلْغَيْبِ
44 These accounts are from the Unseen,

نُوحِيهِ إِلَيْكَ
which We reveal to *you*,

وَمَا كُنتَ لَدَيْهِمْ
and *you* were not with them

إِذْ يُلْقُونَ أَقْلَٰمَهُمْ
when they were casting lots

أَيُّهُمْ
[to see] which of them

يَكْفُلُ مَرْيَمَ
would take charge of Mary's care,

وَمَا كُنتَ لَدَيْهِمْ
nor were *you* with them

إِذْ يَخْتَصِمُونَ ۞
when they were contending.

إِذْ قَالَتِ ٱلْمَلَٰئِكَةُ يَٰمَرْيَمُ
45 When the angels said, 'O Mary,

إِنَّ ٱللَّهَ يُبَشِّرُكِ بِكَلِمَةٍ مِّنْهُ
Allah gives you the good news of a Word from Him

ٱسْمُهُ ٱلْمَسِيحُ عِيسَى ٱبْنُ مَرْيَمَ
whose name is Messiah, Jesus, son of Mary,

وَجِيهًا فِى ٱلدُّنْيَا وَٱلْءَاخِرَةِ
distinguished in the world and the Hereafter,

وَمِنَ ٱلْمُقَرَّبِينَ ۞
and one of those brought near [to Allah].

وَيُكَلِّمُ ٱلنَّاسَ فِى ٱلْمَهْدِ
46 He will speak to people in the cradle

وَكَهْلًا
and in adulthood,

وَمِنَ ٱلصَّٰلِحِينَ ۞
and will be one of the righteous.'

قَالَتْ رَبِّ أَنَّىٰ يَكُونُ لِى وَلَدٌ
47 She said, 'My Lord, how shall I have a child

وَلَمْ يَمْسَسْنِى بَشَرٌ
seeing that no human has ever touched me?'

قَالَ كَذَٰلِكِ ٱللَّهُ
He said, 'So it is that Allah

يَخْلُقُ مَا يَشَآءُ
creates whatever He wishes.

إِذَا قَضَىٰٓ أَمْرًا

When He decides on a matter

فَإِنَّمَا يَقُولُ لَهُۥ كُن فَيَكُونُ ﴿٤٧﴾

He just says to it "Be!" and it is.

وَيُعَلِّمُهُ ٱلْكِتَٰبَ وَٱلْحِكْمَةَ

48 And He will teach him the Book and wisdom,

وَٱلتَّوْرَىٰةَ وَٱلْإِنجِيلَ ﴿٤٨﴾

the Torah and the Evangel,

وَرَسُولًا إِلَىٰ بَنِىٓ إِسْرَٰٓءِيلَ

49 and [he will be] an apostle to the Children of Israel,

أَنِّى قَدْ جِئْتُكُم

[and he will declare,] 'I have certainly brought you

بِـَٔايَةٍ مِّن رَّبِّكُمْ

a sign from your Lord:

أَنِّىٓ أَخْلُقُ لَكُم مِّنَ ٱلطِّينِ

I will create for you out of clay

كَهَيْـَٔةِ ٱلطَّيْرِ

the form of a bird,

فَأَنفُخُ فِيهِ

then I will breathe into it,

فَيَكُونُ طَيْرًۢا بِإِذْنِ ٱللَّهِ

and it will become a bird by Allah's leave.

وَأُبْرِئُ ٱلْأَكْمَهَ وَٱلْأَبْرَصَ

And I heal the blind and the leper

وَأُحْىِ ٱلْمَوْتَىٰ بِإِذْنِ ٱللَّهِ

and I revive the dead by Allah's leave.

وَأُنَبِّئُكُم بِمَا تَأْكُلُونَ

And I will tell you what you have eaten

وَمَا تَدَّخِرُونَ فِى بُيُوتِكُمْ

and what you have stored in your houses.

إِنَّ فِى ذَٰلِكَ لَـَٔايَةً لَّكُمْ

There is indeed a sign in that for you,

إِن كُنتُم مُّؤْمِنِينَ ﴿٤٩﴾

should you be faithful.

وَمُصَدِّقًا

50 And [I come] to confirm [the truth of]

لِّمَا بَيْنَ يَدَىَّ مِنَ ٱلتَّوْرَىٰةِ

that which is before me of the Torah,

وَلِأُحِلَّ لَكُم

and to make lawful for you

بَعْضَ ٱلَّذِى حُرِّمَ عَلَيْكُمْ

some of the things that were forbidden you.

وَجِئْتُكُم بِـَٔايَةٍ مِّن رَّبِّكُمْ

I have brought you a sign from your Lord;

فَٱتَّقُوا۟ ٱللَّهَ وَأَطِيعُونِ ﴿٥٠﴾

so be wary of Allah and obey me.

إِنَّ ٱللَّهَ رَبِّى وَرَبُّكُمْ

51 Indeed Allah is my Lord and your Lord;

فَٱعْبُدُوهُ

so worship Him.

هَٰذَا صِرَٰطٌ مُّسْتَقِيمٌ ﴿٥١﴾ ❖

This is a straight path.'

فَلَمَّآ أَحَسَّ عِيسَىٰ مِنْهُمُ ٱلْكُفْرَ

52 And when Jesus sensed their faithlessness,

قَالَ مَنْ أَنصَارِىٓ إِلَى ٱللَّهِ

he said, 'Who will be my helpers toward Allah?'

قَالَ ٱلْحَوَارِيُّونَ نَحْنُ أَنصَارُ ٱللَّهِ

The Disciples said, 'We will be helpers of Allah.

ءَامَنَّا بِٱللَّهِ

We have faith in Allah,

وَأَشۡهَدۡ بِأَنَّا مُسۡلِمُونَ ۞ and bear witness that we are *muslim*s.

رَبَّنَآ ءَامَنَّا بِمَآ أَنزَلۡتَ 53 Our Lord, we believe in what You have sent down,

وَٱتَّبَعۡنَا ٱلرَّسُولَ and we follow the apostle,

فَٱكۡتُبۡنَا مَعَ ٱلشَّٰهِدِينَ ۞ so write us among the witnesses.'

وَمَكَرُواْ 54 Then they[1] plotted [against Jesus],

وَمَكَرَ ٱللَّهُ and Allah also devised,

وَٱللَّهُ خَيۡرُ ٱلۡمَٰكِرِينَ ۞ and Allah is the best of devisers.

إِذۡ قَالَ ٱللَّهُ يَٰعِيسَىٰٓ إِنِّي مُتَوَفِّيكَ 55 When Allah said, 'O Jesus, I shall take you[r soul],[2]

وَرَافِعُكَ إِلَىَّ and I shall raise you up toward Myself,

وَمُطَهِّرُكَ and I shall clear you

مِنَ ٱلَّذِينَ كَفَرُواْ of [the calumnies of] the faithless,

وَجَاعِلُ ٱلَّذِينَ ٱتَّبَعُوكَ and I shall set those who follow you

فَوۡقَ ٱلَّذِينَ كَفَرُوٓاْ إِلَىٰ يَوۡمِ ٱلۡقِيَٰمَةِ above the faithless until the Day of Resurrection.

ثُمَّ إِلَىَّ مَرۡجِعُكُمۡ Then to Me will be your return,

فَأَحۡكُمُ بَيۡنَكُمۡ whereat I will judge between you

فِيمَا كُنتُمۡ فِيهِ تَخۡتَلِفُونَ ۞ concerning that about which you used to differ.

فَأَمَّا ٱلَّذِينَ كَفَرُواْ 56 As for the faithless,

فَأُعَذِّبُهُمۡ عَذَابًا شَدِيدًا I will punish them with a severe punishment

فِي ٱلدُّنۡيَا وَٱلۡأَخِرَةِ in the world and the Hereafter;

---

[1] That is, the opponents of Jesus among the Jews.

[2] *Tawaffā* means 'to exact fully' something, 'to receive in full,' 'to take one's full share,' and in the present Qur'ānic context it is used in the sense of taking away of the soul, either temporarily, as during sleep (as in 6:60), or permanently, as at the time of death (as in 3:193; 4:97; 6:61; 7:37,126; 8:50; 10:46; 12:101; 13:40; 16:28; 22:5; 32; 32:11; 40:67, 77; 47:27). In verse 39:42, it is used to refer to the taking of the soul both during sleep and death: *'It is Allah who takes (yatawaffā) the souls at death, and those that have not died during their sleep. He retains those for whom He has decreed death, but releases the rest for a specified term.'* The passive form of the verb, *tuwuffiya* means 'to die,' 'to expire,' and to 'pass away.' It occurs in 2:234, 240. In a tradition, Imam 'Alī ibn Mūsā al-Riḍā ('a) explains that Jesus Christ ('a) "was raised alive from the earth to the heaven. Then his soul was taken away between the earth and the heaven. After he was raised to the heaven his soul was restored to his body, and hence the words of God, the Almighty and the Glorious, *'When Allah said: 'O Jesus, I shall take you[r soul], and I shall raise you up to Myself. . .'* " (*'Uyūn akhbār al-Riḍā*, Tehran: Intishārāt-e Jahān, n.d., ed. Sayyid Mahdī al-Ḥusaynī al-Lājwardī, vol. 1, p. 215; cf. *Biḥār al-anwār*, vol. 14, p. 338).

وَمَا لَهُم مِّن نَّصِرِينَ ۝ and they will have no helpers.'

وَأَمَّا ٱلَّذِينَ ءَامَنُوا 57 But as for those who have faith

وَعَمِلُوا ٱلصَّـٰلِحَـٰتِ and do righteous deeds,

فَيُوَفِّيهِمْ أُجُورَهُمْ He will pay them in full their rewards,

وَٱللَّهُ لَا يُحِبُّ ٱلظَّـٰلِمِينَ ۝ and Allah does not like the wrongdoers.

ذَٰلِكَ نَتْلُوهُ عَلَيْكَ 58 These that We recite to you

مِنَ ٱلْـَٔايَـٰتِ وَٱلذِّكْرِ ٱلْحَكِيمِ ۝ are from the signs and the Wise Reminder.[1]

إِنَّ مَثَلَ عِيسَىٰ عِندَ ٱللَّهِ 59 Indeed the case of Jesus with Allah

كَمَثَلِ ءَادَمَ is like the case of Adam:

خَلَقَهُ مِن تُرَابٍ He created him from dust,

ثُمَّ قَالَ لَهُ كُن فَيَكُونُ ۝ then said to him, 'Be,' and he was.

ٱلْحَقُّ مِن رَّبِّكَ 60 This is the truth from your Lord,

فَلَا تَكُن مِّنَ ٱلْمُمْتَرِينَ ۝ so do not be among the skeptics.

فَمَنْ حَآجَّكَ فِيهِ 61 Should anyone argue with *you* concerning him,

مِنۢ بَعْدِ مَا جَآءَكَ مِنَ ٱلْعِلْمِ after the knowledge that has come to *you*,

فَقُلْ تَعَالَوْا نَدْعُ أَبْنَآءَنَا وَأَبْنَآءَكُمْ *say,* 'Come! Let us call our sons and your sons,

وَنِسَآءَنَا وَنِسَآءَكُمْ our women and your women,

وَأَنفُسَنَا وَأَنفُسَكُمْ our souls and your souls,

ثُمَّ نَبْتَهِلْ then let us pray earnestly

فَنَجْعَل لَّعْنَتَ ٱللَّهِ عَلَى ٱلْكَـٰذِبِينَ ۝ and call down Allah's curse upon the liars.'

إِنَّ هَـٰذَا لَهُوَ ٱلْقَصَصُ ٱلْحَقُّ 62 This is indeed the true account, for sure.

وَمَا مِنْ إِلَـٰهٍ إِلَّا ٱللَّهُ There is no god but Allah,

وَإِنَّ ٱللَّهَ لَهُوَ ٱلْعَزِيزُ ٱلْحَكِيمُ ۝ and indeed Allah is the All-mighty, the All-wise.

فَإِن تَوَلَّوْا 63 But if they turn away,

فَإِنَّ ٱللَّهَ عَلِيمٌۢ بِٱلْمُفْسِدِينَ ۝ indeed Allah knows best the agents of corruption.

قُلْ يَـٰٓأَهْلَ ٱلْكِتَـٰبِ 64 *Say,* 'O People of the Book!

تَعَالَوْا إِلَىٰ كَلِمَةٍ سَوَآءٍ بَيْنَنَا وَبَيْنَكُمْ Come to a word common between us and you:

أَلَّا نَعْبُدَ إِلَّا ٱللَّهَ that we will worship no one but Allah,

وَلَا نُشْرِكَ بِهِۦ شَيْـًٔا and that we will not ascribe any partner to Him,

---

[1] Or 'the Definitive Reminder.' This is yet another name of the Holy Qur'ān

وَلَا يَتَّخِذَ بَعْضُنَا بَعْضًا أَرْبَابًا    and that we will not take each other as lords
مِّن دُونِ ٱللَّهِ    besides Allah.'

فَإِن تَوَلَّوْا    But if they turn away,
فَقُولُوا ٱشْهَدُوا بِأَنَّا مُسْلِمُونَ ۞    *say,* 'Be witnesses that we are *muslims.*'[1]

يَـٰٓأَهْلَ ٱلْكِتَـٰبِ    65 O People of the Book!

لِمَ تُحَآجُّونَ فِىٓ إِبْرَٰهِيمَ    Why do you argue concerning Abraham?
وَمَآ أُنزِلَتِ ٱلتَّوْرَىٰةُ وَٱلْإِنجِيلُ    Neither the Torah nor the Evangel were sent down
إِلَّا مِنۢ بَعْدِهِۦٓ    until [long] after him.
أَفَلَا تَعْقِلُونَ ۞    Do you not apply reason?

هَـٰٓأَنتُمْ هَـٰٓؤُلَآءِ حَٰجَجْتُمْ    66 Ah! You are the very ones who argue
فِيمَا لَكُم بِهِۦ عِلْمٌ    about that of which you have knowledge.
فَلِمَ تُحَآجُّونَ    Why then do you argue
فِيمَا لَيْسَ لَكُم بِهِۦ عِلْمٌ    about that of which you have no knowledge?
وَٱللَّهُ يَعْلَمُ وَأَنتُمْ لَا تَعْلَمُونَ ۞    And Allah knows and you do not know.

مَا كَانَ إِبْرَٰهِيمُ يَهُودِيًّا وَلَا نَصْرَانِيًّا    67 Abraham was neither a Jew nor a Christian.
وَلَـٰكِن كَانَ حَنِيفًا مُّسْلِمًا    Rather he was a *ḥanīf,* a *muslim,*
وَمَا كَانَ مِنَ ٱلْمُشْرِكِينَ ۞    and he was not one of the polytheists.

إِنَّ أَوْلَى ٱلنَّاسِ بِإِبْرَٰهِيمَ    68 Indeed the nearest of all people to Abraham
لَلَّذِينَ ٱتَّبَعُوهُ    are those who follow him,
وَهَـٰذَا ٱلنَّبِىُّ وَٱلَّذِينَ ءَامَنُوا    and this prophet and those who have faith,
وَٱللَّهُ وَلِىُّ ٱلْمُؤْمِنِينَ ۞    and Allah is the guardian of the faithful.

وَدَّت طَّآئِفَةٌ مِّنْ أَهْلِ ٱلْكِتَـٰبِ    69 A group of the People of the Book were eager
لَوْ يُضِلُّونَكُمْ    they could lead you astray;
وَمَا يُضِلُّونَ إِلَّآ أَنفُسَهُمْ    yet they lead no one astray except themselves,
وَمَا يَشْعُرُونَ ۞    but they are not aware.

يَـٰٓأَهْلَ ٱلْكِتَـٰبِ    70 O People of the Book!
لِمَ تَكْفُرُونَ بِـَٔايَـٰتِ ٱللَّهِ    Why do you defy Allah's signs
وَأَنتُمْ تَشْهَدُونَ ۞    while you testify [to their truth]?

يَـٰٓأَهْلَ ٱلْكِتَـٰبِ    71 O People of the Book!

---

[1] That is, those who have submitted to Allah.

لِمَ تَلْبِسُونَ ٱلْحَقَّ بِٱلْبَٰطِلِ

Why do you mix the truth with falsehood,

وَتَكْتُمُونَ ٱلْحَقَّ وَأَنتُمْ تَعْلَمُونَ ٧١

and conceal the truth while you know [it]?

وَقَالَت طَّآئِفَةٌ مِّنْ أَهْلِ ٱلْكِتَٰبِ ٧٢

72 A group of the People of the Book say,

ءَامِنُوا بِٱلَّذِىٓ أُنزِلَ عَلَى ٱلَّذِينَ ءَامَنُوا

'Believe in what has been sent down to the faithful

وَجْهَ ٱلنَّهَارِ

at the beginning of the day,

وَٱكْفُرُوٓا ءَاخِرَهُۥ

and disbelieve at its end,

لَعَلَّهُمْ يَرْجِعُونَ ٧٢

so that they may turn back [from their religion].'

وَلَا تُؤْمِنُوٓا ٧٣

73 'And do not believe anyone

إِلَّا لِمَن تَبِعَ دِينَكُمْ

except him who follows your religion.'

قُلْ إِنَّ ٱلْهُدَىٰ هُدَى ٱللَّهِ

*Say*, 'Indeed [true] guidance is the guidance of Allah.'

أَن يُؤْتَىٰٓ أَحَدٌ

'[And do not believe] that anyone may be given

مِّثْلَ مَآ أُوتِيتُمْ

the like of what you were given,

أَوْ يُحَآجُّوكُمْ عِندَ رَبِّكُمْ

or that he may argue with you before your Lord.'[1]

قُلْ إِنَّ ٱلْفَضْلَ بِيَدِ ٱللَّهِ

*Say*, 'Indeed all grace is in Allah's hand;

يُؤْتِيهِ مَن يَشَآءُ

He grants it to whomever He wishes,

وَٱللَّهُ وَٰسِعٌ عَلِيمٌ ٧٣

and Allah is all-bounteous, all-knowing.

يَخْتَصُّ بِرَحْمَتِهِ مَن يَشَآءُ

74 He singles out for His mercy whomever He wishes,

وَٱللَّهُ ذُو ٱلْفَضْلِ ٱلْعَظِيمِ ٧٤

and Allah is dispenser of a great grace.'

وَمِنْ أَهْلِ ٱلْكِتَٰبِ مَنْ

75 And among the People of the Book is he who

إِن تَأْمَنْهُ بِقِنطَارٍ

if you entrust him with a quintal[2]

يُؤَدِّهِۦٓ إِلَيْكَ

will repay it to you,

وَمِنْهُم مَّنْ

and among them is he who,

إِن تَأْمَنْهُ بِدِينَارٍ

if you entrust him with a dinar

---

[1] This is in accordance with 2:76 where the Jews are described as making a similar statement. Alternatively, it may be understood as being part of the reply the Prophet is asked to give to the Jews, in which case the translation will be as follows: '*Say*, "Indeed [true] guidance is the guidance of Allah, so that anyone may be given the like of what you were given, or that he may argue with you before your Lord."'

[2] Quintal: hundredweight. *The American Heritage Dictionary* gives the following history of the English 'quintal': Middle English, a unit of weight, from Old French, from Medieval Latin *quintāle*, from Arabic *qinṭār*, from Late Greek *kentēnarion*, from Late Latin *centēnārium (pondus)*, hundred(weight), from Latin *centēnārius*, of a hundred.

لَّا يُؤَدِّهِۦٓ إِلَيْكَ    will not repay it to you

إِلَّا مَا دُمْتَ عَلَيْهِ قَآئِمًاۗ    unless you stand persistently over him.

ذَٰلِكَ بِأَنَّهُمْ قَالُوا    That is because they say,

لَيْسَ عَلَيْنَا فِى ٱلْأُمِّيِّنَ سَبِيلٌ    'We have no obligation to the non-Jews.'

وَيَقُولُونَ عَلَى ٱللَّهِ ٱلْكَذِبَ    But they speak lies against Allah,

وَهُمْ يَعْلَمُونَ ۝    and they know [it].

بَلَىٰ مَنْ أَوْفَىٰ بِعَهْدِهِۦ    76 Yes, whoever fulfills his commitments

وَٱتَّقَىٰ    and is wary of Allah

فَإِنَّ ٱللَّهَ يُحِبُّ ٱلْمُتَّقِينَ ۝    —Allah indeed loves the Godwary.

إِنَّ ٱلَّذِينَ يَشْتَرُونَ بِعَهْدِ ٱللَّهِ    77 Those who sell Allah's covenant

وَأَيْمَٰنِهِمْ    and their oaths

ثَمَنًا قَلِيلًا    for a paltry gain—

أُوْلَٰٓئِكَ لَا خَلَٰقَ لَهُمْ فِى ٱلْأَخِرَةِ    there shall be no share for them in the Hereafter

وَلَا يُكَلِّمُهُمُ ٱللَّهُ    and Allah will not speak to them

وَلَا يَنظُرُ إِلَيْهِمْ    nor will He [so much as] look at them

يَوْمَ ٱلْقِيَٰمَةِ    on the Day of Resurrection,

وَلَا يُزَكِّيهِمْ    nor will He purify them,

وَلَهُمْ عَذَابٌ أَلِيمٌ ۝    and there is a painful punishment for them.

وَإِنَّ مِنْهُمْ لَفَرِيقًا    78 There is indeed a group of them

يَلْوُۥنَ أَلْسِنَتَهُم بِٱلْكِتَٰبِ    who twist their tongues to mimic the Book,

لِتَحْسَبُوهُ مِنَ ٱلْكِتَٰبِ    that you may suppose that it is from the Book,

وَمَا هُوَ مِنَ ٱلْكِتَٰبِ    though it is not from the Book,

وَيَقُولُونَ هُوَ مِنْ عِندِ ٱللَّهِ    and they say, 'It is from Allah,'

وَمَا هُوَ مِنْ عِندِ ٱللَّهِ    though it is not from Allah,

وَيَقُولُونَ عَلَى ٱللَّهِ ٱلْكَذِبَ    and they attribute lies to Allah,

وَهُمْ يَعْلَمُونَ ۝    and they know [it].

مَا كَانَ لِبَشَرٍ    79 It does not behoove any human

أَن يُؤْتِيَهُ ٱللَّهُ ٱلْكِتَٰبَ    that Allah should give him the Book,

وَٱلْحُكْمَ وَٱلنُّبُوَّةَ    judgement and prophethood,

ثُمَّ يَقُولَ لِلنَّاسِ    and then he should say to the people,

كُونُوا عِبَادًا لِّى مِن دُونِ ٱللَّهِ    'Be my servants instead of Allah.'

وَلَٰكِن كُونُوا رَبَّٰنِيِّـۧنَ    Rather [he would say], 'Be a godly people,

بِمَا كُنتُمْ تُعَلِّمُونَ ٱلْكِتَٰبَ    because of your teaching the Book

وَبِمَا كُنتُمْ تَدْرُسُونَ ۝    and because of your studying it.'

وَلَا يَأْمُرَكُمْ أَن تَتَّخِذُوا    80 And he would not command you to take

ٱلْمَلَٰٓئِكَةَ وَٱلنَّبِيِّـۧنَ أَرْبَابًا    the angels and the prophets for lords.

أَيَأْمُرُكُم بِٱلْكُفْرِ    Would he call you to unfaith

بَعْدَ إِذْ أَنتُم مُّسْلِمُونَ ۝    after you have been *muslim*s?

وَإِذْ أَخَذَ ٱللَّهُ مِيثَٰقَ ٱلنَّبِيِّـۧنَ    81 When Allah took a compact concerning the prophets,

لَمَآ ءَاتَيْتُكُم    [He said,] 'Inasmuch as I have given you

مِّن كِتَٰبٍ وَحِكْمَةٍ    of the Book and wisdom,[1]

ثُمَّ جَآءَكُمْ رَسُولٌ    should an apostle come to you thereafter

مُّصَدِّقٌ لِّمَا مَعَكُمْ    confirming what is with you,

لَتُؤْمِنُنَّ بِهِۦ وَلَتَنصُرُنَّهُۥ    you shall believe in him and help him.'

قَالَ ءَأَقْرَرْتُمْ    He said, 'Do you pledge

وَأَخَذْتُمْ عَلَىٰ ذَٰلِكُمْ إِصْرِى    and accept My covenant on this condition?'

قَالُوٓا أَقْرَرْنَا    They said, 'We pledge.'

قَالَ فَٱشْهَدُوا    He said, 'Then be witnesses,

وَأَنَا۠ مَعَكُم مِّنَ ٱلشَّٰهِدِينَ ۝    and I am also among the witnesses along with you.'

فَمَن تَوَلَّىٰ بَعْدَ ذَٰلِكَ    82 Then whoever turns away after that

فَأُوْلَٰٓئِكَ هُمُ ٱلْفَٰسِقُونَ ۝    —it is they who are the transgressors.

أَفَغَيْرَ دِينِ ٱللَّهِ يَبْغُونَ    83 Do they, then, seek a religion other than Allah's,

وَلَهُۥٓ أَسْلَمَ    while to Him submits

مَن فِى ٱلسَّمَٰوَٰتِ وَٱلْأَرْضِ    whoever there is in the heavens and the earth,

طَوْعًا وَكَرْهًا    willingly or unwillingly,

وَإِلَيْهِ يُرْجَعُونَ ۝    and to Him they will be brought back?

قُلْ ءَامَنَّا بِٱللَّهِ    84 *Say*, 'We have faith in Allah,

وَمَآ أُنزِلَ عَلَيْنَا    and in what has been sent down to us,

---

[1] Or, in accordance with an alternate reading (with *lammā*, instead of *lamā*), 'Since I have given you of the Book and wisdom,' or 'As I have given you . . .'

وَمَآ أُنزِلَ عَلَىٰٓ إِبْرَٰهِيمَ
and what was sent down to Abraham,

وَإِسْمَٰعِيلَ وَإِسْحَٰقَ وَيَعْقُوبَ
Ishmael, Isaac, Jacob

وَٱلْأَسْبَاطِ
and the Tribes,

وَمَآ أُوتِىَ مُوسَىٰ وَعِيسَىٰ
and that which Moses and Jesus were given,

وَٱلنَّبِيُّونَ مِن رَّبِّهِمْ
and the prophets, from their Lord.

لَا نُفَرِّقُ بَيْنَ أَحَدٍ مِّنْهُمْ
We make no distinction between any of them,

وَنَحْنُ لَهُۥ مُسْلِمُونَ ۝
and to Him do we submit.'

وَمَن يَبْتَغِ غَيْرَ ٱلْإِسْلَٰمِ دِينًا
85 Should anyone follow a religion other than Islam,

فَلَن يُقْبَلَ مِنْهُ
it shall never be accepted from him,

وَهُوَ فِى ٱلْءَاخِرَةِ مِنَ ٱلْخَٰسِرِينَ ۝
and he will be among the losers in the Hereafter.

كَيْفَ يَهْدِى ٱللَّهُ قَوْمًا
86 How shall Allah guide a people

كَفَرُواْ بَعْدَ إِيمَٰنِهِمْ
who have disbelieved after their faith

وَشَهِدُوٓاْ أَنَّ ٱلرَّسُولَ حَقٌّ
and [after] bearing witness that the Apostle is true,

وَجَآءَهُمُ ٱلْبَيِّنَٰتُ
and [after] manifest proofs had come to them?

وَٱللَّهُ لَا يَهْدِى ٱلْقَوْمَ ٱلظَّٰلِمِينَ ۝
Allah does not guide the wrongdoing lot.

أُوْلَٰٓئِكَ جَزَآؤُهُمْ أَنَّ عَلَيْهِمْ
87 Their requital is that there shall be upon them

لَعْنَةَ ٱللَّهِ وَٱلْمَلَٰٓئِكَةِ
the curse of Allah, the angels,

وَٱلنَّاسِ أَجْمَعِينَ ۝
and all mankind.

خَٰلِدِينَ فِيهَا
88 They will remain in it [forever],

لَا يُخَفَّفُ عَنْهُمُ ٱلْعَذَابُ
and their punishment shall not be lightened,

وَلَا هُمْ يُنظَرُونَ ۝
nor will they be granted any respite,

إِلَّا ٱلَّذِينَ تَابُواْ مِنۢ بَعْدِ ذَٰلِكَ
89 except such as repent after that

وَأَصْلَحُواْ
and make amends,

فَإِنَّ ٱللَّهَ غَفُورٌ رَّحِيمٌ ۝
for Allah is all-forgiving, all-merciful.

إِنَّ ٱلَّذِينَ كَفَرُواْ بَعْدَ إِيمَٰنِهِمْ
90 Indeed those who turn faithless after their faith,

ثُمَّ ٱزْدَادُواْ كُفْرًا
and then advance in faithlessness,

لَّن تُقْبَلَ تَوْبَتُهُمْ
their repentance will never be accepted,

وَأُوْلَٰٓئِكَ هُمُ ٱلضَّآلُّونَ ۝
and it is they who are the astray.

إِنَّ ٱلَّذِينَ كَفَرُواْ
91 Indeed those who turn faithless,

وَمَاتُواْ وَهُمْ كُفَّارٌ
and die while they are faithless,

فَلَن يُقْبَلَ مِنْ أَحَدِهِم مِّلْءُ الْأَرْضِ ذَهَبًا a world of gold will not be accepted from any of them

وَلَوِ افْتَدَىٰ بِهِ should he offer it for ransom.

أُوْلَـٰئِكَ لَهُمْ عَذَابٌ أَلِيمٌ For such there will be a painful punishment,

وَمَا لَهُم مِّن نَّـٰصِرِينَ ۝ and they will have no helpers.

لَن تَنَالُوا الْبِرَّ 92 You will never attain piety

حَتَّىٰ تُنفِقُوا مِمَّا تُحِبُّونَ until you spend out of what you hold dear,

وَمَا تُنفِقُوا مِن شَىْءٍ and whatever you may spend of anything,

فَإِنَّ اللَّهَ بِهِۦ عَلِيمٌ ۝ ❋ Allah indeed knows it.

[PART 4]

كُلُّ الطَّعَامِ كَانَ حِلًّا لِّبَنِى إِسْرَٰءِيلَ 93 All food was lawful to the Children of Israel

إِلَّا مَا حَرَّمَ إِسْرَٰءِيلُ عَلَىٰ نَفْسِهِۦ except what Israel[1] had forbidden himself

مِن قَبْلِ أَن تُنَزَّلَ التَّوْرَىٰةُ before the Torah was sent down.

قُلْ فَأْتُوا بِالتَّوْرَىٰةِ فَاتْلُوهَا Say, 'Bring the Torah, and read it,

إِن كُنتُمْ صَـٰدِقِينَ ۝ should you be truthful.'

فَمَنِ افْتَرَىٰ عَلَى اللَّهِ الْكَذِبَ 94 So whoever fabricates a lie against Allah

مِنْ بَعْدِ ذَٰلِكَ after that

فَأُوْلَـٰئِكَ هُمُ الظَّـٰلِمُونَ ۝ —it is they who are the wrongdoers.

قُلْ صَدَقَ اللَّهُ 95 Say, 'Allah has spoken the truth;

فَاتَّبِعُوا مِلَّةَ إِبْرَٰهِيمَ حَنِيفًا so follow the creed of Abraham, a ḥanīf,

وَمَا كَانَ مِنَ الْمُشْرِكِينَ ۝ and he was not one of the polytheists.

إِنَّ أَوَّلَ بَيْتٍ وُضِعَ لِلنَّاسِ 96 Indeed the first house to be set up for mankind

لَلَّذِى بِبَكَّةَ is the one at Bakkah,[2]

مُبَارَكًا وَهُدًى لِّلْعَـٰلَمِينَ ۝ blessed and a guidance for all nations.

فِيهِ ءَايَـٰتٌ بَيِّنَـٰتٌ مَّقَامُ إِبْرَٰهِيمَ 97 In it are manifest signs [and] Abraham's Station,

وَمَن دَخَلَهُۥ كَانَ ءَامِنًا and whoever enters it shall be secure.

وَلِلَّهِ عَلَى النَّاسِ And it is the duty of mankind toward Allah

حِجُّ الْبَيْتِ to make pilgrimage to the House

---

[1] That is Jacob (ʿa).
[2] The Holy Mosque or the city of Makkah, or the territory where they stand.

مَنِ ٱسۡتَطَاعَ إِلَيۡهِ سَبِيلًا      —for those who can afford the journey to it—

وَمَن كَفَرَ      and should anyone renege [on his obligation],

فَإِنَّ ٱللَّهَ غَنِيٌّ عَنِ ٱلۡعَٰلَمِينَ ۩      Allah is indeed without need of the creatures.

قُلۡ يَٰٓأَهۡلَ ٱلۡكِتَٰبِ      98 *Say,* 'O People of the Book!

لِمَ تَكۡفُرُونَ بِـَٔايَٰتِ ٱللَّهِ      Why do you defy the signs of Allah,

وَٱللَّهُ شَهِيدٌ عَلَىٰ مَا تَعۡمَلُونَ ۩      while Allah is witness to what you do?'

قُلۡ يَٰٓأَهۡلَ ٱلۡكِتَٰبِ      99 *Say,* 'O People of the Book!

لِمَ تَصُدُّونَ عَن سَبِيلِ ٱللَّهِ مَنۡ ءَامَنَ      why do you bar the faithful from the way of Allah,

تَبۡغُونَهَا عِوَجًا      seeking to make it crooked,

وَأَنتُمۡ شُهَدَآءُ      while you are witnesses [to its truthfulness]?

وَمَا ٱللَّهُ بِغَٰفِلٍ عَمَّا تَعۡمَلُونَ ۩      And Allah is not oblivious of what you do.'

يَٰٓأَيُّهَا ٱلَّذِينَ ءَامَنُوٓاْ      100 O you who have faith,

إِن تُطِيعُواْ فَرِيقًا      if you obey a part

مِّنَ ٱلَّذِينَ أُوتُواْ ٱلۡكِتَٰبَ      of those who were given the Book,

يَرُدُّوكُم بَعۡدَ إِيمَٰنِكُمۡ      they will turn you back, after your faith,

كَٰفِرِينَ ۩      into faithless ones.

وَكَيۡفَ تَكۡفُرُونَ      101 And how would you be faithless

وَأَنتُمۡ تُتۡلَىٰ عَلَيۡكُمۡ ءَايَٰتُ ٱللَّهِ      while the signs of Allah are recited to you

وَفِيكُمۡ رَسُولُهُۥ      and His Apostle is in your midst?

وَمَن يَعۡتَصِم بِٱللَّهِ      And whoever takes recourse in Allah

فَقَدۡ هُدِيَ إِلَىٰ صِرَٰطٍ مُّسۡتَقِيمٍ ۩      is certainly guided to a straight path.

يَٰٓأَيُّهَا ٱلَّذِينَ ءَامَنُواْ      102 O you who have faith!

ٱتَّقُواْ ٱللَّهَ حَقَّ تُقَاتِهِۦ      Be wary of Allah with the wariness due to Him

وَلَا تَمُوتُنَّ إِلَّا وَأَنتُم مُّسۡلِمُونَ ۩      and do not die except as *muslim*s.

وَٱعۡتَصِمُواْ بِحَبۡلِ ٱللَّهِ جَمِيعًا      103 Hold fast, all together, to Allah's cord,

وَلَا تَفَرَّقُواْ      and do not be divided [into sects].

وَٱذۡكُرُواْ نِعۡمَتَ ٱللَّهِ عَلَيۡكُمۡ      And remember Allah's blessing upon you

إِذۡ كُنتُمۡ أَعۡدَآءً      when you were enemies,

فَأَلَّفَ بَيْنَ قُلُوبِكُمْ    then He brought your hearts together,

فَأَصْبَحْتُم بِنِعْمَتِهِ إِخْوَٰنًا    so you became brothers with His blessing.

وَكُنتُمْ عَلَىٰ شَفَا حُفْرَةٍ مِّنَ ٱلنَّارِ    And you were on the brink of a pit of Fire,

فَأَنقَذَكُم مِّنْهَا    whereat He saved you from it.

كَذَٰلِكَ يُبَيِّنُ ٱللَّهُ لَكُمْ ءَايَٰتِهِ    Thus does Allah clarify His signs for you

لَعَلَّكُمْ تَهْتَدُونَ ۝    so that you may be guided.

وَلْتَكُن مِّنكُمْ أُمَّةٌ    104 There has to be a nation among you

يَدْعُونَ إِلَى ٱلْخَيْرِ    summoning to the good,

وَيَأْمُرُونَ بِٱلْمَعْرُوفِ    bidding what is right,

وَيَنْهَوْنَ عَنِ ٱلْمُنكَرِ    and forbidding what is wrong.

وَأُوْلَٰٓئِكَ هُمُ ٱلْمُفْلِحُونَ ۝    It is they who are the felicitous.

وَلَا تَكُونُوا۟ كَٱلَّذِينَ تَفَرَّقُوا۟    105 Do not be like those who became divided [into sects]

وَٱخْتَلَفُوا۟ مِنۢ بَعْدِ مَا جَآءَهُمُ ٱلْبَيِّنَٰتُ    and differed after manifest signs had come to them.

وَأُوْلَٰٓئِكَ لَهُمْ عَذَابٌ عَظِيمٌ ۝    For such there will be a great punishment,

يَوْمَ تَبْيَضُّ وُجُوهٌ    106 on the day when [some] faces will turn white

وَتَسْوَدُّ وُجُوهٌ    and [some] faces will turn black.

فَأَمَّا ٱلَّذِينَ ٱسْوَدَّتْ وُجُوهُهُمْ    As for those whose faces turn black

أَكَفَرْتُم    [it will be said to them], 'Did you disbelieve

بَعْدَ إِيمَٰنِكُمْ    after your faith?

فَذُوقُوا۟ ٱلْعَذَابَ    So taste the punishment

بِمَا كُنتُمْ تَكْفُرُونَ ۝    because of what you used to disbelieve.'

وَأَمَّا ٱلَّذِينَ ٱبْيَضَّتْ وُجُوهُهُمْ    107 But as for those whose faces become white,

فَفِى رَحْمَةِ ٱللَّهِ    they shall dwell in Allah's mercy,

هُمْ فِيهَا خَٰلِدُونَ ۝    and they will remain in it [forever].

تِلْكَ ءَايَٰتُ ٱللَّهِ    108 These are the signs of Allah

نَتْلُوهَا عَلَيْكَ بِٱلْحَقِّ    which We recite to *you* in truth,

وَمَا ٱللَّهُ يُرِيدُ ظُلْمًا    and Allah does not desire any wrong

لِّلْعَٰلَمِينَ ۝    for the creatures.

وَلِلَّهِ مَا فِى ٱلسَّمَٰوَٰتِ    109 To Allah belongs whatever is in the heavens

وَمَا فِى ٱلْأَرْضِ    and whatever is in the earth,

وَإِلَى ٱللَّهِ تُرْجَعُ ٱلْأُمُورُ ۝     and to Allah all matters are returned.

كُنتُمْ خَيْرَ أُمَّةٍ     110 You are the best nation

أُخْرِجَتْ لِلنَّاسِ     [ever] brought forth for mankind:

تَأْمُرُونَ بِٱلْمَعْرُوفِ     you bid what is right

وَتَنْهَوْنَ عَنِ ٱلْمُنكَرِ     and forbid what is wrong,

وَتُؤْمِنُونَ بِٱللَّهِ     and have faith in Allah.

وَلَوْ ءَامَنَ أَهْلُ ٱلْكِتَبِ     And if the People of the Book had believed,

لَكَانَ خَيْرًا لَّهُم     it would have been better for them.

مِّنْهُمُ ٱلْمُؤْمِنُونَ     Among them [some] are faithful,

وَأَكْثَرُهُمُ ٱلْفَسِقُونَ ۝     but most of them are transgressors.

لَن يَضُرُّوكُمْ     111 They[1] will never do you any harm,

إِلَّا أَذَى     except for some hurt;

وَإِن يُقَتِلُوكُمْ     and if they fight you,

يُوَلُّوكُمُ ٱلْأَدْبَارَ     they will turn their backs [to flee],

ثُمَّ لَا يُنصَرُونَ ۝     then they will not be helped.

ضُرِبَتْ عَلَيْهِمُ ٱلذِّلَّةُ     112 Abasement has been stamped upon them

أَيْنَ مَا ثُقِفُوٓا     wherever they are confronted,

إِلَّا بِحَبْلٍ مِّنَ ٱللَّهِ     except for an asylum from Allah

وَحَبْلٍ مِّنَ ٱلنَّاسِ     and an asylum from the people;

وَبَآءُو بِغَضَبٍ مِّنَ ٱللَّهِ     and they earned the wrath of Allah,

وَضُرِبَتْ عَلَيْهِمُ ٱلْمَسْكَنَةُ     and poverty was stamped upon them.

ذَٰلِكَ بِأَنَّهُمْ كَانُوا يَكْفُرُونَ بِـَٔايَتِ ٱللَّهِ     That, because they would defy the signs of Allah

وَيَقْتُلُونَ ٱلْأَنۢبِيَآءَ بِغَيْرِ حَقٍّ     and kill the prophets unjustly.

ذَٰلِكَ بِمَا عَصَوا     That, because they would disobey

وَّكَانُوا يَعْتَدُونَ ۝     and used to commit transgression.

لَيْسُوا سَوَآءً     113 Yet they are not all alike.

مِّنْ أَهْلِ ٱلْكِتَبِ أُمَّةٌ قَآئِمَةٌ     Among the People of the Book is an upright group;

يَتْلُونَ ءَايَتِ ٱللَّهِ ءَانَآءَ ٱلَّيْلِ     they recite Allah's signs in the watches of the night

وَهُمْ يَسْجُدُونَ ۝     and prostrate.

---

[1] That is, the Jews.

يُؤْمِنُونَ بِٱللَّهِ وَٱلْيَوْمِ ٱلْأَخِرِ    114 They have faith in Allah and the Last Day,

وَيَأْمُرُونَ بِٱلْمَعْرُوفِ    and bid what is right

وَيَنْهَوْنَ عَنِ ٱلْمُنكَرِ    and forbid what is wrong,

وَيُسَٰرِعُونَ فِى ٱلْخَيْرَٰتِ    and are active in [performing] good deeds.

وَأُوْلَٰٓئِكَ مِنَ ٱلصَّٰلِحِينَ ۝    They are among the righteous.

وَمَا يَفْعَلُواْ مِنْ خَيْرٍ    115 And whatever good they do,

فَلَن يُكْفَرُوهُ    they will not go unappreciated for it,

وَٱللَّهُ عَلِيمٌۢ بِٱلْمُتَّقِينَ ۝    and Allah knows best the Godwary.

إِنَّ ٱلَّذِينَ كَفَرُواْ    116 As for the faithless,

لَن تُغْنِىَ عَنْهُمْ أَمْوَٰلُهُمْ وَلَآ أَوْلَٰدُهُم    neither their wealth nor their children will avail them

مِّنَ ٱللَّهِ شَيْـًٔا    anything against Allah.

وَأُوْلَٰٓئِكَ أَصْحَٰبُ ٱلنَّارِ    They shall be the inmates of the Fire,

هُمْ فِيهَا خَٰلِدُونَ ۝    and they shall remain in it [forever].

مَثَلُ مَا يُنفِقُونَ    117 The parable of what they spend

فِى هَٰذِهِ ٱلْحَيَوٰةِ ٱلدُّنْيَا    in the life of this world

كَمَثَلِ رِيحٍ فِيهَا صِرٌّ    is that of a cold wind

أَصَابَتْ حَرْثَ قَوْمٍ    that strikes the tillage of a people

ظَلَمُوٓاْ أَنفُسَهُمْ    who wronged themselves,

فَأَهْلَكَتْهُ    destroying it.

وَمَا ظَلَمَهُمُ ٱللَّهُ    Allah does not wrong them,

وَلَٰكِنْ أَنفُسَهُمْ يَظْلِمُونَ ۝    but they wrong themselves.

يَٰٓأَيُّهَا ٱلَّذِينَ ءَامَنُواْ    118 O you who have faith!

لَا تَتَّخِذُواْ بِطَانَةً    Do not take your confidants

مِّن دُونِكُمْ    from others than yourselves;

لَا يَأْلُونَكُمْ خَبَالًا    they will spare nothing to ruin you.

وَدُّواْ مَا عَنِتُّمْ    They are eager to see you in distress.

قَدْ بَدَتِ ٱلْبَغْضَآءُ مِنْ أَفْوَٰهِهِمْ    Hatred has already shown itself from their mouths,

وَمَا تُخْفِى صُدُورُهُمْ أَكْبَرُ    and what their breasts hide [within] is yet worse.

قَدْ بَيَّنَّا لَكُمُ ٱلْأَيَٰتِ    We have certainly made the signs clear for you,

إِن كُنتُم تَعْقِلُونَ ۝ should you apply reason.

هَٰٓأَنتُمْ أُوْلَآءِ تُحِبُّونَهُمْ 119 Ah! You are the ones who bear love towards them,

وَلَا يُحِبُّونَكُمْ while they do not love you,

وَتُؤْمِنُونَ بِٱلْكِتَٰبِ كُلِّهِۦ though you believe in all the Books;

وَإِذَا لَقُوكُمْ قَالُوٓاْ ءَامَنَّا and when they meet you, they say, 'We believe,'

وَإِذَا خَلَوْاْ but when they are alone,

عَضُّواْ عَلَيْكُمُ ٱلْأَنَامِلَ مِنَ ٱلْغَيْظِ they bite their fingertips out of rage at you.

قُلْ مُوتُواْ بِغَيْظِكُمْ *Say*, 'Die of your rage!'

إِنَّ ٱللَّهَ عَلِيمٌ بِذَاتِ ٱلصُّدُورِ ۝ Indeed Allah knows best what is in the breasts.

إِن تَمْسَسْكُمْ حَسَنَةٌ تَسُؤْهُمْ 120 If some good should befall you, it upsets them,

وَإِن تُصِبْكُمْ سَيِّئَةٌ يَفْرَحُواْ بِهَا but if some ill should befall you, they rejoice at it.

وَإِن تَصْبِرُواْ وَتَتَّقُواْ Yet if you are patient and Godwary,

لَا يَضُرُّكُمْ كَيْدُهُمْ شَيْـًٔا their guile will not harm you in any way.

إِنَّ ٱللَّهَ بِمَا يَعْمَلُونَ مُحِيطٌ ۝ Indeed Allah comprehends what they do.

وَإِذْ غَدَوْتَ مِنْ أَهْلِكَ 121 When *you* left *your* family at dawn

تُبَوِّئُ ٱلْمُؤْمِنِينَ مَقَٰعِدَ لِلْقِتَالِ to settle the faithful in their positions for battle

وَٱللَّهُ سَمِيعٌ عَلِيمٌ ۝ —and Allah is all-hearing, all-knowing.

إِذْ هَمَّت طَّآئِفَتَانِ مِنكُمْ 122 When two groups among you were about

أَن تَفْشَلَا to lose courage,

وَٱللَّهُ وَلِيُّهُمَا —though Allah is their guardian,

وَعَلَى ٱللَّهِ فَلْيَتَوَكَّلِ ٱلْمُؤْمِنُونَ ۝ and in Allah let all the faithful put their trust.

وَلَقَدْ نَصَرَكُمُ ٱللَّهُ بِبَدْرٍ 123 Certainly Allah helped you at Badr,

وَأَنتُمْ أَذِلَّةٌ when you were abased [in the enemy's eyes].

فَٱتَّقُواْ ٱللَّهَ لَعَلَّكُمْ تَشْكُرُونَ ۝ So be wary of Allah so that you may give thanks.

إِذْ تَقُولُ لِلْمُؤْمِنِينَ 124 When *you* were saying to the faithful,

أَلَن يَكْفِيَكُمْ 'Is it not enough for you

أَن يُمِدَّكُمْ رَبُّكُم that your Lord should aid you

بِثَلَٰثَةِ ءَالَٰفٍ مِّنَ ٱلْمَلَٰٓئِكَةِ مُنزَلِينَ ۝ with three thousand angels sent down?'

بَلَىٰٓ إِن تَصْبِرُواْ وَتَتَّقُواْ 125 Yes, if you are steadfast and Godwary,

وَيَأۡتُوكُم مِّن فَوۡرِهِمۡ هَـٰذَا and should they come at you suddenly,

يُمۡدِدۡكُمۡ رَبُّكُم your Lord will aid you

بِخَمۡسَةِ ءَالَٰفٍ مِّنَ ٱلۡمَلَـٰٓئِكَةِ مُسَوِّمِينَ ۝ with five thousand marked angels.

وَمَا جَعَلَهُ ٱللَّهُ إِلَّا بُشۡرَىٰ لَكُمۡ 126 Allah did not appoint it but as a good news for you,

وَلِتَطۡمَئِنَّ قُلُوبُكُم بِهِۦۗ and to reassure with it your hearts,

وَمَا ٱلنَّصۡرُ إِلَّا مِنۡ عِندِ ٱللَّهِ and victory[1] comes only from Allah,

ٱلۡعَزِيزِ ٱلۡحَكِيمِ ۝ the All-mighty, the All-wise,

لِيَقۡطَعَ طَرَفًا مِّنَ ٱلَّذِينَ كَفَرُوٓاْ 127 that He may cut down a section of the faithless,

أَوۡ يَكۡبِتَهُمۡ or subdue them,

فَيَنقَلِبُواْ خَآئِبِينَ ۝ so that they retreat disappointed.

لَيۡسَ لَكَ مِنَ ٱلۡأَمۡرِ شَىۡءٌ 128 *You* have no hand in the matter,

أَوۡ يَتُوبَ عَلَيۡهِمۡ whether He accepts their repentance

أَوۡ يُعَذِّبَهُمۡ or punishes them,

فَإِنَّهُمۡ ظَـٰلِمُونَ ۝ for they are indeed wrongdoers.

وَلِلَّهِ مَا فِى ٱلسَّمَـٰوَٰتِ 129 To Allah belongs whatever is in the heavens

وَمَا فِى ٱلۡأَرۡضِۚ and whatever is in the earth:

يَغۡفِرُ لِمَن يَشَآءُ He forgives whomever He wishes

وَيُعَذِّبُ مَن يَشَآءُۚ and punishes whomever He wishes,

وَٱللَّهُ غَفُورٌ رَّحِيمٌ ۝ and Allah is all-forgiving, all-merciful.

يَـٰٓأَيُّهَا ٱلَّذِينَ ءَامَنُواْ 130 O you who have faith!

لَا تَأۡكُلُواْ ٱلرِّبَوٰٓاْ أَضۡعَـٰفًا مُّضَـٰعَفَةًۖ Do not exact usury, twofold and severalfold,

وَٱتَّقُواْ ٱللَّهَ لَعَلَّكُمۡ تُفۡلِحُونَ ۝ and be wary of Allah so that you may be felicitous.

وَٱتَّقُواْ ٱلنَّارَ ٱلَّتِىٓ 131 And beware of the Fire which

أُعِدَّتۡ لِلۡكَـٰفِرِينَ ۝ has been prepared for the faithless,

وَأَطِيعُواْ ٱللَّهَ وَٱلرَّسُولَ 132 and obey Allah and the Apostle

لَعَلَّكُمۡ تُرۡحَمُونَ ۝ ❁ so that you may be granted [His] mercy.

وَسَارِعُوٓاْ إِلَىٰ مَغۡفِرَةٍ مِّن رَّبِّكُمۡ 133 And hasten towards your Lord's forgiveness

وَجَنَّةٍ عَرۡضُهَا ٱلسَّمَـٰوَٰتُ وَٱلۡأَرۡضُ and a paradise as vast as the heavens and the earth,

---

[1] Or 'help.'

أُعِدَّتْ لِلْمُتَّقِينَ ⟨⟩ prepared for the Godwary

ٱلَّذِينَ يُنفِقُونَ فِى ٱلسَّرَّآءِ وَٱلضَّرَّآءِ 134 —those who spend in ease and adversity,

وَٱلْكَظِمِينَ ٱلْغَيْظَ and suppress their anger,

وَٱلْعَافِينَ عَنِ ٱلنَّاسِ and excuse [the faults of] the people,

وَٱللَّهُ يُحِبُّ ٱلْمُحْسِنِينَ ⟨⟩ and Allah loves the virtuous;

وَٱلَّذِينَ إِذَا فَعَلُوا۟ فَحِشَةً 135 and those who, when they commit an indecent act

أَوْ ظَلَمُوٓا۟ أَنفُسَهُمْ or wrong themselves,

ذَكَرُوا۟ ٱللَّهَ remember Allah,

فَٱسْتَغْفَرُوا۟ لِذُنُوبِهِمْ and plead [Allah's] forgiveness for their sins

وَمَن يَغْفِرُ ٱلذُّنُوبَ إِلَّا ٱللَّهُ —and who forgives sins except Allah?—

وَلَمْ يُصِرُّوا۟ عَلَىٰ مَا فَعَلُوا۟ and who do not persist in what they have committed

وَهُمْ يَعْلَمُونَ ⟨⟩ while they know.

أُو۟لَٰٓئِكَ جَزَآؤُهُم مَّغْفِرَةٌ مِّن رَّبِّهِمْ 136 Their reward is forgiveness from their Lord,

وَجَنَّٰتٌ تَجْرِى مِن تَحْتِهَا ٱلْأَنْهَٰرُ and gardens with streams running in them,

خَٰلِدِينَ فِيهَا to remain in them [forever],

وَنِعْمَ أَجْرُ ٱلْعَٰمِلِينَ ⟨⟩ How excellent is the reward of the workers!

قَدْ خَلَتْ مِن قَبْلِكُمْ سُنَنٌ 137 Certain [Divine] precedents have passed before you.

فَسِيرُوا۟ فِى ٱلْأَرْضِ So travel over the land

فَٱنظُرُوا۟ كَيْفَ كَانَ عَٰقِبَةُ ٱلْمُكَذِّبِينَ ⟨⟩ and then observe how was the fate of the deniers.

هَٰذَا بَيَانٌ لِّلنَّاسِ 138 This is an explanation for mankind,

وَهُدًى وَمَوْعِظَةٌ لِّلْمُتَّقِينَ ⟨⟩ and a guidance and advice for the Godwary.

وَلَا تَهِنُوا۟ وَلَا تَحْزَنُوا۟ 139 Do not weaken or grieve:

وَأَنتُمُ ٱلْأَعْلَوْنَ إِن كُنتُم مُّؤْمِنِينَ ⟨⟩ you shall have the upper hand, should you be faithful.

إِن يَمْسَسْكُمْ قَرْحٌ 140 If a wound afflicts you,

فَقَدْ مَسَّ ٱلْقَوْمَ قَرْحٌ مِّثْلُهُۥ a like wound has already afflicted those people;

وَتِلْكَ ٱلْأَيَّامُ نُدَاوِلُهَا بَيْنَ ٱلنَّاسِ and We make such vicissitudes rotate among mankind,

وَلِيَعْلَمَ ٱللَّهُ ٱلَّذِينَ ءَامَنُوا۟ so that Allah may ascertain those who have faith,

وَيَتَّخِذَ مِنكُمْ شُهَدَآءَ
and that He may take martyrs[1] from among you,

وَٱللَّهُ لَا يُحِبُّ ٱلظَّٰلِمِينَ
and Allah does not like the wrongdoers.

وَلِيُمَحِّصَ ٱللَّهُ ٱلَّذِينَ ءَامَنُوا۟
141 And so that Allah may purge those who have faith

وَيَمْحَقَ ٱلْكَٰفِرِينَ
and that He may wipe out the faithless.

أَمْ حَسِبْتُمْ أَن تَدْخُلُوا۟ ٱلْجَنَّةَ
142 Do you suppose that you would enter paradise,

وَلَمَّا يَعْلَمِ ٱللَّهُ
while Allah has not yet ascertained

ٱلَّذِينَ جَٰهَدُوا۟ مِنكُمْ
those of you who have waged jihād

وَيَعْلَمَ ٱلصَّٰبِرِينَ
and not ascertained the steadfast?

وَلَقَدْ كُنتُمْ تَمَنَّوْنَ ٱلْمَوْتَ
143 Certainly you were longing for death

مِن قَبْلِ أَن تَلْقَوْهُ
before you had encountered it.

فَقَدْ رَأَيْتُمُوهُ وَأَنتُمْ تَنظُرُونَ
Then certainly you saw it, as you looked on.

وَمَا مُحَمَّدٌ إِلَّا رَسُولٌ
144 Muḥammad is but an apostle;

قَدْ خَلَتْ مِن قَبْلِهِ ٱلرُّسُلُ
[other] apostles have passed before him.

أَفَإِي۟ن مَّاتَ أَوْ قُتِلَ
If he dies or is slain,

ٱنقَلَبْتُمْ عَلَىٰٓ أَعْقَٰبِكُمْ
will you turn back on your heels?

وَمَن يَنقَلِبْ عَلَىٰ عَقِبَيْهِ
Anyone who turns back on his heels

فَلَن يَضُرَّ ٱللَّهَ شَيْـًٔا
will not harm Allah in any way,

وَسَيَجْزِى ٱللَّهُ ٱلشَّٰكِرِينَ
and Allah will reward the grateful.

وَمَا كَانَ لِنَفْسٍ أَن تَمُوتَ
145 No soul may die

إِلَّا بِإِذْنِ ٱللَّهِ
except by Allah's leave,

كِتَٰبًا مُّؤَجَّلًا
at an appointed time.

وَمَن يُرِدْ ثَوَابَ ٱلدُّنْيَا
Whoever desires the reward of this world,

نُؤْتِهِۦ مِنْهَا
We will give him of it;

وَمَن يُرِدْ ثَوَابَ ٱلْءَاخِرَةِ
and whoever desires the reward of the Hereafter,

نُؤْتِهِۦ مِنْهَا
We will give him of it;

وَسَنَجْزِى ٱلشَّٰكِرِينَ
and We will reward the grateful.

وَكَأَيِّن مِّن نَّبِىٍّ
146 How many a prophet there has been

قَٰتَلَ مَعَهُۥ رِبِّيُّونَ كَثِيرٌ
with whom a multitude of godly men fought.

فَمَا وَهَنُوا۟ لِمَآ أَصَابَهُمْ
They did not falter for what befell them

---

[1] Or 'witnesses.'

فِى سَبِيلِ ٱللَّهِ    in the way of Allah,

وَمَا ضَعُفُواْ    neither did they weaken,

وَمَا ٱسْتَكَانُواْ    nor did they abase themselves;

وَٱللَّهُ يُحِبُّ ٱلصَّـٰبِرِينَ ۝    and Allah loves the steadfast.

وَمَا كَانَ قَوْلَهُمْ إِلَّآ أَن قَالُواْ    147 All that they said was,

رَبَّنَا ٱغْفِرْ لَنَا ذُنُوبَنَا    'Our Lord, forgive us our sins,

وَإِسْرَافَنَا فِى أَمْرِنَا    and our excesses in our affairs,

وَثَبِّتْ أَقْدَامَنَا    and make our feet steady,

وَٱنصُرْنَا عَلَى ٱلْقَوْمِ ٱلْكَـٰفِرِينَ ۝    and help us against the faithless lot.'

فَـَٔاتَىٰهُمُ ٱللَّهُ ثَوَابَ ٱلدُّنْيَا    148 So Allah gave them the reward of this world

وَحُسْنَ ثَوَابِ ٱلْأَخِرَةِ    and the fair reward of the Hereafter;

وَٱللَّهُ يُحِبُّ ٱلْمُحْسِنِينَ ۝    and Allah loves the virtuous.

يَـٰٓأَيُّهَا ٱلَّذِينَ ءَامَنُوٓاْ    149 O you who have faith!

إِن تُطِيعُواْ ٱلَّذِينَ كَفَرُواْ    If you obey the faithless,

يَرُدُّوكُمْ عَلَىٰٓ أَعْقَـٰبِكُمْ    they will turn you back on your heels,

فَتَنقَلِبُواْ خَـٰسِرِينَ ۝    and you will become losers.

بَلِ ٱللَّهُ مَوْلَـٰكُمْ    150 Rather Allah is your Master,

وَهُوَ خَيْرُ ٱلنَّـٰصِرِينَ ۝    and He is the best of helpers.

سَنُلْقِى فِى قُلُوبِ ٱلَّذِينَ كَفَرُواْ ٱلرُّعْبَ    151 We shall cast terror into the hearts of the faithless

بِمَآ أَشْرَكُواْ بِٱللَّهِ    because of their ascribing to Allah partners,

مَا لَمْ يُنَزِّلْ بِهِۦ سُلْطَـٰنًا    for which He has not sent down any authority,

وَمَأْوَىٰهُمُ ٱلنَّارُ    and their refuge shall be the Fire,

وَبِئْسَ مَثْوَى ٱلظَّـٰلِمِينَ ۝    and evil is the [final] abode of the wrongdoers.

وَلَقَدْ صَدَقَكُمُ ٱللَّهُ وَعْدَهُۥٓ    152 Allah certainly fulfilled His promise to you

إِذْ تَحُسُّونَهُم بِإِذْنِهِۦ    when you were slaying them with His leave,

حَتَّىٰٓ إِذَا فَشِلْتُمْ    until you lost courage,

وَتَنَـٰزَعْتُمْ فِى ٱلْأَمْرِ    disputed about the matter,

وَعَصَيْتُم    and disobeyed

مِّنۢ بَعْدِ مَآ أَرَىٰكُم مَّا تُحِبُّونَ    after He showed you what you loved.[1]

---

[1] That is, the spoils of war.

مِنكُم مَّن يُرِيدُ ٱلدُّنْيَا

Some of you desire this world,

وَمِنكُم مَّن يُرِيدُ ٱلْآخِرَةَ

and some of you desire the Hereafter.

ثُمَّ صَرَفَكُمْ عَنْهُمْ

Then He turned you away from them

لِيَبْتَلِيَكُمْ

so that He might test you.

وَلَقَدْ عَفَا عَنكُمْ

Certainly He has excused you,

وَٱللَّهُ ذُو فَضْلٍ عَلَى ٱلْمُؤْمِنِينَ ۞

for Allah is gracious to the faithful.

إِذْ تُصْعِدُونَ

153 When you were fleeing

وَلَا تَلْوُونَ عَلَىٰ أَحَدٍ

without paying any attention to anyone,

وَٱلرَّسُولُ يَدْعُوكُمْ فِي أُخْرَىٰكُمْ

while the Apostle was calling you from your rear,

فَأَثَـٰبَكُمْ غَمًّا بِغَمٍّ

He requited you with grief upon grief,

لِّكَيْلَا تَحْزَنُوا۟ عَلَىٰ مَا فَاتَكُمْ

so that you may not grieve for what escapes you

وَلَا مَآ أَصَـٰبَكُمْ

nor for what befell you,

وَٱللَّهُ خَبِيرٌۢ بِمَا تَعْمَلُونَ ۞

and Allah is well aware of what you do.

ثُمَّ أَنزَلَ عَلَيْكُم مِّنۢ بَعْدِ ٱلْغَمِّ أَمَنَةً

154 Then He sent down to you safety after grief

نُّعَاسًا يَغْشَىٰ طَآئِفَةً مِّنكُمْ

—a drowsiness that came over a group of you—

وَطَآئِفَةٌ قَدْ أَهَمَّتْهُمْ أَنفُسُهُمْ

while another group, anxious only about themselves,

يَظُنُّونَ بِٱللَّهِ غَيْرَ ٱلْحَقِّ

entertained false notions about Allah,

ظَنَّ ٱلْجَـٰهِلِيَّةِ

notions of [pagan] ignorance.

يَقُولُونَ هَل لَّنَا مِنَ ٱلْأَمْرِ مِن شَىْءٍ

They say, 'Do we have any role in the matter?'

قُلْ إِنَّ ٱلْأَمْرَ كُلَّهُۥ لِلَّهِ

Say, 'Indeed the matter belongs totally to Allah.'

يُخْفُونَ فِي أَنفُسِهِم

They hide in their hearts

مَّا لَا يُبْدُونَ لَكَ

what they do not disclose to *you*.

يَقُولُونَ لَوْ كَانَ لَنَا مِنَ ٱلْأَمْرِ شَىْءٌ

They say, 'Had we any role in the matter,

مَّا قُتِلْنَا هَـٰهُنَا

we would not have been slain here.'

قُل لَّوْ كُنتُمْ فِي بُيُوتِكُمْ

Say, 'Even if you had remained in your houses,

لَبَرَزَ ٱلَّذِينَ كُتِبَ عَلَيْهِمُ ٱلْقَتْلُ

those destined to be slain would have set out

إِلَىٰ مَضَاجِعِهِمْ

toward the places where they were laid to rest,

وَلِيَبْتَلِىَ ٱللَّهُ مَا فِي صُدُورِكُمْ

so that Allah may test what is in your breasts,

وَلِيُمَحِّصَ مَا فِي قُلُوبِكُمْ

and that He may purge what is in your hearts,

وَٱللَّهُ عَلِيمٌۢ بِذَاتِ ٱلصُّدُورِ ۞

and Allah knows best what is in the breasts.

إِنَّ ٱلَّذِينَ تَوَلَّوْا۟ مِنكُمْ    155 Those of you who fled

يَوْمَ ٱلْتَقَى ٱلْجَمْعَانِ    on the day when the two hosts met,

إِنَّمَا ٱسْتَزَلَّهُمُ ٱلشَّيْطَنُ    only Satan had made them stumble

بِبَعْضِ مَا كَسَبُوا۟    because of some of their deeds.

وَلَقَدْ عَفَا ٱللَّهُ عَنْهُمْ    Certainly Allah has excused them,

إِنَّ ٱللَّهَ غَفُورٌ حَلِيمٌ ۝    for Allah is all-forgiving, all-forbearing.

يَٰٓأَيُّهَا ٱلَّذِينَ ءَامَنُوا۟    156 O you who have faith!

لَا تَكُونُوا۟ كَٱلَّذِينَ كَفَرُوا۟    Do not be like the faithless

وَقَالُوا۟ لِإِخْوَٰنِهِمْ    who say of their brethren,

إِذَا ضَرَبُوا۟ فِى ٱلْأَرْضِ أَوْ كَانُوا۟ غُزًّى    when they travel in the land or go into battle,

لَّوْ كَانُوا۟ عِندَنَا    'Had they stayed with us

مَا مَاتُوا۟ وَمَا قُتِلُوا۟    they would not have died or been killed,'

لِيَجْعَلَ ٱللَّهُ ذَٰلِكَ حَسْرَةً فِى قُلُوبِهِمْ    so that Allah may make it a regret in their hearts.

وَٱللَّهُ يُحْىِۦ وَيُمِيتُ    But Allah gives life and brings death,

وَٱللَّهُ بِمَا تَعْمَلُونَ بَصِيرٌ ۝    and Allah sees best what you do.

وَلَئِن قُتِلْتُمْ فِى سَبِيلِ ٱللَّهِ أَوْ مُتُّمْ    157 If you are slain in the way of Allah, or die,

لَمَغْفِرَةٌ مِّنَ ٱللَّهِ وَرَحْمَةٌ    surely forgiveness and mercy from Allah

خَيْرٌ مِّمَّا يَجْمَعُونَ ۝    are better than what they amass.

وَلَئِن مُّتُّمْ أَوْ قُتِلْتُمْ    158 And if you die or are slain,

لَإِلَى ٱللَّهِ تُحْشَرُونَ ۝    you will surely be mustered toward Allah.

فَبِمَا رَحْمَةٍ مِّنَ ٱللَّهِ لِنتَ لَهُمْ    159 It is by Allah's mercy that *you* are gentle to them;

وَلَوْ كُنتَ فَظًّا غَلِيظَ ٱلْقَلْبِ    and had *you* been harsh and hardhearted,

لَٱنفَضُّوا۟ مِنْ حَوْلِكَ    surely they would have scattered from around *you*.

فَٱعْفُ عَنْهُمْ وَٱسْتَغْفِرْ لَهُمْ    So *excuse* them, and *plead* for forgiveness for them,

وَشَاوِرْهُمْ فِى ٱلْأَمْرِ    and *consult* them in the affairs,

فَإِذَا عَزَمْتَ فَتَوَكَّلْ عَلَى ٱللَّهِ    and once *you* are resolved, put *your* trust in Allah.

إِنَّ ٱللَّهَ يُحِبُّ ٱلْمُتَوَكِّلِينَ ۝    Indeed Allah loves those who trust in Him.

إِن يَنصُرْكُمُ ٱللَّهُ فَلَا غَالِبَ لَكُمْ    160 If Allah helps you, no one can overcome you,

وَإِن يَخْذُلْكُمْ    but if He forsakes you,

فَمَن ذَا ٱلَّذِى يَنصُرُكُم مِّنۢ بَعْدِهِۦ    who will help you after Him?

وَعَلَى ٱللَّهِ فَلْيَتَوَكَّلِ ٱلْمُؤْمِنُونَ ۞     So in Allah let all the faithful put their trust.

وَمَا كَانَ لِنَبِيٍّ أَن يَغُلَّ     161 A prophet may not breach his trust,

وَمَن يَغْلُلْ     and whoever breaches his trust

يَأْتِ بِمَا غَلَّ يَوْمَ ٱلْقِيَٰمَةِ     will bring his breaches on the Day of Resurrection;

ثُمَّ تُوَفَّىٰ كُلُّ نَفْسٍ     then every soul shall be recompensed fully

مَّا كَسَبَتْ     for what it has earned,

وَهُمْ لَا يُظْلَمُونَ ۞     and they will not be wronged.

أَفَمَنِ ٱتَّبَعَ رِضْوَٰنَ ٱللَّهِ     162 Is he who follows [the course of] Allah's pleasure

كَمَنۢ بَآءَ بِسَخَطٍ مِّنَ ٱللَّهِ     like him who earns Allah's displeasure

وَمَأْوَىٰهُ جَهَنَّمُ     and whose refuge is hell,

وَبِئْسَ ٱلْمَصِيرُ ۞     an evil destination?

هُمْ دَرَجَٰتٌ عِندَ ٱللَّهِ     163 They have ranks with Allah,

وَٱللَّهُ بَصِيرٌۢ بِمَا يَعْمَلُونَ ۞     and Allah sees best what they do.

لَقَدْ مَنَّ ٱللَّهُ عَلَى ٱلْمُؤْمِنِينَ     164 Allah certainly favoured the faithful

إِذْ بَعَثَ فِيهِمْ رَسُولًا     when He raised up among them an apostle

مِّنْ أَنفُسِهِمْ     from among themselves

يَتْلُوا۟ عَلَيْهِمْ ءَايَٰتِهِۦ وَيُزَكِّيهِمْ     to recite to them His signs and to purify them,

وَيُعَلِّمُهُمُ ٱلْكِتَٰبَ وَٱلْحِكْمَةَ     and to teach them the Book and wisdom,

وَإِن كَانُوا۟ مِن قَبْلُ لَفِى ضَلَٰلٍ مُّبِينٍ ۞     and earlier they had indeed been in manifest error.

أَوَلَمَّآ أَصَٰبَتْكُم مُّصِيبَةٌ     165 What, when an affliction visits you

قَدْ أَصَبْتُم مِّثْلَيْهَا     —while you have inflicted twice as much—

قُلْتُمْ أَنَّىٰ هَٰذَا     do you say, 'How is this?'!

قُلْ هُوَ مِنْ عِندِ أَنفُسِكُمْ     *Say,* 'This is from your own souls.'

إِنَّ ٱللَّهَ عَلَىٰ كُلِّ شَىْءٍ قَدِيرٌ ۞     Indeed Allah has power over all things.

وَمَآ أَصَٰبَكُمْ يَوْمَ ٱلْتَقَى ٱلْجَمْعَانِ     166 What befell you on the day when the two hosts met,

فَبِإِذْنِ ٱللَّهِ     was by Allah's permission,

وَلِيَعْلَمَ ٱلْمُؤْمِنِينَ ۞     so that He may ascertain the faithful,

وَلِيَعْلَمَ ٱلَّذِينَ نَافَقُوا۟     167 and ascertain the hypocrites.

وَقِيلَ لَهُمْ تَعَالَوْا۟     [When] they were told: 'Come,

قَٰتِلُوا۟ فِى سَبِيلِ ٱللَّهِ أَوِ ٱدْفَعُوا۟     fight in the way of Allah, or defend [yourselves],

قَالُواْ لَوْ نَعْلَمُ قِتَالًا
they said, 'If we knew any fighting,

لَّٱتَّبَعْنَكُمْ
surely we would have followed you.'

هُمْ لِلْكُفْرِ يَوْمَئِذٍ أَقْرَبُ مِنْهُمْ لِلْإِيمَانِ
That day they were nearer to unfaith than to faith.

يَقُولُونَ بِأَفْوَاهِهِم
They say with their mouths

مَّا لَيْسَ فِى قُلُوبِهِمْ
what is not in their hearts,

وَٱللَّهُ أَعْلَمُ بِمَا يَكْتُمُونَ ۝
and Allah knows best whatever they conceal.

ٱلَّذِينَ قَالُواْ لِإِخْوَٰنِهِمْ
168 Those who said of their brethren,

وَقَعَدُواْ
while they themselves sat back:

لَوْ أَطَاعُونَا
'Had they obeyed us,

مَا قُتِلُواْ
they would not have been killed.'

قُلْ فَٱدْرَءُواْ عَنْ أَنفُسِكُمُ ٱلْمَوْتَ
*Say,* 'Then keep death off from yourselves,

إِن كُنتُمْ صَٰدِقِينَ ۝
should you be truthful.'

وَلَا تَحْسَبَنَّ ٱلَّذِينَ قُتِلُواْ
169 Do not suppose those who were slain

فِى سَبِيلِ ٱللَّهِ
in the way of Allah

أَمْوَٰتًا
to be dead;

بَلْ أَحْيَآءٌ
rather they are living

عِندَ رَبِّهِمْ يُرْزَقُونَ ۝
and provided for near their Lord,

فَرِحِينَ
170 exulting

بِمَآ ءَاتَىٰهُمُ ٱللَّهُ مِن فَضْلِهِۦ
in what Allah has given them out of His grace,

وَيَسْتَبْشِرُونَ بِٱلَّذِينَ لَمْ يَلْحَقُواْ بِهِم
and rejoicing for those who have not yet joined them

مِّنْ خَلْفِهِمْ
from [those left] behind them

أَلَّا خَوْفٌ عَلَيْهِمْ
that they will have no fear,

وَلَا هُمْ يَحْزَنُونَ ۝
nor will they grieve.

يَسْتَبْشِرُونَ بِنِعْمَةٍ مِّنَ ٱللَّهِ وَفَضْلٍ
171 They rejoice in Allah's blessing and grace,

وَأَنَّ ٱللَّهَ لَا يُضِيعُ
and that Allah does not waste

أَجْرَ ٱلْمُؤْمِنِينَ ۝
the reward of the faithful.

ٱلَّذِينَ ٱسْتَجَابُواْ لِلَّهِ وَٱلرَّسُولِ
172 Those who responded to Allah and the Apostle

مِنۢ بَعْدِ مَآ أَصَابَهُمُ ٱلْقَرْحُ
[even] after they had been wounded

لِلَّذِينَ أَحْسَنُواْ مِنْهُمْ
—for those of them who have been virtuous

وَٱتَّقَوْاْ
and Godwary

أَجۡرٌ عَظِيمٌ ۝     there shall be a great reward.

ٱلَّذِينَ قَالَ لَهُمُ ٱلنَّاسُ    173 Those to whom the people said,

إِنَّ ٱلنَّاسَ قَدۡ جَمَعُوا۟ لَكُمۡ    'All the people have gathered against you;

فَٱخۡشَوۡهُمۡ     so fear them.'

فَزَادَهُمۡ إِيمَـٰنٗا     That only increased them in faith,

وَقَالُوا۟ حَسۡبُنَا ٱللَّهُ    and they said, 'Allah is sufficient for us,

وَنِعۡمَ ٱلۡوَكِيلُ ۝     and He is an excellent trustee.'

فَٱنقَلَبُوا۟ بِنِعۡمَةٖ مِّنَ ٱللَّهِ وَفَضۡلٖ   174 So they returned with Allah's blessing and grace,

لَّمۡ يَمۡسَسۡهُمۡ سُوٓءٌ     untouched by any evil.

وَٱتَّبَعُوا۟ رِضۡوَٰنَ ٱللَّهِ     They pursued the pleasure of Allah,

وَٱللَّهُ ذُو فَضۡلٍ عَظِيمٍ ۝   and Allah is dispenser of a great grace.

إِنَّمَا ذَٰلِكُمُ ٱلشَّيۡطَٰنُ يُخَوِّفُ أَوۡلِيَآءَهُۥ   175 That is only Satan frightening his followers!

فَلَا تَخَافُوهُمۡ وَخَافُونِ    So fear them not, and fear Me,

إِن كُنتُم مُّؤۡمِنِينَ ۝     should you be faithful.

وَلَا يَحۡزُنكَ ٱلَّذِينَ يُسَٰرِعُونَ فِى ٱلۡكُفۡرِ   176 *Do not grieve* for those who are active in unfaith;

إِنَّهُمۡ لَن يَضُرُّوا۟ ٱللَّهَ شَيۡـٔٗا    they will not hurt Allah in the least:

يُرِيدُ ٱللَّهُ أَلَّا يَجۡعَلَ لَهُمۡ حَظّٗا   Allah desires to give them no share

فِى ٱلۡآخِرَةِ     in the Hereafter,

وَلَهُمۡ عَذَابٌ عَظِيمٌ ۝   and there is a great punishment for them.

إِنَّ ٱلَّذِينَ ٱشۡتَرَوُا۟ ٱلۡكُفۡرَ بِٱلۡإِيمَٰنِ   177 Those who have bought unfaith for faith

لَن يَضُرُّوا۟ ٱللَّهَ شَيۡـٔٗا    will not hurt Allah in the least,

وَلَهُمۡ عَذَابٌ أَلِيمٌ ۝   and there is a painful punishment for them.

وَلَا يَحۡسَبَنَّ ٱلَّذِينَ كَفَرُوٓا۟   178 Let the faithless not suppose

أَنَّمَا نُمۡلِى لَهُمۡ     that the respite that We grant them

خَيۡرٌ لِّأَنفُسِهِمۡ     is good for their souls:

إِنَّمَا نُمۡلِى لَهُمۡ     We give them respite only

لِيَزۡدَادُوٓا۟ إِثۡمٗا     that they may increase in sin,

وَلَهُمۡ عَذَابٌ مُّهِينٌ ۝   and there is a humiliating punishment for them.

مَّا كَانَ ٱللَّهُ لِيَذَرَ ٱلۡمُؤۡمِنِينَ   179 Allah will not leave the faithful

عَلَىٰ مَآ أَنتُمۡ عَلَيۡهِ     in your present state,

حَتَّىٰ يَمِيزَ ٱلْخَبِيثَ مِنَ ٱلطَّيِّبِ

until He has separated the bad ones from the good.

وَمَا كَانَ ٱللَّهُ لِيُطْلِعَكُمْ عَلَى ٱلْغَيْبِ

Allah will not acquaint you with the Unseen,

وَلَٰكِنَّ ٱللَّهَ يَجْتَبِى مِن رُّسُلِهِ

but Allah chooses from His apostles

مَن يَشَآءُ

whomever He wishes.

فَـَٔامِنُوا بِٱللَّهِ وَرُسُلِهِ

So have faith in Allah and His apostles;

وَإِن تُؤْمِنُوا وَتَتَّقُوا

and if you are faithful and Godwary,

فَلَكُمْ أَجْرٌ عَظِيمٌ ۝

there shall be a great reward for you.

وَلَا يَحْسَبَنَّ ٱلَّذِينَ يَبْخَلُونَ

180 Let the stingy not suppose that [their grudging]

بِمَآ ءَاتَىٰهُمُ ٱللَّهُ مِن فَضْلِهِ

what Allah has given them out of His grace

هُوَ خَيْرًا لَّهُم

is good for them;

بَلْ هُوَ شَرٌّ لَّهُمْ

rather it is bad for them.

سَيُطَوَّقُونَ مَا بَخِلُوا بِهِ

They will be collared with what they grudge

يَوْمَ ٱلْقِيَٰمَةِ

on the Day of Resurrection.

وَلِلَّهِ مِيرَٰثُ ٱلسَّمَٰوَٰتِ

To Allah belongs the heritage of the heavens

وَٱلْأَرْضِ

and the earth,

وَٱللَّهُ بِمَا تَعْمَلُونَ خَبِيرٌ ۝

and Allah is well aware of what you do.

لَّقَدْ سَمِعَ ٱللَّهُ قَوْلَ ٱلَّذِينَ

181 Allah has certainly heard the remark of those

قَالُوٓا إِنَّ ٱللَّهَ فَقِيرٌ وَنَحْنُ أَغْنِيَآءُ

who said, 'Allah is poor and we are rich.'

سَنَكْتُبُ مَا قَالُوا

We will record what they have said,

وَقَتْلَهُمُ ٱلْأَنۢبِيَآءَ بِغَيْرِ حَقٍّ

and their killing of the prophets unjustly,[1]

وَنَقُولُ

and We shall say,

ذُوقُوا عَذَابَ ٱلْحَرِيقِ ۝

'Taste the punishment of the burning.

ذَٰلِكَ بِمَا قَدَّمَتْ أَيْدِيكُمْ

182 That is because of what your hands have sent ahead,

وَأَنَّ ٱللَّهَ لَيْسَ بِظَلَّامٍ لِّلْعَبِيدِ ۝

and because Allah is not tyrannical to the servants.'

ٱلَّذِينَ قَالُوٓا

183 [To] those who say,

إِنَّ ٱللَّهَ عَهِدَ إِلَيْنَآ

'Allah has pledged us

أَلَّا نُؤْمِنَ لِرَسُولٍ

not to believe in any apostle

---

[1] Verses 181-184 are addressed to the Jews. Cf. 2:61, 91; 3:21, 112; 4:115, where the Jews are accused of killing the prophets.

حَتَّىٰ يَأْتِيَنَا بِقُرْبَانٍ تَأْكُلُهُ ٱلنَّارُ

قُلْ قَدْ جَاءَكُمْ رُسُلٌ مِّن قَبْلِى

بِٱلْبَيِّنَٰتِ وَبِٱلَّذِى قُلْتُمْ

فَلِمَ قَتَلْتُمُوهُمْ

إِن كُنتُمْ صَٰدِقِينَ ۩

unless he brings us an offering consumed by fire,'
say, 'Apostles before me certainly brought you
    manifest signs and what you speak of.
    Then why did you kill them,
       should you be truthful?'

فَإِن كَذَّبُوكَ

فَقَدْ كُذِّبَ رُسُلٌ مِّن قَبْلِكَ

جَاءُو بِٱلْبَيِّنَٰتِ وَٱلزُّبُرِ

وَٱلْكِتَٰبِ ٱلْمُنِيرِ ۩

184 But if they deny *you*,
    then before *you* [other] apostles have been denied,
who came with manifest signs, holy writs,
    and an illuminating scripture.

كُلُّ نَفْسٍ ذَآئِقَةُ ٱلْمَوْتِ

وَإِنَّمَا تُوَفَّوْنَ أُجُورَكُمْ

يَوْمَ ٱلْقِيَٰمَةِ

فَمَن زُحْزِحَ عَنِ ٱلنَّارِ

وَأُدْخِلَ ٱلْجَنَّةَ

فَقَدْ فَازَ

وَمَا ٱلْحَيَوٰةُ ٱلدُّنْيَآ

إِلَّا مَتَٰعُ ٱلْغُرُورِ ۩ ٭

185 Every soul shall taste death,
    and you will indeed be paid your full rewards
    on the Day of Resurrection.
Whoever is delivered from the Fire
    and admitted to paradise
       has certainly succeeded.
The life of this world is nothing
    but the wares of delusion.

لَتُبْلَوُنَّ

فِى أَمْوَٰلِكُمْ وَأَنفُسِكُمْ

وَلَتَسْمَعُنَّ

مِنَ ٱلَّذِينَ أُوتُوا۟ ٱلْكِتَٰبَ مِن قَبْلِكُمْ

وَمِنَ ٱلَّذِينَ أَشْرَكُوٓا۟

أَذًى كَثِيرًا

وَإِن تَصْبِرُوا۟ وَتَتَّقُوا۟

فَإِنَّ ذَٰلِكَ مِنْ عَزْمِ ٱلْأُمُورِ ۩

186 You will surely be tested
    in your possessions and your souls,
    and you will surely hear
from those who were given the Book before you
    and from the polytheists
       much affront;
but if you are patient and Godwary,
    that is indeed the steadiest of courses.

وَإِذْ أَخَذَ ٱللَّهُ مِيثَٰقَ

ٱلَّذِينَ أُوتُوا۟ ٱلْكِتَٰبَ

لَتُبَيِّنُنَّهُ لِلنَّاسِ

وَلَا تَكْتُمُونَهُ

فَنَبَذُوهُ وَرَآءَ ظُهُورِهِمْ

187 When Allah made a covenant
    with those who were given the Book:
    'You shall explain it for the people,
       and you shall not conceal it,'
they cast it behind their backs

وَٱشْتَرَوْاْ بِهِۦ ثَمَنًا قَلِيلًا and sold it for a paltry gain.

فَبِئْسَ مَا يَشْتَرُونَ ۱۸۷ How evil is what they buy!

لَا تَحْسَبَنَّ ٱلَّذِينَ 188 Do not suppose those

يَفْرَحُونَ بِمَآ أَتَواْ who exult in what they have done,

وَّيُحِبُّونَ أَن يُحْمَدُواْ بِمَا لَمْ يَفْعَلُواْ and love to be praised for what they have not done

فَلَا تَحْسَبَنَّهُم بِمَفَازَةٍ مِّنَ ٱلْعَذَابِ —do not suppose them saved from punishment,

وَلَهُمْ عَذَابٌ أَلِيمٌ ۱۸۸ and there is a painful punishment for them.

وَلِلَّهِ مُلْكُ ٱلسَّمَـٰوَٰتِ 189 To Allah belongs the kingdom of the heavens

وَٱلْأَرْضِ and the earth,

وَٱللَّهُ عَلَىٰ كُلِّ شَىْءٍ قَدِيرٌ ۱۸۹ and Allah has power over all things.

إِنَّ فِى خَلْقِ ٱلسَّمَـٰوَٰتِ وَٱلْأَرْضِ 190 Indeed in the creation of the heavens and the earth

وَٱخْتِلَـٰفِ ٱلَّيْلِ وَٱلنَّهَارِ and the alternation of night and day,

لَأَيَـٰتٍ لِّأُوْلِى ٱلْأَلْبَـٰبِ ۱۹۰ there are signs for those who possess intellects.

ٱلَّذِينَ يَذْكُرُونَ ٱللَّهَ 191 Those who remember Allah

قِيَـٰمًا وَقُعُودًا وَعَلَىٰ جُنُوبِهِمْ standing, sitting, and lying on their sides,

وَيَتَفَكَّرُونَ فِى خَلْقِ ٱلسَّمَـٰوَٰتِ and reflect on the creation of the heavens

وَٱلْأَرْضِ and the earth [and say],

رَبَّنَا 'Our Lord,

مَا خَلَقْتَ هَـٰذَا بَـٰطِلًا You have not created this in vain!

سُبْحَـٰنَكَ Immaculate are You!

فَقِنَا عَذَابَ ٱلنَّارِ ۱۹۱ Save us from the punishment of the Fire.

رَبَّنَآ 192 Our Lord,

إِنَّكَ مَن تُدْخِلِ ٱلنَّارَ whoever that You make enter the Fire

فَقَدْ أَخْزَيْتَهُۥ will surely have been disgraced by You,

وَمَا لِلظَّـٰلِمِينَ مِنْ أَنصَارٍ ۱۹۲ and the wrongdoers will have no helpers.

رَبَّنَآ 193 Our Lord,

إِنَّنَا سَمِعْنَا مُنَادِيًا we have indeed heard a summoner

يُنَادِى لِلْإِيمَـٰنِ calling to faith,

أَنْ ءَامِنُواْ بِرَبِّكُمْ declaring, "Have faith in your Lord!"

فَـَٔامَنَّا So we believed.

رَبَّنَا     Our Lord,

فَٱغْفِرْ لَنَا ذُنُوبَنَا     forgive us our sins

وَكَفِّرْ عَنَّا سَيِّئَاتِنَا     and absolve us of our misdeeds,

وَتَوَفَّنَا مَعَ ٱلْأَبْرَارِ ۝     and make us die with the pious.

رَبَّنَا وَءَاتِنَا     194 Our Lord, give us

مَا وَعَدتَّنَا عَلَىٰ رُسُلِكَ     what You have promised us through Your apostles,

وَلَا تُخْزِنَا يَوْمَ ٱلْقِيَٰمَةِ ۗ     and do not disgrace us on the Day of Resurrection.

إِنَّكَ لَا تُخْلِفُ ٱلْمِيعَادَ ۝     Indeed You do not break Your promise.'

فَٱسْتَجَابَ لَهُمْ رَبُّهُمْ     195 Then their Lord answered them,

أَنِّى لَآ أُضِيعُ عَمَلَ عَٰمِلٍ مِّنكُم     'I do not waste the work of any worker among you,

مِّن ذَكَرٍ أَوْ أُنثَىٰ ۖ     whether male or female;

بَعْضُكُم مِّنْ بَعْضٍ ۖ     you are all on the same footing.

فَٱلَّذِينَ هَاجَرُواْ     So those who migrated

وَأُخْرِجُواْ مِن دِيَٰرِهِمْ     and were expelled from their homes,

وَأُوذُواْ فِى سَبِيلِى     and were tormented in My way,

وَقَٰتَلُواْ وَقُتِلُواْ     and those who fought and were killed

لَأُكَفِّرَنَّ عَنْهُمْ سَيِّئَاتِهِمْ     —I will surely absolve them of their misdeeds

وَلَأُدْخِلَنَّهُمْ جَنَّٰتٍ تَجْرِى     and I will admit them into gardens

مِن تَحْتِهَا ٱلْأَنْهَٰرُ     with streams running in them,

ثَوَابًا مِّنْ عِندِ ٱللَّهِ ۗ     as a reward from Allah,

وَٱللَّهُ عِندَهُۥ حُسْنُ ٱلثَّوَابِ ۝     and Allah—with Him is the best of rewards.

لَا يَغُرَّنَّكَ تَقَلُّبُ ٱلَّذِينَ كَفَرُواْ     196 Never be misled by the bustle of the faithless

فِى ٱلْبِلَٰدِ ۝     in the towns.

مَتَٰعٌ قَلِيلٌ     197 It is a trivial enjoyment;

ثُمَّ مَأْوَىٰهُمْ جَهَنَّمُ ۚ     then their refuge is hell,

وَبِئْسَ ٱلْمِهَادُ ۝     and it is an evil resting place.

لَٰكِنِ ٱلَّذِينَ ٱتَّقَوْاْ رَبَّهُمْ     198 But those who are wary of their Lord

لَهُمْ جَنَّٰتٌ تَجْرِى     —for them shall be gardens

مِن تَحْتِهَا ٱلْأَنْهَٰرُ     with streams running in them,

خَٰلِدِينَ فِيهَا

to remain in them [forever],

نُزُلًا مِّنْ عِندِ ٱللَّهِ

a hospitality from Allah;

وَمَا عِندَ ٱللَّهِ خَيْرٌ لِّلْأَبْرَارِ ۝

and what is with Allah is better for the pious.

وَإِنَّ مِنْ أَهْلِ ٱلْكِتَٰبِ

199 Indeed among the People of the Book

لَمَن يُؤْمِنُ بِٱللَّهِ

there are surely some who have faith in Allah,

وَمَا أُنزِلَ إِلَيْكُمْ

and in what has been sent down to you,

وَمَا أُنزِلَ إِلَيْهِمْ

and in what has been sent down to them.

خَٰشِعِينَ لِلَّهِ

Humble toward Allah,

لَا يَشْتَرُونَ بِـَٔايَٰتِ ٱللَّهِ ثَمَنًا قَلِيلًا

they do not sell the signs of Allah for a paltry gain.

أُوْلَٰٓئِكَ لَهُمْ أَجْرُهُمْ عِندَ رَبِّهِمْ

They shall have their reward near their Lord;

إِنَّ ٱللَّهَ سَرِيعُ ٱلْحِسَابِ ۝

indeed Allah is swift at reckoning.

يَٰٓأَيُّهَا ٱلَّذِينَ ءَامَنُوا۟

200 O you who have faith!

ٱصْبِرُوا۟ وَصَابِرُوا۟

Be patient, stand firm,

وَرَابِطُوا۟

and close [your] ranks,

وَٱتَّقُوا۟ ٱللَّهَ لَعَلَّكُمْ تُفْلِحُونَ ۝

and be wary of Allah so that you may be felicitous.

## سُوْرَةُ النِّسَاءِ     4. SŪRAT AL-NISĀ'[1]

بِسْمِ ٱللَّهِ

In the Name of Allah,

ٱلرَّحْمَٰنِ ٱلرَّحِيمِ

the All-beneficent, the All-merciful.

يَٰٓأَيُّهَا ٱلنَّاسُ

1 O mankind!

ٱتَّقُوا۟ رَبَّكُمُ

Be wary of your Lord

ٱلَّذِى خَلَقَكُم مِّن نَّفْسٍ وَٰحِدَةٍ

who created you from a single soul,

وَخَلَقَ مِنْهَا زَوْجَهَا

and created its mate from it,

وَبَثَّ مِنْهُمَا رِجَالًا كَثِيرًا

and, from the two of them, scattered numerous men

وَنِسَآءً

and women.

---

[1] The *sūrah* makes frequent reference to matters concerning women (*nisā'*), hence its name.

وَٱتَّقُوا۟ ٱللَّهَ    Be wary of Allah,

ٱلَّذِى تَسَآءَلُونَ بِهِۦ    in whose Name you adjure one another,

وَٱلْأَرْحَامَ    and the wombs.[1]

إِنَّ ٱللَّهَ كَانَ عَلَيْكُمْ رَقِيبًا ۞    Indeed Allah is watchful over you.

وَءَاتُوا۟ ٱلْيَتَـٰمَىٰٓ أَمْوَٰلَهُمْ    2 Give the orphans their property,

وَلَا تَتَبَدَّلُوا۟ ٱلْخَبِيثَ بِٱلطَّيِّبِ    and do not replace the good with the bad,

وَلَا تَأْكُلُوٓا۟ أَمْوَٰلَهُمْ    and do not eat up their property

إِلَىٰٓ أَمْوَٰلِكُمْ    [by mingling it] with your own property,

إِنَّهُۥ كَانَ حُوبًا كَبِيرًا ۞    for that is indeed a great sin.[2]

وَإِنْ خِفْتُمْ أَلَّا تُقْسِطُوا۟    3 If you fear that you may not deal justly

فِى ٱلْيَتَـٰمَىٰ    with the orphans,[3]

فَٱنكِحُوا۟ مَا طَابَ لَكُم مِّنَ ٱلنِّسَآءِ    then marry [other] women that you like,

مَثْنَىٰ وَثُلَـٰثَ وَرُبَـٰعَ    two, three, or four.

فَإِنْ خِفْتُمْ أَلَّا تَعْدِلُوا۟    But if you fear that you may not treat them fairly,

فَوَٰحِدَةً    then [marry only] one,

أَوْ مَا مَلَكَتْ أَيْمَـٰنُكُمْ    or [marry from among] your slave-women.

ذَٰلِكَ أَدْنَىٰٓ أَلَّا تَعُولُوا۟ ۞    That makes it likelier that you will not be unfair.

وَءَاتُوا۟ ٱلنِّسَآءَ صَدُقَـٰتِهِنَّ نِحْلَةً    4 Give women their dowries as an obligation;

فَإِن طِبْنَ لَكُمْ عَن شَىْءٍ مِّنْهُ نَفْسًا    but if they remit anything of it of their own accord,

فَكُلُوهُ هَنِيٓـًٔا مَّرِيٓـًٔا ۞    then consume it as [something] lawful and wholesome.

وَلَا تُؤْتُوا۟ ٱلسُّفَهَآءَ أَمْوَٰلَكُمُ    5 Do not give the feeble-minded your property

ٱلَّتِى جَعَلَ ٱللَّهُ لَكُمْ قِيَـٰمًا    which Allah has assigned you to manage:

وَٱرْزُقُوهُمْ فِيهَا وَٱكْسُوهُمْ    provide for them out of it, and clothe them,

وَقُولُوا۟ لَهُمْ قَوْلًا مَّعْرُوفًا ۞    and speak to them honourable words.

وَٱبْتَلُوا۟ ٱلْيَتَـٰمَىٰ    6 Test the orphans

حَتَّىٰٓ إِذَا بَلَغُوا۟ ٱلنِّكَاحَ    when they reach the age of marriage.

فَإِنْ ءَانَسْتُم مِّنْهُمْ رُشْدًا    Then if you discern in them maturity,

---

[1] That is, 'Be wary of Allah and observe the rights of the blood relations and beware of breaking the ties of kinship.'

[2] See verse 2:220 and the footnote.

[3] That is, girl orphans.

فَٱدْفَعُوٓاْ إِلَيْهِمْ أَمْوَٰلَهُمْ    deliver to them their property.

وَلَا تَأْكُلُوهَآ إِسْرَافًا وَبِدَارًا    And do not consume it lavishly and hastily

أَن يَكْبَرُوٓاْ    lest they should grow up.

وَمَن كَانَ غَنِيًّا فَلْيَسْتَعْفِفْ    As for him who is well-off, let him be abstemious,

وَمَن كَانَ فَقِيرًا    and as for him who is poor,

فَلْيَأْكُلْ بِٱلْمَعْرُوفِ    let him eat in an honourable manner.

فَإِذَا دَفَعْتُمْ إِلَيْهِمْ أَمْوَٰلَهُمْ    And when you deliver to them their property,

فَأَشْهِدُواْ عَلَيْهِمْ    take witnesses over them,

وَكَفَىٰ بِٱللَّهِ حَسِيبًا ۝    and Allah suffices as reckoner.

لِّلرِّجَالِ نَصِيبٌ مِّمَّا تَرَكَ ٱلْوَٰلِدَانِ    7 Men have a share in the heritage left by parents

وَٱلْأَقْرَبُونَ    and near relatives,

وَلِلنِّسَآءِ نَصِيبٌ مِّمَّا تَرَكَ ٱلْوَٰلِدَانِ    and women have a share in the heritage left by parents

وَٱلْأَقْرَبُونَ    and near relatives,

مِمَّا قَلَّ مِنْهُ أَوْ كَثُرَ    whether it be little or much,

نَصِيبًا مَّفْرُوضًا ۝    a share ordained [by Allah].

وَإِذَا حَضَرَ ٱلْقِسْمَةَ أُوْلُواْ ٱلْقُرْبَىٰ    8 And when the division is attended by relatives,

وَٱلْيَتَٰمَىٰ وَٱلْمَسَٰكِينُ    the orphans and the needy,

فَٱرْزُقُوهُم مِّنْهُ    provide for them out of it,

وَقُولُواْ لَهُمْ قَوْلًا مَّعْرُوفًا ۝    and speak to them honourable words.

وَلْيَخْشَ ٱلَّذِينَ    9 Let those fear [the result of mistreating orphans] who,

لَوْ تَرَكُواْ مِنْ خَلْفِهِمْ ذُرِّيَّةً ضِعَٰفًا    were they to leave behind weak offspring,

خَافُواْ عَلَيْهِمْ    would be concerned on their account.

فَلْيَتَّقُواْ ٱللَّهَ    So let them be wary of Allah,

وَلْيَقُولُواْ قَوْلًا سَدِيدًا ۝    and let them speak upright words.

إِنَّ ٱلَّذِينَ يَأْكُلُونَ أَمْوَٰلَ ٱلْيَتَٰمَىٰ    10 Indeed those who consume the property of orphans

ظُلْمًا    wrongfully,

إِنَّمَا يَأْكُلُونَ فِى بُطُونِهِمْ نَارًا    only ingest fire into their bellies,

وَسَيَصْلَوْنَ سَعِيرًا ۝    and soon they will enter the Blaze.

يُوصِيكُمُ ٱللَّهُ فِىٓ أَوْلَٰدِكُمْ    11 Allah enjoins you concerning your children:

لِلذَّكَرِ مِثْلُ    for the male shall be the like of

| | |
|---:|:---|
| حَظِّ ٱلْأُنثَيَيْنِ | the share of two females, |
| فَإِن كُنَّ نِسَآءً فَوْقَ ٱثْنَتَيْنِ | and if there be [two or] more than two females, |
| فَلَهُنَّ ثُلُثَا مَا تَرَكَ | then for them shall be two-thirds of what he[1] leaves; |
| وَإِن كَانَتْ وَٰحِدَةً فَلَهَا ٱلنِّصْفُ | but if she be alone, then for her shall be a half; |
| وَلِأَبَوَيْهِ لِكُلِّ وَٰحِدٍ مِّنْهُمَا | and for each of his parents |
| ٱلسُّدُسُ مِمَّا تَرَكَ | a sixth of what he leaves, |
| إِن كَانَ لَهُۥ وَلَدٌ | if he has children; |
| فَإِن لَّمْ يَكُن لَّهُۥ وَلَدٌ | but if he has no children, |
| وَوَرِثَهُۥٓ أَبَوَاهُ | and his parents are his [sole] heirs, |
| فَلِأُمِّهِ ٱلثُّلُثُ | then it shall be a third for his mother; |
| فَإِن كَانَ لَهُۥٓ إِخْوَةٌ فَلِأُمِّهِ ٱلسُّدُسُ | but if he has brothers, then a sixth for his mother, |
| مِنۢ بَعْدِ وَصِيَّةٍ يُوصِى بِهَآ | after [paying off] any bequest he may have made |
| أَوْ دَيْنٍ | or any debt [he may have incurred]. |
| ءَابَآؤُكُمْ وَأَبْنَآؤُكُمْ | Your parents and your children |
| لَا تَدْرُونَ أَيُّهُمْ | —you do not know which of them |
| أَقْرَبُ لَكُمْ نَفْعًا | is likelier to be beneficial for you. |
| فَرِيضَةً مِّنَ ٱللَّهِ | This is an ordinance from Allah. |
| إِنَّ ٱللَّهَ كَانَ عَلِيمًا حَكِيمًا ۞ | Indeed Allah is all-knowing, all-wise. |
| وَلَكُمْ نِصْفُ مَا تَرَكَ أَزْوَٰجُكُمْ | 12 For you shall be a half of what your wives leave, |
| إِن لَّمْ يَكُن لَّهُنَّ وَلَدٌ | if they have no children; |
| فَإِن كَانَ لَهُنَّ وَلَدٌ | but if they have children, |
| فَلَكُمُ ٱلرُّبُعُ مِمَّا تَرَكْنَ | then for you shall be a fourth of what they leave, |
| مِنۢ بَعْدِ وَصِيَّةٍ يُوصِينَ بِهَآ | after [paying off] any bequest they may have made |
| أَوْ دَيْنٍ | or any debt [they may have incurred]. |
| وَلَهُنَّ ٱلرُّبُعُ مِمَّا تَرَكْتُمْ | And for them [it shall be] a fourth of what you leave, |
| إِن لَّمْ يَكُن لَّكُمْ وَلَدٌ | if you have no children; |
| فَإِن كَانَ لَكُمْ وَلَدٌ | but if you have children, |
| فَلَهُنَّ ٱلثُّمُنُ مِمَّا تَرَكْتُم | then for them shall be an eighth of what you leave, |
| مِّنۢ بَعْدِ وَصِيَّةٍ تُوصُونَ بِهَآ | after [paying off] any bequest you may have made |

---

[1] That is, the deceased person.

أَوْ دَيْنٍ ۚ 
or any debt [you may have incurred].

وَإِن كَانَ رَجُلٌ يُورَثُ كَلَٰلَةً أَوِ ٱمْرَأَةٌ 
If a man or woman is inherited by siblings[1]

وَلَهُۥٓ أَخٌ أَوْ أُخْتٌ 
and has a brother or a sister,

فَلِكُلِّ وَٰحِدٍ مِّنْهُمَا ٱلسُّدُسُ ۚ 
then each of them shall receive a sixth;

فَإِن كَانُوٓاْ أَكْثَرَ مِن ذَٰلِكَ 
but if they are more than that,

فَهُمْ شُرَكَآءُ فِى ٱلثُّلُثِ ۚ 
then they shall share in one third,

مِنۢ بَعْدِ وَصِيَّةٍ يُوصَىٰ بِهَآ 
after [paying off] any bequest he may have made

أَوْ دَيْنٍ 
or any debt [he may have incurred]

غَيْرَ مُضَآرٍّ ۚ 
without prejudice.[2]

وَصِيَّةً مِّنَ ٱللَّهِ ۗ 
[This is] an enjoinment from Allah,

وَٱللَّهُ عَلِيمٌ حَلِيمٌ ۝ 
and Allah is all-knowing, all-forbearing.

تِلْكَ حُدُودُ ٱللَّهِ ۚ 
13 These are Allah's bounds,

وَمَن يُطِعِ ٱللَّهَ وَرَسُولَهُۥ 
and whoever obeys Allah and His Apostle,

يُدْخِلْهُ جَنَّٰتٍ 
He shall admit him to gardens

تَجْرِى مِن تَحْتِهَا ٱلْأَنْهَٰرُ 
with streams running in them,

خَٰلِدِينَ فِيهَا ۚ 
to remain in them [forever].

وَذَٰلِكَ ٱلْفَوْزُ ٱلْعَظِيمُ ۝ 
That is the great success.

وَمَن يَعْصِ ٱللَّهَ وَرَسُولَهُۥ 
14 But whoever disobeys Allah and His Apostle,

وَيَتَعَدَّ حُدُودَهُۥ 
and transgresses the bounds set by Allah,

يُدْخِلْهُ نَارًا 
He shall make him enter a Fire,

خَٰلِدًا فِيهَا 
to remain in it [forever],

وَلَهُۥ عَذَابٌ مُّهِينٌ ۝ 
and there will be a humiliating punishment for him.

وَٱلَّٰتِى يَأْتِينَ ٱلْفَٰحِشَةَ مِن نِّسَآئِكُمْ 
15 Should any of your women commit an indecent act,[3]

فَٱسْتَشْهِدُواْ عَلَيْهِنَّ أَرْبَعَةً مِّنكُمْ ۖ 
produce against them four witness from yourselves,

فَإِن شَهِدُواْ 
and if they testify,

فَأَمْسِكُوهُنَّ فِى ٱلْبُيُوتِ 
detain them[4] in [their] houses

---

[1] *Kalālah* means the siblings of a deceased person without a first-degree heir.

[2] That is, the will should not encroach on the rights of the heirs, for instance by acknowledging a nonexistent debt.

[3] That is, adultery. See verse 4:176 below.

[4] That is, the women against whom testimony has been given.

حَتَّىٰ يَتَوَفَّىٰهُنَّ ٱلْمَوْتُ
until death finishes them,

أَوْ يَجْعَلَ ٱللَّهُ لَهُنَّ سَبِيلًا ۝
or Allah decrees a course for them.[1]

وَٱلَّذَانِ يَأْتِيَٰنِهَا مِنكُمْ
16 Should two among you commit it,[2]

فَـَٔاذُوهُمَا
chastise them both;

فَإِن تَابَا وَأَصْلَحَا فَأَعْرِضُوا عَنْهُمَآ
but if they repent and reform, let them alone.

إِنَّ ٱللَّهَ كَانَ تَوَّابًا رَّحِيمًا ۝
Indeed Allah is all-clement, all-merciful.

إِنَّمَا ٱلتَّوْبَةُ عَلَى ٱللَّهِ لِلَّذِينَ
17 [Acceptance of] repentance by Allah is only for those

يَعْمَلُونَ ٱلسُّوٓءَ بِجَهَٰلَةٍ
who commit evil out of ignorance,

ثُمَّ يَتُوبُونَ مِن قَرِيبٍ
then repent promptly.

فَأُوْلَٰٓئِكَ يَتُوبُ ٱللَّهُ عَلَيْهِمْ
It is such whose repentance Allah will accept,

وَكَانَ ٱللَّهُ عَلِيمًا حَكِيمًا ۝
and Allah is all-knowing, all-wise.

وَلَيْسَتِ ٱلتَّوْبَةُ لِلَّذِينَ
18 But [acceptance of] repentance is not for those

يَعْمَلُونَ ٱلسَّيِّئَاتِ
who go on committing misdeeds:

حَتَّىٰٓ إِذَا حَضَرَ أَحَدَهُمُ ٱلْمَوْتُ
when death approaches any of them,

قَالَ إِنِّي تُبْتُ ٱلْـَٰٔنَ
he says, 'I repent now.'

وَلَا ٱلَّذِينَ يَمُوتُونَ وَهُمْ كُفَّارٌ
Nor is it for those who die while they are faithless.

أُوْلَٰٓئِكَ أَعْتَدْنَا لَهُمْ عَذَابًا أَلِيمًا ۝
For such We have prepared a painful punishment.

يَٰٓأَيُّهَا ٱلَّذِينَ ءَامَنُوا
19 O you who have faith!

لَا يَحِلُّ لَكُمْ أَن تَرِثُوا ٱلنِّسَآءَ كَرْهًا
It is not lawful for you to inherit women forcibly,

وَلَا تَعْضُلُوهُنَّ
and do not press them

لِتَذْهَبُوا بِبَعْضِ مَآ ءَاتَيْتُمُوهُنَّ
to take away part of what you have given them,

إِلَّآ أَن يَأْتِينَ بِفَٰحِشَةٍ مُّبَيِّنَةٍ
unless they commit a gross indecency.[3]

وَعَاشِرُوهُنَّ بِٱلْمَعْرُوفِ
Consort with them in an honourable manner;

فَإِن كَرِهْتُمُوهُنَّ
and should you dislike them,

فَعَسَىٰٓ أَن تَكْرَهُوا شَيْـًٔا
maybe you dislike something

وَيَجْعَلَ ٱللَّهُ فِيهِ خَيْرًا كَثِيرًا ۝
while Allah invests it with an abundant good.

وَإِنْ أَرَدتُّمُ ٱسْتِبْدَالَ زَوْجٍ مَّكَانَ زَوْجٍ
20 If you desire to take a wife in place of another,

---

[1] Superseded by the punishment by stoning for adultery and by verse 24:2 which prescribes the punishment for fornication.

[2] That is, fornication (or sodomy, according to some exegetes).

[3] That is, adultery.

وَءَاتَيْتُمْ إِحْدَىٰهُنَّ قِنطَارًا
and you have given one of them a quintal [of gold],

فَلَا تَأْخُذُواْ مِنْهُ شَيْئًا
do not take anything away from it.

أَتَأْخُذُونَهُۥ بُهْتَٰنًا وَإِثْمًا مُّبِينًا ۝
Would you take it by way of calumny and flagrant sin?!

وَكَيْفَ تَأْخُذُونَهُۥ
21 How could you take it back,

وَقَدْ أَفْضَىٰ بَعْضُكُمْ إِلَىٰ بَعْضٍ
when you have known[1] each other,

وَأَخَذْنَ مِنكُم مِّيثَٰقًا غَلِيظًا ۝
and they have taken from you a solemn covenant?

وَلَا تَنكِحُواْ
22 Do not marry

مَا نَكَحَ ءَابَآؤُكُم مِّنَ ٱلنِّسَآءِ
any of the women whom your fathers had married,

إِلَّا مَا قَدْ سَلَفَ
excluding what is already past.

إِنَّهُۥ كَانَ فَٰحِشَةً
That is indeed an indecency,

وَمَقْتًا وَسَآءَ سَبِيلًا ۝
an outrage and an evil course.

حُرِّمَتْ عَلَيْكُمْ أُمَّهَٰتُكُمْ
23 Forbidden to you are your mothers,

وَبَنَاتُكُمْ وَأَخَوَٰتُكُمْ
your daughters and your sisters,

وَعَمَّٰتُكُمْ وَخَٰلَٰتُكُمْ
your paternal aunts and your maternal aunts,

وَبَنَاتُ ٱلْأَخِ وَبَنَاتُ ٱلْأُخْتِ
your brother's daughters and your sister's daughters,

وَأُمَّهَٰتُكُمُ ٱلَّٰتِىٓ أَرْضَعْنَكُمْ
your [foster-]mothers who have suckled you[2]

وَأَخَوَٰتُكُم مِّنَ ٱلرَّضَٰعَةِ
and your sisters through fosterage,

وَأُمَّهَٰتُ نِسَآئِكُمْ
your wives' mothers,

وَرَبَٰٓئِبُكُمُ ٱلَّٰتِى فِى حُجُورِكُم
and your stepdaughters who are under your care

مِّن نِّسَآئِكُمُ ٱلَّٰتِى دَخَلْتُم بِهِنَّ
[born] of the wives whom you have gone into

فَإِن لَّمْ تَكُونُواْ دَخَلْتُم بِهِنَّ
—but if you have not gone into them

فَلَا جُنَاحَ عَلَيْكُمْ
there is no sin upon you—

وَحَلَٰٓئِلُ أَبْنَآئِكُمُ
and the wives of your sons

ٱلَّذِينَ مِنْ أَصْلَٰبِكُمْ
who are from your own loins,

وَأَن تَجْمَعُواْ بَيْنَ ٱلْأُخْتَيْنِ
and that you should marry two sisters at one time

إِلَّا مَا قَدْ سَلَفَ
—excluding what is already past;

إِنَّ ٱللَّهَ كَانَ غَفُورًا رَّحِيمًا ۝ ❊
indeed Allah is all-forgiving, all-merciful—

---

[1] Know: To have sexual intercourse with (*archaic*).
[2] That is, foster-mothers.

[PART 5]

24 وَٱلْمُحْصَنَتُ مِنَ ٱلنِّسَآءِ

and married women

إِلَّا مَا مَلَكَتْ أَيْمَـٰنُكُمْ

excepting your slave-women.

كِتَـٰبَ ٱللَّهِ عَلَيْكُمْ

This is Allah's ordinance for you.

وَأُحِلَّ لَكُم مَّا وَرَآءَ ذَٰلِكُمْ

As to others than these, it is lawful for you

أَن تَبْتَغُوا۟ بِأَمْوَٰلِكُم

to seek [union with them] with your wealth,

مُّحْصِنِينَ غَيْرَ مُسَـٰفِحِينَ

in wedlock, not in license.

فَمَا ٱسْتَمْتَعْتُم بِهِۦ مِنْهُنَّ

For the enjoyment you have had from them thereby,

فَـَٔاتُوهُنَّ أُجُورَهُنَّ فَرِيضَةً

give them their dowries, by way of settlement,

وَلَا جُنَاحَ عَلَيْكُمْ

and there is no sin upon you

فِيمَا تَرَٰضَيْتُم بِهِۦ مِنۢ بَعْدِ ٱلْفَرِيضَةِ

in what you may agree upon after the settlement.

إِنَّ ٱللَّهَ كَانَ عَلِيمًا حَكِيمًا ٢٤

Indeed Allah is all-knowing, all-wise.

25 وَمَن لَّمْ يَسْتَطِعْ مِنكُمْ طَوْلًا

As for those of you who cannot afford

أَن يَنكِحَ ٱلْمُحْصَنَٰتِ ٱلْمُؤْمِنَٰتِ

to marry faithful free women,

فَمِن مَّا مَلَكَتْ أَيْمَـٰنُكُم

then [let them marry] from what you own,

مِّن فَتَيَـٰتِكُمُ ٱلْمُؤْمِنَٰتِ

from among your faithful slave-women.

وَٱللَّهُ أَعْلَمُ بِإِيمَـٰنِكُم

Your faith is best known [only] to Allah;

بَعْضُكُم مِّنۢ بَعْضٍ

you are all [on a] similar [footing].

فَٱنكِحُوهُنَّ بِإِذْنِ أَهْلِهِنَّ

So marry them with their masters' permission,

وَءَاتُوهُنَّ أُجُورَهُنَّ بِٱلْمَعْرُوفِ

and give them their dowries in an honourable manner

مُحْصَنَٰتٍ

—[such of them] as are chaste women,

غَيْرَ مُسَـٰفِحَٰتٍ وَلَا مُتَّخِذَٰتِ أَخْدَانٍ

not licentious ones or those who take paramours.

فَإِذَآ أُحْصِنَّ فَإِنْ أَتَيْنَ بِفَـٰحِشَةٍ

But on marrying, should they commit an indecent act,

فَعَلَيْهِنَّ

then there shall be for them

نِصْفُ مَا عَلَى ٱلْمُحْصَنَٰتِ مِنَ ٱلْعَذَابِ

[only] half the punishment for free women.

ذَٰلِكَ لِمَنْ خَشِيَ ٱلْعَنَتَ مِنكُمْ

This is for those of you who fear falling into fornication;

وَأَن تَصْبِرُوا۟ خَيْرٌ لَّكُمْ

but it is better that you be continent,[1]

وَٱللَّهُ غَفُورٌ رَّحِيمٌ ٢٥

and Allah is all-forgiving, all-merciful.

يُرِيدُ ٱللَّهُ لِيُبَيِّنَ لَكُمْ

26 Allah desires to explain [the laws] to you,

---

[1] That is, by refraining from marriage with slave-women.

وَيَهْدِيَكُمْ

and to guide you

سُنَنَ ٱلَّذِينَ مِن قَبْلِكُمْ

   to the customs of those who were before you,[1]

وَيَتُوبَ عَلَيْكُمْ

and to turn toward you clemently,

وَٱللَّهُ عَلِيمٌ حَكِيمٌ ۝

   and Allah is all-knowing, all-wise.

وَٱللَّهُ يُرِيدُ أَن يَتُوبَ عَلَيْكُمْ

27 Allah desires to turn toward you clemently,

وَيُرِيدُ ٱلَّذِينَ يَتَّبِعُونَ ٱلشَّهَوَٰتِ

   but those who pursue their [base] appetites desire

أَن تَمِيلُوا۟ مَيْلًا عَظِيمًا ۝

   that you fall into gross waywardness.

يُرِيدُ ٱللَّهُ أَن يُخَفِّفَ عَنكُمْ

28 Allah desires to lighten your burden,

وَخُلِقَ ٱلْإِنسَٰنُ ضَعِيفًا ۝

   for man was created weak.

يَٰٓأَيُّهَا ٱلَّذِينَ ءَامَنُوا۟

29 O you who have faith!

لَا تَأْكُلُوٓا۟ أَمْوَٰلَكُم

Do not eat up your wealth

بَيْنَكُم بِٱلْبَٰطِلِ

   among yourselves unrightfully,[2]

إِلَّآ أَن تَكُونَ تِجَٰرَةً عَن تَرَاضٍ مِّنكُمْ

   but it should be trade by mutual consent.

وَلَا تَقْتُلُوٓا۟ أَنفُسَكُمْ

And do not kill yourselves.[3]

إِنَّ ٱللَّهَ كَانَ بِكُمْ رَحِيمًا ۝

   Indeed Allah is most merciful to you.

وَمَن يَفْعَلْ ذَٰلِكَ عُدْوَٰنًا وَظُلْمًا

30 And whoever does that in aggression and injustice,

فَسَوْفَ نُصْلِيهِ نَارًا

We will soon make him enter the Fire,

وَكَانَ ذَٰلِكَ عَلَى ٱللَّهِ يَسِيرًا ۝

   and that is easy for Allah.

إِن تَجْتَنِبُوا۟ كَبَآئِرَ مَا تُنْهَوْنَ عَنْهُ

31 If you avoid the major sins that you are forbidden,

نُكَفِّرْ عَنكُمْ سَيِّـَٔاتِكُمْ

We will absolve you of your misdeeds,

وَنُدْخِلْكُم مُّدْخَلًا كَرِيمًا ۝

   and admit you to a noble abode.

وَلَا تَتَمَنَّوْا۟ مَا فَضَّلَ ٱللَّهُ بِهِۦ

32 Do not covet the advantage which Allah has given

بَعْضَكُمْ عَلَىٰ بَعْضٍ

   some of you over others.

لِّلرِّجَالِ نَصِيبٌ مِّمَّا ٱكْتَسَبُوا۟

To men belongs a share of what they have earned,

وَلِلنِّسَآءِ نَصِيبٌ مِّمَّا ٱكْتَسَبْنَ

   and to women a share of what they have earned.

---

[1] That is, to the customs of the prophets of the past and their communities.

[2] That is, by way of usury, gambling, usurpation, false claim, or any other illegitimate means.

[3] That is, do not destroy yourselves by consuming wealth acquired through illegitimate means, such as usury, gambling, fraud, theft, bribery, usurpation and so on; or it means, do not commit suicide, or murder, or, do not expose yourselves recklessly to mortal danger.

وَسْتَلُواْ ٱللَّهَ مِن فَضْلِهِۦٓ
And ask Allah for His grace.

إِنَّ ٱللَّهَ كَانَ بِكُلِّ شَيْءٍ عَلِيمًا ٣٢
Indeed Allah has knowledge of all things.

وَلِكُلٍّ جَعَلْنَا مَوَٰلِيَ ٣٣ For everyone We have appointed heirs

مِمَّا تَرَكَ ٱلْوَٰلِدَانِ وَٱلْأَقْرَبُونَ
to what the parents and near relatives leave,

وَٱلَّذِينَ عَقَدَتْ أَيْمَٰنُكُمْ
as well as those with whom you have made a compact;

فَـَٔاتُوهُمْ نَصِيبَهُمْ
so give them their share [of the heritage].

إِنَّ ٱللَّهَ كَانَ عَلَىٰ كُلِّ شَيْءٍ شَهِيدًا ٣٣
Indeed Allah is witness to all things.

ٱلرِّجَالُ قَوَّٰمُونَ عَلَى ٱلنِّسَآءِ ٣٤ Men are the managers of women,

بِمَا فَضَّلَ ٱللَّهُ
because of the advantage Allah has granted

بَعْضَهُمْ عَلَىٰ بَعْضٍ
some of them over others,

وَبِمَآ أَنفَقُواْ مِنْ أَمْوَٰلِهِمْ
and by virtue of their spending out of their wealth.

فَٱلصَّٰلِحَٰتُ قَٰنِتَٰتٌ
So righteous women are obedient,

حَٰفِظَٰتٌ لِّلْغَيْبِ
care-taking in the absence [of their husbands]

بِمَا حَفِظَ ٱللَّهُ
of what Allah has enjoined [them] to guard.

وَٱلَّٰتِي تَخَافُونَ نُشُوزَهُنَّ
As for those [wives] whose misconduct you fear,

فَعِظُوهُنَّ
[first] advise them,

وَٱهْجُرُوهُنَّ فِي ٱلْمَضَاجِعِ
and [if ineffective] keep away from them in the bed,

وَٱضْرِبُوهُنَّ
and [as the last resort] beat them.

فَإِنْ أَطَعْنَكُمْ
Then if they obey you,

فَلَا تَبْغُواْ عَلَيْهِنَّ سَبِيلًا
do not seek any course [of action] against them.

إِنَّ ٱللَّهَ كَانَ عَلِيًّا كَبِيرًا ٣٤
Indeed Allah is all-exalted, all-great.

وَإِنْ خِفْتُمْ شِقَاقَ بَيْنِهِمَا ٣٥ And if you fear a split between the two of them,

فَٱبْعَثُواْ حَكَمًا مِّنْ أَهْلِهِۦ
then appoint an arbiter from his relatives

وَحَكَمًا مِّنْ أَهْلِهَآ
and an arbiter from her relatives.

إِن يُرِيدَآ إِصْلَٰحًا
If they desire reconcilement,

يُوَفِّقِ ٱللَّهُ بَيْنَهُمَآ
Allah shall reconcile them.[1]

إِنَّ ٱللَّهَ كَانَ عَلِيمًا خَبِيرًا ٣٥
Indeed Allah is all-knowing, all-aware.

وَٱعْبُدُواْ ٱللَّهَ وَلَا تُشْرِكُواْ بِهِۦ شَيْـًٔا ٣٦ Worship Allah and do not ascribe any partners to Him,

---

[1] That is, if the arbiters consider it advisable for the couple to remain united in wedlock, Allah will bring out a reconciliation between them.

وَبِٱلْوَٰلِدَيْنِ إِحْسَـٰنًا
and be good to parents,

وَبِذِى ٱلْقُرْبَىٰ وَٱلْيَتَـٰمَىٰ وَٱلْمَسَـٰكِينِ
the relatives, the orphans, the needy,

وَٱلْجَارِ ذِى ٱلْقُرْبَىٰ وَٱلْجَارِ ٱلْجُنُبِ
the near neighbour and the distant neighbour,

وَٱلصَّاحِبِ بِٱلْجَنۢبِ
the companion at your side,

وَٱبْنِ ٱلسَّبِيلِ
the traveller,

وَمَا مَلَكَتْ أَيْمَـٰنُكُمْ
and your slaves.

إِنَّ ٱللَّهَ لَا يُحِبُّ
Indeed Allah does not like

مَن كَانَ مُخْتَالًا فَخُورًا ۝
anyone who is a swaggering braggart.

37 ٱلَّذِينَ يَبْخَلُونَ
Those who are stingy

وَيَأْمُرُونَ ٱلنَّاسَ بِٱلْبُخْلِ
and bid [other] people to be stingy,

وَيَكْتُمُونَ مَآ ءَاتَىٰهُمُ ٱللَّهُ
and conceal whatever Allah has given them

مِن فَضْلِهِ
out of His grace;

وَأَعْتَدْنَا لِلْكَـٰفِرِينَ
and We have prepared for the faithless

عَذَابًا مُّهِينًا ۝
a humiliating punishment.

38 وَٱلَّذِينَ يُنفِقُونَ أَمْوَٰلَهُمْ
And those who spend their wealth

رِئَآءَ ٱلنَّاسِ
to be seen by people,

وَلَا يُؤْمِنُونَ بِٱللَّهِ وَلَا بِٱلْيَوْمِ ٱلْءَاخِرِ
and believe neither in Allah nor in the Last Day.

وَمَن يَكُنِ ٱلشَّيْطَـٰنُ لَهُ قَرِينًا
As for him who has Satan for his companion

فَسَآءَ قَرِينًا ۝
—an evil companion is he!

39 وَمَاذَا عَلَيْهِمْ
What harm would it have done them

لَوْ ءَامَنُوا۟ بِٱللَّهِ
had they believed in Allah

وَٱلْيَوْمِ ٱلْءَاخِرِ
and the Last Day,

وَأَنفَقُوا۟ مِمَّا رَزَقَهُمُ ٱللَّهُ
and spent out of what Allah has provided them?

وَكَانَ ٱللَّهُ بِهِمْ عَلِيمًا ۝
Allah knows them well.

40 إِنَّ ٱللَّهَ لَا يَظْلِمُ
Indeed Allah does not wrong [anyone]

مِثْقَالَ ذَرَّةٍ
[even to the extent of] an atom's weight,

وَإِن تَكُ حَسَنَةً يُضَـٰعِفْهَا
and if it be a good deed He doubles it[s reward],

وَيُؤْتِ مِن لَّدُنْهُ أَجْرًا عَظِيمًا ۝
and gives from Himself a great reward.

41 فَكَيْفَ
So how shall it be,

إِذَا جِئْنَا مِن كُلِّ أُمَّةٍ بِشَهِيدٍ
when We bring from every nation a witness

115

وَجِئْنَا بِكَ عَلَىٰ هَـٰٓؤُلَآءِ شَهِيدًا ۝    and We bring *you* as a witness to them?

يَوْمَئِذٍ    42 On that day

يَوَدُّ ٱلَّذِينَ كَفَرُواْ    those who were faithless

وَعَصَوُاْ ٱلرَّسُولَ    and [who] disobeyed the Apostle will wish

لَوْ تُسَوَّىٰ بِهِمُ ٱلْأَرْضُ    the earth were levelled with them,

وَلَا يَكْتُمُونَ ٱللَّهَ حَدِيثًا ۝    and they will not conceal any matter from Allah.

يَـٰٓأَيُّهَا ٱلَّذِينَ ءَامَنُواْ    43 O you who have faith!

لَا تَقْرَبُواْ ٱلصَّلَوٰةَ وَأَنتُمْ سُكَرَىٰ    Do not approach prayer when you are intoxicated,

حَتَّىٰ تَعْلَمُواْ مَا تَقُولُونَ    [not] until you know what you are saying,

وَلَا جُنُبًا    nor [enter mosques] in the state of ritual impurity

إِلَّا عَابِرِى سَبِيلٍ    —except while passing through—

حَتَّىٰ تَغْتَسِلُواْ    until you have washed yourselves.

وَإِن كُنتُم مَّرْضَىٰ أَوْ عَلَىٰ سَفَرٍ    But if you are sick or on a journey,

أَوْ جَآءَ أَحَدٌ مِّنكُم مِّنَ ٱلْغَآئِطِ    or any of you has come from the toilet,

أَوْ لَـٰمَسْتُمُ ٱلنِّسَآءَ    or you have touched women,[1]

فَلَمْ تَجِدُواْ مَآءً    and you cannot find water,

فَتَيَمَّمُواْ صَعِيدًا طَيِّبًا    then make your ablution on clean ground

فَٱمْسَحُواْ بِوُجُوهِكُمْ وَأَيْدِيكُمْ    and wipe a part of your faces and your hands.

إِنَّ ٱللَّهَ كَانَ عَفُوًّا غَفُورًا ۝    Indeed Allah is all-excusing, all-forgiving.

أَلَمْ تَرَ إِلَى ٱلَّذِينَ أُوتُواْ    44 Have *you* not regarded those who were given

نَصِيبًا مِّنَ ٱلْكِتَـٰبِ    a share of the Book,

يَشْتَرُونَ ٱلضَّلَـٰلَةَ    who purchase error

وَيُرِيدُونَ أَن تَضِلُّواْ ٱلسَّبِيلَ ۝    and desire that you [too] should lose the way?

وَٱللَّهُ أَعْلَمُ بِأَعْدَآئِكُمْ    45 But Allah knows your enemies better,

وَكَفَىٰ بِٱللَّهِ وَلِيًّا    and Allah suffices as guardian,

وَكَفَىٰ بِٱللَّهِ نَصِيرًا ۝    and Allah suffices as helper.

مِّنَ ٱلَّذِينَ هَادُواْ    46 Among the Jews are those who

---

[1] That is, if you have performed sexual intercourse.

تُحَرِّفُونَ ٱلۡكَلِمَ عَن مَّوَاضِعِهِۦ    pervert words from their meanings

وَيَقُولُونَ سَمِعۡنَا وَعَصَيۡنَا    and say, 'We hear and disobey'

وَٱسۡمَعۡ غَيۡرَ مُسۡمَعٖ وَرَٰعِنَا    and 'Hear without listening!' and '*Rā'inā*,'

لَيَّۢا بِأَلۡسِنَتِهِمۡ وَطَعۡنٗا فِى ٱلدِّينِ    twisting their tongues and reviling the faith.

وَلَوۡ أَنَّهُمۡ قَالُوا۟ سَمِعۡنَا وَأَطَعۡنَا    But had they said, 'We hear and obey'

وَٱسۡمَعۡ وَٱنظُرۡنَا    and 'Listen' and '*Unẓurnā*,'

لَكَانَ خَيۡرٗا لَّهُمۡ    it would have been better for them,

وَأَقۡوَمَ    and more upright.[1]

وَلَٰكِن لَّعَنَهُمُ ٱللَّهُ بِكُفۡرِهِمۡ    But Allah has cursed them for their faithlessness,

فَلَا يُؤۡمِنُونَ إِلَّا قَلِيلًا ۝    so they will not believe except a few.

يَٰٓأَيُّهَا ٱلَّذِينَ أُوتُوا۟ ٱلۡكِتَٰبَ    47 O you who were given the Book!

ءَامِنُوا۟ بِمَا نَزَّلۡنَا    Believe in what We have sent down

مُصَدِّقٗا لِّمَا مَعَكُم    confirming what is with you,

مِّن قَبۡلِ أَن نَّطۡمِسَ وُجُوهٗا    before We blot out the faces

فَنَرُدَّهَا عَلَىٰٓ أَدۡبَارِهَآ    and turn them backwards,

أَوۡ نَلۡعَنَهُمۡ    or curse them

كَمَا لَعَنَّآ أَصۡحَٰبَ ٱلسَّبۡتِ    as We cursed the People of the Sabbath,

وَكَانَ أَمۡرُ ٱللَّهِ مَفۡعُولًا ۝    and Allah's command is bound to be fulfilled.

إِنَّ ٱللَّهَ لَا يَغۡفِرُ    48 Indeed Allah does not forgive

أَن يُشۡرَكَ بِهِۦ    that any partner should be ascribed to Him,

وَيَغۡفِرُ مَا دُونَ ذَٰلِكَ    but He forgives anything besides that

لِمَن يَشَآءُ    to whomever He wishes.

وَمَن يُشۡرِكۡ بِٱللَّهِ    And whoever ascribes partners to Allah

فَقَدِ ٱفۡتَرَىٰٓ    has indeed fabricated [a lie]

إِثۡمًا عَظِيمًا ۝    in great sinfulness.

أَلَمۡ تَرَ إِلَى ٱلَّذِينَ    49 Have you not regarded those

يُزَكُّونَ أَنفُسَهُمۡ    who style themselves as pure?

---

[1] See 2:104 and the related footnote.

بَلِ ٱللَّهُ يُزَكِّي مَن يَشَآءُ    Rather it is Allah who purifies whomever He wishes,

وَلَا يُظْلَمُونَ    and they will not be wronged

فَتِيلًا ۝    [so much as] a single date-thread.

ٱنظُرْ كَيْفَ يَفْتَرُونَ عَلَى ٱللَّهِ ٱلْكَذِبَ    50 *Look,* how they fabricate lies against Allah!

وَكَفَىٰ بِهِۦٓ إِثْمًا مُّبِينًا ۝    That suffices for a flagrant sin.

أَلَمْ تَرَ إِلَى ٱلَّذِينَ    51 Have *you* not regarded those

أُوتُواْ نَصِيبًا مِّنَ ٱلْكِتَـٰبِ    who were given a share of the Book[1]

يُؤْمِنُونَ بِٱلْجِبْتِ وَٱلطَّـٰغُوتِ    believing in idols and the Rebel[2]

وَيَقُولُونَ لِلَّذِينَ كَفَرُواْ    and saying of the pagans:

هَـٰٓؤُلَآءِ أَهْدَىٰ    'These are better guided

مِنَ ٱلَّذِينَ ءَامَنُواْ سَبِيلًا ۝    on the way than the faithful'?

أُوْلَـٰٓئِكَ ٱلَّذِينَ لَعَنَهُمُ ٱللَّهُ    52 They are the ones whom Allah has cursed,

وَمَن يَلْعَنِ ٱللَّهُ    and whomever Allah curses,

فَلَن تَجِدَ لَهُۥ نَصِيرًا ۝    you will never find any helper for him.

أَمْ لَهُمْ نَصِيبٌ مِّنَ ٱلْمُلْكِ    53 Or do they have a share in sovereignty?[3]

فَإِذًا لَّا يُؤْتُونَ ٱلنَّاسَ    If so, they will not give the people

نَقِيرًا ۝    [so much as] a speck on a date-stone!

أَمْ يَحْسُدُونَ ٱلنَّاسَ    54 Or do they envy the people

عَلَىٰ مَآ ءَاتَىٰهُمُ ٱللَّهُ مِن فَضْلِهِۦ    for what Allah has given them out of His grace?

فَقَدْ ءَاتَيْنَآ ءَالَ إِبْرَٰهِيمَ    We have certainly given the progeny of Abraham

ٱلْكِتَـٰبَ وَٱلْحِكْمَةَ    the Book and wisdom,

وَءَاتَيْنَٰهُم مُّلْكًا عَظِيمًا ۝    and We have given them a great sovereignty.[4]

فَمِنْهُم مَّنْ ءَامَنَ بِهِۦ    55 Of them[5] are some who believe in *him,*

وَمِنْهُم مَّن صَدَّ عَنْهُ    and of them are some who deter [others] from *him;*

---

[1] That is, the Jews.

[2] Or 'magic and evil spirits.' Cf. footnote at 2:256.

[3] Or 'in the kingdom.'

[4] *Great sovereignty:* a reference to the Imamate, as mentioned in 2:124. According to the traditions of the Imams of the Prophet's descent (i.e., Abraham's progeny, through Ishmael), by the 'great sovereignty' is meant the office of the Imamate, because to obey the Imam is to obey Allah and to disobey the Imam is to disobey Allah. See the commentaries of Furāt al-Kūfī, 'Ayyāshī, Qummī and Ḥibrī.

[5] That is, from among the Jews there are some who believe in the Prophet (ṣ).

وَكَفَىٰ بِجَهَنَّمَ سَعِيرًا ۝    and hell suffices for a blaze!

إِنَّ ٱلَّذِينَ كَفَرُوا۟ بِـَٔايَـٰتِنَا   56 Indeed those who defy Our signs,

سَوْفَ نُصْلِيهِمْ نَارًا     We shall soon make them enter a Fire:

كُلَّمَا نَضِجَتْ جُلُودُهُم    as often as their skins become scorched,

بَدَّلْنَـٰهُمْ جُلُودًا غَيْرَهَا    We shall replace them with other skins,

لِيَذُوقُوا۟ ٱلْعَذَابَ     so that they may taste the punishment.

إِنَّ ٱللَّهَ كَانَ عَزِيزًا حَكِيمًا ۝   Indeed Allah is all-mighty, all-wise.

وَٱلَّذِينَ ءَامَنُوا۟   57 As for those who have faith

وَعَمِلُوا۟ ٱلصَّـٰلِحَـٰتِ    and do righteous deeds,

سَنُدْخِلُهُمْ جَنَّـٰتٍ    We shall admit them into gardens

تَجْرِى مِن تَحْتِهَا ٱلْأَنْهَـٰرُ    with streams running in them,

خَـٰلِدِينَ فِيهَا أَبَدًا     to remain in them forever.

لَّهُمْ فِيهَا أَزْوَٰجٌ مُّطَهَّرَةٌ   In it there will be chaste mates for them,

وَنُدْخِلُهُمْ ظِلًّا ظَلِيلًا ۝ ۞   and We shall admit them into a deep shade.[1]

إِنَّ ٱللَّهَ يَأْمُرُكُمْ أَن تُؤَدُّوا۟ ٱلْأَمَـٰنَـٰتِ   58 Indeed Allah commands you to deliver the trusts

إِلَىٰٓ أَهْلِهَا     to their [rightful] owners,

وَإِذَا حَكَمْتُم بَيْنَ ٱلنَّاسِ   and, when you judge between people,

أَن تَحْكُمُوا۟ بِٱلْعَدْلِ    to judge with fairness.

إِنَّ ٱللَّهَ نِعِمَّا يَعِظُكُم بِهِۦٓ   Excellent indeed is what Allah advises you.

إِنَّ ٱللَّهَ كَانَ سَمِيعًۢا بَصِيرًا ۝   Indeed Allah is all-hearing, all-seeing.

يَـٰٓأَيُّهَا ٱلَّذِينَ ءَامَنُوٓا۟   59 O you who have faith!

أَطِيعُوا۟ ٱللَّهَ وَأَطِيعُوا۟ ٱلرَّسُولَ   Obey Allah and obey the Apostle

وَأُو۟لِى ٱلْأَمْرِ مِنكُمْ   and those vested with authority among you.[2]

فَإِن تَنَـٰزَعْتُمْ فِى شَىْءٍ   And if you dispute concerning anything,

فَرُدُّوهُ إِلَى ٱللَّهِ وَٱلرَّسُولِ   refer it to Allah and the Apostle,

إِن كُنتُمْ تُؤْمِنُونَ بِٱللَّهِ وَٱلْيَوْمِ ٱلْءَاخِرِ   if you have faith in Allah and the Last Day.

ذَٰلِكَ خَيْرٌ وَأَحْسَنُ تَأْوِيلًا ۝   That is better and more favourable in outcome.

---

[1] Or 'into a shady twilight;' see the footnote at **25:45**.

[2] Cf. verse **4:54** above.

أَلَمْ تَرَ إِلَى ٱلَّذِينَ يَزْعُمُونَ 60 Have *you* not regarded those who claim

أَنَّهُمْ ءَامَنُوا بِمَآ أُنزِلَ إِلَيْكَ    that they believe in what has been sent down to *you*,

وَمَآ أُنزِلَ مِن قَبْلِكَ    and what was sent down before *you*?

يُرِيدُونَ أَن يَتَحَاكَمُوٓا إِلَى ٱلطَّٰغُوتِ    They desire to seek the judgment of the Rebel,[1]

وَقَدْ أُمِرُوٓا أَن يَكْفُرُوا بِهِۦ    though they were commanded to defy it,

وَيُرِيدُ ٱلشَّيْطَٰنُ أَن يُضِلَّهُمْ    and Satan desires to lead them astray

ضَلَٰلًۢا بَعِيدًا ۝    into far error.

وَإِذَا قِيلَ لَهُمْ 61 And when they are told,

تَعَالَوْا إِلَىٰ مَآ أَنزَلَ ٱللَّهُ    'Come to what Allah has sent down

وَإِلَى ٱلرَّسُولِ    and [come] to the Apostle,'

رَأَيْتَ ٱلْمُنَٰفِقِينَ يَصُدُّونَ عَنكَ    you see the hypocrites keep away from *you*

صُدُودًا ۝    aversely.

فَكَيْفَ إِذَآ أَصَٰبَتْهُم مُّصِيبَةٌۢ 62 But how will it be when an affliction visits them

بِمَا قَدَّمَتْ أَيْدِيهِمْ    because of what their hands have sent ahead?

ثُمَّ جَآءُوكَ يَحْلِفُونَ بِٱللَّهِ    Then they will come to *you*, swearing by Allah:

إِنْ أَرَدْنَآ إِلَّآ إِحْسَٰنًا وَتَوْفِيقًا ۝    'We desired nothing but benevolence and comity.'

أُوْلَٰٓئِكَ ٱلَّذِينَ يَعْلَمُ ٱللَّهُ 63 They are the ones whom Allah knows

مَا فِى قُلُوبِهِمْ    as to what is in their hearts.

فَأَعْرِضْ عَنْهُمْ وَعِظْهُمْ    So let them alone, and advise them,

وَقُل لَّهُمْ فِىٓ أَنفُسِهِمْ    and speak to them concerning themselves

قَوْلًۢا بَلِيغًا ۝    far-reaching words.

وَمَآ أَرْسَلْنَا مِن رَّسُولٍ 64 We did not send any apostle

إِلَّا لِيُطَاعَ بِإِذْنِ ٱللَّهِ    but to be obeyed by Allah's leave.

وَلَوْ أَنَّهُمْ إِذ ظَّلَمُوٓا أَنفُسَهُمْ    Had they, when they wronged themselves,

جَآءُوكَ فَٱسْتَغْفَرُوا ٱللَّهَ    come to *you* and pleaded Allah for forgiveness,

وَٱسْتَغْفَرَ لَهُمُ ٱلرَّسُولُ    and the Apostle had pleaded for forgiveness for them,

لَوَجَدُوا ٱللَّهَ    they would have surely found Allah

تَوَّابًا رَّحِيمًا ۝    all-clement, all-merciful.

فَلَا وَرَبِّكَ لَا يُؤْمِنُونَ 65 But no, by *your* Lord! They will not believe

---

[1] See footnote at 2:256.

حَتَّىٰ يُحَكِّمُوكَ فِيمَا شَجَرَ بَيْنَهُمْ until they make *you* a judge in their disputes,

ثُمَّ لَا يَجِدُوا۟ فِىٓ أَنفُسِهِمْ حَرَجًا then do not find within their hearts any dissent

مِّمَّا قَضَيْتَ to *your* verdict

وَيُسَلِّمُوا۟ تَسْلِيمًا ۝ and submit in full submission.

وَلَوْ أَنَّا كَتَبْنَا عَلَيْهِمْ 66 Had We prescribed for them, [commanding]:

أَنِ ٱقْتُلُوٓا۟ أَنفُسَكُمْ 'Slay [the guilty among] your folks[1]

أَوِ ٱخْرُجُوا۟ مِن دِيَٰرِكُم or leave your habitations,'

مَّا فَعَلُوهُ they would not have done it,

إِلَّا قَلِيلٌ مِّنْهُمْ except a few of them.

وَلَوْ أَنَّهُمْ فَعَلُوا۟ مَا يُوعَظُونَ بِهِ And if they had done as they were advised

لَكَانَ خَيْرًا لَّهُمْ it would have been better for them,

وَأَشَدَّ تَثْبِيتًا ۝ and firmer in confirming [their faith].

وَإِذًا لَّآتَيْنَٰهُم 67 Then We would surely have given them

مِّن لَّدُنَّآ أَجْرًا عَظِيمًا ۝ a great reward from Us,

وَلَهَدَيْنَٰهُمْ 68 and We would have surely guided them

صِرَٰطًا مُّسْتَقِيمًا ۝ to a straight path.

وَمَن يُطِعِ ٱللَّهَ وَٱلرَّسُولَ 69 Whoever obeys Allah and the Apostle

فَأُو۟لَٰٓئِكَ مَعَ ٱلَّذِينَ أَنْعَمَ ٱللَّهُ عَلَيْهِم —they are with those whom Allah has blessed,

مِّنَ ٱلنَّبِيِّـۧنَ وَٱلصِّدِّيقِينَ including the prophets and the truthful,

وَٱلشُّهَدَآءِ وَٱلصَّٰلِحِينَ the martyrs and the righteous,

وَحَسُنَ أُو۟لَٰٓئِكَ رَفِيقًا ۝ and excellent companions are they!

ذَٰلِكَ ٱلْفَضْلُ مِنَ ٱللَّهِ 70 That is the grace of Allah,

وَكَفَىٰ بِٱللَّهِ عَلِيمًا ۝ and Allah suffices as knower [of His creatures].

يَٰٓأَيُّهَا ٱلَّذِينَ ءَامَنُوا۟ 71 O you who have faith!

خُذُوا۟ حِذْرَكُمْ Take your precautions,

فَٱنفِرُوا۟ ثُبَاتٍ أَوِ ٱنفِرُوا۟ جَمِيعًا ۝ then go forth in companies, or go forth en masse.

وَإِنَّ مِنكُمْ لَمَن لَّيُبَطِّئَنَّ 72 Among you is indeed he who drags his feet,

---

[1] As in the case of the Israelites who were ordered to kill those who were guilty among them of the worship of the Calf. See 2:54.

فَإِنْ أَصَٰبَتْكُم مُّصِيبَةٌ قَالَ
and should an affliction visit you, he says,

قَدْ أَنْعَمَ ٱللَّهُ عَلَىَّ
'It was certainly Allah's blessing

إِذْ لَمْ أَكُن مَّعَهُمْ شَهِيدًا ۞
that I did not accompany them!'

وَلَئِنْ أَصَٰبَكُمْ فَضْلٌ مِّنَ ٱللَّهِ
73 But should a grace from Allah come to you,

لَيَقُولَنَّ
he will surely say,

كَأَن لَّمْ تَكُن بَيْنَكُمْ وَبَيْنَهُۥ مَوَدَّةٌ
as if there were no affection between you and him,

يَٰلَيْتَنِى كُنتُ مَعَهُمْ
'I wish I were with them

فَأَفُوزَ فَوْزًا عَظِيمًا ۞ ❋
so that I had achieved a great success!'

فَلْيُقَٰتِلْ فِى سَبِيلِ ٱللَّهِ
74 Let those fight in the way of Allah

ٱلَّذِينَ يَشْرُونَ ٱلْحَيَوٰةَ ٱلدُّنْيَا بِٱلْأَخِرَةِ
who sell the life of this world for the Hereafter;

وَمَن يُقَٰتِلْ فِى سَبِيلِ ٱللَّهِ
and whoever fights in the way of Allah,

فَيُقْتَلْ أَوْ يَغْلِبْ
and then is slain or conquers,

فَسَوْفَ نُؤْتِيهِ أَجْرًا عَظِيمًا ۞
soon We shall give him a great reward.

وَمَا لَكُمْ لَا تُقَٰتِلُونَ فِى سَبِيلِ ٱللَّهِ
75 Why should you not fight in the way of Allah

وَٱلْمُسْتَضْعَفِينَ مِنَ ٱلرِّجَالِ وَٱلنِّسَآءِ
and the abased men, women,

وَٱلْوِلْدَٰنِ
and children,

ٱلَّذِينَ يَقُولُونَ رَبَّنَآ
who say, 'Our Lord,

أَخْرِجْنَا مِنْ هَٰذِهِ ٱلْقَرْيَةِ
bring us out of this town

ٱلظَّالِمِ أَهْلُهَا
whose people are wrongdoers,

وَٱجْعَل لَّنَا مِن لَّدُنكَ وَلِيًّا
and appoint for us a guardian from You,

وَٱجْعَل لَّنَا مِن لَّدُنكَ نَصِيرًا ۞
and appoint for us a helper from You'?

ٱلَّذِينَ ءَامَنُوا۟ يُقَٰتِلُونَ فِى سَبِيلِ ٱللَّهِ
76 Those who have faith fight in the way of Allah,

وَٱلَّذِينَ كَفَرُوا۟
and those who are faithless

يُقَٰتِلُونَ فِى سَبِيلِ ٱلطَّٰغُوتِ
fight in the way of the Rebel.

فَقَٰتِلُوٓا۟ أَوْلِيَآءَ ٱلشَّيْطَٰنِ
So fight the friends of Satan;

إِنَّ كَيْدَ ٱلشَّيْطَٰنِ كَانَ ضَعِيفًا ۞
indeed the stratagems of Satan are always flimsy.

أَلَمْ تَرَ إِلَى ٱلَّذِينَ قِيلَ لَهُمْ
77 Have *you* not regarded those who were told,

كُفُّوٓا۟ أَيْدِيَكُمْ
'Keep your hands off [from warfare],

وَأَقِيمُوا۟ ٱلصَّلَوٰةَ وَءَاتُوا۟ ٱلزَّكَوٰةَ
and maintain the prayer, and give the *zakāt*?

فَلَمَّا كُتِبَ عَلَيْهِمُ ٱلْقِتَالُ
But when fighting was prescribed for them,

إِذَا فَرِيقٌ مِّنْهُمْ يَخْشَوْنَ ٱلنَّاسَ

behold, a part of them were afraid of people

كَخَشْيَةِ ٱللَّهِ

as if fearing Allah,

أَوْ أَشَدَّ خَشْيَةً

or were even more afraid,

وَقَالُواْ رَبَّنَا

and they said, 'Our Lord!

لِمَ كَتَبْتَ عَلَيْنَا ٱلْقِتَالَ

Why did You prescribe fighting for us?

لَوْلَآ أَخَّرْتَنَآ إِلَىٰ أَجَلٍ قَرِيبٍ

If only You had respited us for a short time!'[1]

قُلْ مَتَٰعُ ٱلدُّنْيَا قَلِيلٌ

*Say*, 'The enjoyment of this world is little

وَٱلْآخِرَةُ خَيْرٌ لِّمَنِ ٱتَّقَىٰ

and the Hereafter is better for the Godwary,

وَلَا تُظْلَمُونَ

and you will not be wronged

فَتِيلًا ۝

so much as a single date-thread.

أَيْنَمَا تَكُونُواْ يُدْرِككُّمُ ٱلْمَوْتُ

78 Wherever you may be, death shall overtake you,

وَلَوْ كُنتُمْ فِى بُرُوجٍ مُّشَيَّدَةٍ

even if you were in fortified towers.'

وَإِن تُصِبْهُمْ حَسَنَةٌ

And if any good befalls them,

يَقُولُواْ هَٰذِهِۦ مِنْ عِندِ ٱللَّهِ

they say, 'This is from Allah;'

وَإِن تُصِبْهُمْ سَيِّئَةٌ

and when an ill befalls them,

يَقُولُواْ هَٰذِهِۦ مِنْ عِندِكَ

they say, 'This is from *you*.'

قُل كُلٌّ مِّنْ عِندِ ٱللَّهِ

*Say*, 'All is from Allah.'

فَمَالِ هَٰٓؤُلَآءِ ٱلْقَوْمِ

What is the matter with these people

لَا يَكَادُونَ يَفْقَهُونَ حَدِيثًا ۝

that they would not understand any matter?

مَّآ أَصَابَكَ مِنْ حَسَنَةٍ فَمِنَ ٱللَّهِ

79 Whatever good befalls *you* is from Allah;

وَمَآ أَصَابَكَ مِن سَيِّئَةٍ فَمِن نَّفْسِكَ

and whatever ill befalls *you* is from *yourself*.

وَأَرْسَلْنَٰكَ لِلنَّاسِ رَسُولًا

We sent *you* as an apostle to mankind,

وَكَفَىٰ بِٱللَّهِ شَهِيدًا ۝

and Allah suffices as a witness.

مَّن يُطِعِ ٱلرَّسُولَ فَقَدْ أَطَاعَ ٱللَّهَ

80 Whoever obeys the Apostle certainly obeys Allah;

وَمَن تَوَلَّىٰ

and as for those who turn their backs [on *you*],

فَمَآ أَرْسَلْنَٰكَ عَلَيْهِمْ حَفِيظًا ۝

We have not sent *you* to keep watch over them.

وَيَقُولُونَ طَاعَةٌ

81 They profess obedience [to *you*],

فَإِذَا بَرَزُواْ مِنْ عِندِكَ

but when they go out from *your* presence,

---

[1] Or 'until an imminent time;' that is, until the time of natural death, which is not far in any case. Cf. 14:44, 63:10-11.

بَيَّتَ طَآئِفَةٌ مِّنْهُمْ — a group of them conspire overnight

غَيْرَ ٱلَّذِى تَقُولُ — [to do] something other than what *you* say.

وَٱللَّهُ يَكْتُبُ مَا يُبَيِّتُونَ — But Allah records what they conspire overnight.

فَأَعْرِضْ عَنْهُمْ وَتَوَكَّلْ عَلَى ٱللَّهِ — So *disregard* them and *put your* trust in Allah,

وَكَفَىٰ بِٱللَّهِ وَكِيلًا ۝ — for Allah suffices as trustee.

أَفَلَا يَتَدَبَّرُونَ ٱلْقُرْءَانَ — 82 Do they not contemplate the Qur'ān?

وَلَوْ كَانَ مِنْ عِندِ غَيْرِ ٱللَّهِ — Had it been from [someone] other than Allah,

لَوَجَدُوا۟ فِيهِ ٱخْتِلَٰفًا كَثِيرًا ۝ — they would have surely found much discrepancy in it.

وَإِذَا جَآءَهُمْ أَمْرٌ مِّنَ ٱلْأَمْنِ أَوِ ٱلْخَوْفِ — 83 When a report of safety or alarm comes to them,

أَذَاعُوا۟ بِهِ — they immediately broadcast it;

وَلَوْ رَدُّوهُ إِلَى ٱلرَّسُولِ — but had they referred it to the Apostle

وَإِلَىٰٓ أُو۟لِى ٱلْأَمْرِ مِنْهُمْ — or to those vested with authority among them,

لَعَلِمَهُ ٱلَّذِينَ يَسْتَنۢبِطُونَهُۥ مِنْهُمْ — those of them who investigate would have ascertained it.

وَلَوْلَا فَضْلُ ٱللَّهِ عَلَيْكُمْ — And were it not for Allah's grace upon you

وَرَحْمَتُهُۥ — and His mercy,

لَٱتَّبَعْتُمُ ٱلشَّيْطَٰنَ — you would have surely followed Satan,

إِلَّا قَلِيلًا ۝ — [all] except a few.

فَقَٰتِلْ فِى سَبِيلِ ٱللَّهِ — 84 So *fight* in the way of Allah:

لَا تُكَلَّفُ إِلَّا نَفْسَكَ — *you* are responsible only for *yourself*,

وَحَرِّضِ ٱلْمُؤْمِنِينَ — but *urge* on the faithful [to fight].

عَسَى ٱللَّهُ أَن يَكُفَّ بَأْسَ ٱلَّذِينَ كَفَرُوا۟ — Maybe Allah will curb the might of the faithless,

وَٱللَّهُ أَشَدُّ بَأْسًا — for Allah is greatest in might

وَأَشَدُّ تَنكِيلًا ۝ — and severest in punishment.

مَّن يَشْفَعْ شَفَٰعَةً حَسَنَةً — 85 Whoever intercedes for a good cause

يَكُن لَّهُۥ نَصِيبٌ مِّنْهَا — shall receive a share of it,

وَمَن يَشْفَعْ شَفَٰعَةً سَيِّئَةً — and whoever intercedes for an evil cause

يَكُن لَّهُۥ كِفْلٌ مِّنْهَا — shall share its burden,

وَكَانَ ٱللَّهُ عَلَىٰ كُلِّ شَىْءٍ مُّقِيتًا ۝ — and Allah is prepotent over all things.

وَإِذَا حُيِّيتُم بِتَحِيَّةٍ 86 When you are greeted with a salute,

فَحَيُّواْ بِأَحْسَنَ مِنْهَآ أَوْ رُدُّوهَآ    greet with a better one than it, or return it;

إِنَّ ٱللَّهَ كَانَ عَلَىٰ كُلِّ شَىْءٍ حَسِيبًا ۝    indeed Allah takes account of all things.

ٱللَّهُ لَآ إِلَٰهَ إِلَّا هُوَ 87 Allah—there is no god except Him—

لَيَجْمَعَنَّكُمْ إِلَىٰ يَوْمِ ٱلْقِيَٰمَةِ    will surely gather you on the Day of Resurrection,

لَا رَيْبَ فِيهِ    in which there is no doubt;

وَمَنْ أَصْدَقُ مِنَ ٱللَّهِ حَدِيثًا ۝ ۞    and who is more truthful in speech than Allah?

فَمَا لَكُمْ فِى ٱلْمُنَٰفِقِينَ فِئَتَيْنِ 88 Why should you be two groups concerning the hypocrites,[1]

وَٱللَّهُ أَرْكَسَهُم    while Allah has made them relapse

بِمَا كَسَبُوٓاْ    because of their deeds?

أَتُرِيدُونَ أَن تَهْدُواْ مَنْ أَضَلَّ ٱللَّهُ    Do you desire to guide someone Allah has led astray?

وَمَن يُضْلِلِ ٱللَّهُ    Whomever Allah leads astray,

فَلَن تَجِدَ لَهُۥ سَبِيلًا ۝    *you* will never find any way for him.

وَدُّواْ لَوْ تَكْفُرُونَ 89 They are eager that you should disbelieve

كَمَا كَفَرُواْ    like they have disbelieved,

فَتَكُونُونَ سَوَآءً    so that you all become alike.

فَلَا تَتَّخِذُواْ مِنْهُمْ أَوْلِيَآءَ    So do not make friends [with anyone] from among them,

حَتَّىٰ يُهَاجِرُواْ فِى سَبِيلِ ٱللَّهِ    until they migrate in the way of Allah.

فَإِن تَوَلَّوْاْ فَخُذُوهُمْ وَٱقْتُلُوهُمْ    But if they turn their backs, seize them and kill them

حَيْثُ وَجَدتُّمُوهُمْ    wherever you find them,

وَلَا تَتَّخِذُواْ مِنْهُمْ وَلِيًّا وَلَا نَصِيرًا ۝    and do not take from among them friends or helpers,

إِلَّا ٱلَّذِينَ يَصِلُونَ إِلَىٰ قَوْمٍ 90 excepting those who join a people

بَيْنَكُمْ وَبَيْنَهُم مِّيثَٰقٌ    between whom and you there is a treaty,

أَوْ جَآءُوكُمْ    or such as come to you

حَصِرَتْ صُدُورُهُمْ أَن يُقَٰتِلُوكُمْ    with hearts reluctant to fight you

أَوْ يُقَٰتِلُواْ قَوْمَهُمْ    or to fight their own people.

---

[1] A reference to the hypocrites of Makkah who feigned sympathy for the Muslims while remaining in Makkah and continuing to work for their enemies.

وَلَوْ شَآءَ ٱللَّهُ

Had Allah wished,

لَسَلَّطَهُمْ عَلَيْكُمْ

He would have imposed them upon you,

فَلَقَتَلُوكُمْ

and then they would have surely fought you.

فَإِنِ ٱعْتَزَلُوكُمْ

So if they keep out of your way

فَلَمْ يُقَٰتِلُوكُمْ وَأَلْقَوْا۟ إِلَيْكُمُ ٱلسَّلَمَ

and do not fight you, and offer you peace,

فَمَا جَعَلَ ٱللَّهُ لَكُمْ

then Allah does not allow you

عَلَيْهِمْ سَبِيلًا ۝

any course [of action] against them.

سَتَجِدُونَ ءَاخَرِينَ

91 You will find others

يُرِيدُونَ أَن يَأْمَنُوكُمْ

desiring to be secure from you,

وَيَأْمَنُوا۟ قَوْمَهُمْ

and secure from their own people;

كُلَّ مَا رُدُّوٓا۟ إِلَى ٱلْفِتْنَةِ

yet whenever they are called back to polytheism,

أُرْكِسُوا۟ فِيهَا

they relapse into it.

فَإِن لَّمْ يَعْتَزِلُوكُمْ

So if they do not keep out of your way,

وَيُلْقُوٓا۟ إِلَيْكُمُ ٱلسَّلَمَ

nor offer you peace,

وَيَكُفُّوٓا۟ أَيْدِيَهُمْ

nor keep their hands off [from fighting],

فَخُذُوهُمْ وَٱقْتُلُوهُمْ

then seize them and kill them

حَيْثُ ثَقِفْتُمُوهُمْ

wherever you confront them,

وَأُو۟لَٰئِكُمْ جَعَلْنَا لَكُمْ عَلَيْهِمْ

and it is such against whom We have given you

سُلْطَٰنًا مُّبِينًا ۝

a clear sanction.

وَمَا كَانَ لِمُؤْمِنٍ أَن يَقْتُلَ مُؤْمِنًا

92 A believer may not kill another believer,

إِلَّا خَطَـًٔا

unless it is by mistake.

وَمَن قَتَلَ مُؤْمِنًا خَطَـًٔا

Anyone who kills a believer by mistake

فَتَحْرِيرُ رَقَبَةٍ مُّؤْمِنَةٍ

should set free a believing slave,

وَدِيَةٌ مُّسَلَّمَةٌ إِلَىٰٓ أَهْلِهِۦٓ

and pay blood-money to his family,[1]

إِلَّآ أَن يَصَّدَّقُوا۟

unless they remit it in charity.

فَإِن كَانَ مِن قَوْمٍ عَدُوٍّ لَّكُمْ

If he[2] belongs to a people that are hostile to you

وَهُوَ مُؤْمِنٌ

but is a believer,

---

[1] That is, to the family of the victim.

[2] That is, the victim.

فَتَحْرِيرُ رَقَبَةٍ مُّؤْمِنَةٍ
then a believing slave is to be set free.

وَإِن كَانَ مِن قَوْمٍ
And if he belongs to a people

بَيْنَكُمْ وَبَيْنَهُم مِّيثَـٰقٌ
with whom you have a treaty,

فَدِيَةٌ مُّسَلَّمَةٌ إِلَىٰٓ أَهْلِهِۦ
the blood-money is to be paid to his family

وَتَحْرِيرُ رَقَبَةٍ مُّؤْمِنَةٍ
and a believing slave is to be set free.

فَمَن لَّمْ يَجِدْ
He who cannot afford [to pay the blood-money],

فَصِيَامُ شَهْرَيْنِ مُتَتَابِعَيْنِ
must fast two successive months

تَوْبَةً مِّنَ ٱللَّهِ
as a penance from Allah,

وَكَانَ ٱللَّهُ عَلِيمًا حَكِيمًا ۝
and Allah is all-knowing, all-wise.

وَمَن يَقْتُلْ مُؤْمِنًا مُّتَعَمِّدًا
93 Should anyone kill a believer intentionally,

فَجَزَآؤُهُۥ جَهَنَّمُ
his requital shall be hell,

خَٰلِدًا فِيهَا
to remain in it [forever];

وَغَضِبَ ٱللَّهُ عَلَيْهِ وَلَعَنَهُۥ
Allah shall be wrathful at him and curse him

وَأَعَدَّ لَهُۥ عَذَابًا عَظِيمًا ۝
and He shall prepare for him a great punishment.

يَـٰٓأَيُّهَا ٱلَّذِينَ ءَامَنُوٓا
94 O you who have faith!

إِذَا ضَرَبْتُمْ فِى سَبِيلِ ٱللَّهِ
When you issue forth in the way of Allah,

فَتَبَيَّنُوا
try to ascertain:

وَلَا تَقُولُوا لِمَنْ أَلْقَىٰٓ إِلَيْكُمُ ٱلسَّلَـٰمَ
do not say to someone who offers you peace,

لَسْتَ مُؤْمِنًا
'You are not a believer,'

تَبْتَغُونَ عَرَضَ ٱلْحَيَوٰةِ ٱلدُّنْيَا
seeking the transitory wares of the life of this world.

فَعِندَ ٱللَّهِ مَغَانِمُ كَثِيرَةٌ
Yet with Allah are plenteous gains.

كَذَٰلِكَ كُنتُم مِّن قَبْلُ
You too were such earlier,

فَمَنَّ ٱللَّهُ عَلَيْكُمْ
but Allah did you a favour.

فَتَبَيَّنُوٓا
Therefore, do ascertain.

إِنَّ ٱللَّهَ كَانَ بِمَا تَعْمَلُونَ خَبِيرًا ۝
Allah is indeed well aware of what you do.

لَّا يَسْتَوِى ٱلْقَـٰعِدُونَ مِنَ ٱلْمُؤْمِنِينَ
95 Not equal are those of the faithful who sit back

غَيْرُ أُولِى ٱلضَّرَرِ
—excepting those who suffer from some disability—

وَٱلْمُجَـٰهِدُونَ فِى سَبِيلِ ٱللَّهِ
and those who wage *jihād* in the way of Allah

بِأَمْوَٰلِهِمْ وَأَنفُسِهِمْ
with their possession and their persons.

فَضَّلَ ٱللَّهُ ٱلْمُجَهِدِينَ    Allah has graced those who wage *jihād*

بِأَمْوَٰلِهِمْ وَأَنفُسِهِمْ    with their possessions and their persons

عَلَى ٱلْقَٰعِدِينَ دَرَجَةً    by a degree over those who sit back;

وَكُلًّا وَعَدَ ٱللَّهُ ٱلْحُسْنَىٰ    yet to each Allah has promised the best reward,

وَفَضَّلَ ٱللَّهُ    and Allah has graced

ٱلْمُجَٰهِدِينَ    those who wage *jihād*

عَلَى ٱلْقَٰعِدِينَ    over those who sit back

أَجْرًا عَظِيمًا ۝    with a great reward:

دَرَجَٰتٍ مِّنْهُ وَمَغْفِرَةً وَرَحْمَةً    96 ranks from Him, forgiveness, and mercy,

وَكَانَ ٱللَّهُ غَفُورًا رَّحِيمًا ۝    and Allah is all-forgiving, all-merciful.

إِنَّ ٱلَّذِينَ تَوَفَّىٰهُمُ ٱلْمَلَٰئِكَةُ    97 Indeed, those whom the angels take away

ظَالِمِىٓ أَنفُسِهِمْ    while they are wronging themselves,

قَالُوا۟ فِيمَ كُنتُمْ    they[1] ask, 'What state were you in?'

قَالُوا۟ كُنَّا مُسْتَضْعَفِينَ فِى ٱلْأَرْضِ    They reply, 'We were abased in the land.'

قَالُوٓا۟ أَلَمْ تَكُنْ أَرْضُ ٱللَّهِ وَٰسِعَةً    They say, 'Was not Allah's earth vast enough

فَتُهَاجِرُوا۟ فِيهَا    so that you might migrate in it?'

فَأُو۟لَٰٓئِكَ مَأْوَىٰهُمْ جَهَنَّمُ    The refuge of such shall be hell,

وَسَآءَتْ مَصِيرًا ۝    and it is an evil destination.

إِلَّا ٱلْمُسْتَضْعَفِينَ مِنَ ٱلرِّجَالِ    98 Except the abased among men,

وَٱلنِّسَآءِ وَٱلْوِلْدَٰنِ    women and children,

لَا يَسْتَطِيعُونَ حِيلَةً    who have neither access to any means

وَلَا يَهْتَدُونَ سَبِيلًا ۝    nor are guided to any way.

فَأُو۟لَٰٓئِكَ عَسَى ٱللَّهُ أَن يَعْفُوَ عَنْهُمْ    99 Maybe Allah will excuse them,

وَكَانَ ٱللَّهُ عَفُوًّا غَفُورًا ۝ ۞    for Allah is all-excusing, all-forgiving.

وَمَن يُهَاجِرْ فِى سَبِيلِ ٱللَّهِ    100 Whoever migrates in the way of Allah

يَجِدْ فِى ٱلْأَرْضِ مُرَٰغَمًا كَثِيرًا وَسَعَةً    will find many havens and plenitude in the earth.

وَمَن يَخْرُجْ مِنۢ بَيْتِهِ    And whoever leaves his home

مُهَاجِرًا إِلَى ٱللَّهِ وَرَسُولِهِ    migrating toward Allah and His Apostle,

ثُمَّ يُدْرِكْهُ ٱلْمَوْتُ    and is then overtaken by death,

---

[1] That is, the angels.

128

فَقَدْ وَقَعَ أَجْرُهُۥ عَلَى ٱللَّهِ ۗ his reward shall certainly fall on Allah,

وَكَانَ ٱللَّهُ غَفُورًا رَّحِيمًا ۝ and Allah is all-forgiving, all-merciful.

وَإِذَا ضَرَبْتُمْ فِى ٱلْأَرْضِ 101 When you journey in the land,

فَلَيْسَ عَلَيْكُمْ جُنَاحٌ there is no sin upon you

أَن تَقْصُرُوا۟ مِنَ ٱلصَّلَوٰةِ in shortening the prayers,

إِنْ خِفْتُمْ أَن يَفْتِنَكُمُ ٱلَّذِينَ كَفَرُوٓا۟ ۚ if you fear that the faithless may trouble you;

إِنَّ ٱلْكَٰفِرِينَ كَانُوا۟ لَكُمْ عَدُوًّا مُّبِينًا ۝ indeed the faithless are your manifest enemies.

وَإِذَا كُنتَ فِيهِمْ فَأَقَمْتَ لَهُمُ ٱلصَّلَوٰةَ 102 When *you* are among them, leading them in prayers,

فَلْتَقُمْ طَآئِفَةٌ مِّنْهُم مَّعَكَ let a group of them stand with *you*

وَلْيَأْخُذُوٓا۟ أَسْلِحَتَهُمْ carrying their weapons.

فَإِذَا سَجَدُوا۟ And when they have done the prostrations,

فَلْيَكُونُوا۟ مِن وَرَآئِكُمْ let them withdraw to the rear,

وَلْتَأْتِ طَآئِفَةٌ أُخْرَىٰ لَمْ يُصَلُّوا۟ then let the other group which has not prayed come

فَلْيُصَلُّوا۟ مَعَكَ and pray with *you*,

وَلْيَأْخُذُوا۟ حِذْرَهُمْ وَأَسْلِحَتَهُمْ ۗ taking their precautions and [bearing] their weapons.

وَدَّ ٱلَّذِينَ كَفَرُوا۟ لَوْ تَغْفُلُونَ The faithless are eager that you should be oblivious

عَنْ أَسْلِحَتِكُمْ وَأَمْتِعَتِكُمْ of your weapons and your baggage,

فَيَمِيلُونَ عَلَيْكُم مَّيْلَةً وَٰحِدَةً ۚ so that they could assault you all at once.

وَلَا جُنَاحَ عَلَيْكُمْ But there is no sin upon you,

إِن كَانَ بِكُمْ أَذًى مِّن مَّطَرٍ if you are troubled by rain

أَوْ كُنتُم مَّرْضَىٰٓ or are sick,

أَن تَضَعُوٓا۟ أَسْلِحَتَكُمْ ۖ to set aside your weapons;

وَخُذُوا۟ حِذْرَكُمْ ۗ but take your precautions.

إِنَّ ٱللَّهَ أَعَدَّ لِلْكَٰفِرِينَ Indeed Allah has prepared for the faithless

عَذَابًا مُّهِينًا ۝ a humiliating punishment.

فَإِذَا قَضَيْتُمُ ٱلصَّلَوٰةَ 103 When you have finished the prayers,

فَٱذْكُرُوا۟ ٱللَّهَ remember Allah,

قِيَٰمًا وَقُعُودًا وَعَلَىٰ جُنُوبِكُمْ ۚ standing, sitting and lying down,

فَإِذَا ٱطْمَأْنَنتُمْ and when you feel secure,

فَأَقِيمُوا۟ ٱلصَّلَوٰةَ ۚ perform the [complete] prayers,

إِنَّ ٱلصَّلَوٰةَ كَانَتْ

for the prayer is indeed

عَلَى ٱلْمُؤْمِنِينَ كِتَٰبًا مَّوْقُوتًا ۞

a timed prescription for the faithful.

وَلَا تَهِنُواْ فِى ٱبْتِغَآءِ ٱلْقَوْمِ

104 Do not slacken in the pursuit of these people.[1]

إِن تَكُونُواْ تَأْلَمُونَ

If you are suffering,

فَإِنَّهُمْ يَأْلَمُونَ كَمَا تَأْلَمُونَ

they are also suffering like you,

وَتَرْجُونَ مِنَ ٱللَّهِ مَا لَا يَرْجُونَ

but you expect from Allah what they do not expect,

وَكَانَ ٱللَّهُ عَلِيمًا حَكِيمًا ۞

and Allah is all-knowing, all-wise.

إِنَّآ أَنزَلْنَآ إِلَيْكَ ٱلْكِتَٰبَ

105 Indeed We have sent down to *you* the Book

بِٱلْحَقِّ

with the truth,

لِتَحْكُمَ بَيْنَ ٱلنَّاسِ

so that *you* may judge between the people

بِمَآ أَرَىٰكَ ٱللَّهُ

by what Allah has shown *you*;

وَلَا تَكُن لِّلْخَآئِنِينَ خَصِيمًا ۞

*do not be* an advocate for the traitors,

وَٱسْتَغْفِرِ ٱللَّهَ

106 and *plead* Allah for forgiveness;

إِنَّ ٱللَّهَ كَانَ غَفُورًا رَّحِيمًا ۞

indeed Allah is all-forgiving, all-merciful.

وَلَا تُجَٰدِلْ عَنِ ٱلَّذِينَ يَخْتَانُونَ أَنفُسَهُمْ

107 And *do not plead* for those who betray themselves;

إِنَّ ٱللَّهَ لَا يُحِبُّ

indeed Allah does not like

مَن كَانَ خَوَّانًا أَثِيمًا ۞

someone who is treacherous and sinful.

يَسْتَخْفُونَ مِنَ ٱلنَّاسِ

108 They try to hide [their real character] from people,

وَلَا يَسْتَخْفُونَ مِنَ ٱللَّهِ

but they do not try to conceal from Allah,

وَهُوَ مَعَهُمْ إِذْ يُبَيِّتُونَ

though He is with them when they conspire overnight

مَا لَا يَرْضَىٰ مِنَ ٱلْقَوْلِ

with a discourse that He does not approve of.

وَكَانَ ٱللَّهُ بِمَا يَعْمَلُونَ مُحِيطًا ۞

And Allah comprehends whatever they do.

هَٰٓأَنتُمْ هَٰٓؤُلَآءِ

109 Aha! There you are,

جَٰدَلْتُمْ عَنْهُمْ فِى ٱلْحَيَوٰةِ ٱلدُّنْيَا

pleading for them in the life of this world!

فَمَن يُجَٰدِلُ ٱللَّهَ عَنْهُمْ

But who will plead for them with Allah

يَوْمَ ٱلْقِيَٰمَةِ

on the Day of Resurrection,

أَم مَّن يَكُونُ عَلَيْهِمْ وَكِيلًا ۞

or will be their defender?

---

[1] That is, the infidels.

وَمَن يَعْمَلْ سُوءًا أَوْ يَظْلِمْ نَفْسَهُ 110 Whoever commits evil or wrongs himself

ثُمَّ يَسْتَغْفِرِ ٱللَّهَ    and then pleads Allah for forgiveness,

يَجِدِ ٱللَّهَ غَفُورًا رَّحِيمًا ۝    will find Allah all-forgiving, al-merciful.

وَمَن يَكْسِبْ إِثْمًا 111 And whoever commits a sin,

فَإِنَّمَا يَكْسِبُهُ عَلَىٰ نَفْسِهِۦ    commits it only against himself;

وَكَانَ ٱللَّهُ عَلِيمًا حَكِيمًا ۝    and Allah is all-knowing, all-wise.

وَمَن يَكْسِبْ خَطِيٓئَةً أَوْ إِثْمًا 112 But someone who commits an iniquity or sin

ثُمَّ يَرْمِ بِهِۦ بَرِيٓئًا    and then accuses an innocent person of it,

فَقَدِ ٱحْتَمَلَ بُهْتَٰنًا    is indeed guilty of calumny

وَإِثْمًا مُّبِينًا ۝    and a flagrant sin.

وَلَوْلَا فَضْلُ ٱللَّهِ عَلَيْكَ وَرَحْمَتُهُ 113 Were it not for Allah's grace and His mercy on *you*,

هَمَّت طَّآئِفَةٌ مِّنْهُمْ أَن يُضِلُّوكَ    a group of them were bent on leading *you* astray;

وَمَا يُضِلُّونَ إِلَّآ أَنفُسَهُمْ    but they do not mislead anyone except themselves,

وَمَا يَضُرُّونَكَ مِن شَىْءٍ    and they cannot do *you* any harm.

وَأَنزَلَ ٱللَّهُ عَلَيْكَ ٱلْكِتَٰبَ وَٱلْحِكْمَةَ    Allah has sent down to *you* the Book and wisdom,

وَعَلَّمَكَ مَا لَمْ تَكُن تَعْلَمُ    and He has taught *you* what *you* did not know,

وَكَانَ فَضْلُ ٱللَّهِ عَلَيْكَ عَظِيمًا ۝ ❊    and great is Allah's grace upon *you*.

لَّا خَيْرَ فِى كَثِيرٍ مِّن نَّجْوَىٰهُمْ 114 There is no good in much of their secret talks,

إِلَّا مَنْ أَمَرَ بِصَدَقَةٍ    excepting him who enjoins charity

أَوْ مَعْرُوفٍ    or what is right

أَوْ إِصْلَٰحٍ بَيْنَ ٱلنَّاسِ    or reconciliation between people,

وَمَن يَفْعَلْ ذَٰلِكَ ٱبْتِغَآءَ مَرْضَاتِ ٱللَّهِ    and whoever does that, seeking Allah's pleasure,

فَسَوْفَ نُؤْتِيهِ أَجْرًا عَظِيمًا ۝    soon We shall give him a great reward.

وَمَن يُشَاقِقِ ٱلرَّسُولَ 115 But whoever defies the Apostle,

مِنۢ بَعْدِ مَا تَبَيَّنَ لَهُ ٱلْهُدَىٰ    after the guidance has become manifest to him,

وَيَتَّبِعْ غَيْرَ سَبِيلِ ٱلْمُؤْمِنِينَ    and follows a way other than that of the faithful,

نُوَلِّهِۦ مَا تَوَلَّىٰ    We shall abandon him to his devices

وَنُصْلِهِۦ جَهَنَّمَ    and We shall make him enter hell,

وَسَآءَتْ مَصِيرًا ۝    and it is an evil destination.

إِنَّ ٱللَّهَ لَا يَغْفِرُ 116 Indeed Allah does not forgive

أَن يُشْرَكَ بِهِ that any partner should be ascribed to Him,

وَيَغْفِرُ مَا دُونَ ذَٰلِكَ but He forgives anything besides that

لِمَن يَشَآءُ to whomever He wishes.

وَمَن يُشْرِكْ بِٱللَّهِ And whoever ascribes partners to Allah

فَقَدْ ضَلَّ ضَلَٰلَۢا بَعِيدًا has certainly strayed into far error.

إِن يَدْعُونَ مِن دُونِهِ إِلَّآ إِنَٰثًا 117 They invoke none but females[1] besides Him,

وَإِن يَدْعُونَ إِلَّا شَيْطَٰنًا مَّرِيدًا and invoke none but a froward Satan,

لَّعَنَهُ ٱللَّهُ 118 whom Allah has cursed,

وَقَالَ لَأَتَّخِذَنَّ مِنْ عِبَادِكَ and who said, 'I will surely take of Your servants

نَصِيبًا مَّفْرُوضًا a settled share,

وَلَأُضِلَّنَّهُمْ 119 and I will lead them astray

وَلَأُمَنِّيَنَّهُمْ and give them [false] hopes,

وَلَأَمُرَنَّهُمْ فَلَيُبَتِّكُنَّ ءَاذَانَ ٱلْأَنْعَٰمِ and prompt them to slit the ears of cattle,[2]

وَلَأَمُرَنَّهُمْ فَلَيُغَيِّرُنَّ خَلْقَ ٱللَّهِ and I will prompt them to alter Allah's creation.'

وَمَن يَتَّخِذِ ٱلشَّيْطَٰنَ وَلِيًّا Whoever takes Satan as a guardian

مِّن دُونِ ٱللَّهِ instead of Allah

فَقَدْ خَسِرَ خُسْرَانًا مُّبِينًا has certainly incurred a manifest loss.

يَعِدُهُمْ 120 He makes them promises

وَيُمَنِّيهِمْ and gives them [false] hopes,

وَمَا يَعِدُهُمُ ٱلشَّيْطَٰنُ إِلَّا غُرُورًا yet Satan does not promise them anything but delusion.

أُوْلَٰٓئِكَ مَأْوَىٰهُمْ جَهَنَّمُ 121 The refuge of such shall be hell,

وَلَا يَجِدُونَ عَنْهَا مَحِيصًا and they will not find any escape from it.

وَٱلَّذِينَ ءَامَنُوا 122 But those who have faith

وَعَمِلُوا ٱلصَّٰلِحَٰتِ and do righteous deeds,

سَنُدْخِلُهُمْ جَنَّٰتٍ We will admit them into gardens

تَجْرِى مِن تَحْتِهَا ٱلْأَنْهَٰرُ with streams running in them,

---

[1] Most of the idols and deities worshipped by Arab pagans had female names, e.g. Lāt, Manāt, 'Uzzā, Nā'ilah, etc.

[2] This refers to the pagan practice of slitting the ears of camels as a sign of their dedication to pagan deities.

خَلِدِينَ فِيهَآ أَبَدًا    to remain in them forever

وَعۡدَ ٱللَّهِ حَقًّا    —a true promise of Allah,

وَمَنۡ أَصۡدَقُ مِنَ ٱللَّهِ قِيلًا ۝    and who is truer in speech than Allah?

لَّيۡسَ بِأَمَانِيِّكُمۡ    123 It will be neither after your hopes

وَلَآ أَمَانِيِّ أَهۡلِ ٱلۡكِتَبِ    nor the hopes of the People of the Book:

مَن يَعۡمَلۡ سُوٓءًا يُجۡزَ بِهِۦ    whoever commits evil shall be requited for it,

وَلَا يَجِدۡ لَهُۥ    and he will not find for himself

مِن دُونِ ٱللَّهِ وَلِيًّا وَلَا نَصِيرًا ۝    any guardian or helper besides Allah.

وَمَن يَعۡمَلۡ مِنَ ٱلصَّلِحَتِ    124 And whoever does righteous deeds,

مِن ذَكَرٍ أَوۡ أُنثَىٰ    whether male or female,

وَهُوَ مُؤۡمِنٌ    should he be faithful

فَأُوْلَٰٓئِكَ يَدۡخُلُونَ ٱلۡجَنَّةَ    —such shall enter paradise

وَلَا يُظۡلَمُونَ    and they will not be wronged

نَقِيرًا ۝    [so much as] the speck on a date-stone.

وَمَنۡ أَحۡسَنُ دِينًا مِّمَّنۡ    125 And who has a better religion than him

أَسۡلَمَ وَجۡهَهُۥ لِلَّهِ وَهُوَ مُحۡسِنٌ    who submits his will to Allah, being virtuous,

وَٱتَّبَعَ مِلَّةَ إِبۡرَٰهِيمَ حَنِيفًا    and follows the creed of Abraham, a *hanif*?

وَٱتَّخَذَ ٱللَّهُ إِبۡرَٰهِيمَ خَلِيلًا ۝    And Allah took Abraham for a dedicated friend.

وَلِلَّهِ مَا فِى ٱلسَّمَٰوَٰتِ    126 To Allah belongs whatever is in the heavens

وَمَا فِى ٱلۡأَرۡضِ    and whatever is on the earth,

وَكَانَ ٱللَّهُ بِكُلِّ شَيۡءٍ مُّحِيطًا ۝    and Allah comprehends all things.

وَيَسۡتَفۡتُونَكَ فِى ٱلنِّسَآءِ    127 They seek *your* ruling concerning women.

قُلِ ٱللَّهُ يُفۡتِيكُمۡ فِيهِنَّ    *Say,* 'Allah gives you a ruling concerning them

وَمَا يُتۡلَىٰ عَلَيۡكُمۡ فِى ٱلۡكِتَبِ    and that which is recited to you in the Book

فِى يَتَٰمَى ٱلنِّسَآءِ    concerning girl orphans

ٱلَّٰتِى لَا تُؤۡتُونَهُنَّ    —whom you do not give

مَا كُتِبَ لَهُنَّ    what has been prescribed for them,

وَتَرۡغَبُونَ أَن تَنكِحُوهُنَّ    and yet you desire to marry them—

وَٱلْمُسْتَضْعَفِينَ مِنَ ٱلْوِلْدَٰنِ and about the weak among children:

وَأَن تَقُومُوا لِلْيَتَٰمَىٰ بِٱلْقِسْطِ that you should maintain the orphans with justice,

وَمَا تَفْعَلُوا مِنْ خَيْرٍ and whatever good you do,

فَإِنَّ ٱللَّهَ كَانَ بِهِۦ عَلِيمًا indeed Allah knows it well.

وَإِنِ ٱمْرَأَةٌ خَافَتْ مِنۢ بَعْلِهَا 128 If a woman fears from her husband

نُشُوزًا أَوْ إِعْرَاضًا misconduct or desertion,

فَلَا جُنَاحَ عَلَيْهِمَآ there is no sin upon the couple

أَن يُصْلِحَا بَيْنَهُمَا صُلْحًا if they reach a reconcilement between themselves;

وَٱلصُّلْحُ خَيْرٌ and reconcilement is better.

وَأُحْضِرَتِ ٱلْأَنفُسُ ٱلشُّحَّ The souls are prone to greed;

وَإِن تُحْسِنُوا وَتَتَّقُوا but if you are virtuous and Godwary,

فَإِنَّ ٱللَّهَ كَانَ بِمَا تَعْمَلُونَ خَبِيرًا Allah is indeed well aware of what you do.

وَلَن تَسْتَطِيعُوا أَن تَعْدِلُوا بَيْنَ ٱلنِّسَآءِ 129 You will not be able to be fair between wives,

وَلَوْ حَرَصْتُمْ even if you are eager to do so.

فَلَا تَمِيلُوا كُلَّ ٱلْمَيْلِ Yet do not turn away from one altogether,

فَتَذَرُوهَا كَٱلْمُعَلَّقَةِ leaving her as if in a suspense.

وَإِن تُصْلِحُوا وَتَتَّقُوا But if you are conciliatory and Godwary,

فَإِنَّ ٱللَّهَ كَانَ غَفُورًا رَّحِيمًا Allah is indeed all-forgiving, all-merciful.

وَإِن يَتَفَرَّقَا 130 But if they separate,

يُغْنِ ٱللَّهُ كُلًّا مِّن سَعَتِهِۦ Allah will suffice each of them out of His bounty,

وَكَانَ ٱللَّهُ وَٰسِعًا حَكِيمًا and Allah is all-bounteous, all-wise.

وَلِلَّهِ مَا فِى ٱلسَّمَٰوَٰتِ 131 To Allah belongs whatever is in the heavens

وَمَا فِى ٱلْأَرْضِ and whatever is on the earth.

وَلَقَدْ وَصَّيْنَا We have certainly enjoined

ٱلَّذِينَ أُوتُوا ٱلْكِتَٰبَ مِن قَبْلِكُمْ those who were given the Book before you,

وَإِيَّاكُمْ and you,

أَنِ ٱتَّقُوا ٱللَّهَ that you should be wary of Allah.

وَإِن تَكْفُرُوا But if you are faithless, [you should know that]

فَإِنَّ لِلَّهِ مَا فِى ٱلسَّمَٰوَٰتِ to Allah indeed belongs whatever is in the heavens

وَمَا فِى ٱلْأَرْضِ

and whatever is on the earth,

وَكَانَ ٱللَّهُ غَنِيًّا حَمِيدًا ۝

and Allah is all-sufficient, all-laudable.

وَلِلَّهِ مَا فِى ٱلسَّمَٰوَٰتِ

132 To Allah belongs whatever is in the heavens

وَمَا فِى ٱلْأَرْضِ

and whatever is on the earth,

وَكَفَىٰ بِٱللَّهِ وَكِيلًا ۝

and Allah suffices as trustee.

إِن يَشَأْ يُذْهِبْكُمْ

133 If He wishes, He will take you away,

أَيُّهَا ٱلنَّاسُ

O mankind,

وَيَأْتِ بِـَٔاخَرِينَ

and bring others [in your place];

وَكَانَ ٱللَّهُ عَلَىٰ ذَٰلِكَ قَدِيرًا ۝

Allah has the power to do that.

مَّن كَانَ يُرِيدُ ثَوَابَ ٱلدُّنْيَا

134 Whoever desires the reward of this world,

فَعِندَ ٱللَّهِ

[should know that] with Allah

ثَوَابُ ٱلدُّنْيَا وَٱلْءَاخِرَةِ

is the reward of this world and the Hereafter,

وَكَانَ ٱللَّهُ سَمِيعًۢا بَصِيرًا ۝ ❁

and Allah is all-hearing, all-seeing.

يَٰٓأَيُّهَا ٱلَّذِينَ ءَامَنُوا

135 O you who have faith!

كُونُوا۟ قَوَّٰمِينَ بِٱلْقِسْطِ

Be maintainers of justice

شُهَدَآءَ لِلَّهِ

and witnesses for the sake of Allah,

وَلَوْ عَلَىٰٓ أَنفُسِكُمْ

even if it should be against yourselves

أَوِ ٱلْوَٰلِدَيْنِ وَٱلْأَقْرَبِينَ

or [your] parents and near relatives,

إِن يَكُنْ غَنِيًّا أَوْ فَقِيرًا

and whether it be [someone] rich or poor,

فَٱللَّهُ أَوْلَىٰ بِهِمَا

for Allah has a greater right over them.

فَلَا تَتَّبِعُوا۟ ٱلْهَوَىٰٓ

So do not follow [your] desires,

أَن تَعْدِلُوا۟

lest you should be unfair,

وَإِن تَلْوُۥٓا۟ أَوْ تُعْرِضُوا۟

and if you distort [the testimony] or disregard [it],

فَإِنَّ ٱللَّهَ كَانَ بِمَا تَعْمَلُونَ خَبِيرًا ۝

Allah is indeed well aware of what you do.

يَٰٓأَيُّهَا ٱلَّذِينَ ءَامَنُوٓا۟

136 O you who have faith!

ءَامِنُوا۟ بِٱللَّهِ وَرَسُولِهِۦ

Have faith in Allah and His Apostle

وَٱلْكِتَٰبِ ٱلَّذِى نَزَّلَ عَلَىٰ رَسُولِهِۦ

and the Book that He has sent down to His Apostle

وَٱلْكِتَٰبِ ٱلَّذِىٓ أَنزَلَ مِن قَبْلُ

and the Book He had sent down earlier.

وَمَن يَكْفُرْ بِٱللَّهِ وَمَلَٰٓئِكَتِهِۦ

Whoever disbelieves in Allah and His angels,

وَكُتُبِهِۦ وَرُسُلِهِۦ وَٱلْيَوْمِ ٱلْءَاخِرِ

His Books and His apostles and the Last Day,

فَقَدْ ضَلَّ ضَلَـٰلَۢا بَعِيدًا ۝

has certainly strayed into far error.

إِنَّ ٱلَّذِينَ ءَامَنُواْ ثُمَّ كَفَرُواْ

137 As for those who believe and then disbelieve,

ثُمَّ ءَامَنُواْ ثُمَّ كَفَرُواْ

then believe [again] and then disbelieve

ثُمَّ ٱزْدَادُواْ كُفْرًا

and then increase in disbelief,

لَّمْ يَكُنِ ٱللَّهُ لِيَغْفِرَ لَهُمْ

Allah shall never forgive them,

وَلَا لِيَهْدِيَهُمْ سَبِيلَۢا ۝

nor shall He guide them to any way.

بَشِّرِ ٱلْمُنَـٰفِقِينَ

138 Inform the hypocrites

بِأَنَّ لَهُمْ عَذَابًا أَلِيمًا ۝

that there is a painful punishment for them

ٱلَّذِينَ يَتَّخِذُونَ ٱلْكَـٰفِرِينَ أَوْلِيَآءَ

139 —those who take the faithless for allies

مِن دُونِ ٱلْمُؤْمِنِينَ

instead of the faithful.

أَيَبْتَغُونَ عِندَهُمُ ٱلْعِزَّةَ

Do they seek honour with them?

فَإِنَّ ٱلْعِزَّةَ لِلَّهِ جَمِيعًا ۝

[If so,] indeed all honour belongs to Allah.

وَقَدْ نَزَّلَ عَلَيْكُمْ فِى ٱلْكِتَـٰبِ

140 Certainly He has sent down to you in the Book

أَنْ إِذَا سَمِعْتُمْ ءَايَـٰتِ ٱللَّهِ يُكْفَرُ بِهَا

that when you hear Allah's signs being disbelieved

وَيُسْتَهْزَأُ بِهَا

and derided,

فَلَا تَقْعُدُواْ مَعَهُمْ

do not sit with them

حَتَّىٰ يَخُوضُواْ فِى حَدِيثٍ غَيْرِهِۦٓ

until they engage in some other discourse,

إِنَّكُمْ إِذًا مِّثْلُهُمْ

or else you [too] will be like them.

إِنَّ ٱللَّهَ جَامِعُ ٱلْمُنَـٰفِقِينَ

Indeed Allah will gather the hypocrites

وَٱلْكَـٰفِرِينَ فِى جَهَنَّمَ جَمِيعًا ۝

and the faithless in hell all together.

ٱلَّذِينَ يَتَرَبَّصُونَ بِكُمْ

141 —Those who lie in wait for you:

فَإِن كَانَ لَكُمْ فَتْحٌ مِّنَ ٱللَّهِ

if there is a victory for you from Allah,

قَالُوٓاْ أَلَمْ نَكُن مَّعَكُمْ

they say, 'Were we not with you?'

وَإِن كَانَ لِلْكَـٰفِرِينَ نَصِيبٌ

But if the faithless get a share [of victory],

قَالُوٓاْ أَلَمْ نَسْتَحْوِذْ عَلَيْكُمْ

they say, 'Did we not prevail upon you

وَنَمْنَعْكُم مِّنَ ٱلْمُؤْمِنِينَ

and defend you against the faithful?'

فَٱللَّهُ يَحْكُمُ بَيْنَكُمْ

Allah will judge between you

يَوْمَ ٱلْقِيَـٰمَةِ

on the Day of Resurrection,

وَلَن يَجْعَلَ ٱللَّهُ لِلْكَـٰفِرِينَ

and Allah will never provide the faithless

عَلَى ٱلْمُؤْمِنِينَ سَبِيلًا ۝     any way [to prevail] over the faithful.

إِنَّ ٱلْمُنَٰفِقِينَ يُخَٰدِعُونَ ٱللَّهَ     142 The hypocrites indeed seek to deceive Allah,

وَهُوَ خَٰدِعُهُمْ     but it is He who outwits them.

وَإِذَا قَامُوٓا۟ إِلَى ٱلصَّلَوٰةِ     When they stand up for prayer,

قَامُوا۟ كُسَالَىٰ يُرَآءُونَ ٱلنَّاسَ     they stand up lazily, showing off to the people

وَلَا يَذْكُرُونَ ٱللَّهَ إِلَّا قَلِيلًا ۝     and not remembering Allah except a little,

مُّذَبْذَبِينَ بَيْنَ ذَٰلِكَ     143 wavering in between:

لَآ إِلَىٰ هَٰٓؤُلَآءِ وَلَآ إِلَىٰ هَٰٓؤُلَآءِ ۚ     neither with these nor with those.

وَمَن يُضْلِلِ ٱللَّهُ     And whomever Allah leads astray,

فَلَن تَجِدَ لَهُۥ سَبِيلًا ۝     you will never find any way for him.

يَٰٓأَيُّهَا ٱلَّذِينَ ءَامَنُوا۟     144 O you who have faith!

لَا تَتَّخِذُوا۟ ٱلْكَٰفِرِينَ أَوْلِيَآءَ     Do not take the faithless for friends

مِن دُونِ ٱلْمُؤْمِنِينَ ۚ     instead of the faithful.

أَتُرِيدُونَ أَن تَجْعَلُوا۟ لِلَّهِ     Do you wish to give Allah

عَلَيْكُمْ سُلْطَٰنًا مُّبِينًا ۝     a clear sanction against yourselves?

إِنَّ ٱلْمُنَٰفِقِينَ     145 Indeed the hypocrites will be

فِى ٱلدَّرْكِ ٱلْأَسْفَلِ مِنَ ٱلنَّارِ     in the lowest reach of the Fire,

وَلَن تَجِدَ لَهُمْ نَصِيرًا ۝     and you will never find any helper for them,

إِلَّا ٱلَّذِينَ تَابُوا۟ وَأَصْلَحُوا۟     146 except for those who repent and reform,

وَٱعْتَصَمُوا۟ بِٱللَّهِ     and hold fast to Allah

وَأَخْلَصُوا۟ دِينَهُمْ لِلَّهِ     and dedicate their religion [exclusively] to Allah.

فَأُو۟لَٰٓئِكَ مَعَ ٱلْمُؤْمِنِينَ ۖ     Those are with the faithful,

وَسَوْفَ يُؤْتِ ٱللَّهُ ٱلْمُؤْمِنِينَ     and soon Allah will give the faithful

أَجْرًا عَظِيمًا ۝     a great reward.

مَّا يَفْعَلُ ٱللَّهُ بِعَذَابِكُمْ     147 Why should Allah punish you

إِن شَكَرْتُمْ وَءَامَنتُمْ ۚ     if you give thanks and be faithful?

وَكَانَ ٱللَّهُ شَاكِرًا عَلِيمًا ۝ ✸     And Allah is appreciative, all-knowing.

[PART 6]

لَّا يُحِبُّ ٱللَّهُ     148 Allah does not like

ٱلْجَهْرَ بِٱلسُّوٓءِ     the broadcasting of [anyone's] evil [conduct]

مِنَ ٱلْقَوْلِ    in speech

إِلَّا مَن ظُلِمَ    except by someone who has been wronged,

وَكَانَ ٱللَّهُ سَمِيعًا عَلِيمًا ۞    and Allah is all-hearing, all-knowing.

إِن تُبْدُواْ خَيْرًا    149 Whether you disclose a good [deed that you do]

أَوْ تُخْفُوهُ أَوْ تَعْفُواْ عَن سُوٓءٍ    or hide it, or excuse an evil [deed],

فَإِنَّ ٱللَّهَ كَانَ عَفُوًّا قَدِيرًا ۞    Allah is indeed all-excusing, all-powerful.

إِنَّ ٱلَّذِينَ يَكْفُرُونَ بِٱللَّهِ وَرُسُلِهِ    150 Those who disbelieve in Allah and His apostles

وَيُرِيدُونَ أَن يُفَرِّقُواْ بَيْنَ ٱللَّهِ وَرُسُلِهِ    and seek to separate Allah from His apostles,

وَيَقُولُونَ نُؤْمِنُ بِبَعْضٍ    and say, 'We believe in some

وَنَكْفُرُ بِبَعْضٍ    and disbelieve in some'

وَيُرِيدُونَ أَن يَتَّخِذُواْ بَيْنَ ذَٰلِكَ سَبِيلًا ۞    and seek to take a way in between

أُوْلَٰٓئِكَ هُمُ ٱلْكَٰفِرُونَ حَقًّا    151 —it is they who are truly faithless,

وَأَعْتَدْنَا لِلْكَٰفِرِينَ    and We have prepared for the faithless

عَذَابًا مُّهِينًا ۞    a humiliating punishment.

وَٱلَّذِينَ ءَامَنُواْ بِٱللَّهِ    152 But those who have faith in Allah

وَرُسُلِهِ    and His apostles

وَلَمْ يُفَرِّقُواْ بَيْنَ أَحَدٍ مِّنْهُمْ    and make no distinction between any of them

أُوْلَٰٓئِكَ سَوْفَ يُؤْتِيهِمْ أُجُورَهُمْ    —them He will soon give their rewards,

وَكَانَ ٱللَّهُ غَفُورًا رَّحِيمًا ۞    and Allah is all-forgiving, all-merciful.

يَسْـَٔلُكَ أَهْلُ ٱلْكِتَٰبِ    153 The People of the Book ask *you*

أَن تُنَزِّلَ عَلَيْهِمْ كِتَٰبًا مِّنَ ٱلسَّمَآءِ    to bring down for them a Book from the sky.

فَقَدْ سَأَلُواْ مُوسَىٰ    Certainly they asked Moses

أَكْبَرَ مِن ذَٰلِكَ    for [something] greater than that,

فَقَالُوٓاْ أَرِنَا ٱللَّهَ جَهْرَةً    for they said, 'Show us Allah visibly,'

فَأَخَذَتْهُمُ ٱلصَّٰعِقَةُ بِظُلْمِهِمْ    whereat a thunderbolt seized them for their wrongdoing.

ثُمَّ ٱتَّخَذُواْ ٱلْعِجْلَ    Then they took up the Calf [for worship],

مِنۢ بَعْدِ مَا جَآءَتْهُمُ ٱلْبَيِّنَٰتُ    after all the manifest proofs that had come to them.

فَعَفَوْنَا عَن ذَٰلِكَ    Yet We excused that,

وَءَاتَيْنَا مُوسَىٰ سُلْطَٰنًا مُّبِينًا ۞    and We gave Moses a manifest authority.

وَرَفَعْنَا فَوْقَهُمُ ٱلطُّورَ    154 And We raised the Mount above them

بِمِيثَـٰقِهِمْ    for the sake of their covenant,

وَقُلْنَا لَهُمُ ٱدْخُلُوا۟ ٱلْبَابَ سُجَّدًا    and We said to them, 'Enter the gate prostrating'

وَقُلْنَا لَهُمْ لَا تَعْدُوا۟ فِى ٱلسَّبْتِ    and We said to them, 'Do not violate the Sabbath,'

وَأَخَذْنَا مِنْهُم مِّيثَـٰقًا غَلِيظًا ۝    and We took from them a solemn covenant.

فَبِمَا نَقْضِهِم مِّيثَـٰقَهُمْ    155 Then because of their breaking their covenant,

وَكُفْرِهِم بِـَٔايَـٰتِ ٱللَّهِ    their defiance of Allah's signs,

وَقَتْلِهِمُ ٱلْأَنۢبِيَآءَ بِغَيْرِ حَقٍّ    their killing of the prophets unjustly

وَقَوْلِهِمْ قُلُوبُنَا غُلْفٌۢ    and for their saying, 'Our hearts are uncircumcised.'[1]

بَلْ طَبَعَ ٱللَّهُ عَلَيْهَا بِكُفْرِهِمْ    Rather Allah has set a seal on them[2] for their unfaith,

فَلَا يُؤْمِنُونَ إِلَّا قَلِيلًا ۝    so they do not have faith except a few.

وَبِكُفْرِهِمْ    156 And for their faithlessness,

وَقَوْلِهِمْ عَلَىٰ مَرْيَمَ بُهْتَـٰنًا عَظِيمًا ۝    and their uttering a monstrous calumny against Mary,

وَقَوْلِهِمْ إِنَّا قَتَلْنَا ٱلْمَسِيحَ    157 and for their saying, 'We killed the Messiah,

عِيسَى ٱبْنَ مَرْيَمَ رَسُولَ ٱللَّهِ    Jesus son of Mary, the apostle of Allah'

وَمَا قَتَلُوهُ    —though they did not kill him

وَمَا صَلَبُوهُ    nor did they crucify him,

وَلَـٰكِن شُبِّهَ لَهُمْ    but so it was made to appear to them.

وَإِنَّ ٱلَّذِينَ ٱخْتَلَفُوا۟ فِيهِ    Indeed those who differ concerning him[3]

لَفِى شَكٍّ مِّنْهُ    are surely in doubt about him:[4]

مَا لَهُم بِهِۦ مِنْ عِلْمٍ    they do not have any knowledge of that

إِلَّا ٱتِّبَاعَ ٱلظَّنِّ    beyond following conjectures,

وَمَا قَتَلُوهُ يَقِينًۢا ۝    and certainly they did not kill him.

بَل رَّفَعَهُ ٱللَّهُ إِلَيْهِ    158 Rather Allah raised him up toward Himself,

وَكَانَ ٱللَّهُ عَزِيزًا حَكِيمًا ۝    and Allah is all-mighty, all-wise.[5]

وَإِن مِّنْ أَهْلِ ٱلْكِتَـٰبِ    159 There is none among the People of the Book

إِلَّا لَيُؤْمِنَنَّ بِهِۦ قَبْلَ مَوْتِهِۦ    but will surely believe in him before his death;

---

[1] Ellipsis. The phrase omitted is: 'We cursed them.' Cf. 5:13, 2:88.

[2] That is, on their hearts.

[3] Or 'it.'

[4] Or 'it.'

[5] See verse 3:55 and the related footnote.

| | |
|---|---|
| وَيَوْمَ ٱلْقِيَـٰمَةِ | and on the Day of Resurrection |
| يَكُونُ عَلَيْهِمْ شَهِيدًا ۞ | he will be a witness against them. [1] |
| فَبِظُلْمٍ مِّنَ ٱلَّذِينَ هَادُواْ | 160 Due to the wrongdoing of the Jews, |
| حَرَّمْنَا عَلَيْهِمْ طَيِّبَـٰتٍ | We prohibited them certain good things |
| أُحِلَّتْ لَهُمْ | that were permitted to them [earlier], |
| وَبِصَدِّهِمْ | and for their barring |
| عَن سَبِيلِ ٱللَّهِ كَثِيرًا ۞ | many [people] from the way of Allah, |
| وَأَخْذِهِمُ ٱلرِّبَوٰاْ | 161 and for their taking usury |
| وَقَدْ نُهُواْ عَنْهُ | —though they had been forbidden from it— |
| وَأَكْلِهِمْ أَمْوَٰلَ ٱلنَّاسِ بِٱلْبَـٰطِلِ | and for eating up the wealth of the people wrongfully. |
| وَأَعْتَدْنَا لِلْكَـٰفِرِينَ مِنْهُمْ | And We have prepared for the faithless among them |
| عَذَابًا أَلِيمًا ۞ | a painful punishment. |
| لَّـٰكِنِ ٱلرَّٰسِخُونَ فِى ٱلْعِلْمِ | 162 But as for those who are firmly grounded in knowledge |
| مِنْهُمْ | from among them, |
| وَٱلْمُؤْمِنُونَ | and the faithful, |
| يُؤْمِنُونَ بِمَآ أُنزِلَ إِلَيْكَ | they believe in what has been sent down to *you*, |
| وَمَآ أُنزِلَ مِن قَبْلِكَ | and what was sent down before *you* |
| وَٱلْمُقِيمِينَ ٱلصَّلَوٰةَ | —those who maintain the prayer, |
| وَٱلْمُؤْتُونَ ٱلزَّكَوٰةَ | give the *zakāt*, |
| وَٱلْمُؤْمِنُونَ بِٱللَّهِ وَٱلْيَوْمِ ٱلْءَاخِرِ | and believe in Allah and the Last Day |
| أُوْلَـٰٓئِكَ سَنُؤْتِيهِمْ أَجْرًا عَظِيمًا ۞ | —them We shall give a great reward. |
| إِنَّآ أَوْحَيْنَآ إِلَيْكَ | 163 We have indeed revealed to *you* |
| كَمَآ أَوْحَيْنَآ إِلَىٰ نُوحٍ | as We revealed to Noah |
| وَٱلنَّبِيِّـۧنَ مِنۢ بَعْدِهِۦ | and the prophets after him, |
| وَأَوْحَيْنَآ إِلَىٰٓ إِبْرَٰهِيمَ وَإِسْمَـٰعِيلَ | and [as] We revealed to Abraham and Ishmael, |
| وَإِسْحَـٰقَ وَيَعْقُوبَ وَٱلْأَسْبَاطِ | Isaac, Jacob, and the Tribes, |
| وَعِيسَىٰ وَأَيُّوبَ | Jesus and Job, |
| وَيُونُسَ وَهَـٰرُونَ وَسُلَيْمَـٰنَ | Jonah, Aaron, and Solomon, |

---

[1] That is, every Jew or Christian, before dying, will believe in the Prophet Muḥammad (ṣ), or, according to another interpretation, in Jesus (ʿa).

وَءَاتَيْنَا دَاوُۥدَ زَبُورًا ۝

—and We gave David the Psalms—

وَرُسُلًا قَدْ قَصَصْنَٰهُمْ عَلَيْكَ مِن قَبْلُ    164

and apostles We have recounted to *you* earlier

وَرُسُلًا لَّمْ نَقْصُصْهُمْ عَلَيْكَ

and apostles We have not recounted to *you*,

وَكَلَّمَ ٱللَّهُ مُوسَىٰ تَكْلِيمًا ۝

—and to Moses Allah spoke directly—

رُّسُلًا مُّبَشِّرِينَ وَمُنذِرِينَ    165

apostles, as bearers of good news and warners,

لِئَلَّا يَكُونَ لِلنَّاسِ

so that mankind may not have

عَلَى ٱللَّهِ حُجَّةٌ

any argument against Allah,

بَعْدَ ٱلرُّسُلِ

after the [sending of the] apostles;

وَكَانَ ٱللَّهُ عَزِيزًا حَكِيمًا ۝

and Allah is all-mighty, all-wise.

لَّٰكِنِ ٱللَّهُ يَشْهَدُ    166

But Allah bears witness

بِمَآ أَنزَلَ إِلَيْكَ

to what He has sent down to *you*

أَنزَلَهُۥ بِعِلْمِهِۦ

—He sent it down with His knowledge—

وَٱلْمَلَٰٓئِكَةُ يَشْهَدُونَ

and the angels bear witness [too],

وَكَفَىٰ بِٱللَّهِ شَهِيدًا ۝

and Allah quite suffices as a witness.

إِنَّ ٱلَّذِينَ كَفَرُوا۟    167

Indeed those who are faithless

وَصَدُّوا۟ عَن سَبِيلِ ٱللَّهِ

and bar [others] from the way of Allah,

قَدْ ضَلُّوا۟ ضَلَٰلًۢا بَعِيدًا ۝

have certainly strayed into far error.

إِنَّ ٱلَّذِينَ كَفَرُوا۟ وَظَلَمُوٓا۟    168

Indeed those who are faithless and do wrong,

لَمْ يَكُنِ ٱللَّهُ لِيَغْفِرَ لَهُمْ

Allah shall never forgive them,

وَلَا لِيَهْدِيَهُمْ طَرِيقًا ۝

nor shall He guide them to any way,

إِلَّا طَرِيقَ جَهَنَّمَ    169

except the way to hell,

خَٰلِدِينَ فِيهَآ أَبَدًا

to remain in it forever,

وَكَانَ ذَٰلِكَ عَلَى ٱللَّهِ يَسِيرًا ۝

and that is easy for Allah.

يَٰٓأَيُّهَا ٱلنَّاسُ    170

O mankind!

قَدْ جَآءَكُمُ ٱلرَّسُولُ

The Apostle has certainly brought you

بِٱلْحَقِّ مِن رَّبِّكُمْ

the truth from your Lord.

فَـَٔامِنُوا۟ خَيْرًا لَّكُمْ

So have faith! That is better for you.

وَإِن تَكْفُرُوا۟

And if you are faithless, [you should know that]

فَإِنَّ لِلَّهِ مَا فِى ٱلسَّمَٰوَٰتِ

to Allah indeed belongs whatever is in the heavens

وَٱلْأَرْضِ

and the earth,

وَكَانَ ٱللَّهُ عَلِيمًا حَكِيمًا ۝ and Allah is all-knowing, all-wise.

يَـٰٓأَهْلَ ٱلْكِتَـٰبِ 171 O People of the Book!

لَا تَغْلُوا۟ فِى دِينِكُمْ Do not exceed the bounds in your religion,

وَلَا تَقُولُوا۟ عَلَى ٱللَّهِ and do not attribute anything to Allah

إِلَّا ٱلْحَقَّ except the truth.

إِنَّمَا ٱلْمَسِيحُ عِيسَى ٱبْنُ مَرْيَمَ The Messiah, Jesus son of Mary, was only

رَسُولُ ٱللَّهِ an apostle of Allah,

وَكَلِمَتُهُۥٓ أَلْقَىٰهَآ إِلَىٰ مَرْيَمَ and His Word that He cast toward Mary

وَرُوحٌ مِّنْهُ and a spirit from Him.

فَـَٔامِنُوا۟ بِٱللَّهِ وَرُسُلِهِۦ So have faith in Allah and His apostles,

وَلَا تَقُولُوا۟ ثَلَـٰثَةٌ and do not say, '[God is] a trinity.'

ٱنتَهُوا۟ خَيْرًا لَّكُمْ Relinquish [such a creed]! That is better for you.

إِنَّمَا ٱللَّهُ إِلَـٰهٌ وَٰحِدٌ Allah is but the One God.

سُبْحَـٰنَهُۥٓ أَن يَكُونَ لَهُۥ وَلَدٌ He is far too immaculate to have any son.

لَّهُۥ مَا فِى ٱلسَّمَـٰوَٰتِ To Him belongs whatever is in the heavens

وَمَا فِى ٱلْأَرْضِ and whatever is on the earth,

وَكَفَىٰ بِٱللَّهِ وَكِيلًا ۝ and Allah suffices as trustee.

لَّن يَسْتَنكِفَ ٱلْمَسِيحُ 172 The Messiah would never disdain

أَن يَكُونَ عَبْدًا لِّلَّهِ being a servant of Allah,

وَلَا ٱلْمَلَـٰٓئِكَةُ ٱلْمُقَرَّبُونَ nor would the angels brought near [to Him].

وَمَن يَسْتَنكِفْ عَنْ عِبَادَتِهِۦ And whoever disdains His worship

وَيَسْتَكْبِرْ and is arrogant,

فَسَيَحْشُرُهُمْ إِلَيْهِ جَمِيعًا ۝ He will gather them all toward Him.

فَأَمَّا ٱلَّذِينَ ءَامَنُوا۟ 173 As for those who have faith

وَعَمِلُوا۟ ٱلصَّـٰلِحَـٰتِ and do righteous deeds,

فَيُوَفِّيهِمْ أُجُورَهُمْ He will pay them in full their rewards,

وَيَزِيدُهُم مِّن فَضْلِهِۦ and He will enhance them out of His grace.

وَأَمَّا ٱلَّذِينَ ٱسْتَنكَفُوا۟ وَٱسْتَكْبَرُوا۟ But those who are disdainful and arrogant,

فَيُعَذِّبُهُمْ عَذَابًا أَلِيمًا He will punish them with a painful punishment,

وَلَا يَجِدُونَ لَهُم مِّن دُونِ ٱللَّهِ and they will not find besides Allah

وَلِيًّا وَلَا نَصِيرًا ۝    any guardian or helper.

يَٰٓأَيُّهَا ٱلنَّاسُ    174 O mankind!

قَدْ جَآءَكُم بُرْهَٰنٌ    Certainly a proof[1] has come to you

مِّن رَّبِّكُمْ    from your Lord,

وَأَنزَلْنَآ إِلَيْكُمْ نُورًا مُّبِينًا ۝    and We have sent down to you a manifest light.[2]

فَأَمَّا ٱلَّذِينَ ءَامَنُوا۟ بِٱللَّهِ    175 As for those who have faith in Allah,

وَٱعْتَصَمُوا۟ بِهِۦ    and hold fast to Him,

فَسَيُدْخِلُهُمْ فِى رَحْمَةٍ مِّنْهُ وَفَضْلٍ    He will admit them to His mercy and grace,

وَيَهْدِيهِمْ إِلَيْهِ صِرَٰطًا مُّسْتَقِيمًا ۝    and He will guide them on a straight path to Him.

يَسْتَفْتُونَكَ    176 They ask *you* for a ruling.

قُلِ ٱللَّهُ يُفْتِيكُمْ    *Say,* 'Allah gives you a ruling

فِى ٱلْكَلَٰلَةِ    concerning the *kalālah*.[3]

إِنِ ٱمْرُؤٌا۟ هَلَكَ لَيْسَ لَهُۥ وَلَدٌ    If a man dies and he has no children [or parents],

وَلَهُۥٓ أُخْتٌ    but has a sister,

فَلَهَا نِصْفُ مَا تَرَكَ    for her shall be a half of what he leaves,

وَهُوَ يَرِثُهَآ    and he shall inherit from her

إِن لَّمْ يَكُن لَّهَا وَلَدٌ    if she has no children.

فَإِن كَانَتَا ٱثْنَتَيْنِ    If there be two sisters,

فَلَهُمَا ٱلثُّلُثَانِ مِمَّا تَرَكَ    then they shall receive two-thirds of what he leaves.

وَإِن كَانُوٓا۟ إِخْوَةً رِّجَالًا وَنِسَآءً    But if there be [several] brothers and sisters,

فَلِلذَّكَرِ مِثْلُ    then for the male shall be the like of

حَظِّ ٱلْأُنثَيَيْنِ    the share of two females.

يُبَيِّنُ ٱللَّهُ لَكُمْ    Allah explains [the laws] for you

أَن تَضِلُّوا۟    lest you should go astray,

وَٱللَّهُ بِكُلِّ شَىْءٍ عَلِيمٌ ۝    and Allah has knowledge of all things.

---

[1] That is, the Prophet Muḥammad (ṣ), or the Qur'ān.

[2] The Qur'ān, according to Mujāhid, Qatādah and Suddī. The *wilāyah* of Imām 'Alī b. Abī Ṭālib ('a) according to traditions from Imām Ja'far b. Muḥammad al-Ṣādiq ('a) and Imām Muḥammad al-Bāqir ('a). See the commentaries of Furāt al-Kūfī and al-'Ayyāshī. under this verse.

[3] See the footnote at verse 4:12 above.

143

سُورَةُ الْمَائِدَة

# 5. SŪRAT AL-MĀ'IDAH[1]

بِسْمِ اللَّهِ
الرَّحْمَٰنِ الرَّحِيمِ

In the Name of Allah,
the All-beneficent, the All-merciful.

يَـٰٓأَيُّهَا ٱلَّذِينَ ءَامَنُوٓا۟
أَوْفُوا۟ بِٱلْعُقُودِ
أُحِلَّتْ لَكُم بَهِيمَةُ ٱلْأَنْعَٰمِ
إِلَّا مَا يُتْلَىٰ عَلَيْكُمْ
غَيْرَ مُحِلِّى ٱلصَّيْدِ
وَأَنتُمْ حُرُمٌ
إِنَّ ٱللَّهَ يَحْكُمُ مَا يُرِيدُ ۞

1 O you who have faith!
Keep your agreements.
You are permitted animals of grazing livestock,
    except what is [now] announced to you,
    disallowing game
    while your are in pilgrim sanctity.[2]
Indeed Allah decrees whatever He desires.

يَـٰٓأَيُّهَا ٱلَّذِينَ ءَامَنُوا۟
لَا تُحِلُّوا۟ شَعَـٰٓئِرَ ٱللَّهِ
وَلَا ٱلشَّهْرَ ٱلْحَرَامَ وَلَا ٱلْهَدْىَ
وَلَا ٱلْقَلَـٰٓئِدَ
وَلَآ ءَآمِّينَ ٱلْبَيْتَ ٱلْحَرَامَ
يَبْتَغُونَ فَضْلًا مِّن رَّبِّهِمْ
وَرِضْوَٰنًا
وَإِذَا حَلَلْتُمْ
فَٱصْطَادُوا۟
وَلَا يَجْرِمَنَّكُمْ شَنَـَٔانُ قَوْمٍ
أَن صَدُّوكُمْ
عَنِ ٱلْمَسْجِدِ ٱلْحَرَامِ

2 O you who have faith!
Do not violate Allah's sacraments,
    neither the sacred month,[3] nor the offering,[4]
    nor the necklaces,
    nor those bound[5] for the Sacred House
    who seek their Lord's grace
    and [His] pleasure.
But when you emerge from pilgrim sanctity
    you may hunt for game.
Ill feeling for a people should not lead you,
    because they barred you
    from [entering] the Sacred Mosque,

---

[1] The *sūrah* takes its name from 'the table' (*al-mā'idah*) mentioned in verses 112-
    115, towards its end.

[2] That is, while you are in a state of *iḥrām*, while performing *ḥajj* or *'umrah*.

[3] That is, the month of *Dhū al-Ḥijjah*, during which the *ḥajj* is performed.

[4] That is, the sheep, camel or cow brought for the sacrifice. The 'necklaces' mean
    the token objects hung around the neck of the sacrificial animal.

[5] That is the pilgrims heading for *ḥajj* or *'umrah*.

أَن تَعْتَدُوا۟

to transgress.

وَتَعَاوَنُوا۟ عَلَى ٱلْبِرِّ وَٱلتَّقْوَىٰ

Cooperate in piety and Godwariness,

وَلَا تَعَاوَنُوا۟ عَلَى ٱلْإِثْمِ وَٱلْعُدْوَٰنِ

but do not cooperate in sin and aggression,

وَٱتَّقُوا۟ ٱللَّهَ

and be wary of Allah.

إِنَّ ٱللَّهَ شَدِيدُ ٱلْعِقَابِ ۝

Indeed Allah is severe in retribution.

حُرِّمَتْ عَلَيْكُمُ ٱلْمَيْتَةُ

3 You are prohibited carrion,

وَٱلدَّمُ وَلَحْمُ ٱلْخِنزِيرِ

blood, the flesh of swine,

وَمَآ أُهِلَّ لِغَيْرِ ٱللَّهِ بِهِۦ

and what has been offered to other than Allah,

وَٱلْمُنْخَنِقَةُ وَٱلْمَوْقُوذَةُ

and the animal strangled or beaten to death,

وَٱلْمُتَرَدِّيَةُ وَٱلنَّطِيحَةُ

and that which dies by falling or is gored to death,

وَمَآ أَكَلَ ٱلسَّبُعُ

and that which is mangled by a beast of prey

إِلَّا مَا ذَكَّيْتُمْ

—barring that which you may purify[1]—

وَمَا ذُبِحَ عَلَى ٱلنُّصُبِ

and what is sacrificed on stone altars [to idols],

وَأَن تَسْتَقْسِمُوا۟ بِٱلْأَزْلَٰمِ

and that you should divide by raffling with arrows.

ذَٰلِكُمْ فِسْقٌ

All that is transgression.

ٱلْيَوْمَ يَئِسَ ٱلَّذِينَ كَفَرُوا۟ مِن دِينِكُمْ

Today the faithless have despaired of your religion.

فَلَا تَخْشَوْهُمْ وَٱخْشَوْنِ

So do not fear them, but fear Me.

ٱلْيَوْمَ أَكْمَلْتُ لَكُمْ دِينَكُمْ

Today I have perfected your religion for you,

وَأَتْمَمْتُ عَلَيْكُمْ نِعْمَتِى

and I have completed My blessing upon you,

وَرَضِيتُ لَكُمُ ٱلْإِسْلَٰمَ دِينًا

and I have approved Islam as your religion.

فَمَنِ ٱضْطُرَّ فِى مَخْمَصَةٍ

But should anyone be compelled by hunger,

غَيْرَ مُتَجَانِفٍ لِّإِثْمٍ

without inclining to sin,

فَإِنَّ ٱللَّهَ غَفُورٌ رَّحِيمٌ ۝

then Allah is indeed all-forgiving, all-merciful.

يَسْـَٔلُونَكَ مَاذَآ أُحِلَّ لَهُمْ

4 They ask *you* as to what is lawful to them.

قُلْ أُحِلَّ لَكُمُ ٱلطَّيِّبَٰتُ

*Say,* 'All the good things are lawful to you.'

وَمَا عَلَّمْتُم مِّنَ ٱلْجَوَارِحِ مُكَلِّبِينَ

As for what you have taught hunting dogs [to catch],

تُعَلِّمُونَهُنَّ مِمَّا عَلَّمَكُمُ ٱللَّهُ

teaching them out of what Allah has taught you,

---

[1] That is, by duly slaughtering the animal wounded by the beast of prey.

فَكُلُواْ مِمَّآ أَمْسَكْنَ عَلَيْكُمْ
eat of what they catch for you

وَٱذْكُرُواْ ٱسْمَ ٱللَّهِ عَلَيْهِ
and mention Allah's Name over it,

وَٱتَّقُواْ ٱللَّهَ
and be wary of Allah.

إِنَّ ٱللَّهَ سَرِيعُ ٱلْحِسَابِ ۝
Indeed Allah is swift at reckoning.

ٱلْيَوْمَ
5 Today

أُحِلَّ لَكُمُ ٱلطَّيِّبَٰتُ
all the good things have been made lawful to you:

وَطَعَامُ ٱلَّذِينَ أُوتُواْ ٱلْكِتَٰبَ
—the food of those who were given the Book

حِلٌّ لَّكُمْ
is lawful to you,

وَطَعَامُكُمْ حِلٌّ لَّهُمْ
and your food is lawful to them—

وَٱلْمُحْصَنَٰتُ مِنَ ٱلْمُؤْمِنَٰتِ
and the chaste ones from among faithful women,

وَٱلْمُحْصَنَٰتُ
and chaste women

مِنَ ٱلَّذِينَ أُوتُواْ ٱلْكِتَٰبَ مِن قَبْلِكُمْ
of those who were given the Book before you,

إِذَآ ءَاتَيْتُمُوهُنَّ أُجُورَهُنَّ
when you have given them their dowries,

مُحْصِنِينَ غَيْرَ مُسَٰفِحِينَ
in wedlock, not in license,

وَلَا مُتَّخِذِىٓ أَخْدَانٍ
nor taking paramours.

وَمَن يَكْفُرْ بِٱلْإِيمَٰنِ
Should anyone renounce his faith,

فَقَدْ حَبِطَ عَمَلُهُ
his work shall fail

وَهُوَ فِى ٱلْأَخِرَةِ مِنَ ٱلْخَٰسِرِينَ ۝
and he will be among the losers in the Hereafter.

يَٰٓأَيُّهَا ٱلَّذِينَ ءَامَنُوٓاْ
6 O you who have faith!

إِذَا قُمْتُمْ إِلَى ٱلصَّلَوٰةِ
When you stand up for prayer,

فَٱغْسِلُواْ وُجُوهَكُمْ
wash your faces

وَأَيْدِيَكُمْ إِلَى ٱلْمَرَافِقِ
and your hands up to the elbows,

وَٱمْسَحُواْ بِرُءُوسِكُمْ وَأَرْجُلَكُمْ
and wipe a part of your heads and your feet,

إِلَى ٱلْكَعْبَيْنِ
up to the ankles.

وَإِن كُنتُمْ جُنُبًا فَٱطَّهَّرُواْ
If you are *junub*, purify yourselves.

وَإِن كُنتُم مَّرْضَىٰٓ أَوْ عَلَىٰ سَفَرٍ
But if you are sick, or on a journey,

أَوْ جَآءَ أَحَدٌ مِّنكُم مِّنَ ٱلْغَآئِطِ
or any of you has come from the toilet,

أَوْ لَٰمَسْتُمُ ٱلنِّسَآءَ
or you have touched women,[1]

فَلَمْ تَجِدُواْ مَآءً
and you cannot find water,

---

[1] That is, if you have had sexual intercourse.

فَتَيَمَّمُواْ صَعِيدًا طَيِّبًا

then make *tayammum* with clean ground

فَٱمْسَحُواْ بِوُجُوهِكُمْ وَأَيْدِيكُم مِّنْهُ

and wipe a part of your faces and your hands
with it.

مَا يُرِيدُ ٱللَّهُ

Allah does not desire

لِيَجْعَلَ عَلَيْكُم مِّنْ حَرَجٍ

to put you to hardship,

وَلَٰكِن يُرِيدُ لِيُطَهِّرَكُمْ

but He desires to purify you,

وَلِيُتِمَّ نِعْمَتَهُۥ عَلَيْكُمْ

and to complete His blessing upon you

لَعَلَّكُمْ تَشْكُرُونَ ۝

so that you may give thanks.

وَٱذْكُرُواْ نِعْمَةَ ٱللَّهِ عَلَيْكُمْ

7 Remember Allah's blessing upon you

وَمِيثَٰقَهُ ٱلَّذِى وَاثَقَكُم بِهِۦٓ

and His covenant with which He has bound you

إِذْ قُلْتُمْ سَمِعْنَا وَأَطَعْنَا

when you said, 'We hear and obey.'

وَٱتَّقُواْ ٱللَّهَ

And be wary of Allah.

إِنَّ ٱللَّهَ عَلِيمٌۢ بِذَاتِ ٱلصُّدُورِ ۝

Indeed Allah knows best what is in the breasts.

يَٰٓأَيُّهَا ٱلَّذِينَ ءَامَنُواْ

8 O you who have faith!

كُونُواْ قَوَّٰمِينَ

Be maintainers,

لِلَّهِ شُهَدَآءَ

as witnesses for the sake of Allah,

بِٱلْقِسْطِ

of justice,[1]

وَلَا يَجْرِمَنَّكُمْ شَنَـَٔانُ قَوْمٍ

and ill feeling for a people should never lead you

عَلَىٰٓ أَلَّا تَعْدِلُواْ

to be unfair.

ٱعْدِلُواْ هُوَ أَقْرَبُ لِلتَّقْوَىٰ

Be fair; that is nearer to Godwariness,

وَٱتَّقُواْ ٱللَّهَ

and be wary of Allah.

إِنَّ ٱللَّهَ خَبِيرٌۢ بِمَا تَعْمَلُونَ ۝

Allah is indeed well aware of what you do.

وَعَدَ ٱللَّهُ ٱلَّذِينَ ءَامَنُواْ

9 Allah has promised those who have faith

وَعَمِلُواْ ٱلصَّٰلِحَٰتِ

and do righteous deeds

هُم مَّغْفِرَةٌ وَأَجْرٌ عَظِيمٌ ۝

forgiveness and a great reward.

وَٱلَّذِينَ كَفَرُواْ وَكَذَّبُواْ بِـَٔايَٰتِنَآ

10 As for those who are faithless and deny Our signs,

أُوْلَٰٓئِكَ أَصْحَٰبُ ٱلْجَحِيمِ ۝

they shall be the inmates of hell.

يَٰٓأَيُّهَا ٱلَّذِينَ ءَامَنُواْ

11 O you who have faith!

ٱذْكُرُواْ نِعْمَتَ ٱللَّهِ عَلَيْكُمْ

Remember Allah's blessing upon you

---

[1] Cf. 4:135.

إِذْ هَمَّ قَوْمٌ
أَن يَبْسُطُوٓاْ إِلَيْكُمْ أَيْدِيَهُمْ
فَكَفَّ أَيْدِيَهُمْ عَنكُمْ
وَٱتَّقُواْ ٱللَّهَ
وَعَلَى ٱللَّهِ فَلْيَتَوَكَّلِ ٱلْمُؤْمِنُونَ ۞

when a people set out

     to extend their hands against you,

       but He withheld their hands from you,

     and be wary of Allah,

     and in Allah let all the faithful put their trust.

وَلَقَدْ أَخَذَ ٱللَّهُ مِيثَٰقَ
بَنِىٓ إِسْرَٰٓءِيلَ
وَبَعَثْنَا مِنْهُمُ ٱثْنَىْ عَشَرَ نَقِيبًا
وَقَالَ ٱللَّهُ إِنِّى مَعَكُمْ
لَئِنْ أَقَمْتُمُ ٱلصَّلَوٰةَ وَءَاتَيْتُمُ ٱلزَّكَوٰةَ
وَءَامَنتُم بِرُسُلِى وَعَزَّرْتُمُوهُمْ
وَأَقْرَضْتُمُ ٱللَّهَ قَرْضًا حَسَنًا
لَّأُكَفِّرَنَّ عَنكُمْ سَيِّـَٔاتِكُمْ
وَلَأُدْخِلَنَّكُمْ جَنَّٰتٍ
تَجْرِى مِن تَحْتِهَا ٱلْأَنْهَٰرُ
فَمَن كَفَرَ بَعْدَ ذَٰلِكَ مِنكُمْ
فَقَدْ ضَلَّ سَوَآءَ ٱلسَّبِيلِ ۞

12 Certainly Allah took a pledge

     from the Children of Israel,

     and We raised among them twelve chiefs.

     And Allah said, 'I am with you!

Surely, if you maintain the prayer and give the *zakāt*

     and have faith in My apostles and support them

     and lend Allah a good loan,

I will surely absolve you of your misdeeds,

     and I will surely admit you into gardens

     with streams running in them.

But whoever of you disbelieves after that

     has certainly strayed from the right way.'

فَبِمَا نَقْضِهِم مِّيثَٰقَهُمْ
لَعَنَّٰهُمْ وَجَعَلْنَا قُلُوبَهُمْ قَٰسِيَةً
يُحَرِّفُونَ ٱلْكَلِمَ عَن مَّوَاضِعِهِۦ
وَنَسُواْ حَظًّا مِّمَّا ذُكِّرُواْ بِهِۦ
وَلَا تَزَالُ تَطَّلِعُ عَلَىٰ خَآئِنَةٍ مِّنْهُمْ
إِلَّا قَلِيلًا مِّنْهُمْ
فَٱعْفُ عَنْهُمْ وَٱصْفَحْ
إِنَّ ٱللَّهَ يُحِبُّ ٱلْمُحْسِنِينَ ۞

13 Then, because of their breaking their covenant

     We cursed them and made their hearts hard:

they pervert words from their meanings,

     and have forgotten a part of what they were reminded.

*You* will not cease to learn of some of their treachery,

     excepting a few of them.

Yet excuse them and forbear.

Indeed Allah loves the virtuous.

وَمِنَ ٱلَّذِينَ قَالُوٓاْ إِنَّا نَصَٰرَىٰٓ
أَخَذْنَا مِيثَٰقَهُمْ
فَنَسُواْ حَظًّا مِّمَّا ذُكِّرُواْ بِهِۦ
فَأَغْرَيْنَا بَيْنَهُمُ ٱلْعَدَاوَةَ وَٱلْبَغْضَآءَ
إِلَىٰ يَوْمِ ٱلْقِيَٰمَةِ

14 Also from those who say, 'We are Christians,'

     We took their pledge;

but they forgot a part of what they were reminded.

So We stirred up enmity and hatred among them

     until the Day of Resurrection,

وَسَوْفَ يُنَبِّئُهُمُ ٱللَّهُ    and soon Allah will inform them

بِمَا كَانُوا۟ يَصْنَعُونَ ۝    concerning what they had been doing.

يَـٰٓأَهْلَ ٱلْكِتَـٰبِ    15 O People of the Book!

قَدْ جَآءَكُمْ رَسُولُنَا    Certainly Our Apostle has come to you,

يُبَيِّنُ لَكُمْ    clarifying for you

كَثِيرًا مِّمَّا كُنتُمْ تُخْفُونَ مِنَ ٱلْكِتَـٰبِ    much of what you used to hide of the Book,

وَيَعْفُوا۟ عَن كَثِيرٍ    and excusing many [an offense of yours].

قَدْ جَآءَكُم مِّنَ ٱللَّهِ نُورٌ    Certainly there has come to you a light from Allah,

وَكِتَـٰبٌ مُّبِينٌ ۝    and a manifest Book.

يَهْدِى بِهِ ٱللَّهُ مَنِ ٱتَّبَعَ    16 With it Allah guides those who follow

رِضْوَٰنَهُۥ    [the course of] His pleasure

سُبُلَ ٱلسَّلَـٰمِ    to the ways of peace,

وَيُخْرِجُهُم مِّنَ ٱلظُّلُمَـٰتِ إِلَى ٱلنُّورِ    and brings them out from darkness into light

بِإِذْنِهِۦ    by His will,

وَيَهْدِيهِمْ إِلَىٰ صِرَٰطٍ مُّسْتَقِيمٍ ۝    and guides them to a straight path.

لَّقَدْ كَفَرَ ٱلَّذِينَ قَالُوٓا۟    17 They are certainly faithless who say,

إِنَّ ٱللَّهَ هُوَ ٱلْمَسِيحُ ٱبْنُ مَرْيَمَ    'Allah is the Messiah, son of Mary.'

قُلْ فَمَن يَمْلِكُ مِنَ ٱللَّهِ شَيْـًٔا    *Say,* 'Who can avail anything against Allah

إِنْ أَرَادَ أَن يُهْلِكَ ٱلْمَسِيحَ ٱبْنَ مَرْيَمَ    should He wish to destroy the Messiah, son of Mary,

وَأُمَّهُۥ وَمَن فِى ٱلْأَرْضِ جَمِيعًا    and his mother, and everyone upon the earth?'

وَلِلَّهِ مُلْكُ ٱلسَّمَـٰوَٰتِ    To Allah belongs the kingdom of the heavens

وَٱلْأَرْضِ    and the earth,

وَمَا بَيْنَهُمَا    and whatever is between them.

يَخْلُقُ مَا يَشَآءُ    He creates whatever He wishes,

وَٱللَّهُ عَلَىٰ كُلِّ شَىْءٍ قَدِيرٌ ۝    and Allah has power over all things.

وَقَالَتِ ٱلْيَهُودُ وَٱلنَّصَـٰرَىٰ    18 The Jews and the Christians say,

نَحْنُ أَبْنَـٰٓؤُا۟ ٱللَّهِ وَأَحِبَّـٰٓؤُهُۥ    'We are Allah's children and His beloved ones.'

قُلْ فَلِمَ يُعَذِّبُكُم بِذُنُوبِكُم    *Say,* 'Then why does He punish you for your sins?'

بَلْ أَنتُم بَشَرٌ مِّمَّنْ خَلَقَ    Rather you are humans from among His creatures.

149

يَغْفِرُ لِمَن يَشَاءُ
He forgives whomever He wishes,

وَيُعَذِّبُ مَن يَشَاءُ
and punishes whomever He wishes,

وَلِلَّهِ مُلْكُ ٱلسَّمَـٰوَٰتِ
and to Allah belongs the kingdom of the heavens

وَٱلْأَرْضِ
and the earth,

وَمَا بَيْنَهُمَا
and whatever is between them,

وَإِلَيْهِ ٱلْمَصِيرُ ۝
and toward Him is the return.

يَـٰٓأَهْلَ ٱلْكِتَـٰبِ
19 O People of the Book!

قَدْ جَآءَكُمْ رَسُولُنَا
Certainly Our Apostle has come to you,

يُبَيِّنُ لَكُمْ
clarifying [the Divine teachings] for you

عَلَىٰ فَتْرَةٍ مِّنَ ٱلرُّسُلِ
after a gap in [the appearance of] the apostles,

أَن تَقُولُوا۟
lest you should say,

مَا جَآءَنَا مِنۢ بَشِيرٍ
'There did not come to us any bearer of good news

وَلَا نَذِيرٍ
nor any warner.'

فَقَدْ جَآءَكُم بَشِيرٌ
Certainly there has come to you

وَنَذِيرٌ
a bearer of good news and a warner.

وَٱللَّهُ عَلَىٰ كُلِّ شَىْءٍ قَدِيرٌ ۝
And Allah has power over all things.

وَإِذْ قَالَ مُوسَىٰ لِقَوْمِهِ
20 When Moses said to his people,

يَـٰقَوْمِ ٱذْكُرُوا۟ نِعْمَةَ ٱللَّهِ عَلَيْكُمْ
'O my people, remember Allah's blessing upon you

إِذْ جَعَلَ فِيكُمْ أَنۢبِيَآءَ
when He appointed prophets among you,

وَجَعَلَكُم مُّلُوكًا
and made you kings,

وَءَاتَىٰكُم
and gave you

مَّا لَمْ يُؤْتِ أَحَدًا مِّنَ ٱلْعَـٰلَمِينَ ۝
what none of the nations were given.

يَـٰقَوْمِ ٱدْخُلُوا۟ ٱلْأَرْضَ ٱلْمُقَدَّسَةَ
21 O my people, enter the Holy Land

ٱلَّتِى كَتَبَ ٱللَّهُ لَكُمْ
which Allah has ordained for you,

وَلَا تَرْتَدُّوا۟ عَلَىٰٓ أَدْبَارِكُمْ
and do not turn your backs

فَتَنقَلِبُوا۟ خَـٰسِرِينَ ۝
or you will become losers.'

قَالُوا۟ يَـٰمُوسَىٰٓ
22 They said, 'O Moses,

إِنَّ فِيهَا قَوْمًا جَبَّارِينَ
there are a tyrannical people in it.

وَإِنَّا لَن نَّدْخُلَهَا حَتَّىٰ يَخْرُجُوا۟ مِنْهَا
We will not enter it until they leave it.

فَإِن يَخْرُجُوا مِنْهَا فَإِنَّا دَٰخِلُونَ ٢٢

But once they leave it, we will go in.'

قَالَ رَجُلَانِ مِنَ ٱلَّذِينَ يَخَافُونَ
23 Said two men from among those who were Godfearing

أَنْعَمَ ٱللَّهُ عَلَيْهِمَا
and whom Allah had blessed:

ٱدْخُلُوا عَلَيْهِمُ ٱلْبَابَ
'Go at them by the gate!

فَإِذَا دَخَلْتُمُوهُ فَإِنَّكُمْ غَٰلِبُونَ
For once you have entered it, you will be victors.

وَعَلَى ٱللَّهِ فَتَوَكَّلُوا إِن كُنتُم مُّؤْمِنِينَ ٢٣
Put your trust in Allah, should you be faithful.'

قَالُوا يَٰمُوسَىٰ
24 They said, 'O Moses,

إِنَّا لَن نَّدْخُلَهَا أَبَدًا مَّا دَامُوا فِيهَا
we will never enter it so long as they remain in it.

فَٱذْهَبْ أَنتَ وَرَبُّكَ فَقَٰتِلَا
Go ahead, you and your Lord, and fight!

إِنَّا هَٰهُنَا قَٰعِدُونَ ٢٤
We will be sitting right here.'

قَالَ رَبِّ
25 He said, 'My Lord!

إِنِّي لَآ أَمْلِكُ إِلَّا نَفْسِي
I have no power over [anyone] except myself

وَأَخِي
and my brother,

فَٱفْرُقْ بَيْنَنَا وَبَيْنَ ٱلْقَوْمِ ٱلْفَٰسِقِينَ ٢٥
so part us from the transgressing lot.'

قَالَ فَإِنَّهَا مُحَرَّمَةٌ عَلَيْهِمْ أَرْبَعِينَ سَنَةً
26 He said, 'It shall be forbidden them for forty years:

يَتِيهُونَ فِي ٱلْأَرْضِ
they shall wander about in the earth.

فَلَا تَأْسَ عَلَى ٱلْقَوْمِ ٱلْفَٰسِقِينَ ٢٦ ۞
So do not grieve for the transgressing lot.'

وَٱتْلُ عَلَيْهِمْ نَبَأَ ٱبْنَيْ ءَادَمَ بِٱلْحَقِّ
27 *Relate* to them truly the account of Adam's two sons.

إِذْ قَرَّبَا قُرْبَانًا
When the two of them offered an offering,

فَتُقُبِّلَ مِنْ أَحَدِهِمَا
it was accepted from one of them

وَلَمْ يُتَقَبَّلْ مِنَ ٱلْآخَرِ
and not accepted from the other.

قَالَ لَأَقْتُلَنَّكَ
[One of them] said, 'Surely I will kill you.'

قَالَ
[The other one] said,

إِنَّمَا يَتَقَبَّلُ ٱللَّهُ مِنَ ٱلْمُتَّقِينَ ٢٧
'Allah accepts only from the Godwary.

لَئِن بَسَطتَ إِلَيَّ يَدَكَ لِتَقْتُلَنِي
28 Even if you extend your hand toward me to kill me,

مَآ أَنَا۠ بِبَاسِطٍ يَدِيَ إِلَيْكَ لِأَقْتُلَكَ
I will not extend my hand toward you to kill you.

إِنِّي أَخَافُ ٱللَّهَ
Indeed I fear Allah,

رَبَّ ٱلْعَٰلَمِينَ ٢٨
the Lord of all the worlds.

إِنِّي أُرِيدُ أَن تَبُوٓأَ
29 I desire that you earn [the burden of]

بِإِثْمِى وَإِثْمِكَ     my sin[1] and your sin,

فَتَكُونَ مِنْ أَصْحَـٰبِ ٱلنَّارِ     to become one of the inmates of the Fire,

وَذَٰلِكَ جَزَٰٓؤُاْ ٱلظَّـٰلِمِينَ ۝     and such is the requital of the wrongdoers.'

فَطَوَّعَتْ لَهُۥ نَفْسُهُۥ قَتْلَ أَخِيهِ     30 So his soul prompted him to kill his brother,

فَقَتَلَهُۥ     and he killed him,

فَأَصْبَحَ مِنَ ٱلْخَـٰسِرِينَ ۝     and thus became one of the losers.

فَبَعَثَ ٱللَّهُ غُرَابًا يَبْحَثُ فِى ٱلْأَرْضِ     31 Then Allah sent a crow, exploring in the ground,

لِيُرِيَهُۥ كَيْفَ يُوَٰرِى سَوْءَةَ أَخِيهِ     to show him how to bury the corpse of his brother.

قَالَ يَـٰوَيْلَتَىٰٓ     He said, 'Woe to me!

أَعَجَزْتُ أَنْ أَكُونَ مِثْلَ هَـٰذَا ٱلْغُرَابِ     Am I unable to be [even] like this crow

فَأُوَٰرِىَ سَوْءَةَ أَخِى     and bury my brother's corpse?'

فَأَصْبَحَ مِنَ ٱلنَّـٰدِمِينَ ۝     Thus he became regretful.

مِنْ أَجْلِ ذَٰلِكَ كَتَبْنَا عَلَىٰ بَنِىٓ إِسْرَٰٓءِيلَ     32 That is why We decreed for the Children of Israel

أَنَّهُۥ مَن قَتَلَ نَفْسًۢا     that whoever kills a soul,[2]

بِغَيْرِ نَفْسٍ     without [its being guilty of] manslaughter

أَوْ فَسَادٍ فِى ٱلْأَرْضِ     or corruption on the earth,

فَكَأَنَّمَا قَتَلَ ٱلنَّاسَ جَمِيعًا     is as though he had killed all mankind,

وَمَنْ أَحْيَاهَا     and whoever saves a life

فَكَأَنَّمَآ أَحْيَا ٱلنَّاسَ جَمِيعًا     is as though he had saved all mankind.

وَلَقَدْ جَآءَتْهُمْ رُسُلُنَا بِٱلْبَيِّنَـٰتِ     Our apostles certainly brought them manifest signs,

ثُمَّ إِنَّ كَثِيرًا مِّنْهُم بَعْدَ ذَٰلِكَ     yet even after that many of them

فِى ٱلْأَرْضِ لَمُسْرِفُونَ ۝     commit excesses on the earth.

إِنَّمَا جَزَٰٓؤُاْ ٱلَّذِينَ يُحَارِبُونَ     33 Indeed the requital of those who wage war

ٱللَّهَ وَرَسُولَهُۥ     against Allah and His Apostle,

وَيَسْعَوْنَ فِى ٱلْأَرْضِ فَسَادًا     and try to cause corruption on the earth,

أَن يُقَتَّلُوٓاْ أَوْ يُصَلَّبُوٓاْ     is that they shall be slain or crucified,

أَوْ تُقَطَّعَ أَيْدِيهِمْ وَأَرْجُلُهُم     or have their hands and feet cut off

مِّنْ خِلَـٰفٍ     from opposite sides

---

[1] That is, the sin of murdering me.

[2] Or 'takes a life.'

أَوْ يُنفَوْاْ مِنَ ٱلْأَرْضِ    or be banished from the land.

ذَٰلِكَ لَهُمْ خِزْىٌ فِى ٱلدُّنْيَا    That is a disgrace for them in this world,

وَلَهُمْ فِى ٱلْءَاخِرَةِ    and in the Hereafter

عَذَابٌ عَظِيمٌ ۝    there is a great punishment for them,

إِلَّا ٱلَّذِينَ تَابُواْ    34 excepting those who repent

مِن قَبْلِ أَن تَقْدِرُواْ عَلَيْهِمْ    before you capture them,

فَٱعْلَمُوٓاْ أَنَّ ٱللَّهَ غَفُورٌ رَّحِيمٌ ۝    and know that Allah is all-forgiving, all-merciful.

يَٰٓأَيُّهَا ٱلَّذِينَ ءَامَنُواْ    35 O you who have faith!

ٱتَّقُواْ ٱللَّهَ    Be wary of Allah,

وَٱبْتَغُوٓاْ إِلَيْهِ ٱلْوَسِيلَةَ    and seek the means of recourse to Him,

وَجَٰهِدُواْ فِى سَبِيلِهِ    and wage *jihād* in His way,

لَعَلَّكُمْ تُفْلِحُونَ ۝    so that you may be felicitous.

إِنَّ ٱلَّذِينَ كَفَرُوٓاْ لَوْ أَنَّ لَهُم    36 Indeed if the faithless possessed

مَّا فِى ٱلْأَرْضِ جَمِيعًا وَمِثْلَهُۥ مَعَهُۥ    all that is on the earth and as much of it besides

لِيَفْتَدُواْ بِهِۦ    to redeem themselves with it

مِنْ عَذَابِ يَوْمِ ٱلْقِيَٰمَةِ    from the punishment of the Day of Resurrection,

مَا تُقُبِّلَ مِنْهُمْ    it shall not be accepted from them,[1]

وَلَهُمْ عَذَابٌ أَلِيمٌ ۝    and there is a painful punishment for them.

يُرِيدُونَ أَن يَخْرُجُواْ مِنَ ٱلنَّارِ    37 They would long to leave the Fire,

وَمَا هُم بِخَٰرِجِينَ مِنْهَا    but they shall never leave it,

وَلَهُمْ عَذَابٌ مُّقِيمٌ ۝    and there is a lasting punishment for them.

وَٱلسَّارِقُ وَٱلسَّارِقَةُ    38 As for the thief, man or woman,

فَٱقْطَعُوٓاْ أَيْدِيَهُمَا    cut off their hands

جَزَآءًۢ بِمَا كَسَبَا    as a requital for what they have earned.

نَكَٰلًا مِّنَ ٱللَّهِ    [That is] an exemplary punishment from Allah,

وَٱللَّهُ عَزِيزٌ حَكِيمٌ ۝    and Allah is all-mighty, all-wise.

فَمَن تَابَ مِنْ بَعْدِ ظُلْمِهِۦ    39 But whoever repents after his wrongdoing,

وَأَصْلَحَ    and reforms,

فَإِنَّ ٱللَّهَ يَتُوبُ عَلَيْهِ    then Allah shall accept his repentance.

---

[1] Cf. 13:18 and 39:47.

إِنَّ ٱللَّهَ غَفُورٌ رَّحِيمٌ ۝    Indeed Allah is all-forgiving, all-merciful.

أَلَمْ تَعْلَمْ    40 Do you not know

أَنَّ ٱللَّهَ لَهُ مُلْكُ ٱلسَّمَٰوَٰتِ    that to Allah belongs the kingdom of the heavens

وَٱلْأَرْضِ    and the earth?

يُعَذِّبُ مَن يَشَآءُ    He punishes whomever He wishes,

وَيَغْفِرُ لِمَن يَشَآءُ    and forgives whomever He wishes,

وَٱللَّهُ عَلَىٰ كُلِّ شَىْءٍ قَدِيرٌ ۝    and Allah has power over all things.

يَٰٓأَيُّهَا ٱلرَّسُولُ لَا يَحْزُنكَ    41 O Apostle! *Do not grieve*

ٱلَّذِينَ يُسَٰرِعُونَ فِى ٱلْكُفْرِ    for those who are active in [promoting] unfaith,

مِنَ ٱلَّذِينَ قَالُوٓاْ ءَامَنَّا بِأَفْوَٰهِهِمْ    such as those who say, 'We believe' with their mouths,

وَلَمْ تُؤْمِن قُلُوبُهُمْ    but whose hearts have no faith,

وَمِنَ ٱلَّذِينَ هَادُواْ    and the Jews

سَمَّٰعُونَ لِلْكَذِبِ    who eavesdrop with the aim of [telling] lies [against *you*]

سَمَّٰعُونَ لِقَوْمٍ ءَاخَرِينَ لَمْ يَأْتُوكَ    and eavesdrop for other people who do not come to *you*.

يُحَرِّفُونَ ٱلْكَلِمَ مِنۢ بَعْدِ مَوَاضِعِهِۦ    They pervert words from their meanings,

يَقُولُونَ إِنْ أُوتِيتُمْ هَٰذَا فَخُذُوهُ    [and] say, 'If you are given this, take it,

وَإِن لَّمْ تُؤْتَوْهُ فَٱحْذَرُواْ    but if you are not given this, beware!'

وَمَن يُرِدِ ٱللَّهُ فِتْنَتَهُ    Yet whomever Allah wishes to mislead,[1]

فَلَن تَمْلِكَ لَهُ مِنَ ٱللَّهِ شَيْـًٔا    you cannot avail him anything against Allah.

أُوْلَٰٓئِكَ ٱلَّذِينَ    They are the ones

لَمْ يُرِدِ ٱللَّهُ أَن يُطَهِّرَ قُلُوبَهُمْ    whose hearts Allah did not desire to purify.

هُمْ فِى ٱلدُّنْيَا خِزْىٌ    For them is disgrace in this world,

وَلَهُمْ فِى ٱلْأَخِرَةِ عَذَابٌ عَظِيمٌ ۝    and there is a great punishment for them in the Hereafter.

سَمَّٰعُونَ لِلْكَذِبِ    42 Eavesdroppers with the aim of [telling] lies,

أَكَّٰلُونَ لِلسُّحْتِ    eaters of the unlawful

فَإِن جَآءُوكَ فَٱحْكُم بَيْنَهُمْ    —if they come to *you*, judge between them,

أَوْ أَعْرِضْ عَنْهُمْ    or disregard them.

وَإِن تُعْرِضْ عَنْهُمْ    If *you* disregard them,

فَلَن يَضُرُّوكَ شَيْـًٔا    they will not harm *you* in any way.

---

[1] Or 'to punish.'

وَإِنْ حَكَمْتَ فَٱحْكُم بَيْنَهُم بِٱلْقِسْطِ

But if *you* judge, judge between them with justice.

إِنَّ ٱللَّهَ يُحِبُّ ٱلْمُقْسِطِينَ ۝

Indeed Allah loves the just.

43 وَكَيْفَ يُحَكِّمُونَكَ

43 And how should they make *you* a judge,

وَعِندَهُمُ ٱلتَّوْرَىٰةُ

while with them is the Torah,

فِيهَا حُكْمُ ٱللَّهِ

in which is Allah's judgement?

ثُمَّ يَتَوَلَّوْنَ مِنۢ بَعْدِ ذَٰلِكَ

Yet in spite of that they turn their backs [on Him]

وَمَآ أُوْلَٰٓئِكَ بِٱلْمُؤْمِنِينَ ۝

and they are not believers.

44 إِنَّآ أَنزَلْنَا ٱلتَّوْرَىٰةَ

44 We sent down the Torah

فِيهَا هُدًى وَنُورٌ

containing guidance and light.

يَحْكُمُ بِهَا ٱلنَّبِيُّونَ ٱلَّذِينَ أَسْلَمُواْ

The prophets, who had submitted,[1] judged by it

لِلَّذِينَ هَادُواْ

for the Jews,

وَٱلرَّبَّٰنِيُّونَ وَٱلْأَحْبَارُ

and so did the rabbis and the scribes,

بِمَا ٱسْتُحْفِظُواْ مِن كِتَٰبِ ٱللَّهِ

as they were charged to preserve the Book of Allah

وَكَانُواْ عَلَيْهِ شُهَدَآءَ

and were witnesses to it.

فَلَا تَخْشَوُاْ ٱلنَّاسَ وَٱخْشَوْنِ

So do not fear the people, but fear Me,

وَلَا تَشْتَرُواْ بِـَٔايَٰتِى ثَمَنًا قَلِيلًا

and do not sell My signs for a paltry gain.

وَمَن لَّمْ يَحْكُم بِمَآ أَنزَلَ ٱللَّهُ

Those who do not judge by what Allah has sent down

فَأُوْلَٰٓئِكَ هُمُ ٱلْكَٰفِرُونَ ۝

—it is they who are the faithless.

45 وَكَتَبْنَا عَلَيْهِمْ فِيهَآ

45 And in it We prescribed for them:

أَنَّ ٱلنَّفْسَ بِٱلنَّفْسِ

a life for a life,

وَٱلْعَيْنَ بِٱلْعَيْنِ

an eye for an eye,

وَٱلْأَنفَ بِٱلْأَنفِ وَٱلْأُذُنَ بِٱلْأُذُنِ

a nose for a nose, and an ear for an ear,

وَٱلسِّنَّ بِٱلسِّنِّ وَٱلْجُرُوحَ قِصَاصٌ

a tooth for a tooth, and retaliation for wounds.

فَمَن تَصَدَّقَ بِهِۦ

Yet whoever remits it out of charity,

فَهُوَ كَفَّارَةٌ لَّهُۥ

that shall be an atonement for him.

وَمَن لَّمْ يَحْكُم بِمَآ أَنزَلَ ٱللَّهُ

Those who do not judge by what Allah has sent down

فَأُوْلَٰٓئِكَ هُمُ ٱلظَّٰلِمُونَ ۝

—it is they who are the wrongdoers.

46 وَقَفَّيْنَا عَلَىٰٓ ءَاثَٰرِهِم بِعِيسَى ٱبْنِ مَرْيَمَ

46 And We followed them with Jesus son of Mary,

مُصَدِّقًا لِّمَا بَيْنَ يَدَيْهِ مِنَ ٱلتَّوْرَىٰةِ

to confirm that which was before him of the Torah,

---

[1] That is, to Allah's commandments as revealed to Moses.

وَءَاتَيْنَـٰهُ ٱلْإِنجِيلَ
and We gave him the Evangel

فِيهِ هُدًى وَنُورٌ
containing guidance and light,

وَمُصَدِّقًا لِّمَا بَيْنَ يَدَيْهِ مِنَ ٱلتَّوْرَىٰةِ
confirming what was before it of the Torah,

وَهُدًى وَمَوْعِظَةً لِّلْمُتَّقِينَ ۝
and as guidance and advice for the Godwary.

وَلْيَحْكُمْ أَهْلُ ٱلْإِنجِيلِ
47 Let the people of the Evangel judge

بِمَآ أَنزَلَ ٱللَّهُ فِيهِ
by what Allah has sent down in it.

وَمَن لَّمْ يَحْكُم بِمَآ أَنزَلَ ٱللَّهُ
Those who do not judge by what Allah has sent down

فَأُوْلَـٰئِكَ هُمُ ٱلْفَـٰسِقُونَ ۝
—it is they who are the transgressors.

وَأَنزَلْنَآ إِلَيْكَ ٱلْكِتَـٰبَ بِٱلْحَقِّ
48 We have sent down to *you* the Book with the truth,

مُصَدِّقًا لِّمَا بَيْنَ يَدَيْهِ مِنَ ٱلْكِتَـٰبِ
confirming what was before it of the Book

وَمُهَيْمِنًا عَلَيْهِ
and as a guardian over it.

فَٱحْكُم بَيْنَهُم بِمَآ أَنزَلَ ٱللَّهُ
So *judge* between them by what Allah has sent down,

وَلَا تَتَّبِعْ أَهْوَآءَهُمْ
and *do not follow* their desires

عَمَّا جَآءَكَ مِنَ ٱلْحَقِّ
against the truth that has come to *you*.

لِكُلٍّ جَعَلْنَا مِنكُمْ
For each [community] among you We had appointed

شِرْعَةً وَمِنْهَاجًا
a code [of law] and a path,[1]

وَلَوْ شَآءَ ٱللَّهُ
and had Allah wished

لَجَعَلَكُمْ أُمَّةً وَٰحِدَةً
He would have made you one community,

وَلَـٰكِن لِّيَبْلُوَكُمْ
but [His purposes required] that He should test you

فِى مَآ ءَاتَـٰكُمْ
in respect to what He has given you.

فَٱسْتَبِقُواْ ٱلْخَيْرَٰتِ
So take the lead in all good works.

إِلَى ٱللَّهِ مَرْجِعُكُمْ جَمِيعًا
To Allah shall be the return of you all,

فَيُنَبِّئُكُم
whereat He will inform you

بِمَا كُنتُمْ فِيهِ تَخْتَلِفُونَ ۝
concerning that about which you used to differ.

وَأَنِ ٱحْكُم بَيْنَهُم بِمَآ أَنزَلَ ٱللَّهُ
49 *Judge* between them by what Allah has sent down,

وَلَا تَتَّبِعْ أَهْوَآءَهُمْ
and *do not follow* their desires.

وَٱحْذَرْهُمْ أَن يَفْتِنُوكَ
*Beware* of them lest they should beguile *you*

عَنۢ بَعْضِ مَآ أَنزَلَ ٱللَّهُ إِلَيْكَ
from part of what Allah has sent down to *you*.

---

[1] Or, 'For everyone of you We have appointed a way of approach, whereby he comes' (reading *minhā jā'a*, instead of *minhāja*).

فَإِن تَوَلَّوْاْ

    But if they turn their backs [on *you*],

فَاعْلَمْ أَنَّمَا يُرِيدُ ٱللَّهُ أَن يُصِيبَهُم

        then *know* that Allah desires to punish them

بِبَعْضِ ذُنُوبِهِمْ

            for some of their sins,

وَإِنَّ كَثِيرًا مِّنَ ٱلنَّاسِ لَفَٰسِقُونَ ۝

    and indeed many of the people are transgressors.

أَفَحُكْمَ ٱلْجَٰهِلِيَّةِ يَبْغُونَ

50 Do they seek the judgement of [pagan] ignorance?

وَمَنْ أَحْسَنُ مِنَ ٱللَّهِ حُكْمًا

    But who is better than Allah in judgement

لِّقَوْمٍ يُوقِنُونَ ۝ ۞

        for a people who have certainty?

يَٰٓأَيُّهَا ٱلَّذِينَ ءَامَنُواْ

51 O you who have faith!

لَا تَتَّخِذُواْ ٱلْيَهُودَ وَٱلنَّصَٰرَىٰٓ أَوْلِيَآءَ

    Do not take the Jews and the Christians for friends:

بَعْضُهُمْ أَوْلِيَآءُ بَعْضٍ

        they are friends of each other.

وَمَن يَتَوَلَّهُم مِّنكُمْ

    Any of you who takes them as friends

فَإِنَّهُۥ مِنْهُمْ

    is indeed one of them.

إِنَّ ٱللَّهَ لَا يَهْدِى ٱلْقَوْمَ ٱلظَّٰلِمِينَ ۝

    Indeed Allah does not guide the wrongdoing lot.

فَتَرَى ٱلَّذِينَ فِى قُلُوبِهِم مَّرَضٌ

52 Yet *you* see those in whose hearts is a sickness

يُسَٰرِعُونَ فِيهِمْ

        rushing to them,

يَقُولُونَ نَخْشَىٰٓ أَن تُصِيبَنَا دَآئِرَةٌ

    saying, 'We fear lest a turn of fortune should visit us.'

فَعَسَى ٱللَّهُ أَن يَأْتِىَ بِٱلْفَتْحِ

    Maybe Allah will bring about a victory,

أَوْ أَمْرٍ مِّنْ عِندِهِۦ

        or a command from Him,

فَيُصْبِحُواْ

    and then they will be

عَلَىٰ مَآ أَسَرُّواْ فِىٓ أَنفُسِهِمْ نَٰدِمِينَ ۝

    regretful for what they kept secret in their hearts,

وَيَقُولُ ٱلَّذِينَ ءَامَنُوٓاْ

53 and the faithful will say,

أَهَٰٓؤُلَآءِ ٱلَّذِينَ أَقْسَمُواْ بِٱللَّهِ

    'Are these the ones who swore by Allah

جَهْدَ أَيْمَٰنِهِمْ إِنَّهُمْ لَمَعَكُمْ

    with solemn oaths that they were with you?!'

حَبِطَتْ أَعْمَٰلُهُمْ

Their works have failed,

فَأَصْبَحُواْ خَٰسِرِينَ ۝

    and they have become losers.

يَٰٓأَيُّهَا ٱلَّذِينَ ءَامَنُواْ

54 O you who have faith!

مَن يَرْتَدَّ مِنكُمْ عَن دِينِهِۦ

Should any of you desert his religion,

فَسَوْفَ يَأْتِى ٱللَّهُ بِقَوْمٍ يُحِبُّهُمْ

Allah will soon bring a people whom He loves

وَيُحِبُّونَهُۥٓ

    and who love Him,

أَذِلَّةٍ عَلَى ٱلْمُؤْمِنِينَ

    [who will be] humble towards the faithful,

أَعِزَّةٍ عَلَى ٱلْكَفِرِينَ     stern towards the faithless,

يُجَهِدُونَ فِى سَبِيلِ ٱللَّهِ     wage *jihād* in the way of Allah,

وَلَا يَخَافُونَ لَوْمَةَ لَآبِمٍ     not fearing the blame of any blamer.

ذَٰلِكَ فَضْلُ ٱللَّهِ     That is Allah's grace

يُؤْتِيهِ مَن يَشَآءُ     which He grants to whomever He wishes,

وَٱللَّهُ وَسِعٌ عَلِيمٌ ۝     and Allah is all-bounteous, all-knowing.

إِنَّمَا وَلِيُّكُمُ ٱللَّهُ وَرَسُولُهُ     55 Your guardian is only Allah, His Apostle,

وَٱلَّذِينَ ءَامَنُوا ٱلَّذِينَ يُقِيمُونَ ٱلصَّلَوٰةَ     and the faithful who maintain the prayer

وَيُؤْتُونَ ٱلزَّكَوٰةَ وَهُمْ رَٰكِعُونَ ۝     and give the *zakāt* while bowing down.

وَمَن يَتَوَلَّ ٱللَّهَ     56 Whoever takes for his guardians Allah,

وَرَسُولَهُ وَٱلَّذِينَ ءَامَنُوا     His Apostle and the faithful [should know that]

فَإِنَّ حِزْبَ ٱللَّهِ هُمُ ٱلْغَٰلِبُونَ ۝     the confederates of Allah are indeed the victorious.

يَٰٓأَيُّهَا ٱلَّذِينَ ءَامَنُوا     57 O you who have faith!

لَا تَتَّخِذُوا ٱلَّذِينَ ٱتَّخَذُوا دِينَكُمْ     Do not take those who take your religion

هُزُوًا وَلَعِبًا     in derision and play,

مِّنَ ٱلَّذِينَ أُوتُوا ٱلْكِتَٰبَ     from among those who were given the Book

مِن قَبْلِكُمْ     before you,

وَٱلْكُفَّارَ     and the infidels,

أَوْلِيَآءَ     as friends,

وَٱتَّقُوا ٱللَّهَ إِن كُنتُم مُّؤْمِنِينَ ۝     and be wary of Allah, should you be faithful.

وَإِذَا نَادَيْتُمْ إِلَى ٱلصَّلَوٰةِ     58 When you call to prayer,

ٱتَّخَذُوهَا هُزُوًا وَلَعِبًا     they take it in derision and play.

ذَٰلِكَ بِأَنَّهُمْ     That is because they are

قَوْمٌ لَّا يَعْقِلُونَ ۝     a people who do not apply reason.

قُلْ يَٰٓأَهْلَ ٱلْكِتَٰبِ     59 *Say*, 'O People of the Book!

هَلْ تَنقِمُونَ مِنَّا     Are you vindictive toward us[1]

إِلَّآ أَنْ ءَامَنَّا بِٱللَّهِ     for any reason except that we have faith in Allah

وَمَآ أُنزِلَ إِلَيْنَا     and in what has been sent down to us,

وَمَآ أُنزِلَ مِن قَبْلُ     and in what was sent down before,

---

[1] Or 'Do you find fault with us. . . .'

وَأَنَّ أَكْثَرَكُمْ فَٰسِقُونَ ۝    and that most of you are transgressors?'

قُلْ هَلْ أُنَبِّئُكُم    60 *Say,* 'Shall I inform you

بِشَرٍّ مِّن ذَٰلِكَ    concerning something worse than that

مَثُوبَةً عِندَ ٱللَّهِ    as a requital from Allah?

مَن لَّعَنَهُ ٱللَّهُ    Those whom Allah has cursed

وَغَضِبَ عَلَيْهِ    and with whom He is wrathful,

وَجَعَلَ مِنْهُمُ ٱلْقِرَدَةَ وَٱلْخَنَازِيرَ    and turned some of whom into apes and swine,

وَعَبَدَ ٱلطَّٰغُوتَ    and worshippers[1] of the Rebel!

أُوْلَٰٓئِكَ شَرٌّ مَّكَانًا    Such are in a worse situation,

وَأَضَلُّ عَن سَوَآءِ ٱلسَّبِيلِ ۝    and more astray from the right way.'

وَإِذَا جَآءُوكُمْ    61 When they come to you,

قَالُوٓاْ ءَامَنَّا    they say, 'We believe.'

وَقَد دَّخَلُواْ بِٱلْكُفْرِ    Certainly they enter with disbelief

وَهُمْ قَدْ خَرَجُواْ بِهِۦ    and leave with it,

وَٱللَّهُ أَعْلَمُ    and Allah knows best

بِمَا كَانُواْ يَكْتُمُونَ ۝    as to what they have been concealing.

وَتَرَىٰ كَثِيرًا مِّنْهُمْ يُسَٰرِعُونَ فِى ٱلْإِثْمِ    62 *You* see many of them actively engaged in sin

وَٱلْعُدْوَٰنِ    and aggression,

وَأَكْلِهِمُ ٱلسُّحْتَ    and consuming illicit gains.

لَبِئْسَ مَا كَانُواْ يَعْمَلُونَ ۝    Surely, evil is what they have been doing.

لَوْلَا يَنْهَٰهُمُ ٱلرَّبَّٰنِيُّونَ وَٱلْأَحْبَارُ    63 Why do not the rabbis and the scribes forbid them

عَن قَوْلِهِمُ ٱلْإِثْمَ    from sinful speech

وَأَكْلِهِمُ ٱلسُّحْتَ    and consuming illicit gains?

لَبِئْسَ مَا كَانُواْ يَصْنَعُونَ ۝    Surely, evil is what they have been working.

وَقَالَتِ ٱلْيَهُودُ يَدُ ٱللَّهِ مَغْلُولَةٌ    64 The Jews say, 'Allah's hand is tied up.'

غُلَّتْ أَيْدِيهِمْ    Tied up be their hands,

وَلُعِنُواْ بِمَا قَالُواْ    and cursed be they for what they say!

بَلْ يَدَاهُ مَبْسُوطَتَانِ    Rather, His hands are wide open:

يُنفِقُ كَيْفَ يَشَآءُ    He bestows as He wishes.

---

[1] Or 'slaves.'

وَلَيَزِيدَنَّ كَثِيرًا مِّنْهُم

Surely many of them will be increased

مَّآ أُنزِلَ إِلَيْكَ مِن رَّبِّكَ

by what has been sent to *you* from *your* Lord

طُغْيَٰنًا وَكُفْرًا

in rebellion and unfaith,

وَأَلْقَيْنَا بَيْنَهُمُ ٱلْعَدَٰوَةَ وَٱلْبَغْضَآءَ

and We have cast enmity and hatred amongst them

إِلَىٰ يَوْمِ ٱلْقِيَٰمَةِ

until the Day of Resurrection.

كُلَّمَآ أَوْقَدُوا۟ نَارًا لِّلْحَرْبِ

Every time they ignite the flames of war,

أَطْفَأَهَا ٱللَّهُ

Allah puts them out.

وَيَسْعَوْنَ فِى ٱلْأَرْضِ فَسَادًا

They seek to cause corruption on the earth,

وَٱللَّهُ لَا يُحِبُّ ٱلْمُفْسِدِينَ ۞

and Allah does not like the agents of corruption.

وَلَوْ أَنَّ أَهْلَ ٱلْكِتَٰبِ ءَامَنُوا۟

65 Had the People of the Book believed

وَٱتَّقَوْا۟

and been Godwary,

لَكَفَّرْنَا عَنْهُمْ سَيِّـَٔاتِهِمْ

We would surely have absolved them of their misdeeds

وَلَأَدْخَلْنَٰهُمْ جَنَّٰتِ ٱلنَّعِيمِ ۞

and admitted them into gardens of bliss.

وَلَوْ أَنَّهُمْ أَقَامُوا۟ ٱلتَّوْرَىٰةَ وَٱلْإِنجِيلَ

66 Had they observed the Torah and the Evangel,

وَمَآ أُنزِلَ إِلَيْهِم مِّن رَّبِّهِمْ

and what was sent down to them from their Lord,

لَأَكَلُوا۟

they would surely have drawn nourishment

مِن فَوْقِهِمْ وَمِن تَحْتِ أَرْجُلِهِم

from above them and from beneath their feet.

مِّنْهُمْ أُمَّةٌ مُّقْتَصِدَةٌ

There is an upright group among them,

وَكَثِيرٌ مِّنْهُمْ سَآءَ مَا يَعْمَلُونَ ۞ ۞

but evil is what many of them do.

يَٰٓأَيُّهَا ٱلرَّسُولُ

67 O Apostle!

بَلِّغْ مَآ أُنزِلَ إِلَيْكَ

Communicate that which has been sent down to *you*

مِن رَّبِّكَ

from *your* Lord,

وَإِن لَّمْ تَفْعَلْ

and if *you* do not,

فَمَا بَلَّغْتَ رِسَالَتَهُۥ

*you* will not have communicated His message,

وَٱللَّهُ يَعْصِمُكَ مِنَ ٱلنَّاسِ

and Allah shall protect *you* from the people.

إِنَّ ٱللَّهَ لَا يَهْدِى ٱلْقَوْمَ ٱلْكَٰفِرِينَ ۞

Indeed Allah does not guide the faithless lot.

قُلْ يَٰٓأَهْلَ ٱلْكِتَٰبِ

68 *Say,* 'O People of the Book!

لَسْتُمْ عَلَىٰ شَىْءٍ

You do not stand on anything

حَتَّىٰ تُقِيمُوا۟ ٱلتَّوْرَىٰةَ وَٱلْإِنجِيلَ    until you observe the Torah and the Evangel

وَمَآ أُنزِلَ إِلَيْكُم مِّن رَّبِّكُمْ    and what was sent down to you from your Lord.'

وَلَيَزِيدَنَّ كَثِيرًا مِّنْهُم    Surely many of them will be increased

مَّآ أُنزِلَ إِلَيْكَ مِن رَّبِّكَ    by what has been sent down to *you* from *your* Lord

طُغْيَٰنًا وَكُفْرًا    in rebellion and unfaith.

فَلَا تَأْسَ عَلَى ٱلْقَوْمِ ٱلْكَٰفِرِينَ ﴿٦٨﴾    So *do not grieve* for the faithless lot.

إِنَّ ٱلَّذِينَ ءَامَنُوا۟    69 Indeed the faithful,

وَٱلَّذِينَ هَادُوا۟ وَٱلصَّٰبِـُٔونَ وَٱلنَّصَٰرَىٰ    the Jews, the Sabaeans, and the Christians

مَنْ ءَامَنَ بِٱللَّهِ وَٱلْيَوْمِ ٱلْأَخِرِ    —those who have faith in Allah and the Last Day

وَعَمِلَ صَٰلِحًا    and act righteously—

فَلَا خَوْفٌ عَلَيْهِمْ    they will have no fear,

وَلَا هُمْ يَحْزَنُونَ ﴿٦٩﴾    nor will they grieve.

لَقَدْ أَخَذْنَا مِيثَٰقَ بَنِىٓ إِسْرَٰٓءِيلَ    70 Certainly We took a pledge from the Children of Israel,

وَأَرْسَلْنَآ إِلَيْهِمْ رُسُلًا    and We sent apostles to them.

كُلَّمَا جَآءَهُمْ رَسُولٌ    Whenever an apostle brought them

بِمَا لَا تَهْوَىٰٓ أَنفُسُهُمْ    that which was not to their liking,

فَرِيقًا كَذَّبُوا۟    they would impugn a part of them,

وَفَرِيقًا يَقْتُلُونَ ﴿٧٠﴾    and a part they would slay.

وَحَسِبُوٓا۟ أَلَّا تَكُونَ فِتْنَةٌ    71 They supposed there would be no testing,

فَعَمُوا۟ وَصَمُّوا۟    so they became blind and deaf.

ثُمَّ تَابَ ٱللَّهُ عَلَيْهِمْ    Thereafter Allah accepted their repentance,

ثُمَّ عَمُوا۟ وَصَمُّوا۟ كَثِيرٌ مِّنْهُمْ    yet [again] many of them became blind and deaf,

وَٱللَّهُ بَصِيرٌ بِمَا يَعْمَلُونَ ﴿٧١﴾    and Allah sees best what they do.

لَقَدْ كَفَرَ ٱلَّذِينَ قَالُوٓا۟    72 They are certainly faithless who say,

إِنَّ ٱللَّهَ هُوَ ٱلْمَسِيحُ ٱبْنُ مَرْيَمَ    'Allah is the Messiah, son of Mary.'

وَقَالَ ٱلْمَسِيحُ يَٰبَنِىٓ إِسْرَٰٓءِيلَ    But the Messiah had said, 'O Children of Israel!

ٱعْبُدُوا۟ ٱللَّهَ رَبِّى وَرَبَّكُمْ    Worship Allah, my Lord and your Lord.

إِنَّهُۥ مَن يُشْرِكْ بِٱللَّهِ

Indeed whoever ascribes partners to Allah,

فَقَدْ حَرَّمَ ٱللَّهُ عَلَيْهِ ٱلْجَنَّةَ

Allah shall forbid him [entry into] paradise,

وَمَأْوَىٰهُ ٱلنَّارُ

and his refuge shall be the Fire,

وَمَا لِلظَّـٰلِمِينَ مِنْ أَنصَارٍ ٧٢

and the wrongdoers will not have any helpers.'

لَّقَدْ كَفَرَ ٱلَّذِينَ قَالُوٓا۟ 73

They are certainly faithless who say,

إِنَّ ٱللَّهَ ثَالِثُ ثَلَـٰثَةٍ

'Allah is the third [person] of a trinity,'

وَمَا مِنْ إِلَـٰهٍ إِلَّآ إِلَـٰهٌ وَٰحِدٌ

while there is no god except the One God.

وَإِن لَّمْ يَنتَهُوا۟ عَمَّا يَقُولُونَ

If they do not relinquish what they say,

لَيَمَسَّنَّ ٱلَّذِينَ كَفَرُوا۟ مِنْهُمْ

there shall befall the faithless among them

عَذَابٌ أَلِيمٌ ٧٣

a painful punishment.

أَفَلَا يَتُوبُونَ إِلَى ٱللَّهِ 74

Will they not repent to Allah

وَيَسْتَغْفِرُونَهُۥ

and plead Him for forgiveness?

وَٱللَّهُ غَفُورٌ رَّحِيمٌ ٧٤

Yet Allah is all-forgiving, all-merciful.

مَّا ٱلْمَسِيحُ ٱبْنُ مَرْيَمَ إِلَّا رَسُولٌ 75

The Messiah, son of Mary, is but an apostle.

قَدْ خَلَتْ مِن قَبْلِهِ ٱلرُّسُلُ

Certainly [other] apostles have passed before him,

وَأُمُّهُۥ صِدِّيقَةٌ

and his mother was a truthful one.

كَانَا يَأْكُلَانِ ٱلطَّعَامَ

Both of them would eat food.

ٱنظُرْ كَيْفَ نُبَيِّنُ لَهُمُ ٱلْأَيَـٰتِ

*Look* how We clarify the signs for them,

ثُمَّ ٱنظُرْ أَنَّىٰ يُؤْفَكُونَ ٧٥

and yet, *look*, how they go astray!

قُلْ أَتَعْبُدُونَ مِن دُونِ ٱللَّهِ 76

*Say*, 'Do you worship, besides Allah,

مَا لَا يَمْلِكُ لَكُمْ ضَرًّا وَلَا نَفْعًا

what has no power to bring you any benefit or harm,

وَٱللَّهُ هُوَ ٱلسَّمِيعُ ٱلْعَلِيمُ ٧٦

while Allah—He is the All-hearing, the All-knowing?!'

قُلْ يَـٰٓأَهْلَ ٱلْكِتَـٰبِ 77

*Say*, 'O People of the Book!

لَا تَغْلُوا۟ فِى دِينِكُمْ غَيْرَ ٱلْحَقِّ

Do not unduly exceed the bounds in your religion

وَلَا تَتَّبِعُوٓا۟

and do not follow

أَهْوَآءَ قَوْمٍ قَدْ ضَلُّوا۟ مِن قَبْلُ

the fancies of a people who went astray in the past,

وَأَضَلُّوا۟ كَثِيرًا

and led many astray,

وَضَلُّوا۟ عَن سَوَآءِ ٱلسَّبِيلِ ٧٧

and [themselves] strayed from the right path.'

لُعِنَ ٱلَّذِينَ كَفَرُوا۟ مِنۢ بَنِىٓ إِسْرَٰٓءِيلَ 78

The faithless among the Children of Israel were cursed

عَلَىٰ لِسَانِ دَاوُۥدَ وَعِيسَى ٱبْنِ مَرْيَمَ

on the tongue of David and Jesus son of Mary.

ذَٰلِكَ بِمَا عَصَوا

That, because they would disobey

وَّكَانُواْ يَعْتَدُونَ ۝

and used to commit transgression.

كَانُواْ لَا يَتَنَاهَوْنَ 79 They would not forbid one another

عَن مُّنكَرٍ فَعَلُوهُ

from the wrongs that they committed.

لَبِئْسَ مَا كَانُواْ يَفْعَلُونَ ۝

Surely, evil is what they had been doing.

تَرَىٰ كَثِيرًا مِّنْهُمْ 80 *You* see many of them

يَتَوَلَّوْنَ ٱلَّذِينَ كَفَرُواْ

fraternizing with the faithless.

لَبِئْسَ مَا قَدَّمَتْ هُمْ أَنفُسُهُمْ

Surely evil is what they have sent ahead for their souls,

أَن سَخِطَ ٱللَّهُ عَلَيْهِمْ

as Allah is displeased with them

وَفِى ٱلْعَذَابِ هُمْ خَٰلِدُونَ ۝

and they shall remain in punishment [forever].

وَلَوْ كَانُواْ يُؤْمِنُونَ بِٱللَّهِ وَٱلنَّبِيِّ 81 Had they believed in Allah and the Prophet

وَمَآ أُنزِلَ إِلَيْهِ

and what has been sent down to him,

مَا ٱتَّخَذُوهُمْ أَوْلِيَآءَ

they would not have taken them for allies.

وَلَٰكِنَّ كَثِيرًا مِّنْهُمْ فَٰسِقُونَ ۝ ❖

But most of them are transgressors.

[PART 7]

لَتَجِدَنَّ 82 Surely *You* will find

أَشَدَّ ٱلنَّاسِ عَدَٰوَةً لِّلَّذِينَ ءَامَنُواْ

the most hostile of all people towards the faithful

ٱلْيَهُودَ وَٱلَّذِينَ أَشْرَكُواْ

to be the Jews and the polytheists,

وَلَتَجِدَنَّ

and surely *you* will find

أَقْرَبَهُم مَّوَدَّةً لِّلَّذِينَ ءَامَنُواْ

the nearest of them in affection to the faithful

ٱلَّذِينَ قَالُوٓاْ إِنَّا نَصَٰرَىٰ

to be those who say 'We are Christians.'

ذَٰلِكَ بِأَنَّ

That is because

مِنْهُمْ قِسِّيسِينَ وَرُهْبَانًا

there are priests and monks among them,

وَأَنَّهُمْ لَا يَسْتَكْبِرُونَ ۝

and because they are not arrogant.

وَإِذَا سَمِعُواْ مَآ أُنزِلَ إِلَى ٱلرَّسُولِ 83 When they hear what has been revealed to the Apostle,

تَرَىٰ أَعْيُنَهُمْ تَفِيضُ مِنَ ٱلدَّمْعِ

*you* see their eyes fill with tears

مِمَّا عَرَفُواْ مِنَ ٱلْحَقِّ

because of the truth that they recognize.

يَقُولُونَ رَبَّنَآ ءَامَنَّا

They say, 'Our Lord, we believe;

فَٱكْتُبْنَا مَعَ ٱلشَّٰهِدِينَ ۝

so write us down among the witnesses.

وَمَا لَنَا لَا نُؤْمِنُ بِٱللَّهِ 84 Why should we not believe in Allah

وَمَا جَآءَنَا مِنَ ٱلْحَقِّ
and the truth that has come to us,

وَنَطْمَعُ أَن يُدْخِلَنَا رَبُّنَا
eager as we are that our Lord should admit us

مَعَ ٱلْقَوْمِ ٱلصَّـٰلِحِينَ ۝
among the righteous people?'

فَأَثَـٰبَهُمُ ٱللَّهُ بِمَا قَالُوا۟
85 So, for what they said, Allah requited them

جَنَّـٰتٍ تَجْرِى مِن تَحْتِهَا ٱلْأَنْهَـٰرُ
with gardens with streams running in them,

خَـٰلِدِينَ فِيهَا
to remain in them [forever],

وَذَٰلِكَ جَزَآءُ ٱلْمُحْسِنِينَ ۝
and that is the reward of the virtuous.

وَٱلَّذِينَ كَفَرُوا۟ وَكَذَّبُوا۟ بِـَٔايَـٰتِنَآ
86 But those who are faithless and deny Our signs

أُو۟لَـٰٓئِكَ أَصْحَـٰبُ ٱلْجَحِيمِ ۝
—they shall be the inmates of hell.

يَـٰٓأَيُّهَا ٱلَّذِينَ ءَامَنُوا۟
87 O you who have faith!

لَا تُحَرِّمُوا۟ طَيِّبَـٰتِ
Do not prohibit the good things

مَآ أَحَلَّ ٱللَّهُ لَكُمْ
that Allah has made lawful to you,

وَلَا تَعْتَدُوٓا۟
and do not transgress.

إِنَّ ٱللَّهَ لَا يُحِبُّ ٱلْمُعْتَدِينَ ۝
Indeed Allah does not like the transgressors.

وَكُلُوا۟
88 Eat

مِمَّا رَزَقَكُمُ ٱللَّهُ حَلَـٰلًا طَيِّبًا
the lawful and good things Allah has provided you,

وَٱتَّقُوا۟ ٱللَّهَ ٱلَّذِىٓ أَنتُم بِهِۦ مُؤْمِنُونَ ۝
and be wary of Allah in whom you have faith.

لَا يُؤَاخِذُكُمُ ٱللَّهُ
89 Allah shall not take you to task

بِٱللَّغْوِ فِىٓ أَيْمَـٰنِكُمْ
for what is frivolous in your oaths;

وَلَـٰكِن يُؤَاخِذُكُم
but He shall take you to task

بِمَا عَقَّدتُّمُ ٱلْأَيْمَـٰنَ
for what you pledge in earnest.

فَكَفَّـٰرَتُهُۥٓ إِطْعَامُ عَشَرَةِ مَسَـٰكِينَ
The atonement for it is to feed ten needy persons

مِنْ أَوْسَطِ مَا تُطْعِمُونَ أَهْلِيكُمْ
with the average food you give to your families,

أَوْ كِسْوَتُهُمْ أَوْ تَحْرِيرُ رَقَبَةٍ
or their clothing, or the freeing of a slave.

فَمَن لَّمْ يَجِدْ
He who cannot afford [any of these]

فَصِيَامُ ثَلَـٰثَةِ أَيَّامٍ
shall fast for three days.

ذَٰلِكَ كَفَّـٰرَةُ أَيْمَـٰنِكُمْ إِذَا حَلَفْتُمْ
That is the atonement for your oaths when you vow.

وَٱحْفَظُوٓا۟ أَيْمَـٰنَكُمْ
But keep your oaths.

كَذَٰلِكَ يُبَيِّنُ ٱللَّهُ لَكُمْ ءَايَـٰتِهِۦ
Thus does Allah clarify His signs for you

لَعَلَّكُمْ تَشْكُرُونَ ۝
so that you may give thanks.

يَـٰٓأَيُّهَا ٱلَّذِينَ ءَامَنُوٓاْ 90 O you who have faith!

إِنَّمَا ٱلْخَمْرُ وَٱلْمَيْسِرُ وَٱلْأَنصَابُ Indeed wine, gambling, idols

وَٱلْأَزْلَـٰمُ and the divining arrows

رِجْسٌ مِّنْ عَمَلِ ٱلشَّيْطَـٰنِ are abominations of Satan's doing,

فَٱجْتَنِبُوهُ لَعَلَّكُمْ تُفْلِحُونَ so avoid them, so that you may be felicitous.

إِنَّمَا يُرِيدُ ٱلشَّيْطَـٰنُ 91 Indeed Satan seeks

أَن يُوقِعَ بَيْنَكُمُ ٱلْعَدَٰوَةَ وَٱلْبَغْضَآءَ to cast enmity and hatred among you

فِى ٱلْخَمْرِ وَٱلْمَيْسِرِ through wine and gambling,

وَيَصُدَّكُمْ عَن ذِكْرِ ٱللَّهِ and to hinder you from the remembrance of Allah

وَعَنِ ٱلصَّلَوٰةِ and from prayer.

فَهَلْ أَنتُم مُّنتَهُونَ Will you, then, relinquish?

وَأَطِيعُواْ ٱللَّهَ وَأَطِيعُواْ ٱلرَّسُولَ 92 And obey Allah and obey the Apostle,

وَٱحْذَرُواْ and beware;

فَإِن تَوَلَّيْتُمْ but if you turn your backs,

فَٱعْلَمُوٓاْ أَنَّمَا عَلَىٰ رَسُولِنَا then know that Our Apostle's duty is only

ٱلْبَلَـٰغُ ٱلْمُبِينُ to communicate in clear terms.

لَيْسَ عَلَى ٱلَّذِينَ ءَامَنُواْ 93 There will be no sin upon those who have faith

وَعَمِلُواْ ٱلصَّـٰلِحَـٰتِ and do righteous deeds

جُنَاحٌ فِيمَا طَعِمُوٓاْ in regard to what they have eaten [in the past]

إِذَا مَا ٱتَّقَواْ وَّءَامَنُواْ so long as they are Godwary and faithful

وَعَمِلُواْ ٱلصَّـٰلِحَـٰتِ and do righteous deeds,

ثُمَّ ٱتَّقَواْ وَّءَامَنُواْ and are further Godwary and faithful,

ثُمَّ ٱتَّقَواْ وَّأَحْسَنُواْ and are further Godwary and virtuous.

وَٱللَّهُ يُحِبُّ ٱلْمُحْسِنِينَ And Allah loves the virtuous.

يَـٰٓأَيُّهَا ٱلَّذِينَ ءَامَنُواْ 94 O you who have faith!

لَيَبْلُوَنَّكُمُ ٱللَّهُ بِشَىْءٍ مِّنَ ٱلصَّيْدِ Allah will surely test you with some of the game

تَنَالُهُۥٓ أَيْدِيكُمْ وَرِمَاحُكُمْ within the reach of your hands and spears,

لِيَعْلَمَ ٱللَّهُ so that Allah may know

مَن يَخَافُهُۥ بِٱلْغَيْبِ those who fear Him in secret.

فَمَنِ ٱعۡتَدَىٰ بَعۡدَ ذَٰلِكَ
So whoever transgresses after that,

فَلَهُۥ عَذَابٌ أَلِيمٞ
there is a painful punishment for him.

يَـٰٓأَيُّهَا ٱلَّذِينَ ءَامَنُواْ
95 O you who have faith!

لَا تَقۡتُلُواْ ٱلصَّيۡدَ وَأَنتُمۡ حُرُمٞ
Do not kill any game when you are in pilgrim sanctity.

وَمَن قَتَلَهُۥ مِنكُم مُّتَعَمِّدٗا
Should any of you kill it intentionally,

فَجَزَآءٞ
its atonement,

مِّثۡلُ مَا قَتَلَ مِنَ ٱلنَّعَمِ
the counterpart from cattle of what he has killed,

تَحۡكُمُ بِهِۦ ذَوَا عَدۡلٖ مِّنكُمۡ
as judged by two fair men among you,

هَدۡيَۢا بَٰلِغَ ٱلۡكَعۡبَةِ
will be an offering brought to the Ka'bah,

أَوۡ كَفَّٰرَةٞ طَعَامُ مَسَٰكِينَ
or an atonement by feeding a needy person,

أَوۡ عَدۡلُ ذَٰلِكَ صِيَامٗا
or its equivalent in fasting,

لِّيَذُوقَ
that he may taste

وَبَالَ أَمۡرِهِۦۗ
the evil consequences of his conduct.

عَفَا ٱللَّهُ عَمَّا سَلَفَۚ
Allah has excused what is already past;

وَمَنۡ عَادَ
but should anyone resume,

فَيَنتَقِمُ ٱللَّهُ مِنۡهُۚ
Allah shall take vengeance on him,

وَٱللَّهُ عَزِيزٞ ذُو ٱنتِقَامٍ
for Allah is all-mighty, avenger.

أُحِلَّ لَكُمۡ صَيۡدُ ٱلۡبَحۡرِ وَطَعَامُهُۥ
96 You are permitted the game of the sea and its food,

مَتَٰعٗا لَّكُمۡ وَلِلسَّيَّارَةِۖ
a provision for you and for the caravans,

وَحُرِّمَ عَلَيۡكُمۡ صَيۡدُ ٱلۡبَرِّ
but you are forbidden the game of the land

مَا دُمۡتُمۡ حُرُمٗاۗ
so long as you remain in pilgrim sanctity,

وَٱتَّقُواْ ٱللَّهَ
and be wary of Allah

ٱلَّذِىٓ إِلَيۡهِ تُحۡشَرُونَ
toward whom you will be gathered.

جَعَلَ ٱللَّهُ ٱلۡكَعۡبَةَ ٱلۡبَيۡتَ ٱلۡحَرَامَ
97 Allah has made the Ka'bah, the Sacred House,

قِيَٰمٗا لِّلنَّاسِ
a [means of] sustentation for mankind,

وَٱلشَّهۡرَ ٱلۡحَرَامَ وَٱلۡهَدۡىَ
and [also] the sacred month, the offering

وَٱلۡقَلَـٰٓئِدَۚ
and the garlands,

ذَٰلِكَ لِتَعۡلَمُوٓاْ
so that you may know

أَنَّ ٱللَّهَ يَعۡلَمُ مَا فِى ٱلسَّمَٰوَٰتِ
that Allah knows whatever there is in the heavens

وَمَا فِى ٱلۡأَرۡضِ
and whatever there is in the earth,

166

وَأَنَّ ٱللَّهَ بِكُلِّ شَىْءٍ عَلِيمٌ ۝    and that Allah has knowledge of all things.

أَعْلَمُوٓاْ أَنَّ ٱللَّهَ شَدِيدُ ٱلْعِقَابِ    98 Know that Allah is severe in retribution,

وَأَنَّ ٱللَّهَ غَفُورٌ رَّحِيمٌ ۝    and that Allah is all-forgiving, all-merciful.

مَّا عَلَى ٱلرَّسُولِ إِلَّا ٱلْبَلَٰغُ    99 The Apostle's duty is only to communicate

وَٱللَّهُ يَعْلَمُ مَا تُبْدُونَ    and Allah knows whatever you disclose

وَمَا تَكْتُمُونَ ۝    and whatever you conceal.

قُل لَّا يَسْتَوِى ٱلْخَبِيثُ وَٱلطَّيِّبُ    100 *Say,* 'The good and the bad are not equal,

وَلَوْ أَعْجَبَكَ كَثْرَةُ ٱلْخَبِيثِ    though the abundance of the bad should amaze you.'

فَٱتَّقُواْ ٱللَّهَ يَٰٓأُوْلِى ٱلْأَلْبَٰبِ    So be wary of Allah, O you who possess intellect,

لَعَلَّكُمْ تُفْلِحُونَ ۝    so that you may be felicitous!

يَٰٓأَيُّهَا ٱلَّذِينَ ءَامَنُواْ    101 O you who have faith!

لَا تَسْـَٔلُواْ عَنْ أَشْيَآءَ    Do not ask about things

إِن تُبْدَ لَكُمْ تَسُؤْكُمْ    which, if they are disclosed to you, will upset you.

وَإِن تَسْـَٔلُواْ عَنْهَا    Yet if you ask about them

حِينَ يُنَزَّلُ ٱلْقُرْءَانُ    while the Qurʾān is being sent down,

تُبْدَ لَكُمْ    they shall be disclosed to you.

عَفَا ٱللَّهُ عَنْهَا    Allah has excused it,

وَٱللَّهُ غَفُورٌ حَلِيمٌ ۝    and Allah is all-forgiving, all-forbearing.

قَدْ سَأَلَهَا قَوْمٌ مِّن قَبْلِكُمْ    102 Certainly some people asked about them before you

ثُمَّ أَصْبَحُواْ بِهَا كَٰفِرِينَ ۝    and then came to disbelieve in them.

مَا جَعَلَ ٱللَّهُ مِنۢ بَحِيرَةٍ    103 Allah has not prescribed any such thing as *Baḥīrah,*

وَلَا سَآئِبَةٍ وَلَا وَصِيلَةٍ وَلَا حَامٍ    *Sāʾibah, Waṣīlah,* or *Hām;*[1]

وَلَٰكِنَّ ٱلَّذِينَ كَفَرُواْ    but those who are faithless

يَفْتَرُونَ عَلَى ٱللَّهِ ٱلْكَذِبَ    fabricate lies against Allah,

وَأَكْثَرُهُمْ لَا يَعْقِلُونَ ۝    and most of them do not apply reason.

وَإِذَا قِيلَ لَهُمْ    104 And when they are told,

---

[1] The pre-Islamic Arabs used these terms for individual camels and sheep, which were subject to such practices as slitting of ears, forbidding their use for burden, dedication to idols, and restriction of their flesh to males. The commentators give different descriptions of these primitive customs and their significance, reflecting probably their varying practice among pre-Islamic Arabs.

| | |
|---|---|
| تَعَالَوْا۟ إِلَىٰ مَآ أَنزَلَ ٱللَّهُ | 'Come to what Allah has sent down |
| وَإِلَى ٱلرَّسُولِ | and [come] to the Apostle,' |
| قَالُوا۟ حَسْبُنَا | they say, 'Sufficient for us |
| مَا وَجَدْنَا عَلَيْهِ ءَابَآءَنَآ | is what we have found our fathers following.' |
| أَوَلَوْ كَانَ ءَابَآؤُهُمْ لَا يَعْلَمُونَ شَيْـًٔا | What, even if their fathers did not know anything |
| وَلَا يَهْتَدُونَ ۝ | and were not guided?! |
| يَـٰٓأَيُّهَا ٱلَّذِينَ ءَامَنُوا۟ عَلَيْكُمْ أَنفُسَكُمْ | 105 O you who have faith! Take care of your own souls. |
| لَا يَضُرُّكُم مَّن ضَلَّ | He who goes strays cannot hurt you |
| إِذَا ٱهْتَدَيْتُمْ | if you are guided. |
| إِلَى ٱللَّهِ مَرْجِعُكُمْ جَمِيعًا | To Allah will be the return of you all, |
| فَيُنَبِّئُكُم | whereat He will inform you |
| بِمَا كُنتُمْ تَعْمَلُونَ ۝ | concerning what you used to do. |
| يَـٰٓأَيُّهَا ٱلَّذِينَ ءَامَنُوا۟ | 106 O you who have faith! |
| شَهَٰدَةُ بَيْنِكُمْ | The witness between you, |
| إِذَا حَضَرَ أَحَدَكُمُ ٱلْمَوْتُ | when death approaches any of you, |
| حِينَ ٱلْوَصِيَّةِ | while making a bequest, |
| ٱثْنَانِ ذَوَا عَدْلٍ مِّنكُمْ | shall be two fair men from among yourselves |
| أَوْ ءَاخَرَانِ مِنْ غَيْرِكُمْ | —or two from among others,[1] |
| إِنْ أَنتُمْ ضَرَبْتُمْ فِى ٱلْأَرْضِ | if you are journeying in the land |
| فَأَصَٰبَتْكُم مُّصِيبَةُ ٱلْمَوْتِ | and the affliction of death visits you. |
| تَحْبِسُونَهُمَا مِنۢ بَعْدِ ٱلصَّلَوٰةِ | You shall detain the two of them after the prayer, |
| فَيُقْسِمَانِ بِٱللَّهِ إِنِ ٱرْتَبْتُمْ | and, if you have any doubt, they shall vow by Allah, |
| لَا نَشْتَرِى بِهِۦ ثَمَنًا | 'We will not sell it for any gain, |
| وَلَوْ كَانَ ذَا قُرْبَىٰ | even if it were a relative, |
| وَلَا نَكْتُمُ شَهَٰدَةَ ٱللَّهِ | nor will we conceal the testimony of Allah, |
| إِنَّآ إِذًا لَّمِنَ ٱلْءَاثِمِينَ ۝ | for then we would indeed be among the sinners.' |
| فَإِنْ عُثِرَ عَلَىٰٓ أَنَّهُمَا ٱسْتَحَقَّآ إِثْمًا | 107 But if it is found that both of them were guilty of a sin,[2] |

---

[1] That is, from among non-Muslims, on non-availability of Muslim witnesses during journey.

[2] That is, of the sin of perjury.

فَآخَرَانِ يَقُومَانِ مَقَامَهُمَا

then two others shall stand up in their place

مِنَ ٱلَّذِينَ ٱسْتَحَقَّ عَلَيْهِمُ ٱلْأَوْلَيَٰنِ

from among those nearest in kinship to the claimants

فَيُقْسِمَانِ بِٱللَّهِ

and swear by Allah:

لَشَهَٰدَتُنَآ أَحَقُّ مِن شَهَٰدَتِهِمَا

'Our testimony is surely truer than their testimony,

وَمَا ٱعْتَدَيْنَآ

and we have not transgressed,

إِنَّآ إِذًا لَّمِنَ ٱلظَّٰلِمِينَ ۝

for then we would indeed be among the wrongdoers.'

ذَٰلِكَ أَدْنَىٰٓ أَن يَأْتُوا۟ بِٱلشَّهَٰدَةِ

108 That makes it likelier that they give the testimony

عَلَىٰ وَجْهِهَآ

in its genuine form,

أَوْ يَخَافُوٓا۟ أَن تُرَدَّ أَيْمَٰنٌۢ بَعْدَ أَيْمَٰنِهِمْ

or fear that other oaths will be taken after their oaths.

وَٱتَّقُوا۟ ٱللَّهَ وَٱسْمَعُوا۟

Be wary of Allah and listen,

وَٱللَّهُ لَا يَهْدِى ٱلْقَوْمَ ٱلْفَٰسِقِينَ ۝ ❉

and Allah does not guide the transgressing lot.

يَوْمَ يَجْمَعُ ٱللَّهُ ٱلرُّسُلَ

109 The day Allah will gather the apostles

فَيَقُولُ مَاذَآ أُجِبْتُمْ

and say, 'What was the response to you?'

قَالُوا۟ لَا عِلْمَ لَنَآ

They will say, 'We have no knowledge.

إِنَّكَ أَنتَ عَلَّٰمُ ٱلْغُيُوبِ ۝

Indeed You are knower of all that is Unseen.'

إِذْ قَالَ ٱللَّهُ يَٰعِيسَى ٱبْنَ مَرْيَمَ

110 When Allah will say, O Jesus son of Mary,

ٱذْكُرْ نِعْمَتِى عَلَيْكَ

remember My blessing upon you

وَعَلَىٰ وَٰلِدَتِكَ

and upon your mother,

إِذْ أَيَّدتُّكَ بِرُوحِ ٱلْقُدُسِ

when I strengthened you with the Holy Spirit,

تُكَلِّمُ ٱلنَّاسَ فِى ٱلْمَهْدِ

so you would speak to the people in the cradle

وَكَهْلًا

and in adulthood,

وَإِذْ عَلَّمْتُكَ ٱلْكِتَٰبَ وَٱلْحِكْمَةَ

and when I taught you the Book and wisdom,

وَٱلتَّوْرَىٰةَ وَٱلْإِنجِيلَ

the Torah and the Evangel,

وَإِذْ تَخْلُقُ مِنَ ٱلطِّينِ

and when you would create from clay

كَهَيْـَٔةِ ٱلطَّيْرِ بِإِذْنِى

the form of a bird, with My leave,

فَتَنفُخُ فِيهَا

and you would breathe into it

فَتَكُونُ طَيْرًۢا بِإِذْنِى

and it would become a bird, with My leave;

وَتُبْرِئُ ٱلْأَكْمَهَ وَٱلْأَبْرَصَ

and you would heal the blind and the leper,

بِإِذْنِى

with My leave,

وَإِذْ تُخْرِجُ ٱلْمَوْتَىٰ بِإِذْنِى

and you would raise the dead, with My leave;

وَإِذْ كَفَفْتُ بَنِىٓ إِسْرَٰٓءِيلَ عَنكَ

and when I held off [the evil of] the Children of Israel from you

إِذْ جِئْتَهُم بِٱلْبَيِّنَٰتِ

when you brought them manifest proofs,

فَقَالَ ٱلَّذِينَ كَفَرُوا۟ مِنْهُمْ

whereat the faithless among them said,

إِنْ هَٰذَآ إِلَّا سِحْرٌ مُّبِينٌ ۝

'This is nothing but plain magic.'

وَإِذْ أَوْحَيْتُ إِلَى ٱلْحَوَارِيِّۦنَ

111 And when I inspired the Disciples,

أَنْ ءَامِنُوا۟ بِى وَبِرَسُولِى

[saying], 'Have faith in Me and My apostle,'

قَالُوٓا۟ ءَامَنَّا

they said, 'We have faith.

وَٱشْهَدْ بِأَنَّنَا مُسْلِمُونَ ۝

Bear witness that we are *muslims.*'

إِذْ قَالَ ٱلْحَوَارِيُّونَ يَٰعِيسَى ٱبْنَ مَرْيَمَ

112 When the Disciples said, 'O Jesus son of Mary!

هَلْ يَسْتَطِيعُ رَبُّكَ أَن يُنَزِّلَ عَلَيْنَا مَآئِدَةً مِّنَ ٱلسَّمَآءِ

Can your Lord send down to us a table[1] from the sky?'

قَالَ ٱتَّقُوا۟ ٱللَّهَ

Said he, 'Be wary of Allah,

إِن كُنتُم مُّؤْمِنِينَ ۝

should you be faithful.'

قَالُوا۟ نُرِيدُ أَن نَّأْكُلَ مِنْهَا

113 They said, 'We desire to eat from it,

وَتَطْمَئِنَّ قُلُوبُنَا

and our hearts will be at rest:

وَنَعْلَمَ أَن قَدْ صَدَقْتَنَا

we shall know that you have told us the truth,

وَنَكُونَ عَلَيْهَا مِنَ ٱلشَّٰهِدِينَ ۝

and we shall be among the witnesses to it.'

قَالَ عِيسَى ٱبْنُ مَرْيَمَ ٱللَّهُمَّ رَبَّنَآ

114 Said Jesus son of Mary, 'O Allah! Our Lord!

أَنزِلْ عَلَيْنَا مَآئِدَةً مِّنَ ٱلسَّمَآءِ

Send down to us a table from the sky,

تَكُونُ لَنَا عِيدًا

to be a festival for us,

لِّأَوَّلِنَا وَءَاخِرِنَا

for the first ones and the last ones among us

وَءَايَةً مِّنكَ

and as a sign from You,

وَٱرْزُقْنَا

and provide for us;

وَأَنتَ خَيْرُ ٱلرَّٰزِقِينَ ۝

for You are the best of providers.'

قَالَ ٱللَّهُ إِنِّى مُنَزِّلُهَا عَلَيْكُمْ

115 Allah said, 'I will indeed send it down to you.

فَمَن يَكْفُرْ بَعْدُ مِنكُمْ

But should any of you disbelieves after this,

فَإِنِّىٓ أُعَذِّبُهُۥ عَذَابًا

I will indeed punish him with a punishment

لَّآ أُعَذِّبُهُۥٓ أَحَدًا مِّنَ ٱلْعَٰلَمِينَ ۝

such as I do not punish anyone in all creation.'

---

[1] Table: The food and drink served at meals.

وَإِذْ قَالَ اللَّهُ يَعِيسَى ابْنَ مَرْيَمَ
116 And when Allah will say, 'O Jesus son of Mary!

ءَأَنتَ قُلْتَ لِلنَّاسِ
Were it you who said to the people,

اتَّخِذُونِي وَأُمِّيَ إِلَهَيْنِ مِن دُونِ اللَّهِ
"Take me and my mother for gods besides Allah"?'

قَالَ سُبْحَنَكَ
He will say, 'Immaculate are You!

مَا يَكُونُ لِي أَنْ أَقُولَ
It does not behoove me to say

مَا لَيْسَ لِي بِحَقٍّ
what I have no right to [say].

إِن كُنتُ قُلْتُهُ فَقَدْ عَلِمْتَهُ
Had I said it, You would certainly have known it:

تَعْلَمُ مَا فِي نَفْسِي
You know whatever is in my self,

وَلَا أَعْلَمُ مَا فِي نَفْسِكَ
and I do not know what is in Your Self.

إِنَّكَ أَنتَ عَلَّمُ الْغُيُوبِ ۝
Indeed You are knower of all that is Unseen.

مَا قُلْتُ لَهُمْ
117 I did not say to them [anything]

إِلَّا مَا أَمَرْتَنِي بِهِ
except what You had commanded me [to say]:

أَنِ اعْبُدُواْ اللَّهَ رَبِّي وَرَبَّكُمْ
"Worship Allah, my Lord and your Lord."

وَكُنتُ عَلَيْهِمْ شَهِيدًا
And I was a witness to them

مَا دُمْتُ فِيهِمْ
so long as I was among them.

فَلَمَّا تَوَفَّيْتَنِي
But when You had taken me away,

كُنتَ أَنتَ الرَّقِيبَ عَلَيْهِمْ
You Yourself were watchful over them,

وَأَنتَ عَلَى كُلِّ شَيْءٍ شَهِيدٌ ۝
and You are witness to all things.

إِن تُعَذِّبْهُمْ فَإِنَّهُمْ عِبَادُكَ
118 If You punish them, they are indeed Your creatures;

وَإِن تَغْفِرْ لَهُمْ
but if You forgive them,

فَإِنَّكَ أَنتَ الْعَزِيزُ الْحَكِيمُ ۝
You are indeed the All-mighty, the All-wise.'

قَالَ اللَّهُ
119 Allah will say,

هَذَا يَوْمُ يَنفَعُ الصَّدِقِينَ صِدْقُهُمْ
'This day truthfulness shall benefit the truthful.

لَهُمْ جَنَّتٌ
For them there will be gardens

تَجْرِي مِن تَحْتِهَا الْأَنْهَرُ
with streams running in them,

خَلِدِينَ فِيهَا أَبَدًا
to remain in them forever.

رَضِيَ اللَّهُ عَنْهُمْ
Allah is pleased with them

وَرَضُواْ عَنْهُ
and they are pleased with Him.

ذَلِكَ الْفَوْزُ الْعَظِيمُ ۝
That is the great success.'

لِلَّهِ مُلْكُ ٱلسَّمَـٰوَٰتِ 120 To Allah belongs the kingdom of the heavens

وَٱلْأَرْضِ and the earth

وَمَا فِيهِنَّ and whatever there is in them,

وَهُوَ عَلَىٰ كُلِّ شَىْءٍ قَدِيرٌ ۞ and He has power over all things.

# سُورَةُ ٱلْأَنْعَام

# 6. SŪRAT AL-AN'ĀM[1]

بِسْمِ ٱللَّهِ In the Name of Allah,

ٱلرَّحْمَـٰنِ ٱلرَّحِيمِ the All-beneficent, the All-merciful.

ٱلْحَمْدُ لِلَّهِ 1 All praise belongs to Allah

ٱلَّذِى خَلَقَ ٱلسَّمَـٰوَٰتِ وَٱلْأَرْضَ who created the heavens and the earth

وَجَعَلَ ٱلظُّلُمَـٰتِ وَٱلنُّورَ and made the darknesses and the light.

ثُمَّ ٱلَّذِينَ كَفَرُواْ بِرَبِّهِمْ يَعْدِلُونَ ۞ Yet the faithless equate [others] with their Lord.

هُوَ ٱلَّذِى خَلَقَكُم مِّن طِينٍ 2 It is He who created you from clay,

ثُمَّ قَضَىٰ أَجَلاً then ordained the term [of your life]

وَأَجَلٌ مُّسَمًّى عِندَهُۥ —the specified term is with Him—

ثُمَّ أَنتُمْ تَمْتَرُونَ ۞ and yet you are in doubt.

وَهُوَ ٱللَّهُ فِى ٱلسَّمَـٰوَٰتِ وَفِى ٱلْأَرْضِ 3 He is Allah in the heavens and on the earth:

يَعْلَمُ سِرَّكُمْ وَجَهْرَكُمْ He knows your secret and your overt [matters],

وَيَعْلَمُ مَا تَكْسِبُونَ ۞ and He knows what you earn.

وَمَا تَأْتِيهِم مِّنْ ءَايَةٍ 4 There did not come to them any sign

مِّنْ ءَايَـٰتِ رَبِّهِمْ from among the signs of their Lord,

إِلَّا كَانُواْ عَنْهَا مُعْرِضِينَ ۞ but that they used to disregard it.

فَقَدْ كَذَّبُواْ بِٱلْحَقِّ لَمَّا جَآءَهُمْ 5 They certainly denied the truth when it came to them,

فَسَوْفَ يَأْتِيهِمْ أَنۢبَـٰٓؤُاْ but soon there will come to them the news

مَا كَانُواْ بِهِۦ يَسْتَهْزِءُونَ ۞ of what they have been deriding.

أَلَمْ يَرَوْاْ 6 Have they not regarded

---

[1] The *sūrah* takes its name from 'the cattle' (*al-an'ām*) mentioned in verses 136-146 which deal with pagan superstitions and certain regulations related to cattle.

كَمْ أَهْلَكْنَا مِن قَبْلِهِم مِن قَرْنٍ how many a generation We have destroyed before them

مَّكَّنَّهُمْ فِى ٱلأَرْضِ whom We had granted power in the land

مَا لَمْ نُمَكِّن لَّكُمْ in respects that We did not grant you,

وَأَرْسَلْنَا ٱلسَّمَآءَ عَلَيْهِم مِّدْرَارًا and We sent abundant rains for them from the sky

وَجَعَلْنَا ٱلأَنْهَرَ تَجْرِى مِن تَحْتِهِمْ and made streams run for them.

فَأَهْلَكْنَهُم بِذُنُوبِهِمْ Then We destroyed them for their sins,

وَأَنشَأْنَا مِنْ بَعْدِهِمْ قَرْنًا ءَاخَرِينَ ۝ and brought forth another generation after them.

وَلَوْ نَزَّلْنَا عَلَيْكَ كِتَبًا فِى قِرْطَاسٍ 7 Had We sent down to *you* a Book on paper

فَلَمَسُوهُ بِأَيْدِيهِمْ so they could touch it with their [own] hands,

لَقَالَ ٱلَّذِينَ كَفَرُوٓاْ [still] the faithless would have said,

إِنْ هَذَآ إِلَّا سِحْرٌ مُّبِينٌ ۝ 'This is nothing but plain magic.'

وَقَالُواْ 8 And they say,

لَوْلَآ أُنزِلَ عَلَيْهِ مَلَكٌ 'Why has not an angel been sent down to him?'

وَلَوْ أَنزَلْنَا مَلَكًا Were We to sent down an angel,

لَّقُضِىَ ٱلأَمْرُ the matter would surely be decided,

ثُمَّ لَا يُنظَرُونَ ۝ and then they would not be granted any respite.

وَلَوْ جَعَلْنَهُ مَلَكًا 9 And had We made him[1] an angel,

لَّجَعَلْنَهُ رَجُلًا We would have surely made him a man,

وَلَلَبَسْنَا عَلَيْهِم and we would have surely confounded them

مَّا يَلْبِسُونَ ۝ in regard to [the truth] that they confound.

وَلَقَدِ ٱسْتُهْزِئَ بِرُسُلٍ مِّن قَبْلِكَ 10 Apostles were certainly derided before *you*.

فَحَاقَ بِٱلَّذِينَ سَخِرُواْ مِنْهُم Then those who ridiculed them were besieged

مَّا كَانُواْ بِهِۦ يَسْتَهْزِءُونَ ۝ by what they used to deride.

قُلْ سِيرُواْ فِى ٱلأَرْضِ 11 *Say,* 'Travel over the land,

ثُمَّ ٱنظُرُواْ and then observe

كَيْفَ كَانَ عَقِبَةُ ٱلْمُكَذِّبِينَ ۝ how was the fate of the deniers.'

قُل لِّمَن مَّا فِى ٱلسَّمَوَتِ 12 *Say,* 'To whom belongs whatever is in the heavens

وَٱلأَرْضِ and the earth?

قُل لِّلَّهِ *Say,* 'To Allah.

---

[1] That is, the apostle.

173

كَتَبَ عَلَىٰ نَفْسِهِ ٱلرَّحْمَةَ  He has made mercy incumbent upon Himself.

لَيَجْمَعَنَّكُمْ إِلَىٰ يَوْمِ ٱلْقِيَٰمَةِ  He will surely gather you on the Day of Resurrection,

لَا رَيْبَ فِيهِ  in which there is no doubt.

ٱلَّذِينَ خَسِرُوٓاْ أَنفُسَهُمْ  Those who have ruined their souls[1]

فَهُمْ لَا يُؤْمِنُونَ ۝  will not have faith.'

وَلَهُۥ مَا سَكَنَ فِى ٱلَّيْلِ  13 To Him belongs whatever abides in the night

وَٱلنَّهَارِ  and the day,

وَهُوَ ٱلسَّمِيعُ ٱلْعَلِيمُ ۝  and He is the All-hearing, the All-knowing.

قُلْ أَغَيْرَ ٱللَّهِ أَتَّخِذُ وَلِيًّا  14 Say, 'Shall I take for guardian [anyone] other than Allah,

فَاطِرِ ٱلسَّمَٰوَٰتِ وَٱلْأَرْضِ  the originator of the heavens and the earth,

وَهُوَ يُطْعِمُ وَلَا يُطْعَمُ  who feeds and is not fed?'

قُلْ إِنِّىٓ أُمِرْتُ  Say, 'I have been commanded

أَنْ أَكُونَ أَوَّلَ مَنْ أَسْلَمَ  to be the first of those who submit [to Allah],'

وَلَا تَكُونَنَّ مِنَ ٱلْمُشْرِكِينَ ۝  and never be one of the polytheists.

قُلْ إِنِّىٓ أَخَافُ إِنْ عَصَيْتُ رَبِّى  15 Say, 'Indeed, should I disobey my Lord, I fear

عَذَابَ يَوْمٍ عَظِيمٍ ۝  the punishment of a tremendous day.'

مَّن يُصْرَفْ عَنْهُ يَوْمَئِذٍ  16 Whoever is spared of it on that day,

فَقَدْ رَحِمَهُۥ  He has certainly been merciful to him,

وَذَٰلِكَ ٱلْفَوْزُ ٱلْمُبِينُ ۝  and that is the manifest success.

وَإِن يَمْسَسْكَ ٱللَّهُ بِضُرٍّ  17 Should Allah visit you with some distress

فَلَا كَاشِفَ لَهُۥٓ إِلَّا هُوَ  there is no one to remove it except Him;

وَإِن يَمْسَسْكَ بِخَيْرٍ  and should He bring you some good,

فَهُوَ عَلَىٰ كُلِّ شَىْءٍ قَدِيرٌ ۝  then He has power over all things.

وَهُوَ ٱلْقَاهِرُ فَوْقَ عِبَادِهِۦ  18 And He is the All-dominant over His servants,

وَهُوَ ٱلْحَكِيمُ ٱلْخَبِيرُ ۝  and He is the All-wise, the All-aware.

قُلْ أَىُّ شَىْءٍ أَكْبَرُ شَهَٰدَةً  19 Say, 'What thing is greatest as witness?'

قُلِ ٱللَّهُ  Say, 'Allah!

شَهِيدٌۢ بَيْنِى وَبَيْنَكُمْ  [He is] witness between me and you,

---

[1] Or 'themselves.'

وَأُوحِيَ إِلَيَّ هَـٰذَا ٱلْقُرْءَانُ

and this Qurʾān has been revealed to me

لِأُنذِرَكُم بِهِۦ

that I may warn thereby you

وَمَنۢ بَلَغَ

and whomever it may reach.'

أَئِنَّكُمْ لَتَشْهَدُونَ

'Do you indeed bear witness

أَنَّ مَعَ ٱللَّهِ ءَالِهَةً أُخْرَىٰ

that there are other gods besides Allah?'

قُل لَّآ أَشْهَدُ

*Say*, 'I do not bear witness [to any such thing].'

قُلْ إِنَّمَا هُوَ إِلَـٰهٌ وَٰحِدٌ

*Say*, 'Indeed He is the One God,

وَإِنَّنِي بَرِىٓءٌ مِّمَّا تُشْرِكُونَ ۝

and I indeed disown what you associate [with Him].'

ٱلَّذِينَ ءَاتَيْنَـٰهُمُ ٱلْكِتَـٰبَ

20 Those whom We have given the Book

يَعْرِفُونَهُۥ

recognize *him*

كَمَا يَعْرِفُونَ أَبْنَآءَهُمُ

just as they recognize their sons.[1]

ٱلَّذِينَ خَسِرُوٓا۟ أَنفُسَهُمْ

Those who have ruined their souls

فَهُمْ لَا يُؤْمِنُونَ ۝

will not have faith.

وَمَنْ أَظْلَمُ مِمَّنِ

21 Who is a greater wrongdoer than him

ٱفْتَرَىٰ عَلَى ٱللَّهِ كَذِبًا

who fabricates a lie against Allah,

أَوْ كَذَّبَ بِـَٔايَـٰتِهِۦٓ

or denies His signs?

إِنَّهُۥ لَا يُفْلِحُ ٱلظَّـٰلِمُونَ ۝

Indeed the wrongdoers will not be felicitous.

وَيَوْمَ نَحْشُرُهُمْ جَمِيعًا

22 On the day when We gather them all together,

ثُمَّ نَقُولُ لِلَّذِينَ أَشْرَكُوٓا۟

We shall say to those who ascribed partners [to Allah]

أَيْنَ شُرَكَآؤُكُمُ ٱلَّذِينَ كُنتُمْ تَزْعُمُونَ ۝

'Where are your partners that you used to claim?'

ثُمَّ لَمْ تَكُن فِتْنَتُهُمْ إِلَّآ أَن قَالُوا۟

23 Then their only excuse will be to say,

وَٱللَّهِ رَبِّنَا مَا كُنَّا مُشْرِكِينَ ۝

'By Allah, our Lord, we were not polytheists.'

ٱنظُرْ كَيْفَ كَذَبُوا۟ عَلَىٰٓ أَنفُسِهِمْ

24 *Look*, how they forswear themselves,

وَضَلَّ عَنْهُم مَّا كَانُوا۟ يَفْتَرُونَ ۝

and what they used to fabricate has forsaken them.

وَمِنْهُم مَّن يَسْتَمِعُ إِلَيْكَ

25 There are some of them who prick up their ears at *you*,

وَجَعَلْنَا عَلَىٰ قُلُوبِهِمْ أَكِنَّةً

but We have cast veils on their hearts

أَن يَفْقَهُوهُ

lest they should understand it,

---

[1] That is, the Prophet's genuineness is quite evident to the Jews and the Christians because of the prophesies concerning the Prophet's advent and his description in their scriptures.

وَفِىٓ ءَاذَانِهِمْ وَقْرًا

and a deafness into their ears;

وَإِن يَرَوْاْ كُلَّ ءَايَةٍ

and though they should see every sign,

لَّا يُؤْمِنُواْ بِهَا

they will not believe in it.

حَتَّىٰٓ إِذَا جَآءُوكَ يُجَٰدِلُونَكَ

When they come to *you,* to dispute with *you,*

يَقُولُ ٱلَّذِينَ كَفَرُوٓاْ

the faithless say,

إِنْ هَٰذَآ إِلَّآ أَسَٰطِيرُ ٱلْأَوَّلِينَ ۝

'These are nothing but myths of the ancients.'

وَهُمْ يَنْهَوْنَ عَنْهُ

26 They dissuade [others] from [following] *him,*

وَيَنْـَٔوْنَ عَنْهُ

and [themselves] avoid *him*;

وَإِن يُهْلِكُونَ إِلَّآ أَنفُسَهُمْ

yet they destroy no one except themselves,

وَمَا يَشْعُرُونَ ۝

but they are not aware.

وَلَوْ تَرَىٰٓ

27 Were *you* to see

إِذْ وُقِفُواْ عَلَى ٱلنَّارِ

when they are brought to a halt by the Fire,

فَقَالُواْ

whereupon they will say,

يَٰلَيْتَنَا نُرَدُّ

'If only we were sent back [into the world]!

وَلَا نُكَذِّبَ بِـَٔايَٰتِ رَبِّنَا

Then we will not deny the signs of our Lord,

وَنَكُونَ مِنَ ٱلْمُؤْمِنِينَ ۝

and we will be among the faithful!'

بَلْ بَدَا لَهُم

28 Rather, now has become evident to them

مَّا كَانُواْ يُخْفُونَ مِن قَبْلُ

what they used to hide before.

وَلَوْ رُدُّواْ

But were they to be sent back

لَعَادُواْ لِمَا نُهُواْ عَنْهُ

they would revert to what they were forbidden,

وَإِنَّهُمْ لَكَٰذِبُونَ ۝

and they are indeed liars.

وَقَالُوٓاْ إِنْ هِىَ إِلَّا حَيَاتُنَا ٱلدُّنْيَا

29 They say, 'There is nothing but our life of this world,

وَمَا نَحْنُ بِمَبْعُوثِينَ ۝

and we shall not be resurrected.'

وَلَوْ تَرَىٰٓ

30 Were *you* to see

إِذْ وُقِفُواْ عَلَىٰ رَبِّهِمْ

when they are stationed before their Lord.

قَالَ أَلَيْسَ هَٰذَا بِٱلْحَقِّ

He will say, 'Is this not the truth?'

قَالُواْ بَلَىٰ وَرَبِّنَا

They will say, 'Yes, by our Lord!'

قَالَ فَذُوقُواْ ٱلْعَذَابَ

He will say, 'So taste the punishment

بِمَا كُنتُمْ تَكْفُرُونَ ۝

because of what you used to disbelieve.'

قَدْ خَسِرَ ٱلَّذِينَ كَذَّبُواْ

31 They are certainly losers who deny

بِلِقَآءِ ٱللَّهِ ۚ

the encounter with Allah.

حَتَّىٰ إِذَا جَآءَتْهُمُ ٱلسَّاعَةُ بَغْتَةً

When the Hour overtakes them suddenly,

قَالُوا۟ يَـٰحَسْرَتَنَا عَلَىٰ مَا فَرَّطْنَا فِيهَا

they will say, 'Alas for us, for what we neglected in it!'

وَهُمْ يَحْمِلُونَ أَوْزَارَهُمْ عَلَىٰ ظُهُورِهِمْ ۚ

And they will bear their burdens on their backs.

أَلَا سَآءَ مَا يَزِرُونَ ۝

Look! Evil is what they bear!

وَمَا ٱلْحَيَوٰةُ ٱلدُّنْيَآ

32 The life of the world is nothing

إِلَّا لَعِبٌ وَلَهْوٌ ۖ

but play and diversion,

وَلَلدَّارُ ٱلْآخِرَةُ خَيْرٌ

and the abode of the Hereafter is surely better

لِّلَّذِينَ يَتَّقُونَ ۗ

for those who are Godwary.

أَفَلَا تَعْقِلُونَ ۝

Do you not apply reason?

قَدْ نَعْلَمُ إِنَّهُ لَيَحْزُنُكَ ٱلَّذِى يَقُولُونَ ۖ

33 We certainly know that what they say grieves *you*.

فَإِنَّهُمْ لَا يُكَذِّبُونَكَ

Yet it is not *you* that they deny,

وَلَـٰكِنَّ ٱلظَّـٰلِمِينَ بِـَٔايَـٰتِ ٱللَّهِ يَجْحَدُونَ ۝

but it is Allah's signs that the wrongdoers impugn.

وَلَقَدْ كُذِّبَتْ رُسُلٌ مِّن قَبْلِكَ

34 Apostles were certainly denied before *you*,

فَصَبَرُوا۟ عَلَىٰ مَا كُذِّبُوا۟ وَأُوذُوا۟

yet they patiently bore being denied and tormented

حَتَّىٰ أَتَىٰهُمْ نَصْرُنَا ۚ

until Our help came to them.

وَلَا مُبَدِّلَ لِكَلِمَـٰتِ ٱللَّهِ ۚ

Nothing can change the words of Allah,

وَلَقَدْ جَآءَكَ

and there have certainly come to *you*

مِن نَّبَإِ ٱلْمُرْسَلِينَ ۝

some of the accounts of the apostles.

وَإِن كَانَ كَبُرَ عَلَيْكَ إِعْرَاضُهُمْ

35 And should their aversion be hard on *you*,

فَإِنِ ٱسْتَطَعْتَ أَن تَبْتَغِىَ نَفَقًا فِى ٱلْأَرْضِ

find, if *you* can, a tunnel into the ground,

أَوْ سُلَّمًا فِى ٱلسَّمَآءِ

or a ladder into sky,

فَتَأْتِيَهُم بِـَٔايَةٍ ۚ

that *you* may bring them a sign.

وَلَوْ شَآءَ ٱللَّهُ

Had Allah wished,

لَجَمَعَهُمْ عَلَى ٱلْهُدَىٰ ۚ

He would have brought them together on guidance.

فَلَا تَكُونَنَّ مِنَ ٱلْجَـٰهِلِينَ ۝ ۞

So *do not be* one of the ignorant.

إِنَّمَا يَسْتَجِيبُ ٱلَّذِينَ يَسْمَعُونَ ۘ

36 Only those who listen will respond [to *you*].

وَٱلْمَوْتَىٰ يَبْعَثُهُمُ ٱللَّهُ

As for the dead, Allah will resurrect them,

ثُمَّ إِلَيْهِ يُرْجَعُونَ ۝

then they will be brought back to Him.

وَقَالُوا۟

37 They say,

لَوْلَا نُزِّلَ عَلَيْهِ ءَايَةٌ 'Why has not a sign been sent down to him

مِّن رَّبِّهِ from his Lord?'

قُلْ إِنَّ ٱللَّهَ قَادِرٌ عَلَىٰ أَن يُنَزِّلَ ءَايَةً *Say,* 'Allah is indeed able to send down a sign,'

وَلَٰكِنَّ أَكْثَرَهُمْ لَا يَعْلَمُونَ ۝ but most of them do not know.

وَمَا مِن دَآبَّةٍ فِى ٱلْأَرْضِ 38 There is no animal on land,

وَلَا طَٰٓئِرٍ يَطِيرُ بِجَنَاحَيْهِ nor a bird that flies with its wings,

إِلَّآ أُمَمٌ أَمْثَالُكُم but they are communities like yourselves.

مَّا فَرَّطْنَا فِى ٱلْكِتَٰبِ مِن شَىْءٍ We have not omitted anything from the Book.

ثُمَّ إِلَىٰ رَبِّهِمْ يُحْشَرُونَ ۝ Then they will be mustered toward their Lord.

وَٱلَّذِينَ كَذَّبُوا۟ بِـَٔايَٰتِنَا صُمٌّ وَبُكْمٌ 39 Those who deny Our signs are deaf and dumb,

فِى ٱلظُّلُمَٰتِ in a manifold darkness.

مَن يَشَإِ ٱللَّهُ يُضْلِلْهُ Allah leads astray whomever He wishes,

وَمَن يَشَأْ and whomever He wishes

يَجْعَلْهُ عَلَىٰ صِرَٰطٍ مُّسْتَقِيمٍ ۝ He puts him on a straight path.

قُلْ أَرَءَيْتَكُمْ 40 *Say,* 'Tell me,

إِنْ أَتَىٰكُمْ عَذَابُ ٱللَّهِ should Allah's punishment overtake you,

أَوْ أَتَتْكُمُ ٱلسَّاعَةُ or should the Hour overtake you,

أَغَيْرَ ٱللَّهِ تَدْعُونَ will you supplicate anyone other than Allah,

إِن كُنتُمْ صَٰدِقِينَ ۝ should you be truthful?

بَلْ إِيَّاهُ تَدْعُونَ 41 Rather, Him you will supplicate,

فَيَكْشِفُ and He will remove

مَا تَدْعُونَ إِلَيْهِ that for which you supplicated Him,

إِن شَآءَ if He wishes,

وَتَنسَوْنَ and you will forget

مَا تُشْرِكُونَ ۝ what you ascribe [to Him] as [His] partners.'

وَلَقَدْ أَرْسَلْنَآ إِلَىٰٓ أُمَمٍ 42 We have certainly sent [apostles] to nations

مِّن قَبْلِكَ before *you,*

فَأَخَذْنَٰهُم بِٱلْبَأْسَآءِ وَٱلضَّرَّآءِ then We seized them with stress and distress

لَعَلَّهُمْ يَتَضَرَّعُونَ ۝ so that they might entreat [Us].

فَلَوْلَآ 43 Why did they not

إِذْ جَاءَهُم بَأْسُنَا تَضَرَّعُواْ
entreat when Our might overtook them!

وَلَكِن قَسَتْ قُلُوبُهُمْ
But their hearts had hardened,

وَزَيَّنَ لَهُمُ ٱلشَّيْطَنُ
and Satan had made to seem decorous to them

مَا كَانُواْ يَعْمَلُونَ ۝
what they had been doing.

فَلَمَّا نَسُواْ مَا ذُكِّرُواْ بِهِ
44 So when they forgot what they had been admonished of,

فَتَحْنَا عَلَيْهِمْ أَبْوَبَ كُلِّ شَىْءٍ
We opened for them the gates of all [good] things.

حَتَّىٰ إِذَا فَرِحُواْ بِمَآ أُوتُوٓاْ
When they rejoiced in what they were given,

أَخَذْنَهُم بَغْتَةً
We seized them suddenly,

فَإِذَا هُم مُّبْلِسُونَ ۝
whereat, behold, they were despondent.

فَقُطِعَ دَابِرُ ٱلْقَوْمِ ٱلَّذِينَ ظَلَمُواْ
45 Thus the wrongdoing lot were rooted out,

وَٱلْحَمْدُ لِلَّهِ
and all praise belongs to Allah,

رَبِّ ٱلْعَلَمِينَ ۝
the Lord of all the worlds.

قُلْ أَرَءَيْتُمْ إِنْ أَخَذَ ٱللَّهُ سَمْعَكُمْ
46 Say, 'Tell me, should Allah take away your hearing

وَأَبْصَرَكُمْ
and your sight

وَخَتَمَ عَلَىٰ قُلُوبِكُم
and set a seal on your hearts,

مَّنْ إِلَهٌ غَيْرُ ٱللَّهِ
which god other than Allah

يَأْتِيكُم بِهِ
can bring it [back] to you?'

ٱنظُرْ كَيْفَ نُصَرِّفُ ٱلْآيَتِ
Look, how We paraphrase the signs variously;

ثُمَّ هُمْ يَصْدِفُونَ ۝
nevertheless they turn away.

قُلْ أَرَءَيْتَكُمْ إِنْ أَتَىٰكُمْ عَذَابُ ٱللَّهِ
47 Say, 'Tell me, should Allah's punishment overtake you

بَغْتَةً أَوْ جَهْرَةً
suddenly or visibly,

هَلْ يُهْلَكُ إِلَّا ٱلْقَوْمُ ٱلظَّلِمُونَ ۝
will anyone be destroyed except the wrongdoing lot?'

وَمَا نُرْسِلُ ٱلْمُرْسَلِينَ
48 We do not send the apostles

إِلَّا مُبَشِّرِينَ وَمُنذِرِينَ
except as bearers of good news and warners.

فَمَنْ ءَامَنَ وَأَصْلَحَ
As for those who are faithful and righteous,

فَلَا خَوْفٌ عَلَيْهِمْ
they will have no fear,

وَلَا هُمْ يَحْزَنُونَ ۝
nor will they grieve.

وَٱلَّذِينَ كَذَّبُواْ بِآيَتِنَا
49 But as for those who deny Our signs,

يَمَسُّهُمُ ٱلْعَذَابُ
the punishment shall befall them

بِمَا كَانُواْ يَفْسُقُونَ ۝
because of the transgressions they used to commit.

179

قُل لَّآ أَقُولُ لَكُمْ    50 *Say,* 'I do not say to you

عِندِى خَزَآئِنُ ٱللَّهِ    that I possess the treasures of Allah,

وَلَآ أَعْلَمُ ٱلْغَيْبَ    nor do I know the Unseen,

وَلَآ أَقُولُ لَكُمْ إِنِّى مَلَكٌ    nor do I say to you that I am an angel.

إِنْ أَتَّبِعُ إِلَّا مَا يُوحَىٰٓ إِلَىَّ    I follow only what is revealed to me.'

قُلْ هَلْ يَسْتَوِى ٱلْأَعْمَىٰ وَٱلْبَصِيرُ    *Say,* 'Are the blind one and the seer equal?

أَفَلَا تَتَفَكَّرُونَ ۝    So do you not reflect?'

وَأَنذِرْ بِهِ ٱلَّذِينَ يَخَافُونَ    51 And *warn* by its[1] means those who fear

أَن يُحْشَرُوٓاْ إِلَىٰ رَبِّهِمْ    being mustered toward their Lord,

لَيْسَ لَهُم مِّن دُونِهِۦ وَلِىٌّ    besides whom they shall have neither any guardian

وَلَا شَفِيعٌ    nor any intercessor,

لَّعَلَّهُمْ يَتَّقُونَ ۝    so that they may be Godwary.

وَلَا تَطْرُدِ ٱلَّذِينَ يَدْعُونَ رَبَّهُم    52 Do not drive away those who supplicate their Lord

بِٱلْغَدَوٰةِ وَٱلْعَشِىِّ    morning and evening

يُرِيدُونَ وَجْهَهُۥ    desiring His face.[2]

مَا عَلَيْكَ مِنْ حِسَابِهِم مِّن شَىْءٍ    Neither are *you* accountable for them in any way,

وَمَا مِنْ حِسَابِكَ عَلَيْهِم مِّن شَىْءٍ    nor are they accountable for *you* in any way,

فَتَطْرُدَهُمْ    so that *you* may drive them away

فَتَكُونَ مِنَ ٱلظَّٰلِمِينَ ۝    and thus become one of the wrongdoers.

وَكَذَٰلِكَ فَتَنَّا بَعْضَهُم بِبَعْضٍ    53 Thus do We test them by means of one another

لِّيَقُولُوٓاْ    so that they should say,

أَهَٰٓؤُلَآءِ مَنَّ ٱللَّهُ عَلَيْهِم    'Are these the ones whom Allah has favoured

مِّنۢ بَيْنِنَآ    from among us?!'

أَلَيْسَ ٱللَّهُ بِأَعْلَمَ بِٱلشَّٰكِرِينَ ۝    Does not Allah know best the grateful?!

وَإِذَا جَآءَكَ ٱلَّذِينَ يُؤْمِنُونَ بِـَٔايَٰتِنَا    54 When those who have faith in Our signs come to *you,*

فَقُلْ سَلَٰمٌ عَلَيْكُمْ    *say,* 'Peace to you!

---

[1] That is, the Qur'ān, referred to in the preceding verse: 'I follow only what is revealed to me.'

[2] Or 'desiring only Him.' The phrase '*yurīdūna wajha*' has been interpreted variously as meaning 'seeking His nearness,' 'seeking His presence,' 'desiring His reward,' 'seeking His pleasure,' and 'pursuing His path.' Cf. 17:28.

كَتَبَ رَبُّكُمْ عَلَىٰ نَفْسِهِ ٱلرَّحْمَةَ ۖ
أَنَّهُۥ مَنْ عَمِلَ مِنكُمْ سُوٓءًۢا
بِجَهَٰلَةٍ
ثُمَّ تَابَ مِنۢ بَعْدِهِۦ وَأَصْلَحَ
فَأَنَّهُۥ غَفُورٌ رَّحِيمٌ ۝

Your Lord has made mercy incumbent upon Himself:
    whoever of you commits an evil [deed]
        out of ignorance
    and then repents after that and reforms,
    then He is indeed all-forgiving, all-merciful.'

وَكَذَٰلِكَ نُفَصِّلُ ٱلْءَايَٰتِ
وَلِتَسْتَبِينَ سَبِيلُ ٱلْمُجْرِمِينَ ۝

55 Thus do We elaborate[1] the signs,
    so that the way of the guilty may be exposed.

قُلْ إِنِّى نُهِيتُ أَنْ أَعْبُدَ
ٱلَّذِينَ تَدْعُونَ مِن دُونِ ٱللَّهِ ۚ

56 Say, 'I have been forbidden to worship
    those whom you invoke besides Allah.'

قُل لَّآ أَتَّبِعُ أَهْوَآءَكُمْ ۙ
قَدْ ضَلَلْتُ إِذًا
وَمَآ أَنَا۠ مِنَ ٱلْمُهْتَدِينَ ۝

Say, 'I do not follow your desires,
    for then I will have gone astray,
    and I will not be among the [rightly] guided.'

قُلْ إِنِّى عَلَىٰ بَيِّنَةٍ
مِّن رَّبِّى
وَكَذَّبْتُم بِهِۦ ۚ

57 Say, 'Indeed I stand on a manifest proof
    from my Lord
    and you have denied it.

مَا عِندِى مَا تَسْتَعْجِلُونَ بِهِۦٓ ۚ
إِنِ ٱلْحُكْمُ إِلَّا لِلَّهِ ۖ
يَقُصُّ ٱلْحَقَّ ۖ
وَهُوَ خَيْرُ ٱلْفَٰصِلِينَ ۝

What you seek to hasten is not up to me.
Judgement belongs only to Allah;
    He expounds the truth
    and He is the best of judges.'

قُل لَّوْ أَنَّ عِندِى مَا تَسْتَعْجِلُونَ بِهِۦ
لَقُضِىَ ٱلْأَمْرُ
بَيْنِى وَبَيْنَكُمْ ۗ
وَٱللَّهُ أَعْلَمُ بِٱلظَّٰلِمِينَ ۝

58 Say, 'If what you seek to hasten were with me,
    the matter would surely have been decided
    between you and me,
    and Allah knows best the wrongdoers.'

وَعِندَهُۥ مَفَاتِحُ ٱلْغَيْبِ
لَا يَعْلَمُهَآ إِلَّا هُوَ ۚ
وَيَعْلَمُ مَا فِى ٱلْبَرِّ وَٱلْبَحْرِ ۚ
وَمَا تَسْقُطُ مِن وَرَقَةٍ إِلَّا يَعْلَمُهَا

59 With Him are the treasures of the Unseen;[2]
    no one knows them except Him.
He knows whatever there is in land and sea.
No leaf falls without His knowing it,

---

1 Or 'articulate.' Cf. 6:97, 98, 126, 154; 7:32, 52, 145, 174; 9:10; 10:5, 24, 37;
  11:1; 13:2; 30:28; 41:3, 44.

2 Or 'the keys of the Unseen.'

وَلَا حَبَّةٍ فِى ظُلُمَتِ ٱلْأَرْضِ nor is there a grain in the darkness of the earth,

وَلَا رَطْبٍ وَلَا يَابِسٍ nor anything fresh or withered

إِلَّا فِى كِتَبٍ مُبِينٍ ۞ but it is in a manifest Book.

وَهُوَ ٱلَّذِى يَتَوَفَّىٰكُم بِٱلَّيْلِ 60 It is He who takes your souls by night,

وَيَعْلَمُ مَا جَرَحْتُم بِٱلنَّهَارِ and He knows what you do by day,

ثُمَّ يَبْعَثُكُمْ فِيهِ then He reanimates you therein

لِيُقْضَىٰ أَجَلٌ مُّسَمًّى so that a specified term may be completed.

ثُمَّ إِلَيْهِ مَرْجِعُكُمْ Then to Him will be your return,

ثُمَّ يُنَبِّئُكُم whereat He will inform you

بِمَا كُنتُمْ تَعْمَلُونَ ۞ concerning what you used to do.

وَهُوَ ٱلْقَاهِرُ فَوْقَ عِبَادِهِۦ 61 He is the All-dominant over His servants,

وَيُرْسِلُ عَلَيْكُمْ حَفَظَةً and He sends guards to [protect] you.

حَتَّىٰ إِذَا جَآءَ أَحَدَكُمُ ٱلْمَوْتُ When death approaches anyone of you,

تَوَفَّتْهُ رُسُلُنَا Our messengers take him away

وَهُمْ لَا يُفَرِّطُونَ ۞ and they do not neglect [their duty].

ثُمَّ رُدُّوٓا۟ إِلَى ٱللَّهِ مَوْلَىٰهُمُ ٱلْحَقِّ 62 Then they are returned to Allah, their real master.

أَلَا لَهُ ٱلْحُكْمُ Look! All judgement belongs to Him,

وَهُوَ أَسْرَعُ ٱلْحَٰسِبِينَ ۞ and He is the swiftest of reckoners.

قُلْ مَن يُنَجِّيكُم مِّن ظُلُمَٰتِ 63 Say, 'Who delivers you from the darkness

ٱلْبَرِّ وَٱلْبَحْرِ of land and sea,

تَدْعُونَهُۥ تَضَرُّعًا وَخُفْيَةً [when] You invoke Him suppliantly and secretly:

لَّئِنْ أَنجَىٰنَا مِنْ هَٰذِهِۦ "If He delivers us from this,

لَنَكُونَنَّ مِنَ ٱلشَّٰكِرِينَ ۞ we will surely be among the grateful"?'

قُلِ ٱللَّهُ يُنَجِّيكُم مِّنْهَا 64 Say, 'It is Allah who delivers you from them

وَمِن كُلِّ كَرْبٍ and from every agony,

ثُمَّ أَنتُمْ تُشْرِكُونَ ۞ [but] then you ascribe partners [to Him].'

قُلْ هُوَ ٱلْقَادِرُ عَلَىٰٓ أَن يَبْعَثَ عَلَيْكُمْ 65 Say, 'He is able to send upon you

عَذَابًا مِّن فَوْقِكُمْ a punishment from above you

أَوْ مِن تَحْتِ أَرْجُلِكُمْ or from under your feet,

أَوْ يَلْبِسَكُمْ شِيَعًا or confound you as [hostile] factions,

وَيُذِيقَ بَعْضَكُم بَأْسَ بَعْضٍ

and make you taste one another's violence.

ٱنظُرْ كَيْفَ نُصَرِّفُ ٱلْءَايَٰتِ

*Look*, how We paraphrase the signs variously

لَعَلَّهُمْ يَفْقَهُونَ ۝

so that they may understand.

وَكَذَّبَ بِهِۦ قَوْمُكَ وَهُوَ ٱلْحَقُّ

66 *Your* people have denied it, though it is the truth.

قُل لَّسْتُ عَلَيْكُم بِوَكِيلٍ ۝

*Say*, 'It is not my business to watch over you.'

لِّكُلِّ نَبَإٍ مُّسْتَقَرٌّ

67 For every prophecy there is a [preordained] setting,

وَسَوْفَ تَعْلَمُونَ ۝

and soon you will know.

وَإِذَا رَأَيْتَ ٱلَّذِينَ

68 When you see those who

يَخُوضُونَ فِىٓ ءَايَٰتِنَا

gossip impiously about Our signs,

فَأَعْرِضْ عَنْهُمْ حَتَّىٰ يَخُوضُوا۟

avoid them until they engage

فِى حَدِيثٍ غَيْرِهِۦ

in some other discourse;

وَإِمَّا يُنسِيَنَّكَ ٱلشَّيْطَٰنُ

but if Satan makes you forget,

فَلَا تَقْعُدْ بَعْدَ ٱلذِّكْرَىٰ

then, after remembering, do not sit

مَعَ ٱلْقَوْمِ ٱلظَّٰلِمِينَ ۝

with the wrongdoing lot.

وَمَا عَلَى ٱلَّذِينَ يَتَّقُونَ

69 Those who are Godwary

مِنْ حِسَابِهِم مِّن شَىْءٍ

are in no way accountable for them,[1]

وَلَٰكِن ذِكْرَىٰ

but this is merely for admonition's sake,

لَعَلَّهُمْ يَتَّقُونَ ۝

so that they may beware.[2]

وَذَرِ ٱلَّذِينَ ٱتَّخَذُوا۟

70 *Leave alone* those who take

دِينَهُمْ لَعِبًا وَلَهْوًا

their religion for play and diversion

وَغَرَّتْهُمُ ٱلْحَيَوٰةُ ٱلدُّنْيَا

and whom the life of this world has deceived,

وَذَكِّرْ بِهِۦ

and admonish with it,

أَن تُبْسَلَ نَفْسٌ

lest any soul should perish

بِمَا كَسَبَتْ

because of what it has earned:

لَيْسَ لَهَا مِن دُونِ ٱللَّهِ وَلِىٌّ

It shall not have any guardian besides Allah,

وَلَا شَفِيعٌ

nor any intercessor;

وَإِن تَعْدِلْ كُلَّ عَدْلٍ

and though it should offer every kind of ransom,

لَّا يُؤْخَذْ مِنْهَآ

it shall not be accepted from it.

---

[1] That is, for those who deride Allah's signs.

[2] That is, of the company of those who deride Allah's signs.

أُوْلَٰئِكَ ٱلَّذِينَ أُبْسِلُواْ

They are the ones who perish

بِمَا كَسَبُواْ

because of what they have earned;

لَهُمْ شَرَابٌ مِّنْ حَمِيمٍ

they shall have boiling water for drink

وَعَذَابٌ أَلِيمٌ

and a painful punishment

بِمَا كَانُواْ يَكْفُرُونَ ٧٠

because of what they used to defy.

قُلْ أَنَدْعُواْ مِن دُونِ ٱللَّهِ 71

*Say,* 'Shall we invoke besides Allah

مَا لَا يَنفَعُنَا وَلَا يَضُرُّنَا

that which can neither benefit us nor harm us,

وَنُرَدُّ عَلَىٰ أَعْقَابِنَا بَعْدَ إِذْ هَدَىٰنَا ٱللَّهُ

and turn back on our heels after Allah has guided us,

كَٱلَّذِي ٱسْتَهْوَتْهُ ٱلشَّيَٰطِينُ

like someone seduced by the devils

فِي ٱلْأَرْضِ حَيْرَانَ

and bewildered on the earth,

لَهُۥ أَصْحَٰبٌ يَدْعُونَهُۥٓ إِلَى ٱلْهُدَى

who has companions that invite him to guidance,

ٱئْتِنَا

[saying,] "Come to us!"?'

قُلْ إِنَّ هُدَى ٱللَّهِ

*Say,* 'Indeed it is the guidance of Allah

هُوَ ٱلْهُدَى

which is [true] guidance.

وَأُمِرْنَا لِنُسْلِمَ

and we have been commanded to submit

لِرَبِّ ٱلْعَٰلَمِينَ ٧١

to the Lord of all the worlds,

وَأَنْ أَقِيمُواْ ٱلصَّلَوٰةَ وَٱتَّقُوهُ 72

and that "Maintain the prayer and be wary of Him,

وَهُوَ ٱلَّذِي إِلَيْهِ تُحْشَرُونَ ٧٢

and it is He toward whom you will be gathered."'

وَهُوَ ٱلَّذِي خَلَقَ ٱلسَّمَٰوَٰتِ وَٱلْأَرْضَ 73

It is He who created the heavens and the earth

بِٱلْحَقِّ

with the truth;

وَيَوْمَ يَقُولُ كُن فَيَكُونُ

and the day He says [to something], 'Be!' it is.

قَوْلُهُ ٱلْحَقُّ وَلَهُ ٱلْمُلْكُ

His word is the truth, and to Him belongs all sovereignty

يَوْمَ يُنفَخُ فِي ٱلصُّورِ

on the day when the Trumpet will be blown.

عَٰلِمُ ٱلْغَيْبِ وَٱلشَّهَٰدَةِ

Knower of the sensible and the Unseen,

وَهُوَ ٱلْحَكِيمُ ٱلْخَبِيرُ ٧٣

He is the All-wise, the All-aware.

وَإِذْ قَالَ إِبْرَٰهِيمُ لِأَبِيهِ ءَازَرَ 74

When Abraham said to Azar, his father,

أَتَتَّخِذُ أَصْنَامًا ءَالِهَةً

'Do you take idols for gods?

إِنِّي أَرَىٰكَ وَقَوْمَكَ فِي ضَلَٰلٍ مُّبِينٍ ٧٤

Indeed I see you and your people in manifest error.'

وَكَذَٰلِكَ نُرِي إِبْرَٰهِيمَ 75

Thus did We show Abraham

مَلَكُوتَ ٱلسَّمَـٰوَٰتِ وَٱلْأَرْضِ
the dominions of the heavens and the earth,

وَلِيَكُونَ مِنَ ٱلْمُوقِنِينَ ۝
that he might be of those who possess certitude.

فَلَمَّا جَنَّ عَلَيْهِ ٱلَّيْلُ رَءَا كَوْكَبًا
76 When night darkened over him, he saw a star

قَالَ هَـٰذَا رَبِّى
and said, 'This is my Lord!'

فَلَمَّا أَفَلَ
But when it set,

قَالَ لَآ أُحِبُّ ٱلْأَفِلِينَ ۝
he said, 'I do not like those who set.'

فَلَمَّا رَءَا ٱلْقَمَرَ بَازِغًا
77 Then, when he saw the moon rising,

قَالَ هَـٰذَا رَبِّى
he said, 'This is my Lord!'

فَلَمَّا أَفَلَ
But when it set,

قَالَ لَئِن لَّمْ يَهْدِنِى رَبِّى
he said, 'Had my Lord not guided me,

لَأَكُونَنَّ مِنَ ٱلْقَوْمِ ٱلضَّآلِّينَ ۝
I would surely have been among the astray lot.'

فَلَمَّا رَءَا ٱلشَّمْسَ بَازِغَةً
78 Then, when he saw the sun rising,

قَالَ هَـٰذَا رَبِّى هَـٰذَآ أَكْبَرُ
he said, 'This is my Lord! This is bigger!'

فَلَمَّآ أَفَلَتْ قَالَ يَـٰقَوْمِ
But when it set, he said, 'O my people,

إِنِّى بَرِىٓءٌ مِّمَّا تُشْرِكُونَ ۝
indeed I disown what you take as [His] partners.'

إِنِّى وَجَّهْتُ وَجْهِىَ
79 Indeed I have turned my face

لِلَّذِى فَطَرَ ٱلسَّمَـٰوَٰتِ وَٱلْأَرْضَ
toward Him who originated the heavens and the earth,

حَنِيفًا
as a *hanif*,

وَمَآ أَنَا۠ مِنَ ٱلْمُشْرِكِينَ ۝
and I am not one of the polytheists.'

وَحَآجَّهُۥ قَوْمُهُۥ
80 His people argued with him.

قَالَ أَتُحَـٰجُّوٓنِّى فِى ٱللَّهِ
He said, 'Do you argue with me concerning Allah,

وَقَدْ هَدَٰنِ
while He has guided me for certain?

وَلَآ أَخَافُ
I do not fear

مَا تُشْرِكُونَ بِهِۦٓ
what you ascribe to Him as [His] partners,

إِلَّآ أَن يَشَآءَ رَبِّى شَيْئًا
excepting anything that my Lord may wish.

وَسِعَ رَبِّى كُلَّ شَىْءٍ عِلْمًا
My Lord embraces all things in [His] knowledge.

أَفَلَا تَتَذَكَّرُونَ ۝
Will you not then take admonition?

وَكَيْفَ أَخَافُ
81 How could I fear

مَآ أَشْرَكْتُمْ
what you ascribe [to Him] as [His] partners,

وَلَا تَخَافُونَ أَنَّكُمْ أَشْرَكْتُم بِٱللَّهِ
when you do not fear ascribing to Allah partners

مَا لَمْ يُنَزِّلْ بِهِۦ عَلَيْكُمْ سُلْطَـٰنًا for which He has not sent down any authority to you?

فَأَىُّ ٱلْفَرِيقَيْنِ So [tell me,] which of the two sides

أَحَقُّ بِٱلْأَمْنِ has a greater right to safety,

إِن كُنتُمْ تَعْلَمُونَ ۝ if you know?

ٱلَّذِينَ ءَامَنُوا 82 Those who have faith

وَلَمْ يَلْبِسُوٓا۟ إِيمَـٰنَهُم بِظُلْمٍ and do not taint their faith with wrongdoing

أُو۟لَـٰٓئِكَ لَهُمُ ٱلْأَمْنُ —for such there shall be safety,

وَهُم مُّهْتَدُونَ ۝ and they are the [rightly] guided.'

وَتِلْكَ حُجَّتُنَآ ءَاتَيْنَـٰهَآ إِبْرَٰهِيمَ 83 This was Our argument that We gave to Abraham

عَلَىٰ قَوْمِهِۦ against his people.

نَرْفَعُ دَرَجَـٰتٍ مَّن نَّشَآءُ We raise in rank whomever We wish.

إِنَّ رَبَّكَ حَكِيمٌ عَلِيمٌ ۝ Indeed *your* Lord is all-wise, all-knowing.

وَوَهَبْنَا لَهُۥٓ إِسْحَـٰقَ وَيَعْقُوبَ 84 And We gave him Isaac and Jacob

كُلًّا هَدَيْنَا and guided each of them.

وَنُوحًا هَدَيْنَا مِن قَبْلُ And Noah We had guided before,

وَمِن ذُرِّيَّتِهِۦ دَاوُۥدَ وَسُلَيْمَـٰنَ and from his offspring, David and Solomon,

وَأَيُّوبَ وَيُوسُفَ وَمُوسَىٰ وَهَـٰرُونَ Job, Joseph, Moses and Aaron

وَكَذَٰلِكَ نَجْزِى ٱلْمُحْسِنِينَ ۝ —thus do We reward the virtuous—

وَزَكَرِيَّا وَيَحْيَىٰ وَعِيسَىٰ وَإِلْيَاسَ 85 and Zechariah, John, Jesus and Ilyās,

كُلٌّ مِّنَ ٱلصَّـٰلِحِينَ ۝ —each of them among the righteous—

وَإِسْمَـٰعِيلَ وَٱلْيَسَعَ وَيُونُسَ وَلُوطًا 86 and Ishmael, Elisha, Jonah and Lot

وَكُلًّا فَضَّلْنَا عَلَى ٱلْعَـٰلَمِينَ ۝ —each We graced over all the nations—

وَمِنْ ءَابَآئِهِمْ 87 and from among their fathers,

وَذُرِّيَّـٰتِهِمْ وَإِخْوَٰنِهِمْ their descendants and brethren

وَٱجْتَبَيْنَـٰهُمْ —We chose them

وَهَدَيْنَـٰهُمْ إِلَىٰ صِرَٰطٍ مُّسْتَقِيمٍ ۝ and guided them to a straight path.

ذَٰلِكَ هُدَى ٱللَّهِ 88 That is Allah's guidance:

يَهْدِى بِهِۦ with it He guides

مَن يَشَآءُ مِنْ عِبَادِهِۦ whomever He wishes of His servants.

وَلَوْ أَشْرَكُوا۟ But were they to ascribe any partners [to Allah],

لَحَبِطَ عَنْهُم مَّا كَانُوا يَعْمَلُونَ ۞ what they used to do would not avail them.

أُوْلَٰٓئِكَ ٱلَّذِينَ ءَاتَيْنَٰهُمُ ٱلْكِتَٰبَ 89 They are the ones whom We gave the Book,

وَٱلْحُكْمَ وَٱلنُّبُوَّةَ the judgement and prophethood.

فَإِن يَكْفُرْ بِهَا هَٰٓؤُلَآءِ So if these disbelieve in them,

فَقَدْ وَكَّلْنَا بِهَا قَوْمًا We have certainly entrusted them to a people

لَّيْسُوا بِهَا بِكَٰفِرِينَ ۞ who will never disbelieve in them.

أُوْلَٰٓئِكَ ٱلَّذِينَ هَدَى ٱللَّهُ 90 They are the ones whom Allah has guided.

فَبِهُدَىٰهُمُ ٱقْتَدِهْ So *follow* their guidance.

قُل لَّآ أَسْـَٔلُكُمْ عَلَيْهِ أَجْرًا *Say*, 'I do not ask you any recompense for it.

إِنْ هُوَ إِلَّا ذِكْرَىٰ لِلْعَٰلَمِينَ ۞ It is just an admonition for all the nations.'

وَمَا قَدَرُوا ٱللَّهَ حَقَّ قَدْرِهِۦٓ 91 They did not regard Allah with the regard due to Him

إِذْ قَالُوا when they said,

مَآ أَنزَلَ ٱللَّهُ عَلَىٰ بَشَرٍ مِّن شَىْءٍ 'Allah has not sent down anything to any human.'

قُلْ مَنْ أَنزَلَ ٱلْكِتَٰبَ ٱلَّذِى *Say*, 'Who had sent down the Book

جَآءَ بِهِ مُوسَىٰ that was brought by Moses

نُورًا وَهُدًى لِّلنَّاسِ as a light and guidance for the people,

تَجْعَلُونَهُۥ قَرَاطِيسَ تُبْدُونَهَا which You make into parchments that you display,

وَتُخْفُونَ كَثِيرًا while you conceal much of it,

وَعُلِّمْتُم and [by means of which] you were taught

مَّا لَمْ تَعْلَمُوٓا what you did not know,

أَنتُمْ وَلَآ ءَابَآؤُكُمْ [neither] you nor your fathers?'

قُلِ ٱللَّهُ *Say*, 'Allah!'

ثُمَّ ذَرْهُمْ فِى خَوْضِهِمْ يَلْعَبُونَ ۞ Then leave them to play around in their impious gossip.

وَهَٰذَا كِتَٰبٌ أَنزَلْنَٰهُ مُبَارَكٌ 92 Blessed is this Book which We have sent down,

مُّصَدِّقُ ٱلَّذِى بَيْنَ يَدَيْهِ confirming what was [revealed] before it,

وَلِتُنذِرَ أُمَّ ٱلْقُرَىٰ so that *you* may warn the Mother of Cities[1]

وَمَنْ حَوْلَهَا and those around it.

وَٱلَّذِينَ يُؤْمِنُونَ بِٱلْأَخِرَةِ يُؤْمِنُونَ بِهِۦ Those who believe in the Hereafter believe in it,

وَهُمْ عَلَىٰ صَلَاتِهِمْ يُحَافِظُونَ ۞ and they are watchful of their prayers.

---

[1] That is, the people of Makkah, known at the time as 'the Mother of the Cities.'

وَمَنْ أَظْلَمُ مِمَّنِ 93 Who is a greater wrongdoer than him

افْتَرَى عَلَى اللَّهِ كَذِبًا who fabricates a lie against Allah,

أَوْ قَالَ أُوحِيَ إِلَيَّ or says, 'It has been revealed to me,'

وَلَمْ يُوحَ إِلَيْهِ شَيْءٌ while nothing was revealed to him,

وَمَن قَالَ and he who says,

سَأُنزِلُ مِثْلَ مَا أَنزَلَ اللَّهُ 'I will bring the like of what Allah has sent down?'

وَلَوْ تَرَى إِذِ الظَّالِمُونَ Were *you* to see when the wrongdoers

فِي غَمَرَاتِ الْمَوْتِ are in the throes of death,

وَالْمَلَائِكَةُ بَاسِطُوا أَيْدِيهِمْ and the angels extend their hands [saying]:

أَخْرِجُوا أَنفُسَكُمُ 'Give up your souls!

الْيَوْمَ تُجْزَوْنَ Today you shall be requited

عَذَابَ الْهُونِ with a humiliating punishment

بِمَا كُنتُمْ تَقُولُونَ عَلَى اللَّهِ because of what you used to attribute to Allah

غَيْرَ الْحَقِّ untruly,

وَكُنتُمْ عَنْ آيَاتِهِ تَسْتَكْبِرُونَ ۝ and for your being disdainful towards His signs.'

وَلَقَدْ جِئْتُمُونَا فُرَادَى 94 'Certainly you have come to Us alone,

كَمَا خَلَقْنَاكُمْ أَوَّلَ مَرَّةٍ just as We created you the first time,

وَتَرَكْتُم مَّا خَوَّلْنَاكُمْ وَرَاءَ ظُهُورِكُمْ and left behind whatever We had bestowed on you.

وَمَا نَرَى مَعَكُمْ شُفَعَاءَكُمُ We do not see your intercessors with you

الَّذِينَ زَعَمْتُمْ —those whom you claimed

أَنَّهُمْ فِيكُمْ شُرَكَاءُ to be [Our] partners in [deciding] you[r] [fate].

لَقَد تَّقَطَّعَ بَيْنَكُمْ Certainly all links between you have been cut,

وَضَلَّ عَنكُم مَّا كُنتُمْ تَزْعُمُونَ ۝ and what you used to claim has forsaken you!'

إِنَّ اللَّهَ فَالِقُ الْحَبِّ وَالنَّوَى 95 Indeed Allah is the splitter of the grain and the pit.[1]

يُخْرِجُ الْحَيَّ مِنَ الْمَيِّتِ He brings forth the living from the dead

وَمُخْرِجُ الْمَيِّتِ مِنَ الْحَيِّ and He brings forth the dead from the living.

ذَٰلِكُمُ اللَّهُ That is Allah!

---

[1] That is, the single, central kernel or stone of certain fruits, such as a date, peach or cherry.

فَأَنَّىٰ تُؤْفَكُونَ ۝    Then where do you stray?

فَالِقُ ٱلْإِصْبَاحِ    96 Splitter of the dawn,

وَجَعَلَ ٱلَّيْلَ سَكَنًا    He has made the night for rest,

وَٱلشَّمْسَ وَٱلْقَمَرَ حُسْبَانًا    and the sun and the moon for calculation.[1]

ذَٰلِكَ تَقْدِيرُ ٱلْعَزِيزِ    That is the ordaining of the All-mighty,

ٱلْعَلِيمِ ۝    the All-knowing.

وَهُوَ ٱلَّذِى جَعَلَ لَكُمُ ٱلنُّجُومَ    97 It is He who made the stars for you,

لِتَهْتَدُوا۟ بِهَا    so that you may be guided by them

فِى ظُلُمَٰتِ ٱلْبَرِّ وَٱلْبَحْرِ    in the darkness of land and sea.

قَدْ فَصَّلْنَا ٱلْءَايَٰتِ    We have certainly elaborated the signs

لِقَوْمٍ يَعْلَمُونَ ۝    for a people who have knowledge.

وَهُوَ ٱلَّذِى أَنشَأَكُم    98 It is He who created you

مِّن نَّفْسٍ وَٰحِدَةٍ    from a single soul,

فَمُسْتَقَرٌّ    then there is the [enduring] abode

وَمُسْتَوْدَعٌ    and the place of temporary lodging.[2]

قَدْ فَصَّلْنَا ٱلْءَايَٰتِ    We have certainly elaborated the signs

لِقَوْمٍ يَفْقَهُونَ ۝    for a people who understand.

وَهُوَ ٱلَّذِى أَنزَلَ مِنَ ٱلسَّمَآءِ مَآءً    99 It is He who sends down water from the sky,

فَأَخْرَجْنَا بِهِۦ نَبَاتَ كُلِّ شَىْءٍ    and brings forth with it every kind of growing thing.

فَأَخْرَجْنَا مِنْهُ خَضِرًا    Then from it We bring forth vegetation

نُّخْرِجُ مِنْهُ حَبًّا مُّتَرَاكِبًا    from which We produce the grain, in clusters,

وَمِنَ ٱلنَّخْلِ مِن طَلْعِهَا    and from the palm-tree, from the spathes of it,

قِنْوَانٌ دَانِيَةٌ    low-hanging clusters [of dates],

وَجَنَّٰتٍ مِّنْ أَعْنَابٍ وَٱلزَّيْتُونَ    and gardens of grapes, olives

---

[1] That is, of time: days, months and years.

[2] The terms *mustaqarr* and *mustawdaʿ* (alternatively read as *mustaqirr* and *mustawdiʿ*) have been interpreted variously. According to one interpretation, they refer to the mother's womb (*raḥm*) and the father's loins (*ṣulb*) respectively. ʿAyyāshī cites several traditions under this verse from the Imams Muḥammad al-Bāqir, Jaʿfar al-Ṣādiq, Mūsā al-Kāẓim and ʿAlī al-Hādī, which interpret *mustaqarr* (or *mustaqirr*) as the heart of someone whose faith is constant and permanent, and *mustawdaʿ* as that of one whose faith is temporary, passing away at or before death. (Cf. *al-Tafsīr al-Burhān* and *al-Tafsīr al-Ṣāfī*)

وَٱلرُّمَّانَ

and pomegranates,

مُشْتَبِهًا وَغَيْرَ مُتَشَـٰبِهٍۗ

similar and dissimilar.

ٱنظُرُوٓاْ إِلَىٰ ثَمَرِهِۦٓ إِذَآ أَثْمَرَ وَيَنْعِهِۦٓ

Look at its fruit as it fructifies and ripens.

إِنَّ فِى ذَٰلِكُمْ لَأَيَـٰتٍ

Indeed there are signs in that

لِّقَوْمٍ يُؤْمِنُونَ ٩٩

for a people who have faith.

وَجَعَلُواْ لِلَّهِ شُرَكَآءَ ٱلْجِنَّ

100 They make the jinn partners of Allah,

وَخَلَقَهُمْۖ

though He has created them,

وَخَرَقُواْ لَهُۥ بَنِينَ وَبَنَـٰتٍ

and carve out sons and daughters for Him,

بِغَيْرِ عِلْمٍۚ

without any knowledge.

سُبْحَـٰنَهُۥ وَتَعَـٰلَىٰ

Immaculate is He and exalted

عَمَّا يَصِفُونَ ١٠٠

above what they allege [concerning Him]!

بَدِيعُ ٱلسَّمَـٰوَٰتِ وَٱلْأَرْضِۖ

101 The originator of the heavens and the earth

أَنَّىٰ يَكُونُ لَهُۥ وَلَدٌ

—how could He have a son

وَلَمْ تَكُن لَّهُۥ صَـٰحِبَةٌۖ

when He has had no spouse?

وَخَلَقَ كُلَّ شَىْءٍۖ

He created all things

وَهُوَ بِكُلِّ شَىْءٍ عَلِيمٌ ١٠١

and He has knowledge of all things.

ذَٰلِكُمُ ٱللَّهُ رَبُّكُمْۖ

102 That is Allah, your Lord,

لَآ إِلَـٰهَ إِلَّا هُوَۖ

there is no god except Him,

خَـٰلِقُ كُلِّ شَىْءٍ

the creator of all things;

فَٱعْبُدُوهُۚ

so worship Him.

وَهُوَ عَلَىٰ كُلِّ شَىْءٍ وَكِيلٌ ١٠٢

He watches over all things.

لَّا تُدْرِكُهُ ٱلْأَبْصَـٰرُ

103 The sights do not apprehend Him,

وَهُوَ يُدْرِكُ ٱلْأَبْصَـٰرَۖ

yet He apprehends the sights,

وَهُوَ ٱللَّطِيفُ ٱلْخَبِيرُ ١٠٣

and He is the All-attentive,[1] the All-aware.

قَدْ جَآءَكُم بَصَآئِرُ

104 [Say,] 'Certainly insights have come to you

مِن رَّبِّكُمْۖ

from your Lord.

فَمَنْ أَبْصَرَ فَلِنَفْسِهِۦۖ

So whoever sees, it is to the benefit of his own soul,

---

[1] Or 'All-gracious.' Cf. 22:63; 31:16; 33:34; 67:14.

وَمَنْ عَمِيَ

and whoever remains blind,

فَعَلَيْهَا

it is to its detriment,

وَمَآ أَنَا۠ عَلَيْكُم بِحَفِيظٍ ۝

and I am not a keeper over you.'

وَكَذَٰلِكَ نُصَرِّفُ ٱلْأَيَـٰتِ

105 Thus do We paraphrase the signs variously,

وَلِيَقُولُواْ دَرَسْتَ

lest they should say, '*You* have received instruction,'

وَلِنُبَيِّنَهُۥ

and so that We may make it clear

لِقَوْمٍ يَعْلَمُونَ ۝

for a people who have knowledge.

ٱتَّبِعْ مَآ أُوحِىَ إِلَيْكَ

106 *Follow* that which has been revealed to *you*

مِن رَّبِّكَ

from *your* Lord,

لَآ إِلَـٰهَ إِلَّا هُوَ

there is no god except Him,

وَأَعْرِضْ عَنِ ٱلْمُشْرِكِينَ ۝

and *turn away* from the polytheists.

وَلَوْ شَآءَ ٱللَّهُ

107 Had Allah wished

مَآ أَشْرَكُواْ

they would not have ascribed partners [to Him].

وَمَا جَعَلْنَـٰكَ عَلَيْهِمْ حَفِيظًا

We have not made *you* a caretaker for them,

وَمَآ أَنتَ عَلَيْهِم بِوَكِيلٍ ۝

nor is it your duty to watch over them.

وَلَا تَسُبُّواْ ٱلَّذِينَ يَدْعُونَ

108 Do not abuse those whom they invoke

مِن دُونِ ٱللَّهِ

besides Allah,

فَيَسُبُّواْ ٱللَّهَ عَدْوًا

lest they should abuse Allah out of hostility,[1]

بِغَيْرِ عِلْمٍ

without any knowledge.

كَذَٰلِكَ

That is how

زَيَّنَّا لِكُلِّ أُمَّةٍ عَمَلَهُمْ

to every people We have made their conduct seem decorous.

ثُمَّ إِلَىٰ رَبِّهِم مَّرْجِعُهُمْ

Then their return will be to their Lord

فَيُنَبِّئُهُم

and He will inform them

بِمَا كَانُواْ يَعْمَلُونَ ۝

concerning what they used to do.

وَأَقْسَمُواْ بِٱللَّهِ جَهْدَ أَيْمَـٰنِهِمْ

109 They swear by Allah with solemn oaths

لَئِن جَآءَتْهُمْ ءَايَةٌ

that were a sign to come to them

لَّيُؤْمِنُنَّ بِهَا

they would surely believe in it.

قُلْ إِنَّمَا ٱلْأَيَـٰتُ عِندَ ٱللَّهِ

*Say*, 'The signs are only with Allah,'

---

[1] Or 'out of transgression,' or 'wrongfully.'

وَمَا يُشْعِرُكُمْ    and what will bring home to you[1]

أَنَّهَآ إِذَا جَآءَتْ لَا يُؤْمِنُونَ ۱۰۹    that they will not believe even if they came?

وَنُقَلِّبُ أَفْئِدَتَهُمْ وَأَبْصَـٰرَهُمْ    110 We transform their hearts and their visions

كَمَا لَمْ يُؤْمِنُوا۟ بِهِۦٓ أَوَّلَ مَرَّةٍ    as they did not believe in it the first time,

وَنَذَرُهُمْ فِى طُغْيَـٰنِهِمْ يَعْمَهُونَ ۱۱۰ ✻    and We leave them bewildered in their rebellion.

**[PART 8]**

وَلَوْ أَنَّنَا نَزَّلْنَآ إِلَيْهِمُ ٱلْمَلَـٰٓئِكَةَ    111 Even if We had sent down angels to them,

وَكَلَّمَهُمُ ٱلْمَوْتَىٰ    and the dead had spoken to them,

وَحَشَرْنَا عَلَيْهِمْ كُلَّ شَىْءٍ    and We had gathered before them all things

قُبُلًا    manifestly,[2]

مَّا كَانُوا۟ لِيُؤْمِنُوٓا۟ إِلَّآ أَن يَشَآءَ ٱللَّهُ    they would [still] not believe unless Allah wished.

وَلَـٰكِنَّ أَكْثَرَهُمْ يَجْهَلُونَ ۱۱۱    But most of them are ignorant.

وَكَذَٰلِكَ    112 That is how

جَعَلْنَا لِكُلِّ نَبِىٍّ عَدُوًّا    for every prophet We appointed as enemy

شَيَـٰطِينَ ٱلْإِنسِ وَٱلْجِنِّ    the devils from among humans and jinn,

يُوحِى بَعْضُهُمْ إِلَىٰ بَعْضٍ    who inspire each other

زُخْرُفَ ٱلْقَوْلِ    with flashy words,

غُرُورًا    deceptively.

وَلَوْ شَآءَ رَبُّكَ    Had *your* Lord wished,

مَا فَعَلُوهُ    they would not have done it.

فَذَرْهُمْ وَمَا يَفْتَرُونَ ۱۱۲    So *leave* them with what they fabricate,

وَلِتَصْغَىٰٓ إِلَيْهِ أَفْئِدَةُ    113 so that toward it may incline the hearts

ٱلَّذِينَ لَا يُؤْمِنُونَ بِٱلْأَخِرَةِ    of those who do not believe in the Hereafter,

وَلِيَرْضَوْهُ    and so that they may be pleased with it

وَلِيَقْتَرِفُوا۟ مَا هُم مُّقْتَرِفُونَ ۱۱۳    and commit what they commit.

أَفَغَيْرَ ٱللَّهِ أَبْتَغِى حَكَمًا    114 [*Say,*] 'Shall I seek a judge other than Allah,

وَهُوَ ٱلَّذِىٓ أَنزَلَ إِلَيْكُمُ ٱلْكِتَـٰبَ    while it is He who has sent down to you the Book,

مُفَصَّلًا    well-elaborated?'

---

[1] That is, to the faithful.

[2] Or, 'in [their] diversity.'

وَٱلَّذِينَ ءَاتَيْنَهُمُ ٱلْكِتَبَ

Those whom We have given the Book

يَعْلَمُونَ أَنَّهُ مُنَزَّلٌ مِّن رَّبِّكَ

know that it has been sent down from *your* Lord

بِٱلْحَقِّ

with the truth;

فَلَا تَكُونَنَّ مِنَ ٱلْمُمْتَرِينَ ۝

so do not be one of the skeptics.

وَتَمَّتْ كَلِمَتُ رَبِّكَ

115 The word of *your* Lord has been fulfilled

صِدْقًا وَعَدْلًا

in truth and justice.

لَّا مُبَدِّلَ لِكَلِمَتِهِۦ

Nothing can change His words,

وَهُوَ ٱلسَّمِيعُ ٱلْعَلِيمُ ۝

and He is the All-hearing, the All-knowing.

وَإِن تُطِعْ أَكْثَرَ مَن فِى ٱلْأَرْضِ

116 If you obey most of those on the earth,

يُضِلُّوكَ عَن سَبِيلِ ٱللَّهِ

they will lead you astray from the way of Allah.

إِن يَتَّبِعُونَ إِلَّا ٱلظَّنَّ

They follow nothing but conjectures

وَإِنْ هُمْ إِلَّا يَخْرُصُونَ ۝

and they do nothing but surmise.

إِنَّ رَبَّكَ هُوَ أَعْلَمُ مَن يَضِلُّ

117 Indeed your Lord knows best those who stray

عَن سَبِيلِهِۦ

from His way;

وَهُوَ أَعْلَمُ بِٱلْمُهْتَدِينَ ۝

and He knows best those who are guided.

فَكُلُوا۟ مِمَّا

118 Eat from that

ذُكِرَ ٱسْمُ ٱللَّهِ عَلَيْهِ

over which Allah's Name has been mentioned,

إِن كُنتُم بِـَٔايَتِهِۦ مُؤْمِنِينَ ۝

if you are believers in His signs.

وَمَا لَكُمْ أَلَّا تَأْكُلُوا۟

119 Why should you not eat

مِمَّا ذُكِرَ ٱسْمُ ٱللَّهِ عَلَيْهِ

that over which Allah's Name has been mentioned,

وَقَدْ فَصَّلَ لَكُم

while He has already elaborated for you

مَّا حَرَّمَ عَلَيْكُمْ

whatever He has forbidden you,

إِلَّا مَا ٱضْطُرِرْتُمْ إِلَيْهِ

excepting what you may be compelled to [eat]?

وَإِنَّ كَثِيرًا لَّيُضِلُّونَ بِأَهْوَائِهِم

Indeed many mislead [others] by their fancies,

بِغَيْرِ عِلْمٍ

without any knowledge.

إِنَّ رَبَّكَ هُوَ أَعْلَمُ بِٱلْمُعْتَدِينَ ۝

Indeed *your* Lord knows best the transgressors.

وَذَرُوا۟ ظَهَرَ ٱلْإِثْمِ وَبَاطِنَهُۥ

120 Renounce outward sins and the inward ones.

إِنَّ ٱلَّذِينَ يَكْسِبُونَ ٱلْإِثْمَ

Indeed those who commit sins

سَيُجْزَوْنَ بِمَا كَانُوا۟ يَقْتَرِفُونَ ۝

shall be requited for what they used to commit.

وَلَا تَأْكُلُوا۟

121 Do not eat

مِمَّا
[anything] of that

لَمْ يُذْكَرِ ٱسْمُ ٱللَّهِ عَلَيْهِ
over which Allah's Name has not been mentioned,

وَإِنَّهُ لَفِسْقٌ
and that is indeed transgression.

وَإِنَّ ٱلشَّيَـٰطِينَ لَيُوحُونَ إِلَىٰٓ أَوْلِيَآئِهِمْ
Indeed the satans inspire their friends

لِيُجَـٰدِلُوكُمْ
to dispute with you;

وَإِنْ أَطَعْتُمُوهُمْ
and if you obey them,

إِنَّكُمْ لَمُشْرِكُونَ ۝
you will indeed be polytheists.

أَوَمَن كَانَ مَيْتًا فَأَحْيَيْنَـٰهُ
122 Is he who was lifeless, then We gave him life

وَجَعَلْنَا لَهُ نُورًا
and provided him with a light

يَمْشِى بِهِۦ فِى ٱلنَّاسِ
by which he walks among the people,

كَمَن مَّثَلُهُۥ فِى ٱلظُّلُمَـٰتِ
like one who dwells in a manifold darkness

لَيْسَ بِخَارِجٍ مِّنْهَا
which he cannot leave?

كَذَٰلِكَ زُيِّنَ لِلْكَـٰفِرِينَ
To the faithless is thus presented as decorous

مَا كَانُوا۟ يَعْمَلُونَ ۝
what they have been doing.

وَكَذَٰلِكَ جَعَلْنَا فِى كُلِّ قَرْيَةٍ
123 Thus have We installed in every town

أَكَـٰبِرَ مُجْرِمِيهَا
its major criminals

لِيَمْكُرُوا۟ فِيهَا
that they may plot therein.

وَمَا يَمْكُرُونَ إِلَّا بِأَنفُسِهِمْ
Yet they do not plot except against their own souls,

وَمَا يَشْعُرُونَ ۝
but they are not aware.

وَإِذَا جَآءَتْهُمْ ءَايَةٌ قَالُوا۟
124 And when a sign comes to them, they say,

لَن نُّؤْمِنَ حَتَّىٰ نُؤْتَىٰ
'We will not believe until we are given

مِثْلَ مَآ أُوتِىَ رُسُلُ ٱللَّهِ
the like of what was given to Allah's apostles.'

ٱللَّهُ أَعْلَمُ حَيْثُ يَجْعَلُ رِسَالَتَهُۥ
Allah knows best where to place His apostleship!

سَيُصِيبُ ٱلَّذِينَ أَجْرَمُوا۟
Soon the guilty will be visited by

صَغَارٌ عِندَ ٱللَّهِ
a degradation before Allah

وَعَذَابٌ شَدِيدٌۢ
and a severe punishment

بِمَا كَانُوا۟ يَمْكُرُونَ ۝
because of the plots they used to devise.

فَمَن يُرِدِ ٱللَّهُ أَن يَهْدِيَهُۥ
125 Whomever Allah desires to guide,

يَشْرَحْ صَدْرَهُۥ لِلْإِسْلَـٰمِ
He opens his breast to Islam,

وَمَن يُرِدْ أَن يُضِلَّهُۥ
and whomever He desires to lead astray,

تَجْعَلْ صَدْرَهُ ضَيِّقًا حَرَجًا

He makes his breast narrow and straitened

كَأَنَّمَا يَصَّعَّدُ فِى ٱلسَّمَآءِ

as if he were climbing to a height.[1]

كَذَٰلِكَ يَجْعَلُ ٱللَّهُ ٱلرِّجْسَ

Thus does Allah lay [spiritual] defilement

عَلَى ٱلَّذِينَ لَا يُؤْمِنُونَ ۝

on those who do not have faith.

وَهَٰذَا صِرَاطُ رَبِّكَ مُسْتَقِيمًا

126 This is the straight path of *your* Lord.

قَدْ فَصَّلْنَا ٱلْآيَٰتِ

We have already elaborated the signs

لِقَوْمٍ يَذَّكَّرُونَ ۝ ✱

for a people who take admonition.

هُمْ

127 For them shall be

دَارُ ٱلسَّلَٰمِ عِندَ رَبِّهِمْ

the abode of peace near their Lord

وَهُوَ وَلِيُّهُم

and He will be their guardian

بِمَا كَانُوا۟ يَعْمَلُونَ ۝

because of what they used to do.

وَيَوْمَ يَحْشُرُهُمْ جَمِيعًا

128 On the day He will gather them all together,

يَٰمَعْشَرَ ٱلْجِنِّ

[He will say], 'O company of jinn!

قَدِ ٱسْتَكْثَرْتُم مِّنَ ٱلْإِنسِ

You claimed many of the humans.'

وَقَالَ أَوْلِيَآؤُهُم مِّنَ ٱلْإِنسِ

Their friends from among the humans will say,

رَبَّنَا ٱسْتَمْتَعَ بَعْضُنَا بِبَعْضٍ

'Our Lord, we used each other,

وَبَلَغْنَا أَجَلَنَا

and we completed our term

ٱلَّذِىٓ أَجَّلْتَ لَنَا

which You had appointed for us.'

قَالَ ٱلنَّارُ مَثْوَىٰكُمْ

He will say, 'The Fire is your abode,

خَٰلِدِينَ فِيهَآ

to remain in it [forever],

إِلَّا مَا شَآءَ ٱللَّهُ

except what Allah may wish.'

إِنَّ رَبَّكَ حَكِيمٌ عَلِيمٌ ۝

Indeed *your* Lord is all-wise, all-knowing.

وَكَذَٰلِكَ

129 That is how

نُوَلِّى بَعْضَ ٱلظَّٰلِمِينَ بَعْضًا

We make the wrongdoers one another's friends

بِمَا كَانُوا۟ يَكْسِبُونَ ۝

because of what they used to earn.

يَٰمَعْشَرَ ٱلْجِنِّ وَٱلْإِنسِ

130 'O company of jinn and humans!

أَلَمْ يَأْتِكُمْ رُسُلٌ مِّنكُمْ

Did there not come to you apostles from yourselves,

يَقُصُّونَ عَلَيْكُمْ ءَايَٰتِى

recounting to you My signs

وَيُنذِرُونَكُمْ لِقَآءَ يَوْمِكُمْ هَٰذَا

and warning you of the encounter of this Day?'

---

[1] That is, makes his spiritual and intellectual capacities shrink.

قَالُوا شَهِدْنَا عَلَىٰٓ أَنفُسِنَا ۖ They will say, 'We testify against ourselves.'

وَغَرَّتْهُمُ ٱلْحَيَوٰةُ ٱلدُّنْيَا The life of this world had deceived them,

وَشَهِدُوا عَلَىٰٓ أَنفُسِهِمْ and they will testify against themselves

أَنَّهُمْ كَانُوا كَـٰفِرِينَ ۝ that they had been faithless.

ذَٰلِكَ أَن لَّمْ يَكُن رَّبُّكَ 131 This is because *your* Lord would never

مُهْلِكَ ٱلْقُرَىٰ destroy the towns

بِظُلْمٍ unjustly

وَأَهْلُهَا غَـٰفِلُونَ ۝ while their people were unaware.

وَلِكُلٍّ دَرَجَـٰتٌ 132 For everyone there are ranks

مِّمَّا عَمِلُوا ۚ in accordance with what they have done;

وَمَا رَبُّكَ بِغَـٰفِلٍ عَمَّا يَعْمَلُونَ ۝ and *your* Lord is not oblivious of what they do.

وَرَبُّكَ ٱلْغَنِىُّ 133 *Your* Lord is the All-sufficient

ذُو ٱلرَّحْمَةِ ۚ dispenser of mercy.

إِن يَشَأْ يُذْهِبْكُمْ If He wishes, He will take you away,

وَيَسْتَخْلِفْ مِنۢ بَعْدِكُم مَّا يَشَآءُ and make whomever He wishes succeed you,

كَمَآ أَنشَأَكُم just as He produced you

مِّن ذُرِّيَّةِ قَوْمٍ ءَاخَرِينَ ۝ from the descendants of another people.

إِنَّ مَا تُوعَدُونَ لَـَٔاتٍ ۖ 134 Indeed what you are promised will surely come,

وَمَآ أَنتُم بِمُعْجِزِينَ ۝ and you will not be able to thwart it.

قُلْ يَـٰقَوْمِ 135 *Say*, 'O my people,

ٱعْمَلُوا عَلَىٰ مَكَانَتِكُمْ Act according to your ability;

إِنِّى عَامِلٌ ۖ I too am acting.

فَسَوْفَ تَعْلَمُونَ Soon you will know

مَن تَكُونُ لَهُۥ عَـٰقِبَةُ ٱلدَّارِ ۗ in whose favour the outcome of that abode will be.

إِنَّهُۥ لَا يُفْلِحُ ٱلظَّـٰلِمُونَ ۝ Indeed the wrongdoers will not be felicitous.'

وَجَعَلُوا لِلَّهِ 136 They dedicate to Allah

مِمَّا ذَرَأَ مِنَ ٱلْحَرْثِ وَٱلْأَنْعَـٰمِ out of what He has created of the crops and cattle

نَصِيبًا a portion,

فَقَالُوا هَـٰذَا لِلَّهِ بِزَعْمِهِمْ and say, 'This is for Allah,' so do they maintain,

وَهَـٰذَا لِشُرَكَآئِنَا ۖ 'and this is for our partners.'

فَمَا كَانَ لِشُرَكَآئِهِمْ

But what is for their partners

فَلَا يَصِلُ إِلَى اللَّهِ

does not reach Allah,

وَمَا كَانَ لِلَّهِ

and what is for Allah

فَهُوَ يَصِلُ إِلَى شُرَكَآئِهِمْ

reaches their partners.

سَآءَ مَا يَحْكُمُونَ ۞

Evil is the judgement that they make.

وَكَذَٰلِكَ 137

That is how

زَيَّنَ لِكَثِيرٍ مِّنَ ٱلْمُشْرِكِينَ

to most of the polytheists is presented as decorous

قَتْلَ أَوْلَٰدِهِمْ

the slaying of their children

شُرَكَآؤُهُمْ

by those whom they ascribe as partners [to Allah],

لِيُرْدُوهُمْ

that they may ruin them

وَلِيَلْبِسُوا عَلَيْهِمْ دِينَهُمْ

and confound their religion for them.

وَلَوْ شَآءَ ٱللَّهُ مَا فَعَلُوهُ

Had Allah wished, they would not have done it.

فَذَرْهُمْ وَمَا يَفْتَرُونَ ۞

So *leave* them with what they fabricate.

وَقَالُوا 138

And they say,

هَٰذِهِۦ أَنْعَٰمٌ وَحَرْثٌ حِجْرٌ

'These cattle and tillage are a taboo:

لَّا يَطْعَمُهَآ إِلَّا مَن نَّشَآءُ

none may eat them except whom we please,'

بِزَعْمِهِمْ

so they maintain,

وَأَنْعَٰمٌ حُرِّمَتْ ظُهُورُهَا

and there are cattle whose backs are forbidden

وَأَنْعَٰمٌ لَّا يَذْكُرُونَ ٱسْمَ ٱللَّهِ عَلَيْهَا

and cattle over which they do not mention Allah's Name,

ٱفْتِرَآءً عَلَيْهِ

fabricating a lie against Him.

سَيَجْزِيهِم

Soon He will requite them

بِمَا كَانُوا يَفْتَرُونَ ۞

for what they used to fabricate.

وَقَالُوا 139

And they say,

مَا فِى بُطُونِ هَٰذِهِ ٱلْأَنْعَٰمِ

'That which is in the bellies of these cattle

خَالِصَةٌ لِّذُكُورِنَا

is exclusively for our males

وَمُحَرَّمٌ عَلَىٰٓ أَزْوَٰجِنَا

and forbidden to our wives.

وَإِن يَكُن مَّيْتَةً فَهُمْ فِيهِ شُرَكَآءُ

But if it be still-born, they will all share it.'

سَيَجْزِيهِمْ وَصْفَهُمْ

Soon He will requite them for their allegations.

إِنَّهُ حَكِيمٌ عَلِيمٌ ۞

Indeed He is all-wise, all-knowing.

قَدْ خَسِرَ ٱلَّذِينَ 140

They are certainly losers

قَتَلُوٓا۟ أَوْلَٰدَهُمْ سَفَهًۢا　who slay their children foolishly

بِغَيْرِ عِلْمٍ　without knowledge,

وَحَرَّمُوا۟ مَا رَزَقَهُمُ ٱللَّهُ　and forbid what Allah has provided them,

ٱفْتِرَآءً عَلَى ٱللَّهِ　fabricating a lie against Allah.

قَدْ ضَلُّوا۟ وَمَا كَانُوا۟ مُهْتَدِينَ ۝　Certainly, they have gone astray and are not guided.

وَهُوَ ٱلَّذِىٓ أَنشَأَ جَنَّٰتٍ　141 It is He who produces gardens

مَّعْرُوشَٰتٍ وَغَيْرَ مَعْرُوشَٰتٍ　trellised and without trellises,

وَٱلنَّخْلَ وَٱلزَّرْعَ مُخْتَلِفًا أُكُلُهُۥ　and palm-trees and crops of diverse produce,

وَٱلزَّيْتُونَ وَٱلرُّمَّانَ　olives and pomegranates,

مُتَشَٰبِهًا وَغَيْرَ مُتَشَٰبِهٍۢ　similar and dissimilar.

كُلُوا۟ مِن ثَمَرِهِۦٓ إِذَآ أَثْمَرَ　Eat of its fruits when it fructifies,

وَءَاتُوا۟ حَقَّهُۥ يَوْمَ حَصَادِهِۦ　and give its due on the day of harvest,

وَلَا تُسْرِفُوٓا۟　and do not be wasteful;

إِنَّهُۥ لَا يُحِبُّ ٱلْمُسْرِفِينَ ۝　indeed Allah does not like the wasteful.

وَمِنَ ٱلْأَنْعَٰمِ حَمُولَةً　142 Of the cattle [some] are for burden

وَفَرْشًا　and [some] for slaughter.

كُلُوا۟ مِمَّا رَزَقَكُمُ ٱللَّهُ　Eat of what Allah has provided you

وَلَا تَتَّبِعُوا۟ خُطُوَٰتِ ٱلشَّيْطَٰنِ　and do not follow in Satan's footsteps;

إِنَّهُۥ لَكُمْ عَدُوٌّ مُّبِينٌ ۝　he is indeed your manifest enemy.

ثَمَٰنِيَةَ أَزْوَٰجٍ　143 Eight mates:[1]

مِّنَ ٱلضَّأْنِ ٱثْنَيْنِ　two of sheep,

وَمِنَ ٱلْمَعْزِ ٱثْنَيْنِ　and two of goats.

قُلْ ءَآلذَّكَرَيْنِ حَرَّمَ　*Say*, 'Is it the two males that He has forbidden

أَمِ ٱلْأُنثَيَيْنِ　or the two females,

أَمَّا ٱشْتَمَلَتْ عَلَيْهِ　or what is contained

أَرْحَامُ ٱلْأُنثَيَيْنِ　in the wombs of the two females?

نَبِّـُٔونِى بِعِلْمٍ إِن كُنتُمْ صَٰدِقِينَ ۝　Inform me with knowledge, should you be truthful.'

وَمِنَ ٱلْإِبِلِ ٱثْنَيْنِ وَمِنَ ٱلْبَقَرِ ٱثْنَيْنِ　144 And two of camels and two of oxen.

قُلْ ءَآلذَّكَرَيْنِ حَرَّمَ　*Say*, 'Is it the two males that He has forbidden

---

[1] Cf. 39:6.

أَمِ ٱلْأُنثَيَيْنِ

or the two females,

أَمَّا ٱشْتَمَلَتْ عَلَيْهِ

or what is contained

أَرْحَامُ ٱلْأُنثَيَيْنِ

in the wombs of the two females?

أَمْ كُنتُمْ شُهَدَآءَ

Were you witnesses

إِذْ وَصَّىٰكُمُ ٱللَّهُ بِهَـٰذَا

when Allah enjoined this upon you?"

فَمَنْ أَظْلَمُ

So who is a greater wrongdoer

مِمَّنِ ٱفْتَرَىٰ عَلَى ٱللَّهِ كَذِبًا

than him who fabricates a lie against Allah

لِيُضِلَّ ٱلنَّاسَ بِغَيْرِ عِلْمٍ

to mislead the people without any knowledge?

إِنَّ ٱللَّهَ لَا يَهْدِى ٱلْقَوْمَ ٱلظَّـٰلِمِينَ ۞

Indeed Allah does not guide the wrongdoing lot.

قُل لَّآ أَجِدُ فِى مَآ أُوحِىَ إِلَىَّ

145 *Say,* 'I do not find in what has been revealed to me

مُحَرَّمًا عَلَىٰ طَاعِمٍ يَطْعَمُهُۥٓ

that anyone be forbidden to eat anything

إِلَّآ أَن يَكُونَ مَيْتَةً أَوْ دَمًا مَّسْفُوحًا

except carrion or spilt blood,

أَوْ لَحْمَ خِنزِيرٍ

or the flesh of swine

فَإِنَّهُۥ رِجْسٌ

—for that is indeed unclean—

أَوْ فِسْقًا أُهِلَّ لِغَيْرِ ٱللَّهِ بِهِۦ

or an impiety offered to other than Allah.

فَمَنِ ٱضْطُرَّ

But should someone be compelled,

غَيْرَ بَاغٍ وَلَا عَادٍ

without being rebellious or aggressive,

فَإِنَّ رَبَّكَ غَفُورٌ رَّحِيمٌ ۞

indeed *your* Lord is all-forgiving, all-merciful.

وَعَلَى ٱلَّذِينَ هَادُواْ حَرَّمْنَا

146 To the Jews We forbade

كُلَّ ذِى ظُفُرٍ

every animal having an undivided hoof,

وَمِنَ ٱلْبَقَرِ وَٱلْغَنَمِ

and of oxen and sheep

حَرَّمْنَا عَلَيْهِمْ شُحُومَهُمَآ

We forbade them their fat,

إِلَّا مَا حَمَلَتْ ظُهُورُهُمَآ أَوِ ٱلْحَوَايَا

except what is borne by their backs or the entrails

أَوْ مَا ٱخْتَلَطَ بِعَظْمٍ

or what is attached to the bones.

ذَٰلِكَ جَزَيْنَـٰهُم بِبَغْيِهِمْ

We requited them with that for their rebelliousness,

وَإِنَّا لَصَـٰدِقُونَ ۞

and We indeed speak the truth.

فَإِن كَذَّبُوكَ

147 But if they deny *you,*

فَقُل

*say,*

رَّبُّكُمْ ذُو رَحْمَةٍ وَٰسِعَةٍ

'Your Lord is dispenser of an all-embracing mercy,

وَلَا يُرَدُّ بَأْسُهُۥ

but His punishment will not be averted

عَنِ ٱلْقَوْمِ ٱلْمُجْرِمِينَ ۝    from the guilty lot.'

سَيَقُولُ ٱلَّذِينَ أَشْرَكُوا    148 The polytheists will say,

لَوْ شَآءَ ٱللَّهُ    'Had Allah wished

مَآ أَشْرَكْنَا    we would not have ascribed any partner [to Him],

وَلَآ ءَابَاؤُنَا    nor our fathers,

وَلَا حَرَّمْنَا مِن شَيْءٍ    nor would we have forbidden anything.'

كَذَٰلِكَ كَذَّبَ ٱلَّذِينَ مِن قَبْلِهِمْ    Those who were before them had denied[1] likewise

حَتَّىٰ ذَاقُوا بَأْسَنَا    until they tasted Our punishment.

قُلْ هَلْ عِندَكُم مِّنْ عِلْمٍ    Say, 'Do you have any [revealed] knowledge

فَتُخْرِجُوهُ لَنَآ    that you can produce before us?

إِن تَتَّبِعُونَ إِلَّا ٱلظَّنَّ    You follow nothing but conjectures,

وَإِنْ أَنتُمْ إِلَّا تَخْرُصُونَ ۝    and you do nothing but surmise.'

قُلْ فَلِلَّهِ ٱلْحُجَّةُ ٱلْبَٰلِغَةُ    149 Say, 'To Allah belongs the conclusive argument.

فَلَوْ شَآءَ    Had He wished,

لَهَدَىٰكُمْ أَجْمَعِينَ ۝    He would have surely guided you all.'

قُلْ هَلُمَّ شُهَدَآءَكُمُ    150 Say, 'Bring your witnesses

ٱلَّذِينَ يَشْهَدُونَ أَنَّ ٱللَّهَ حَرَّمَ هَٰذَا    who may testify that Allah has forbidden this.'

فَإِن شَهِدُوا فَلَا تَشْهَدْ مَعَهُمْ    So if they testify, do not testify with them,

وَلَا تَتَّبِعْ أَهْوَآءَ ٱلَّذِينَ    and do not follow the desires of those

كَذَّبُوا بِآيَٰتِنَا    who deny Our signs,

وَٱلَّذِينَ لَا يُؤْمِنُونَ بِٱلْآخِرَةِ    and those who do not believe in the Hereafter

وَهُم بِرَبِّهِمْ يَعْدِلُونَ ۝    and equate [others] with their Lord.

قُل تَعَالَوْا أَتْلُ    151 Say, 'Come, I will recount

مَا حَرَّمَ رَبُّكُمْ عَلَيْكُمْ    what your Lord has forbidden you from.

أَلَّا تُشْرِكُوا بِهِ شَيْئًا    That you shall not ascribe any partners to Him,

وَبِٱلْوَٰلِدَيْنِ إِحْسَٰنًا    and you shall be good to the parents,

وَلَا تَقْتُلُوا أَوْلَٰدَكُم مِّنْ إِمْلَٰقٍ    you shall not kill your children due to penury

نَّحْنُ نَرْزُقُكُمْ وَإِيَّاهُمْ    —We will provide for you and for them—

---

[1] Or 'those who were before them had lied likewise,' in accordance with an alternate reading. (see al-Zamakhsharī, al-Rāzī, and al-Ṭabrisī)

وَلَا تَقْرَبُوا۟ ٱلْفَوَٰحِشَ

you shall not approach indecencies,

مَا ظَهَرَ مِنْهَا وَمَا بَطَنَ

the outward among them and the inward ones,

وَلَا تَقْتُلُوا۟ ٱلنَّفْسَ ٱلَّتِى

and you shall not kill a soul

حَرَّمَ ٱللَّهُ

[whose life] Allah has made inviolable,

إِلَّا بِٱلْحَقِّ

except with due cause.

ذَٰلِكُمْ وَصَّىٰكُم بِهِۦ

This is what He has enjoined upon you

لَعَلَّكُمْ تَعْقِلُونَ ۝

so that you may apply reason.

وَلَا تَقْرَبُوا۟ مَالَ ٱلْيَتِيمِ 152 Do not approach the orphan's property,

إِلَّا بِٱلَّتِى هِىَ أَحْسَنُ

except in the best [possible] manner,

حَتَّىٰ يَبْلُغَ أَشُدَّهُۥ

until he comes of age.

وَأَوْفُوا۟ ٱلْكَيْلَ وَٱلْمِيزَانَ

And observe fully the measure and the balance[1]

بِٱلْقِسْطِ

with justice.

لَا نُكَلِّفُ نَفْسًا إِلَّا وُسْعَهَا

We task no soul except according to its capacity.

وَإِذَا قُلْتُمْ فَٱعْدِلُوا۟

And when you speak, be fair,

وَلَوْ كَانَ ذَا قُرْبَىٰ

even if it were a relative;

وَبِعَهْدِ ٱللَّهِ أَوْفُوا۟

and fulfill Allah's covenant.

ذَٰلِكُمْ وَصَّىٰكُم بِهِۦ

This is what He enjoins upon you

لَعَلَّكُمْ تَذَكَّرُونَ ۝

so that you may take admonition.

وَأَنَّ هَٰذَا صِرَٰطِى مُسْتَقِيمًا 153 This indeed is my straight path,

فَٱتَّبِعُوهُ

so follow it,

وَلَا تَتَّبِعُوا۟ ٱلسُّبُلَ

and do not follow [other] ways,

فَتَفَرَّقَ بِكُمْ عَن سَبِيلِهِۦ

for they will separate you from His way.

ذَٰلِكُمْ وَصَّىٰكُم بِهِۦ

This is what He enjoins upon you

لَعَلَّكُمْ تَتَّقُونَ ۝

so that you may be Godwary.'

ثُمَّ ءَاتَيْنَا مُوسَى ٱلْكِتَٰبَ 154 Then We gave Moses the Book,

تَمَامًا عَلَى ٱلَّذِىٓ أَحْسَنَ

completing [Our blessing] on him who is virtuous,

وَتَفْصِيلًا لِّكُلِّ شَىْءٍ

and as an elaboration[2] of all things,

---

[1] That is, weights and measures.

[2] Or 'articulation.'

وَهُدًى وَرَحْمَةً and as a guidance and mercy,

لَعَلَّهُم so that they may

بِلِقَآءِ رَبِّهِمْ يُؤْمِنُونَ ۝ believe in the encounter with their Lord.

وَهَـٰذَا كِتَـٰبٌ أَنزَلْنَـٰهُ 155 And this Book that We have sent down

مُبَارَكٌ is a blessed one;

فَٱتَّبِعُوهُ so follow it,

وَٱتَّقُواْ and be Godwary

لَعَلَّكُمْ تُرْحَمُونَ ۝ so that you may receive [His] mercy.

أَن تَقُولُوٓاْ 156 Lest you should say,

إِنَّمَآ أُنزِلَ ٱلْكِتَـٰبُ 'The Book was sent down only

عَلَىٰ طَآئِفَتَيْنِ مِن قَبْلِنَا to two communities before us,[1]

وَإِن كُنَّا عَن دِرَاسَتِهِمْ لَغَـٰفِلِينَ ۝ and we were indeed unaware of their studies,'

أَوْ تَقُولُوٓاْ 157 or [lest] you should say,

لَوْ أَنَّآ أُنزِلَ عَلَيْنَا ٱلْكِتَـٰبُ 'If the Book had been sent down to us,

لَكُنَّآ أَهْدَىٰ مِنْهُمْ surely we would have been better-guided than them.'

فَقَدْ جَآءَكُم بَيِّنَةٌ There has already come to you a manifest proof

مِّن رَّبِّكُمْ from your Lord

وَهُدًى وَرَحْمَةٌ and a guidance and mercy.

فَمَنْ أَظْلَمُ So who is a greater wrongdoer

مِمَّن كَذَّبَ بِـَٔايَـٰتِ ٱللَّهِ than him who denies the signs of Allah,

وَصَدَفَ عَنْهَا and turns away from them?

سَنَجْزِى ٱلَّذِينَ يَصْدِفُونَ Soon We shall requite those who turn away

عَنْ ءَايَـٰتِنَا from Our signs

سُوٓءَ ٱلْعَذَابِ with a terrible punishment

بِمَا كَانُواْ يَصْدِفُونَ ۝ because of what they used to evade.

هَلْ يَنظُرُونَ إِلَّآ 158 Do they await anything but

أَن تَأْتِيَهُمُ ٱلْمَلَـٰٓئِكَةُ that the angels should come to them,

أَوْ يَأْتِىَ رَبُّكَ or *your* Lord should come,

أَوْ يَأْتِىَ بَعْضُ ءَايَـٰتِ رَبِّكَ or some of *your* Lord's signs should come?

---

[1] That is, Jews and Christians.

يَوْمَ يَأْتِي بَعْضُ ءَايَتِ رَبِّكَ The day when some of *your* Lord signs do come,

لَا يَنفَعُ نَفْسًا إِيمَنُهَا faith shall not benefit any soul

لَمْ تَكُنْ ءَامَنَتْ مِن قَبْلُ that had not believed beforehand

أَوْ كَسَبَتْ فِي إِيمَنِهَا خَيْرًا and had not earned some goodness in its faith.

قُلِ ٱنتَظِرُوٓاْ إِنَّا مُنتَظِرُونَ ۝ *Say*, 'Wait! We too are waiting!'

إِنَّ ٱلَّذِينَ فَرَّقُواْ دِينَهُمْ 159 Indeed those who split up their religion

وَكَانُواْ شِيَعًا and become sects,

لَّسْتَ مِنْهُمْ فِي شَىْءٍ *you* will not have anything to do with them.

إِنَّمَآ أَمْرُهُمْ إِلَى ٱللَّهِ Their matter rests only with Allah;

ثُمَّ يُنَبِّئُهُم then He will inform them

بِمَا كَانُواْ يَفْعَلُونَ ۝ concerning what they used to do.

مَن جَآءَ بِٱلْحَسَنَةِ 160 Whoever brings virtue

فَلَهُۥ عَشْرُ أَمْثَالِهَا shall receive ten times its like;

وَمَن جَآءَ بِٱلسَّيِّئَةِ but whoever brings vice

فَلَا يُجْزَىٰٓ إِلَّا مِثْلَهَا shall not be requited except with its like,

وَهُمْ لَا يُظْلَمُونَ ۝ and they will not be wronged.[1]

قُلْ إِنَّنِي هَدَىٰنِي رَبِّىٓ 161 *Say*, 'Indeed my Lord has guided me

إِلَىٰ صِرَٰطٍ مُّسْتَقِيمٍ to a straight path,

دِينًا قِيَمًا the upright religion,

مِّلَّةَ إِبْرَٰهِيمَ حَنِيفًا the creed of Abraham, a *hanīf*,

وَمَا كَانَ مِنَ ٱلْمُشْرِكِينَ ۝ and he was not one of the polytheists.'

قُلْ إِنَّ صَلَاتِى وَنُسُكِى 162 *Say*, 'Indeed my prayer and my worship,

وَمَحْيَاىَ وَمَمَاتِى my life and my death

لِلَّهِ رَبِّ ٱلْعَٰلَمِينَ ۝ are for the sake of Allah, the Lord of all the worlds.

لَا شَرِيكَ لَهُۥ 163 He has no partner,

وَبِذَٰلِكَ أُمِرْتُ and this [creed] I have been commanded [to follow],

وَأَنَا۠ أَوَّلُ ٱلْمُسْلِمِينَ ۝ and I am the first of those who submit [to Allah].'

قُلْ أَغَيْرَ ٱللَّهِ أَبْغِى رَبًّا 164 *Say*, 'Shall I seek a Lord other than Allah,

وَهُوَ رَبُّ كُلِّ شَىْءٍ while He is the Lord of all things?'

---

[1] Cf. 27:89; 28:84.

وَلَا تَكْسِبُ كُلُّ نَفْسٍ إِلَّا عَلَيْهَا
No soul does evil except against itself,

وَلَا تَزِرُ وَازِرَةٌ وِزْرَ أُخْرَىٰ
and no bearer shall bear another's burden;

ثُمَّ إِلَىٰ رَبِّكُم مَّرْجِعُكُمْ
then to your Lord will be your return,

فَيُنَبِّئُكُم
whereat He will inform you

بِمَا كُنتُمْ فِيهِ تَخْتَلِفُونَ ۝
concerning that about which you used to differ.

وَهُوَ ٱلَّذِى جَعَلَكُمْ خَلَـٰئِفَ ٱلْأَرْضِ
165 It is He who has made you successors on the earth,

وَرَفَعَ بَعْضَكُمْ فَوْقَ بَعْضٍ دَرَجَـٰتٍ
and raised some of you in rank above others

لِّيَبْلُوَكُمْ
so that He may test you

فِى مَآ ءَاتَىٰكُمْ
in respect to what He has given you.

إِنَّ رَبَّكَ سَرِيعُ ٱلْعِقَابِ
Indeed *your* Lord is swift in retribution,

وَإِنَّهُ لَغَفُورٌ رَّحِيمٌ ۝
and indeed He is all-forgiving, all-merciful.

# سُورَةُ الأَعْرَافِ     7. SŪRAT AL-A'RĀF[1]

بِسْمِ ٱللَّهِ
In the Name of Allah,

ٱلرَّحْمَـٰنِ ٱلرَّحِيمِ
the All-beneficent, the All-merciful.

الٓمٓصٓ ۝ 1 *Alif, Lām, Mīm, Ṣād.*

كِتَـٰبٌ أُنزِلَ إِلَيْكَ 2 [This is] a Book that has been sent down to *you*

فَلَا يَكُن فِى صَدْرِكَ حَرَجٌ
—so let there be no disquiet in *your* heart

مِّنْهُ
on its account

لِتُنذِرَ بِهِ
that *you* may warn thereby—

وَذِكْرَىٰ لِلْمُؤْمِنِينَ ۝ and as an admonition for the faithful.

ٱتَّبِعُوا۟ مَآ أُنزِلَ إِلَيْكُم 3 Follow what has been sent down to you

مِّن رَّبِّكُمْ
from your Lord,

وَلَا تَتَّبِعُوا۟ مِن دُونِهِ أَوْلِيَآءَ
and do not follow any masters besides Him.

قَلِيلًا مَّا تَذَكَّرُونَ ۝ Little is the admonition that you take!

وَكَم مِّن قَرْيَةٍ أَهْلَكْنَـٰهَا 4 How many a town We have destroyed!

فَجَآءَهَا بَأْسُنَا بَيَـٰتًا
Our punishment came to it at night,

---

[1] The *sūrah* takes its name from 'the Elevation' (*al-A'rāf*) mentioned in verses 46-8.

أَوْ هُمْ قَآئِلُونَ ۝　　or while they were taking a midday nap.

فَمَا كَانَ دَعْوَىٰهُمْ 5 Then their cry,

إِذْ جَآءَهُم بَأْسُنَآ　　when Our punishment overtook them,

إِلَّآ أَن قَالُوٓاْ　　was only that they said,

إِنَّا كُنَّا ظَٰلِمِينَ ۝　　'We have indeed been wrongdoers!'

فَلَنَسْـَٔلَنَّ ٱلَّذِينَ 6 We will surely question those

أُرْسِلَ إِلَيْهِمْ　　to whom the apostles were sent,

وَلَنَسْـَٔلَنَّ ٱلْمُرْسَلِينَ ۝　　and We will surely question the apostles.

فَلَنَقُصَّنَّ عَلَيْهِم بِعِلْمٍ 7 Then We will surely recount to them with knowledge,

وَمَا كُنَّا غَآئِبِينَ ۝　　for We had not been absent.

وَٱلْوَزْنُ يَوْمَئِذٍ ٱلْحَقُّ 8 The weighing [of deeds] on that Day is a truth.

فَمَن ثَقُلَتْ مَوَٰزِينُهُۥ　　As for those whose deeds weigh heavy in the scales

فَأُوْلَٰٓئِكَ هُمُ ٱلْمُفْلِحُونَ ۝　　—it is they who are the felicitous.

وَمَنْ خَفَّتْ مَوَٰزِينُهُۥ 9 As for those whose deeds weigh light in the scales,

فَأُوْلَٰٓئِكَ ٱلَّذِينَ خَسِرُوٓاْ أَنفُسَهُم　　—it is they who have ruined their souls,

بِمَا كَانُواْ بِـَٔايَٰتِنَا يَظْلِمُونَ ۝　　because they used to wrong Our signs.

وَلَقَدْ مَكَّنَّٰكُمْ فِى ٱلْأَرْضِ 10 Certainly We have established you on the earth,

وَجَعَلْنَا لَكُمْ فِيهَا مَعَٰيِشَ　　and made in it [various] means of livelihood for you.

قَلِيلًا مَّا تَشْكُرُونَ ۝　　Little do you thank.

وَلَقَدْ خَلَقْنَٰكُمْ ثُمَّ صَوَّرْنَٰكُمْ 11 Certainly We created you, then We formed you,

ثُمَّ قُلْنَا لِلْمَلَٰٓئِكَةِ　　then We said to the angels,

ٱسْجُدُواْ لِـَٔادَمَ　　'Prostrate before Adam.'

فَسَجَدُوٓاْ إِلَّآ إِبْلِيسَ　　So they [all] prostrated, except Iblis:

لَمْ يَكُن مِّنَ ٱلسَّٰجِدِينَ ۝　　he was not among those who prostrated.

قَالَ مَا مَنَعَكَ أَلَّا تَسْجُدَ 12 Said He, 'What prevented you from prostrating,

إِذْ أَمَرْتُكَ　　when I commanded you?'

قَالَ أَنَا۠ خَيْرٌ مِّنْهُ　　'I am better than him,' he said.

خَلَقْتَنِى مِن نَّارٍ　　'You created me from fire

وَخَلَقْتَهُۥ مِن طِينٍ ۝　　and You created him from clay.'

قَالَ فَٱهْبِطْ مِنْهَا 13 'Get down from it!' He said.

205

فَمَا يَكُونُ لَكَ أَن تَتَكَبَّرَ فِيهَا

'It is not for you to be arrogant therein.

فَٱخْرُجْ

Begone!

إِنَّكَ مِنَ ٱلصَّٰغِرِينَ ۞

You are indeed among the degraded ones.'

قَالَ 14 He said,

أَنظِرْنِى إِلَىٰ يَوْمِ يُبْعَثُونَ ۞

'Respite me till the day they will be resurrected.'

قَالَ إِنَّكَ مِنَ ٱلْمُنظَرِينَ ۞ 15 Said He, 'You are indeed among the reprieved.'

قَالَ فَبِمَآ أَغْوَيْتَنِى 16 'As You have consigned me to perversity,' he said,

لَأَقْعُدَنَّ لَهُمْ

'I will surely lie in wait for them

صِرَٰطَكَ ٱلْمُسْتَقِيمَ ۞

on Your straight path.

ثُمَّ لَآتِيَنَّهُم مِّنۢ بَيْنِ أَيْدِيهِمْ 17 Then I will come at them from their front

وَمِنْ خَلْفِهِمْ

and from their rear,

وَعَنْ أَيْمَٰنِهِمْ وَعَن شَمَآئِلِهِمْ

and from their right and their left,

وَلَا تَجِدُ أَكْثَرَهُمْ شَٰكِرِينَ ۞

and You will not find most of them to be grateful.'

قَالَ ٱخْرُجْ مِنْهَا مَذْءُومًا مَّدْحُورًا 18 Said He, 'Begone hence, blameful, banished!

لَّمَن تَبِعَكَ مِنْهُمْ

Whoever of them follows you,

لَأَمْلَأَنَّ جَهَنَّمَ مِنكُمْ أَجْمَعِينَ ۞

I will surely fill hell with you all.'

وَيَٰٓـَٔادَمُ 19 [Then He said to Adam,] 'O Adam,

ٱسْكُنْ أَنتَ وَزَوْجُكَ ٱلْجَنَّةَ

dwell with your mate in paradise,

فَكُلَا مِنْ حَيْثُ شِئْتُمَا

and eat thereof whence you wish;

وَلَا تَقْرَبَا هَٰذِهِ ٱلشَّجَرَةَ

but do not approach this tree,

فَتَكُونَا مِنَ ٱلظَّٰلِمِينَ ۞

lest you should be among the wrongdoers.'

فَوَسْوَسَ لَهُمَا ٱلشَّيْطَٰنُ 20 Then Satan tempted them,

لِيُبْدِىَ لَهُمَا

to expose to them

مَا وُۥرِىَ عَنْهُمَا مِن سَوْءَٰتِهِمَا

what was hidden from them of their nakedness,

وَقَالَ

and he said,

مَا نَهَٰكُمَا رَبُّكُمَا عَنْ هَٰذِهِ ٱلشَّجَرَةِ

'Your Lord has only forbidden you from this tree

إِلَّآ أَن تَكُونَا مَلَكَيْنِ

lest you should become angels,

أَوْ تَكُونَا مِنَ ٱلْخَٰلِدِينَ ۞

or lest you become immortal.'

وَقَاسَمَهُمَآ 21 And he swore to them,

إِنِّى لَكُمَا لَمِنَ ٱلنَّٰصِحِينَ ۞

'I am indeed your well-wisher.'

206

فَدَلَّىٰهُمَا بِغُرُورٍ 22 Thus he brought about their fall by deception.

فَلَمَّا ذَاقَا ٱلشَّجَرَةَ     So when they tasted of the tree,

بَدَتْ لَهُمَا سَوْءَٰتُهُمَا     their nakedness became exposed to them,

وَطَفِقَا يَخْصِفَانِ عَلَيْهِمَا     and they began to stitch over themselves

مِن وَرَقِ ٱلْجَنَّةِ     with the leaves of paradise.

وَنَادَىٰهُمَا رَبُّهُمَآ     Their Lord called out to them,

أَلَمْ أَنْهَكُمَا عَن تِلْكُمَا ٱلشَّجَرَةِ     'Did I not forbid you from that tree,

وَأَقُل لَّكُمَآ     and tell you,

إِنَّ ٱلشَّيْطَٰنَ لَكُمَا عَدُوٌّ مُّبِينٌ ۞     "Satan is indeed your manifest enemy?" '

قَالَا رَبَّنَا ظَلَمْنَآ أَنفُسَنَا 23 They said, 'Our Lord, we have wronged ourselves!

وَإِن لَّمْ تَغْفِرْ لَنَا وَتَرْحَمْنَا     If You do not forgive us and have mercy upon us,

لَنَكُونَنَّ مِنَ ٱلْخَٰسِرِينَ ۞     we will surely be among the losers.'

قَالَ ٱهْبِطُواْ 24 He said, 'Get down,

بَعْضُكُمْ لِبَعْضٍ عَدُوٌّ     being enemies of one another!

وَلَكُمْ فِى ٱلْأَرْضِ مُسْتَقَرٌّ     On the earth shall be your abode

وَمَتَٰعٌ إِلَىٰ حِينٍ ۞     and sustenance for a time.'

قَالَ فِيهَا تَحْيَوْنَ 25 He said, 'In it you will live,

وَفِيهَا تَمُوتُونَ     and in it you will die;

وَمِنْهَا تُخْرَجُونَ ۞     and from it you will be raised [from the dead].'

يَٰبَنِىٓ ءَادَمَ 26 'O Children of Adam!

قَدْ أَنزَلْنَا عَلَيْكُمْ لِبَاسًا     We have certainly sent down to you garments

يُوَٰرِى سَوْءَٰتِكُمْ وَرِيشًا     to cover your nakedness, and for adornment.

وَلِبَاسُ ٱلتَّقْوَىٰ ذَٰلِكَ خَيْرٌ     Yet the garment of Godwariness—that is the best.

ذَٰلِكَ مِنْ ءَايَٰتِ ٱللَّهِ     That is [one] of Allah's signs,

لَعَلَّهُمْ يَذَّكَّرُونَ ۞     so that they may take admonition.

يَٰبَنِىٓ ءَادَمَ 27 O Children of Adam!

لَا يَفْتِنَنَّكُمُ ٱلشَّيْطَٰنُ     Do not let Satan tempt you,

كَمَآ أَخْرَجَ أَبَوَيْكُم مِّنَ ٱلْجَنَّةِ     like he expelled your parents from paradise,

يَنزِعُ عَنْهُمَا لِبَاسَهُمَا     stripping them of their garments

لِيُرِيَهُمَا سَوْءَٰتِهِمَآ     to expose to them their nakedness.

إِنَّهُۥ يَرَىٰكُمْ هُوَ وَقَبِيلُهُۥ
Indeed he sees you—he and his hosts—

مِنْ حَيْثُ لَا تَرَوْنَهُمْ
whence you do not see them.

إِنَّا جَعَلْنَا ٱلشَّيَـٰطِينَ أَوْلِيَآءَ
We have indeed made the devils friends

لِلَّذِينَ لَا يُؤْمِنُونَ ٢٧
of those who have no faith.

وَإِذَا فَعَلُواْ فَـٰحِشَةً قَالُواْ
28 When they commit an indecency, they say,

وَجَدْنَا عَلَيْهَآ ءَابَآءَنَا
'We found our fathers practising it,

وَٱللَّهُ أَمَرَنَا بِهَا
and Allah has enjoined it upon us.'

قُلْ إِنَّ ٱللَّهَ لَا يَأْمُرُ بِٱلْفَحْشَآءِ
Say, 'Indeed Allah does not enjoin indecencies.

أَتَقُولُونَ عَلَى ٱللَّهِ مَا لَا تَعْلَمُونَ ٢٨
Do you attribute to Allah what you do not know?'

قُلْ أَمَرَ رَبِّى بِٱلْقِسْطِ
29 Say, 'My Lord has enjoined justice,'

وَأَقِيمُواْ وُجُوهَكُمْ
and [He has enjoined,] 'Set your heart [on Him]

عِندَ كُلِّ مَسْجِدٍ
at every occasion of prayer,

وَٱدْعُوهُ
and invoke Him,

مُخْلِصِينَ لَهُ ٱلدِّينَ
putting your exclusive faith in Him.

كَمَا بَدَأَكُمْ
Even as He brought you forth in the beginning,

تَعُودُونَ ٢٩
so will you return.'

فَرِيقًا هَدَىٰ
30 A part [of mankind] He has guided

وَفَرِيقًا حَقَّ عَلَيْهِمُ ٱلضَّلَـٰلَةُ
and a part has deserved [to be consigned to] error,

إِنَّهُمُ ٱتَّخَذُواْ ٱلشَّيَـٰطِينَ أَوْلِيَآءَ
for they took devils for guardians

مِن دُونِ ٱللَّهِ
instead of Allah,

وَيَحْسَبُونَ أَنَّهُم مُّهْتَدُونَ ٣٠
and supposed they were guided.

يَـٰبَنِىٓ ءَادَمَ
31 O Children of Adam!

خُذُواْ زِينَتَكُمْ عِندَ كُلِّ مَسْجِدٍ
Put on your adornment on every occasion of prayer,

وَكُلُواْ وَٱشْرَبُواْ وَلَا تُسْرِفُوٓاْ
and eat and drink, but do not waste;

إِنَّهُۥ لَا يُحِبُّ ٱلْمُسْرِفِينَ ٣١
indeed Allah does not like the wasteful.

قُلْ مَنْ حَرَّمَ زِينَةَ ٱللَّهِ
32 Say, 'Who has forbidden the adornment of Allah

ٱلَّتِىٓ أَخْرَجَ لِعِبَادِهِۦ
which He has brought forth for His servants,

وَٱلطَّيِّبَـٰتِ مِنَ ٱلرِّزْقِ
and the good things of [His] provision?'

*Say,* 'These are for the faithful

     in the life of this world,

and exclusively for them on the Day of Resurrection.'

Thus do We elaborate the signs

     for a people who have knowledge.

33 *Say,* 'My Lord has only forbidden indecencies,

     the outward among them and the inward ones,

and sin and undue aggression,

and that you should ascribe to Allah partners

     for which He has not sent down any authority,

and that you should attribute to Allah

     what you do not know.

34 There is a [preordained] time for every nation:

     when their time comes,

     they shall not defer it by a single hour

     nor shall they advance it.

35 O Children of Adam!

     If there come to you apostles from among yourselves,

     recounting to you My signs,

     then those who are Godwary and righteous

     will have no fear,

     nor will they grieve.

36 But those who deny Our signs

     and are disdainful of them,

     they shall be the inmates of the Fire

     and they shall remain in it [forever].

37 So who is a greater wrongdoer than him

أَفۡتَرَىٰ عَلَى ٱللَّهِ كَذِبًا who fabricates a lie against Allah,

أَوۡ كَذَّبَ بِـَٔايَـٰتِهِۦ or denies His signs?

أُوْلَـٰٓئِكَ يَنَالُهُمۡ نَصِيبُهُم مِّنَ ٱلۡكِتَـٰبِ Their share, as decreed in the Book, shall reach them.

حَتَّىٰٓ إِذَا جَآءَتۡهُمۡ رُسُلُنَا يَتَوَفَّوۡنَهُمۡ When Our messengers[1] come to take them away,

قَالُوٓاْ they will say,

أَيۡنَ مَا كُنتُمۡ تَدۡعُونَ 'Where is that which you used to invoke

مِن دُونِ ٱللَّهِ besides Allah?'

قَالُواْ ضَلُّواْ عَنَّا They will say, 'They have forsaken us,'

وَشَهِدُواْ عَلَىٰٓ أَنفُسِهِمۡ and they will testify against themselves

أَنَّهُمۡ كَانُواْ كَـٰفِرِينَ ٣٧ that they were faithless.

قَالَ ٱدۡخُلُواْ فِىٓ أُمَمٍ 38 He will say, 'Enter, along with the nations

قَدۡ خَلَتۡ مِن قَبۡلِكُم who passed before you

مِّنَ ٱلۡجِنِّ وَٱلۡإِنسِ of jinn and humans,

فِى ٱلنَّارِ into the Fire!'

كُلَّمَا دَخَلَتۡ أُمَّةٌ Every time that a nation enters [hell],

لَّعَنَتۡ أُخۡتَهَا it will curse its sister [nation].

حَتَّىٰٓ إِذَا ٱدَّارَكُواْ فِيهَا جَمِيعًا When they all rejoin in it,

قَالَتۡ أُخۡرَىٰهُمۡ لِأُولَىٰهُمۡ the last of them will say about the first of them,

رَبَّنَا هَـٰٓؤُلَآءِ أَضَلُّونَا 'Our Lord, it was they who led us astray;

فَـَٔاتِهِمۡ عَذَابًا ضِعۡفًا مِّنَ ٱلنَّارِ so give them a double punishment of the Fire.'

قَالَ لِكُلٍّ ضِعۡفٌ He will say, 'It is double for each [of you],

وَلَـٰكِن لَّا تَعۡلَمُونَ ٣٨ but you do not know.'

وَقَالَتۡ أُولَىٰهُمۡ لِأُخۡرَىٰهُمۡ 39 And the first of them will say to the last of them,

فَمَا كَانَ لَكُمۡ عَلَيۡنَا مِن فَضۡلٍ 'You have no advantage over us!

فَذُوقُواْ ٱلۡعَذَابَ So taste the punishment

بِمَا كُنتُمۡ تَكۡسِبُونَ ٣٩ because of what you used to earn.'

إِنَّ ٱلَّذِينَ كَذَّبُواْ بِـَٔايَـٰتِنَا 40 Indeed, those who deny Our signs

وَٱسۡتَكۡبَرُواْ عَنۡهَا and are disdainful of them—

لَا تُفَتَّحُ لَهُمۡ أَبۡوَٰبُ ٱلسَّمَآءِ the gates of the heaven will not be opened for them,

---

[1] That is, the angels of death.

وَلَا يَدْخُلُونَ ٱلْجَنَّةَ

 nor shall they enter paradise

حَتَّىٰ يَلِجَ ٱلْجَمَلُ فِى سَمِّ ٱلْخِيَاطِ

 until the camel passes through the needle's eye,[1]

وَكَذَٰلِكَ نَجْزِى ٱلْمُجْرِمِينَ ۝

 and thus do We requite the guilty.

هُم مِّن جَهَنَّمَ مِهَادٌ

41 They shall have hell for their resting place,

وَمِن فَوْقِهِمْ غَوَاشٍ

 and over them shall be sheets [of fire],

وَكَذَٰلِكَ نَجْزِى ٱلظَّٰلِمِينَ ۝

 and thus do We requite the wrongdoers.

وَٱلَّذِينَ ءَامَنُوا۟

42 As for those who have faith

وَعَمِلُوا۟ ٱلصَّٰلِحَٰتِ

 and do righteous deeds

لَا نُكَلِّفُ نَفْسًا

  —We task no soul

إِلَّا وُسْعَهَآ

 except according to its capacity—

أُو۟لَٰٓئِكَ أَصْحَٰبُ ٱلْجَنَّةِ

 they shall be the inhabitants of paradise,

هُمْ فِيهَا خَٰلِدُونَ ۝

 and they shall remain in it [forever].

وَنَزَعْنَا

43 We will remove

مَا فِى صُدُورِهِم مِّنْ غِلٍّ

 whatever rancour there is in their breasts,

تَجْرِى مِن تَحْتِهِمُ ٱلْأَنْهَٰرُ

 and streams will run for them.

وَقَالُوا۟ ٱلْحَمْدُ لِلَّهِ

 They will say, 'All praise belongs to Allah,

ٱلَّذِى هَدَىٰنَا لِهَٰذَا

 who guided us to this.

وَمَا كُنَّا لِنَهْتَدِىَ

 We would have never been guided

لَوْلَآ أَنْ هَدَىٰنَا ٱللَّهُ

 had not Allah guided us.

لَقَدْ جَآءَتْ رُسُلُ رَبِّنَا بِٱلْحَقِّ

 Our Lord's apostles had certainly brought the truth.'

وَنُودُوٓا۟

 And the call would be made to them:

أَن تِلْكُمُ ٱلْجَنَّةُ أُورِثْتُمُوهَا

 'This is paradise, which you have been given to inherit

بِمَا كُنتُمْ تَعْمَلُونَ ۝

 because of what you used to do!'

وَنَادَىٰٓ أَصْحَٰبُ ٱلْجَنَّةِ

44 The inhabitants of paradise will call out

أَصْحَٰبَ ٱلنَّارِ

 to the inmates of the Fire,

أَن قَدْ وَجَدْنَا مَا وَعَدَنَا رَبُّنَا حَقًّا

 'We found what our Lord promised us to be true;

فَهَلْ وَجَدتُّم مَّا وَعَدَ رَبُّكُمْ حَقًّا

 did you find what your Lord promised you to be true?'

قَالُوا۟ نَعَمْ

 'Yes,' they will say.

فَأَذَّنَ مُؤَذِّنٌۢ بَيْنَهُمْ

 Then an caller will announce in their midst,

---

[1] Or, 'until the cable passes through the needle's eye.'

211

أَن لَّعْنَةُ ٱللَّهِ عَلَى ٱلظَّٰلِمِينَ ۝    'May Allah's curse be on the wrongdoers!'

ٱلَّذِينَ يَصُدُّونَ عَن سَبِيلِ ٱللَّهِ    45 —Those who bar [others] from the way of Allah,

وَيَبْغُونَهَا عِوَجًا    and seek to make it crooked,

وَهُم بِٱلْءَاخِرَةِ كَٰفِرُونَ ۝    and disbelieve in the Hereafter.

وَبَيْنَهُمَا حِجَابٌ    46 And there will be a veil between them.

وَعَلَى ٱلْأَعْرَافِ رِجَالٌ    And on the Elevations will be certain men

يَعْرِفُونَ كُلًّا بِسِيمَٰهُمْ    who recognize each of them by their mark.

وَنَادَوْاْ أَصْحَٰبَ ٱلْجَنَّةِ    They will call out to the inhabitants of paradise,

أَن سَلَٰمٌ عَلَيْكُمْ    'Peace be to you!'

لَمْ يَدْخُلُوهَا    (They[1] will not have entered it,

وَهُمْ يَطْمَعُونَ ۝    though they would be eager to do so.

وَإِذَا صُرِفَتْ أَبْصَٰرُهُمْ    47 And when their look is turned

تِلْقَآءَ أَصْحَٰبِ ٱلنَّارِ    toward the inmates of the Fire,

قَالُواْ رَبَّنَا    they will say, 'Our Lord,

لَا تَجْعَلْنَا مَعَ ٱلْقَوْمِ ٱلظَّٰلِمِينَ ۝    do not put us among the wrongdoing lot!')

وَنَادَىٰٓ أَصْحَٰبُ ٱلْأَعْرَافِ    48 And the occupants of the Elevations will call out

رِجَالًا يَعْرِفُونَهُم بِسِيمَٰهُمْ    to certain men whom they recognize by their marks,

قَالُواْ مَآ أَغْنَىٰ عَنكُمْ جَمْعُكُمْ    'Your rallying[2] did not avail you,

وَمَا كُنتُمْ تَسْتَكْبِرُونَ ۝    nor what you used to disdain.

أَهَٰٓؤُلَآءِ ٱلَّذِينَ أَقْسَمْتُمْ    49 Are these[3] the ones concerning whom you swore

لَا يَنَالُهُمُ ٱللَّهُ بِرَحْمَةٍ    that Allah will not extend them any mercy?'

ٱدْخُلُواْ ٱلْجَنَّةَ    'Enter paradise![4]

لَا خَوْفٌ عَلَيْكُمْ    You shall have no fear,

وَلَآ أَنتُمْ تَحْزَنُونَ ۝    nor shall you grieve.'

وَنَادَىٰٓ أَصْحَٰبُ ٱلنَّارِ    50 The inmates of the Fire will call out

أَصْحَٰبَ ٱلْجَنَّةِ    to the inhabitants of paradise,

أَنْ أَفِيضُواْ عَلَيْنَا مِنَ ٱلْمَآءِ    'Pour on us some water,

---

[1] That is, the people of paradise.

[2] Or 'your amassing.'

[3] That is, the people who will be about to enter paradise.

[4] Addressed to the people about to enter paradise?

أَوْ مِمَّا رَزَقَكُمُ ٱللَّهُ    or something of what Allah has provided you.'

قَالُوٓاْ    They will say,

إِنَّ ٱللَّهَ حَرَّمَهُمَا    'Allah has indeed forbidden these two

عَلَى ٱلْكَٰفِرِينَ ۝    to the faithless!'

ٱلَّذِينَ ٱتَّخَذُواْ دِينَهُمْ لَهْوًا وَلَعِبًا    51 Those who took their religion for diversion and play

وَغَرَّتْهُمُ ٱلْحَيَوٰةُ ٱلدُّنْيَا    and whom the life of the world had deceived.

فَٱلْيَوْمَ نَنسَٰهُمْ    So today We will forget them

كَمَا نَسُواْ لِقَآءَ يَوْمِهِمْ هَٰذَا    as they forgot the encounter of this day of theirs,

وَمَا كَانُواْ بِـَٔايَٰتِنَا يَجْحَدُونَ ۝    and as they used to impugn Our signs.

وَلَقَدْ جِئْنَٰهُم بِكِتَٰبٍ    52 Certainly We have brought them a Book,

فَصَّلْنَٰهُ عَلَىٰ عِلْمٍ    which We have elaborated with knowledge,

هُدًى وَرَحْمَةً    as a guidance and mercy

لِّقَوْمٍ يُؤْمِنُونَ ۝    for a people who have faith.

هَلْ يَنظُرُونَ إِلَّا تَأْوِيلَهُۥ    53 Do they await anything but its fulfillment?

يَوْمَ يَأْتِى تَأْوِيلُهُۥ    The day when its fulfillment comes,

يَقُولُ ٱلَّذِينَ نَسُوهُ مِن قَبْلُ    those who had forgotten it before will say,

قَدْ جَآءَتْ رُسُلُ رَبِّنَا بِٱلْحَقِّ    'Our Lord's apostles had certainly brought the truth.

فَهَل لَّنَا مِن شُفَعَآءَ فَيَشْفَعُواْ لَنَآ    If only we had some intercessors to intercede for us,

أَوْ نُرَدُّ    or we would be returned,

فَنَعْمَلَ غَيْرَ ٱلَّذِى كُنَّا نَعْمَلُ    so that we may do differently from what we did!'

قَدْ خَسِرُوٓاْ أَنفُسَهُمْ    They have certainly ruined their souls,

وَضَلَّ عَنْهُم مَّا كَانُواْ يَفْتَرُونَ ۝    and what they used to fabricate has forsaken them.

إِنَّ رَبَّكُمُ ٱللَّهُ    54 Indeed your Lord is Allah,

ٱلَّذِى خَلَقَ ٱلسَّمَٰوَٰتِ وَٱلْأَرْضَ    who created the heavens and the earth

فِى سِتَّةِ أَيَّامٍ    in six days,

ثُمَّ ٱسْتَوَىٰ عَلَى ٱلْعَرْشِ    and then settled on the Throne.

يُغْشِى ٱلَّيْلَ ٱلنَّهَارَ    He draws the night's cover over the day,

يَطْلُبُهُۥ حَثِيثًا    which pursues it swiftly,

وَٱلشَّمْسَ وَٱلْقَمَرَ وَٱلنُّجُومَ    and [He created] the sun, the moon, and the stars,

مُسَخَّرَٰتٍ بِأَمْرِهِۦٓ    [all of them] disposed by His command.

أَلَا لَهُ ٱلْخَلْقُ وَٱلْأَمْرُ    Look! All creation and command belong to Him.

تَبَارَكَ ٱللَّهُ رَبُّ ٱلْعَٰلَمِينَ ۝    Blessed is Allah, the Lord of all the worlds.

ٱدْعُوا۟ رَبَّكُمْ تَضَرُّعًا وَخُفْيَةً    55 Supplicate your Lord, beseechingly and secretly.

إِنَّهُۥ لَا يُحِبُّ ٱلْمُعْتَدِينَ ۝    Indeed He does not like the transgressors.

وَلَا تُفْسِدُوا۟ فِى ٱلْأَرْضِ    56 And do not cause corruption on the earth

بَعْدَ إِصْلَٰحِهَا    after its restoration,

وَٱدْعُوهُ خَوْفًا وَطَمَعًا    and supplicate Him with fear and hope:

إِنَّ رَحْمَتَ ٱللَّهِ    indeed Allah's mercy

قَرِيبٌ مِّنَ ٱلْمُحْسِنِينَ ۝    is close to the virtuous.

وَهُوَ ٱلَّذِى يُرْسِلُ ٱلرِّيَٰحَ    57 It is He who sends forth the winds

بُشْرًۢا بَيْنَ يَدَىْ رَحْمَتِهِۦ    as harbingers of His mercy.

حَتَّىٰٓ إِذَآ أَقَلَّتْ سَحَابًا ثِقَالًا    When they bear [rain-]laden clouds,

سُقْنَٰهُ لِبَلَدٍ مَّيِّتٍ    We drive them toward a dead land

فَأَنزَلْنَا بِهِ ٱلْمَآءَ    and send down water on it,

فَأَخْرَجْنَا بِهِۦ مِن كُلِّ ٱلثَّمَرَٰتِ    and with it We bring forth all kinds of crops.

كَذَٰلِكَ نُخْرِجُ ٱلْمَوْتَىٰ    Thus shall We raise the dead;

لَعَلَّكُمْ تَذَكَّرُونَ ۝    maybe you will take admonition.

وَٱلْبَلَدُ ٱلطَّيِّبُ يَخْرُجُ نَبَاتُهُۥ    58 The good land—its vegetation comes out

بِإِذْنِ رَبِّهِۦ    by the permission of its Lord,

وَٱلَّذِى خَبُثَ    and as for that which is bad,

لَا يَخْرُجُ إِلَّا نَكِدًا    it does not come out except sparsely.

كَذَٰلِكَ نُصَرِّفُ ٱلْءَايَٰتِ    Thus do We paraphrase the signs variously

لِقَوْمٍ يَشْكُرُونَ ۝    for a people who give thanks.

لَقَدْ أَرْسَلْنَا نُوحًا إِلَىٰ قَوْمِهِۦ    59 Certainly We sent Noah to his people.

فَقَالَ يَٰقَوْمِ ٱعْبُدُوا۟ ٱللَّهَ    He said, 'O my people, worship Allah!

مَا لَكُم مِّنْ إِلَٰهٍ غَيْرُهُۥٓ    You have no other god besides Him.

إِنِّىٓ أَخَافُ عَلَيْكُمْ عَذَابَ    Indeed I fear for you the punishment

يَوْمٍ عَظِيمٍ ۝    of a tremendous day.'

قَالَ ٱلْمَلَأُ مِن قَوْمِهِۦٓ 60 The elite of his people said,

إِنَّا لَنَرَىٰكَ فِى ضَلَٰلٍ مُّبِينٍ ۝    'Indeed we see you in manifest error.'

قَالَ يَٰقَوْمِ لَيْسَ بِى ضَلَٰلَةٌ 61 He said, 'O my people, I am not in error.

وَلَٰكِنِّى رَسُولٌ مِّن رَّبِّ ٱلْعَٰلَمِينَ ۝    Rather I am an apostle from the Lord of all the worlds.

أُبَلِّغُكُمْ رِسَٰلَٰتِ رَبِّى 62 I communicate to you the messages of my Lord,

وَأَنصَحُ لَكُمْ    and I am your well-wisher,

وَأَعْلَمُ مِنَ ٱللَّهِ مَا لَا تَعْلَمُونَ ۝    and I know from Allah what you do not know.

أَوَعَجِبْتُمْ 63 Do you consider it odd

أَن جَآءَكُمْ ذِكْرٌ مِّن رَّبِّكُمْ    that a reminder from your Lord should come to you

عَلَىٰ رَجُلٍ مِّنكُمْ    through a man from among yourselves,

لِيُنذِرَكُمْ    to warn you

وَلِتَتَّقُوا    so that you may be Godwary

وَلَعَلَّكُمْ تُرْحَمُونَ ۝    and so that you may receive His mercy?'

فَكَذَّبُوهُ 64 But they denied him.

فَأَنجَيْنَٰهُ    So We delivered him

وَٱلَّذِينَ مَعَهُۥ فِى ٱلْفُلْكِ    and those who were with him in the ark,

وَأَغْرَقْنَا ٱلَّذِينَ كَذَّبُوا بِـَٔايَٰتِنَآ    and We drowned those who denied Our signs.

إِنَّهُمْ كَانُوا قَوْمًا عَمِينَ ۝ ◆    Indeed they were a blind lot.

وَإِلَىٰ عَادٍ أَخَاهُمْ هُودًا 65 And to [the people of] 'Ād, Hūd, their brother.

قَالَ يَٰقَوْمِ ٱعْبُدُوا ٱللَّهَ    He said, 'O my people, worship Allah!

مَا لَكُم مِّنْ إِلَٰهٍ غَيْرُهُۥٓ    You have no other god besides Him.

أَفَلَا تَتَّقُونَ ۝    Will you not then be wary [of Him]?'

قَالَ ٱلْمَلَأُ ٱلَّذِينَ كَفَرُوا مِن قَوْمِهِۦٓ 66 The elite of his people who were faithless said,

إِنَّا لَنَرَىٰكَ فِى سَفَاهَةٍ    'Indeed we see you to be in folly,

وَإِنَّا لَنَظُنُّكَ مِنَ ٱلْكَٰذِبِينَ ۝    and indeed we consider you to be a liar.'

قَالَ يَٰقَوْمِ لَيْسَ بِى سَفَاهَةٌ 67 He said, 'O my people, I am not in folly.

وَلَٰكِنِّى رَسُولٌ مِّن رَّبِّ ٱلْعَٰلَمِينَ ۝    Rather I am an apostle from the Lord of all the worlds.

أُبَلِّغُكُمْ رِسَٰلَٰتِ رَبِّى 68 I communicate to you the messages of my Lord

وَأَنَا۠ لَكُمْ نَاصِحٌ أَمِينٌ ۝ and I am a trustworthy well-wisher for you.

أَوَعَجِبْتُمْ 69 Do you consider it odd that

أَن جَآءَكُمْ ذِكْرٌ مِّن رَّبِّكُمْ there should come to you a reminder from your Lord

عَلَىٰ رَجُلٍ مِّنكُمْ through a man from among yourselves,

لِيُنذِرَكُمْ so that he may warn you?

وَاذْكُرُوٓاْ إِذْ جَعَلَكُمْ خُلَفَآءَ Remember when He made you successors

مِنۢ بَعْدِ قَوْمِ نُوحٍ after the people of Noah,

وَزَادَكُمْ فِى ٱلْخَلْقِ بَصْۜطَةً and increased you vastly in creation.

فَاذْكُرُوٓاْ ءَالَآءَ ٱللَّهِ So remember Allah's bounties

لَعَلَّكُمْ تُفْلِحُونَ ۝ so that you may be felicitous.'

قَالُوٓاْ أَجِئْتَنَا 70 They said, 'Have you come to [tell] us

لِنَعْبُدَ ٱللَّهَ وَحْدَهُ that we should worship Allah alone

وَنَذَرَ مَا كَانَ يَعْبُدُ ءَابَآؤُنَا and abandon what our fathers have been worshiping?

فَأْتِنَا بِمَا تَعِدُنَآ Then bring us what you threaten us with,

إِن كُنتَ مِنَ ٱلصَّٰدِقِينَ ۝ should you be truthful.'

قَالَ قَدْ وَقَعَ عَلَيْكُم 71 He said, 'There has become due against you

مِّن رَّبِّكُمْ رِجْسٌ وَغَضَبٌ a punishment and wrath from your Lord.

أَتُجَٰدِلُونَنِى فِىٓ أَسْمَآءٍ Do you dispute with me regarding names

سَمَّيْتُمُوهَآ which you have named

أَنتُمْ وَءَابَآؤُكُم —you and your fathers—

مَّا نَزَّلَ ٱللَّهُ بِهَا مِن سُلْطَٰنٍ for which Allah has not sent down any authority?

فَٱنتَظِرُوٓاْ So wait!

إِنِّى مَعَكُم مِّنَ ٱلْمُنتَظِرِينَ ۝ I too am waiting along with you.'

فَأَنجَيْنَٰهُ وَٱلَّذِينَ مَعَهُ 72 Then We delivered him and those who were with him

بِرَحْمَةٍ مِّنَّا by a mercy from Us,

وَقَطَعْنَا دَابِرَ ٱلَّذِينَ كَذَّبُواْ بِـَٔايَٰتِنَا and We rooted out those who denied Our signs

وَمَا كَانُواْ مُؤْمِنِينَ ۝ and were not faithful.

وَإِلَىٰ ثَمُودَ أَخَاهُمْ صَٰلِحًا 73 And to [the people of] Thamūd, Ṣāliḥ, their brother.

قَالَ يَٰقَوْمِ ٱعْبُدُواْ ٱللَّهَ He said, 'O my people, worship Allah!

مَا لَكُم مِّنْ إِلَٰهٍ غَيْرُهُ You have no other god besides Him.

قَدْ جَآءَتْكُم بَيِّنَةٌ
There has certainly come to you a manifest proof

مِّن رَّبِّكُمْ
from your Lord.

هَـٰذِهِۦ نَاقَةُ ٱللَّهِ لَكُمْ ءَايَةً
This she-camel of Allah is a sign for you.

فَذَرُوهَا تَأْكُلْ فِىٓ أَرْضِ ٱللَّهِ
Let her alone to graze [freely] in Allah's land,

وَلَا تَمَسُّوهَا بِسُوٓءٍ
and do not cause her any harm,[1]

فَيَأْخُذَكُمْ عَذَابٌ أَلِيمٌ ٧٣
for then you shall be seized by a painful punishment.

وَٱذْكُرُوٓاْ إِذْ جَعَلَكُمْ خُلَفَآءَ
74 Remember when He made you successors

مِنۢ بَعْدِ عَادٍ
after [the people of] 'Ād,

وَبَوَّأَكُمْ فِى ٱلْأَرْضِ
and settled you in the land:

تَتَّخِذُونَ مِن سُهُولِهَا قُصُورًا
you build palaces in its plains,

وَتَنْحِتُونَ ٱلْجِبَالَ بُيُوتًا
and hew houses out of the mountains.

فَٱذْكُرُوٓاْ ءَالَآءَ ٱللَّهِ
So remember Allah's bounties,

وَلَا تَعْثَوْاْ فِى ٱلْأَرْضِ
and do not act wickedly on the earth,

مُفْسِدِينَ ٧٤
causing corruption.'

قَالَ ٱلْمَلَأُ ٱلَّذِينَ ٱسْتَكْبَرُواْ مِن قَوْمِهِۦ
75 The elite of his people who were arrogant said

لِلَّذِينَ ٱسْتُضْعِفُواْ
to those who were abased

لِمَنْ ءَامَنَ مِنْهُمْ
—to those among them who had faith—

أَتَعْلَمُونَ أَنَّ صَـٰلِحًا مُّرْسَلٌ مِّن رَّبِّهِۦ
'Do you know that Ṣāliḥ has been sent by his Lord?'

قَالُوٓاْ
They said,

إِنَّا بِمَآ أُرْسِلَ بِهِۦ مُؤْمِنُونَ ٧٥
'We indeed believe in what he has been sent with.'

قَالَ ٱلَّذِينَ ٱسْتَكْبَرُوٓاْ
76 Those who were arrogant said,

إِنَّا بِٱلَّذِىٓ ءَامَنتُم بِهِۦ كَـٰفِرُونَ ٧٦
'We indeed disbelieve in what you have believed.'

فَعَقَرُواْ ٱلنَّاقَةَ
77 So they hamstrung the She-camel

وَعَتَوْاْ عَنْ أَمْرِ رَبِّهِمْ
and defied the command of their Lord,

وَقَالُواْ
and they said,

يَـٰصَـٰلِحُ ٱئْتِنَا بِمَا تَعِدُنَآ
'O Ṣāliḥ, bring us what you threaten us with,

إِن كُنتَ مِنَ ٱلْمُرْسَلِينَ ٧٧
if you are one of the apostles.'

فَأَخَذَتْهُمُ ٱلرَّجْفَةُ
78 So the earthquake seized them,

فَأَصْبَحُواْ فِى دَارِهِمْ جَـٰثِمِينَ ٧٨
and they lay lifeless prostrate in their homes.

---

[1] Or 'do not touch her with malice.'

فَتَوَلَّىٰ عَنْهُمْ وَقَالَ
79 So he abandoned them [to their fate], and said,

يَـٰقَوْمِ
'O my people!

لَقَدْ أَبْلَغْتُكُمْ
Certainly I communicated to you

رِسَالَةَ رَبِّى
the message of my Lord,

وَنَصَحْتُ لَكُمْ
and I was your well-wisher,

وَلَـٰكِن لَّا تُحِبُّونَ ٱلنَّـٰصِحِينَ ۝
but you did not like well-wishers.'

وَلُوطًا إِذْ قَالَ لِقَوْمِهِ
80 And Lot, when he said to his people,

أَتَأْتُونَ ٱلْفَـٰحِشَةَ
'What! Do you commit an outrage

مَا سَبَقَكُم بِهَا مِنْ أَحَدٍ مِّنَ ٱلْعَـٰلَمِينَ ۝
none in the world ever committed before you?!

إِنَّكُمْ لَتَأْتُونَ ٱلرِّجَالَ شَهْوَةً
81 Indeed you come to men with desire[1]

مِّن دُونِ ٱلنِّسَآءِ
instead of women!

بَلْ أَنتُمْ قَوْمٌ مُّسْرِفُونَ ۝
Rather you are a profligate lot.

وَمَا كَانَ جَوَابَ قَوْمِهِ إِلَّآ أَن قَالُوٓا۟
82 But the only answer of his people was that they said,

أَخْرِجُوهُم مِّن قَرْيَتِكُمْ
'Expel them from your town!

إِنَّهُمْ أُنَاسٌ يَتَطَهَّرُونَ ۝
They are indeed a puritanical lot.'

فَأَنجَيْنَـٰهُ وَأَهْلَهُۥٓ إِلَّا ٱمْرَأَتَهُۥ
83 So We delivered him and his family, except his wife;

كَانَتْ مِنَ ٱلْغَـٰبِرِينَ ۝
she was one of those who remained behind.

وَأَمْطَرْنَا عَلَيْهِم مَّطَرًا
84 Then We poured down upon them a rain [of stones].

فَٱنظُرْ كَيْفَ كَانَ عَـٰقِبَةُ ٱلْمُجْرِمِينَ ۝
So *observe* how was the fate of the guilty!

وَإِلَىٰ مَدْيَنَ أَخَاهُمْ شُعَيْبًا
85 And to [the people of] Midian, Shuʿayb, their brother.

قَالَ يَـٰقَوْمِ ٱعْبُدُوا۟ ٱللَّهَ
He said, 'O my people, worship Allah!

مَا لَكُم مِّنْ إِلَـٰهٍ غَيْرُهُۥ
You have no other god besides Him.

قَدْ جَآءَتْكُم بَيِّنَةٌ
There has certainly come to you a manifest proof

مِّن رَّبِّكُمْ
from your Lord.

فَأَوْفُوا۟ ٱلْكَيْلَ وَٱلْمِيزَانَ
Observe fully the measure and the balance,

وَلَا تَبْخَسُوا۟ ٱلنَّاسَ أَشْيَآءَهُمْ
and do not cheat the people of their goods,[2]

---

[1] Desire: sexual appetite or a sexual urge.

[2] That is, by employing short weights and measures.

وَلَا تُفْسِدُوا فِى ٱلْأَرْضِ    and do not cause corruption on the earth

بَعْدَ إِصْلَٰحِهَا    after its restoration.

ذَٰلِكُمْ خَيْرٌ لَّكُمْ إِن كُنتُم مُّؤْمِنِينَ    That is better for you, if you are faithful.

وَلَا تَقْعُدُوا بِكُلِّ صِرَٰطٍ    86 And do not lie in wait on every road

تُوعِدُونَ وَتَصُدُّونَ عَن سَبِيلِ ٱللَّهِ    to threaten and bar from the way of Allah

مَنْ ءَامَنَ بِهِۦ    those who have faith in Him,

وَتَبْغُونَهَا عِوَجًا    seeking to make it crooked.

وَٱذْكُرُوا إِذْ كُنتُمْ قَلِيلًا    And remember when you were few,

فَكَثَّرَكُمْ    and He multiplied you,

وَٱنظُرُوا    and observe

كَيْفَ كَانَ عَٰقِبَةُ ٱلْمُفْسِدِينَ    how was the fate of the agents of corruption.

وَإِن كَانَ طَآئِفَةٌ مِّنكُمْ ءَامَنُوا    87 If a group of you have believed

بِٱلَّذِى أُرْسِلْتُ بِهِۦ    in what I have been sent with,

وَطَآئِفَةٌ لَّمْ يُؤْمِنُوا    and a group have not believed,

فَٱصْبِرُوا حَتَّىٰ يَحْكُمَ ٱللَّهُ بَيْنَنَا    be patient until Allah judges between us,

وَهُوَ خَيْرُ ٱلْحَٰكِمِينَ    and He is the best of judges.'

[PART 9]

قَالَ ٱلْمَلَأُ ٱلَّذِينَ ٱسْتَكْبَرُوا مِن قَوْمِهِۦ    88 The elite of his people who were arrogant said,

لَنُخْرِجَنَّكَ يَٰشُعَيْبُ    'O Shu'ayb, we will surely expel you

وَٱلَّذِينَ ءَامَنُوا مَعَكَ    and the faithful who are with you

مِن قَرْيَتِنَآ    from our town,

أَوْ لَتَعُودُنَّ فِى مِلَّتِنَا    or else you shall revert to our creed.'

قَالَ أَوَلَوْ كُنَّا كَٰرِهِينَ    He said, 'What! Even if we should be unwilling?!

قَدِ ٱفْتَرَيْنَا عَلَى ٱللَّهِ كَذِبًا    89 We would be fabricating a lie against Allah

إِنْ عُدْنَا فِى مِلَّتِكُم    should we revert to your creed

بَعْدَ إِذْ نَجَّىٰنَا ٱللَّهُ مِنْهَا    after Allah had delivered us from it.

وَمَا يَكُونُ لَنَآ أَن نَّعُودَ فِيهَا    It does not behoove us to return to it,

إِلَّآ أَن يَشَآءَ ٱللَّهُ رَبُّنَا    unless Allah, our Lord, should wish so.

وَسِعَ رَبُّنَا كُلَّ شَىْءٍ عِلْمًا    Our Lord embraces all things in [His] knowledge.

عَلَى ٱللَّهِ تَوَكَّلْنَا    In Allah we have put our trust.'

رَبَّنَا ٱفْتَحْ بَيْنَنَا وَبَيْنَ قَوْمِنَا بِٱلْحَقِّ
'Our Lord! Judge justly between us and our people,

وَأَنتَ خَيْرُ ٱلْفَٰتِحِينَ
and You are the best of judges!'

٩٠ وَقَالَ ٱلْمَلَأُ ٱلَّذِينَ كَفَرُوا۟ مِن قَوْمِهِۦ
90 The elite of his people who were faithless said,

لَئِنِ ٱتَّبَعْتُمْ شُعَيْبًا
'If you follow Shu'ayb,

إِنَّكُمْ إِذًا لَّخَٰسِرُونَ
you will indeed be losers.'

٩١ فَأَخَذَتْهُمُ ٱلرَّجْفَةُ
91 So the earthquake seized them,

فَأَصْبَحُوا۟ فِى دَارِهِمْ جَٰثِمِينَ
and they lay lifeless prostrate in their homes.

٩٢ ٱلَّذِينَ كَذَّبُوا۟ شُعَيْبًا
92 Those who impugned Shu'ayb

كَأَن لَّمْ يَغْنَوْا۟ فِيهَا
became as if they had never lived there.

ٱلَّذِينَ كَذَّبُوا۟ شُعَيْبًا
Those who impugned Shu'ayb

كَانُوا۟ هُمُ ٱلْخَٰسِرِينَ
were themselves the losers.

٩٣ فَتَوَلَّىٰ عَنْهُمْ
93 So he abandoned them [to their fate]

وَقَالَ يَٰقَوْمِ
and said, 'O my people!

لَقَدْ أَبْلَغْتُكُمْ
Certainly I communicated to you

رِسَٰلَٰتِ رَبِّى
the messages of my Lord,

وَنَصَحْتُ لَكُمْ
and I was your well-wisher.

فَكَيْفَ ءَاسَىٰ عَلَىٰ قَوْمٍ كَٰفِرِينَ
So how should I grieve for a faithless lot?'

٩٤ وَمَآ أَرْسَلْنَا فِى قَرْيَةٍ مِّن نَّبِىٍّ
94 We did not send a prophet to any town

إِلَّآ أَخَذْنَآ أَهْلَهَا بِٱلْبَأْسَآءِ وَٱلضَّرَّآءِ
without visiting its people with stress and distress

لَعَلَّهُمْ يَضَّرَّعُونَ
so that they might entreat [for Allah's forgiveness].

٩٥ ثُمَّ بَدَّلْنَا مَكَانَ ٱلسَّيِّئَةِ ٱلْحَسَنَةَ
95 Then We changed the ill [conditions] to good

حَتَّىٰ عَفَوا۟ وَّقَالُوا۟
until they multiplied [in numbers] and said,

قَدْ مَسَّ ءَابَآءَنَا ٱلضَّرَّآءُ وَٱلسَّرَّآءُ
'Adversity and ease befell our fathers [too].'

فَأَخَذْنَٰهُم بَغْتَةً
Then We seized them suddenly

وَهُمْ لَا يَشْعُرُونَ
while they were unaware.

٩٦ وَلَوْ أَنَّ أَهْلَ ٱلْقُرَىٰٓ ءَامَنُوا۟
96 If the people of the towns had been faithful

وَٱتَّقَوْا۟
and Godwary,

لَفَتَحْنَا عَلَيْهِم بَرَكَٰتٍ
We would have opened to them blessings

مِّنَ ٱلسَّمَآءِ وَٱلْأَرْضِ
from the heaven and the earth.

وَلَٰكِن كَذَّبُوا But they denied;

فَأَخَذْنَٰهُم so We seized them

بِمَا كَانُوا يَكْسِبُونَ ۞ because of what they used to earn.

أَفَأَمِنَ أَهْلُ ٱلْقُرَىٰ 97 Do the people of the towns feel secure

أَن يَأْتِيَهُم بَأْسُنَا بَيَٰتًا from Our punishment overtaking them at night

وَهُمْ نَآئِمُونَ ۞ while they are asleep?

أَوَأَمِنَ أَهْلُ ٱلْقُرَىٰ 98 Do the people of the towns feel secure

أَن يَأْتِيَهُم بَأْسُنَا ضُحًى from Our punishment overtaking them at midday

وَهُمْ يَلْعَبُونَ ۞ while they are playing around?

أَفَأَمِنُوا مَكْرَ ٱللَّهِ 99 Do they feel secure from Allah's devising?

فَلَا يَأْمَنُ مَكْرَ ٱللَّهِ No one feels secure from Allah's devising

إِلَّا ٱلْقَوْمُ ٱلْخَٰسِرُونَ ۞ except the people who are losers.

أَوَلَمْ يَهْدِ لِلَّذِينَ يَرِثُونَ ٱلْأَرْضَ 100 Does it not dawn upon those who inherited the earth

مِنۢ بَعْدِ أَهْلِهَآ after its [former] inhabitants

أَن لَّوْ نَشَآءُ أَصَبْنَٰهُم بِذُنُوبِهِمْ that if We wish We will punish them for their sins,

وَنَطْبَعُ عَلَىٰ قُلُوبِهِمْ and set a seal on their hearts

فَهُمْ لَا يَسْمَعُونَ ۞ so they would not hear?

تِلْكَ ٱلْقُرَىٰ 101 These are the towns

نَقُصُّ عَلَيْكَ مِنْ أَنۢبَآئِهَا some of whose accounts We recount to *you.*

وَلَقَدْ جَآءَتْهُمْ رُسُلُهُم Their apostles certainly brought them

بِٱلْبَيِّنَٰتِ manifest proofs,

فَمَا كَانُوا لِيُؤْمِنُوا but they were not the ones to believe

بِمَا كَذَّبُوا مِن قَبْلُ in what they had denied earlier.

كَذَٰلِكَ يَطْبَعُ ٱللَّهُ Thus does Allah put a seal

عَلَىٰ قُلُوبِ ٱلْكَٰفِرِينَ ۞ on the hearts of the faithless.

وَمَا وَجَدْنَا لِأَكْثَرِهِم 102 We did not find in most of them

مِّنْ عَهْدٍ any [loyalty to] covenants.

وَإِن وَجَدْنَآ أَكْثَرَهُمْ لَفَٰسِقِينَ ۞ Indeed We found most of them to be transgressors.

ثُمَّ بَعَثْنَا مِنۢ بَعْدِهِم مُّوسَىٰ بِـَٔايَٰتِنَآ 103 Then after them We sent Moses with Our signs

إِلَىٰ فِرْعَوْنَ وَمَلَإِيْهِۦ        to Pharaoh and his elite,

فَظَلَمُوا۟ بِهَا     but they wronged them.

فَٱنظُرْ     So *observe*

كَيْفَ كَانَ عَٰقِبَةُ ٱلْمُفْسِدِينَ ١٣     how was the fate of the agents of corruption!

وَقَالَ مُوسَىٰ 104 And Moses said,

يَٰفِرْعَوْنُ     'O Pharaoh,

إِنِّى رَسُولٌ مِّن رَّبِّ ٱلْعَٰلَمِينَ ١٤ I am indeed an apostle from the Lord of all the worlds.'

حَقِيقٌ عَلَىٰٓ أَن لَّآ أَقُولَ عَلَى ٱللَّهِ 105 It behooves me to say nothing about Allah

إِلَّا ٱلْحَقَّ     except the truth.

قَدْ جِئْتُكُم بِبَيِّنَةٍ     I certainly bring you a manifest proof

مِّن رَّبِّكُمْ        from your Lord.

فَأَرْسِلْ مَعِىَ بَنِىٓ إِسْرَٰٓءِيلَ ١٥ So let the Children of Israel go with me.'

قَالَ إِن كُنتَ جِئْتَ بِـَٔايَةٍ 106 He said, 'If you have brought a sign,

فَأْتِ بِهَآ        produce it,

إِن كُنتَ مِنَ ٱلصَّٰدِقِينَ ١٦     should you be truthful.'

فَأَلْقَىٰ عَصَاهُ 107 Thereat he threw down his staff,

فَإِذَا هِىَ ثُعْبَانٌ مُّبِينٌ ١٧     and behold, it became a manifest python.

وَنَزَعَ يَدَهُۥ 108 Then he drew out his hand,

فَإِذَا هِىَ بَيْضَآءُ لِلنَّٰظِرِينَ ١٨     and behold, it was white to the onlookers.

قَالَ ٱلْمَلَأُ مِن قَوْمِ فِرْعَوْنَ 109 The elite of Pharaoh's people said,

إِنَّ هَٰذَا لَسَٰحِرٌ عَلِيمٌ ١٩     'This is indeed an expert magician;

يُرِيدُ أَن يُخْرِجَكُم مِّنْ أَرْضِكُمْ 110 he seeks to expel you from your land.'

فَمَاذَا تَأْمُرُونَ ٢٠     'So what do you advise?'

قَالُوٓا۟ أَرْجِهْ وَأَخَاهُ 111 They said, 'Put him and his brother off for a while,

وَأَرْسِلْ فِى ٱلْمَدَآئِنِ حَٰشِرِينَ ٢١     and send heralds to the cities,

يَأْتُوكَ بِكُلِّ سَٰحِرٍ عَلِيمٍ ٢٢ 112 to bring you every expert magician.'

وَجَآءَ ٱلسَّحَرَةُ فِرْعَوْنَ 113 And the magicians came to Pharaoh.

قَالُوٓا۟     They said,

إِنَّ لَنَا لَأَجْرًا     'We shall indeed have a reward

إِن كُنَّا نَحْنُ ٱلْغَٰلِبِينَ ۝    if we were to be the victors?'[1]

قَالَ نَعَمْ    114 He said, 'Of course!

وَإِنَّكُمْ لَمِنَ ٱلْمُقَرَّبِينَ ۝    And indeed you shall be among those near [to me].'

قَالُوا۟ يَٰمُوسَىٰٓ    115 They said, 'O Moses,

إِمَّآ أَن تُلْقِىَ    will you throw [first],

وَإِمَّآ أَن نَّكُونَ نَحْنُ ٱلْمُلْقِينَ ۝    or shall we throw?'

قَالَ أَلْقُوا۟    116 He said, 'Throw [yours].'

فَلَمَّآ أَلْقَوْا۟    So when they threw,

سَحَرُوٓا۟ أَعْيُنَ ٱلنَّاسِ    they bewitched the people's eyes

وَٱسْتَرْهَبُوهُمْ    and overawed them,

وَجَآءُو بِسِحْرٍ عَظِيمٍ ۝    producing a tremendous magic.

وَأَوْحَيْنَآ إِلَىٰ مُوسَىٰٓ    117 And We signalled to Moses:

أَنْ أَلْقِ عَصَاكَ    'Throw down your staff.'

فَإِذَا هِىَ تَلْقَفُ مَا يَأْفِكُونَ ۝    And behold, it was swallowing what they had faked.

فَوَقَعَ ٱلْحَقُّ    118 So the truth came out,

وَبَطَلَ مَا كَانُوا۟ يَعْمَلُونَ ۝    and what they had wrought was reduced to naught.

فَغُلِبُوا۟ هُنَالِكَ    119 Thereat they were vanquished,

وَٱنقَلَبُوا۟ صَٰغِرِينَ ۝    and they retreated, humiliated.

وَأُلْقِىَ ٱلسَّحَرَةُ سَٰجِدِينَ ۝    120 And the magicians fell down in prostration.

قَالُوٓا۟    121 They said,

ءَامَنَّا بِرَبِّ ٱلْعَٰلَمِينَ ۝    'We have believed in the Lord of all the worlds,

رَبِّ مُوسَىٰ وَهَٰرُونَ ۝    122    the Lord of Moses and Aaron.'

قَالَ فِرْعَوْنُ    123 Pharaoh said,

ءَامَنتُم بِهِۦ قَبْلَ أَنْ ءَاذَنَ لَكُمْ    'Do you profess faith in Him before I may permit you?

إِنَّ هَٰذَا لَمَكْرٌ مَّكَرْتُمُوهُ فِى ٱلْمَدِينَةِ    It is indeed a plot you have devised in the city

لِتُخْرِجُوا۟ مِنْهَآ أَهْلَهَا    to expel its people from it.

---

[1] This is in accordance with the reading of Ḥafṣ and that of the Ḥijāzī *qārīs*. However, in accordance with an alternate reading (with an interrogative *hamzah* before *inna*, exactly as in 26:41, a parallel verse) the translation will be, 'Shall we indeed have a reward if we were to be the victors?' (see *Mu'jam al-Qirā'āt al-Qur'āniyyah*, ii, pp. 388-389).

فَسَوۡفَ تَعۡلَمُونَ ۝

Soon you will know [the consequences]!

لَأُقَطِّعَنَّ أَيۡدِيَكُمۡ وَأَرۡجُلَكُم 124 Surely I will cut off your hands and feet

مِّنۡ خِلَٰفٖ　on opposite sides,

ثُمَّ لَأُصَلِّبَنَّكُمۡ أَجۡمَعِينَ ۝　and then I will surely crucify all of you.'

قَالُوٓاْ إِنَّآ إِلَىٰ رَبِّنَا مُنقَلِبُونَ ۝ 125 They said, 'Indeed we shall return to our Lord.

وَمَا تَنقِمُ مِنَّآ إِلَّآ 126 You are vindictive toward us only

أَنۡ ءَامَنَّا　because we have believed

بِـَٔايَٰتِ رَبِّنَا لَمَّا جَآءَتۡنَا　in the signs of our Lord, when they came to us.'

رَبَّنَآ أَفۡرِغۡ عَلَيۡنَا صَبۡرٗا　'Our Lord! Pour patience upon us,

وَتَوَفَّنَا مُسۡلِمِينَ ۝　and grant us to die as *muslim*s.'

وَقَالَ ٱلۡمَلَأُ مِن قَوۡمِ فِرۡعَوۡنَ 127 The elite of Pharaoh's people said,

أَتَذَرُ مُوسَىٰ وَقَوۡمَهُۥ　'Will you leave Moses and his people

لِيُفۡسِدُواْ فِي ٱلۡأَرۡضِ　to cause corruption in the land,

وَيَذَرَكَ وَءَالِهَتَكَۚ　and to abandon you and your gods?'

قَالَ سَنُقَتِّلُ أَبۡنَآءَهُمۡ　He said, 'We will kill their sons

وَنَسۡتَحۡيِۦ نِسَآءَهُمۡ　and spare their women,

وَإِنَّا فَوۡقَهُمۡ قَٰهِرُونَ ۝　and indeed we are dominant over them.'

قَالَ مُوسَىٰ لِقَوۡمِهِ 128 Moses said to his people,

ٱسۡتَعِينُواْ بِٱللَّهِ وَٱصۡبِرُوٓاْۖ　'Turn to Allah for help and be patient.

إِنَّ ٱلۡأَرۡضَ لِلَّهِ　The earth indeed belongs to Allah,

يُورِثُهَا مَن يَشَآءُ　and He gives its inheritance to whomever He wishes

مِنۡ عِبَادِهِۦۖ　of His servants,

وَٱلۡعَٰقِبَةُ لِلۡمُتَّقِينَ ۝　and the outcome will be in favour of the Godwary.'

قَالُوٓاْ 129 They said,

أُوذِينَا مِن قَبۡلِ أَن تَأۡتِيَنَا　'We were tormented before you came to us

وَمِنۢ بَعۡدِ مَا جِئۡتَنَاۚ　and [also] after you came to us.'

قَالَ عَسَىٰ رَبُّكُمۡ أَن يُهۡلِكَ عَدُوَّكُمۡ　He said, 'Maybe your Lord will destroy your enemy

وَيَسۡتَخۡلِفَكُمۡ فِي ٱلۡأَرۡضِ　and make you successors in the land,

فَيَنظُرَ كَيۡفَ تَعۡمَلُونَ ۝　and then He will see how you act.'

وَلَقَدۡ أَخَذۡنَآ ءَالَ فِرۡعَوۡنَ 130 Certainly We afflicted Pharaoh's clan

بِٱلسِّنِينَ وَنَقْصٍ مِّنَ ٱلثَّمَرَٰتِ
with droughts and loss of produce,

لَعَلَّهُمْ يَذَّكَّرُونَ ۝
so that they may take admonition.

فَإِذَا جَآءَتْهُمُ ٱلْحَسَنَةُ 131
131 But whenever any good came to them,

قَالُوا۟ لَنَا هَٰذِهِ ۖ
they would say, 'This is our due.'

وَإِن تُصِبْهُمْ سَيِّئَةٌ
And if any ill visited them,

يَطَّيَّرُوا۟ بِمُوسَىٰ
they took it for ill omens attending Moses

وَمَن مَّعَهُۥٓ ۗ
and those who were with him.

أَلَآ
(Look!

إِنَّمَا طَٰٓئِرُهُمْ عِندَ ٱللَّهِ
Indeed the cause of their ill omens is with Allah,

وَلَٰكِنَّ أَكْثَرَهُمْ لَا يَعْلَمُونَ ۝
but most of them do not know.)

وَقَالُوا۟ 132
132 And they said,

مَهْمَا تَأْتِنَا بِهِۦ مِنْ ءَايَةٍ لِّتَسْحَرَنَا بِهَا
'Whatever sign you may bring us to bewitch us,

فَمَا نَحْنُ لَكَ بِمُؤْمِنِينَ ۝
we are not going to believe you.'

فَأَرْسَلْنَا عَلَيْهِمُ ٱلطُّوفَانَ وَٱلْجَرَادَ 133
133 So We sent against them a flood and locusts,

وَٱلْقُمَّلَ وَٱلضَّفَادِعَ وَٱلدَّمَ
lice, frogs and blood,

ءَايَٰتٍ مُّفَصَّلَٰتٍ
as distinct signs.

فَٱسْتَكْبَرُوا۟
But they acted arrogantly,

وَكَانُوا۟ قَوْمًا مُّجْرِمِينَ ۝
and they were a guilty lot.

وَلَمَّا وَقَعَ عَلَيْهِمُ ٱلرِّجْزُ قَالُوا۟ 134
134 Whenever a plague fell upon them, they would say,

يَٰمُوسَى ٱدْعُ لَنَا رَبَّكَ
'O Moses, invoke your Lord for us

بِمَا عَهِدَ عِندَكَ ۖ
by the covenant He has made with you.

لَئِن كَشَفْتَ عَنَّا ٱلرِّجْزَ
If you remove the plague from us,

لَنُؤْمِنَنَّ لَكَ
we will certainly believe in you

وَلَنُرْسِلَنَّ مَعَكَ بَنِىٓ إِسْرَٰٓءِيلَ ۝
and let the Children of Israel go along with you.'

فَلَمَّا كَشَفْنَا عَنْهُمُ ٱلرِّجْزَ 135
135 But when We had removed the plague from them

إِلَىٰٓ أَجَلٍ هُم بَٰلِغُوهُ
until a term that they should have completed,

إِذَا هُمْ يَنكُثُونَ ۝
behold, they broke their promise.

فَٱنتَقَمْنَا مِنْهُمْ 136
136 So We took vengeance on them

فَأَغْرَقْنَٰهُمْ فِى ٱلْيَمِّ
and drowned them in the sea,

بِأَنَّهُمْ كَذَّبُوا۟ بِـَٔايَٰتِنَا
for they denied Our signs

وَكَانُواْ عَنْهَا غَفِلِينَ ۞

and were oblivious to them.

وَأَوْرَثْنَا ٱلْقَوْمَ ٱلَّذِينَ كَانُواْ يُسْتَضْعَفُونَ

137 We made the people who were abased the heirs

مَشَٰرِقَ ٱلْأَرْضِ وَمَغَٰرِبَهَا

to the east and west of the land

ٱلَّتِى بَٰرَكْنَا فِيهَا

which We had blessed,

وَتَمَّتْ كَلِمَتُ رَبِّكَ ٱلْحُسْنَىٰ

and your Lord's best word [of promise] was fulfilled

عَلَىٰ بَنِىٓ إِسْرَٰٓءِيلَ

for the Children of Israel

بِمَا صَبَرُواْ

because of their patience,

وَدَمَّرْنَا

and We destroyed

مَا كَانَ يَصْنَعُ فِرْعَوْنُ وَقَوْمُهُۥ

what Pharaoh and his people had built

وَمَا كَانُواْ يَعْرِشُونَ ۞

and what they used to erect.

وَجَٰوَزْنَا بِبَنِىٓ إِسْرَٰٓءِيلَ ٱلْبَحْرَ

138 We carried the Children of Israel across the sea,

فَأَتَوْاْ عَلَىٰ قَوْمٍ

whereat they came upon a people

يَعْكُفُونَ عَلَىٰٓ أَصْنَامٍ لَّهُمْ

cleaving to certain idols that they had.

قَالُواْ يَٰمُوسَى ٱجْعَل لَّنَآ إِلَٰهًا

They said, 'O Moses, make for us a god

كَمَا لَهُمْ ءَالِهَةٌ

like the gods that they have.'

قَالَ إِنَّكُمْ قَوْمٌ تَجْهَلُونَ ۞

He said, 'You are indeed an ignorant lot.

إِنَّ هَٰٓؤُلَآءِ مُتَبَّرٌ مَّا هُمْ فِيهِ

139 What they are engaged in is indeed bound to perish,

وَبَٰطِلٌ مَّا كَانُواْ يَعْمَلُونَ ۞

and what they have been doing shall come to naught.'

قَالَ أَغَيْرَ ٱللَّهِ أَبْغِيكُمْ إِلَٰهًا

140 He said, 'Shall I find you a god other than Allah,

وَهُوَ فَضَّلَكُمْ

while He has graced you

عَلَى ٱلْعَٰلَمِينَ ۞

over all the nations?'

وَإِذْ أَنجَيْنَٰكُم مِّنْ ءَالِ فِرْعَوْنَ

141 And when We delivered you from Pharaoh's clan

يَسُومُونَكُمْ سُوٓءَ ٱلْعَذَابِ

who inflicted on you a terrible torment,

يُقَتِّلُونَ أَبْنَآءَكُمْ

slaughtering your sons

وَيَسْتَحْيُونَ نِسَآءَكُمْ

and sparing your women,

وَفِى ذَٰلِكُم بَلَآءٌ مِّن رَّبِّكُمْ عَظِيمٌ ۞

and there was a great test in that from your Lord.

وَوَٰعَدْنَا مُوسَىٰ

142 And We made an appointment with Moses

ثَلَٰثِينَ لَيْلَةً

for thirty nights,

وَأَتْمَمْنَٰهَا بِعَشْرٍ

and completed them with ten [more];

فَتَمَّ مِيقَٰتُ رَبِّهِۦٓ أَرْبَعِينَ لَيْلَةً    thus the tryst of his Lord was completed in forty nights.

وَقَالَ مُوسَىٰ لِأَخِيهِ هَٰرُونَ    And Moses said to Aaron, his brother,

ٱخْلُفْنِى فِى قَوْمِى    'Be my successor among my people,

وَأَصْلِحْ    and set things right

وَلَا تَتَّبِعْ    and do not follow

سَبِيلَ ٱلْمُفْسِدِينَ ۝    the way of the agents of corruption.'

وَلَمَّا جَآءَ مُوسَىٰ لِمِيقَٰتِنَا    143 When Moses arrived at Our tryst

وَكَلَّمَهُۥ رَبُّهُۥ    and his Lord spoke to him,

قَالَ رَبِّ أَرِنِىٓ    he said, 'My Lord, show [Yourself] to me,

أَنظُرْ إِلَيْكَ    that I may look at You!'

قَالَ لَن تَرَىٰنِى    He said, 'You shall not see Me.

وَلَٰكِنِ ٱنظُرْ إِلَى ٱلْجَبَلِ    But look at the mountain:

فَإِنِ ٱسْتَقَرَّ مَكَانَهُۥ فَسَوْفَ تَرَىٰنِى    if it abides in its place, then you will see Me.'

فَلَمَّا تَجَلَّىٰ رَبُّهُۥ لِلْجَبَلِ    So when his Lord disclosed Himself to the mountain,

جَعَلَهُۥ دَكًّا    He levelled it,[1]

وَخَرَّ مُوسَىٰ صَعِقًا    and Moses fell down swooning.

فَلَمَّآ أَفَاقَ قَالَ    And when he recovered, he said,

سُبْحَٰنَكَ تُبْتُ إِلَيْكَ    'Immaculate are You! I turn to You in penitence,

وَأَنَا۠ أَوَّلُ ٱلْمُؤْمِنِينَ ۝    and I am the first of the faithful.'

قَالَ يَٰمُوسَىٰٓ    144 He said, 'O Moses,

إِنِّى ٱصْطَفَيْتُكَ عَلَى ٱلنَّاسِ    I have chosen you over the people

بِرِسَٰلَٰتِى وَبِكَلَٰمِى    with My messages and My speech.

فَخُذْ مَآ ءَاتَيْتُكَ    So take what I give you,

وَكُن مِّنَ ٱلشَّٰكِرِينَ ۝    and be among the grateful.'

وَكَتَبْنَا لَهُۥ فِى ٱلْأَلْوَاحِ    145 And We wrote for him in the Tablets

مِن كُلِّ شَىْءٍ مَّوْعِظَةً    advice concerning all things

وَتَفْصِيلًا لِّكُلِّ شَىْءٍ    and an elaboration of all things,

فَخُذْهَا بِقُوَّةٍ    [and We said], 'Hold on to them with power,

وَأْمُرْ قَوْمَكَ    and bid your people

---

[1] Or 'He made it crumble.'

يَأْخُذُوا بِأَحْسَنِهَا

to hold on to the best of [what is in] them.

سَأُوْرِيكُمْ دَارَ ٱلْفَسِقِينَ ۝

Soon I shall show you the abode of the transgressors.

سَأَصْرِفُ عَنْ ءَايَتِىَ

146 Soon I shall turn away from My signs

ٱلَّذِينَ يَتَكَبَّرُونَ فِى ٱلْأَرْضِ بِغَيْرِ ٱلْحَقِّ

those who are unduly arrogant in the earth:

وَإِن يَرَوْا كُلَّ ءَايَةٍ

[even] though they should see every sign,

لَّا يُؤْمِنُوا بِهَا

they will not believe in it,

وَإِن يَرَوْا سَبِيلَ ٱلرُّشْدِ

and if they see the way of rectitude

لَا يَتَّخِذُوهُ سَبِيلًا

they will not take it as [their] way,

وَإِن يَرَوْا سَبِيلَ ٱلْغَىِّ

and if they see the way of error

يَتَّخِذُوهُ سَبِيلًا

they will take it as [their] way.

ذَٰلِكَ بِأَنَّهُمْ كَذَّبُوا بِـَٔايَتِنَا

That is because they deny Our signs

وَكَانُوا عَنْهَا غَفِلِينَ ۝

and are oblivious to them.'

وَٱلَّذِينَ كَذَّبُوا بِـَٔايَتِنَا

147 Those who deny Our signs

وَلِقَآءِ ٱلْأَخِرَةِ

and the encounter of the Hereafter,

حَبِطَتْ أَعْمَلُهُمْ

their works have failed.

هَلْ يُجْزَوْنَ إِلَّا مَا كَانُوا يَعْمَلُونَ ۝

Shall they be requited except for what they used to do?

وَٱتَّخَذَ قَوْمُ مُوسَىٰ مِنۢ بَعْدِهِۦ

148 The people of Moses took up in his absence

مِنْ حُلِيِّهِمْ عِجْلًا

a calf [cast] from their ornaments

جَسَدًا لَّهُۥ خُوَارٌ

—a body with a low.

أَلَمْ يَرَوْا أَنَّهُۥ لَا يُكَلِّمُهُمْ

Did they not regard that it did not speak to them,

وَلَا يَهْدِيهِمْ سَبِيلًا

nor did it guide them to any way?

ٱتَّخَذُوهُ

They took it up [for worship]

وَكَانُوا ظَلِمِينَ ۝

and they were wrongdoers.

وَلَمَّا سُقِطَ فِىٓ أَيْدِيهِمْ

149 But when they became remorseful

وَرَأَوْا أَنَّهُمْ قَدْ ضَلُّوا

and realised they had gone astray,

قَالُوا لَئِن لَّمْ يَرْحَمْنَا رَبُّنَا

they said, 'Should our Lord have no mercy on us,

وَيَغْفِرْ لَنَا

and forgive us,

لَنَكُونَنَّ مِنَ ٱلْخَسِرِينَ ۝

we will be surely among the losers.'

وَلَمَّا رَجَعَ مُوسَىٰٓ إِلَىٰ قَوْمِهِۦ

150 And when Moses returned to his people,

غَضْبَٰنَ أَسِفًا

angry and indignant,

قَالَ بِئْسَمَا خَلَفْتُمُونِى مِنۢ بَعْدِىٓ

he said, 'Evil has been your conduct in my absence!

أَعَجِلْتُمْ أَمْرَ رَبِّكُمْ

Would you hasten on the edict of your Lord?'

وَأَلْقَى ٱلْأَلْوَاحَ

He threw down the tablets

وَأَخَذَ بِرَأْسِ أَخِيهِ

and seized his brother by the head,

يَجُرُّهُۥٓ إِلَيْهِ

pulling him towards himself.

قَالَ ٱبْنَ أُمَّ

He said, 'Son of my mother,

إِنَّ ٱلْقَوْمَ ٱسْتَضْعَفُونِى

indeed this people thought me to be weak,

وَكَادُوا۟ يَقْتُلُونَنِى

and they were about to kill me.

فَلَا تُشْمِتْ بِىَ ٱلْأَعْدَآءَ

So do not let the enemies gloat over me,

وَلَا تَجْعَلْنِى مَعَ ٱلْقَوْمِ ٱلظَّٰلِمِينَ ۝

and do not take me with the wrongdoing lot.'

قَالَ رَبِّ ٱغْفِرْ لِى وَلِأَخِى

151 He said, 'My Lord, forgive me and my brother,

وَأَدْخِلْنَا فِى رَحْمَتِكَ

and admit us into Your mercy,

وَأَنتَ أَرْحَمُ ٱلرَّٰحِمِينَ ۝

for You are the most merciful of the merciful.

إِنَّ ٱلَّذِينَ ٱتَّخَذُوا۟ ٱلْعِجْلَ

152 Indeed those who took up the calf [for worship]

سَيَنَالُهُمْ غَضَبٌ مِّن رَّبِّهِمْ

shall be overtaken by their Lord's wrath

وَذِلَّةٌ فِى ٱلْحَيَوٰةِ ٱلدُّنْيَا

and abasement in the life of the world.'

وَكَذَٰلِكَ نَجْزِى ٱلْمُفْتَرِينَ ۝

Thus do We requite the fabricators [of lies].

وَٱلَّذِينَ عَمِلُوا۟ ٱلسَّيِّئَاتِ

153 Yet [to] those who commit misdeeds

ثُمَّ تَابُوا۟ مِنۢ بَعْدِهَا وَءَامَنُوٓا۟

but repent after that, and believe,

إِنَّ رَبَّكَ مِنۢ بَعْدِهَا

—indeed, after that, your Lord

لَغَفُورٌ رَّحِيمٌ ۝

shall surely be all-forgiving, all-merciful.

وَلَمَّا سَكَتَ عَن مُّوسَى ٱلْغَضَبُ

154 And when Moses' indignation abated,

أَخَذَ ٱلْأَلْوَاحَ

he picked up the tablets

وَفِى نُسْخَتِهَا هُدًى وَرَحْمَةٌ

whose inscriptions contained guidance and mercy

لِّلَّذِينَ هُمْ لِرَبِّهِمْ يَرْهَبُونَ ۝

for those who are in awe of their Lord.

وَٱخْتَارَ مُوسَىٰ قَوْمَهُۥ سَبْعِينَ رَجُلًا

155 Moses chose seventy men from his people

لِّمِيقَٰتِنَا

for Our tryst,

فَلَمَّآ أَخَذَتْهُمُ ٱلرَّجْفَةُ

and when the earthquake seized them,

قَالَ رَبِّ لَوْ شِئْتَ

he said, 'My Lord, had You wished,

أَهْلَكْتَهُم مِّن قَبْلُ وَإِيَّىٰىَ

You would have destroyed them and me before.

أَتُهْلِكُنَا

Will You destroy us

بِمَا فَعَلَ ٱلسُّفَهَآءُ مِنَّآ

because of what the fools amongst us have done?

إِنْ هِىَ إِلَّا فِتْنَتُكَ

It is only Your test

تُضِلُّ بِهَا مَن تَشَآءُ

by which You lead astray whomever You wish

وَتَهْدِى مَن تَشَآءُ

and guide whomever You wish.

أَنتَ وَلِيُّنَا

You are our master,

فَٱغْفِرْ لَنَا وَٱرْحَمْنَا

so forgive us and have mercy on us,

وَأَنتَ خَيْرُ ٱلْغَفِرِينَ ۝

for You are the best of those who forgive.

156   وَٱكْتُبْ لَنَا فِى هَٰذِهِ ٱلدُّنْيَا حَسَنَةً

156   And appoint goodness for us in this world

وَفِى ٱلْآخِرَةِ

and the Hereafter,

إِنَّا هُدْنَآ إِلَيْكَ

for indeed we have come back to You.'

قَالَ عَذَابِىٓ أُصِيبُ بِهِۦ مَنْ أَشَآءُ

Said He, 'I visit My punishment on whomever I wish,

وَرَحْمَتِى وَسِعَتْ كُلَّ شَىْءٍ

but My mercy embraces all things.[1]

فَسَأَكْتُبُهَا لِلَّذِينَ يَتَّقُونَ

Soon I shall appoint it for those who are Godwary

وَيُؤْتُونَ ٱلزَّكَوٰةَ

and give the *zakāt*

وَٱلَّذِينَ هُم بِـَٔايَٰتِنَا يُؤْمِنُونَ ۝

and those who believe in Our signs

157   ٱلَّذِينَ يَتَّبِعُونَ ٱلرَّسُولَ

157   —those who follow the Apostle,

ٱلنَّبِىَّ ٱلْأُمِّىَّ

the uninstructed prophet,

ٱلَّذِى يَجِدُونَهُۥ مَكْتُوبًا عِندَهُمْ

whose mention they find written with them

فِى ٱلتَّوْرَىٰةِ وَٱلْإِنجِيلِ

in the Torah and the Evangel,

يَأْمُرُهُم بِٱلْمَعْرُوفِ

who bids them to do what is right

وَيَنْهَىٰهُمْ عَنِ ٱلْمُنكَرِ

and forbids them from what is wrong,

وَيُحِلُّ لَهُمُ ٱلطَّيِّبَٰتِ

makes lawful to them all the good things

وَيُحَرِّمُ عَلَيْهِمُ ٱلْخَبَٰئِثَ

and forbids them from all vicious things,

وَيَضَعُ عَنْهُمْ إِصْرَهُمْ

and relieves them of their burdens

وَٱلْأَغْلَٰلَ ٱلَّتِى كَانَتْ عَلَيْهِمْ

and the shackles that were upon them

فَٱلَّذِينَ ءَامَنُواْ بِهِۦ

—those who believe in him,

وَعَزَّرُوهُ وَنَصَرُوهُ

honour him, and help him

---

[1] Cf. 6:12.

and follow the light

that has been sent down with him,[1]

they are the felicitous.'

وَٱتَّبَعُوا ٱلنُّورَ
ٱلَّذِىٓ أُنزِلَ مَعَهُۥٓ
أُوْلَٰٓئِكَ هُمُ ٱلْمُفْلِحُونَ ۝

158 *Say,* 'O mankind!

I am the Apostle of Allah to you all, [of Him]

to whom belongs the kingdom of the heavens

and the earth.

There is no god except Him.

He gives life and brings death.'

So have faith in Allah and His Apostle,

the uninstructed prophet,

who has faith in Allah and His words,

and follow him so that you may be guided.

قُلْ يَٰٓأَيُّهَا ٱلنَّاسُ
إِنِّى رَسُولُ ٱللَّهِ إِلَيْكُمْ جَمِيعًا
ٱلَّذِى لَهُۥ مُلْكُ ٱلسَّمَٰوَٰتِ
وَٱلْأَرْضِ
لَآ إِلَٰهَ إِلَّا هُوَ
يُحْىِۦ وَيُمِيتُ
فَـَٔامِنُوا بِٱللَّهِ وَرَسُولِهِ
ٱلنَّبِىِّ ٱلْأُمِّىِّ
ٱلَّذِى يُؤْمِنُ بِٱللَّهِ وَكَلِمَٰتِهِۦ
وَٱتَّبِعُوهُ لَعَلَّكُمْ تَهْتَدُونَ ۝

159 Among the people of Moses is a group

who guide [the people] by the truth

and do justice thereby.

وَمِن قَوْمِ مُوسَىٰٓ أُمَّةٌ
يَهْدُونَ بِٱلْحَقِّ
وَبِهِۦ يَعْدِلُونَ ۝

160 We split them up into twelve tribal communities,

and We revealed to Moses,

when his people asked him for water,

[saying], 'Strike the rock with your staff,'

whereat twelve fountains gushed forth from it.

Every tribe came to know its drinking-place.

And We shaded them with clouds,

and We sent down to them manna and quails:

'Eat of the good things We have provided you.'

And they did not wrong Us,

but they used to wrong [only] themselves.

وَقَطَّعْنَٰهُمُ ٱثْنَتَىْ عَشْرَةَ أَسْبَاطًا أُمَمًا
وَأَوْحَيْنَآ إِلَىٰ مُوسَىٰٓ
إِذِ ٱسْتَسْقَىٰهُ قَوْمُهُۥٓ
أَنِ ٱضْرِب بِّعَصَاكَ ٱلْحَجَرَ
فَٱنۢبَجَسَتْ مِنْهُ ٱثْنَتَا عَشْرَةَ عَيْنًا
قَدْ عَلِمَ كُلُّ أُنَاسٍ مَّشْرَبَهُمْ
وَظَلَّلْنَا عَلَيْهِمُ ٱلْغَمَٰمَ
وَأَنزَلْنَا عَلَيْهِمُ ٱلْمَنَّ وَٱلسَّلْوَىٰ
كُلُوا مِن طَيِّبَٰتِ مَا رَزَقْنَٰكُمْ
وَمَا ظَلَمُونَا
وَلَٰكِن كَانُوٓا أَنفُسَهُمْ يَظْلِمُونَ ۝

161 And when they were told,

'Settle in this town

وَإِذْ قِيلَ لَهُمُ
ٱسْكُنُوا هَٰذِهِ ٱلْقَرْيَةَ

---
[1] Cf. 4:174.

وَكُلُوا۟ مِنْهَا حَيْثُ شِئْتُمْ

and eat thereof whence you wish;

وَقُولُوا۟ حِطَّةٌ

and say, "Relieve [us of the burden of our sins],"

وَٱدْخُلُوا۟ ٱلْبَابَ سُجَّدًا

and enter prostrating at the gate,

نَّغْفِرْ لَكُمْ خَطِيٓـَٰتِكُمْ

that We may forgive your iniquities,

سَنَزِيدُ ٱلْمُحْسِنِينَ ۝

and soon We shall enhance the virtuous.'[1]

فَبَدَّلَ ٱلَّذِينَ ظَلَمُوا۟ مِنْهُمْ قَوْلًا

162 But the wrongdoers changed the saying

غَيْرَ ٱلَّذِى قِيلَ لَهُمْ

with other than what they had been told.

فَأَرْسَلْنَا عَلَيْهِمْ رِجْزًا مِّنَ ٱلسَّمَآءِ

So We sent against them a plague from the sky

بِمَا كَانُوا۟ يَظْلِمُونَ ۝

because of the transgressions they used to commit.

وَسْـَٔلْهُمْ

163 Ask them[2]

عَنِ ٱلْقَرْيَةِ ٱلَّتِى كَانَتْ حَاضِرَةَ ٱلْبَحْرِ

about the town that was situated on the seaside,

إِذْ يَعْدُونَ فِى ٱلسَّبْتِ

when they violated the Sabbath,

إِذْ تَأْتِيهِمْ حِيتَانُهُمْ

when their fish would come to them

يَوْمَ سَبْتِهِمْ

on the Sabbath day,

شُرَّعًا

visibly on the shore,

وَيَوْمَ لَا يَسْبِتُونَ

but on days when they were not keeping Sabbath

لَا تَأْتِيهِمْ

they would not come to them.

كَذَٰلِكَ نَبْلُوهُم

Thus did We test them

بِمَا كَانُوا۟ يَفْسُقُونَ ۝

because of the transgressions they used to commit.

وَإِذْ قَالَتْ أُمَّةٌ مِّنْهُمْ

164 When a group of them said,

لِمَ تَعِظُونَ قَوْمًا ٱللَّهُ مُهْلِكُهُمْ

'Why do you advise a people whom Allah will destroy

أَوْ مُعَذِّبُهُمْ عَذَابًا شَدِيدًا

or punish with a severe punishment?'

قَالُوا۟ مَعْذِرَةً إِلَىٰ رَبِّكُمْ

They said, 'As an excuse before your Lord,

وَلَعَلَّهُمْ يَتَّقُونَ ۝

and [with the hope] that they may be Godwary.'

فَلَمَّا نَسُوا۟ مَا ذُكِّرُوا۟ بِهِۦٓ

165 So when they forgot what they had been reminded of

أَنجَيْنَا ٱلَّذِينَ يَنْهَوْنَ عَنِ ٱلسُّوٓءِ

We delivered those who forbade evil [conduct]

وَأَخَذْنَا ٱلَّذِينَ ظَلَمُوا۟ بِعَذَابٍۭ بَئِيسٍۭ

and seized the wrongdoers with a terrible punishment

بِمَا كَانُوا۟ يَفْسُقُونَ ۝

because of the transgressions they used to commit.

---

[1] Cf. 2:58.

[2] That is, the Jews, to whom the following passages relate, up to verse 171.

فَلَمَّا عَتَوْاْ   166 When they defied [the command pertaining to]

عَن مَّا نُهُواْ عَنْهُ    what they were forbidden from,

قُلْنَا لَهُمْ كُونُواْ قِرَدَةً خَسِئِينَ ۝    We said to them, 'Be you spurned apes.'[1]

وَإِذْ تَأَذَّنَ رَبُّكَ   167 And when *your* Lord proclaimed

لَيَبْعَثَنَّ عَلَيْهِمْ    that He would surely send against them,[2]

إِلَىٰ يَوْمِ ٱلْقِيَٰمَةِ    until the Day of Resurrection,

مَن يَسُومُهُمْ سُوٓءَ ٱلْعَذَابِ    those who would inflict on them a terrible punishment.

إِنَّ رَبَّكَ لَسَرِيعُ ٱلْعِقَابِ    Indeed your Lord is swift in retribution,

وَإِنَّهُ لَغَفُورٌ رَّحِيمٌ ۝    and indeed He is all-forgiving, all-merciful.

وَقَطَّعْنَٰهُمْ فِى ٱلْأَرْضِ أُمَمًا   168 We dispersed them into communities around the earth:

مِّنْهُمُ ٱلصَّٰلِحُونَ    some of them were righteous,

وَمِنْهُمْ دُونَ ذَٰلِكَ    and some of them otherwise,

وَبَلَوْنَٰهُم بِٱلْحَسَنَٰتِ وَٱلسَّيِّئَاتِ    and We tested them with good and bad [times]

لَعَلَّهُمْ يَرْجِعُونَ ۝    so that they may come back.

فَخَلَفَ مِنۢ بَعْدِهِمْ خَلْفٌ   169 Then they were succeeded by an evil posterity

وَرِثُواْ ٱلْكِتَٰبَ    which inherited the Book:

يَأْخُذُونَ عَرَضَ هَٰذَا ٱلْأَدْنَىٰ    they grab the transitory gains of this lower world,[3]

وَيَقُولُونَ سَيُغْفَرُ لَنَا    and say, 'It will be forgiven us.'

وَإِن يَأْتِهِمْ عَرَضٌ مِّثْلُهُ    And if similar transitory gains were to come their way,

يَأْخُذُوهُ    they would grab them too.

أَلَمْ يُؤْخَذْ عَلَيْهِم مِّيثَٰقُ ٱلْكِتَٰبِ    Was not the covenant of the Book taken with them

أَن لَّا يَقُولُواْ عَلَى ٱللَّهِ    that they shall not attribute anything to Allah

إِلَّا ٱلْحَقَّ    except the truth?

وَدَرَسُواْ مَا فِيهِ    They have studied what is in it,

وَٱلدَّارُ ٱلْأَخِرَةُ خَيْرٌ    and [know that] the abode of the Hereafter is better

لِّلَّذِينَ يَتَّقُونَ ۝    for those who are Godwary.

أَفَلَا تَعْقِلُونَ ۝    Do you not apply reason?

---

[1] Cf. 2:65.

[2] That is, the Jews.

[3] That is, in return for sinful actions.

وَٱلَّذِينَ يُمَسِّكُونَ بِٱلۡكِتَٰبِ

170 As for those who hold fast to the Book

وَأَقَامُوا۟ ٱلصَّلَوٰةَ

and maintain the prayer

إِنَّا لَا نُضِيعُ

—indeed We do not waste

أَجۡرَ ٱلۡمُصۡلِحِينَ ۞

the reward of those who bring about reform.

وَإِذۡ نَتَقۡنَا ٱلۡجَبَلَ

171 When We plucked the mountain

فَوۡقَهُمۡ كَأَنَّهُۥ ظُلَّةٌ

[and held it] above them as if it were a canopy

وَظَنُّوٓا۟ أَنَّهُۥ وَاقِعٌۢ بِهِمۡ

(and they thought it was about to fall on them):

خُذُوا۟ مَآ ءَاتَيۡنَٰكُم بِقُوَّةٍ

'Hold on with power to what We have given you

وَٱذۡكُرُوا۟ مَا فِيهِ

and remember that which is in it,

لَعَلَّكُمۡ تَتَّقُونَ ۞

so that you may be Godwary.'

وَإِذۡ أَخَذَ رَبُّكَ مِنۢ بَنِىٓ ءَادَمَ

172 When your Lord took from the Children of Adam,

مِن ظُهُورِهِمۡ

from their loins, their descendants

ذُرِّيَّتَهُمۡ وَأَشۡهَدَهُمۡ عَلَىٰٓ أَنفُسِهِمۡ

and made them bear witness over themselves,

أَلَسۡتُ بِرَبِّكُمۡ

[He said to them,] 'Am I not your Lord?'

قَالُوا۟ بَلَىٰ شَهِدۡنَآ

They said, 'Yes indeed! We bear witness.'

أَن تَقُولُوا۟ يَوۡمَ ٱلۡقِيَٰمَةِ

[This,] lest you should say on the Day of Resurrection,

إِنَّا كُنَّا عَنۡ هَٰذَا غَٰفِلِينَ ۞

'Indeed we were unaware of this,'

أَوۡ تَقُولُوٓا۟

173 or lest you should say,

إِنَّمَآ أَشۡرَكَ ءَابَآؤُنَا مِن قَبۡلُ

'Our fathers ascribed partners [to Allah] before [us]

وَكُنَّا ذُرِّيَّةً مِّنۢ بَعۡدِهِمۡ

and we were descendants after them.

أَفَتُهۡلِكُنَا

Will You then destroy us

بِمَا فَعَلَ ٱلۡمُبۡطِلُونَ ۞

because of what the falsifiers have done?'

وَكَذَٰلِكَ نُفَصِّلُ ٱلۡءَايَٰتِ

174 Thus do We elaborate the signs,

وَلَعَلَّهُمۡ يَرۡجِعُونَ ۞

so that they may come back.

وَٱتۡلُ عَلَيۡهِمۡ نَبَأَ ٱلَّذِىٓ

175 *Relate* to them an account of him

ءَاتَيۡنَٰهُ ءَايَٰتِنَا فَٱنسَلَخَ مِنۡهَا

to whom We gave Our signs, but he cast them off.

فَأَتۡبَعَهُ ٱلشَّيۡطَٰنُ

Thereupon Satan pursued him,

فَكَانَ مِنَ ٱلۡغَاوِينَ ۞

and he became one of the perverse.

وَلَوۡ شِئۡنَا

176 Had We wished,

لَرَفَعۡنَٰهُ بِهَا

We would have surely raised him by their means,

وَلَٰكِنَّهُۥٓ أَخْلَدَ إِلَى ٱلْأَرْضِ

but he clung to the earth

وَٱتَّبَعَ هَوَىٰهُ

and followed his [base] desires.

فَمَثَلُهُۥ كَمَثَلِ ٱلْكَلْبِ

So his parable is that of a dog:

إِن تَحْمِلْ عَلَيْهِ يَلْهَثْ

if you make for it, it lolls out its tongue,

أَوْ تَتْرُكْهُ يَلْهَثْ

and if you let it alone, it lolls out its tongue.

ذَّٰلِكَ مَثَلُ ٱلْقَوْمِ ٱلَّذِينَ

Such is the parable of the people who

كَذَّبُوا۟ بِـَٔايَٰتِنَا

deny Our signs.

فَٱقْصُصِ ٱلْقَصَصَ

So recount these narratives,

لَعَلَّهُمْ يَتَفَكَّرُونَ ۝

so that they may reflect.

سَآءَ مَثَلًا ٱلْقَوْمُ ٱلَّذِينَ كَذَّبُوا۟ بِـَٔايَٰتِنَا

177 Evil is the parable of the people who deny Our signs

وَأَنفُسَهُمْ كَانُوا۟ يَظْلِمُونَ ۝

and wrong themselves.

مَن يَهْدِ ٱللَّهُ فَهُوَ ٱلْمُهْتَدِى

178 Whomever Allah guides is rightly guided,

وَمَن يُضْلِلْ

and whomever He leads astray

فَأُو۟لَٰٓئِكَ هُمُ ٱلْخَٰسِرُونَ ۝

—it is they who are the losers.

وَلَقَدْ ذَرَأْنَا لِجَهَنَّمَ

179 Certainly We have created for hell

كَثِيرًا مِّنَ ٱلْجِنِّ وَٱلْإِنسِ

many of the jinn and humans:

لَهُمْ قُلُوبٌ لَّا يَفْقَهُونَ بِهَا

they have hearts with which they do not understand,

وَلَهُمْ أَعْيُنٌ لَّا يُبْصِرُونَ بِهَا

they have eyes with which they do not see,

وَلَهُمْ ءَاذَانٌ لَّا يَسْمَعُونَ بِهَآ

they have ears with which they do not hear.

أُو۟لَٰٓئِكَ كَٱلْأَنْعَٰمِ

They are like cattle;

بَلْ هُمْ أَضَلُّ

rather they are more astray.

أُو۟لَٰٓئِكَ هُمُ ٱلْغَٰفِلُونَ ۝

It is they who are the heedless.[1]

وَلِلَّهِ ٱلْأَسْمَآءُ ٱلْحُسْنَىٰ

180 To Allah belong the Best Names,

فَٱدْعُوهُ بِهَا

so supplicate Him by them,

وَذَرُوا۟ ٱلَّذِينَ يُلْحِدُونَ

and abandon those who commit sacrilege

فِىٓ أَسْمَٰٓئِهِۦ

in His names.

سَيُجْزَوْنَ مَا كَانُوا۟ يَعْمَلُونَ ۝

Soon they shall be requited for what they used to do.

وَمِمَّنْ خَلَقْنَآ أُمَّةٌ

181 Among those We have created are a nation

يَهْدُونَ بِٱلْحَقِّ

who guide by the truth

---

[1] Cf. 8:21-24, 55, 25:44.

235

وَبِهِۦ يَعْدِلُونَ ۞    and act justly thereby.

وَالَّذِينَ كَذَّبُواْ بِـَٔايَٰتِنَا    182 As for those who deny Our signs,

سَنَسْتَدْرِجُهُم    We will draw them imperceptibly [into ruin],

مِّنْ حَيْثُ لَا يَعْلَمُونَ ۞    whence they do not know.

وَأُمْلِى لَهُمْ    183 And I will grant them respite,

إِنَّ كَيْدِى مَتِينٌ ۞    for My devising is indeed sure.

أَوَلَمْ يَتَفَكَّرُواْ    184 Have they not reflected

مَا بِصَاحِبِهِم مِّن جِنَّةٍ    that there is no madness in their companion,[1]

إِنْ هُوَ إِلَّا نَذِيرٌ مُّبِينٌ ۞    [and that] he is just a manifest warner?

أَوَلَمْ يَنظُرُواْ فِى    185 Have they not contemplated

مَلَكُوتِ ٱلسَّمَٰوَٰتِ وَٱلْأَرْضِ    the dominions of the heavens and the earth,

وَمَا خَلَقَ ٱللَّهُ مِن شَىْءٍ    and whatever things Allah has created,

وَأَنْ عَسَىٰٓ أَن يَكُونَ قَدِ ٱقْتَرَبَ أَجَلُهُمْ    and that maybe their time[2] has already drawn near?

فَبِأَىِّ حَدِيثٍ بَعْدَهُۥ يُؤْمِنُونَ ۞    So what discourse will they believe after this?![3]

مَن يُضْلِلِ ٱللَّهُ    186 Whomever Allah leads astray

فَلَا هَادِىَ لَهُۥ    has no guide,

وَيَذَرُهُمْ فِى طُغْيَٰنِهِمْ يَعْمَهُونَ ۞    and He leaves them bewildered in their rebellion.

يَسْـَٔلُونَكَ عَنِ ٱلسَّاعَةِ    187 They question *you* concerning the Hour,

أَيَّانَ مُرْسَىٰهَا    when it will set in.

قُلْ إِنَّمَا عِلْمُهَا عِندَ رَبِّى    *Say,* 'Its knowledge is only with my Lord:

لَا يُجَلِّيهَا لِوَقْتِهَآ إِلَّا هُوَ    none except Him shall manifest it at its time.

ثَقُلَتْ فِى ٱلسَّمَٰوَٰتِ وَٱلْأَرْضِ    It will weigh heavy on the heavens and the earth.

لَا تَأْتِيكُمْ إِلَّا بَغْتَةً    It will not overtake you but suddenly.'

يَسْـَٔلُونَكَ كَأَنَّكَ حَفِىٌّ عَنْهَا    They ask *you* as if *you* were in the know of it.

قُلْ إِنَّمَا عِلْمُهَا عِندَ ٱللَّهِ    *Say,* 'Its knowledge is only with Allah,

وَلَٰكِنَّ أَكْثَرَ ٱلنَّاسِ لَا يَعْلَمُونَ ۞    but most people do not know.'

قُل لَّآ أَمْلِكُ لِنَفْسِى نَفْعًا    188 *Say,* 'I have no control over any benefit for myself

---

[1] That is, the Prophet.

[2] That is, death.

[3] That is, the Qurʾān.

وَلَا ضَرًّا — nor [over] any harm

إِلَّا مَا شَاءَ ٱللَّهُ — except what Allah may wish.

وَلَوْ كُنتُ أَعْلَمُ ٱلْغَيْبَ — Had I known the Unseen,

لَٱسْتَكْثَرْتُ مِنَ ٱلْخَيْرِ — I would have acquired much good,

وَمَا مَسَّنِيَ ٱلسُّوٓءُ — and no ill would have befallen me.

إِنْ أَنَا۠ إِلَّا نَذِيرٌ وَبَشِيرٌ — I am only a warner and a bearer of good news

لِّقَوْمٍ يُؤْمِنُونَ — to a people who have faith.'

هُوَ ٱلَّذِى خَلَقَكُم مِّن نَّفْسٍ وَٰحِدَةٍ — 189 It is He who created you from a single soul,

وَجَعَلَ مِنْهَا زَوْجَهَا — and made from it its mate,

لِيَسْكُنَ إِلَيْهَا — that he might find comfort with her.

فَلَمَّا تَغَشَّىٰهَا — So when he had covered[1] her,

حَمَلَتْ حَمْلًا خَفِيفًا — she bore a light burden

فَمَرَّتْ بِهِۦ — and passed [some time] with it.

فَلَمَّآ أَثْقَلَت — When she had grown heavy,

دَّعَوَا ٱللَّهَ رَبَّهُمَا — they both invoked Allah, their Lord:

لَئِنْ ءَاتَيْتَنَا صَٰلِحًا — 'If You give us a healthy [child],

لَّنَكُونَنَّ مِنَ ٱلشَّٰكِرِينَ — we will be surely grateful.'

فَلَمَّآ ءَاتَىٰهُمَا صَٰلِحًا — 190 Then when He gave them a healthy [child],

جَعَلَا لَهُۥ شُرَكَآءَ — they ascribed partners to Him

فِيمَآ ءَاتَىٰهُمَا — in what He had given them.

فَتَعَٰلَى ٱللَّهُ — Exalted is Allah

عَمَّا يُشْرِكُونَ — above [having] any partners that they ascribe [to Him].

أَيُشْرِكُونَ مَا لَا يَخْلُقُ شَيْئًا — 191 Do they ascribe [to Him] partners that create nothing

وَهُمْ يُخْلَقُونَ — and have been created themselves,

وَلَا يَسْتَطِيعُونَ لَهُمْ نَصْرًا — 192 and can neither help them,

وَلَآ أَنفُسَهُمْ يَنصُرُونَ — nor help themselves?

وَإِن تَدْعُوهُمْ إِلَى ٱلْهُدَىٰ — 193 And if you call them to guidance,

لَا يَتَّبِعُوكُمْ — they will not follow you:

---

[1] Cover: to copulate with.

237

سَوَآءٌ عَلَيْكُمْ أَدَعَوْتُمُوهُمْ
it is the same to you whether you call them

أَمْ أَنتُمْ صَامِتُونَ ۝
or whether you are silent.

إِنَّ ٱلَّذِينَ تَدْعُونَ مِن دُونِ ٱللَّهِ
194 Indeed those whom you invoke besides Allah

عِبَادٌ أَمْثَالُكُمْ
are creatures like you.

فَٱدْعُوهُمْ
So invoke them:

فَلْيَسْتَجِيبُوا۟ لَكُمْ
they should answer you,

إِن كُنتُمْ صَادِقِينَ ۝
if you are truthful.

أَلَهُمْ أَرْجُلٌ يَمْشُونَ بِهَآ
195 Do they have any feet to walk with?

أَمْ لَهُمْ أَيْدٍ يَبْطِشُونَ بِهَآ
Do they have any hands to grasp with?

أَمْ لَهُمْ أَعْيُنٌ يُبْصِرُونَ بِهَآ
Do they have any eyes to see with?

أَمْ لَهُمْ ءَاذَانٌ يَسْمَعُونَ بِهَآ
Do they have any ears to hear with?

قُلِ ٱدْعُوا۟ شُرَكَآءَكُمْ
*Say*, 'Invoke your partners [that you ascribe to Allah]

ثُمَّ كِيدُونِ
and try out your stratagems[1] against me

فَلَا تُنظِرُونِ ۝
without granting me any respite.

إِنَّ وَلِيِّـۧ ٱللَّهُ
196 My guardian is indeed Allah

ٱلَّذِى نَزَّلَ ٱلْكِتَٰبَ
who sent down the Book,

وَهُوَ يَتَوَلَّى ٱلصَّٰلِحِينَ ۝
and He takes care of the righteous.

وَٱلَّذِينَ تَدْعُونَ مِن دُونِهِ
197 Those whom you invoke besides Him

لَا يَسْتَطِيعُونَ نَصْرَكُمْ
can neither help you,

وَلَآ أَنفُسَهُمْ يَنصُرُونَ ۝
nor help themselves.'

وَإِن تَدْعُوهُمْ إِلَى ٱلْهُدَىٰ لَا يَسْمَعُوا۟
198 If *you* call them to guidance, they will not hear.

وَتَرَىٰهُمْ يَنظُرُونَ إِلَيْكَ
*You* see them observing *you*,

وَهُمْ لَا يُبْصِرُونَ ۝
but they do not perceive.

خُذِ ٱلْعَفْوَ
199 *Adopt* [a policy of] excusing [the faults of people],

وَأْمُرْ بِٱلْعُرْفِ
*bid* what is right,

وَأَعْرِضْ عَنِ ٱلْجَٰهِلِينَ ۝
and *turn away* from the ignorant.

وَإِمَّا يَنزَغَنَّكَ مِنَ ٱلشَّيْطَٰنِ نَزْغٌ
200 Should a temptation from Satan disturb *you*,

فَٱسْتَعِذْ بِٱللَّهِ
invoke the protection of Allah;

إِنَّهُ سَمِيعٌ عَلِيمٌ ۝
indeed He is all-hearing, all-knowing.

---

[1] Or 'try out your guile against me.' Cf. 11:55.

إِنَّ ٱلَّذِينَ ٱتَّقَوۡاْ إِذَا مَسَّهُمۡ 201 **When those who are Godwary are touched**

طَـٰٓئِفٌ مِّنَ ٱلشَّيۡطَـٰنِ 　　　**by a visitation[1] of Satan,**

تَذَكَّرُواْ 　　　　　**they remember [Allah]**

فَإِذَا هُم مُّبۡصِرُونَ ٢٠١ 　**and, behold, they perceive.**

وَإِخۡوَٰنُهُمۡ 202 **But their brethren,[2]**

يَمُدُّونَهُمۡ فِى ٱلۡغَىِّ 　　**they draw them into error,**

ثُمَّ لَا يُقۡصِرُونَ ٢٠٢ 　**and then they do not spare [any harm].**

وَإِذَا لَمۡ تَأۡتِهِم بِـَٔايَةٍ 203 **When *you* do not bring them a sign,**

قَالُواْ لَوۡلَا ٱجۡتَبَيۡتَهَا 　　**they say, 'Why do you not improvise one?'**

قُلۡ إِنَّمَآ أَتَّبِعُ مَا يُوحَىٰٓ إِلَىَّ 　**Say, 'I only follow what is revealed to me**

مِن رَّبِّى 　　　　　**from my Lord;**

هَـٰذَا بَصَآئِرُ مِن رَّبِّكُمۡ 　**these are insights from your Lord,**

وَهُدًى وَرَحۡمَةٌ 　　　**and a guidance and mercy**

لِّقَوۡمٍ يُؤۡمِنُونَ ٢٠٣ 　**for a people who have faith.'**

وَإِذَا قُرِئَ ٱلۡقُرۡءَانُ 204 **When the Qur'ān is recited,**

فَٱسۡتَمِعُواْ لَهُۥ وَأَنصِتُواْ 　**listen to it and be silent,**

لَعَلَّكُمۡ تُرۡحَمُونَ ٢٠٤ 　**maybe you will receive [Allah's] mercy.**

وَٱذۡكُر رَّبَّكَ فِى نَفۡسِكَ 205 **And remember *your* Lord within your heart**

تَضَرُّعًا وَخِيفَةً 　　　**beseechingly and reverentially,**

وَدُونَ ٱلۡجَهۡرِ مِنَ ٱلۡقَوۡلِ 　　**without being loud,**

بِٱلۡغُدُوِّ وَٱلۡءَاصَالِ 　　**morning and evening,**

وَلَا تَكُن مِّنَ ٱلۡغَـٰفِلِينَ ٢٠٥ **and *do not be* among the heedless.**

إِنَّ ٱلَّذِينَ عِندَ رَبِّكَ 206 **Indeed those who are [stationed] near *your* Lord**

لَا يَسۡتَكۡبِرُونَ عَنۡ عِبَادَتِهِۦ 　**do not disdain to worship Him.**

وَيُسَبِّحُونَهُۥ 　　　**They glorify Him**

وَلَهُۥ يَسۡجُدُونَ ۩ ٢٠٦ 　**and prostrate to Him.**

---

[1] Or 'insinuation.'

[2] That is, the polytheists, who are referred to as brethren of Satans.

# سُورَةُ الأنفَالِ     8. SŪRAT AL-ANFĀL[1]

بِسْمِ اللَّهِ

In the Name of Allah,

الرَّحْمَٰنِ الرَّحِيمِ

the All-beneficent, the All-merciful.

يَسْـَٔلُونَكَ عَنِ ٱلْأَنفَالِ

1 They ask *you* concerning the *anfāl*.[2]

قُلِ ٱلْأَنفَالُ لِلَّهِ وَٱلرَّسُولِ

Say, 'The *anfāl* belong to Allah and the Apostle.'

فَٱتَّقُوا۟ ٱللَّهَ وَأَصْلِحُوا۟ ذَاتَ بَيْنِكُمْ

So be wary of Allah and settle your differences,

وَأَطِيعُوا۟ ٱللَّهَ وَرَسُولَهُ

and obey Allah and His Apostle,

إِن كُنتُم مُّؤْمِنِينَ ۝

should you be faithful.

إِنَّمَا ٱلْمُؤْمِنُونَ ٱلَّذِينَ

2 The faithful are only those

إِذَا ذُكِرَ ٱللَّهُ وَجِلَتْ قُلُوبُهُمْ

whose hearts tremble [with awe] when Allah is mentioned,

وَإِذَا تُلِيَتْ عَلَيْهِمْ ءَايَٰتُهُ

and when His signs are recited to them,

زَادَتْهُمْ إِيمَٰنًا

they[3] increase their faith,

وَعَلَىٰ رَبِّهِمْ يَتَوَكَّلُونَ ۝

and who put their trust in their Lord,

ٱلَّذِينَ يُقِيمُونَ ٱلصَّلَوٰةَ

3 maintain the prayer

وَمِمَّا رَزَقْنَٰهُمْ يُنفِقُونَ ۝

and spend out of what We have provided them.

أُو۟لَٰٓئِكَ هُمُ ٱلْمُؤْمِنُونَ حَقًّا

4 It is they who are truly the faithful.

لَّهُمْ دَرَجَٰتٌ عِندَ رَبِّهِمْ

They shall have ranks near their Lord,

وَمَغْفِرَةٌ وَرِزْقٌ كَرِيمٌ ۝

forgiveness and a noble provision.

كَمَآ أَخْرَجَكَ رَبُّكَ مِنۢ بَيْتِكَ

5 As *your* Lord brought *you* out from *your* home

بِٱلْحَقِّ

with truth,

وَإِنَّ فَرِيقًا مِّنَ ٱلْمُؤْمِنِينَ

a part of the faithful were indeed

لَكَٰرِهُونَ ۝

reluctant.

يُجَٰدِلُونَكَ فِى ٱلْحَقِّ

6 They disputed with *you* concerning the truth

---

[1] The *sūrah* takes its name from the term *al-anfāl* mentioned in verse 1.

[2] Or, 'They ask *you* for the *anfāl*,' according to an alternate reading (*yas'alūnaka al-anfāl*).

[3] That is, the signs of Allah, when they are recited to the faithful.

بَعْدَ مَا تَبَيَّنَ

after it had become clear,

كَأَنَّمَا يُسَاقُونَ إِلَى ٱلْمَوْتِ

as if they were being driven towards death

وَهُمْ يَنظُرُونَ ۝

as they looked on.

وَإِذْ يَعِدُكُمُ ٱللَّهُ

7 When Allah promised you [victory over]

إِحْدَى ٱلطَّآئِفَتَيْنِ أَنَّهَا لَكُمْ

one of the two companies, [saying], 'It is for you,'

وَتَوَدُّونَ

you were eager

أَنَّ غَيْرَ ذَاتِ ٱلشَّوْكَةِ تَكُونُ لَكُمْ

that it should be the one that was unarmed.[1]

وَيُرِيدُ ٱللَّهُ أَن يُحِقَّ ٱلْحَقَّ

But Allah desires to confirm the truth

بِكَلِمَـٰتِهِۦ

with His words,

وَيَقْطَعَ دَابِرَ ٱلْكَـٰفِرِينَ ۝

and to root out the faithless,

لِيُحِقَّ ٱلْحَقَّ

8 so that He may confirm the truth

وَيُبْطِلَ ٱلْبَـٰطِلَ

and bring falsehood to naught,

وَلَوْ كَرِهَ ٱلْمُجْرِمُونَ ۝

though the guilty should be averse.

إِذْ تَسْتَغِيثُونَ رَبَّكُمْ

9 When you appealed to your Lord for help,

فَٱسْتَجَابَ لَكُمْ أَنِّي مُمِدُّكُم

He answered you: 'I will aid you

بِأَلْفٍ مِّنَ ٱلْمَلَـٰٓئِكَةِ مُرْدِفِينَ ۝

with a thousand angels in a file.'

وَمَا جَعَلَهُ ٱللَّهُ إِلَّا بُشْرَىٰ

10 Allah did not appoint it but as a good news,

وَلِتَطْمَئِنَّ بِهِۦ قُلُوبُكُمْ

and to reassure your hearts.

وَمَا ٱلنَّصْرُ إِلَّا مِنْ عِندِ ٱللَّهِ

Victory[2] comes only from Allah.

إِنَّ ٱللَّهَ عَزِيزٌ حَكِيمٌ ۝

Indeed Allah is all-mighty, all-wise.

إِذْ يُغَشِّيكُمُ ٱلنُّعَاسَ

11 When He covered you with a trance

أَمَنَةً مِّنْهُ

as a [sense of] security from Him,

وَيُنَزِّلُ عَلَيْكُم مِّنَ ٱلسَّمَآءِ مَآءً

and He sent down water from the sky

لِّيُطَهِّرَكُم بِهِۦ

to purify you with it,

وَيُذْهِبَ عَنكُمْ رِجْزَ ٱلشَّيْطَـٰنِ

and to repel from you the defilement of Satan,

وَلِيَرْبِطَ عَلَىٰ قُلُوبِكُمْ

and to fortify your hearts,

وَيُثَبِّتَ بِهِ ٱلْأَقْدَامَ ۝

and to make [your] feet steady with it.

---

[1] Literally, 'one that was free of thorns.' That is, one which was unarmed and, therefore, easy to encounter.

[2] Or 'help.'

إِذْ يُوحِى رَبُّكَ إِلَى ٱلْمَلَٰئِكَةِ 12 Then your Lord signaled to the angels:

أَنِّى مَعَكُمْ 'I am indeed with you;

فَثَبِّتُوا ٱلَّذِينَ ءَامَنُوا ۚ so steady the faithful.

سَأُلْقِى فِى قُلُوبِ ٱلَّذِينَ كَفَرُوا ٱلرُّعْبَ I will cast terror into the hearts of the faithless.

فَٱضْرِبُوا فَوْقَ ٱلْأَعْنَاقِ So strike their necks,

وَٱضْرِبُوا مِنْهُمْ كُلَّ بَنَانٍ ۝ and strike each of their fingertips!'

ذَٰلِكَ بِأَنَّهُمْ شَآقُّوا ٱللَّهَ وَرَسُولَهُۥ ۚ 13 That, because they defied Allah and His Apostle.

وَمَن يُشَاقِقِ ٱللَّهَ وَرَسُولَهُۥ And whoever defies Allah and His Apostle,

فَإِنَّ ٱللَّهَ شَدِيدُ ٱلْعِقَابِ ۝ Allah is indeed severe in retribution.

ذَٰلِكُمْ فَذُوقُوهُ وَأَنَّ 14 Taste this, and [know] that

لِلْكَٰفِرِينَ عَذَابَ ٱلنَّارِ ۝ for the faithless is the punishment of the Fire.

يَٰٓأَيُّهَا ٱلَّذِينَ ءَامَنُوٓا 15 O you who have faith!

إِذَا لَقِيتُمُ When you encounter

ٱلَّذِينَ كَفَرُوا زَحْفًا the faithless advancing [for battle],

فَلَا تُوَلُّوهُمُ ٱلْأَدْبَارَ ۝ do not turn your backs [to flee] from them.

وَمَن يُوَلِّهِمْ يَوْمَئِذٍ دُبُرَهُۥٓ 16 Whoever turns his back [to flee] from them that day

إِلَّا مُتَحَرِّفًا لِّقِتَالٍ —unless [he is] diverting to fight

أَوْ مُتَحَيِّزًا إِلَىٰ فِئَةٍ or retiring towards another troop—

فَقَدْ بَآءَ بِغَضَبٍ مِّنَ ٱللَّهِ shall certainly earn Allah's wrath,

وَمَأْوَىٰهُ جَهَنَّمُ ۖ وَبِئْسَ ٱلْمَصِيرُ ۝ and his refuge shall be hell, an evil destination.

فَلَمْ تَقْتُلُوهُمْ 17 You did not kill them;

وَلَٰكِنَّ ٱللَّهَ قَتَلَهُمْ ۚ rather it was Allah who killed them;

وَمَا رَمَيْتَ إِذْ رَمَيْتَ and *you* did not throw when *you* threw,[1]

وَلَٰكِنَّ ٱللَّهَ رَمَىٰ ۚ rather it was Allah who threw,

وَلِيُبْلِىَ ٱلْمُؤْمِنِينَ that He might test the faithful

مِنْهُ بَلَآءً حَسَنًا ۚ with a good test from Himself.[2]

---

[1] According to tradition, at the outset of the battle of Badr, the Prophet (ṣ) took a handful of dust, containing sand and pebbles, and threw it at the enemy troops. It struck in the face every warrior of the enemy, entering their eyes, noses and mouths, disconcerting them, resulting ultimately in their being routed by the small Muslim force.

[2] Or 'that He might grant the faithful a splendid award from Himself.'

إِنَّ ٱللَّهَ سَمِيعٌ عَلِيمٌ ۝    Indeed Allah is all-hearing, all-knowing.

ذَٰلِكُمْ وَأَنَّ    18 Such is the case, and [know] that

ٱللَّهَ مُوهِنُ كَيْدِ ٱلْكَٰفِرِينَ ۝    Allah undermines the stratagems of the faithless.

إِن تَسْتَفْتِحُوا    19 If you sought a verdict,

فَقَدْ جَآءَكُمُ ٱلْفَتْحُ    the verdict has certainly come to you;[1]

وَإِن تَنتَهُوا    and if you relinquish [faithlessness],

فَهُوَ خَيْرٌ لَّكُمْ    it is better for you,

وَإِن تَعُودُوا نَعُدْ    but if you revert, We [too] shall return

وَلَن تُغْنِىَ عَنكُمْ فِئَتُكُمْ شَيْـًٔا    and your troops will never avail you

وَلَوْ كَثُرَتْ    though they should be ever so many,

وَأَنَّ ٱللَّهَ مَعَ ٱلْمُؤْمِنِينَ ۝    and [know] that Allah is with the faithful.

يَٰٓأَيُّهَا ٱلَّذِينَ ءَامَنُوا    20 O you who have faith!

أَطِيعُوا ٱللَّهَ وَرَسُولَهُ    Obey Allah and His Apostle,

وَلَا تَوَلَّوْا عَنْهُ وَأَنتُمْ تَسْمَعُونَ ۝    and do not turn away from him while you hear [him].

وَلَا تَكُونُوا كَٱلَّذِينَ قَالُوا    21 Do not be like those who say,

سَمِعْنَا وَهُمْ لَا يَسْمَعُونَ ۝ ۞    'We hear,' though they do not hear.

إِنَّ شَرَّ ٱلدَّوَآبِّ عِندَ ٱللَّهِ    22 Indeed the worst of beasts in Allah's sight

ٱلصُّمُّ ٱلْبُكْمُ ٱلَّذِينَ لَا يَعْقِلُونَ ۝    are the deaf and the dumb who do not apply reason.

وَلَوْ عَلِمَ ٱللَّهُ فِيهِمْ خَيْرًا    23 Had Allah known any good in them,

لَّأَسْمَعَهُمْ    surely He would have made them hear,

وَلَوْ أَسْمَعَهُمْ    and were He to make them hear,

لَتَوَلَّوا وَّهُم مُّعْرِضُونَ ۝    surely they would turn away, being disregardful.

يَٰٓأَيُّهَا ٱلَّذِينَ ءَامَنُوا    24 O you who have faith!

ٱسْتَجِيبُوا لِلَّهِ وَلِلرَّسُولِ    Answer Allah and the Apostle

إِذَا دَعَاكُمْ لِمَا يُحْيِيكُمْ    when he summons you to that which will give you life.

وَٱعْلَمُوا أَنَّ ٱللَّهَ يَحُولُ    Know that Allah intervenes

بَيْنَ ٱلْمَرْءِ وَقَلْبِهِ    between a man and his heart

---

[1] Addressed to the faithless.

وَأَنَّهُمْ إِلَيْهِ تُحْشَرُونَ ۝ and that toward Him you will be mustered.

وَٱتَّقُواْ فِتْنَةً 25 And beware of a punishment

لَا تُصِيبَنَّ ٱلَّذِينَ ظَلَمُواْ مِنكُمْ which shall not visit the wrongdoers among you

خَاصَّةً exclusively,

وَٱعْلَمُوٓاْ أَنَّ ٱللَّهَ شَدِيدُ ٱلْعِقَابِ ۝ and know that Allah is severe in retribution.

وَٱذْكُرُوٓاْ إِذْ أَنتُمْ قَلِيلٌ 26 Remember when you were few,

مُّسْتَضْعَفُونَ فِى ٱلْأَرْضِ abased in the land,

تَخَافُونَ أَن يَتَخَطَّفَكُمُ ٱلنَّاسُ and feared lest the people should despoil you,

فَـَٔاوَىٰكُمْ and He gave you refuge,

وَأَيَّدَكُم بِنَصْرِهِۦ and strengthened you with His help,

وَرَزَقَكُم مِّنَ ٱلطَّيِّبَٰتِ and provided you with all the good things

لَعَلَّكُمْ تَشْكُرُونَ ۝ so that you may give thanks.

يَـٰٓأَيُّهَا ٱلَّذِينَ ءَامَنُواْ 27 O you who have faith!

لَا تَخُونُواْ ٱللَّهَ وَٱلرَّسُولَ Do not betray Allah and the Apostle,

وَتَخُونُوٓاْ أَمَٰنَٰتِكُمْ وَأَنتُمْ تَعْلَمُونَ ۝ and do not betray your trusts knowingly.

وَٱعْلَمُوٓاْ أَنَّمَآ أَمْوَٰلُكُمْ وَأَوْلَٰدُكُمْ 28 Know that your possessions and children are only

فِتْنَةٌ a test,

وَأَنَّ ٱللَّهَ عِندَهُۥٓ أَجْرٌ عَظِيمٌ ۝ and that Allah—with Him is a great reward.

يَـٰٓأَيُّهَا ٱلَّذِينَ ءَامَنُوٓاْ 29 O you who have faith!

إِن تَتَّقُواْ ٱللَّهَ If you are wary of Allah,

يَجْعَل لَّكُمْ فُرْقَانًا He shall appoint a criterion[1] for you,

وَيُكَفِّرْ عَنكُمْ سَيِّـَٔاتِكُمْ and absolve you of your misdeeds,

وَيَغْفِرْ لَكُمْ and forgive you,

وَٱللَّهُ ذُو ٱلْفَضْلِ ٱلْعَظِيمِ ۝ for Allah is dispenser of a great grace.

وَإِذْ يَمْكُرُ بِكَ ٱلَّذِينَ كَفَرُواْ 30 When the faithless plotted against *you*

لِيُثْبِتُوكَ أَوْ يَقْتُلُوكَ أَوْ يُخْرِجُوكَ to take *you* captive, or to kill or expel *you*.

وَيَمْكُرُونَ وَيَمْكُرُ ٱللَّهُ They plotted and Allah devised,

---

[1] That is, a knowledge which will enable you to distinguish between truth and falsehood.

وَٱللَّهُ خَيْرُ ٱلْمَٰكِرِينَ ۞    and Allah is the best of devisers.

وَإِذَا تُتْلَىٰ عَلَيْهِمْ ءَايَٰتُنَا 31 When Our signs are recited to them,

قَالُوا۟ قَدْ سَمِعْنَا    they say, 'We have heard already.

لَوْ نَشَآءُ لَقُلْنَا مِثْلَ هَٰذَآ     If we want, we [too] can say like this.

إِنْ هَٰذَآ إِلَّآ أَسَٰطِيرُ ٱلْأَوَّلِينَ ۞     These are nothing but myths of the ancients.'

وَإِذْ قَالُوا۟ 32 And when they said,

ٱللَّهُمَّ    'O Allah,

إِن كَانَ هَٰذَا هُوَ ٱلْحَقَّ مِنْ عِندِكَ     if this be the truth from You,

فَأَمْطِرْ عَلَيْنَا حِجَارَةً مِّنَ ٱلسَّمَآءِ     rain down upon us stones from the sky,

أَوِ ٱئْتِنَا بِعَذَابٍ أَلِيمٍ ۞     or bring us a painful punishment.'

وَمَا كَانَ ٱللَّهُ لِيُعَذِّبَهُمْ 33 But Allah will not punish them

وَأَنتَ فِيهِمْ    while *you* are in their midst,

وَمَا كَانَ ٱللَّهُ مُعَذِّبَهُمْ    nor will Allah punish them

وَهُمْ يَسْتَغْفِرُونَ ۞    while they plead for forgiveness.

وَمَا لَهُمْ 34 What [excuse] have they

أَلَّا يُعَذِّبَهُمُ ٱللَّهُ     that Allah should not punish them,

وَهُمْ يَصُدُّونَ عَنِ ٱلْمَسْجِدِ ٱلْحَرَامِ   when they bar [the faithful] from the Holy Mosque,

وَمَا كَانُوٓا۟ أَوْلِيَآءَهُۥٓ    and they are not its custodians?

إِنْ أَوْلِيَآؤُهُۥٓ إِلَّا ٱلْمُتَّقُونَ    Its custodians are only the Godwary,

وَلَٰكِنَّ أَكْثَرَهُمْ لَا يَعْلَمُونَ ۞    but most of them do not know.

وَمَا كَانَ صَلَاتُهُمْ عِندَ ٱلْبَيْتِ 35 Their prayer at the House is nothing

إِلَّا مُكَآءً وَتَصْدِيَةً    but whistling and clapping.

فَذُوقُوا۟ ٱلْعَذَابَ    So taste the punishment

بِمَا كُنتُمْ تَكْفُرُونَ ۞    because of what you used to defy.

إِنَّ ٱلَّذِينَ كَفَرُوا۟ يُنفِقُونَ أَمْوَٰلَهُمْ 36 Indeed the faithless spend their wealth

لِيَصُدُّوا۟ عَن سَبِيلِ ٱللَّهِ    to bar from the way of Allah.

فَسَيُنفِقُونَهَا    Soon they will have spent it,

ثُمَّ تَكُونُ عَلَيْهِمْ حَسْرَةً     then it will be a cause of regret to them,

ثُمَّ يُغْلَبُونَ     then they will be overcome,

وَٱلَّذِينَ كَفَرُوٓا۟ إِلَىٰ جَهَنَّمَ يُحْشَرُونَ ۞   and the faithless will be gathered toward Hell,

لِيَمِيزَ ٱللَّهُ ٱلْخَبِيثَ    37 so that Allah may separate the bad ones

مِنَ ٱلطَّيِّبِ    from the good,

وَيَجْعَلَ ٱلْخَبِيثَ بَعْضَهُۥ عَلَىٰ بَعْضٍ    and place the bad on one another,

فَيَرْكُمَهُۥ جَمِيعًا    and pile them up together,

فَيَجْعَلَهُۥ فِى جَهَنَّمَ    and cast them into hell.

أُوْلَٰٓئِكَ هُمُ ٱلْخَٰسِرُونَ ۝    It is they who are the losers.

قُل لِّلَّذِينَ كَفَرُوٓاْ    38 *Say* to the faithless,

إِن يَنتَهُواْ    if they relinquish [faithlessness],

يُغْفَرْ لَهُم مَّا قَدْ سَلَفَ    what is already past shall be forgiven them.

وَإِن يَعُودُواْ    But if they revert [to faithlessness],

فَقَدْ مَضَتْ سُنَّتُ ٱلْأَوَّلِينَ ۝    then the precedent of the ancients has already passed.

وَقَٰتِلُوهُمْ حَتَّىٰ لَا تَكُونَ فِتْنَةٌ    39 Fight them until faithlessness[1] is no more,

وَيَكُونَ ٱلدِّينُ كُلُّهُۥ لِلَّهِ    and religion becomes exclusively for Allah.

فَإِنِ ٱنتَهَوْاْ    But if they relinquish,

فَإِنَّ ٱللَّهَ بِمَا يَعْمَلُونَ بَصِيرٌ ۝    Allah indeed sees best what they do.

وَإِن تَوَلَّوْاْ    40 And if they turn away,

فَٱعْلَمُوٓاْ أَنَّ ٱللَّهَ مَوْلَىٰكُمْ    then know that Allah is your master:

نِعْمَ ٱلْمَوْلَىٰ وَنِعْمَ ٱلنَّصِيرُ ۝ ❈    an excellent master and an excellent helper!

[PART 10]

وَٱعْلَمُوٓاْ أَنَّمَا غَنِمْتُم مِّن شَىْءٍ    41 Know that whatever thing you may come by,

فَأَنَّ لِلَّهِ خُمُسَهُۥ وَلِلرَّسُولِ    a fifth of it is for Allah and the Apostle,

وَلِذِى ٱلْقُرْبَىٰ وَٱلْيَتَٰمَىٰ    for the relatives and the orphans,

وَٱلْمَسَٰكِينِ وَٱبْنِ ٱلسَّبِيلِ    for the needy and the traveller,

إِن كُنتُمْ ءَامَنتُم بِٱللَّهِ    if you have faith in Allah

وَمَآ أَنزَلْنَا عَلَىٰ عَبْدِنَا    and what We sent down to Our servant

يَوْمَ ٱلْفُرْقَانِ    on the Day of Separation,[2]

يَوْمَ ٱلْتَقَى ٱلْجَمْعَانِ    the day when the two hosts met;

وَٱللَّهُ عَلَىٰ كُلِّ شَىْءٍ قَدِيرٌ ۝    and Allah has power over all things.

---

[1] Or 'polytheism.' Cf. 2:193.

[2] That is, the day on which the Battle of Badr took place.

إِذْ أَنتُم بِٱلْعُدْوَةِ ٱلدُّنْيَا ٤٢ **When you were on the nearer side,**[1]

وَهُم بِٱلْعُدْوَةِ ٱلْقُصْوَىٰ and they[2] on the farther side,

وَٱلرَّكْبُ أَسْفَلَ مِنكُمْ while the caravan was below you,

وَلَوْ تَوَاعَدتُّمْ and had you agreed together on an encounter,

لَٱخْتَلَفْتُمْ فِى ٱلْمِيعَٰدِ you would have certainly failed to keep the tryst,[3]

وَلَٰكِن لِّيَقْضِىَ ٱللَّهُ but in order that Allah may carry through

أَمْرًا كَانَ مَفْعُولًا a matter that was bound to be fulfilled,

لِّيَهْلِكَ مَنْ هَلَكَ so that he who perishes might perish

عَنۢ بَيِّنَةٍ by a manifest proof,

وَيَحْيَىٰ مَنْ حَىَّ and he who lives may live on

عَنۢ بَيِّنَةٍ by a manifest proof,

وَإِنَّ ٱللَّهَ لَسَمِيعٌ عَلِيمٌ and Allah is indeed all-hearing, all-knowing.

إِذْ يُرِيكَهُمُ ٱللَّهُ ٤٣ **When Allah showed them**[4] **to** *you*

فِى مَنَامِكَ قَلِيلًا as few in *your* dream,

وَلَوْ أَرَىٰكَهُمْ كَثِيرًا and had He shown them as many,

لَّفَشِلْتُمْ you would have lost heart,

وَلَتَنَٰزَعْتُمْ فِى ٱلْأَمْرِ and disputed about the matter.

وَلَٰكِنَّ ٱللَّهَ سَلَّمَ But Allah spared you.

إِنَّهُۥ عَلِيمٌۢ بِذَاتِ ٱلصُّدُورِ Indeed He knows well what is in the breasts.

وَإِذْ يُرِيكُمُوهُمْ ٤٤ **And when He showed them to you**

إِذِ ٱلْتَقَيْتُمْ —when you met them [on the battlefield]—

فِى أَعْيُنِكُمْ قَلِيلًا as few in your eyes,

وَيُقَلِّلُكُمْ فِى أَعْيُنِهِمْ and He made you [appear] few in their eyes

لِيَقْضِىَ ٱللَّهُ in order that Allah may carry through

أَمْرًا كَانَ مَفْعُولًا a matter that was bound to be fulfilled,

وَإِلَى ٱللَّهِ تُرْجَعُ ٱلْأُمُورُ and to Allah all matters are returned.

يَٰٓأَيُّهَا ٱلَّذِينَ ءَامَنُوٓا ٤٥ **O you who have faith!**

[1] That is, on the side of the valley nearer to Madinah.
[2] That is, the army of the polytheists of Makkah.
[3] Or 'you would have not not kept the tryst.'
[4] That is, the enemy troops.

247

إِذَا لَقِيتُمْ فِئَةً

When you meet a host [in battle],

فَٱثْبُتُوا۟ وَٱذْكُرُوا۟ ٱللَّهَ كَثِيرًا

then stand firm, and remember Allah greatly

لَّعَلَّكُمْ تُفْلِحُونَ ۝

so that you may be felicitous.

وَأَطِيعُوا۟ ٱللَّهَ وَرَسُولَهُۥ

46 And obey Allah and His Apostle,

وَلَا تَنَـٰزَعُوا۟

and do not dispute,

فَتَفْشَلُوا۟ وَتَذْهَبَ رِيحُكُمْ ۖ

or you will lose heart and your power will be gone.

وَٱصْبِرُوٓا۟ ۚ

And be patient;

إِنَّ ٱللَّهَ مَعَ ٱلصَّـٰبِرِينَ ۝

indeed Allah is with the patient.

وَلَا تَكُونُوا۟

47 Do not be

كَٱلَّذِينَ خَرَجُوا۟ مِن دِيَـٰرِهِم

like those who left their homes

بَطَرًا وَرِئَآءَ ٱلنَّاسِ

vainly and to show off to the people,

وَيَصُدُّونَ عَن سَبِيلِ ٱللَّهِ ۚ

and to bar [other people] from the way of Allah,

وَٱللَّهُ بِمَا يَعْمَلُونَ مُحِيطٌ ۝

and Allah comprehends what they do.

وَإِذْ زَيَّنَ لَهُمُ ٱلشَّيْطَـٰنُ أَعْمَـٰلَهُمْ

48 When Satan made their deeds seem decorous to them,

وَقَالَ لَا غَالِبَ لَكُمُ ٱلْيَوْمَ

and said, 'No one shall overcome you today

مِنَ ٱلنَّاسِ

from among all mankind,

وَإِنِّى جَارٌ لَّكُمْ ۖ

and I will stand by you.'

فَلَمَّا تَرَآءَتِ ٱلْفِئَتَانِ

But when the two hosts sighted each other,

نَكَصَ عَلَىٰ عَقِبَيْهِ وَقَالَ

he took to his heels, saying,

إِنِّى بَرِىٓءٌ مِّنكُمْ

'Indeed I am quit of you.

إِنِّىٓ أَرَىٰ مَا لَا تَرَوْنَ

I see what you do not see.

إِنِّىٓ أَخَافُ ٱللَّهَ ۚ

Indeed I fear Allah,

وَٱللَّهُ شَدِيدُ ٱلْعِقَابِ ۝

and Allah is severe in retribution.'

إِذْ يَقُولُ ٱلْمُنَـٰفِقُونَ

49 When the hypocrites said,

وَٱلَّذِينَ فِى قُلُوبِهِم مَّرَضٌ

and [also] those in whose hearts is a sickness,

غَرَّ هَـٰٓؤُلَآءِ دِينُهُمْ ۗ

'Their religion has deceived them.'

وَمَن يَتَوَكَّلْ عَلَى ٱللَّهِ

But whoever puts his trust in Allah,

فَإِنَّ ٱللَّهَ عَزِيزٌ حَكِيمٌ ۝

then Allah is indeed all-mighty, all-wise.

وَلَوْ تَرَىٰٓ

50 Were *you* to see

إِذْ يَتَوَفَّى ٱلَّذِينَ كَفَرُوا۟ ٱلْمَلَـٰٓئِكَةُ

when the angels take away the faithless,

يَضْرِبُونَ وُجُوهَهُمْ وَأَدْبَـٰرَهُمْ    striking their faces and their backs,

وَذُوقُواْ عَذَابَ ٱلْحَرِيقِ ۝    [saying], 'Taste the punishment of the burning.

ذَٰلِكَ بِمَا قَدَّمَتْ أَيْدِيكُمْ 51 That is because of what your hands have sent ahead,

وَأَنَّ ٱللَّهَ لَيْسَ بِظَلَّٰمٍ لِّلْعَبِيدِ ۝    and because Allah is not tyrannical to the servants.'

كَدَأْبِ ءَالِ فِرْعَوْنَ 52 Like the precedent of Pharaoh's clan

وَٱلَّذِينَ مِن قَبْلِهِمْ    and those who were before them,

كَفَرُواْ بِـَٔايَٰتِ ٱللَّهِ    who defied Allah's signs,

فَأَخَذَهُمُ ٱللَّهُ بِذُنُوبِهِمْ    so Allah seized them for their sins.

إِنَّ ٱللَّهَ قَوِيٌّ شَدِيدُ ٱلْعِقَابِ ۝    Indeed Allah is all-strong, severe in retribution.

ذَٰلِكَ بِأَنَّ ٱللَّهَ لَمْ يَكُ مُغَيِّرًا نِّعْمَةً 53 That is because Allah never changes a blessing

أَنْعَمَهَا عَلَىٰ قَوْمٍ    that He has bestowed on a people

حَتَّىٰ يُغَيِّرُواْ مَا بِأَنفُسِهِمْ    unless they change what is in their own souls,

وَأَنَّ ٱللَّهَ سَمِيعٌ عَلِيمٌ ۝    and Allah is all-hearing, all-knowing:

كَدَأْبِ ءَالِ فِرْعَوْنَ 54 Like the precedent of Pharaoh's clan

وَٱلَّذِينَ مِن قَبْلِهِمْ    and those who were before them,

كَذَّبُواْ بِـَٔايَٰتِ رَبِّهِمْ    who denied the signs of their Lord;

فَأَهْلَكْنَٰهُم بِذُنُوبِهِمْ    so We destroyed them for their sins,

وَأَغْرَقْنَآ ءَالَ فِرْعَوْنَ    and We drowned Pharaoh's clan;

وَكُلٌّ كَانُواْ ظَٰلِمِينَ ۝    and they were all wrongdoers.

إِنَّ شَرَّ ٱلدَّوَآبِّ عِندَ ٱللَّهِ 55 Indeed the worst of beasts in Allah's sight

ٱلَّذِينَ كَفَرُواْ    are those who are faithless;

فَهُمْ لَا يُؤْمِنُونَ ۝    so they will not have faith.

ٱلَّذِينَ عَٰهَدتَّ مِنْهُمْ 56 —Those with whom *you* made a treaty,

ثُمَّ يَنقُضُونَ عَهْدَهُمْ فِى كُلِّ مَرَّةٍ    and who violated their treaty every time,

وَهُمْ لَا يَتَّقُونَ ۝    and who are not Godwary.

فَإِمَّا تَثْقَفَنَّهُمْ فِى ٱلْحَرْبِ 57 So if you confront them in battle,

فَشَرِّدْ بِهِم    treat them [in such a wise] as to disperse

مَّنْ خَلْفَهُمْ    those who are behind them,

لَعَلَّهُمْ يَذَّكَّرُونَ ۝    so that they may take admonition.

وَإِمَّا تَخَافَنَّ مِن قَوْمٍ خِيَانَةً 58 And if you fear treachery from a people,

فَأَنۢبِذۡ إِلَيۡهِمۡ عَلَىٰ سَوَآءٍ       break off [the treaty] with them in a like manner.

إِنَّ ٱللَّهَ لَا يُحِبُّ ٱلۡخَآئِنِينَ ۝       Indeed Allah does not like the treacherous.

وَلَا يَحۡسَبَنَّ ٱلَّذِينَ كَفَرُواْ       59 Let the faithless not suppose

سَبَقُوٓاْ       that they have outmaneuvered [Allah].

إِنَّهُمۡ لَا يُعۡجِزُونَ ۝       Indeed they cannot thwart [His power].

وَأَعِدُّواْ لَهُم مَّا ٱسۡتَطَعۡتُم       60 Prepare against them whatever you can

مِّن قُوَّةٍ وَمِن رِّبَاطِ ٱلۡخَيۡلِ       of [military] power and war-horses,

تُرۡهِبُونَ بِهِۦ عَدُوَّ ٱللَّهِ       awing thereby the enemy of Allah,

وَعَدُوَّكُمۡ       and your enemy,

وَءَاخَرِينَ مِن دُونِهِمۡ       and others besides them,

لَا تَعۡلَمُونَهُمُ       whom you do not know,

ٱللَّهُ يَعۡلَمُهُمۡ       but Allah knows them.

وَمَا تُنفِقُواْ مِن شَيۡءٍ فِى سَبِيلِ ٱللَّهِ       And whatever you spend in the way of Allah

يُوَفَّ إِلَيۡكُمۡ       will be repaid to you in full,

وَأَنتُمۡ لَا تُظۡلَمُونَ ۝ ۞       and you will not be wronged.

وَإِن جَنَحُواْ لِلسَّلۡمِ       61 And if they incline toward peace,

فَٱجۡنَحۡ لَهَا       then *you* [too] incline toward it,

وَتَوَكَّلۡ عَلَى ٱللَّهِ       and *put your* trust in Allah.

إِنَّهُۥ هُوَ ٱلسَّمِيعُ ٱلۡعَلِيمُ ۝       Indeed He is the All-hearing, the All-knowing.

وَإِن يُرِيدُوٓاْ أَن يَخۡدَعُوكَ       62 But if they desire to deceive *you*,

فَإِنَّ حَسۡبَكَ ٱللَّهُ       Allah is indeed sufficient for *you*.

هُوَ ٱلَّذِىٓ أَيَّدَكَ بِنَصۡرِهِۦ       It is He who strengthened *you* with His help

وَبِٱلۡمُؤۡمِنِينَ ۝       and with the means of the faithful,

وَأَلَّفَ بَيۡنَ قُلُوبِهِمۡ       63 and united their hearts.

لَوۡ أَنفَقۡتَ مَا فِى ٱلۡأَرۡضِ جَمِيعًا       Had *you* spent all that is in the earth,

مَّآ أَلَّفۡتَ بَيۡنَ قُلُوبِهِمۡ       *you* could not have united their hearts,

وَلَٰكِنَّ ٱللَّهَ أَلَّفَ بَيۡنَهُمۡ       but Allah united them together.

إِنَّهُۥ عَزِيزٌ حَكِيمٌ ۝       Indeed He is all-mighty, all-wise.

يَٰٓأَيُّهَا ٱلنَّبِىُّ       64 O Prophet!

حَسۡبُكَ ٱللَّهُ       Sufficient for *you* is Allah

وَمَنِ ٱتَّبَعَكَ مِنَ ٱلْمُؤْمِنِينَ ۝ and those of the faithful who follow *you*.

يَٰٓأَيُّهَا ٱلنَّبِىُّ 65 O Prophet!

حَرِّضِ ٱلْمُؤْمِنِينَ عَلَى ٱلْقِتَالِ *Urge* on the faithful to fight:

إِن يَكُن مِّنكُمْ عِشْرُونَ صَٰبِرُونَ If there be twenty patient men among you,

يَغْلِبُوا۟ مِا۟ئَتَيْنِ they shall overcome two hundred;

وَإِن يَكُن مِّنكُم مِّا۟ئَةٌ and if there be a hundred of you,

يَغْلِبُوٓا۟ أَلْفًا مِّنَ ٱلَّذِينَ كَفَرُوا۟ they shall overcome a thousand of the faithless,

بِأَنَّهُمْ قَوْمٌ لَّا يَفْقَهُونَ ۝ for they are a lot who do not understand.

ٱلْـَٰٔنَ خَفَّفَ ٱللَّهُ عَنكُمْ 66 Now Allah has lightened your burden,

وَعَلِمَ أَنَّ فِيكُمْ ضَعْفًا knowing that there is weakness in you.

فَإِن يَكُن مِّنكُم مِّا۟ئَةٌ صَابِرَةٌ So if there be a hundred patient men among you,

يَغْلِبُوا۟ مِا۟ئَتَيْنِ they shall overcome two hundred;

وَإِن يَكُن مِّنكُمْ أَلْفٌ and if there be a thousand,

يَغْلِبُوٓا۟ أَلْفَيْنِ they shall overcome two thousand,

بِإِذْنِ ٱللَّهِ by Allah's leave;

وَٱللَّهُ مَعَ ٱلصَّٰبِرِينَ ۝ and Allah is with the patient.

مَا كَانَ لِنَبِىٍّ أَن يَكُونَ لَهُۥٓ أَسْرَىٰ 67 A prophet may not take captives

حَتَّىٰ يُثْخِنَ until he has thoroughly decimated [the enemy]

فِى ٱلْأَرْضِ in the land.

تُرِيدُونَ عَرَضَ ٱلدُّنْيَا You desire the transitory gains of this world,

وَٱللَّهُ يُرِيدُ while Allah desires [for you]

ٱلْـَٔاخِرَةَ [the reward of] the Hereafter,

وَٱللَّهُ عَزِيزٌ حَكِيمٌ ۝ and Allah is all-mighty, all-wise.

لَّوْلَا كِتَٰبٌ مِّنَ ٱللَّهِ سَبَقَ 68 Had it not been for a prior decree of Allah,

لَمَسَّكُمْ surely there would have befallen you

فِيمَآ أَخَذْتُمْ عَذَابٌ عَظِيمٌ ۝ a great punishment for what you took.

فَكُلُوا۟ مِمَّا غَنِمْتُمْ 69 Avail yourselves of the spoils you have taken

حَلَٰلًا طَيِّبًا as lawful and good,

وَٱتَّقُوا۟ ٱللَّهَ and be wary of Allah.

إِنَّ ٱللَّهَ غَفُورٌ رَّحِيمٌ ۝ Indeed Allah is all-forgiving, all-merciful.

يَـٰٓأَيُّهَا ٱلنَّبِىُّ 70 O Prophet!

قُل لِّمَن فِىٓ أَيْدِيكُم مِّنَ ٱلْأَسْرَىٰٓ Say to the captives who are in your hands,

إِن يَعْلَمِ ٱللَّهُ فِى قُلُوبِكُمْ خَيْرًا 'If Allah finds any good in your hearts,

يُؤْتِكُمْ خَيْرًا He will give you [something which is] better

مِّمَّآ أُخِذَ مِنكُمْ than what has been taken away from you,

وَيَغْفِرْ لَكُمْ and He will forgive you,

وَٱللَّهُ غَفُورٌ رَّحِيمٌ ۝ and Allah is all-forgiving, al-merciful.'

وَإِن يُرِيدُواْ خِيَانَتَكَ 71 But if they seek to betray you,

فَقَدْ خَانُواْ ٱللَّهَ مِن قَبْلُ then they have already betrayed Allah earlier,

فَأَمْكَنَ مِنْهُمْ and He gave [you] power over them;

وَٱللَّهُ عَلِيمٌ حَكِيمٌ ۝ and Allah is all-knowing, all-wise.

إِنَّ ٱلَّذِينَ ءَامَنُواْ وَهَاجَرُواْ 72 Indeed those who have believed and migrated

وَجَـٰهَدُواْ بِأَمْوَٰلِهِمْ وَأَنفُسِهِمْ and waged *jihād* with their possessions and persons

فِى سَبِيلِ ٱللَّهِ in the way of Allah,

وَٱلَّذِينَ ءَاوَواْ وَّنَصَرُوٓاْ and those who gave [them] shelter and help

أُوْلَـٰٓئِكَ بَعْضُهُمْ أَوْلِيَآءُ بَعْضٍ —they are heirs of one another.

وَٱلَّذِينَ ءَامَنُواْ وَلَمْ يُهَاجِرُواْ As for those who have believed but did not migrate,

مَا لَكُم مِّن وَلَـٰيَتِهِم مِّن شَىْءٍ you have no heirdom in relation to them whatsoever

حَتَّىٰ يُهَاجِرُواْ until they migrate.

وَإِنِ ٱسْتَنصَرُوكُمْ فِى ٱلدِّينِ Yet if they ask your help for the sake of religion,

فَعَلَيْكُمُ ٱلنَّصْرُ it is incumbent on you to help them,

إِلَّا عَلَىٰ قَوْمٍ excepting against a people

بَيْنَكُمْ وَبَيْنَهُم مِّيثَـٰقٌ with whom you have a treaty;

وَٱللَّهُ بِمَا تَعْمَلُونَ بَصِيرٌ ۝ and Allah see best what you do.

وَٱلَّذِينَ كَفَرُواْ بَعْضُهُمْ أَوْلِيَآءُ بَعْضٍ 73 As for the faithless, they are heirs of one another.

إِلَّا تَفْعَلُوهُ Unless you do the same,

تَكُن فِتْنَةٌ فِى ٱلْأَرْضِ there will be tribulation in the earth

وَفَسَادٌ كَبِيرٌ ۝ and a great corruption.

وَٱلَّذِينَ ءَامَنُواْ وَهَاجَرُواْ 74 Those who have believed, migrated,

وَجَهَدُواْ فِى سَبِيلِ ٱللَّهِ    and waged *jihād* in the way of Allah,

وَٱلَّذِينَ ءَاوَواْ وَنَصَرُواْ    and those who gave them shelter and help,

أُوْلَٰئِكَ هُمُ ٱلْمُؤْمِنُونَ حَقًّا    it is they who are truly the faithful.

هُم مَّغْفِرَةٌ وَرِزْقٌ كَرِيمٌ ٧٤    For them shall be forgiveness and a noble provision.

وَٱلَّذِينَ ءَامَنُواْ مِنۢ بَعْدُ وَهَاجَرُواْ 75 And those who believed afterwards and migrated,

وَجَهَدُواْ مَعَكُمْ    and waged *jihād* along with you,

فَأُوْلَٰئِكَ مِنكُمْ    they belong to you;

وَأُوْلُواْ ٱلْأَرْحَامِ    but the blood relatives

بَعْضُهُمْ أَوْلَىٰ بِبَعْضٍ    are more entitled to inherit from one another

فِى كِتَٰبِ ٱللَّهِ    in the Book of Allah.[1]

إِنَّ ٱللَّهَ بِكُلِّ شَىْءٍ عَلِيمٌ ٧٥    Indeed Allah has knowledge of all things.

## سُورَةُ التَّوبَةِ    9. SŪRAT AL-TAWBAH[2]

بَرَآءَةٌ مِّنَ ٱللَّهِ 1 [This is] a [declaration of] repudiation by Allah

وَرَسُولِهِۦ    and His Apostle [addressed]

إِلَى ٱلَّذِينَ عَٰهَدتُّم مِّنَ ٱلْمُشْرِكِينَ    to the polytheists with whom you had made a treaty:

فَسِيحُواْ فِى ٱلْأَرْضِ أَرْبَعَةَ أَشْهُرٍ 2 Travel [unmolested] in the land for four months,

وَٱعْلَمُوٓاْ أَنَّكُمْ غَيْرُ مُعْجِزِى ٱللَّهِ    but know that you cannot thwart Allah,

وَأَنَّ ٱللَّهَ مُخْزِى ٱلْكَٰفِرِينَ    and that Allah shall disgrace the faithless.

وَأَذَٰنٌ مِّنَ ٱللَّهِ 3 [This is] an announcement from Allah

وَرَسُولِهِۦ    and His Apostle

إِلَى ٱلنَّاسِ    to all the people

يَوْمَ ٱلْحَجِّ ٱلْأَكْبَرِ    on the day of the greater *ḥajj*:[3]

أَنَّ ٱللَّهَ    that Allah

بَرِىٓءٌ مِّنَ ٱلْمُشْرِكِينَ وَرَسُولُهُۥ    and His Apostle repudiate the polytheists:

---

[1] Cf. 33:6.

[2] The *sūrah* is named after 'repentance' (*tawbah*), mentioned in verses 3 & 5.

[3] That is, the tenth of Dhū al-Ḥijjah, the day on which the pilgrims perform some of the major rites of the ḥajj in Minā.

فَإِن تُبْتُمْ فَهُوَ خَيْرٌ لَّكُمْ

If you repent[1] that is better for you;

وَإِن تَوَلَّيْتُمْ

but if you turn your backs [on Allah],

فَٱعْلَمُوٓاْ أَنَّكُمْ غَيْرُ مُعْجِزِى ٱللَّهِ

know that you cannot thwart Allah,

وَبَشِّرِ ٱلَّذِينَ كَفَرُواْ بِعَذَابٍ أَلِيمٍ ۝

and *inform* the faithless of a painful punishment

إِلَّا ٱلَّذِينَ عَٰهَدتُّم مِّنَ ٱلْمُشْرِكِينَ

4 (barring the polytheists with whom you have made a treaty

ثُمَّ لَمْ يَنقُصُوكُمْ شَيْـًٔا

and who did not violate any [of its terms] with you,

وَلَمْ يُظَٰهِرُواْ عَلَيْكُمْ أَحَدًا

nor backed anyone against you.

فَأَتِمُّوٓاْ إِلَيْهِمْ عَهْدَهُمْ إِلَىٰ مُدَّتِهِمْ

So fulfill the treaty with them until [the end of] its term.

إِنَّ ٱللَّهَ يُحِبُّ ٱلْمُتَّقِينَ ۝

Indeed Allah loves the Godwary).

فَإِذَا ٱنسَلَخَ ٱلْأَشْهُرُ ٱلْحُرُمُ

5 Then, when the sacred months have passed,

فَٱقْتُلُواْ ٱلْمُشْرِكِينَ حَيْثُ وَجَدتُّمُوهُمْ

kill the polytheists wherever you find them,

وَخُذُوهُمْ وَٱحْصُرُوهُمْ

capture them and besiege them,

وَٱقْعُدُواْ لَهُمْ كُلَّ مَرْصَدٍ

and lie in wait for them at every ambush.

فَإِن تَابُواْ

But if they repent,

وَأَقَامُواْ ٱلصَّلَوٰةَ وَءَاتَوُاْ ٱلزَّكَوٰةَ

and maintain the prayer and give the *zakāt*,

فَخَلُّواْ سَبِيلَهُمْ

then let them alone.

إِنَّ ٱللَّهَ غَفُورٌ رَّحِيمٌ ۝

Indeed Allah is all-forgiving, all-merciful.

وَإِنْ أَحَدٌ مِّنَ ٱلْمُشْرِكِينَ ٱسْتَجَارَكَ

6 If any of the polytheists seeks asylum from *you*,

فَأَجِرْهُ حَتَّىٰ يَسْمَعَ كَلَٰمَ ٱللَّهِ

*grant* him asylum until he hears the Word of Allah.

ثُمَّ أَبْلِغْهُ مَأْمَنَهُۥ

Then convey him to his place of safety.

ذَٰلِكَ بِأَنَّهُمْ قَوْمٌ لَّا يَعْلَمُونَ ۝

That is because they are a people who do not know.

كَيْفَ يَكُونُ لِلْمُشْرِكِينَ عَهْدٌ

7 How shall the polytheists have any [valid] treaty

عِندَ ٱللَّهِ وَعِندَ رَسُولِهِۦٓ

with Allah and His Apostle?!

إِلَّا ٱلَّذِينَ عَٰهَدتُّمْ

(Barring those with whom you made a treaty

عِندَ ٱلْمَسْجِدِ ٱلْحَرَامِ

at the Holy Mosque;

فَمَا ٱسْتَقَٰمُواْ لَكُمْ

so long as they are steadfast with you,

فَٱسْتَقِيمُواْ لَهُمْ

be steadfast with them.

إِنَّ ٱللَّهَ يُحِبُّ ٱلْمُتَّقِينَ ۝

Indeed Allah loves the Godwary.)

كَيْفَ وَإِن يَظْهَرُواْ عَلَيْكُمْ

8 How? For if they get the better of you,

---

[1] That is, abandon idolatry.

لَا يَرْقُبُواْ فِيكُمْ إِلَّا    they will observe toward you neither kinship

وَلَا ذِمَّةً    nor covenant.

يُرْضُونَكُم بِأَفْوَٰهِهِمْ    They please you with their mouths

وَتَأْبَىٰ قُلُوبُهُمْ    while their hearts spurn you;

وَأَكْثَرُهُمْ فَٰسِقُونَ ۝    and most of them are transgressors.

ٱشْتَرَوْاْ بِـَٔايَٰتِ ٱللَّهِ ثَمَنًا قَلِيلًا    9 They have sold the signs of Allah for a paltry gain,

فَصَدُّواْ عَن سَبِيلِهِ    and have barred [the people] from His way.

إِنَّهُمْ سَآءَ مَا كَانُواْ يَعْمَلُونَ ۝    Evil indeed is what they have been doing.

لَا يَرْقُبُونَ فِى مُؤْمِنٍ إِلَّا    10 They observe toward a believer neither kinship

وَلَا ذِمَّةً    nor covenant,

وَأُوْلَٰٓئِكَ هُمُ ٱلْمُعْتَدُونَ ۝    and it is they who are the transgressors.

فَإِن تَابُواْ    11 Yet if they repent

وَأَقَامُواْ ٱلصَّلَوٰةَ وَءَاتَوُاْ ٱلزَّكَوٰةَ    and maintain the prayer and give the *zakāt*,

فَإِخْوَٰنُكُمْ فِى ٱلدِّينِ    then they are your brethren in faith.

وَنُفَصِّلُ ٱلْءَايَٰتِ    We elaborate the signs

لِقَوْمٍ يَعْلَمُونَ ۝    for a people who have knowledge.

وَإِن نَّكَثُوٓاْ أَيْمَٰنَهُم    12 But if they break their pledges

مِّنۢ بَعْدِ عَهْدِهِمْ    after their having made a treaty

وَطَعَنُواْ فِى دِينِكُمْ    and revile your religion,

فَقَٰتِلُوٓاْ أَئِمَّةَ ٱلْكُفْرِ    then fight the leaders of unfaith

إِنَّهُمْ لَآ أَيْمَٰنَ لَهُمْ    —indeed they have no [commitment to] pledges—

لَعَلَّهُمْ يَنتَهُونَ ۝    maybe they will relinquish.

أَلَا تُقَٰتِلُونَ قَوْمًا    13 Will you not make war on a people

نَّكَثُوٓاْ أَيْمَٰنَهُمْ    who broke their pledges

وَهَمُّواْ بِإِخْرَاجِ ٱلرَّسُولِ    and resolved to expel the Apostle,

وَهُم بَدَءُوكُمْ أَوَّلَ مَرَّةٍ    and opened [hostilities] against you initially?

أَتَخْشَوْنَهُمْ    Do you fear them?

فَٱللَّهُ أَحَقُّ أَن تَخْشَوْهُ    But Allah is worthier of being feared by you,

إِن كُنتُم مُّؤْمِنِينَ ۝    should you be faithful.

قَٰتِلُوهُمْ    14 Make war on them

يُعَذِّبْهُمُ ٱللَّهُ بِأَيْدِيكُمْ
so that Allah may punish them by your hands

وَيُخْزِهِمْ
and humiliate them,

وَيَنصُرْكُمْ عَلَيْهِمْ
and help you against them,

وَيَشْفِ صُدُورَ قَوْمٍ مُّؤْمِنِينَ ۝
and heal the hearts of a faithful folk,

15 وَيُذْهِبْ غَيْظَ قُلُوبِهِمْ
and remove rage from their hearts,

وَيَتُوبُ ٱللَّهُ
and Allah turns clemently

عَلَىٰ مَن يَشَآءُ
to whomever He wishes,

وَٱللَّهُ عَلِيمٌ حَكِيمٌ ۝
and Allah is all-knowing, all-wise

16 أَمْ حَسِبْتُمْ أَن تُتْرَكُوا۟
16 Do you suppose that you will be let off

وَلَمَّا يَعْلَمِ ٱللَّهُ
while Allah has not yet ascertained

ٱلَّذِينَ جَٰهَدُوا۟ مِنكُمْ
those of you who wage *jihād*

وَلَمْ يَتَّخِذُوا۟
and those who do not take,

مِن دُونِ ٱللَّهِ وَلَا رَسُولِهِ
besides Allah and His Apostle

وَلَا ٱلْمُؤْمِنِينَ
and the faithful,

وَلِيجَةً
anyone as [their] confidant?

وَٱللَّهُ خَبِيرٌ بِمَا تَعْمَلُونَ ۝
Allah is well aware of what you do.

17 مَا كَانَ لِلْمُشْرِكِينَ أَن يَعْمُرُوا۟
17 The polytheists may not maintain

مَسَٰجِدَ ٱللَّهِ
Allah's mosques

شَٰهِدِينَ عَلَىٰ أَنفُسِهِم بِٱلْكُفْرِ
while they are witness to their own unfaith.

أُو۟لَٰٓئِكَ حَبِطَتْ أَعْمَٰلُهُمْ
Their works have failed,

وَفِى ٱلنَّارِ هُمْ خَٰلِدُونَ ۝
and they shall remain in the Fire [forever].

18 إِنَّمَا يَعْمُرُ مَسَٰجِدَ ٱللَّهِ
18 Only those shall maintain Allah's mosques

مَنْ ءَامَنَ بِٱللَّهِ وَٱلْيَوْمِ ٱلْأَخِرِ
who believe in Allah and the Last Day,

وَأَقَامَ ٱلصَّلَوٰةَ وَءَاتَى ٱلزَّكَوٰةَ
and maintain the prayer and give the *zakāt*,

وَلَمْ يَخْشَ إِلَّا ٱللَّهَ
and fear no one except Allah.

فَعَسَىٰٓ أُو۟لَٰٓئِكَ أَن يَكُونُوا۟
They, hopefully, will be

مِنَ ٱلْمُهْتَدِينَ ۝ ۞
among the guided.

19 أَجَعَلْتُمْ سِقَايَةَ ٱلْحَآجِّ
19 Do you regard the providing of water to ḥajj pilgrims

وَعِمَارَةَ ٱلْمَسْجِدِ ٱلْحَرَامِ
and the maintenance of the Holy Mosque

كَمَنْ ءَامَنَ بِٱللَّهِ
as similar [in worth] to someone who has faith in Allah

وَٱلۡيَوۡمِ ٱلۡأٓخِرِ
and [believes in] the Last Day

وَجَٰهَدَ فِى سَبِيلِ ٱللَّهِ
and wages *jihād* in the way of Allah?

لَا يَسۡتَوُۥنَ عِندَ ٱللَّهِ
They are not equal with Allah,

وَٱللَّهُ لَا يَهۡدِى ٱلۡقَوۡمَ ٱلظَّٰلِمِينَ ۝
and Allah does not guide the wrongdoing lot.

ٱلَّذِينَ ءَامَنُواْ وَهَاجَرُواْ
20 Those who have believed and migrated,

وَجَٰهَدُواْ فِى سَبِيلِ ٱللَّهِ
and waged *jihād* in the way of Allah

بِأَمۡوَٰلِهِمۡ وَأَنفُسِهِمۡ
with their possessions and persons

أَعۡظَمُ دَرَجَةً عِندَ ٱللَّهِ
have a greater rank near Allah,

وَأُوْلَٰٓئِكَ هُمُ ٱلۡفَآئِزُونَ ۝
and it is they who are the triumphant.

يُبَشِّرُهُمۡ رَبُّهُم بِرَحۡمَةٍ مِّنۡهُ
21 Their Lord gives them the good news of His mercy

وَرِضۡوَٰنٍ
and [His] pleasure,

وَجَنَّٰتٍ لَّهُمۡ فِيهَا نَعِيمٌ مُّقِيمٌ ۝
and for them there will be gardens with lasting bliss,

خَٰلِدِينَ فِيهَآ أَبَدًا
22 to remain in them forever.

إِنَّ ٱللَّهَ عِندَهُۥٓ أَجۡرٌ عَظِيمٌ ۝
With Allah indeed is a great reward.

يَٰٓأَيُّهَا ٱلَّذِينَ ءَامَنُواْ
23 O you who have faith!

لَا تَتَّخِذُوٓاْ ءَابَآءَكُمۡ وَإِخۡوَٰنَكُمۡ أَوۡلِيَآءَ
Do not befriend your fathers and brothers[1]

إِنِ ٱسۡتَحَبُّواْ ٱلۡكُفۡرَ عَلَى ٱلۡإِيمَٰنِ
if they prefer faithlessness to faith.

وَمَن يَتَوَلَّهُم مِّنكُمۡ
Those of you who befriend them

فَأُوْلَٰٓئِكَ هُمُ ٱلظَّٰلِمُونَ ۝
—it is they who are the wrongdoers.

قُلۡ إِن كَانَ ءَابَآؤُكُمۡ وَأَبۡنَآؤُكُمۡ
24 *Say,* 'If your fathers and your sons,

وَإِخۡوَٰنُكُمۡ وَأَزۡوَٰجُكُمۡ وَعَشِيرَتُكُمۡ
your brethren, your spouses, and your kinsfolk,

وَأَمۡوَٰلٌ ٱقۡتَرَفۡتُمُوهَا
the possessions that you have acquired,

وَتِجَٰرَةٌ تَخۡشَوۡنَ كَسَادَهَا
the business you fear may suffer,

وَمَسَٰكِنُ تَرۡضَوۡنَهَآ
and the dwellings you are fond of,

أَحَبَّ إِلَيۡكُم مِّنَ ٱللَّهِ وَرَسُولِهِۦ
are dearer to you than Allah and His Apostle

وَجِهَادٍ فِى سَبِيلِهِۦ
and to waging *jihād* in His way,

فَتَرَبَّصُواْ حَتَّىٰ يَأۡتِىَ ٱللَّهُ بِأَمۡرِهِۦ
then wait until Allah issues His edict,

وَٱللَّهُ لَا يَهۡدِى ٱلۡقَوۡمَ ٱلۡفَٰسِقِينَ ۝
and Allah does not guide the transgressing lot.

لَقَدۡ نَصَرَكُمُ ٱللَّهُ
25 Allah has certainly helped you

---

[1] Or 'Do not take your fathers and brothers for intimates.'

| | |
|---|---|
| فِى مَوَاطِنَ كَثِيرَةٍ | in many situations, |
| وَيَوْمَ حُنَيْنٍ | and on the day of Ḥunayn, |
| إِذْ أَعْجَبَتْكُمْ كَثْرَتُكُمْ | when your great number impressed you, |
| فَلَمْ تُغْنِ عَنكُمْ شَيْئًا | but it did not avail you in any way, |
| وَضَاقَتْ عَلَيْكُمُ ٱلْأَرْضُ | and the earth became narrow for you |
| بِمَا رَحُبَتْ | in spite of its expanse,[1] |
| ثُمَّ وَلَّيْتُم مُّدْبِرِينَ ٢٥ | whereupon you turned your backs [to flee]. |
| ثُمَّ أَنزَلَ ٱللَّهُ سَكِينَتَهُ عَلَىٰ رَسُولِهِ | 26 Then Allah sent down His composure |
| وَعَلَى ٱلْمُؤْمِنِينَ | upon His Apostle and upon the faithful, |
| وَأَنزَلَ جُنُودًا لَّمْ تَرَوْهَا | and He sent down hosts you did not see, |
| وَعَذَّبَ ٱلَّذِينَ كَفَرُواْ | and He punished the faithless, |
| وَذَٰلِكَ جَزَآءُ ٱلْكَٰفِرِينَ ٢٦ | and that is the requital of the faithless. |
| ثُمَّ يَتُوبُ ٱللَّهُ مِنۢ بَعْدِ ذَٰلِكَ | 27 Then Allah shall turn clemently after that |
| عَلَىٰ مَن يَشَآءُ | to whomever He wishes. |
| وَٱللَّهُ غَفُورٌ رَّحِيمٌ ٢٧ | Indeed Allah is all-forgiving, all-merciful. |
| يَٰٓأَيُّهَا ٱلَّذِينَ ءَامَنُوٓاْ | 28 O you who have faith! |
| إِنَّمَا ٱلْمُشْرِكُونَ نَجَسٌ | The polytheists are indeed unclean: |
| فَلَا يَقْرَبُواْ ٱلْمَسْجِدَ ٱلْحَرَامَ | so let them not approach the Holy Mosque |
| بَعْدَ عَامِهِمْ هَٰذَا | after this year. |
| وَإِنْ خِفْتُمْ عَيْلَةً | Should you fear poverty, |
| فَسَوْفَ يُغْنِيكُمُ ٱللَّهُ مِن فَضْلِهِ | Allah will enrich you out of His grace, |
| إِن شَآءَ | if He wishes. |
| إِنَّ ٱللَّهَ عَلِيمٌ حَكِيمٌ ٢٨ | Indeed Allah is all-knowing, all-wise. |
| قَٰتِلُواْ ٱلَّذِينَ لَا يُؤْمِنُونَ بِٱللَّهِ | 29 Fight those who do not have faith in Allah |
| وَلَا بِٱلْيَوْمِ ٱلْءَاخِرِ | nor [believe] in the Last Day, |
| وَلَا يُحَرِّمُونَ | nor forbid |
| مَا حَرَّمَ ٱللَّهُ وَرَسُولُهُ | what Allah and His Apostle have forbidden, |
| وَلَا يَدِينُونَ دِينَ ٱلْحَقِّ | nor practise the true religion, |

---

[1] That is, you were at a complete loss and at the end of your wits.

مِنَ ٱلَّذِينَ أُوتُوا۟ ٱلْكِتَٰبَ
from among those who were given the Book,

حَتَّىٰ يُعْطُوا۟ ٱلْجِزْيَةَ عَن يَدٍ
until they pay the tribute out of hand,

وَهُمْ صَٰغِرُونَ ۩
degraded.

٣٠ وَقَالَتِ ٱلْيَهُودُ عُزَيْرٌ ٱبْنُ ٱللَّهِ
30 The Jews say, 'Ezra is the son of Allah,'

وَقَالَتِ ٱلنَّصَٰرَى ٱلْمَسِيحُ ٱبْنُ ٱللَّهِ
and the Christians say, 'Christ is the son of Allah.'

ذَٰلِكَ قَوْلُهُم بِأَفْوَٰهِهِمْ
That is an opinion that they mouth,

يُضَٰهِـُٔونَ
imitating

قَوْلَ ٱلَّذِينَ كَفَرُوا۟ مِن قَبْلُ
the opinions of the faithless of former times.

قَٰتَلَهُمُ ٱللَّهُ أَنَّىٰ يُؤْفَكُونَ ۩
May Allah assail them, where do they stray?!

٣١ ٱتَّخَذُوٓا۟ أَحْبَارَهُمْ وَرُهْبَٰنَهُمْ
31 They have taken their scribes and their monks

أَرْبَابًا مِّن دُونِ ٱللَّهِ
as lords besides Allah,

وَٱلْمَسِيحَ ٱبْنَ مَرْيَمَ
and also Christ, Mary's son;

وَمَآ أُمِرُوٓا۟ إِلَّا لِيَعْبُدُوٓا۟
though they were commanded to worship only

إِلَٰهًا وَٰحِدًا
the One God,

لَّآ إِلَٰهَ إِلَّا هُوَ
there is no god except Him;

سُبْحَٰنَهُ
He is far too immaculate

عَمَّا يُشْرِكُونَ ۩
to have any partners that they ascribe [to Him].

٣٢ يُرِيدُونَ أَن يُطْفِـُٔوا۟ نُورَ ٱللَّهِ
32 They desire to put out the light of Allah

بِأَفْوَٰهِهِمْ
with their mouths,

وَيَأْبَى ٱللَّهُ إِلَّآ أَن يُتِمَّ نُورَهُ
but Allah is intent on perfecting His light

وَلَوْ كَرِهَ ٱلْكَٰفِرُونَ ۩
though the faithless should be averse.

٣٣ هُوَ ٱلَّذِىٓ أَرْسَلَ رَسُولَهُ بِٱلْهُدَىٰ
33 It is He who has sent His Apostle with the guidance

وَدِينِ ٱلْحَقِّ
and the religion of truth,

لِيُظْهِرَهُ عَلَى ٱلدِّينِ كُلِّهِۦ
that He may make it prevail over all religions,

وَلَوْ كَرِهَ ٱلْمُشْرِكُونَ ۩ ۞
though the polytheists should be averse.

٣٤ يَٰٓأَيُّهَا ٱلَّذِينَ ءَامَنُوٓا۟
34 O you who have faith!

إِنَّ كَثِيرًا مِّنَ ٱلْأَحْبَارِ وَٱلرُّهْبَانِ
Indeed many of the scribes and monks

لَيَأْكُلُونَ أَمْوَٰلَ ٱلنَّاسِ بِٱلْبَٰطِلِ
wrongfully eat up the people's wealth,

وَيَصُدُّونَ عَن سَبِيلِ ٱللَّهِ
and bar [them] from the way of Allah.

وَٱلَّذِينَ يَكْنِزُونَ ٱلذَّهَبَ وَٱلْفِضَّةَ
Those who treasure up gold and silver,

وَلَا يُنفِقُونَهَا فِى سَبِيلِ ٱللَّهِ    and do not spend it in the way of Allah,

فَبَشِّرْهُم بِعَذَابٍ أَلِيمٍ ۝    inform them of a painful punishment

يَوْمَ يُحْمَىٰ عَلَيْهَا فِى نَارِ جَهَنَّمَ   35   on the day when these shall be heated in hellfire

فَتُكْوَىٰ بِهَا جِبَاهُهُمْ    and therewith branded on their foreheads,

وَجُنُوبُهُمْ وَظُهُورُهُمْ    their sides and their backs [and told]:

هَٰذَا مَا كَنَزْتُمْ لِأَنفُسِكُمْ    'This is what you treasured up for yourselves!

فَذُوقُوا۟ مَا كُنتُمْ تَكْنِزُونَ ۝    So taste what you have treasured!'

إِنَّ عِدَّةَ ٱلشُّهُورِ عِندَ ٱللَّهِ   36   Indeed the number of months with Allah

ٱثْنَا عَشَرَ شَهْرًا    is twelve months

فِى كِتَٰبِ ٱللَّهِ    in Allah's Book,

يَوْمَ خَلَقَ ٱلسَّمَٰوَٰتِ    the day when He created the heavens

وَٱلْأَرْضَ    and the earth.

مِنْهَآ أَرْبَعَةٌ حُرُمٌ    Of these, four are sacred.

ذَٰلِكَ ٱلدِّينُ ٱلْقَيِّمُ    That is the upright religion.

فَلَا تَظْلِمُوا۟ فِيهِنَّ أَنفُسَكُمْ    So do not wrong yourselves during them.[1]

وَقَٰتِلُوا۟ ٱلْمُشْرِكِينَ كَآفَّةً    Fight all the polytheists,

كَمَا يُقَٰتِلُونَكُمْ كَآفَّةً    just as they fight you all,

وَٱعْلَمُوٓا۟ أَنَّ ٱللَّهَ مَعَ ٱلْمُتَّقِينَ ۝    and know that Allah is with the Godwary.

إِنَّمَا ٱلنَّسِىٓءُ زِيَادَةٌ فِى ٱلْكُفْرِ   37   Indeed *nasī* is an increase in unfaith,

يُضَلُّ بِهِ ٱلَّذِينَ كَفَرُوا۟    whereby the faithless are led [further] astray.

يُحِلُّونَهُۥ عَامًا وَيُحَرِّمُونَهُۥ عَامًا    They allow it in one year and forbid it another year,

لِّيُوَاطِـُٔوا۟ عِدَّةَ    so as to fit in with the number

مَا حَرَّمَ ٱللَّهُ    which Allah has made inviolable,

فَيُحِلُّوا۟ مَا حَرَّمَ ٱللَّهُ    thus permitting what Allah has forbidden.

زُيِّنَ لَهُمْ سُوٓءُ أَعْمَٰلِهِمْ    Their evil deeds appear to them as decorous,

وَٱللَّهُ لَا يَهْدِى ٱلْقَوْمَ ٱلْكَٰفِرِينَ ۝    and Allah does not guide the faithless lot.

يَٰٓأَيُّهَا ٱلَّذِينَ ءَامَنُوا۟   38   O you who have faith!

مَا لَكُمْ    What is the matter with you

---

[1] The sacred months are Muḥarram, Rajab, Dhū al-Qaʿdah and Dhū al-Ḥijjah.

إِذَا قِيلَ لَكُمُ
    that when you are told:

ٱنفِرُواْ فِى سَبِيلِ ٱللَّهِ
    'Go forth in the way of Allah,'

ٱثَّاقَلْتُمْ إِلَى ٱلْأَرْضِ
    you sink heavily to the ground?

أَرَضِيتُم بِٱلْحَيَوٰةِ ٱلدُّنْيَا
    Are you pleased with the life of this world

مِنَ ٱلْآخِرَةِ
    instead of the Hereafter?

فَمَا مَتَٰعُ ٱلْحَيَوٰةِ ٱلدُّنْيَا
    But the wares of the life of this world

فِى ٱلْآخِرَةِ
    compared with the Hereafter

إِلَّا قَلِيلٌ ۝
    are but insignificant.

إِلَّا تَنفِرُواْ
    39 If you do not go forth,

يُعَذِّبْكُمْ عَذَابًا أَلِيمًا
    He will punish you with a painful punishment,

وَيَسْتَبْدِلْ قَوْمًا غَيْرَكُمْ
    and replace you with another people,

وَلَا تَضُرُّوهُ شَيْئًا
    and you will not hurt Him in any wise,

وَٱللَّهُ عَلَىٰ كُلِّ شَىْءٍ قَدِيرٌ ۝
    and Allah has power over all things.

إِلَّا تَنصُرُوهُ
    40 If you do not help him,[1]

فَقَدْ نَصَرَهُ ٱللَّهُ
    then Allah has already helped him

إِذْ أَخْرَجَهُ ٱلَّذِينَ كَفَرُواْ
    when the faithless expelled him,

ثَانِىَ ٱثْنَيْنِ
    as one of two [refugees],

إِذْ هُمَا فِى ٱلْغَارِ
    when the two of them were in the cave,

إِذْ يَقُولُ لِصَٰحِبِهِ
    he said to his companion,

لَا تَحْزَنْ إِنَّ ٱللَّهَ مَعَنَا
    'Do not grieve; Allah is indeed with us.'

فَأَنزَلَ ٱللَّهُ سَكِينَتَهُ عَلَيْهِ
    Then Allah sent down His composure upon him,

وَأَيَّدَهُ بِجُنُودٍ لَّمْ تَرَوْهَا
    and strengthened him with hosts you did not see,

وَجَعَلَ كَلِمَةَ ٱلَّذِينَ كَفَرُواْ ٱلسُّفْلَىٰ
    and He made the word of the faithless the lowest;

وَكَلِمَةُ ٱللَّهِ هِىَ ٱلْعُلْيَا
    and the word of Allah is the highest;

وَٱللَّهُ عَزِيزٌ حَكِيمٌ ۝
    and Allah is all-mighty, all-wise.

ٱنفِرُواْ خِفَافًا وَثِقَالاً
    41 Go forth, whether [armed] lightly or heavily,

وَجَٰهِدُواْ بِأَمْوَٰلِكُمْ وَأَنفُسِكُمْ
    and wage *jihād* with your possessions and persons

فِى سَبِيلِ ٱللَّهِ
    in the way of Allah.

ذَٰلِكُمْ خَيْرٌ لَّكُمْ إِن كُنتُمْ تَعْلَمُونَ ۝
    That is better for you, should you know.

---

[1] That is, the Prophet (*s*).

لَوْ كَانَ عَرَضًا قَرِيبًا 42 Were it an accessible gain

وَسَفَرًا قَاصِدًا or a short journey,

لَّآتَّبَعُوكَ they would have surely followed *you*;

وَلَٰكِنۢ بَعُدَتْ عَلَيْهِمُ ٱلشُّقَّةُ but the distance seemed too far to them.

وَسَيَحْلِفُونَ بِٱللَّهِ Yet they will swear by Allah:

لَوِ ٱسْتَطَعْنَا 'If we could,

لَخَرَجْنَا مَعَكُمْ surely we would have gone forth with you.'

يُهْلِكُونَ أَنفُسَهُمْ They [merely] destroy themselves.

وَٱللَّهُ يَعْلَمُ إِنَّهُمْ لَكَٰذِبُونَ ۝ Allah knows that they are indeed liars.

عَفَا ٱللَّهُ عَنكَ 43 May Allah excuse *you*!

لِمَ أَذِنتَ لَهُمْ Why did *you* grant them leave [to stay behind]

حَتَّىٰ يَتَبَيَّنَ لَكَ ٱلَّذِينَ صَدَقُوا۟ before those who told the truth were evident to *you*

وَتَعْلَمَ ٱلْكَٰذِبِينَ ۝ and *you* had ascertained the liars?

لَا يَسْتَـْٔذِنُكَ ٱلَّذِينَ 44 Those who believe in Allah and the Last Day

يُؤْمِنُونَ بِٱللَّهِ وَٱلْيَوْمِ ٱلْءَاخِرِ do not ask *you* for leave [exempting them]

أَن يُجَٰهِدُوا۟ بِأَمْوَٰلِهِمْ from waging *jihād* with their possessions

وَأَنفُسِهِمْ and their persons,

وَٱللَّهُ عَلِيمٌۢ بِٱلْمُتَّقِينَ ۝ and Allah knows best the Godwary.

إِنَّمَا يَسْتَـْٔذِنُكَ ٱلَّذِينَ 45 Only those seek a leave [of exemption] from *you*

لَا يُؤْمِنُونَ بِٱللَّهِ وَٱلْيَوْمِ ٱلْءَاخِرِ who do not believe in Allah and the Last Day,

وَٱرْتَابَتْ قُلُوبُهُمْ and whose hearts are in doubt,

فَهُمْ فِى رَيْبِهِمْ يَتَرَدَّدُونَ ۝ ۞ so they waver in their doubt.

وَلَوْ أَرَادُوا۟ ٱلْخُرُوجَ 46 Had they desired to go forth,

لَأَعَدُّوا۟ لَهُۥ عُدَّةً they would have surely made some preparations for it;

وَلَٰكِن كَرِهَ ٱللَّهُ ٱنۢبِعَاثَهُمْ but Allah was averse to arouse them,

فَثَبَّطَهُمْ so He held them back,

وَقِيلَ and it was said [to them],

ٱقْعُدُوا۟ مَعَ ٱلْقَٰعِدِينَ ۝ 'Be seated with those who sit back.'

لَوْ خَرَجُوا۟ فِيكُم 47 Had they gone forth with you,

مَّا زَادُوكُمْ إِلَّا خَبَالًا they would have only added to your troubles,

وَلَأَوْضَعُوا۟    and they would have surely spread rumours

خِلَلَكُمْ    in your midst,

يَبْغُونَكُمُ ٱلْفِتْنَةَ    seeking to cause sedition among you.

وَفِيكُمْ سَمَّٰعُونَ لَهُمْ    They have some spies among you,

وَٱللَّهُ عَلِيمٌۢ بِٱلظَّٰلِمِينَ ۝    and Allah knows best the wrongdoers.

لَقَدِ ٱبْتَغَوُا۟ ٱلْفِتْنَةَ مِن قَبْلُ    48 They certainly sought to cause sedition earlier,

وَقَلَّبُوا۟ لَكَ ٱلْأُمُورَ    and upset the matters for *you*,

حَتَّىٰ جَآءَ ٱلْحَقُّ وَظَهَرَ أَمْرُ ٱللَّهِ    until the truth came and Allah's command prevailed,

وَهُمْ كَٰرِهُونَ ۝    much as they were averse.

وَمِنْهُم مَّن يَقُولُ    49 Among them there are some who say,

ٱئْذَن لِّى وَلَا تَفْتِنِّىٓ    'Give me leave, and do not put me to temptation.'[1]

أَلَا فِى ٱلْفِتْنَةِ سَقَطُوا۟    Look! They have already fallen into temptation[2]

وَإِنَّ جَهَنَّمَ لَمُحِيطَةٌۢ بِٱلْكَٰفِرِينَ ۝    and indeed hell besieges the faithless.

إِن تُصِبْكَ حَسَنَةٌ تَسُؤْهُمْ    50 If some good should befall you, it upsets them;

وَإِن تُصِبْكَ مُصِيبَةٌ    but if an adversity befalls *you*,

يَقُولُوا۟    they say,

قَدْ أَخَذْنَآ أَمْرَنَا مِن قَبْلُ    'We had already taken our precautions in advance,'

وَيَتَوَلَّوا۟ وَّهُمْ فَرِحُونَ ۝    and they go away exulting.

قُل لَّن يُصِيبَنَآ    51 *Say*, 'Nothing will befall us

إِلَّا مَا كَتَبَ ٱللَّهُ لَنَا    except what Allah has ordained for us.

هُوَ مَوْلَىٰنَا    He is our master,

وَعَلَى ٱللَّهِ فَلْيَتَوَكَّلِ ٱلْمُؤْمِنُونَ ۝    and in Allah let all the faithful put their trust.'

قُلْ هَلْ تَرَبَّصُونَ بِنَآ    52 *Say*, 'Do you await anything to befall us

إِلَّآ إِحْدَى ٱلْحُسْنَيَيْنِ    except one of the two excellences?'[3]

وَنَحْنُ نَتَرَبَّصُ بِكُمْ    But we await

أَن يُصِيبَكُمُ ٱللَّهُ    that Allah shall visit on you

---

[1] Or 'do not push me into sinfulness (or unfaith),' or 'do not put me in a predicament." Cf. Ṭabarī and Ṭūsī.

[2] Or 'sinfulness (or unfaith),' or 'a predicament,' based on how the word '*fitnah*' is interpreted in the preceding sentence.

[3] That is, victory or martyrdom.

بِعَذَابٍ مِّنْ عِندِهِۦٓ a punishment, from Him,

أَوْ بِأَيْدِينَا or by our hands.

فَتَرَبَّصُوٓا۟ So wait!

إِنَّا مَعَكُم مُّتَرَبِّصُونَ We too are waiting along with you.'

٥٣ قُلْ أَنفِقُوا۟ طَوْعًا أَوْ كَرْهًا 53 *Say*, 'Spend willingly or unwillingly,

لَّن يُتَقَبَّلَ مِنكُمْ it shall never be accepted from you;

إِنَّكُمْ كُنتُمْ قَوْمًا فَـٰسِقِينَ for you are indeed a transgressing lot.'

٥٤ وَمَا مَنَعَهُمْ أَن تُقْبَلَ مِنْهُمْ نَفَقَـٰتُهُمْ 54 Nothing stops their charities from being accepted

إِلَّآ أَنَّهُمْ كَفَرُوا۟ بِٱللَّهِ except that they have no faith in Allah

وَبِرَسُولِهِۦ and His Apostle

وَلَا يَأْتُونَ ٱلصَّلَوٰةَ إِلَّا وَهُمْ كُسَالَىٰ and do not perform the prayer but lazily,

وَلَا يُنفِقُونَ إِلَّا وَهُمْ كَٰرِهُونَ and do not spend but reluctantly.

٥٥ فَلَا تُعْجِبْكَ أَمْوَٰلُهُمْ وَلَآ أَوْلَـٰدُهُمْ 55 So let not their wealth and children impress *you*:

إِنَّمَا يُرِيدُ ٱللَّهُ لِيُعَذِّبَهُم بِهَا Allah only desires to punish them with these

فِى ٱلْحَيَوٰةِ ٱلدُّنْيَا in the life of this world,

وَتَزْهَقَ أَنفُسُهُمْ وَهُمْ كَٰفِرُونَ and that their souls may depart while they are faithless.

وَيَحْلِفُونَ بِٱللَّهِ إِنَّهُمْ لَمِنكُمْ 56 They swear by Allah that they belong to you,[1]

وَمَا هُم مِّنكُمْ but they do not belong to you.

وَلَـٰكِنَّهُمْ قَوْمٌ يَفْرَقُونَ Rather they are a frightened lot.

٥٧ لَوْ يَجِدُونَ مَلْجَـًٔا أَوْ مَغَـٰرَٰتٍ 57 If they could find a refuge, or a hideout,

أَوْ مُدَّخَلًا or a hole [to creep into],

لَّوَلَّوْا۟ إِلَيْهِ وَهُمْ يَجْمَحُونَ they would turn to it in frantic haste.

وَمِنْهُم مَّن يَلْمِزُكَ 58 There are some of them who blame *you*

فِى ٱلصَّدَقَـٰتِ regarding [the distribution of] the charities:

فَإِنْ أُعْطُوا۟ مِنْهَا رَضُوا۟ if they are given from them, they are pleased,

وَإِن لَّمْ يُعْطَوْا۟ مِنْهَآ but if they are not given from them,

إِذَا هُمْ يَسْخَطُونَ behold, they are displeased.

٥٩ وَلَوْ أَنَّهُمْ رَضُوا۟ 59 [It would have been better] if they had been pleased

مَآ ءَاتَىٰهُمُ ٱللَّهُ وَرَسُولُهُۥ with what Allah and His Apostle gave them,

---

[1] That is, to the faithful.

وَقَالُوا۟
and had said,

حَسۡبُنَا ٱللَّهُ
'Allah is sufficient for us;

سَيُؤۡتِينَا ٱللَّهُ مِن فَضۡلِهِۦ وَرَسُولُهُۥٓ
Allah will give us out of His grace, and His Apostle.

إِنَّآ إِلَى ٱللَّهِ رَٰغِبُونَ ۝
Indeed to Allah do we eagerly turn.'

إِنَّمَا ٱلصَّدَقَٰتُ لِلۡفُقَرَآءِ وَٱلۡمَسَٰكِينِ
60 Charities are only for the poor and the needy,

وَٱلۡعَٰمِلِينَ عَلَيۡهَا
and those employed to collect them,

وَٱلۡمُؤَلَّفَةِ قُلُوبُهُمۡ
and those whose hearts are to be reconciled,

وَفِى ٱلرِّقَابِ وَٱلۡغَٰرِمِينَ
and for [the freedom of] the slaves and the debtors,

وَفِى سَبِيلِ ٱللَّهِ
and in the way of Allah,

وَٱبۡنِ ٱلسَّبِيلِ
and for the traveller.

فَرِيضَةً مِّنَ ٱللَّهِ
[This is] an ordinance from Allah,

وَٱللَّهُ عَلِيمٌ حَكِيمٌ ۝
and Allah is all-knowing, all-wise.

وَمِنۡهُمُ ٱلَّذِينَ يُؤۡذُونَ ٱلنَّبِىَّ
61 Among them are those who torment the Prophet,

وَيَقُولُونَ هُوَ أُذُنٌ
and say, 'He is an ear.'[1]

قُلۡ أُذُنُ خَيۡرٍ لَّكُمۡ
*Say*, 'An ear that is good for you.

يُؤۡمِنُ بِٱللَّهِ وَيُؤۡمِنُ لِلۡمُؤۡمِنِينَ
He has faith in Allah and trusts the faithful,

وَرَحۡمَةٌ لِّلَّذِينَ ءَامَنُوا۟ مِنكُمۡ
and is a mercy for those of you who have faith.'

وَٱلَّذِينَ يُؤۡذُونَ رَسُولَ ٱللَّهِ
As for those who torment the Apostle of Allah,

هُمۡ عَذَابٌ أَلِيمٌ ۝
there is a painful punishment for them.

يَحۡلِفُونَ بِٱللَّهِ لَكُمۡ لِيُرۡضُوكُمۡ
62 They swear to you by Allah, to please you;

وَٱللَّهُ وَرَسُولُهُۥٓ أَحَقُّ
but Allah and His Apostle are worthier

أَن يُرۡضُوهُ
that they should please Him,

إِن كَانُوا۟ مُؤۡمِنِينَ ۝
should they be faithful.

أَلَمۡ يَعۡلَمُوٓا۟ أَنَّهُۥ مَن يُحَادِدِ ٱللَّهَ
63 Do they not know that whoever opposes Allah

وَرَسُولَهُۥ
and His Apostle,

فَأَنَّ لَهُۥ نَارَ جَهَنَّمَ
there awaits him the Fire of hell,

خَٰلِدًا فِيهَا
to remain in it [forever]?

ذَٰلِكَ ٱلۡخِزۡىُ ٱلۡعَظِيمُ ۝
That is the great disgrace.

يَحۡذَرُ ٱلۡمُنَٰفِقُونَ
64 The hypocrites are apprehensive

---

[1] That is, easily persuadable, unquestioning and naive

265

أَن تُنَزَّلَ عَلَيْهِمْ سُورَةٌ     lest a *sūrah* should be sent down against them,

تُنَبِّئُهُم بِمَا فِى قُلُوبِهِمْ     informing them about what is in their hearts.

قُلِ ٱسْتَهْزِءُوٓاْ     *Say,* 'Go on deriding.

إِنَّ ٱللَّهَ مُخْرِجٌ     Allah will indeed disclose

مَّا تَحْذَرُونَ ۝     what you are apprehensive of.'

وَلَئِن سَأَلْتَهُمْ     65 If you question them [regarding their conduct],

لَيَقُولُنَّ     they will surely say,

إِنَّمَا كُنَّا نَخُوضُ وَنَلْعَبُ     'We were just gossiping and amusing ourselves.'

قُلْ أَبِٱللَّهِ وَءَايَٰتِهِ وَرَسُولِهِ     *Say,* 'Were you deriding Allah, His signs,

كُنتُمْ تَسْتَهْزِءُونَ ۝     and His apostles?

لَا تَعْتَذِرُواْ     66 Do not make excuses.

قَدْ كَفَرْتُم بَعْدَ إِيمَٰنِكُمْ     You have disbelieved after your faith.'

إِن نَّعْفُ عَن طَآئِفَةٍ مِّنكُمْ     If We forgive a group among you,

نُعَذِّبْ طَآئِفَةً     We will punish another group,

بِأَنَّهُمْ كَانُواْ مُجْرِمِينَ ۝     for they have been guilty.

ٱلْمُنَٰفِقُونَ وَٱلْمُنَٰفِقَٰتُ     67 The hypocrites, men and women,

بَعْضُهُم مِّنۢ بَعْضٍ     are all alike:

يَأْمُرُونَ بِٱلْمُنكَرِ     they bid what is wrong

وَيَنْهَوْنَ عَنِ ٱلْمَعْرُوفِ     and forbid what is right;

وَيَقْبِضُونَ أَيْدِيَهُمْ     and are tight-fisted.[1]

نَسُواْ ٱللَّهَ     They have forgotten Allah,

فَنَسِيَهُمْ     so He has forgotten them.

إِنَّ ٱلْمُنَٰفِقِينَ هُمُ ٱلْفَٰسِقُونَ ۝     The hypocrites are indeed the transgressors.

وَعَدَ ٱللَّهُ ٱلْمُنَٰفِقِينَ وَٱلْمُنَٰفِقَٰتِ     68 Allah has promised the hypocrites, men and women,

وَٱلْكُفَّارَ     and the faithless,

نَارَ جَهَنَّمَ     the Fire of hell,

خَٰلِدِينَ فِيهَا     to remain in it [forever].

هِىَ حَسْبُهُمْ     That suffices them.

وَلَعَنَهُمُ ٱللَّهُ     Allah has cursed them,

---

[1] That is, they are reluctant to spend in the way of Allah.

وَلَهُمْ عَذَابٌ مُّقِيمٌ ۞ and there is a lasting punishment for them.

كَٱلَّذِينَ 69 [Hypocrites! Your case is] similar to those who were

مِن قَبْلِكُمْ before you,

كَانُوٓاْ أَشَدَّ مِنكُمْ قُوَّةً who were more powerful than you

وَأَكْثَرَ أَمْوَٰلاً وَأَوْلَٰدًا and more abounding in wealth and children:

فَٱسْتَمْتَعُواْ بِخَلَٰقِهِمْ they enjoyed their share [of worldly existence];

فَٱسْتَمْتَعْتُم بِخَلَٰقِكُمْ you too enjoy your share,

كَمَا ٱسْتَمْتَعَ ٱلَّذِينَ مِن قَبْلِكُم just like those who were before you enjoyed

بِخَلَٰقِهِمْ their share,

وَخُضْتُمْ كَٱلَّذِى خَاضُوٓاْ and you have gossiped [impiously] as they gossiped.

أُوْلَٰٓئِكَ حَبِطَتْ أَعْمَٰلُهُمْ فِى ٱلدُّنْيَا They are the ones whose works have failed

وَٱلْءَاخِرَةِ in this world and the Hereafter;

وَأُوْلَٰٓئِكَ هُمُ ٱلْخَٰسِرُونَ ۞ and it is they who are the losers.

أَلَمْ يَأْتِهِمْ 70 Has there not come to them

نَبَأُ ٱلَّذِينَ مِن قَبْلِهِمْ the account of those who were before them

قَوْمِ نُوحٍ وَعَادٍ وَثَمُودَ —the people of Noah, 'Ād, and Thamūd,

وَقَوْمِ إِبْرَٰهِيمَ and the people of Abraham,

وَأَصْحَٰبِ مَدْيَنَ the inhabitants of Midian,

وَٱلْمُؤْتَفِكَٰتِ and the towns that were overturned?[1]

أَتَتْهُمْ رُسُلُهُم بِٱلْبَيِّنَٰتِ Their apostles brought them manifest proofs.

فَمَا كَانَ ٱللَّهُ لِيَظْلِمَهُمْ So it was not Allah who wronged them,

وَلَٰكِن كَانُوٓاْ أَنفُسَهُمْ يَظْلِمُونَ ۞ but it was they who used to wrong themselves.

وَٱلْمُؤْمِنُونَ وَٱلْمُؤْمِنَٰتُ 71 But the faithful, men and women,

بَعْضُهُمْ أَوْلِيَآءُ بَعْضٍ are comrades of one another:

يَأْمُرُونَ بِٱلْمَعْرُوفِ they bid what is right

وَيَنْهَوْنَ عَنِ ٱلْمُنكَرِ and forbid what is wrong

وَيُقِيمُونَ ٱلصَّلَوٰةَ and maintain the prayer,

وَيُؤْتُونَ ٱلزَّكَوٰةَ give the *zakāt*,

وَيُطِيعُونَ ٱللَّهَ وَرَسُولَهُ and obey Allah and His Apostle.

---

[1] That is, the towns of the people of Lot. Cf. 53:53, 69:9.

أُوْلَـٰٓئِكَ سَيَرْحَمُهُمُ ٱللَّهُ
It is they to whom Allah will soon grant His mercy.

إِنَّ ٱللَّهَ عَزِيزٌ حَكِيمٌ ۝
Indeed Allah is all-mighty, all-wise.

وَعَدَ ٱللَّهُ ٱلْمُؤْمِنِينَ وَٱلْمُؤْمِنَٰتِ
72 Allah has promised the faithful, men and women,

جَنَّٰتٍ تَجْرِى مِن تَحْتِهَا ٱلْأَنْهَٰرُ
gardens with streams running in them,

خَٰلِدِينَ فِيهَا
to remain in them [forever],

وَمَسَٰكِنَ طَيِّبَةً فِى جَنَّٰتِ عَدْنٍ
and good dwellings in the Gardens of Eden.[1]

وَرِضْوَٰنٌ مِّنَ ٱللَّهِ أَكْبَرُ
Yet Allah's pleasure is greater [than all these];

ذَٰلِكَ هُوَ ٱلْفَوْزُ ٱلْعَظِيمُ ۝
that is the great success.

يَٰٓأَيُّهَا ٱلنَّبِىُّ
73 O Prophet!

جَٰهِدِ ٱلْكُفَّارَ وَٱلْمُنَٰفِقِينَ
*Wage jihād* against the faithless and the hypocrites,

وَٱغْلُظْ عَلَيْهِمْ
and *be* severe with them.

وَمَأْوَىٰهُمْ جَهَنَّمُ
Their refuge shall be hell,

وَبِئْسَ ٱلْمَصِيرُ ۝
and it is an evil destination.

يَحْلِفُونَ بِٱللَّهِ مَا قَالُوا۟
74 They swear by Allah that they did not say it.

وَلَقَدْ قَالُوا۟ كَلِمَةَ ٱلْكُفْرِ
But they certainly did utter the word of unfaith

وَكَفَرُوا۟ بَعْدَ إِسْلَٰمِهِمْ
and renounced faith after their *islam*.

وَهَمُّوا۟ بِمَا لَمْ يَنَالُوا۟
They contemplated what they could not achieve,

وَمَا نَقَمُوٓا۟ إِلَّآ
and they were vindictive only

أَنْ أَغْنَىٰهُمُ ٱللَّهُ وَرَسُولُهُ
because Allah and His Apostle had enriched them

مِن فَضْلِهِۦ
out of His grace.

فَإِن يَتُوبُوا۟ يَكُ خَيْرًا لَّهُمْ
Yet if they repent, it will be better for them;

وَإِن يَتَوَلَّوْا۟
but if they turn away,

يُعَذِّبْهُمُ ٱللَّهُ عَذَابًا أَلِيمًا
Allah shall punish them with a painful punishment

فِى ٱلدُّنْيَا وَٱلْأَخِرَةِ
in this world and the Hereafter,

وَمَا لَهُمْ فِى ٱلْأَرْضِ
and they shall not find on the earth

مِن وَلِىٍّ وَلَا نَصِيرٍ ۝ ۞
any guardian or helper.

وَمِنْهُم مَّنْ عَٰهَدَ ٱللَّهَ
75 Among them are those who made a pledge with Allah:

لَئِنْ ءَاتَىٰنَا مِن فَضْلِهِۦ
'If He gives us out of His grace,

---

[1] Or 'eternal [or everlasting] gardens.' Cf. 13:23; 16:31; 18:31; 19:61; 20:76; 35:33; 38:50; 40:8; 61:12; 98:8.

لَنَصَّدَّقَنَّ     we will surely give the *zakāt*

وَلَنَكُونَنَّ مِنَ ٱلصَّـٰلِحِينَ ٧٥     and we will surely be among the righteous.'

فَلَمَّآ ءَاتَىٰهُم مِّن فَضْلِهِۦ ٧٦ But when He gave them out of His grace,

بَخِلُوا۟ بِهِۦ     they grudged it

وَتَوَلَّوا۟ وَّهُم مُّعْرِضُونَ ٧٦     and turned away, being disregardful.

فَأَعْقَبَهُمْ نِفَاقًا فِى قُلُوبِهِمْ ٧٧ So He caused hypocrisy to ensue in their hearts

إِلَىٰ يَوْمِ يَلْقَوْنَهُۥ     until the day they will encounter Him,

بِمَآ أَخْلَفُوا۟     because of their going back

ٱللَّهَ مَا وَعَدُوهُ     on what they had promised Allah

وَبِمَا كَانُوا۟ يَكْذِبُونَ ٧٧     and because of the lies they used to tell.

أَلَمْ يَعْلَمُوٓا۟ أَنَّ ٱللَّهَ يَعْلَمُ ٧٨ Do they not know that Allah knows

سِرَّهُمْ وَنَجْوَىٰهُمْ     their secret [thoughts] and [hears] their secret talks,

وَأَنَّ ٱللَّهَ عَلَّـٰمُ ٱلْغُيُوبِ ٧٨     and that Allah is knower of all that is Unseen?

ٱلَّذِينَ يَلْمِزُونَ ٱلْمُطَّوِّعِينَ ٧٩ Those who blame the voluntary donors

مِنَ ٱلْمُؤْمِنِينَ     from among the faithful

فِى ٱلصَّدَقَـٰتِ     concerning the charities—

وَٱلَّذِينَ لَا يَجِدُونَ     and as for those who do not find

إِلَّا جُهْدَهُمْ     [anything] except [what] their means [permit],

فَيَسْخَرُونَ مِنْهُمْ     they ridicule them—

سَخِرَ ٱللَّهُ مِنْهُمْ     Allah shall put them to ridicule,

وَلَهُمْ عَذَابٌ أَلِيمٌ ٧٩     and there is a painful punishment for them.

ٱسْتَغْفِرْ لَهُمْ ٨٠ Whether *you* plead forgiveness for them

أَوْ لَا تَسْتَغْفِرْ لَهُمْ     or do not plead forgiveness for them,

إِن تَسْتَغْفِرْ لَهُمْ     even if *you* plead forgiveness for them

سَبْعِينَ مَرَّةً     seventy times,

فَلَن يَغْفِرَ ٱللَّهُ لَهُمْ     Allah shall never forgive them

ذَٰلِكَ بِأَنَّهُمْ كَفَرُوا۟ بِٱللَّهِ وَرَسُولِهِۦ     because they defied Allah and His Apostle;

وَٱللَّهُ لَا يَهْدِى ٱلْقَوْمَ ٱلْفَـٰسِقِينَ ٨٠     and Allah does not guide the transgressing lot.

فَرِحَ ٱلْمُخَلَّفُونَ ٨١ Those who were left behind[1] exulted

---

[1] That is, those who were kept from participating in *jihād* with the Prophet (ṣ). Cf. verse 46.

بِمَقْعَدِهِمْ    for their sitting back

خِلَٰفَ رَسُولِ ٱللَّهِ    against [the command of] the Apostle of Allah,[1]

وَكَرِهُوٓاْ أَن يُجَٰهِدُواْ    and were reluctant to wage *jihād*

بِأَمْوَٰلِهِمْ وَأَنفُسِهِمْ    with their possessions and persons

فِى سَبِيلِ ٱللَّهِ    in the way of Allah,

وَقَالُواْ لَا تَنفِرُواْ فِى ٱلْحَرِّ    and they said, 'Do not go forth in this heat.'

قُلْ نَارُ جَهَنَّمَ أَشَدُّ حَرًّا    *Say,* The fire of hell is severer in heat,

لَّوْ كَانُواْ يَفْقَهُونَ ۝    should they understand.

فَلْيَضْحَكُواْ قَلِيلًا وَلْيَبْكُواْ كَثِيرًا    82 So let them laugh a little; much will they weep

جَزَآءًۢ بِمَا كَانُواْ يَكْسِبُونَ ۝    as a requital for what they used to earn.

فَإِن رَّجَعَكَ ٱللَّهُ    83 If Allah brings *you* back [from the battlefront]

إِلَىٰ طَآئِفَةٍ مِّنْهُمْ    to a group of them

فَٱسْتَـْٔذَنُوكَ لِلْخُرُوجِ    and they seek *your* permission to go forth,

فَقُل لَّن تَخْرُجُواْ مَعِىَ أَبَدًا    *say,* 'You shall never go forth with me,

وَلَن تُقَٰتِلُواْ مَعِىَ عَدُوًّا    and you shall not fight with me against any enemy.

إِنَّكُمْ رَضِيتُم بِٱلْقُعُودِ أَوَّلَ مَرَّةٍ    You were indeed pleased to sit back the first time,

فَٱقْعُدُواْ مَعَ ٱلْخَٰلِفِينَ ۝    so sit back with those who stay behind.'

وَلَا تُصَلِّ عَلَىٰٓ أَحَدٍ مِّنْهُم مَّاتَ أَبَدًا    84 And never *pray* over any of them when he dies,

وَلَا تَقُمْ عَلَىٰ قَبْرِهِۦٓ    nor *stand* on his graveside.

إِنَّهُمْ كَفَرُواْ بِٱللَّهِ وَرَسُولِهِۦ    They indeed defied Allah and His Apostle

وَمَاتُواْ وَهُمْ فَٰسِقُونَ ۝    and died as transgressors.

وَلَا تُعْجِبْكَ أَمْوَٰلُهُمْ وَأَوْلَٰدُهُمْ    85 Let not their possessions or their children impress *you.*

إِنَّمَا يُرِيدُ ٱللَّهُ أَن يُعَذِّبَهُم بِهَا    Allah only desires to punish them with these

فِى ٱلدُّنْيَا    in this world,

وَتَزْهَقَ أَنفُسُهُمْ    and that their souls may depart

وَهُمْ كَٰفِرُونَ ۝    while they are faithless.

وَإِذَآ أُنزِلَتْ سُورَةٌ    86 When a *sūrah* is sent down

أَنْ ءَامِنُواْ بِٱللَّهِ    [declaring]: 'Have faith in Allah,

وَجَٰهِدُواْ مَعَ رَسُولِهِ    and wage *jihād* along with His Apostle,

---

[1] Or 'for their staying away from [the expedition of] the Apostle of Allah.'

أَسْتَغْذَنَكَ أُوْلُوا الطَّوْلِ مِنْهُمْ     the affluent among them ask *you* for leave,

وَقَالُوا ذَرْنَا نَكُن مَّعَ الْقَاعِدِينَ ۞     and say, 'Let us remain with those who sit back.'

رَضُوا بِأَن يَكُونُوا مَعَ الْخَوَالِفِ     87 They are pleased to be with those who stay back,[1]

وَطُبِعَ عَلَىٰ قُلُوبِهِمْ     and their hearts have been sealed.

فَهُمْ لَا يَفْقَهُونَ ۞     So they do not understand.

لَكِنِ الرَّسُولُ وَالَّذِينَ ءَامَنُوا مَعَهُ     88 But the Apostle and the faithful who are with him

جَهَدُوا بِأَمْوَٰلِهِمْ وَأَنفُسِهِمْ     wage *jihād* with their possessions and persons,

وَأُوْلَٰٓئِكَ لَهُمُ الْخَيْرَٰتُ     and to such belong all the blessings,

وَأُوْلَٰٓئِكَ هُمُ الْمُفْلِحُونَ ۞     and it is they who are the felicitous.

أَعَدَّ اللَّهُ لَهُمْ جَنَّٰتٍ     89 Allah has prepared for them gardens

تَجْرِى مِن تَحْتِهَا الْأَنْهَٰرُ     with streams running in them,

خَٰلِدِينَ فِيهَا     to remain in them [forever].

ذَٰلِكَ الْفَوْزُ الْعَظِيمُ ۞     That is the great success.

وَجَآءَ الْمُعَذِّرُونَ مِنَ الْأَعْرَابِ     90 Some of the Bedouins who sought to be excused came

لِيُؤْذَنَ لَهُمْ     so that they may be granted leave [to stay back];

وَقَعَدَ الَّذِينَ كَذَبُوا اللَّهَ وَرَسُولَهُۥ     while those who lied to Allah and His Apostle sat back.

سَيُصِيبُ الَّذِينَ كَفَرُوا مِنْهُمْ     Soon there shall visit the faithless among them

عَذَابٌ أَلِيمٌ ۞     a painful punishment.

لَّيْسَ عَلَى الضُّعَفَآءِ     91 There is no blame on the weak,

وَلَا عَلَى الْمَرْضَىٰ     nor on the sick,

وَلَا عَلَى الَّذِينَ     nor on those

لَا يَجِدُونَ مَا يُنفِقُونَ حَرَجٌ     who do not find anything to spend,

إِذَا نَصَحُوا لِلَّهِ     so long as they are sincere to Allah

وَرَسُولِهِۦ     and His Apostle.

مَا عَلَى الْمُحْسِنِينَ مِن سَبِيلٍ     There is no [cause for] blaming the virtuous,

وَاللَّهُ غَفُورٌ رَّحِيمٌ ۞     and Allah is all-forgiving, all-merciful.

وَلَا عَلَى الَّذِينَ     92 Nor [is there any blame] on those to whom,

إِذَا مَآ أَتَوْكَ لِتَحْمِلَهُمْ     when they came to *you* to provide them with a mount,

قُلْتَ لَآ أَجِدُ مَآ أَحْمِلُكُمْ عَلَيْهِ     *you* said, 'I do not find any mount for you,'

---

[1] That is, along with women and children, the invalid and the decrepit.

تَوَلَّوا وَّأَعۡيُنُهُمۡ تَفِيضُ مِنَ ٱلدَّمۡعِ حَزَنًا  and they turned back, their eyes flowing with tears, grieved

أَلَّا يَجِدُوا مَا يُنفِقُونَ ۝  because they did not find any means to spend.

[PART 11]

93 إِنَّمَا ٱلسَّبِيلُ عَلَى ٱلَّذِينَ  The blame lies only on those

يَسۡتَـٔۡذِنُونَكَ  who ask leave of *you* [to stay behind]

وَهُمۡ أَغۡنِيَآءُ  though they are well-off.

رَضُوا بِأَن يَكُونُوا مَعَ ٱلۡخَوَالِفِ  They are pleased to be with those who stay back;

وَطَبَعَ ٱللَّهُ عَلَىٰ قُلُوبِهِمۡ  Allah has set a seal on their hearts,

فَهُمۡ لَا يَعۡلَمُونَ ۝  so they do not know [the outcome of their conduct].

94 يَعۡتَذِرُونَ إِلَيۡكُمۡ  They will offer you excuses

إِذَا رَجَعۡتُمۡ إِلَيۡهِمۡ  when you return to them.

قُل لَّا تَعۡتَذِرُوا  *Say,* 'Do not make excuses;

لَن نُّؤۡمِنَ لَكُمۡ  we will never believe you.

قَدۡ نَبَّأَنَا ٱللَّهُ مِنۡ أَخۡبَارِكُمۡ  Allah has informed us of your state of affairs.

وَسَيَرَى ٱللَّهُ عَمَلَكُمۡ وَرَسُولُهُ  Allah and His Apostle will observe your conduct,

ثُمَّ تُرَدُّونَ  then you will be returned

إِلَىٰ عَٰلِمِ ٱلۡغَيۡبِ وَٱلشَّهَٰدَةِ  to the Knower of the sensible and the Unseen,

فَيُنَبِّئُكُم  and He will inform you

بِمَا كُنتُمۡ تَعۡمَلُونَ ۝  concerning what you used to do.

95 سَيَحۡلِفُونَ بِٱللَّهِ لَكُمۡ  They will swear to you by Allah,

إِذَا ٱنقَلَبۡتُمۡ إِلَيۡهِمۡ  when you return to them,

لِتُعۡرِضُوا عَنۡهُمۡ  that you may leave them alone.

فَأَعۡرِضُوا عَنۡهُمۡ  So leave them alone.

إِنَّهُمۡ رِجۡسٌ  They are indeed filth,

وَمَأۡوَىٰهُمۡ جَهَنَّمُ  and their refuge shall be hell,

جَزَآءً بِمَا كَانُوا يَكۡسِبُونَ ۝  a requital for what they used to earn.

96 يَحۡلِفُونَ لَكُمۡ  They swear to you

لِتَرۡضَوۡا عَنۡهُمۡ  that you may be reconciled to them.

فَإِن تَرۡضَوۡا عَنۡهُمۡ  But even if you are reconciled to them

فَإِنَّ ٱللَّهَ لَا يَرْضَىٰ
Allah shall not be reconciled

عَنِ ٱلْقَوْمِ ٱلْفَٰسِقِينَ ٩٧
to the transgressing lot.

ٱلْأَعْرَابُ أَشَدُّ كُفْرًا
97 The Bedouins are more obdurate in unfaith

وَنِفَاقًا
and hypocrisy,

وَأَجْدَرُ أَلَّا يَعْلَمُوا حُدُودَ
and more apt to be ignorant of the precepts

مَآ أَنزَلَ ٱللَّهُ عَلَىٰ رَسُولِهِ
that Allah has sent down to His Apostle,

وَٱللَّهُ عَلِيمٌ حَكِيمٌ ٩٧
and Allah is all-knowing, all-wise.

وَمِنَ ٱلْأَعْرَابِ مَن يَتَّخِذُ
98 Among the Bedouins are those who regard

مَا يُنفِقُ مَغْرَمًا
what they spend as a loss,

وَيَتَرَبَّصُ بِكُمُ ٱلدَّوَآئِرَ
and they watch for a reversal of your fortunes.

عَلَيْهِمْ دَآئِرَةُ ٱلسَّوْءِ
Theirs shall be an adverse turn of fortune,

وَٱللَّهُ سَمِيعٌ عَلِيمٌ ٩٨
and Allah is all-hearing, all-knowing.

وَمِنَ ٱلْأَعْرَابِ
99 Yet among the Bedouins are [also]

مَن يُؤْمِنُ بِٱللَّهِ وَٱلْيَوْمِ ٱلْأَخِرِ
those who believe in Allah and the Last Day,

وَيَتَّخِذُ مَا يُنفِقُ
and regard what they spend

قُرُبَٰتٍ عِندَ ٱللَّهِ
as [a means of attaining] nearness to Allah

وَصَلَوَٰتِ ٱلرَّسُولِ
and the blessings of the Apostle.

أَلَآ إِنَّهَا قُرْبَةٌ لَّهُمْ
Look! It shall indeed bring them nearness,

سَيُدْخِلُهُمُ ٱللَّهُ فِى رَحْمَتِهِ
and Allah will admit them into His mercy.

إِنَّ ٱللَّهَ غَفُورٌ رَّحِيمٌ ٩٩
Indeed Allah is all-forgiving, all-merciful.

وَٱلسَّٰبِقُونَ ٱلْأَوَّلُونَ
100 The early vanguard

مِنَ ٱلْمُهَٰجِرِينَ وَٱلْأَنصَارِ
of the Emigrants and the Helpers

وَٱلَّذِينَ ٱتَّبَعُوهُم بِإِحْسَٰنٍ
and those who followed them in virtue,

رَّضِىَ ٱللَّهُ عَنْهُمْ
—Allah is pleased with them

وَرَضُوا عَنْهُ
and they are pleased with Him,

وَأَعَدَّ لَهُمْ جَنَّٰتٍ
and He has prepared for them gardens

تَجْرِى تَحْتَهَا ٱلْأَنْهَٰرُ
with streams running in them,

خَٰلِدِينَ فِيهَآ أَبَدًا
to remain in them forever.

ذَٰلِكَ ٱلْفَوْزُ ٱلْعَظِيمُ ١٠٠
That is the great success.

101 There are hypocrites among the Bedouins around you

and among the townspeople of Madinah,

steeped in hypocrisy.

You do not know them;

We know them,

and We will punish them twice,

then they shall be consigned to a great punishment.

102 [There are] others who have confessed to their sins,

having mixed up righteous conduct

with other that was evil.

Maybe Allah will accept their repentance.

Indeed Allah is all-forgiving, all-merciful.

103 *Take* charity from their possessions

to cleanse them and purify them thereby,

and bless them.

Indeed *your* blessing is a comfort to them,

and Allah is all-hearing, all-knowing.

104 Do they not know

that it is Allah who accepts the repentance

of His servants

and receives the charities,

and that it is Allah who is the All-clement,

the All-merciful?

105 And *say,* 'Go on working:

Allah will see your conduct,

and His Apostle and the faithful [as well],

and you will be returned

to the Knower of the sensible and the Unseen,

and He will inform you

بِمَا كُنتُمۡ تَعۡمَلُونَ ۝    concerning what you used to do.

وَءَاخَرُونَ مُرۡجَوۡنَ لِأَمۡرِ ٱللَّهِ    106 [There are] others waiting Allah's edict:

إِمَّا يُعَذِّبُهُمۡ    either He shall punish them,

وَإِمَّا يَتُوبُ عَلَيۡهِمۡ    or turn to them clemently,

وَٱللَّهُ عَلِيمٌ حَكِيمٌ ۝    and Allah is all-knowing, all-wise.

وَٱلَّذِينَ ٱتَّخَذُواْ مَسۡجِدًا ضِرَارًا وَكُفۡرًا    107 As for those who took to a mosque for sabotage and for defiance,

وَتَفۡرِيقَۢا بَيۡنَ ٱلۡمُؤۡمِنِينَ    and to cause division among the faithful,

وَإِرۡصَادًا    and for the purpose of ambush

لِّمَنۡ حَارَبَ ٱللَّهَ    [used] by those who have fought Allah

وَرَسُولَهُۥ مِن قَبۡلُ    and His Apostle before

وَلَيَحۡلِفُنَّ    —they will surely swear:

إِنۡ أَرَدۡنَآ إِلَّا ٱلۡحُسۡنَىٰ    'We desired nothing but good,'

وَٱللَّهُ يَشۡهَدُ إِنَّهُمۡ لَكَٰذِبُونَ ۝    and Allah bears witness that they are indeed liars.

لَا تَقُمۡ فِيهِ أَبَدًا    108 *Do not stand* in it ever!

لَّمَسۡجِدٌ أُسِّسَ عَلَى ٱلتَّقۡوَىٰ    A mosque founded on Godwariness

مِنۡ أَوَّلِ يَوۡمٍ    from the [very] first day

أَحَقُّ أَن تَقُومَ فِيهِ    is worthier that *you* stand in it [for prayer].

فِيهِ رِجَالٌ يُحِبُّونَ أَن يَتَطَهَّرُواْ    Therein are men who love to keep pure,

وَٱللَّهُ يُحِبُّ ٱلۡمُطَّهِّرِينَ ۝    and Allah loves those who keep pure.

أَفَمَنۡ أَسَّسَ بُنۡيَٰنَهُۥ    109 Is he who founds his building

عَلَىٰ تَقۡوَىٰ مِنَ ٱللَّهِ    on Godwariness

وَرِضۡوَٰنٍ    and [the pursuit of Allah's] pleasure

خَيۡرٌ    better-off

أَم مَّنۡ أَسَّسَ بُنۡيَٰنَهُۥ    or he who founds his building

عَلَىٰ شَفَا جُرُفٍ هَارٍ    on the brink of a collapsing bank

فَٱنۡهَارَ بِهِۦ فِي نَارِ جَهَنَّمَ    which collapses with him into the fire of hell?

وَٱللَّهُ لَا يَهۡدِي ٱلۡقَوۡمَ ٱلظَّٰلِمِينَ ۝    And Allah does not guide the wrongdoing lot.

لَا يَزَالُ بُنۡيَٰنُهُمُ ٱلَّذِي بَنَوۡاْ    110 The building they have built will never cease

رِيبَةً فِى قُلُوبِهِمْ to be [a source of] disquiet in their hearts

إِلَّا أَن تَقَطَّعَ قُلُوبُهُمْ until their hearts are cut into pieces,

وَٱللَّهُ عَلِيمٌ حَكِيمٌ ۞ and Allah is all-knowing, all-wise.

إِنَّ ٱللَّهَ ٱشْتَرَىٰ مِنَ ٱلْمُؤْمِنِينَ 111 Indeed Allah has bought from the faithful

أَنفُسَهُمْ وَأَمْوَٰلَهُم their souls and their possessions

بِأَنَّ لَهُمُ ٱلْجَنَّةَ for paradise to be theirs:

يُقَٰتِلُونَ فِى سَبِيلِ ٱللَّهِ they fight in the way of Allah,

فَيَقْتُلُونَ وَيُقْتَلُونَ kill, and are killed.

وَعْدًا عَلَيْهِ حَقًّا A promise binding upon Him

فِى ٱلتَّوْرَىٰةِ وَٱلْإِنجِيلِ وَٱلْقُرْءَانِ in the Torah and the Evangel and the Qur'ān.

وَمَنْ أَوْفَىٰ بِعَهْدِهِۦ مِنَ ٱللَّهِ And who is truer to his promise than Allah?

فَٱسْتَبْشِرُوا بِبَيْعِكُمُ ٱلَّذِى بَايَعْتُم بِهِۦ So rejoice in the bargain you have made with Him,

وَذَٰلِكَ هُوَ ٱلْفَوْزُ ٱلْعَظِيمُ ۞ and that is the great success.

ٱلتَّٰٓئِبُونَ ٱلْعَٰبِدُونَ 112 [The faithful are] penitent, devout,

ٱلْحَٰمِدُونَ celebrators of Allah's praise,

ٱلسَّٰٓئِحُونَ wayfarers,[1]

ٱلرَّٰكِعُونَ who bow

ٱلسَّٰجِدُونَ [and] prostrate [in prayer],

ٱلْءَامِرُونَ بِٱلْمَعْرُوفِ bid what is right

وَٱلنَّاهُونَ عَنِ ٱلْمُنكَرِ and forbid what is wrong,

وَٱلْحَٰفِظُونَ لِحُدُودِ ٱللَّهِ and keep Allah's bounds

وَبَشِّرِ ٱلْمُؤْمِنِينَ ۞ —and *give* good news to the faithful.

مَا كَانَ لِلنَّبِىِّ وَٱلَّذِينَ ءَامَنُوٓا 113 The Prophet and the faithful may not

أَن يَسْتَغْفِرُوا لِلْمُشْرِكِينَ plead forgiveness for the polytheists,

وَلَوْ كَانُوٓا أُو۟لِى قُرْبَىٰ even if they should be [their] relatives,

مِنۢ بَعْدِ مَا تَبَيَّنَ لَهُمْ after it has become clear to them

أَنَّهُمْ أَصْحَٰبُ ٱلْجَحِيمِ ۞ that they will be the inmates of hell.

وَمَا كَانَ ٱسْتِغْفَارُ إِبْرَٰهِيمَ لِأَبِيهِ 114 Abraham's pleading forgiveness for his father

---

[1] Or 'those who fast.'

إِلَّا عَن مَّوْعِدَةٍ وَعَدَهَآ إِيَّاهُ
was only to fulfill a promise he had made him.[1]

فَلَمَّا تَبَيَّنَ لَهُۥٓ
So when it became manifest to him

أَنَّهُۥ عَدُوٌّ لِلَّهِ
that he was an enemy of God,

تَبَرَّأَ مِنْهُ
he repudiated him.

إِنَّ إِبْرَٰهِيمَ لَأَوَّٰهٌ
Indeed Abraham was most plaintive

حَلِيمٌ ۝
and forbearing.

وَمَا كَانَ ٱللَّهُ لِيُضِلَّ قَوْمًا
115 Allah does not lead any people astray

بَعْدَ إِذْ هَدَىٰهُمْ
after He has guided them

حَتَّىٰ يُبَيِّنَ لَهُم
until He has made clear to them

مَّا يَتَّقُونَ ۝
what they should beware of.

إِنَّ ٱللَّهَ بِكُلِّ شَىْءٍ عَلِيمٌ ۝
Indeed Allah has knowledge of all things.

إِنَّ ٱللَّهَ لَهُۥ مُلْكُ ٱلسَّمَٰوَٰتِ
116 Indeed to Allah belongs the kingdom of the heavens

وَٱلْأَرْضِ
and the earth.

يُحْىِۦ وَيُمِيتُ
He gives life and brings death.

وَمَا لَكُم مِّن دُونِ ٱللَّهِ
And besides Allah you do not have

مِن وَلِيٍّ وَلَا نَصِيرٍ ۝
any guardian or helper.

لَّقَد تَّابَ ٱللَّهُ عَلَى ٱلنَّبِىِّ
117 Certainly Allah turned clemently to the Prophet

وَٱلْمُهَٰجِرِينَ وَٱلْأَنصَارِ
and the Emigrants and the Helpers,

ٱلَّذِينَ ٱتَّبَعُوهُ فِى سَاعَةِ ٱلْعُسْرَةِ
who followed him in the hour of difficulty,

مِنۢ بَعْدِ مَا كَادَ يَزِيغُ قُلُوبُ فَرِيقٍ مِّنْهُمْ
after the hearts of a part of them were about to swerve.

ثُمَّ تَابَ عَلَيْهِمْ
Then He turned clemently to them

إِنَّهُۥ بِهِمْ رَءُوفٌ رَّحِيمٌ ۝
—indeed He is most kind and merciful to them—

وَعَلَى ٱلثَّلَٰثَةِ ٱلَّذِينَ خُلِّفُوا
118 and to the three who were left behind.

حَتَّىٰٓ إِذَا ضَاقَتْ عَلَيْهِمُ ٱلْأَرْضُ
When the earth became narrow for them

بِمَا رَحُبَتْ
with [all] its expanse,

وَضَاقَتْ عَلَيْهِمْ أَنفُسُهُمْ
and their own souls weighed heavily on them,[2]

---

[1] Cf. 19:47, 60:4.

[2] That is, they were at a complete loss and were oppressed by a feeling of guilt.

وَظَنُّوٓا أَن لَّا مَلْجَأَ مِنَ ٱللَّهِ    and they knew that there was no refuge from Allah

إِلَّآ إِلَيْهِ    except in Him,

ثُمَّ تَابَ عَلَيْهِمْ    then He turned clemently toward them

لِيَتُوبُوٓا    so that they might be penitent.

إِنَّ ٱللَّهَ هُوَ ٱلتَّوَّابُ ٱلرَّحِيمُ ۝    Indeed Allah is the All-clement, the All-merciful.

يَٰٓأَيُّهَا ٱلَّذِينَ ءَامَنُوا    119 O you who have faith!

ٱتَّقُوا ٱللَّهَ وَكُونُوا مَعَ ٱلصَّٰدِقِينَ ۝    Be wary of Allah, and be with the Truthful.

مَا كَانَ لِأَهْلِ ٱلْمَدِينَةِ    120 It is not fitting for the people of Madinah

وَمَنْ حَوْلَهُم مِّنَ ٱلْأَعْرَابِ    and the Bedouins around them

أَن يَتَخَلَّفُوا عَن رَّسُولِ ٱللَّهِ    to hang back behind the Apostle of Allah[1]

وَلَا يَرْغَبُوا بِأَنفُسِهِمْ عَن نَّفْسِهِ    and prefer their own lives to his life.

ذَٰلِكَ بِأَنَّهُمْ لَا يُصِيبُهُمْ ظَمَأٌ    That is because there does experience any thirst,

وَلَا نَصَبٌ وَلَا مَخْمَصَةٌ    nor fatigue, nor hunger,

فِى سَبِيلِ ٱللَّهِ    in the way of Allah,

وَلَا يَطَـُٔونَ مَوْطِئًا يَغِيظُ ٱلْكُفَّارَ    nor do they tread any ground enraging the faithless,

وَلَا يَنَالُونَ مِنْ عَدُوٍّ نَّيْلًا    nor do they gain any ground against an enemy

إِلَّا كُتِبَ لَهُم بِهِ عَمَلٌ صَٰلِحٌ    but a righteous deed is written for them on its account.

إِنَّ ٱللَّهَ لَا يُضِيعُ أَجْرَ ٱلْمُحْسِنِينَ ۝    Indeed Allah does not waste the reward of the virtuous.

وَلَا يُنفِقُونَ نَفَقَةً    121 And neither do they incur any expense,

صَغِيرَةً وَلَا كَبِيرَةً    big or small,

وَلَا يَقْطَعُونَ وَادِيًا    nor do they cross any valley,

إِلَّا كُتِبَ لَهُمْ    but it is written to their account,

لِيَجْزِيَهُمُ ٱللَّهُ    so that Allah may reward them

أَحْسَنَ مَا كَانُوا يَعْمَلُونَ ۝ ❁    by the best of what they used to do.

وَمَا كَانَ ٱلْمُؤْمِنُونَ لِيَنفِرُوا كَآفَّةً    122 Yet it is not for the faithful to go forth en masse.[2]

---

[1] That is, by failing to accompany the Apostle of Allah during his campaigns.

[2] That is, it is not feasible, or reasonable, for all the faithful to set out for Madinah, the Prophet's city, for the study of the religious sciences.

فَلَوْلَا نَفَرَ
But why should not there go forth

مِن كُلِّ فِرْقَةٍ مِّنْهُمْ طَآئِفَةٌ
a group from each of their sections

لِّيَتَفَقَّهُواْ فِى ٱلدِّينِ
to become learned in religion,

وَلِيُنذِرُواْ قَوْمَهُمْ
and to warn their people

إِذَا رَجَعُوٓاْ إِلَيْهِمْ
when they return to them,

لَعَلَّهُمْ يَحْذَرُونَ ۝
so that they may beware?

يَـٰٓأَيُّهَا ٱلَّذِينَ ءَامَنُواْ
123 O you who have faith!

قَـٰتِلُواْ ٱلَّذِينَ يَلُونَكُم مِّنَ ٱلْكُفَّارِ
Fight the faithless who are in your vicinity,

وَلْيَجِدُواْ فِيكُمْ غِلْظَةً
and let them find severity in you,

وَٱعْلَمُوٓاْ أَنَّ ٱللَّهَ مَعَ ٱلْمُتَّقِينَ ۝
and know that Allah is with the Godwary.

وَإِذَا مَآ أُنزِلَتْ سُورَةٌ
124 Whenever a *sūrah* is sent down,

فَمِنْهُم مَّن يَقُولُ
there are some of them[1] who say,

أَيُّكُمْ زَادَتْهُ هَـٰذِهِۦٓ إِيمَـٰنًا
'Which of you did it increase in faith?'

فَأَمَّا ٱلَّذِينَ ءَامَنُواْ
As for those who have faith,

فَزَادَتْهُمْ إِيمَـٰنًا
it increases them in faith,

وَهُمْ يَسْتَبْشِرُونَ ۝
and they rejoice.

وَأَمَّا ٱلَّذِينَ فِى قُلُوبِهِم مَّرَضٌ
125 But as for those in whose heart is a sickness,

فَزَادَتْهُمْ رِجْسًا إِلَىٰ رِجْسِهِمْ
it only adds defilement to their defilement,

وَمَاتُواْ وَهُمْ كَـٰفِرُونَ ۝
and they die while they are faithless.

أَوَلَا يَرَوْنَ أَنَّهُمْ
126 Do they not see that they

يُفْتَنُونَ فِى كُلِّ عَامٍ مَّرَّةً أَوْ مَرَّتَيْنِ
are tried once or twice every year?

ثُمَّ لَا يَتُوبُونَ
Yet they neither repent,

وَلَا هُمْ يَذَّكَّرُونَ ۝
nor do they take admonition.

وَإِذَا مَآ أُنزِلَتْ سُورَةٌ
127 And whenever a *sūrah* is sent down,

نَّظَرَ بَعْضُهُمْ إِلَىٰ بَعْضٍ
they look at one another:

هَلْ يَرَىٰكُم مِّنْ أَحَدٍ
'Is anybody observing you?'

ثُمَّ ٱنصَرَفُواْ
Then they slip away.

---

[1] That is, the hypocrites.

صَرَفَ آللَّهُ قُلُوبَهُم   Allah has turned aside their hearts,

بِأَنَّهُمْ قَوْمٌ لَّا يَفْقَهُونَ ۝   for they are a people who do not understand.

لَقَدْ جَاءَكُمْ رَسُولٌ   128 There has certainly come to you an apostle

مِّنْ أَنفُسِكُمْ   from among yourselves.

عَزِيزٌ عَلَيْهِ مَا عَنِتُّمْ   Grievous to him is your distress;

حَرِيصٌ عَلَيْكُم   he has deep concern for you,

بِالْمُؤْمِنِينَ رَءُوفٌ رَّحِيمٌ ۝   and is most kind and merciful to the faithful.

فَإِن تَوَلَّوْا۟   129 But if they turn their backs [on *you*],

فَقُلْ حَسْبِيَ آللَّهُ   *say,* 'Allah is sufficient for me.

لَآ إِلَٰهَ إِلَّا هُوَ   There is no god except Him.

عَلَيْهِ تَوَكَّلْتُ   In Him I have put my trust

وَهُوَ رَبُّ الْعَرْشِ الْعَظِيمِ ۝   and He is the Lord of the Great Throne.

## سُورَةُ يُونُسَ    10. SŪRAT YŪNUS[1]

بِسْمِ آللَّهِ   In the Name of Allah,

آلرَّحْمَٰنِ آلرَّحِيمِ   the All-beneficent, the All-merciful.

الٓر   1 *Alif, Lām, Rā.*

تِلْكَ ءَايَتُ آلْكِتَٰبِ آلْحَكِيمِ ۝   These are the signs of the Wise[2] Book.

أَكَانَ لِلنَّاسِ عَجَبًا   2 Does it seem odd to these people

أَنْ أَوْحَيْنَآ إِلَىٰ رَجُلٍ   that We have revealed to a man

مِّنْهُمْ   from among themselves,

أَنْ أَنذِرِ آلنَّاسَ   [declaring], 'Warn mankind,

وَبَشِّرِ آلَّذِينَ ءَامَنُوٓا۟   and give good news to the faithful

أَنَّ لَهُمْ قَدَمَ صِدْقٍ عِندَ رَبِّهِمْ   that they are in good standing with their Lord'?

قَالَ آلْكَٰفِرُونَ   The faithless say,

---

[1] 'Yūnus' is the Arabic for 'Jonah,' the prophet whose account appears in this *sūrah*.
[2] Or 'Definitive.'

إِنَّ هَـٰذَا لَسِحْرٌ مُّبِينٌ ۞    'This is indeed a plain magician.'

إِنَّ رَبَّكُمُ ٱللَّهُ    3 Indeed your Lord is Allah,

ٱلَّذِى خَلَقَ ٱلسَّمَـٰوَٰتِ    who created the heavens

وَٱلْأَرْضَ    and the earth

فِى سِتَّةِ أَيَّامٍ    in six days,

ثُمَّ ٱسْتَوَىٰ عَلَى ٱلْعَرْشِ    and then settled on the Throne,

يُدَبِّرُ ٱلْأَمْرَ    directing the command.[1]

مَا مِن شَفِيعٍ إِلَّا مِنۢ بَعْدِ إِذْنِهِ    There is no intercessor, except by His leave.

ذَٰلِكُمُ ٱللَّهُ رَبُّكُمْ فَٱعْبُدُوهُ    That is Allah, your Lord! So worship Him.

أَفَلَا تَذَكَّرُونَ ۞    Will you not then take admonition?

إِلَيْهِ مَرْجِعُكُمْ جَمِيعًا    4 To Him will be the return of you all

وَعْدَ ٱللَّهِ حَقًّا    —[that is] Allah's true promise.

إِنَّهُۥ يَبْدَؤُاْ ٱلْخَلْقَ    Indeed He originates the creation,

ثُمَّ يُعِيدُهُۥ    then He will bring it back

لِيَجْزِىَ ٱلَّذِينَ ءَامَنُواْ    that He may reward those who have faith

وَعَمِلُواْ ٱلصَّـٰلِحَـٰتِ    and do righteous deeds

بِٱلْقِسْطِ    with justice.

وَٱلَّذِينَ كَفَرُواْ    As for the faithless,

لَهُمْ شَرَابٌ مِّنْ حَمِيمٍ    they shall have boiling water for drink,

وَعَذَابٌ أَلِيمٌ    and a painful punishment

بِمَا كَانُواْ يَكْفُرُونَ ۞    because of what they used to defy.

هُوَ ٱلَّذِى جَعَلَ ٱلشَّمْسَ ضِيَآءً    5 It is He who made the sun a radiance

وَٱلْقَمَرَ نُورًا    and the moon a light,

وَقَدَّرَهُۥ مَنَازِلَ    and ordained its phases

لِتَعْلَمُواْ عَدَدَ ٱلسِّنِينَ    that you might know the number of years

وَٱلْحِسَابَ    and the calculation [of time].

مَا خَلَقَ ٱللَّهُ ذَٰلِكَ إِلَّا بِٱلْحَقِّ    Allah did not create all that except with the Truth.

يُفَصِّلُ ٱلْآيَـٰتِ    He elaborates the signs

لِقَوْمٍ يَعْلَمُونَ ۞    for a people who have knowledge.

---

[1] Cf. 32:5, 13:2.

إِنَّ فِى ٱخْتِلَٰفِ ٱلَّيْلِ وَٱلنَّهَارِ    6 Indeed in the alternation of night and day,

وَمَا خَلَقَ ٱللَّهُ فِى ٱلسَّمَٰوَٰتِ    and whatever Allah has created in the heavens

وَٱلْأَرْضِ    and the earth,

لَءَايَٰتٍ لِّقَوْمٍ يَتَّقُونَ ۝    there are surely signs for a people who are Godwary.

إِنَّ ٱلَّذِينَ لَا يَرْجُونَ لِقَآءَنَا    7 Indeed those who do not expect to encounter Us

وَرَضُوا۟ بِٱلْحَيَوٰةِ ٱلدُّنْيَا    and who are pleased with the life of this world

وَٱطْمَأَنُّوا۟ بِهَا    and satisfied with it,

وَٱلَّذِينَ هُمْ عَنْ ءَايَٰتِنَا غَٰفِلُونَ ۝    and those who are oblivious of Our signs

أُو۟لَٰٓئِكَ مَأْوَىٰهُمُ ٱلنَّارُ    8 —it is they whose refuge shall be the Fire

بِمَا كَانُوا۟ يَكْسِبُونَ ۝    because of what they used to earn.

إِنَّ ٱلَّذِينَ ءَامَنُوا۟    9 Indeed those who have faith

وَعَمِلُوا۟ ٱلصَّٰلِحَٰتِ    and do righteous deeds,

يَهْدِيهِمْ رَبُّهُم بِإِيمَٰنِهِمْ    their Lord guides them by the means of their faith.

تَجْرِى مِن تَحْتِهِمُ ٱلْأَنْهَٰرُ    Streams will run for them

فِى جَنَّٰتِ ٱلنَّعِيمِ ۝    in gardens of bliss.

دَعْوَىٰهُمْ فِيهَا    10 Their call therein will be,

سُبْحَٰنَكَ ٱللَّهُمَّ    'O Allah! Immaculate are You!'

وَتَحِيَّتُهُمْ فِيهَا سَلَٰمٌ    and their greeting therein will be, 'Peace!'

وَءَاخِرُ دَعْوَىٰهُمْ    and their concluding call,

أَنِ ٱلْحَمْدُ لِلَّهِ    'All praise belongs to Allah,

رَبِّ ٱلْعَٰلَمِينَ ۝ ✦    the Lord of all the worlds.'

وَلَوْ يُعَجِّلُ ٱللَّهُ لِلنَّاسِ ٱلشَّرَّ    11 Were Allah to hasten ill[1] for mankind

ٱسْتِعْجَالَهُم بِٱلْخَيْرِ    with their haste for good,

لَقُضِىَ إِلَيْهِمْ أَجَلُهُمْ    their term would have been over.

فَنَذَرُ ٱلَّذِينَ لَا يَرْجُونَ    But We leave those who do not expect

لِقَآءَنَا    to encounter Us

فِى طُغْيَٰنِهِمْ يَعْمَهُونَ ۝    bewildered in their rebellion.

وَإِذَا مَسَّ ٱلْإِنسَٰنَ ٱلضُّرُّ    12 When distress befalls man,

دَعَانَا    he supplicates Us,

---

[1] That is, punishment.

لِجَنبِهِ أَوْ قَاعِدًا أَوْ قَآئِمًا [lying] on his side, sitting, or standing;

فَلَمَّا كَشَفْنَا عَنْهُ ضُرَّهُ but when We remove his distress,

مَرَّ كَأَن لَّمْ يَدْعُنَا he passes on as if he had never supplicated Us

إِلَىٰ ضُرٍّ مَّسَّهُ concerning the distress that had befallen him.

كَذَٰلِكَ زُيِّنَ لِلْمُسْرِفِينَ To the profligate is thus presented as decorous

مَا كَانُوا۟ يَعْمَلُونَ ۝ what they have been doing.

وَلَقَدْ أَهْلَكْنَا ٱلْقُرُونَ 13 Certainly We destroyed [several] generations

مِن قَبْلِكُمْ before you

لَمَّا ظَلَمُوا۟ when they perpetrated wrongs:

وَجَآءَتْهُمْ رُسُلُهُم بِٱلْبَيِّنَٰتِ their apostles brought them manifest proofs,

وَمَا كَانُوا۟ لِيُؤْمِنُوا۟ but they would not have faith.

كَذَٰلِكَ نَجْزِى ٱلْقَوْمَ ٱلْمُجْرِمِينَ ۝ Thus do We requite the guilty lot.

ثُمَّ جَعَلْنَٰكُمْ خَلَٰئِفَ فِى ٱلْأَرْضِ 14 Then We made you successors on the earth

مِنۢ بَعْدِهِمْ after them

لِنَنظُرَ كَيْفَ تَعْمَلُونَ ۝ that We may observe how you will act.

وَإِذَا تُتْلَىٰ عَلَيْهِمْ ءَايَاتُنَا بَيِّنَٰتٍ 15 When Our manifest signs are recited to them,

قَالَ ٱلَّذِينَ لَا يَرْجُونَ لِقَآءَنَا those who do not expect to encounter Us say,

ٱئْتِ بِقُرْءَانٍ غَيْرِ هَٰذَآ 'Bring a Qur'ān other than this,

أَوْ بَدِّلْهُ or alter it.'

قُل مَّا يَكُونُ لِىٓ أَنْ أُبَدِّلَهُ Say, 'I may not alter it

مِن تِلْقَآئِ نَفْسِىٓ of my own accord.

إِنْ أَتَّبِعُ إِلَّا مَا يُوحَىٰٓ إِلَىَّ I follow only what is revealed to me.

إِنِّىٓ أَخَافُ إِنْ عَصَيْتُ رَبِّى Indeed should I disobey my Lord, I fear

عَذَابَ يَوْمٍ عَظِيمٍ ۝ the punishment of a tremendous day.

قُل لَّوْ شَآءَ ٱللَّهُ 16 Say, 'Had Allah [so] wished,

مَا تَلَوْتُهُ عَلَيْكُمْ I would not have recited it to you,

وَلَآ أَدْرَىٰكُم بِهِ nor would He have made it known to you,

فَقَدْ لَبِثْتُ فِيكُمْ عُمُرًا مِّن قَبْلِهِ for I have dwelled among you for a lifetime before it.

أَفَلَا تَعْقِلُونَ ۝ Do you not apply reason?'

فَمَنْ أَظْلَمُ مِمَّنِ 17 So who is a greater wrongdoer than him

أَفْتَرَىٰ عَلَى ٱللَّهِ كَذِبًا

who fabricates a lie against Allah,

أَوْ كَذَّبَ بِـَٔايَٰتِهِۦٓ

or denies His signs?

إِنَّهُۥ لَا يُفْلِحُ ٱلْمُجْرِمُونَ ۝

Indeed the guilty will not be felicitous.

وَيَعْبُدُونَ مِن دُونِ ٱللَّهِ

18 They worship besides Allah

مَا لَا يَضُرُّهُمْ

that which neither causes them any harm,

وَلَا يَنفَعُهُمْ

nor brings them any benefit,

وَيَقُولُونَ

and they say,

هَٰٓؤُلَآءِ شُفَعَٰٓؤُنَا عِندَ ٱللَّهِ

'These are our intercessors with Allah.'

قُلْ أَتُنَبِّـُٔونَ ٱللَّهَ

*Say,* 'Will you inform Allah

بِمَا لَا يَعْلَمُ

about something He does not know

فِى ٱلسَّمَٰوَٰتِ وَلَا فِى ٱلْأَرْضِ

in the heavens or on the earth?

سُبْحَٰنَهُۥ وَتَعَٰلَىٰ

Immaculate is He and exalted

عَمَّا يُشْرِكُونَ ۝

above [having] any partners that they ascribe [to Him].

وَمَا كَانَ ٱلنَّاسُ إِلَّآ أُمَّةً وَٰحِدَةً

19 Mankind were but a single [religious] community;

فَٱخْتَلَفُوا۟

then they differed.

وَلَوْلَا كَلِمَةٌ سَبَقَتْ مِن رَّبِّكَ

And were it not for a prior decree of *your* Lord,

لَقُضِىَ بَيْنَهُمْ

decision would have been made between them

فِيمَا فِيهِ يَخْتَلِفُونَ ۝

concerning that about which they differ.

وَيَقُولُونَ

20 They say,

لَوْلَآ أُنزِلَ عَلَيْهِ ءَايَةٌ

'Why has not some sign[1] been sent down to him

مِّن رَّبِّهِۦ

from his Lord?'

فَقُلْ

*Say,* '[The knowledge of]

إِنَّمَا ٱلْغَيْبُ لِلَّهِ

the Unseen belongs only to Allah.

فَٱنتَظِرُوٓا۟

So wait.

إِنِّى مَعَكُم مِّنَ ٱلْمُنتَظِرِينَ ۝

I too am waiting along with you.'

وَإِذَآ أَذَقْنَا ٱلنَّاسَ رَحْمَةً

21 When We let people taste [Our] mercy

مِّنۢ بَعْدِ ضَرَّآءَ مَسَّتْهُمْ

after a distress that has befallen them,

إِذَا لَهُم مَّكْرٌ فِىٓ ءَايَاتِنَا

behold, they scheme against Our signs!

---

[1] That is, miracle.

قُل ٱللَّهُ أَسْرَعُ مَكْرًا

*Say*, 'Allah is more swift at devising.'

إِنَّ رُسُلَنَا يَكْتُبُونَ مَا تَمْكُرُونَ

Indeed Our messengers write down what you scheme.

هُوَ ٱلَّذِى يُسَيِّرُكُمْ فِى ٱلْبَرِّ وَٱلْبَحْرِ

22 It is He who carries you across land and sea.

حَتَّىٰٓ إِذَا كُنتُمْ فِى ٱلْفُلْكِ

When you are in the ships,

وَجَرَيْنَ بِهِم بِرِيحٍ طَيِّبَةٍ

and they sail with them with a favourable wind,

وَفَرِحُواْ بِهَا

rejoicing in it,

جَآءَتْهَا رِيحٌ عَاصِفٌ

there comes upon them a tempestuous wind

وَجَآءَهُمُ ٱلْمَوْجُ مِن كُلِّ مَكَانٍ

and waves assail them from every side,

وَظَنُّوٓاْ أَنَّهُمْ أُحِيطَ بِهِمْ

and they think that they are besieged,

دَعَوُاْ ٱللَّهَ مُخْلِصِينَ لَهُ ٱلدِّينَ

they invoke Allah putting exclusive faith in Him,

لَئِنْ أَنجَيْتَنَا مِنْ هَٰذِهِۦ

'If You deliver us from this,

لَنَكُونَنَّ مِنَ ٱلشَّٰكِرِينَ

we will surely be among the grateful.'

فَلَمَّآ أَنجَىٰهُمْ

23 But when He delivers them,

إِذَا هُمْ يَبْغُونَ فِى ٱلْأَرْضِ

behold, they commit violations on the earth

بِغَيْرِ ٱلْحَقِّ

unduly!

يَٰٓأَيُّهَا ٱلنَّاسُ

O mankind!

إِنَّمَا بَغْيُكُمْ عَلَىٰٓ أَنفُسِكُم

Your violations are only to your own detriment.

مَّتَٰعَ ٱلْحَيَوٰةِ ٱلدُّنْيَا

[These are] the wares of the life of this world;

ثُمَّ إِلَيْنَا مَرْجِعُكُمْ

then to Us will be your return,

فَنُنَبِّئُكُم

whereat We will inform you

بِمَا كُنتُمْ تَعْمَلُونَ

concerning that which you used to do.

إِنَّمَا مَثَلُ ٱلْحَيَوٰةِ ٱلدُّنْيَا كَمَآءٍ

24 The parable of the life of this world is that of water

أَنزَلْنَٰهُ مِنَ ٱلسَّمَآءِ

which We send down from the sky.

فَٱخْتَلَطَ بِهِۦ نَبَاتُ ٱلْأَرْضِ

It mingles with the earth's vegetation

مِمَّا يَأْكُلُ ٱلنَّاسُ وَٱلْأَنْعَٰمُ

from which humans and cattle eat.

حَتَّىٰٓ إِذَآ أَخَذَتِ ٱلْأَرْضُ زُخْرُفَهَا

When the earth puts on its luster

وَٱزَّيَّنَتْ

and is adorned,

وَظَنَّ أَهْلُهَآ أَنَّهُمْ قَٰدِرُونَ عَلَيْهَآ

and its inhabitants think they have power over it,

أَتَىٰهَآ أَمْرُنَا

Our edict comes to it,

لَيْلًا أَوْ نَهَارًا

by night or day,

فَجَعَلْنَٰهَا حَصِيدًا

whereat We turn it into a mown field,

كَأَن لَّمْ تَغْنَ بِٱلْأَمْسِ

as if it did not flourish the day before.

كَذَٰلِكَ نُفَصِّلُ ٱلْءَايَٰتِ

Thus do We elaborate the signs

لِقَوْمٍ يَتَفَكَّرُونَ ٢٤

for a people who reflect.

وَٱللَّهُ يَدْعُوٓاْ إِلَىٰ دَارِ ٱلسَّلَٰمِ

25 Allah invites to the abode of peace,

وَيَهْدِى مَن يَشَآءُ

and He guides whomever He wishes

إِلَىٰ صِرَٰطٍ مُّسْتَقِيمٍ ٢٥

to a straight path.

لِّلَّذِينَ أَحْسَنُواْ ٱلْحُسْنَىٰ

26 Those who are virtuous shall receive the best reward

وَزِيَادَةٌ

and an enhancement.

وَلَا يَرْهَقُ وُجُوهَهُمْ قَتَرٌ وَلَا ذِلَّةٌ

Neither dust nor abasement shall overcast their faces.

أُوْلَٰٓئِكَ أَصْحَٰبُ ٱلْجَنَّةِ

They shall be the inhabitants of paradise,

هُمْ فِيهَا خَٰلِدُونَ ٢٦

and they shall remain in it [forever].

وَٱلَّذِينَ كَسَبُواْ ٱلسَّيِّـَٔاتِ

27 For those who have committed misdeeds,

جَزَآءُ سَيِّئَةٍ بِمِثْلِهَا

the requital of a misdeed shall be its like,

وَتَرْهَقُهُمْ ذِلَّةٌ

and they shall be overcast by abasement.

مَّا لَهُم مِّنَ ٱللَّهِ مِنْ عَاصِمٍ

They shall have no one to protect [them] from Allah.

كَأَنَّمَآ أُغْشِيَتْ وُجُوهُهُمْ

[They will be] as if their faces were covered

قِطَعًا مِّنَ ٱلَّيْلِ مُظْلِمًا

with dark patches of the night.

أُوْلَٰٓئِكَ أَصْحَٰبُ ٱلنَّارِ

They shall be the inmates of the Fire,

هُمْ فِيهَا خَٰلِدُونَ ٢٧

and they shall remain in it [forever].

وَيَوْمَ نَحْشُرُهُمْ جَمِيعًا

28 On the day when We gather them all together,

ثُمَّ نَقُولُ لِلَّذِينَ أَشْرَكُواْ

We shall say to those who ascribe partners [to Allah],

مَكَانَكُمْ

'Stay where you are

أَنتُمْ وَشُرَكَآؤُكُمْ

—you and your partners!'

فَزَيَّلْنَا بَيْنَهُمْ

Then We shall set them apart from one another,

وَقَالَ شُرَكَآؤُهُم

and their partners[1] will say,

مَّا كُنتُمْ إِيَّانَا تَعْبُدُونَ ٢٨

'It was not us that you worshipped.

---

[1] That is, the false gods whom the polytheists associated with Allah.

فَكَفَىٰ بِٱللَّهِ شَهِيدًا بَيْنَنَا وَبَيْنَكُمْ

29 Allah suffices as a witness between you and us.

إِن كُنَّا عَنْ عِبَادَتِكُمْ لَغَٰفِلِينَ

We were indeed unaware of your worship.'

هُنَالِكَ

30 There

تَبْلُواْ كُلُّ نَفْسٍ مَّا أَسْلَفَتْ

every soul will examine what it has sent in advance,

وَرُدُّوٓاْ إِلَى ٱللَّهِ

and they will be returned to Allah,

مَوْلَىٰهُمُ ٱلْحَقِّ

their real master,

وَضَلَّ عَنْهُم مَّا كَانُواْ يَفْتَرُونَ

and what they used to fabricate will forsake them.

قُلْ مَن يَرْزُقُكُم مِّنَ ٱلسَّمَآءِ

31 Say, 'Who provides for you out of the sky

وَٱلْأَرْضِ

and the earth?

أَمَّن يَمْلِكُ ٱلسَّمْعَ وَٱلْأَبْصَٰرَ

Who controls [your] hearing and sight,

وَمَن يُخْرِجُ ٱلْحَىَّ مِنَ ٱلْمَيِّتِ

and who brings forth the living from the dead

وَيُخْرِجُ ٱلْمَيِّتَ مِنَ ٱلْحَىِّ

and brings forth the dead from the living,

وَمَن يُدَبِّرُ ٱلْأَمْرَ

and who directs the command?

فَسَيَقُولُونَ ٱللَّهُ

They will say, 'Allah.'

فَقُلْ أَفَلَا تَتَّقُونَ

Say, 'Will you not then be wary [of Him]?

فَذَٰلِكُمُ ٱللَّهُ رَبُّكُمُ ٱلْحَقُّ

32 That, then, is Allah, your true Lord.

فَمَاذَا بَعْدَ ٱلْحَقِّ إِلَّا ٱلضَّلَٰلُ

So what is there after the truth except error?

فَأَنَّىٰ تُصْرَفُونَ

Then where are you being led away?

كَذَٰلِكَ حَقَّتْ كَلِمَتُ رَبِّكَ

33 Thus the word of *your* Lord became due

عَلَى ٱلَّذِينَ فَسَقُوٓاْ

against those who transgress

أَنَّهُمْ لَا يُؤْمِنُونَ

that they shall not have faith.

قُلْ هَلْ مِن شُرَكَآئِكُم

34 Say, 'Is there anyone among your partners

مَّن يَبْدَؤُاْ ٱلْخَلْقَ ثُمَّ يُعِيدُهُۥ

who originates the creation and then brings it back?'

قُلِ ٱللَّهُ يَبْدَؤُاْ ٱلْخَلْقَ

Say, 'Allah originates the creation,

ثُمَّ يُعِيدُهُۥ

then He will bring it back.'

فَأَنَّىٰ تُؤْفَكُونَ

Then where do you stray?

قُلْ هَلْ مِن شُرَكَآئِكُم

35 Say, 'Is there anyone among your partners

مَّن يَهْدِىٓ إِلَى ٱلْحَقِّ

who may guide to the truth?'

قُلِ ٱللَّهُ يَهْدِى لِلْحَقِّ

Say, 'Allah guides to the truth.

أَفَمَن يَهْدِىٓ إِلَى ٱلْحَقِّ

Is He who guides to the truth

أَحَقُّ أَن يُتَّبَعَ    worthier to be followed,

أَمَّن لَّا يَهِدِّىٓ إِلَّآ أَن يُهْدَىٰ    or he who guides not unless he is [himself] guided?

فَمَا لَكُمْ    What is the matter with you?

كَيْفَ تَحْكُمُونَ ۩    How do you judge?'

وَمَا يَتَّبِعُ أَكْثَرُهُمْ إِلَّا ظَنًّا    36 Most of them just follow conjecture;

إِنَّ ٱلظَّنَّ لَا يُغْنِى مِنَ ٱلْحَقِّ شَيْـًٔا    indeed conjecture is no substitute for the truth.

إِنَّ ٱللَّهَ عَلِيمٌ بِمَا يَفْعَلُونَ ۩    Indeed Allah knows best what they do.

وَمَا كَانَ هَٰذَا ٱلْقُرْءَانُ أَن يُفْتَرَىٰ    37 This Qur'ān could not have been fabricated

مِن دُونِ ٱللَّهِ    by anyone besides Allah;

وَلَٰكِن تَصْدِيقَ ٱلَّذِى    rather it is a confirmation of what was [revealed]

بَيْنَ يَدَيْهِ    before it,

وَتَفْصِيلَ ٱلْكِتَٰبِ    and an elaboration of the Book,

لَا رَيْبَ فِيهِ    there is no doubt in it,

مِن رَّبِّ ٱلْعَٰلَمِينَ ۩    from the Lord of all the worlds.

أَمْ يَقُولُونَ ٱفْتَرَىٰهُ    38 Do they say, 'He has fabricated it?'

قُلْ فَأْتُوا۟ بِسُورَةٍ مِّثْلِهِۦ    *Say*, 'Then bring a *sūrah* like it,

وَٱدْعُوا۟ مَنِ ٱسْتَطَعْتُم    and invoke whomever you can,

مِّن دُونِ ٱللَّهِ    besides Allah,

إِن كُنتُمْ صَٰدِقِينَ ۩    should you be truthful.'

بَلْ كَذَّبُوا۟    39 Rather, they deny

بِمَا لَمْ يُحِيطُوا۟ بِعِلْمِهِۦ    that whose knowledge they do not comprehend,

وَلَمَّا يَأْتِهِمْ تَأْوِيلُهُۥ    and whose explanation has not yet come to them.

كَذَٰلِكَ كَذَّبَ ٱلَّذِينَ مِن قَبْلِهِمْ    Those who were before them denied likewise.

فَٱنظُرْ كَيْفَ كَانَ عَٰقِبَةُ ٱلظَّٰلِمِينَ ۩    So *observe* how was the fate of the wrongdoers!

وَمِنْهُم مَّن يُؤْمِنُ بِهِۦ    40 Some of them believe in it,

وَمِنْهُم مَّن لَّا يُؤْمِنُ بِهِۦ    and some of them do not believe in it,

وَرَبُّكَ أَعْلَمُ بِٱلْمُفْسِدِينَ ۩    and *your* Lord best knows the agents of corruption.

وَإِن كَذَّبُوكَ    41 If they deny *you*,

فَقُل لِّى عَمَلِى    *say*, 'My deeds belong to me

وَلَكُمْ عَمَلُكُمْ    and your deeds belong to you:

أَنتُم بَرِيُّونَ مِمَّا أَعْمَلُ     you are absolved of what I do

وَأَنَا۠ بَرِىٓءٌ مِّمَّا تَعْمَلُونَ ۝     and I am absolved of what you do.'

وَمِنْهُم مَّن يَسْتَمِعُونَ إِلَيْكَ     42 There are some of them who prick up their ears at *you*.

أَفَأَنتَ تُسْمِعُ ٱلصُّمَّ     But can *you* make the deaf hear

وَلَوْ كَانُوا۟ لَا يَعْقِلُونَ ۝     even if they do not apply reason?

وَمِنْهُم مَّن يَنظُرُ إِلَيْكَ     43 And there are some of them who observe *you*.

أَفَأَنتَ تَهْدِى ٱلْعُمْىَ     But can *you* guide the blind

وَلَوْ كَانُوا۟ لَا يُبْصِرُونَ ۝     even if they do not perceive?

إِنَّ ٱللَّهَ لَا يَظْلِمُ ٱلنَّاسَ شَيْـًٔا     44 Indeed Allah does not wrong people in the least;

وَلَـٰكِنَّ ٱلنَّاسَ أَنفُسَهُمْ يَظْلِمُونَ ۝     rather it is people who wrong themselves.

وَيَوْمَ يَحْشُرُهُمْ     45 On the day He will gather them

كَأَن لَّمْ يَلْبَثُوٓا۟     [it will be] as if they had not remained [in the world]

إِلَّا سَاعَةً مِّنَ ٱلنَّهَارِ     except for an hour of the day

يَتَعَارَفُونَ بَيْنَهُمْ     getting acquainted with one another.

قَدْ خَسِرَ ٱلَّذِينَ كَذَّبُوا۟     They are certainly losers who deny

بِلِقَآءِ ٱللَّهِ     the encounter with Allah,

وَمَا كَانُوا۟ مُهْتَدِينَ ۝     and they are not guided.

وَإِمَّا نُرِيَنَّكَ     46 Whether We show *you*

بَعْضَ ٱلَّذِى نَعِدُهُمْ     a part of what We promise them,

أَوْ نَتَوَفَّيَنَّكَ     or take *you* away [before that],

فَإِلَيْنَا مَرْجِعُهُمْ     [in any case] their return will be to Us.

ثُمَّ ٱللَّهُ شَهِيدٌ عَلَىٰ مَا يَفْعَلُونَ ۝     Then Allah will be witness to what they do.

وَلِكُلِّ أُمَّةٍ رَّسُولٌ     47 There is an apostle[1] for every nation;

فَإِذَا جَآءَ رَسُولُهُمْ     so when their apostle comes,

قُضِىَ بَيْنَهُم بِٱلْقِسْطِ     judgement is made between them with justice,

وَهُمْ لَا يُظْلَمُونَ ۝     and they are not wronged.

وَيَقُولُونَ مَتَىٰ هَـٰذَا ٱلْوَعْدُ     48 They say, 'When will this promise be fulfilled,

إِن كُنتُمْ صَـٰدِقِينَ ۝     should you be truthful?'

---

[1] Or 'There is a messenger.'

قُل لَّآ أَمۡلِكُ لِنَفۡسِى ضَرًّا 49 *Say*, 'I have no control over any benefit for myself

وَلَا نَفۡعًا     nor [over] any harm

إِلَّا مَا شَآءَ ٱللَّهُ     except what Allah may wish.

لِكُلِّ أُمَّةٍ أَجَلٌ     There is a time for every nation:

إِذَا جَآءَ أَجَلُهُمۡ     when their time comes,

فَلَا يَسۡتَـٔۡخِرُونَ سَاعَةً     they shall not defer it by a single hour

وَلَا يَسۡتَقۡدِمُونَ ۝     nor shall they advance it.'

قُلۡ أَرَءَيۡتُمۡ إِنۡ أَتَىٰكُمۡ عَذَابُهُۥ 50 *Say*, 'Tell me, should His punishment overtake you

بَيَٰتًا أَوۡ نَهَارًا     by night or day, [you will not be able to avert it];

مَّاذَا يَسۡتَعۡجِلُ مِنۡهُ ٱلۡمُجۡرِمُونَ ۝     so what part of it do the guilty seek to hasten?'

أَثُمَّ إِذَا مَا وَقَعَ ءَامَنتُم بِهِۦٓ 51 'What! Do you believe it when it has befallen?

ءَآلۡـَٰٔنَ     Now?

وَقَدۡ كُنتُم بِهِۦ تَسۡتَعۡجِلُونَ ۝     While you would seek to hasten it [earlier]?!'

ثُمَّ قِيلَ لِلَّذِينَ ظَلَمُوٓا 52 Then it will be said to those who were wrongdoers,

ذُوقُوا عَذَابَ ٱلۡخُلۡدِ     'Taste the everlasting punishment.

هَلۡ تُجۡزَوۡنَ     Shall you be requited

إِلَّا بِمَا كُنتُمۡ تَكۡسِبُونَ ۝ ❊     except for what you used to earn?'

وَيَسۡتَنۢبِـُٔونَكَ أَحَقٌّ هُوَ 53 They inquire of *you*, 'Is it true?'

قُلۡ إِى وَرَبِّىٓ إِنَّهُۥ لَحَقٌّ     *Say*, 'Yes! By my Lord, it is true,

وَمَآ أَنتُم بِمُعۡجِزِينَ ۝     and you cannot thwart [Him].'

وَلَوۡ أَنَّ لِكُلِّ نَفۡسٍ ظَلَمَتۡ 54 Were any soul that has done wrong to possess

مَا فِى ٱلۡأَرۡضِ     whatever there is on the earth,

لَٱفۡتَدَتۡ بِهِۦ     it would surely offer it for ransom.

وَأَسَرُّوا ٱلنَّدَامَةَ     They will hide their remorse

لَمَّا رَأَوُا ٱلۡعَذَابَ     when they sight the punishment;

وَقُضِىَ بَيۡنَهُم     and judgement will be made between them

بِٱلۡقِسۡطِ     with justice

وَهُمۡ لَا يُظۡلَمُونَ ۝     and they will not be wronged.

أَلَآ إِنَّ لِلَّهِ 55 Look! To Allah indeed belongs

مَا فِى ٱلسَّمَٰوَٰتِ وَٱلۡأَرۡضِ     whatever is in the heavens and the earth.

أَلَآ إِنَّ وَعۡدَ ٱللَّهِ حَقٌّ Look! Allah's promise is indeed true;

وَلَٰكِنَّ أَكۡثَرَهُمۡ لَا يَعۡلَمُونَ but most of them do not know.

هُوَ يُحۡىِۦ وَيُمِيتُ 56 It is He who gives life and brings death,

وَإِلَيۡهِ تُرۡجَعُونَ and to Him you shall be brought back.

يَٰٓأَيُّهَا ٱلنَّاسُ 57 O mankind!

قَدۡ جَآءَتۡكُم مَّوۡعِظَةٌ There has certainly come to you an advice

مِّن رَّبِّكُمۡ from your Lord,

وَشِفَآءٌ لِّمَا فِى ٱلصُّدُورِ and a cure for what is in the breasts,

وَهُدًى وَرَحۡمَةٌ لِّلۡمُؤۡمِنِينَ and a guidance and mercy for the faithful.

قُلۡ بِفَضۡلِ ٱللَّهِ وَبِرَحۡمَتِهِۦ 58 Say, 'In Allah's grace and His mercy—

فَبِذَٰلِكَ فَلۡيَفۡرَحُواْ let them rejoice in that!

هُوَ خَيۡرٌ مِّمَّا يَجۡمَعُونَ It is better than what they amass.'

قُلۡ أَرَءَيۡتُم مَّآ أَنزَلَ ٱللَّهُ 59 Say, 'Have you regarded what Allah has sent down

لَكُم مِّن رِّزۡقٍ for you of [His] provision,

فَجَعَلۡتُم مِّنۡهُ حَرَامًا whereupon you made some of it unlawful

وَحَلَٰلًا and [some] lawful?'

قُلۡ ءَآللَّهُ أَذِنَ لَكُمۡ Say, 'Did Allah give you the sanction [to do so],

أَمۡ عَلَى ٱللَّهِ تَفۡتَرُونَ or do you fabricate a lie against Allah?'

وَمَا ظَنُّ ٱلَّذِينَ 60 What is the idea of those

يَفۡتَرُونَ عَلَى ٱللَّهِ ٱلۡكَذِبَ who fabricate lies against Allah [concerning

يَوۡمَ ٱلۡقِيَٰمَةِ their situation] on the Day of Resurrection?

إِنَّ ٱللَّهَ لَذُو فَضۡلٍ عَلَى ٱلنَّاسِ Indeed Allah is gracious to mankind,

وَلَٰكِنَّ أَكۡثَرَهُمۡ لَا يَشۡكُرُونَ but most of them do not give thanks.

وَمَا تَكُونُ فِى شَأۡنٍ 61 You do not engage in any work,

وَمَا تَتۡلُواْ مِنۡهُ مِن قُرۡءَانٍ neither do you recite any part of the Qur'ān,

وَلَا تَعۡمَلُونَ مِنۡ عَمَلٍ nor do you perform any deed

إِلَّا كُنَّا عَلَيۡكُمۡ شُهُودًا without Our being witness over you

إِذۡ تُفِيضُونَ فِيهِ when you are engaged therein.

وَمَا يَعۡزُبُ عَن رَّبِّكَ مِن مِّثۡقَالِ ذَرَّةٍ Not an atom's weight escapes your Lord

فِى ٱلۡأَرۡضِ وَلَا فِى ٱلسَّمَآءِ in the earth or in the sky,

وَلَآ أَصْغَرَ مِن ذَٰلِكَ وَلَآ أَكْبَرَ
nor [is there] anything smaller than that nor bigger,

إِلَّا فِى كِتَـٰبٍ مُّبِينٍ ۝
but it is in a manifest Book.

أَلَآ إِنَّ أَوْلِيَآءَ ٱللَّهِ لَا خَوْفٌ عَلَيْهِمْ
62 Look! The friends of Allah will indeed have no fear

وَلَا هُمْ يَحْزَنُونَ ۝
nor will they grieve.

ٱلَّذِينَ ءَامَنُوا۟
63 —Those who have faith,

وَكَانُوا۟ يَتَّقُونَ ۝
and are Godwary.

لَهُمُ ٱلْبُشْرَىٰ فِى ٱلْحَيَوٰةِ ٱلدُّنْيَا
64 For them is good news in the life of this world

وَفِى ٱلْءَاخِرَةِ
and in the Hereafter.

لَا تَبْدِيلَ لِكَلِمَـٰتِ ٱللَّهِ
(There is no altering the words of Allah.)

ذَٰلِكَ هُوَ ٱلْفَوْزُ ٱلْعَظِيمُ ۝
That is the great success.

وَلَا يَحْزُنكَ قَوْلُهُمْ
65 Do not grieve at their remarks;

إِنَّ ٱلْعِزَّةَ لِلَّهِ جَمِيعًا
indeed all might belongs to Allah;

هُوَ ٱلسَّمِيعُ ٱلْعَلِيمُ ۝
He is the All-hearing, the All-knowing.

أَلَآ
66 Look!

إِنَّ لِلَّهِ مَن فِى ٱلسَّمَـٰوَٰتِ
To Allah indeed belongs whoever is in the heavens

وَمَن فِى ٱلْأَرْضِ
and whoever is on the earth.

وَمَا يَتَّبِعُ ٱلَّذِينَ يَدْعُونَ
And what do they pursue who invoke

مِن دُونِ ٱللَّهِ شُرَكَآءَ
partners besides Allah?

إِن يَتَّبِعُونَ إِلَّا ٱلظَّنَّ
They merely follow conjectures

وَإِنْ هُمْ إِلَّا يَخْرُصُونَ ۝
and they just make surmises.

هُوَ ٱلَّذِى جَعَلَ لَكُمُ ٱلَّيْلَ
67 It is He who made the night for you,

لِتَسْكُنُوا۟ فِيهِ
that you may rest in it,

وَٱلنَّهَارَ مُبْصِرًا
and the day to provide visibility.

إِنَّ فِى ذَٰلِكَ لَءَايَـٰتٍ لِّقَوْمٍ يَسْمَعُونَ ۝
There are indeed signs in that for people who listen.

قَالُوا۟ ٱتَّخَذَ ٱللَّهُ وَلَدًا
68 They say, 'Allah has taken a son!'

سُبْحَـٰنَهُ
Immaculate is He!

هُوَ ٱلْغَنِىُّ
He is the All-sufficient.

لَهُ مَا فِى ٱلسَّمَـٰوَٰتِ
To Him belongs whatever is in the heavens

وَمَا فِى ٱلْأَرْضِ
and whatever is in the earth.

إِنْ عِندَكُم مِّن سُلْطَـٰنٍ بِهَـٰذَآ
You have no authority for this [statement].

أَتَقُولُونَ عَلَى ٱللَّهِ مَا لَا تَعْلَمُونَ ۝ Do you attribute to Allah what you do not know?

قُلْ إِنَّ ٱلَّذِينَ يَفْتَرُونَ 69 *Say*, 'Indeed those who fabricate

عَلَى ٱللَّهِ ٱلْكَذِبَ lies against Allah

لَا يُفْلِحُونَ ۝ will not be felicitous.'

مَتَٰعٌ فِى ٱلدُّنْيَا 70 An enjoyment in this world;

ثُمَّ إِلَيْنَا مَرْجِعُهُمْ then to Us shall be their return,

ثُمَّ نُذِيقُهُمُ ٱلْعَذَابَ ٱلشَّدِيدَ then We shall make them taste the severe punishment

بِمَا كَانُوا۟ يَكْفُرُونَ ۝ because of what they used to defy.

وَٱتْلُ عَلَيْهِمْ نَبَأَ نُوحٍ 71 *Relate* to them the account of Noah

إِذْ قَالَ لِقَوْمِهِ when he said to his people,

يَٰقَوْمِ 'O my people!

إِن كَانَ كَبُرَ عَلَيْكُم مَّقَامِى If my stay [among you] be hard on you

وَتَذْكِيرِى بِـَٔايَٰتِ ٱللَّهِ and [also] my reminding you of Allah's signs,

فَعَلَى ٱللَّهِ تَوَكَّلْتُ [for my part] I have put my trust in Allah.

فَأَجْمِعُوا۟ أَمْرَكُمْ وَشُرَكَاءَكُمْ So conspire together, along with your partners,[1]

ثُمَّ لَا يَكُنْ أَمْرُكُمْ عَلَيْكُمْ غُمَّةً leaving nothing vague in your plan,

ثُمَّ ٱقْضُوا۟ إِلَىَّ then carry it out against me

وَلَا تُنظِرُونِ ۝ without giving me any respite.

فَإِن تَوَلَّيْتُمْ 72 If you turn your back [on me],

فَمَا سَأَلْتُكُم مِّنْ أَجْرٍ I do not ask any reward from you;

إِنْ أَجْرِىَ إِلَّا عَلَى ٱللَّهِ my reward lies only with Allah

وَأُمِرْتُ and I have been commanded

أَنْ أَكُونَ مِنَ ٱلْمُسْلِمِينَ ۝ to be of those who submit [to Allah].'

فَكَذَّبُوهُ 73 But they impugned him.

فَنَجَّيْنَٰهُ وَمَن مَّعَهُ So We delivered him and those who were with him

فِى ٱلْفُلْكِ in the ark

وَجَعَلْنَٰهُمْ خَلَٰئِفَ and We made them the successors,[2]

---

[1] That is, the false deities whom you worship besides Allah.

[2] That is, of those who perished in the Flood, and heirs to all that belonged to them.

and We drowned those who denied Our signs.

So *observe*

how was the fate of those who were warned!

74 Then after him We sent [other] apostles

to their people.

They brought them manifest proofs,

but they would not believe

something they had denied before.

Thus do We seal the hearts of the transgressors.

75 Then, after them, We sent Moses and Aaron

to Pharaoh and his elite

with Our signs,

but they acted arrogantly

and they were a guilty lot.

76 When the truth from Us came to them,

they said, 'This is indeed plain magic!'

77 Moses said, 'Do you say of the truth

when it comes to you [that it is magic]?

Is this magic?

Magicians do not find salvation.'

78 They said, 'Have you come to us

to turn us away

from what we found our fathers following,

so that supremacy may be yours in the land?

We will not believe in the two of you.'[1]

79 Pharaoh said,

'Bring me every expert magician.'

80 So when the magicians came,

---

[1] That is, Moses and Aaron ('a).

قَالَ لَهُم مُّوسَىٰ    Moses said to them,

أَلْقُوا مَآ أَنتُم مُّلْقُونَ ۝    'Throw down what you have to throw.'

فَلَمَّآ أَلْقَوْا    81 So when they threw down [their sticks and ropes],

قَالَ مُوسَىٰ مَا جِئْتُم بِهِ ٱلسِّحْرُ    Moses said, 'What you have produced is magic.

إِنَّ ٱللَّهَ سَيُبْطِلُهُۥٓ    Indeed Allah will bring it to naught presently.

إِنَّ ٱللَّهَ لَا يُصْلِحُ عَمَلَ    Indeed Allah does not ratify the conduct

ٱلْمُفْسِدِينَ ۝    of those who cause corruption.

وَيُحِقُّ ٱللَّهُ ٱلْحَقَّ بِكَلِمَـٰتِهِۦ    82 Allah will confirm the truth with His words,

وَلَوْ كَرِهَ ٱلْمُجْرِمُونَ ۝    though the guilty should be averse.'

فَمَآ ءَامَنَ لِمُوسَىٰٓ    83 But none believed in Moses

إِلَّا ذُرِّيَّةٌ مِّن قَوْمِهِۦ    except some youths from among his people,

عَلَىٰ خَوْفٍ مِّن فِرْعَوْنَ وَمَلَإِيْهِمْ    for the fear of Pharaoh and his elite

أَن يَفْتِنَهُمْ    that he would persecute them.

وَإِنَّ فِرْعَوْنَ لَعَالٍ فِى ٱلْأَرْضِ    For Pharaoh was indeed a tyrant in the land,

وَإِنَّهُۥ لَمِنَ ٱلْمُسْرِفِينَ ۝    and indeed he was an unrestrained [despot].

وَقَالَ مُوسَىٰ يَـٰقَوْمِ    84 And Moses said, 'O my people!

إِن كُنتُمْ ءَامَنتُم بِٱللَّهِ فَعَلَيْهِ تَوَكَّلُوٓا    If you have faith in Allah, put your trust in Him

إِن كُنتُم مُّسْلِمِينَ ۝    if you are among those who submit [to Him].

فَقَالُوا عَلَى ٱللَّهِ تَوَكَّلْنَا    85 Whereat they said, 'In Allah we have put our trust.'

رَبَّنَا    'Our Lord!

لَا تَجْعَلْنَا فِتْنَةً    Do not make us a [means of] test

لِّلْقَوْمِ ٱلظَّـٰلِمِينَ ۝    for the wrongdoing lot,

وَنَجِّنَا بِرَحْمَتِكَ    86 and deliver us by Your mercy

مِنَ ٱلْقَوْمِ ٱلْكَـٰفِرِينَ ۝    from the faithless lot.'

وَأَوْحَيْنَآ إِلَىٰ مُوسَىٰ وَأَخِيهِ    87 We revealed to Moses and his brother

أَن تَبَوَّءَا لِقَوْمِكُمَا بِمِصْرَ بُيُوتًا    [saying], 'Settle your people in the city,[1]

وَٱجْعَلُوا بُيُوتَكُمْ قِبْلَةً    and let your houses face each other,[2]

---

[1] That is, Bayt al-Maqdis, in accordance with a tradition of Imam al-Ṣādiq ('a) (*Tafsīr al-Qummī*). Alternatively, 'Provide houses for your people in Egypt.'

[2] Or 'Make your homes places of worship.'

وَأَقِيمُواْ ٱلصَّلَوٰةَ

and maintain the prayer,

وَبَشِّرِ ٱلْمُؤْمِنِينَ ۝

and give good news to the faithful.'

وَقَالَ مُوسَىٰ 88 Moses said,

رَبَّنَآ

'Our Lord!

إِنَّكَ ءَاتَيْتَ فِرْعَوْنَ وَمَلَأَهُ

You have given Pharaoh and his elite

زِينَةً وَأَمْوَٰلًا فِى ٱلْحَيَوٰةِ ٱلدُّنْيَا

glamour and wealth in the life of this world,

رَبَّنَا

Our Lord,

لِيُضِلُّواْ عَن سَبِيلِكَ

that they may lead [people] astray from Your way!

رَبَّنَا

Our Lord!

ٱطْمِسْ عَلَىٰ أَمْوَٰلِهِمْ

Blot out their wealth

وَٱشْدُدْ عَلَىٰ قُلُوبِهِمْ

and harden their hearts

فَلَا يُؤْمِنُواْ

so that they do not believe

حَتَّىٰ يَرَوُاْ ٱلْعَذَابَ ٱلْأَلِيمَ ۝

until they see the painful punishment.'

قَالَ 89 Said He,

قَدْ أُجِيبَت دَّعْوَتُكُمَا

'Your[1] supplication has already been granted.

فَٱسْتَقِيمَا

So be steadfast,

وَلَا تَتَّبِعَآنِّ

and do not follow

سَبِيلَ ٱلَّذِينَ لَا يَعْلَمُونَ ۝

the way of those who do not know.'

وَجَوَزْنَا بِبَنِىٓ إِسْرَٰٓءِيلَ ٱلْبَحْرَ 90 We carried the Children of Israel across the sea,

فَأَتْبَعَهُمْ فِرْعَوْنُ وَجُنُودُهُ

whereat Pharaoh and his troops pursued them

بَغْيًا وَعَدْوًا

out of defiance and aggression.

حَتَّىٰٓ إِذَآ أَدْرَكَهُ ٱلْغَرَقُ قَالَ

When overtaken by drowning, he called out,

ءَامَنتُ أَنَّهُ لَآ إِلَٰهَ إِلَّا ٱلَّذِىٓ

'I believe that there is no god except Him

ءَامَنَتْ بِهِۦ بَنُوٓاْ إِسْرَٰٓءِيلَ

in whom the Children of Israel believe,

وَأَنَا۠ مِنَ ٱلْمُسْلِمِينَ ۝

and I am one of those who submit [to Him]!'

ءَآلْـَٰٔنَ 91 [He was told,] 'What! Now?

وَقَدْ عَصَيْتَ قَبْلُ

When you have been disobedient heretofore

وَكُنتَ مِنَ ٱلْمُفْسِدِينَ ۝

and were among the agents of corruption?!

فَٱلْيَوْمَ نُنَجِّيكَ بِبَدَنِكَ 92 So today We shall deliver your body

---

[1] That is, of Moses and Aaron (ﷺ).

لِتَكُونَ لِمَنْ خَلْفَكَ ءَايَةً    so that you may be a sign for those who come after you.'

وَإِنَّ كَثِيرًا مِّنَ ٱلنَّاسِ    Indeed many of the people

عَنْ ءَايَتِنَا لَغَفِلُونَ ۝    are oblivious to Our signs.

وَلَقَدْ بَوَّأْنَا بَنِى إِسْرَٰٓءِيلَ 93   Certainly We settled the Children of Israel

مُبَوَّأَ صِدْقٍ    in a worthy settlement

وَرَزَقْنَٰهُم مِّنَ ٱلطَّيِّبَٰتِ    and We provided them with all the good things,

فَمَا ٱخْتَلَفُوا    and they did not differ

حَتَّىٰ جَآءَهُمُ ٱلْعِلْمُ    until [after] the knowledge had come to them.

إِنَّ رَبَّكَ يَقْضِى بَيْنَهُمْ    *Your* Lord will indeed judge between them

يَوْمَ ٱلْقِيَٰمَةِ    on the Day of Resurrection

فِيمَا كَانُوا فِيهِ يَخْتَلِفُونَ ۝    concerning that about which they used to differ.

فَإِن كُنتَ فِى شَكٍّ 94   So if *you* are in doubt

مِّمَّآ أَنزَلْنَآ إِلَيْكَ    about what We have sent down to *you*,

فَسْـَٔلِ ٱلَّذِينَ يَقْرَءُونَ ٱلْكِتَٰبَ    *ask* those who read the Book

مِن قَبْلِكَ    [revealed] before *you*.

لَقَدْ جَآءَكَ ٱلْحَقُّ مِن رَّبِّكَ    The truth has certainly come to *you* from *your* Lord;

فَلَا تَكُونَنَّ مِنَ ٱلْمُمْتَرِينَ ۝    so *do not be* among the skeptics.

وَلَا تَكُونَنَّ مِنَ ٱلَّذِينَ كَذَّبُوا 95   And *do not be* of those who deny

بِـَٔايَٰتِ ٱللَّهِ    the signs of Allah,

فَتَكُونَ مِنَ ٱلْخَٰسِرِينَ ۝    [for] then *you* shall be among the losers.

إِنَّ ٱلَّذِينَ 96   Indeed those

حَقَّتْ عَلَيْهِمْ كَلِمَتُ رَبِّكَ    against whom *your* Lord's judgement has become due

لَا يُؤْمِنُونَ ۝    will not have faith,

وَلَوْ جَآءَتْهُمْ كُلُّ ءَايَةٍ 97   even though every sign were to come to them,

حَتَّىٰ يَرَوُا ٱلْعَذَابَ ٱلْأَلِيمَ ۝    until they sight the painful punishment.

فَلَوْلَا كَانَتْ قَرْيَةٌ ءَامَنَتْ 98   Why has there not been any town that might believe,

فَنَفَعَهَآ إِيمَٰنُهَآ    so that its belief might benefit it,

إِلَّا قَوْمَ يُونُسَ    except the people of Jonah?

لَمَّآ ءَامَنُوا    When they believed,

كَشَفْنَا عَنْهُمْ عَذَابَ ٱلْخِزْيِ We removed from them the punishment of disgrace

فِى ٱلْحَيَوٰةِ ٱلدُّنْيَا in the life of this world,

وَمَتَّعْنَٰهُمْ إِلَىٰ حِينٍ ۝ and We provided for them for a while.

وَلَوْ شَآءَ رَبُّكَ 99 And had *your* Lord wished,

لَءَامَنَ مَن فِى ٱلْأَرْضِ كُلُّهُمْ جَمِيعًا all those who are on earth would have believed.

أَفَأَنتَ تُكْرِهُ ٱلنَّاسَ Would *you* then force people

حَتَّىٰ يَكُونُوا مُؤْمِنِينَ ۝ until they become faithful?

وَمَا كَانَ لِنَفْسٍ أَن تُؤْمِنَ 100 No soul may have faith

إِلَّا بِإِذْنِ ٱللَّهِ except by Allah's leave,

وَيَجْعَلُ ٱلرِّجْسَ and He lays defilement

عَلَى ٱلَّذِينَ لَا يَعْقِلُونَ ۝ on those who do not apply reason.

قُلِ ٱنظُرُوا مَاذَا فِى ٱلسَّمَٰوَٰتِ 101 *Say,* 'Observe what is in the heavens

وَٱلْأَرْضِ and the earth.'

وَمَا تُغْنِى ٱلْءَايَٰتُ وَٱلنُّذُرُ But neither signs nor warnings avail

عَن قَوْمٍ لَّا يُؤْمِنُونَ ۝ a people who have no faith.

فَهَلْ يَنتَظِرُونَ إِلَّا مِثْلَ أَيَّامِ 102 Do they await anything except the like of the days

ٱلَّذِينَ خَلَوْا مِن قَبْلِهِمْ of those who passed away before them?

قُلْ فَٱنتَظِرُوا *Say,* 'Then wait!

إِنِّى مَعَكُم مِّنَ ٱلْمُنتَظِرِينَ ۝ I too am waiting along with you.'

ثُمَّ نُنَجِّى رُسُلَنَا 103 Then We shall deliver Our apostles

وَٱلَّذِينَ ءَامَنُوا and those who have faith.

كَذَٰلِكَ حَقًّا عَلَيْنَا نُنجِ ٱلْمُؤْمِنِينَ ۝ Thus it is a must for Us to deliver the faithful.

قُلْ يَٰٓأَيُّهَا ٱلنَّاسُ 104 *Say,* 'O people!

إِن كُنتُمْ فِى شَكٍّ مِّن دِينِى if you are in doubt about my religion,

فَلَآ أَعْبُدُ ٱلَّذِينَ then [know that] I do not worship those whom

تَعْبُدُونَ مِن دُونِ ٱللَّهِ you worship besides Allah.

وَلَٰكِنْ أَعْبُدُ ٱللَّهَ Rather I worship only Allah,

ٱلَّذِى يَتَوَفَّىٰكُمْ who causes you to die,

وَأُمِرْتُ أَنْ أَكُونَ and I have been commanded to be

مِنَ ٱلْمُؤْمِنِينَ ﴿٤﴾    among the faithful,

وَأَنْ   105   and that:

أَقِمْ وَجْهَكَ لِلدِّينِ    "*Dedicate yourself* to the religion,

حَنِيفًا    as a *ḥanīf,*

وَلَا تَكُونَنَّ مِنَ ٱلْمُشْرِكِينَ ﴿٥﴾    and *never be* one of the polytheists.

وَلَا تَدْعُ مِن دُونِ ٱللَّهِ   106   Nor *invoke* besides Allah

مَا لَا يَنفَعُكَ    that which neither benefits *you*

وَلَا يَضُرُّكَ    nor can do *you* any harm.

فَإِن فَعَلْتَ    For if *you* do so,

فَإِنَّكَ إِذًا مِّنَ ٱلظَّٰلِمِينَ ﴿٦﴾    then *you* will indeed be among the wrongdoers." '

وَإِن يَمْسَسْكَ ٱللَّهُ بِضُرٍّ   107   Should Allah visit you with some distress,

فَلَا كَاشِفَ لَهُۥ إِلَّا هُوَ    there is no one to remove it except Him;

وَإِن يُرِدْكَ بِخَيْرٍ    and should He desire any good for you,

فَلَا رَآدَّ لِفَضْلِهِۦ    none can stand in the way of His grace:

يُصِيبُ بِهِۦ مَن يَشَآءُ مِنْ عِبَادِهِۦ    He grants it to whomever He wishes of His servants,

وَهُوَ ٱلْغَفُورُ ٱلرَّحِيمُ ﴿٧﴾    and He is the All-forgiving, the All-merciful.

قُلْ يَٰٓأَيُّهَا ٱلنَّاسُ   108   *Say,* 'O mankind!

قَدْ جَآءَكُمُ ٱلْحَقُّ مِن رَّبِّكُمْ    The truth has already come to you from your Lord.

فَمَنِ ٱهْتَدَىٰ    Whoever is guided,

فَإِنَّمَا يَهْتَدِى لِنَفْسِهِۦ    is guided only for [the good of] his own soul,

وَمَن ضَلَّ    and whoever goes astray,

فَإِنَّمَا يَضِلُّ عَلَيْهَا    goes astray only to its detriment,

وَمَآ أَنَا۠ عَلَيْكُم بِوَكِيلٍ ﴿٨﴾    and it is not my business to watch over you.'

وَٱتَّبِعْ مَا يُوحَىٰٓ إِلَيْكَ   109   And *follow* that which is revealed to *you*,

وَٱصْبِرْ حَتَّىٰ يَحْكُمَ ٱللَّهُ    and *be patient* until Allah issues [His] judgement,

وَهُوَ خَيْرُ ٱلْحَٰكِمِينَ ﴿٩﴾    and He is the best of judges.

سُورَةُ هُودٍ      # 11. SŪRAT HŪD[1]

بِسْمِ ٱللَّهِ
ٱلرَّحْمَٰنِ ٱلرَّحِيمِ

In the Name of Allah,
the All-beneficent, the All-merciful.

الٓرٓ    1   *Alif, Lām Rā.*

كِتَٰبٌ    [This is] a Book,

أُحْكِمَتْ ءَايَٰتُهُۥ    whose signs have been made definitive[2]

ثُمَّ فُصِّلَتْ    and then elaborated,[3]

مِن لَّدُنْ حَكِيمٍ خَبِيرٍ ۞    from One [who is] all-wise, all-aware,

أَلَّا تَعْبُدُوٓا۟ إِلَّا ٱللَّهَ    2   declaring: 'Worship no one but Allah.

إِنَّنِى لَكُم مِّنْهُ نَذِيرٌ    I am indeed a warner from Him to you

وَبَشِيرٌ ۞    and a bearer of good news.

وَأَنِ ٱسْتَغْفِرُوا۟ رَبَّكُمْ    3   Plead with your Lord for forgiveness,

ثُمَّ تُوبُوٓا۟ إِلَيْهِ    then turn to Him penitently.

يُمَتِّعْكُم مَّتَٰعًا حَسَنًا    He will provide you with a good provision

إِلَىٰٓ أَجَلٍ مُّسَمًّى    for a specified term

وَيُؤْتِ كُلَّ ذِى فَضْلٍ فَضْلَهُۥ    and grant His grace to every meritorious person.

وَإِن تَوَلَّوْا۟    But if you turn your backs [on Him],

فَإِنِّىٓ أَخَافُ عَلَيْكُمْ    indeed I fear for you

عَذَابَ يَوْمٍ كَبِيرٍ ۞    the punishment of a terrible day.

إِلَى ٱللَّهِ مَرْجِعُكُمْ    4   To Allah will be your return,

وَهُوَ عَلَىٰ كُلِّ شَىْءٍ قَدِيرٌ ۞    and He has power over all things.'

أَلَآ إِنَّهُمْ يَثْنُونَ صُدُورَهُمْ    5   Look! They fold up their breasts[4]

لِيَسْتَخْفُوا۟ مِنْهُ    to hide [their secret feelings] from him

---

[1] The *sūrah* is named after Hūd ('a), whose account is given in verses 50-60.

[2] Cf. 3:7.

[3] Or 'articulated.'

[4] 'To fold up one's breast' is an idiomatic phrase, meaning to conceal one's spite within one's heart.

أَلَا حِينَ يَسْتَغْشُونَ ثِيَابَهُمْ

Look! When they draw their cloaks over their heads,[1]

يَعْلَمُ مَا يُسِرُّونَ

He knows whatever they keep secret

وَمَا يُعْلِنُونَ

and whatever they disclose.

إِنَّهُ عَلِيمٌ بِذَاتِ ٱلصُّدُورِ ۞

Indeed He knows best whatever is in the breasts.

[PART 12]

وَمَا مِن دَآبَّةٍ فِى ٱلْأَرْضِ 6

There is no animal on the earth,

إِلَّا عَلَى ٱللَّهِ رِزْقُهَا

but that its sustenance lies with Allah,

وَيَعْلَمُ مُسْتَقَرَّهَا

and He knows its [enduring] abode

وَمُسْتَوْدَعَهَا

and its temporary place of lodging.

كُلٌّ فِى كِتَبٍ مُّبِينٍ ۞

Everything is in a manifest Book.

وَهُوَ ٱلَّذِى خَلَقَ ٱلسَّمَوَتِ 7

It is He who created the heavens

وَٱلْأَرْضَ

and the earth

فِى سِتَّةِ أَيَّامٍ

in six days

وَكَانَ عَرْشُهُ عَلَى ٱلْمَآءِ

—and His Throne was [then] upon the waters—

لِيَبْلُوَكُمْ

that He may test you [to see]

أَيُّكُمْ أَحْسَنُ عَمَلًا

which of you is best in conduct.

وَلَئِن قُلْتَ

Yet if *you* say,

إِنَّكُم مَّبْعُوثُونَ

'You will indeed be raised up

مِنۢ بَعْدِ ٱلْمَوْتِ

after death,'

لَيَقُولَنَّ ٱلَّذِينَ كَفَرُوٓا۟

the faithless will surely say,

إِنْ هَذَآ إِلَّا سِحْرٌ مُّبِينٌ ۞

'This is nothing but plain magic.'

وَلَئِنْ أَخَّرْنَا عَنْهُمُ ٱلْعَذَابَ 8

And if We defer their punishment

إِلَىٰٓ أُمَّةٍ مَّعْدُودَةٍ

until a certain time,

لَّيَقُولُنَّ مَا يَحْبِسُهُ

they will surely say, 'What holds it back?'

أَلَا يَوْمَ يَأْتِيهِمْ

Look! On the day it overtakes them

لَيْسَ مَصْرُوفًا عَنْهُمْ

it shall not be turned away from them,

وَحَاقَ بِهِم

and they will be besieged

مَّا كَانُوا۟ بِهِۦ يَسْتَهْزِءُونَ ۞

by what they used to deride.

وَلَئِنْ أَذَقْنَا ٱلْإِنسَنَ مِنَّا رَحْمَةً 9

If We let man taste a mercy from Us,

---

[1] So that they may not be recognized. Cf. 71:7.

ثُمَّ نَزَعْنَهَا مِنْهُ    and then withdraw it from him,

إِنَّهُ لَيَؤُوسٌ كَفُورٌ ۞    he becomes despondent, ungrateful.

وَلَئِنْ أَذَقْنَهُ نَعْمَآءَ    10 And if We let him have a taste of Our blessings

بَعْدَ ضَرَّآءَ مَسَّتْهُ    after adversities have befallen him,

لَيَقُولَنَّ    he will surely say,

ذَهَبَ ٱلسَّيِّئَاتُ عَنِّي    'All ills have left me.'

إِنَّهُ لَفَرِحٌ فَخُورٌ ۞    Indeed he becomes an exultant braggart,

إِلَّا ٱلَّذِينَ صَبَرُوا    11 excepting those who are patient

وَعَمِلُوا ٱلصَّٰلِحَٰتِ    and do righteous deeds.

أُوْلَٰٓئِكَ لَهُم مَّغْفِرَةٌ    For such there will be forgiveness

وَأَجْرٌ كَبِيرٌ ۞    and a great reward.

فَلَعَلَّكَ تَارِكٌ    12 [Look out] lest *you* should disregard

بَعْضَ مَا يُوحَىٰٓ إِلَيْكَ    aught of what has been revealed to *you*,

وَضَآئِقٌ بِهِۦ صَدْرُكَ أَن يَقُولُوا    and be upset because they say,

لَوْلَآ أُنزِلَ عَلَيْهِ كَنزٌ    'Why has not a treasure been sent down to him,

أَوْ جَآءَ مَعَهُۥ مَلَكٌ    or [why does] not an angel accompany him?'

إِنَّمَآ أَنتَ نَذِيرٌ    *You* are only a warner,

وَٱللَّهُ عَلَىٰ كُلِّ شَىْءٍ وَكِيلٌ ۞    and Allah watches over all things.

أَمْ يَقُولُونَ ٱفْتَرَىٰهُ    13 Do they say, 'He has fabricated it?'

قُلْ فَأْتُوا بِعَشْرِ سُوَرٍ مِّثْلِهِۦ    *Say*, 'Then bring ten *sūrah*s like it,

مُفْتَرَيَٰتٍ    fabricated,

وَٱدْعُوا مَنِ ٱسْتَطَعْتُم مِّن دُونِ ٱللَّهِ    and invoke whomever you can, besides Allah,

إِن كُنتُمْ صَٰدِقِينَ ۞    should you be truthful.'

فَإِلَّمْ يَسْتَجِيبُوا لَكُمْ    14 But if they do not respond to you,

فَٱعْلَمُوٓا أَنَّمَآ أُنزِلَ    know that it has been sent down

بِعِلْمِ ٱللَّهِ    by Allah's knowledge,

وَأَن لَّآ إِلَٰهَ إِلَّا هُوَ    and that there is no god except Him.

فَهَلْ أَنتُم مُّسْلِمُونَ ۞    Will you, then, submit [to Allah]?

مَن كَانَ يُرِيدُ ٱلْحَيَوٰةَ ٱلدُّنْيَا    15 As for those who desire the life of this world

وَزِينَتَهَا    and its glitter,

نُوَفِّ إِلَيْهِمْ أَعْمَٰلَهُمْ فِيهَا
We will recompense them fully for their works therein,

وَهُمْ فِيهَا لَا يُبْخَسُونَ ۝
and they shall not be underpaid in it.

أُوْلَٰٓئِكَ ٱلَّذِينَ لَيْسَ لَهُمْ
16 They are the ones for whom there shall be nothing

فِى ٱلْأَخِرَةِ
in the Hereafter

إِلَّا ٱلنَّارُ
but Fire:

وَحَبِطَ مَا صَنَعُواْ فِيهَا
what they had accomplished in the world has failed,

وَبَٰطِلٌ مَّا كَانُواْ يَعْمَلُونَ ۝
and their works have come to naught.

أَفَمَن كَانَ عَلَىٰ بَيِّنَةٍ مِّن رَّبِّهِۦ
17 Is he who stands on a manifest proof from his Lord,

وَيَتْلُوهُ شَاهِدٌ مِّنْهُ
and whom a witness of his own [family] follows?[1]

وَمِن قَبْلِهِۦ كِتَٰبُ مُوسَىٰٓ
And before him[2] there was the Book of Moses,

إِمَامًا وَرَحْمَةً
a guide and mercy.

أُوْلَٰٓئِكَ يُؤْمِنُونَ بِهِۦ
It is they who have faith in it,

وَمَن يَكْفُرْ بِهِۦ مِنَ ٱلْأَحْزَابِ
and whoever defies him from among the factions,

فَٱلنَّارُ مَوْعِدُهُۥ
the Fire is their tryst.

فَلَا تَكُ فِى مِرْيَةٍ مِّنْهُ
So *do not be* in doubt about it;

إِنَّهُ ٱلْحَقُّ مِن رَّبِّكَ
it is the truth from *your* Lord,

وَلَٰكِنَّ أَكْثَرَ ٱلنَّاسِ لَا يُؤْمِنُونَ ۝
but most people do not have faith.

وَمَنْ أَظْلَمُ مِمَّنِ
18 And who is a greater wrongdoer than him

ٱفْتَرَىٰ عَلَى ٱللَّهِ كَذِبًا
who fabricates a lie against Allah?

أُوْلَٰٓئِكَ يُعْرَضُونَ عَلَىٰ رَبِّهِمْ
They shall be presented before their Lord,

وَيَقُولُ ٱلْأَشْهَٰدُ
and the witnesses will say,

هَٰٓؤُلَآءِ ٱلَّذِينَ كَذَبُواْ عَلَىٰ رَبِّهِمْ
'It is these who lied against their Lord.'

أَلَا لَعْنَةُ ٱللَّهِ عَلَى ٱلظَّٰلِمِينَ ۝
Look! The curse of Allah is upon the wrongdoers

ٱلَّذِينَ يَصُدُّونَ عَن سَبِيلِ ٱللَّهِ
19 —those who bar [others] from the way of Allah,

وَيَبْغُونَهَا عِوَجًا
and seek to make it crooked,

وَهُم بِٱلْأَخِرَةِ هُمْ كَٰفِرُونَ ۝
and disbelieve in the Hereafter.

أُوْلَٰٓئِكَ لَمْ يَكُونُواْ مُعْجِزِينَ
20 They cannot thwart [Allah]

---

[1] Ellipsis. That is, is such a person like someone who is not such? Or, can such one be deterred by the denial of the ignorant?

[2] Or 'before it,' that is, the Qur'ān.

فِى ٱلْأَرْضِ    on the earth,

وَمَا كَانَ لَهُم مِّن دُونِ ٱللَّهِ    nor do they have besides Allah

مِنْ أَوْلِيَآءَ    any guardian.

يُضَٰعَفُ لَهُمُ ٱلْعَذَابُ    For them the punishment shall be doubled,

مَا كَانُوا۟ يَسْتَطِيعُونَ ٱلسَّمْعَ    for they could neither listen,

وَمَا كَانُوا۟ يُبْصِرُونَ ٢٠    nor did they use to see.

أُو۟لَٰٓئِكَ ٱلَّذِينَ خَسِرُوٓا۟ أَنفُسَهُمْ    21 They are the ones who have ruined their souls,

وَضَلَّ عَنْهُم مَّا كَانُوا۟ يَفْتَرُونَ ٢١    and what they used to fabricate has forsaken them.

لَا جَرَمَ أَنَّهُمْ    22 Undoubtedly, they are the ones

فِى ٱلْءَاخِرَةِ هُمُ ٱلْأَخْسَرُونَ ٢٢    who will be the biggest losers in the Hereafter.

إِنَّ ٱلَّذِينَ ءَامَنُوا۟    23 Indeed those who have faith

وَعَمِلُوا۟ ٱلصَّٰلِحَٰتِ    and do righteous deeds

وَأَخْبَتُوٓا۟ إِلَىٰ رَبِّهِمْ    and are humble before their Lord

أُو۟لَٰٓئِكَ أَصْحَٰبُ ٱلْجَنَّةِ    —they shall be the inhabitants of paradise,

هُمْ فِيهَا خَٰلِدُونَ ٢٣ ۞    and they shall remain in it [forever].

مَثَلُ ٱلْفَرِيقَيْنِ    24 The parable of the two parties

كَٱلْأَعْمَىٰ وَٱلْأَصَمِّ    is that of one who is blind and deaf

وَٱلْبَصِيرِ وَٱلسَّمِيعِ    and one who sees and hears.

هَلْ يَسْتَوِيَانِ مَثَلًا    Are they equal in comparison?

أَفَلَا تَذَكَّرُونَ ٢٤    Will you not then take admonition?

وَلَقَدْ أَرْسَلْنَا نُوحًا إِلَىٰ قَوْمِهِۦٓ    25 Certainly We sent Noah to his people [to declare]:

إِنِّى لَكُمْ نَذِيرٌ مُّبِينٌ ٢٥    'Indeed I am a manifest warner to you,

أَن لَّا تَعْبُدُوٓا۟ إِلَّا ٱللَّهَ    26 Worship none but Allah.

إِنِّىٓ أَخَافُ عَلَيْكُمْ عَذَابَ    Indeed I fear for you the punishment

يَوْمٍ أَلِيمٍ ٢٦    of a painful day.'

فَقَالَ ٱلْمَلَأُ ٱلَّذِينَ كَفَرُوا۟ مِن قَوْمِهِۦ    27 But the elite of the faithless from among his people said,

مَا نَرَىٰكَ    'We do not see you to be

إِلَّا بَشَرًا مِّثْلَنَا    anything but a human being like ourselves,

وَمَا نَرَىٰكَ ٱتَّبَعَكَ    and we do not see anyone following you

إِلَّا ٱلَّذِينَ هُمۡ    except those who are

أَرَاذِلُنَا بَادِيَ ٱلرَّأۡيِ    simpleminded riffraff from our midst.

وَمَا نَرَىٰ لَكُمۡ عَلَيۡنَا مِن فَضۡلِۭ    Nor do we see that you have any merit over us.

بَلۡ نَظُنُّكُمۡ كَٰذِبِينَ ٢٧    Rather we consider you to be liars.'

قَالَ يَٰقَوۡمِ أَرَءَيۡتُمۡ    28 He said, 'O my people! Tell me,

إِن كُنتُ عَلَىٰ بَيِّنَةٖ مِّن رَّبِّي    should I stand on a manifest proof from my Lord,

وَءَاتَىٰنِي رَحۡمَةٗ مِّنۡ عِندِهِۦ    and He has granted me His own mercy

فَعُمِّيَتۡ عَلَيۡكُمۡ    —though it should be invisible to you—

أَنُلۡزِمُكُمُوهَا    shall we force it upon you

وَأَنتُمۡ لَهَا كَٰرِهُونَ ٢٨    while you are averse to it?

وَيَٰقَوۡمِ    29 O my people!

لَآ أَسۡـَٔلُكُمۡ عَلَيۡهِ مَالًا    I do not ask you any material reward for it.

إِنۡ أَجۡرِيَ إِلَّا عَلَى ٱللَّهِ    My reward lies only with Allah.

وَمَآ أَنَا۠ بِطَارِدِ ٱلَّذِينَ ءَامَنُوٓاْ    But I will not drive away those who have faith.

إِنَّهُم مُّلَٰقُواْ رَبِّهِمۡ    Indeed they will encounter their Lord.

وَلَٰكِنِّيٓ أَرَىٰكُمۡ قَوۡمٗا تَجۡهَلُونَ ٢٩    But I see that you are an ignorant lot.

وَيَٰقَوۡمِ    30 O my people!

مَن يَنصُرُنِي مِنَ ٱللَّهِ    Who would come to my help against Allah

إِن طَرَدتُّهُمۡ    were I to drive them away?

أَفَلَا تَذَكَّرُونَ ٣٠    Will you not then take admonition?

وَلَآ أَقُولُ لَكُمۡ    31 I do not say to you

عِندِي خَزَآئِنُ ٱللَّهِ    that I possess the treasuries of Allah,

وَلَآ أَعۡلَمُ ٱلۡغَيۡبَ    neither do I know the Unseen.

وَلَآ أَقُولُ إِنِّي مَلَكٞ    I do not claim to be an angel,

وَلَآ أَقُولُ    neither do I say

لِلَّذِينَ تَزۡدَرِيٓ أَعۡيُنُكُمۡ    of those who are despicable in your eyes

لَن يُؤۡتِيَهُمُ ٱللَّهُ خَيۡرًا    that Allah will not grant them any good

ٱللَّهُ أَعۡلَمُ بِمَا فِيٓ أَنفُسِهِمۡ    —Allah knows best what is in their hearts—

إِنِّيٓ إِذٗا لَّمِنَ ٱلظَّٰلِمِينَ ٣١    for then I would indeed be a wrongdoer.'

قَالُواْ يَٰنُوحُ    32 They said, 'O Noah,

305

قَدْ جَـٰدَلْتَنَا
you have disputed with us already,

فَأَكْثَرْتَ جِدَٰلَنَا
and you have disputed with us exceedingly.

فَأْتِنَا بِمَا تَعِدُنَآ
Now bring us what you threaten us with

إِن كُنتَ مِنَ ٱلصَّـٰدِقِينَ ٣٢
should you be truthful.

قَالَ إِنَّمَا يَأْتِيكُم بِهِ ٱللَّهُ
33 He said, 'Allah will indeed bring it on you

إِن شَآءَ
if He wishes,

وَمَآ أَنتُم بِمُعْجِزِينَ ٣٣
and you cannot thwart [Him].

وَلَا يَنفَعُكُمْ نُصْحِىٓ
34 My exhorting will not benefit you,

إِنْ أَرَدتُّ أَنْ أَنصَحَ لَكُمْ
much as I may seek to exhort you,

إِن كَانَ ٱللَّهُ يُرِيدُ أَن يُغْوِيَكُمْ
if Allah desires to consign you to perversity.

هُوَ رَبُّكُمْ
He is your Lord,

وَإِلَيْهِ تُرْجَعُونَ ٣٤
and to Him you shall be brought back.'

أَمْ يَقُولُونَ ٱفْتَرَىٰهُ
35 Do they say, 'He has fabricated it?'

قُلْ إِنِ ٱفْتَرَيْتُهُۥ
Say, 'Should I have fabricated it,

فَعَلَىَّ إِجْرَامِى
then my guilt will be upon me,

وَأَنَا۠ بَرِىٓءٌ مِّمَّا تُجْرِمُونَ ٣٥
and I am absolved of your guilty conduct.'

وَأُوحِىَ إِلَىٰ نُوحٍ
36 It was revealed to Noah:

أَنَّهُۥ لَن يُؤْمِنَ مِن قَوْمِكَ
'None of your people will believe

إِلَّا مَن قَدْ ءَامَنَ
except those who already have faith;

فَلَا تَبْتَئِسْ بِمَا كَانُوا۟ يَفْعَلُونَ ٣٦
so do not sorrow for what they used to do.

وَٱصْنَعِ ٱلْفُلْكَ بِأَعْيُنِنَا
37 Build the ark before Our eyes

وَوَحْيِنَا
and by Our revelation,

وَلَا تُخَـٰطِبْنِى
and do not plead with Me

فِى ٱلَّذِينَ ظَلَمُوٓا۟
for those who are wrongdoers:

إِنَّهُم مُّغْرَقُونَ ٣٧
they shall indeed be drowned.'

وَيَصْنَعُ ٱلْفُلْكَ
38 As he was building the ark,

وَكُلَّمَا مَرَّ عَلَيْهِ مَلَأٌ مِّن قَوْمِهِۦ
whenever the elders of his people passed by him,

سَخِرُوا۟ مِنْهُ
they would ridicule him.

قَالَ إِن تَسْخَرُواْ مِنَّا

He said, 'If you ridicule us [today],

فَإِنَّا نَسْخَرُ مِنكُمْ

we shall ridicule you [tomorrow]

كَمَا تَسْخَرُونَ ۝

just as you ridicule us [now].

فَسَوْفَ تَعْلَمُونَ 39

39 Soon you will know

مَن يَأْتِيهِ عَذَابٌ يُخْزِيهِ

whom a disgraceful punishment will overtake

وَيَحِلُّ عَلَيْهِ عَذَابٌ مُّقِيمٌ ۝

and on whom a lasting punishment will descend.'

حَتَّىٰ إِذَا جَآءَ أَمْرُنَا 40

40 When Our edict came

وَفَارَ ٱلتَّنُّورُ

and the oven gushed [a stream of water],

قُلْنَا ٱحْمِلْ فِيهَا

We said, 'Carry in it

مِن كُلٍّ زَوْجَيْنِ ٱثْنَيْنِ

a pair[1] of every kind [of animal],

وَأَهْلَكَ

along with your family

إِلَّا مَن

—except those [of them]

سَبَقَ عَلَيْهِ ٱلْقَوْلُ

against whom the edict has already been given—

وَمَنْ ءَامَنَ

and those who have faith.'

وَمَآ ءَامَنَ مَعَهُۥٓ إِلَّا قَلِيلٌ ۝

And none believed with him except a few.

وَقَالَ ٱرْكَبُواْ فِيهَا 41

41 He said, 'Board it:

بِسْمِ ٱللَّهِ مَجْرٜىٰهَا وَمُرْسَىٰهَآ

In the Name of Allah it shall set sail and cast anchor.

إِنَّ رَبِّى لَغَفُورٌ رَّحِيمٌ ۝

Indeed my Lord is all-forgiving, all-merciful.'

وَهِىَ تَجْرِى بِهِمْ فِى مَوْجٍ 42

42 And it sailed along with them amid waves

كَٱلْجِبَالِ

[rising] like mountains.

وَنَادَىٰ نُوحٌ ٱبْنَهُۥ وَكَانَ فِى مَعْزِلٍ

Noah called out to his son, who stood aloof,

يَٰبُنَىَّ ٱرْكَب مَّعَنَا

'O my son! 'Board with us,

وَلَا تَكُن مَّعَ ٱلْكَٰفِرِينَ ۝

and do not be with the faithless!'

قَالَ سَـَٔاوِىٓ إِلَىٰ جَبَلٍ 43

43 He said, 'I shall take refuge on a mountain;

يَعْصِمُنِى مِنَ ٱلْمَآءِ

it will protect me from the flood.'

قَالَ لَا عَاصِمَ ٱلْيَوْمَ

He said, 'There is none today who can protect

مِنْ أَمْرِ ٱللَّهِ

from Allah's edict,

إِلَّا مَن رَّحِمَ

except someone upon whom He has mercy.'

وَحَالَ بَيْنَهُمَا ٱلْمَوْجُ

Then the waves came between them,

---

[1] That is, male and female. Cf. 23:27.

307

فَكَانَ مِنَ ٱلْمُغْرَقِينَ ٤٣     and he was among those who were drowned.

وَقِيلَ يَـٰٓأَرْضُ ٱبْلَعِى مَآءَكِ ٤٤   Then it was said, 'O earth, swallow your water!

وَيَـٰسَمَآءُ أَقْلِعِى        O sky, leave off!'

وَغِيضَ ٱلْمَآءُ         The waters receded;

وَقُضِىَ ٱلْأَمْرُ         the edict was carried out,

وَٱسْتَوَتْ عَلَى ٱلْجُودِىِّ    and it[1] settled on [Mount] Judi.

وَقِيلَ بُعْدًا لِّلْقَوْمِ ٱلظَّـٰلِمِينَ ٤٤   Then it was said, 'Away with the wrongdoing lot!'

وَنَادَىٰ نُوحٌ رَّبَّهُۥ ٤٥   Noah called out to his Lord,

فَقَالَ رَبِّ        and said, 'My Lord!

إِنَّ ٱبْنِى مِنْ أَهْلِى    My son is indeed from my family.

وَإِنَّ وَعْدَكَ ٱلْحَقُّ     Your promise is indeed true,

وَأَنتَ أَحْكَمُ ٱلْحَـٰكِمِينَ ٤٥   and You are the fairest of all judges.'

قَالَ يَـٰنُوحُ ٤٦   Said He, 'O Noah!

إِنَّهُۥ لَيْسَ مِنْ أَهْلِكَ    Indeed He is not of your family.

إِنَّهُۥ عَمَلٌ غَيْرُ صَـٰلِحٍ   Indeed he is [personification of] unrighteous conduct.

فَلَا تَسْـَٔلْنِ        So do not ask Me

مَا لَيْسَ لَكَ بِهِۦ عِلْمٌ   [something] of which you have no knowledge.

إِنِّىٓ أَعِظُكَ       I advise you

أَن تَكُونَ مِنَ ٱلْجَـٰهِلِينَ ٤٦   lest you should be among the ignorant.'

قَالَ رَبِّ ٤٧   He said, 'My Lord!

إِنِّىٓ أَعُوذُ بِكَ     I seek Your protection

أَنْ أَسْـَٔلَكَ       lest I should ask You

مَا لَيْسَ لِى بِهِۦ عِلْمٌ   something of which I have no knowledge.

وَإِلَّا تَغْفِرْ لِى وَتَرْحَمْنِىٓ   If You do not forgive me and have mercy upon me

أَكُن مِّنَ ٱلْخَـٰسِرِينَ ٤٧   I shall be among the losers.'

قِيلَ يَـٰنُوحُ ٤٨   It was said, 'O Noah!

---

[1] That is, the Ark of Noah.

اَهْبِطْ

Disembark

بِسَلَمٍ مِّنَّا وَبَرَكَتٍ

in peace from Us and with [Our] blessings

عَلَيْكَ وَعَلَىٰٓ أُمَمٍ

upon you and upon nations

مِّمَّن مَّعَكَ

[to descend] from those who are with you,

وَأُمَمٌ سَنُمَتِّعُهُمْ

and nations whom We shall provide for,

ثُمَّ يَمَسُّهُم مِّنَّا عَذَابٌ أَلِيمٌ ۝

then a painful punishment from Us shall befall them.'

تِلْكَ مِنْ أَنۢبَآءِ ٱلْغَيْبِ

49 These are accounts of the Unseen

نُوحِيهَآ إِلَيْكَ

which We reveal to *you*.

مَا كُنتَ تَعْلَمُهَآ أَنتَ وَلَا قَوْمُكَ

Neither *you* nor *your* people used to know them

مِن قَبْلِ هَـٰذَا

before this.

فَٱصْبِرْ

So *be patient*.

إِنَّ ٱلْعَـٰقِبَةَ لِلْمُتَّقِينَ ۝

Indeed the outcome will be in favour of the Godwary.

وَإِلَىٰ عَادٍ أَخَاهُمْ هُودًا

50 And to 'Ād [We sent] Hūd, their brother.

قَالَ يَـٰقَوْمِ

He said, 'O my people!

ٱعْبُدُوا۟ ٱللَّهَ

Worship Allah.

مَا لَكُم مِّنْ إِلَـٰهٍ غَيْرُهُۥٓ

You have no other god besides Him:

إِنْ أَنتُمْ إِلَّا مُفْتَرُونَ ۝

you merely fabricate [the gods that you worship].

يَـٰقَوْمِ

51 'O my people!

لَآ أَسْـَٔلُكُمْ عَلَيْهِ أَجْرًا

I do not ask you any reward for it.

إِنْ أَجْرِىَ إِلَّا عَلَى ٱلَّذِى

My reward lies only with Him

فَطَرَنِىٓ

who originated me.

أَفَلَا تَعْقِلُونَ ۝

Do you not apply reason?

وَيَـٰقَوْمِ

52 'O my people!

ٱسْتَغْفِرُوا۟ رَبَّكُمْ

Plead with your Lord for forgiveness,

ثُمَّ تُوبُوٓا۟ إِلَيْهِ

then turn to Him penitently:

يُرْسِلِ ٱلسَّمَآءَ عَلَيْكُم مِّدْرَارًا

He will send copious rains for you from the sky,

وَيَزِدْكُمْ قُوَّةً إِلَىٰ قُوَّتِكُمْ

and add power to your [present] power.

وَلَا تَتَوَلَّوْا۟ مُجْرِمِينَ ۝

So do not turn your backs [on Him] as guilty ones.'

قَالُواْ يَٰهُودُ 53 They said, 'O Hūd,

مَا جِئْتَنَا بِبَيِّنَةٍ    you have not brought us any manifest proof.

وَمَا نَحْنُ بِتَارِكِيٓ ءَالِهَتِنَا    We are not going to abandon our gods

عَن قَوْلِكَ    for what you say,

وَمَا نَحْنُ لَكَ بِمُؤْمِنِينَ ۝    and we are not going to believe you.

إِن نَّقُولُ إِلَّا ٱعْتَرَىٰكَ بَعْضُ ءَالِهَتِنَا 54 All we say is that some of our gods have visited you

بِسُوٓءٍ    with an evil.'

قَالَ إِنِّيٓ أُشْهِدُ ٱللَّهَ    He said, 'I call Allah to witness

وَٱشْهَدُوٓاْ    —and you too be [my] witnesses—

أَنِّي بَرِيٓءٌ مِّمَّا تُشْرِكُونَ ۝    that I repudiate what you take as [His] partners

مِن دُونِهِۦ 55    besides Him.

فَكِيدُونِي جَمِيعًا    Now try out your stratagems against me, together,

ثُمَّ لَا تُنظِرُونِ ۝    without granting me any respite.

إِنِّي تَوَكَّلْتُ عَلَى ٱللَّهِ 56 Indeed I have put my trust in Allah,

رَبِّي وَرَبِّكُم    my Lord and your Lord.

مَّا مِن دَآبَّةٍ    There is no living being

إِلَّا هُوَ ءَاخِذُۢ بِنَاصِيَتِهَآ    but He holds it by its forelock.

إِنَّ رَبِّي عَلَىٰ صِرَٰطٍ مُّسْتَقِيمٍ ۝    Indeed my Lord is on a straight path.

فَإِن تَوَلَّوْاْ 57 But if you turn your backs [on me],

فَقَدْ أَبْلَغْتُكُم    then [know that] I have communicated to you

مَّآ أُرْسِلْتُ بِهِۦٓ إِلَيْكُمْ    whatever I was sent to you with.

وَيَسْتَخْلِفُ رَبِّي قَوْمًا غَيْرَكُمْ    My Lord will make another people succeed you,

وَلَا تَضُرُّونَهُۥ شَيْئًا    and you will not hurt Allah in the least.

إِنَّ رَبِّي عَلَىٰ كُلِّ شَىْءٍ حَفِيظٌ ۝    Indeed my Lord is watchful over all things.'

وَلَمَّا جَآءَ أَمْرُنَا 58 And when Our edict came,

نَجَّيْنَا هُودًا وَٱلَّذِينَ ءَامَنُواْ مَعَهُۥ    We delivered Hūd and the faithful who were with him,

بِرَحْمَةٍ مِّنَّا    by a mercy from Us,

وَنَجَّيْنَٰهُم مِّنْ عَذَابٍ غَلِيظٍ ۝    and We delivered them from a harsh punishment.

وَتِلْكَ عَادٌ 59 Such were [the people of] Ād:

جَحَدُواْ بِـَٔايَٰتِ رَبِّهِمْ    they impugned the signs of their Lord

وَعَصَوْا۟ رُسُلَهُۥ    and disobeyed His apostles,

وَٱتَّبَعُوٓا۟ أَمْرَ كُلِّ جَبَّارٍ عَنِيدٍ ۞    and followed the dictates of every obdurate tyrant.

وَأُتْبِعُوا۟ فِى هَٰذِهِ ٱلدُّنْيَا لَعْنَةً    60 So they were pursued by a curse in this world

وَيَوْمَ ٱلْقِيَٰمَةِ    and on the Day of Resurrection.

أَلَآ إِنَّ عَادًا كَفَرُوا۟ رَبَّهُمْ    Look! Indeed 'Ād defied their Lord.

أَلَا بُعْدًا لِّعَادٍ قَوْمِ هُودٍ ۞ ۞    Look! Away with 'Ād, the people of Hud!

وَإِلَىٰ ثَمُودَ أَخَاهُمْ صَٰلِحًا    61 And to Thamūd [We sent] Ṣāliḥ, their brother.

قَالَ يَٰقَوْمِ    He said, 'O my people!

ٱعْبُدُوا۟ ٱللَّهَ    Worship Allah.

مَا لَكُم مِّنْ إِلَٰهٍ غَيْرُهُۥ    You have no other god besides Him.

هُوَ أَنشَأَكُم مِّنَ ٱلْأَرْضِ    He brought you forth from the earth

وَٱسْتَعْمَرَكُمْ فِيهَا    and made it your habitation.

فَٱسْتَغْفِرُوهُ    So plead with Him for forgiveness,

ثُمَّ تُوبُوٓا۟ إِلَيْهِ    then turn to Him penitently.

إِنَّ رَبِّى قَرِيبٌ مُّجِيبٌ ۞    My Lord is indeed nearmost [and] responsive.'

قَالُوا۟ يَٰصَٰلِحُ    62 They said, 'O Ṣāliḥ!

قَدْ كُنتَ فِينَا مَرْجُوًّا    You were a source of hope to us

قَبْلَ هَٰذَآ    before this.

أَتَنْهَىٰنَآ أَن نَّعْبُدَ    Do you forbid us to worship

مَا يَعْبُدُ ءَابَآؤُنَا    what our fathers have been worshiping?

وَإِنَّنَا لَفِى شَكٍّ مِّمَّا    Indeed we have grave doubts concerning

تَدْعُونَآ إِلَيْهِ مُرِيبٍ ۞    that to which you invite us.'

قَالَ يَٰقَوْمِ أَرَءَيْتُمْ    63 He said, 'O my people! Tell me,

إِن كُنتُ عَلَىٰ بَيِّنَةٍ مِّن رَّبِّى    should I stand on a manifest proof from my Lord,

وَءَاتَىٰنِى مِنْهُ رَحْمَةً    and He has granted me His own mercy,

فَمَن يَنصُرُنِى مِنَ ٱللَّهِ    who will protect me from Allah

إِنْ عَصَيْتُهُۥ    should I disobey Him?

فَمَا تَزِيدُونَنِى غَيْرَ تَخْسِيرٍ ۞    For then you will increase me in nothing but loss.

وَيَٰقَوْمِ    64 O my people!

هَـٰذِهِۦ نَاقَةُ ٱللَّهِ لَكُمْ ءَايَةً

This she-camel of Allah is a sign for you.

فَذَرُوهَا تَأْكُلْ فِىٓ أَرْضِ ٱللَّهِ

Let her graze [freely] in Allah's land,

وَلَا تَمَسُّوهَا بِسُوٓءٍ

and do not cause her any harm,

فَيَأْخُذَكُمْ عَذَابٌ قَرِيبٌ ۝

for then you shall be seized by a prompt punishment.'

فَعَقَرُوهَا

65 But they hamstrung her,

فَقَالَ

whereupon he said,

تَمَتَّعُوا۟ فِى دَارِكُمْ ثَلَـٰثَةَ أَيَّامٍ

'Enjoy yourselves in your homes for three days:

ذَٰلِكَ وَعْدٌ غَيْرُ مَكْذُوبٍ ۝

that is a promise not untrue!'

فَلَمَّا جَآءَ أَمْرُنَا

66 So when Our edict came,

نَجَّيْنَا صَـٰلِحًا

We delivered Ṣāliḥ

وَٱلَّذِينَ ءَامَنُوا۟ مَعَهُۥ

and the faithful who were with him

بِرَحْمَةٍ مِّنَّا

by a mercy from Us,

وَمِنْ خِزْىِ يَوْمِئِذٍ

and from the [punishment and] disgrace of that day.

إِنَّ رَبَّكَ هُوَ ٱلْقَوِىُّ ٱلْعَزِيزُ ۝

Your Lord is indeed the All-strong, the All-mighty.

وَأَخَذَ ٱلَّذِينَ ظَلَمُوا۟ ٱلصَّيْحَةُ

67 The Cry seized those who were wrongdoers,

فَأَصْبَحُوا۟ فِى دِيَـٰرِهِمْ جَـٰثِمِينَ ۝

and they lay lifeless prostrate in their homes,

كَأَن لَّمْ يَغْنَوْا۟ فِيهَآ

68 as if they had never lived there.

أَلَآ إِنَّ ثَمُودَا۟ كَفَرُوا۟ رَبَّهُمْ

Look! Indeed Thamūd defied their Lord.

أَلَا بُعْدًا لِّثَمُودَ ۝

Look! Away with Thamūd!

وَلَقَدْ جَآءَتْ رُسُلُنَآ إِبْرَٰهِيمَ

69 Certainly Our messengers came to Abraham

بِٱلْبُشْرَىٰ

with the good news,

قَالُوا۟ سَلَـٰمًا

and said, 'Peace!'

قَالَ سَلَـٰمٌ

'Peace!' He replied.

فَمَا لَبِثَ أَن جَآءَ بِعِجْلٍ حَنِيذٍ ۝

Presently he brought [for them] a roasted calf.

فَلَمَّا رَءَآ أَيْدِيَهُمْ لَا تَصِلُ إِلَيْهِ

70 But when he saw their hands not reaching for it,

نَكِرَهُمْ وَأَوْجَسَ مِنْهُمْ خِيفَةً

he took them amiss and felt a fear of them.

قَالُوا۟ لَا تَخَفْ

They said, 'Do not be afraid.

إِنَّآ أُرْسِلْنَآ إِلَىٰ قَوْمِ لُوطٍ ۝

We have been sent to the people of Lot.'

وَٱمْرَأَتُهُۥ قَآئِمَةٌ فَضَحِكَتْ

71 His wife, standing by, laughed

فَبَشَّرْنَهَا بِإِسْحَقَ     as We gave her the good news of [the birth of] Isaac,

وَمِن وَرَآءِ إِسْحَقَ يَعْقُوبَ ۝     and of Jacob, after Isaac.

قَالَتْ يَوَيْلَتَىٰٓ     72 She said, 'Oh, my!

ءَأَلِدُ وَأَنَا۠ عَجُوزٌ     Shall I, an old woman, bear [children],

وَهَذَا بَعْلِى شَيْخًا     and [while] this husband of mine is an old man?!

إِنَّ هَذَا لَشَىْءٌ عَجِيبٌ ۝     That is indeed an odd thing!'

قَالُوٓا۟ أَتَعْجَبِينَ مِنْ أَمْرِ ٱللَّهِ     73 They said, 'Are you amazed at Allah's dispensation?

رَحْمَتُ ٱللَّهِ وَبَرَكَٰتُهُۥ عَلَيْكُمْ     [That is] Allah's mercy and His blessings upon you,

أَهْلَ ٱلْبَيْتِ     members of the household.

إِنَّهُۥ حَمِيدٌ مَّجِيدٌ ۝     Indeed He is all-laudable, all-glorious.'

فَلَمَّا ذَهَبَ عَنْ إِبْرَٰهِيمَ ٱلرَّوْعُ     74 So when the awe had left Abraham

وَجَآءَتْهُ ٱلْبُشْرَىٰ     and the good news had reached him,

يُجَٰدِلُنَا فِى قَوْمِ لُوطٍ ۝     he pleaded with Us concerning the people of Lot.

إِنَّ إِبْرَٰهِيمَ لَحَلِيمٌ     75 Abraham was indeed most forbearing,

أَوَّٰهٌ مُّنِيبٌ ۝     plaintive, [and] penitent.

يَٰٓإِبْرَٰهِيمُ أَعْرِضْ عَنْ هَٰذَآ     76 'O Abraham, let this matter alone!

إِنَّهُۥ قَدْ جَآءَ أَمْرُ رَبِّكَ     Your Lord's edict has certainly come,

وَإِنَّهُمْ ءَاتِيهِمْ عَذَابٌ غَيْرُ مَرْدُودٍ ۝     and an irrevocable punishment shall overtake them.'

وَلَمَّا جَآءَتْ رُسُلُنَا لُوطًا     77 When Our messengers came to Lot,

سِىٓءَ بِهِمْ     he was distressed on their account

وَضَاقَ بِهِمْ ذَرْعًا     and in a predicament for their sake,

وَقَالَ     and he said,

هَٰذَا يَوْمٌ عَصِيبٌ ۝     'This is a terrible day!'

وَجَآءَهُۥ قَوْمُهُۥ يُهْرَعُونَ إِلَيْهِ     78 Then his people came running toward him,

وَمِن قَبْلُ كَانُوا۟ يَعْمَلُونَ ٱلسَّيِّئَاتِ     and they had been committing misdeeds aforetime.

قَالَ يَٰقَوْمِ هَٰٓؤُلَآءِ بَنَاتِى     He said, 'O my people, these are my daughters:

هُنَّ أَطْهَرُ لَكُمْ     they are purer for you.[1]

فَٱتَّقُوا۟ ٱللَّهَ     Be wary of Allah

وَلَا تُخْزُونِ فِى ضَيْفِى     and do not humiliate me with regard to my guests.

---

[1] That is, it would be purer for you to get married to them.

أَلَيْسَ مِنكُمْ رَجُلٌ رَّشِيدٌ ۝ Is there not a right-minded man among you?'

قَالُواْ لَقَدْ عَلِمْتَ 79 They said, 'You certainly know

مَا لَنَا فِى بَنَاتِكَ مِنْ حَقٍّ that we have no interest in your daughters,

وَإِنَّكَ لَتَعْلَمُ مَا نُرِيدُ ۝ and indeed you know what we want.'

قَالَ لَوْ أَنَّ لِى بِكُمْ قُوَّةً 80 He said, 'If only I had the power to deter you,

أَوْ ءَاوِى إِلَىٰ رُكْنٍ شَدِيدٍ ۝ or could take refuge in a mighty support!'

قَالُواْ يَٰلُوطُ 81 They said, 'O Lot,

إِنَّا رُسُلُ رَبِّكَ we are messengers of your Lord.

لَن يَصِلُواْ إِلَيْكَ They will never get at you.

فَأَسْرِ بِأَهْلِكَ بِقِطْعٍ مِّنَ ٱلَّيْلِ Set out with your family in a watch of the night;

وَلَا يَلْتَفِتْ مِنكُمْ أَحَدٌ and none of you shall turn round,

إِلَّا ٱمْرَأَتَكَ except your wife;

إِنَّهُۥ مُصِيبُهَا مَآ أَصَابَهُمْ indeed she will be struck by what strikes them.

إِنَّ مَوْعِدَهُمُ ٱلصُّبْحُ Indeed their tryst is the dawn.

أَلَيْسَ ٱلصُّبْحُ بِقَرِيبٍ ۝ Is not the dawn [already] near?'

فَلَمَّا جَآءَ أَمْرُنَا 82 So when Our edict came,

جَعَلْنَا عَٰلِيَهَا سَافِلَهَا We made its[1] topmost part its nethermost,

وَأَمْطَرْنَا عَلَيْهَا حِجَارَةً and We rained on it stones

مِّن سِجِّيلٍ مَّنضُودٍ ۝ of laminar shale,

مُّسَوَّمَةً عِندَ رَبِّكَ 83 targeted[2] with your Lord [for the profligate],[3]

وَمَا هِىَ مِنَ ٱلظَّٰلِمِينَ بِبَعِيدٍ ۝ never far from the wrongdoers.

وَإِلَىٰ مَدْيَنَ أَخَاهُمْ شُعَيْبًا 84 And to Midian [We sent] Shu'ayb, their brother.

قَالَ يَٰقَوْمِ He said, 'O my people!

ٱعْبُدُواْ ٱللَّهَ Worship Allah.

مَا لَكُم مِّنْ إِلَٰهٍ غَيْرُهُۥ You have no other god besides Him.

وَلَا تَنقُصُواْ ٱلْمِكْيَالَ وَٱلْمِيزَانَ Do not diminish the measure or the balance.

---

[1] That is, of the city of Sodom.

[2] Or 'marked.'

[3] Cf. 51:34.

إِنِّى أَرَىٰكُم بِخَيْرٍ

Indeed I see that you are faring well,

وَإِنِّى أَخَافُ عَلَيْكُمْ عَذَابَ

but I fear for you the punishment

يَوْمٍ مُحِيطٍ ۞

of an all-embracing day.'

85 وَيَٰقَوْمِ

85 'O my people!

أَوْفُوا ٱلْمِكْيَالَ وَٱلْمِيزَانَ بِٱلْقِسْطِ

Observe fully the measure and the balance, with justice,

وَلَا تَبْخَسُوا ٱلنَّاسَ أَشْيَآءَهُمْ

and do not cheat the people of their goods,[1]

وَلَا تَعْثَوْا فِى ٱلْأَرْضِ

and do not act wickedly on the earth,

مُفْسِدِينَ ۞

causing corruption.'

بَقِيَّتُ ٱللَّهِ خَيْرٌ لَّكُمْ

86 What remains of Allah's provision[2] is better for you,

إِن كُنتُم مُّؤْمِنِينَ

should you be faithful,

وَمَآ أَنَا۠ عَلَيْكُم بِحَفِيظٍ ۞

and I am not a keeper over you.

قَالُوا يَٰشُعَيْبُ

87 They said, 'O Shu'ayb,

أَصَلَوٰتُكَ تَأْمُرُكَ

does your worship require

أَن نَّتْرُكَ

that we abandon

مَا يَعْبُدُ ءَابَآؤُنَآ

what our fathers have been worshiping,

أَوْ أَن نَّفْعَلَ فِىٓ أَمْوَٰلِنَا

or that we should not do with our means

مَا نَشَٰٓؤُا۟

whatever we wish?

إِنَّكَ لَأَنتَ ٱلْحَلِيمُ ٱلرَّشِيدُ ۞

You are indeed [a] gentle and sensible [person].'

قَالَ يَٰقَوْمِ أَرَءَيْتُمْ

88 He said, 'O my people! Have you considered,

إِن كُنتُ عَلَىٰ بَيِّنَةٍ مِّن رَّبِّى

should I stand on a manifest proof from my Lord,

وَرَزَقَنِى مِنْهُ رِزْقًا حَسَنًا

who has provided me a good provision from Himself?[3]

وَمَآ أُرِيدُ أَنْ أُخَالِفَكُمْ

I do not wish to oppose you

إِلَىٰ مَآ أَنْهَىٰكُمْ عَنْهُ

by what I forbid you.

إِنْ أُرِيدُ إِلَّا ٱلْإِصْلَٰحَ

I only desire to put things in order,

مَا ٱسْتَطَعْتُ

as far as I can,

---

[1] That is, by employing short weights and measures.

[2] That is, of your lawful earnings.

[3] That is, 'If I stand on a clear proof from my Lord, who has provided me with lawful means of livelihood, is it a right thing for you to reject my call to faith in Allah and fair dealing?'

وَمَا تَوْفِيقِىَ إِلَّا بِٱللَّهِ    and my success lies only with Allah:

عَلَيْهِ تَوَكَّلْتُ    in Him I have put my trust,

وَإِلَيْهِ أُنِيبُ ۞    and to Him I turn penitently.

وَيَٰقَوْمِ    89 O my people,

لَا يَجْرِمَنَّكُمْ شِقَاقِى    do not let your defiance toward me lead you

أَن يُصِيبَكُم مِّثْلُ مَآ أَصَابَ    to be visited by the like of what was visited on

قَوْمَ نُوحٍ    the people of Noah,

أَوْ قَوْمَ هُودٍ    or the people of Hūd,

أَوْ قَوْمَ صَٰلِحٍ    or the people of Ṣāliḥ,

وَمَا قَوْمُ لُوطٍ مِّنكُم بِبَعِيدٍ ۞    and the people of Lot are not distant from you.

وَٱسْتَغْفِرُوا۟ رَبَّكُمْ    90 Plead with your Lord for forgiveness,

ثُمَّ تُوبُوٓا۟ إِلَيْهِ    then turn to Him penitently.

إِنَّ رَبِّى رَحِيمٌ وَدُودٌ ۞    My Lord is indeed all-merciful, all-affectionate.'

قَالُوا۟ يَٰشُعَيْبُ    91 They said, 'O Shu'ayb,

مَا نَفْقَهُ كَثِيرًا مِّمَّا تَقُولُ    we do not understand much of what you say.

وَإِنَّا لَنَرَىٰكَ فِينَا ضَعِيفًا    Indeed we see you are weak amongst us ,

وَلَوْلَا رَهْطُكَ    and were it not for your tribe,

لَرَجَمْنَٰكَ    we would have stoned you,

وَمَآ أَنتَ عَلَيْنَا بِعَزِيزٍ ۞    and you are not venerable to us.'

قَالَ يَٰقَوْمِ    92 He said, 'O my people!

أَرَهْطِىٓ أَعَزُّ عَلَيْكُم مِّنَ ٱللَّهِ    Is my tribe more venerable in your sight than Allah,

وَٱتَّخَذْتُمُوهُ وَرَآءَكُمْ ظِهْرِيًّا    to whom you pay no regard?

إِنَّ رَبِّى بِمَا تَعْمَلُونَ مُحِيطٌ ۞    Indeed my Lord comprehends whatever you do.

وَيَٰقَوْمِ    93 O my people!

ٱعْمَلُوا۟ عَلَىٰ مَكَانَتِكُمْ    Act according to your ability;

إِنِّى عَٰمِلٌ    I too am acting.

سَوْفَ تَعْلَمُونَ مَن يَأْتِيهِ    Soon you will know who will be overtaken by

عَذَابٌ يُخْزِيهِ    a punishment that will disgrace him,

وَمَنْ هُوَ كَٰذِبٌ    and who is a liar.

وَٱرْتَقِبُوٓا۟    So be on the watch;

إِنِّي مَعَكُمْ رَقِيبٌ ۝
I too will be watching along with you.'

وَلَمَّا جَآءَ أَمْرُنَا 94 And when Our edict came,

نَجَّيْنَا شُعَيْبًا
We delivered Shu'ayb

وَٱلَّذِينَ ءَامَنُوا۟ مَعَهُۥ
and the faithful who were with him

بِرَحْمَةٍ مِّنَّا
by a mercy from Us.

وَأَخَذَتِ ٱلَّذِينَ ظَلَمُوا۟ ٱلصَّيْحَةُ
And the Cry seized those who were wrongdoers,

فَأَصْبَحُوا۟ فِي دِيَٰرِهِمْ جَٰثِمِينَ ۝
whereat they lay lifeless prostrate in their homes,

كَأَن لَّمْ يَغْنَوْا۟ فِيهَآ 95
as if they had never lived there.

أَلَا بُعْدًا لِّمَدْيَنَ
Look! Away with Midian!

كَمَا بَعِدَتْ ثَمُودُ ۝
—just as Thamūd was done away with!

وَلَقَدْ أَرْسَلْنَا مُوسَىٰ بِـَٔايَٰتِنَا 96 Certainly We sent Moses with Our signs

وَسُلْطَٰنٍ مُّبِينٍ ۝
and a manifest authority,

إِلَىٰ فِرْعَوْنَ وَمَلَإِي۟هِۦ 97 to Pharaoh and his elite,

فَٱتَّبَعُوٓا۟ أَمْرَ فِرْعَوْنَ
but they followed Pharaoh's dictates,

وَمَآ أَمْرُ فِرْعَوْنَ بِرَشِيدٍ ۝
and Pharaoh's dictates were not right-minded.

يَقْدُمُ قَوْمَهُۥ يَوْمَ ٱلْقِيَٰمَةِ 98 On the Day of Resurrection he will lead his people

فَأَوْرَدَهُمُ ٱلنَّارَ
and conduct them into the Fire:

وَبِئْسَ ٱلْوِرْدُ ٱلْمَوْرُودُ ۝
an evil goal for the incoming![1]

وَأُتْبِعُوا۟ فِي هَٰذِهِۦ لَعْنَةً 99 They were pursued by a curse in this [world],

وَيَوْمَ ٱلْقِيَٰمَةِ
as well as on the Day of Resurrection;

بِئْسَ ٱلرِّفْدُ ٱلْمَرْفُودُ ۝
evil is the award conferred [upon them]!

ذَٰلِكَ مِنْ أَنۢبَآءِ ٱلْقُرَىٰ 100 These are from the accounts of the townships

نَقُصُّهُۥ عَلَيْكَ
which We recount to *you*.

مِنْهَا قَآئِمٌ
Of them there are some that still stand,

وَحَصِيدٌ ۝
and some that have been mown down.

وَمَا ظَلَمْنَٰهُمْ 101 We did not wrong them,

وَلَٰكِن ظَلَمُوٓا۟ أَنفُسَهُمْ
but they wronged themselves.

---

[1] Or 'an evil watering place for the thirsty.'

فَمَآ أَغْنَتْ عَنْهُمْ ءَالِهَتُهُمُ ٱلَّتِى
Of no avail to them were their gods whom

يَدْعُونَ مِن دُونِ ٱللَّهِ مِن شَىْءٍ
they would invoke besides Allah, in any wise,

لَّمَّا جَآءَ أَمْرُ رَبِّكَ
when *your* Lord's edict came,

وَمَا زَادُوهُمْ
and they[1] did not increase them in anything

غَيْرَ تَتْبِيبٍ ۞
but ruin.

وَكَذَٰلِكَ أَخْذُ رَبِّكَ
102 Such is the seizing of *your* Lord

إِذَآ أَخَذَ ٱلْقُرَىٰ وَهِىَ ظَٰلِمَةٌ
when He seizes the townships that are wrongdoing.

إِنَّ أَخْذَهُۥٓ أَلِيمٌ شَدِيدٌ ۞
Indeed His seizing is painful, severe.

إِنَّ فِى ذَٰلِكَ لَءَايَةً
103 There is indeed a sign in that

لِّمَنْ خَافَ عَذَابَ ٱلْءَاخِرَةِ
for him who fears the punishment of the Hereafter.

ذَٰلِكَ يَوْمٌ مَّجْمُوعٌ لَّهُ ٱلنَّاسُ
That is a day on which all mankind will be gathered,

وَذَٰلِكَ يَوْمٌ مَّشْهُودٌ ۞
and it is a day witnessed [by all creatures].

وَمَا نُؤَخِّرُهُۥٓ
104 And We do not defer it

إِلَّا لِأَجَلٍ مَّعْدُودٍ ۞
but for a determinate term.

يَوْمَ يَأْتِ
105 The day it comes,

لَا تَكَلَّمُ نَفْسٌ إِلَّا بِإِذْنِهِۦ
no one shall speak except by His leave.

فَمِنْهُمْ شَقِىٌّ
[On that day,] some of them will be wretched

وَسَعِيدٌ ۞
and [some] felicitous.

فَأَمَّا ٱلَّذِينَ شَقُوا۟
106 As for the wretched,

فَفِى ٱلنَّارِ
they shall be in the Fire:

لَهُمْ فِيهَا زَفِيرٌ وَشَهِيقٌ ۞
their lot therein will be groaning and wailing.

خَٰلِدِينَ فِيهَا
107 They shall remain in it

مَا دَامَتِ ٱلسَّمَٰوَٰتُ وَٱلْأَرْضُ
for as long as the heavens and the earth endure

إِلَّا مَا شَآءَ رَبُّكَ
—except what *your* Lord may wish;

إِنَّ رَبَّكَ فَعَّالٌ لِّمَا يُرِيدُ ۞ ۞
indeed *your* Lord does whatever He desires.

وَأَمَّا ٱلَّذِينَ سُعِدُوا۟
108 As for the felicitous,

فَفِى ٱلْجَنَّةِ
they will be in paradise.

خَٰلِدِينَ فِيهَا
They will remain in it

مَا دَامَتِ ٱلسَّمَٰوَٰتُ وَٱلْأَرْضُ
for as long as the heavens and the earth endure

---

[1] That is, their false gods.

إِلَّا مَا شَآءَ رَبُّكَ

—except what *your* Lord may wish—

عَطَآءً غَيْرَ مَجْذُوذٍ ۝

an endless bounty.

فَلَا تَكُ فِى مِرْيَةٍ مِّمَّا يَعْبُدُ هَٰٓؤُلَآءِ

109 So *do not be* in doubt about what these[1] worship:

مَا يَعْبُدُونَ إِلَّا كَمَا يَعْبُدُ ءَابَآؤُهُم

they worship just as their fathers worshiped

مِّن قَبْلُ

before,

وَإِنَّا لَمُوَفُّوهُمْ نَصِيبَهُمْ

and We shall surely pay them their full share,

غَيْرَ مَنقُوصٍ ۝

undiminished.

وَلَقَدْ ءَاتَيْنَا مُوسَى ٱلْكِتَٰبَ

110 Certainly We gave Moses the Book,

فَٱخْتُلِفَ فِيهِ

but differences arose about it,

وَلَوْلَا كَلِمَةٌ سَبَقَتْ مِن رَّبِّكَ

and were it not for a prior decree of *your* Lord,

لَقُضِىَ بَيْنَهُمْ

a decision would have been made between them;

وَإِنَّهُمْ لَفِى شَكٍّ مِّنْهُ مُرِيبٍ ۝

indeed they are in grave doubt concerning it.

وَإِنَّ كُلًّا لَّمَّا لَيُوَفِّيَنَّهُمْ رَبُّكَ

111 *Your* Lord will indeed recompense everyone fully

أَعْمَٰلَهُمْ

for their works.

إِنَّهُ بِمَا يَعْمَلُونَ خَبِيرٌ ۝

Indeed He is well aware of what they do.

فَٱسْتَقِمْ كَمَآ أُمِرْتَ

112 So *be steadfast*, just as *you* have been commanded—

وَمَن تَابَ مَعَكَ

[*you*] and whoever has turned [to Allah] with *you*—

وَلَا تَطْغَوْاْ

and do not overstep the bounds.

إِنَّهُ بِمَا تَعْمَلُونَ بَصِيرٌ ۝

Indeed He sees best what you do.

وَلَا تَرْكَنُوٓاْ إِلَى ٱلَّذِينَ ظَلَمُواْ

113 And do not incline toward the wrongdoers,

فَتَمَسَّكُمُ ٱلنَّارُ

lest the Fire should touch you,

وَمَا لَكُم مِّن دُونِ ٱللَّهِ مِنْ أَوْلِيَآءَ

and you will not have any friend besides Allah,

ثُمَّ لَا تُنصَرُونَ ۝

then you will not be helped.

وَأَقِمِ ٱلصَّلَوٰةَ طَرَفَىِ ٱلنَّهَارِ

114 *Maintain* the prayer at the two ends of the day,[2]

وَزُلَفًا مِّنَ ٱلَّيْلِ

and during the early hours of the night.

إِنَّ ٱلْحَسَنَٰتِ يُذْهِبْنَ ٱلسَّيِّئَاتِ

Indeed good deeds efface misdeeds.[3]

---

[1] That is, the idolaters of Arabia.

[2] That is, at dawn and sunset.

[3] Or 'Indeed good deeds remove ills,' or 'Indeed virtues efface vices.'

ذَٰلِكَ ذِكْرَىٰ لِلذَّٰكِرِينَ ۝     That is an admonition for the mindful.

وَٱصْبِرْ ۝     115 And *be* patient;

فَإِنَّ ٱللَّهَ لَا يُضِيعُ     indeed Allah does not waste

أَجْرَ ٱلْمُحْسِنِينَ ۝     the reward of the virtuous.

فَلَوْلَا كَانَ مِنَ ٱلْقُرُونِ     116 Why were there not among the generations

مِن قَبْلِكُمْ     before you

أُوْلُوا بَقِيَّةٍ     a remnant [of the wise]

يَنْهَوْنَ عَنِ ٱلْفَسَادِ فِى ٱلْأَرْضِ     who might forbid from corruption in the earth,

إِلَّا قَلِيلًا     except a few

مِّمَّنْ أَنجَيْنَا مِنْهُمْ     of those whom We delivered from among them?

وَٱتَّبَعَ ٱلَّذِينَ ظَلَمُوا     Those who were wrongdoers pursued

مَآ أُتْرِفُوا فِيهِ     that in which they had been granted affluence,

وَكَانُوا مُجْرِمِينَ ۝     and they were a guilty lot.

وَمَا كَانَ رَبُّكَ لِيُهْلِكَ ٱلْقُرَىٰ     117 *Your* Lord would never destroy the townships

بِظُلْمٍ     unjustly

وَأَهْلُهَا مُصْلِحُونَ ۝     while their inhabitants were bringing about reform.

وَلَوْ شَآءَ رَبُّكَ     118 Had *your* Lord wished,

لَجَعَلَ ٱلنَّاسَ أُمَّةً وَٰحِدَةً     He would have made mankind one community;

وَلَا يَزَالُونَ مُخْتَلِفِينَ ۝     but they continue to differ,

إِلَّا مَن رَّحِمَ رَبُّكَ     119 except those on whom *your* Lord has mercy

وَلِذَٰلِكَ خَلَقَهُمْ     —and that is why He created them—

وَتَمَّتْ كَلِمَةُ رَبِّكَ     and the word of your Lord has been fulfilled:

لَأَمْلَأَنَّ جَهَنَّمَ     'I will surely fill hell

مِنَ ٱلْجِنَّةِ وَٱلنَّاسِ أَجْمَعِينَ ۝     with jinn and humans, all together!'[1]

وَكُلًّا نَّقُصُّ عَلَيْكَ     120 Whatever We relate to you

مِنْ أَنبَآءِ ٱلرُّسُلِ     of the accounts of the apostles

مَا نُثَبِّتُ بِهِ فُؤَادَكَ     are those by which We strengthen *your* heart,

وَجَآءَكَ فِى هَٰذِهِ ٱلْحَقُّ     and there has come to *you* in this [*sūrah*] the truth

---

[1] That is, all of those who are followers of Satan. See 38:85

وَمَوْعِظَةٌ وَذِكْرَىٰ لِلْمُؤْمِنِينَ ۞    and an advice and admonition for the faithful.

وَقُل لِّلَّذِينَ لَا يُؤْمِنُونَ    121 And *say* to those who do not have faith,

ٱعْمَلُوا عَلَىٰ مَكَانَتِكُمْ    'Act according to your ability;

إِنَّا عَمِلُونَ ۞    we too are acting.

وَٱنتَظِرُوا    122 And wait!

إِنَّا مُنتَظِرُونَ ۞    We too are waiting.'

وَلِلَّهِ غَيْبُ ٱلسَّمَٰوَٰتِ    123 To Allah belongs the Unseen of the heavens

وَٱلْأَرْضِ    and the earth,

وَإِلَيْهِ يُرْجَعُ ٱلْأَمْرُ كُلُّهُۥ    and to Him all matters are returned.

فَٱعْبُدْهُ    So *worship* Him

وَتَوَكَّلْ عَلَيْهِ    and trust in Him.

وَمَا رَبُّكَ بِغَٰفِلٍ عَمَّا تَعْمَلُونَ ۞    *Your* Lord is not oblivious of what you do.

# سُورَةُ يُوسُفَ      12. SŪRAT YŪSUF[1]

بِسْمِ ٱللَّهِ    In the Name of Allah,

ٱلرَّحْمَٰنِ ٱلرَّحِيمِ    the All-beneficent, the All-merciful.

الٓر    1 *Alf, Lām, Rā.*

تِلْكَ ءَايَٰتُ ٱلْكِتَٰبِ ٱلْمُبِينِ ۞    These are the signs of the Manifest Book.

إِنَّا أَنزَلْنَٰهُ قُرْءَٰنًا عَرَبِيًّا    2 Indeed We have sent it down as an Arabic Qur'ān

لَّعَلَّكُمْ تَعْقِلُونَ ۞    so that you may apply reason.

نَحْنُ نَقُصُّ عَلَيْكَ    3 We will recount to *you*

أَحْسَنَ ٱلْقَصَصِ    the best of narratives[2]

بِمَا أَوْحَيْنَا إِلَيْكَ هَٰذَا ٱلْقُرْءَانَ    in what We have revealed to *you* of this Qur'ān,

وَإِن كُنتَ مِن قَبْلِهِۦ    and indeed prior to it *you* were

لَمِنَ ٱلْغَٰفِلِينَ ۞    among those who are unaware [of it].

إِذْ قَالَ يُوسُفُ لِأَبِيهِ    4 When Joseph said to his father,

---

[1] 'Yūsuf' is the Arabic for 'Joseph,' whose well-known story is told in this *sūrah*.

[2] Or 'We will tell *you* a story in the best style of narration.'

يَتَأَبَتِ 'Father!

إِنِّى رَأَيْتُ أَحَدَ عَشَرَ كَوْكَبًا    I saw eleven planets,[1]

وَٱلشَّمْسَ وَٱلْقَمَرَ     and the sun and the moon:

رَأَيْتُهُمْ لِى سَٰجِدِينَ ۝     I saw them prostrating themselves before me.'

قَالَ يَٰبُنَىَّ 5 He said, 'My son,

لَا تَقْصُصْ رُءْيَاكَ عَلَىٰٓ إِخْوَتِكَ   do not recount your dream to your brothers,

فَيَكِيدُواْ لَكَ كَيْدًا     lest they should devise schemes against you.

إِنَّ ٱلشَّيْطَٰنَ لِلْإِنسَٰنِ عَدُوٌّ مُّبِينٌ ۝   Satan is indeed man's manifest enemy.

وَكَذَٰلِكَ يَجْتَبِيكَ رَبُّكَ 6 That is how your Lord will choose you,

وَيُعَلِّمُكَ مِن تَأْوِيلِ ٱلْأَحَادِيثِ    and teach you the interpretation of dreams,[2]

وَيُتِمُّ نِعْمَتَهُۥ عَلَيْكَ     and complete His blessing upon you

وَعَلَىٰٓ ءَالِ يَعْقُوبَ     and upon the house of Jacob,

كَمَآ أَتَمَّهَا عَلَىٰٓ أَبَوَيْكَ مِن قَبْلُ   just as He completed it earlier for your fathers,

إِبْرَٰهِيمَ وَإِسْحَٰقَ     Abraham and Isaac.

إِنَّ رَبَّكَ عَلِيمٌ حَكِيمٌ ۝ ✹   Your Lord is indeed all-knowing, all-wise.'

لَّقَدْ كَانَ فِى يُوسُفَ وَإِخْوَتِهِۦٓ 7 In Joseph and his brothers there are certainly

ءَايَٰتٌ لِّلسَّآئِلِينَ ۝     signs for the seekers.

إِذْ قَالُواْ 8 When they[3] said,

لَيُوسُفُ وَأَخُوهُ     'Surely Joseph and his brother[4]

أَحَبُّ إِلَىٰٓ أَبِينَا مِنَّا    are dearer to our father than [the rest of] us,

وَنَحْنُ عُصْبَةٌ     though we are a hardy group.

إِنَّ أَبَانَا لَفِى ضَلَٰلٍ مُّبِينٍ ۝   Our father is indeed in manifest error.'

ٱقْتُلُواْ يُوسُفَ أَوِ ٱطْرَحُوهُ أَرْضًا 9 'Kill Joseph or cast him away into some [distant] land,

يَخْلُ لَكُمْ وَجْهُ أَبِيكُمْ    so that your father's love may be exclusively yours,

وَتَكُونُواْ مِنۢ بَعْدِهِۦ قَوْمًا صَٰلِحِينَ ۝   and that you may become a righteous lot after that.'

قَالَ قَآئِلٌ مِّنْهُمْ لَا تَقْتُلُواْ يُوسُفَ 10 One of them said, 'Do not kill Joseph,

وَأَلْقُوهُ فِى غَيَٰبَتِ ٱلْجُبِّ    but throw him into the recess of some well

---

[1] Or 'stars.'

[2] Or 'the interpretation of visions.'

[3] That is, the brothers of Joseph ('a).

[4] That is, Benjamin.

يَلْتَقِطْهُ بَعْضُ ٱلسَّيَّارَةِ    so that some caravan may pick him up,

إِن كُنتُمْ فَـٰعِلِينَ ⑩    if you are to do [anything].'

قَالُوا يَـٰٓأَبَانَا   11 They said, 'Father!

مَا لَكَ لَا تَأْمَنَّا عَلَىٰ يُوسُفَ    Why is it that you do not trust us with Joseph?

وَإِنَّا لَهُۥ لَنَـٰصِحُونَ ⑪    We are indeed his well-wishers.

أَرْسِلْهُ مَعَنَا غَدًا   12 Let him go with us tomorrow

يَرْتَعْ وَيَلْعَبْ    so that he may eat lots of fruits and play,

وَإِنَّا لَهُۥ لَحَـٰفِظُونَ ⑫    and we will indeed take [good] care of him.'

قَالَ إِنِّى لَيَحْزُنُنِىٓ   13 He said, 'It really upsets me

أَن تَذْهَبُوا بِهِۦ    that you should take him away,

وَأَخَافُ أَن يَأْكُلَهُ ٱلذِّئْبُ    and I fear the wolf may eat him

وَأَنتُمْ عَنْهُ غَـٰفِلُونَ ⑬    while you are oblivious of him.'

قَالُوا لَئِنْ أَكَلَهُ ٱلذِّئْبُ   14 They said, 'Should the wolf eat him

وَنَحْنُ عُصْبَةٌ    while we are a hardy group,

إِنَّآ إِذًا لَّخَـٰسِرُونَ ⑭    then we will indeed be losers!'

فَلَمَّا ذَهَبُوا بِهِۦ   15 So when they took him away

وَأَجْمَعُوٓا أَن يَجْعَلُوهُ    and conspired to put him

فِى غَيَـٰبَتِ ٱلْجُبِّ    into the recess of a well,

وَأَوْحَيْنَآ إِلَيْهِ    We revealed to him, '[A day will come when]

لَتُنَبِّئَنَّهُم بِأَمْرِهِمْ هَـٰذَا    you will surely inform them about this affair of theirs

وَهُمْ لَا يَشْعُرُونَ ⑮    while they are not aware [of your identity].'

وَجَآءُوٓ أَبَاهُمْ عِشَآءً يَبْكُونَ ⑯   16 In the evening, they came weeping to their father.

قَالُوا يَـٰٓأَبَانَآ   17 They said, 'Father!

إِنَّا ذَهَبْنَا نَسْتَبِقُ    We had gone racing

وَتَرَكْنَا يُوسُفَ عِندَ مَتَـٰعِنَا    and left Joseph with our things,

فَأَكَلَهُ ٱلذِّئْبُ    whereat the wolf ate him.

وَمَآ أَنتَ بِمُؤْمِنٍ لَّنَا    But you will not believe us

وَلَوْ كُنَّا صَـٰدِقِينَ ⑰    even if we spoke truly.'

وَجَآءُو عَلَىٰ قَمِيصِهِۦ بِدَمٍ كَذِبٍ   18 And they produced sham blood on his shirt.

قَالَ بَلْ    He said, 'Rather

سَوَّلَتْ لَكُمْ أَنفُسُكُمْ أَمْرًا

your souls have made a matter seem decorous to you.

فَصَبْرٌ جَمِيلٌ

Yet patience is graceful,

وَٱللَّهُ ٱلْمُسْتَعَانُ عَلَىٰ مَا تَصِفُونَ ⟨١٨⟩

and Allah is my resort against what you allege.'

وَجَآءَتْ سَيَّارَةٌ

19 And there came a caravan,

فَأَرْسَلُوا۟ وَارِدَهُمْ

and they sent their water-drawer,

فَأَدْلَىٰ دَلْوَهُۥ

who let down his bucket.

قَالَ يَٰبُشْرَىٰ هَٰذَا غُلَٰمٌ

'Good news!' he said. 'This is a young boy!'

وَأَسَرُّوهُ بِضَٰعَةً

So they hid him as [a piece of] merchandise,

وَٱللَّهُ عَلِيمٌ بِمَا يَعْمَلُونَ ⟨١٩⟩

and Allah knew best what they were doing.

وَشَرَوْهُ بِثَمَنٍۭ بَخْسٍ

20 And they sold him for a cheap price,

دَرَٰهِمَ مَعْدُودَةٍ

a few dirhams,

وَكَانُوا۟ فِيهِ مِنَ ٱلزَّٰهِدِينَ ⟨٢٠⟩

for they set small store by him.

وَقَالَ ٱلَّذِى ٱشْتَرَىٰهُ مِن مِّصْرَ

21 The man from Egypt who had bought him said

لِٱمْرَأَتِهِۦٓ

to his wife,

أَكْرِمِى مَثْوَىٰهُ

'Give him an honourable place [in the household].[1]

عَسَىٰٓ أَن يَنفَعَنَآ

Maybe he will be useful to us,

أَوْ نَتَّخِذَهُۥ وَلَدًا

or we may adopt him as a son.'

وَكَذَٰلِكَ مَكَّنَّا لِيُوسُفَ فِى ٱلْأَرْضِ

Thus We established Joseph in the land

وَلِنُعَلِّمَهُۥ

and that We might teach him

مِن تَأْوِيلِ ٱلْأَحَادِيثِ

the interpretation of dreams.

وَٱللَّهُ غَالِبٌ عَلَىٰٓ أَمْرِهِۦ

Allah has [full] command of His affairs,

وَلَٰكِنَّ أَكْثَرَ ٱلنَّاسِ لَا يَعْلَمُونَ ⟨٢١⟩

but most people do not know.

وَلَمَّا بَلَغَ أَشُدَّهُۥٓ

22 When he came of age,

ءَاتَيْنَٰهُ حُكْمًا وَعِلْمًا

We gave him judgement and [sacred] knowledge,

وَكَذَٰلِكَ نَجْزِى ٱلْمُحْسِنِينَ ⟨٢٢⟩

and thus do We reward the virtuous.

وَرَٰوَدَتْهُ ٱلَّتِى هُوَ فِى بَيْتِهَا

23 The woman in whose house he was solicited

عَن نَّفْسِهِۦ

him.

وَغَلَّقَتِ ٱلْأَبْوَٰبَ

She closed the doors

---

[1] Or 'Keep him in a respectable manner.'

وَقَالَتْ هَيْتَ لَكَ    and said, 'Come!!'

قَالَ مَعَاذَ ٱللَّهِ    He said, 'God forbid!

إِنَّهُۥ رَبِّى    Indeed He is my Lord;

أَحْسَنَ مَثْوَاىَ    He has given me a good abode.[1]

إِنَّهُۥ لَا يُفْلِحُ ٱلظَّـٰلِمُونَ ۝    Indeed the wrongdoers are not felicitous.'

وَلَقَدْ هَمَّتْ بِهِۦ    24 She certainly made for him;

وَهَمَّ بِهَا    and he would have made for her [too]

لَوْلَآ أَن رَّءَا بُرْهَـٰنَ رَبِّهِۦ    had he not beheld the proof of his Lord.

كَذَٰلِكَ    So it was,

لِنَصْرِفَ عَنْهُ    that We might turn away from him

ٱلسُّوٓءَ وَٱلْفَحْشَآءَ    all evil and indecency.

إِنَّهُۥ مِنْ عِبَادِنَا ٱلْمُخْلَصِينَ ۝    He was indeed one of Our dedicated servants.

وَٱسْتَبَقَا ٱلْبَابَ    25 They raced to the door,

وَقَدَّتْ قَمِيصَهُۥ مِن دُبُرٍ    and she tore his shirt from behind,

وَأَلْفَيَا سَيِّدَهَا لَدَا ٱلْبَابِ    and they ran into her husband at the door.

قَالَتْ مَا جَزَآءُ مَنْ    She said, 'What is to be the requital of him

أَرَادَ بِأَهْلِكَ سُوٓءًا    who has evil intentions for your wife

إِلَّآ أَن يُسْجَنَ أَوْ عَذَابٌ أَلِيمٌ ۝    except imprisonment or a painful punishment?'

قَالَ هِىَ رَٰوَدَتْنِى عَن نَّفْسِى    26 He said, 'It was she who solicited me.'

وَشَهِدَ شَاهِدٌ مِّنْ أَهْلِهَا    A witness of her own household testified:

إِن كَانَ قَمِيصُهُۥ قُدَّ مِن قُبُلٍ    'If his shirt is torn from the front,

فَصَدَقَتْ وَهُوَ مِنَ ٱلْكَـٰذِبِينَ ۝    she tells the truth and he lies.

وَإِن كَانَ قَمِيصُهُۥ قُدَّ مِن دُبُرٍ    27 But if his shirt is torn from behind,

فَكَذَبَتْ وَهُوَ مِنَ ٱلصَّـٰدِقِينَ ۝    then she lies and he tells the truth.'

فَلَمَّا رَءَا قَمِيصَهُۥ قُدَّ مِن دُبُرٍ    28 So when he saw that his shirt was torn from behind,

قَالَ إِنَّهُۥ مِن كَيْدِكُنَّ    he said, 'This is [a case] of you women's guile!

إِنَّ كَيْدَكُنَّ عَظِيمٌ ۝    Your guile is great indeed!

يُوسُفُ أَعْرِضْ عَنْ هَـٰذَا    29 Joseph, let this matter alone,

وَٱسْتَغْفِرِى لِذَنۢبِكِ    and you, woman, plead for forgiveness for your sin,

---

[1] Or 'Indeed he is my master; he has kept me in a nice manner.'

إِنَّكِ كُنتِ مِنَ ٱلْخَاطِئِينَ ۞ ۞

for you have indeed been erring.'

وَقَالَ نِسْوَةٌ فِى ٱلْمَدِينَةِ 30 Some of the townswomen said,

ٱمْرَأَتُ ٱلْعَزِيزِ

'The chieftain's wife

تُرَٰوِدُ فَتَىٰهَا عَن نَّفْسِهِۦ

has solicited her slave boy!

قَدْ شَغَفَهَا حُبًّا

He has captivated her love.

إِنَّا لَنَرَىٰهَا فِى ضَلَٰلٍ مُّبِينٍ ۞

Indeed we see her to be in manifest error.'

فَلَمَّا سَمِعَتْ بِمَكْرِهِنَّ 31 When she heard of their machinations,

أَرْسَلَتْ إِلَيْهِنَّ

she sent for them

وَأَعْتَدَتْ هُنَّ مُتَّكَـًٔا

and arranged a repast,

وَءَاتَتْ كُلَّ وَٰحِدَةٍ مِّنْهُنَّ سِكِّينًا

and gave each of them a knife,

وَقَالَتِ ٱخْرُجْ عَلَيْهِنَّ

and said [to Joseph], 'Come out before them.'

فَلَمَّا رَأَيْنَهُۥ أَكْبَرْنَهُۥ

So when they saw him, they marveled at him

وَقَطَّعْنَ أَيْدِيَهُنَّ

and cut their hands [absent-mindedly],

وَقُلْنَ حَٰشَ لِلَّهِ

and they said, 'Good heavens!

مَا هَٰذَا بَشَرًا

This is not a human being!

إِنْ هَٰذَآ إِلَّا مَلَكٌ كَرِيمٌ ۞

This is but a noble angel!'

قَالَتْ 32 She said,

فَذَٰلِكُنَّ ٱلَّذِى لُمْتُنَّنِى فِيهِ

'He is the one on whose account you blamed me.

وَلَقَدْ رَٰوَدتُّهُۥ عَن نَّفْسِهِۦ

Certainly I did solicit him,

فَٱسْتَعْصَمَ

but he was continent,

وَلَئِن لَّمْ يَفْعَلْ مَآ ءَامُرُهُۥ

and if he does not do what I bid him,

لَيُسْجَنَنَّ

surely he shall be imprisoned

وَلَيَكُونًا مِّنَ ٱلصَّٰغِرِينَ ۞

and he will be among the wretched.'

قَالَ رَبِّ ٱلسِّجْنُ أَحَبُّ إِلَىَّ 33 He said, 'My Lord! The prison is dearer to me

مِمَّا يَدْعُونَنِى إِلَيْهِ

than to what they invite me.

وَإِلَّا تَصْرِفْ

If You do not turn away

عَنِّى كَيْدَهُنَّ

their schemes from me,

أَصْبُ إِلَيْهِنَّ

then I will incline towards them

وَأَكُن مِّنَ ٱلْجَٰهِلِينَ ۞

and become one of the senseless.'

فَٱسْتَجَابَ لَهُۥ رَبُّهُۥ 34 So his Lord answered him

فَصَرَفَ عَنْهُ كَيْدَهُنَّ
and turned away their stratagems from him.

إِنَّهُ هُوَ ٱلسَّمِيعُ ٱلْعَلِيمُ ﴿٣٤﴾
Indeed He is the All-hearing, the All-knowing.

ثُمَّ بَدَا لَهُم
35 Then it appeared to them,[1]

مِّنۢ بَعْدِ مَا رَأَوُاْ ٱلْءَايَـٰتِ
after they had seen all the signs [of his innocence],

لَيَسْجُنُنَّهُۥ حَتَّىٰ حِينٍ ﴿٣٥﴾
that they should confine him for some time.

وَدَخَلَ مَعَهُ ٱلسِّجْنَ فَتَيَانِ
36 There entered the prison two youths along with him.

قَالَ أَحَدُهُمَآ
One of them said,

إِنِّىٓ أَرَىٰنِىٓ أَعْصِرُ خَمْرًا
'I dreamt that I am pressing grapes.'

وَقَالَ ٱلْءَاخَرُ
The other said,

إِنِّىٓ أَرَىٰنِىٓ أَحْمِلُ فَوْقَ رَأْسِى خُبْزًا
'I dreamt that I am carrying bread on my head

تَأْكُلُ ٱلطَّيْرُ مِنْهُ
from which the birds are eating.'

نَبِّئْنَا بِتَأْوِيلِهِۦٓ
'Inform us of its interpretation,' [they said],

إِنَّا نَرَىٰكَ مِنَ ٱلْمُحْسِنِينَ ﴿٣٦﴾
'for indeed we see you to be a virtuous man.'

قَالَ
37 He said,

لَا يَأْتِيكُمَا طَعَامٌ تُرْزَقَانِهِۦٓ
'Before the meals you are served come to you

إِلَّا نَبَّأْتُكُمَا بِتَأْوِيلِهِۦ قَبْلَ أَن يَأْتِيَكُمَا
I will inform you of its interpretation.

ذَٰلِكُمَا مِمَّا عَلَّمَنِى رَبِّىٓ
That is among things my Lord has taught me.

إِنِّى تَرَكْتُ مِلَّةَ قَوْمٍ
Indeed I renounce the creed of the people

لَّا يُؤْمِنُونَ بِٱللَّهِ
who have no faith in Allah

وَهُم بِٱلْءَاخِرَةِ هُمْ كَـٰفِرُونَ ﴿٣٧﴾
and who [also] disbelieve in the Hereafter.

وَٱتَّبَعْتُ مِلَّةَ ءَابَآءِىٓ
38 I follow the creed of my fathers,

إِبْرَٰهِيمَ وَإِسْحَـٰقَ وَيَعْقُوبَ
Abraham, Isaac and Jacob.

مَا كَانَ لَنَآ
It is not for us

أَن نُّشْرِكَ بِٱللَّهِ مِن شَىْءٍ
to ascribe any partner to Allah.

ذَٰلِكَ مِن فَضْلِ ٱللَّهِ عَلَيْنَا
That is by virtue of Allah's grace upon us

وَعَلَى ٱلنَّاسِ
and upon all mankind,

وَلَـٰكِنَّ أَكْثَرَ ٱلنَّاسِ لَا يَشْكُرُونَ ﴿٣٨﴾
but most people do not give thanks.

يَـٰصَـٰحِبَىِ ٱلسِّجْنِ
39 O my prison mates!

ءَأَرْبَابٌ مُّتَفَرِّقُونَ خَيْرٌ
Are different masters better,

---

[1] That is, the menfolk.

or Allah, the One, the All-paramount?

مَا تَعْبُدُونَ مِن دُونِهِۦٓ إِلَّآ أَسْمَآءً 40 You do not worship besides Him but [mere] names

سَمَّيْتُمُوهَآ أَنتُمْ وَءَابَآؤُكُم     that you and your fathers have coined,

مَّآ أَنزَلَ ٱللَّهُ بِهَا مِن سُلْطَٰنٍ     for which Allah has not sent down any authority.

إِنِ ٱلْحُكْمُ إِلَّا لِلَّهِ     Sovereignty belongs only to Allah.

أَمَرَ أَلَّا تَعْبُدُوٓا۟ إِلَّآ إِيَّاهُ     He has commanded you to worship none except Him.

ذَٰلِكَ ٱلدِّينُ ٱلْقَيِّمُ     That is the upright religion,

وَلَٰكِنَّ أَكْثَرَ ٱلنَّاسِ لَا يَعْلَمُونَ ۝     but most people do not know.

يَٰصَٰحِبَيِ ٱلسِّجْنِ 41 O my prison mates!

أَمَّآ أَحَدُكُمَا     As for one of you,

فَيَسْقِى رَبَّهُۥ خَمْرًا     he will serve wine to his master,

وَأَمَّا ٱلْءَاخَرُ     and as for the other,

فَيُصْلَبُ     he will be crucified,

فَتَأْكُلُ ٱلطَّيْرُ مِن رَّأْسِهِۦ     and vultures will eat from his head.

قُضِىَ ٱلْأَمْرُ ٱلَّذِى فِيهِ تَسْتَفْتِيَانِ ۝     The matter about which you inquire has been decided.'

وَقَالَ لِلَّذِى ظَنَّ 42 Then he said to the one whom he knew

أَنَّهُۥ نَاجٍ مِّنْهُمَا     would be delivered from among the two:

ٱذْكُرْنِى عِندَ رَبِّكَ     'Mention me to your master.'

فَأَنسَىٰهُ ٱلشَّيْطَٰنُ     But Satan caused him to forget

ذِكْرَ رَبِّهِۦ     mentioning [it] to his master.

فَلَبِثَ فِى ٱلسِّجْنِ بِضْعَ سِنِينَ ۝     So he remained in the prison for several years.

وَقَالَ ٱلْمَلِكُ 43 [One day] the king said,

إِنِّىٓ أَرَىٰ سَبْعَ بَقَرَٰتٍ سِمَانٍ     'I saw [in a dream] seven fat cows

يَأْكُلُهُنَّ سَبْعٌ عِجَافٌ     being devoured by seven lean ones,

وَسَبْعَ سُنۢبُلَٰتٍ خُضْرٍ     and seven green ears

وَأُخَرَ يَابِسَٰتٍ     and [seven] others [that were] dry.

يَٰٓأَيُّهَا ٱلْمَلَأُ أَفْتُونِى فِى رُءْيَٰىَ     O courtiers, give me your opinion about my dream,

إِن كُنتُمْ لِلرُّءْيَا تَعْبُرُونَ ۝     if you can interpret dreams.'

قَالُوٓا۟ أَضْغَٰثُ أَحْلَٰمٍ 44 They said, '[These are] confused nightmares,

وَمَا نَحْنُ بِتَأْوِيلِ ٱلْأَحْلَٰمِ بِعَٰلِمِينَ ٤٤    and we do not know the interpretation of nightmares.'

وَقَالَ ٱلَّذِى نَجَا مِنْهُمَا ٤٥    45 Said the one of the two who had been delivered,

وَٱدَّكَرَ بَعْدَ أُمَّةٍ    remembering [Joseph] after a along time:

أَنَا۠ أُنَبِّئُكُم بِتَأْوِيلِهِۦ    'I will inform you of its interpretation;

فَأَرْسِلُونِ ٤٥    so let me go [to meet Joseph in the prison].'

يُوسُفُ أَيُّهَا ٱلصِّدِّيقُ ٤٦    46 'Joseph,' [he said], 'O truthful one,

أَفْتِنَا فِى سَبْعِ بَقَرَٰتٍ سِمَانٍ    give us your opinion concerning seven fat cows

يَأْكُلُهُنَّ سَبْعٌ عِجَافٌ    who are eaten by seven lean ones,

وَسَبْعِ سُنۢبُلَٰتٍ خُضْرٍ    and seven green ears

وَأُخَرَ يَابِسَٰتٍ    and [seven] others dry,

لَّعَلِّىٓ أَرْجِعُ إِلَى ٱلنَّاسِ    that I may return to the people

لَعَلَّهُمْ يَعْلَمُونَ ٤٦    so that they may know [the truth of the matter].'

قَالَ تَزْرَعُونَ سَبْعَ سِنِينَ دَأَبًا ٤٧    47 He said, 'You will sow for seven consecutive years.

فَمَا حَصَدتُّمْ فَذَرُوهُ فِى سُنۢبُلِهِۦٓ    Then leave in the ear whatever [grain] you harvest,

إِلَّا قَلِيلًا مِّمَّا تَأْكُلُونَ ٤٧    except a little that you eat.

ثُمَّ يَأْتِى مِنۢ بَعْدِ ذَٰلِكَ سَبْعٌ شِدَادٌ ٤٨    48 Then after that there will come seven hard years

يَأْكُلْنَ    which will eat up

مَا قَدَّمْتُمْ لَهُنَّ    whatever you have set aside for them

إِلَّا قَلِيلًا مِّمَّا تُحْصِنُونَ ٤٨    —all except a little which you preserve [for seed].

ثُمَّ يَأْتِى مِنۢ بَعْدِ ذَٰلِكَ عَامٌ ٤٩    49 Then after that there will come a year

فِيهِ يُغَاثُ ٱلنَّاسُ    wherein the people will be granted relief

وَفِيهِ يَعْصِرُونَ ٤٩    and provided with rains therein.[1]

وَقَالَ ٱلْمَلِكُ ٱئْتُونِى بِهِۦ ٥٠    50 The king said, 'Bring him to me!'

فَلَمَّا جَآءَهُ ٱلرَّسُولُ    When the messenger came to him,[2]

قَالَ ٱرْجِعْ إِلَىٰ رَبِّكَ    he said, 'Go back to your master,

---

[1] The translation given here is in accordance with the reading *yuʿṣarūn* narrated from al-Imam al-Ṣādiq; see *Majmaʿ al-Bayān* and *Tafsīr al-Qummī*; see also *Lisān al-ʿArab*, under *ʿaṣr*. The same reading is attributed to al-Aʿraj and ʿĪsā al-Baṣrī (*Muʿjam al-Qirāʾāt al-Qurʾāniyyah*). However, in accordance with the reading *yaʿṣirūn*, the meaning will be 'they will press [i.e. grapes or oil seeds, for juice and oil] therein.'

[2] That is, to Joseph (ʿa).

فَسْـَٔلْهُ مَا بَالُ ٱلنِّسْوَةِ

and ask him about the affair of women

ٱلَّـٰتِى قَطَّعْنَ أَيْدِيَهُنَّ

who cut their hands.

إِنَّ رَبِّى بِكَيْدِهِنَّ عَلِيمٌ ۝

My Lord is indeed well aware of their stratagems.'

قَالَ مَا خَطْبُكُنَّ 51 The king said, 'What was your business, women,

إِذْ رَٰوَدتُّنَّ يُوسُفَ عَن نَّفْسِهِۦ

when you solicited Joseph?'

قُلْنَ حَـٰشَ لِلَّهِ

They said, 'Heaven be praised!

مَا عَلِمْنَا عَلَيْهِ مِن سُوٓءٍ

We know of no evil in him.'

قَالَتِ ٱمْرَأَتُ ٱلْعَزِيزِ

The prince's wife said,

ٱلْـَٔـٰنَ حَصْحَصَ ٱلْحَقُّ

'Now the truth has come to light!

أَنَا۠ رَٰوَدتُّهُۥ عَن نَّفْسِهِۦ

It was I who solicited him,

وَإِنَّهُۥ لَمِنَ ٱلصَّـٰدِقِينَ ۝

and he is indeed telling the truth.'

ذَٰلِكَ 52 [Joseph said], [I initiated] this [inquiry],

لِيَعْلَمَ أَنِّى لَمْ أَخُنْهُ

that he[1] may know that I did not betray him

بِٱلْغَيْبِ

in his absence,

وَأَنَّ ٱللَّهَ لَا يَهْدِى

and that Allah does not further

كَيْدَ ٱلْخَآئِنِينَ ۝ ۞

the schemes of the treacherous.

[PART 13]

وَمَآ أُبَرِّئُ نَفْسِىٓ 53 Yet I do not absolve my [own carnal] soul,

إِنَّ ٱلنَّفْسَ لَأَمَّارَةٌۢ بِٱلسُّوٓءِ

for the [carnal] soul indeed prompts [men] to evil,

إِلَّا مَا رَحِمَ رَبِّىٓ

except inasmuch as my Lord has mercy.

إِنَّ رَبِّى غَفُورٌ رَّحِيمٌ ۝

Indeed my Lord is all-forgiving, all-merciful.'

وَقَالَ ٱلْمَلِكُ ٱئْتُونِى بِهِۦٓ 54 The king said, 'Bring him to me,

أَسْتَخْلِصْهُ لِنَفْسِى

I will make him my favourite.'

فَلَمَّا كَلَّمَهُۥ قَالَ

Then, when he had spoken with him, he said,

إِنَّكَ ٱلْيَوْمَ

'Indeed today [onwards]

لَدَيْنَا مَكِينٌ أَمِينٌ ۝

you will be honoured and trustworthy with us.'

قَالَ 55 He said,

ٱجْعَلْنِى عَلَىٰ خَزَآئِنِ ٱلْأَرْضِ

'Put me in charge of the country's granaries.

إِنِّى حَفِيظٌ عَلِيمٌ ۝

I am indeed fastidious [and] well-informed.'

---

[1] That is, the Egyptian nobleman in whose house Joseph ('a) was living.

وَكَذَٰلِكَ مَكَّنَّا لِيُوسُفَ فِى ٱلْأَرْضِ 56 That is how We established Joseph in the land

يَتَبَوَّأُ مِنْهَا حَيْثُ يَشَآءُ that he may settle in it wherever he wished.

نُصِيبُ بِرَحْمَتِنَا مَن نَّشَآءُ We confer Our mercy on whomever We wish,

وَلَا نُضِيعُ أَجْرَ ٱلْمُحْسِنِينَ ۝ and We do not waste the reward of the virtuous.

وَلَأَجْرُ ٱلْأَخِرَةِ خَيْرٌ 57 And the reward of the Hereafter is surely better

لِّلَّذِينَ ءَامَنُوا۟ وَكَانُوا۟ يَتَّقُونَ ۝ for those who have faith and are Godwary.

وَجَآءَ إِخْوَةُ يُوسُفَ 58 [After some years] the brothers of Joseph came

فَدَخَلُوا۟ عَلَيْهِ and entered his presence.

فَعَرَفَهُمْ He recognized them,

وَهُمْ لَهُۥ مُنكِرُونَ ۝ but they did not recognize him.

وَلَمَّا جَهَّزَهُم بِجَهَازِهِمْ 59 When he had furnished them with their provision,

قَالَ ٱئْتُونِى بِأَخٍ لَّكُم he said, 'Bring me a brother that you have

مِّنْ أَبِيكُمْ through your father.

أَلَا تَرَوْنَ أَنِّى أُوفِى ٱلْكَيْلَ Do you not see that I give the full measure

وَأَنَا۠ خَيْرُ ٱلْمُنزِلِينَ ۝ and that I am the best of hosts?

فَإِن لَّمْ تَأْتُونِى بِهِۦ 60 But if you do not bring him to me,

فَلَا كَيْلَ لَكُمْ عِندِى then there will be no rations for you with me,

وَلَا تَقْرَبُونِ ۝ and don't [ever] come near me.'

قَالُوا۟ سَنُرَٰوِدُ عَنْهُ أَبَاهُ 61 They said, 'We will solicit him from his father.

وَإِنَّا لَفَٰعِلُونَ ۝ [That] we will surely do.'

وَقَالَ لِفِتْيَٰنِهِ 62 He said to his servants,

ٱجْعَلُوا۟ بِضَٰعَتَهُمْ فِى رِحَالِهِمْ 'Put their money in their saddlebags.

لَعَلَّهُمْ يَعْرِفُونَهَآ Maybe they will recognize it

إِذَا ٱنقَلَبُوٓا۟ إِلَىٰٓ أَهْلِهِمْ when they return to their folks,

لَعَلَّهُمْ يَرْجِعُونَ ۝ and maybe they will come back [again].'

فَلَمَّا رَجَعُوٓا۟ إِلَىٰٓ أَبِيهِمْ قَالُوا۟ 63 So when they returned to their father, they said,

يَٰٓأَبَانَا مُنِعَ مِنَّا ٱلْكَيْلُ 'Father, the measure has been withheld from us,

فَأَرْسِلْ مَعَنَآ أَخَانَا so let our brother go with us

نَكْتَلْ so that we may obtain the measure,

وَإِنَّا لَهُۥ لَحَٰفِظُونَ ۝ and we will indeed take [good] care of him.'

قَالَ هَلْ ءَامَنُكُمْ عَلَيْهِ    64 He said, 'Should I trust you with him

إِلَّا كَمَآ أَمِنتُكُمْ عَلَىٰٓ أَخِيهِ    just as I trusted you with his brother

مِن قَبْلُ    before?

فَٱللَّهُ خَيْرٌ حَفِظًا    Yet Allah is the best of protectors,

وَهُوَ أَرْحَمُ ٱلرَّٰحِمِينَ ۝    and He is the most merciful of merciful ones.'

وَلَمَّا فَتَحُوا۟ مَتَٰعَهُمْ    65 And when they opened their baggage,

وَجَدُوا۟ بِضَٰعَتَهُمْ رُدَّتْ إِلَيْهِمْ    they found their money restored to them.

قَالُوا۟ يَٰٓأَبَانَا مَا نَبْغِى    They said, 'Father, what [more] do we want?!

هَٰذِهِۦ بِضَٰعَتُنَا رُدَّتْ إِلَيْنَا    This is our money, restored to us!

وَنَمِيرُ أَهْلَنَا    We will get provisions for our family

وَنَحْفَظُ أَخَانَا    and take care of our brother,

وَنَزْدَادُ كَيْلَ بَعِيرٍ    and add another camel-load of rations.

ذَٰلِكَ كَيْلٌ يَسِيرٌ ۝    These are meagre rations.'

قَالَ لَنْ أُرْسِلَهُۥ مَعَكُمْ    66 He said, 'I will not let him go with you

حَتَّىٰ تُؤْتُونِ مَوْثِقًا مِّنَ ٱللَّهِ    until you give me a [solemn] pledge by Allah

لَتَأْتُنَّنِى بِهِۦٓ    that you will surely bring him back to me,

إِلَّآ أَن يُحَاطَ بِكُمْ    unless you are made to perish.'

فَلَمَّآ ءَاتَوْهُ مَوْثِقَهُمْ    When they had given him their [solemn] pledge,

قَالَ ٱللَّهُ عَلَىٰ مَا نَقُولُ وَكِيلٌ ۝    he said, 'Allah is witness over what we say.'

وَقَالَ يَٰبَنِىَّ    67 And he said, 'My sons,

لَا تَدْخُلُوا۟ مِنۢ بَابٍ وَٰحِدٍ    do not enter by one gate,

وَٱدْخُلُوا۟ مِنْ أَبْوَٰبٍ مُّتَفَرِّقَةٍ    but enter by separate gates,

وَمَآ أُغْنِى عَنكُم    though I cannot avail you

مِّنَ ٱللَّهِ مِن شَىْءٍ    anything against Allah.

إِنِ ٱلْحُكْمُ إِلَّا لِلَّهِ    Sovereignty belongs only to Allah.

عَلَيْهِ تَوَكَّلْتُ    In Him I have put my trust;

وَعَلَيْهِ فَلْيَتَوَكَّلِ ٱلْمُتَوَكِّلُونَ ۝    and in Him let all the trusting put their trust.'

وَلَمَّا دَخَلُوا۟    68 When they entered

مِنْ حَيْثُ أَمَرَهُمْ أَبُوهُم    whence their father had bidden them,

مَّا كَانَ يُغْنِى عَنْهُم    it did not avail them

مِّنَ ٱللَّهِ مِن شَىْءٍ    anything against Allah,

إِلَّا حَاجَةً فِى نَفْسِ يَعْقُوبَ قَضَىٰهَا    but only fulfilled a wish in Jacob's heart.

وَإِنَّهُ لَذُو عِلْمٍ    Indeed he had the knowledge

لِّمَا عَلَّمْنَٰهُ    of what We had taught him,

وَلَٰكِنَّ أَكْثَرَ ٱلنَّاسِ لَا يَعْلَمُونَ ۝    but most people do not know.

وَلَمَّا دَخَلُوا۟ عَلَىٰ يُوسُفَ 69   And when they entered into the presence of Joseph,

ءَاوَىٰٓ إِلَيْهِ أَخَاهُ قَالَ    he set his brother close to himself, and said,

إِنِّىٓ أَنَا۠ أَخُوكَ    'Indeed I am your brother,

فَلَا تَبْتَئِسْ بِمَا كَانُوا۟ يَعْمَلُونَ ۝    so do not sorrow for what they used to do.'

فَلَمَّا جَهَّزَهُم بِجَهَازِهِمْ 70   When he had furnished them with their provision,

جَعَلَ ٱلسِّقَايَةَ فِى رَحْلِ أَخِيهِ    he put the drinking-cup into his brother's saddlebag.

ثُمَّ أَذَّنَ مُؤَذِّنٌ    Then a herald shouted:

أَيَّتُهَا ٱلْعِيرُ    'O [men of the] caravan!

إِنَّكُمْ لَسَٰرِقُونَ ۝    You are indeed thieves!'

قَالُوا۟ وَأَقْبَلُوا۟ عَلَيْهِم 71   They said, as they turned towards them,

مَّاذَا تَفْقِدُونَ ۝    'What are you missing?'

قَالُوا۟ نَفْقِدُ صُوَاعَ ٱلْمَلِكِ 72   They said, 'We miss the king's goblet.'

وَلِمَن جَآءَ بِهِۦ حِمْلُ بَعِيرٍ    'Whoever brings it shall have a camel-load [of grain],'

وَأَنَا۠ بِهِۦ زَعِيمٌ ۝    [said the steward], 'I will guarantee that.'

قَالُوا۟ تَٱللَّهِ 73   They said, 'By Allah!

لَقَدْ عَلِمْتُم مَّا جِئْنَا    You certainly know that we did not come

لِنُفْسِدَ فِى ٱلْأَرْضِ    to make trouble in this country,

وَمَا كُنَّا سَٰرِقِينَ ۝    and we are not thieves.'

قَالُوا۟ فَمَا جَزَآؤُهُۥٓ 74   They said, 'What shall be its requital

إِن كُنتُمْ كَٰذِبِينَ ۝    if you [prove to] be lying?'

قَالُوا۟ جَزَٰٓؤُهُۥ 75   They said, 'The requital for it

مَن وُجِدَ فِى رَحْلِهِۦ    shall be that he in whose saddlebag it is found

فَهُوَ جَزَٰٓؤُهُۥ    shall give himself over as its requital.

كَذَٰلِكَ نَجْزِى ٱلظَّٰلِمِينَ ۝    Thus do we requite the wrongdoers.'

فَبَدَأَ بِأَوْعِيَتِهِمْ 76   Then he began with their sacks,

333

قَبْلَ وِعَآءِ أَخِيهِ before [opening] his brother's sack.

ثُمَّ ٱسْتَخْرَجَهَا مِن وِعَآءِ أَخِيهِ Then he took it out from his brother's sack.

كَذَٰلِكَ كِدْنَا لِيُوسُفَ Thus did We devise for Joseph's sake.

مَا كَانَ لِيَأْخُذَ أَخَاهُ He could not have held his brother

فِى دِينِ ٱلْمَلِكِ under the king's law

إِلَّآ أَن يَشَآءَ ٱللَّهُ unless Allah willed [otherwise].

نَرْفَعُ دَرَجَٰتٍ مَّن نَّشَآءُ We raise in rank whomever We please,

وَفَوْقَ كُلِّ ذِى عِلْمٍ and above every man of knowledge

عَلِيمٌ ۞ ۞ is One who knows best.[1]

قَالُوٓاْ إِن يَسْرِقْ 77 They said, 'If he has stolen [there is no wonder];

فَقَدْ سَرَقَ أَخٌ لَّهُۥ مِن قَبْلُ a brother of his had stolen before.'

فَأَسَرَّهَا يُوسُفُ فِى نَفْسِهِ Thereupon Joseph kept the matter to himself

وَلَمْ يُبْدِهَا لَهُمْ and he did not disclose it to them.

قَالَ أَنتُمْ شَرٌّ مَّكَانًا He said, 'Your are in a worse state!

وَٱللَّهُ أَعْلَمُ بِمَا تَصِفُونَ ۞ And Allah knows best what you allege.'

قَالُوٓاْ يَٰٓأَيُّهَا ٱلْعَزِيزُ 78 They said, 'O emir!

إِنَّ لَهُۥٓ أَبًا شَيْخًا كَبِيرًا Indeed he has a father, a very old man;

فَخُذْ أَحَدَنَا مَكَانَهُۥٓ so take one of us in his place.

إِنَّا نَرَىٰكَ مِنَ ٱلْمُحْسِنِينَ ۞ Indeed we see that you are a virtuous man.'

قَالَ مَعَاذَ ٱللَّهِ أَن نَّأْخُذَ 79 He said, 'God forbid that we should take

إِلَّا مَن وَجَدْنَا مَتَٰعَنَا عِندَهُۥٓ anyone except him with whom we found our wares,

إِنَّآ إِذًا لَّظَٰلِمُونَ ۞ for then we would indeed be wrongdoers.'

فَلَمَّا ٱسْتَيْـَٔسُواْ مِنْهُ 80 When they had despaired of [moving] him,

خَلَصُواْ نَجِيًّا they withdrew to confer privately.

قَالَ كَبِيرُهُمْ The eldest of them said,

أَلَمْ تَعْلَمُوٓاْ أَنَّ أَبَاكُمْ 'Don't you know that your father

قَدْ أَخَذَ عَلَيْكُم مَّوْثِقًا مِّنَ ٱللَّهِ has taken a [solemn] pledge from you by Allah,

وَمِن قَبْلُ مَا فَرَّطتُمْ and earlier you have neglected your duty

فِى يُوسُفَ in regard to Joseph?

---

[1] Or 'above every man of knowledge is one who knows better.'

فَلَنْ أَبْرَحَ ٱلْأَرْضَ    So I will never leave this land

حَتَّىٰ يَأْذَنَ لِىٓ أَبِىٓ    until my father permits me,

أَوْ يَحْكُمَ ٱللَّهُ لِى    or Allah passes a judgement for me,

وَهُوَ خَيْرُ ٱلْحَـٰكِمِينَ ۞    and He is the best of judges.

۞ ٱرْجِعُوٓا۟ إِلَىٰٓ أَبِيكُمْ    81 Go back to your father,

فَقُولُوا۟ يَـٰٓأَبَانَآ    and say, "Father!

إِنَّ ٱبْنَكَ سَرَقَ    Your son has indeed committed theft,

وَمَا شَهِدْنَآ إِلَّا بِمَا عَلِمْنَا    and we testified only to what we knew,[1]

وَمَا كُنَّا لِلْغَيْبِ حَـٰفِظِينَ ۞    and we could not have forestalled the unseen.

وَسْـَٔلِ ٱلْقَرْيَةَ ٱلَّتِى كُنَّا فِيهَا    82 Ask [the people of] the town we were in,

وَٱلْعِيرَ ٱلَّتِىٓ أَقْبَلْنَا فِيهَا    and the caravan with which we came.

وَإِنَّا لَصَـٰدِقُونَ ۞    We indeed speak the truth." '

قَالَ    83 He[2] said, 'Rather

بَلْ سَوَّلَتْ لَكُمْ أَنفُسُكُمْ أَمْرًا    your souls have made a matter seem decorous to you.

فَصَبْرٌ جَمِيلٌ    Yet patience is graceful.

عَسَى ٱللَّهُ أَن يَأْتِيَنِى بِهِمْ جَمِيعًا    Maybe Allah will bring them all [back] to me.

إِنَّهُۥ هُوَ ٱلْعَلِيمُ ٱلْحَكِيمُ ۞    Indeed He is the All-knowing, the All-wise.'

وَتَوَلَّىٰ عَنْهُمْ وَقَالَ    84 And he turned away from them and said,

يَـٰٓأَسَفَىٰ عَلَىٰ يُوسُفَ    'Alas for Joseph!'

وَٱبْيَضَّتْ عَيْنَاهُ مِنَ ٱلْحُزْنِ    His eyes had turned white with grief,

فَهُوَ كَظِيمٌ ۞    and he choked with suppressed agony.

قَالُوا۟ تَٱللَّهِ    85 They said, 'By Allah!

تَفْتَؤُا۟ تَذْكُرُ يُوسُفَ    You will go on remembering Joseph

حَتَّىٰ تَكُونَ حَرَضًا    until you wreck your health

أَوْ تَكُونَ مِنَ ٱلْهَـٰلِكِينَ ۞    or perish.'

قَالَ    86 He said,

إِنَّمَآ أَشْكُوا۟ بَثِّى وَحُزْنِى    'I complain of my anguish and grief only

---

[1] That is, concerning the penalty for theft according to the custom of the Canaanites.

[2] That is, Jacob ( 'a), after hearing what his sons had told him.

إِلَى ٱللَّهِ to Allah.

وَأَعْلَمُ مِنَ ٱللَّهِ مَا لَا تَعْلَمُونَ ٨٦ I know from Allah what you do not know.'

يَـٰبَنِىَّ ٱذْهَبُوا 87 'Go, my sons,

فَتَحَسَّسُوا مِن يُوسُفَ and look for Joseph

وَأَخِيهِ and his brother,

وَلَا تَا۟يْـَٔسُوا مِن رَّوْحِ ٱللَّهِ and do not despair of Allah's mercy.

إِنَّهُۥ لَا يَا۟يْـَٔسُ مِن رَّوْحِ ٱللَّهِ Indeed no one despairs of Allah's mercy

إِلَّا ٱلْقَوْمُ ٱلْكَـٰفِرُونَ ٨٧ except the faithless lot.'

فَلَمَّا دَخَلُوا عَلَيْهِ 88 Then, when they entered into his presence,

قَالُوا يَـٰٓأَيُّهَا ٱلْعَزِيزُ they said, 'O emir!

مَسَّنَا وَأَهْلَنَا ٱلضُّرُّ Distress has befallen our family, and us,

وَجِئْنَا بِبِضَـٰعَةٍ مُّزْجَىٰةٍ and we have brought [just] a meager sum.

فَأَوْفِ لَنَا ٱلْكَيْلَ Yet grant us the full measure,

وَتَصَدَّقْ عَلَيْنَآ and be charitable to us!

إِنَّ ٱللَّهَ يَجْزِى ٱلْمُتَصَدِّقِينَ ٨٨ Indeed Allah rewards the charitable.'

قَالَ 89 He said,

هَلْ عَلِمْتُم مَّا فَعَلْتُم بِيُوسُفَ 'Have you realized what you did to Joseph

وَأَخِيهِ and his brother,

إِذْ أَنتُمْ جَـٰهِلُونَ ٨٩ when you were senseless?'

قَالُوٓا أَءِنَّكَ لَأَنتَ يُوسُفُ ٩٠ They said, 'Are you really Joseph?!'

قَالَ أَنَا۠ يُوسُفُ وَهَـٰذَآ أَخِى He said, 'I am Joseph, and this is my brother.

قَدْ مَنَّ ٱللَّهُ عَلَيْنَآ Certainly Allah has shown us favour.

إِنَّهُۥ مَن يَتَّقِ وَيَصْبِرْ Indeed if one is Godwary and patient

فَإِنَّ ٱللَّهَ لَا يُضِيعُ Allah does not waste

أَجْرَ ٱلْمُحْسِنِينَ ٩٠ the reward of the virtuous.'

قَالُوا تَٱللَّهِ 91 They said, 'By Allah,

لَقَدْ ءَاثَرَكَ ٱللَّهُ عَلَيْنَا Allah has certainly preferred you over us,

وَإِن كُنَّا لَخَـٰطِـِٔينَ ٩١ and we have indeed been erring.'

قَالَ لَا تَثْرِيبَ عَلَيْكُمُ ٱلْيَوْمَ 92 He said, 'There shall be no reproach on you today.

يَغْفِرُ ٱللَّهُ لَكُمْ Allah will forgive you,

وَهُوَ أَرْحَمُ ٱلرَّٰحِمِينَ ۝     and He is the most merciful of the merciful.

٩٣ ٱذْهَبُوا بِقَمِيصِى هَـٰذَا     93 Take this shirt of mine,

فَأَلْقُوهُ عَلَىٰ وَجْهِ أَبِى     and cast it upon my father's face;

يَأْتِ بَصِيرًا     he will regain his sight,

وَأْتُونِى بِأَهْلِكُمْ أَجْمَعِينَ ۝     and bring me all your folks.'

وَلَمَّا فَصَلَتِ ٱلْعِيرُ قَالَ أَبُوهُمْ     94 As the caravan set off, their father said,

إِنِّى لَأَجِدُ رِيحَ يُوسُفَ     'I sense the scent of Joseph,

لَوْلَا أَن تُفَنِّدُونِ ۝     if you will not consider me a dotard.'

قَالُوا تَٱللَّهِ     95 They said, 'By God,

إِنَّكَ لَفِى ضَلَـٰلِكَ ٱلْقَدِيمِ ۝     you persist in your inveterate error.'

فَلَمَّا أَن جَآءَ ٱلْبَشِيرُ     96 When the bearer of good news arrived,

أَلْقَىٰهُ عَلَىٰ وَجْهِهِ     he cast it[1] on his face,

فَٱرْتَدَّ بَصِيرًا     and he regained his sight.

قَالَ أَلَمْ أَقُل لَّكُمْ     He said, 'Did I not tell you,

إِنِّىٓ أَعْلَمُ مِنَ ٱللَّهِ مَا لَا تَعْلَمُونَ ۝     "I know from Allah what you do not know?" '

قَالُوا يَـٰٓأَبَانَا     97 They said, 'Father!

ٱسْتَغْفِرْ لَنَا ذُنُوبَنَآ     Plead [with Allah] for forgiveness of our sins!

إِنَّا كُنَّا خَـٰطِـِٔينَ ۝     We have indeed been erring.'

قَالَ     98 He said,

سَوْفَ أَسْتَغْفِرُ لَكُمْ رَبِّىٓ     'I shall plead with my Lord to forgive you;

إِنَّهُ هُوَ ٱلْغَفُورُ ٱلرَّحِيمُ ۝     indeed He is the All-forgiving, the All-merciful.'

فَلَمَّا دَخَلُوا عَلَىٰ يُوسُفَ     99 When they entered into the presence of Joseph,

ءَاوَىٰٓ إِلَيْهِ أَبَوَيْهِ     he set his parents close to himself,

وَقَالَ ٱدْخُلُوا مِصْرَ     and said, 'Welcome to Egypt,

إِن شَآءَ ٱللَّهُ ءَامِنِينَ ۝     in safety, God willing!'

وَرَفَعَ أَبَوَيْهِ عَلَى ٱلْعَرْشِ     100 And he seated his parents high upon the throne,

وَخَرُّوا لَهُ سُجَّدًا     and they fell down prostrate before him.

وَقَالَ يَـٰٓأَبَتِ     He said, 'Father!

هَـٰذَا تَأْوِيلُ رُءْيَـٰىَ مِن قَبْلُ     This is the fulfillment of my dream of long ago,

---

[1] That is, the shirt of Joseph ('a).

337

قَدْ جَعَلَهَا رَبِّى حَقًّا     which my Lord has made come true.

وَقَدْ أَحْسَنَ بِى     He was certainly gracious to me

إِذْ أَخْرَجَنِى مِنَ ٱلسِّجْنِ     when He brought me out of the prison

وَجَآءَ بِكُم مِّنَ ٱلْبَدْوِ     and brought you over from the desert

مِنۢ بَعْدِ أَن نَّزَغَ ٱلشَّيْطَٰنُ     after that Satan had incited ill feeling

بَيْنِى وَبَيْنَ إِخْوَتِىٓ     between me and my brothers.

إِنَّ رَبِّى لَطِيفٌ     Indeed my Lord is all-attentive

لِّمَا يَشَآءُ     in bringing about what He wishes.

إِنَّهُۥ هُوَ ٱلْعَلِيمُ ٱلْحَكِيمُ ۞     Indeed He is the All-knowing, the All-wise.'

رَبِّ     101 'My Lord!

قَدْ ءَاتَيْتَنِى مِنَ ٱلْمُلْكِ     You have granted me a share in the kingdom,

وَعَلَّمْتَنِى مِن تَأْوِيلِ ٱلْأَحَادِيثِ     and taught me the interpretation of dreams.

فَاطِرَ ٱلسَّمَٰوَٰتِ وَٱلْأَرْضِ     Originator of the heavens and earth!

أَنتَ وَلِىِّۦ فِى ٱلدُّنْيَا     You are my guardian in this world

وَٱلْأَخِرَةِ     and the Hereafter!

تَوَفَّنِى مُسْلِمًا     Let my death be in submission [to You],

وَأَلْحِقْنِى بِٱلصَّٰلِحِينَ ۞     and unite me with the Righteous.'

ذَٰلِكَ مِنْ أَنۢبَآءِ ٱلْغَيْبِ     102 These are accounts of the Unseen

نُوحِيهِ إِلَيْكَ     which We reveal to *you*,

وَمَا كُنتَ لَدَيْهِمْ     and *you* were not with them

إِذْ أَجْمَعُوٓا۟ أَمْرَهُمْ وَهُمْ يَمْكُرُونَ ۞     when they conspired together and schemed.

وَمَآ أَكْثَرُ ٱلنَّاسِ     103 Yet most people

وَلَوْ حَرَصْتَ بِمُؤْمِنِينَ ۞     will not have faith, however eager *you* should be.

وَمَا تَسْـَٔلُهُمْ عَلَيْهِ مِنْ أَجْرٍ     104 *You* do not ask them any reward for it:

إِنْ هُوَ إِلَّا ذِكْرٌ لِّلْعَٰلَمِينَ ۞     it[1] is just a reminder for all the nations.

وَكَأَيِّن مِّنْ ءَايَةٍ فِى ٱلسَّمَٰوَٰتِ     105 How many a sign there is in the heavens

وَٱلْأَرْضِ     and the earth

يَمُرُّونَ عَلَيْهَا     that they pass by

---

[1] That is, the Qur'ān.

وَهُمْ عَنْهَا مُعْرِضُونَ ۝

while they are disregardful of it!

وَمَا يُؤْمِنُ أَكْثَرُهُم بِٱللَّهِ

106 And most of them do not believe in Allah

إِلَّا وَهُم مُّشْرِكُونَ ۝

without ascribing partners to Him.

أَفَأَمِنُوٓاْ أَن تَأْتِيَهُمْ

107 Do they feel secure from being overtaken

غَٰشِيَةٌ مِّنْ عَذَابِ ٱللَّهِ

by a blanket punishment from Allah,

أَوْ تَأْتِيَهُمُ ٱلسَّاعَةُ بَغْتَةً

or being overtaken by the Hour, suddenly,

وَهُمْ لَا يَشْعُرُونَ ۝

while they are unaware?

قُلْ هَٰذِهِۦ سَبِيلِىٓ

108 *Say,* 'This is my way.

أَدْعُوٓاْ إِلَى ٱللَّهِ عَلَىٰ بَصِيرَةٍ

I summon to Allah with insight

أَنَا۠ وَمَنِ ٱتَّبَعَنِى

—I and he who follows me.

وَسُبْحَٰنَ ٱللَّهِ

Immaculate is Allah,

وَمَآ أَنَا۠ مِنَ ٱلْمُشْرِكِينَ ۝

and I am not one of the polytheists.'

وَمَآ أَرْسَلْنَا مِن قَبْلِكَ

109 We did not send [any apostles] before *you*

إِلَّا رِجَالًا نُّوحِىٓ إِلَيْهِم

except as men to whom We revealed

مِّنْ أَهْلِ ٱلْقُرَىٰٓ

from among the people of the towns.

أَفَلَمْ يَسِيرُواْ فِى ٱلْأَرْضِ

Have they not traveled over the land

فَيَنظُرُواْ

so that they may observe

كَيْفَ كَانَ عَٰقِبَةُ ٱلَّذِينَ مِن قَبْلِهِمْ

how was the fate of those who were before them?

وَلَدَارُ ٱلْءَاخِرَةِ خَيْرٌ

And the abode of the Hereafter is surely better

لِّلَّذِينَ ٱتَّقَوْاْ

for those who are Godwary.

أَفَلَا تَعْقِلُونَ ۝

Do you not apply reason?

حَتَّىٰٓ إِذَا ٱسْتَيْـَٔسَ ٱلرُّسُلُ

110 When the apostles lost hope[1]

وَظَنُّوٓاْ أَنَّهُمْ قَدْ كُذِبُواْ

and they thought that they had been told lies,[2]

جَآءَهُمْ نَصْرُنَا

Our help came to them,

فَنُجِّىَ مَن نَّشَآءُ

and We delivered whomever We wished,

وَلَا يُرَدُّ بَأْسُنَا

and Our punishment will not be averted

عَنِ ٱلْقَوْمِ ٱلْمُجْرِمِينَ ۝

from the guilty lot.

---

[1] That is, when the apostles lost hopes of bringing their people to the right path.

[2] That is, the people to whom the apostles had been sent thought that the apostles had been told lies concerning the impending punishment of the infidels.

لَقَدْ كَانَ فِى قَصَصِهِمْ عِبْرَةٌ ١١١ There is certainly a moral in their accounts

لِّأُوْلِى ٱلْأَلْبَبِ for those who possess intellect.

مَا كَانَ حَدِيثًا يُفْتَرَى This [Qur'ān] is not a fabricated discourse;

وَلَـكِن تَصْدِيقَ ٱلَّذِى rather it is a confirmation of what was [revealed]

بَيْنَ يَدَيْهِ before it,

وَتَفْصِيلَ كُلِّ شَىْءٍ and an elaboration[1] of all things,

وَهُدًى وَرَحْمَةً and a guidance and mercy

لِّقَوْمٍ يُؤْمِنُونَ ۝ for a people who have faith.

# سُورَةُ الرَّعْد     13. SŪRAT AL-RA'D[2]

بِسْمِ ٱللَّهِ In the Name of Allah,

ٱلرَّحْمَـٰنِ ٱلرَّحِيمِ the All-beneficent, the All-merciful.

الٓمٓر ١ *Alif, Lām, Mīm, Rā.*

تِلْكَ ءَايَـٰتُ ٱلْكِتَـٰبِ These are the signs of the Book.

وَٱلَّذِى أُنزِلَ إِلَيْكَ مِن رَّبِّكَ That which has been sent down to *you* from *your* Lord

ٱلْحَقُّ is the truth,

وَلَـٰكِنَّ أَكْثَرَ ٱلنَّاسِ لَا يُؤْمِنُونَ ۝ but most people do not believe [in it].

ٱللَّهُ ٱلَّذِى رَفَعَ ٱلسَّمَـٰوَٰتِ ٢ It is Allah who raised the heavens

بِغَيْرِ عَمَدٍ تَرَوْنَهَا without any pillars that you see,

ثُمَّ ٱسْتَوَىٰ عَلَى ٱلْعَرْشِ and then presided over the Throne.

وَسَخَّرَ ٱلشَّمْسَ وَٱلْقَمَرَ He disposed the sun and the moon,

كُلٌّ يَجْرِى لِأَجَلٍ مُّسَمًّى each moving for a specified term.[3]

يُدَبِّرُ ٱلْأَمْرَ He directs the command,

يُفَصِّلُ ٱلْآيَـٰتِ [and] elaborates[4] the signs

لَعَلَّكُم بِلِقَآءِ رَبِّكُمْ تُوقِنُونَ ۝ that you may be certain of encountering your Lord.

---

[1] Or 'unravelling.'

[2] The *sūrah* takes its name from thunder (*al-ra'd*), mentioned in verse 13.

[3] Or 'until a specified time.'

[4] Or 'unravels.'

وَهُوَ ٱلَّذِى مَدَّ ٱلْأَرْضَ  3 It is He who has spread out the earth

وَجَعَلَ فِيهَا رَوَاسِىَ وَأَنْهَرًا       and set in it firm mountains and streams,

وَمِن كُلِّ ٱلثَّمَرَتِ       and of every fruit

جَعَلَ فِيهَا زَوْجَيْنِ ٱثْنَيْنِ       He has made in it two kinds.[1]

يُغْشِى ٱلَّيْلَ ٱلنَّهَارَ       He draws the night's cover over the day.

إِنَّ فِى ذَلِكَ لَأَيَتٍ       There are indeed signs in that

لِّقَوْمٍ يَتَفَكَّرُونَ ۝       for a people who reflect.

وَفِى ٱلْأَرْضِ قِطَعٌ مُّتَجَوِرَتٌ  4 In the earth are neighbouring terrains [of diverse kinds]

وَجَنَّتٌ مِّنْ أَعْنَبٍ وَزَرْعٌ       and vineyards, farms,

وَنَخِيلٌ       and date palms

صِنْوَانٌ وَغَيْرُ صِنْوَانٍ       growing from the same root and from diverse roots,

يُسْقَىٰ بِمَآءٍ وَحِدٍ       [all] irrigated by the same water,

وَنُفَضِّلُ بَعْضَهَا عَلَىٰ بَعْضٍ       and We give some of them an advantage over others

فِى ٱلْأُكُلِ       in flavour.

إِنَّ فِى ذَلِكَ لَأَيَتٍ       There are indeed signs in that

لِّقَوْمٍ يَعْقِلُونَ ۞       for a people who apply reason.

وَإِن تَعْجَبْ  5 If *you* are to wonder [at anything],

فَعَجَبٌ قَوْلُهُمْ       then wonderful[2] is their remark,

أَءِذَا كُنَّا تُرَبًا       'When we have become dust,

أَءِنَّا لَفِى خَلْقٍ جَدِيدٍ       shall we be [ushered] into a new creation?'

أُوْلَٰٓئِكَ ٱلَّذِينَ كَفَرُوا۟ بِرَبِّهِمْ       They are the ones who defy their Lord;

وَأُوْلَٰٓئِكَ ٱلْأَغْلَلُ فِى أَعْنَاقِهِمْ       they shall have iron collars around their necks,

وَأُوْلَٰٓئِكَ أَصْحَبُ ٱلنَّارِ       they shall be the inhabitants of the Fire,

هُمْ فِيهَا خَلِدُونَ ۝       and they shall remain in it [forever].

وَيَسْتَعْجِلُونَكَ بِٱلسَّيِّئَةِ  6 They would press *you* for evil

قَبْلَ ٱلْحَسَنَةِ       sooner than for good,[3]

وَقَدْ خَلَتْ مِن قَبْلِهِمُ       though there have already gone by before them

---

[1] Or 'a pair,' or 'two mates.'

[2] That is, odd, astonishing.

[3] That is, they ask you to bring about the Divine punishment with which you have threatened them, instead of pleading for Divine mercy and forgiveness.

ٱلْمَثُلَتُ    exemplary punishments.

وَإِنَّ رَبَّكَ لَذُو مَغْفِرَةٍ لِّلنَّاسِ    Indeed *your* Lord is forgiving to mankind

عَلَىٰ ظُلْمِهِمْ    despite their wrongdoing,

وَإِنَّ رَبَّكَ لَشَدِيدُ ٱلْعِقَابِ ٦    and indeed *your* Lord is severe in retribution.

وَيَقُولُ ٱلَّذِينَ كَفَرُواْ    7 The faithless say,

لَوْلَآ أُنزِلَ عَلَيْهِ ءَايَةٌ    'Why has not some sign been sent down to him

مِّن رَّبِّهِۦٓ    from his Lord?'

إِنَّمَآ أَنتَ مُنذِرٌ    *You* are only a warner,

وَلِكُلِّ قَوْمٍ هَادٍ ٧    and there is a guide for every people.

ٱللَّهُ يَعْلَمُ مَا تَحْمِلُ كُلُّ أُنثَىٰ    8 Allah knows what every female carries [in her womb],

وَمَا تَغِيضُ ٱلْأَرْحَامُ    and what the wombs reduce

وَمَا تَزْدَادُ    and what they increase,[1]

وَكُلُّ شَىْءٍ عِندَهُۥ بِمِقْدَارٍ ٨    and everything is by [precise] measure with Him,

عَٰلِمُ ٱلْغَيْبِ وَٱلشَّهَٰدَةِ    9 the Knower of the sensible and the Unseen,

ٱلْكَبِيرُ ٱلْمُتَعَالِ ٩    the All-great, the All-sublime.

سَوَآءٌ مِّنكُم مَّنْ أَسَرَّ ٱلْقَوْلَ    10 It is the same [to Him] whether any of you speaks secretly,

وَمَن جَهَرَ بِهِۦ    or does so loudly,

وَمَنْ هُوَ مُسْتَخْفٍ بِٱلَّيْلِ    or whether he lurks in the night,

وَسَارِبٌ بِٱلنَّهَارِ ١٠    or is open to view in daytime.[2]

لَهُۥ مُعَقِّبَٰتٌ مِّنۢ بَيْنِ يَدَيْهِ    11 He has guardian angels, to his front

وَمِنْ خَلْفِهِۦ    and his rear,

يَحْفَظُونَهُۥ مِنْ أَمْرِ ٱللَّهِ    who guard him by Allah's command.

إِنَّ ٱللَّهَ لَا يُغَيِّرُ مَا بِقَوْمٍ    Indeed Allah does not change a people's lot,

حَتَّىٰ يُغَيِّرُواْ مَا بِأَنفُسِهِمْ    unless they change what is in their souls.

وَإِذَآ أَرَادَ ٱللَّهُ بِقَوْمٍ سُوٓءًا    And when Allah wishes to visit ill on a people,

فَلَا مَرَدَّ لَهُۥ    there is nothing that can avert it,

وَمَا لَهُم مِّن دُونِهِۦ مِن وَالٍ ١١    and they have no protector besides Him.

---

[1] That is, what the wombs reduce or increase of the embryo or the foetus or the time of gestation.

[2] Or 'marches in daytime.'

هُوَ ٱلَّذِى يُرِيكُمُ ٱلْبَرْقَ    12 It is He who shows you the lightning,

خَوْفًا وَطَمَعًا    inspiring fear and hope,

وَيُنشِئُ ٱلسَّحَابَ ٱلثِّقَالَ ۝    and He produces the clouds heavy [with rain].

وَيُسَبِّحُ ٱلرَّعْدُ بِحَمْدِهِۦ    13 The Thunder celebrates His praise,

وَٱلْمَلَٰٓئِكَةُ مِنْ خِيفَتِهِۦ    and the angels [too], in awe of Him,

وَيُرْسِلُ ٱلصَّوَٰعِقَ    and He releases the thunderbolts

فَيُصِيبُ بِهَا مَن يَشَآءُ    and strikes with them whomever He wishes.

وَهُمْ يُجَٰدِلُونَ فِى ٱللَّهِ    Yet they dispute concerning Allah,

وَهُوَ شَدِيدُ ٱلْمِحَالِ ۝    though He is great in might.[1]

لَهُۥ دَعْوَةُ ٱلْحَقِّ    14 [Only] to Him belongs the true invocation;[2]

وَٱلَّذِينَ يَدْعُونَ مِن دُونِهِۦ    and those whom they invoke besides Him

لَا يَسْتَجِيبُونَ لَهُم بِشَىْءٍ    do not answer them in any wise—

إِلَّا كَبَٰسِطِ كَفَّيْهِ إِلَى ٱلْمَآءِ    like someone who stretches his hands towards water

لِيَبْلُغَ فَاهُ    [desiring] that it should reach his mouth,

وَمَا هُوَ بِبَٰلِغِهِۦ    but it does not reach it—

وَمَا دُعَآءُ ٱلْكَٰفِرِينَ إِلَّا فِى ضَلَٰلٍ ۝    and the invocations of the faithless only go awry.

وَلِلَّهِ يَسْجُدُ مَن فِى ٱلسَّمَٰوَٰتِ    15 To Allah prostrates whoever there is in the heavens

وَٱلْأَرْضِ    and the earth,

طَوْعًا وَكَرْهًا    willingly or unwillingly,

وَظِلَٰلُهُم بِٱلْغُدُوِّ وَٱلْءَاصَالِ ۝ ۩    and their shadows at sunrise and sunset.

قُل    16 Say,

مَن رَّبُّ ٱلسَّمَٰوَٰتِ وَٱلْأَرْضِ    'Who is the Lord of the heavens and the earth?'

قُلِ ٱللَّهُ    Say, 'Allah!'

قُلْ أَفَٱتَّخَذْتُم مِّن دُونِهِۦٓ    Say, 'Have you then taken others besides Him

أَوْلِيَآءَ    for guardians,

لَا يَمْلِكُونَ لِأَنفُسِهِمْ نَفْعًا    who have no control over their own benefit

وَلَا ضَرًّا    or harm?'

قُلْ    Say,

---

[1] Or 'though He is severe in punishment.'

[2] Or 'His is the invitation to the truth,' or 'His is the true invitation.'

هَلْ يَسْتَوِى ٱلْأَعْمَىٰ وَٱلْبَصِيرُ

'Are the blind one and the seer equal?

أَمْ هَلْ تَسْتَوِى ٱلظُّلُمَٰتُ وَٱلنُّورُ

Or are the darkness and the light equal?'

أَمْ جَعَلُوا۟ لِلَّهِ شُرَكَآءَ

Have they set up for Allah partners

خَلَقُوا۟ كَخَلْقِهِۦ

who have created like His creation,

فَتَشَٰبَهَ ٱلْخَلْقُ عَلَيْهِمْ

so that the creations seemed confusable to them?

قُلِ ٱللَّهُ خَٰلِقُ كُلِّ شَىْءٍ

*Say,* 'Allah is the creator of all things,

وَهُوَ ٱلْوَٰحِدُ ٱلْقَهَّٰرُ ۝

and He is the One, the All-paramount.'

أَنزَلَ مِنَ ٱلسَّمَآءِ مَآءً

17 He sends down water from the sky

فَسَالَتْ أَوْدِيَةٌۢ

whereat the valleys are flooded

بِقَدَرِهَا

to [the extent of] their capacity,

فَٱحْتَمَلَ ٱلسَّيْلُ زَبَدًا رَّابِيًا

and the flood carries along a swelling scum.

وَمِمَّا يُوقِدُونَ عَلَيْهِ فِى ٱلنَّارِ

And from what they smelt in the fire

ٱبْتِغَآءَ حِلْيَةٍ أَوْ مَتَٰعٍ

for the purpose of [making] ornaments or wares,

زَبَدٌ مِّثْلُهُۥ

[there arises] a similar scum.

كَذَٰلِكَ يَضْرِبُ ٱللَّهُ ٱلْحَقَّ

That is how Allah compares the truth

وَٱلْبَٰطِلَ

and falsehood.

فَأَمَّا ٱلزَّبَدُ فَيَذْهَبُ جُفَآءً

As for the scum, it leaves as dross,

وَأَمَّا مَا يَنفَعُ ٱلنَّاسَ

and that which profits the people

فَيَمْكُثُ فِى ٱلْأَرْضِ

remains in the earth.

كَذَٰلِكَ يَضْرِبُ ٱللَّهُ ٱلْأَمْثَالَ ۝

That is how Allah draws comparisons.

لِلَّذِينَ ٱسْتَجَابُوا۟ لِرَبِّهِمُ

18 For those who answer [the summons of] their Lord

ٱلْحُسْنَىٰ

there shall be the best [of rewards].

وَٱلَّذِينَ لَمْ يَسْتَجِيبُوا۟ لَهُ

But those who do not answer Him,

لَوْ أَنَّ لَهُم مَّا فِى ٱلْأَرْضِ جَمِيعًا

even if they possessed all that is on the earth

وَمِثْلَهُۥ مَعَهُۥ

and as much of it besides,

لَٱفْتَدَوْا۟

they would surely offer it to redeem themselves

بِهِۦ

with it.[1]

أُو۟لَٰٓئِكَ لَهُمْ سُوٓءُ ٱلْحِسَابِ

For such there shall be an adverse reckoning,

وَمَأْوَىٰهُمْ جَهَنَّمُ

and their refuge shall be hell,

---

[1] Cf. 5:36 & 39:47.

وَبِئْسَ ٱلْمِهَادُ ۝   and it is an evil resting place.

أَفَمَن يَعْلَمُ 19   Is someone who knows

أَنَّمَا أُنزِلَ إِلَيْكَ مِن رَّبِّكَ   that what has been sent down to *you* from *your* Lord

ٱلْحَقُّ   is the truth,

كَمَنْ هُوَ أَعْمَىٰ   like someone who is blind?

إِنَّمَا يَتَذَكَّرُ أُوْلُوا۟ ٱلْأَلْبَٰبِ ۝   Only those who possess intellect take admonition

ٱلَّذِينَ يُوفُونَ بِعَهْدِ ٱللَّهِ 20   —those who fulfill Allah's covenant

وَلَا يَنقُضُونَ ٱلْمِيثَٰقَ ۝   and do not break the pledge solemnly made,

وَٱلَّذِينَ يَصِلُونَ 21   and those who join

مَآ أَمَرَ ٱللَّهُ بِهِۦٓ أَن يُوصَلَ   what Allah has commanded to be joined,

وَيَخْشَوْنَ رَبَّهُمْ   and fear their Lord,

وَيَخَافُونَ سُوٓءَ ٱلْحِسَابِ ۝   and are afraid of an adverse reckoning

وَٱلَّذِينَ صَبَرُوا۟ 22   —those who are patient

ٱبْتِغَآءَ وَجْهِ رَبِّهِمْ   for the sake of their Lord's pleasure,

وَأَقَامُوا۟ ٱلصَّلَوٰةَ   maintain the prayer,

وَأَنفَقُوا۟ مِمَّا رَزَقْنَٰهُمْ   and spend out of what We have provided them,

سِرًّا وَعَلَانِيَةً   secretly and openly,

وَيَدْرَءُونَ بِٱلْحَسَنَةِ ٱلسَّيِّئَةَ   and repel evil [conduct] with good.

أُو۟لَٰٓئِكَ لَهُمْ عُقْبَى ٱلدَّارِ ۝   For such will be the reward of the [ultimate] abode:

جَنَّٰتُ عَدْنٍ 23   the Gardens of Eden,

يَدْخُلُونَهَا   which they will enter

وَمَن صَلَحَ   along with whoever is righteous

مِنْ ءَابَآئِهِمْ   from among their forebears,

وَأَزْوَٰجِهِمْ وَذُرِّيَّٰتِهِمْ   their spouses, and their descendents,

وَٱلْمَلَٰٓئِكَةُ يَدْخُلُونَ عَلَيْهِم   and the angels will call on them

مِّن كُلِّ بَابٍ ۝   from every door:

سَلَٰمٌ عَلَيْكُم بِمَا صَبَرْتُمْ 24   'Peace be to you, for your patience.'

فَنِعْمَ عُقْبَى ٱلدَّارِ ۝   How excellent is the reward of the [ultimate] abode!

وَٱلَّذِينَ يَنقُضُونَ عَهْدَ ٱللَّهِ 25   But as for those who break Allah's compact

مِنۢ بَعْدِ مِيثَٰقِهِۦ   after having pledged it solemnly,

345

وَيَقْطَعُونَ      and sever

مَا أَمَرَ ٱللَّهُ بِهِۦ أَن يُوصَلَ      what Allah has commanded to be joined,

وَيُفْسِدُونَ فِى ٱلْأَرْضِ      and cause corruption in the earth

أُوْلَٰٓئِكَ لَهُمُ ٱللَّعْنَةُ      —it is such on whom the curse will lie,

وَهُمْ سُوٓءُ ٱلدَّارِ ۝      and for them will be the ills of the [ultimate] abode.

ٱللَّهُ يَبْسُطُ ٱلرِّزْقَ    26 Allah expands the provision

لِمَن يَشَآءُ      for whomever He wishes,

وَيَقْدِرُ      and tightens it.

وَفَرِحُوا بِٱلْحَيَوٰةِ ٱلدُّنْيَا      They exult in the life of this world,

وَمَا ٱلْحَيَوٰةُ ٱلدُّنْيَا فِى ٱلْأَخِرَةِ      but compared with the Hereafter the life of this world

إِلَّا مَتَٰعٌ ۝      is but a [trifling] enjoyment.

وَيَقُولُ ٱلَّذِينَ كَفَرُوا    27 The faithless say,

لَوْلَآ أُنزِلَ عَلَيْهِ ءَايَةٌ      'Why has not some sign been sent down to him

مِّن رَّبِّهِۦ      from his Lord?'

قُلْ إِنَّ ٱللَّهَ يُضِلُّ مَن يَشَآءُ      *Say,* 'Indeed Allah leads astray whomever He wishes,

وَيَهْدِىٓ إِلَيْهِ      and guides to Himself

مَنْ أَنَابَ ۝      those who turn penitently [to Him]

ٱلَّذِينَ ءَامَنُوا    28 —those who have faith,

وَتَطْمَئِنُّ قُلُوبُهُم      and whose hearts find rest

بِذِكْرِ ٱللَّهِ      in the remembrance of Allah.

أَلَا بِذِكْرِ ٱللَّهِ تَطْمَئِنُّ ٱلْقُلُوبُ ۝      Look! The hearts find rest in Allah's remembrance!

ٱلَّذِينَ ءَامَنُوا وَعَمِلُوا ٱلصَّٰلِحَٰتِ    29 Those who have faith and do righteous deeds

طُوبَىٰ لَهُمْ      —happy are they

وَحُسْنُ مَآبٍ ۝      and good is their [ultimate] destination.

كَذَٰلِكَ أَرْسَلْنَٰكَ فِىٓ أُمَّةٍ    30 Thus have We sent *you* to a nation

قَدْ خَلَتْ مِن قَبْلِهَآ أُمَمٌ      before which many nations have passed away,

لِّتَتْلُوَا۟ عَلَيْهِمُ      that *you* may recite to them

ٱلَّذِىٓ أَوْحَيْنَآ إِلَيْكَ      what We have revealed to *you.*

وَهُمْ يَكْفُرُونَ بِٱلرَّحْمَٰنِ      Yet they defy the All-beneficent.

قُلْ هُوَ رَبِّي

*Say*, 'He is my Lord;

لَا إِلَهَ إِلَّا هُوَ

    there is no god except Him;

عَلَيْهِ تَوَكَّلْتُ

in Him I have put my trust,

وَإِلَيْهِ مَتَابِ ۝

    and to Him will be my return.'

وَلَوْ أَنَّ قُرْءَانًا

31 If only it were a Qur'ān[1]

سُيِّرَتْ بِهِ الْجِبَالُ

    whereby the mountains could be moved,

أَوْ قُطِّعَتْ بِهِ الْأَرْضُ

    or the earth could be split,

أَوْ كُلِّمَ بِهِ الْمَوْتَى

    or the dead could be spoken to . . . .[2]

بَل لِلَّهِ الْأَمْرُ جَمِيعًا

Rather all dispensation belongs to Allah.

أَفَلَمْ يَايْئَسِ الَّذِينَ ءَامَنُوا

Have not the faithful yet realised

أَن لَّوْ يَشَاءُ اللَّهُ

    that had Allah wished

لَهَدَى النَّاسَ جَمِيعًا

    He would have guided mankind all together?

وَلَا يَزَالُ الَّذِينَ كَفَرُوا تُصِيبُهُم

The faithless will continue to be visited

بِمَا صَنَعُوا قَارِعَةٌ

    by catastrophes because of their doings

أَوْ تَحُلُّ قَرِيبًا مِّن دَارِهِمْ

    —or they[3] will land near their habitations—

حَتَّى يَأْتِيَ وَعْدُ اللَّهِ

    until Allah's promise comes to pass.

إِنَّ اللَّهَ لَا يُخْلِفُ الْمِيعَادَ ۝

Indeed Allah does not break His promise.

وَلَقَدِ اسْتُهْزِئَ بِرُسُلٍ مِّن قَبْلِكَ

32 Apostles were certainly derided at before *you*.

فَأَمْلَيْتُ لِلَّذِينَ كَفَرُوا

    But then I gave respite to those who were faithless,

ثُمَّ أَخَذْتُهُمْ

    then I seized them;

فَكَيْفَ كَانَ عِقَابِ ۝

    so how was My retribution?

أَفَمَنْ هُوَ قَآئِمٌ عَلَى كُلِّ نَفْسٍ

33 Is He who sustains every soul[4]

بِمَا كَسَبَتْ

    in spite of what it earns [comparable to the idols]?

وَجَعَلُوا لِلَّهِ شُرَكَاءَ

And yet they ascribe partners to Allah!

قُلْ سَمُّوهُمْ

*Say*, 'Name them!'

---

[1] Or 'Even if it were a Qur'ān.'

[2] Ellipsis. The phrase omitted is 'all unbelievers would have embraced the faith.' Or 'still they would not have embraced the faith.' Cf. 6:111.

[3] That is, the disasters.

[4] Or 'Is He who maintains every soul in spite of what it earns. Or 'Is He who is vigilant over every soul as to what it earns.' See 9:25, where *bimā* is used in the sense of 'in spite of.'

أَمْ تُنَبِّئُونَهُ    Will you inform Him

بِمَا لَا يَعْلَمُ فِى ٱلْأَرْضِ    of something He does not know about on the earth,

أَم بِظَٰهِرٍ مِّنَ ٱلْقَوْلِ    or of [what are] mere words?

بَلْ    Rather

زُيِّنَ لِلَّذِينَ كَفَرُوا۟ مَكْرُهُمْ    their scheming is presented as decorous to the faithless,

وَصُدُّوا۟ عَنِ ٱلسَّبِيلِ    and they have been barred from the [right] way;

وَمَن يُضْلِلِ ٱللَّهُ    and whomever Allah leads astray,

فَمَا لَهُۥ مِنْ هَادٍ ۩    has no guide.

هُّم عَذَابٌ فِى ٱلْحَيَوٰةِ ٱلدُّنْيَا    34 There is a punishment for them in the life of this world,

وَلَعَذَابُ ٱلْأَٰخِرَةِ    and the punishment of the Hereafter will surely be

أَشَقُّ    harder,

وَمَا لَهُم مِّنَ ٱللَّهِ مِن وَاقٍ ۞    and they have no defender against Allah.

مَّثَلُ ٱلْجَنَّةِ ٱلَّتِى    35 A description of the paradise

وُعِدَ ٱلْمُتَّقُونَ    promised to the Godwary:

تَجْرِى مِن تَحْتِهَا ٱلْأَنْهَٰرُ    streams run in it,

أُكُلُهَا دَآئِمٌ وَظِلُّهَا    its fruits and shade are everlasting.

تِلْكَ عُقْبَى ٱلَّذِينَ ٱتَّقَوا۟    Such is the requital of those who are Godwary;

وَّعُقْبَى ٱلْكَٰفِرِينَ ٱلنَّارُ ۞    and the requital of the faithless is the Fire.

وَٱلَّذِينَ ءَاتَيْنَٰهُمُ ٱلْكِتَٰبَ    36 Those whom We have given the Book[1]

يَفْرَحُونَ بِمَآ أُنزِلَ إِلَيْكَ    rejoice in what has been sent down to *you*.

وَمِنَ ٱلْأَحْزَابِ مَن يُنكِرُ بَعْضَهُۥ    Among the factions[2] are those who deny a part of it.

قُلْ إِنَّمَآ أُمِرْتُ أَنْ أَعْبُدَ ٱللَّهَ    *Say,* 'Indeed I have been commanded to worship Allah

وَلَآ أُشْرِكَ بِهِۦٓ    and not to ascribe any partner to Him.

إِلَيْهِ أَدْعُوا۟    To Him do I summon [all mankind]

وَإِلَيْهِ مَتَابِ ۞    and to Him will be my return.'

وَكَذَٰلِكَ أَنزَلْنَٰهُ    37 Thus We have sent it down

---

[1] That is, the Jews and the Christians, or the faithful who followed the Prophet (*s*).

[2] That is, from among those belonging to Jewish and Christian sects, or the Arab polytheists.

حُكْمًا عَرَبِيًّا    as a dispensation[1] in Arabic;

وَلَئِنِ ٱتَّبَعْتَ أَهْوَآءَهُم    and should *you* follow their desires

بَعْدَمَا جَآءَكَ مِنَ ٱلْعِلْمِ    after the knowledge that has come to *you,*

مَا لَكَ مِنَ ٱللَّهِ    *you* shall have against Allah neither

مِن وَلِيٍّ وَلَا وَاقٍ ۝    any guardian nor any defender.

وَلَقَدْ أَرْسَلْنَا رُسُلًا مِّن قَبْلِكَ    38 Certainly We have sent apostles before *you,*

وَجَعَلْنَا لَهُمْ أَزْوَٰجًا    and We appointed for them wives

وَذُرِّيَّةً    and descendants;

وَمَا كَانَ لِرَسُولٍ أَن يَأْتِيَ بِـَٔايَةٍ    and an apostle may not bring a sign

إِلَّا بِإِذْنِ ٱللَّهِ    except by Allah's leave.

لِكُلِّ أَجَلٍ كِتَابٌ ۝    There is a book for every term:

يَمْحُوا۟ ٱللَّهُ مَا يَشَآءُ وَيُثْبِتُ    39 Allah effaces and confirms whatever He wishes

وَعِندَهُۥٓ أُمُّ ٱلْكِتَٰبِ ۝    and with Him is the Mother of the Book.[2]

وَإِن مَّا نُرِيَنَّكَ بَعْضَ ٱلَّذِى    40 Whether We show *you* a part of what

نَعِدُهُمْ    We promise them,[3]

أَوْ نَتَوَفَّيَنَّكَ    or take *you* away [before that],

فَإِنَّمَا عَلَيْكَ ٱلْبَلَٰغُ    *your* duty is only to communicate,

وَعَلَيْنَا ٱلْحِسَابُ ۝    and it is for Us to do the reckoning.

أَوَلَمْ يَرَوْا۟ أَنَّا نَأْتِى ٱلْأَرْضَ    41 Have they not seen how We visit the land

نَنقُصُهَا مِنْ أَطْرَافِهَا    diminishing it at its edges?

وَٱللَّهُ يَحْكُمُ    Allah judges,

لَا مُعَقِّبَ لِحُكْمِهِۦ    and there is none who may repeal His judgement,

وَهُوَ سَرِيعُ ٱلْحِسَابِ ۝    and He is swift at reckoning.

وَقَدْ مَكَرَ ٱلَّذِينَ مِن قَبْلِهِمْ    42 Those who were before them [also] schemed;[4]

فَلِلَّهِ ٱلْمَكْرُ جَمِيعًا    yet all devising belongs to Allah.

يَعْلَمُ مَا تَكْسِبُ كُلُّ نَفْسٍ    He knows what every soul earns.

وَسَيَعْلَمُ ٱلْكُفَّٰرُ    Soon the faithless will know

---

[1] Cf. 2:213; 5:43-49.

[2] Cf. 43:4.

[3] That is, the punishment.

[4] Ellipsis. The omitted phrase is 'but their plotting was of no avail to them.'

349

لِمَنْ عُقْبَى ٱلدَّارِ ۞    in whose favour the outcome of that abode will be.

وَيَقُولُ ٱلَّذِينَ كَفَرُوا    43 The faithless say,

لَسْتَ مُرْسَلًا    'You have not been sent [by Allah].'

قُلْ كَفَىٰ بِٱللَّهِ شَهِيدًا بَيْنِى    Say, 'Allah suffices as a witness between me

وَبَيْنَكُمْ    and you,

وَمَنْ عِندَهُۥ عِلْمُ ٱلْكِتَٰبِ ۞    and he who possesses the knowledge of the Book.

## سُورَةُ إِبْرَاهِيمَ    14. SŪRAT IBRĀHĪM[1]

بِسْمِ ٱللَّهِ    In the Name of Allah,

ٱلرَّحْمَٰنِ ٱلرَّحِيمِ    the All-beneficent, the All-merciful.

الٓرۚ    1 *Alif, Lām, Rā.*

كِتَٰبٌ أَنزَلْنَٰهُ إِلَيْكَ    [This is] a Book We have sent down to *you*

لِتُخْرِجَ ٱلنَّاسَ مِنَ ٱلظُّلُمَٰتِ    that *you* may bring mankind out from darkness

إِلَى ٱلنُّورِ    into light,

بِإِذْنِ رَبِّهِمْ    by the command of their Lord,

إِلَىٰ صِرَٰطِ ٱلْعَزِيزِ ٱلْحَمِيدِ ۞    to the path of the All-mighty, the All-laudable

ٱللَّهِ    2 —Allah,

ٱلَّذِى لَهُۥ مَا فِى ٱلسَّمَٰوَٰتِ    to whom belongs whatever is in the heavens

وَمَا فِى ٱلْأَرْضِ    and whatever is on the earth.

وَوَيْلٌ لِّلْكَٰفِرِينَ مِنْ عَذَابٍ شَدِيدٍ ۞    And woe to the faithless for a severe punishment

ٱلَّذِينَ يَسْتَحِبُّونَ ٱلْحَيَوٰةَ ٱلدُّنْيَا    3 —those who prefer the life of this world

عَلَى ٱلْءَاخِرَةِ    to the Hereafter,

وَيَصُدُّونَ عَن سَبِيلِ ٱللَّهِ    and bar [others] from the way of Allah,

وَيَبْغُونَهَا عِوَجًا    and seek to make it crooked.

أُوْلَٰٓئِكَ فِى ضَلَٰلٍ بَعِيدٍ ۞    They are in extreme error.

وَمَآ أَرْسَلْنَا مِن رَّسُولٍ    4 We did not send any apostle

إِلَّا بِلِسَانِ قَوْمِهِۦ    except with the language of his people,

---

[1] The *sūrah* is named after Abraham, whose prayer appears in verses 35-41.

لِيُبَيِّنَ لَهُمۡ so that he might make [Our messages] clear to them.

فَيُضِلُّ ٱللَّهُ مَن يَشَآءُ Then Allah leads astray whomever He wishes,

وَيَهۡدِى مَن يَشَآءُ and He guides whomsoever He wishes,

وَهُوَ ٱلۡعَزِيزُ ٱلۡحَكِيمُ and He is the All-mighty, the All-wise.

وَلَقَدۡ أَرۡسَلۡنَا مُوسَىٰ بِـَٔايَٰتِنَآ 5 Certainly We sent Moses with Our signs:

أَنۡ أَخۡرِجۡ قَوۡمَكَ مِنَ ٱلظُّلُمَٰتِ 'Bring your people out from darkness

إِلَى ٱلنُّورِ into light

وَذَكِّرۡهُم بِأَيَّىٰمِ ٱللَّهِ and remind them of Allah's [holy] days.

إِنَّ فِى ذَٰلِكَ لَأَيَٰتٍ There are indeed signs in that

لِّكُلِّ صَبَّارٍ شَكُورٍ for every patient and grateful [servant].'

وَإِذۡ قَالَ مُوسَىٰ لِقَوۡمِهِ 6 When Moses said to his people,

ٱذۡكُرُواْ نِعۡمَةَ ٱللَّهِ عَلَيۡكُمۡ 'Remember Allah's blessing upon you

إِذۡ أَنجَىٰكُم مِّنۡ ءَالِ فِرۡعَوۡنَ when He delivered you from Pharaoh's clan

يَسُومُونَكُمۡ سُوٓءَ ٱلۡعَذَابِ who inflicted a terrible torment on you,

وَيُذَبِّحُونَ أَبۡنَآءَكُمۡ and slaughtered your sons

وَيَسۡتَحۡيُونَ نِسَآءَكُمۡ and spared your women,

وَفِى ذَٰلِكُم and in that there was

بَلَآءٌ مِّن رَّبِّكُمۡ عَظِيمٌ a great test from your Lord.'

وَإِذۡ تَأَذَّنَ رَبُّكُمۡ 7 And when your Lord proclaimed,

لَئِن شَكَرۡتُمۡ 'If you are grateful,

لَأَزِيدَنَّكُمۡ I will surely enhance you [in blessing],

وَلَئِن كَفَرۡتُمۡ but if you are ungrateful,

إِنَّ عَذَابِى لَشَدِيدٌ My punishment is indeed severe.'

وَقَالَ مُوسَىٰ 8 And Moses said,

إِن تَكۡفُرُوٓاْ 'Should you be faithless

أَنتُمۡ وَمَن فِى ٱلۡأَرۡضِ جَمِيعًا —you and everyone on the earth, all together—

فَإِنَّ ٱللَّهَ لَغَنِىٌّ حَمِيدٌ indeed Allah is all-sufficient, all-laudable.'

أَلَمۡ يَأۡتِكُمۡ 9 Has there not come to you

نَبَؤُاْ ٱلَّذِينَ مِن قَبۡلِكُمۡ the account of those who were before you

قَوْمِ نُوحٍ وَعَادٍ وَثَمُودَ

—the people of Noah, ʿĀd and Thamūd,

وَٱلَّذِينَ مِنْ بَعْدِهِمْ

and those who were after them,

لَا يَعْلَمُهُمْ إِلَّا ٱللَّهُ

whom no one knows [well] except Allah?

جَآءَتْهُمْ رُسُلُهُم بِٱلْبَيِّنَٰتِ

Their apostles brought them manifest proofs,

فَرَدُّوٓاْ أَيْدِيَهُمْ فِىٓ أَفْوَٰهِهِمْ

but they did not respond to them,[1]

وَقَالُوٓاْ

and said,

إِنَّا كَفَرْنَا بِمَآ أُرْسِلْتُم بِهِۦ

'We disbelieve in what you have been sent with.

وَإِنَّا لَفِى شَكٍّ مِّمَّا

Indeed we have grave doubts concerning

تَدْعُونَنَآ إِلَيْهِ مُرِيبٍ ۞

that to which you invite us.'

قَالَتْ رُسُلُهُمْ أَفِى ٱللَّهِ شَكٌّ

10 Their apostles said, 'Is there any doubt about Allah,

فَاطِرِ ٱلسَّمَٰوَٰتِ وَٱلْأَرْضِ

the originator of the heavens and the earth?!

يَدْعُوكُمْ لِيَغْفِرَ لَكُم مِّن ذُنُوبِكُمْ

He calls you to forgive you a part of your sins,

وَيُؤَخِّرَكُمْ إِلَىٰٓ أَجَلٍ مُّسَمًّى

and grants you respite until a specified time.'[2]

قَالُوٓاْ إِنْ أَنتُمْ إِلَّا بَشَرٌ مِّثْلُنَا

They said, 'You are nothing but humans like us

تُرِيدُونَ أَن تَصُدُّونَا

who desire to bar us

عَمَّا كَانَ يَعْبُدُ ءَابَآؤُنَا

from what our fathers used to worship.

فَأْتُونَا بِسُلْطَٰنٍ مُّبِينٍ

So bring us a manifest authority.'

قَالَتْ لَهُمْ رُسُلُهُمْ

11 Their apostles said to them,

إِن نَّحْنُ إِلَّا بَشَرٌ مِّثْلُكُمْ

'Indeed we are just human beings like yourselves;

وَلَٰكِنَّ ٱللَّهَ يَمُنُّ عَلَىٰ

but Allah favours

مَن يَشَآءُ مِنْ عِبَادِهِۦ

whomever of His servants that He wishes.

وَمَا كَانَ لَنَآ أَن نَّأْتِيَكُم بِسُلْطَٰنٍ

We may not bring you an authority

إِلَّا بِإِذْنِ ٱللَّهِ

except by Allah's leave,

وَعَلَى ٱللَّهِ فَلْيَتَوَكَّلِ ٱلْمُؤْمِنُونَ

and in Allah let all the faithful put their trust.

وَمَا لَنَآ أَلَّا نَتَوَكَّلَ عَلَى ٱللَّهِ

12 And why should we not put our trust in Allah,

وَقَدْ هَدَىٰنَا سُبُلَنَا

seeing that He has guided us in our ways?

وَلَنَصْبِرَنَّ

Surely, we will put up patiently

---

[1] Literally, 'they put their hands into their mouths,' an idiomatic expression that has been interpreted variously. See Ṭabrisī and Ṭabarī.

[2] Or 'for a specified term.'

عَلَىٰ مَآ ءَاذَيْتُمُونَا   with whatever torment you may inflict upon us,

وَعَلَى ٱللَّهِ فَلْيَتَوَكَّلِ ٱلْمُتَوَكِّلُونَ ۝   and in Allah let all the trusting put their trust.'

وَقَالَ ٱلَّذِينَ كَفَرُواْ لِرُسُلِهِمْ   13 But the faithless said to their apostles,

لَنُخْرِجَنَّكُم مِّنْ أَرْضِنَآ   'Surely we will expel you from our land,

أَوْ لَتَعُودُنَّ فِى مِلَّتِنَا   or you should revert to our creed.'

فَأَوْحَىٰ إِلَيْهِمْ رَبُّهُمْ   Thereat their Lord revealed to them:

لَنُهْلِكَنَّ ٱلظَّٰلِمِينَ ۝   'We will surely destroy the wrongdoers,

وَلَنُسْكِنَنَّكُمُ ٱلْأَرْضَ   14 and surely We will settle you in the land

مِنۢ بَعْدِهِمْ   after them.

ذَٰلِكَ لِمَنْ   This [promise] is for someone

خَافَ مَقَامِى   who is awed to stand before Me

وَخَافَ وَعِيدِ ۝   and fears My threat.'

وَٱسْتَفْتَحُواْ   15 They[1] prayed for victory[2] [against the infidels],

وَخَابَ كُلُّ جَبَّارٍ عَنِيدٍ ۝   and every obdurate tyrant has failed,

مِّن وَرَآئِهِ جَهَنَّمُ   16 with hell lying ahead of him,[3]

وَيُسْقَىٰ   [where] he shall be given to drink

مِن مَّآءٍ صَدِيدٍ ۝   of a purulent fluid,

يَتَجَرَّعُهُ   17 gulping it down,

وَلَا يَكَادُ يُسِيغُهُ   but hardly swallowing it:

وَيَأْتِيهِ ٱلْمَوْتُ مِن كُلِّ مَكَانٍ   death will assail him from every side,

وَمَا هُوَ بِمَيِّتٍ   but he will not die,

وَمِن وَرَآئِهِ عَذَابٌ غَلِيظٌ ۝   and there is [yet] a harsh punishment ahead of him.

مَّثَلُ ٱلَّذِينَ كَفَرُواْ بِرَبِّهِمْ   18 A parable of those who defy their Lord:

أَعْمَٰلُهُمْ كَرَمَادٍ   their deeds are like ashes

ٱشْتَدَّتْ بِهِ ٱلرِّيحُ   over which the wind blows hard

فِى يَوْمٍ عَاصِفٍ   on a tempestuous day:

لَّا يَقْدِرُونَ مِمَّا كَسَبُواْ عَلَىٰ شَىْءٍ   they have no power over anything they have earned.

---

[1] That is, the apostles.

[2] Or 'verdict;' that is, the verdict of Allah against the unbelievers.

[3] That is, with hell waiting for him.

ذَٰلِكَ هُوَ ٱلضَّلَـٰلُ ٱلْبَعِيدُ ۝

That is extreme error.

أَلَمْ تَرَ أَنَّ ٱللَّهَ خَلَقَ ٱلسَّمَـٰوَٰتِ

19 Have you not regarded that Allah created the heavens

وَٱلْأَرْضَ

and the earth

بِٱلْحَقِّ

with the Truth.

إِن يَشَأْ يُذْهِبْكُمْ

If He wishes, He will take you away,

وَيَأْتِ بِخَلْقٍ جَدِيدٍ ۝

and bring about a new creation,

وَمَا ذَٰلِكَ عَلَى ٱللَّهِ بِعَزِيزٍ ۝

20 and that is not a hard thing for Allah.

وَبَرَزُواْ لِلَّهِ جَمِيعًا

21 Together they will be presented before Allah.

فَقَالَ ٱلضُّعَفَـٰٓؤُاْ

Then those who were weak will say

لِلَّذِينَ ٱسْتَكْبَرُوٓاْ

to those who were arrogant,

إِنَّا كُنَّا لَكُمْ تَبَعًا

'Indeed we were your followers.

فَهَلْ أَنتُم مُّغْنُونَ عَنَّا

So will you avail us

مِنْ عَذَابِ ٱللَّهِ

against Allah's punishment

مِن شَىْءٍ

in any wise?'

قَالُواْ لَوْ هَدَىٰنَا ٱللَّهُ

They will say, 'Had Allah guided us,

لَهَدَيْنَـٰكُمْ

surely we would have guided you.

سَوَآءٌ عَلَيْنَآ أَجَزِعْنَآ

It is the same to us whether we are restless

أَمْ صَبَرْنَا

or patient:

مَا لَنَا مِن مَّحِيصٍ ۝

there is no escape for us.'

وَقَالَ ٱلشَّيْطَـٰنُ لَمَّا قُضِىَ ٱلْأَمْرُ

22 When the matter has been decided, Satan will say,

إِنَّ ٱللَّهَ وَعَدَكُمْ وَعْدَ ٱلْحَقِّ

'Indeed Allah made you a promise that was true

وَوَعَدتُّكُمْ فَأَخْلَفْتُكُمْ

and I [too] made you a promise, but I failed you.

وَمَا كَانَ لِىَ عَلَيْكُم مِّن سُلْطَـٰنٍ

I had no authority over you,

إِلَّآ أَن دَعَوْتُكُمْ فَٱسْتَجَبْتُمْ لِى

except that I called you and you responded to me.

فَلَا تَلُومُونِى وَلُومُوٓاْ أَنفُسَكُم

So do not blame me, but blame yourselves.

مَّآ أَنَا۠ بِمُصْرِخِكُمْ

I cannot respond to your distress calls,

وَمَآ أَنتُم بِمُصْرِخِىَّ

neither can you respond to my distress calls.

إِنِّى كَفَرْتُ

Indeed I disavow

بِمَآ أَشْرَكْتُمُونِ مِن قَبْلُ

your taking me for [Allah's] partner aforetime.

إِنَّ ٱلظَّـٰلِمِينَ لَهُمْ عَذَابٌ أَلِيمٌ ۝

There is indeed a painful punishment for the wrongdoer

وَأُدْخِلَ ٱلَّذِينَ ءَامَنُواْ وَعَمِلُواْ 23 Those who have faith and do righteous deeds

ٱلصَّٰلِحَٰتِ      will be admitted

جَنَّٰتٍ تَجْرِى مِن تَحْتِهَا ٱلْأَنْهَٰرُ      into gardens with streams running in them,

خَٰلِدِينَ فِيهَا      to remain in them [forever],

بِإِذْنِ رَبِّهِمْ      by the leave of their Lord.

تَحِيَّتُهُمْ فِيهَا سَلَٰمٌ ۝      Their greeting therein will be 'Peace!'

أَلَمْ تَرَ 24 Have you not regarded

كَيْفَ ضَرَبَ ٱللَّهُ مَثَلًا      how Allah has drawn a parable?

كَلِمَةً طَيِّبَةً كَشَجَرَةٍ طَيِّبَةٍ      A good word is like a good tree:

أَصْلُهَا ثَابِتٌ      its roots are steady

وَفَرْعُهَا فِى ٱلسَّمَآءِ ۝      and its branches are in the sky?

تُؤْتِىٓ أُكُلَهَا كُلَّ حِينٍ 25 It gives its fruit every season

بِإِذْنِ رَبِّهَا      by the leave of its Lord.

وَيَضْرِبُ ٱللَّهُ ٱلْأَمْثَالَ لِلنَّاسِ      Allah draws these parables for mankind

لَعَلَّهُمْ يَتَذَكَّرُونَ ۝      so that they may take admonition.

وَمَثَلُ كَلِمَةٍ خَبِيثَةٍ 26 And the parable of a bad word

كَشَجَرَةٍ خَبِيثَةٍ      is that of a bad tree:

ٱجْتُثَّتْ مِن فَوْقِ ٱلْأَرْضِ      uprooted from the ground,

مَا لَهَا مِن قَرَارٍ ۝      it has no stability.

يُثَبِّتُ ٱللَّهُ ٱلَّذِينَ ءَامَنُواْ 27 Allah fortifies those who have faith

بِٱلْقَوْلِ ٱلثَّابِتِ      with an immutable word

فِى ٱلْحَيَوٰةِ ٱلدُّنْيَا      in the life of this world

وَفِى ٱلْءَاخِرَةِ      and in the Hereafter,

وَيُضِلُّ ٱللَّهُ ٱلظَّٰلِمِينَ      and Allah leads astray the wrongdoers,

وَيَفْعَلُ ٱللَّهُ مَا يَشَآءُ ۝      and Allah does whatever He wishes.

أَلَمْ تَرَ إِلَى ٱلَّذِينَ بَدَّلُواْ 28 Have you not regarded those who have changed

نِعْمَتَ ٱللَّهِ كُفْرًا      Allah's blessing with ingratitude,

وَأَحَلُّواْ قَوْمَهُمْ دَارَ ٱلْبَوَارِ ۝      and landed their people in the house of ruin?

جَهَنَّمَ يَصْلَوْنَهَا ۖ 29 —hell, which they shall enter,

وَبِئْسَ ٱلْقَرَارُ ۝    and it is an evil abode!

وَجَعَلُوا۟ لِلَّهِ أَندَادًا 30 They have set up equals to Allah,

لِّيُضِلُّوا۟ عَن سَبِيلِهِۦ ۗ    to lead [people] astray from His way.

قُلْ تَمَتَّعُوا۟    *Say,* 'Enjoy [for a while],

فَإِنَّ مَصِيرَكُمْ إِلَى ٱلنَّارِ ۝    for indeed your destination is toward the Fire!'

قُل لِّعِبَادِىَ ٱلَّذِينَ ءَامَنُوا۟ 31 *Tell* My servants who have faith

يُقِيمُوا۟ ٱلصَّلَوٰةَ    to maintain the prayer

وَيُنفِقُوا۟    and to spend

مِمَّا رَزَقْنَٰهُمْ    out of what We have provided them with,

سِرًّا وَعَلَانِيَةً    secretly and openly,

مِّن قَبْلِ أَن يَأْتِىَ يَوْمٌ    before there comes a day

لَّا بَيْعٌ فِيهِ    on which there will be neither any bargaining

وَلَا خِلَٰلٌ ۝    nor friendship.

ٱللَّهُ ٱلَّذِى خَلَقَ ٱلسَّمَٰوَٰتِ 32 It is Allah who created the heavens

وَٱلْأَرْضَ    and the earth,

وَأَنزَلَ مِنَ ٱلسَّمَآءِ مَآءً    and He sends down water from the sky

فَأَخْرَجَ بِهِۦ مِنَ ٱلثَّمَرَٰتِ    and with it He brings forth crops

رِزْقًا لَّكُمْ ۖ    for your sustenance.

وَسَخَّرَ لَكُمُ ٱلْفُلْكَ    And He disposed the ships for you[r benefit]

لِتَجْرِىَ فِى ٱلْبَحْرِ بِأَمْرِهِۦ ۖ    so that they may sail at sea by His command,

وَسَخَّرَ لَكُمُ ٱلْأَنْهَٰرَ ۝    and He disposed the rivers for you.

وَسَخَّرَ لَكُمُ ٱلشَّمْسَ وَٱلْقَمَرَ 33 He disposed the sun and moon for you,

دَآئِبَيْنِ ۖ    constant [in their courses],

وَسَخَّرَ لَكُمُ ٱلَّيْلَ وَٱلنَّهَارَ ۝    and He disposed the night and the day,

وَءَاتَىٰكُم مِّن كُلِّ مَا سَأَلْتُمُوهُ ۚ 34 and He gave you all that you had asked Him.[1]

---

[1] That is, He provided you with everything demanded by your nature and your original capacities.

وَإِن تَعُدُّواْ نِعْمَتَ ٱللَّهِ    If you enumerate Allah's blessings,

لَا تُحْصُوهَآ    you will not be able to count them.

إِنَّ ٱلْإِنسَـٰنَ لَظَلُومٌ كَفَّارٌ ۝    Indeed man is most unfair and ungrateful!

وَإِذْ قَالَ إِبْرَٰهِيمُ    35 When Abraham said,

رَبِّ ٱجْعَلْ هَـٰذَا ٱلْبَلَدَ ءَامِنًا    'My Lord! Make this city a sanctuary,

وَٱجْنُبْنِى وَبَنِىَّ    and save me and my children

أَن نَّعْبُدَ ٱلْأَصْنَامَ ۝    from worshiping idols.

رَبِّ إِنَّهُنَّ أَضْلَلْنَ كَثِيرًا مِّنَ ٱلنَّاسِ    36 My Lord! Indeed they have misled many people.

فَمَن تَبِعَنِى فَإِنَّهُۥ مِنِّى    So whoever follows me indeed belongs to me,

وَمَنْ عَصَانِى    and as for someone who disobeys me,

فَإِنَّكَ غَفُورٌ رَّحِيمٌ ۝    well, You are indeed all-forgiving, all-merciful.

رَّبَّنَآ    37 Our Lord!

إِنِّىٓ أَسْكَنتُ مِن ذُرِّيَّتِى    I have settled part of my descendants

بِوَادٍ غَيْرِ ذِى زَرْعٍ    in a barren valley,

عِندَ بَيْتِكَ ٱلْمُحَرَّمِ رَبَّنَا    by Your sacred House, our Lord,

لِيُقِيمُواْ ٱلصَّلَوٰةَ    that they may maintain the prayer.

فَٱجْعَلْ أَفْـِٔدَةً مِّنَ ٱلنَّاسِ    So make the hearts of a part of the people

تَهْوِىٓ إِلَيْهِمْ    fond of them,

وَٱرْزُقْهُم مِّنَ ٱلثَّمَرَٰتِ    and provide them with fruits,

لَعَلَّهُمْ يَشْكُرُونَ ۝    that they may give thanks.

رَّبَّنَآ    38 Our Lord!

إِنَّكَ تَعْلَمُ مَا نُخْفِى    Indeed You know whatever we hide

وَمَا نُعْلِنُ    and whatever we disclose,

وَمَا يَخْفَىٰ عَلَى ٱللَّهِ مِن شَىْءٍ    and nothing is hidden from Allah

فِى ٱلْأَرْضِ    on the earth

وَلَا فِى ٱلسَّمَآءِ ۝    or in the sky.

ٱلْحَمْدُ لِلَّهِ    39 All praise belongs to Allah,

ٱلَّذِى وَهَبَ لِى عَلَى ٱلْكِبَرِ    who, despite [my] old age, gave me

إِسْمَـٰعِيلَ وَإِسْحَـٰقَ    Ishmael and Isaac.

إِنَّ رَبِّى لَسَمِيعُ ٱلدُّعَآءِ ۝

Indeed my Lord hears all supplications.

رَبِّ 40 My Lord!

ٱجْعَلْنِى مُقِيمَ ٱلصَّلَوٰةِ

Make me a maintainer of the prayer,

وَمِن ذُرِّيَّتِى

and my descendants [too].

رَبَّنَا

Our Lord,

وَتَقَبَّلْ دُعَآءِ ۝

accept my supplication.

رَبَّنَا 41 Our Lord!

ٱغْفِرْ لِى وَلِوَٰلِدَىَّ

Forgive me and my parents,

وَلِلْمُؤْمِنِينَ

and all the faithful,

يَوْمَ يَقُومُ ٱلْحِسَابُ ۝

on the day when the reckoning is held.'

وَلَا تَحْسَبَنَّ ٱللَّهَ غَٰفِلاً 42 Do not suppose that Allah is oblivious

عَمَّا يَعْمَلُ ٱلظَّٰلِمُونَ

to what the wrongdoers are doing.

إِنَّمَا يُؤَخِّرُهُمْ

He is only granting them respite

لِيَوْمٍ تَشْخَصُ فِيهِ ٱلْأَبْصَرُ ۝

until the day when the eyes will be glazed.

مُهْطِعِينَ مُقْنِعِى رُءُوسِهِمْ 43 Scrambling with their heads upturned,

لَا يَرْتَدُّ إِلَيْهِمْ طَرْفُهُمْ

there will be a fixed gaze in their eyes

وَأَفْئِدَتُهُمْ هَوَآءٌ ۝

and their hearts will be vacant.

وَأَنذِرِ ٱلنَّاسَ يَوْمَ 44 *Warn* the people of the day when

يَأْتِيهِمُ ٱلْعَذَابُ

the punishment will overtake them,

فَيَقُولُ ٱلَّذِينَ ظَلَمُواْ

whereat the wrongdoers will say,

رَبَّنَآ أَخِّرْنَآ إِلَىٰٓ أَجَلٍ قَرِيبٍ

'Our Lord! Respite us for a brief while

نُجِبْ دَعْوَتَكَ

so that we may respond to Your call,

وَنَتَّبِعِ ٱلرُّسُلَ

and follow the apostles.'[1]

أَوَلَمْ تَكُونُوٓاْ أَقْسَمْتُم مِّن قَبْلُ

[They will be told,] 'Did you not use to swear earlier

مَا لَكُم مِّن زَوَالٍ ۝

that there would be no reverse for you,

وَسَكَنتُمْ فِى مَسَٰكِنِ 45 while you dwelt in the dwellings

ٱلَّذِينَ ظَلَمُوٓاْ أَنفُسَهُمْ

of those who had wronged themselves [before],

---

[1] The appeal for respite made by the wrongdoers indicates that the punishment mentioned here is one that will befall them in the life of this world.

وَتَبَيَّنَ لَكُمْ
and it had been made clear to you

كَيْفَ فَعَلْنَا بِهِمْ
how We had dealt with them [before you],

وَضَرَبْنَا لَكُمُ ٱلْأَمْثَالَ ﴿٤٥﴾
and We had [also] cited examples for you?'

وَقَدْ مَكَرُواْ مَكْرَهُمْ
46 They certainly devised their schemes,

وَعِندَ ٱللَّهِ مَكْرُهُمْ
but their schemes are known to Allah,

وَإِن كَانَ مَكْرُهُمْ
and their schemes are not such

لِتَزُولَ مِنْهُ ٱلْجِبَالُ ﴿٤٦﴾
as to dislodge the mountains.[1]

فَلَا تَحْسَبَنَّ ٱللَّهَ
47 So do not suppose that Allah

مُخْلِفَ وَعْدِهِ رُسُلَهُ
will break His promise to His apostles.

إِنَّ ٱللَّهَ عَزِيزٌ ذُو ٱنتِقَامٍ ﴿٤٧﴾
Indeed Allah is all-mighty, avenger.

يَوْمَ تُبَدَّلُ ٱلْأَرْضُ غَيْرَ ٱلْأَرْضِ
48 The day the earth is transformed into another earth

وَٱلسَّمَٰوَٰتُ
and the heavens [as well],

وَبَرَزُواْ لِلَّهِ
and they are presented before Allah,

ٱلْوَٰحِدِ ٱلْقَهَّارِ ﴿٤٨﴾
the One, the All-paramount.

وَتَرَى ٱلْمُجْرِمِينَ يَوْمَئِذٍ
49 On that day *you* will see the guilty

مُقَرَّنِينَ فِى ٱلْأَصْفَادِ ﴿٤٩﴾
bound together in chains,

سَرَابِيلُهُم مِّن قَطِرَانٍ
50 their garments made of pitch,[2]

وَتَغْشَىٰ وُجُوهَهُمُ ٱلنَّارُ ﴿٥٠﴾
and the Fire covering their faces,

لِيَجْزِىَ ٱللَّهُ كُلَّ نَفْسٍ
51 so that Allah may reward every soul

مَّا كَسَبَتْ
for what it has earned.[3]

إِنَّ ٱللَّهَ سَرِيعُ ٱلْحِسَابِ ﴿٥١﴾
Indeed Allah is swift at reckoning.

هَٰذَا بَلَٰغٌ لِّلنَّاسِ
52 This is a proclamation for mankind

وَلِيُنذَرُواْ بِهِۦ
so that they may be warned thereby,

وَلِيَعْلَمُوٓاْ أَنَّمَا هُوَ إِلَٰهٌ وَٰحِدٌ
and know that He is indeed the One God,

وَلِيَذَّكَّرَ أُوْلُواْ ٱلْأَلْبَٰبِ ﴿٥٢﴾
and those who possess intellect may take admonition.

---

[1] According to an alternate reading (with *la-tazūlu*), the meaning will be 'their schemes are indeed such as to dislodge (or annihilate) [even] the mountains.'

[2] Or 'of molten copper.'

[3] Or, perhaps preferably, 'so that Allah may requite every soul with what it has earned,' which implies that deeds are identical with their recompense, or that deeds are their own recompense.

[PART 14]

سُورَةُ الْحِجْرِ

**15. SŪRAT AL-ḤIJR[1]**

بِسْمِ اللَّهِ          In the Name of Allah,

الرَّحْمَٰنِ الرَّحِيمِ          the All-beneficent, the All-merciful.

الٓرٰ ١          1 *Alif, Lām, Rā.*

تِلْكَ ءَايَٰتُ ٱلْكِتَٰبِ          These are the signs of the Book

وَقُرْءَانٍ مُّبِينٍ ۝          and a manifest Qur'ān.

رُّبَمَا يَوَدُّ ٱلَّذِينَ كَفَرُوا ٢          2 Much will the faithless wish

لَوْ كَانُوا مُسْلِمِينَ ۝          that they had been *muslim*s.

ذَرْهُمْ يَأْكُلُوا وَيَتَمَتَّعُوا ٣          3 *Leave* them to eat and enjoy

وَيُلْهِهِمُ ٱلْأَمَلُ          and to be diverted by longings.

فَسَوْفَ يَعْلَمُونَ ۝          Soon they will know.

وَمَا أَهْلَكْنَا مِن قَرْيَةٍ ٤          4 We did not destroy any town

إِلَّا وَلَهَا كِتَابٌ مَّعْلُومٌ ۝          but that it had a known term.

مَّا تَسْبِقُ مِنْ أُمَّةٍ أَجَلَهَا ٥          5 No nation can advance its time

وَمَا يَسْتَـْٔخِرُونَ ۝          nor can it defer it.

وَقَالُوا ٦          6 They said,

يَٰٓأَيُّهَا ٱلَّذِى          'O you,

نُزِّلَ عَلَيْهِ ٱلذِّكْرُ          to whom the Reminder has been sent down,

إِنَّكَ لَمَجْنُونٌ ۝          you are indeed crazy.

لَّوْ مَا تَأْتِينَا بِٱلْمَلَٰٓئِكَةِ ٧          7 Why do you not bring us the angels

إِن كُنتَ مِنَ ٱلصَّٰدِقِينَ ۝          should you be truthful?!'

مَا نُنَزِّلُ ٱلْمَلَٰٓئِكَةَ ٨          8 We do not send down the angels

إِلَّا بِٱلْحَقِّ          except with due reason,

وَمَا كَانُوا إِذًا مُّنظَرِينَ ۝          and then they will not be granted any respite.

---

[1] The *sūrah* takes its name from Ḥijr (mentioned in verse 80), a place or region said to be inhabited by the people of Thamūd.

إِنَّا نَحْنُ نَزَّلْنَا ٱلذِّكْرَ 9 Indeed We have sent down the Reminder,[1]

وَإِنَّا لَهُۥ لَحَٰفِظُونَ ۝ and indeed We will preserve it.

وَلَقَدْ أَرْسَلْنَا مِن قَبْلِكَ 10 Certainly We sent [apostles] before *you*

فِى شِيَعِ ٱلْأَوَّلِينَ ۝ to former communities,

وَمَا يَأْتِيهِم مِّن رَّسُولٍ 11 and there did not come to them any apostle

إِلَّا كَانُواْ بِهِۦ يَسْتَهْزِءُونَ ۝ but that they used to deride him.

كَذَٰلِكَ نَسْلُكُهُۥ 12 That is how We let it pass

فِى قُلُوبِ ٱلْمُجْرِمِينَ ۝ through the hearts of the guilty:

لَا يُؤْمِنُونَ بِهِۦ 13 they do not believe in it,

وَقَدْ خَلَتْ سُنَّةُ ٱلْأَوَّلِينَ ۝ and the precedent of the ancients has already passed.

وَلَوْ فَتَحْنَا عَلَيْهِم 14 Were We to open for them

بَابًا مِّنَ ٱلسَّمَآءِ a gate of the sky,

فَظَلُّواْ فِيهِ يَعْرُجُونَ ۝ so that they could go on ascending through it,

لَقَالُوٓاْ 15 they would surely say,

إِنَّمَا سُكِّرَتْ أَبْصَٰرُنَا 'Indeed a spell has been cast on our eyes;

بَلْ نَحْنُ قَوْمٌ مَّسْحُورُونَ ۝ rather we are a bewitched lot.'

وَلَقَدْ جَعَلْنَا فِى ٱلسَّمَآءِ بُرُوجًا 16 Certainly We have appointed houses[2] in the sky

وَزَيَّنَّٰهَا لِلنَّٰظِرِينَ ۝ and adorned them for the onlookers,

وَحَفِظْنَٰهَا 17 and We have guarded them

مِن كُلِّ شَيْطَٰنٍ رَّجِيمٍ ۝ from every outcast Satan,

إِلَّا مَنِ ٱسْتَرَقَ ٱلسَّمْعَ 18 except someone who may eavesdrop,

فَأَتْبَعَهُۥ شِهَابٌ مُّبِينٌ ۝ whereat there pursues him a manifest flame.[3]

وَٱلْأَرْضَ مَدَدْنَٰهَا 19 And We spread out the earth,

وَأَلْقَيْنَا فِيهَا رَوَٰسِىَ and cast in it firm mountains,

وَأَنۢبَتْنَا فِيهَا and We grew in it

مِن كُلِّ شَىْءٍ مَّوْزُونٍ ۝ every kind of balanced thing,

---

[1] That is, the Qur'ān.

[2] House: One of the 12 parts into which the heavens are divided in astrology. Cf. 25:61; 85:1.

[3] Or 'meteor.'

وَجَعَلْنَا لَكُمْ فِيهَا مَعَيِشَ 20 and made in it [various] means of livelihood for you

وَمَن لَّسْتُمْ لَهُ بِرَزِقِينَ ۝ and for those whom you do not provide for.

وَإِن مِّن شَىْءٍ 21 There is not a thing

إِلَّا عِندَنَا خَزَآئِنُهُ but that its sources are with Us,

وَمَا نُنَزِّلُهُ and We do not send it down

إِلَّا بِقَدَرٍ مَّعْلُومٍ ۝ except in a known measure.

وَأَرْسَلْنَا ٱلرِّيَٰحَ لَوَٰقِحَ 22 And We send the fertilizing winds

فَأَنزَلْنَا مِنَ ٱلسَّمَآءِ مَآءً and send down water from the sky

فَأَسْقَيْنَٰكُمُوهُ providing it for you to drink

وَمَآ أَنتُمْ لَهُ بِخَٰزِنِينَ ۝ and you are not maintainers of its resources.

وَإِنَّا لَنَحْنُ نُحْيِۦ 23 Indeed it is We who give life

وَنُمِيتُ and bring death

وَنَحْنُ ٱلْوَٰرِثُونَ ۝ and We are the inheritors.

وَلَقَدْ عَلِمْنَا ٱلْمُسْتَقْدِمِينَ مِنكُمْ 24 Certainly We know the predecessors among you

وَلَقَدْ عَلِمْنَا ٱلْمُسْتَـْٔخِرِينَ ۝ and certainly We know the successors,

وَإِنَّ رَبَّكَ هُوَ يَحْشُرُهُمْ 25 and indeed it is *your* Lord who will resurrect them.

إِنَّهُ حَكِيمٌ عَلِيمٌ ۝ Indeed He is all-wise, all-knowing.

وَلَقَدْ خَلَقْنَا ٱلْإِنسَٰنَ 26 Certainly We created man

مِن صَلْصَٰلٍ out of a dry clay[1]

مِّنْ حَمَإٍ مَّسْنُونٍ ۝ [drawn] from an aging mud,

وَٱلْجَآنَّ خَلَقْنَٰهُ مِن قَبْلُ 27 and We created the jinn earlier

مِن نَّارِ ٱلسَّمُومِ ۝ out of a piercing fire.

وَإِذْ قَالَ رَبُّكَ لِلْمَلَٰئِكَةِ 28 When your Lord said to the angels,

إِنِّى خَٰلِقٌ بَشَرًا 'Indeed I am going to create a human

مِّن صَلْصَٰلٍ مِّنْ حَمَإٍ مَّسْنُونٍ ۝ out of a dry clay [drawn] from an aging mud.

فَإِذَا سَوَّيْتُهُ 29 So when I have proportioned him

وَنَفَخْتُ فِيهِ مِن رُّوحِى and breathed into him of My spirit,

---

[1] Or 'clinking clay,' that is, giving a clinking sound due to being hard and dry. Cf. 15:28

then fall down in prostration before him.'

فَسَجَدَ ٱلْمَلَـٰٓئِكَةُ 30 Thereat the angels prostrated,

كُلُّهُمْ أَجْمَعُونَ ۝      all of them together,

إِلَّآ إِبْلِيسَ 31      except Iblis:

أَبَىٰٓ أَن يَكُونَ مَعَ ٱلسَّـٰجِدِينَ ۝    he refused to be among those who prostrated.

قَالَ يَـٰٓإِبْلِيسُ 32 He said, 'O Iblis!

مَا لَكَ أَلَّا تَكُونَ      What kept you from being

مَعَ ٱلسَّـٰجِدِينَ ۝      among those who have prostrated?'

قَالَ لَمْ أَكُن لِّأَسْجُدَ لِبَشَرٍ 33 Said he, 'I will not prostrate before a human

خَلَقْتَهُۥ      whom You have created

مِن صَلْصَـٰلٍ مِّنْ حَمَإٍ مَّسْنُونٍ ۝    out of a dry clay [drawn] from an aging mud.'

قَالَ فَٱخْرُجْ مِنْهَا 34 He said, 'Begone hence,

فَإِنَّكَ رَجِيمٌ ۝      for you are indeed an outcast,

وَإِنَّ عَلَيْكَ ٱللَّعْنَةَ 35    and indeed the curse shall lie on you

إِلَىٰ يَوْمِ ٱلدِّينِ ۝      until the Day of Retribution.'[1]

قَالَ رَبِّ 36 He said, 'My Lord!

فَأَنظِرْنِىٓ إِلَىٰ يَوْمِ يُبْعَثُونَ ۝    Respite me till the day they will be resurrected.'

قَالَ فَإِنَّكَ مِنَ ٱلْمُنظَرِينَ ۝ 37 Said He, 'You are indeed among the reprieved

إِلَىٰ يَوْمِ ٱلْوَقْتِ ٱلْمَعْلُومِ ۝ 38   until the day of the known time.'

قَالَ رَبِّ 39 He said, 'My Lord!

بِمَآ أَغْوَيْتَنِى      As You have consigned me to perversity,

لَأُزَيِّنَنَّ لَهُمْ فِى ٱلْأَرْضِ      I will surely glamorize [evil] for them on the earth,

وَلَأُغْوِيَنَّهُمْ أَجْمَعِينَ ۝      and I will surely pervert them,

إِلَّا عِبَادَكَ مِنْهُمُ ٱلْمُخْلَصِينَ ۝ 40   except Your exclusive servants among them.'

قَالَ 41 He said,

هَـٰذَا صِرَٰطٌ عَلَىَّ مُسْتَقِيمٌ ۝    'This is the path [leading] straight to Me.[2]

---

[1] Or 'the Day of Judgement.'

[2] Read alternatively as *hādhā ṣirāṭun ʿaliyyun mustaqīm*, meaning 'this is an exalted straight path.' This reading is narrated from al-Imam al-Ṣādiq (*Majmaʿ al-Bayān*) and from thirteen other authorities, among them Yaʿqūb, al-Ḍaḥḥāk, Mujāhid, Qatādah, and Ibn Sīrīn. (See *Muʿjam al-Qirāʾāt al-Qurʾāniyyah*)

إِنَّ عِبَادِى 42 Indeed as for My servants

لَيْسَ لَكَ عَلَيْهِمْ سُلْطَنٌ   you do not have any authority over them,

إِلَّا مَنِ ٱتَّبَعَكَ مِنَ ٱلْغَاوِينَ ۝   except the perverse who follow you,

وَإِنَّ جَهَنَّمَ لَمَوْعِدُهُمْ أَجْمَعِينَ ۝ 43   and indeed hell is the tryst of them all.

لَهَا سَبْعَةُ أَبْوَابٍ 44 It has seven gates,

لِّكُلِّ بَابٍ مِّنْهُمْ جُزْءٌ مَّقْسُومٌ ۝   and to each gate belongs a separate portion of them.'

إِنَّ ٱلْمُتَّقِينَ 45 Indeed the Godwary will be

فِى جَنَّـٰتٍ وَعُيُونٍ ۝   amid gardens and springs.

ٱدْخُلُوهَا بِسَلَـٰمٍ ءَامِنِينَ ۝ 46 "Enter it in peace and safety!"

وَنَزَعْنَا 47 We will remove

مَا فِى صُدُورِهِم مِّنْ غِلٍّ   whatever rancour there is in their breasts;

إِخْوَٰنًا   [intimate like] brothers, [they will be reclining]

عَلَىٰ سُرُرٍ مُّتَقَـٰبِلِينَ ۝   on couches, facing one another.

لَا يَمَسُّهُمْ فِيهَا نَصَبٌ 48 Therein neither weariness shall touch them,

وَمَا هُم مِّنْهَا بِمُخْرَجِينَ ۝ ✴   nor will they [ever] be expelled from it.

نَبِّئْ عِبَادِى 49 *Inform* my servants

أَنِّى أَنَا ٱلْغَفُورُ ٱلرَّحِيمُ ۝   that I am indeed the All-forgiving, the All-merciful,

وَأَنَّ عَذَابِى هُوَ ٱلْعَذَابُ ٱلْأَلِيمُ ۝ 50   and that My punishment is a painful punishment.

وَنَبِّئْهُمْ عَن ضَيْفِ إِبْرَٰهِيمَ ۝ 51 And *inform* them about the guests of Abraham,

إِذْ دَخَلُوا۟ عَلَيْهِ 52   when they entered into his presence

فَقَالُوا۟ سَلَـٰمًا   and said, 'Peace!'

قَالَ إِنَّا مِنكُمْ وَجِلُونَ ۝   He said, 'We are indeed afraid of you.'

قَالُوا۟ لَا تَوْجَلْ 53 They said, 'Do not be afraid.

إِنَّا نُبَشِّرُكَ بِغُلَـٰمٍ عَلِيمٍ ۝   Indeed we give you the good news of a wise son.'

قَالَ أَبَشَّرْتُمُونِى 54 He said, 'Do you give me good news

عَلَىٰ أَن مَّسَّنِىَ ٱلْكِبَرُ   though old age has befallen me?

فَبِمَ تُبَشِّرُونَ ۝   What is the good news that you bring me?"

قَالُوا۟ بَشَّرْنَـٰكَ بِٱلْحَقِّ 55 They said, 'We bring you good news in truth;

فَلَا تَكُن مِّنَ ٱلْقَـٰنِطِينَ ۝   so do not be among the despondent.'

قَالَ وَمَن يَقْنَطُ مِن رَّحْمَةِ رَبِّهِ 56 He said, 'Who despairs of his Lord's mercy

إِلَّا ٱلضَّآلُّونَ ۝      except those who are astray?!'

قَالَ فَمَا خَطْبُكُمْ أَيُّهَا ٱلْمُرْسَلُونَ ۝ 57 He said, 'O messengers, what is now your errand?'

قَالُوٓا۟ إِنَّآ أُرْسِلْنَآ 58 They said, 'We have been sent

إِلَىٰ قَوْمٍ مُّجْرِمِينَ ۝      toward a guilty people,

إِلَّآ ءَالَ لُوطٍ 59 [who shall perish] except the family of Lot.

إِنَّا لَمُنَجُّوهُمْ أَجْمَعِينَ ۝      We will indeed deliver all of them,

إِلَّا ٱمْرَأَتَهُ 60 except his wife,

قَدَّرْنَآ      [who], We have ordained,

إِنَّهَا لَمِنَ ٱلْغَٰبِرِينَ ۝      will indeed be among those who remain behind.'

فَلَمَّا جَآءَ ءَالَ لُوطٍ ٱلْمُرْسَلُونَ ۝ 61 So when the messengers came to Lot's family,

قَالَ إِنَّكُمْ قَوْمٌ مُّنكَرُونَ ۝ 62 he said, 'You are indeed strangers [to me].'

قَالُوا۟ بَلْ جِئْنَٰكَ 63 They said, 'Rather we bring you

بِمَا كَانُوا۟ فِيهِ يَمْتَرُونَ ۝      what they used to doubt.

وَأَتَيْنَٰكَ بِٱلْحَقِّ 64 We bring you the truth,

وَإِنَّا لَصَٰدِقُونَ ۝      and indeed we speak the truth.

فَأَسْرِ بِأَهْلِكَ 65 Take your family

بِقِطْعٍ مِّنَ ٱلَّيْلِ      in a watch of the night;

وَٱتَّبِعْ أَدْبَٰرَهُمْ      and follow in their rear,

وَلَا يَلْتَفِتْ مِنكُمْ أَحَدٌ      and none of you should turn round,

وَٱمْضُوا۟ حَيْثُ تُؤْمَرُونَ ۝      and proceed as you are bidden.'

وَقَضَيْنَآ إِلَيْهِ ذَٰلِكَ ٱلْأَمْرَ 66 We apprised him of the matter

أَنَّ دَابِرَ هَٰٓؤُلَآءِ مَقْطُوعٌ      that these[1] will be rooted out

مُّصْبِحِينَ ۝      by dawn.

وَجَآءَ أَهْلُ ٱلْمَدِينَةِ 67 The people of the city came,

يَسْتَبْشِرُونَ ۝      rejoicing.

قَالَ إِنَّ هَٰٓؤُلَآءِ ضَيْفِى 68 He said, 'These are indeed my guests.

فَلَا تَفْضَحُونِ ۝      Do not bring dishonour on me.

وَٱتَّقُوا۟ ٱللَّهَ 69 Be wary of Allah

---

[1] That is, the people of Sodom.

وَلَا تُخْزُونِ ۩

and do not humiliate me.'

قَالُوٓاْ أَوَلَمْ نَنْهَكَ

70 They said, 'Did we not forbid you

عَنِ ٱلْعَلَمِينَ ۩

from [defending[1]] strangers?

قَالَ هَٰٓؤُلَآءِ بَنَاتِىٓ

71 He said, 'These are my daughters, [marry them]

إِن كُنتُمْ فَعِلِينَ ۩

if you should do anything.'

لَعَمْرُكَ

72 By *your* life,

إِنَّهُمْ لَفِى سَكْرَتِهِمْ يَعْمَهُونَ ۩

they were bewildered in their drunkenness.

فَأَخَذَتْهُمُ ٱلصَّيْحَةُ مُشْرِقِينَ ۩

73 So the Cry seized them at sunrise,

فَجَعَلْنَا عَلِيَهَا سَافِلَهَا

74 and We made its[2] topmost part its nethermost,

وَأَمْطَرْنَا عَلَيْهِم

and rained on them

حِجَارَةً مِّن سِجِّيلٍ ۩

stones of shale.

إِنَّ فِى ذَٰلِكَ لَأَيَٰتٍ لِّلْمُتَوَسِّمِينَ ۩

75 There are indeed signs in that for the percipient.

وَإِنَّهَا لَبِسَبِيلٍ مُّقِيمٍ ۩

76 Indeed it is on a standing road,

إِنَّ فِى ذَٰلِكَ لَأَيَةً لِّلْمُؤْمِنِينَ ۩

77 and there is indeed a sign in that for the faithful.

وَإِن كَانَ أَصْحَٰبُ ٱلْأَيْكَةِ

78 Indeed the inhabitants of Aykah[3]

لَظَٰلِمِينَ ۩

were wrongdoers.

فَٱنتَقَمْنَا مِنْهُمْ

79 So We took vengeance on them,

وَإِنَّهُمَا

and indeed the two of them[4]

لَبِإِمَامٍ مُّبِينٍ ۩

are on an open highway.

وَلَقَدْ كَذَّبَ أَصْحَٰبُ ٱلْحِجْرِ

80 Certainly the inhabitants of Ḥijr denied

ٱلْمُرْسَلِينَ ۩

the apostles.

وَءَاتَيْنَٰهُمْ ءَايَٰتِنَا

81 We had given them Our signs

فَكَانُواْ عَنْهَا مُعْرِضِينَ ۩

but they disregarded them.

وَكَانُواْ يَنْحِتُونَ مِنَ ٱلْجِبَالِ بُيُوتًا

82 They used to hew out dwellings from mountains

---

[1] Or, from entertaining.

[2] That is, of the city of Sodom.

[3] Apparently, one of the towns to which the prophet Shuʿayb (ʿa) was sent. Cf. 26:176; 38:13; 50:14.

[4] That is, Sodom and Aykah.

ءَامِنِينَ ۝    feeling secure.

فَأَخَذَتْهُمُ ٱلصَّيْحَةُ مُصْبِحِينَ ۝    83 So the Cry seized them at dawn,

فَمَآ أَغْنَىٰ عَنْهُم مَّا كَانُوا۟ يَكْسِبُونَ ۝    84 and what they used to earn did not avail them.

وَمَا خَلَقْنَا ٱلسَّمَـٰوَٰتِ وَٱلْأَرْضَ    85 We did not create the heavens and the earth

وَمَا بَيْنَهُمَآ    and whatever is between them

إِلَّا بِٱلْحَقِّ    except with the Truth,

وَإِنَّ ٱلسَّاعَةَ لَآتِيَةٌ    and indeed the Hour is bound to come.

فَٱصْفَحِ ٱلصَّفْحَ ٱلْجَمِيلَ ۝    So *forbear* with a graceful forbearance.

إِنَّ رَبَّكَ هُوَ ٱلْخَلَّـٰقُ ٱلْعَلِيمُ ۝    86 Indeed *your* Lord is the All-creator, the All-knowing.

وَلَقَدْ ءَاتَيْنَـٰكَ    87 Certainly We have given *you*

سَبْعًا مِّنَ ٱلْمَثَانِي    [the *sūrah* of] the seven oft-repeated verses[1]

وَٱلْقُرْءَانَ ٱلْعَظِيمَ ۝    and the great Qur'ān.

لَا تَمُدَّنَّ عَيْنَيْكَ    88 Do not extend *your* glance

إِلَىٰ مَا مَتَّعْنَا بِهِۦٓ    toward what We have provided to

أَزْوَٰجًا مِّنْهُمْ    certain groups of them,

وَلَا تَحْزَنْ عَلَيْهِمْ    and do not grieve for them,

وَٱخْفِضْ جَنَاحَكَ لِلْمُؤْمِنِينَ ۝    and lower *your* wing to the faithful,[2]

وَقُلْ إِنِّىٓ أَنَا ٱلنَّذِيرُ ٱلْمُبِينُ ۝    89 and say, 'I am indeed a manifest warner.'

كَمَآ أَنزَلْنَا عَلَى ٱلْمُقْتَسِمِينَ ۝    90 Even as We sent down on the dividers,[3]

ٱلَّذِينَ جَعَلُوا۟ ٱلْقُرْءَانَ عِضِينَ ۝    91 who reduced the Qur'ān into pieces,

فَوَرَبِّكَ    92 by your Lord,

لَنَسْـَٔلَنَّهُمْ أَجْمَعِينَ ۝    We will question them all

عَمَّا كَانُوا۟ يَعْمَلُونَ ۝    93 concerning what they used to do.

فَٱصْدَعْ بِمَا تُؤْمَرُ    94 So *proclaim* what *you* have been commanded,

وَأَعْرِضْ عَنِ ٱلْمُشْرِكِينَ ۝    and *turn away* from the polytheists.

إِنَّا كَفَيْنَـٰكَ ٱلْمُسْتَهْزِءِينَ ۝    95 Indeed We will suffice *you* against the deriders

---

[1] That is, the Sūrat al-Fātiḥah, the opening *sūrah* of the Qur'ān.

[2] That is, be humble and gracious towards them. Cf. 17:24; 26:215.

[3] Or 'swearers.'

96 ٱلَّذِينَ يَجْعَلُونَ مَعَ ٱللَّهِ —those who set up besides Allah
إِلَٰهًا ءَاخَرَ another god.
فَسَوْفَ يَعْلَمُونَ ۩ Soon they will know!

97 وَلَقَدْ نَعْلَمُ أَنَّكَ يَضِيقُ صَدْرُكَ Certainly We know that *you* become upset
بِمَا يَقُولُونَ ۩ because of what they say.

98 فَسَبِّحْ بِحَمْدِ رَبِّكَ So *celebrate* the praise of *your* Lord
وَكُن مِّنَ ٱلسَّٰجِدِينَ ۩ and *be* among those who prostrate,

99 وَٱعْبُدْ رَبَّكَ and worship *your* Lord
حَتَّىٰ يَأْتِيَكَ ٱلْيَقِينُ ۩ until certainty[1] comes to *you*.

# سُورَةُ النَّحْلِ

# 16. SŪRAT AL-NAHL[2]

بِسْمِ ٱللَّهِ In the Name of Allah,
ٱلرَّحْمَٰنِ ٱلرَّحِيمِ the All-beneficent, the All-merciful.

1 أَتَىٰ أَمْرُ ٱللَّهِ Allah's edict is coming!
فَلَا تَسْتَعْجِلُوهُ So do not seek to hasten it.
سُبْحَٰنَهُ وَتَعَٰلَىٰ Immaculate is He and exalted
عَمَّا يُشْرِكُونَ ۩ above [having] any partners that they ascribe [to Him].

2 يُنَزِّلُ ٱلْمَلَٰئِكَةَ He sends down the angels
بِٱلرُّوحِ مِنْ أَمْرِهِ with the Spirit of His command[3]
عَلَىٰ مَن يَشَآءُ مِنْ عِبَادِهِ to whomever He wishes of His servants:
أَنْ أَنذِرُوٓا۟ أَنَّهُۥ لَآ إِلَٰهَ إِلَّآ أَنَا۠ 'Warn [the people] that there is no god except Me;
فَٱتَّقُونِ ۩ so be wary of Me.'

3 خَلَقَ ٱلسَّمَٰوَٰتِ وَٱلْأَرْضَ He created the heavens and the earth
بِٱلْحَقِّ with the Truth.
تَعَٰلَىٰ He is above

---

[1] Or 'death.'

[2] The *sūrah* takes its name from the honey bee (*al-nahl*) mentioned in verses 68-69.

[3] Or 'Law.'

عَمَّا يُشْرِكُونَ ۞    having any partners that they ascribe [to Him].

خَلَقَ ٱلْإِنسَـٰنَ مِن نُّطْفَةٍ    4 He created man from a drop of [seminal] fluid,[1]

فَإِذَا هُوَ خَصِيمٌ مُّبِينٌ ۞    and, behold, he is an open contender![2]

وَٱلْأَنْعَـٰمَ خَلَقَهَا    5 He created the cattle,

لَكُمْ فِيهَا دِفْءٌ وَمَنَـٰفِعُ    in which there is warmth[3] for you and [other] uses

وَمِنْهَا تَأْكُلُونَ ۞    and some of them you eat.

وَلَكُمْ فِيهَا جَمَالٌ    6 There is in them a beauty for you

حِينَ تُرِيحُونَ    when you bring them home for rest

وَحِينَ تَسْرَحُونَ ۞    and when you drive them forth to pasture.

وَتَحْمِلُ أَثْقَالَكُمْ إِلَىٰ بَلَدٍ    7 And they bear your burdens to towns

لَّمْ تَكُونُوا۟ بَـٰلِغِيهِ    which you could not reach

إِلَّا بِشِقِّ ٱلْأَنفُسِ    except by straining yourselves.

إِنَّ رَبَّكُمْ لَرَءُوفٌ رَّحِيمٌ ۞    Indeed your Lord is most kind and merciful.

وَٱلْخَيْلَ وَٱلْبِغَالَ وَٱلْحَمِيرَ    8 And horses, mules and asses,

لِتَرْكَبُوهَا وَزِينَةً    for you to ride them, and for adornment,

وَيَخْلُقُ مَا لَا تَعْلَمُونَ ۞    and He creates what you do not know.

وَعَلَى ٱللَّهِ قَصْدُ ٱلسَّبِيلِ    9 With Allah rests guidance to the straight path,[4]

وَمِنْهَا جَآئِرٌ    and some of them[5] are devious,

وَلَوْ شَآءَ لَهَدَىٰكُمْ أَجْمَعِينَ ۞    and had He wished He would have guided you all.

هُوَ ٱلَّذِىٓ أَنزَلَ مِنَ ٱلسَّمَآءِ مَآءً    10 It is He who sends down water from the sky:

لَّكُم مِّنْهُ شَرَابٌ    from it you get your drink

وَمِنْهُ شَجَرٌ    and from it are [sustained] the plants

فِيهِ تُسِيمُونَ ۞    wherein you pasture your herds.

يُنۢبِتُ لَكُم بِهِ ٱلزَّرْعَ    11 With it He makes the crops grow for you

وَٱلزَّيْتُونَ وَٱلنَّخِيلَ وَٱلْأَعْنَـٰبَ    and olives, date palms, vines,

---

[1] Or 'from a drop of semen;' cf. 18:37; 22:5; 23:13-14; 35:11; 36:77; 40:67; 53:46; 75:37; 76:2; 80:19.

[2] Or 'a lucid debater,' or 'an open adversary;' cf. 36:77.

[3] That is, in the garments made from wool and leather.

[4] Cf. 20:50; 76:3; 99:12.

[5] That is, some of the paths. Cf. 6:153

وَمِن كُلِّ ٱلثَّمَرَٰتِ     and fruits of all kinds.

إِنَّ فِى ذَٰلِكَ لَآيَةً لِّقَوْمٍ يَتَفَكَّرُونَ ۝     There is indeed a sign in that for a people who reflect.

وَسَخَّرَ لَكُمُ ٱلَّيْلَ وَٱلنَّهَارَ     12 He disposed the night and the day for you,

وَٱلشَّمْسَ وَٱلْقَمَرَ وَٱلنُّجُومُ     and the sun, the moon and the stars

مُسَخَّرَٰتٌ بِأَمْرِهِۦ     are disposed by His command.

إِنَّ فِى ذَٰلِكَ لَآيَٰتٍ     There is indeed a sign in that

لِّقَوْمٍ يَعْقِلُونَ ۝     for a people who apply reason.

وَمَا ذَرَأَ لَكُمْ فِى ٱلْأَرْضِ     13 And whatever He has created for you in the earth

مُخْتَلِفًا أَلْوَٰنُهُۥٓ     of diverse hues

إِنَّ فِى ذَٰلِكَ لَآيَةً     —there is indeed a sign in that

لِّقَوْمٍ يَذَّكَّرُونَ ۝     for a people who take admonition.

وَهُوَ ٱلَّذِى سَخَّرَ ٱلْبَحْرَ     14 It is He who disposed the sea [for your benefit]

لِتَأْكُلُوا۟ مِنْهُ لَحْمًا طَرِيًّا     that you may eat from it fresh meat,

وَتَسْتَخْرِجُوا۟ مِنْهُ حِلْيَةً تَلْبَسُونَهَا     and obtain from it ornaments, which you wear

وَتَرَى ٱلْفُلْكَ مَوَاخِرَ فِيهِ     —and *you* see the ships plowing through it—

وَلِتَبْتَغُوا۟ مِن فَضْلِهِۦ     and that you may seek of His grace,

وَلَعَلَّكُمْ تَشْكُرُونَ ۝     and that you may give thanks.

وَأَلْقَىٰ فِى ٱلْأَرْضِ رَوَٰسِىَ     15 He cast in the earth firm mountains

أَن تَمِيدَ بِكُمْ     lest it should shake with you,

وَأَنْهَٰرًا وَسُبُلًا     and [made] streams and ways,

لَّعَلَّكُمْ تَهْتَدُونَ ۝     so that you may be guided

وَعَلَٰمَٰتٍ     16 —and the landmarks [as well],

وَبِٱلنَّجْمِ هُمْ يَهْتَدُونَ ۝     and by the stars they are guided.

أَفَمَن يَخْلُقُ كَمَن لَّا يَخْلُقُ     17 Is He who creates like one who does not create?

أَفَلَا تَذَكَّرُونَ ۝     Will you not then take admonition?

وَإِن تَعُدُّوا۟ نِعْمَةَ ٱللَّهِ     18 If you enumerate Allah's blessings,

لَا تُحْصُوهَآ     you will not be able to count them.

إِنَّ ٱللَّهَ لَغَفُورٌ رَّحِيمٌ ۝     Indeed Allah is all-forgiving, all-merciful.

وَٱللَّهُ يَعْلَمُ مَا تُسِرُّونَ     19 Allah knows whatever you hide

وَمَا تُعْلِنُونَ ۝     and whatever you disclose.

وَٱلَّذِينَ يَدْعُونَ مِن دُونِ ٱللَّهِ 20 Those whom they invoke besides Allah

لَا يَخْلُقُونَ شَيْئًا    do not create anything

وَهُمْ يُخْلَقُونَ ۝    and are themselves created.

أَمْوَٰتٌ غَيْرُ أَحْيَآءٍ 21 They are dead, not living,

وَمَا يَشْعُرُونَ أَيَّانَ يُبْعَثُونَ ۝    and are not aware when they will be resurrected.

إِلَٰهُكُمْ إِلَٰهٌ وَٰحِدٌ 22 Your God is the One God.

فَٱلَّذِينَ لَا يُؤْمِنُونَ بِٱلْأَخِرَةِ    Those who do not believe in the Hereafter,

قُلُوبُهُم مُّنكِرَةٌ    their hearts are amiss,[1]

وَهُم مُّسْتَكْبِرُونَ ۝    and they are arrogant.

لَا جَرَمَ أَنَّ ٱللَّهَ يَعْلَمُ مَا يُسِرُّونَ 23 Undoubtedly, Allah knows whatever they hide

وَمَا يُعْلِنُونَ    and whatever they disclose.

إِنَّهُ لَا يُحِبُّ ٱلْمُسْتَكْبِرِينَ ۝    Indeed He does not like the arrogant.

وَإِذَا قِيلَ لَهُم 24 When they are told,

مَّاذَآ أَنزَلَ رَبُّكُمْ    'What is it that your Lord has sent down?'

قَالُوٓا۟ أَسَٰطِيرُ ٱلْأَوَّلِينَ ۝    They say, 'Myths of the ancients,'

لِيَحْمِلُوٓا۟ أَوْزَارَهُمْ كَامِلَةً 25    that they may bear their entire burdens

يَوْمَ ٱلْقِيَٰمَةِ    on the Day of Resurrection,

وَمِنْ أَوْزَارِ ٱلَّذِينَ    along with some of the burdens of those

يُضِلُّونَهُم بِغَيْرِ عِلْمٍ    whom they lead astray without any knowledge.

أَلَا سَآءَ مَا يَزِرُونَ ۝    Look! Evil is what they bear!

قَدْ مَكَرَ ٱلَّذِينَ مِن قَبْلِهِمْ 26 Those who were before them [had also] schemed.

فَأَتَى ٱللَّهُ بُنْيَٰنَهُم مِّنَ ٱلْقَوَاعِدِ    Then Allah razed their edifice from the foundations

فَخَرَّ عَلَيْهِمُ ٱلسَّقْفُ مِن فَوْقِهِمْ    and the roof collapsed upon them from above

وَأَتَىٰهُمُ ٱلْعَذَابُ    and the punishment overtook them

مِنْ حَيْثُ لَا يَشْعُرُونَ ۝    whence they were not aware of.

ثُمَّ يَوْمَ ٱلْقِيَٰمَةِ يُخْزِيهِمْ 27 Then He will disgrace them on the Day of Resurrection,

وَيَقُولُ أَيْنَ شُرَكَآءِىَ ٱلَّذِينَ    and say, 'Where are My partners

كُنتُمْ تُشَٰقُّونَ فِيهِمْ    for whose sake you used to defy [Allah]?'

قَالَ ٱلَّذِينَ أُوتُوا۟ ٱلْعِلْمَ    Those who were given knowledge will say,

---

[1] Or 'their hearts are disbelieving.'

إِنَّ ٱلْخِزْىَ ٱلْيَوْمَ وَٱلسُّوٓءَ 'Indeed today disgrace and distress

عَلَى ٱلْكَـٰفِرِينَ ۝ pursue the faithless.'

ٱلَّذِينَ تَتَوَفَّىٰهُمُ ٱلْمَلَـٰٓئِكَةُ 28 —Those whom the angels take away

ظَالِمِىٓ أَنفُسِهِمْ while they are wronging themselves.

فَأَلْقَوُا۟ ٱلسَّلَمَ Thereat they submit:

مَا كُنَّا نَعْمَلُ مِن سُوٓءٍۭ 'We were not doing any evil!'

بَلَىٰٓ إِنَّ ٱللَّهَ عَلِيمٌۢ 'Yes, indeed Allah knows best

بِمَا كُنتُمْ تَعْمَلُونَ ۝ what you used to do!

فَٱدْخُلُوٓا۟ أَبْوَٰبَ جَهَنَّمَ 29 Enter the gates of hell

خَـٰلِدِينَ فِيهَا to remain in it [forever].

فَلَبِئْسَ مَثْوَى ٱلْمُتَكَبِّرِينَ ۝ ❖ Evil is the [final] abode of the arrogant.'

وَقِيلَ لِلَّذِينَ ٱتَّقَوْا۟ 30 But to those who were Godwary it will be said,

مَاذَآ أَنزَلَ رَبُّكُمْ 'What is it that your Lord has sent down?'

قَالُوا۟ خَيْرًا They will say, 'Good.'

لِّلَّذِينَ أَحْسَنُوا۟ فِى هَـٰذِهِ ٱلدُّنْيَا For those who do good in this world

حَسَنَةٌ there will be a good [reward],

وَلَدَارُ ٱلْءَاخِرَةِ خَيْرٌ and the abode of the Hereafter is better,

وَلَنِعْمَ دَارُ ٱلْمُتَّقِينَ ۝ and the abode of the Godwary is surely excellent:

جَنَّـٰتُ عَدْنٍ يَدْخُلُونَهَا 31 the Gardens of Eden, which they will enter,

تَجْرِى مِن تَحْتِهَا ٱلْأَنْهَـٰرُ with streams running in them.

لَهُمْ فِيهَا مَا يَشَآءُونَ There they will have whatever they wish,

كَذَٰلِكَ يَجْزِى ٱللَّهُ ٱلْمُتَّقِينَ ۝ and thus does Allah reward the Godwary

ٱلَّذِينَ تَتَوَفَّىٰهُمُ ٱلْمَلَـٰٓئِكَةُ 32 —those whom the angels take away

طَيِّبِينَ while they are pure.

يَقُولُونَ سَلَـٰمٌ عَلَيْكُمُ They say [to them], 'Peace be to you!

ٱدْخُلُوا۟ ٱلْجَنَّةَ بِمَا كُنتُمْ تَعْمَلُونَ ۝ Enter paradise because of what you used to do.'

هَلْ يَنظُرُونَ إِلَّآ 33 Do they await anything but

أَن تَأْتِيَهُمُ ٱلْمَلَـٰٓئِكَةُ that the angels should come to them,

أَوْ يَأْتِىَ أَمْرُ رَبِّكَ or your Lord's edict should come?

كَذَٰلِكَ فَعَلَ ٱلَّذِينَ مِن قَبْلِهِمْ Those who were before them had acted likewise;

وَمَا ظَلَمَهُمُ ٱللَّهُ Allah did not wrong them,

وَلَـٰكِن كَانُوٓاْ أَنفُسَهُمْ يَظْلِمُونَ ٣٣ but they used to wrong themselves.

فَأَصَابَهُمْ سَيِّئَاتُ مَا عَمِلُواْ 34 So the evils of what they had earned visited them,

وَحَاقَ بِهِم and they were besieged by

مَّا كَانُواْ بِهِۦ يَسْتَهْزِءُونَ ٣٤ what they used to deride.

وَقَالَ ٱلَّذِينَ أَشْرَكُواْ 35 The polytheists say,

لَوْ شَآءَ ٱللَّهُ 'Had Allah wished,

مَا عَبَدْنَا مِن دُونِهِۦ مِن شَىْءٍ we would not have worshiped anything besides Him

نَّحْنُ وَلَآ ءَابَآؤُنَا —neither we, nor our fathers—

وَلَا حَرَّمْنَا مِن دُونِهِۦ مِن شَىْءٍ nor would we have held anything holy besides Him.'[1]

كَذَٰلِكَ فَعَلَ ٱلَّذِينَ مِن قَبْلِهِمْ Those who were before them had acted likewise.

فَهَلْ عَلَى ٱلرُّسُلِ Is the apostles' duty

إِلَّا ٱلْبَلَـٰغُ ٱلْمُبِينُ ٣٥ anything but to communicate in clear terms?

وَلَقَدْ بَعَثْنَا فِى كُلِّ أُمَّةٍ رَّسُولًا 36 Certainly We raised an apostle in every nation

أَنِ ٱعْبُدُواْ ٱللَّهَ [to preach:] 'Worship Allah,

وَٱجْتَنِبُواْ ٱلطَّـٰغُوتَ and keep away from the Rebel.'

فَمِنْهُم مَّنْ هَدَى ٱللَّهُ Then among them were some whom Allah guided,

وَمِنْهُم مَّنْ and among them were some

حَقَّتْ عَلَيْهِ ٱلضَّلَـٰلَةُ who deserved to be in error.

فَسِيرُواْ فِى ٱلْأَرْضِ So travel over the land

فَٱنظُرُواْ and then observe

كَيْفَ كَانَ عَـٰقِبَةُ ٱلْمُكَذِّبِينَ ٣٦ how was the fate of the deniers.

إِن تَحْرِصْ عَلَىٰ هُدَىٰهُمْ 37 If you are eager for them to be guided,

فَإِنَّ ٱللَّهَ لَا يَهْدِى indeed Allah does not guide

مَن يُضِلُّ those who mislead [others],

وَمَا لَهُم مِّن نَّـٰصِرِينَ ٣٧ and they will have no helpers.

وَأَقْسَمُواْ بِٱللَّهِ جَهْدَ أَيْمَـٰنِهِمْ 38 They swear by Allah with solemn oaths

---

[1] Or 'nor we would have forbidden anything without Him (that is, without His permission).' Cf. 6:148.

لَا يَبْعَثُ ٱللَّهُ مَن يَمُوتُ     that Allah will not resurrect those who die.

بَلَىٰ وَعْدًا عَلَيْهِ حَقًّا     Yes indeed, it is a promise binding upon Him,

وَلَٰكِنَّ أَكْثَرَ ٱلنَّاسِ لَا يَعْلَمُونَ ۝     but most people do not know.

لِيُبَيِّنَ لَهُمُ ٱلَّذِى يَخْتَلِفُونَ فِيهِ     39 That He may clarify for them what they differ about,

وَلِيَعْلَمَ ٱلَّذِينَ كَفَرُوٓا۟     and that the faithless may know

أَنَّهُمْ كَانُوا۟ كَٰذِبِينَ ۝     that they were liars.

إِنَّمَا قَوْلُنَا لِشَىْءٍ إِذَآ أَرَدْنَٰهُ     40 All that We say to a thing, when We will it,

أَن نَّقُولَ لَهُۥ كُن فَيَكُونُ ۝     is to say to it 'Be!' and it is.

وَٱلَّذِينَ هَاجَرُوا۟ فِى ٱللَّهِ     41 Those who migrate for the sake of Allah

مِنۢ بَعْدِ مَا ظُلِمُوا۟     after they have been wronged,

لَنُبَوِّئَنَّهُمْ فِى ٱلدُّنْيَا حَسَنَةً     We will surely settle them in a good place in the world,

وَلَأَجْرُ ٱلْآخِرَةِ أَكْبَرُ     and the reward of the Hereafter is surely greater,

لَوْ كَانُوا۟ يَعْلَمُونَ ۝     had they known.

ٱلَّذِينَ صَبَرُوا۟     42 —Those who are patient

وَعَلَىٰ رَبِّهِمْ يَتَوَكَّلُونَ ۝     and put their trust in their Lord.

وَمَآ أَرْسَلْنَا مِن قَبْلِكَ     43 We did not send [any apostles] before *you*

إِلَّا رِجَالًا نُّوحِىٓ إِلَيْهِمْ     except as men to whom We revealed

فَسْـَٔلُوٓا۟ أَهْلَ ٱلذِّكْرِ     —ask the People of the Reminder

إِن كُنتُمْ لَا تَعْلَمُونَ ۝     if you do not know—

بِٱلْبَيِّنَٰتِ وَٱلزُّبُرِ     44 [and sent them] with manifest proofs and scriptures.

وَأَنزَلْنَآ إِلَيْكَ ٱلذِّكْرَ     We have sent down the reminder to *you*

لِتُبَيِّنَ لِلنَّاسِ     so that *you* may clarify for the people

مَا نُزِّلَ إِلَيْهِمْ     that which has been sent down to them,

وَلَعَلَّهُمْ يَتَفَكَّرُونَ ۝     so that they may reflect.

أَفَأَمِنَ ٱلَّذِينَ مَكَرُوا۟ ٱلسَّيِّـَٔاتِ     45 Do those who make evil schemes feel secure

أَن يَخْسِفَ ٱللَّهُ بِهِمُ ٱلْأَرْضَ     that Allah will not make the earth swallow them,

أَوْ يَأْتِيَهُمُ ٱلْعَذَابُ     or the punishment will not overtake them

مِنْ حَيْثُ لَا يَشْعُرُونَ ۝     whence they are not aware of?

أَوْ يَأْخُذَهُمْ     46 Or that He will not seize them

فِى تَقَلُّبِهِمْ　in the midst of their bustle,

فَمَا هُم بِمُعْجِزِينَ ۝　whereupon they will not be able to thwart [Him]?

أَوْ يَأْخُذَهُمْ　47 Or that He will not visit them

عَلَىٰ تَخَوُّفٍ　with attrition?[1]

فَإِنَّ رَبَّكُمْ لَرَءُوفٌ رَّحِيمٌ ۝　Indeed your Lord is most kind and merciful.

أَوَلَمْ يَرَوْاْ إِلَىٰ　48 Have they not regarded

مَا خَلَقَ ٱللَّهُ مِن شَىْءٍ　that whatever thing Allah has created

يَتَفَيَّؤُاْ ظِلَـٰلُهُ عَنِ ٱلْيَمِينِ　casts its shadow to the right

وَٱلشَّمَآئِلِ　and to the left,

سُجَّدًا لِّلَّهِ وَهُمْ دَٰخِرُونَ ۝　prostrating to Allah in utter humility?

وَلِلَّهِ يَسْجُدُ مَا فِى ٱلسَّمَـٰوَٰتِ　49 To Allah prostrates whatever is in the heavens

وَمَا فِى ٱلْأَرْضِ　and whatever is on the earth,

مِن دَآبَّةٍ وَٱلْمَلَـٰٓئِكَةُ　including animals and angels,

وَهُمْ لَا يَسْتَكْبِرُونَ ۝　and they are not arrogant.

يَخَافُونَ رَبَّهُم مِّن فَوْقِهِمْ　50 They fear their Lord above them,

وَيَفْعَلُونَ مَا يُؤْمَرُونَ ۩ ۝　and do what they are commanded.

وَقَالَ ٱللَّهُ　51 And Allah has said,

لَا تَتَّخِذُوٓاْ إِلَـٰهَيْنِ ٱثْنَيْنِ　'Do not worship two gods.

إِنَّمَا هُوَ إِلَـٰهٌ وَٰحِدٌ　Indeed He is the One God,

فَإِيَّـٰىَ فَٱرْهَبُونِ ۝　so be in awe of Me [alone].'

وَلَهُۥ مَا فِى ٱلسَّمَـٰوَٰتِ　52 To Him belongs whatever is in the heavens

وَٱلْأَرْضِ　and the earth,

وَلَهُ ٱلدِّينُ وَاصِبًا　and to Him belongs the enduring religion.

أَفَغَيْرَ ٱللَّهِ تَتَّقُونَ ۝　Will you, then, be wary of other than Allah?

وَمَا بِكُم مِّن نِّعْمَةٍ فَمِنَ ٱللَّهِ　53 Whatever blessing you have is from Allah,

ثُمَّ إِذَا مَسَّكُمُ ٱلضُّرُّ　then when a distress befalls you,

فَإِلَيْهِ تَجْـَٔرُونَ ۝　you make entreaties to Him.

ثُمَّ إِذَا كَشَفَ ٱلضُّرَّ عَنكُمْ　54 Then when He removes the distress from you,

---

[1] Or 'amid panic.'

إِذَا فَرِيقٌ مِّنكُم بِرَبِّهِمْ يُشْرِكُونَ ۝    behold, a part of them ascribe partners to their Lord,

لِيَكْفُرُواْ بِمَآ ءَاتَيْنَهُمْ    55 being unthankful for what We have given them.

فَتَمَتَّعُواْ فَسَوْفَ تَعْلَمُونَ ۝    So let them enjoy. Soon they shall know!

وَيَجْعَلُونَ لِمَا لَا يَعْلَمُونَ    56 To what they do not know, they attribute

نَصِيبًا مِّمَّا رَزَقْنَهُمْ    a share in what We have provided them with.

تَاللَّهِ لَتُسْـَٔلُنَّ    By Allah, you will surely be questioned

عَمَّا كُنتُمْ تَفْتَرُونَ ۝    concerning what you used to fabricate.

وَيَجْعَلُونَ لِلَّهِ ٱلْبَنَـٰتِ    57 And they attribute daughters to Allah

سُبْحَـٰنَهُۥ    —immaculate is He—

وَلَهُم مَّا يَشْتَهُونَ ۝    while they will have what they desire!

وَإِذَا بُشِّرَ أَحَدُهُم    58 When one of them is brought the news

بِٱلْأُنثَىٰ    of a female [newborn],

ظَلَّ وَجْهُهُۥ مُسْوَدًّا    his face becomes darkened

وَهُوَ كَظِيمٌ ۝    and he chokes with suppressed agony.

يَتَوَٰرَىٰ مِنَ ٱلْقَوْمِ    59 He hides from the people

مِن سُوٓءِ مَا بُشِّرَ بِهِۦٓ    out of distress at the news he has been brought:

أَيُمْسِكُهُۥ عَلَىٰ هُونٍ    shall he retain it in humiliation,

أَمْ يَدُسُّهُۥ فِى ٱلتُّرَابِ    or bury it in the ground!¹

أَلَا سَآءَ مَا يَحْكُمُونَ ۝    Look! Evil is the judgement that they make.

لِلَّذِينَ لَا يُؤْمِنُونَ بِٱلْأَخِرَةِ    60 For those who do not believe in the Hereafter

مَثَلُ ٱلسَّوْءِ    there is an evil description,

وَلِلَّهِ ٱلْمَثَلُ ٱلْأَعْلَىٰ    and the loftiest description belongs to Allah,

وَهُوَ ٱلْعَزِيزُ ٱلْحَكِيمُ ۝    and He is the All-mighty, the All-wise.

وَلَوْ يُؤَاخِذُ ٱللَّهُ ٱلنَّاسَ    61 Were Allah to take mankind to task

بِظُلْمِهِم    for their wrongdoing,

مَّا تَرَكَ عَلَيْهَا مِن دَآبَّةٍ    He would not leave any living being upon it.²

وَلَـٰكِن يُؤَخِّرُهُمْ إِلَىٰٓ أَجَلٍ مُّسَمًّى    But He respites them until a specified time;

---

¹ This refers to the practice of pre-Islamic Arabs of burying their newborn daughters alive.

² That is, on the surface of the earth.

فَإِذَا جَآءَ أَجَلُهُمْ

so when their time comes

لَا يَسْتَخِرُونَ سَاعَةً

they shall not defer it by a single hour

وَلَا يَسْتَقْدِمُونَ ٦١

nor shall they advance it.

وَيَجْعَلُونَ لِلَّهِ

62 They attribute to Allah

مَا يَكْرَهُونَ

what they dislike [for themselves],

وَتَصِفُ أَلْسِنَتُهُمُ ٱلْكَذِبَ

and their tongues assert the lie

أَنَّ لَهُمُ ٱلْحُسْنَىٰ

that the best reward will be theirs.

لَا جَرَمَ أَنَّ لَهُمُ ٱلنَّارَ

Undoubtedly, the Fire shall be their lot

وَأَنَّهُم مُّفْرَطُونَ ٦٢

and they will be foremost [in entering it].[1]

تَٱللَّهِ

63 By Allah,

لَقَدْ أَرْسَلْنَآ إِلَىٰٓ أُمَمٍ

We have certainly sent [apostles] to nations

مِّن قَبْلِكَ

before *you.*

فَزَيَّنَ لَهُمُ ٱلشَّيْطَٰنُ أَعْمَٰلَهُمْ

But Satan made their deeds seem decorous to them.

فَهُوَ وَلِيُّهُمُ ٱلْيَوْمَ

So he is their master[2] today

وَلَهُمْ عَذَابٌ أَلِيمٌ ٦٣

and there is a painful punishment for them.

وَمَآ أَنزَلْنَا عَلَيْكَ ٱلْكِتَٰبَ

64 We did not send down the Book to *you*

إِلَّا لِتُبَيِّنَ لَهُمُ

except [for the purpose] that *you* may clarify for them

ٱلَّذِى ٱخْتَلَفُوا۟ فِيهِ

what they differ about,

وَهُدًى وَرَحْمَةً

and as a guidance and mercy

لِّقَوْمٍ يُؤْمِنُونَ ٦٤

for a people who have faith.

وَٱللَّهُ أَنزَلَ مِنَ ٱلسَّمَآءِ مَآءً

65 Allah sends down water from the sky

فَأَحْيَا بِهِ ٱلْأَرْضَ بَعْدَ مَوْتِهَآ

with which He revives the earth after its death.

إِنَّ فِى ذَٰلِكَ لَءَايَةً لِّقَوْمٍ يَسْمَعُونَ ٦٥

There is indeed a sign in that for a people who listen.

وَإِنَّ لَكُمْ فِى ٱلْأَنْعَٰمِ لَعِبْرَةً

66 There is indeed a moral for you in the cattle:

نُّسْقِيكُم مِّمَّا فِى بُطُونِهِ

We give you to drink of that which is in their bellies

مِنۢ بَيْنِ فَرْثٍ وَدَمٍ

from between [intestinal] waste and blood,

لَّبَنًا خَالِصًا سَآئِغًا لِّلشَّٰرِبِينَ ٦٦

as pure milk, pleasant to those who drink.

وَمِن ثَمَرَٰتِ ٱلنَّخِيلِ وَٱلْأَعْنَٰبِ

67 And of the fruits of date palms and vines,

---

[1] Or 'they will be left to languish in it.'

[2] Or 'guardian,' or 'friend.'

تَتَّخِذُونَ مِنْهُ سَكَرًا وَرِزْقًا حَسَنًا    from which you draw wine and goodly provision.

إِنَّ فِى ذَٰلِكَ لَآيَةً    There are indeed signs in that

لِقَوْمٍ يَعْقِلُونَ ۝    for a people who apply reason.

وَأَوْحَىٰ رَبُّكَ إِلَى ٱلنَّحْلِ    68 And *your* Lord inspired the bee [saying]:

أَنِ ٱتَّخِذِى مِنَ ٱلْجِبَالِ بُيُوتًا    'Make your home in the mountains,

وَمِنَ ٱلشَّجَرِ    and on the trees

وَمِمَّا يَعْرِشُونَ ۝    and the trellises that they erect.

ثُمَّ كُلِى مِن كُلِّ ٱلثَّمَرَٰتِ    69 Then eat from every [kind of] fruit

فَٱسْلُكِى سُبُلَ رَبِّكِ ذُلُلًا    and follow meekly the ways of your Lord.'

يَخْرُجُ مِنْ بُطُونِهَا    There issues from its belly

شَرَابٌ مُّخْتَلِفٌ أَلْوَٰنُهُ    a juice of diverse hues

فِيهِ شِفَآءٌ لِّلنَّاسِ    in which there is cure for the people.

إِنَّ فِى ذَٰلِكَ لَآيَةً لِّقَوْمٍ يَتَفَكَّرُونَ ۝    There is indeed a sign in that for a people who reflect.

وَٱللَّهُ خَلَقَكُمْ    70 Allah has created you,

ثُمَّ يَتَوَفَّىٰكُمْ    then He takes you away,

وَمِنكُم مَّن يُرَدُّ    and there are some among you who are relegated

إِلَىٰ أَرْذَلِ ٱلْعُمُرِ    to the nethermost age

لِكَىْ لَا يَعْلَمَ    so that he knows nothing

بَعْدَ عِلْمٍ شَيْئًا    after [having possessed] some knowledge.

إِنَّ ٱللَّهَ عَلِيمٌ قَدِيرٌ ۝    Indeed Allah is all-knowing, all-powerful.

وَٱللَّهُ فَضَّلَ بَعْضَكُمْ عَلَىٰ بَعْضٍ    71 Allah has granted some of you an advantage over others

فِى ٱلرِّزْقِ    in [respect of] provision.

فَمَا ٱلَّذِينَ فُضِّلُوا    Those who have been granted an advantage do not

بِرَآدِّى رِزْقِهِمْ    give over their provision

عَلَىٰ مَا مَلَكَتْ أَيْمَٰنُهُمْ    to their slaves

فَهُمْ فِيهِ سَوَآءٌ    so that they become equal in its respect.

أَفَبِنِعْمَةِ ٱللَّهِ يَجْحَدُونَ ۝    What, will they dispute the blessing of Allah?

وَٱللَّهُ جَعَلَ لَكُم مِّنْ أَنفُسِكُمْ أَزْوَٰجًا    72 Allah made for you mates from your own selves

وَجَعَلَ لَكُم مِّنْ أَزْوَٰجِكُم    and appointed for you, from your mates,

بَنِينَ وَحَفَدَةً children and grandchildren,

وَرَزَقَكُم مِّنَ ٱلطَّيِّبَٰتِ and We provided you with all the good things.

أَفَبِٱلْبَٰطِلِ يُؤْمِنُونَ What, will they believe in falsehood

وَبِنِعْمَتِ ٱللَّهِ هُمْ يَكْفُرُونَ ۝ while they deny the blessing of Allah?

وَيَعْبُدُونَ مِن دُونِ ٱللَّهِ 73 They worship besides Allah

مَا لَا يَمْلِكُ لَهُمْ رِزْقًا what has no power to provide them

مِّنَ ٱلسَّمَٰوَٰتِ وَٱلْأَرْضِ شَيْـًٔا with anything from the heavens and the earth,

وَلَا يَسْتَطِيعُونَ ۝ nor are they capable [of doing that].

فَلَا تَضْرِبُوا۟ لِلَّهِ ٱلْأَمْثَالَ 74 So do not draw comparisons for Allah:

إِنَّ ٱللَّهَ يَعْلَمُ وَأَنتُمْ لَا تَعْلَمُونَ ۝ ❋ indeed Allah knows and you do not know.

ضَرَبَ ٱللَّهُ مَثَلًا 75 Allah draws a parable:

عَبْدًا مَّمْلُوكًا لَّا يَقْدِرُ عَلَىٰ شَىْءٍ a chattel who has no power over anything,

وَمَن رَّزَقْنَٰهُ مِنَّا رِزْقًا حَسَنًا and one whom We have provided a goodly provision

فَهُوَ يُنفِقُ مِنْهُ and who spends out of it

سِرًّا وَجَهْرًا secretly and openly.

هَلْ يَسْتَوُۥنَ Are they equal?

ٱلْحَمْدُ لِلَّهِ All praise belongs to Allah.

بَلْ أَكْثَرُهُمْ لَا يَعْلَمُونَ ۝ But most of them do not know.

وَضَرَبَ ٱللَّهُ مَثَلًا 76 Allah draws [another] parable:

رَّجُلَيْنِ أَحَدُهُمَآ أَبْكَمُ Two men, one of whom is dumb,

لَا يَقْدِرُ عَلَىٰ شَىْءٍ having no power over anything

وَهُوَ كَلٌّ عَلَىٰ مَوْلَىٰهُ and who is a liability to his master:

أَيْنَمَا يُوَجِّههُّ wherever he directs him

لَا يَأْتِ بِخَيْرٍ he does not bring any good.

هَلْ يَسْتَوِى هُوَ وَمَن يَأْمُرُ بِٱلْعَدْلِ Is he equal to someone who enjoins justice

وَهُوَ عَلَىٰ صِرَٰطٍ مُّسْتَقِيمٍ ۝ and is [steady] on a straight path?

وَلِلَّهِ غَيْبُ ٱلسَّمَٰوَٰتِ 77 To Allah belongs the Unseen of the heavens

وَٱلْأَرْضِ and the earth.

وَمَآ أَمْرُ ٱلسَّاعَةِ إِلَّا The matter of the Hour is just

كَلَمۡحِ ٱلۡبَصَرِ    like the twinkling of an eye,

أَوۡ هُوَ أَقۡرَبُ    or [even] swifter.

إِنَّ ٱللَّهَ عَلَىٰ كُلِّ شَىۡءٍ قَدِيرٌ ۝    Indeed Allah has power over all things.

وَٱللَّهُ أَخۡرَجَكُم    78 Allah has brought you forth

مِّنۢ بُطُونِ أُمَّهَٰتِكُمۡ    from the bellies of your mothers

لَا تَعۡلَمُونَ شَيۡـًٔا    while you did not know anything.

وَجَعَلَ لَكُمُ ٱلسَّمۡعَ وَٱلۡأَبۡصَٰرَ وَٱلۡأَفۡـِٔدَةَ    He made for you hearing, eyesight, and hearts

لَعَلَّكُمۡ تَشۡكُرُونَ ۝    so that you may give thanks.

أَلَمۡ يَرَوۡاْ إِلَى ٱلطَّيۡرِ    79 Have they not regarded the birds

مُسَخَّرَٰتٍ فِى جَوِّ ٱلسَّمَآءِ    disposed in the air of the sky:

مَا يُمۡسِكُهُنَّ إِلَّا ٱللَّهُ    no one sustains them except Allah.

إِنَّ فِى ذَٰلِكَ لَـَٔايَٰتٍ    There are indeed signs in that

لِّقَوۡمٍ يُؤۡمِنُونَ ۝    for a people who have faith.

وَٱللَّهُ جَعَلَ لَكُم    80 It is Allah who has made for you

مِّنۢ بُيُوتِكُمۡ سَكَنًا    your homes as a place of rest

وَجَعَلَ لَكُم    and He made for you

مِّن جُلُودِ ٱلۡأَنۡعَٰمِ بُيُوتًا    homes out of the skins of the cattle

تَسۡتَخِفُّونَهَا    which you find portable

يَوۡمَ ظَعۡنِكُمۡ    on the day of your shifting

وَيَوۡمَ إِقَامَتِكُمۡ    and on the day of your halt,

وَمِنۡ أَصۡوَافِهَا    and out of their wool,

وَأَوۡبَارِهَا وَأَشۡعَارِهَآ    their fur and hair

أَثَٰثًا وَمَتَٰعًا إِلَىٰ حِينٍ ۝    furniture and wares [enduring] for a while.

وَٱللَّهُ جَعَلَ لَكُم    81 It is Allah who has made for you

مِّمَّا خَلَقَ ظِلَٰلًا    shade from what He created,

وَجَعَلَ لَكُم مِّنَ ٱلۡجِبَالِ أَكۡنَٰنًا    and made for you retreats in the mountains,

وَجَعَلَ لَكُمۡ سَرَٰبِيلَ    and made for you garments

تَقِيكُمُ ٱلۡحَرَّ    that protect you from heat

وَسَرَٰبِيلَ تَقِيكُم    and garments that protect you

بِأْسِكُمْ from your [mutual] violence.

كَذَٰلِكَ يُتِمُّ نِعْمَتَهُ عَلَيْكُمْ That is how He completes His blessing upon you

لَعَلَّكُمْ تُسْلِمُونَ so that you may submit [to Him].

فَإِن تَوَلَّوْا 82 But if they turn their backs [on you],

فَإِنَّمَا عَلَيْكَ ٱلْبَلَٰغُ ٱلْمُبِينُ *your* duty is only to communicate in clear terms.

يَعْرِفُونَ نِعْمَتَ ٱللَّهِ 83 They recognize the blessing of Allah

ثُمَّ يُنكِرُونَهَا and then deny it,

وَأَكْثَرُهُمُ ٱلْكَٰفِرُونَ and most of them are faithless.

وَيَوْمَ نَبْعَثُ مِن كُلِّ أُمَّةٍ شَهِيدًا 84 The day We shall raise a witness from every nation,

ثُمَّ لَا يُؤْذَنُ لِلَّذِينَ كَفَرُوا then the faithless will not be permitted [to speak],[1]

وَلَا هُمْ يُسْتَعْتَبُونَ nor will they be asked to propitiate [Allah].

وَإِذَا رَأَى ٱلَّذِينَ ظَلَمُوا ٱلْعَذَابَ 85 And when the wrongdoers sight the punishment,

فَلَا يُخَفَّفُ عَنْهُمْ it shall not be lightened for them,

وَلَا هُمْ يُنظَرُونَ nor will they be granted any respite.

وَإِذَا رَأَى ٱلَّذِينَ أَشْرَكُوا شُرَكَآءَهُمْ 86 When the polytheists sight their partners,

قَالُوا رَبَّنَا they will say, 'Our Lord!

هَٰٓؤُلَآءِ شُرَكَآؤُنَا ٱلَّذِينَ كُنَّا نَدْعُوا These are our partners whom we used to invoke

مِن دُونِكَ besides You.'

فَأَلْقَوْا إِلَيْهِمُ ٱلْقَوْلَ But they will retort to them,

إِنَّكُمْ لَكَٰذِبُونَ 'You are indeed liars!'

وَأَلْقَوْا إِلَى ٱللَّهِ يَوْمَئِذٍ ٱلسَّلَمَ 87 They will submit to Allah on that day,

وَضَلَّ عَنْهُم مَّا كَانُوا يَفْتَرُونَ and what they used to fabricate will forsake them.

ٱلَّذِينَ كَفَرُوا 88 Those who are faithless

وَصَدُّوا عَن سَبِيلِ ٱللَّهِ and bar from the way of Allah

زِدْنَٰهُمْ عَذَابًا فَوْقَ ٱلْعَذَابِ —We shall add punishment to their punishment

بِمَا كَانُوا يُفْسِدُونَ because of the corruption they used to cause.

وَيَوْمَ نَبْعَثُ فِى كُلِّ أُمَّةٍ 89 The day We raise in every nation

شَهِيدًا عَلَيْهِم مِّنْ أَنفُسِهِمْ a witness against them from among themselves,

وَجِئْنَا بِكَ شَهِيدًا عَلَىٰ هَٰٓؤُلَآءِ We shall bring *you* as a witness against these.

---

[1] Cf. 11:105; 23:108; 36:65; 78:38.

وَنَزَّلْنَا عَلَيْكَ ٱلْكِتَـٰبَ

We have sent down the Book to *you*

تِبْيَـٰنًا لِّكُلِّ شَىْءٍ

as a clarification of all things

وَهُدًى وَرَحْمَةً

and as a guidance and mercy

وَبُشْرَىٰ لِلْمُسْلِمِينَ ۝

and good news for the *muslim*s.

إِنَّ ٱللَّهَ يَأْمُرُ بِٱلْعَدْلِ وَٱلْإِحْسَـٰنِ

90 Indeed Allah enjoins justice and kindness

وَإِيتَآئِ ذِى ٱلْقُرْبَىٰ

and generosity towards relatives,

وَيَنْهَىٰ عَنِ ٱلْفَحْشَآءِ وَٱلْمُنكَرِ

and He forbids indecency, wrong,

وَٱلْبَغْىِ

and aggression.

يَعِظُكُمْ

He advises you,

لَعَلَّكُمْ تَذَكَّرُونَ ۝

so that you may take admonition.

وَأَوْفُوا۟ بِعَهْدِ ٱللَّهِ إِذَا عَـٰهَدتُّمْ

91 Fulfill Allah's covenant when you pledge,

وَلَا تَنقُضُوا۟ ٱلْأَيْمَـٰنَ

and do not break [your] oaths

بَعْدَ تَوْكِيدِهَا

after pledging them solemnly

وَقَدْ جَعَلْتُمُ ٱللَّهَ عَلَيْكُمْ كَفِيلًا

and having made Allah a witness over yourselves.

إِنَّ ٱللَّهَ يَعْلَمُ مَا تَفْعَلُونَ ۝

Indeed Allah knows what you do.

وَلَا تَكُونُوا۟ كَٱلَّتِى نَقَضَتْ غَزْلَهَا

92 Do not be like her who would undo her yarn,

مِنۢ بَعْدِ قُوَّةٍ أَنكَـٰثًا

breaking it up after [spinning it to] strength,

تَتَّخِذُونَ أَيْمَـٰنَكُمْ دَخَلًۢا

by making your oaths a means of [mutual] deceit

بَيْنَكُمْ

among yourselves,

أَن تَكُونَ أُمَّةٌ هِىَ أَرْبَىٰ

so that one community may become more affluent

مِنْ أُمَّةٍ

than another community.[1]

إِنَّمَا يَبْلُوكُمُ ٱللَّهُ بِهِۦ

Allah only tests you thereby,

وَلَيُبَيِّنَنَّ لَكُمْ

and He will surely clarify for you

يَوْمَ ٱلْقِيَـٰمَةِ

on the Day of Resurrection

مَا كُنتُمْ فِيهِ تَخْتَلِفُونَ ۝

what you used to differ about.

وَلَوْ شَآءَ ٱللَّهُ

93 Had Allah wished,

لَجَعَلَكُمْ أُمَّةً وَٰحِدَةً

He would have made you one community,

وَلَـٰكِن يُضِلُّ مَن يَشَآءُ

but He leads astray whomever He wishes

---

[1] Or 'for one community may be more numerous (or more affluent) than another community.'

وَيَهْدِى مَن يَشَآءُ ۚ and guides whomever He wishes,

وَلَتُسْـَٔلُنَّ and you will surely be questioned

عَمَّا كُنتُمْ تَعْمَلُونَ ۝ concerning what you used to do.

وَلَا تَتَّخِذُوٓا۟ أَيْمَـٰنَكُمْ دَخَلًۢا 94 Do not make your oaths a means of [mutual] deceit

بَيْنَكُمْ among yourselves

فَتَزِلَّ قَدَمٌۢ بَعْدَ ثُبُوتِهَا lest feet should stumble after being steady

وَتَذُوقُوا۟ ٱلسُّوٓءَ بِمَا صَدَدتُّمْ and [lest] you suffer ill for barring

عَن سَبِيلِ ٱللَّهِ ۖ from the way of Allah

وَلَكُمْ عَذَابٌ عَظِيمٌ ۝ and there be a great punishment for you.

وَلَا تَشْتَرُوا۟ بِعَهْدِ ٱللَّهِ ثَمَنًا قَلِيلًا ۚ 95 Do not sell Allah's covenant for a paltry gain.

إِنَّمَا عِندَ ٱللَّهِ هُوَ خَيْرٌ لَّكُمْ Indeed what is with Allah is better for you,

إِن كُنتُمْ تَعْلَمُونَ ۝ should you know.

مَا عِندَكُمْ يَنفَدُ ۖ 96 That which is with you will be spent

وَمَا عِندَ ٱللَّهِ بَاقٍ ۗ but what is with Allah shall last,

وَلَنَجْزِيَنَّ ٱلَّذِينَ صَبَرُوٓا۟ أَجْرَهُم and We will surely pay the patient their reward

بِأَحْسَنِ مَا كَانُوا۟ يَعْمَلُونَ ۝ by the best of what they used to do.

مَنْ عَمِلَ صَـٰلِحًا 97 Whoever acts righteously,

مِّن ذَكَرٍ أَوْ أُنثَىٰ وَهُوَ مُؤْمِنٌ [whether] male or female, should he be faithful,

فَلَنُحْيِيَنَّهُۥ حَيَوٰةً طَيِّبَةً ۖ —We shall revive him with a good life

وَلَنَجْزِيَنَّهُمْ أَجْرَهُم and pay them their reward

بِأَحْسَنِ مَا كَانُوا۟ يَعْمَلُونَ ۝ by the best of what they used to do.

فَإِذَا قَرَأْتَ ٱلْقُرْءَانَ 98 When *you* recite the Qur'ān,

فَٱسْتَعِذْ بِٱللَّهِ *seek* the protection of Allah

مِنَ ٱلشَّيْطَـٰنِ ٱلرَّجِيمِ ۝ against the outcast Satan.

إِنَّهُۥ لَيْسَ لَهُۥ سُلْطَـٰنٌ 99 Indeed he does not have any authority

عَلَى ٱلَّذِينَ ءَامَنُوا۟ over those who have faith

وَعَلَىٰ رَبِّهِمْ يَتَوَكَّلُونَ ۝ and put their trust in their Lord.

إِنَّمَا سُلْطَـٰنُهُۥ عَلَى ٱلَّذِينَ يَتَوَلَّوْنَهُۥ 100 His authority is only over those who befriend him

وَٱلَّذِينَ هُم بِهِۦ مُشْرِكُونَ ۝ and those who make him a partner [of Allah].

وَإِذَا بَدَّلْنَآ ءَايَةً مَّكَانَ ءَايَةٍ 101 When We change a sign with another in its place

وَٱللَّهُ أَعْلَمُ بِمَا يُنَزِّلُ       —and Allah knows best what He sends down—

قَالُوٓاْ إِنَّمَآ أَنتَ مُفْتَرٍ       they say, '*You* are just a fabricator.'

بَلْ أَكْثَرُهُمْ لَا يَعْلَمُونَ ۝    Rather most of them do not know.

قُلْ نَزَّلَهُۥ رُوحُ ٱلْقُدُسِ 102 *Say,* the Holy Spirit has brought it down

مِن رَّبِّكَ بِٱلْحَقِّ         duly from *your* Lord

لِيُثَبِّتَ ٱلَّذِينَ ءَامَنُواْ      to fortify those who have faith

وَهُدًى وَبُشْرَىٰ لِلْمُسْلِمِينَ ۝   and as a guidance and good news for the *muslims*.

وَلَقَدْ نَعْلَمُ أَنَّهُمْ يَقُولُونَ 103 We certainly know that they say,

إِنَّمَا يُعَلِّمُهُۥ بَشَرٌ        'It is only a human that instructs him.'

لِّسَانُ ٱلَّذِى يُلْحِدُونَ إِلَيْهِ   The language of him to whom they refer

أَعْجَمِيٌّ               is non-Arabic,

وَهَٰذَا لِسَانٌ عَرَبِيٌّ مُّبِينٌ ۝    while this is a clear Arabic language.

إِنَّ ٱلَّذِينَ لَا يُؤْمِنُونَ بِـَٔايَٰتِ ٱللَّهِ 104 Indeed those who do not believe in the signs of Allah

لَا يَهْدِيهِمُ ٱللَّهُ        —Allah shall not guide them

وَلَهُمْ عَذَابٌ أَلِيمٌ ۝     and there is a painful punishment for them.

إِنَّمَا يَفْتَرِى ٱلْكَذِبَ 105 Only those fabricate lies

ٱلَّذِينَ لَا يُؤْمِنُونَ بِـَٔايَٰتِ ٱللَّهِ   who do not believe in the signs of Allah,

وَأُوْلَٰٓئِكَ هُمُ ٱلْكَٰذِبُونَ ۝   and it is they who are the liars.

مَن كَفَرَ بِٱللَّهِ 106 Whoever renounces faith in Allah

مِنۢ بَعْدِ إِيمَٰنِهِۦ       after [affirming] his faith

إِلَّا مَنْ أُكْرِهَ         —barring someone who is compelled

وَقَلْبُهُۥ مُطْمَئِنٌّۢ بِٱلْإِيمَٰنِ    while his heart is at rest in faith—

وَلَٰكِن مَّن شَرَحَ بِٱلْكُفْرِ صَدْرًا   but those who open up their breasts to unfaith,

فَعَلَيْهِمْ غَضَبٌ مِّنَ ٱللَّهِ    upon such shall be Allah's wrath,

وَلَهُمْ عَذَابٌ عَظِيمٌ ۝     and there is a great punishment for them.

ذَٰلِكَ بِأَنَّهُمُ ٱسْتَحَبُّواْ ٱلْحَيَوٰةَ ٱلدُّنْيَا 107 That, because they preferred the life of the world

عَلَى ٱلْأَخِرَةِ         to the Hereafter

وَأَنَّ ٱللَّهَ لَا يَهْدِى ٱلْقَوْمَ ٱلْكَٰفِرِينَ ۝   and that Allah does not guide the faithless lot.

أُوْلَٰٓئِكَ ٱلَّذِينَ طَبَعَ ٱللَّهُ عَلَىٰ قُلُوبِهِمْ 108 They are the ones on whose hearts Allah has set a seal,

وَسَمْعِهِمْ وَأَبْصَرِهِمْ ۖ and on their hearing and their sight [as well],

وَأُوْلَـٰٓئِكَ هُمُ ٱلْغَـٰفِلُونَ ۝ and it is they who are the heedless.

لَا جَرَمَ أَنَّهُمْ 109 Undoubtedly, they are the ones

فِى ٱلْـَٔاخِرَةِ هُمُ ٱلْخَـٰسِرُونَ ۝ who will be the losers in the Hereafter.

ثُمَّ إِنَّ رَبَّكَ 110 Then indeed your Lord,

لِلَّذِينَ هَاجَرُوا۟ مِنۢ بَعْدِ مَا فُتِنُوا۟ to those who migrated, after they were persecuted,

ثُمَّ جَـٰهَدُوا۟ وَصَبَرُوٓا۟ and waged *jihād* and were patient

إِنَّ رَبَّكَ مِنۢ بَعْدِهَا —indeed, after that, your Lord

لَغَفُورٌ رَّحِيمٌ ۝ will surely be all-forgiving, all-merciful.

يَوْمَ تَأْتِى كُلُّ نَفْسٍ 111 The day when every soul will come

تُجَـٰدِلُ عَن نَّفْسِهَا pleading for itself

وَتُوَفَّىٰ كُلُّ نَفْسٍ and every soul will be recompensed fully

مَّا عَمِلَتْ for what it has done,

وَهُمْ لَا يُظْلَمُونَ ۝ and they will not be wronged.

وَضَرَبَ ٱللَّهُ مَثَلًا 112 Allah draws a parable:

قَرْيَةً كَانَتْ ءَامِنَةً مُّطْمَئِنَّةً A town secure and peaceful.

يَأْتِيهَا رِزْقُهَا رَغَدًا مِّن كُلِّ مَكَانٍ Its provision came abundantly from every place.

فَكَفَرَتْ بِأَنْعُمِ ٱللَّهِ But it was ungrateful toward Allah's blessings.

فَأَذَٰقَهَا ٱللَّهُ لِبَاسَ ٱلْجُوعِ وَٱلْخَوْفِ So Allah made it taste hunger and fear

بِمَا كَانُوا۟ يَصْنَعُونَ ۝ because of what they used to do.

وَلَقَدْ جَآءَهُمْ رَسُولٌ 113 There had certainly come to them an apostle

مِّنْهُمْ from among themselves,

فَكَذَّبُوهُ but they impugned him,

فَأَخَذَهُمُ ٱلْعَذَابُ so the punishment seized them

وَهُمْ ظَـٰلِمُونَ ۝ while they were wrongdoers.

فَكُلُوا۟ مِمَّا رَزَقَكُمُ ٱللَّهُ 114 So eat out of what Allah has provided you

حَلَـٰلًا طَيِّبًا as lawful and good,

وَٱشْكُرُوا۟ نِعْمَتَ ٱللَّهِ and give thanks for Allah's blessing,

إِن كُنتُمْ إِيَّاهُ تَعْبُدُونَ ۝ if it is Him that you worship.

115 He has forbidden you only carrion,

blood, the flesh of the swine,

and that which has been offered to other than Allah.

But should someone be compelled,

without being rebellious or aggressive,

indeed Allah is all-forgiving, all-merciful.[1]

116 Do not say,

asserting falsely with your tongues,

'This is lawful, and this is unlawful,'

to fabricate lies against Allah.

Indeed those who fabricate lies against Allah

will not be felicitous.

117 A trifling enjoyment,

and there will be a painful punishment for them.

118 We forbade to the Jews

what We have recounted to *you* earlier,

and We did not wrong them,

but they used to wrong themselves.

119 Then indeed *your* Lord,

to those who commit evil out of ignorance

and then repent after that, and reform

—indeed, after that, your Lord

will surely be all-forgiving, all-merciful.

120 Indeed Abraham was a nation

obedient to Allah,

a *ḥanīf*,

and he was not one of the polytheists.

121 Grateful [as he was] for His blessings,

---

[1] Cf. 2:173; 5:3; 6:145.

أَجْتَبَـٰهُ

He chose him

وَهَدَنٰهُ إِلَىٰ صِرَٰطٍ مُّسْتَقِيمٍ

and guided him to a straight path.

وَءَاتَيْنَـٰهُ فِى ٱلدُّنْيَا حَسَنَةً

122 We gave him good in this world,

وَإِنَّهُۥ فِى ٱلْءَاخِرَةِ

and in the Hereafter he will indeed be

لَمِنَ ٱلصَّـٰلِحِينَ

among the Righteous.

ثُمَّ أَوْحَيْنَآ إِلَيْكَ

123 Then We revealed to *you* [saying],

أَنِ ٱتَّبِعْ مِلَّةَ إِبْرَٰهِيمَ حَنِيفًا

'Follow the creed of Abraham, a *ḥanīf*,

وَمَا كَانَ مِنَ ٱلْمُشْرِكِينَ

and he was not one of the polytheists.'

إِنَّمَا جُعِلَ ٱلسَّبْتُ

124 The Sabbath was only prescribed

عَلَى ٱلَّذِينَ ٱخْتَلَفُوا۟ فِيهِ

for those who differed about it.

وَإِنَّ رَبَّكَ لَيَحْكُمُ بَيْنَهُمْ

*Your* Lord will indeed judge between them

يَوْمَ ٱلْقِيَٰمَةِ

on the Day of Resurrection

فِيمَا كَانُوا۟ فِيهِ يَخْتَلِفُونَ

concerning that about which they used to differ.

ٱدْعُ إِلَىٰ سَبِيلِ رَبِّكَ بِٱلْحِكْمَةِ

125 *Invite* to the way of *your* Lord with wisdom

وَٱلْمَوْعِظَةِ ٱلْحَسَنَةِ

and good advice

وَجَـٰدِلْهُم بِٱلَّتِى هِىَ أَحْسَنُ

and *dispute* with them in a manner that is best.

إِنَّ رَبَّكَ هُوَ أَعْلَمُ

Indeed *your* Lord knows best

بِمَن ضَلَّ عَن سَبِيلِهِۦ

those who stray from His way,

وَهُوَ أَعْلَمُ بِٱلْمُهْتَدِينَ

and He knows best those who are guided.

وَإِنْ عَاقَبْتُمْ

126 And if you retaliate,

فَعَاقِبُوا۟

retaliate with the like of

بِمِثْلِ مَا عُوقِبْتُم بِهِۦ

what you have been made to suffer,

وَلَئِن صَبَرْتُمْ

but if you are patient

لَهُوَ خَيْرٌ لِّلصَّـٰبِرِينَ

that is surely better for the patient.

وَٱصْبِرْ

127 So *be patient,*

وَمَا صَبْرُكَ إِلَّا بِٱللَّهِ

and *you* cannot be patient except with Allah['s help].

وَلَا تَحْزَنْ عَلَيْهِمْ

And *do not grieve* for them,

وَلَا تَكُ فِى ضَيْقٍ مِّمَّا يَمْكُرُونَ

nor be upset by their guile.

إِنَّ ٱللَّهَ مَعَ ٱلَّذِينَ ٱتَّقَوا۟

128 Indeed Allah is with those who are Godwary

وَٱلَّذِينَ هُم مُّحْسِنُونَ

and those who are virtuous.

[PART 15]

# سُورَةُ الْإِسْرَاءِ

## 17. SŪRAT AL-ISRĀ'[1]

بِسْمِ اللَّهِ
الرَّحْمَٰنِ الرَّحِيمِ

In the Name of Allah,
the All-beneficent, the All-merciful.

| | |
|---|---|
| سُبْحَٰنَ ٱلَّذِى | 1 Immaculate is He who |
| أَسْرَىٰ بِعَبْدِهِۦ لَيْلًا | carried His servant on a journey by night |
| مِّنَ ٱلْمَسْجِدِ ٱلْحَرَامِ | from the Sacred Mosque |
| إِلَى ٱلْمَسْجِدِ ٱلْأَقْصَا | to the Farthest Mosque |
| ٱلَّذِى بَٰرَكْنَا حَوْلَهُۥ | whose environs We have blessed, |
| لِنُرِيَهُۥ مِنْ ءَايَٰتِنَآ | that We might show him some of Our signs. |
| إِنَّهُۥ هُوَ ٱلسَّمِيعُ ٱلْبَصِيرُ ۝ | Indeed He is the All-hearing, the All-seeing. |

| | |
|---|---|
| وَءَاتَيْنَا مُوسَى ٱلْكِتَٰبَ | 2 We gave Moses the Book, |
| وَجَعَلْنَٰهُ هُدًى لِّبَنِىٓ إِسْرَٰٓءِيلَ | and made it a guide for the Children of Israel |
| أَلَّا تَتَّخِذُوا۟ مِن دُونِى وَكِيلًا ۝ | —[saying,] 'Do not take any trustee besides Me'— |
| ذُرِّيَّةَ مَنْ حَمَلْنَا | 3 descendants of those whom We carried |
| مَعَ نُوحٍ | [in the ark] with Noah. |
| إِنَّهُۥ كَانَ عَبْدًا شَكُورًا ۝ | Indeed he was a grateful servant. |

| | |
|---|---|
| وَقَضَيْنَآ إِلَىٰ بَنِىٓ إِسْرَٰٓءِيلَ | 4 We revealed to the Children of Israel |
| فِى ٱلْكِتَٰبِ | in the Book: |
| لَتُفْسِدُنَّ فِى ٱلْأَرْضِ مَرَّتَيْنِ | 'Twice you will cause corruption on the earth, |
| وَلَتَعْلُنَّ عُلُوًّا كَبِيرًا ۝ | and you will perpetrate great tyranny.' |
| فَإِذَا جَآءَ وَعْدُ أُولَىٰهُمَا | 5 So when the first occasion of the two [prophecies] came, |
| بَعَثْنَا عَلَيْكُمْ | We aroused against you |
| عِبَادًا لَّنَآ أُو۟لِى بَأْسٍ شَدِيدٍ | Our servants possessing great might, |

---

[1] The *sūrah* takes its name from the subject of verse 1, *isrā'* (lit. 'taking s.o. on a night journey'), relating to the celestial journey (*mi'rāj*) of the Prophet (ṣ).

فَجَاسُواْ خِلَلَ ٱلدِّيَارِ    and they ransacked [your] habitations,

وَكَانَ وَعْدًا مَّفْعُولًا ۝    and the promise was bound to be fulfilled.

ثُمَّ رَدَدْنَا لَكُمُ ٱلْكَرَّةَ عَلَيْهِمْ    6 Then We gave you back the turn [to prevail] over them,

وَأَمْدَدْنَكُم بِأَمْوَلٍ وَبَنِينَ    and We aided you with children and wealth,

وَجَعَلْنَكُمْ أَكْثَرَ نَفِيرًا ۝    and made you greater in number,

إِنْ أَحْسَنتُمْ    7    [saying,] 'If you do good,

أَحْسَنتُمْ لِأَنفُسِكُمْ    you will do good to your [own] souls,

وَإِنْ أَسَأْتُمْ    and if you do evil,

فَلَهَا    it will be [evil] for them.'

فَإِذَا جَاءَ وَعْدُ ٱلْآخِرَةِ    So when the occasion for the other [prophecy] comes,

لِيَسُوءُواْ وُجُوهَكُمْ    they will make your faces[1] wretched,

وَلِيَدْخُلُواْ ٱلْمَسْجِدَ    and enter the Temple

كَمَا دَخَلُوهُ أَوَّلَ مَرَّةٍ    just as they entered it the first time,

وَلِيُتَبِّرُواْ مَا عَلَوْاْ تَتْبِيرًا ۝    and utterly destroy whatever they come upon.

عَسَىٰ رَبُّكُمْ أَن يَرْحَمَكُمْ    8 Maybe your Lord will have mercy on you,

وَإِنْ عُدتُّمْ عُدْنَا    but if you revert, We [too] will revert,

وَجَعَلْنَا جَهَنَّمَ لِلْكَفِرِينَ حَصِيرًا ۝    and We have made hell a prison for the faithless.'

إِنَّ هَذَا ٱلْقُرْءَانَ يَهْدِى    9 Indeed this Qur'ān guides

لِلَّتِى هِىَ أَقْوَمُ    to what is most upright,

وَيُبَشِّرُ ٱلْمُؤْمِنِينَ    and gives the good news to the faithful

ٱلَّذِينَ يَعْمَلُونَ ٱلصَّلِحَتِ    who do righteous deeds

أَنَّ لَهُمْ أَجْرًا كَبِيرًا ۝    that there is a great reward for them.

وَأَنَّ ٱلَّذِينَ لَا يُؤْمِنُونَ بِٱلْآخِرَةِ    10 As for those who do not believe in the Hereafter,

أَعْتَدْنَا لَهُمْ عَذَابًا أَلِيمًا ۝    We have prepared a painful punishment for them.

وَيَدْعُ ٱلْإِنسَنُ بِٱلشَّرِّ    11 Man prays for ill

دُعَاءَهُ بِٱلْخَيْرِ    as [avidly as] he prays for good,

وَكَانَ ٱلْإِنسَنُ عَجُولًا ۝    and man is overhasty.

---

[1] Or 'notables.'

وَجَعَلْنَا ٱلَّيْلَ وَٱلنَّهَارَ ءَايَتَيْنِ 12 We made the night and the day two signs.

فَمَحَوْنَآ ءَايَةَ ٱلَّيْلِ       Then We effaced the sign of the night,

وَجَعَلْنَآ ءَايَةَ ٱلنَّهَارِ مُبْصِرَةً      and made the sign of the day lightsome

لِتَبْتَغُواْ فَضْلًا مِّن رَّبِّكُمْ      that you may seek grace from your Lord

وَلِتَعْلَمُواْ عَدَدَ ٱلسِّنِينَ      and that you may know the number of years

وَٱلْحِسَابَ            and the calculation [of time],

وَكُلَّ شَىْءٍ فَصَّلْنَهُ تَفْصِيلًا ۝     and We have elaborated everything in detail.[1]

وَكُلَّ إِنسَنٍ أَلْزَمْنَهُ طَـٰٓئِرَهُۥ 13 We have attached every person's omen

فِى عُنُقِهِۦ         to his neck,

وَنُخْرِجُ لَهُۥ       and We shall bring it out for him

يَوْمَ ٱلْقِيَمَةِ       on the Day of Resurrection

كِتَبًا يَلْقَىٰهُ مَنشُورًا ۝     as a wide open book that he will encounter.

ٱقْرَأْ كِتَبَكَ 14 'Read your book!

كَفَىٰ بِنَفْسِكَ ٱلْيَوْمَ عَلَيْكَ حَسِيبًا ۝   Today your soul suffices as your own reckoner.'[2]

مَّنِ ٱهْتَدَىٰ 15 Whoever is guided

فَإِنَّمَا يَهْتَدِى لِنَفْسِهِۦ     is guided only to [the good of] his own soul,

وَمَن ضَلَّ       and whoever goes astray,

فَإِنَّمَا يَضِلُّ عَلَيْهَا     goes astray only to its detriment.

وَلَا تَزِرُ وَازِرَةٌ وِزْرَ أُخْرَىٰ    No bearer shall bear another's burden.

وَمَا كُنَّا مُعَذِّبِينَ      We do not punish [any community]

حَتَّىٰ نَبْعَثَ رَسُولًا ۝     until We have sent [it] an apostle.

وَإِذَآ أَرَدْنَآ أَن نُّهْلِكَ قَرْيَةً 16 And when We desire to destroy a town

أَمَرْنَا مُتْرَفِيهَا      We command its affluent ones [to obey Allah].

فَفَسَقُواْ فِيهَا      But they commit transgression in it,

فَحَقَّ عَلَيْهَا ٱلْقَوْلُ     and so the word becomes due against it,

فَدَمَّرْنَهَا تَدْمِيرًا ۝     and We destroy it utterly.

وَكَمْ أَهْلَكْنَا مِنَ ٱلْقُرُونِ 17 How many generations We have destroyed

مِنۢ بَعْدِ نُوحٍ      since Noah!

---

[1] Or 'articulated everything distinctly.'

[2] Or 'today you suffice as your own reckoner.'

وَكَفَىٰ بِرَبِّكَ    *Your* Lord suffices

بِذُنُوبِ عِبَادِهِۦ خَبِيرًۢا بَصِيرًا ۝    as one all-aware, all-seeing about His servants' sins.

مَّن كَانَ يُرِيدُ ٱلْعَاجِلَةَ   18 Whoever desires this transitory life,

عَجَّلْنَا لَهُۥ فِيهَا    We expedite for him therein

مَا نَشَآءُ    whatever We wish,

لِمَن نُّرِيدُ    for whomever We desire.

ثُمَّ جَعَلْنَا لَهُۥ جَهَنَّمَ    Then We appoint hell for him,

يَصْلَىٰهَا مَذْمُومًا مَّدْحُورًا ۝    to enter it, blameful and spurned.

وَمَنْ أَرَادَ ٱلْءَاخِرَةَ   19 Whoever desires the Hereafter

وَسَعَىٰ لَهَا سَعْيَهَا    and strives for it with an endeavour worthy of it,

وَهُوَ مُؤْمِنٌ    should he be faithful

فَأُوْلَـٰٓئِكَ كَانَ سَعْيُهُم مَّشْكُورًا ۝    —the endeavour of such will be well-appreciated.

كُلًّا نُّمِدُّ هَـٰٓؤُلَآءِ وَهَـٰٓؤُلَآءِ   20 To these and to those—to all We extend

مِنْ عَطَآءِ رَبِّكَ    the bounty of *your* Lord,

وَمَا كَانَ عَطَآءُ رَبِّكَ مَحْظُورًا ۝    and the bounty of *your* Lord is not confined.

ٱنظُرْ   21 *Observe*

كَيْفَ فَضَّلْنَا بَعْضَهُمْ    how We have given some of them an advantage

عَلَىٰ بَعْضٍ    over some others;

وَلَلْءَاخِرَةُ أَكْبَرُ دَرَجَـٰتٍ    yet the Hereafter is surely greater in respect of ranks

وَأَكْبَرُ تَفْضِيلًا ۝    and greater in respect of relative merit.[1]

لَّا تَجْعَلْ مَعَ ٱللَّهِ إِلَـٰهًا ءَاخَرَ   22 Do not set up another god besides Allah,

فَتَقْعُدَ مَذْمُومًا مَّخْذُولًا ۝ ❋    or you will sit blameworthy, forsaken.

وَقَضَىٰ رَبُّكَ   23 *Your* Lord has decreed

أَلَّا تَعْبُدُوٓا۟ إِلَّآ إِيَّاهُ    that you shall not worship anyone except Him,

وَبِٱلْوَٰلِدَيْنِ إِحْسَـٰنًا    and [He has enjoined] kindness to parents.

إِمَّا يَبْلُغَنَّ عِندَكَ ٱلْكِبَرَ    Should they reach old age at your side

أَحَدُهُمَآ أَوْ كِلَاهُمَا    —one of them or both—

---

[1] Or 'greater in respect of preferment.'

فَلَا تَقُل لَّهُمَآ أُفٍّ     do not say to them, 'Fie!'[1]

وَلَا تَنْهَرْهُمَا     And do not chide them,

وَقُل لَّهُمَا قَوْلًا كَرِيمًا ۞     but speak to them noble words.

24 وَٱخْفِضْ لَهُمَا جَنَاحَ ٱلذُّلِّ     24 Lower the wing of humility to them,

مِنَ ٱلرَّحْمَةِ     out of mercy,

وَقُل رَّبِّ ٱرْحَمْهُمَا     and say, 'My Lord! Have mercy on them,

كَمَا رَبَّيَانِى صَغِيرًا ۞     just as they reared me when I was [a] small ]child]!'

رَّبُّكُمْ أَعْلَمُ بِمَا فِى نُفُوسِكُمْ     25 Your Lord knows best what is in your hearts.

إِن تَكُونُوا۟ صَٰلِحِينَ     Should you be righteous,

فَإِنَّهُۥ كَانَ لِلْأَوَّٰبِينَ غَفُورًا ۞     He is indeed most forgiving toward penitents.

وَءَاتِ ذَا ٱلْقُرْبَىٰ حَقَّهُۥ     26 *Give* the relatives their [due] right,

وَٱلْمِسْكِينَ وَٱبْنَ ٱلسَّبِيلِ     and the needy and the traveller [as well],

وَلَا تُبَذِّرْ تَبْذِيرًا ۞     but do not squander wastefully.

إِنَّ ٱلْمُبَذِّرِينَ كَانُوٓا۟ إِخْوَٰنَ ٱلشَّيَٰطِينِ     27 Indeed the wasteful are brothers of satans,

وَكَانَ ٱلشَّيْطَٰنُ لِرَبِّهِۦ كَفُورًا ۞     and Satan is ungrateful to his Lord.

وَإِمَّا تُعْرِضَنَّ عَنْهُمُ     28 And if you have to overlook them [for now],

ٱبْتِغَآءَ رَحْمَةٍ مِّن رَّبِّكَ     seeking the mercy of your Lord

تَرْجُوهَا     which you expect [in the future],

فَقُل لَّهُمْ قَوْلًا مَّيْسُورًا ۞     speak to them gentle words.

وَلَا تَجْعَلْ يَدَكَ مَغْلُولَةً     29 Do not keep your hand chained

إِلَىٰ عُنُقِكَ     to your neck,

وَلَا تَبْسُطْهَا كُلَّ ٱلْبَسْطِ     nor open it all together,[2]

فَتَقْعُدَ مَلُومًا مَّحْسُورًا ۞     or you will sit blameworthy, regretful.

إِنَّ رَبَّكَ يَبْسُطُ ٱلرِّزْقَ     30 Indeed your Lord expands the provision

لِمَن يَشَآءُ     for whomever He wishes,

وَيَقْدِرُ     and tightens it.

إِنَّهُۥ كَانَ بِعِبَادِهِۦ خَبِيرًۢا بَصِيرًا ۞     Indeed He is all-aware, all-seeing about His servants.

---

[1] That is, do not grumble or speak to them in an ill-tempered manner. *Uff* is an interjection expressing displeasure and exasperation, indicating that one has been put out of patience.

[2] That is, neither be miserly nor be a spendthrift.

وَلَا تَقْتُلُوٓا۟ أَوْلَٰدَكُمْ   31 Do not kill your children

خَشْيَةَ إِمْلَٰقٍ      for the fear of penury:

نَّحْنُ نَرْزُقُهُمْ وَإِيَّاكُمْ      We will provide for them and for you.

إِنَّ قَتْلَهُمْ كَانَ خِطْـًٔا كَبِيرًا ۩      Killing them is indeed a great iniquity.

وَلَا تَقْرَبُوا۟ ٱلزِّنَىٰٓ   32 Do not approach fornication.

إِنَّهُۥ كَانَ فَٰحِشَةً وَسَآءَ سَبِيلًا ۩      It is indeed an indecency and an evil way.

وَلَا تَقْتُلُوا۟ ٱلنَّفْسَ ٱلَّتِى   33 Do not kill a soul

حَرَّمَ ٱللَّهُ      [whose life] Allah has made inviolable,

إِلَّا بِٱلْحَقِّ      except with due cause,

وَمَن قُتِلَ مَظْلُومًا      and whoever is killed wrongfully,

فَقَدْ جَعَلْنَا لِوَلِيِّهِۦ سُلْطَٰنًا      We have certainly given his heir an authority.

فَلَا يُسْرِف فِّى ٱلْقَتْلِ      But let him not commit any excess in killing,[1]

إِنَّهُۥ كَانَ مَنصُورًا ۩      for he enjoys the support [of law].

وَلَا تَقْرَبُوا۟ مَالَ ٱلْيَتِيمِ   34 Do not approach the orphan's property

إِلَّا بِٱلَّتِى هِىَ أَحْسَنُ      except in the best manner

حَتَّىٰ يَبْلُغَ أَشُدَّهُۥ      until he comes of age.

وَأَوْفُوا۟ بِٱلْعَهْدِ      And fulfill the covenants;

إِنَّ ٱلْعَهْدَ كَانَ مَسْـُٔولًا ۩      indeed all covenants are accountable.

وَأَوْفُوا۟ ٱلْكَيْلَ إِذَا كِلْتُمْ   35 When you measure, observe fully the measure,

وَزِنُوا۟ بِٱلْقِسْطَاسِ ٱلْمُسْتَقِيمِ      [and] weigh with an even balance.

ذَٰلِكَ خَيْرٌ وَأَحْسَنُ تَأْوِيلًا ۩      That is better and fairer in outcome.

وَلَا تَقْفُ مَا لَيْسَ لَكَ بِهِۦ عِلْمٌ   36 Do not follow that of which you have no knowledge.

إِنَّ ٱلسَّمْعَ وَٱلْبَصَرَ وَٱلْفُؤَادَ      Indeed the hearing, the eyesight, and the heart

كُلُّ أُو۟لَٰٓئِكَ كَانَ عَنْهُ مَسْـُٔولًا ۩      —all of these are accountable.

وَلَا تَمْشِ فِى ٱلْأَرْضِ مَرَحًا   37 Do not walk exultantly on the earth.

إِنَّكَ لَن تَخْرِقَ ٱلْأَرْضَ      Indeed you will neither pierce the earth,

وَلَن تَبْلُغَ ٱلْجِبَالَ طُولًا ۩      nor reach the mountains in height.

كُلُّ ذَٰلِكَ كَانَ سَيِّئُهُۥ   38 The evil of all these is

---

[1] Such as mutilating the body of the murderer, or killing someone other than the guilty person for the sake of vengeance.

عِندَ رَبِّكَ مَكْرُوهًا ۞ detestable to *your* Lord.

ذَٰلِكَ مِمَّآ 39 These are among [precepts] that

أَوْحَىٰٓ إِلَيْكَ رَبُّكَ مِنَ ٱلْحِكْمَةِ *your* Lord has revealed to *you* of wisdom.

وَلَا تَجْعَلْ مَعَ ٱللَّهِ إِلَٰهًا ءَاخَرَ Do not set up another god besides Allah,

فَتُلْقَىٰ فِى جَهَنَّمَ or you will be cast into hell,

مَلُومًا مَّدْحُورًا ۞ blameworthy, banished.

أَفَأَصْفَىٰكُمْ رَبُّكُم بِٱلْبَنِينَ 40 Did your Lord prefer you with sons,

وَٱتَّخَذَ مِنَ ٱلْمَلَٰٓئِكَةِ إِنَٰثًا and [Himself] adopt females from among the angels?[1]

إِنَّكُمْ لَتَقُولُونَ قَوْلًا عَظِيمًا ۞ Indeed you say a monstrous word!

وَلَقَدْ صَرَّفْنَا 41 Certainly We have paraphrased

فِى هَٰذَا ٱلْقُرْءَانِ [the principles of guidance] in this Qur'ān

لِيَذَّكَّرُوا۟ so that they may take admonition,

وَمَا يَزِيدُهُمْ إِلَّا نُفُورًا ۞ but it increases them only in aversion.

قُل لَّوْ كَانَ مَعَهُۥٓ ءَالِهَةٌ 42 Say, 'Were there [other] gods besides Him,

كَمَا يَقُولُونَ as they say,

إِذًا لَّٱبْتَغَوْا۟ إِلَىٰ ذِى ٱلْعَرْشِ سَبِيلًا ۞ they would surely encroach on the Lord of the Throne.

سُبْحَٰنَهُۥ 43 Immaculate is He,

وَتَعَٰلَىٰ عَمَّا يَقُولُونَ عُلُوًّا كَبِيرًا ۞ and greatly exalted above what they say!'

تُسَبِّحُ لَهُ ٱلسَّمَٰوَٰتُ ٱلسَّبْعُ 44 The seven heavens glorify Him,

وَٱلْأَرْضُ and the earth [too],

وَمَن فِيهِنَّ and whoever is in them.

وَإِن مِّن شَىْءٍ إِلَّا يُسَبِّحُ بِحَمْدِهِۦ There is not a thing but celebrates His praise,

وَلَٰكِن لَّا تَفْقَهُونَ تَسْبِيحَهُمْ but you do not understand their glorification.

إِنَّهُۥ كَانَ حَلِيمًا غَفُورًا ۞ Indeed He is all-forbearing, all-forgiving.

وَإِذَا قَرَأْتَ ٱلْقُرْءَانَ 45 When *you* recite the Qur'ān,

جَعَلْنَا بَيْنَكَ We draw between *you*

وَبَيْنَ ٱلَّذِينَ لَا يُؤْمِنُونَ بِٱلْءَاخِرَةِ and those who do not believe in the Hereafter

---

[1] Cf. 4:117, 37:150, 43:19, 53:21, 27.

حِجَابًا مَّسْتُورًا ۝

a hidden curtain,

وَجَعَلْنَا عَلَىٰ قُلُوبِهِمْ أَكِنَّةً 46

and We cast veils on their hearts,

أَن يَفْقَهُوهُ

lest they should understand it,

وَفِىٓ ءَاذَانِهِمْ وَقْرًا

and a deafness into their ears.

وَإِذَا ذَكَرْتَ رَبَّكَ فِى ٱلْقُرْءَانِ وَحْدَهُۥ

When you mention *your* Lord alone in the Qur'ān,

وَلَّوْا۟ عَلَىٰٓ أَدْبَٰرِهِمْ نُفُورًا ۝

they turn their backs in aversion.

نَّحْنُ أَعْلَمُ بِمَا يَسْتَمِعُونَ بِهِۦٓ 47

47 We know best what they listen for,

إِذْ يَسْتَمِعُونَ إِلَيْكَ

when they listen to *you*,

وَإِذْ هُمْ نَجْوَىٰٓ

and when they hold secret talks,

إِذْ يَقُولُ ٱلظَّٰلِمُونَ

when the wrongdoers say,

إِن تَتَّبِعُونَ إِلَّا

'[If you follow him] You will be following just

رَجُلًا مَّسْحُورًا ۝

a bewitched man.'

ٱنظُرْ كَيْفَ ضَرَبُوا۟ لَكَ ٱلْأَمْثَٰلَ 48

48 *Look,* how they draw comparisons for *you*;

فَضَلُّوا۟

so they go astray,

فَلَا يَسْتَطِيعُونَ سَبِيلًا ۝

and cannot find a way.

وَقَالُوٓا۟ أَءِذَا كُنَّا عِظَٰمًا 49

49 They say, 'What, when we have become bones

وَرُفَٰتًا

and dust,

أَءِنَّا لَمَبْعُوثُونَ خَلْقًا جَدِيدًا ۝ ۞

shall we really be raised in a new creation?

قُلْ كُونُوا۟ حِجَارَةً أَوْ حَدِيدًا ۝ 50

50 *Say,* 'Should you be stones, or iron,

أَوْ خَلْقًا مِّمَّا يَكْبُرُ فِى صُدُورِكُمْ 51

51 or a creature more fantastic to your minds!'

فَسَيَقُولُونَ مَن يُعِيدُنَا

They will say, 'Who will bring us back?'

قُلِ ٱلَّذِى فَطَرَكُمْ أَوَّلَ مَرَّةٍ

*Say,* 'He who originated you the first time.'

فَسَيُنْغِضُونَ إِلَيْكَ رُءُوسَهُمْ

They will nod their heads at you,

وَيَقُولُونَ مَتَىٰ هُوَ

and say, 'When will that be?

قُلْ عَسَىٰٓ أَن يَكُونَ قَرِيبًا ۝

*Say,* 'Maybe it is near!

يَوْمَ يَدْعُوكُمْ 52

52 The day He calls you,

فَتَسْتَجِيبُونَ بِحَمْدِهِۦ

you will respond to Him, praising Him,

وَتَظُنُّونَ إِن لَّبِثْتُمْ إِلَّا قَلِيلًا ۝

and you will think you remained only a little.'

وَقُل لِّعِبَادِى 53

53 *Tell* My servants

يَقُولُواْ ٱلَّتِى هِىَ أَحْسَنُ

to speak in a manner which is the best.

إِنَّ ٱلشَّيْطَـٰنَ يَنزَغُ بَيْنَهُمْ

Indeed Satan incites ill feeling between them,

إِنَّ ٱلشَّيْطَـٰنَ كَانَ لِلْإِنسَـٰنِ

and Satan is indeed man's

عَدُوًّا مُّبِينًا ۝

manifest enemy.

رَّبُّكُمْ أَعْلَمُ بِكُمْ

54 Your Lord knows you best.

إِن يَشَأْ يَرْحَمْكُمْ

He will have mercy on you, if He wishes,

أَوْ إِن يَشَأْ يُعَذِّبْكُمْ

or punish you, if He wishes,

وَمَآ أَرْسَلْنَـٰكَ عَلَيْهِمْ وَكِيلًا ۝

and We did not send *you* to watch over them.

وَرَبُّكَ أَعْلَمُ بِمَن فِى ٱلسَّمَـٰوَٰتِ

55 Your Lord knows best whoever is in the heavens

وَٱلْأَرْضِ

and the earth.

وَلَقَدْ فَضَّلْنَا بَعْضَ ٱلنَّبِيِّـۧنَ

Certainly We gave some prophets an advantage

عَلَىٰ بَعْضٍ

over others,

وَءَاتَيْنَا دَاوُۥدَ زَبُورًا ۝

and We gave David the Psalms.

قُلِ ٱدْعُواْ ٱلَّذِينَ زَعَمْتُم

56 *Say*, 'Invoke those whom you claim [to be gods]

مِّن دُونِهِۦ

besides Him.

فَلَا يَمْلِكُونَ كَشْفَ ٱلضُّرِّ عَنكُمْ

They have no power to remove your distress

وَلَا تَحْوِيلًا ۝

nor to bring about any change [in your state].

أُوْلَـٰٓئِكَ ٱلَّذِينَ يَدْعُونَ

57 They [themselves] are the ones who supplicate,[1]

يَبْتَغُونَ إِلَىٰ رَبِّهِمُ ٱلْوَسِيلَةَ

seeking a recourse to their Lord,

أَيُّهُمْ أَقْرَبُ

whoever is nearer [to Him],

وَيَرْجُونَ رَحْمَتَهُۥ

expecting His mercy

وَيَخَافُونَ عَذَابَهُۥٓ

and fearing His punishment.'

إِنَّ عَذَابَ رَبِّكَ

Indeed *your* Lord's punishment

كَانَ مَحْذُورًا ۝

is a thing to beware of.

وَإِن مِّن قَرْيَةٍ إِلَّا نَحْنُ مُهْلِكُوهَا

58 There is not a town but We will destroy it

قَبْلَ يَوْمِ ٱلْقِيَـٰمَةِ

before the Day of Resurrection,

أَوْ مُعَذِّبُوهَا عَذَابًا شَدِيدًا

or punish it with a severe punishment.

---

[1] Or 'Those whom they (i.e. the polytheists) invoke, themselves seek a recourse to their Lord. . . .'

كَانَ ذَٰلِكَ فِى ٱلْكِتَٰبِ مَسْطُورًا ۝     That has been written in the Book.

وَمَا مَنَعَنَا أَن نُّرْسِلَ بِٱلْآيَٰتِ   59 Nothing keeps Us from sending signs

إِلَّا أَن كَذَّبَ بِهَا ٱلْأَوَّلُونَ     except that the ancients denied them.

وَءَاتَيْنَا ثَمُودَ ٱلنَّاقَةَ مُبْصِرَةً     We gave Thamūd the she-camel as an eye-opener,

فَظَلَمُوا۟ بِهَا     but they wronged her.

وَمَا نُرْسِلُ بِٱلْآيَٰتِ إِلَّا تَخْوِيفًا ۝     We do not send the signs except for deterrence.

وَإِذْ قُلْنَا لَكَ   60 When We said to *you*,

إِنَّ رَبَّكَ أَحَاطَ بِٱلنَّاسِ     'Indeed *your* Lord comprehends all mankind,'

وَمَا جَعَلْنَا ٱلرُّءْيَا ٱلَّتِىٓ أَرَيْنَٰكَ     We did not appoint the vision that We showed *you*

إِلَّا فِتْنَةً لِّلنَّاسِ     except as a test for the people

وَٱلشَّجَرَةَ ٱلْمَلْعُونَةَ فِى ٱلْقُرْءَانِ     and the tree cursed in the Qur'ān.

وَنُخَوِّفُهُمْ     We deter them,

فَمَا يَزِيدُهُمْ إِلَّا طُغْيَٰنًا كَبِيرًا ۝     but it only increases them in great rebellion.

وَإِذْ قُلْنَا لِلْمَلَٰئِكَةِ   61 When We said to the angels,

ٱسْجُدُوا۟ لِءَادَمَ     'Prostrate before Adam,'

فَسَجَدُوٓا۟ إِلَّآ إِبْلِيسَ     they [all] prostrated, except Iblis:

قَالَ ءَأَسْجُدُ     Said he, 'Shall I prostrate before someone

لِمَنْ خَلَقْتَ طِينًا ۝     whom You have created from clay?'

قَالَ أَرَءَيْتَكَ هَٰذَا ٱلَّذِى   62 Said he, 'Do You see this one whom

كَرَّمْتَ عَلَىَّ     You have honoured above me?

لَئِنْ أَخَّرْتَنِ إِلَىٰ يَوْمِ ٱلْقِيَٰمَةِ     If You respite me until the Day of Resurrection,

لَأَحْتَنِكَنَّ ذُرِّيَّتَهُۥٓ     I will surely destroy his progeny,

إِلَّا قَلِيلًا ۝     [all] except a few.'

قَالَ ٱذْهَبْ   63 Said He, 'Begone!

فَمَن تَبِعَكَ مِنْهُمْ     Whoever of them follows you,

فَإِنَّ جَهَنَّمَ جَزَآؤُكُمْ     indeed the hell shall be your requital,

جَزَآءً مَّوْفُورًا ۝     an ample reward.

وَٱسْتَفْزِزْ مَنِ ٱسْتَطَعْتَ مِنْهُم   64 Instigate whomever of them you can

بِصَوْتِكَ    with your voice; [1]

وَأَجْلِبْ عَلَيْهِم بِخَيْلِكَ    and rally against them your cavalry

وَرَجِلِكَ    and your infantry,

وَشَارِكْهُمْ فِي ٱلْأَمْوَٰلِ وَٱلْأَوْلَٰدِ    and share with them in wealth and children,

وَعِدْهُمْ    and make promises to them!'

وَمَا يَعِدُهُمُ ٱلشَّيْطَٰنُ إِلَّا غُرُورًا ۝    But Satan promises them nothing but delusion.

إِنَّ عِبَادِى    65 'As for My servants,

لَيْسَ لَكَ عَلَيْهِمْ سُلْطَٰنٌ    you shall have no authority over them.'

وَكَفَىٰ بِرَبِّكَ وَكِيلًا ۝    And *your* Lord suffices as trustee.

رَّبُّكُمُ ٱلَّذِى يُزْجِى لَكُمُ ٱلْفُلْكَ    66 Your Lord is He who drives for you the ships

فِى ٱلْبَحْرِ    in the sea,

لِتَبْتَغُواْ مِن فَضْلِهِ    that you may seek His grace.

إِنَّهُ كَانَ بِكُمْ رَحِيمًا ۝    Indeed He is most merciful to you.

وَإِذَا مَسَّكُمُ ٱلضُّرُّ فِى ٱلْبَحْرِ    67 And when distress befalls you at sea,

ضَلَّ مَن تَدْعُونَ إِلَّا إِيَّاهُ    those whom you invoke besides Him are forsaken.

فَلَمَّا نَجَّىٰكُمْ إِلَى ٱلْبَرِّ    But when He delivers you to land,

أَعْرَضْتُمْ    you are disregardful [of Him].

وَكَانَ ٱلْإِنسَٰنُ كَفُورًا ۝    And man is very ungrateful.

أَفَأَمِنتُمْ    68 Do you feel secure

أَن يَخْسِفَ بِكُمْ جَانِبَ ٱلْبَرِّ    that He will not make the coastland swallow you,

أَوْ يُرْسِلَ عَلَيْكُمْ حَاصِبًا    or He will not unleash upon you a rain of stones?

ثُمَّ لَا تَجِدُواْ لَكُمْ وَكِيلًا ۝    Then you will not find any defender for yourselves.

أَمْ أَمِنتُمْ    69 Do you feel secure

أَن يُعِيدَكُمْ فِيهِ تَارَةً أُخْرَىٰ    that He will not send you back into it another time

فَيُرْسِلَ عَلَيْكُمْ قَاصِفًا مِّنَ ٱلرِّيحِ    and unleash against you a shattering gale

فَيُغْرِقَكُم بِمَا كَفَرْتُمْ    and drown you because of your unfaith?

ثُمَّ لَا تَجِدُواْ لَكُمْ    Then you will not find for yourselves

عَلَيْنَا بِهِۦ تَبِيعًا ۝    any redresser against Us.

---

[1] Or 'Tempt whomever . . . .'

وَلَقَدْ كَرَّمْنَا بَنِى ءَادَمَ 70 Certainly We have honoured the Children of Adam,

وَحَمَلْنَهُمْ فِى ٱلْبَرِّ وَٱلْبَحْرِ    and carried them over land and sea,

وَرَزَقْنَهُم مِّنَ ٱلطَّيِّبَتِ    and provided them with all the good things,

وَفَضَّلْنَهُمْ    and given them an advantage

عَلَىٰ كَثِيرٍ مِّمَّنْ خَلَقْنَا    over many of those We have created

تَفْضِيلًا ۝    with a complete preference.

يَوْمَ نَدْعُوا۟ كُلَّ أُنَاسٍ 71 The day We shall summon every group of people

بِإِمَـٰمِهِمْ    with their *imam*,[1]

فَمَنْ أُوتِىَ كِتَـٰبَهُۥ بِيَمِينِهِۦ    then whoever is given his book in his right hand

فَأُو۟لَـٰٓئِكَ يَقْرَءُونَ كِتَـٰبَهُمْ    —they will read it,

وَلَا يُظْلَمُونَ    and they will not be wronged

فَتِيلًا ۝    so much as a single date-thread.

وَمَن كَانَ فِى هَـٰذِهِۦٓ أَعْمَىٰ 72 But whoever has been blind in this [world],

فَهُوَ فِى ٱلْأَخِرَةِ أَعْمَىٰ    will be blind in the Hereafter,

وَأَضَلُّ سَبِيلًا ۝    and [even] more astray from the [right] way.

وَإِن كَادُوا۟ لَيَفْتِنُونَكَ 73 They were about to beguile *you*

عَنِ ٱلَّذِىٓ أَوْحَيْنَآ إِلَيْكَ    from what Allah has revealed to *you*

لِتَفْتَرِىَ عَلَيْنَا    so that *you* may fabricate against Us

غَيْرَهُۥ    something other than that,

وَإِذًا لَّٱتَّخَذُوكَ خَلِيلًا ۝    whereat they would have befriended *you*.

وَلَوْلَآ أَن ثَبَّتْنَـٰكَ 74 Had We not fortified *you*,

لَقَدْ كِدتَّ تَرْكَنُ إِلَيْهِمْ    certainly *you* might have inclined toward them

شَيْـًٔا قَلِيلًا ۝    a bit.

إِذًا لَّأَذَقْنَـٰكَ 75 Then We would have surely made *you* taste

ضِعْفَ ٱلْحَيَوٰةِ    a double [punishment] in this life

وَضِعْفَ ٱلْمَمَاتِ    and a double [punishment] after death,

ثُمَّ لَا تَجِدُ لَكَ    and then *you* would have not found for *yourself*

---

[1] That is, leader.

عَلَيْنَا نَصِيرًا ۝    any helper against Us.

وَإِن كَادُواْ لَيَسْتَفِزُّونَكَ مِنَ ٱلْأَرْضِ    76 They were about to hound you out of the land,

لِيُخْرِجُوكَ مِنْهَا    to expel you from it,

وَإِذًا لَّا يَلْبَثُونَ خِلَٰفَكَ    but then they would not have stayed after you

إِلَّا قَلِيلًا ۝    but a little.

سُنَّةَ مَن قَدْ أَرْسَلْنَا    77 A precedent of those We have sent

قَبْلَكَ مِن رُّسُلِنَا ۖ    from among Our apostles before *you*,

وَلَا تَجِدُ لِسُنَّتِنَا تَحْوِيلًا ۝    and *you* will not find any change in Our precedent.

أَقِمِ ٱلصَّلَوٰةَ لِدُلُوكِ ٱلشَّمْسِ    78 *Maintain* the prayer from the sun's decline[1]

إِلَىٰ غَسَقِ ٱلَّيْلِ    till the darkness of the night,

وَقُرْءَانَ ٱلْفَجْرِ ۖ    and [*observe* particularly] the dawn recital.

إِنَّ قُرْءَانَ ٱلْفَجْرِ كَانَ مَشْهُودًا ۝    Indeed the dawn recital is attended [by angels].

وَمِنَ ٱلَّيْلِ فَتَهَجَّدْ بِهِۦ    79 And *keep vigil* for a part of the night,

نَافِلَةً لَّكَ    as a supererogatory [devotion] for *you*.

عَسَىٰٓ أَن يَبْعَثَكَ رَبُّكَ    It may be that *your* Lord will raise *you*

مَقَامًا مَّحْمُودًا ۝    to a praiseworthy station.

وَقُل رَّبِّ    80 And *say,* 'My Lord!

أَدْخِلْنِى مُدْخَلَ صِدْقٍ    'Admit me with a worthy entrance,

وَأَخْرِجْنِى مُخْرَجَ صِدْقٍ    and bring me out with a worthy departure,

وَٱجْعَل لِّى    and render me

مِن لَّدُنكَ سُلْطَٰنًا نَّصِيرًا ۝    a favourable authority from Yourself.'

وَقُلْ جَآءَ ٱلْحَقُّ    81 And *say,* 'The truth has come,

وَزَهَقَ ٱلْبَٰطِلُ ۚ    and falsehood has vanished.

إِنَّ ٱلْبَٰطِلَ كَانَ زَهُوقًا ۝    Indeed falsehood is bound to vanish.'

وَنُنَزِّلُ مِنَ ٱلْقُرْءَانِ    82 We send down in the Qur'ān

مَا هُوَ شِفَآءٌ وَرَحْمَةٌ لِّلْمُؤْمِنِينَ ۙ    that which is a cure and mercy for the faithful;

وَلَا يَزِيدُ ٱلظَّٰلِمِينَ إِلَّا خَسَارًا ۝    and it increases the wrongdoers only in loss.

---

[1] That is, from noon onwards, when the sun crosses the meridian.

وَإِذَآ أَنْعَمْنَا عَلَى ٱلْإِنسَـٰنِ    83 When We bless man,

أَعْرَضَ وَنَـَٔا بِجَانِبِهِۦ         he is disregardful and turns aside;

وَإِذَا مَسَّهُ ٱلشَّرُّ كَانَ يَـُٔوسًا ۝    but when an ill befalls him, he is despondent.

قُلْ كُلٌّ يَعْمَلُ عَلَىٰ شَاكِلَتِهِۦ    84 *Say,* 'Everyone acts according to his character.'

فَرَبُّكُمْ أَعْلَمُ         Your Lord knows best

بِمَنْ هُوَ أَهْدَىٰ سَبِيلًا ۝         who is better guided with regard to the way.

وَيَسْـَٔلُونَكَ عَنِ ٱلرُّوحِ    85 They question *you* concerning the Spirit.

قُلِ ٱلرُّوحُ مِنْ أَمْرِ رَبِّى         *Say,* 'The Spirit is of the command of my Lord,[1]

وَمَآ أُوتِيتُم مِّنَ ٱلْعِلْمِ         and you have not been given of the knowledge

إِلَّا قَلِيلًا ۝         except a few [of you].'[2]

وَلَئِن شِئْنَا    86 If We wish,

لَنَذْهَبَنَّ         We would take away

بِٱلَّذِىٓ أَوْحَيْنَآ إِلَيْكَ         what We have revealed to *you.*

ثُمَّ لَا تَجِدُ لَكَ بِهِۦ         Then *you* would not find for *yourself*

عَلَيْنَا وَكِيلًا ۝         any defender against Us,

إِلَّا رَحْمَةً مِّن رَّبِّكَ    87    except a mercy from *your* Lord.

إِنَّ فَضْلَهُۥ كَانَ عَلَيْكَ كَبِيرًا ۝    Indeed His grace has been great upon *you.*

قُل    88 *Say,*

لَّئِنِ ٱجْتَمَعَتِ ٱلْإِنسُ وَٱلْجِنُّ         'Should all humans and jinn rally

عَلَىٰٓ أَن يَأْتُوا۟         to bring

بِمِثْلِ هَـٰذَا ٱلْقُرْءَانِ         the like of this Qur'ān,

لَا يَأْتُونَ بِمِثْلِهِۦ         they will not bring the like of it,

وَلَوْ كَانَ بَعْضُهُمْ لِبَعْضٍ ظَهِيرًا ۝    even if they assisted one another.

وَلَقَدْ صَرَّفْنَا لِلنَّاسِ    89 We have certainly interspersed for the people

فِى هَـٰذَا ٱلْقُرْءَانِ مِن كُلِّ مَثَلٍ         this Qur'ān with every [kind of] parable,

فَأَبَىٰٓ أَكْثَرُ ٱلنَّاسِ إِلَّا كُفُورًا ۝    but most people are only intent on ingratitude.[3]

وَقَالُوا۟    90 They say,

---

[1] Or 'the Spirit relates to the command of my Lord.' Or 'the Spirit proceeds from the command of my Lord.'

[2] Or 'you have not been given of the knowledge except a little.'

[3] Or 'faithlessness.' Cf. 17:99 below and 25:50.

لَن نُّؤْمِنَ لَكَ حَتَّىٰ 'We will not believe *you* until

تَفْجُرَ لَنَا مِنَ ٱلْأَرْضِ يَنۢبُوعًا ۝ *you* make a spring gush forth for us from the ground.

أَوْ تَكُونَ لَكَ جَنَّةٌ 91 Or until *you* have a garden

مِّن نَّخِيلٍ وَعِنَبٍ of date palms and vines

فَتُفَجِّرَ ٱلْأَنْهَٰرَ خِلَٰلَهَا تَفْجِيرًا ۝ and *you* make streams gush through it.

أَوْ تُسْقِطَ ٱلسَّمَآءَ 92 Or until *you* cause the sky to fall

كَمَا زَعَمْتَ عَلَيْنَا كِسَفًا in fragments upon us, just as you would aver.

أَوْ تَأْتِىَ بِٱللَّهِ وَٱلْمَلَٰٓئِكَةِ Or until you bring Allah and the angels

قَبِيلًا ۝ [right] in front of us.

أَوْ يَكُونَ لَكَ بَيْتٌ مِّن زُخْرُفٍ 93 Or until *you* have a house of gold,

أَوْ تَرْقَىٰ فِى ٱلسَّمَآءِ or *you* ascend into the sky.

وَلَن نُّؤْمِنَ لِرُقِيِّكَ And we will not believe *your* ascension

حَتَّىٰ تُنَزِّلَ عَلَيْنَا كِتَٰبًا نَّقْرَؤُهُ ۥ until *you* bring down for us a book that we may read.'

قُلْ سُبْحَانَ رَبِّى *Say*, 'Immaculate is my Lord!

هَلْ كُنتُ إِلَّا بَشَرًا رَّسُولًا ۝ Am I anything but a human, an apostle?!'

وَمَا مَنَعَ ٱلنَّاسَ أَن يُؤْمِنُوٓا۟ 94 Nothing kept the people from believing

إِذْ جَآءَهُمُ ٱلْهُدَىٰٓ when guidance came to them,

إِلَّآ أَن قَالُوٓا۟ but their saying,

أَبَعَثَ ٱللَّهُ بَشَرًا رَّسُولًا ۝ 'Has Allah sent a human as an apostle?!'

قُل لَّوْ كَانَ فِى ٱلْأَرْضِ مَلَٰٓئِكَةٌ 95 *Say*, 'Had there been angels in the earth,

يَمْشُونَ walking around

مُطْمَئِنِّينَ and residing [in it like humans do],

لَنَزَّلْنَا عَلَيْهِم مِّنَ ٱلسَّمَآءِ We would have sent down to them from the heaven

مَلَكًا رَّسُولًا ۝ an angel as apostle.'

قُلْ كَفَىٰ بِٱللَّهِ شَهِيدًۢا 96 *Say*, 'Allah suffices as a witness

بَيْنِى وَبَيْنَكُمْ ۚ between me and you.

إِنَّهُۥ كَانَ بِعِبَادِهِۦ خَبِيرًۢا بَصِيرًا ۝ Indeed He is all-aware, all-seeing about His servants.'

وَمَن يَهْدِ ٱللَّهُ فَهُوَ ٱلْمُهْتَدِ 97 Whomever Allah guides is rightly guided,

وَمَن يُضْلِلْ and whomever He leads astray

فَلَن تَجِدَ لَهُمْ أَوْلِيَآءَ مِن دُونِهِۦ ۖ *you* will never find them any guardians besides Him.

وَنَحْشُرُهُمْ يَوْمَ ٱلْقِيَمَةِ On the Day of Resurrection, We shall muster them

عَلَىٰ وُجُوهِهِمْ [scrambling] on their faces,[1]

عُمْيًا وَبُكْمًا وَصُمًّا blind, dumb, and deaf.

مَّأْوَىٰهُمْ جَهَنَّمُ Their refuge shall be hell.

كُلَّمَا خَبَتْ Whenever it subsides,

زِدْنَٰهُمْ سَعِيرًا ۩ We shall intensify the blaze for them.

ذَٰلِكَ جَزَآؤُهُم 98 That is their requital

بِأَنَّهُمْ كَفَرُوا۟ بِـَٔايَٰتِنَا because they defied Our signs

وَقَالُوٓا۟ أَءِذَا كُنَّا عِظَٰمًا and said, 'What, when we have become bones

وَرُفَٰتًا and dust,

أَءِنَّا لَمَبْعُوثُونَ خَلْقًا جَدِيدًا ۩ shall we really be raised in a new creation?'

أَوَلَمْ يَرَوْا۟ أَنَّ ٱللَّهَ 99 Do they not see that Allah,

ٱلَّذِى خَلَقَ ٱلسَّمَٰوَٰتِ وَٱلْأَرْضَ who created the heavens and the earth,

قَادِرٌ عَلَىٰٓ أَن يَخْلُقَ مِثْلَهُمْ is able to create the like of them?

وَجَعَلَ لَهُمْ أَجَلًا He has appointed for them a term,

لَّا رَيْبَ فِيهِ in which there is no doubt;

فَأَبَى ٱلظَّٰلِمُونَ إِلَّا كُفُورًا ۩ yet the wrongdoers are only intent on ingratitude.[2]

قُل لَّوْ أَنتُمْ تَمْلِكُونَ 100 Say, 'Even if you possessed

خَزَآئِنَ رَحْمَةِ رَبِّىٓ the treasuries of my Lord's mercy,

إِذًا لَّأَمْسَكْتُمْ خَشْيَةَ ٱلْإِنفَاقِ you would withhold them for the fear of being spent,

وَكَانَ ٱلْإِنسَٰنُ قَتُورًا ۩ and man is very niggardly.'

وَلَقَدْ ءَاتَيْنَا مُوسَىٰ 101 Certainly We gave Moses

تِسْعَ ءَايَٰتٍۭ بَيِّنَٰتٍ nine manifest signs.

فَسْـَٔلْ بَنِىٓ إِسْرَٰٓءِيلَ So ask the children of Israel.

إِذْ جَآءَهُمْ When he came to them,

فَقَالَ لَهُۥ فِرْعَوْنُ Pharaoh said to him,

إِنِّى لَأَظُنُّكَ يَٰمُوسَىٰ مَسْحُورًا ۩ 'O Moses, indeed I think you are bewitched.'

---

[1] Cf. 25:34, 54:48.

[2] Or 'faithlessness.'

قَالَ 102 He said,

لَقَدْ عَلِمْتَ مَآ أَنزَلَ هَٰٓؤُلَآءِ     'You certainly know that no one has sent these [signs]

إِلَّا رَبُّ ٱلسَّمَٰوَٰتِ وَٱلْأَرْضِ     except the Lord of the heavens and the earth

بَصَآئِرَ     as eye-openers,

وَإِنِّى لَأَظُنُّكَ يَٰفِرْعَوْنُ مَثْبُورًا ۝     and I, O Pharaoh, indeed think you are doomed.'

فَأَرَادَ أَن يَسْتَفِزَّهُم مِّنَ ٱلْأَرْضِ     103 He desired to exterminate them from the land,

فَأَغْرَقْنَٰهُ     so We drowned him

وَمَن مَّعَهُۥ جَمِيعًا ۝     and all those who were with him.

وَقُلْنَا مِنۢ بَعْدِهِۦ لِبَنِىٓ إِسْرَٰٓءِيلَ     104 After him We said to the children of Israel,

ٱسْكُنُوا۟ ٱلْأَرْضَ     'Take up residence in the land,

فَإِذَا جَآءَ وَعْدُ ٱلْءَاخِرَةِ     and when the occasion of the other [promise] comes,[1]

جِئْنَا بِكُمْ لَفِيفًا ۝     We shall gather you in mixed company.'[2]

وَبِٱلْحَقِّ أَنزَلْنَٰهُ     105 With the truth did We send it down,

وَبِٱلْحَقِّ نَزَلَ     and with the truth did it descend,

وَمَآ أَرْسَلْنَٰكَ     and We did not send *you*

إِلَّا مُبَشِّرًا وَنَذِيرًا ۝     except as a bearer of good news and as a warner.

وَقُرْءَانًا فَرَقْنَٰهُ     106 We have sent the Qur'ān in [discrete] parts

لِتَقْرَأَهُۥ عَلَى ٱلنَّاسِ     so that *you* may read it to the people

عَلَىٰ مُكْثٍ     a little at a time,

وَنَزَّلْنَٰهُ تَنزِيلًا ۝     and We have sent it down piecemeal.

قُلْ ءَامِنُوا۟ بِهِۦٓ     107 *Say*, 'Whether you believe in it,

أَوْ لَا تُؤْمِنُوٓا۟     or do not believe in it,

إِنَّ ٱلَّذِينَ أُوتُوا۟ ٱلْعِلْمَ     indeed those who were given knowledge

مِن قَبْلِهِۦٓ     before it

إِذَا يُتْلَىٰ عَلَيْهِمْ     when it is recited to them,

يَخِرُّونَ لِلْأَذْقَانِ سُجَّدًا ۝     fall down in prostration on their faces,

وَيَقُولُونَ سُبْحَٰنَ رَبِّنَآ     108 and say, "Immaculate is our Lord!

---

[1] Or 'when the promise of the Hereafter comes.'

[2] Or 'We shall bring you all together.' Or 'We shall bring you from all places.'

إِن كَانَ وَعْدُ رَبِّنَا لَمَفْعُولًا ۝    Indeed Our Lord's promise is bound to be fulfilled."

وَيَخِرُّونَ لِلْأَذْقَانِ يَبْكُونَ    109 Weeping, they fall down on their faces,

وَيَزِيدُهُمْ خُشُوعًا ۩ ۝    and it increases them in humility.'

قُلِ ٱدْعُوا۟ ٱللَّهَ أَوِ ٱدْعُوا۟ ٱلرَّحْمَٰنَ    110 Say, 'Invoke "Allah" or invoke "the All-beneficent."

أَيًّا مَّا تَدْعُوا۟    Whichever [of His Names] you may invoke,

فَلَهُ ٱلْأَسْمَاءُ ٱلْحُسْنَىٰ    to Him belong the Best Names.'

وَلَا تَجْهَرْ بِصَلَاتِكَ وَلَا تُخَافِتْ بِهَا    *Be* neither loud in *your* prayer, nor murmur it,

وَٱبْتَغِ بَيْنَ ذَٰلِكَ سَبِيلًا ۝    but *follow* a middle course between these,

وَقُلِ ٱلْحَمْدُ لِلَّهِ    111 and *say*, 'All praise belongs to Allah,

ٱلَّذِى لَمْ يَتَّخِذْ وَلَدًا    who has neither taken any son,

وَلَمْ يَكُن لَّهُۥ شَرِيكٌ فِى ٱلْمُلْكِ    nor has He any partner in sovereignty,

وَلَمْ يَكُن لَّهُۥ وَلِىٌّ مِّنَ ٱلذُّلِّ    nor has He [taken] any ally out of weakness,'

وَكَبِّرْهُ تَكْبِيرًا ۝    and *magnify* Him with a magnification [worthy of Him].

## سُورَةُ الكَهْف     18. SŪRAT AL-KAHF[1]

بِسْمِ ٱللَّهِ    In the Name of Allah,

ٱلرَّحْمَٰنِ ٱلرَّحِيمِ    the All-beneficent, the All-merciful.

ٱلْحَمْدُ لِلَّهِ ٱلَّذِى    1 All praise belongs to Allah,

أَنزَلَ عَلَىٰ عَبْدِهِ ٱلْكِتَٰبَ    who has sent down the Book to His servant

وَلَمْ يَجْعَل لَّهُۥ عِوَجَا ۝    and did not let any crookedness be in it,

قَيِّمًا    2 [a Book] upright,

لِّيُنذِرَ بَأْسًا شَدِيدًا مِّن لَّدُنْهُ    to warn of a severe punishment from Him,

وَيُبَشِّرَ ٱلْمُؤْمِنِينَ    and to give good news to the faithful

ٱلَّذِينَ يَعْمَلُونَ ٱلصَّٰلِحَٰتِ    who do righteous deeds,

أَنَّ لَهُمْ أَجْرًا حَسَنًا ۝    that there shall be for them a good reward,

مَّٰكِثِينَ فِيهِ أَبَدًا ۝    3 to abide in it forever,

---

[1] The *sūrah* derives its name from the story of the Companions of the Cave (*aṣḥāb al-kahf*) told at its beginning.

وَيُنذِرَ ٱلَّذِينَ قَالُوا 4   and to warn those who say,

ٱتَّخَذَ ٱللَّهُ وَلَدًا ۝   'Allah has taken a son.'

مَّا هُم بِهِۦ مِنْ عِلْمٍ 5   They do not have any knowledge of that,

وَلَا لِآبَآئِهِمْ   nor did their fathers.

كَبُرَتْ كَلِمَةً   Monstrous is the utterance

تَخْرُجُ مِنْ أَفْوَٰهِهِمْ   that comes out of their mouths,

إِن يَقُولُونَ إِلَّا كَذِبًا ۝   and they say nothing but a lie.

فَلَعَلَّكَ بَٰخِعٌ نَّفْسَكَ 6   *You* are liable to imperil *your* life

عَلَىٰٓ ءَاثَٰرِهِمْ   for their sake,

إِن لَّمْ يُؤْمِنُوا   if they should not believe

بِهَٰذَا ٱلْحَدِيثِ أَسَفًا ۝   this discourse,[1] out of grief.

إِنَّا جَعَلْنَا مَا عَلَى ٱلْأَرْضِ 7   Indeed We have made whatever is on the earth

زِينَةً لَّهَا   an adornment for it

لِنَبْلُوَهُمْ   that We may test them [to see]

أَيُّهُمْ أَحْسَنُ عَمَلًا ۝   which of them is best in conduct.

وَإِنَّا لَجَٰعِلُونَ مَا عَلَيْهَا 8   And indeed We will turn whatever is on it

صَعِيدًا جُرُزًا ۝   into a barren plain.

أَمْ حَسِبْتَ أَنَّ أَصْحَٰبَ ٱلْكَهْفِ 9   Do *you* suppose that the Companions of the Cave

وَٱلرَّقِيمِ   and the Inscription

كَانُوا مِنْ ءَايَٰتِنَا عَجَبًا ۝   were among Our wonderful signs?

إِذْ أَوَى ٱلْفِتْيَةُ إِلَى ٱلْكَهْفِ 10   When the youths took refuge in the Cave,

فَقَالُوا رَبَّنَآ   they said, 'Our Lord!

ءَاتِنَا مِن لَّدُنكَ رَحْمَةً   Grant us a mercy from Yourself,

وَهَيِّئْ لَنَا مِنْ أَمْرِنَا رَشَدًا ۝   and help us on to rectitude in our affair.'

فَضَرَبْنَا عَلَىٰٓ ءَاذَانِهِمْ فِى ٱلْكَهْفِ 11   So We put them to sleep[2] in the Cave

سِنِينَ عَدَدًا ۝   for several years.

ثُمَّ بَعَثْنَٰهُمْ لِنَعْلَمَ 12   Then We aroused them that We might know

---

[1] That is, the Qur'ān.

[2] Literally: 'struck on their ears,' or 'drew a curtain (or veil) on their ears.'

أَىُّ ٱلْحِزْبَيْنِ
which of the two groups

أَحْصَىٰ لِمَا لَبِثُوٓا۟ أَمَدًا ۝
better reckoned the period they had stayed.

13 نَّحْنُ نَقُصُّ عَلَيْكَ نَبَأَهُم بِٱلْحَقِّ
13 We relate to *you* their account in truth.

إِنَّهُمْ فِتْيَةٌ ءَامَنُوا۟ بِرَبِّهِمْ
They were indeed youths who had faith in their Lord,

وَزِدْنَٰهُمْ هُدًى ۝
and We had enhanced them in guidance,

14 وَرَبَطْنَا عَلَىٰ قُلُوبِهِمْ
14 and fortified their hearts,

إِذْ قَامُوا۟ فَقَالُوا۟
when they stood up and said,

رَبُّنَا رَبُّ ٱلسَّمَٰوَٰتِ وَٱلْأَرْضِ
'Our Lord is the Lord of the heavens and the earth.

لَن نَّدْعُوَا۟ مِن دُونِهِۦٓ إِلَٰهًا
We will never invoke any god besides Him,

لَّقَدْ قُلْنَآ إِذًا شَطَطًا ۝
for then we shall certainly have said an atrocious lie.

15 هَٰٓؤُلَآءِ قَوْمُنَا
15 These—our people—

ٱتَّخَذُوا۟ مِن دُونِهِۦٓ ءَالِهَةً
have taken gods besides Him.

لَّوْلَا يَأْتُونَ
Why do they not bring

عَلَيْهِم بِسُلْطَٰنٍ بَيِّنٍ
any clear authority touching them?

فَمَنْ أَظْلَمُ
So who is a greater wrongdoer

مِمَّنِ ٱفْتَرَىٰ عَلَى ٱللَّهِ كَذِبًا ۝
than he who fabricates a lie against Allah?

16 وَإِذِ ٱعْتَزَلْتُمُوهُمْ
16 When you have dissociated yourselves from them

وَمَا يَعْبُدُونَ إِلَّا ٱللَّهَ
and from what they worship except Allah,

فَأْوُۥٓا۟ إِلَى ٱلْكَهْفِ
then take refuge in the Cave.

يَنشُرْ لَكُمْ رَبُّكُم مِّن رَّحْمَتِهِۦ
Your Lord will unfold His mercy for you,

وَيُهَيِّئْ لَكُم
and He will help you on

مِّنْ أَمْرِكُم مِّرْفَقًا ۝ ۞
to ease in your affair.'

17 وَتَرَى ٱلشَّمْسَ إِذَا طَلَعَت
17 *You* may see the sun, when it rises,

تَّزَٰوَرُ عَن كَهْفِهِمْ ذَاتَ ٱلْيَمِينِ
slanting toward the right of their cave,

وَإِذَا غَرَبَت
and, when it sets,

تَّقْرِضُهُمْ ذَاتَ ٱلشِّمَالِ
cut across them towards the left,

وَهُمْ فِى فَجْوَةٍ مِّنْهُ
while they are in a cavern within it.

ذَٰلِكَ مِنْ ءَايَٰتِ ٱللَّهِ
That is one of Allah's signs.

مَن يَهْدِ ٱللَّهُ فَهُوَ ٱلْمُهْتَدِ
Whomever Allah guides is rightly guided,

وَمَن يُضْلِلْ
and whomever He leads astray,

فَلَن تَجِدَ لَهُۥ وَلِيًّا مُّرْشِدًا ۝    you will never find for him any guardian or guide.

وَتَحْسَبُهُمْ أَيْقَاظًا    18 You will suppose them to be awake,

وَهُمْ رُقُودٌ    although they are asleep.

وَنُقَلِّبُهُمْ ذَاتَ ٱلْيَمِينِ    We turn them to the right

وَذَاتَ ٱلشِّمَالِ    and to the left,

وَكَلْبُهُم بَٰسِطٌ ذِرَاعَيْهِ    and their dog [lies] stretching its forelegs

بِٱلْوَصِيدِ    at the threshold.

لَوِ ٱطَّلَعْتَ عَلَيْهِمْ    If you come upon them,

لَوَلَّيْتَ مِنْهُمْ فِرَارًا    you will surely turn to flee from them,

وَلَمُلِئْتَ مِنْهُمْ رُعْبًا ۝    and you will surely be filled with a terror of them.

وَكَذَٰلِكَ بَعَثْنَٰهُمْ    19 So it was that We aroused them [from sleep]

لِيَتَسَآءَلُوا۟ بَيْنَهُمْ    so that they might question one another.

قَالَ قَآئِلٌ مِّنْهُمْ    One of them said,

كَمْ لَبِثْتُمْ    'How long have you stayed [here]?'

قَالُوا۟ لَبِثْنَا يَوْمًا    They said, 'We have stayed a day, or part of a day.'

أَوْ بَعْضَ يَوْمٍ قَالُوا۟ رَبُّكُمْ أَعْلَمُ    They said, 'Your Lord knows best

بِمَا لَبِثْتُمْ    how long you have stayed.

فَٱبْعَثُوٓا۟ أَحَدَكُم    Send one of you

بِوَرِقِكُمْ هَٰذِهِۦٓ إِلَى ٱلْمَدِينَةِ    to the city with this money.

فَلْيَنظُرْ أَيُّهَآ أَزْكَىٰ طَعَامًا    Let him observe which of them has the purest food,

فَلْيَأْتِكُم بِرِزْقٍ مِّنْهُ    and bring you provisions from there.

وَلْيَتَلَطَّفْ    Let him be attentive,[1]

وَلَا يُشْعِرَنَّ بِكُمْ أَحَدًا ۝    and let him not make anyone aware of you.

إِنَّهُمْ إِن يَظْهَرُوا۟ عَلَيْكُمْ    20 Indeed should they prevail over you,

يَرْجُمُوكُمْ    they will [either] stone you [to death],

أَوْ يُعِيدُوكُمْ فِى مِلَّتِهِمْ    or force you back into their creed,

وَلَن تُفْلِحُوٓا۟ إِذًا أَبَدًا ۝    and then you will never be saved.

وَكَذَٰلِكَ أَعْثَرْنَا عَلَيْهِمْ    21 So it was that We let them come upon them,[2]

---

[1] Or 'careful.'

[2] That is, We let the people discover the cave where the Men of the Cave were.

لِيَعْلَمُوٓا أَنَّ وَعْدَ ٱللَّهِ حَقٌّ

that they might know that Allah's promise is true,

وَأَنَّ ٱلسَّاعَةَ لَا رَيْبَ فِيهَآ

and that there is no doubt in the Hour.

إِذْ يَتَنَٰزَعُونَ بَيْنَهُمْ

As they were disputing among themselves

أَمْرَهُمْ

about their matter,

فَقَالُوا ٱبْنُوا عَلَيْهِم بُنْيَٰنًا

they said, 'Build a building over them.

رَّبُّهُمْ أَعْلَمُ بِهِمْ

Their Lord knows them best.'

قَالَ ٱلَّذِينَ غَلَبُوا عَلَىٰٓ أَمْرِهِمْ

Those who had the say in their matter said,

لَنَتَّخِذَنَّ عَلَيْهِم مَّسْجِدًا ۝

'We will set up a place of worship over them.'

سَيَقُولُونَ ثَلَٰثَةٌ

22 They will say, '[They are] three;

رَّابِعُهُمْ كَلْبُهُمْ

their dog is the fourth of them.

وَيَقُولُونَ خَمْسَةٌ

They will say, '[They are] five,

سَادِسُهُمْ كَلْبُهُمْ

their dog is the sixth of them,'

رَجْمًا بِٱلْغَيْبِ

taking a shot at the invisible.[1]

وَيَقُولُونَ سَبْعَةٌ

They will say, '[They are] seven,

وَثَامِنُهُمْ كَلْبُهُمْ

their dog is the eighth of them.'

قُل رَّبِّىٓ أَعْلَمُ بِعِدَّتِهِم

*Say*, 'My Lord knows best their number,

مَّا يَعْلَمُهُمْ إِلَّا قَلِيلٌ

and none knows them except a few.'

فَلَا تُمَارِ فِيهِمْ

So do not dispute concerning them,

إِلَّا مِرَآءً ظَٰهِرًا

except for a seeming dispute,

وَلَا تَسْتَفْتِ فِيهِم

and do not question about them

مِّنْهُمْ أَحَدًا ۝

any of them.

وَلَا تَقُولَنَّ لِشَاْىْءٍ

23 *Do not say* about anything,

إِنِّى فَاعِلٌ ذَٰلِكَ غَدًا ۝

'I will indeed do it tomorrow,'

إِلَّآ أَن يَشَآءَ ٱللَّهُ

24 without [adding], 'if Allah wishes.'

وَٱذْكُر رَّبَّكَ إِذَا نَسِيتَ

And when you forget, remember your Lord,

وَقُلْ عَسَىٰٓ أَن يَهْدِيَنِ رَبِّى

and say, 'Maybe my Lord will guide me

لِأَقْرَبَ مِنْ هَٰذَا رَشَدًا ۝

to [something] more akin to rectitude than this.

---

[1] That is, making a wild guess.

وَلَبِثُوا۟ فِى كَهْفِهِمْ 25 They remained in the Cave

ثَلَٰثَ مِا۟ئَةٍ سِنِينَ    for three hundred years,

وَٱزْدَادُوا۟ تِسْعًا ۩    and added nine more [to that number].

قُلِ ٱللَّهُ أَعْلَمُ بِمَا لَبِثُوا۟ 26 *Say,* 'Allah knows best how long they remained.

لَهُۥ غَيْبُ ٱلسَّمَٰوَٰتِ    To Him belongs the Unseen of the heavens

وَٱلْأَرْضِ    and the earth.

أَبْصِرْ بِهِۦ    How well does He see!

وَأَسْمِعْ    How well does He hear!

مَا لَهُم مِّن دُونِهِۦ مِن وَلِىٍّ    They have no guardian besides Him,

وَلَا يُشْرِكُ فِى حُكْمِهِۦٓ أَحَدًا ۩    and none shares with Him in His judgement.

وَٱتْلُ مَآ أُوحِىَ إِلَيْكَ 27 *Recite* what has been revealed to *you*

مِن كِتَابِ رَبِّكَ    from *your* Lord's Book.

لَا مُبَدِّلَ لِكَلِمَٰتِهِۦ    Nothing can change His words,

وَلَن تَجِدَ مِن دُونِهِۦ مُلْتَحَدًا ۩    and *you* will never find any refuge besides Him.

وَٱصْبِرْ نَفْسَكَ مَعَ ٱلَّذِينَ 28 *Content yourself* with the company of those who

يَدْعُونَ رَبَّهُم    supplicate their Lord

بِٱلْغَدَوٰةِ وَٱلْعَشِىِّ    morning and evening,

يُرِيدُونَ وَجْهَهُۥ    desiring His Face,

وَلَا تَعْدُ عَيْنَاكَ عَنْهُمْ    and *do not loose sight* of them,

تُرِيدُ زِينَةَ ٱلْحَيَوٰةِ ٱلدُّنْيَا    desiring the glitter of the life of this world.[1]

وَلَا تُطِعْ    And *Do not obey*

مَنْ أَغْفَلْنَا قَلْبَهُۥ    him whose heart We have made oblivious

عَن ذِكْرِنَا    to Our remembrance,

وَٱتَّبَعَ هَوَىٰهُ    and who follows his own desires,

وَكَانَ أَمْرُهُۥ فُرُطًا ۩    and whose conduct is [mere] profligacy.

وَقُلِ ٱلْحَقُّ مِن رَّبِّكُمْ 29 And *say,* '[This is] the truth from your Lord:

فَمَن شَآءَ فَلْيُؤْمِن    let anyone who wishes believe it,

وَمَن شَآءَ فَلْيَكْفُرْ    and let anyone who wishes disbelieve it.'

---

[1] Cf. 6:52.

إِنَّآ أَعْتَدْنَا لِلظَّٰلِمِينَ نَارًا
Indeed We have prepared for the wrongdoers a Fire

أَحَاطَ بِهِمْ سُرَادِقُهَا
whose curtains will surround them [on all sides].

وَإِن يَسْتَغِيثُوا۟
If they cry out for help,

يُغَاثُوا۟ بِمَآءٍ كَٱلْمُهْلِ
they will be helped with a water like molten copper

يَشْوِى ٱلْوُجُوهَ
which will scald the faces.

بِئْسَ ٱلشَّرَابُ
What an evil drink,

وَسَآءَتْ مُرْتَفَقًا ۝
and how ill a resting place!

إِنَّ ٱلَّذِينَ ءَامَنُوا۟
30 As for those who have faith

وَعَمِلُوا۟ ٱلصَّٰلِحَٰتِ
and do righteous deeds

إِنَّا لَا نُضِيعُ أَجْرَ
—indeed We do not waste the reward

مَنْ أَحْسَنَ عَمَلًا ۝
of those who are good in deeds.

أُو۟لَٰٓئِكَ هُمْ جَنَّٰتُ عَدْنٍ
31 For such there will be the Gardens of Eden

تَجْرِى مِن تَحْتِهِمُ ٱلْأَنْهَٰرُ
with streams running in them.

يُحَلَّوْنَ فِيهَا
They will be adorned therein

مِنْ أَسَاوِرَ مِن ذَهَبٍ
with bracelets of gold

وَيَلْبَسُونَ ثِيَابًا خُضْرًا
and wear green garments

مِّن سُندُسٍ وَإِسْتَبْرَقٍ
of silk and brocade,

مُّتَّكِئِينَ فِيهَا عَلَى ٱلْأَرَآئِكِ
reclining therein on couches.

نِعْمَ ٱلثَّوَابُ
How excellent a reward,

وَحَسُنَتْ مُرْتَفَقًا ۝ ۞
and how good a resting place!

وَٱضْرِبْ لَهُم مَّثَلًا رَّجُلَيْنِ
32 *Draw* for them the parable of two men

جَعَلْنَا لِأَحَدِهِمَا
for each of whom We had made

جَنَّتَيْنِ مِنْ أَعْنَٰبٍ
two gardens of vines,

وَحَفَفْنَٰهُمَا بِنَخْلٍ
and We had surrounded them with date palms,

وَجَعَلْنَا بَيْنَهُمَا زَرْعًا ۝
and placed crops between them.

كِلْتَا ٱلْجَنَّتَيْنِ ءَاتَتْ أُكُلَهَا
33 Both gardens yielded their produce

وَلَمْ تَظْلِم مِّنْهُ شَيْئًا
without stinting anything of it.

وَفَجَّرْنَا خِلَٰلَهُمَا نَهَرًا ۝
And We had set a stream gushing through them.

وَكَانَ لَهُۥ ثَمَرٌ
34 He had abundant fruits,

| | |
|---|---|
| فَقَالَ لِصَـٰحِبِهِۦ | so he said to his companion, |
| وَهُوَ يُحَاوِرُهُۥٓ | as he conversed with him: |
| أَنَا۠ أَكْثَرُ مِنكَ مَالًا | 'I have more wealth than you, |
| وَأَعَزُّ نَفَرًا ۝ | and am stronger with respect to numbers.'[1] |
| وَدَخَلَ جَنَّتَهُۥ | 35 He entered his garden |
| وَهُوَ ظَالِمٌ لِّنَفْسِهِۦ | while he wronged himself. |
| قَالَ | He said, |
| مَآ أَظُنُّ أَن تَبِيدَ هَـٰذِهِۦٓ أَبَدًا ۝ | 'I do not think that this will ever perish, |
| وَمَآ أَظُنُّ ٱلسَّاعَةَ قَآئِمَةً | 36 and I do not think that the Hour will ever set in. |
| وَلَئِن رُّدِدتُّ إِلَىٰ رَبِّى | And even if I am returned to my Lord |
| لَأَجِدَنَّ خَيْرًا مِّنْهَا مُنقَلَبًا ۝ | I will surely find a resort better than this.' |
| قَالَ لَهُۥ صَاحِبُهُۥ | 37 His companion said to him, |
| وَهُوَ يُحَاوِرُهُۥٓ | as he conversed with him: |
| أَكَفَرْتَ بِٱلَّذِى خَلَقَكَ | 'Do you disbelieve in Him who created you |
| مِن تُرَابٍ | from dust, |
| ثُمَّ مِن نُّطْفَةٍ | then from a drop of [seminal] fluid, |
| ثُمَّ سَوَّىٰكَ رَجُلًا ۝ | then fashioned you as a man? |
| لَّـٰكِنَّا۠ هُوَ ٱللَّهُ رَبِّى | 38 But I [say], "He is Allah, my Lord," |
| وَلَآ أُشْرِكُ بِرَبِّىٓ أَحَدًا ۝ | and I do not ascribe any partner to my Lord. |
| وَلَوْلَآ إِذْ دَخَلْتَ جَنَّتَكَ قُلْتَ | 39 Why did you not say, when you entered your garden, |
| مَا شَآءَ ٱللَّهُ | "[This is] as Allah has wished! |
| لَا قُوَّةَ إِلَّا بِٱللَّهِ | There is no power except by Allah!" |
| إِن تَرَنِ أَنَا۠ أَقَلَّ مِنكَ مَالًا | If you see that I have lesser wealth than you |
| وَوَلَدًا ۝ | and children, |
| فَعَسَىٰ رَبِّىٓ أَن يُؤْتِيَنِ | 40 maybe my Lord will give me |
| خَيْرًا مِّن جَنَّتِكَ | [something] better than your garden, |
| وَيُرْسِلَ عَلَيْهَا حُسْبَانًا | and He will unleash upon it bolts |
| مِّنَ ٱلسَّمَآءِ | from the sky, |

---

[1] That is, in respect to the number of servants and attendants and the size of family and clan.

فَتُصْبِحَ صَعِيدًا زَلَقًا ۝　　　so that it becomes a bare plain.

٤١ أَوْ يُصْبِحَ مَاؤُهَا غَوْرًا　　Or its water will sink down,

فَلَن تَسْتَطِيعَ لَهُ طَلَبًا ۝　　so that you cannot obtain it.'

وَأُحِيطَ بِثَمَرِهِ ٤٢　And ruin closed in on his produce,

فَأَصْبَحَ يُقَلِّبُ كَفَّيْهِ　　and he began to wring his hands

عَلَىٰ مَا أَنفَقَ فِيهَا　　for what he had spent on it,

وَهِىَ خَاوِيَةٌ عَلَىٰ عُرُوشِهَا　　as it lay fallen on its trellises.

وَيَقُولُ　　He was saying,

يَٰلَيْتَنِى لَمْ أُشْرِكْ بِرَبِّى أَحَدًا ۝　'I wish I had not ascribed any partner to my Lord.'

وَلَمْ تَكُن لَّهُ فِئَةٌ يَنصُرُونَهُ ٤٣　He had no party to help him,

مِن دُونِ ٱللَّهِ　　besides Allah,

وَمَا كَانَ مُنتَصِرًا ۝　　nor could he help himself.

هُنَالِكَ ٱلْوَلَٰيَةُ لِلَّهِ ٤٤　There all guardianship belongs to Allah,

ٱلْحَقِّ　　the Real.

هُوَ خَيْرٌ ثَوَابًا　　He is best in rewarding,

وَخَيْرٌ عُقْبًا ۝　　and best in requiting.

وَٱضْرِبْ لَهُم ٤٥　*Draw* for them

مَّثَلَ ٱلْحَيَوٰةِ ٱلدُّنْيَا　　the parable of the life of this world:

كَمَاءٍ أَنزَلْنَٰهُ مِنَ ٱلسَّمَاءِ　　[It is] like the water We send down from the sky.

فَٱخْتَلَطَ بِهِۦ نَبَاتُ ٱلْأَرْضِ　　Then the earth's vegetation mingles with it.

فَأَصْبَحَ هَشِيمًا تَذْرُوهُ ٱلرِّيَٰحُ　　Then it becomes chaff, scattered by the wind.

وَكَانَ ٱللَّهُ عَلَىٰ كُلِّ شَىْءٍ مُّقْتَدِرًا ۝　And Allah is omnipotent over all things.

ٱلْمَالُ وَٱلْبَنُونَ ٤٦　Wealth and children

زِينَةُ ٱلْحَيَوٰةِ ٱلدُّنْيَا　　are an adornment of the life of the world,

وَٱلْبَٰقِيَٰتُ ٱلصَّٰلِحَٰتُ　　but lasting righteous deeds

خَيْرٌ عِندَ رَبِّكَ ثَوَابًا　　are better with *your* Lord in reward

وَخَيْرٌ أَمَلًا ۝　　and better in hope.

وَيَوْمَ نُسَيِّرُ ٱلْجِبَالَ ٤٧　The day We shall set the mountains moving

وَتَرَى ٱلْأَرْضَ بَارِزَةً　　and *you* will see the earth in full view,

وَحَشَرْنَٰهُمْ

We shall muster them,

فَلَمْ نُغَادِرْ مِنْهُمْ أَحَدًا ۝

and We will not leave out anyone of them.

وَعُرِضُواْ عَلَىٰ رَبِّكَ صَفًّا

48 They will be presented before *your* Lord in ranks:

لَّقَدْ جِئْتُمُونَا

'Certainly you have come to Us

كَمَا خَلَقْنَٰكُمْ أَوَّلَ مَرَّةٍ

just as We created you the first time.

بَلْ زَعَمْتُمْ

Rather you maintained

أَلَّن نَّجْعَلَ لَكُم مَّوْعِدًا ۝

that We had not appointed a tryst for you.'

وَوُضِعَ ٱلْكِتَٰبُ

49 The Book will be set up.

فَتَرَى ٱلْمُجْرِمِينَ

Then *you* will see the guilty

مُشْفِقِينَ مِمَّا فِيهِ

apprehensive of what is in it.

وَيَقُولُونَ يَٰوَيْلَتَنَا

They will say, 'Woe to us!

مَالِ هَٰذَا ٱلْكِتَٰبِ

What a book is this!

لَا يُغَادِرُ صَغِيرَةً وَلَا كَبِيرَةً

It omits nothing, big or small,

إِلَّآ أَحْصَىٰهَا

without enumerating it.'

وَوَجَدُواْ مَا عَمِلُواْ حَاضِرًا

They will find present whatever they had done,

وَلَا يَظْلِمُ رَبُّكَ أَحَدًا ۝

and your Lord does not wrong anyone.

وَإِذْ قُلْنَا لِلْمَلَٰٓئِكَةِ

50 When We said to the angels,

ٱسْجُدُواْ لِءَادَمَ

'Prostrate before Adam,'

فَسَجَدُوٓاْ إِلَّآ إِبْلِيسَ

they prostrated, except Iblis.

كَانَ مِنَ ٱلْجِنِّ

He was one of the jinn,

فَفَسَقَ عَنْ أَمْرِ رَبِّهِۦٓ

so he transgressed against his Lord's command.

أَفَتَتَّخِذُونَهُۥ وَذُرِّيَّتَهُۥٓ أَوْلِيَآءَ

Will you then take him and his offspring for guardians

مِن دُونِى

in My stead,

وَهُمْ لَكُمْ عَدُوٌّ

though they are your enemies?

بِئْسَ لِلظَّٰلِمِينَ بَدَلًا ۝

How evil a substitute for the wrongdoers!

مَّآ أَشْهَدتُّهُمْ خَلْقَ

51 I did not make them a witness to the creation

ٱلسَّمَٰوَٰتِ وَٱلْأَرْضِ

of the heavens and the earth,

وَلَا خَلْقَ أَنفُسِهِمْ

nor to their own creation,

وَمَا كُنتُ مُتَّخِذَ ٱلْمُضِلِّينَ عَضُدًا ۝

nor do I take those who mislead as assistants.

414

وَيَوْمَ يَقُولُ 52 The day He will say,

نَادُواْ شُرَكَآءِىَ ٱلَّذِينَ زَعَمْتُمْ   'Call those whom you maintained to be My partners,'

فَدَعَوْهُمْ    they will call them,

فَلَمْ يَسْتَجِيبُواْ لَهُمْ    but they will not respond to them,

وَجَعَلْنَا بَيْنَهُم مَّوْبِقًا ۝    for We shall place an abyss between them.

وَرَءَا ٱلْمُجْرِمُونَ ٱلنَّارَ   53 The guilty will sight the Fire

فَظَنُّوٓاْ أَنَّهُم مُّوَاقِعُوهَا    and know that they will fall into it,

وَلَمْ يَجِدُواْ عَنْهَا مَصْرِفًا ۝    for they will find no means to circumvent it.

وَلَقَدْ صَرَّفْنَا فِى هَٰذَا ٱلْقُرْءَانِ   54 Certainly We have made this Qur'ān interspersed

لِلنَّاسِ مِن كُلِّ مَثَلٍ    with every kind of parable for mankind.

وَكَانَ ٱلْإِنسَٰنُ أَكْثَرَ شَىْءٍ جَدَلًا ۝    But man is the most disputatious of creatures.

وَمَا مَنَعَ ٱلنَّاسَ أَن يُؤْمِنُوٓاْ   55 People do not refuse to have faith

إِذْ جَآءَهُمُ ٱلْهُدَىٰ    when guidance comes to them

وَيَسْتَغْفِرُواْ رَبَّهُمْ    and to plead to their Lord for forgiveness,

إِلَّآ أَن تَأْتِيَهُمْ    without being overtaken

سُنَّةُ ٱلْأَوَّلِينَ    by the precedent of the ancients,

أَوْ يَأْتِيَهُمُ ٱلْعَذَابُ قُبُلًا ۝    or confronting the punishment.[1]

وَمَا نُرْسِلُ ٱلْمُرْسَلِينَ   56 We do not send the apostles

إِلَّا مُبَشِّرِينَ وَمُنذِرِينَ    except as bearers of good news and as warners,

وَيُجَٰدِلُ ٱلَّذِينَ كَفَرُواْ    but those who are faithless dispute

بِٱلْبَٰطِلِ    fallaciously

لِيُدْحِضُواْ بِهِ ٱلْحَقَّ    to refute thereby the truth,

وَٱتَّخَذُوٓاْ ءَايَٰتِى    having taken My signs

وَمَآ أُنذِرُواْ    and what they are warned of

هُزُوًا ۝    in derision.

وَمَنْ أَظْلَمُ   57 Who is a greater wrongdoer

مِمَّن ذُكِّرَ    than he who is reminded

بِـَٔايَٰتِ رَبِّهِۦ    of the signs of his Lord,

فَأَعْرَضَ عَنْهَا    whereat he disregards them

---

[1] Or, 'being overtaken by diverse punishments.'

| | |
|---|---|
| وَنَسِىَ مَا قَدَّمَتْ يَدَاهُ | and forgets what his hands have sent ahead? |
| إِنَّا جَعَلْنَا عَلَىٰ قُلُوبِهِمْ أَكِنَّةً | Indeed We have cast veils on their hearts |
| أَن يَفْقَهُوهُ | lest they should understand it, |
| وَفِىٓ ءَاذَانِهِمْ وَقْرًا | and a deafness into their ears; |
| وَإِن تَدْعُهُمْ إِلَى ٱلْهُدَىٰ | and if *you* invite them to guidance |
| فَلَن يَهْتَدُوٓا۟ إِذًا أَبَدًا | they will never [let themselves] be guided. |
| وَرَبُّكَ ٱلْغَفُورُ ذُو ٱلرَّحْمَةِ | 58 *Your* Lord is the All-forgiving dispenser of mercy. |
| لَوْ يُؤَاخِذُهُم | Were He to take them to task |
| بِمَا كَسَبُوا۟ | because of what they have committed, |
| لَعَجَّلَ لَهُمُ ٱلْعَذَابَ | He would have surely hastened their punishment. |
| بَل لَّهُم مَّوْعِدٌ | But they have a tryst, |
| لَّن يَجِدُوا۟ مِن دُونِهِۦ مَوْئِلًا | [when] they will not find a refuge besides Him.[1] |
| وَتِلْكَ ٱلْقُرَىٰٓ أَهْلَكْنَٰهُمْ | 59 Those are the towns that We destroyed |
| لَمَّا ظَلَمُوا۟ | when they were wrongdoers, |
| وَجَعَلْنَا لِمَهْلِكِهِم مَّوْعِدًا | and We appointed a tryst for their destruction. |
| وَإِذْ قَالَ مُوسَىٰ لِفَتَىٰهُ | 60 When Moses said to his lad, |
| لَآ أَبْرَحُ | 'I will go on [journeying] |
| حَتَّىٰٓ أَبْلُغَ مَجْمَعَ ٱلْبَحْرَيْنِ | until I have reached the confluence of the two seas, |
| أَوْ أَمْضِىَ حُقُبًا | or have spent a long time [travelling].' |
| فَلَمَّا بَلَغَا مَجْمَعَ بَيْنِهِمَا | 61 So when they reached the confluence between them, |
| نَسِيَا حُوتَهُمَا | they forgot their fish, |
| فَٱتَّخَذَ سَبِيلَهُۥ فِى ٱلْبَحْرِ سَرَبًا | which found its way into the sea, sneaking away. |
| فَلَمَّا جَاوَزَا | 62 So when they had passed on, |
| قَالَ لِفَتَىٰهُ | he said to his lad, |
| ءَاتِنَا غَدَآءَنَا | 'Bring us our meal. |
| لَقَدْ لَقِينَا | We have certainly encountered |
| مِن سَفَرِنَا هَٰذَا نَصَبًا | much fatigue on this journey of ours.' |
| قَالَ أَرَءَيْتَ | 63 He said, 'Did you see?! |

---

[1] Or 'from which they will not find any refuge.'

إِذْ أَوَيْنَآ إِلَى ٱلصَّخْرَةِ    When we took shelter at the rock,

فَإِنِّى نَسِيتُ ٱلْحُوتَ    indeed I forgot about the fish

وَمَآ أَنسَىٰنِيهُ إِلَّا ٱلشَّيْطَٰنُ    —and none but Satan made me forget

أَنْ أَذْكُرَهُ    to mention it!—

وَٱتَّخَذَ سَبِيلَهُ فِى ٱلْبَحْرِ عَجَبًا ۝    and it made its way into the sea in an amazing manner!'

قَالَ ذَٰلِكَ مَا كُنَّا نَبْغِ   64 He said, 'That is what we were after!'

فَٱرْتَدَّا عَلَىٰٓ ءَاثَارِهِمَا قَصَصًا ۝    So they returned, retracing their footsteps.

فَوَجَدَا عَبْدًا مِّنْ عِبَادِنَآ   65 [There] they found one of Our servants

ءَاتَيْنَٰهُ رَحْمَةً مِّنْ عِندِنَا    whom We had granted a mercy from Ourselves,

وَعَلَّمْنَٰهُ مِن لَّدُنَّا عِلْمًا ۝    and taught him a knowledge from Our own.

قَالَ لَهُ مُوسَىٰ هَلْ أَتَّبِعُكَ   66 Moses said to him, 'May I follow you

عَلَىٰٓ أَن تُعَلِّمَنِ    for the purpose that you teach me

مِمَّا عُلِّمْتَ رُشْدًا ۝    some of the probity you have been taught?'

قَالَ   67 He said,

إِنَّكَ لَن تَسْتَطِيعَ مَعِىَ صَبْرًا ۝    'Indeed you cannot have patience with me!

وَكَيْفَ تَصْبِرُ   68 And how can you have patience

عَلَىٰ مَا لَمْ تُحِطْ بِهِۦ خُبْرًا ۝    about something you are not in the know of?'

قَالَ سَتَجِدُنِىٓ   69 He said, 'You will find me,

إِن شَآءَ ٱللَّهُ صَابِرًا    God willing, to be patient,

وَلَآ أَعْصِى لَكَ أَمْرًا ۝    and I will not disobey you in any matter.'

قَالَ فَإِنِ ٱتَّبَعْتَنِى   70 He said, 'If you follow me,

فَلَا تَسْـَٔلْنِى عَن شَىْءٍ    do not question me concerning anything

حَتَّىٰٓ أُحْدِثَ لَكَ مِنْهُ ذِكْرًا ۝    until I [myself] make a mention of it to you.'

فَٱنطَلَقَا   71 So they went on.

حَتَّىٰٓ إِذَا رَكِبَا فِى ٱلسَّفِينَةِ    When they boarded the boat,

خَرَقَهَا    he made a hole in it.

قَالَ أَخَرَقْتَهَا    He said, 'Did you make a hole in it

لِتُغْرِقَ أَهْلَهَا    to drown its people?

لَقَدْ جِئْتَ شَيْـًٔا إِمْرًا ۝    You have certainly done a monstrous thing!'

قَالَ أَلَمْ أَقُلْ   72 He said, 'Did I not say,

إِنَّكَ لَن تَسْتَطِيعَ مَعِيَ صَبْرًا ۞    indeed you cannot have patience with me?'

قَالَ لَا تُؤَاخِذْنِي بِمَا نَسِيتُ   73 He said, 'Do not take me to task for my forgetting,

وَلَا تُرْهِقْنِي مِنْ أَمْرِي عُسْرًا ۞    and do not be hard upon me.'

فَٱنطَلَقَا   74 So they went on.

حَتَّىٰ إِذَا لَقِيَا غُلَٰمًا فَقَتَلَهُۥ    When they encountered a boy, he slew him.

قَالَ أَقَتَلْتَ نَفْسًا زَكِيَّةً    He said, 'Did you slay an innocent soul,

بِغَيْرِ نَفْسٍ    without [his having slain] anyone?

لَّقَدْ جِئْتَ شَيْئًا نُّكْرًا ۞ ۞    You have certainly done a dire thing!'

[PART 16]

قَالَ أَلَمْ أَقُل لَّكَ   75 He said, 'Did I not tell you,

إِنَّكَ لَن تَسْتَطِيعَ مَعِيَ صَبْرًا ۞    indeed you cannot have patience with me?'

قَالَ إِن سَأَلْتُكَ عَن شَيْءٍ بَعْدَهَا   76 He said, 'If I question you about anything after this,

فَلَا تُصَٰحِبْنِي    do not keep me in your company.

قَدْ بَلَغْتَ مِن لَّدُنِّي عُذْرًا ۞    You have already got sufficient excuse on my part.'

فَٱنطَلَقَا   77 So they went on.

حَتَّىٰ إِذَآ أَتَيَآ أَهْلَ قَرْيَةٍ    When they came to the people of a town,

ٱسْتَطْعَمَآ أَهْلَهَا    they asked its people for food,

فَأَبَوْا أَن يُضَيِّفُوهُمَا    but they refused to extend them any hospitality.

فَوَجَدَا فِيهَا جِدَارًا    There they found a wall

يُرِيدُ أَن يَنقَضَّ    which was about to collapse,

فَأَقَامَهُۥ    so he erected it.

قَالَ لَوْ شِئْتَ    He said, 'Had you wished,

لَتَّخَذْتَ عَلَيْهِ أَجْرًا ۞    you could have taken a wage for it.'

قَالَ هَٰذَا فِرَاقُ بَيْنِي وَبَيْنِكَ   78 He said, 'This is where you and I shall part.

سَأُنَبِّئُكَ بِتَأْوِيلِ    I will inform you about the interpretation

مَا لَمْ تَسْتَطِع عَّلَيْهِ صَبْرًا ۞    of that over which you could not maintain patience.

أَمَّا ٱلسَّفِينَةُ فَكَانَتْ لِمَسَٰكِينَ   79 As for the boat, it belonged to some poor people

يَعْمَلُونَ فِي ٱلْبَحْرِ    who work on the sea.

فَأَرَدتُّ أَنْ أَعِيبَهَا    I wanted to make it defective,

وَكَانَ وَرَآءَهُم مَّلِكٌ    for behind them was a king

يَأْخُذُ كُلَّ سَفِينَةٍ غَصْبًا ۝

seizing every ship usurpingly.

وَأَمَّا ٱلْغُلَـٰمُ 80 As for the boy,

فَكَانَ أَبَوَاهُ مُؤْمِنَيْنِ

his parents were faithful [persons],

فَخَشِينَآ أَن يُرْهِقَهُمَا

and We feared he would overwhelm them

طُغْيَـٰنًا وَكُفْرًا ۝

with rebellion and unfaith.

فَأَرَدْنَآ 81 So We desired

أَن يُبْدِلَهُمَا رَبُّهُمَا

that their Lord should give them in exchange

خَيْرًا مِّنْهُ زَكَوٰةً

one better than him in respect of purity

وَأَقْرَبَ رُحْمًا ۝

and closer in mercy.

وَأَمَّا ٱلْجِدَارُ 82 As for the wall,

فَكَانَ لِغُلَـٰمَيْنِ يَتِيمَيْنِ

it belonged to two boy orphans

فِى ٱلْمَدِينَةِ

in the city.

وَكَانَ تَحْتَهُ كَنزٌ لَّهُمَا

Under it there was a treasure belonging to them.

وَكَانَ أَبُوهُمَا صَـٰلِحًا

Their father had been a righteous man.

فَأَرَادَ رَبُّكَ أَن يَبْلُغَآ أَشُدَّهُمَا

So your Lord desired that they should come of age

وَيَسْتَخْرِجَا كَنزَهُمَا

and take out their treasure

رَحْمَةً مِّن رَّبِّكَ

—as a mercy from your Lord.

وَمَا فَعَلْتُهُ عَنْ أَمْرِى

I did not do that out of my own accord.

ذَٰلِكَ تَأْوِيلُ

This is the interpretation

مَا لَمْ تَسْطِع عَّلَيْهِ صَبْرًا ۝

of that over which you could not maintain patience.'

وَيَسْـَٔلُونَكَ عَن ذِى ٱلْقَرْنَيْنِ 83 They question *you* concerning Dhul Qarnayn.

قُلْ سَأَتْلُوا۟ عَلَيْكُم مِّنْهُ ذِكْرًا ۝

*Say*, 'I will relate to you an account of him.'

إِنَّا مَكَّنَّا لَهُ فِى ٱلْأَرْضِ 84 Indeed We had granted him power in the land

وَءَاتَيْنَـٰهُ مِن كُلِّ شَىْءٍ سَبَبًا ۝

and given him the means to all things.

فَأَتْبَعَ سَبَبًا ۝ 85 So he followed a means.

حَتَّىٰٓ إِذَا بَلَغَ مَغْرِبَ ٱلشَّمْسِ 86 When he reached the place where the sun sets,

وَجَدَهَا تَغْرُبُ فِى عَيْنٍ حَمِئَةٍ

he found it setting in a muddy spring,

وَوَجَدَ عِندَهَا قَوْمًا

and by it he found a people.

قُلْنَا يَـٰذَا ٱلْقَرْنَيْنِ

We said, 'O Dhul Qarnayn!

إِمَّا أَن تُعَذِّبَ

You may either punish them,

وَإِمَّا أَن تَتَّخِذَ فِيهِمْ حُسْنًا ۝

or treat them with kindness.'

قَالَ أَمَّا مَن ظَلَمَ 87 He said, 'As for him who is a wrongdoer,

فَسَوْفَ نُعَذِّبُهُ

we will punish him.

ثُمَّ يُرَدُّ إِلَىٰ رَبِّهِ

Then he shall be returned to his Lord

فَيُعَذِّبُهُ عَذَابًا نُّكْرًا ۝

and He will punish him with a dire punishment.

وَأَمَّا مَنْ ءَامَنَ وَعَمِلَ صَٰلِحًا 88 But as for him who has faith and acts righteously,

فَلَهُۥ جَزَآءً ٱلْحُسْنَىٰ

he shall have the best reward,

وَسَنَقُولُ لَهُۥ مِنْ أَمْرِنَا يُسْرًا ۝

and we will speak to him gently of our command.'

ثُمَّ أَتْبَعَ سَبَبًا ۝ 89 Then he followed a means.

حَتَّىٰ إِذَا بَلَغَ مَطْلِعَ ٱلشَّمْسِ 90 When he reached the place where the sun rises,

وَجَدَهَا تَطْلُعُ عَلَىٰ قَوْمٍ

he found it rising on a people

لَّمْ نَجْعَل لَّهُم مِّن دُونِهَا سِتْرًا ۝

for whom We had not provided any shield against it.

كَذَٰلِكَ 91 So it was,

وَقَدْ أَحَطْنَا بِمَا لَدَيْهِ خُبْرًا ۝

and We comprehended whatever pertained to him.

ثُمَّ أَتْبَعَ سَبَبًا ۝ 92 Then he followed a means.

حَتَّىٰ إِذَا بَلَغَ بَيْنَ ٱلسَّدَّيْنِ 93 When he reached [the place] between the two barriers,

وَجَدَ مِن دُونِهِمَا قَوْمًا

he found between them a people

لَّا يَكَادُونَ يَفْقَهُونَ قَوْلًا ۝

who could hardly understand a word.

قَالُوا يَٰذَا ٱلْقَرْنَيْنِ 94 They said, 'O Dhul Qarnayn!

إِنَّ يَأْجُوجَ وَمَأْجُوجَ

Indeed Gog and Magog

مُفْسِدُونَ فِى ٱلْأَرْضِ

are causing corruption in the land.

فَهَلْ نَجْعَلُ لَكَ خَرْجًا

Shall we pay you a tribute

عَلَىٰ أَن تَجْعَلَ

on condition that you build

بَيْنَنَا وَبَيْنَهُمْ سَدًّا ۝

a barrier between them and us?'

قَالَ 95 He said,

مَا مَكَّنِّى فِيهِ رَبِّى خَيْرٌ

'What my Lord has furnished me is better.

فَأَعِينُونِى بِقُوَّةٍ

Yet help me with some power,

أَجْعَلْ بَيْنَكُمْ وَبَيْنَهُمْ رَدْمًا ۝

and I will make a bulwark between you and them.

ءَاتُونِى زُبَرَ ٱلْحَدِيدِ 96 Bring me pieces of iron!'

حَتَّىٰ إِذَا سَاوَىٰ بَيْنَ ٱلصَّدَفَيْنِ

When he had levelled up between the flanks,

قَالَ ٱنفُخُوا ۖ

he said, 'Blow!'

حَتَّىٰ إِذَا جَعَلَهُۥ نَارًا

When he had turned it into fire,

قَالَ ءَاتُونِىٓ أُفْرِغْ عَلَيْهِ قِطْرًا ۞

he said, 'Bring me molten copper to pour over it.'

فَمَا ٱسْطَٰعُوٓا۟ أَن يَظْهَرُوهُ

97 So they could neither scale it,

وَمَا ٱسْتَطَٰعُوا۟ لَهُۥ نَقْبًا ۞

nor could they make a hole in it.

قَالَ هَٰذَا رَحْمَةٌ مِّن رَّبِّى ۖ

98 He said, 'This is a mercy from my Lord.

فَإِذَا جَآءَ وَعْدُ رَبِّى

But when the promise of my Lord is fulfilled,

جَعَلَهُۥ دَكَّآءَ ۖ

He will level it;[1]

وَكَانَ وَعْدُ رَبِّى حَقًّا ۞ ✱

and my Lord's promise is true.'

وَتَرَكْنَا بَعْضَهُمْ يَوْمَئِذٍ

99 That day We shall let them

يَمُوجُ فِى بَعْضٍ ۖ

surge over one another,

وَنُفِخَ فِى ٱلصُّورِ

and the Trumpet will be blown,

فَجَمَعْنَٰهُمْ جَمْعًا ۞

and We shall gather them all,

وَعَرَضْنَا جَهَنَّمَ يَوْمَئِذٍ

100 and that day We shall bring hell into view

لِّلْكَٰفِرِينَ عَرْضًا ۞

visibly for the faithless.

ٱلَّذِينَ كَانَتْ أَعْيُنُهُمْ فِى غِطَآءٍ

101 —Those whose eyes were blindfolded

عَن ذِكْرِى

to My remembrance

وَكَانُوا۟ لَا يَسْتَطِيعُونَ سَمْعًا ۞

and who could not hear.

أَفَحَسِبَ ٱلَّذِينَ كَفَرُوٓا۟

102 Do the faithless suppose

أَن يَتَّخِذُوا۟ عِبَادِى

that they have taken My servants

مِن دُونِىٓ أَوْلِيَآءَ ۚ

for guardians in My stead?

إِنَّآ أَعْتَدْنَا جَهَنَّمَ

Indeed We have prepared hell

لِلْكَٰفِرِينَ نُزُلًا ۞

for the hospitality of the faithless.

قُلْ هَلْ نُنَبِّئُكُم بِٱلْأَخْسَرِينَ

103 Say, 'Shall we inform you about the biggest losers

أَعْمَٰلًا ۞

in regard to works?

ٱلَّذِينَ ضَلَّ سَعْيُهُمْ

104 Those whose endeavour goes awry

فِى ٱلْحَيَوٰةِ ٱلدُّنْيَا

in the life of the world,

وَهُمْ يَحْسَبُونَ

while they suppose

---

[1] Or, 'He will make it crumble.'

أَهُمْ يُحْسِنُونَ صُنْعًا ۝    they are doing good.'

أُوْلَٰٓئِكَ ٱلَّذِينَ كَفَرُواْ    105 They are the ones who deny

بِـَٔايَٰتِ رَبِّهِمْ    the signs of their Lord

وَلِقَآئِهِۦ    and the encounter with Him

فَحَبِطَتْ أَعْمَٰلُهُمْ    So their works have failed.

فَلَا نُقِيمُ لَهُمْ يَوْمَ ٱلْقِيَٰمَةِ    On the Day of Resurrection We will not set for them

وَزْنًا ۝    any weight.

ذَٰلِكَ جَزَآؤُهُمْ جَهَنَّمُ    106 That is their requital—hell—

بِمَا كَفَرُواْ    because of their faithlessness

وَٱتَّخَذُوٓاْ ءَايَٰتِى وَرُسُلِى هُزُوًا ۝    and taking My signs and My apostles in derision.

إِنَّ ٱلَّذِينَ ءَامَنُواْ    107 As for those who have faith

وَعَمِلُواْ ٱلصَّٰلِحَٰتِ    and do righteous deeds

كَانَتْ لَهُمْ جَنَّٰتُ ٱلْفِرْدَوْسِ    they shall have the gardens of Firdaws[1]

نُزُلًا ۝    for abode,[2]

خَٰلِدِينَ فِيهَا    108 to remain [forever] in them,

لَا يَبْغُونَ عَنْهَا حِوَلًا ۝    from where they will not seek to shift.

قُل لَّوْ كَانَ ٱلْبَحْرُ مِدَادًا لِّكَلِمَٰتِ رَبِّى    109 *Say,* 'If the sea were ink for the words of my Lord,

لَنَفِدَ ٱلْبَحْرُ    the sea would be spent

قَبْلَ أَن تَنفَدَ كَلِمَٰتُ رَبِّى    before the words of my Lord are spent,

وَلَوْ جِئْنَا بِمِثْلِهِۦ مَدَدًا ۝    though We brought another like it for replenishment.

قُلْ إِنَّمَآ أَنَا۠ بَشَرٌ مِّثْلُكُمْ    110 *Say,* 'I am just a human being like you.

يُوحَىٰٓ إِلَىَّ    It has been revealed to me

أَنَّمَآ إِلَٰهُكُمْ إِلَٰهٌ وَٰحِدٌ    that your God is the One God.

فَمَن كَانَ يَرْجُواْ لِقَآءَ رَبِّهِۦ    So whoever expects to encounter his Lord

فَلْيَعْمَلْ عَمَلًا صَٰلِحًا    —let him act righteously,

وَلَا يُشْرِكْ    and not associate

بِعِبَادَةِ رَبِّهِۦٓ أَحَدًا ۝    anyone with the worship of his Lord.'

---

[1] Said to be the highest and choicest part of paradise. See Ṭabarī, Baḥrānī and Qummī.

[2] Or 'hospitality.'

# 19. SŪRAT MARYAM[1]

In the Name of Allah,
the All-beneficent, the All-merciful.

1 *Kāf, Hā, Yā, 'Ayn, Ṣād.*

2 [This is] an account[2] of *your* Lord's mercy
on His servant, Zechariah,

3 when he called out to his Lord with a secret cry.

4 He said, 'My Lord!
Indeed my bones have become feeble,
and my head has turned white with age,
yet never have I,
my Lord, been disappointed in supplicating You!

5 Indeed I fear my kinsmen,
after me,
and my wife is barren.
So grant me from Yourself an heir

6 who may inherit from me
and inherit from the House of Jacob,
and make him, my Lord, pleasing [to You]!'

7 'O Zechariah!
Indeed We give you the good news of a son,
whose name is "John."
Never before have We made anyone his namesake.'

8 He said, 'My Lord!
How shall I have a son,

---

[1] The *sūrah* takes its name from the story of Mary ( 'a) told in verses 16-34.
[2] Or 'a mention,' 'a reminder,' or 'a recollection.'

وَكَانَتِ ٱمْرَأَتِى عَاقِرًا

when my wife is barren,

وَقَدْ بَلَغْتُ مِنَ ٱلْكِبَرِ عِتِيًّا ۞

and I am already advanced in age?'

قَالَ كَذَلِكَ 9

9 He said, 'So shall it be.

قَالَ رَبُّكَ هُوَ عَلَىَّ هَيِّنٌ

Your Lord has said, "It is simple for Me."

وَقَدْ خَلَقْتُكَ مِن قَبْلُ

Certainly I created you before

وَلَمْ تَكُ شَيْئًا ۞

when you were nothing.'

قَالَ رَبِّ 10

10 He said, 'My Lord!

ٱجْعَل لِّىٓ ءَايَةً

Appoint a sign for me.'

قَالَ ءَايَتُكَ

He said, 'Your sign is that

أَلَّا تُكَلِّمَ ٱلنَّاسَ

you will not speak to the people

ثَلَثَ لَيَالٍ سَوِيًّا ۞

for three complete nights.'

فَخَرَجَ عَلَىٰ قَوْمِهِ 11

11 So he emerged before his people

مِنَ ٱلْمِحْرَابِ

from the Temple,

فَأَوْحَىٰٓ إِلَيْهِمْ

and signaled to them

أَن سَبِّحُواْ

that they should glorify [Allah]

بُكْرَةً وَعَشِيًّا ۞

morning and evening.

يَٰيَحْيَىٰ 12

12 'O John!' [We said,]

خُذِ ٱلْكِتَبَ بِقُوَّةٍ

'Hold on with power to the Book!'

وَءَاتَيْنَهُ ٱلْحُكْمَ صَبِيًّا ۞

And We gave him judgement while still a child,

وَحَنَانًا مِّن لَّدُنَّا وَزَكَوٰةً 13

13 and a compassion and purity from Us.

وَكَانَ تَقِيًّا ۞

He was Godwary,

وَبَرًّۢا بِوَٰلِدَيْهِ 14

14 and good to his parents,

وَلَمْ يَكُن جَبَّارًا عَصِيًّا ۞

and was not self-willed or disobedient.

وَسَلَٰمٌ عَلَيْهِ 15

15 Peace be to him,

يَوْمَ وُلِدَ

the day he was born,

وَيَوْمَ يَمُوتُ

and the day he dies,

وَيَوْمَ يُبْعَثُ حَيًّا ۞

and the day he is raised alive!

وَٱذْكُرْ فِى ٱلْكِتَبِ مَرْيَمَ 16

16 And *mention* in the Book Mary,

إِذِ ٱنتَبَذَتْ مِنْ أَهْلِهَا

when she withdrew from her family

مَكَانًا شَرْقِيًّا ۝     to an easterly place.

فَٱتَّخَذَتْ مِن دُونِهِمْ حِجَابًا    17 Thus did she seclude herself from them,

فَأَرْسَلْنَآ إِلَيْهَا رُوحَنَا     whereupon We sent to her Our Spirit[1]

فَتَمَثَّلَ لَهَا     and he became incarnate for her

بَشَرًا سَوِيًّا ۝     as a well-proportioned human.

قَالَتْ إِنِّىٓ أَعُوذُ بِٱلرَّحْمَٰنِ    18 She said, 'I seek the protection of the All-beneficent

مِنكَ     from you,

إِن كُنتَ تَقِيًّا ۝     should you be Godwary!'

قَالَ إِنَّمَآ أَنَا۠ رَسُولُ رَبِّكِ    19 He said, 'I am only a messenger of your Lord

لِأَهَبَ لَكِ غُلَٰمًا زَكِيًّا ۝     that I may give you a pure son.'

قَالَتْ أَنَّىٰ يَكُونُ لِى غُلَٰمٌ    20 She said, 'How shall I have a child

وَلَمْ يَمْسَسْنِى بَشَرٌ     seeing that no human being has ever touched me,

وَلَمْ أَكُ بَغِيًّا ۝     nor have I been unchaste?'

قَالَ كَذَٰلِكِ    21 He said, 'So shall it be.

قَالَ رَبُّكِ هُوَ عَلَىَّ هَيِّنٌ     Your Lord says, "It is simple for Me."

وَلِنَجْعَلَهُۥٓ ءَايَةً لِّلنَّاسِ     And so that We may make him a sign for mankind

وَرَحْمَةً مِّنَّا     and a mercy from Us,

وَكَانَ أَمْرًا مَّقْضِيًّا ۝ ۞     and it is a matter [already] decided.'

فَحَمَلَتْهُ    22 Thus she conceived him,

فَٱنتَبَذَتْ بِهِۦ مَكَانًا قَصِيًّا ۝     then withdrew with him to a distant place.

فَأَجَآءَهَا ٱلْمَخَاضُ    23 The birth pangs brought her

إِلَىٰ جِذْعِ ٱلنَّخْلَةِ     to the trunk of a date palm.

قَالَتْ يَٰلَيْتَنِى مِتُّ قَبْلَ هَٰذَا     She said, 'I wish I had died before this

وَكُنتُ نَسْيًا مَّنسِيًّا ۝     and become a forgotten thing, beyond recall.'

فَنَادَىٰهَا مِن تَحْتِهَآ    24 Thereupon he[2] called her from below her [saying,]

أَلَّا تَحْزَنِى     'Do not grieve!

قَدْ جَعَلَ رَبُّكِ تَحْتَكِ سَرِيًّا ۝     Your Lord has made a spring to flow at your feet.

وَهُزِّىٓ إِلَيْكِ بِجِذْعِ ٱلنَّخْلَةِ    25 Shake the trunk of the palm tree,

---

[1] That is, Gabriel ('a).

[2] That is, the angel Gabriel, or the baby Jesus, whom she was carrying in her belly.

تُسْقِطْ عَلَيْكِ رُطَبًا جَنِيًّا ٢٥    freshly picked dates will drop upon you.

فَكُلِى وَٱشْرَبِى وَقَرِّى عَيْنًا    26 Eat, drink, and be comforted.

فَإِمَّا تَرَيِنَّ مِنَ ٱلْبَشَرِ أَحَدًا    Then if you see any human,

فَقُولِىٓ    say,

إِنِّى نَذَرْتُ لِلرَّحْمَٰنِ صَوْمًا    "Indeed I have vowed a fast to the All-beneficent,

فَلَنْ أُكَلِّمَ ٱلْيَوْمَ إِنسِيًّا ٢٦    so I will not speak to any human today." '

فَأَتَتْ بِهِۦ قَوْمَهَا تَحْمِلُهُۥ    27 Then carrying him she brought him to her people.

قَالُواْ يَٰمَرْيَمُ    They said, 'O Mary,

لَقَدْ جِئْتِ شَيْئًا فَرِيًّا ٢٧    you have certainly come up with an odd thing!

يَٰٓأُخْتَ هَٰرُونَ    28 O sister of Aaron['s lineage]!

مَا كَانَ أَبُوكِ ٱمْرَأَ سَوْءٍ    Your father was not an evil man,

وَمَا كَانَتْ أُمُّكِ بَغِيًّا ٢٨    nor was your mother unchaste.'

فَأَشَارَتْ إِلَيْهِ    29 Thereat she pointed to him.

قَالُواْ كَيْفَ نُكَلِّمُ    They said, 'How can we speak

مَن كَانَ فِى ٱلْمَهْدِ صَبِيًّا ٢٩    to one who is yet a baby in the cradle?'

قَالَ إِنِّى عَبْدُ ٱللَّهِ    30 He said, 'Indeed I am a servant of Allah!

ءَاتَىٰنِىَ ٱلْكِتَٰبَ    He has given me the Book

وَجَعَلَنِى نَبِيًّا ٣٠    and made me a prophet.

وَجَعَلَنِى مُبَارَكًا    31 He has made me blessed,

أَيْنَ مَا كُنتُ    wherever I may be,

وَأَوْصَٰنِى بِٱلصَّلَوٰةِ    and He has enjoined me to [maintain] the prayer

وَٱلزَّكَوٰةِ    and to [pay] the zakāt

مَا دُمْتُ حَيًّا ٣١    as long as I live,

وَبَرًّۢا بِوَٰلِدَتِى    32 and to be good to my mother,

وَلَمْ يَجْعَلْنِى جَبَّارًا شَقِيًّا ٣٢    and He has not made me self-willed and wretched.

وَٱلسَّلَٰمُ عَلَىَّ    33 Peace is to me

يَوْمَ وُلِدتُّ    the day I was born,

وَيَوْمَ أَمُوتُ    and the day I die,

وَيَوْمَ أُبْعَثُ حَيًّا ٣٣    and the day I am raised alive.'

ذَٰلِكَ عِيسَى ٱبْنُ مَرْيَمَ    34 That is Jesus, son of Mary,

قَوْلَ ٱلْحَقِّ

a Word of the Real

ٱلَّذِى فِيهِ يَمْتَرُونَ ﴿٣٤﴾

concerning whom they are in doubt.

مَا كَانَ لِلَّهِ أَن يَتَّخِذَ مِن وَلَدٍ

35 It is not for Allah to take a son.

سُبْحَٰنَهُۥٓ

Immaculate is He!

إِذَا قَضَىٰٓ أَمْرًا

When He decides on a matter,

فَإِنَّمَا يَقُولُ لَهُۥ كُن فَيَكُونُ ﴿٣٥﴾

He just says to it, 'Be!' and it is.

وَإِنَّ ٱللَّهَ رَبِّى وَرَبُّكُمْ

36 'Indeed Allah is my Lord and your Lord.

فَٱعْبُدُوهُ

So worship Him.

هَٰذَا صِرَٰطٌ مُّسْتَقِيمٌ ﴿٣٦﴾

This is a straight path.'

فَٱخْتَلَفَ ٱلْأَحْزَابُ مِنۢ بَيْنِهِمْ

37 But the factions differed among themselves.

فَوَيْلٌ لِّلَّذِينَ كَفَرُوا۟

So woe to the faithless

مِن مَّشْهَدِ يَوْمٍ عَظِيمٍ ﴿٣٧﴾

at the scene of a tremendous day.

أَسْمِعْ بِهِمْ

38 How well they will hear

وَأَبْصِرْ

and how well they will see

يَوْمَ يَأْتُونَنَا

on the day when they come to Us!

لَٰكِنِ ٱلظَّٰلِمُونَ ٱلْيَوْمَ

But today the wrongdoers are

فِى ضَلَٰلٍ مُّبِينٍ ﴿٣٨﴾

in manifest error.

وَأَنذِرْهُمْ يَوْمَ ٱلْحَسْرَةِ

39 *Warn* them of the Day of Regret,[1]

إِذْ قُضِىَ ٱلْأَمْرُ

when the matter will be decided,

وَهُمْ فِى غَفْلَةٍ

while they are [yet] heedless

وَهُمْ لَا يُؤْمِنُونَ ﴿٣٩﴾

and do not have faith.

إِنَّا نَحْنُ نَرِثُ ٱلْأَرْضَ

40 Indeed We shall inherit the earth

وَمَنْ عَلَيْهَا

and whoever there is on it,

وَإِلَيْنَا يُرْجَعُونَ ﴿٤٠﴾

and to Us they shall be brought back.

وَٱذْكُرْ فِى ٱلْكِتَٰبِ إِبْرَٰهِيمَ

41 And *mention* in the Book Abraham.

إِنَّهُۥ كَانَ صِدِّيقًا نَّبِيًّا ﴿٤١﴾

Indeed he was a truthful one, a prophet.

إِذْ قَالَ لِأَبِيهِ يَٰٓأَبَتِ

42 When he said to his father, 'Father!

لِمَ تَعْبُدُ

Why do you worship

---

[1] Another name for the Day of Judgement.

مَا لَا يَسْمَعُ وَلَا يُبْصِرُ
that which neither hears nor sees,

وَلَا يُغْنِي عَنكَ شَيْئًا ٤٢
and is of no avail to you in any way?

يَـٰٓأَبَتِ ٤٣ Father!

إِنِّى قَدْ جَآءَنِى مِنَ ٱلْعِلْمِ
Indeed a knowledge has already come to me

مَا لَمْ يَأْتِكَ
which has not come to you.

فَٱتَّبِعْنِىٓ أَهْدِكَ صِرَٰطًا سَوِيًّا ٤٣
So follow me that I may guide you to a right path.

يَـٰٓأَبَتِ ٤٤ Father!

لَا تَعْبُدِ ٱلشَّيْطَـٰنَ
Do not worship Satan.

إِنَّ ٱلشَّيْطَـٰنَ كَانَ لِلرَّحْمَـٰنِ عَصِيًّا ٤٤
Indeed Satan is disobedient to the All-beneficent.

يَـٰٓأَبَتِ ٤٥ Father!

إِنِّىٓ أَخَافُ
I am indeed afraid

أَن يَمَسَّكَ عَذَابٌ مِّنَ ٱلرَّحْمَـٰنِ
that a punishment from the All-beneficent will befall you,

فَتَكُونَ لِلشَّيْطَـٰنِ وَلِيًّا ٤٥
and you will become Satan's accomplice.'

قَالَ ٤٦ He said,

أَرَاغِبٌ أَنتَ عَنْ ءَالِهَتِى يَـٰٓإِبْرَٰهِيمُ
'Abraham! Are you renouncing my gods?

لَئِن لَّمْ تَنتَهِ لَأَرْجُمَنَّكَ
If you do not relinquish, I will stone you.

وَٱهْجُرْنِى مَلِيًّا ٤٦
Keep away from me for a long while.'[1]

قَالَ سَلَـٰمٌ عَلَيْكَ ٤٧ He said, 'Peace be to you!

سَأَسْتَغْفِرُ لَكَ رَبِّىٓ
I shall plead with my Lord to forgive you.

إِنَّهُۥ كَانَ بِى حَفِيًّا ٤٧
Indeed He is gracious to me.

وَأَعْتَزِلُكُمْ ٤٨ I dissociate myself from you

وَمَا تَدْعُونَ مِن دُونِ ٱللَّهِ
and whatever you invoke besides Allah.

وَأَدْعُوا۟ رَبِّى
I will supplicate my Lord.

عَسَىٰٓ أَلَّآ أَكُونَ
Hopefully, I will not be

بِدُعَآءِ رَبِّى شَقِيًّا ٤٨
disappointed in supplicating my Lord.'

فَلَمَّا ٱعْتَزَلَهُمْ ٤٩ So when he had left them

وَمَا يَعْبُدُونَ مِن دُونِ ٱللَّهِ
and what they worshipped besides Allah,

وَهَبْنَا لَهُۥٓ إِسْحَـٰقَ وَيَعْقُوبَ
We gave him Isaac and Jacob,

وَكُلًّا جَعَلْنَا نَبِيًّا ٤٩
and each We made a prophet.

---

[1] That is, 'Go away. Stop annoying me.'

وَوَهَبْنَا لَهُم مِّن رَّحْمَتِنَا 50 And We gave them out of Our mercy,

وَجَعَلْنَا لَهُمْ لِسَانَ صِدْقٍ عَلِيًّا ۝ and conferred on them a worthy and lofty repute.

وَاذْكُرْ فِى ٱلْكِتَٰبِ مُوسَىٰٓ 51 And *mention* in the Book Moses.

إِنَّهُۥ كَانَ مُخْلَصًا Indeed he was exclusively dedicated [to Allah],

وَكَانَ رَسُولًا نَّبِيًّا ۝ and an apostle and a prophet.

وَنَٰدَيْنَٰهُ 52 We called him

مِن جَانِبِ ٱلطُّورِ ٱلْأَيْمَنِ from the right side of the Mount

وَقَرَّبْنَٰهُ نَجِيًّا ۝ and We drew him near for confidential discourse.

وَوَهَبْنَا لَهُۥ مِن رَّحْمَتِنَآ 53 And We gave him out of Our mercy

أَخَاهُ هَٰرُونَ نَبِيًّا ۝ his brother Aaron, a prophet.

وَاذْكُرْ فِى ٱلْكِتَٰبِ إِسْمَٰعِيلَ 54 And *mention* in the Book Ishmael.

إِنَّهُۥ كَانَ صَادِقَ ٱلْوَعْدِ Indeed he was true to his promise,

وَكَانَ رَسُولًا نَّبِيًّا ۝ and an apostle and a prophet.

وَكَانَ يَأْمُرُ أَهْلَهُۥ بِٱلصَّلَوٰةِ 55 He used to bid his family to [maintain] the prayer

وَٱلزَّكَوٰةِ and to [pay] the *zakāt*,

وَكَانَ عِندَ رَبِّهِۦ مَرْضِيًّا ۝ and was pleasing to his Lord.

وَاذْكُرْ فِى ٱلْكِتَٰبِ إِدْرِيسَ 56 And *mention* in the Book Idrīs.

إِنَّهُۥ كَانَ صِدِّيقًا نَّبِيًّا ۝ Indeed he was a truthful one, a prophet,

وَرَفَعْنَٰهُ مَكَانًا عَلِيًّا ۝ 57 and We raised him to a station exalted.

أُو۟لَٰٓئِكَ ٱلَّذِينَ أَنْعَمَ ٱللَّهُ عَلَيْهِم 58 They are the ones whom Allah has blessed

مِّنَ ٱلنَّبِيِّۦنَ مِن ذُرِّيَّةِ ءَادَمَ from among the prophets of Adam's progeny,

وَمِمَّنْ حَمَلْنَا مَعَ نُوحٍ and from [the progeny of] those We carried with Noah,

وَمِن ذُرِّيَّةِ إِبْرَٰهِيمَ وَإِسْرَٰٓءِيلَ and from among the progeny of Abraham and Israel,

وَمِمَّنْ هَدَيْنَا وَٱجْتَبَيْنَآ and from among those We guided and chose.

إِذَا تُتْلَىٰ عَلَيْهِمْ ءَايَٰتُ ٱلرَّحْمَٰنِ When the signs of the All-beneficent were recited to them,

خَرُّوا۟ سُجَّدًا وَبُكِيًّا ۩ ۝ they would fall down weeping in prostration.

خَلَفَ مِنۢ بَعْدِهِمْ خَلْفٌ 59 But they were succeeded by an evil posterity

أَضَاعُواْ ٱلصَّلَوٰةَ     who neglected the prayer,

وَٱتَّبَعُواْ ٱلشَّهَوَٰتِ     and followed [their base] appetites.

فَسَوْفَ يَلْقَوْنَ غَيًّا     So they will soon encounter [the reward of] perversity,

إِلَّا مَن تَابَ وَءَامَنَ   60   barring those who repent, believe,

وَعَمِلَ صَٰلِحًا     and act righteously.

فَأُوْلَٰٓئِكَ يَدْخُلُونَ ٱلْجَنَّةَ     Such will enter paradise,

وَلَا يُظْلَمُونَ شَيْـًٔا     and they will not be wronged in the least.

جَنَّٰتِ عَدْنٍ ٱلَّتِى وَعَدَ ٱلرَّحْمَٰنُ   61   Gardens of Eden promised by the All-beneficent

عِبَادَهُۥ بِٱلْغَيْبِ     to His servants, [while they were still] unseen.

إِنَّهُۥ كَانَ وَعْدُهُۥ مَأْتِيًّا     Indeed His promise is bound to come to pass.

لَّا يَسْمَعُونَ فِيهَا لَغْوًا   62   Therein they will not hear vain talk,

إِلَّا سَلَٰمًا     but only 'Peace!'

وَلَهُمْ رِزْقُهُمْ فِيهَا     And therein they will have their provision

بُكْرَةً وَعَشِيًّا     morning and evening.

تِلْكَ ٱلْجَنَّةُ ٱلَّتِى نُورِثُ   63   This is the paradise We will give as inheritance

مِنْ عِبَادِنَا مَن كَانَ تَقِيًّا     to those of Our servants who are Godwary.

وَمَا نَتَنَزَّلُ   64   'We do not descend

إِلَّا بِأَمْرِ رَبِّكَ     except by the command of *your* Lord.

لَهُۥ مَا بَيْنَ أَيْدِينَا     To Him belongs whatever is before us

وَمَا خَلْفَنَا     and whatever is behind us

وَمَا بَيْنَ ذَٰلِكَ     and whatever is in between that,

وَمَا كَانَ رَبُّكَ نَسِيًّا     and *your* Lord is not forgetful.

رَّبُّ ٱلسَّمَٰوَٰتِ وَٱلْأَرْضِ   65   The Lord of the heavens and the earth

وَمَا بَيْنَهُمَا     and whatever is between them.

فَٱعْبُدْهُ وَٱصْطَبِرْ لِعِبَٰدَتِهِۦ     So *worship* Him and *be steadfast* in His worship.

هَلْ تَعْلَمُ لَهُۥ سَمِيًّا     Do *you* know anyone who could be His namesake?'

وَيَقُولُ ٱلْإِنسَٰنُ أَءِذَا مَا مِتُّ   66   Man says, 'Shall I, when I have died,

لَسَوْفَ أُخْرَجُ حَيًّا     be brought forth alive?'

أَوَلَا يَذْكُرُ ٱلْإِنسَٰنُ    67 Does not man remember

أَنَّا خَلَقْنَٰهُ مِن قَبْلُ      that We created him before

وَلَمْ يَكُ شَيْـًٔا ۝         when he was nothing?

فَوَرَبِّكَ لَنَحْشُرَنَّهُمْ    68 By your Lord, We will surely gather them

وَٱلشَّيَٰطِينَ         and the devils;

ثُمَّ لَنُحْضِرَنَّهُمْ حَوْلَ جَهَنَّمَ    then We will surely bring them up around hell

جِثِيًّا ۝         [scrambling] on their knees.[1]

ثُمَّ لَنَنزِعَنَّ مِن كُلِّ شِيعَةٍ    69 Then from every group We shall draw

أَيُّهُمْ         whichever of them

أَشَدُّ عَلَى ٱلرَّحْمَٰنِ عِتِيًّا ۝      was more defiant to the All-beneficent.

ثُمَّ لَنَحْنُ أَعْلَمُ    70 Then surely We will know best

بِٱلَّذِينَ هُمْ أَوْلَىٰ بِهَا صِلِيًّا ۝      those who deserve most to enter it.

وَإِن مِّنكُمْ إِلَّا وَارِدُهَا    71 There is none of you but will come to it:[2]

كَانَ عَلَىٰ رَبِّكَ حَتْمًا مَّقْضِيًّا ۝      a [matter that is a] decided certainty with *your* Lord.

ثُمَّ نُنَجِّى ٱلَّذِينَ ٱتَّقَواْ    72 Then We will deliver those who are Godwary,

وَنَذَرُ ٱلظَّٰلِمِينَ فِيهَا جِثِيًّا ۝      and leave the wrongdoers in it, fallen on their knees.

وَإِذَا تُتْلَىٰ عَلَيْهِمْ ءَايَٰتُنَا بَيِّنَٰتٍ    73 When Our manifest signs are recited to them,

قَالَ ٱلَّذِينَ كَفَرُواْ لِلَّذِينَ ءَامَنُوٓاْ      the faithless say to the faithful,

أَىُّ ٱلْفَرِيقَيْنِ خَيْرٌ مَّقَامًا      'Which of the two sides is superior in station[3]

وَأَحْسَنُ نَدِيًّا ۝         and better with respect to company?'[4]

وَكَمْ أَهْلَكْنَا قَبْلَهُم مِّن قَرْنٍ    74 How many a generation We have destroyed before them,

هُمْ أَحْسَنُ أَثَٰثًا وَرِءْيًا ۝      who were superior in furniture and appearance!

قُلْ مَن كَانَ فِى ٱلضَّلَٰلَةِ    75 *Say,* 'Whoever abides in error,

فَلْيَمْدُدْ لَهُ ٱلرَّحْمَٰنُ مَدًّا      the All-beneficent shall prolong his respite

حَتَّىٰ إِذَا رَأَوْاْ مَا يُوعَدُونَ      until they sight what they have been promised:

إِمَّا ٱلْعَذَابَ وَإِمَّا ٱلسَّاعَةَ      either punishment, or the Hour.

---

[1] Or 'in groups.'

[2] That is, they will approach it, without entering it.

[3] Or 'superior with respect to dwelling.'

[4] Or 'better with respect to gatherings.'

فَسَيَعْلَمُونَ مَنْ هُوَ شَرٌّ مَّكَانًا

Then they will know whose position is worse,

وَأَضْعَفُ جُندًا ۝

and whose host is weaker.

76 Allah enhances in guidance those who are [rightly] guided

وَيَزِيدُ ٱللَّهُ ٱلَّذِينَ ٱهْتَدَوْا هُدًى

وَٱلْبَٰقِيَٰتُ ٱلصَّٰلِحَٰتُ

and lasting righteous deeds

خَيْرٌ عِندَ رَبِّكَ ثَوَابًا

are better with *your* Lord in reward,

وَخَيْرٌ مَّرَدًّا ۝

and better with respect to return [to Allah].

77 Have *you* not regarded him who defies Our signs,

أَفَرَءَيْتَ ٱلَّذِى كَفَرَ بِـَٔايَٰتِنَا

and says, 'I will surely be given wealth and children'?

وَقَالَ لَأُوتَيَنَّ مَالًا وَوَلَدًا ۝

78 Has he come to know the Unseen,

أَطَّلَعَ ٱلْغَيْبَ

or taken a promise from the All-beneficent?

أَمِ ٱتَّخَذَ عِندَ ٱلرَّحْمَٰنِ عَهْدًا ۝

79 No indeed! We will write down what he says,

كَلَّا سَنَكْتُبُ مَا يَقُولُ

and We will prolong his punishment endlessly.

وَنَمُدُّ لَهُۥ مِنَ ٱلْعَذَابِ مَدًّا ۝

80 We shall take over from him what he talks about, [1]

وَنَرِثُهُۥ مَا يَقُولُ

and he will come to Us alone.

وَيَأْتِينَا فَرْدًا ۝

81 They have taken gods besides Allah

وَٱتَّخَذُوا مِن دُونِ ٱللَّهِ ءَالِهَةً

that they may be a [source of] might to them:

لِّيَكُونُوا لَهُمْ عِزًّا ۝

82 No Indeed!

كَلَّا

Soon they will disown their worship,

سَيَكْفُرُونَ بِعِبَادَتِهِمْ

and they will become their opponents.

وَيَكُونُونَ عَلَيْهِمْ ضِدًّا ۝

83 Have *you* not regarded

أَلَمْ تَرَ

that We unleash the devils

أَنَّا أَرْسَلْنَا ٱلشَّيَٰطِينَ

upon the faithless

عَلَى ٱلْكَٰفِرِينَ

to urge them impetuously?

تَؤُزُّهُمْ أَزًّا ۝

84 So *do not make haste* against them;

فَلَا تَعْجَلْ عَلَيْهِمْ

indeed We are counting[2] for them, a counting [down].

إِنَّمَا نَعُدُّ لَهُمْ عَدًّا ۝

85 The day We shall gather the Godwary

يَوْمَ نَحْشُرُ ٱلْمُتَّقِينَ

toward the All-beneficent, on mounts,[3]

إِلَى ٱلرَّحْمَٰنِ وَفْدًا ۝

---

[1] That is, 'He will depart unaccompanied from the world, leaving in Our possession the wealth and children that he talks about.'

[2] That is, the number of their breaths.

[3] Or 'as incoming guests.'

وَنَسُوقُ ٱلْمُجْرِمِينَ 86 and drive the guilty

إِلَىٰ جَهَنَّمَ وِرْدًا as a thirsty herd towards hell.

لَّا يَمْلِكُونَ ٱلشَّفَـٰعَةَ 87 No one will have the power to intercede [with Allah],

إِلَّا مَنِ ٱتَّخَذَ except for him who has taken

عِندَ ٱلرَّحْمَـٰنِ عَهْدًا a covenant with the All-beneficent.

وَقَالُوا۟ ٱتَّخَذَ ٱلرَّحْمَـٰنُ وَلَدًا 88 They say, 'The All-beneficent has taken a son!'

لَّقَدْ جِئْتُمْ شَيْـًٔا إِدًّا 89 You have certainly advanced something hideous!

تَكَادُ ٱلسَّمَـٰوَٰتُ يَتَفَطَّرْنَ مِنْهُ 90 The heavens are about to be rent apart at it,

وَتَنشَقُّ ٱلْأَرْضُ the earth to split open,

وَتَخِرُّ ٱلْجِبَالُ هَدًّا and the mountains to collapse into bits,

أَن دَعَوْا۟ لِلرَّحْمَـٰنِ وَلَدًا 91 that they should ascribe a son to the All-beneficent!

وَمَا يَنۢبَغِى لِلرَّحْمَـٰنِ 92 It does not behoove the All-beneficent

أَن يَتَّخِذَ وَلَدًا to take a son.

إِن كُلُّ مَن فِى ٱلسَّمَـٰوَٰتِ وَٱلْأَرْضِ 93 There is none in the heavens and the earth

إِلَّآ ءَاتِى ٱلرَّحْمَـٰنِ عَبْدًا but he comes to the All-beneficent as a servant.

لَّقَدْ أَحْصَىٰهُمْ 94 Certainly He has counted them [all]

وَعَدَّهُمْ عَدًّا and numbered them precisely,

وَكُلُّهُمْ ءَاتِيهِ 95 and each of them will come to Him

يَوْمَ ٱلْقِيَـٰمَةِ فَرْدًا alone on the Day of Resurrection.

إِنَّ ٱلَّذِينَ ءَامَنُوا۟ وَعَمِلُوا۟ ٱلصَّـٰلِحَـٰتِ 96 Indeed those who have faith and do righteous deeds

سَيَجْعَلُ لَهُمُ ٱلرَّحْمَـٰنُ وُدًّا —the All-beneficent will endear them [to His creation].

فَإِنَّمَا يَسَّرْنَـٰهُ بِلِسَانِكَ 97 Indeed We have made it simple in *your* language

لِتُبَشِّرَ بِهِ ٱلْمُتَّقِينَ so that *you* may give good news thereby to the Godwary

وَتُنذِرَ بِهِ قَوْمًا لُّدًّا and *warn* with it a disputatious lot.

وَكَمْ أَهْلَكْنَا قَبْلَهُم مِّن قَرْنٍ 98 How many a generation We have destroyed before them!

هَلْ تُحِسُّ مِنْهُم مِّنْ أَحَدٍ Can *you* descry any one of them,

أَوْ تَسْمَعُ لَهُمْ رِكْزًۢا or hear from them so much as a murmur?

# سُورَةُ طه

# 20. SŪRAT ṬĀ HĀ

بِسمِ ٱللَّهِ
ٱلرَّحْمَٰنِ ٱلرَّحِيمِ

In the Name of Allah,
the All-beneficent, the All-merciful.

طه ١ *Ṭā Hā!*[1]

مَآ أَنزَلْنَا عَلَيْكَ ٱلْقُرْءَانَ ٢ We did not send down to *you* the Qurʾān

لِتَشْقَىٰ that *you* should be miserable,

إِلَّا تَذْكِرَةً ٣ but only as an admonition

لِّمَن يَخْشَىٰ to him who fears [his Lord].

تَنزِيلًا مِّمَّنْ ٤ A sending down [of the Revelation] from Him

خَلَقَ ٱلْأَرْضَ who created the earth

وَٱلسَّمَٰوَٰتِ ٱلْعُلَى and the lofty heavens.

ٱلرَّحْمَٰنُ عَلَى ٱلْعَرْشِ ٱسْتَوَىٰ ٥ The All-beneficent, settled on the Throne.

لَهُۥ مَا فِى ٱلسَّمَٰوَٰتِ ٦ To Him belongs whatever is in the heavens

وَمَا فِى ٱلْأَرْضِ and whatever is on the earth,

وَمَا بَيْنَهُمَا and whatever is between them,

وَمَا تَحْتَ ٱلثَّرَىٰ and whatever is under the ground.

وَإِن تَجْهَرْ بِٱلْقَوْلِ ٧ Whether you speak loudly [or in secret tones]

فَإِنَّهُۥ يَعْلَمُ ٱلسِّرَّ He indeed knows the secret

وَأَخْفَى and what is still more hidden.

ٱللَّهُ لَآ إِلَٰهَ إِلَّا هُوَ ٨ Allah—there is no god except Him—

لَهُ ٱلْأَسْمَآءُ ٱلْحُسْنَىٰ to Him belong the Best Names.

وَهَلْ أَتَىٰكَ حَدِيثُ مُوسَىٰ ٩ Did the story of Moses come to *you*,

إِذْ رَءَا نَارًا ١٠ when he sighted a fire,

فَقَالَ لِأَهْلِهِ ٱمْكُثُوٓا۟ and said to his family, 'Wait!

---

[1] Like *Yā Sīn*, *Ṭā Hā* is said to be one of the names of the Prophet (ṣ). *Maʿānī al-akhbār*, p. 22.

إِنِّىٓ ءَانَسْتُ نَارًا

Indeed I descry a fire!

لَّعَلِّىٓ ءَاتِيكُم مِّنْهَا بِقَبَسٍ

Maybe I will bring you a brand from it,

أَوْ أَجِدُ عَلَى ٱلنَّارِ هُدًى ۝

or find some guidance at the fire.'

فَلَمَّآ أَتَىٰهَا

11 So when he came to it,

نُودِىَ يَـٰمُوسَىٰٓ ۝

he was called, 'O Moses!

إِنِّىٓ أَنَا۠ رَبُّكَ

12 Indeed I am your Lord!

فَٱخْلَعْ نَعْلَيْكَ ۖ

So take off your sandals.

إِنَّكَ بِٱلْوَادِ ٱلْمُقَدَّسِ طُوًى ۝

You are indeed in the sacred valley of Ṭuwā.

وَأَنَا ٱخْتَرْتُكَ

13 I have chosen you;

فَٱسْتَمِعْ لِمَا يُوحَىٰٓ ۝

so listen to what is revealed.

إِنَّنِىٓ أَنَا ٱللَّهُ

14 Indeed I am Allah

لَآ إِلَـٰهَ إِلَّآ أَنَا۠

—there is no god except Me.

فَٱعْبُدْنِى

So worship Me,

وَأَقِمِ ٱلصَّلَوٰةَ لِذِكْرِىٓ ۝

and maintain the prayer for My remembrance.

إِنَّ ٱلسَّاعَةَ ءَاتِيَةٌ

15 Indeed the Hour is bound to come:

أَكَادُ أُخْفِيهَا

I will have it hidden,

لِتُجْزَىٰ كُلُّ نَفْسٍ

so that every soul may be rewarded

بِمَا تَسْعَىٰ ۝

for what it strives for.

فَلَا يَصُدَّنَّكَ عَنْهَا

16 So do not let yourself be distracted from it

مَن لَّا يُؤْمِنُ بِهَا

by those who do not believe in it

وَٱتَّبَعَ هَوَىٰهُ

and who follow their desires,

فَتَرْدَىٰ ۝

lest you should perish.

وَمَا تِلْكَ بِيَمِينِكَ يَـٰمُوسَىٰ ۝

17 Moses, what is that in your right hand?'

قَالَ هِىَ عَصَاىَ

18 He said, 'It is my staff.

أَتَوَكَّؤُا۟ عَلَيْهَا

I lean upon it,

وَأَهُشُّ بِهَا عَلَىٰ غَنَمِى

and with it I beat down leaves for my sheep;

وَلِىَ فِيهَا مَـَٔارِبُ أُخْرَىٰ ۝

and I have other uses for it.'

قَالَ أَلْقِهَا يَـٰمُوسَىٰ ۝

19 He said, 'Moses, throw it down.'

فَأَلْقَىٰهَا

20 So he threw it down,

فَإِذَا هِىَ حَيَّةٌ تَسْعَىٰ ۝

and behold, it was a snake, moving swiftly.

21 He said, 'Take hold of it, and do not fear.

We will restore it to its former state.

22 Now clasp your hand to your armpit:

it will emerge white, without any fault.

[This is yet] another sign,

23 that We may show you some of Our great signs.

24 Go to Pharaoh.

He has indeed rebelled.'

25 He said, 'My Lord!

Open my breast for me.

26 Make my affair easy for me.

27 Remove the hitch from my tongue,[1]

28 [so that] they may understand my discourse.

29 Appoint for me a minister from my family,

30 Aaron, my brother.

31 Strengthen my back through him,[2]

32 and make him my associate in my affair,

33 so that we may glorify You greatly,

34 and remember You greatly.

35 Indeed You see us best.'

36 He said,

'Moses, your request has been granted!

37 Certainly, We have done you a favour another time,

38 when We revealed to your mother

whatever that was revealed:

39 "Put him in the casket,

and cast it into the river.

Then the river will cast it on the bank,

---

[1] That is, 'Grant me clarity of speech.'

[2] That is, 'reinforce my strength through him.'

436

يَأْخُذْهُ عَدُوٌّ لِّي   and he shall be picked up by an enemy of Mine

وَعَدُوٌّ لَّهُ   and an enemy of his."

وَأَلْقَيْتُ عَلَيْكَ مَحَبَّةً مِّنِّي   And I cast upon you a love from Me,[1]

وَلِتُصْنَعَ عَلَىٰ عَيْنِي ۝   and that you might be reared under My eyes.

إِذْ تَمْشِي أُخْتُكَ   40 When your sister walked up [to Pharaoh's palace]

فَتَقُولُ   saying,

هَلْ أَدُلُّكُمْ عَلَىٰ مَن يَكْفُلُهُ   "Shall I show you someone who will take care of him?"

فَرَجَعْنَاكَ إِلَىٰ أُمِّكَ   Then We restored you to your mother,

كَيْ تَقَرَّ عَيْنُهَا وَلَا تَحْزَنَ   that she might be comforted and not grieve.

وَقَتَلْتَ نَفْسًا   Then you slew a soul,

فَنَجَّيْنَاكَ مِنَ ٱلْغَمِّ   whereupon We delivered you from anguish,

وَفَتَنَّاكَ فُتُونًا   and We tried you with various ordeals.

فَلَبِثْتَ سِنِينَ   Then you stayed for several years

فِي أَهْلِ مَدْيَنَ   among the people of Midian.

ثُمَّ جِئْتَ عَلَىٰ قَدَرٍ يَٰمُوسَىٰ ۝   Then you turned up as ordained, O Moses!

وَٱصْطَنَعْتُكَ لِنَفْسِي ۝   41 And I chose you for Myself.

ٱذْهَبْ أَنتَ وَأَخُوكَ بِـَٔايَٰتِي   42 Go ahead, you and your brother, with My signs

وَلَا تَنِيَا فِي ذِكْرِي ۝   and do not flag in My remembrance.

ٱذْهَبَا إِلَىٰ فِرْعَوْنَ   43 Let the two of you go to Pharaoh.

إِنَّهُ طَغَىٰ ۝   Indeed he has rebelled.

فَقُولَا لَهُ قَوْلًا لَّيِّنًا   44 Speak to him in a soft manner;

لَّعَلَّهُ يَتَذَكَّرُ أَوْ يَخْشَىٰ ۝   maybe he will take admonition or fear.'

قَالَا رَبَّنَا   45 The two of them said, 'Our Lord!

إِنَّنَا نَخَافُ أَن يَفْرُطَ عَلَيْنَا   We are indeed afraid that he will forestall us

أَوْ أَن يَطْغَىٰ ۝   or will overstep the bounds.'

قَالَ لَا تَخَافَا   46 He said, 'Do not be afraid,

إِنَّنِي مَعَكُمَا   for I will be with the two of you,

أَسْمَعُ وَأَرَىٰ ۝   hearing and seeing [whatever happens].

فَأْتِيَاهُ فَقُولَا   47 So approach him and say,

---

[1] That is, 'I made you endearing' (to people, or to Allah).

إِنَّا رَسُولَا رَبِّكَ     "We are the apostles of your Lord.

فَأَرْسِلْ مَعَنَا بَنِىٓ إِسْرَٰٓءِيلَ     Let the Children of Israel go with us,

وَلَا تُعَذِّبْهُمْ     and do not torture them!

قَدْ جِئْنَٰكَ     We certainly bring you

بِـَٔايَةٍ مِّن رَّبِّكَ     a sign from your Lord,

وَٱلسَّلَٰمُ عَلَىٰ     and may peace be upon

مَنِ ٱتَّبَعَ ٱلْهُدَىٰٓ ۝     him who follows guidance!

إِنَّا قَدْ أُوحِىَ إِلَيْنَآ 48     Indeed it has been revealed to us

أَنَّ ٱلْعَذَابَ عَلَىٰ     that the punishment shall befall

مَن كَذَّبَ وَتَوَلَّىٰ ۝     those who deny and turn their backs [on us]." '

قَالَ فَمَن رَّبُّكُمَا يَٰمُوسَىٰ ۝ 49     He said, 'Who is your Lord, Moses?'

قَالَ رَبُّنَا ٱلَّذِىٓ 50     He said, 'Our Lord is He

أَعْطَىٰ كُلَّ شَىْءٍ خَلْقَهُۥ     who gave everything its creation

ثُمَّ هَدَىٰ ۝     and then guided it.'

قَالَ فَمَا بَالُ ٱلْقُرُونِ ٱلْأُولَىٰ ۝ 51     He said, 'What about the former generations?'

قَالَ عِلْمُهَا عِندَ رَبِّى 52     He said, 'Their knowledge is with my Lord,

فِى كِتَٰبٍ     in a Book.

لَّا يَضِلُّ رَبِّى وَلَا يَنسَى ۝     My Lord neither makes any error nor forgets.'

ٱلَّذِى جَعَلَ لَكُمُ ٱلْأَرْضَ مَهْدًا 53     He who made the earth for you a cradle,

وَسَلَكَ لَكُمْ فِيهَا سُبُلًا     and in it threaded for you ways,

وَأَنزَلَ مِنَ ٱلسَّمَآءِ مَآءً     and sent down water from the sky,

فَأَخْرَجْنَا بِهِۦٓ     and with it We brought forth

أَزْوَٰجًا مِّن نَّبَاتٍ شَتَّىٰ ۝     various kinds of vegetation.

كُلُوا۟ وَٱرْعَوْا۟ أَنْعَٰمَكُمْ 54     'Eat and pasture your cattle.'

إِنَّ فِى ذَٰلِكَ لَءَايَٰتٍ     There are indeed signs in that

لِّأُو۟لِى ٱلنُّهَىٰ ۝ ❋     for those who have sense.

مِنْهَا خَلَقْنَٰكُمْ 55     From it did We create you,

وَفِيهَا نُعِيدُكُمْ     into it shall We return you,

وَمِنْهَا نُخْرِجُكُمْ     and from it shall We bring you forth

تَارَةً أُخْرَىٰ ۝     another time.

وَلَقَدْ أَرَيْنَـٰهُ ءَايَـٰتِنَا كُلَّهَا 56 Certainly We showed him all Our signs.

فَكَذَّبَ وَأَبَىٰ But he denied [them] and refused [to believe them].

قَالَ أَجِئْتَنَا 57 He said, 'Have you come to us,

لِتُخْرِجَنَا مِنْ أَرْضِنَا بِسِحْرِكَ يَـٰمُوسَىٰ Moses, to expel us from our land with your magic?

فَلَنَأْتِيَنَّكَ بِسِحْرٍ مِّثْلِهِۦ 58 Yet we [too] will bring you a magic like it!

فَٱجْعَلْ بَيْنَنَا وَبَيْنَكَ مَوْعِدًا So fix a tryst between us and you,

لَّا نُخْلِفُهُۥ نَحْنُ وَلَآ أَنتَ which neither we shall fail nor you,

مَكَانًا سُوًى at a middle place.'[1]

قَالَ مَوْعِدُكُمْ يَوْمُ ٱلزِّينَةِ 59 He said, 'Your tryst shall be the Day of Adornment,

وَأَن يُحْشَرَ ٱلنَّاسُ ضُحًى and let the people be assembled in early forenoon.'

فَتَوَلَّىٰ فِرْعَوْنُ 60 Then Pharaoh withdrew [to consult privately],

فَجَمَعَ كَيْدَهُۥ summoned up his guile,

ثُمَّ أَتَىٰ and then arrived [at the scene of the contest].

قَالَ لَهُم مُّوسَىٰ وَيْلَكُمْ 61 Moses said to them, 'Woe to you!

لَا تَفْتَرُوا۟ عَلَى ٱللَّهِ كَذِبًا Do not fabricate a lie against Allah,

فَيُسْحِتَكُم بِعَذَابٍ lest He should annihilate you with a punishment.

وَقَدْ خَابَ مَنِ ٱفْتَرَىٰ Whoever fabricates lies certainly fails.'

فَتَنَـٰزَعُوٓا۟ أَمْرَهُم بَيْنَهُمْ 62 So they disputed their matter among themselves,

وَأَسَرُّوا۟ ٱلنَّجْوَىٰ and kept their confidential talks secret.

قَالُوٓا۟ إِنْ هَـٰذَٰنِ لَسَـٰحِرَٰنِ 63 They said, 'These two are indeed magicians

يُرِيدَانِ أَن يُخْرِجَاكُم who intend to expel you

مِّنْ أَرْضِكُم بِسِحْرِهِمَا from your land with their magic,

وَيَذْهَبَا بِطَرِيقَتِكُمُ ٱلْمُثْلَىٰ and to abolish your excellent tradition![2]

فَأَجْمِعُوا۟ كَيْدَكُمْ 64 So summon up your ingenuity,

ثُمَّ ٱئْتُوا۟ صَفًّا then come in ranks.

وَقَدْ أَفْلَحَ ٱلْيَوْمَ مَنِ ٱسْتَعْلَىٰ Today he who has the upper hand will be saved!'

قَالُوا۟ يَـٰمُوسَىٰٓ 65 They said, 'O Moses!

إِمَّآ أَن تُلْقِىَ Either you will throw down,

---

[1] Or 'at a neutral location,' or 'on a level ground.'
[2] Cf. 40:26.

وَإِمَّآ أَن نَّكُونَ أَوَّلَ مَنْ أَلْقَىٰ ۝　　or we shall be the first to throw.'

قَالَ بَلْ أَلْقُوا۟ ۖ　　66 He said, 'Rather you throw down first.'

فَإِذَا حِبَالُهُمْ وَعِصِيُّهُمْ يُخَيَّلُ إِلَيْهِ　　Behold, their ropes and staffs appeared to him

مِن سِحْرِهِمْ　　by their magic

أَنَّهَا تَسْعَىٰ ۝　　to wriggle swiftly.

فَأَوْجَسَ فِى نَفْسِهِۦ خِيفَةً مُّوسَىٰ ۝　　67 Then Moses felt a fear within his heart.

قُلْنَا لَا تَخَفْ　　68 We said, 'Do not be afraid.

إِنَّكَ أَنتَ ٱلْأَعْلَىٰ ۝　　Indeed you will have the upper hand.

وَأَلْقِ مَا فِى يَمِينِكَ　　69 Throw down what is in your right hand,

تَلْقَفْ مَا صَنَعُوٓا۟ ۖ　　and it will swallow what they have conjured.

إِنَّمَا صَنَعُوا۟ كَيْدُ سَٰحِرٍ ۖ　　What they have conjured is only a magician's trick,

وَلَا يُفْلِحُ ٱلسَّاحِرُ　　and the magician is not successful

حَيْثُ أَتَىٰ ۝　　wherever he may go.'

فَأُلْقِىَ ٱلسَّحَرَةُ سُجَّدًا　　70 Thereat the magicians fell down prostrating.

قَالُوٓا۟ ءَامَنَّا بِرَبِّ هَٰرُونَ　　They said, 'We have believed in the Lord of Aaron

وَمُوسَىٰ ۝　　and Moses!'

قَالَ ءَامَنتُمْ لَهُۥ　　71 He said, 'Do you profess faith in Him

قَبْلَ أَنْ ءَاذَنَ لَكُمْ ۖ　　before I may permit you?

إِنَّهُۥ لَكَبِيرُكُمُ ٱلَّذِى عَلَّمَكُمُ ٱلسِّحْرَ ۖ　　He is indeed your chief who has taught you magic!

فَلَأُقَطِّعَنَّ أَيْدِيَكُمْ وَأَرْجُلَكُم　　Surely I will cut off your hands and feet

مِّنْ خِلَٰفٍ　　from opposite sides,

وَلَأُصَلِّبَنَّكُمْ فِى جُذُوعِ ٱلنَّخْلِ　　and I will crucify you on the trunks of palm trees.

وَلَتَعْلَمُنَّ　　So you will know

أَيُّنَآ أَشَدُّ عَذَابًا　　which of us can inflict a punishment severer

وَأَبْقَىٰ ۝　　and more lasting.'

قَالُوا۟ لَن نُّؤْثِرَكَ　　72 They said, 'We will never prefer you

عَلَىٰ مَا جَآءَنَا مِنَ ٱلْبَيِّنَٰتِ　　to the manifest proofs which have come to us

وَٱلَّذِى فَطَرَنَا ۖ　　and [to] Him who originated us.

فَٱقْضِ مَآ أَنتَ قَاضٍ ۖ　　Decide whatever you may.

إِنَّمَا تَقْضِى هَٰذِهِ ٱلْحَيَوٰةَ ٱلدُّنْيَآ ۝　　You can only decide about the life of this world.

إِنَّا ءَامَنَّا بِرَبِّنَا 73 We have indeed believed in our Lord

لِيَغْفِرَ لَنَا خَطَـٰيَـٰنَا that He may forgive us our iniquities

وَمَا أَكْرَهْتَنَا عَلَيْهِ مِنَ ٱلسِّحْرِ and the magic you compelled us to perform.

وَٱللَّهُ خَيْرٌ وَأَبْقَىٰ ۝ Allah is better and more lasting.'

إِنَّهُۥ مَن يَأْتِ رَبَّهُۥ مُجْرِمًا 74 Whoever comes to his Lord laden with guilt,

فَإِنَّ لَهُۥ جَهَنَّمَ indeed for him shall be hell

لَا يَمُوتُ فِيهَا وَلَا يَحْيَىٰ ۝ where he will neither live nor die.

وَمَن يَأْتِهِۦ مُؤْمِنًا 75 But whoever comes to Him with faith

قَدْ عَمِلَ ٱلصَّـٰلِحَـٰتِ and he has done righteous deeds,

فَأُوْلَـٰٓئِكَ لَهُمُ ٱلدَّرَجَـٰتُ ٱلْعُلَىٰ ۝ for such shall be the highest ranks

جَنَّـٰتُ عَدْنٍ 76 —the Gardens of Eden,

تَجْرِى مِن تَحْتِهَا ٱلْأَنْهَـٰرُ with streams running in them,

خَـٰلِدِينَ فِيهَا to abide in them [forever],

وَذَٰلِكَ جَزَآءُ مَن تَزَكَّىٰ ۝ and that is the reward of him who keeps pure.

وَلَقَدْ أَوْحَيْنَآ إِلَىٰ مُوسَىٰٓ 77 Certainly We revealed to Moses,

أَنْ أَسْرِ بِعِبَادِى [saying], 'Take My servants on a journey by night.

فَٱضْرِبْ لَهُمْ طَرِيقًا فِى ٱلْبَحْرِ يَبَسًا Then strike out for them a dry path through the sea.

لَّا تَخَـٰفُ دَرَكًا Do not be afraid of being overtaken,

وَلَا تَخْشَىٰ ۝ and have no fear [of getting drowned].

فَأَتْبَعَهُمْ فِرْعَوْنُ بِجُنُودِهِۦ 78 Then Pharaoh pursued them with his troops,

فَغَشِيَهُم whereat they were engulfed

مِّنَ ٱلْيَمِّ مَا غَشِيَهُمْ ۝ by what engulfed them of the sea.

وَأَضَلَّ فِرْعَوْنُ قَوْمَهُۥ 79 Pharaoh led his people astray

وَمَا هَدَىٰ ۝ and did not guide them.

يَـٰبَنِىٓ إِسْرَٰٓءِيلَ 80 O Children of Israel!

قَدْ أَنجَيْنَـٰكُم مِّنْ عَدُوِّكُمْ We delivered you from your enemy,

وَوَٰعَدْنَـٰكُمْ and We appointed with you a tryst

جَانِبَ ٱلطُّورِ ٱلْأَيْمَنَ on the right side of the Mount

وَنَزَّلْنَا عَلَيْكُمُ ٱلْمَنَّ وَٱلسَّلْوَىٰ ۝ and We sent down to you manna and quails:

كُلُوا۟ مِن طَيِّبَـٰتِ مَا رَزَقْنَـٰكُمْ 81 'Eat of the good things We have provided you,

وَلَا تَطْغَوْا فِيهِ     but do not overstep the bounds therein,

فَيَحِلَّ عَلَيْكُمْ غَضَبِي     lest My wrath should descend on you.

وَمَن يَحْلِلْ عَلَيْهِ غَضَبِي     And he on whom My wrath descends

فَقَدْ هَوَىٰ ۝     certainly perishes.[1]

وَإِنِّي لَغَفَّارٌ لِّمَن تَابَ    82 Indeed I am all-forgiver toward him who repents,

وَءَامَنَ وَعَمِلَ صَـٰلِحًا     becomes faithful and acts righteously,

ثُمَّ ٱهْتَدَىٰ ۝ ❉     and then follows guidance.'

وَمَآ أَعْجَلَكَ عَن قَوْمِكَ يَـٰمُوسَىٰ ۝    83 'What has hurried you from your people, O Moses?'

قَالَ هُمْ أُوْلَآءِ عَلَىٰ أَثَرِي    84 He said, 'They are close upon my heels,

وَعَجِلْتُ إِلَيْكَ رَبِّ     and I hurried on to You, my Lord,

لِتَرْضَىٰ ۝     that You may be pleased.'

قَالَ فَإِنَّا قَدْ فَتَنَّا قَوْمَكَ    85 He said, 'Indeed We tried your people

مِنۢ بَعْدِكَ     in your absence,

وَأَضَلَّهُمُ ٱلسَّامِرِىُّ ۝     and the Sāmirī[2] has led them astray.'

فَرَجَعَ مُوسَىٰٓ إِلَىٰ قَوْمِهِ    86 Thereupon Moses returned to his people,

غَضْبَـٰنَ أَسِفًا     indignant and grieved.

قَالَ يَـٰقَوْمِ     He said, 'O my people!

أَلَمْ يَعِدْكُمْ رَبُّكُمْ وَعْدًا حَسَنًا     Did not your Lord give you a true promise?

أَفَطَالَ عَلَيْكُمُ ٱلْعَهْدُ     Did the period [of my absence] seem too long to you?

أَمْ أَرَدتُّمْ     Or did you desire

أَن يَحِلَّ عَلَيْكُمْ غَضَبٌ مِّن رَّبِّكُمْ     that your Lord's wrath should descend on you

فَأَخْلَفْتُم مَّوْعِدِي ۝     and so you failed your tryst with me?'

قَالُوا۟ مَآ أَخْلَفْنَا مَوْعِدَكَ    87 They said, 'We did not fail our tryst with you

بِمَلْكِنَا     of our own accord,

وَلَـٰكِنَّا حُمِّلْنَآ أَوْزَارًا     but we were laden with the weight

مِّن زِينَةِ ٱلْقَوْمِ     of the people's ornaments,

فَقَذَفْنَـٰهَا     and we cast them [into the fire]

---

[1] Or 'falls' (that is, into hell).

[2] Apparently one of the Israelites accompanying Moses ('a).

فَكَذَٰلِكَ أَلْقَى ٱلسَّامِرِيُّ ۞    and so did the Sāmirī throw.'

فَأَخْرَجَ لَهُمْ عِجْلًا    88 Then he produced for them a calf

جَسَدًا لَّهُ خُوَارٌ    —a [lifeless] body with a low—

فَقَالُوا هَٰذَآ إِلَٰهُكُمْ    and they said, This is your god

وَإِلَٰهُ مُوسَىٰ    and the God of Moses,

فَنَسِىَ ۞    so he[1] forgot!

أَفَلَا يَرَوْنَ أَلَّا يَرْجِعُ إِلَيْهِمْ قَوْلًا    89 Did they not see that it did not answer them,

وَلَا يَمْلِكُ لَهُمْ ضَرًّا وَلَا نَفْعًا ۞    nor could it bring them any benefit or harm?

وَلَقَدْ قَالَ لَهُمْ هَٰرُونُ مِن قَبْلُ    90 Aaron had certainly told them earlier,

يَٰقَوْمِ    'O my people!

إِنَّمَا فُتِنتُم بِهِۦ    You are only being tested by it.

وَإِنَّ رَبَّكُمُ ٱلرَّحْمَٰنُ    Indeed your Lord is the All-beneficent.

فَٱتَّبِعُونِى وَأَطِيعُوٓا أَمْرِى ۞    So follow me and obey my command!'

قَالُوا لَن نَّبْرَحَ عَلَيْهِ عَٰكِفِينَ    91 They had said, 'We will keep on clinging to it

حَتَّىٰ يَرْجِعَ إِلَيْنَا مُوسَىٰ ۞    until Moses returns to us.'

قَالَ يَٰهَٰرُونُ    92 He said, 'O Aaron!

مَا مَنَعَكَ    What kept you,

إِذْ رَأَيْتَهُمْ ضَلُّوٓا ۞    when you saw them going astray,

أَلَّا تَتَّبِعَنِ    93 from following me?

أَفَعَصَيْتَ أَمْرِى ۞    Did you disobey my command?'

قَالَ يَبْنَؤُمَّ    94 He said, 'O son of my mother!

لَا تَأْخُذْ بِلِحْيَتِى وَلَا بِرَأْسِىٓ    Do not hold my beard or my head!

إِنِّى خَشِيتُ أَن تَقُولَ    I feared lest you should say,

فَرَّقْتَ بَيْنَ بَنِىٓ إِسْرَٰٓءِيلَ    "You have caused a rift among the Children of Israel,

وَلَمْ تَرْقُبْ قَوْلِى ۞    and did not heed my word [of advice]." '

قَالَ فَمَا خَطْبُكَ يَٰسَٰمِرِيُّ ۞    95 He said, 'What is your business, O Sāmirī?'

قَالَ بَصُرْتُ بِمَا لَمْ يَبْصُرُوا بِهِۦ    96 He said, 'I saw what they did not see.

---

[1] That is, either the Sāmirī, who forgot Moses' teaching about the worship of God, or, alternately, Moses who is said to have left behind his god and gone away in search of him.

فَقَبَضْتُ قَبْضَةً مِّنْ أَثَرِ ٱلرَّسُولِ
فَنَبَذْتُهَا

I took a handful [of dust] from the messenger's trail
and threw it.

وَكَذَٰلِكَ سَوَّلَتْ لِي نَفْسِى ۩

That is how my soul prompted me.'

قَالَ فَٱذْهَبْ

97 He said, 'Begone!

فَإِنَّ لَكَ فِى ٱلْحَيَوٰةِ أَن تَقُولَ
لَا مِسَاسَ

It shall be your [lot] throughout life to say,
"Do not touch me!"

وَإِنَّ لَكَ مَوْعِدًا
لَّن تُخْلَفَهُۥ

Indeed there is a tryst for you
which you will not fail to keep!

وَٱنظُرْ إِلَىٰ إِلَٰهِكَ
ٱلَّذِى ظَلْتَ عَلَيْهِ عَاكِفًا

Now look at your god
to whom you went on clinging.

لَّنُحَرِّقَنَّهُۥ

We will burn it down

ثُمَّ لَنَنسِفَنَّهُۥ فِى ٱلْيَمِّ نَسْفًا ۩

and then scatter it[s ashes] into the sea.

إِنَّمَآ إِلَٰهُكُمُ ٱللَّهُ

98 Indeed your God is Allah.

ٱلَّذِى لَآ إِلَٰهَ إِلَّا هُوَ ۚ

There is no god except Him.

وَسِعَ كُلَّ شَىْءٍ عِلْمًا ۩

He embraces all things in [His] knowledge.'

كَذَٰلِكَ نَقُصُّ عَلَيْكَ

99 Thus do We relate to *you*

مِنْ أَنۢبَآءِ مَا قَدْ سَبَقَ ۚ

some accounts of what is past.

وَقَدْ ءَاتَيْنَٰكَ

Certainly We have given *you*

مِن لَّدُنَّا ذِكْرًا ۩

a Reminder from Ourselves.

مَّنْ أَعْرَضَ عَنْهُ

100 Whoever disregards it

فَإِنَّهُۥ يَحْمِلُ يَوْمَ ٱلْقِيَٰمَةِ وِزْرًا ۩

shall bear its onus on the Day of Resurrection,

خَٰلِدِينَ فِيهِ ۖ

101 remaining in it [forever].

وَسَآءَ لَهُمْ يَوْمَ ٱلْقِيَٰمَةِ حِمْلًا ۩

Evil is their burden on the Day of Resurrection

يَوْمَ يُنفَخُ فِى ٱلصُّورِ ۚ

102 —the day the Trumpet will be blown—

وَنَحْشُرُ ٱلْمُجْرِمِينَ يَوْمَئِذٍ
زُرْقًا ۩

on that day We shall muster the guilty
with blind eyes.[1]

يَتَخَٰفَتُونَ بَيْنَهُمْ

103 They will whisper to one another:

إِن لَّبِثْتُمْ إِلَّا عَشْرًا ۩

'You have stayed only for ten [days].'

---

[1] Literally, 'with blued eyes.' Cf. 17:72, 97; 20:124–125.

نَّحْنُ أَعْلَمُ بِمَا يَقُولُونَ 104 We know best what they will say,

إِذْ يَقُولُ أَمْثَلُهُمْ طَرِيقَةً    when the best of them in conduct will say,

إِن لَّبِثْتُمْ إِلَّا يَوْمًا    'You stayed only a day!'

وَيَسْأَلُونَكَ عَنِ ٱلْجِبَالِ 105 They question *you* concerning the mountains.

فَقُلْ يَنسِفُهَا رَبِّى نَسْفًا    *Say,* 'My Lord will scatter them [like dust].

فَيَذَرُهَا قَاعًا صَفْصَفًا 106 Then He will leave it[1] a level plain.

لَّا تَرَىٰ فِيهَا عِوَجًا وَلَآ أَمْتًا 107 You will not see any crookedness or unevenness in it.

يَوْمَئِذٍ يَتَّبِعُونَ ٱلدَّاعِىَ 108 On that day they will follow a summoner

لَا عِوَجَ لَهُ    in whom there will be no deviousness.

وَخَشَعَتِ ٱلْأَصْوَاتُ لِلرَّحْمَٰنِ    The voices will be muted before the All-beneficent,

فَلَا تَسْمَعُ إِلَّا هَمْسًا    and *you* will hear nothing but a murmur.

يَوْمَئِذٍ لَّا تَنفَعُ ٱلشَّفَٰعَةُ 109 Intercession will not avail that day

إِلَّا مَنْ أَذِنَ لَهُ ٱلرَّحْمَٰنُ    except from him whom the All-beneficent allows

وَرَضِىَ لَهُۥ قَوْلًا    and approves of his word.

يَعْلَمُ مَا بَيْنَ أَيْدِيهِمْ 110 He knows that which is before them

وَمَا خَلْفَهُمْ    and that which is behind them,

وَلَا يُحِيطُونَ بِهِۦ عِلْمًا    but they cannot comprehend Him in their knowledge.

وَعَنَتِ ٱلْوُجُوهُ 111 All faces shall be humbled

لِلْحَىِّ ٱلْقَيُّومِ    before the Living One, the All-sustainer,

وَقَدْ خَابَ    and he will fail

مَنْ حَمَلَ ظُلْمًا    who bears [the onus of] wrongdoing.

وَمَن يَعْمَلْ مِنَ ٱلصَّٰلِحَٰتِ 112 But whoever does righteous deeds,

وَهُوَ مُؤْمِنٌ    should he be faithful,

فَلَا يَخَافُ ظُلْمًا وَلَا هَضْمًا    shall neither fear any wrong nor detraction.

وَكَذَٰلِكَ أَنزَلْنَٰهُ قُرْءَانًا عَرَبِيًّا 113 Thus We have sent it down as an Arabic Qur'ān

وَصَرَّفْنَا فِيهِ مِنَ ٱلْوَعِيدِ    and We have paraphrased the threats in it

لَعَلَّهُمْ يَتَّقُونَ    so that they may be Godwary

---

[1] That is, the earth.

or it may evoke remembrance for them.

114 So exalted is Allah, the True Sovereign.

*Do not hasten* with the Qur'ān

before its revelation is completed for *you*,

and *say*, 'My Lord! Increase me in knowledge.'

115 Certainly We had enjoined Adam earlier;

but he forgot,

and We did not find any resoluteness in him.

116 When We said to the angels,

'Prostrate before Adam,'

they prostrated, except Iblis:

he refused.

117 We said, 'O Adam!

This is indeed an enemy of yours and your mate's.

So do not let him expel you from paradise,

or you will be miserable.

118 Indeed you will neither be hungry in it nor naked.

119 Indeed you will neither be thirsty in it,

nor suffer from the sun.

120 Then Satan tempted him.

He said, 'O Adam!

Shall I show you the tree of immortality,

and an imperishable kingdom?'

121 So they both ate of it,

and their nakedness became exposed to them,

and they began to stitch over themselves

with the leaves of paradise.

Adam disobeyed his Lord,

and went amiss.

ثُمَّ ٱجْتَبَـٰهُ رَبُّهُ 122 Then his Lord chose him,

فَتَابَ عَلَيْهِ     and turned to him clemently,

وَهَدَىٰ ۞     and guided him.

قَالَ 123 He said,

ٱهْبِطَا مِنْهَا جَمِيعًۢا     'Get down both of you[1] from it, all together,

بَعْضُكُمْ لِبَعْضٍ عَدُوٌّ     being enemies of one another!

فَإِمَّا يَأْتِيَنَّكُم مِّنِّى هُدًى     Yet, should any guidance come to you from Me,

فَمَنِ ٱتَّبَعَ هُدَاىَ     those who follow My guidance

فَلَا يَضِلُّ وَلَا يَشْقَىٰ ۞     will not go astray, nor will they be miserable.

وَمَنْ أَعْرَضَ عَن ذِكْرِى 124 But whoever disregards My remembrance,

فَإِنَّ لَهُۥ مَعِيشَةً ضَنكًا     his shall be a wretched life,

وَنَحْشُرُهُۥ يَوْمَ ٱلْقِيَـٰمَةِ     and on the Day of Resurrection We shall raise him

أَعْمَىٰ ۞     blind.

قَالَ رَبِّ 125 He will say, 'My Lord!

لِمَ حَشَرْتَنِىٓ أَعْمَىٰ     Why have You raised me blind,

وَقَدْ كُنتُ بَصِيرًا ۞     though I used to see?'

قَالَ كَذَٰلِكَ 126 He will say: 'So it is.

أَتَتْكَ ءَايَـٰتُنَا فَنَسِيتَهَا     Our signs came to you, but you forgot them,

وَكَذَٰلِكَ ٱلْيَوْمَ تُنسَىٰ ۞     and thus you will be forgotten today.'

وَكَذَٰلِكَ نَجْزِى مَنْ أَسْرَفَ 127 Thus do We requite him who is a profligate

وَلَمْ يُؤْمِنۢ بِـَٔايَـٰتِ رَبِّهِۦ     and does not believe in the signs of his Lord.

وَلَعَذَابُ ٱلْءَاخِرَةِ أَشَدُّ     And the punishment of the Hereafter is severer

وَأَبْقَىٰٓ ۞     and more lasting.

أَفَلَمْ يَهْدِ لَهُمْ 128 Does it not dawn upon them

كَمْ أَهْلَكْنَا قَبْلَهُم مِّنَ ٱلْقُرُونِ     how many generations We have destroyed before them,

يَمْشُونَ فِى مَسَـٰكِنِهِمْ     amid [the ruins of] whose dwellings they walk?

إِنَّ فِى ذَٰلِكَ لَءَايَـٰتٍ     There are indeed signs in this

لِّأُوْلِى ٱلنُّهَىٰ ۞     for those who have reason.

وَلَوْلَا كَلِمَةٌ سَبَقَتْ مِن رَّبِّكَ 129 And were it not for a prior decree of *your* Lord

---

[1] That is, Adam and Eve, or Adam and Iblīs.

447

لَكَانَ لِزَامًا وَأَجَلٌ مُّسَمًّى ۞

and a specified time, it was inevitable.

فَٱصْبِرْ عَلَىٰ مَا يَقُولُونَ

130 So *be patient* with what they say,

وَسَبِّحْ بِحَمْدِ رَبِّكَ

and *celebrate* the praise of *your* Lord

قَبْلَ طُلُوعِ ٱلشَّمْسِ

before the rising of the sun

وَقَبْلَ غُرُوبِهَا

and before the sunset,

وَمِنْ ءَانَآئِ ٱلَّيْلِ فَسَبِّحْ

and *glorify* Him in watches of the night

وَأَطْرَافَ ٱلنَّهَارِ

and at the day's ends,

لَعَلَّكَ تَرْضَىٰ ۞

that *you* may be pleased.

وَلَا تَمُدَّنَّ عَيْنَيْكَ

131 Do not extend *your* glance

إِلَىٰ مَا مَتَّعْنَا بِهِۦٓ أَزْوَٰجًا مِّنْهُمْ

toward what We have provided certain groups of them

زَهْرَةَ ٱلْحَيَوٰةِ ٱلدُّنْيَا

as a glitter of the life of this world,

لِنَفْتِنَهُمْ فِيهِ

so that We may test them thereby.

وَرِزْقُ رَبِّكَ خَيْرٌ

And the provision of *your* Lord is better

وَأَبْقَىٰ ۞

and more lasting.

وَأْمُرْ أَهْلَكَ بِٱلصَّلَوٰةِ

132 And bid *your* family to prayer

وَٱصْطَبِرْ عَلَيْهَا

and *be* steadfast in its maintenance.

لَا نَسْـَٔلُكَ رِزْقًا

We do not ask any provision of *you*.

نَّحْنُ نَرْزُقُكَ

It is We who provide for *you*,

وَٱلْعَٰقِبَةُ لِلتَّقْوَىٰ ۞

and the outcome will be in favour of Godwariness.

وَقَالُوا۟ لَوْلَا يَأْتِينَا

133 They say, 'Why does he not bring us

بِـَٔايَةٍ مِّن رَّبِّهِۦ

a sign from his Lord?'

أَوَلَمْ تَأْتِهِم بَيِّنَةُ

Has there not come to them a manifest proof

مَا فِى ٱلصُّحُفِ ٱلْأُولَىٰ ۞

in that which is in the former scriptures?

وَلَوْ أَنَّآ أَهْلَكْنَٰهُم

134 Had We destroyed them

بِعَذَابٍ مِّن قَبْلِهِۦ

with a punishment before it,[1]

لَقَالُوا۟ رَبَّنَا

they would have surely said, 'Our Lord!

لَوْلَآ أَرْسَلْتَ إِلَيْنَا رَسُولًا

Why did You not send us an apostle

فَنَتَّبِعَ ءَايَٰتِكَ

so that we might follow Your signs

مِن قَبْلِ أَن نَّذِلَّ وَنَخْزَىٰ ۞

before we were abased and disgraced?'

---

[1] That is, before the revelation of the Qur'ān.

قُل كُلٌّ مُّتَرَبِّصٌ    135 *Say,* 'Each [of us] is waiting.

فَتَرَبَّصُواْ    So wait!

فَسَتَعْلَمُونَ    Soon you will know

مَنْ أَصْحَابُ ٱلصِّرَاطِ ٱلسَّوِيِّ    who are the people of the right path,

وَمَنِ ٱهْتَدَىٰ ۝    and who is [rightly] guided.'

[PART 17]

# سُورَةُ الأَنبِيَاء    21. SŪRAT AL-ANBIYĀ'[1]

بِسْمِ ٱللَّهِ    In the Name of Allah,

ٱلرَّحْمَٰنِ ٱلرَّحِيمِ    the All-beneficent, the All-merciful.

ٱقْتَرَبَ لِلنَّاسِ حِسَابُهُمْ    1 Mankind's reckoning has drawn near to them,

وَهُمْ فِى غَفْلَةٍ مُّعْرِضُونَ ۝    yet they are disregardful in [their] obliviousness.

مَا يَأْتِيهِم    2 There does not come to them

مِّن ذِكْرٍ مِّن رَّبِّهِم مُّحْدَثٍ    any new reminder from their Lord

إِلَّا ٱسْتَمَعُوهُ وَهُمْ يَلْعَبُونَ ۝    but they listen to it as they play around,

لَاهِيَةً قُلُوبُهُمْ    3 their hearts set on diversions.

وَأَسَرُّواْ ٱلنَّجْوَى ٱلَّذِينَ ظَلَمُواْ    The wrongdoers secretly whisper together, [saying],

هَلْ هَٰذَا إِلَّا بَشَرٌ مِّثْلُكُمْ    'Is not this [man] just a human being like yourselves?

أَفَتَأْتُونَ ٱلسِّحْرَ وَأَنتُمْ تُبْصِرُونَ ۝    Will you give in to magic with open eyes?'

قَالَ رَبِّى يَعْلَمُ    4 He said, 'My Lord knows

ٱلْقَوْلَ فِى ٱلسَّمَاءِ وَٱلْأَرْضِ    every word [spoken] in the sky and the earth,

وَهُوَ ٱلسَّمِيعُ ٱلْعَلِيمُ ۝    and He is the All-hearing, the All-knowing.'

بَلْ قَالُوٓاْ أَضْغَٰثُ أَحْلَٰمٍ    5 Rather they said, '[They are] confused nightmares!'

بَلِ ٱفْتَرَىٰهُ    'Rather he has fabricated it!'

بَلْ هُوَ شَاعِرٌ    'Rather he is a poet!'

فَلْيَأْتِنَا بِـَٔايَةٍ كَمَآ أُرْسِلَ ٱلْأَوَّلُونَ ۝    'Let him bring us a sign, like those sent to the ancients.'

مَآ ءَامَنَتْ قَبْلَهُم مِّن قَرْيَةٍ أَهْلَكْنَٰهَآ    6 No town that We destroyed before them believed.[2]

---

[1] Accounts of several prophets (*anbiyā'*) appear in this *sūrah*, hence its name.

[2] That is, they did not believe even after miracles were shown to them.

أَفَهُمْ يُؤْمِنُونَ ۝    Will these then have faith [if they are sent signs]?

وَمَآ أَرْسَلْنَا قَبْلَكَ   7 We did not send [any apostles] before *you*

إِلَّا رِجَالًا نُّوحِىٓ إِلَيْهِمْ    except as men, to whom We revealed.

فَسْـَٔلُوٓاْ أَهْلَ ٱلذِّكْرِ    Ask the People of the Reminder[1]

إِن كُنتُمْ لَا تَعْلَمُونَ ۝    if you do not know.

وَمَا جَعَلْنَٰهُمْ جَسَدًا   8 We did not make them bodies

لَّا يَأْكُلُونَ ٱلطَّعَامَ    that did not eat food,

وَمَا كَانُواْ خَٰلِدِينَ ۝    and they were not immortal.

ثُمَّ صَدَقْنَٰهُمُ ٱلْوَعْدَ   9 Then We fulfilled Our promise to them,

فَأَنجَيْنَٰهُمْ وَمَن نَّشَآءُ    and We delivered them and whomever We wished,

وَأَهْلَكْنَا ٱلْمُسْرِفِينَ ۝    and We destroyed the profligates.

لَقَدْ أَنزَلْنَآ إِلَيْكُمْ كِتَٰبًا   10 Certainly We have sent down to you a Book

فِيهِ ذِكْرُكُمْ    in which there is an admonition for you.

أَفَلَا تَعْقِلُونَ ۝    Do you not apply reason?

وَكَمْ قَصَمْنَا مِن قَرْيَةٍ   11 How many a town We have smashed

كَانَتْ ظَالِمَةً    that had been wrongdoing,

وَأَنشَأْنَا بَعْدَهَا قَوْمًا ءَاخَرِينَ ۝    and We brought forth another people after it.

فَلَمَّآ أَحَسُّواْ بَأْسَنَآ   12 So when they sighted Our punishment,

إِذَا هُم مِّنْهَا يَرْكُضُونَ ۝    behold, they ran away from it.

لَا تَرْكُضُواْ   13 'Do not run away!

وَٱرْجِعُوٓاْ إِلَىٰ مَآ أُتْرِفْتُمْ فِيهِ    Return to the opulence you were given to enjoy

وَمَسَٰكِنِكُمْ    and to your dwellings

لَعَلَّكُمْ تُسْـَٔلُونَ ۝    so that you may be questioned!'

قَالُواْ يَٰوَيْلَنَآ   14 They said, 'Woe to us!

إِنَّا كُنَّا ظَٰلِمِينَ ۝    We have indeed been wrongdoers!'

فَمَا زَالَت تِّلْكَ دَعْوَىٰهُمْ   15 That remained their cry

حَتَّىٰ جَعَلْنَٰهُمْ حَصِيدًا    until We turned them into a mown field,

خَٰمِدِينَ ۝    stilled [like burnt ashes].

وَمَا خَلَقْنَا ٱلسَّمَآءَ وَٱلْأَرْضَ   16 We did not create the sky and the earth

---

[1] Cf. 16:43.

وَمَا بَيْنَهُمَا لَـٰعِبِينَ ۝    and whatever is between them for play.

لَوْ أَرَدْنَا أَن نَّتَّخِذَ لَهْوًا    17 Had We desired to take up some diversion

لَّاتَّخَذْنَـٰهُ مِن لَّدُنَّا    We would have surely taken it up with Ourselves,

إِن كُنَّا فَـٰعِلِينَ ۝    were We to do [so].

بَلْ نَقْذِفُ بِٱلْحَقِّ عَلَى ٱلْبَـٰطِلِ    18 Rather We hurls the truth against falsehood,

فَيَدْمَغُهُ    and it crushes its head,

فَإِذَا هُوَ زَاهِقٌ    and behold, falsehood vanishes!

وَلَكُمُ ٱلْوَيْلُ مِمَّا تَصِفُونَ ۝    And woe to you for what you allege [about Allah].

وَلَهُۥ مَن فِى ٱلسَّمَـٰوَٰتِ    19 To Him belongs whatever is in the heavens

وَٱلْأَرْضِ    and the earth,

وَمَنْ عِندَهُۥ    and those who are near Him

لَا يَسْتَكْبِرُونَ عَنْ عِبَادَتِهِۦ    do not disdain to worship Him,

وَلَا يَسْتَحْسِرُونَ ۝    nor do they become weary.

يُسَبِّحُونَ ٱلَّيْلَ وَٱلنَّهَارَ    20 They glorify [Him] night and day,

لَا يَفْتُرُونَ ۝    and they do not flag.

أَمِ ٱتَّخَذُوٓاْ ءَالِهَةً مِّنَ ٱلْأَرْضِ    21 Have they taken gods from the earth

هُمْ يُنشِرُونَ ۝    who raise [the dead]?

لَوْ كَانَ فِيهِمَآ ءَالِهَةٌ إِلَّا ٱللَّهُ    22 Had there been gods in them[1] other than Allah,

لَفَسَدَتَا    they would surely have fallen apart.

فَسُبْحَـٰنَ ٱللَّهِ رَبِّ ٱلْعَرْشِ    Clear is Allah, the Lord of the Throne,

عَمَّا يَصِفُونَ ۝    of what they allege [concerning Him].

لَا يُسْـَٔلُ عَمَّا يَفْعَلُ    23 He is not questioned concerning what He does,

وَهُمْ يُسْـَٔلُونَ ۝    but they are questioned.

أَمِ ٱتَّخَذُوٓاْ مِن دُونِهِۦٓ ءَالِهَةً    24 Have they taken gods besides Him?

قُلْ هَاتُواْ بُرْهَـٰنَكُمْ    Say, 'Produce your evidence!

هَـٰذَا ذِكْرُ مَن مَّعِىَ    This is a reminder for those who are with me,

وَذِكْرُ مَن قَبْلِى    and a reminder for those [who went] before me.'

بَلْ أَكْثَرُهُمْ لَا يَعْلَمُونَ ٱلْحَقَّ    Rather most of them do not know the truth,

فَهُم مُّعْرِضُونَ ۝    and so they are disregardful.

---

[1] That is, in the heavens and the earth.

وَمَآ أَرْسَلْنَا مِن قَبْلِكَ مِن رَّسُولٍ   25 We did not send any apostle before *you*

إِلَّا نُوحِىٓ إِلَيْهِ    but We revealed to him

أَنَّهُۥ لَآ إِلَٰهَ إِلَّآ أَنَا۠    that 'There is no god except Me;

فَٱعْبُدُونِ ۞    so worship Me.'

وَقَالُوا۟ ٱتَّخَذَ ٱلرَّحْمَٰنُ وَلَدًا   26 They say, 'The All-beneficent has taken offsprings.'

سُبْحَٰنَهُۥ    Immaculate is He!

بَلْ عِبَادٌ مُّكْرَمُونَ ۞    Rather they are [His] honoured servants.

لَا يَسْبِقُونَهُۥ بِٱلْقَوْلِ   27 They do not venture to speak ahead of Him,

وَهُم بِأَمْرِهِۦ يَعْمَلُونَ ۞    and they act by His command.

يَعْلَمُ مَا بَيْنَ أَيْدِيهِمْ   28 He knows that which is before them

وَمَا خَلْفَهُمْ    and that which is behind them,

وَلَا يَشْفَعُونَ    and they do not intercede

إِلَّا لِمَنِ ٱرْتَضَىٰ    except for someone He approves of,

وَهُم مِّنْ خَشْيَتِهِۦ مُشْفِقُونَ ۞ ❋    and they are apprehensive for the fear of Him.

وَمَن يَقُلْ مِنْهُمْ   29 Should any of them say,

إِنِّىٓ إِلَٰهٌ مِّن دُونِهِۦ    'I am a god besides Him,'

فَذَٰلِكَ نَجْزِيهِ جَهَنَّمَ    We will requite him with hell.

كَذَٰلِكَ نَجْزِى ٱلظَّٰلِمِينَ ۞    Thus do We requite the wrongdoers.

أَوَلَمْ يَرَ ٱلَّذِينَ كَفَرُوٓا۟   30 Have the faithless not regarded

أَنَّ ٱلسَّمَٰوَٰتِ وَٱلْأَرْضَ كَانَتَا رَتْقًا    that the heavens and the earth were interwoven

فَفَتَقْنَٰهُمَا    and We disjoined them,

وَجَعَلْنَا مِنَ ٱلْمَآءِ كُلَّ شَىْءٍ حَىٍّ    and We made every living thing out of water?

أَفَلَا يُؤْمِنُونَ ۞    Will they not then have faith?

وَجَعَلْنَا فِى ٱلْأَرْضِ رَوَٰسِىَ   31 We set firm mountains in the earth

أَن تَمِيدَ بِهِمْ    lest it should shake with them,

وَجَعَلْنَا فِيهَا فِجَاجًا سُبُلًا    and We made broad ways in them

لَّعَلَّهُمْ يَهْتَدُونَ ۞    so that they may be guided [to their destinations].

وَجَعَلْنَا ٱلسَّمَآءَ سَقْفًا مَّحْفُوظًا   32 We made the sky a preserved roof

وَهُمْ عَنْ ءَايَٰتِهَا مُعْرِضُونَ ۞    and yet they are disregardful of its signs.

وَهُوَ ٱلَّذِى خَلَقَ ٱلَّيْلَ وَٱلنَّهَارَ   33 It is He who created the night and the day,

وَٱلشَّمْسَ وَٱلْقَمَرَ　the sun and the moon,

كُلٌّ فِى فَلَكٍ يَسْبَحُونَ ۝　each swimming in an orbit.

وَمَا جَعَلْنَا لِبَشَرٍ مِّن قَبْلِكَ ٱلْخُلْدَ　34 We did not give immortality to any human before *you*.

أَفَإِن مِّتَّ فَهُمُ ٱلْخَٰلِدُونَ ۝　If *you* are fated to die, will they live on forever?

كُلُّ نَفْسٍ ذَآئِقَةُ ٱلْمَوْتِ　35 Every soul shall taste death,

وَنَبْلُوكُم بِٱلشَّرِّ وَٱلْخَيْرِ　and We will test you with good and ill

فِتْنَةً　by way of test,

وَإِلَيْنَا تُرْجَعُونَ ۝　and to Us you will be brought back.

وَإِذَا رَءَاكَ ٱلَّذِينَ كَفَرُوٓا　36 Whenever the faithless see *you*

إِن يَتَّخِذُونَكَ إِلَّا هُزُوًا　they only take *you* in derision:

أَهَٰذَا ٱلَّذِى يَذْكُرُ ءَالِهَتَكُمْ　'Is this the one who speaks ill of your gods?'

وَهُم بِذِكْرِ ٱلرَّحْمَٰنِ هُمْ كَٰفِرُونَ ۝　And they defy the remembrance of the All-beneficent.

خُلِقَ ٱلْإِنسَٰنُ مِنْ عَجَلٍ　37 Man is a creature of hastiness.

سَأُو۟رِيكُمْ ءَايَٰتِى　Soon I will show you My signs.

فَلَا تَسْتَعْجِلُونِ ۝　So do not ask Me to hasten.

وَيَقُولُونَ مَتَىٰ هَٰذَا ٱلْوَعْدُ　38 And they say, 'When will this promise be fulfilled,

إِن كُنتُمْ صَٰدِقِينَ ۝　should you be truthful?'

لَوْ يَعْلَمُ ٱلَّذِينَ كَفَرُوا۟ حِينَ　39 If only the faithless knew of the time when

لَا يَكُفُّونَ عَن وُجُوهِهِمُ ٱلنَّارَ　they will not be able to keep the Fire off their faces

وَلَا عَن ظُهُورِهِمْ　and their backs,

وَلَا هُمْ يُنصَرُونَ ۝　nor will they be helped![1]

بَلْ تَأْتِيهِم بَغْتَةً　40 Rather it will overtake them suddenly,

فَتَبْهَتُهُمْ　dumbfounding them.

فَلَا يَسْتَطِيعُونَ رَدَّهَا　So neither will they be able to avert it,

وَلَا هُمْ يُنظَرُونَ ۝　nor will they be granted any respite.

وَلَقَدِ ٱسْتُهْزِئَ بِرُسُلٍ مِّن قَبْلِكَ　41 Apostles were certainly derided at before *you*;

فَحَاقَ بِٱلَّذِينَ سَخِرُوا۟ مِنْهُم　but those who ridiculed them were besieged

مَّا كَانُوا۟ بِهِ يَسْتَهْزِءُونَ ۝　by what they had been deriding.

---

[1] That is, had the faithless known their state in hell, they would not ask for the punishment to be hastened.

قُل مَن يَكْلَؤُكُم بِٱلَّيْلِ وَٱلنَّهَارِ  42 *Say,* 'Who can guard you, day and night,

مِنَ ٱلرَّحْمَٰنِ  from [the punishment of] the All-beneficent?'

بَلْ هُمْ عَن ذِكْرِ رَبِّهِم مُّعْرِضُونَ ۝  Rather they are disregardful of their Lord's remembrance.

أَمْ لَهُمْ ءَالِهَةٌ تَمْنَعُهُم مِّن دُونِنَا  43 Do they have gods besides Us to defend them?

لَا يَسْتَطِيعُونَ نَصْرَ أَنفُسِهِمْ  Neither can they help themselves,

وَلَا هُم مِّنَّا يُصْحَبُونَ ۝  nor can they provide them with an escort against Us.

بَلْ مَتَّعْنَا هَٰؤُلَآءِ وَءَابَآءَهُمْ  44 Rather We have provided for them and their fathers

حَتَّىٰ طَالَ عَلَيْهِمُ ٱلْعُمُرُ  until they lived on for long years.

أَفَلَا يَرَوْنَ أَنَّا نَأْتِي ٱلْأَرْضَ  Do they not see how We visit the land

نَنقُصُهَا مِنْ أَطْرَافِهَآ  diminishing it at its edges?[1]

أَفَهُمُ ٱلْغَٰلِبُونَ ۝  Are they the ones who will prevail?

قُلْ إِنَّمَآ أُنذِرُكُم بِٱلْوَحْيِ  45 *Say,* 'I indeed warn you by the means of revelation.'

وَلَا يَسْمَعُ ٱلصُّمُّ ٱلدُّعَآءَ  But the deaf do not hear the call

إِذَا مَا يُنذَرُونَ ۝  when they are warned.

وَلَئِن مَّسَّتْهُمْ نَفْحَةٌ مِّنْ عَذَابِ رَبِّكَ  46 Should a whiff of your Lord's punishment touch them,

لَيَقُولُنَّ يَٰوَيْلَنَآ  they will surely say, 'Woe to us!

إِنَّا كُنَّا ظَٰلِمِينَ ۝  We have indeed been wrongdoers!'

وَنَضَعُ ٱلْمَوَٰزِينَ ٱلْقِسْطَ  47 We shall set up the scales of justice

لِيَوْمِ ٱلْقِيَٰمَةِ  on the Day of Resurrection,

فَلَا تُظْلَمُ نَفْسٌ شَيْئًا  and no soul will be wronged in the least.

وَإِن كَانَ مِثْقَالَ حَبَّةٍ مِّنْ خَرْدَلٍ  Even if it be the weight of a mustard seed

أَتَيْنَا بِهَا  We shall produce it

وَكَفَىٰ بِنَا حَٰسِبِينَ ۝  and We suffice as reckoners.

وَلَقَدْ ءَاتَيْنَا مُوسَىٰ وَهَٰرُونَ  48 Certainly We gave Moses and Aaron

ٱلْفُرْقَانَ  the Distinguisher,

وَضِيَآءً وَذِكْرًا لِّلْمُتَّقِينَ ۝  as a light and reminder for the Godwary.

ٱلَّذِينَ يَخْشَوْنَ رَبَّهُم بِٱلْغَيْبِ  49 Those who fear their Lord in secret,

وَهُم مِّنَ ٱلسَّاعَةِ مُشْفِقُونَ ۝  and who are apprehensive of the Hour.

---

[1] Cf. 13:41.

وَهَٰذَا ذِكْرٌ مُّبَارَكٌ أَنزَلْنَٰهُ ۚ 50 This is a blessed reminder which We have sent down.

أَفَأَنتُمْ لَهُۥ مُنكِرُونَ ۝     Will you then deny it?

وَلَقَدْ ءَاتَيْنَآ إِبْرَٰهِيمَ رُشْدَهُۥ 51 Certainly We had given Abraham his rectitude

مِن قَبْلُ     before,

وَكُنَّا بِهِۦ عَٰلِمِينَ ۝     and We knew him

إِذْ قَالَ لِأَبِيهِ وَقَوْمِهِ 52     when he said to his father and his people,

مَا هَٰذِهِ ٱلتَّمَاثِيلُ ٱلَّتِىٓ     'What are these images

أَنتُمْ لَهَا عَٰكِفُونَ ۝     to which you keep on clinging?'

قَالُوا۟ وَجَدْنَآ ءَابَآءَنَا لَهَا عَٰبِدِينَ ۝ 53 They said, 'We found our fathers worshipping them.'

قَالَ لَقَدْ كُنتُمْ أَنتُمْ وَءَابَآؤُكُمْ 54 He said, 'Certainly you and your fathers have been

فِى ضَلَٰلٍ مُّبِينٍ ۝     in manifest error.

قَالُوٓا۟ أَجِئْتَنَا بِٱلْحَقِّ 55 They said, 'Are you telling the truth,[1]

أَمْ أَنتَ مِنَ ٱللَّٰعِبِينَ ۝     or are you [just] kidding?'

قَالَ بَل رَّبُّكُمْ رَبُّ ٱلسَّمَٰوَٰتِ 56 He said, 'Rather your Lord is the Lord of the heavens

وَٱلْأَرْضِ     and the earth,

ٱلَّذِى فَطَرَهُنَّ     who originated them,

وَأَنَا۠ عَلَىٰ ذَٰلِكُم مِّنَ ٱلشَّٰهِدِينَ ۝     and I am a witness to this.

وَتَٱللَّهِ لَأَكِيدَنَّ أَصْنَٰمَكُم 57     By Allah, I will devise a stratagem against your idols

بَعْدَ أَن تُوَلُّوا۟ مُدْبِرِينَ ۝     after you have gone away.'

فَجَعَلَهُمْ جُذَٰذًا 58 So he broke them into pieces,

إِلَّا كَبِيرًا لَّهُمْ     —all except the biggest of them—

لَعَلَّهُمْ إِلَيْهِ يَرْجِعُونَ ۝     so that they might come back to it.

قَالُوا۟ مَن فَعَلَ هَٰذَا بِـَٔالِهَتِنَآ 59 They said, 'Whoever has done this to Our gods?!

إِنَّهُۥ لَمِنَ ٱلظَّٰلِمِينَ ۝     He is indeed a wrongdoer!'

قَالُوا۟ سَمِعْنَا فَتًى يَذْكُرُهُمْ 60 They said, 'We heard a young man speaking ill of them.

يُقَالُ لَهُۥٓ إِبْرَٰهِيمُ ۝     He is called "Abraham."'

قَالُوا۟ فَأْتُوا۟ بِهِۦ عَلَىٰٓ أَعْيُنِ ٱلنَّاسِ 61 They said, 'Bring him before the people's eyes

لَعَلَّهُمْ يَشْهَدُونَ ۝     so that they may bear witness [against him].'

---

[1] Or 'Are you speaking seriously.'

قَالُوٓاْ ءَأَنتَ فَعَلْتَ هَٰذَا بِـَٔالِهَتِنَا يَٰإِبْرَٰهِيمُ ۝ 62 They said, 'Were it you who did this to our gods, O Abraham?'

قَالَ بَلْ فَعَلَهُۥ كَبِيرُهُمْ هَٰذَا فَسْـَٔلُوهُمْ إِن كَانُواْ يَنطِقُونَ ۝ 63 He said, 'Rather it was this biggest of them who did it! Ask them, if they can speak.'

فَرَجَعُوٓاْ إِلَىٰٓ أَنفُسِهِمْ فَقَالُوٓاْ إِنَّكُمْ أَنتُمُ ٱلظَّٰلِمُونَ ۝ 64 Thereat they came to themselves and said [to one another], 'Indeed it is you who are the wrongdoers!'

ثُمَّ نُكِسُواْ عَلَىٰ رُءُوسِهِمْ لَقَدْ عَلِمْتَ مَا هَٰٓؤُلَآءِ يَنطِقُونَ ۝ 65 Then they hung their heads. [They said], 'You certainly know that they cannot speak.'

قَالَ أَفَتَعْبُدُونَ مِن دُونِ ٱللَّهِ مَا لَا يَنفَعُكُمْ شَيْـًٔا وَلَا يَضُرُّكُمْ ۝ 66 He said, 'Do you then worship, besides Allah, that which cannot cause you any benefit or harm?

أُفٍّ لَّكُمْ وَلِمَا تَعْبُدُونَ مِن دُونِ ٱللَّهِ أَفَلَا تَعْقِلُونَ ۝ 67 Fie on you and what you worship besides Allah! Do you not apply reason?'

قَالُواْ حَرِّقُوهُ وَٱنصُرُوٓاْ ءَالِهَتَكُمْ إِن كُنتُمْ فَٰعِلِينَ ۝ 68 They said, 'Burn him, and help your gods, if you are to do anything!'

قُلْنَا يَٰنَارُ كُونِى بَرْدًا وَسَلَٰمًا عَلَىٰٓ إِبْرَٰهِيمَ ۝ 69 We said, 'O fire! Be cool and safe for Abraham!'

وَأَرَادُواْ بِهِۦ كَيْدًا فَجَعَلْنَٰهُمُ ٱلْأَخْسَرِينَ ۝ 70 They sought to outmaneuver him, but We made them the biggest losers.

وَنَجَّيْنَٰهُ وَلُوطًا إِلَى ٱلْأَرْضِ ٱلَّتِى بَٰرَكْنَا فِيهَا لِلْعَٰلَمِينَ ۝ 71 We delivered him and Lot toward the land which We have blessed for all nations.[1]

وَوَهَبْنَا لَهُۥٓ إِسْحَٰقَ وَيَعْقُوبَ نَافِلَةً وَكُلًّا جَعَلْنَا صَٰلِحِينَ ۝ 72 And We gave him Isaac, and Jacob as well for a grandson,[2] and each of them We made righteous.

وَجَعَلْنَٰهُمْ أَئِمَّةً يَهْدُونَ بِأَمْرِنَا وَأَوْحَيْنَآ إِلَيْهِمْ 73 We made them *imams*, guiding by Our command, and We revealed to them

---

[1] That is, Canaan.

[2] In a tradition of al-Imam al-Ṣādiq ('a), *nāfilatan* here is interpreted as meaning *walad al-walad nāfilatan*. Cf. *Maʿānī al-akhbār*, p. 225.

فِعْلَ ٱلْخَيْرَٰتِ     the performance of good deeds,

وَإِقَامَ ٱلصَّلَوٰةِ     the maintenance of prayers,

وَإِيتَآءَ ٱلزَّكَوٰةِ     and the giving of *zakāt*,

وَكَانُوا۟ لَنَا عَٰبِدِينَ ۞     and they used to worship Us.

وَلُوطًا ءَاتَيْنَٰهُ حُكْمًا     74 We gave judgement and knowledge to Lot,

وَعِلْمًا وَنَجَّيْنَٰهُ مِنَ ٱلْقَرْيَةِ     and We delivered him from the town

ٱلَّتِى كَانَت تَّعْمَلُ ٱلْخَبَٰٓئِثَ     which used to commit vicious acts.

إِنَّهُمْ كَانُوا۟ قَوْمَ سَوْءٍ فَٰسِقِينَ ۞     Indeed they were an evil and profligate lot.

وَأَدْخَلْنَٰهُ فِى رَحْمَتِنَآ     75 And We admitted him into Our mercy.

إِنَّهُۥ مِنَ ٱلصَّٰلِحِينَ ۞     Indeed he was one of the righteous.

وَنُوحًا إِذْ نَادَىٰ مِن قَبْلُ     76 And before that Noah, when he called out,

فَٱسْتَجَبْنَا لَهُۥ     We responded to him

فَنَجَّيْنَٰهُ وَأَهْلَهُۥ     and delivered him and his family

مِنَ ٱلْكَرْبِ ٱلْعَظِيمِ ۞     from the great agony.

وَنَصَرْنَٰهُ مِنَ ٱلْقَوْمِ     77 And We helped him against the people

ٱلَّذِينَ كَذَّبُوا۟ بِـَٔايَٰتِنَآ     who denied Our signs.

إِنَّهُمْ كَانُوا۟ قَوْمَ سَوْءٍ     They were indeed an evil lot;

فَأَغْرَقْنَٰهُمْ أَجْمَعِينَ ۞     so We drowned them all.

وَدَاوُۥدَ وَسُلَيْمَٰنَ     78 And David and Solomon

إِذْ يَحْكُمَانِ فِى ٱلْحَرْثِ     when they gave judgement concerning the tillage

إِذْ نَفَشَتْ فِيهِ غَنَمُ ٱلْقَوْمِ     when the sheep of some people strayed into it by night,

وَكُنَّا لِحُكْمِهِمْ شَٰهِدِينَ ۞     and We were witness to their judgement.

فَفَهَّمْنَٰهَا سُلَيْمَٰنَ     79 We gave its understanding to Solomon,

وَكُلًّا ءَاتَيْنَا حُكْمًا وَعِلْمًا     and to each We gave judgement and knowledge.

وَسَخَّرْنَا     And We disposed

مَعَ دَاوُۥدَ ٱلْجِبَالَ يُسَبِّحْنَ وَٱلطَّيْرَ     the mountains and the birds to glorify [Him] with David,

وَكُنَّا فَٰعِلِينَ ۞     and We have been the doer [of such things].

وَعَلَّمْنَهُ صَنْعَةَ لَبُوسٍ لَّكُمْ 80 We taught him the making of coats of mail for you,

لِتُحْصِنَكُم مِّنۢ بَأْسِكُمْ     to protect you from your [own] violence.

فَهَلْ أَنتُمْ شَٰكِرُونَ ۝     Will you then be grateful?

وَلِسُلَيْمَٰنَ ٱلرِّيحَ عَاصِفَةً 81 And for Solomon [We disposed] the tempestuous wind

تَجْرِى بِأَمْرِهِۦ     which blew by his command

إِلَى ٱلْأَرْضِ ٱلَّتِى بَٰرَكْنَا فِيهَا     toward the land which We have blessed,

وَكُنَّا بِكُلِّ شَىْءٍ عَٰلِمِينَ ۝     and We have knowledge of all things.

وَمِنَ ٱلشَّيَٰطِينِ مَن يَغُوصُونَ لَهُۥ 82 Among the devils were some who dived for him

وَيَعْمَلُونَ عَمَلًا دُونَ ذَٰلِكَ     and performed tasks other than that,

وَكُنَّا لَهُمْ حَٰفِظِينَ ۝     and We were watchful over them.

وَأَيُّوبَ إِذْ نَادَىٰ رَبَّهُۥٓ 83 And Job, when he called out to his Lord,

أَنِّى مَسَّنِىَ ٱلضُّرُّ     'Indeed distress has befallen me,

وَأَنتَ أَرْحَمُ ٱلرَّٰحِمِينَ ۝     and You are the most merciful of the merciful.'

فَٱسْتَجَبْنَا لَهُۥ 84 So We answered his prayer

فَكَشَفْنَا مَا بِهِۦ مِن ضُرٍّ     and removed his distress,

وَءَاتَيْنَٰهُ أَهْلَهُۥ     and We gave him [back] his family

وَمِثْلَهُم مَّعَهُمْ     along with others like them,

رَحْمَةً مِّنْ عِندِنَا     as a mercy from Us,

وَذِكْرَىٰ لِلْعَٰبِدِينَ ۝     and an admonition for the devout.

وَإِسْمَٰعِيلَ وَإِدْرِيسَ وَذَا ٱلْكِفْلِ 85 And Ishmael, Idris, and Dhul-Kifl

كُلٌّ مِّنَ ٱلصَّٰبِرِينَ ۝     —each of them was among the patient.

وَأَدْخَلْنَٰهُمْ فِى رَحْمَتِنَآ 86 We admitted them into Our mercy.

إِنَّهُم مِّنَ ٱلصَّٰلِحِينَ ۝     Indeed they were among the righteous.

وَذَا ٱلنُّونِ إِذ ذَّهَبَ مُغَٰضِبًا 87 And the Man of the Fish, when he left in a rage,

فَظَنَّ أَن لَّن نَّقْدِرَ عَلَيْهِ     thinking that We would not put him to hardship.

فَنَادَىٰ فِى ٱلظُّلُمَٰتِ     Then he cried out in the darkness,

أَن لَّآ إِلَٰهَ إِلَّآ أَنتَ     'There is no god except You!

سُبْحَـٰنَكَ    You are immaculate!

إِنِّى كُنتُ مِنَ ٱلظَّـٰلِمِينَ ۝    I have indeed been among the wrongdoers!'

فَٱسْتَجَبْنَا    88 So We answered his prayer

لَهُۥ وَنَجَّيْنَـٰهُ مِنَ ٱلْغَمِّ    and delivered him from the agony;

وَكَذَٰلِكَ نُـۨجِى ٱلْمُؤْمِنِينَ ۝    and thus do We deliver the faithful.

وَزَكَرِيَّآ إِذْ نَادَىٰ رَبَّهُۥ    89 And Zechariah, when he cried out to his Lord,

رَبِّ    'My Lord!

لَا تَذَرْنِى فَرْدًا    Do not leave me without an heir,

وَأَنتَ خَيْرُ ٱلْوَٰرِثِينَ ۝    and You are the best of inheritors.'

فَٱسْتَجَبْنَا لَهُۥ    90 So We answered his prayer,

وَوَهَبْنَا لَهُۥ يَحْيَىٰ    and gave him John,

وَأَصْلَحْنَا لَهُۥ زَوْجَهُۥٓ    and remedied his wife['s infertility] for him.

إِنَّهُمْ كَانُوا۟ يُسَـٰرِعُونَ    Indeed they were active

فِى ٱلْخَيْرَٰتِ    in [performing] good works,

وَيَدْعُونَنَا    and they would supplicate Us

رَغَبًا وَرَهَبًا    with eagerness and awe

وَكَانُوا۟ لَنَا خَـٰشِعِينَ ۝    and were humble before Us.

وَٱلَّتِىٓ أَحْصَنَتْ فَرْجَهَا    91 And her who guarded her chastity,

فَنَفَخْنَا فِيهَا مِن رُّوحِنَا    so We breathed into her Our spirit.[1]

وَجَعَلْنَـٰهَا وَٱبْنَهَآ ءَايَةً لِّلْعَـٰلَمِينَ ۝    and made her and her son a sign for all the nations.

إِنَّ هَـٰذِهِۦٓ أُمَّتُكُمْ أُمَّةً وَٰحِدَةً    92 Indeed this community of yours is one community,

وَأَنَا۠ رَبُّكُمْ    and I am your Lord.

فَٱعْبُدُونِ ۝    So worship Me.

وَتَقَطَّعُوٓا۟ أَمْرَهُم بَيْنَهُمْ    93 They[2] have fragmented their religion among themselves.

كُلٌّ إِلَيْنَا رَٰجِعُونَ ۝    Everyone of them will return to Us.

فَمَن يَعْمَلْ مِنَ ٱلصَّـٰلِحَـٰتِ    94 Whoever does righteous deeds,

---

[1] Or 'of Our spirit.'

[2] That is, the earlier religious communities, such as Jews and Christians. Cf. 23:53

وَهُوَ مُؤْمِنٌ
should he be faithful,

فَلَا كُفْرَانَ لِسَعْيِهِ
his endeavour shall not go unappreciated,

وَإِنَّا لَهُ كَـٰتِبُونَ ۝
and We will indeed write it for him.

وَحَرَمٌ عَلَىٰ قَرْيَةٍ ٩٥
95 It is forbidden for [the people of] any town

أَهْلَكْنَـٰهَآ
that We have destroyed [to return to the world]:

أَنَّهُمْ لَا يَرْجِعُونَ ۝
they shall not return.

حَتَّىٰ إِذَا فُتِحَتْ يَأْجُوجُ وَمَأْجُوجُ
96 When Gog and Magog are let loose,

وَهُم مِّن كُلِّ حَدَبٍ يَنسِلُونَ ۝
and they race down from every slope,[1]

وَٱقْتَرَبَ ٱلْوَعْدُ ٱلْحَقُّ
97 and the true promise draws near [to its fulfillment],

فَإِذَا هِيَ شَـٰخِصَةٌ أَبْصَـٰرُ ٱلَّذِينَ كَفَرُوا
behold, the faithless will look on with a fixed gaze:

يَـٰوَيْلَنَا
'Woe to us!

قَدْ كُنَّا فِي غَفْلَةٍ مِّنْ هَـٰذَا
We have certainly been oblivious to this!

بَلْ كُنَّا ظَـٰلِمِينَ ۝
Rather we have been wrongdoers!'

إِنَّكُمْ وَمَا تَعْبُدُونَ مِن دُونِ ٱللَّهِ
98 Indeed you and what you worship besides Allah

حَصَبُ جَهَنَّمَ
shall be fuel for hell,

أَنتُمْ لَهَا وَٰرِدُونَ ۝
and you will come to it

لَوْ كَانَ هَـٰٓؤُلَآءِ ءَالِهَةً
99 —had they been gods,

مَّا وَرَدُوهَا
they would not have come to it—

وَكُلٌّ فِيهَا خَـٰلِدُونَ ۝
and they will all remain in it [forever].

لَهُمْ فِيهَا زَفِيرٌ
100 Their lot therein will be groaning,

وَهُمْ فِيهَا لَا يَسْمَعُونَ ۝
and they will not hear anything in it.

إِنَّ ٱلَّذِينَ سَبَقَتْ لَهُم
101 Indeed those to whom there has gone beforehand

مِّنَّا ٱلْحُسْنَىٰٓ
[the promise of] the best reward from Us

أُوْلَـٰٓئِكَ عَنْهَا مُبْعَدُونَ ۝
will be kept away from it.

لَا يَسْمَعُونَ حَسِيسَهَا
102 They will not hear even its faint sound

وَهُمْ فِي مَا ٱشْتَهَتْ أَنفُسُهُمْ خَـٰلِدُونَ ۝
and they will remain [forever] in what their souls desire.

لَا يَحْزُنُهُمُ ٱلْفَزَعُ ٱلْأَكْبَرُ
103 The Great Terror will not upset them,

وَتَتَلَقَّاهُمُ ٱلْمَلَـٰٓئِكَةُ
and the angels will receive them [saying]:

---

[1] Or, according to a less familiar reading (*jadath,* for *ḥadab*), 'they will be scrambling out of every grave.' Cf. 37:51.

هَٰذَا يَوْمُكُمُ ٱلَّذِى كُنتُمْ تُوعَدُونَ ۞    'This is your day which you were promised.'

يَوْمَ نَطْوِى ٱلسَّمَآءَ    104 The day We shall roll up the sky,

كَطَىِّ ٱلسِّجِلِّ لِلْكُتُبِ    like the rolling of the scrolls for writings.

كَمَا بَدَأْنَآ أَوَّلَ خَلْقٍ نُّعِيدُهُۥ    We will bring it back as We began the first creation

وَعْدًا عَلَيْنَآ    —a promise [binding] on Us.

إِنَّا كُنَّا فَٰعِلِينَ ۞    [That] indeed We will do.

وَلَقَدْ كَتَبْنَا فِى ٱلزَّبُورِ    105 Certainly We wrote in the Psalms,

مِنۢ بَعْدِ ٱلذِّكْرِ    after the Torah:

أَنَّ ٱلْأَرْضَ يَرِثُهَا عِبَادِىَ ٱلصَّٰلِحُونَ ۞    'Indeed My righteous servants shall inherit the earth.'

إِنَّ فِى هَٰذَا    106 There is indeed in this

لَبَلَٰغًا لِّقَوْمٍ عَٰبِدِينَ ۞    a proclamation for a devout people.

وَمَآ أَرْسَلْنَٰكَ    107 We did not send *you*

إِلَّا رَحْمَةً لِّلْعَٰلَمِينَ ۞    but as a mercy to all the nations.[1]

قُلْ إِنَّمَا يُوحَىٰٓ إِلَىَّ    108 *Say,* 'It has been revealed to me

أَنَّمَآ إِلَٰهُكُمْ إِلَٰهٌ وَٰحِدٌ    that your God is the One God.

فَهَلْ أَنتُم مُّسْلِمُونَ ۞    So will you submit?'

فَإِن تَوَلَّوْا۟    109 But if they turn away,

فَقُلْ ءَاذَنتُكُمْ عَلَىٰ سَوَآءٍ    say, 'I have proclaimed to you all alike,

وَإِنْ أَدْرِىٓ    and I do not know

أَقَرِيبٌ أَم بَعِيدٌ مَّا تُوعَدُونَ ۞    whether what you have been promised is far or near.

إِنَّهُۥ يَعْلَمُ ٱلْجَهْرَ مِنَ ٱلْقَوْلِ    110 Indeed He knows whatever is spoken aloud,

وَيَعْلَمُ مَا تَكْتُمُونَ ۞    and He knows whatever you conceal.

وَإِنْ أَدْرِى    111 I do not know

لَعَلَّهُۥ فِتْنَةٌ لَّكُمْ    —maybe it is a trial for you

وَمَتَٰعٌ إِلَىٰ حِينٍ ۞    and an enjoyment for a while.'

قَٰلَ رَبِّ ٱحْكُم بِٱلْحَقِّ    112 He said,[2] 'My Lord! Judge with justice.'

وَرَبُّنَا ٱلرَّحْمَٰنُ    'Our Lord is the All-beneficent;

ٱلْمُسْتَعَانُ عَلَىٰ مَا تَصِفُونَ ۞    [He is our] resort against what you allege.'

---

[1] Or 'to all the worlds.'

[2] Or 'Say,' according to an alternate reading (*qul* instead of *qāla*).

# 22. SŪRAT AL-ḤAJJ[1]

بِسْمِ اللّٰهِ

In the Name of Allah,

الرَّحْمٰنِ الرَّحِيمِ

the All-beneficent, the All-merciful.

يَـٰٓأَيُّهَا ٱلنَّاسُ ٱتَّقُواْ رَبَّكُمْ ۚ

1 O mankind! Be wary of your Lord!

إِنَّ زَلْزَلَةَ ٱلسَّاعَةِ شَىْءٌ عَظِيمٌ ۝

Indeed the quake of the Hour is a terrible thing.

يَوْمَ تَرَوْنَهَا

2 The day that you will see it,

تَذْهَلُ كُلُّ مُرْضِعَةٍ عَمَّآ أَرْضَعَتْ

every suckling female will neglect what she suckled,

وَتَضَعُ كُلُّ ذَاتِ حَمْلٍ حَمْلَهَا

and every pregnant female will deliver her burden,

وَتَرَى ٱلنَّاسَ سُكَـٰرَىٰ

and *you* will see the people drunk,

وَمَا هُم بِسُكَـٰرَىٰ

yet they will not be drunken,

وَلَـٰكِنَّ عَذَابَ ٱللّٰهِ شَدِيدٌ ۝

but Allah's punishment is severe.

وَمِنَ ٱلنَّاسِ مَن يُجَـٰدِلُ فِى ٱللّٰهِ

3 Among the people are those who dispute about Allah

بِغَيْرِ عِلْمٍ

without any knowledge,

وَيَتَّبِعُ كُلَّ شَيْطَـٰنٍ مَّرِيدٍ ۝

and follow every froward devil,

كُتِبَ عَلَيْهِ

4 about whom it has been decreed

أَنَّهُۥ مَن تَوَلَّاهُ

that should anyone take him for a friend,

فَأَنَّهُۥ يُضِلُّهُۥ

he will lead him astray,

وَيَهْدِيهِ إِلَىٰ عَذَابِ ٱلسَّعِيرِ ۝

and conduct him toward the punishment of the Blaze.

يَـٰٓأَيُّهَا ٱلنَّاسُ

5 O people!

إِن كُنتُمْ فِى رَيْبٍ مِّنَ ٱلْبَعْثِ

If you are in doubt about the resurrection,

فَإِنَّا خَلَقْنَـٰكُم مِّن تُرَابٍ

[consider that] We indeed created you from dust,

ثُمَّ مِن نُّطْفَةٍ

then from a drop of [seminal] fluid,

ثُمَّ مِنْ عَلَقَةٍ

then from a clinging mass,[2]

ثُمَّ مِن مُّضْغَةٍ

then from a fleshy tissue,[3]

---

[1] Verses 26-37 of this *sūrah* relate to the *ḥajj* pilgrimage, after which it is named.

[2] That is, an embryo; cf. 23:13-14, 40:67, 75:37.

[3] That is, the fetus in the early stages of its development; cf. 23:13.

مُّخَلَّقَةٍ وَغَيْرِ مُخَلَّقَةٍ    partly formed and partly unformed,

لِنُبَيِّنَ لَكُمْ    so that We may manifest [Our power] to you.

وَنُقِرُّ فِى ٱلْأَرْحَامِ مَا نَشَآءُ    We establish in the wombs whatever We wish

إِلَىٰٓ أَجَلٍ مُّسَمًّى    for a specified term,

ثُمَّ نُخْرِجُكُمْ طِفْلًا    then We bring you forth as infants,

ثُمَّ لِتَبْلُغُوٓا۟ أَشُدَّكُمْ    then [We rear you] so that you may come of age.

وَمِنكُم مَّن يُتَوَفَّىٰ    [Then] there are some of you who are taken away,

وَمِنكُم مَّن يُرَدُّ    and there are some of you who are relegated

إِلَىٰٓ أَرْذَلِ ٱلْعُمُرِ    to the nethermost age,

لِكَيْلَا يَعْلَمَ    so that he knows nothing

مِنۢ بَعْدِ عِلْمٍ شَيْـًٔا    after [having possessed] some knowledge.

وَتَرَى ٱلْأَرْضَ هَامِدَةً    And you see the earth torpid,

فَإِذَآ أَنزَلْنَا عَلَيْهَا ٱلْمَآءَ    yet when We send down water upon it,

ٱهْتَزَّتْ وَرَبَتْ    it stirs and swells,

وَأَنۢبَتَتْ مِن كُلِّ زَوْجٍۭ بَهِيجٍ ۝    and grows every delightful kind [of plant].

ذَٰلِكَ بِأَنَّ ٱللَّهَ هُوَ ٱلْحَقُّ    6 That is because Allah is the Reality

وَأَنَّهُۥ يُحْىِ ٱلْمَوْتَىٰ    and it is He who revives the dead,

وَأَنَّهُۥ عَلَىٰ كُلِّ شَىْءٍ قَدِيرٌ ۝    and He has power over all things,

وَأَنَّ ٱلسَّاعَةَ ءَاتِيَةٌ    7 and the Hour is bound to come,

لَّا رَيْبَ فِيهَا    there is no doubt in it,

وَأَنَّ ٱللَّهَ يَبْعَثُ مَن فِى ٱلْقُبُورِ ۝    and Allah will resurrect those who are in the graves.

وَمِنَ ٱلنَّاسِ مَن يُجَٰدِلُ    8 Among the people are those who dispute

فِى ٱللَّهِ    concerning Allah

بِغَيْرِ عِلْمٍ وَلَا هُدًى    without any knowledge or guidance,

وَلَا كِتَٰبٍ مُّنِيرٍ ۝    or an enlightening Book,

ثَانِىَ عِطْفِهِۦ    9 turning aside disdainfully

لِيُضِلَّ عَن سَبِيلِ ٱللَّهِ    to lead [others] astray from the way of Allah.

لَهُۥ فِى ٱلدُّنْيَا خِزْىٌ    For such there is disgrace in this world,

وَنُذِيقُهُۥ يَوْمَ ٱلْقِيَٰمَةِ    and on the Day of Resurrection We will make him taste

عَذَابَ ٱلْحَرِيقِ ۝    the punishment of the burning:

ذَٰلِكَ بِمَا قَدَّمَتْ يَدَاكَ 10 'That is because of what your hands have sent ahead,[1]

وَأَنَّ ٱللَّهَ لَيْسَ بِظَلَّٰمٍ لِّلْعَبِيدِ ۝ and because Allah is not tyrannical to the servants.'

وَمِنَ ٱلنَّاسِ مَن يَعْبُدُ ٱللَّهَ 11 And among the people are those who worship Allah

عَلَىٰ حَرْفٍ on the [very] fringe:

فَإِنْ أَصَابَهُۥ خَيْرٌ ٱطْمَأَنَّ بِهِۦ if good fortune befalls him, he is content with it;

وَإِنْ أَصَابَتْهُ فِتْنَةٌ but if an ordeal visits him

ٱنقَلَبَ عَلَىٰ وَجْهِهِۦ he makes a turnabout,

خَسِرَ ٱلدُّنْيَا وَٱلْآخِرَةَ to become a loser in the world and the Hereafter.

ذَٰلِكَ هُوَ ٱلْخُسْرَانُ ٱلْمُبِينُ ۝ That is the manifest loss.

يَدْعُواْ مِن دُونِ ٱللَّهِ 12 He invokes besides Allah

مَا لَا يَضُرُّهُۥ وَمَا لَا يَنفَعُهُۥ that which can bring him neither benefit nor harm.

ذَٰلِكَ هُوَ ٱلضَّلَٰلُ ٱلْبَعِيدُ ۝ That is extreme error.

يَدْعُواْ لَمَن ضَرُّهُۥ 13 He invokes someone whose harm is surely

أَقْرَبُ مِن نَّفْعِهِۦ likelier than his benefit.

لَبِئْسَ ٱلْمَوْلَىٰ وَلَبِئْسَ ٱلْعَشِيرُ ۝ Surely an evil ally and an evil companion!

إِنَّ ٱللَّهَ يُدْخِلُ ٱلَّذِينَ ءَامَنُواْ 14 Allah will indeed admit those who have faith

وَعَمِلُواْ ٱلصَّٰلِحَٰتِ and do righteous deeds

جَنَّٰتٍ تَجْرِى مِن تَحْتِهَا ٱلْأَنْهَٰرُ into gardens with streams running in them.

إِنَّ ٱللَّهَ يَفْعَلُ مَا يُرِيدُ ۝ Indeed Allah does whatever He desires.

مَن كَانَ يَظُنُّ 15 Whoever thinks

أَن لَّن يَنصُرَهُ ٱللَّهُ that Allah will not help *him*

فِى ٱلدُّنْيَا وَٱلْآخِرَةِ in this world and the Hereafter,

فَلْيَمْدُدْ بِسَبَبٍ إِلَى ٱلسَّمَآءِ let him extend a rope to the ceiling

ثُمَّ لْيَقْطَعْ and hang himself,

فَلْيَنظُرْ and see

هَلْ يُذْهِبَنَّ كَيْدُهُۥ مَا يَغِيظُ ۝ if his artifice would remove his rage.

وَكَذَٰلِكَ أَنزَلْنَٰهُ ءَايَٰتٍ بَيِّنَٰتٍ 16 Thus have We sent it down as manifest signs,

وَأَنَّ ٱللَّهَ يَهْدِى مَن يُرِيدُ ۝ and indeed Allah guides whomever He desires.

---

[1] Or 'prepared,' or 'committed.'

إِنَّ ٱلَّذِينَ ءَامَنُوا    17 Indeed the faithful,

وَٱلَّذِينَ هَادُوا وَٱلصَّٰبِئِينَ    the Jews, the Sabaeans,

وَٱلنَّصَٰرَىٰ وَٱلۡمَجُوسَ    the Christians, the Magians

وَٱلَّذِينَ أَشۡرَكُوٓا    and the polytheists

إِنَّ ٱللَّهَ يَفۡصِلُ بَيۡنَهُمۡ    —Allah will indeed judge between them

يَوۡمَ ٱلۡقِيَٰمَةِ    on the Day of Resurrection.

إِنَّ ٱللَّهَ عَلَىٰ كُلِّ شَيۡءٍ شَهِيدٌ ۝    Indeed Allah is witness to all things.

أَلَمۡ تَرَ أَنَّ ٱللَّهَ يَسۡجُدُ لَهُ    18 Have you not regarded that to Allah prostrates

مَن فِى ٱلسَّمَٰوَٰتِ    whoever is in the heavens

وَمَن فِى ٱلۡأَرۡضِ    and whoever is on the earth,

وَٱلشَّمۡسُ وَٱلۡقَمَرُ وَٱلنُّجُومُ    and the sun, the moon, and the stars,

وَٱلۡجِبَالُ وَٱلشَّجَرُ وَٱلدَّوَآبُّ    the mountains, the trees, and the animals

وَكَثِيرٌ مِّنَ ٱلنَّاسِ    and many of mankind,

وَكَثِيرٌ حَقَّ عَلَيۡهِ ٱلۡعَذَابُ    and for many the punishment has become due.

وَمَن يُهِنِ ٱللَّهُ    Whomever Allah humiliates

فَمَا لَهُۥ مِن مُّكۡرِمٍ    will find no one who may bring him honour.

إِنَّ ٱللَّهَ يَفۡعَلُ مَا يَشَآءُ ۝ ۩ ✿    Indeed Allah does whatever He wishes.

۞ هَٰذَانِ خَصۡمَانِ    19 These two contenders contend

ٱخۡتَصَمُوا فِى رَبِّهِمۡ    concerning their Lord.

فَٱلَّذِينَ كَفَرُوا    As for those who are faithless,

قُطِّعَتۡ لَهُمۡ ثِيَابٌ مِّن نَّارٍ    cloaks of fire will be cut out for them,

يُصَبُّ مِن فَوۡقِ رُءُوسِهِمُ ٱلۡحَمِيمُ ۝    and boiling water will be poured over their heads,

يُصۡهَرُ بِهِۦ مَا فِى بُطُونِهِمۡ وَٱلۡجُلُودُ ۝    20 with which their skins and entrails will be fused,

وَلَهُم مَّقَٰمِعُ مِنۡ حَدِيدٍ ۝    21 and there will be clubs of iron for them.

كُلَّمَآ أَرَادُوٓا    22 Whenever they desire

أَن يَخۡرُجُوا مِنۡهَا مِنۡ غَمٍّ    to leave it out of anguish,

أُعِيدُوا فِيهَا    they will be turned back into it

وَذُوقُوا عَذَابَ ٱلۡحَرِيقِ ۝    [and told]: 'Taste the punishment of the burning!'

إِنَّ ٱللَّهَ يُدْخِلُ ٱلَّذِينَ ءَامَنُواْ

23 Indeed Allah will admit those who have faith

وَعَمِلُواْ ٱلصَّٰلِحَٰتِ

and do righteous deeds

جَنَّٰتٍ تَجْرِى مِن تَحْتِهَا ٱلْأَنْهَٰرُ

into gardens with streams running in them,

يُحَلَّوْنَ فِيهَا مِنْ أَسَاوِرَ

adorned therein with bracelets

مِن ذَهَبٍ وَلُؤْلُؤًا

of gold and pearl,

وَلِبَاسُهُمْ فِيهَا حَرِيرٌ ۝

and their dress therein will be silk.

وَهُدُوٓاْ إِلَى ٱلطَّيِّبِ مِنَ ٱلْقَوْلِ

24 They shall be guided to the purest speech,

وَهُدُوٓاْ إِلَىٰ صِرَٰطِ ٱلْحَمِيدِ ۝

and guided to the path of the All-laudable.

إِنَّ ٱلَّذِينَ كَفَرُواْ

25 Indeed those who are faithless

وَيَصُدُّونَ عَن سَبِيلِ ٱللَّهِ

and who bar from the way of Allah

وَٱلْمَسْجِدِ ٱلْحَرَامِ

and the Sacred Mosque,

ٱلَّذِى جَعَلْنَٰهُ لِلنَّاسِ

which We have assigned for all the people,

سَوَآءً ٱلْعَٰكِفُ فِيهِ وَٱلْبَادِ

the native and the visitor being equal therein

وَمَن يُرِدْ فِيهِ بِإِلْحَادٍ

—whoever seeks to commit therein sacrilege

بِظُلْمٍ

with the intent of wrongdoing,

نُذِقْهُ مِنْ عَذَابٍ أَلِيمٍ ۝

We shall make him taste a painful punishment.

وَإِذْ بَوَّأْنَا لِإِبْرَٰهِيمَ مَكَانَ ٱلْبَيْتِ

26 When We settled for Abraham the site of the House

أَن لَّا تُشْرِكْ بِى شَيْـًٔا

[saying], Do not ascribe any partners to Me,

وَطَهِّرْ بَيْتِىَ لِلطَّآئِفِينَ

and purify My House for those who go around it,

وَٱلْقَآئِمِينَ

and those who stand [in it for prayer],

وَٱلرُّكَّعِ ٱلسُّجُودِ ۝

and those who bow and prostrate.

وَأَذِّن فِى ٱلنَّاسِ بِٱلْحَجِّ

27 And proclaim the ḥajj to people:

يَأْتُوكَ رِجَالًا

they shall come to you on foot

وَعَلَىٰ كُلِّ ضَامِرٍ

and on lean camels

يَأْتِينَ مِن كُلِّ فَجٍّ عَمِيقٍ ۝

coming from distant places,

لِّيَشْهَدُواْ مَنَٰفِعَ لَهُمْ

28 that they may witness the benefits for them,

وَيَذْكُرُواْ ٱسْمَ ٱللَّهِ

and mention Allah's Name

فِىٓ أَيَّامٍ مَّعْلُومَٰتٍ

during the known days

عَلَىٰ مَا رَزَقَهُم مِّنۢ بَهِيمَةِ ٱلْأَنْعَٰمِ

over the livestock He has provided them.

فَكُلُوا۟ مِنْهَا     So eat thereof,

وَأَطْعِمُوا۟ ٱلْبَآئِسَ ٱلْفَقِيرَ ۩     and feed the destitute.

ثُمَّ لْيَقْضُوا۟ تَفَثَهُمْ     29 Then let them do away with their untidiness,[1]

وَلْيُوفُوا۟ نُذُورَهُمْ     and fulfill their vows,

وَلْيَطَّوَّفُوا۟ بِٱلْبَيْتِ ٱلْعَتِيقِ ۩     and go around the Ancient House.[2]

ذَٰلِكَ     30 That.

وَمَن يُعَظِّمْ حُرُمَٰتِ ٱللَّهِ     And whoever venerates the sacraments of Allah,

فَهُوَ خَيْرٌ لَّهُۥ عِندَ رَبِّهِۦ     that is better for him with his Lord.

وَأُحِلَّتْ لَكُمُ ٱلْأَنْعَٰمُ     You are permitted [animals of] grazing livestock

إِلَّا مَا يُتْلَىٰ عَلَيْكُمْ     except for what will be recited to you.

فَٱجْتَنِبُوا۟ ٱلرِّجْسَ مِنَ ٱلْأَوْثَٰنِ     So avoid the abomination of idols,

وَٱجْتَنِبُوا۟ قَوْلَ ٱلزُّورِ ۩     and avoid false speech,

حُنَفَآءَ لِلَّهِ     31 as persons having pure faith in Allah,

غَيْرَ مُشْرِكِينَ بِهِۦ     not ascribing partners to Him.

وَمَن يُشْرِكْ بِٱللَّهِ     Whoever ascribes partners to Allah

فَكَأَنَّمَا خَرَّ مِنَ ٱلسَّمَآءِ     is as though he had fallen from a height

فَتَخْطَفُهُ ٱلطَّيْرُ     to be devoured by vultures,

أَوْ تَهْوِى بِهِ ٱلرِّيحُ     or to be blown away by the wind

فِى مَكَانٍ سَحِيقٍ ۩     far and wide.

ذَٰلِكَ     32 That.

وَمَن يُعَظِّمْ شَعَٰئِرَ ٱللَّهِ     And whoever venerates the sacraments of Allah

فَإِنَّهَا مِن تَقْوَى ٱلْقُلُوبِ ۩     —indeed that arises from the Godwariness of hearts.

لَكُمْ فِيهَا مَنَٰفِعُ إِلَىٰٓ أَجَلٍ مُّسَمًّى     33 You may benefit from them until a specified time.[3]

ثُمَّ مَحِلُّهَآ إِلَى ٱلْبَيْتِ ٱلْعَتِيقِ ۩     Then their place of sacrifice is by the Ancient House.

وَلِكُلِّ أُمَّةٍ جَعَلْنَا مَنسَكًا     34 For every nation We have appointed a rite

---

[1] According to the commentators, the phrase *li yaqḍū tafathahum* implies egress from the state of *iḥrām* (after shortening the hair or the nails, and taking the bath), and relief from its restrictions. Or it means 'let them perform their rites.'

[2] Or, 'the Free House,' that is, free from bondage of anyone's ownership.

[3] That is, you may benefit from the sacrificial animals, such as by using them as mounts or milking them, until they arrive at the place where they are to be sacrificed.

لِيَذْكُرُوا اسْمَ اللَّهِ    that they might mention Allah's Name

عَلَىٰ مَا رَزَقَهُم مِّنْ بَهِيمَةِ الْأَنْعَامِ    over the livestock He has provided them.

فَإِلَٰهُكُمْ إِلَٰهٌ وَاحِدٌ    Your God is the One God.

فَلَهُۥ أَسْلِمُوا    So submit to Him.

وَبَشِّرِ الْمُخْبِتِينَ ۝    And *give* good news to the humble

الَّذِينَ 35 —those

إِذَا ذُكِرَ اللَّهُ وَجِلَتْ قُلُوبُهُمْ    whose hearts tremble with awe when Allah is mentioned,

وَالصَّابِرِينَ عَلَىٰ مَا أَصَابَهُمْ    and who are patient through whatever visits them,

وَالْمُقِيمِى الصَّلَوٰةِ    and who maintain the prayer

وَمِمَّا رَزَقْنَاهُمْ يُنفِقُونَ ۝    and spend out of what We have provided them.

وَالْبُدْنَ جَعَلْنَاهَا لَكُم 36 We have appointed for you the [sacrificial] camels

مِّن شَعَائِرِ اللَّهِ    as one of Allah's sacraments.

لَكُمْ فِيهَا خَيْرٌ    There is good for you in them.

فَاذْكُرُوا اسْمَ اللَّهِ عَلَيْهَا صَوَافَّ    So mention the Name of Allah over them as they stand.

فَإِذَا وَجَبَتْ جُنُوبُهَا    And when they have fallen on their flanks,

فَكُلُوا مِنْهَا    eat from them,

وَأَطْعِمُوا الْقَانِعَ    and feed the self-contained needy

وَالْمُعْتَرَّ    and the mendicant.

كَذَٰلِكَ سَخَّرْنَاهَا    Thus have We disposed them for your benefit

لَكُمْ لَعَلَّكُمْ تَشْكُرُونَ ۝    so that you may give thanks.

لَن يَنَالَ اللَّهَ لُحُومُهَا وَلَا دِمَاؤُهَا 37 It is not their flesh or their blood that reaches Allah.

وَلَٰكِن يَنَالُهُ التَّقْوَىٰ مِنكُمْ    Rather it is your Godwariness that reaches Him.

كَذَٰلِكَ سَخَّرَهَا لَكُمْ    Thus has He disposed them for your benefit

لِتُكَبِّرُوا اللَّهَ عَلَىٰ مَا هَدَىٰكُمْ    so that you may magnify Allah for His guiding you.

وَبَشِّرِ الْمُحْسِنِينَ ۝    And *give* good news to the virtuous.

إِنَّ اللَّهَ يُدَافِعُ عَنِ الَّذِينَ آمَنُوا 38 Allah indeed defends those who have faith.

إِنَّ اللَّهَ لَا يُحِبُّ كُلَّ خَوَّانٍ كَفُورٍ ۝    Indeed Allah does not like any ingrate traitor.

أُذِنَ لِلَّذِينَ يُقَاتَلُونَ 39 Those who are fought against are permitted [to fight]

بِأَنَّهُمْ ظُلِمُوا    because they have been wronged,

وَإِنَّ ٱللَّهَ عَلَىٰ نَصْرِهِمْ لَقَدِيرٌ ۝

and Allah is indeed able to help them.

ٱلَّذِينَ أُخْرِجُوا۟ مِن دِيَٰرِهِم

40 —Those who were expelled from their homes

بِغَيْرِ حَقٍّ

unjustly,

إِلَّآ أَن يَقُولُوا۟ رَبُّنَا ٱللَّهُ

only because they said, 'Allah is our Lord.'

وَلَوْلَا دَفْعُ ٱللَّهِ ٱلنَّاسَ

Had not Allah repulsed the people

بَعْضَهُم بِبَعْضٍ

from one another,

لَّهُدِّمَتْ صَوَٰمِعُ وَبِيَعٌ

ruin would have befallen the monasteries, churches,

وَصَلَوَٰتٌ وَمَسَٰجِدُ

synagogues and mosques

يُذْكَرُ فِيهَا ٱسْمُ ٱللَّهِ كَثِيرًا

in which Allah's Name is mentioned greatly.

وَلَيَنصُرَنَّ ٱللَّهُ مَن يَنصُرُهُۥٓ

Allah will surely help those who help Him.

إِنَّ ٱللَّهَ لَقَوِيٌّ عَزِيزٌ ۝

Indeed Allah is all-strong, all-mighty.

ٱلَّذِينَ إِن مَّكَّنَّٰهُمْ فِى ٱلْأَرْضِ

41 Those who, if We granted them power in the land,

أَقَامُوا۟ ٱلصَّلَوٰةَ

maintain the prayer,

وَءَاتَوُا۟ ٱلزَّكَوٰةَ

give the *zakāt*,

وَأَمَرُوا۟ بِٱلْمَعْرُوفِ

and bid what is right

وَنَهَوْا۟ عَنِ ٱلْمُنكَرِ

and forbid what is wrong.

وَلِلَّهِ عَٰقِبَةُ ٱلْأُمُورِ ۝

And with Allah rests the outcome of all matters.

وَإِن يُكَذِّبُوكَ

42 If they impugn *you*,

فَقَدْ كَذَّبَتْ قَبْلَهُمْ قَوْمُ نُوحٍ

the people of Noah have impugned before them

وَعَادٌ وَثَمُودُ ۝

and 'Ād and Thamūd

وَقَوْمُ إِبْرَٰهِيمَ

43 [as well as] the people of Abraham

وَقَوْمُ لُوطٍ ۝

and the people of Lot,

وَأَصْحَٰبُ مَدْيَنَ

44 and the inhabitants of Midian,

وَكُذِّبَ مُوسَىٰ

and Moses was also impugned.

فَأَمْلَيْتُ لِلْكَٰفِرِينَ

But I gave the faithless a respite,

ثُمَّ أَخَذْتُهُمْ

then I seized them

فَكَيْفَ كَانَ نَكِيرِ ۝

and how was My rebuttal!

فَكَأَيِّن مِّن قَرْيَةٍ أَهْلَكْنَٰهَا

45 How many towns We have destroyed

وَهِىَ ظَالِمَةٌ

while they were wrongdoers!

فَهِيَ خَاوِيَةٌ عَلَىٰ عُرُوشِهَا So they lie fallen on their trellises,

وَبِئْرٍ مُّعَطَّلَةٍ their wells neglected

وَقَصْرٍ مَّشِيدٍ and their lofty palaces [desolate]!

أَفَلَمْ يَسِيرُوا۟ فِى ٱلْأَرْضِ 46 Have they not traveled over the land

فَتَكُونَ لَهُمْ قُلُوبٌ so that they may have hearts

يَعْقِلُونَ بِهَآ by which they may apply reason,

أَوْ ءَاذَانٌ يَسْمَعُونَ بِهَا or ears by which they may hear?

فَإِنَّهَا لَا تَعْمَى ٱلْأَبْصَٰرُ Indeed it is not the eyes that turn blind,

وَلَٰكِن تَعْمَى ٱلْقُلُوبُ but the hearts turn blind

ٱلَّتِى فِى ٱلصُّدُورِ —those which are in the breasts!

وَيَسْتَعْجِلُونَكَ بِٱلْعَذَابِ 47 They ask *you* to hasten the punishment,

وَلَن يُخْلِفَ ٱللَّهُ وَعْدَهُۥ though Allah shall never break His promise.

وَإِنَّ يَوْمًا عِندَ رَبِّكَ Indeed a day with *your* Lord

كَأَلْفِ سَنَةٍ مِّمَّا تَعُدُّونَ is like a thousand years of your reckoning.

وَكَأَيِّن مِّن قَرْيَةٍ أَمْلَيْتُ لَهَا 48 To how many a town did I give respite

وَهِىَ ظَالِمَةٌ while it was wrongdoing.

ثُمَّ أَخَذْتُهَا Then I seized it,

وَإِلَىَّ ٱلْمَصِيرُ and toward Me is the destination.

قُل يَٰٓأَيُّهَا ٱلنَّاسُ 49 *Say,* 'O mankind!

إِنَّمَآ أَنَا۠ لَكُمْ نَذِيرٌ مُّبِينٌ I am only a manifest warner to you!'

فَٱلَّذِينَ ءَامَنُوا۟ وَعَمِلُوا۟ ٱلصَّٰلِحَٰتِ 50 As for those who have faith and do righteous deeds,

لَهُم مَّغْفِرَةٌ وَرِزْقٌ كَرِيمٌ for them is forgiveness and a noble provision.

وَٱلَّذِينَ سَعَوْا۟ فِىٓ ءَايَٰتِنَا 51 But as for those who contend with Our signs,

مُعَٰجِزِينَ seeking to thwart [their purpose],

أُو۟لَٰٓئِكَ أَصْحَٰبُ ٱلْجَحِيمِ they shall be the inmates of hell.

وَمَآ أَرْسَلْنَا مِن قَبْلِكَ 52 We did not send before *you*

مِن رَّسُولٍ وَلَا نَبِىٍّ any apostle or prophet

إِلَّآ إِذَا تَمَنَّىٰٓ but that when he recited [the scripture]

أَلْقَى ٱلشَّيْطَٰنُ فِىٓ أُمْنِيَّتِهِۦ Satan interjected [something] in his recitation.

فَيَنسَخُ ٱللَّهُ مَا يُلْقِى ٱلشَّيْطَـٰنُ

Thereat Allah nullifies whatever Satan has interjected,

ثُمَّ يُحْكِمُ ٱللَّهُ ءَايَـٰتِهِۦ

[and] then Allah confirms His signs,

وَٱللَّهُ عَلِيمٌ حَكِيمٌ ۝

and Allah is All-knowing, All-wise.

لِّيَجْعَلَ مَا يُلْقِى ٱلشَّيْطَـٰنُ

53 That He may make what Satan has thrown in

فِتْنَةً لِّلَّذِينَ فِى قُلُوبِهِم مَّرَضٌ

a trial for those in whose hearts is a sickness

وَٱلْقَاسِيَةِ قُلُوبُهُمْ

and those whose hearts have hardened.

وَإِنَّ ٱلظَّـٰلِمِينَ لَفِى شِقَاقٍ بَعِيدٍ ۝

Indeed the wrongdoers are steeped in extreme defiance.

وَلِيَعْلَمَ ٱلَّذِينَ أُوتُوا۟ ٱلْعِلْمَ

54 That those who have been given knowledge may know

أَنَّهُ ٱلْحَقُّ مِن رَّبِّكَ

that it is the truth from your Lord,

فَيُؤْمِنُوا۟ بِهِۦ

and so they may have faith in it,

فَتُخْبِتَ لَهُۥ قُلُوبُهُمْ

and their hearts may be humbled before Him.

وَإِنَّ ٱللَّهَ لَهَادِ ٱلَّذِينَ ءَامَنُوٓا۟

Indeed Allah guides those who have faith

إِلَىٰ صِرَٰطٍ مُّسْتَقِيمٍ ۝

to a straight path.

وَلَا يَزَالُ ٱلَّذِينَ كَفَرُوا۟

55 Those who are faithless persist

فِى مِرْيَةٍ مِّنْهُ

in their doubt about it,

حَتَّىٰ تَأْتِيَهُمُ ٱلسَّاعَةُ بَغْتَةً

until the Hour overtakes them suddenly,

أَوْ يَأْتِيَهُمْ عَذَابُ

or they are overtaken by the punishment

يَوْمٍ عَقِيمٍ ۝

of an inauspicious day.

ٱلْمُلْكُ يَوْمَئِذٍ لِّلَّهِ

56 On that day all sovereignty will belong to Allah:

يَحْكُمُ بَيْنَهُمْ

He will judge between them.

فَٱلَّذِينَ ءَامَنُوا۟ وَعَمِلُوا۟ ٱلصَّـٰلِحَـٰتِ

Then those who have faith and do righteous deeds

فِى جَنَّـٰتِ ٱلنَّعِيمِ ۝

will be in gardens of bliss,

وَٱلَّذِينَ كَفَرُوا۟

57 and those who are faithless

وَكَذَّبُوا۟ بِـَٔايَـٰتِنَا

and who deny Our signs

فَأُو۟لَـٰٓئِكَ لَهُمْ عَذَابٌ مُّهِينٌ ۝

—for such there will be a humiliating punishment.

وَٱلَّذِينَ هَاجَرُوا۟ فِى سَبِيلِ ٱللَّهِ

58 Those who migrate in the way of Allah

ثُمَّ قُتِلُوٓا۟ أَوْ مَاتُوا۟

and then are slain, or die,

لَيَرْزُقَنَّهُمُ ٱللَّهُ رِزْقًا حَسَنًا

Allah will surely provide them with a good provision.

وَإِنَّ ٱللَّهَ لَهُوَ خَيْرُ ٱلرَّٰزِقِينَ ۝

Allah is indeed the best of providers.

لِيُدْخِلَنَّهُم مُّدْخَلًا    59 He will admit them into an abode

يَرْضَوْنَهُ    they are pleased with.

وَإِنَّ ٱللَّهَ لَعَلِيمٌ حَلِيمٌ ۝    Indeed Allah is all-knowing, all-forbearing.

ذَٰلِكَ وَمَنْ عَاقَبَ    60 That; and whoever retaliates

بِمِثْلِ    with the like of

مَا عُوقِبَ بِهِ    what he has been made to suffer,

ثُمَّ بُغِيَ عَلَيْهِ    and then is [again] aggressed against,

لَيَنصُرَنَّهُ ٱللَّهُ    Allah will surely help him.

إِنَّ ٱللَّهَ لَعَفُوٌّ غَفُورٌ ۝    Indeed Allah is all-excusing, all-forgiving.

ذَٰلِكَ بِأَنَّ ٱللَّهَ يُولِجُ ٱلَّيْلَ    61 That is because Allah makes the night pass

فِى ٱلنَّهَارِ    into the day

وَيُولِجُ ٱلنَّهَارَ فِى ٱلَّيْلِ    and makes the day pass into the night,

وَأَنَّ ٱللَّهَ سَمِيعٌ بَصِيرٌ ۝    and because Allah is all-hearing, all-seeing.

ذَٰلِكَ بِأَنَّ ٱللَّهَ هُوَ ٱلْحَقُّ    62 That is because Allah is the Reality,

وَأَنَّ مَا يَدْعُونَ مِن دُونِهِ    and what they invoke besides Him

هُوَ ٱلْبَٰطِلُ    is nullity,

وَأَنَّ ٱللَّهَ هُوَ ٱلْعَلِىُّ ٱلْكَبِيرُ ۝    and because Allah is the All-exalted, the All-great.

أَلَمْ تَرَ    63 Have *you* not regarded

أَنَّ ٱللَّهَ أَنزَلَ مِنَ ٱلسَّمَاءِ مَاءً    that Allah sends down water from the sky,

فَتُصْبِحُ ٱلْأَرْضُ مُخْضَرَّةً    whereupon the earth turns green?

إِنَّ ٱللَّهَ لَطِيفٌ خَبِيرٌ ۝    Indeed Allah is all-attentive, all-aware.

لَهُ مَا فِى ٱلسَّمَٰوَٰتِ    64 To Him belongs whatever is in the heavens

وَمَا فِى ٱلْأَرْضِ    and whatever is in the earth,

وَإِنَّ ٱللَّهَ لَهُوَ ٱلْغَنِىُّ ٱلْحَمِيدُ ۝    Indeed Allah is the All-sufficient, the All-laudable.

أَلَمْ تَرَ    65 Have you not regarded

أَنَّ ٱللَّهَ سَخَّرَ لَكُم    that Allah has disposed for you[r benefit]

مَّا فِى ٱلْأَرْضِ    whatever there is in the earth,

وَٱلْفُلْكَ تَجْرِى فِى ٱلْبَحْرِ بِأَمْرِهِ    and [that] the ships sail at sea by His command,

وَيُمْسِكُ ٱلسَّمَاءَ    and He sustains the sky

أَن تَقَعَ عَلَى ٱلْأَرْضِ    lest it should fall on the earth,

إِلَّا بِإِذْنِهِ

excepting [when it does so] by His leave?

إِنَّ ٱللَّهَ بِٱلنَّاسِ لَرَءُوفٌ رَّحِيمٌ ۩

Indeed Allah is most kind and merciful to mankind.

وَهُوَ ٱلَّذِىٓ أَحْيَاكُمْ

66 It is He who gave you life

ثُمَّ يُمِيتُكُمْ

then He makes you die,

ثُمَّ يُحْيِيكُمْ

then He brings you to life.

إِنَّ ٱلْإِنسَـٰنَ لَكَفُورٌ ۩

Indeed man is very ungrateful.

لِّكُلِّ أُمَّةٍ جَعَلْنَا مَنسَكًا

67 For every nation We had appointed a rite [of worship]

هُمْ نَاسِكُوهُ

which they used to observe;

فَلَا يُنَـٰزِعُنَّكَ فِى ٱلْأَمْرِ

so let them not dispute with *you* about the matter.[1]

وَٱدْعُ إِلَىٰ رَبِّكَ

And *invite* to your Lord.

إِنَّكَ لَعَلَىٰ هُدًى مُّسْتَقِيمٍ ۩

Indeed *you* are on a straight guidance.

وَإِن جَـٰدَلُوكَ

68 And if they dispute with *you*,

فَقُلِ ٱللَّهُ أَعْلَمُ بِمَا تَعْمَلُونَ ۩

*say*, 'Allah knows best what you are doing.

ٱللَّهُ يَحْكُمُ بَيْنَكُمْ

69 Allah will judge between you

يَوْمَ ٱلْقِيَـٰمَةِ

on the Day of Resurrection

فِيمَا كُنتُمْ فِيهِ تَخْتَلِفُونَ ۩

concerning that about which you used to differ.'

أَلَمْ تَعْلَمْ أَنَّ ٱللَّهَ يَعْلَمُ

70 Do you not know that Allah knows

مَا فِى ٱلسَّمَآءِ وَٱلْأَرْضِ

whatever there is in the sky and the earth?

إِنَّ ذَٰلِكَ فِى كِتَـٰبٍ

That is indeed in a Book.

إِنَّ ذَٰلِكَ عَلَى ٱللَّهِ يَسِيرٌ ۩

That is indeed easy for Allah.'

وَيَعْبُدُونَ مِن دُونِ ٱللَّهِ

71 They worship besides Allah

مَا لَمْ يُنَزِّلْ بِهِۦ سُلْطَـٰنًا

that for which He has not sent down any authority,

وَمَا لَيْسَ لَهُم بِهِۦ عِلْمٌ

and of which they have no knowledge.

وَمَا لِلظَّـٰلِمِينَ مِن نَّصِيرٍ ۩

And the wrongdoers shall have no helper.

وَإِذَا تُتْلَىٰ عَلَيْهِمْ ءَايَـٰتُنَا بَيِّنَـٰتٍ

72 When Our manifest signs are recited to them,

تَعْرِفُ

*you* perceive

فِى وُجُوهِ ٱلَّذِينَ كَفَرُوا ٱلْمُنكَرَ

denial on the faces of the faithless:

يَكَادُونَ يَسْطُونَ

they would almost pounce

---

[1] Or 'the Law.'

بِٱلَّذِينَ يَتْلُونَ عَلَيْهِمْ ءَايَٰتِنَا
upon those who recite Our signs to them.

قُلْ أَفَأُنَبِّئُكُم
*Say,* 'Shall I inform you

بِشَرٍّ مِّن ذَٰلِكُمْ
about something worse than that?

ٱلنَّارُ وَعَدَهَا ٱللَّهُ ٱلَّذِينَ كَفَرُوا۟
The Fire which Allah has promised the faithless.

وَبِئْسَ ٱلْمَصِيرُ ۝
And it is an evil destination.'

يَٰٓأَيُّهَا ٱلنَّاسُ 73 O mankind!

ضُرِبَ مَثَلٌ فَٱسْتَمِعُوا۟ لَهُۥٓ
Listen to a parable that is being drawn:

إِنَّ ٱلَّذِينَ تَدْعُونَ مِن دُونِ ٱللَّهِ
Indeed those whom you invoke besides Allah

لَن يَخْلُقُوا۟ ذُبَابًا
will never create [even] a fly

وَلَوِ ٱجْتَمَعُوا۟ لَهُۥ
even if they all rallied to do so!

وَإِن يَسْلُبْهُمُ ٱلذُّبَابُ شَيْئًا
And if a fly should take away something from them,

لَّا يَسْتَنقِذُوهُ مِنْهُ
they can not recover that from it.

ضَعُفَ ٱلطَّالِبُ وَٱلْمَطْلُوبُ ۝
Feeble is the seeker and the sought!

مَا قَدَرُوا۟ ٱللَّهَ حَقَّ قَدْرِهِۦٓ 74 They do not regard Allah with the regard due to Him.

إِنَّ ٱللَّهَ لَقَوِىٌّ عَزِيزٌ ۝
Indeed Allah is all-strong, all-mighty.

ٱللَّهُ يَصْطَفِى مِنَ ٱلْمَلَٰٓئِكَةِ رُسُلًا 75 Allah chooses messengers from angles

وَمِنَ ٱلنَّاسِ
and from mankind.

إِنَّ ٱللَّهَ سَمِيعٌ بَصِيرٌ ۝
Indeed Allah is all-hearing, all-seeing.

يَعْلَمُ مَا بَيْنَ أَيْدِيهِمْ 76 He knows that which is before them

وَمَا خَلْفَهُمْ
and that which is behind them,

وَإِلَى ٱللَّهِ تُرْجَعُ ٱلْأُمُورُ ۝
and to Allah all matters are returned.

يَٰٓأَيُّهَا ٱلَّذِينَ ءَامَنُوا۟ 77 O you who have faith!

ٱرْكَعُوا۟ وَٱسْجُدُوا۟
Bow down and prostrate yourselves,

وَٱعْبُدُوا۟ رَبَّكُمْ
and worship your Lord,

وَٱفْعَلُوا۟ ٱلْخَيْرَ
and do good,

لَعَلَّكُمْ تُفْلِحُونَ ۩ ۝
so that you may be felicitous.

وَجَٰهِدُوا۟ فِى ٱللَّهِ 78 And wage *jihād* for the sake of Allah,

حَقَّ جِهَادِهِۦ
a *jihād* which is worthy of Him.

هُوَ ٱجۡتَبَىٰكُمۡ

He has chosen you

وَمَا جَعَلَ عَلَيۡكُمۡ

and has not placed for you

فِى ٱلدِّينِ مِنۡ حَرَجٍ

any obstacle in the religion,

مِّلَّةَ أَبِيكُمۡ إِبۡرَٰهِيمَ

the faith of your father, Abraham.

هُوَ سَمَّىٰكُمُ ٱلۡمُسۡلِمِينَ

He named you 'muslims'

مِن قَبۡلُ وَفِى هَٰذَا

before, and in this,[1]

لِيَكُونَ ٱلرَّسُولُ شَهِيدًا عَلَيۡكُمۡ

so that the Apostle may be a witness to you,

وَتَكُونُواْ شُهَدَآءَ عَلَى ٱلنَّاسِ

and that you may be witnesses to mankind.

فَأَقِيمُواْ ٱلصَّلَوٰةَ

So maintain the prayer,

وَءَاتُواْ ٱلزَّكَوٰةَ

give the zakāt,

وَٱعۡتَصِمُواْ بِٱللَّهِ

and hold fast to Allah.

هُوَ مَوۡلَىٰكُمۡ

He is your master

فَنِعۡمَ ٱلۡمَوۡلَىٰ وَنِعۡمَ ٱلنَّصِيرُ ۝

—an excellent master and an excellent helper.

[PART 18]

سُورَةُ ٱلۡمُؤۡمِنُونَ

# 23. SŪRAT AL-MU'MINŪN[2]

بِسۡمِ ٱللَّهِ

In the Name of Allah,

ٱلرَّحۡمَٰنِ ٱلرَّحِيمِ

the All-beneficent, the All-merciful.

١ قَدۡ أَفۡلَحَ ٱلۡمُؤۡمِنُونَ ۝

1 Certainly, the faithful have attained salvation

٢ ٱلَّذِينَ هُمۡ فِى صَلَاتِهِمۡ خَٰشِعُونَ ۝

2 —those who are humble in their prayers,

٣ وَٱلَّذِينَ هُمۡ عَنِ ٱللَّغۡوِ مُعۡرِضُونَ ۝

3 who avoid vain talk,

٤ وَٱلَّذِينَ هُمۡ لِلزَّكَوٰةِ فَٰعِلُونَ ۝

4 who carry out their [duty of] zakāt,

٥ وَٱلَّذِينَ هُمۡ لِفُرُوجِهِمۡ حَٰفِظُونَ ۝

5 who guard their private parts[3]

٦ إِلَّا عَلَىٰ أَزۡوَٰجِهِمۡ

6 (except from their spouses

أَوۡ مَا مَلَكَتۡ أَيۡمَٰنُهُمۡ

or their slave women,

فَإِنَّهُمۡ غَيۡرُ مَلُومِينَ ۝

for then they are not blameworthy;

---

[1] That is, in the earlier scriptures and in the present one, that is, the Qur'ān.

[2] The *sūrah* takes its name from verse 1 which mentions the faithful (*mu'minūn*).

[3] That is, those who refrain from unlawful sexual relations and cover their private parts properly, except in the state of privacy with their spouses.

7 فَمَنِ ٱبْتَغَىٰ وَرَآءَ ذَٰلِكَ but whoever seeks [anything] beyond that
فَأُوْلَٰئِكَ هُمُ ٱلْعَادُونَ ۝     —it is they who are transgressors)

8 وَٱلَّذِينَ هُمْ and those who
لِأَمَٰنَٰتِهِمْ وَعَهْدِهِمْ رَٰعُونَ ۝     keep their trusts and covenants,

9 وَٱلَّذِينَ هُمْ and who
عَلَىٰ صَلَوَٰتِهِمْ يُحَافِظُونَ ۝     are watchful of their prayers.

10 أُوْلَٰئِكَ هُمُ ٱلْوَٰرِثُونَ ۝ It is they who will be the inheritors,
11 ٱلَّذِينَ يَرِثُونَ ٱلْفِرْدَوْسَ who shall inherit paradise,
هُمْ فِيهَا خَٰلِدُونَ ۝     and will remain in it [forever].[1]

12 وَلَقَدْ خَلَقْنَا ٱلْإِنسَٰنَ Certainly We created man
مِن سُلَٰلَةٍ مِّن طِينٍ ۝     from an extract of clay.

13 ثُمَّ جَعَلْنَٰهُ نُطْفَةً Then We made him a drop of [seminal] fluid
فِى قَرَارٍ مَّكِينٍ ۝     [lodged] in a secure abode.

14 ثُمَّ خَلَقْنَا ٱلنُّطْفَةَ عَلَقَةً Then We created the drop of fluid as a clinging mass.
فَخَلَقْنَا ٱلْعَلَقَةَ مُضْغَةً Then We created the clinging mass as a fleshy tissue.
فَخَلَقْنَا ٱلْمُضْغَةَ عِظَٰمًا Then We created the fleshy tissue as bones.
فَكَسَوْنَا ٱلْعِظَٰمَ لَحْمًا Then We clothed the bones with flesh.
ثُمَّ أَنشَأْنَٰهُ خَلْقًا ءَاخَرَ Then We produced him as [yet] another creature.
فَتَبَارَكَ ٱللَّهُ أَحْسَنُ ٱلْخَٰلِقِينَ ۝ So blessed is Allah, the best of creators!

15 ثُمَّ إِنَّكُم بَعْدَ ذَٰلِكَ لَمَيِّتُونَ ۝ Then indeed you die after that.
16 ثُمَّ إِنَّكُمْ Then you will indeed
يَوْمَ ٱلْقِيَٰمَةِ تُبْعَثُونَ ۝     be raised up on the Day of Resurrection.

17 وَلَقَدْ خَلَقْنَا فَوْقَكُمْ سَبْعَ طَرَآئِقَ Certainly We created above you the seven tiers[2]
وَمَا كُنَّا عَنِ ٱلْخَلْقِ غَٰفِلِينَ ۝ and We have not been oblivious of creation.

18 وَأَنزَلْنَا مِنَ ٱلسَّمَآءِ مَآءً We sent down water from the sky
بِقَدَرٍ in a measured manner,
فَأَسْكَنَّٰهُ فِى ٱلْأَرْضِ and We lodged it within the ground,

---

[1] Cf. 70:22-35

[2] Or, 'seven tracks;' this, apparently, refers to the seven heavens.

وَإِنَّا عَلَىٰ ذَهَابٍ بِهِۦ لَقَٰدِرُونَ ۞    and We are indeed able to take it away.

فَأَنشَأْنَا لَكُم بِهِۦ    19 Then with it We produced for you

جَنَّٰتٍ مِّن نَّخِيلٍ وَأَعْنَٰبٍ    gardens of date palms and vines.

لَّكُمْ فِيهَا فَوَٰكِهُ كَثِيرَةٌ    There are abundant fruits in them for you,

وَمِنْهَا تَأْكُلُونَ ۞    and you eat from them.

وَشَجَرَةً تَخْرُجُ مِن طُورِ سَيْنَآءَ    20 And a tree that grows on Mount Sinai

تَنۢبُتُ بِالدُّهْنِ وَصِبْغٍ    which produces oil and a seasoning

لِّلْءَاكِلِينَ ۞    for those who eat.

وَإِنَّ لَكُمْ فِى ٱلْأَنْعَٰمِ لَعِبْرَةً    21 There is indeed a moral for you in the cattle:

نُّسْقِيكُم مِّمَّا فِى بُطُونِهَا    We give you to drink of that which is in their bellies,

وَلَكُمْ فِيهَا مَنَٰفِعُ كَثِيرَةٌ    and you have many uses in them,

وَمِنْهَا تَأْكُلُونَ ۞    and you eat some of them,

وَعَلَيْهَا وَعَلَى ٱلْفُلْكِ تُحْمَلُونَ ۞    22 and you are carried on them and on ships.

وَلَقَدْ أَرْسَلْنَا نُوحًا إِلَىٰ قَوْمِهِۦ    23 Certainly We sent Noah to his people,

فَقَالَ يَٰقَوْمِ ٱعْبُدُوا۟ ٱللَّهَ    and he said, 'O my people! Worship Allah!

مَا لَكُم مِّنْ إِلَٰهٍ غَيْرُهُۥٓ    You have no other god besides Him.

أَفَلَا تَتَّقُونَ ۞    Will you not then be wary [of Him]?'

فَقَالَ ٱلْمَلَؤُا۟ ٱلَّذِينَ كَفَرُوا۟ مِن قَوْمِهِۦ    24 But the elite of the faithless from among his people said,

مَا هَٰذَآ إِلَّا بَشَرٌ مِّثْلُكُمْ    'This is just a human being like you,

يُرِيدُ أَن يَتَفَضَّلَ عَلَيْكُمْ    who seeks to dominate you.

وَلَوْ شَآءَ ٱللَّهُ    Had Allah wished,

لَأَنزَلَ مَلَٰٓئِكَةً    He would have sent down angels.

مَّا سَمِعْنَا بِهَٰذَا    We never heard of such a thing

فِىٓ ءَابَآئِنَا ٱلْأَوَّلِينَ ۞    among our forefathers.

إِنْ هُوَ إِلَّا رَجُلٌۢ بِهِۦ جِنَّةٌ    25 He is just a man possessed by madness.

فَتَرَبَّصُوا۟ بِهِۦ حَتَّىٰ حِينٍ ۞    So bear with him for a while.'

قَالَ رَبِّ    26 He said, 'My Lord!

ٱنصُرْنِى بِمَا كَذَّبُونِ ۞    Help me, as they impugn me.'

فَأَوْحَيْنَآ إِلَيْهِ    27 So We revealed to him:

أَنِ ٱصْنَعِ ٱلْفُلْكَ بِأَعْيُنِنَا    'Build the ark before Our eyes

وَوَحْيِنَا    and by Our revelation.

فَإِذَا جَآءَ أَمْرُنَا    When Our edict comes

وَفَارَ ٱلتَّنُّورُ    and the oven gushes [a stream of water],

فَٱسْلُكْ فِيهَا مِن كُلٍّ زَوْجَيْنِ ٱثْنَيْنِ    bring into it a pair of every kind[1] [of animal],

وَأَهْلَكَ    and your family,

إِلَّا    except

مَن سَبَقَ عَلَيْهِ ٱلْقَوْلُ مِنْهُمْ    those of them against whom the decree has gone beforehand

وَلَا تُخَٰطِبْنِى    and do not plead with Me

فِى ٱلَّذِينَ ظَلَمُوٓاْ    for those who are wrongdoers:

إِنَّهُم مُّغْرَقُونَ ٢٧    they shall indeed be drowned.'

فَإِذَا ٱسْتَوَيْتَ أَنتَ وَمَن مَّعَكَ    28 When you, and those who are with you, are settled

عَلَى ٱلْفُلْكِ    in the ark,

فَقُلِ ٱلْحَمْدُ لِلَّهِ    say, "All praise belongs to Allah,

ٱلَّذِى نَجَّىٰنَا    who has delivered us

مِنَ ٱلْقَوْمِ ٱلظَّٰلِمِينَ ٢٨    from the wrongdoing lot."

وَقُل رَّبِّ    29 And say, "My Lord!

أَنزِلْنِى مُنزَلًا مُّبَارَكًا    Land me with a blessed landing,

وَأَنتَ خَيْرُ ٱلْمُنزِلِينَ ٢٩    for You are the best of those who bring ashore." '

إِنَّ فِى ذَٰلِكَ لَءَايَٰتٍ    30 There are indeed signs in this;

وَإِن كُنَّا لَمُبْتَلِينَ ٣٠    and indeed We have been testing.

ثُمَّ أَنشَأْنَا مِنۢ بَعْدِهِمْ    31 Then after them We brought forth

قَرْنًا ءَاخَرِينَ ٣١    another generation,

فَأَرْسَلْنَا فِيهِمْ رَسُولًا مِّنْهُمْ    32 and We sent them an apostle from among themselves,

أَنِ ٱعْبُدُواْ ٱللَّهَ    saying, 'Worship Allah!

مَا لَكُم مِّنْ إِلَٰهٍ غَيْرُهُۥٓ    You have no other god besides Him.

أَفَلَا تَتَّقُونَ ٣٢    Will you not then be wary [of Him]?'

وَقَالَ ٱلْمَلَأُ مِن قَوْمِهِ    33 Said the elite of his people,

---

[1] Or 'bring into it, of every kind [of animal], two mates.'

الَّذِينَ كَفَرُوا    who were faithless

وَكَذَّبُوا بِلِقَآءِ ٱلْآخِرَةِ    and who denied the encounter of the Hereafter

وَأَتْرَفْنَهُمْ    and whom We had given affluence

فِي ٱلْحَيَوٰةِ ٱلدُّنْيَا    in the life of the world:

مَا هَذَآ إِلَّا بَشَرٌ مِّثْلُكُمْ    'This is just a human being like you:

يَأْكُلُ مِمَّا تَأْكُلُونَ مِنْهُ    he eats what you eat,

وَيَشْرَبُ مِمَّا تَشْرَبُونَ ۝    and drinks what you drink.

وَلَئِنْ أَطَعْتُم بَشَرًا مِّثْلَكُمْ    34 If you obey a human being like yourselves,

إِنَّكُمْ إِذًا لَّخَسِرُونَ ۝    you will indeed be losers.

أَيَعِدُكُمْ أَنَّكُمْ إِذَا مِتُّمْ    35 Does he promise you that when you have died

وَكُنتُمْ تُرَابًا وَعِظَامًا    and become dust and bones

أَنَّكُم مُّخْرَجُونَ ۝    you will indeed be raised [from the dead]?

هَيْهَاتَ هَيْهَاتَ لِمَا تُوعَدُونَ ۝    36 Far-fetched, far-fetched is what you are promised!

إِنْ هِيَ إِلَّا حَيَاتُنَا ٱلدُّنْيَا    37 There is nothing but the life of this world:

نَمُوتُ وَنَحْيَا    we live and we die,

وَمَا نَحْنُ بِمَبْعُوثِينَ ۝    and we shall not be resurrected.

إِنْ هُوَ إِلَّا رَجُلٌ    38 He is just a man

ٱفْتَرَىٰ عَلَى ٱللَّهِ كَذِبًا    who has fabricated a lie against Allah,

وَمَا نَحْنُ لَهُ بِمُؤْمِنِينَ ۝    and we will not believe in him.'

قَالَ رَبِّ    39 He said, 'My Lord!

ٱنصُرْنِي بِمَا كَذَّبُونِ ۝    Help me, as they impugn me.'

قَالَ عَمَّا قَلِيلٍ    40 He said, 'In a little while

لَّيُصْبِحُنَّ نَادِمِينَ ۝    they will become regretful.'

فَأَخَذَتْهُمُ ٱلصَّيْحَةُ بِٱلْحَقِّ    41 So the Cry seized them justifiably

فَجَعَلْنَاهُمْ غُثَآءً    and We turned them into a scum.

فَبُعْدًا لِّلْقَوْمِ ٱلظَّالِمِينَ ۝    So away with the wrongdoing lot!

ثُمَّ أَنشَأْنَا مِنْ بَعْدِهِمْ    42 Then after them We brought forth

قُرُونًا ءَاخَرِينَ ۝    other generations.

مَا تَسْبِقُ مِنْ أُمَّةٍ أَجَلَهَا    43 No nation can advance its time

وَمَا يَسْتَأْخِرُونَ ۝    nor can it defer it.

ثُمَّ أَرْسَلْنَا رُسُلَنَا تَتْرَا    44 Then We sent Our apostles successively.

كُلَّ مَا جَاءَ أُمَّةً رَّسُولُهَا    Whenever there came to a nation its apostle,

كَذَّبُوهُ    they impugned him,

فَأَتْبَعْنَا بَعْضَهُم بَعْضًا    so We made them follow one another [to extinction]

وَجَعَلْنَهُمْ أَحَادِيثَ    and We turned them into folktales.

فَبُعْدًا لِّقَوْمٍ لَّا يُؤْمِنُونَ ۝    So away with the faithless lot!

ثُمَّ أَرْسَلْنَا مُوسَىٰ وَأَخَاهُ هَرُونَ    45 Then We sent Moses and Aaron, his brother,

بِآيَتِنَا وَسُلْطَنٍ مُّبِينٍ ۝    with Our signs and a manifest authority,

إِلَىٰ فِرْعَوْنَ وَمَلَإِيْهِ    46 to Pharaoh and his elites;

فَٱسْتَكْبَرُوا    but they acted arrogantly

وَكَانُوا قَوْمًا عَالِينَ ۝    and they were a tyrannical lot.

فَقَالُوا أَنُؤْمِنُ لِبَشَرَيْنِ مِثْلِنَا    47 They said, 'Shall we believe two humans like ourselves,

وَقَوْمُهُمَا لَنَا عَبِدُونَ ۝    while their people are our slaves?'

فَكَذَّبُوهُمَا    48 So they impugned the two of them,

فَكَانُوا مِنَ ٱلْمُهْلَكِينَ ۝    whereat they were among those who were destroyed.

وَلَقَدْ ءَاتَيْنَا مُوسَى ٱلْكِتَبَ    49 Certainly We gave Moses the Book

لَعَلَّهُمْ يَهْتَدُونَ ۝    so that they might be guided,

وَجَعَلْنَا ٱبْنَ مَرْيَمَ    50 and We made the son of Mary

وَأُمَّهُ    and his mother

ءَايَةً    a sign,

وَءَاوَيْنَهُمَا إِلَىٰ رَبْوَةٍ    and sheltered them in a highland,

ذَاتِ قَرَارٍ وَمَعِينٍ ۝    level and watered by a stream.

يَٰٓأَيُّهَا ٱلرُّسُلُ    51 O apostles!

كُلُوا مِنَ ٱلطَّيِّبَتِ    Eat of the good things

وَٱعْمَلُوا صَلِحًا    and act righteously.

إِنِّي بِمَا تَعْمَلُونَ عَلِيمٌ ۝    Indeed I know best what you do.

وَإِنَّ هَٰذِهِۦٓ أُمَّتُكُمْ أُمَّةً وَٰحِدَةً    52 Indeed this community of yours is one community,

وَأَنَا۠ رَبُّكُمْ    and I am your Lord,

فَٱتَّقُونِ ۝    so be wary of Me.

فَتَقَطَّعُوٓا أَمْرَهُم بَيْنَهُمْ زُبُرًا  53 But they fragmented their religion among themselves,

كُلُّ حِزْبٍ بِمَا لَدَيْهِمْ فَرِحُونَ  each party exulting in what it had.

فَذَرْهُمْ فِى غَمْرَتِهِمْ حَتَّىٰ حِينٍ  54 So *leave* them in their stupor for a while.

أَيَحْسَبُونَ أَنَّمَا نُمِدُّهُم بِهِۦ  55 Do they suppose that whatever aid We provide them

مِن مَّالٍ وَبَنِينَ  in regard to wealth and children [is because]

نُسَارِعُ لَهُمْ فِى ٱلْخَيْرَٰتِ  56 We are eager to bring them good?

بَل لَّا يَشْعُرُونَ  Rather they are not aware!

إِنَّ ٱلَّذِينَ هُم  57 Indeed those who are

مِّنْ خَشْيَةِ رَبِّهِم مُّشْفِقُونَ  apprehensive for the fear of their Lord,

وَٱلَّذِينَ هُم بِـَٔايَٰتِ رَبِّهِمْ يُؤْمِنُونَ  58 and who believe in the signs of their Lord,

وَٱلَّذِينَ هُم بِرَبِّهِمْ لَا يُشْرِكُونَ  59 and who do not ascribe partners to their Lord;

وَٱلَّذِينَ يُؤْتُونَ مَآ ءَاتَوا۟  60 and who give whatever they give

وَّقُلُوبُهُمْ وَجِلَةٌ  while their hearts tremble with awe

أَنَّهُمْ إِلَىٰ رَبِّهِمْ رَٰجِعُونَ  that they are going to return to their Lord

أُو۟لَٰٓئِكَ يُسَٰرِعُونَ  61 —it is they who are zealous

فِى ٱلْخَيْرَٰتِ  in [performing] good works,

وَهُمْ لَهَا سَٰبِقُونَ  and take the lead in them.

وَلَا نُكَلِّفُ نَفْسًا إِلَّا وُسْعَهَا  62 We task no soul except according to its capacity,

وَلَدَيْنَا كِتَٰبٌ يَنطِقُ بِٱلْحَقِّ  and with Us is a book that speaks the truth,

وَهُمْ لَا يُظْلَمُونَ  and they will not be wronged.

بَلْ قُلُوبُهُمْ فِى غَمْرَةٍ مِّنْ هَٰذَا  63 Rather their hearts are in a stupor in regard to this,

وَلَهُمْ أَعْمَٰلٌ مِّن دُونِ ذَٰلِكَ  and there are their other deeds besides

هُمْ لَهَا عَٰمِلُونَ  which they perpetrate.

حَتَّىٰٓ إِذَآ أَخَذْنَا مُتْرَفِيهِم بِٱلْعَذَابِ  64 When We seize their affluent ones with punishment,

إِذَا هُمْ يَجْـَٔرُونَ  behold, they make entreaties [to Us].

لَا تَجْـَٔرُوا۟ ٱلْيَوْمَ  65 'Do not make entreaties today!

إِنَّكُم مِّنَّا لَا تُنصَرُونَ  Indeed you will not receive any help from Us.

قَدْ كَانَتْ ءَايَٰتِى تُتْلَىٰ عَلَيْكُمْ  66 Certainly My signs used to be recited to you,

فَكُنتُمْ عَلَىٰٓ أَعْقَٰبِكُمْ تَنكِصُونَ  but you used to take to your heels,

مُسْتَكْبِرِينَ بِهِۦ   67 being disdainful of it,[1]

سَٰمِرًا تَهْجُرُونَ ۝   talking nonsense in your nightly sessions.'

أَفَلَمْ يَدَّبَّرُوا۟ ٱلْقَوْلَ   68 Have they not contemplated the discourse,[2]

أَمْ جَآءَهُم   or has anything come to them [in it]

مَّا لَمْ يَأْتِ ءَابَآءَهُمُ ٱلْأَوَّلِينَ ۝   that did not come to their forefathers?

أَمْ لَمْ يَعْرِفُوا۟ رَسُولَهُمْ   69 Is it that they do not recognize their apostle,[3]

فَهُمْ لَهُۥ مُنكِرُونَ ۝   and so they deny him?[4]

أَمْ يَقُولُونَ بِهِۦ جِنَّةٌۢ   70 Do they say, 'There is madness in him'?

بَلْ جَآءَهُم بِٱلْحَقِّ   Rather he has brought them the truth,

وَأَكْثَرُهُمْ لِلْحَقِّ كَٰرِهُونَ ۝   and most of them are averse to the truth.

وَلَوِ ٱتَّبَعَ ٱلْحَقُّ أَهْوَآءَهُمْ   71 Had the Truth followed their desires,

لَفَسَدَتِ ٱلسَّمَٰوَٰتُ وَٱلْأَرْضُ   the heavens and the earth would have surely fallen apart

وَمَن فِيهِنَّ   [along] with those who are in them.

بَلْ أَتَيْنَٰهُم بِذِكْرِهِمْ   Rather We have brought them their reminder,

فَهُمْ عَن ذِكْرِهِم مُّعْرِضُونَ ۝   but they are disregardful of their reminder.

أَمْ تَسْـَٔلُهُمْ خَرْجًا   72 Do *you* ask a recompense from them?

فَخَرَاجُ رَبِّكَ خَيْرٌ   Yet *your* Lord's recompense is better,

وَهُوَ خَيْرُ ٱلرَّٰزِقِينَ ۝   and He is the best of providers.

وَإِنَّكَ لَتَدْعُوهُمْ   73 Indeed *you* invite them

إِلَىٰ صِرَٰطٍ مُّسْتَقِيمٍ ۝   to a straight path,

وَإِنَّ ٱلَّذِينَ لَا يُؤْمِنُونَ   74 and indeed those who do not believe

بِٱلْءَاخِرَةِ   in the Hereafter

عَنِ ٱلصِّرَٰطِ لَنَٰكِبُونَ ۝ ❈   surely deviate from the path.

وَلَوْ رَحِمْنَٰهُمْ   75 Should We have mercy upon them

وَكَشَفْنَا مَا بِهِم مِّن ضُرٍّ   and remove their distress from them,

لَّلَجُّوا۟   they would surely persist,

---

[1] That is, the Qur'ān. Or, 'him,' that is of the Prophet.

[2] That is, the Qur'ān. Cf. 4:82, 47:24.

[3] That is, 'Is the Apostle a stranger of an unknown background and a person unknown to them?'

[4] Or 'and so they are not at home with him.'

فِى طُغْيَـٰنِهِمْ يَعْمَهُونَ ٧٥     bewildered in their rebellion.

وَلَقَدْ أَخَذْنَـٰهُم بِٱلْعَذَابِ ٧٦ Certainly We have seized them with punishment,

فَمَا ٱسْتَكَانُوا۟ لِرَبِّهِمْ     yet they neither humbled themselves to their Lord,

وَمَا يَتَضَرَّعُونَ ٧٦     nor did they entreat [Him for mercy].

حَتَّىٰٓ إِذَا فَتَحْنَا عَلَيْهِم بَابًا ٧٧ When We opened on them the door

ذَا عَذَابٍ شَدِيدٍ     of a severe punishment,

إِذَا هُمْ فِيهِ مُبْلِسُونَ ٧٧     behold, they are despondent in it.

وَهُوَ ٱلَّذِىٓ أَنشَأَ لَكُمُ ٱلسَّمْعَ ٧٨ It is He who made for you hearing,

وَٱلْأَبْصَـٰرَ وَٱلْأَفْـِٔدَةَ     eyesight, and hearts.

قَلِيلًا مَّا تَشْكُرُونَ ٧٨     Little do you thank.

وَهُوَ ٱلَّذِى ذَرَأَكُمْ فِى ٱلْأَرْضِ ٧٩ It is He who created you on the earth,

وَإِلَيْهِ تُحْشَرُونَ ٧٩     and you will be mustered toward Him.

وَهُوَ ٱلَّذِى يُحْىِۦ وَيُمِيتُ ٨٠ And it is He who gives life and brings death

وَلَهُ ٱخْتِلَـٰفُ ٱلَّيْلِ وَٱلنَّهَارِ     and due to Him are the alternation of day and night.

أَفَلَا تَعْقِلُونَ ٨٠     Do you not apply reason?

بَلْ قَالُوا۟ مِثْلَ مَا قَالَ ٱلْأَوَّلُونَ ٨١ Rather they say just like what the ancients said.

قَالُوٓا۟ أَءِذَا مِتْنَا ٨٢ They said, 'What, when we are dead

وَكُنَّا تُرَابًا وَعِظَـٰمًا     and become dust and bones,

أَءِنَّا لَمَبْعُوثُونَ ٨٢     shall we be resurrected?'

لَقَدْ وُعِدْنَا نَحْنُ وَءَابَآؤُنَا هَـٰذَا ٨٣ Certainly we and our fathers were promised this

مِن قَبْلُ     before.

إِنْ هَـٰذَآ إِلَّآ أَسَـٰطِيرُ ٱلْأَوَّلِينَ ٨٣     [But] these are nothing but myths of the ancients.'

قُل لِّمَنِ ٱلْأَرْضُ ٨٤ Say, 'To whom does the earth belong

وَمَن فِيهَآ     and whoever it contains,

إِن كُنتُمْ تَعْلَمُونَ ٨٤     if you know?'

سَيَقُولُونَ لِلَّهِ ٨٥ They will say, 'To Allah.'

قُلْ أَفَلَا تَذَكَّرُونَ ٨٥     Say, 'Will you not then take admonition?'

قُلْ مَن رَّبُّ ٱلسَّمَـٰوَٰتِ ٱلسَّبْعِ ٨٦ Say, 'Who is the Lord of the seven heavens

وَرَبُّ ٱلْعَرْشِ ٱلْعَظِيمِ ٨٦     and the Lord of the Great Throne?'

سَيَقُولُونَ لِلَّهِ    87 They will say, '[They belong] to Allah.'

قُلْ أَفَلَا تَتَّقُونَ    Say, 'Will you not then be wary [of Him]?'

قُلْ مَنْ بِيَدِهِ مَلَكُوتُ كُلِّ شَيْءٍ    88 Say, 'In whose hand is the dominion of all things,

وَهُوَ يُجِيرُ    and who shelters

وَلَا يُجَارُ عَلَيْهِ    and no shelter can be provided from Him,

إِن كُنتُمْ تَعْلَمُونَ    if you know?'

سَيَقُولُونَ لِلَّهِ    89 They will say, '[They all belong] to Allah.'

قُلْ فَأَنَّىٰ تُسْحَرُونَ    Say, 'Then how are you being deluded?'[1]

بَلْ أَتَيْنَهُم بِالْحَقِّ    90 Rather We have brought them the truth,

وَإِنَّهُمْ لَكَذِبُونَ    and they are indeed liars.

مَا ٱتَّخَذَ ٱللَّهُ مِن وَلَدٍ    91 Allah has not taken any offspring,

وَمَا كَانَ مَعَهُ مِنْ إِلَٰهٍ    neither is there any god besides Him,

إِذًا لَّذَهَبَ كُلُّ إِلَٰهٍ بِمَا خَلَقَ    for then each god would take away what he created,

وَلَعَلَا بَعْضُهُمْ عَلَىٰ بَعْضٍ    and some of them would surely rise up against others.

سُبْحَٰنَ ٱللَّهِ عَمَّا يَصِفُونَ    Clear is Allah of what they allege!

عَٰلِمِ ٱلْغَيْبِ وَٱلشَّهَٰدَةِ    92 The Knower of the sensible and the Unseen,

فَتَعَٰلَىٰ    He is above

عَمَّا يُشْرِكُونَ    having any partners that they ascribe [to Him].

قُل رَّبِّ    93 Say, 'My Lord!

إِمَّا تُرِيَنِّي مَا يُوعَدُونَ    If You should show me what they are promised,

رَبِّ فَلَا تَجْعَلْنِي    94 then do not put me, my Lord,

فِي ٱلْقَوْمِ ٱلظَّٰلِمِينَ    among the wrongdoing lot.'

وَإِنَّا عَلَىٰ أَن نُّرِيَكَ مَا نَعِدُهُمْ لَقَٰدِرُونَ    95 We are indeed able to show *you* what We promise them.

ٱدْفَعْ بِٱلَّتِي هِيَ أَحْسَنُ ٱلسَّيِّئَةَ    96 *Repel* ill [conduct] with that which is the best.

نَحْنُ أَعْلَمُ بِمَا يَصِفُونَ    We know best whatever they allege.

وَقُل رَّبِّ    97 And *say*, 'My Lord!

أَعُوذُ بِكَ    I seek Your protection

---

[1] Or 'How are you being misled,' or 'How are you being rendered blind.'

مِنْ هَمَزَاتِ ٱلشَّيَٰطِينِ ۝          from the promptings of devils;

وَأَعُوذُ بِكَ رَبِّ   98              and I seek Your protection, my Lord,

أَن يَحْضُرُونِ ۝                     from their presence near me.'

حَتَّىٰ إِذَا جَآءَ أَحَدَهُمُ ٱلْمَوْتُ   99   When death comes to one of them,

قَالَ رَبِّ                           he says, 'My Lord!

ٱرْجِعُونِ ۝                          Take me back,

لَعَلِّىٓ أَعْمَلُ صَٰلِحًا فِيمَا تَرَكْتُ   100   that I may act righteously in what I have left behind.'

كَلَّآ                                'By no means!

إِنَّهَا كَلِمَةٌ هُوَ قَآئِلُهَا          These are mere words that he says.'

وَمِن وَرَآئِهِم بَرْزَخٌ                And ahead of them is a barrier

إِلَىٰ يَوْمِ يُبْعَثُونَ ۝             until the day they will be resurrected

فَإِذَا نُفِخَ فِى ٱلصُّورِ   101       And when the Trumpet is blown,

فَلَآ أَنسَابَ بَيْنَهُمْ يَوْمَئِذٍ     there will be no ties between them on that day,

وَلَا يَتَسَآءَلُونَ ۝                 nor will they ask [about] each other.[1]

فَمَن ثَقُلَتْ مَوَٰزِينُهُۥ   102       Then those whose deeds weigh heavy in the scales

فَأُوْلَٰٓئِكَ هُمُ ٱلْمُفْلِحُونَ ۝    —it is they who are the felicitous.

وَمَنْ خَفَّتْ مَوَٰزِينُهُۥ   103       As for those whose deeds weigh light in the scales,

فَأُوْلَٰٓئِكَ ٱلَّذِينَ خَسِرُوٓا۟ أَنفُسَهُمْ   —they will be the ones who have ruined their souls,

فِى جَهَنَّمَ خَٰلِدُونَ ۝            [and] they will remain in hell [forever].

تَلْفَحُ وُجُوهَهُمُ ٱلنَّارُ   104      The Fire will scorch their faces,

وَهُمْ فِيهَا كَٰلِحُونَ ۝            and they will be morose in it.

أَلَمْ تَكُنْ ءَايَٰتِى تُتْلَىٰ عَلَيْكُمْ   105   'Was it not that My signs were recited to you

فَكُنتُم بِهَا تُكَذِّبُونَ ۝         but you would deny them?'

قَالُوا۟ رَبَّنَا   106                 They will say, 'Our Lord!

غَلَبَتْ عَلَيْنَا شِقْوَتُنَا          Our wretchedness overcame us,

وَكُنَّا قَوْمًا ضَآلِّينَ ۝          and we were an astray lot.

رَبَّنَآ أَخْرِجْنَا مِنْهَا   107         Our Lord! Bring us out of this!

فَإِنْ عُدْنَا فَإِنَّا ظَٰلِمُونَ ۝      Then, if we revert, we will indeed be wrongdoers.'

---

[1] Cf. 70:10.

قَالَ ٱخْسَئُوا۟ فِيهَا 108 He will say, 'Begone in it,

وَلَا تُكَلِّمُونِ ۝ and do not speak to Me!

إِنَّهُۥ كَانَ فَرِيقٌ مِّنْ عِبَادِى 109 Indeed there was a part of My servants

يَقُولُونَ رَبَّنَآ who would say, "Our Lord!

ءَامَنَّا We have believed.

فَٱغْفِرْ لَنَا وَٱرْحَمْنَا So forgive us, and have mercy on us,

وَأَنتَ خَيْرُ ٱلرَّٰحِمِينَ ۝ and You are the best of the merciful."

فَٱتَّخَذْتُمُوهُمْ سِخْرِيًّا 110 But then you took them by ridicule

حَتَّىٰٓ أَنسَوْكُمْ ذِكْرِى until they made you forget My remembrance,[1]

وَكُنتُم مِّنْهُمْ تَضْحَكُونَ ۝ and you used to laugh at them.

إِنِّى جَزَيْتُهُمُ ٱلْيَوْمَ بِمَا صَبَرُوٓا۟ 111 Indeed I have rewarded them today for their patience.

أَنَّهُمْ هُمُ ٱلْفَآئِزُونَ ۝ They are indeed the triumphant.'

قَٰلَ 112 He will say,

كَمْ لَبِثْتُمْ فِى ٱلْأَرْضِ عَدَدَ سِنِينَ 'How many years did you remain on earth?'

قَالُوا۟ لَبِثْنَا يَوْمًا 113 They will say, 'We remained for a day,

أَوْ بَعْضَ يَوْمٍ or part of a day;

فَسْـَٔلِ ٱلْعَآدِّينَ ۝ yet ask those who keep the count.'

قَٰلَ إِن لَّبِثْتُمْ إِلَّا قَلِيلًا 114 He will say, 'You only remained a little;

لَّوْ أَنَّكُمْ كُنتُمْ تَعْلَمُونَ ۝ if only you had known.

أَفَحَسِبْتُمْ أَنَّمَا خَلَقْنَٰكُمْ عَبَثًا 115 Did you suppose that We created you aimlessly,

وَأَنَّكُمْ إِلَيْنَا لَا تُرْجَعُونَ ۝ and that you will not be brought back to Us?'

فَتَعَٰلَى ٱللَّهُ ٱلْمَلِكُ ٱلْحَقُّ 116 So exalted is Allah, the True Sovereign,

لَآ إِلَٰهَ إِلَّا هُوَ There is no god except Him,

رَبُّ ٱلْعَرْشِ ٱلْكَرِيمِ ۝ the Lord of the Noble Throne.

وَمَن يَدْعُ مَعَ ٱللَّهِ إِلَٰهًا ءَاخَرَ 117 Whoever invokes besides Allah another god

لَا بُرْهَٰنَ لَهُۥ بِهِۦ of which he has no proof,

فَإِنَّمَا حِسَابُهُۥ عِندَ رَبِّهِۦٓ his reckoning will indeed rest with his Lord.

إِنَّهُۥ لَا يُفْلِحُ ٱلْكَٰفِرُونَ ۝ Indeed the faithless will not be felicitous.

---

[1] That is, 'your contemptuous attitude towards them made you oblivious of Me and My reminders and warnings.'

وَقُل رَّبِّ 118 *Say,* 'My Lord,

اغْفِرْ وَارْحَمْ     forgive and have mercy,

وَأَنتَ خَيْرُ ٱلرَّحِمِينَ ۝     and You are the best of the merciful.'

سُورَةُ النُّورِ         24. SŪRAT AL-NŪR[1]

بِسْمِ ٱللَّهِ        In the Name of Allah,

ٱلرَّحْمَٰنِ ٱلرَّحِيمِ     the All-beneficent, the All-merciful.

سُورَةٌ أَنزَلْنَٰهَا 1 [This is] a *sūrah* which We have sent down,

وَفَرَضْنَٰهَا     and prescribed it,

وَأَنزَلْنَا فِيهَآ ءَايَٰتٍ بَيِّنَٰتٍ     and We have sent down in it manifest signs

لَّعَلَّكُمْ تَذَكَّرُونَ ۝     so that you may take admonition.

ٱلزَّانِيَةُ وَٱلزَّانِى 2 As for the fornicatress and the fornicator,

فَٱجْلِدُواْ كُلَّ وَٰحِدٍ مِّنْهُمَا     strike each of them

مِائَةَ جَلْدَةٍ       a hundred lashes,

وَلَا تَأْخُذْكُم بِهِمَا رَأْفَةٌ     and let not pity for them overcome you

فِى دِينِ ٱللَّهِ        in Allah's law,

إِن كُنتُمْ تُؤْمِنُونَ بِٱللَّهِ     if you believe in Allah

وَٱلْيَوْمِ ٱلْءَاخِرِ       and the Last Day,

وَلْيَشْهَدْ عَذَابَهُمَا     and let their punishment be witnessed

طَآئِفَةٌ مِّنَ ٱلْمُؤْمِنِينَ ۝     by a group of the faithful.

ٱلزَّانِى لَا يَنكِحُ إِلَّا زَانِيَةً 3 The fornicator shall not marry anyone but a fornicatress

أَوْ مُشْرِكَةً      or an idolatress,

وَٱلزَّانِيَةُ لَا يَنكِحُهَآ     and the fornicatress shall be married by none

إِلَّا زَانٍ أَوْ مُشْرِكٌ     except a fornicator or an idolater,

وَحُرِّمَ ذَٰلِكَ عَلَى ٱلْمُؤْمِنِينَ ۝     and that is forbidden to the faithful.

وَٱلَّذِينَ يَرْمُونَ ٱلْمُحْصَنَٰتِ 4 As for those who accuse honourable women

ثُمَّ لَمْ يَأْتُواْ بِأَرْبَعَةِ شُهَدَآءَ     and do not bring four witnesses,

---

[1] The *sūrah* is named after the famous 'Light Verse,' which occurs in it (24:35).

فَٱجْلِدُوهُمْ ثَمَٰنِينَ جَلْدَةً    strike them eighty lashes,

وَلَا تَقْبَلُواْ لَهُمْ شَهَٰدَةً أَبَدًا    and never accept any testimony from them after that,

وَأُوْلَٰٓئِكَ هُمُ ٱلْفَٰسِقُونَ ۝    and they are transgressors,

إِلَّا ٱلَّذِينَ تَابُواْ مِنۢ بَعْدِ ذَٰلِكَ  5    excepting those who repent after that

وَأَصْلَحُواْ    and reform,

فَإِنَّ ٱللَّهَ غَفُورٌ رَّحِيمٌ ۝    for Allah is indeed all-forgiving, all-merciful.

وَٱلَّذِينَ يَرْمُونَ أَزْوَٰجَهُمْ  6    As for those who accuse their wives,

وَلَمْ يَكُن لَّهُمْ شُهَدَآءُ إِلَّآ أَنفُسُهُمْ    but have no witnesses except themselves,

فَشَهَٰدَةُ أَحَدِهِمْ    then the testimony of one of them

أَرْبَعُ شَهَٰدَٰتِۭ بِٱللَّهِ    shall be a fourfold testimony [sworn] by Allah

إِنَّهُۥ لَمِنَ ٱلصَّٰدِقِينَ ۝    that he is indeed stating the truth,

وَٱلْخَٰمِسَةُ أَنَّ لَعْنَتَ ٱللَّهِ عَلَيْهِ  7    and a fifth [oath] that Allah's wrath shall be upon him

إِن كَانَ مِنَ ٱلْكَٰذِبِينَ ۝    if he were lying.

وَيَدْرَؤُاْ عَنْهَا ٱلْعَذَابَ  8    The punishment shall be averted from her

أَن تَشْهَدَ أَرْبَعَ شَهَٰدَٰتِۭ بِٱللَّهِ    by her testifying with four oaths [sworn] by Allah

إِنَّهُۥ لَمِنَ ٱلْكَٰذِبِينَ ۝    that he is indeed lying,

وَٱلْخَٰمِسَةَ أَنَّ غَضَبَ ٱللَّهِ عَلَيْهَآ  9    and a fifth [oath] that Allah's wrath shall be upon her

إِن كَانَ مِنَ ٱلصَّٰدِقِينَ ۝    if he were stating the truth.

وَلَوْلَا فَضْلُ ٱللَّهِ عَلَيْكُمْ وَرَحْمَتُهُۥ  10    Were it not for Allah's grace and His mercy upon you,

وَأَنَّ ٱللَّهَ تَوَّابٌ حَكِيمٌ ۝    and that Allah is all-clement, all-wise. . . .[1]

إِنَّ ٱلَّذِينَ جَآءُو بِٱلْإِفْكِ  11    Indeed those who initiated the calumny

عُصْبَةٌ مِّنكُمْ    are a band from among yourselves.

لَا تَحْسَبُوهُ شَرًّا لَّكُم    Do not suppose it is bad for you.

بَلْ هُوَ خَيْرٌ لَّكُمْ    Rather it is for your good.

لِكُلِّ ٱمْرِئٍ مِّنْهُم    Each man among them bears [the onus for]

مَّا ٱكْتَسَبَ مِنَ ٱلْإِثْمِ    his share in the sin,

وَٱلَّذِى تَوَلَّىٰ كِبْرَهُۥ    and as for him who assumed its major burden

مِنْهُمْ    from among them

لَهُۥ عَذَابٌ عَظِيمٌ ۝    there is a great punishment for him.

---

[1] Ellipsis. For the omitted part of the sentence see verses 14 & 21 below.

لَوْلَا إِذْ سَمِعْتُمُوهُ  12 When you [first] heard about it, why did not

ظَنَّ ٱلْمُؤْمِنُونَ وَٱلْمُؤْمِنَـٰتُ  the faithful, men and women, think

بِأَنفُسِهِمْ خَيْرًا  well of their folks,

وَقَالُوا هَـٰذَآ إِفْكٌ مُّبِينٌ ۝  and say, 'This is an obvious calumny'?

لَوْلَا جَآءُو عَلَيْهِ بِأَرْبَعَةِ شُهَدَآءَ  13 Why did they[1] not bring four witnesses to it?

فَإِذْ لَمْ يَأْتُوا بِٱلشُّهَدَآءِ  So when they could not bring the witnesses,

فَأُوْلَـٰئِكَ عِندَ ٱللَّهِ هُمُ ٱلْكَـٰذِبُونَ ۝  they are liars in Allah's sight.

وَلَوْلَا فَضْلُ ٱللَّهِ عَلَيْكُمْ وَرَحْمَتُهُ  14 Were it not for Allah's grace and His mercy upon you

فِى ٱلدُّنْيَا وَٱلْـَٔاخِرَةِ  in this world and the Hereafter,

لَمَسَّكُمْ  there would have befallen you

فِى مَآ أَفَضْتُمْ فِيهِ عَذَابٌ عَظِيمٌ ۝  a great punishment for what you ventured into,

إِذْ تَلَقَّوْنَهُ بِأَلْسِنَتِكُمْ  15 when you were receiving it on your tongues,

وَتَقُولُونَ بِأَفْوَاهِكُم  and were mouthing

مَّا لَيْسَ لَكُم بِهِۦ عِلْمٌ  something of which you had no knowledge,

وَتَحْسَبُونَهُ هَيِّنًا  supposing it to be a light matter,

وَهُوَ عِندَ ٱللَّهِ عَظِيمٌ ۝  while it is was a grave [matter] with Allah.

وَلَوْلَا إِذْ سَمِعْتُمُوهُ قُلْتُم  16 And why did you not, when you heard it, say,

مَّا يَكُونُ لَنَآ أَن نَّتَكَلَّمَ بِهَـٰذَا  'It is not for us to say such a thing.

سُبْحَـٰنَكَ  [O Allah!] You are immaculate!

هَـٰذَا بُهْتَـٰنٌ عَظِيمٌ ۝  This is a monstrous calumny!'

يَعِظُكُمُ ٱللَّهُ  17 Allah advises you

أَن تَعُودُوا لِمِثْلِهِۦٓ أَبَدًا  lest you should ever repeat the like of it,

إِن كُنتُم مُّؤْمِنِينَ ۝  should you be faithful.

وَيُبَيِّنُ ٱللَّهُ لَكُمُ ٱلْـَٔايَـٰتِ  18 Allah clarifies the signs for you,

وَٱللَّهُ عَلِيمٌ حَكِيمٌ ۝  and Allah is all-knowing, all-wise.

إِنَّ ٱلَّذِينَ يُحِبُّونَ أَن تَشِيعَ ٱلْفَـٰحِشَةُ  19 Indeed those who want indecency to spread

فِى ٱلَّذِينَ ءَامَنُوا  among the faithful

لَهُمْ عَذَابٌ أَلِيمٌ  —there is a painful punishment for them

---

[1] That is, those who had spread the slander accusing the Prophet's wife and one of the Companions.

فِى ٱلدُّنْيَا وَٱلْءَاخِرَةِ

in the world and the Hereafter,

وَٱللَّهُ يَعْلَمُ وَأَنتُمْ لَا تَعْلَمُونَ ﴿١٩﴾

and Allah knows and you do not know.

وَلَوْلَا فَضْلُ ٱللَّهِ عَلَيْكُمْ وَرَحْمَتُهُۥ

20 Were it not for Allah's grace and His mercy upon you,

وَأَنَّ ٱللَّهَ رَءُوفٌ رَّحِيمٌ ﴿٢٠﴾ ❂

and that Allah is all-kind, all-merciful.

يَٰٓأَيُّهَا ٱلَّذِينَ ءَامَنُوا

21 O you who have faith!

لَا تَتَّبِعُوا خُطُوَٰتِ ٱلشَّيْطَٰنِ

Do not follow in Satan's steps.

وَمَن يَتَّبِعْ خُطُوَٰتِ ٱلشَّيْطَٰنِ

Whoever follows in Satan's steps [should know that]

فَإِنَّهُۥ يَأْمُرُ بِٱلْفَحْشَآءِ

he indeed prompts [you to commit] indecent acts

وَٱلْمُنكَرِ

and wrong.

وَلَوْلَا فَضْلُ ٱللَّهِ عَلَيْكُمْ وَرَحْمَتُهُۥ

Were it not for Allah's grace and His mercy upon you,

مَا زَكَىٰ مِنكُم مِّنْ أَحَدٍ أَبَدًا

not one of you would ever be pure.

وَلَٰكِنَّ ٱللَّهَ يُزَكِّى مَن يَشَآءُ

But Allah purifies whomever He wishes,

وَٱللَّهُ سَمِيعٌ عَلِيمٌ ﴿٢١﴾

and Allah is all-hearing, all-knowing.

وَلَا يَأْتَلِ أُو۟لُوا۟ ٱلْفَضْلِ مِنكُمْ وَٱلسَّعَةِ

22 Let the well-off and the opulent among you not vow[1]

أَن يُؤْتُوٓا۟ أُو۟لِى ٱلْقُرْبَىٰ وَٱلْمَسَٰكِينَ

not to give to the relatives and the needy,

وَٱلْمُهَٰجِرِينَ فِى سَبِيلِ ٱللَّهِ

and to those who have migrated in the way of Allah,

وَلْيَعْفُوا۟ وَلْيَصْفَحُوٓا۟

and let them excuse and forbear.

أَلَا تُحِبُّونَ أَن يَغْفِرَ ٱللَّهُ لَكُمْ

Do you not love that Allah should forgive you?

وَٱللَّهُ غَفُورٌ رَّحِيمٌ ﴿٢٢﴾

And Allah is all-forgiving, all-merciful.

إِنَّ ٱلَّذِينَ يَرْمُونَ

23 Indeed those who accuse

ٱلْمُحْصَنَٰتِ ٱلْغَٰفِلَٰتِ ٱلْمُؤْمِنَٰتِ

honourable and unwary faithful women

لُعِنُوا۟ فِى ٱلدُّنْيَا وَٱلْءَاخِرَةِ

shall be cursed in this world and the Hereafter,

وَهُمْ عَذَابٌ عَظِيمٌ ﴿٢٣﴾

and there shall be a great punishment for them

يَوْمَ تَشْهَدُ عَلَيْهِمْ

24 on the day when witness shall be given against them

أَلْسِنَتُهُمْ وَأَيْدِيهِمْ وَأَرْجُلُهُم

by their tongues, their hands, and their feet

بِمَا كَانُوا۟ يَعْمَلُونَ ﴿٢٤﴾

concerning what they used to do.

يَوْمَئِذٍ يُوَفِّيهِمُ ٱللَّهُ

25 On that day Allah will pay them in full

---

[1] Or 'Let the well-to-do and the opulent among you not fail to give. . . . '

دِينَهُمُ ٱلْحَقَّ    their due recompense,

وَيَعْلَمُونَ    and they shall know

أَنَّ ٱللَّهَ هُوَ ٱلْحَقُّ ٱلْمُبِينُ ۝    that Allah is the Manifest Reality.

ٱلْخَبِيثَٰتُ لِلْخَبِيثِينَ   26 Vicious women are for vicious men,

وَٱلْخَبِيثُونَ لِلْخَبِيثَٰتِ    and vicious men for vicious women.

وَٱلطَّيِّبَٰتُ لِلطَّيِّبِينَ    Good women are for good men,

وَٱلطَّيِّبُونَ لِلطَّيِّبَٰتِ    and good men for good women.[1]

أُوْلَٰٓئِكَ مُبَرَّءُونَ مِمَّا يَقُولُونَ   These are absolved of what they say [about them].[2]

لَهُم مَّغْفِرَةٌ وَرِزْقٌ كَرِيمٌ ۝   For them is forgiveness and a noble provision.

يَٰٓأَيُّهَا ٱلَّذِينَ ءَامَنُوا۟   27 O you who have faith!

لَا تَدْخُلُوا۟ بُيُوتًا غَيْرَ بُيُوتِكُمْ    Do not enter houses other than your own

حَتَّىٰ تَسْتَأْنِسُوا۟    until you have announced [your arrival]

وَتُسَلِّمُوا۟ عَلَىٰٓ أَهْلِهَا    and greeted their occupants.

ذَٰلِكُمْ خَيْرٌ لَّكُمْ    That is better for you.

لَعَلَّكُمْ تَذَكَّرُونَ ۝    Maybe you will take admonition.

فَإِن لَّمْ تَجِدُوا۟ فِيهَآ أَحَدًا   28 But if you do not find anyone in them,

فَلَا تَدْخُلُوهَا    do not enter them

حَتَّىٰ يُؤْذَنَ لَكُمْ    until you are given permission,

وَإِن قِيلَ لَكُمُ ٱرْجِعُوا۟ فَٱرْجِعُوا۟   and if you are told: 'Turn back,' then do turn back.

هُوَ أَزْكَىٰ لَكُمْ    That is more decent for you.

وَٱللَّهُ بِمَا تَعْمَلُونَ عَلِيمٌ ۝   And Allah knows best what you do.

لَّيْسَ عَلَيْكُمْ جُنَاحٌ   29 There will be no sin upon you

---

[1] Or, 'Vicious words (or deeds) come from vicious persons, and vicious persons are worthy of vicious words (or deeds). Good words (or deeds) come from good people, and good people are worthy of good words (or deeds).' According to this interpretation, this verse is similar in meaning to 17:84. This interpretation is also supported by the last part of the verse: 'They are absolved of what they say [about them].' However in accordance with the translation given above, the meaning of the verse will be similar to verse 24:3, at the beginning of this *sūrah*.

[2] That is, persons of good repute among the faithful legally stand absolved of any kind of allegations against them unless there is valid evidence to the contrary.

أَن تَدْخُلُوا    in entering [without announcing]

بُيُوتًا غَيْرَ مَسْكُونَةٍ    uninhabited houses

فِيهَا مَتَـٰعٌ لَّكُمْ    wherein you have goods belonging to you.

وَٱللَّهُ يَعْلَمُ مَا تُبْدُونَ    And Allah knows whatever you disclose

وَمَا تَكْتُمُونَ ﴿٢٩﴾    and whatever you conceal.

قُل لِّلْمُؤْمِنِينَ يَغُضُّوا مِنْ أَبْصَٰرِهِمْ    30 *Tell* the faithful men to cast down their looks

وَيَحْفَظُوا فُرُوجَهُمْ    and to guard their private parts.

ذَٰلِكَ أَزْكَىٰ لَهُمْ    That is more decent for them.

إِنَّ ٱللَّهَ خَبِيرٌ بِمَا يَصْنَعُونَ ﴿٣٠﴾    Allah is indeed well aware of what they do.

وَقُل لِّلْمُؤْمِنَٰتِ    31 And *tell* the faithful women

يَغْضُضْنَ مِنْ أَبْصَٰرِهِنَّ    to cast down their looks

وَيَحْفَظْنَ فُرُوجَهُنَّ    and to guard their private parts,

وَلَا يُبْدِينَ زِينَتَهُنَّ    and not to display their charms,

إِلَّا مَا ظَهَرَ مِنْهَا    except for what is outward,

وَلْيَضْرِبْنَ بِخُمُرِهِنَّ عَلَىٰ جُيُوبِهِنَّ    and let them draw their veils over their bosoms,

وَلَا يُبْدِينَ زِينَتَهُنَّ    and not display their charms

إِلَّا لِبُعُولَتِهِنَّ    except to their husbands,

أَوْ ءَابَآئِهِنَّ    or their fathers,

أَوْ ءَابَآءِ بُعُولَتِهِنَّ    or their husband's fathers,

أَوْ أَبْنَآئِهِنَّ    or their sons,

أَوْ أَبْنَآءِ بُعُولَتِهِنَّ    or their husband's sons,

أَوْ إِخْوَٰنِهِنَّ    or their brothers,

أَوْ بَنِىٓ إِخْوَٰنِهِنَّ    or their brothers' sons,

أَوْ بَنِىٓ أَخَوَٰتِهِنَّ    or their sisters' sons,

أَوْ نِسَآئِهِنَّ    or their women,[1]

أَوْ مَا مَلَكَتْ أَيْمَٰنُهُنَّ    or their slave girls,

---

[1] That is, Muslim women. Hence it is not lawful for Muslim women to expose their charms before non-Muslim women, who may possibly describe what they see to their men.

أَوِ ٱلتَّـٰبِعِينَ غَيْرِ أُوْلِي ٱلْإِرْبَةِ مِنَ ٱلرِّجَالِ

or male dependants lacking [sexual] desire,

أَوِ ٱلطِّفْلِ ٱلَّذِينَ لَمْ يَظْهَرُوا۟

or children uninitiated

عَلَىٰ عَوْرَٰتِ ٱلنِّسَآءِ

to women's parts.[1]

وَلَا يَضْرِبْنَ بِأَرْجُلِهِنَّ

And let them not thump their feet

لِيُعْلَمَ مَا يُخْفِينَ مِن زِينَتِهِنَّ

to make known their hidden ornaments.

وَتُوبُوٓا۟ إِلَى ٱللَّهِ جَمِيعًا

Rally to Allah in repentance,

أَيُّهَ ٱلْمُؤْمِنُونَ

O faithful,

لَعَلَّكُمْ تُفْلِحُونَ ۝

so that you may be felicitous.

وَأَنكِحُوا۟ ٱلْأَيَـٰمَىٰ مِنكُمْ

32 Marry off those who are single among you

وَٱلصَّـٰلِحِينَ مِنْ عِبَادِكُمْ

and the upright[2] among your male slaves

وَإِمَآئِكُمْ

and your female slaves.

إِن يَكُونُوا۟ فُقَرَآءَ

If they are poor,

يُغْنِهِمُ ٱللَّهُ مِن فَضْلِهِۦ

Allah will enrich them out of His grace,

وَٱللَّهُ وَٰسِعٌ عَلِيمٌ ۝

and Allah is all-bounteous, all-knowing.

وَلْيَسْتَعْفِفِ ٱلَّذِينَ لَا يَجِدُونَ نِكَاحًا

33 Those who cannot afford marriage should be continent

حَتَّىٰ يُغْنِيَهُمُ ٱللَّهُ مِن فَضْلِهِۦ

until Allah enriches them out of His grace.

وَٱلَّذِينَ يَبْتَغُونَ ٱلْكِتَـٰبَ

As for those who seek an emancipation deal

مِمَّا مَلَكَتْ أَيْمَـٰنُكُمْ

from among your slaves,

فَكَاتِبُوهُمْ

make such a deal with them

إِنْ عَلِمْتُمْ فِيهِمْ خَيْرًا

if you know any good in them,

وَءَاتُوهُم مِّن مَّالِ ٱللَّهِ

and give them out of the wealth of Allah

ٱلَّذِىٓ ءَاتَىٰكُمْ

which He has given you.

وَلَا تُكْرِهُوا۟ فَتَيَـٰتِكُمْ عَلَى ٱلْبِغَآءِ

Do not compel your female slaves to prostitution

إِنْ أَرَدْنَ تَحَصُّنًا

when they desire to be chaste,

لِّتَبْتَغُوا۟ عَرَضَ ٱلْحَيَوٰةِ ٱلدُّنْيَا

seeking the transitory wares of the life of this world.

وَمَن يُكْرِههُّنَّ

Should anyone compel them,

فَإِنَّ ٱللَّهَ مِنۢ بَعْدِ إِكْرَٰهِهِنَّ

then after their compulsion Allah is indeed

---

[1] That is, boys who have not reached the age of virility.

[2] That is, those who are faithful, or honest and chaste.

غَفُورٌ رَّحِيمٌ ۝     all-forgiving, all-merciful.

وَلَقَدْ أَنزَلْنَآ إِلَيْكُمْ ءَايَٰتٍ مُّبَيِّنَٰتٍ    34 Certainly We have sent down to you manifest signs

وَمَثَلًا مِّنَ ٱلَّذِينَ خَلَوْا۟ مِن قَبْلِكُمْ    and a description of those who passed before you,

وَمَوْعِظَةً لِّلْمُتَّقِينَ ۝ ۞    and an advice for the Godwary.

ٱللَّهُ نُورُ ٱلسَّمَٰوَٰتِ وَٱلْأَرْضِ    35 Allah is the Light of the heavens and the earth.

مَثَلُ نُورِهِۦ كَمِشْكَوٰةٍ فِيهَا مِصْبَاحٌ    The parable of His Light is a niche wherein is a lamp

ٱلْمِصْبَاحُ فِى زُجَاجَةٍ    —the lamp is in a glass,

ٱلزُّجَاجَةُ كَأَنَّهَا كَوْكَبٌ دُرِّىٌّ    the glass as it were a glittering star—

يُوقَدُ مِن شَجَرَةٍ مُّبَٰرَكَةٍ زَيْتُونَةٍ    lit from a blessed olive tree,

لَّا شَرْقِيَّةٍ وَلَا غَرْبِيَّةٍ    neither eastern nor western,

يَكَادُ زَيْتُهَا يُضِىٓءُ    whose oil almost lights up,

وَلَوْ لَمْ تَمْسَسْهُ نَارٌ    though fire should not touch it.

نُّورٌ عَلَىٰ نُورٍ    Light upon light.

يَهْدِى ٱللَّهُ لِنُورِهِۦ مَن يَشَآءُ    Allah guides to His Light whomever He wishes.

وَيَضْرِبُ ٱللَّهُ ٱلْأَمْثَٰلَ لِلنَّاسِ    Allah draws parables for mankind,

وَٱللَّهُ بِكُلِّ شَىْءٍ عَلِيمٌ ۝    and Allah has knowledge of all things.

فِى بُيُوتٍ أَذِنَ ٱللَّهُ أَن تُرْفَعَ    36 In houses Allah has allowed to be raised

وَيُذْكَرَ فِيهَا ٱسْمُهُ    and wherein His Name is celebrated,

يُسَبِّحُ لَهُۥ فِيهَا بِٱلْغُدُوِّ وَٱلْءَاصَالِ ۝    He is glorified therein, morning and evening,

رِجَالٌ    37 by men

لَّا تُلْهِيهِمْ تِجَٰرَةٌ وَلَا بَيْعٌ    whom neither trading nor bargaining distracts

عَن ذِكْرِ ٱللَّهِ    from the remembrance of Allah,

وَإِقَامِ ٱلصَّلَوٰةِ    and the maintenance of prayer

وَإِيتَآءِ ٱلزَّكَوٰةِ    and the giving of zakāt.

يَخَافُونَ يَوْمًا    They are fearful of a day

تَتَقَلَّبُ فِيهِ ٱلْقُلُوبُ وَٱلْأَبْصَٰرُ ۝    wherein the heart and the sight will be transformed,

لِيَجْزِيَهُمُ ٱللَّهُ    38 so that Allah may reward them

أَحْسَنَ مَا عَمِلُوا۟    for the best of what they have done,

وَيَزِيدَهُم مِّن فَضْلِهِۦ    and enhance them out of His grace,

وَٱللَّهُ يَرْزُقُ مَن يَشَاءُ

and Allah provides for whomever He wishes

بِغَيْرِ حِسَابٍ ۝

without any reckoning.

وَٱلَّذِينَ كَفَرُوٓاْ

39 As for the faithless,

أَعْمَٰلُهُمْ كَسَرَابٍ بِقِيعَةٍ

their works are like a mirage in a plain,

يَحْسَبُهُ ٱلظَّمْـَٔانُ مَآءً

which the thirsty man supposes to be water.

حَتَّىٰٓ إِذَا جَآءَهُۥ

When he comes to it,

لَمْ يَجِدْهُ شَيْـًٔا

he finds it to be nothing;

وَوَجَدَ ٱللَّهَ عِندَهُۥ

but there he finds Allah,

فَوَفَّىٰهُ حِسَابَهُۥ ۗ

who will pay him his full account,

وَٱللَّهُ سَرِيعُ ٱلْحِسَابِ ۝

and Allah is swift at reckoning.

أَوْ كَظُلُمَٰتٍ فِى بَحْرٍ لُّجِّىٍّ

40 Or like the manifold darkness in a deep sea,

يَغْشَىٰهُ مَوْجٌ مِّن فَوْقِهِۦ مَوْجٌ

covered by billow upon billow,

مِّن فَوْقِهِۦ سَحَابٌ ۚ

overcast by clouds,

ظُلُمَٰتٌۢ

manifold [layers of] darkness,

بَعْضُهَا فَوْقَ بَعْضٍ

one on the top of another:

إِذَآ أَخْرَجَ يَدَهُۥ

when he brings out his hand,

لَمْ يَكَدْ يَرَىٰهَا ۗ

he can hardly see it,

وَمَن لَّمْ يَجْعَلِ ٱللَّهُ لَهُۥ نُورًا

and one whom Allah has not granted any light

فَمَا لَهُۥ مِن نُّورٍ ۝

has no light.

أَلَمْ تَرَ أَنَّ

41 Have you not regarded

ٱللَّهَ يُسَبِّحُ لَهُۥ مَن فِى ٱلسَّمَٰوَٰتِ

that Allah is glorified by everyone in the heavens

وَٱلْأَرْضِ

and the earth,

وَٱلطَّيْرُ صَٰٓفَّٰتٍ ۖ

and the birds spreading their wings.

كُلٌّ قَدْ عَلِمَ صَلَاتَهُۥ وَتَسْبِيحَهُۥ ۗ

Each knows his prayer and glorification,

وَٱللَّهُ عَلِيمٌۢ بِمَا يَفْعَلُونَ ۝

and Allah knows best what they do.

وَلِلَّهِ مُلْكُ ٱلسَّمَٰوَٰتِ

42 To Allah belongs the kingdom of the heavens

وَٱلْأَرْضِ ۖ

and the earth,

وَإِلَى ٱللَّهِ ٱلْمَصِيرُ ۝

and toward Allah is the destination.

أَلَمْ تَرَ أَنَّ ٱللَّهَ يُزْجِى سَحَابًا

43 Have you not regarded that Allah drives the clouds,

ثُمَّ يُؤَلِّفُ بَيْنَهُۥ

then He composes them,

| | |
|---|---|
| ثُمَّ يَجْعَلُهُ رُكَامًا | then He piles them up, |
| فَتَرَى ٱلْوَدْقَ يَخْرُجُ مِنْ خِلَلِهِۦ | whereat you see the rain issuing from its midst? |
| وَيُنَزِّلُ مِنَ ٱلسَّمَآءِ | And He sends down from the sky |
| مِن جِبَالٍ فِيهَا مِنۢ بَرَدٍ | hail, out of the mountains[1] that are in it, |
| فَيُصِيبُ بِهِۦ مَن يَشَآءُ | and He strikes with it whomever He wishes, |
| وَيَصْرِفُهُۥ عَن مَّن يَشَآءُ | and turns it away from whomever He wishes. |
| يَكَادُ سَنَا بَرْقِهِۦ | The brilliance of its lightening almost |
| يَذْهَبُ بِٱلْأَبْصَٰرِ ۝ | takes away the sight. |
| يُقَلِّبُ ٱللَّهُ ٱلَّيْلَ وَٱلنَّهَارَ | 44 Allah alternates the night and the day. |
| إِنَّ فِى ذَٰلِكَ لَعِبْرَةً | There is indeed a moral in that |
| لِّأُو۟لِى ٱلْأَبْصَٰرِ ۝ | for those who have insight. |
| وَٱللَّهُ خَلَقَ كُلَّ دَآبَّةٍ مِّن مَّآءٍ | 45 Allah created every animal from water. |
| فَمِنْهُم مَّن يَمْشِى عَلَىٰ بَطْنِهِۦ | Among them are some that creep upon their bellies, |
| وَمِنْهُم مَّن يَمْشِى عَلَىٰ رِجْلَيْنِ | and among them are some that walk on two feet, |
| وَمِنْهُم مَّن يَمْشِى عَلَىٰٓ أَرْبَعٍ | and among them are some that walk on four. |
| يَخْلُقُ ٱللَّهُ مَا يَشَآءُ | Allah creates whatever He wishes. |
| إِنَّ ٱللَّهَ عَلَىٰ كُلِّ شَىْءٍ قَدِيرٌ ۝ | Indeed Allah has power over all things. |
| لَّقَدْ أَنزَلْنَآ ءَايَٰتٍ مُّبَيِّنَٰتٍ | 46 Certainly We have sent down manifest signs, |
| وَٱللَّهُ يَهْدِى مَن يَشَآءُ | and Allah guides whomever He wishes |
| إِلَىٰ صِرَٰطٍ مُّسْتَقِيمٍ ۝ | to a straight path. |
| وَيَقُولُونَ ءَامَنَّا بِٱللَّهِ وَبِٱلرَّسُولِ وَأَطَعْنَا | 47 They say, 'We have faith in Allah and His Apostle, and we obey.' |
| ثُمَّ يَتَوَلَّىٰ فَرِيقٌ مِّنْهُم مِّنۢ بَعْدِ ذَٰلِكَ وَمَآ أُو۟لَٰٓئِكَ بِٱلْمُؤْمِنِينَ ۝ | Then after that a part of them refuse to comply, and they do not have faith. |
| وَإِذَا دُعُوٓا۟ إِلَى ٱللَّهِ وَرَسُولِهِۦ لِيَحْكُمَ بَيْنَهُمْ | 48 When they are summoned to Allah and His Apostle that He may judge between them, |
| إِذَا فَرِيقٌ مِّنْهُم مُّعْرِضُونَ ۝ | behold, a part of them turn aside. |
| وَإِن يَكُن لَّهُمُ ٱلْحَقُّ | 49 But if justice be on their side, |

---

[1] A metaphorical reference to the clouds.

يَأْتُوٓا إِلَيْهِ مُذْعِنِينَ ⑤    they come compliantly to him.

أَفِى قُلُوبِهِم مَّرَضٌ    50 Is there a sickness in their hearts?

أَمِ ٱرْتَابُوٓا    Or do they have doubts

أَمْ يَخَافُونَ    or fear

أَن يَحِيفَ ٱللَّهُ عَلَيْهِمْ وَرَسُولُهُۥ    that Allah and His Apostle will be unjust to them?

بَلْ أُوْلَٰٓئِكَ هُمُ ٱلظَّٰلِمُونَ ⑤    Rather it is they who are the wrongdoers.

إِنَّمَا كَانَ قَوْلَ ٱلْمُؤْمِنِينَ    51 All the response of the faithful,

إِذَا دُعُوٓا إِلَى ٱللَّهِ وَرَسُولِهِۦ    when they are summoned to Allah and His Apostle

لِيَحْكُمَ بَيْنَهُمْ    that He may judge between them,

أَن يَقُولُوا سَمِعْنَا وَأَطَعْنَا    is to say, 'We hear and obey.'

وَأُوْلَٰٓئِكَ هُمُ ٱلْمُفْلِحُونَ ⑤    It is they who are the felicitous.

وَمَن يُطِعِ ٱللَّهَ وَرَسُولَهُۥ    52 Whoever obeys Allah and His Apostle,

وَيَخْشَ ٱللَّهَ وَيَتَّقْهِ    and fears Allah and is wary of Him

فَأُوْلَٰٓئِكَ هُمُ ٱلْفَآئِزُونَ ⑤ ✸    —it is they who will be the triumphant.

وَأَقْسَمُوا بِٱللَّهِ جَهْدَ أَيْمَٰنِهِمْ    53 They swear by Allah with solemn oaths

لَئِنْ أَمَرْتَهُمْ    that if *you* order them

لَيَخْرُجُنَّ    they will surely go forth.

قُل لَّا تُقْسِمُوا    *Say,* 'Do not swear!

طَاعَةٌ مَّعْرُوفَةٌ    Honourable obedience [is all that is expected of you].

إِنَّ ٱللَّهَ خَبِيرٌ بِمَا تَعْمَلُونَ ⑤    Allah is indeed well aware of what you do.'

قُلْ أَطِيعُوا ٱللَّهَ وَأَطِيعُوا ٱلرَّسُولَ    54 *Say,* 'Obey Allah, and obey the Apostle.'

فَإِن تَوَلَّوْا    But if you turn your backs, [you should know that]

فَإِنَّمَا عَلَيْهِ مَا حُمِّلَ    he is only responsible for *his* burden

وَعَلَيْكُم مَّا حُمِّلْتُمْ    and you are responsible for your burden,

وَإِن تُطِيعُوهُ تَهْتَدُوا    and if you obey *him,* you shall be guided,

وَمَا عَلَى ٱلرَّسُولِ إِلَّا    and the Apostle's duty is only

ٱلْبَلَٰغُ ٱلْمُبِينُ ⑤    to communicate in clear terms.

وَعَدَ ٱللَّهُ ٱلَّذِينَ ءَامَنُوا مِنكُمْ    55 Allah has promised those of you who have faith

وَعَمِلُوا ٱلصَّٰلِحَٰتِ    and do righteous deeds

لَيَسْتَخْلِفَنَّهُمْ فِى ٱلْأَرْضِ    that He will surely make them successors in the earth,

كَمَا ٱسْتَخْلَفَ ٱلَّذِينَ مِن قَبْلِهِمْ
just as He made those who were before them successors,

وَلَيُمَكِّنَنَّ لَهُمْ
and He will surely establish for them

دِينَهُمُ ٱلَّذِى ٱرْتَضَىٰ لَهُمْ
their religion which He has approved for them,

وَلَيُبَدِّلَنَّهُم
and that He will surely change their state

مِّنۢ بَعْدِ خَوْفِهِمْ أَمْنًا
to security after their fear,

يَعْبُدُونَنِى
while they worship Me,

لَا يُشْرِكُونَ بِى شَيْئًا
not ascribing any partners to Me.

وَمَن كَفَرَ بَعْدَ ذَٰلِكَ
And whoever is ungrateful after that

فَأُو۟لَٰٓئِكَ هُمُ ٱلْفَٰسِقُونَ ۝
—it is they who are the transgressors.

وَأَقِيمُوا۟ ٱلصَّلَوٰةَ وَءَاتُوا۟ ٱلزَّكَوٰةَ
56 Maintain the prayer and give the *zakāt*,

وَأَطِيعُوا۟ ٱلرَّسُولَ
and obey the Apostle

لَعَلَّكُمْ تُرْحَمُونَ ۝
so that you may receive [Allah's] mercy.

لَا تَحْسَبَنَّ ٱلَّذِينَ كَفَرُوا۟
57 Do not suppose that those who are faithless

مُعْجِزِينَ فِى ٱلْأَرْضِ
can thwart [Allah] on the earth.

وَمَأْوَىٰهُمُ ٱلنَّارُ
Their refuge shall be the Fire,

وَلَبِئْسَ ٱلْمَصِيرُ ۝
and it is surely an evil destination.

يَٰٓأَيُّهَا ٱلَّذِينَ ءَامَنُوا۟
58 O you who have faith!

لِيَسْتَـْٔذِنكُمُ ٱلَّذِينَ مَلَكَتْ أَيْمَٰنُكُمْ
Let your permission be sought by your slaves

وَٱلَّذِينَ لَمْ يَبْلُغُوا۟ ٱلْحُلُمَ مِنكُمْ
and those of you who have not reached puberty

ثَلَٰثَ مَرَّٰتٍ
three times:

مِّن قَبْلِ صَلَوٰةِ ٱلْفَجْرِ
before the dawn prayer,

وَحِينَ تَضَعُونَ ثِيَابَكُم مِّنَ ٱلظَّهِيرَةِ
and when you put off your garments at noon,

وَمِنۢ بَعْدِ صَلَوٰةِ ٱلْعِشَآءِ
and after the night prayer.

ثَلَٰثُ عَوْرَٰتٍ لَّكُمْ
These are three times of privacy for you.

لَيْسَ عَلَيْكُمْ وَلَا عَلَيْهِمْ جُنَاحٌۢ بَعْدَهُنَّ
Apart from these, it is not sinful of you or them

طَوَّٰفُونَ عَلَيْكُم بَعْضُكُمْ عَلَىٰ بَعْضٍ
to frequent one another [freely].

كَذَٰلِكَ يُبَيِّنُ ٱللَّهُ لَكُمُ ٱلْءَايَٰتِ
Thus does Allah clarify the signs for you,

وَٱللَّهُ عَلِيمٌ حَكِيمٌ ۝
and Allah is all-knowing, all-wise.

وَإِذَا بَلَغَ ٱلْأَطْفَٰلُ مِنكُمُ ٱلْحُلُمَ
59 When your children reach puberty,

فَلْيَسْتَـٔذِنُوا۟    let them ask permission [at all times]

كَمَا ٱسْتَـٔذَنَ ٱلَّذِينَ مِن قَبْلِهِمْ    just as those who asked permission before them.

كَذَٰلِكَ يُبَيِّنُ ٱللَّهُ لَكُمْ ءَايَٰتِهِۦ    Thus does Allah clarify His signs for you,

وَٱللَّهُ عَلِيمٌ حَكِيمٌ ۝    and Allah is all-knowing, all-wise.

وَٱلْقَوَٰعِدُ مِنَ ٱلنِّسَآءِ    60 As for women advanced in years

ٱلَّٰتِى لَا يَرْجُونَ نِكَاحًا    who do not expect to marry,

فَلَيْسَ عَلَيْهِنَّ جُنَاحٌ    there will be no sin upon them

أَن يَضَعْنَ ثِيَابَهُنَّ    if they put off their cloaks,

غَيْرَ مُتَبَرِّجَٰتٍ بِزِينَةٍ    without displaying their adornment.

وَأَن يَسْتَعْفِفْنَ خَيْرٌ لَّهُنَّ    But it is better for them to be continent,

وَٱللَّهُ سَمِيعٌ عَلِيمٌ ۝    and Allah is all-hearing, all-knowing.

لَّيْسَ عَلَى ٱلْأَعْمَىٰ حَرَجٌ    61 There is no blame upon the blind,

وَلَا عَلَى ٱلْأَعْرَجِ حَرَجٌ    nor any blame upon the lame,

وَلَا عَلَى ٱلْمَرِيضِ حَرَجٌ    nor any blame upon the sick,

وَلَا عَلَىٰٓ أَنفُسِكُمْ    nor upon yourselves

أَن تَأْكُلُوا۟ مِنۢ بُيُوتِكُمْ    if you eat from your own houses,

أَوْ بُيُوتِ ءَابَآئِكُمْ    or your fathers' houses,

أَوْ بُيُوتِ أُمَّهَٰتِكُمْ    or your mothers' houses,

أَوْ بُيُوتِ إِخْوَٰنِكُمْ    or your brothers' houses,

أَوْ بُيُوتِ أَخَوَٰتِكُمْ    or your sisters' houses,

أَوْ بُيُوتِ أَعْمَٰمِكُمْ    or the houses of your paternal uncles,

أَوْ بُيُوتِ عَمَّٰتِكُمْ    or the houses of your paternal aunts,

أَوْ بُيُوتِ أَخْوَٰلِكُمْ    or the houses of your maternal uncles,

أَوْ بُيُوتِ خَٰلَٰتِكُمْ    or the houses of your maternal aunts,

أَوْ مَا مَلَكْتُم مَّفَاتِحَهُۥٓ    or those whose keys are in your possession,

أَوْ صَدِيقِكُمْ    or those of your friends.

لَيْسَ عَلَيْكُمْ جُنَاحٌ    There will be no blame on you

أَن تَأْكُلُوا۟ جَمِيعًا أَوْ أَشْتَاتًا    whether you eat together or separately.

فَإِذَا دَخَلْتُم بُيُوتًا    So when you enter houses,

فَسَلِّمُواْ عَلَىٰٓ أَنفُسِكُمْ     greet yourselves[1]

تَحِيَّةً مِّنْ عِندِ ٱللَّهِ     with a salutation from Allah,

مُبَٰرَكَةً طَيِّبَةً     blessed and good.

كَذَٰلِكَ يُبَيِّنُ ٱللَّهُ لَكُمُ ٱلْءَايَٰتِ     Thus does Allah clarify His signs for you

لَعَلَّكُمْ تَعْقِلُونَ ۝     so that you may apply reason.

إِنَّمَا ٱلْمُؤْمِنُونَ ٱلَّذِينَ ءَامَنُواْ     62 Indeed the faithful are those who have faith

بِٱللَّهِ وَرَسُولِهِۦ     in Allah and His Apostle,

وَإِذَا كَانُواْ مَعَهُۥ عَلَىٰٓ أَمْرٍ جَامِعٍ     and when they are with him in a collective affair,

لَّمْ يَذْهَبُواْ     they do not leave

حَتَّىٰ يَسْتَـْٔذِنُوهُ     until they have sought his permission.

إِنَّ ٱلَّذِينَ يَسْتَـْٔذِنُونَكَ     Indeed those who seek *your* permission

أُوْلَٰٓئِكَ ٱلَّذِينَ يُؤْمِنُونَ بِٱللَّهِ     —it is they who have faith in Allah

وَرَسُولِهِۦ     and His Apostle.

فَإِذَا ٱسْتَـْٔذَنُوكَ     So when they seek *your* permission

لِبَعْضِ شَأْنِهِمْ     for some work of theirs,

فَأْذَن لِّمَن شِئْتَ مِنْهُمْ     give permission to whomever of them *you* wish

وَٱسْتَغْفِرْ لَهُمُ ٱللَّهَ     and *plead* with Allah to forgive them.

إِنَّ ٱللَّهَ غَفُورٌ رَّحِيمٌ ۝     Indeed Allah is all-forgiving, all-merciful.

لَّا تَجْعَلُواْ دُعَآءَ ٱلرَّسُولِ بَيْنَكُمْ     63 Do not consider the Apostle's summons amongst you

كَدُعَآءِ بَعْضِكُم بَعْضًا     to be like your summoning one another.

قَدْ يَعْلَمُ ٱللَّهُ ٱلَّذِينَ     Allah certainly knows those

يَتَسَلَّلُونَ مِنكُمْ لِوَاذًا     of you who slip away under cover.

فَلْيَحْذَرِ ٱلَّذِينَ يُخَالِفُونَ عَنْ أَمْرِهِۦٓ     So let those who disobey his orders beware

أَن تُصِيبَهُمْ فِتْنَةٌ     lest an ordeal should visit them

أَوْ يُصِيبَهُمْ عَذَابٌ أَلِيمٌ ۝     or a painful punishment should visit them.

أَلَآ     64 Look!

إِنَّ لِلَّهِ مَا فِى ٱلسَّمَٰوَٰتِ     To Allah indeed belongs whatever is in the heavens

وَٱلْأَرْضِ     and the earth.

---

[1] Or 'greet your folks.'

قَدْ يَعْلَمُ مَآ أَنتُمْ عَلَيْهِ

He certainly knows what you are up to,

وَيَوْمَ يُرْجَعُونَ إِلَيْهِ

and the day they are brought back to Him

فَيُنَبِّئُهُم بِمَا عَمِلُواْ

He will inform them about what they have done,

وَٱللَّهُ بِكُلِّ شَيْءٍ عَلِيمٌ ۝

and Allah has knowledge of all things.

سُورَةُ الفُرْقَانِ

## 25. SŪRAT AL-FURQĀN[1]

بِسْمِ ٱللَّهِ

In the Name of Allah,

ٱلرَّحْمَٰنِ ٱلرَّحِيمِ

the All-beneficent, the All-merciful.

تَبَارَكَ ٱلَّذِى ₁ Blessed is He

نَزَّلَ ٱلْفُرْقَانَ عَلَىٰ عَبْدِهِ

who sent down the Criterion to His servant

لِيَكُونَ لِلْعَٰلَمِينَ نَذِيرًا ۝

that he may be a warner to all the nations.

ٱلَّذِى لَهُۥ مُلْكُ ٱلسَّمَٰوَٰتِ ₂ He, to whom belongs the sovereignty of the heavens

وَٱلْأَرْضِ    and the earth,

وَلَمْ يَتَّخِذْ وَلَدًا    and who did not take a son,

وَلَمْ يَكُن لَّهُۥ شَرِيكٌ فِى ٱلْمُلْكِ    nor has He any partner in sovereignty,

وَخَلَقَ كُلَّ شَيْءٍ    and He created everything,

فَقَدَّرَهُۥ تَقْدِيرًا ۝    and then determined it in a precise measure.

وَٱتَّخَذُواْ مِن دُونِهِۦٓ ءَالِهَةً ₃ Yet they have taken gods besides Him

لَّا يَخْلُقُونَ شَيْئًا    who create nothing

وَهُمْ يُخْلَقُونَ    and have themselves been created,

وَلَا يَمْلِكُونَ لِأَنفُسِهِمْ ضَرًّا    and who have no control over their own harm

وَلَا نَفْعًا    or benefit

وَلَا يَمْلِكُونَ مَوْتًا    and have no control over [their own] death,

وَلَا حَيَوٰةً    or life,

وَلَا نُشُورًا ۝    or resurrection.

وَقَالَ ٱلَّذِينَ كَفَرُواْ ₄ The faithless say,

---

[1] The *sūrah* takes its name from verse 1, which refers to the Qur'ān as "*al-Furqān*" (*lit.* 'the Distinguisher,' or 'the Separator,' i.e. between truth and falsehood).

إِنْ هَـٰذَآ إِلَّآ إِفۡكٌ ٱفۡتَرَىٰهُ 'This is nothing but a lie that he has fabricated,

وَأَعَانَهُۥ عَلَيۡهِ قَوۡمٌ ءَاخَرُونَ and other people have abetted him in it.'

فَقَدۡ جَآءُو Thus they have certainly come out with

ظُلۡمًا وَزُورًا ۝ wrongdoing and falsehood.

وَقَالُوٓاْ أَسَٰطِيرُ ٱلۡأَوَّلِينَ ٱكۡتَتَبَهَا 5 They say, 'He has taken down myths of the ancients,

فَهِيَ تُمۡلَىٰ عَلَيۡهِ بُكۡرَةً وَأَصِيلًا ۝ and they are dictated to him morning and evening.'

قُلۡ أَنزَلَهُ ٱلَّذِى 6 *Say*, 'It has been sent down by Him

يَعۡلَمُ ٱلسِّرَّ فِى ٱلسَّمَٰوَٰتِ who knows the hidden in the heavens

وَٱلۡأَرۡضِ and the earth.

إِنَّهُۥ كَانَ غَفُورًا رَّحِيمًا ۝ Indeed He is all-forgiving, all-merciful.'

وَقَالُواْ مَالِ هَٰذَا ٱلرَّسُولِ 7 And they say, 'What sort of apostle is this

يَأۡكُلُ ٱلطَّعَامَ who eats food

وَيَمۡشِى فِى ٱلۡأَسۡوَاقِ and walks in the marketplaces?

لَوۡلَآ أُنزِلَ إِلَيۡهِ مَلَكٌ Why has not an angel been sent down to him

فَيَكُونَ مَعَهُۥ نَذِيرًا ۝ so as to be a warner along with him?'

أَوۡ يُلۡقَىٰٓ إِلَيۡهِ كَنزٌ 8 Or, '[Why is not] a treasure thrown to him,

أَوۡ تَكُونُ لَهُۥ جَنَّةٌ or [why does] he [not] have a garden

يَأۡكُلُ مِنۡهَا from which he may eat?'

وَقَالَ ٱلظَّٰلِمُونَ And the wrongdoers say,

إِن تَتَّبِعُونَ إِلَّا رَجُلًا مَّسۡحُورًا ۝ 'You are just following a bewitched man.'

ٱنظُرۡ كَيۡفَ ضَرَبُواْ لَكَ ٱلۡأَمۡثَٰلَ 9 *Look*, how they draw comparisons for *you*;

فَضَلُّواْ so they go astray,

فَلَا يَسۡتَطِيعُونَ سَبِيلًا ۝ and cannot find the way.

تَبَارَكَ ٱلَّذِى 10 Blessed is He

إِن شَآءَ جَعَلَ لَكَ خَيۡرًا مِّن ذَٰلِكَ who will grant *you* better than that if He wishes

جَنَّٰتٍ تَجۡرِى مِن تَحۡتِهَا ٱلۡأَنۡهَٰرُ —gardens with streams running in them,

وَيَجۡعَل لَّكَ قُصُورًا ۝ and He will give *you* palaces.

بَلۡ كَذَّبُواْ بِٱلسَّاعَةِ 11 Rather they deny the Hour,

وَأَعۡتَدۡنَا and We have prepared

لِمَن كَذَّبَ بِٱلسَّاعَةِ سَعِيرًا ۝ a Blaze for those who deny the Hour.

إِذَا رَأَتْهُم مِّن مَّكَانٍ بَعِيدٍ 12 When it[1] sights them from a distant place,

سَمِعُوا لَهَا تَغَيُّظًا وَزَفِيرًا they will hear it raging and roaring.

وَإِذَآ أُلْقُوا مِنْهَا مَكَانًا ضَيِّقًا 13 And when they are cast into a narrow place in it,

مُّقَرَّنِينَ bound together [in chains],

دَعَوْا هُنَالِكَ ثُبُورًا they will pray for [their own] annihilation.[2]

لَّا تَدْعُوا 14 [They will be told:] 'Do not pray

ٱلْيَوْمَ ثُبُورًا وَٰحِدًا for a single annihilation today,

وَٱدْعُوا ثُبُورًا كَثِيرًا but pray for many annihilations!'

قُلْ أَذَٰلِكَ خَيْرٌ 15 Say, 'Is that better,

أَمْ جَنَّةُ ٱلْخُلْدِ ٱلَّتِى وُعِدَ ٱلْمُتَّقُونَ or the everlasting paradise promised to the Godwary,

كَانَتْ لَهُمْ جَزَآءً وَمَصِيرًا which will be their reward and destination?'

هُمْ فِيهَا مَا يَشَآءُونَ 16 There they will have whatever they wish,

خَٰلِدِينَ abiding [forever],

كَانَ عَلَىٰ رَبِّكَ وَعْدًا مَّسْـُٔولًا a promise [much] besought, [binding] on *your* Lord.[3]

وَيَوْمَ يَحْشُرُهُمْ 17 On the day that He will muster them

وَمَا يَعْبُدُونَ مِن دُونِ ٱللَّهِ and those whom they worship besides Allah,

فَيَقُولُ He will say,

ءَأَنتُمْ أَضْلَلْتُمْ عِبَادِى هَٰٓؤُلَآءِ 'Were it you who led astray these servants of Mine,

أَمْ هُمْ ضَلُّوا ٱلسَّبِيلَ or did they themselves stray from the way?'

قَالُوا سُبْحَٰنَكَ 18 They will say, 'Immaculate are You!

مَا كَانَ يَنۢبَغِى لَنَآ It does not behoove us

أَن نَّتَّخِذَ مِن دُونِكَ مِنْ أَوْلِيَآءَ to take any guardians in Your stead!

وَلَٰكِن مَّتَّعْتَهُمْ وَءَابَآءَهُمْ But You provided them and their fathers

حَتَّىٰ نَسُوا ٱلذِّكْرَ until they forgot the Reminder,

وَكَانُوا قَوْمًۢا بُورًا and they were a ruined lot.'

فَقَدْ كَذَّبُوكُم بِمَا تَقُولُونَ 19 So they will certainly impugn you in what you say,

فَمَا تَسْتَطِيعُونَ صَرْفًا and you will neither be able to circumvent [punishment]

---

[1] That is, hell.

[2] Cf. 43:77, 78:40.

[3] Cf. 3:194: 'Our Lord, grant us what You have promised us through Your apostles.'

وَلَا نَصْرًا    nor find help,

وَمَن يَظْلِم مِّنكُمْ    and whoever of you does wrong,

نُذِقْهُ عَذَابًا كَبِيرًا ۝    We shall make him taste a terrible punishment.

وَمَآ أَرْسَلْنَا قَبْلَكَ مِنَ ٱلْمُرْسَلِينَ    20 We did not send any apostles before *you*

إِلَّآ إِنَّهُمْ لَيَأْكُلُونَ ٱلطَّعَامَ    but that they indeed ate food

وَيَمْشُونَ فِى ٱلْأَسْوَاقِ    and walked in the marketplaces.

وَجَعَلْنَا بَعْضَكُمْ لِبَعْضٍ فِتْنَةً    We have made you a trial for one another,

أَتَصْبِرُونَ    [to see] if you will be patient,

وَكَانَ رَبُّكَ بَصِيرًا ۝    and *your* Lord is all-seeing.

[PART 19]

وَقَالَ ٱلَّذِينَ لَا يَرْجُونَ لِقَآءَنَا    21 Those who do not expect to encounter Us say,

لَوْلَآ أُنزِلَ عَلَيْنَا ٱلْمَلَٰٓئِكَةُ    'Why have not angels been sent down to us,

أَوْ نَرَىٰ رَبَّنَا    or why do we not see our Lord?'

لَقَدِ ٱسْتَكْبَرُوا۟ فِىٓ أَنفُسِهِمْ    Certainly they are full of arrogance within their souls

وَعَتَوْ عُتُوًّا كَبِيرًا ۝    and have become terribly defiant.

يَوْمَ يَرَوْنَ ٱلْمَلَٰٓئِكَةَ    22 The day when they see the angels,

لَا بُشْرَىٰ يَوْمَئِذٍ لِّلْمُجْرِمِينَ    there will be no good news for the guilty that day,

وَيَقُولُونَ حِجْرًا مَّحْجُورًا ۝    and they[1] will say, 'Keep off [from paradise]!'

وَقَدِمْنَآ إِلَىٰ مَا عَمِلُوا۟ مِنْ عَمَلٍ    23 Then We shall attend to the works they have done

فَجَعَلْنَٰهُ هَبَآءً مَّنثُورًا ۝    and then turn them into scattered dust.

أَصْحَٰبُ ٱلْجَنَّةِ يَوْمَئِذٍ    24 On that day the inhabitants of paradise

خَيْرٌ مُّسْتَقَرًّا    will be in the best abode

وَأَحْسَنُ مَقِيلًا ۝    and an excellent resting place.

وَيَوْمَ تَشَقَّقُ ٱلسَّمَآءُ    25 The day when the sky will be split open

بِٱلْغَمَٰمِ    with the clouds,

وَنُزِّلَ ٱلْمَلَٰٓئِكَةُ    and the angels will be sent down

---

[1] That is, the angels, who will say this to the faithless. According to another interpretation, during pre-Islamic days, whenever, during one of the holy months in which warfare was prohibited by custom, an Arab felt threatened by someone belonging to a belligerent tribe, he would say, *Ḥijran mahjūrā*, thus telling the member of the hostile tribe to keep distance by appealing to the sanctity of the holy month. On this basis, it is the faithless who ask the angels to keep off.

تَنزِيلًا ۝

**26** on that day true sovereignty

ٱلْمُلْكُ يَوْمَئِذٍ ٱلْحَقُّ

will belong to the All-beneficent,

لِلرَّحْمَٰنِ

and it will be a hard day for the faithless.[1]

وَكَانَ يَوْمًا عَلَى ٱلْكَٰفِرِينَ عَسِيرًا ۝

**27** A day when the wrongdoer will bite his hands,

وَيَوْمَ يَعَضُّ ٱلظَّالِمُ عَلَىٰ يَدَيْهِ

saying, 'I wish

يَقُولُ يَٰلَيْتَنِى

I had followed the Apostle's way!

ٱتَّخَذْتُ مَعَ ٱلرَّسُولِ سَبِيلًا ۝

**28** Woe to me!

يَٰوَيْلَتَىٰ

I wish I had not taken so and so as friend!

لَيْتَنِى لَمْ أَتَّخِذْ فُلَانًا خَلِيلًا ۝

**29** Certainly He led me astray from the Reminder

لَّقَدْ أَضَلَّنِى عَنِ ٱلذِّكْرِ

after it had come to me,

بَعْدَ إِذْ جَآءَنِى

and Satan is a deserter of man.'

وَكَانَ ٱلشَّيْطَٰنُ لِلْإِنسَٰنِ خَذُولًا ۝

**30** And the Apostle will say, 'O my Lord!

وَقَالَ ٱلرَّسُولُ يَٰرَبِّ

Indeed my people

إِنَّ قَوْمِى

consigned this Qur'ān to oblivion.'

ٱتَّخَذُوا۟ هَٰذَا ٱلْقُرْءَانَ مَهْجُورًا ۝

**31** That is how for every prophet We assigned an enemy

وَكَذَٰلِكَ جَعَلْنَا لِكُلِّ نَبِىٍّ عَدُوًّا

from among the guilty,

مِّنَ ٱلْمُجْرِمِينَ

and *your* Lord suffices as helper and guide.

وَكَفَىٰ بِرَبِّكَ هَادِيًا وَنَصِيرًا ۝

**32** The faithless say,

وَقَالَ ٱلَّذِينَ كَفَرُوا۟

'Why has not the Qur'ān been sent down to him

لَوْلَا نُزِّلَ عَلَيْهِ ٱلْقُرْءَانُ

all at once?'

جُمْلَةً وَٰحِدَةً

So it is, that We may strengthen *your* heart with it,

كَذَٰلِكَ لِنُثَبِّتَ بِهِۦ فُؤَادَكَ

and We have recited it [to *you*]

وَرَتَّلْنَٰهُ

in a measured tone.

تَرْتِيلًا ۝

**33** They do not bring *you* any poser

وَلَا يَأْتُونَكَ بِمَثَلٍ

but that We bring *you* the truth [in reply to them]

إِلَّا جِئْنَٰكَ بِٱلْحَقِّ

and the best exposition.

وَأَحْسَنَ تَفْسِيرًا ۝

**34** Those who will be mustered on their faces

ٱلَّذِينَ يُحْشَرُونَ عَلَىٰ وُجُوهِهِمْ

toward hell,

إِلَىٰ جَهَنَّمَ

---

[1] Cf. 74:9.

أُو۟لَـٰٓئِكَ شَرٌّ مَّكَانًا    they are the worse situated

وَأَضَلُّ سَبِيلًا ۩    and further astray from the [right] way.

وَلَقَدْ ءَاتَيْنَا مُوسَى ٱلْكِتَـٰبَ    35 Certainly We gave Moses the Book

وَجَعَلْنَا مَعَهُۥٓ أَخَاهُ هَـٰرُونَ    and We made Aaron, his brother, accompany him

وَزِيرًا ۩    as a minister.

فَقُلْنَا ٱذْهَبَآ    36 Then We said, 'Let the two of you go

إِلَى ٱلْقَوْمِ ٱلَّذِينَ كَذَّبُوا۟ بِـَٔايَـٰتِنَا    to the people who have denied Our signs.'

فَدَمَّرْنَـٰهُمْ تَدْمِيرًا ۩    Then We destroyed them utterly.

وَقَوْمَ نُوحٍ    37 And Noah's people,

لَّمَّا كَذَّبُوا۟ ٱلرُّسُلَ أَغْرَقْنَـٰهُمْ    We drowned them when they impugned the apostles,

وَجَعَلْنَـٰهُمْ لِلنَّاسِ ءَايَةً    and We made them a sign for mankind,

وَأَعْتَدْنَا لِلظَّـٰلِمِينَ    and We have prepared for the wrongdoers

عَذَابًا أَلِيمًا ۩    a painful punishment.

وَعَادًا وَثَمُودَا۟    38 And 'Ād and Thamūd,

وَأَصْحَـٰبَ ٱلرَّسِّ    and the inhabitants of Rass,

وَقُرُونًۢا بَيْنَ ذَٰلِكَ كَثِيرًا ۩    and many generations between them.

وَكُلًّا ضَرَبْنَا لَهُ ٱلْأَمْثَـٰلَ    39 For each of them We drew examples,

وَكُلًّا تَبَّرْنَا تَتْبِيرًا ۩    and each We destroyed utterly.

وَلَقَدْ أَتَوْا۟ عَلَى    40 Certainly they must have passed

ٱلْقَرْيَةِ ٱلَّتِىٓ أُمْطِرَتْ مَطَرَ ٱلسَّوْءِ    the town on which an evil shower was rained.

أَفَلَمْ يَكُونُوا۟ يَرَوْنَهَا    Have they not seen it?

بَلْ كَانُوا۟ لَا يَرْجُونَ نُشُورًا ۩    Rather they did not expect resurrection.

وَإِذَا رَأَوْكَ إِن يَتَّخِذُونَكَ إِلَّا هُزُوًا    41 When they see *you* they just take *you* in derision:

أَهَـٰذَا ٱلَّذِى بَعَثَ ٱللَّهُ رَسُولًا ۩    'Is this the one whom Allah has sent as an apostle!?

إِن كَادَ لَيُضِلُّنَا    42 Indeed he was about to lead us astray

عَنْ ءَالِهَتِنَا    from our gods,

لَوْلَآ أَن صَبَرْنَا عَلَيْهَا    had we not stood by them.'

وَسَوْفَ يَعْلَمُونَ    Soon they will know,

حِينَ يَرَوْنَ ٱلْعَذَابَ    when they sight the punishment,

مَنْ أَضَلُّ سَبِيلًا ۝    who is further astray from the [right] way.

أَرَءَيْتَ مَنِ ٱتَّخَذَ    43 Have *you* seen him who has taken

إِلَـٰهَهُۥ هَوَىٰهُ    his desire to be his god?

أَفَأَنتَ تَكُونُ عَلَيْهِ وَكِيلًا ۝    Is it *your* duty to watch over him?

أَمْ تَحْسَبُ    44 Do *you* suppose

أَنَّ أَكْثَرَهُمْ يَسْمَعُونَ أَوْ يَعْقِلُونَ    that most of them listen or apply reason?

إِنْ هُمْ إِلَّا كَٱلْأَنْعَـٰمِ    They are just like cattle;

بَلْ هُمْ أَضَلُّ سَبِيلًا ۝    rather they are further astray from the way.

أَلَمْ تَرَ    45 Have *you* not regarded

إِلَىٰ رَبِّكَ كَيْفَ مَدَّ ٱلظِّلَّ    how *your* Lord spreads the twilight?[1]

وَلَوْ شَآءَ لَجَعَلَهُۥ سَاكِنًا    (Had He wished He would have made it still.)

ثُمَّ جَعَلْنَا ٱلشَّمْسَ عَلَيْهِ دَلِيلًا ۝    Then We made the sun a beacon for it.

ثُمَّ قَبَضْنَـٰهُ إِلَيْنَا    46 Then We retract it toward Ourselves,

قَبْضًا يَسِيرًا ۝    with a gentle retracting.

وَهُوَ ٱلَّذِى جَعَلَ لَكُمُ ٱلَّيْلَ لِبَاسًا    47 It is He who made for you the night as a covering

وَٱلنَّوْمَ سُبَاتًا    and sleep for rest

وَجَعَلَ ٱلنَّهَارَ نُشُورًا ۝    and He made the day a recall to life.

وَهُوَ ٱلَّذِى أَرْسَلَ ٱلرِّيَـٰحَ    48 And it is He who sends the winds

بُشْرًۢا بَيْنَ يَدَىْ رَحْمَتِهِۦ    as harbingers of His mercy,

وَأَنزَلْنَا مِنَ ٱلسَّمَآءِ مَآءً طَهُورًا ۝    and We send down from the sky purifying water,

لِّنُحْـِۧىَ بِهِۦ بَلْدَةً مَّيْتًا    49 with which We revive a dead country

وَنُسْقِيَهُۥ    and provide water to

مِمَّا خَلَقْنَآ أَنْعَـٰمًا وَأَنَاسِىَّ كَثِيرًا ۝    many of the cattle and humans We have created.

وَلَقَدْ صَرَّفْنَـٰهُ بَيْنَهُمْ    50 Certainly We distribute it among them

لِيَذَّكَّرُوا۟    so that they may take admonition.

فَأَبَىٰٓ أَكْثَرُ ٱلنَّاسِ إِلَّا كُفُورًا ۝    But most people are only intent on ingratitude.

وَلَوْ شِئْنَا    51 Had We wished,

---

[1] This is in accordance with a tradition of al-Imam al-Bāqir ('a) in which *ẓill* is explained as the light during the hours between daybreak and sunrise (see *Tafsīr al-Qummī*). Or 'extends the shadow.'

لَبَعَثْنَا فِى كُلِّ قَرْيَةٍ نَّذِيرًا ۝    We would have sent a warner to every town.

فَلَا تُطِعِ ٱلْكَـٰفِرِينَ    52 So *do not obey* the faithless,

وَجَـٰهِدْهُم بِهِۦ جِهَادًا كَبِيرًا ۝    but *wage* against them a great *jihād* with it.[1]

۞ وَهُوَ ٱلَّذِى مَرَجَ ٱلْبَحْرَيْنِ    53 It is He who merged the two seas:

هَـٰذَا عَذْبٌ فُرَاتٌ    this one sweet and agreeable,

وَهَـٰذَا مِلْحٌ أُجَاجٌ    and that one briny and bitter,

وَجَعَلَ بَيْنَهُمَا بَرْزَخًا    and between the two He set a barrier

وَحِجْرًا مَّحْجُورًا ۝    and a forbidding hindrance.

وَهُوَ ٱلَّذِى خَلَقَ مِنَ ٱلْمَآءِ بَشَرًا    54 It is He who created the human being from water,

فَجَعَلَهُۥ نَسَبًا وَصِهْرًا    then invested him with ties of blood and marriage,

وَكَانَ رَبُّكَ قَدِيرًا ۝    and *your* Lord is all-powerful.

وَيَعْبُدُونَ مِن دُونِ ٱللَّهِ    55 They worship besides Allah

مَا لَا يَنفَعُهُمْ    that which neither brings them any benefit

وَلَا يَضُرُّهُمْ    nor causes them any harm,

وَكَانَ ٱلْكَافِرُ عَلَىٰ رَبِّهِۦ ظَهِيرًا ۝    and the faithless one is ever an abettor against his Lord.

وَمَآ أَرْسَلْنَـٰكَ    56 We did not send *you*

إِلَّا مُبَشِّرًا وَنَذِيرًا ۝    except as a bearer of good news and as a warner.

قُلْ مَآ أَسْـَٔلُكُمْ عَلَيْهِ مِنْ أَجْرٍ    57 *Say,* 'I do not ask you any reward for it,

إِلَّا مَن شَآءَ أَن يَتَّخِذَ    except that anyone who wishes should take

إِلَىٰ رَبِّهِۦ سَبِيلًا ۝    the way to his Lord.'

وَتَوَكَّلْ عَلَى ٱلْحَىِّ    58 Put *your* trust in the Living One

ٱلَّذِى لَا يَمُوتُ    who does not die,

وَسَبِّحْ بِحَمْدِهِۦ    and *celebrate* His praise.

وَكَفَىٰ بِهِۦ بِذُنُوبِ عِبَادِهِۦ خَبِيرًا ۝    He suffices as one all-aware of the sins of His servants.

ٱلَّذِى خَلَقَ ٱلسَّمَـٰوَٰتِ وَٱلْأَرْضَ    59 He, who created the heavens and the earth

وَمَا بَيْنَهُمَا    and whatever is between them

فِى سِتَّةِ أَيَّامٍ    in six days,

---

[1] That is, with the help of the Qur'ān.

ثُمَّ ٱسۡتَوَىٰ عَلَى ٱلۡعَرۡشِۚ    and then settled on the Throne,

ٱلرَّحۡمَـٰنُ    the All-beneficent;

فَسۡـَٔلۡ بِهِۦ خَبِيرًا ۝    so ask about Him[1] someone who is well aware.

وَإِذَا قِيلَ لَهُمُ   60 When they are told:

ٱسۡجُدُواْ لِلرَّحۡمَـٰنِ    'Prostrate yourselves before the All-beneficent,'

قَالُواْ وَمَا ٱلرَّحۡمَـٰنُ    they say, 'What is "the All-beneficent"?

أَنَسۡجُدُ    Shall we prostrate ourselves

لِمَا تَأۡمُرُنَا    before whatever you bid us?'

وَزَادَهُمۡ نُفُورًا ۩ ۝    And it increases their aversion.

تَبَارَكَ ٱلَّذِى   61 Blessed is He who

جَعَلَ فِى ٱلسَّمَآءِ بُرُوجًا    appointed houses in the sky

وَجَعَلَ فِيهَا سِرَٰجًا    and set in it a lamp

وَقَمَرًا مُّنِيرًا ۝    and a shining moon.

وَهُوَ ٱلَّذِى جَعَلَ   62 It is He who made

ٱلَّيۡلَ وَٱلنَّهَارَ خِلۡفَةً    the night and the day alternate

لِّمَنۡ أَرَادَ أَن يَذَّكَّرَ    for one who desires to take admonition,

أَوۡ أَرَادَ شُكُورًا ۝    or desires to give thanks.

وَعِبَادُ ٱلرَّحۡمَـٰنِ ٱلَّذِينَ   63 The servants of the All-beneficent are those who

يَمۡشُونَ عَلَى ٱلۡأَرۡضِ هَوۡنًا    walk humbly on the earth,

وَإِذَا خَاطَبَهُمُ ٱلۡجَـٰهِلُونَ    and when the ignorant address them,

قَالُواْ سَلَـٰمًا ۝    say, 'Peace!'

وَٱلَّذِينَ يَبِيتُونَ لِرَبِّهِمۡ   64 Those who spend the night with their Lord,

سُجَّدًا وَقِيَـٰمًا ۝    prostrating and standing [in worship].

وَٱلَّذِينَ يَقُولُونَ رَبَّنَا   65 Those who say, 'Our Lord!

ٱصۡرِفۡ عَنَّا عَذَابَ جَهَنَّمَۖ    Turn away from us the punishment of hell.

إِنَّ عَذَابَهَا كَانَ غَرَامًا ۝    Indeed its punishment is enduring.

---

[1] Or, 'ask about it,' that is, about the creation of the heavens and the earth, or the meaning of the Throne.

إِنَّهَا سَآءَتْ مُسْتَقَرًّا وَمُقَامًا ۝    66 Indeed it is an evil abode and place.'

وَالَّذِينَ إِذَآ أَنفَقُوا۟    67 Those who, when spending,

لَمْ يُسْرِفُوا۟ وَلَمْ يَقْتُرُوا۟    are neither wasteful nor tightfisted,

وَكَانَ بَيْنَ ذَٰلِكَ قَوَامًا ۝    and moderation lies between these [extremes].

وَالَّذِينَ لَا يَدْعُونَ مَعَ ٱللَّهِ إِلَٰهًا ءَاخَرَ    68 Those who do not invoke another god besides Allah,

وَلَا يَقْتُلُونَ ٱلنَّفْسَ ٱلَّتِى    and do not kill a soul

حَرَّمَ ٱللَّهُ    [whose life] Allah has made inviolable,

إِلَّا بِٱلْحَقِّ    except with due cause,

وَلَا يَزْنُونَ ۚ    and do not commit fornication.

وَمَن يَفْعَلْ ذَٰلِكَ    (Whoever does that

يَلْقَ أَثَامًا ۝    shall encounter its retribution,

يُضَٰعَفْ لَهُ ٱلْعَذَابُ    69 the punishment being doubled for him

يَوْمَ ٱلْقِيَٰمَةِ    on the Day of Resurrection.

وَيَخْلُدْ فِيهِۦ مُهَانًا ۝    In it he will abide in humiliation forever,

إِلَّا مَن تَابَ وَءَامَنَ    70 excepting those who repent, attain faith,

وَعَمِلَ عَمَلًا صَٰلِحًا    and act righteously.

فَأُو۟لَٰٓئِكَ    For such,

يُبَدِّلُ ٱللَّهُ سَيِّـَٔاتِهِمْ حَسَنَٰتٍ ۗ    Allah will replace their misdeeds with good deeds,[1]

وَكَانَ ٱللَّهُ غَفُورًا رَّحِيمًا ۝    and Allah is all-forgiving, all-merciful.

وَمَن تَابَ    71 And whoever repents

وَعَمِلَ صَٰلِحًا    and acts righteously

فَإِنَّهُۥ يَتُوبُ إِلَى ٱللَّهِ مَتَابًا ۝    indeed turns to Allah with due penitence).

وَالَّذِينَ لَا يَشْهَدُونَ ٱلزُّورَ    72 Those who do not give false testimony,[2]

وَإِذَا مَرُّوا۟ بِٱللَّغْوِ    and when they come upon vain talk,

مَرُّوا۟ كِرَامًا ۝    pass by nobly.

وَالَّذِينَ إِذَا ذُكِّرُوا۟ بِـَٔايَٰتِ رَبِّهِمْ    73 Those who, when reminded of the signs of their Lord,

لَمْ يَخِرُّوا۟ عَلَيْهَا صُمًّا وَعُمْيَانًا ۝    do not turn a deaf ear and a blind eye to them.

---

[1] Or 'their vices with virtues.'

[2] Or, 'those who do not participate in humbug.' That is, those who do not attend music parties or take part in senseless and sinful gatherings and amusements. (See *Tafsīr al-Qummī, Manhaj al-Ṣādiqīn*)

وَٱلَّذِينَ يَقُولُونَ رَبَّنَا 74 And those who say, 'Our Lord!

هَبْ لَنَا    Grant us

مِنْ أَزْوَٰجِنَا وَذُرِّيَّٰتِنَا قُرَّةَ أَعْيُنٍ    comfort in our spouses and descendants,

وَٱجْعَلْنَا لِلْمُتَّقِينَ إِمَامًا ٧٤    and make us *imam*s of the Godwary.'

أُوْلَٰٓئِكَ يُجْزَوْنَ ٱلْغُرْفَةَ 75 Those shall be rewarded with sublime abodes

بِمَا صَبَرُوا۟    for their patience,

وَيُلَقَّوْنَ فِيهَا تَحِيَّةً    and they shall be met there with greetings

وَسَلَٰمًا ٧٥    and 'Peace,'

خَٰلِدِينَ فِيهَا 76    to abide in them [forever],

حَسُنَتْ مُسْتَقَرًّا وَمُقَامًا ٧٦    an excellent abode and place.


قُلْ مَا يَعْبَؤُا۟ بِكُمْ رَبِّى 77 *Say,* 'What store my Lord would set by you

لَوْلَا دُعَآؤُكُمْ    were it not for your supplication?'[1]

فَقَدْ كَذَّبْتُمْ    But you impugned [me and my advice],

فَسَوْفَ يَكُونُ لِزَامًا ٧٧    so that will continue to haunt you.'


## سُورَةُ ٱلشُّعَرَآءِ                 26. SŪRAT AL-SHU'ARĀ'[2]

بِسْمِ ٱللَّهِ    In the Name of Allah,

ٱلرَّحْمَٰنِ ٱلرَّحِيمِ    the All-beneficent, the All-merciful.


طسٓمٓ ١ 1 *Ṭā, Sīn, Mīm.*

تِلْكَ ءَايَٰتُ ٱلْكِتَٰبِ ٱلْمُبِينِ ٢ 2 These are the signs of the Manifest Book.

لَعَلَّكَ بَٰخِعٌ نَّفْسَكَ 3 *You* might kill *yourself* [out of distress]

أَلَّا يَكُونُوا۟ مُؤْمِنِينَ ٣    that they will not have faith.

إِن نَّشَأْ نُنَزِّلْ عَلَيْهِم 4 If We wish We will send down to them

مِّنَ ٱلسَّمَآءِ ءَايَةً    a sign from the sky

فَظَلَّتْ أَعْنَٰقُهُمْ لَهَا خَٰضِعِينَ ٤    before which their heads will remain bowed in humility.

---

[1] Or 'were it not for your invitation.'

[2] The *sūrah* takes its name from verses 224-227 concerning the poets (*shu'arā'*).

وَمَا يَأْتِيهِم 5 There would not come to them

مِّن ذِكْرٍ مِّنَ ٱلرَّحْمَٰنِ مُحْدَثٍ     any new reminder from the All-beneficent

إِلَّا كَانُوا عَنْهُ مُعْرِضِينَ ٥     but that they used to disregard it.

فَقَدْ كَذَّبُوا 6 They have certainly denied [the truth],

فَسَيَأْتِيهِمْ أَنۢبَٰٓؤُا۟     but soon there will come to them the news

مَا كَانُوا بِهِۦ يَسْتَهْزِءُونَ ٦     of what they have been deriding.

أَوَلَمْ يَرَوْا إِلَى ٱلْأَرْضِ 7 Have they not regarded the earth,

كَمْ أَنۢبَتْنَا فِيهَا     how many We have caused to grow in it

مِن كُلِّ زَوْجٍ كَرِيمٍ ٧     of every splendid kind [of vegetation]?

إِنَّ فِى ذَٰلِكَ لَءَايَةً 8 There is indeed a sign in that;

وَمَا كَانَ أَكْثَرُهُم مُّؤْمِنِينَ ٨     but most of them do not have faith.

وَإِنَّ رَبَّكَ لَهُوَ ٱلْعَزِيزُ ٱلرَّحِيمُ ٩ 9 Indeed *your* Lord is the All-mighty, the All-merciful.

وَإِذْ نَادَىٰ رَبُّكَ مُوسَىٰٓ 10 When *your* Lord called out to Moses:

أَنِ ٱئْتِ ٱلْقَوْمَ ٱلظَّٰلِمِينَ ١٠     [saying,] 'Go to the wrongdoing people,

قَوْمَ فِرْعَوْنَ 11     the people of Pharaoh.

أَلَا يَتَّقُونَ ١١     Will they not be wary [of Allah]?'

قَالَ رَبِّ 12 He said, 'My Lord!

إِنِّىٓ أَخَافُ أَن يُكَذِّبُونِ ١٢     I fear they will impugn me,

وَيَضِيقُ صَدْرِى 13     and I will become upset,

وَلَا يَنطَلِقُ لِسَانِى     and my tongue will fail me.

فَأَرْسِلْ إِلَىٰ هَٰرُونَ ١٣     So send [Your messenger] to Aaron.

وَلَهُمْ عَلَىَّ ذَنۢبٌ 14 Also they have a charge against me,

فَأَخَافُ أَن يَقْتُلُونِ ١٤     and I fear they will kill me.'

قَالَ كَلَّا 15 He said, 'Certainly not!

فَٱذْهَبَا بِـَٔايَٰتِنَآ     Let the two of you go with Our signs:

إِنَّا مَعَكُم مُّسْتَمِعُونَ ١٥     We will indeed be with you, hearing [everything].

فَأْتِيَا فِرْعَوْنَ فَقُولَآ 16 So approach Pharaoh and say,

إِنَّا رَسُولُ رَبِّ ٱلْعَٰلَمِينَ ١٦     "We are indeed envoys of the Lord of the worlds

أَنْ أَرْسِلْ مَعَنَا بَنِىٓ إِسْرَٰٓءِيلَ ١٧ 17     that you let the Children of Israel go with us."'

قَالَ أَلَمْ نُرَبِّكَ فِينَا وَلِيدًا 18 He said, 'Did we not rear you as a child among us,

وَلَبِثْتَ فِينَا مِنْ عُمُرِكَ سِنِينَ and did you not stay with us for years of your life?

وَفَعَلْتَ فَعْلَتَكَ ٱلَّتِي فَعَلْتَ 19 Then you committed that deed of yours,

وَأَنتَ مِنَ ٱلْكَفِرِينَ and you are an ingrate.'

قَالَ فَعَلْتُهَآ إِذًا وَأَنَا۟ مِنَ ٱلضَّآلِّينَ 20 He said, 'I did that when I was astray.

فَفَرَرْتُ مِنكُمْ لَمَّا خِفْتُكُمْ 21 So I fled from you, as I was afraid of you.

فَوَهَبَ لِي رَبِّي حُكْمًا Then my Lord gave me judgement

وَجَعَلَنِي مِنَ ٱلْمُرْسَلِينَ and made me one of the apostles.

وَتِلْكَ نِعْمَةٌ 22 As for that favour,

تَمُنُّهَا عَلَيَّ you remind me of it reproachfully

أَنْ عَبَّدتَّ بَنِي إِسْرَٰٓءِيلَ because your have enslaved the Children of Israel.'

قَالَ فِرْعَوْنُ وَمَا رَبُّ ٱلْعَٰلَمِينَ 23 He said, 'And what is "the Lord of all the worlds?" '

قَالَ رَبُّ ٱلسَّمَٰوَٰتِ وَٱلْأَرْضِ 24 He said, 'The Lord of the heavens and the earth

وَمَا بَيْنَهُمَآ and whatever is between them,

إِن كُنتُم مُّوقِنِينَ —should you have conviction.'

قَالَ لِمَنْ حَوْلَهُ 25 He said to those who were around him,

أَلَا تَسْتَمِعُونَ 'Don't you hear?!'

قَالَ رَبُّكُمْ 26 He said, 'Your Lord,

وَرَبُّ ءَابَآئِكُمُ ٱلْأَوَّلِينَ and the Lord of your forefathers!'

قَالَ 27 He said,

إِنَّ رَسُولَكُمُ ٱلَّذِىٓ أُرْسِلَ إِلَيْكُمْ 'Indeed your messenger, who has been sent to you,

لَمَجْنُونٌ is surely crazy!'

قَالَ رَبُّ ٱلْمَشْرِقِ وَٱلْمَغْرِبِ 28 He said, 'The Lord of the east and the west

وَمَا بَيْنَهُمَآ and whatever is between them

إِن كُنتُمْ تَعْقِلُونَ —should you apply reason.'

قَالَ لَئِنِ ٱتَّخَذْتَ إِلَٰهًا غَيْرِى 29 He said, 'If you take up any god other than me,

لَأَجْعَلَنَّكَ مِنَ ٱلْمَسْجُونِينَ I will surely make you a prisoner!'

قَالَ أَوَلَوْ جِئْتُكَ بِشَىْءٍ مُّبِينٍ 30 He said, 'What if I bring you something manifest?'

قَالَ فَأْتِ بِهِۦٓ 31 He said, 'Then bring it,

إِن كُنتَ مِنَ ٱلصَّٰدِقِينَ should you be truthful.'

فَأَلْقَىٰ عَصَاهُ 32 Thereat he threw down his staff,

فَإِذَا هِيَ ثُعْبَانٌ مُّبِينٌ ۝     and behold, it was a manifest python.

وَنَزَعَ يَدَهُ 33 Then he drew out his hand,

فَإِذَا هِيَ بَيْضَآءُ لِلنَّـٰظِرِينَ ۝     and behold, it was white to the onlookers.

قَالَ لِلْمَلَإِ حَوْلَهُ 34 He said to the elite [who stood] around him,

إِنَّ هَـٰذَا لَسَـٰحِرٌ عَلِيمٌ ۝     'This is indeed an expert magician

يُرِيدُ أَن يُخْرِجَكُم مِّنْ أَرْضِكُم 35     who seeks to expel you from your land

بِسِحْرِهِۦ     with his magic.

فَمَاذَا تَأْمُرُونَ ۝     So what do you advise?'

قَالُوٓا۟ أَرْجِهْ وَأَخَاهُ 36 They said, 'Put him and his brother off for a while,

وَٱبْعَثْ فِى ٱلْمَدَآئِنِ حَـٰشِرِينَ ۝     and send heralds to the cities

يَأْتُوكَ بِكُلِّ سَحَّارٍ عَلِيمٍ ۝ 37     to bring you every expert magician.'

فَجُمِعَ ٱلسَّحَرَةُ 38 So the magicians were gathered

لِمِيقَـٰتِ يَوْمٍ مَّعْلُومٍ ۝     for the tryst of a known day,

وَقِيلَ لِلنَّاسِ 39 and the people were told:

هَلْ أَنتُم مُّجْتَمِعُونَ ۝     'Will you gather?!'

لَعَلَّنَا نَتَّبِعُ ٱلسَّحَرَةَ 40     'Maybe we will follow the magicians,

إِن كَانُوا۟ هُمُ ٱلْغَـٰلِبِينَ ۝     should they be the victors!'

فَلَمَّا جَآءَ ٱلسَّحَرَةُ 41 So when the magicians came,

قَالُوا۟ لِفِرْعَوْنَ     they said to Pharaoh,

أَئِنَّ لَنَا لَأَجْرًا     'Shall we indeed have a reward

إِن كُنَّا نَحْنُ ٱلْغَـٰلِبِينَ ۝     if we were to be the victors?'

قَالَ نَعَمْ 42 He said, ' Of course;

وَإِنَّكُمْ إِذًا لَّمِنَ ٱلْمُقَرَّبِينَ ۝     and indeed you shall be among those near [to me].'

قَالَ لَهُم مُّوسَىٰٓ 43 Moses said to them,

أَلْقُوا۟ مَآ أَنتُم مُّلْقُونَ ۝     'Throw down what you have to throw!'

فَأَلْقَوْا۟ حِبَالَهُمْ وَعِصِيَّهُمْ 44 So they threw down their sticks and ropes,

وَقَالُوا۟ بِعِزَّةِ فِرْعَوْنَ     and said, 'By the might of Pharaoh,

إِنَّا لَنَحْنُ ٱلْغَـٰلِبُونَ ۝     we shall surely be the victors!'

فَأَلْقَىٰ مُوسَىٰ عَصَاهُ 45 Thereat Moses threw down his staff,

فَإِذَا

and behold,

هِىَ تَلْقَفُ مَا يَأْفِكُونَ ۝

it was swallowing what they had faked.

فَأُلْقِىَ ٱلسَّحَرَةُ سَٰجِدِينَ ۝ 46 Thereat the magicians fell down prostrating.

قَالُوٓاْ 47 They said,

ءَامَنَّا بِرَبِّ ٱلْعَٰلَمِينَ ۝

'We believe in the Lord of all the worlds,

رَبِّ مُوسَىٰ وَهَٰرُونَ ۝ 48 the Lord of Moses and Aaron.'

قَالَ 49 He said,

ءَامَنتُمْ لَهُۥ قَبْلَ أَنْ ءَاذَنَ لَكُمْ

'Do you profess faith in Him before I permit you?

إِنَّهُۥ لَكَبِيرُكُمُ ٱلَّذِى عَلَّمَكُمُ ٱلسِّحْرَ

He is indeed your chief who has taught you magic!

فَلَسَوْفَ تَعْلَمُونَ

Soon you will surely know!

لَأُقَطِّعَنَّ أَيْدِيَكُمْ وَأَرْجُلَكُم

Surely I will cut off your hands and feet

مِّنْ خِلَٰفٍ

from opposite sides,

وَلَأُصَلِّبَنَّكُمْ أَجْمَعِينَ ۝

and I will surely crucify you all.'

قَالُواْ لَا ضَيْرَ 50 They said, '[There is] no harm [in that]!

إِنَّآ إِلَىٰ رَبِّنَا مُنقَلِبُونَ ۝

Indeed we shall return to our Lord.

إِنَّا نَطْمَعُ 51 Indeed we hope

أَن يَغْفِرَ لَنَا رَبُّنَا خَطَٰيَٰنَآ

our Lord will forgive us our iniquities

أَن كُنَّآ أَوَّلَ ٱلْمُؤْمِنِينَ ۝ ٭

for being the first to believe.'

وَأَوْحَيْنَآ إِلَىٰ مُوسَىٰٓ 52 Then We revealed to Moses,

أَنْ أَسْرِ بِعِبَادِىٓ [saying], 'Take My servants on a journey by night,

إِنَّكُم مُّتَّبَعُونَ ۝ for you will be pursued.

فَأَرْسَلَ فِرْعَوْنُ 53 Then Pharaoh sent

فِى ٱلْمَدَآئِنِ حَٰشِرِينَ ۝ heralds to the cities,

إِنَّ هَٰٓؤُلَآءِ لَشِرْذِمَةٌ قَلِيلُونَ ۝ 54 [announcing:] 'These[1] are indeed a small gang.

وَإِنَّهُمْ لَنَا لَغَآئِظُونَ ۝ 55 They have surely aroused our wrath,

وَإِنَّا لَجَمِيعٌ حَٰذِرُونَ ۝ 56 and indeed We are all on our guard.'[2]

فَأَخْرَجْنَٰهُم مِّن جَنَّٰتٍ وَعُيُونٍ ۝ 57 So We expelled them from gardens and springs,

وَكُنُوزٍ وَمَقَامٍ كَرِيمٍ ۝ 58 and [from] treasures and splendid places.

---

[1] That is, the Israelites.

[2] Or, 'Surely We are all a well-armed host.'

كَذَٰلِكَ 59 So it was;

وَأَوْرَثْنَٰهَا بَنِىٓ إِسْرَٰٓءِيلَ ۞   and We bequeathed them to the Children of Israel.

فَأَتْبَعُوهُم مُّشْرِقِينَ ۞ 60 Then they pursued them at sunrise.

فَلَمَّا تَرَٰٓءَا ٱلْجَمْعَانِ 61 When the two hosts sighted each other,

قَالَ أَصْحَٰبُ مُوسَىٰٓ   the companions of Moses said,

إِنَّا لَمُدْرَكُونَ ۞   'Indeed we have been caught up.'

قَالَ كَلَّآ 62 He said, 'Certainly not!

إِنَّ مَعِىَ رَبِّى   Indeed my Lord is with me.

سَيَهْدِينِ ۞   He will guide me.'

فَأَوْحَيْنَآ إِلَىٰ مُوسَىٰٓ 63 Thereupon We revealed to Moses:

أَنِ ٱضْرِب بِّعَصَاكَ ٱلْبَحْرَ   'Strike the sea with your staff!'

فَٱنفَلَقَ   Whereupon it parted,

فَكَانَ كُلُّ فِرْقٍ كَٱلطَّوْدِ ٱلْعَظِيمِ ۞   and each part was as if it were a great mountain.

وَأَزْلَفْنَا ثَمَّ ٱلْءَاخَرِينَ ۞ 64 There, We brought the others near.

وَأَنجَيْنَا مُوسَىٰ 65 And We delivered Moses

وَمَن مَّعَهُۥٓ أَجْمَعِينَ ۞   and all those who were with him.

ثُمَّ أَغْرَقْنَا ٱلْءَاخَرِينَ ۞ 66 Then We drowned the others.

إِنَّ فِى ذَٰلِكَ لَءَايَةً 67 There is indeed a sign in that,

وَمَا كَانَ أَكْثَرُهُم مُّؤْمِنِينَ ۞   but most of them do not have faith.

وَإِنَّ رَبَّكَ لَهُوَ ٱلْعَزِيزُ ٱلرَّحِيمُ ۞ 68 Indeed *your* Lord is the All-mighty, the All-merciful.

وَٱتْلُ عَلَيْهِمْ نَبَأَ إِبْرَٰهِيمَ ۞ 69 *Relate* to them the account of Abraham

إِذْ قَالَ لِأَبِيهِ وَقَوْمِهِ 70 when he said to his father and his people,

مَا تَعْبُدُونَ ۞   'What is it that you are worshiping?!'

قَالُوا۟ نَعْبُدُ أَصْنَامًا 71 They said, 'We worship idols,

فَنَظَلُّ لَهَا عَٰكِفِينَ ۞   and we will go on clinging to them.'

قَالَ هَلْ يَسْمَعُونَكُمْ إِذْ تَدْعُونَ ۞ 72 He said, 'Do they hear you when you call them?

أَوْ يَنفَعُونَكُمْ 73 Or do they bring you any benefit,

أَوْ يَضُرُّونَ ۞   or cause you any harm?'

قَالُوا۟ 74 They said,

بَلْ وَجَدْنَآ ءَابَآءَنَا كَذَٰلِكَ يَفْعَلُونَ ۝     'Rather we found our fathers acting likewise.'

قَالَ 75 He said,

أَفَرَءَيْتُم مَّا كُنتُمْ تَعْبُدُونَ ۝     'Have you regarded what you have been worshipping,

أَنتُمْ وَءَابَآؤُكُمُ ٱلْأَقْدَمُونَ ۝ 76     you and your ancestors?

فَإِنَّهُمْ عَدُوٌّ لِّىٓ 77 They are indeed hateful to me,

إِلَّا رَبَّ ٱلْعَٰلَمِينَ ۝     but the Lord of all the worlds,

ٱلَّذِى خَلَقَنِى 78 who created me,

فَهُوَ يَهْدِينِ ۝     it is He who guides me,

وَٱلَّذِى هُوَ يُطْعِمُنِى وَيَسْقِينِ ۝ 79     and provides me with food and drink,

وَإِذَا مَرِضْتُ فَهُوَ يَشْفِينِ ۝ 80     and when I get sick, it is He who cures me;

وَٱلَّذِى يُمِيتُنِى 81 who will make me die,

ثُمَّ يُحْيِينِ ۝     then He will bring me to life,

وَٱلَّذِىٓ أَطْمَعُ أَن يَغْفِرَ لِى خَطِيٓـَٔتِى 82     and who, I hope, will forgive me my iniquities

يَوْمَ ٱلدِّينِ ۝     on the Day of Retribution.'[1]

رَبِّ هَبْ لِى حُكْمًا 83 'My Lord! Grant me [unerring] judgement,

وَأَلْحِقْنِى بِٱلصَّٰلِحِينَ ۝     and unite me with the Righteous.

وَٱجْعَل لِّى لِسَانَ صِدْقٍ 84 Confer on me a worthy repute

فِى ٱلْءَاخِرِينَ ۝     among the posterity,

وَٱجْعَلْنِى مِن وَرَثَةِ جَنَّةِ ٱلنَّعِيمِ ۝ 85 and make me one of the heirs to the paradise of bliss.

وَٱغْفِرْ لِأَبِىٓ 86 Forgive my father,

إِنَّهُۥ كَانَ مِنَ ٱلضَّآلِّينَ ۝     for he is one of those who are astray.

وَلَا تُخْزِنِى 87 Do not disgrace me

يَوْمَ يُبْعَثُونَ ۝     on the day that they will be resurrected,

يَوْمَ لَا يَنفَعُ مَالٌ وَلَا بَنُونَ ۝ 88 the day when neither wealth nor children will avail,

إِلَّا مَنْ أَتَى ٱللَّهَ بِقَلْبٍ سَلِيمٍ ۝ 89 except him who comes to Allah with a sound heart,'[2]

وَأُزْلِفَتِ ٱلْجَنَّةُ لِلْمُتَّقِينَ ۝ 90 and paradise will be brought near for the Godwary,

وَبُرِّزَتِ ٱلْجَحِيمُ لِلْغَاوِينَ ۝ 91 and hell will be brought into view for the perverse,

وَقِيلَ لَهُمْ 92 and they shall be told:

---

[1] Or 'the Day of Judgement.'

[2] That is, a heart that is free from the love of the world.

أَيْنَ مَا كُنتُمْ تَعْبُدُونَ ۝ 'Where is that which you used to worship

مِن دُونِ ٱللَّهِ 93    besides Allah?

هَلْ يَنصُرُونَكُمْ أَوْ يَنتَصِرُونَ ۝ Do they help you, or do they help each other?'

فَكُبْكِبُوا فِيهَا 94 Then they will be cast into it on their faces

هُمْ وَٱلْغَاوُونَ ۝    —they and the perverse,

وَجُنُودُ إِبْلِيسَ أَجْمَعُونَ ۝ 95    and the hosts of Iblis all together.

قَالُوا وَهُمْ فِيهَا يَخْتَصِمُونَ ۝ 96 They will say, as they wrangle in it [together],

تَٱللَّهِ إِن كُنَّا لَفِى ضَلَٰلٍ مُّبِينٍ ۝ 97    'By Allah, we had indeed been in manifest error,

إِذْ نُسَوِّيكُم بِرَبِّ ٱلْعَٰلَمِينَ ۝ 98    when we equated you with the Lord of all the worlds!

وَمَا أَضَلَّنَا إِلَّا ٱلْمُجْرِمُونَ ۝ 99    And no one led us astray except the guilty.

فَمَا لَنَا مِن شَٰفِعِينَ ۝ 100    Now we have no intercessors,

وَلَا صَدِيقٍ حَمِيمٍ ۝ 101    nor do we have any sympathetic friend.

فَلَوْ أَنَّ لَنَا كَرَّةً 102    Had there been another turn for us,

فَنَكُونَ مِنَ ٱلْمُؤْمِنِينَ ۝    we would be among the faithful.'

إِنَّ فِى ذَٰلِكَ لَآيَةً 103 There is indeed a sign in that;

وَمَا كَانَ أَكْثَرُهُم مُّؤْمِنِينَ ۝    but most of them do not have faith.

وَإِنَّ رَبَّكَ لَهُوَ ٱلْعَزِيزُ ٱلرَّحِيمُ ۝ 104 Indeed *your* Lord is the All-mighty, the All-merciful.

كَذَّبَتْ قَوْمُ نُوحٍ ٱلْمُرْسَلِينَ ۝ 105 The people of Noah impugned the apostles

إِذْ قَالَ لَهُمْ أَخُوهُمْ نُوحٌ 106 when Noah, their brother, said to them,

أَلَا تَتَّقُونَ ۝    'Will you not be wary [of Allah]?

إِنِّى لَكُمْ رَسُولٌ أَمِينٌ ۝ 107 Indeed I am a trusted apostle [sent] to you.

فَٱتَّقُوا ٱللَّهَ وَأَطِيعُونِ ۝ 108 So be wary of Allah and obey me.

وَمَا أَسْـَٔلُكُمْ عَلَيْهِ مِنْ أَجْرٍ 109 I do not ask you any reward for it;

إِنْ أَجْرِىَ إِلَّا عَلَىٰ رَبِّ ٱلْعَٰلَمِينَ ۝    my reward lies only with the Lord of all the worlds.

فَٱتَّقُوا ٱللَّهَ وَأَطِيعُونِ ۝ ۞ 110 So be wary of Allah and obey me.'

قَالُوا أَنُؤْمِنُ لَكَ 111 They said, 'Shall we believe in you,

وَٱتَّبَعَكَ ٱلْأَرْذَلُونَ ۝    when it is the riffraff who follow you?'

قَالَ وَمَا عِلْمِى 112 He said, 'What do I know

بِمَا كَانُوا يَعْمَلُونَ ۝    as to what they used to do?

إِنْ حِسَابُهُمْ إِلَّا عَلَى رَبِّى   113 Their reckoning is only with my Lord,

لَوْ تَشْعُرُونَ ۝   should you be aware.

وَمَا أَنَا بِطَارِدِ ٱلْمُؤْمِنِينَ ۝   114 I will not drive away the faithful.

إِنْ أَنَا إِلَّا نَذِيرٌ مُّبِينٌ ۝   115 I am just a manifest warner.'

قَالُوا لَئِن لَّمْ تَنتَهِ يَٰنُوحُ   116 They said, 'Noah, if you do not relinquish,

لَتَكُونَنَّ مِنَ ٱلْمَرْجُومِينَ ۝   you will certainly be stoned [to death].'

قَالَ رَبِّ   117 He said, 'My Lord!

إِنَّ قَوْمِى كَذَّبُونِ ۝   Indeed my people have impugned me.

فَٱفْتَحْ بَيْنِى وَبَيْنَهُمْ فَتْحًا   118 So judge conclusively between me and them,

وَنَجِّنِى وَمَن مَّعِىَ مِنَ ٱلْمُؤْمِنِينَ ۝   and deliver me and the faithful who are with me.'

فَأَنجَيْنَٰهُ   119 Thereupon We delivered him

وَمَن مَّعَهُ فِى ٱلْفُلْكِ ٱلْمَشْحُونِ ۝   and those who were with him in the laden ark.

ثُمَّ أَغْرَقْنَا بَعْدُ ٱلْبَاقِينَ ۝   120 Then We drowned the rest.

إِنَّ فِى ذَٰلِكَ لَآيَةً   121 There is indeed a sign in that;

وَمَا كَانَ أَكْثَرُهُم مُّؤْمِنِينَ ۝   but most of them do not have faith.

وَإِنَّ رَبَّكَ لَهُوَ ٱلْعَزِيزُ ٱلرَّحِيمُ ۝   122 Indeed *your* Lord is the All-mighty, the All-merciful.

كَذَّبَتْ عَادٌ ٱلْمُرْسَلِينَ ۝   123 [The people of] ‘Ād impugned the apostles,

إِذْ قَالَ لَهُمْ أَخُوهُمْ هُودٌ   124 when Hūd, their brother, said to them,

أَلَا تَتَّقُونَ ۝   'Will you not be wary [of Allah]?

إِنِّى لَكُمْ رَسُولٌ أَمِينٌ ۝   125 Indeed I am a trusted apostle [sent] to you.

فَٱتَّقُوا ٱللَّهَ وَأَطِيعُونِ ۝   126 So be wary of Allah and obey me.

وَمَا أَسْـَٔلُكُمْ عَلَيْهِ مِنْ أَجْرٍ   127 I do not ask you any reward for it;

إِنْ أَجْرِىَ إِلَّا عَلَىٰ رَبِّ ٱلْعَٰلَمِينَ ۝   my reward lies only with the Lord of all the worlds.

أَتَبْنُونَ بِكُلِّ رِيعٍ ءَايَةً تَعْبَثُونَ ۝   128 Do you futilely build a sign on every prominence?

وَتَتَّخِذُونَ مَصَانِعَ لَعَلَّكُمْ تَخْلُدُونَ ۝   129 You set up structures as if you will be immortal,

وَإِذَا بَطَشْتُم   130 and when you seize [someone for punishment],

بَطَشْتُمْ جَبَّارِينَ ۝   you seize [him] like tyrants.

فَٱتَّقُوا ٱللَّهَ وَأَطِيعُونِ ۝   131 So be wary of Allah and obey me.

وَٱتَّقُوا ٱلَّذِى   132 And be wary of Him

أُمَدَّكُم بِمَا تَعْلَمُونَ ۞    who has provided you with what you know,

أُمَدَّكُم بِأَنْعَمٍ وَبَنِينَ ۞   133   and aided you with sons and with cattle,

وَجَنَّتٍ وَعُيُونٍ ۞   134     gardens and springs.

إِنِّى أَخَافُ عَلَيْكُمْ   135   Indeed I fear for you

عَذَابَ يَوْمٍ عَظِيمٍ ۞     the punishment of a tremendous day.'

قَالُوا سَوَآءٌ عَلَيْنَآ   136 They said, 'It is the same to us

أَوَعَظْتَ أَمْ لَمْ تَكُن مِّنَ ٱلْوَٰعِظِينَ ۞     whether you advise us or not.

إِنْ هَٰذَآ إِلَّا خُلُقُ ٱلْأَوَّلِينَ ۞   137   This is nothing but the ethos of the ancients,[1]

وَمَا نَحْنُ بِمُعَذَّبِينَ ۞   138    and we will not be punished.'

فَكَذَّبُوهُ   139 So they impugned him,

فَأَهْلَكْنَٰهُمْ     whereupon We destroyed them.

إِنَّ فِى ذَٰلِكَ لَآيَةً     There is indeed a sign in that;

وَمَا كَانَ أَكْثَرُهُم مُّؤْمِنِينَ ۞     but most of them do not have faith.

وَإِنَّ رَبَّكَ لَهُوَ ٱلْعَزِيزُ ٱلرَّحِيمُ ۞   140 Indeed *your* Lord is the All-mighty, the All-merciful.

كَذَّبَتْ ثَمُودُ ٱلْمُرْسَلِينَ ۞   141 [The people of] Thamūd impugned the apostles

إِذْ قَالَ لَهُمْ أَخُوهُمْ صَٰلِحٌ   142 when Ṣāliḥ, their brother, said to them,

أَلَا تَتَّقُونَ ۞     'Will you not be wary [of Allah]?

إِنِّى لَكُمْ رَسُولٌ أَمِينٌ ۞   143     Indeed I am a trusted apostle [sent] to you.

فَٱتَّقُوا ٱللَّهَ وَأَطِيعُونِ ۞   144    So be wary of Allah and obey me.

وَمَآ أَسْـَٔلُكُمْ عَلَيْهِ مِنْ أَجْرٍ   145 I do not ask you any reward for it;

إِنْ أَجْرِىَ إِلَّا عَلَىٰ رَبِّ ٱلْعَٰلَمِينَ ۞     my reward lies only with the Lord of all the worlds.

أَتُتْرَكُونَ فِى مَا هَٰهُنَآ ءَامِنِينَ ۞   146 Will you be left secure in that which is here

فِى جَنَّٰتٍ وَعُيُونٍ ۞   147   —amid gardens and springs,

وَزُرُوعٍ وَنَخْلٍ طَلْعُهَا هَضِيمٌ ۞   148 farms and date palms with dainty spathes?

وَتَنْحِتُونَ مِنَ ٱلْجِبَالِ بُيُوتًا فَٰرِهِينَ ۞   149 And you hue houses out of the mountains skillfully.[2]

فَٱتَّقُوا ٱللَّهَ وَأَطِيعُونِ ۞   150 So be wary of Allah and obey me,

---

[1] Or, 'This is nothing but a fabrication of the ancients,' according to an alternate reading (*khaluq*, instead of *khuluq*).

[2] Or, 'exultantly.'

وَلَا تُطِيعُوٓا۟ أَمْرَ ٱلْمُسْرِفِينَ ۝ 151 and do not obey the dictates of the profligate,

ٱلَّذِينَ يُفْسِدُونَ فِى ٱلْأَرْضِ 152 who cause corruption in the land

وَلَا يُصْلِحُونَ ۝ and do not bring about reform.'

قَالُوٓا۟ إِنَّمَآ أَنتَ مِنَ ٱلْمُسَحَّرِينَ ۝ 153 They said, 'Indeed you are one of the bewitched.

مَآ أَنتَ إِلَّا بَشَرٌ مِّثْلُنَا 154 You are just a human being like us.

فَأْتِ بِـَٔايَةٍ إِن كُنتَ مِنَ ٱلصَّٰدِقِينَ ۝ So bring us a sign, should you be truthful.'

قَالَ هَٰذِهِۦ نَاقَةٌ 155 He said, 'This is a she-camel;

لَّهَا شِرْبٌ وَلَكُمْ شِرْبُ يَوْمٍ مَّعْلُومٍ ۝ she shall drink and you shall drink on known days.

وَلَا تَمَسُّوهَا بِسُوٓءٍ 156 Do not cause her any harm,

فَيَأْخُذَكُمْ عَذَابُ for then you shall be seized by the punishment

يَوْمٍ عَظِيمٍ ۝ of a terrible day.'

فَعَقَرُوهَا 157 But they hamstrung her,

فَأَصْبَحُوا۟ نَٰدِمِينَ ۝ whereupon they became regretful.

فَأَخَذَهُمُ ٱلْعَذَابُ 158 So the punishment seized them.

إِنَّ فِى ذَٰلِكَ لَـَٔايَةً There is indeed a sign in that;

وَمَا كَانَ أَكْثَرُهُم مُّؤْمِنِينَ ۝ but most of them do not have faith.

وَإِنَّ رَبَّكَ لَهُوَ ٱلْعَزِيزُ ٱلرَّحِيمُ ۝ 159 Indeed *your* Lord is the All-mighty, the All-merciful.

كَذَّبَتْ قَوْمُ لُوطٍ ٱلْمُرْسَلِينَ ۝ 160 The people of Lot impugned the apostles

إِذْ قَالَ لَهُمْ أَخُوهُمْ لُوطٌ 161 when Lot, their brother, said to them,

أَلَا تَتَّقُونَ ۝ 'Will you not be wary [of Allah]?

إِنِّى لَكُمْ رَسُولٌ أَمِينٌ ۝ 162 Indeed I am a trusted apostle [sent] to you.

فَٱتَّقُوا۟ ٱللَّهَ وَأَطِيعُونِ ۝ 163 So be wary of Allah and obey me.

وَمَآ أَسْـَٔلُكُمْ عَلَيْهِ مِنْ أَجْرٍ 164 I do not ask you any reward for it;

إِنْ أَجْرِىَ إِلَّا عَلَىٰ رَبِّ ٱلْعَٰلَمِينَ ۝ my reward lies only with the Lord of all the worlds.

أَتَأْتُونَ ٱلذُّكْرَانَ مِنَ ٱلْعَٰلَمِينَ ۝ 165 What! Of all people do you come to males,

وَتَذَرُونَ 166 abandoning

مَا خَلَقَ لَكُمْ رَبُّكُم مِّنْ أَزْوَٰجِكُم your wives your Lord has created for you?

بَلْ أَنتُمْ قَوْمٌ عَادُونَ ۝ Rather you are a transgressing lot.'

قَالُوا۟ لَئِن لَّمْ تَنتَهِ يَٰلُوطُ 167 They said, 'Lot, if you do not relinquish,

لَتَكُونَنَّ مِنَ ٱلْمُخْرَجِينَ ۝    you will surely be banished.'

قَالَ 168 He said,

إِنِّى لِعَمَلِكُم مِّنَ ٱلْقَالِينَ ۝    'Indeed I detest your conduct.'

رَبِّ 169    'My Lord!

نَجِّنِى وَأَهْلِى مِمَّا يَعْمَلُونَ ۝    Deliver me and my family from what they do.'

فَنَجَّيْنَهُ وَأَهْلَهُ أَجْمَعِينَ ۝ 170 So We delivered him and all his family,

إِلَّا عَجُوزًا فِى ٱلْغَبِرِينَ ۝ 171 except an old woman who remained behind.

ثُمَّ دَمَّرْنَا ٱلْآخَرِينَ ۝ 172 Then We destroyed [all] the others,

وَأَمْطَرْنَا عَلَيْهِم مَّطَرًا 173    and rained down upon them a rain [of stones].

فَسَآءَ مَطَرُ ٱلْمُنذَرِينَ ۝    Evil was the rain of those who were warned!

إِنَّ فِى ذَلِكَ لَآيَةً 174 There is indeed a sign in that;

وَمَا كَانَ أَكْثَرُهُم مُّؤْمِنِينَ ۝    but most of them do not have faith.

وَإِنَّ رَبَّكَ لَهُوَ ٱلْعَزِيزُ ٱلرَّحِيمُ ۝ 175 Indeed *your* Lord is the All-mighty, the All-merciful.

كَذَّبَ أَصْحَبُ لْئَيْكَةِ ٱلْمُرْسَلِينَ ۝ 176 The inhabitants of Aykah impugned the apostles,

إِذْ قَالَ لَهُمْ شُعَيْبٌ 177 when Shuʿayb said to them,

أَلَا تَتَّقُونَ ۝    'Will you not be wary [of Allah]?

إِنِّى لَكُمْ رَسُولٌ أَمِينٌ ۝ 178 Indeed I am a trusted apostle [sent] to you.

فَٱتَّقُوا ٱللَّهَ وَأَطِيعُونِ ۝ 179 So be wary of Allah and obey me.

وَمَآ أَسْئَلُكُمْ عَلَيْهِ مِنْ أَجْرٍ 180 I do not ask you any reward for it;

إِنْ أَجْرِىَ إِلَّا عَلَى رَبِّ ٱلْعَلَمِينَ ۝ ❖    my reward lies only with the Lord of all the worlds.

أَوْفُوا ٱلْكَيْلَ 181 Observe fully the measure,

وَلَا تَكُونُوا مِنَ ٱلْمُخْسِرِينَ ۝    and do not be of those who give short measure.

وَزِنُوا بِٱلْقِسْطَاسِ ٱلْمُسْتَقِيمِ ۝ 182 Weigh with an even balance,

وَلَا تَبْخَسُوا ٱلنَّاسَ أَشْيَآءَهُمْ 183    and do not cheat the people of their goods.

وَلَا تَعْثَوْا فِى ٱلْأَرْضِ    Do not act wickedly on the earth,

مُفْسِدِينَ ۝    causing corruption.

وَٱتَّقُوا ٱلَّذِى خَلَقَكُمْ 184 Be wary of Him who created you

وَٱلْجِبِلَّةَ ٱلْأَوَّلِينَ ۝    and the earlier generations.'

قَالُوٓا إِنَّمَآ أَنتَ مِنَ ٱلْمُسَحَّرِينَ ۝ 185 They said, 'Indeed you are one of the bewitched.

وَمَآ أَنتَ إِلَّا بَشَرٌ مِّثْلُنَا 186 You are just a human being like us,

وَإِن نَّظُنُّكَ لَمِنَ ٱلْكَٰذِبِينَ ۝ and we indeed consider you to be a liar.

فَأَسْقِطْ عَلَيْنَا كِسَفًا مِّنَ ٱلسَّمَآءِ 187 Then make a fragment fall upon us from the sky,

إِن كُنتَ مِنَ ٱلصَّٰدِقِينَ ۝ should you be truthful.'

قَالَ رَبِّىٓ أَعْلَمُ بِمَا تَعْمَلُونَ ۝ 188 He said, 'My Lord knows best what you are doing.'

فَكَذَّبُوهُ 189 So they impugned him,

فَأَخَذَهُمْ and then they were seized

عَذَابُ يَوْمِ ٱلظُّلَّةِ by the punishment of the day of the shady cloud.

إِنَّهُۥ كَانَ عَذَابَ يَوْمٍ عَظِيمٍ ۝ It was indeed the punishment of a tremendous day.

إِنَّ فِى ذَٰلِكَ لَءَايَةً 190 There is indeed a sign in that;

وَمَا كَانَ أَكْثَرُهُم مُّؤْمِنِينَ ۝ but most of them do not have faith.

وَإِنَّ رَبَّكَ لَهُوَ ٱلْعَزِيزُ ٱلرَّحِيمُ ۝ 191 Indeed *your* Lord is the All-mighty, the All-merciful.

وَإِنَّهُۥ لَتَنزِيلُ 192 This is indeed [a Book] sent down

رَبِّ ٱلْعَٰلَمِينَ ۝ by the Lord of all the worlds,

نَزَلَ بِهِ ٱلرُّوحُ ٱلْأَمِينُ ۝ 193 brought down by the Trustworthy Spirit,

عَلَىٰ قَلْبِكَ 194 upon *your* heart,

لِتَكُونَ مِنَ ٱلْمُنذِرِينَ ۝ (so that *you* may be one of the warners),

بِلِسَانٍ عَرَبِىٍّ مُّبِينٍ ۝ 195 in a clear Arabic language.

وَإِنَّهُۥ لَفِى زُبُرِ ٱلْأَوَّلِينَ ۝ 196 It is indeed [foretold] in the scriptures of the ancients.

أَوَلَمْ يَكُن لَّهُمْ ءَايَةً 197 Is it not a sign for them

أَن يَعْلَمَهُۥ عُلَمَٰٓؤُا۟ بَنِىٓ إِسْرَٰٓءِيلَ ۝ that the learned the Children of Israel recognize it?

وَلَوْ نَزَّلْنَٰهُ عَلَىٰ بَعْضِ ٱلْأَعْجَمِينَ ۝ 198 Had We sent it down upon some non-Arab

فَقَرَأَهُۥ عَلَيْهِم 199 and had he recited it to them,

مَّا كَانُوا۟ بِهِۦ مُؤْمِنِينَ ۝ they would not have believed in it.

كَذَٰلِكَ سَلَكْنَٰهُ 200 This is how We let it pass

فِى قُلُوبِ ٱلْمُجْرِمِينَ ۝ through the hearts of the guilty:

لَا يُؤْمِنُونَ بِهِۦ 201 they do not believe in it

حَتَّىٰ يَرَوُا۟ ٱلْعَذَابَ ٱلْأَلِيمَ ۝ until they sight the painful punishment.

فَيَأْتِيَهُم بَغْتَةً 202 It will overtake them suddenly

وَهُمْ لَا يَشْعُرُونَ ۝     while they are unaware.

فَيَقُولُوا ۝ 203 Thereupon they will say,

هَلْ نَحْنُ مُنظَرُونَ ۝     'Shall we be granted any respite?'

أَفَبِعَذَابِنَا يَسْتَعْجِلُونَ ۝ 204 So do they seek to hasten on Our punishment?

أَفَرَءَيْتَ 205 Do *you* see,

إِن مَّتَّعْنَٰهُمْ سِنِينَ ۝     should We let them enjoy for some years,

ثُمَّ جَآءَهُم 206 then there comes to them

مَّا كَانُوا يُوعَدُونَ ۝     what they have been promised,

مَآ أَغْنَىٰ عَنْهُم 207    of what avail to them will be

مَّا كَانُوا يُمَتَّعُونَ ۝     that which they were given to enjoy?

وَمَآ أَهْلَكْنَا مِن قَرْيَةٍ 208 We have not destroyed any town

إِلَّا لَهَا مُنذِرُونَ ۝     without its having warners,

ذِكْرَىٰ 209    for the sake of admonition,

وَمَا كُنَّا ظَٰلِمِينَ ۝     and We were not unjust.

وَمَا تَنَزَّلَتْ بِهِ ٱلشَّيَٰطِينُ ۝ 210 It[1] has not been brought down by the devils.

وَمَا يَنۢبَغِى لَهُمْ 211 Neither does it behoove them,

وَمَا يَسْتَطِيعُونَ ۝     nor are they capable [of doing that].

إِنَّهُمْ عَنِ ٱلسَّمْعِ لَمَعْزُولُونَ ۝ 212 Indeed they are kept at bay [even] from hearing it.

فَلَا تَدْعُ مَعَ ٱللَّهِ إِلَٰهًا ءَاخَرَ 213 So *do not invoke* any god besides Allah,

فَتَكُونَ مِنَ ٱلْمُعَذَّبِينَ ۝     lest *you* should be among the punished.

وَأَنذِرْ عَشِيرَتَكَ ٱلْأَقْرَبِينَ ۝ 214 *Warn* the nearest of your kinsfolk,

وَٱخْفِضْ جَنَاحَكَ 215    and lower *your* wing

لِمَنِ ٱتَّبَعَكَ مِنَ ٱلْمُؤْمِنِينَ ۝     to the faithful who follow *you*.

فَإِنْ عَصَوْكَ 216 But if they disobey you,

فَقُلْ إِنِّى بَرِىٓءٌ مِّمَّا تَعْمَلُونَ ۝     say, 'I am absolved of what you do.'

وَتَوَكَّلْ عَلَى ٱلْعَزِيزِ ٱلرَّحِيمِ ۝ 217 And put *your* trust in the All-mighty, the All-merciful,

ٱلَّذِى يَرَىٰكَ حِينَ تَقُومُ ۝ 218 who sees *you* when *you* stand [for prayer],

---

[1] That is, the Qur’ān.

وَتَقَلُّبَكَ فِي ٱلسَّٰجِدِينَ ۝ 219 and your going about among those who prostrate.

إِنَّهُۥ هُوَ ٱلسَّمِيعُ ٱلْعَلِيمُ ۝ 220 Indeed He is the All-hearing, the All-knowing.

هَلْ أُنَبِّئُكُمْ 221 Should I inform you

عَلَىٰ مَن تَنَزَّلُ ٱلشَّيَٰطِينُ ۝     on whom the devils descend?

تَنَزَّلُ عَلَىٰ كُلِّ أَفَّاكٍ أَثِيمٍ ۝ 222 They descend on every sinful liar.

يُلْقُونَ ٱلسَّمْعَ ۝ 223 They eavesdrop,

وَأَكْثَرُهُمْ كَٰذِبُونَ ۝     and most of them are liars.

وَٱلشُّعَرَآءُ يَتَّبِعُهُمُ ٱلْغَاوُۥنَ ۝ 224 As for the poets, [only] the perverse follow them.

أَلَمْ تَرَ أَنَّهُمْ فِي كُلِّ وَادٍ يَهِيمُونَ ۝ 225 Have *you* not regarded that they rove in every valley,

وَأَنَّهُمْ يَقُولُونَ مَا لَا يَفْعَلُونَ ۝ 226 and that they say what they do not do?

إِلَّا ٱلَّذِينَ ءَامَنُوا وَعَمِلُوا ٱلصَّٰلِحَٰتِ 227 Barring those who have faith and do righteous deeds

وَذَكَرُوا ٱللَّهَ كَثِيرًا     and remember Allah greatly,

وَٱنتَصَرُوا مِنۢ بَعْدِ مَا ظُلِمُوا ۗ     and aid each other after they have been wronged.

وَسَيَعْلَمُ ٱلَّذِينَ ظَلَمُوٓا     And the wrongdoers will soon know

أَىَّ مُنقَلَبٍ يَنقَلِبُونَ ۝     at what goal they will end up.

## سُورَةُ ٱلنَّمْلِ     27. SŪRAT AL-NAML[1]

بِسْمِ ٱللَّهِ     In the Name of Allah,

ٱلرَّحْمَٰنِ ٱلرَّحِيمِ     the All-beneficent, the All-merciful.

طسٓ 1 *Tā, Sīn.*

تِلْكَ ءَايَٰتُ ٱلْقُرْءَانِ وَكِتَابٍ مُّبِينٍ ۝ These are the signs of the Qur'ān and a manifest Book,

هُدًى وَبُشْرَىٰ لِلْمُؤْمِنِينَ ۝ 2 a guidance and good news for the faithful

ٱلَّذِينَ يُقِيمُونَ ٱلصَّلَوٰةَ 3 —those who maintain the prayer

وَيُؤْتُونَ ٱلزَّكَوٰةَ     and pay the *zakāt,*

---

[1] The *sūrah* takes its name from the story of Solomon and the ant (*naml*), mentioned in verses 15-19

وَهُم بِٱلۡآخِرَةِ هُمۡ يُوقِنُونَ ۝

and who are certain of the Hereafter.

إِنَّ ٱلَّذِينَ لَا يُؤۡمِنُونَ بِٱلۡآخِرَةِ ٤

4 As for those who do not believe in the Hereafter,

زَيَّنَّا لَهُمۡ أَعۡمَٰلَهُمۡ

We have made their deeds seem decorous to them,

فَهُمۡ يَعۡمَهُونَ ۝

and so they are bewildered.

أُوْلَٰٓئِكَ ٱلَّذِينَ هُمۡ ٥

5 They are the ones for whom there is

سُوٓءُ ٱلۡعَذَابِ

a terrible punishment,

وَهُمۡ

and they are the ones

فِى ٱلۡآخِرَةِ هُمُ ٱلۡأَخۡسَرُونَ ۝

who will be the biggest losers in the Hereafter.

وَإِنَّكَ لَتُلَقَّى ٱلۡقُرۡءَانَ ٦

6 Indeed *you* receive the Qur'ān

مِن لَّدُنۡ حَكِيمٍ عَلِيمٍ ۝

from One who is all-wise, all-knowing.

إِذۡ قَالَ مُوسَىٰ لِأَهۡلِهِۦٓ ٧

7 When Moses said to his family,

إِنِّىٓ ءَانَسۡتُ نَارًا

'Indeed I descry a fire!

سَـَٔاتِيكُم مِّنۡهَا بِخَبَرٍ

I will bring you some news from it,

أَوۡ ءَاتِيكُم بِشِهَابٍ قَبَسٍ

or bring you a firebrand

لَّعَلَّكُمۡ تَصۡطَلُونَ ۝

so that you may warm yourselves.'

فَلَمَّا جَآءَهَا ٨

8 So when he came to it,

نُودِىَ أَنۢ بُورِكَ مَن فِى ٱلنَّارِ

he was called: 'Blessed is He who is in the fire

وَمَنۡ حَوۡلَهَا

and who is [as well] around it,

وَسُبۡحَٰنَ ٱللَّهِ رَبِّ ٱلۡعَٰلَمِينَ ۝

and immaculate is Allah, the Lord of all the worlds!'

يَٰمُوسَىٰٓ إِنَّهُۥٓ أَنَا ٱللَّهُ ٩

9 'O Moses! Indeed I am Allah,

ٱلۡعَزِيزُ ٱلۡحَكِيمُ ۝

the All-mighty, the All-wise.'

وَأَلۡقِ عَصَاكَ ١٠

10 'Throw down your staff!'

فَلَمَّا رَءَاهَا تَهۡتَزُّ كَأَنَّهَا جَآنٌّ

And when he saw it wriggling, as if it were a snake,

وَلَّىٰ مُدۡبِرًا وَلَمۡ يُعَقِّبۡ

he turned his back [to flee], without looking back.

يَٰمُوسَىٰ لَا تَخَفۡ

'O Moses! 'Do not be afraid.

إِنِّى لَا يَخَافُ لَدَىَّ ٱلۡمُرۡسَلُونَ ۝

Indeed the apostles are not afraid before Me,

إِلَّا مَن ظَلَمَ ١١

11 barring someone who does wrong

ثُمَّ بَدَّلَ حُسۡنًۢا بَعۡدَ سُوٓءٍ

and then makes up with goodness for [his] fault,

فَإِنِّي غَفُورٌ رَّحِيمٌ ۝

وَأَدْخِلْ يَدَكَ فِي جَيْبِكَ

تَخْرُجْ بَيْضَآءَ مِنْ غَيْرِ سُوٓءٍ

فِي تِسْعِ ءَايَـٰتٍ إِلَىٰ فِرْعَوْنَ وَقَوْمِهِۦٓ

إِنَّهُمْ كَانُوا۟ قَوْمًا فَـٰسِقِينَ ۝

فَلَمَّا جَآءَتْهُمْ ءَايَـٰتُنَا مُبْصِرَةً

قَالُوا۟ هَـٰذَا سِحْرٌ مُّبِينٌ ۝

وَجَحَدُوا۟ بِهَا

وَٱسْتَيْقَنَتْهَآ أَنفُسُهُمْ

ظُلْمًا وَعُلُوًّا

فَٱنظُرْ

كَيْفَ كَانَ عَـٰقِبَةُ ٱلْمُفْسِدِينَ ۝

وَلَقَدْ ءَاتَيْنَا دَاوُۥدَ وَسُلَيْمَـٰنَ عِلْمًا

وَقَالَا ٱلْحَمْدُ لِلَّهِ

ٱلَّذِى فَضَّلَنَا

عَلَىٰ كَثِيرٍ مِّنْ عِبَادِهِ ٱلْمُؤْمِنِينَ ۝

وَوَرِثَ سُلَيْمَـٰنُ دَاوُۥدَ

وَقَالَ يَـٰٓأَيُّهَا ٱلنَّاسُ

عُلِّمْنَا مَنطِقَ ٱلطَّيْرِ

وَأُوتِينَا مِن كُلِّ شَىْءٍ

إِنَّ هَـٰذَا لَهُوَ ٱلْفَضْلُ ٱلْمُبِينُ ۝

وَحُشِرَ لِسُلَيْمَـٰنَ جُنُودُهُۥ

مِنَ ٱلْجِنِّ وَٱلْإِنسِ وَٱلطَّيْرِ

فَهُمْ يُوزَعُونَ ۝

حَتَّىٰٓ إِذَآ أَتَوْا۟ عَلَىٰ وَادِ ٱلنَّمْلِ

قَالَتْ نَمْلَةٌ يَـٰٓأَيُّهَا ٱلنَّمْلُ

ٱدْخُلُوا۟ مَسَـٰكِنَكُمْ

لَا يَحْطِمَنَّكُمْ سُلَيْمَـٰنُ وَجُنُودُهُۥ

وَهُمْ لَا يَشْعُرُونَ ۝

for indeed I am all-forgiving, all-merciful.'

12 'Insert your hand into your bosom.

It will emerge white, without any fault,

—among nine signs for Pharaoh and his people.

Indeed they are a transgressing lot.'

13 But when Our signs came to them, as eye-openers,

they said, 'This is plain magic.'

14 They impugned them

—though they were convinced in their hearts—

wrongfully and defiantly.

So *observe*

how was the fate of the agents of corruption!

15 Certainly We gave David and Solomon knowledge,

and they said, 'All praise belongs to Allah,

who granted us an advantage

over many of His faithful servants.'

16 Solomon inherited from David,

and he said, 'O people!

We have been taught the speech of the birds,

and we have been given out of everything.

Indeed this is a manifest advantage.'

17 [Once] Solomon's hosts were marched out [of their camp],

comprising jinn, humans, and birds,

and they were held in check.

18 When they came to the Valley of Ants,

an ant said, 'O ants!

Enter your dwellings,

lest Solomon and his hosts should trample on you

while they are unaware.'

فَتَبَسَّمَ ضَاحِكًا مِّن قَوْلِهَا    19 Whereat he smiled, amused at its words,

وَقَالَ رَبِّ    and he said, 'My Lord!

أَوْزِعْنِي أَنْ أَشْكُرَ نِعْمَتَكَ    Inspire me to give thanks for Your blessing

ٱلَّتِي أَنْعَمْتَ عَلَيَّ وَعَلَىٰ وَٰلِدَيَّ    with which You have blessed me and my parents,

وَأَنْ أَعْمَلَ صَٰلِحًا    and that I may do righteous deeds

تَرْضَٰهُ    which may please You,

وَأَدْخِلْنِي بِرَحْمَتِكَ    and admit me, by Your mercy,

فِي عِبَادِكَ ٱلصَّٰلِحِينَ ۩    among Your righteous servants.'

وَتَفَقَّدَ ٱلطَّيْرَ    20 [One day] he reviewed the birds,

فَقَالَ مَا لِيَ لَآ أَرَى ٱلْهُدْهُدَ    and said, 'Why do I not see the hoopoe?

أَمْ كَانَ مِنَ ٱلْغَآئِبِينَ ۩    Or is he absent?'

لَأُعَذِّبَنَّهُ عَذَابًا شَدِيدًا    21 'I will surely punish him with a severe punishment,

أَوْ لَأَاذْبَحَنَّهُ    or I will surely behead him,

أَوْ لَيَأْتِيَنِّي بِسُلْطَٰنٍ مُّبِينٍ ۩    unless he brings a clear-cut excuse.'

فَمَكَثَ غَيْرَ بَعِيدٍ    22 He did not stay for long [before he turned up]

فَقَالَ أَحَطتُ بِمَا    and said, 'I have alighted on something

لَمْ تُحِطْ بِهِۦ    which you have not alighted on,

وَجِئْتُكَ مِن سَبَإٍ بِنَبَإٍ يَقِينٍ ۩    and I have brought you from Sheba a definite report.

إِنِّي وَجَدتُّ ٱمْرَأَةً تَمْلِكُهُمْ    23 I found a woman ruling over them,

وَأُوتِيَتْ مِن كُلِّ شَيْءٍ    and she has been given everything,

وَلَهَا عَرْشٌ عَظِيمٌ ۩    and she has a great throne.

وَجَدتُّهَا وَقَوْمَهَا يَسْجُدُونَ لِلشَّمْسِ    24 I found her and her people prostrating to the sun

مِن دُونِ ٱللَّهِ    instead of Allah,

وَزَيَّنَ لَهُمُ ٱلشَّيْطَٰنُ أَعْمَٰلَهُمْ    and Satan has made their deeds seem decorous to them

فَصَدَّهُمْ عَنِ ٱلسَّبِيلِ    —thus he has barred them from the way [of Allah],

فَهُمْ لَا يَهْتَدُونَ ۩    so they are not guided—

أَلَّا يَسْجُدُوا۟ لِلَّهِ    25 so that they do not prostrate themselves to Allah,

ٱلَّذِي يُخْرِجُ ٱلْخَبْءَ فِي ٱلسَّمَٰوَٰتِ    who brings out the hidden in the heavens

وَٱلْأَرْضِ    and the earth,

وَيَعْلَمُ مَا تُخْفُونَ    and He knows whatever you hide

وَمَا تُعْلِنُونَ ۝    and whatever you disclose.

ٱللَّهُ لَآ إِلَهَ إِلَّا هُوَ    26 Allah—there is no god except Him—

رَبُّ ٱلْعَرْشِ ٱلْعَظِيمِ ۝    is the Lord of the Great Throne.'

قَالَ سَنَنظُرُ أَصَدَقْتَ    27 He said, 'We shall see whether you are truthful,

أَمْ كُنتَ مِنَ ٱلْكَذِبِينَ ۝    or if you are one of the liars.'

ٱذْهَب بِّكِتَبِي هَذَا فَأَلْقِهْ إِلَيْهِمْ    28 Take this letter of mine and deliver it to them.

ثُمَّ تَوَلَّ عَنْهُمْ    Then draw away from them

فَٱنظُرْ مَاذَا يَرْجِعُونَ ۝    and observe what [response] they return.'

قَالَتْ يَٰٓأَيُّهَا ٱلْمَلَؤُاْ    29 She said, 'O [members of the] elite!

إِنِّىٓ أُلْقِىَ إِلَىَّ كِتَبٌ كَرِيمٌ ۝    Indeed a noble letter has been delivered to me.

إِنَّهُۥ مِن سُلَيْمَنَ    30 It is from Solomon,

وَإِنَّهُۥ بِسْمِ ٱللَّهِ    and it begins in the name of Allah,

ٱلرَّحْمَنِ ٱلرَّحِيمِ ۝    the All-beneficent, the All-merciful.

أَلَّا تَعْلُواْ عَلَىَّ    31 [It states,] "Do not defy me,

وَأْتُونِى مُسْلِمِينَ ۝    and come to me in submission." '

قَالَتْ يَٰٓأَيُّهَا ٱلْمَلَؤُاْ    32 She said, 'O [members of the] elite!

أَفْتُونِى فِى أَمْرِى    Give me your opinion concerning my matter.

مَا كُنتُ قَاطِعَةً أَمْرًا    I do not decide any matter

حَتَّىٰ تَشْهَدُونِ ۝    until you are present.'

قَالُواْ    33 They said,

نَحْنُ أُوْلُواْ قُوَّةٍ وَأُوْلُواْ بَأْسٍ شَدِيدٍ    'We are powerful and possess a great might.

وَٱلْأَمْرُ إِلَيْكِ    But it is up to you to command.

فَٱنظُرِى مَاذَا تَأْمُرِينَ ۝    So see what you will command.'

قَالَتْ إِنَّ ٱلْمُلُوكَ إِذَا دَخَلُواْ قَرْيَةً    34 She said, 'Indeed when kings enter a town,

أَفْسَدُوهَا    they devastate it,

وَجَعَلُوٓاْ أَعِزَّةَ أَهْلِهَآ    and reduce the mightiest of its people

أَذِلَّةً    to the most abased.

وَكَذَلِكَ يَفْعَلُونَ ۝    That is how they act.

وَإِنِّى مُرْسِلَةٌ إِلَيْهِم بِهَدِيَّةٍ    35 I will send them a gift,

فَنَاظِرَةٌۢ بِمَ يَرْجِعُ ٱلْمُرْسَلُونَ ۝    and I shall see what the envoys bring back.'

فَلَمَّا جَآءَ سُلَيۡمَٰنَ 36 So when he[1] came to Solomon,

قَالَ أَتُمِدُّونَنِ بِمَالٍ    he said, 'Are you aiding me with wealth?

فَمَآ ءَاتَىٰنِۦَ ٱللَّهُ    What Allah has given me

خَيۡرٌ مِّمَّآ ءَاتَىٰكُم    is better than what He has given you.

بَلۡ أَنتُم بِهَدِيَّتِكُمۡ تَفۡرَحُونَ ۩    Rather you are exultant over your gift!

ٱرۡجِعۡ إِلَيۡهِمۡ 37    Go back to them,

فَلَنَأۡتِيَنَّهُم بِجُنُودٍ    for we will come at them with hosts

لَّا قِبَلَ لَهُم بِهَا    which they cannot face,

وَلَنُخۡرِجَنَّهُم مِّنۡهَآ أَذِلَّةً    and we will expel them from it, abased,

وَهُمۡ صَٰغِرُونَ ۩    and they shall be degraded.'

قَالَ يَٰٓأَيُّهَا ٱلۡمَلَؤُاْ 38 He said, 'O [members of the] elite!

أَيُّكُمۡ يَأۡتِينِي بِعَرۡشِهَا    Which of you will bring me her throne

قَبۡلَ أَن يَأۡتُونِي مُسۡلِمِينَ ۩    before they come to me in submission?'

قَالَ عِفۡرِيتٌ مِّنَ ٱلۡجِنِّ 39 An afreet[2] from among the jinn said,

أَنَا۠ ءَاتِيكَ بِهِۦ    'I will bring it to you

قَبۡلَ أَن تَقُومَ مِن مَّقَامِكَ    before you rise from your place.

وَإِنِّي عَلَيۡهِ لَقَوِيٌّ أَمِينٌ ۩    Indeed I have the power for it and am trustworthy.'

قَالَ ٱلَّذِي عِندَهُۥ عِلۡمٌ مِّنَ ٱلۡكِتَٰبِ 40 The one who had knowledge of the Book[3] said,

أَنَا۠ ءَاتِيكَ بِهِۦ    'I will bring it to you

قَبۡلَ أَن يَرۡتَدَّ إِلَيۡكَ طَرۡفُكَ    in the twinkling of an eye.'

فَلَمَّا رَءَاهُ مُسۡتَقِرًّا عِندَهُۥ    So when he saw it set near him,

قَالَ هَٰذَا مِن فَضۡلِ رَبِّي    he said, 'This is by the grace of my Lord,

لِيَبۡلُوَنِيٓ ءَأَشۡكُرُ أَمۡ أَكۡفُرُ    to test me if I will give thanks or be ungrateful.

وَمَن شَكَرَ    And whoever gives thanks,

فَإِنَّمَا يَشۡكُرُ لِنَفۡسِهِۦ    gives thanks only for his own sake.

وَمَن كَفَرَ    And whoever is ungrateful [should know that]

فَإِنَّ رَبِّي غَنِيٌّ كَرِيمٌ ۩    my Lord is indeed all-sufficient, all-generous.'

---

[1] That is, the envoy.

[2] *Ifrīt* (noun): devil, demon, giant, rebel; (adj.) cunning, sly, wily, smart, mischievous, rebellious, defiant.

[3] He is said to have been Solomon's vizier and successor, Āṣif ibn Barkhiyā.

قَالَ نَكِّرُواْ لَهَا عَرْشَهَا 41 He said, 'Disguise her throne for her,

نَنظُرْ أَتَهْتَدِىٓ      so that we may see whether she is discerning

أَمْ تَكُونُ مِنَ ٱلَّذِينَ لَا يَهْتَدُونَ ﴿﴾    or if she is one of the undiscerning ones.'

فَلَمَّا جَآءَتْ قِيلَ 42 So when she came, it was said [to her],

أَهَـٰكَذَا عَرْشُكِ      'Is your throne like this one?'

قَالَتْ كَأَنَّهُۥ هُوَ      She said, 'It seems to be the same,

وَأُوتِينَا ٱلْعِلْمَ مِن قَبْلِهَا    and we were informed before it,[1]

وَكُنَّا مُسْلِمِينَ ﴿﴾      and we had submitted.'

وَصَدَّهَا 43 She had been barred [from the way of Allah]

مَا كَانَت تَّعْبُدُ مِن دُونِ ٱللَّهِ    by what she used to worship besides Allah,

إِنَّهَا كَانَتْ مِن قَوْمٍ كَـٰفِرِينَ ﴿﴾    for she belonged to a faithless people.

قِيلَ لَهَا ٱدْخُلِى ٱلصَّرْحَ 44 It was said to her, 'Enter the palace.'

فَلَمَّا رَأَتْهُ      So when she saw it,

حَسِبَتْهُ لُجَّةً      she supposed it to be a pool of water,

وَكَشَفَتْ عَن سَاقَيْهَا    and she bared her shanks.

قَالَ إِنَّهُۥ صَرْحٌ مُّمَرَّدٌ مِّن قَوَارِيرَ   He said, 'It is a palace paved with crystal.'

قَالَتْ رَبِّ      She said, 'My Lord!

إِنِّى ظَلَمْتُ نَفْسِى      Indeed I have wronged myself,

وَأَسْلَمْتُ مَعَ سُلَيْمَـٰنَ لِلَّهِ    and I submit with Solomon to Allah,

رَبِّ ٱلْعَـٰلَمِينَ ﴿﴾      the Lord of all the worlds.'

وَلَقَدْ أَرْسَلْنَآ إِلَىٰ ثَمُودَ أَخَاهُمْ صَـٰلِحًا 45 Certainly We sent to Thamūd Ṣāliḥ, their brother,

أَنِ ٱعْبُدُواْ ٱللَّهَ      [with the summons:] 'Worship Allah!'

فَإِذَا هُمْ فَرِيقَانِ      But thereat they became two groups

يَخْتَصِمُونَ ﴿﴾      contending with each other.

قَالَ يَـٰقَوْمِ 46 He said, 'O My people!

لِمَ تَسْتَعْجِلُونَ      Why do you press

بِٱلسَّيِّئَةِ قَبْلَ ٱلْحَسَنَةِ    for evil sooner than for good?

لَوْلَا تَسْتَغْفِرُونَ ٱللَّهَ    Why do you not plead to Allah for forgiveness

---

[1] That is, 'we had knowledge of Solomon's extraordinary authority even before we saw such feats, and we had submitted ourselves to him.'

لَعَلَّكُمْ تُرْحَمُونَ ۝    so that you may receive His mercy?'

قَالُوٓاْ ٱطَّيَّرْنَا بِكَ    47 They said, 'We take for a bad omen you

وَبِمَن مَّعَكَ    and those who are with you.'

قَالَ طَـٰٓئِرُكُمْ عِندَ ٱللَّهِ    He said, 'Your bad omens are with Allah.

بَلْ أَنتُمْ قَوْمٌ تُفْتَنُونَ ۝    Rather you are a people being tested.'

وَكَانَ فِى ٱلْمَدِينَةِ تِسْعَةُ رَهْطٍ    48 There were nine persons[1] in the city

يُفْسِدُونَ فِى ٱلْأَرْضِ    who caused corruption in the land,

وَلَا يُصْلِحُونَ ۝    and did not bring about any reform.

قَالُواْ تَقَاسَمُواْ بِٱللَّهِ    49 They said, '[Let us] swear together by Allah

لَنُبَيِّتَنَّهُۥ وَأَهْلَهُۥ    that we will attack him and his family by night.

ثُمَّ لَنَقُولَنَّ لِوَلِيِّهِۦ    Then we will surely tell his heir

مَا شَهِدْنَا مَهْلِكَ أَهْلِهِۦ    that we were not present at the murder of his family

وَإِنَّا لَصَـٰدِقُونَ ۝    and we indeed speak the truth.'

وَمَكَرُواْ مَكْرًا    50 They devised a plot,

وَمَكَرْنَا مَكْرًا    and We [too] devised a plan,

وَهُمْ لَا يَشْعُرُونَ ۝    but they were not aware.

فَٱنظُرْ كَيْفَ كَانَ عَـٰقِبَةُ مَكْرِهِمْ    51 So *observe* how was the outcome of their plotting,

أَنَّا دَمَّرْنَـٰهُمْ وَقَوْمَهُمْ أَجْمَعِينَ ۝    as We destroyed them and all their people.

فَتِلْكَ بُيُوتُهُمْ خَاوِيَةًۢ    52 So there lay their houses, fallen in ruin,

بِمَا ظَلَمُوٓاْ    because of their wrongdoing.

إِنَّ فِى ذَٰلِكَ لَأٓيَةً    There is indeed a sign in that

لِّقَوْمٍ يَعْلَمُونَ ۝    for a people who have knowledge.

وَأَنجَيْنَا ٱلَّذِينَ ءَامَنُواْ    53 And We delivered those who had faith

وَكَانُواْ يَتَّقُونَ ۝    and were Godwary.

وَلُوطًا إِذْ قَالَ لِقَوْمِهِۦٓ    54 And Lot, when he said to his people,

أَتَأْتُونَ ٱلْفَـٰحِشَةَ    'What! Do you commit this indecency

وَأَنتُمْ تُبْصِرُونَ ۝    while you see [with your own eyes]?

أَئِنَّكُمْ لَتَأْتُونَ ٱلرِّجَالَ شَهْوَةً    55 Do you approach men with [sexual] desire

---

[1] Or 'nine families' (or gangs).

مِّن دُونِ ٱلنِّسَآءِ     instead of women?!

بَلۡ أَنتُمۡ قَوۡمٌ تَجۡهَلُونَ ۝    Rather you are a senseless lot!'

[PART 20]

فَمَا كَانَ جَوَابَ قَوۡمِهِۦٓ إِلَّآ أَن قَالُوٓاْ    56 But the only answer of his people was that they said,

أَخۡرِجُوٓاْ ءَالَ لُوطٖ مِّن قَرۡيَتِكُمۡۖ    'Expel Lot's family from your town!

إِنَّهُمۡ أُنَاسٌ يَتَطَهَّرُونَ ۝    They are indeed a puritanical lot.'

فَأَنجَيۡنَٰهُ وَأَهۡلَهُۥٓ إِلَّا ٱمۡرَأَتَهُۥ    57 So We delivered him and his family, except his wife.

قَدَّرۡنَٰهَا    We ordained her to be

مِنَ ٱلۡغَٰبِرِينَ ۝    among those who remained behind.

وَأَمۡطَرۡنَا عَلَيۡهِم مَّطَرٗاۖ    58 Then We poured down upon them a rain [of stones].

فَسَآءَ مَطَرُ ٱلۡمُنذَرِينَ ۝    So evil was the rain of those who were warned!

قُلِ ٱلۡحَمۡدُ لِلَّهِ    59 *Say*, 'All praise belongs to Allah,

وَسَلَٰمٌ عَلَىٰ عِبَادِهِ    and Peace be to His servants

ٱلَّذِينَ ٱصۡطَفَىٰٓۗ    whom He has chosen.'

ءَآللَّهُ خَيۡرٌ أَمَّا يُشۡرِكُونَ ۝    Is Allah better, or the partners they ascribe [to Him]?

أَمَّنۡ خَلَقَ ٱلسَّمَٰوَٰتِ وَٱلۡأَرۡضَ    60 Is He who created the heavens and the earth,

وَأَنزَلَ لَكُم مِّنَ ٱلسَّمَآءِ مَآءٗ    and sends down for you water from the sky,

فَأَنۢبَتۡنَا بِهِۦ حَدَآئِقَ ذَاتَ بَهۡجَةٖ    whereby We grow delightful gardens,

مَّا كَانَ لَكُمۡ أَن تُنۢبِتُواْ شَجَرَهَآ    whose trees you could never cause to grow. . . ?[1]

أَءِلَٰهٌ مَّعَ ٱللَّهِ    What! Is there a god besides Allah?

بَلۡ هُمۡ قَوۡمٞ يَعۡدِلُونَ ۝    Rather they are a lot who equate [others with Allah].

أَمَّن جَعَلَ ٱلۡأَرۡضَ قَرَارٗا    61 Is He who made the earth an abode [for you],

وَجَعَلَ خِلَٰلَهَآ أَنۡهَٰرٗا    and made rivers [flowing] through it,

وَجَعَلَ لَهَا رَوَٰسِيَ    and set firm mountains for it,

وَجَعَلَ بَيۡنَ ٱلۡبَحۡرَيۡنِ حَاجِزًاۗ    and set a barrier between the two seas. . . ?

أَءِلَٰهٌ مَّعَ ٱللَّهِ    What! Is there a god besides Allah?

بَلۡ أَكۡثَرُهُمۡ لَا يَعۡلَمُونَ ۝    Rather most of them do not know.

أَمَّن يُجِيبُ ٱلۡمُضۡطَرَّ    62 Is He who answers the call of the distressed [person]

---

[1] Ellipsis. The omitted phrase here and in the following verses (61-64) is 'better or the partners they ascribe to Him.'

إِذَا دَعَاهُ — when he invokes Him

وَيَكْشِفُ ٱلسُّوٓءَ — and removes his distress,

وَيَجْعَلُكُمْ خُلَفَآءَ ٱلْأَرْضِ — and makes you the earth's successors...?

أَءِلَٰهٌ مَّعَ ٱللَّهِ — What! Is there a god besides Allah?

قَلِيلًا مَّا تَذَكَّرُونَ ⦿ — Little is the admonition that you take.

63 أَمَّن يَهْدِيكُمْ — Is He who guides you

فِى ظُلُمَٰتِ ٱلْبَرِّ وَٱلْبَحْرِ — in the darkness of land and sea

وَمَن يُرْسِلُ ٱلرِّيَٰحَ — and who sends the winds

بُشْرًۢا بَيْنَ يَدَىْ رَحْمَتِهِۦٓ — as harbingers of His mercy...?

أَءِلَٰهٌ مَّعَ ٱللَّهِ — What! Is there a god besides Allah?

تَعَٰلَى ٱللَّهُ — Exalted is Allah

عَمَّا يُشْرِكُونَ ⦿ — above [having] any partners they ascribe [to Him].

64 أَمَّن يَبْدَؤُا۟ ٱلْخَلْقَ — Is He who originates the creation,

ثُمَّ يُعِيدُهُۥ — then He will bring it back,

وَمَن يَرْزُقُكُم مِّنَ ٱلسَّمَآءِ — and who provides for you from the sky

وَٱلْأَرْضِ — and the earth...?

أَءِلَٰهٌ مَّعَ ٱللَّهِ — What! Is there a god besides Allah?

قُلْ هَاتُوا۟ بُرْهَٰنَكُمْ — Say, 'Produce your evidence,

إِن كُنتُمْ صَٰدِقِينَ ⦿ — should you be truthful.'

65 قُل — Say,

لَّا يَعْلَمُ مَن فِى ٱلسَّمَٰوَٰتِ وَٱلْأَرْضِ — 'No one in the heavens or the earth knows

ٱلْغَيْبَ — the Unseen

إِلَّا ٱللَّهُ — except Allah,

وَمَا يَشْعُرُونَ — and they are not aware

أَيَّانَ يُبْعَثُونَ ⦿ — when they will be resurrected.'

66 بَلِ ٱدَّٰرَكَ عِلْمُهُمْ فِى ٱلْءَاخِرَةِ — Do they comprehend the knowledge of the Hereafter?

بَلْ هُمْ فِى شَكٍّ مِّنْهَا — No, they are in doubt about it.

بَلْ هُم مِّنْهَا عَمُونَ ⦿ — Rather they are blind to it.

وَقَالَ ٱلَّذِينَ كَفَرُوٓاْ 67 The faithless say,

أَءِذَا كُنَّا تُرَٰبًا وَءَابَآؤُنَآ    'What! When we and our fathers have become dust

أَئِنَّا لَمُخْرَجُونَ ۝      shall we indeed be raised [from the dead]?

لَقَدْ وُعِدْنَا هَٰذَا نَحْنُ وَءَابَآؤُنَا 68 Certainly we and our fathers were promised this

مِن قَبْلُ      before.

إِنْ هَٰذَآ إِلَّآ أَسَٰطِيرُ ٱلْأَوَّلِينَ ۝      [But] these are just myths of the ancients.'

قُلْ سِيرُواْ فِى ٱلْأَرْضِ 69 *Say,* 'Travel over the land

فَٱنظُرُواْ      and then observe

كَيْفَ كَانَ عَٰقِبَةُ ٱلْمُجْرِمِينَ ۝      how was the fate of the guilty.'

وَلَا تَحْزَنْ عَلَيْهِمْ 70 *Do not grieve* for them,

وَلَا تَكُن فِى ضَيْقٍ مِّمَّا يَمْكُرُونَ ۝    and do not be upset by their guile.

وَيَقُولُونَ مَتَىٰ هَٰذَا ٱلْوَعْدُ 71 They say, 'When will this promise be fulfilled,

إِن كُنتُمْ صَٰدِقِينَ ۝      should you be truthful?

قُلْ عَسَىٰٓ أَن يَكُونَ رَدِفَ لَكُم 72 *Say,* 'Perhaps right behind you there is

بَعْضُ ٱلَّذِى تَسْتَعْجِلُونَ ۝      some of what you seek to hasten.'

وَإِنَّ رَبَّكَ لَذُو فَضْلٍ عَلَى ٱلنَّاسِ 73 Indeed *your* Lord is gracious to mankind,

وَلَٰكِنَّ أَكْثَرَهُمْ لَا يَشْكُرُونَ ۝      but most of them do not give thanks.

وَإِنَّ رَبَّكَ لَيَعْلَمُ 74 *Your* Lord indeed knows

مَا تُكِنُّ صُدُورُهُمْ      whatever their breasts conceal,

وَمَا يُعْلِنُونَ ۝      and whatever they disclose.

وَمَا مِنْ غَآئِبَةٍ فِى ٱلسَّمَآءِ 75 There is no invisible thing in the heaven

وَٱلْأَرْضِ      and the earth

إِلَّا فِى كِتَٰبٍ مُّبِينٍ ۝      but it is in a manifest Book.[1]

إِنَّ هَٰذَا ٱلْقُرْءَانَ يَقُصُّ 76 Indeed this Qur'ān recounts

عَلَىٰ بَنِىٓ إِسْرَٰٓءِيلَ      to the Children of Israel

أَكْثَرَ ٱلَّذِى هُمْ فِيهِ يَخْتَلِفُونَ ۝      most of what they differ about,

وَإِنَّهُ لَهُدًى وَرَحْمَةٌ 77 and it is indeed a guidance and mercy

لِّلْمُؤْمِنِينَ ۝      for the faithful.

إِنَّ رَبَّكَ يَقْضِى بَيْنَهُم 78 Indeed *your* Lord will decide between them

---

[1] That is, in 'the Guarded Tablet.'

بِحُكْمِهِۦ

وَهُوَ ٱلْعَزِيزُ ٱلْعَلِيمُ ۝ by His judgement,

and He is the All-mighty, the All-knowing.

فَتَوَكَّلْ عَلَى ٱللَّهِ 79 So put *your* trust in Allah,

إِنَّكَ عَلَى ٱلْحَقِّ ٱلْمُبِينِ ۝     for *you* indeed stand on the manifest truth.

إِنَّكَ لَا تُسْمِعُ ٱلْمَوْتَىٰ 80 Indeed *you* cannot make the dead hear,

وَلَا تُسْمِعُ ٱلصُّمَّ ٱلدُّعَآءَ     nor can *you* make the deaf hear the call

إِذَا وَلَّوْا۟ مُدْبِرِينَ ۝     when they turn their backs [upon *you*],

وَمَآ أَنتَ بِهَـٰدِى ٱلْعُمْىِ 81 nor can *you* lead the blind

عَن ضَلَـٰلَتِهِمْ     out of their error.

إِن تُسْمِعُ إِلَّا مَن     *You* can make only those hear

يُؤْمِنُ بِـَٔايَـٰتِنَا فَهُم مُّسْلِمُونَ ۝ ❁     who believe in Our signs and who have submitted.

وَإِذَا وَقَعَ ٱلْقَوْلُ عَلَيْهِمْ 82 And when the word [of judgement] falls upon them,

أَخْرَجْنَا هُمْ دَآبَّةً مِّنَ ٱلْأَرْضِ     We shall bring out for them an Animal[1] from the earth

تُكَلِّمُهُمْ     who shall speak to them

أَنَّ ٱلنَّاسَ كَانُوا۟ بِـَٔايَـٰتِنَا لَا يُوقِنُونَ ۝     that the people had no faith in Our signs.

وَيَوْمَ نَحْشُرُ مِن كُلِّ أُمَّةٍ 83 The day We shall resurrect[2] from every nation

فَوْجًا مِّمَّن يُكَذِّبُ بِـَٔايَـٰتِنَا     a group of those who denied Our signs,

فَهُمْ يُوزَعُونَ ۝     and they shall be held in check.

حَتَّىٰٓ إِذَا جَآءُو 84 When they come,

قَالَ أَكَذَّبْتُم بِـَٔايَـٰتِى     He will say, 'Did you deny My signs

وَلَمْ تُحِيطُوا۟ بِهَا عِلْمًا     without comprehending them in knowledge?

أَمَّاذَا كُنتُمْ تَعْمَلُونَ ۝     What was it that you used to do?'

وَوَقَعَ ٱلْقَوْلُ عَلَيْهِم 85 And the word [of judgement] shall fall upon them

بِمَا ظَلَمُوا۟     for their wrongdoing,

فَهُمْ لَا يَنطِقُونَ ۝     and they will not speak.

أَلَمْ يَرَوْا۟ أَنَّا جَعَلْنَا ٱلَّيْلَ 86 Do they not see that We made the night

لِيَسْكُنُوا۟ فِيهِ     that they may rest in it,

---

[1] Or 'a beast.'

[2] See 20:124-125 where *hashr* is used in the sense of resurrection.

وَٱلنَّهَارَ مُبْصِرًا    and the day to provide visibility.

إِنَّ فِى ذَٰلِكَ لَـَٔايَٰتٍ    There are indeed signs in that

لِّقَوْمٍ يُؤْمِنُونَ ۝    for a people who have faith.

وَيَوْمَ يُنفَخُ فِى ٱلصُّورِ    87 The day when the trumpet will be blown,

فَفَزِعَ مَن فِى ٱلسَّمَٰوَٰتِ    whoever is in the heavens will be terrified

وَمَن فِى ٱلْأَرْضِ    and whoever is on the earth,

إِلَّا مَن شَآءَ ٱللَّهُ    except whomever Allah may wish,

وَكُلٌّ أَتَوْهُ دَٰخِرِينَ ۝    and all will come to Him in utter humility.

وَتَرَى ٱلْجِبَالَ    88 And *you* see the mountains,

تَحْسَبُهَا جَامِدَةً    which *you* suppose to be stationary,

وَهِىَ تَمُرُّ مَرَّ ٱلسَّحَابِ    while they drift like passing clouds

صُنْعَ ٱللَّهِ    —the handiwork of Allah

ٱلَّذِىٓ أَتْقَنَ كُلَّ شَىْءٍ    who has made everything faultless.

إِنَّهُۥ خَبِيرٌۢ بِمَا تَفْعَلُونَ ۝    He is indeed well aware of what you do.

مَن جَآءَ بِٱلْحَسَنَةِ    89 Whoever brings virtue

فَلَهُۥ خَيْرٌ مِّنْهَا    shall receive [a reward] better than it;

وَهُم مِّن فَزَعٍ يَوْمَئِذٍ ءَامِنُونَ ۝    and they shall be secure from terror on that day.

وَمَن جَآءَ بِٱلسَّيِّئَةِ    90 And whoever brings vice

فَكُبَّتْ وُجُوهُهُمْ فِى ٱلنَّارِ    —they shall be cast on their faces into the Fire

هَلْ تُجْزَوْنَ    [and told:] 'Shall you be requited

إِلَّا مَا كُنتُمْ تَعْمَلُونَ ۝    except with what you used to do?'

إِنَّمَآ أُمِرْتُ    91 'Indeed I have been commanded

أَنْ أَعْبُدَ رَبَّ هَٰذِهِ ٱلْبَلْدَةِ    to worship the Lord of this city[1]

ٱلَّذِى حَرَّمَهَا    who has made it inviolable[2]

وَلَهُۥ كُلُّ شَىْءٍ    and to whom all things belong,

وَأُمِرْتُ    and I have been commanded

---

[1] That is, the holy city of Makkah.
[2] Or 'sacred.'

أَنْ أَكُونَ مِنَ ٱلْمُسْلِمِينَ ۝    to be among those who submit [to Allah],

92 وَأَنْ أَتْلُوَا ٱلْقُرْءَانَ    and to recite the Qur'ān.'

فَمَنِ ٱهْتَدَىٰ    So whoever is guided

فَإِنَّمَا يَهْتَدِى لِنَفْسِهِ    is guided only for his own sake,

وَمَن ضَلَّ    and as for him who goes astray,

فَقُلْ إِنَّمَآ أَنَا۟ مِنَ ٱلْمُنذِرِينَ ۝    say, 'I am just one of the warners.'

93 وَقُلِ ٱلْحَمْدُ لِلَّهِ    And say, 'All praise belongs to Allah.

سَيُرِيكُمْ ءَايَٰتِهِ    Soon He will show you His signs,

فَتَعْرِفُونَهَا    and you will recognize them.'

وَمَا رَبُّكَ بِغَٰفِلٍ عَمَّا تَعْمَلُونَ ۝    And *your* Lord is not oblivious of what you do.

## سُورَةُ الْقَصَصِ    28. SŪRAT AL-QAṢAṢ[1]

بِسْمِ ٱللَّهِ    In the Name of Allah,

ٱلرَّحْمَٰنِ ٱلرَّحِيمِ    the All-beneficent, the All-merciful.

1 طسٓمٓ ۝    *Ṭā, Sīn, Mīm.*

2 تِلْكَ ءَايَٰتُ ٱلْكِتَٰبِ ٱلْمُبِينِ ۝    These are the signs of the Manifest Book.

3 نَتْلُوا۟ عَلَيْكَ    We relate to *you*

مِن نَّبَإِ مُوسَىٰ وَفِرْعَوْنَ بِٱلْحَقِّ    truly some of the account of Moses and Pharaoh

لِقَوْمٍ يُؤْمِنُونَ ۝    for a people who have faith.

4 إِنَّ فِرْعَوْنَ عَلَا فِى ٱلْأَرْضِ    Indeed Pharaoh domineered in the land,

وَجَعَلَ أَهْلَهَا شِيَعًا    reducing its people into factions,

يَسْتَضْعِفُ طَآئِفَةً مِّنْهُمْ    abasing one group of them,

يُذَبِّحُ أَبْنَآءَهُمْ وَيَسْتَحْىِۦ نِسَآءَهُمْ    slaughtering their sons and sparing their women.

إِنَّهُۥ كَانَ مِنَ ٱلْمُفْسِدِينَ ۝    Indeed He was one of the agents of corruption.

5 وَنُرِيدُ أَن نَّمُنَّ    And We desired to show favour

عَلَى ٱلَّذِينَ ٱسْتُضْعِفُوا۟ فِى ٱلْأَرْضِ    to those who were abased in the land,

وَنَجْعَلَهُمْ أَئِمَّةً    and to make them *imams*,

---

[1] The *sūrah* takes its name from verse 25 wherein the word *qaṣaṣ* (story) occurs.

| | |
|---|---|
| وَنَجْعَلَهُمُ ٱلْوَٰرِثِينَ ۝ | and to make them the heirs, |
| وَنُمَكِّنَ لَهُمْ فِى ٱلْأَرْضِ | 6 and to establish them in the land, |
| وَنُرِىَ فِرْعَوْنَ وَهَٰمَٰنَ | and to show Pharaoh and Hāmān |
| وَجُنُودَهُمَا | and their hosts |
| مِنْهُم | from them[1] |
| مَّا كَانُوا۟ يَحْذَرُونَ ۝ | that of which they were apprehensive. |
| وَأَوْحَيْنَآ إِلَىٰٓ أُمِّ مُوسَىٰٓ | 7 We revealed to Moses' mother, |
| أَنْ أَرْضِعِيهِ | [saying], 'Nurse him; |
| فَإِذَا خِفْتِ عَلَيْهِ فَأَلْقِيهِ فِى ٱلْيَمِّ | then, when you fear for him, cast him into the river, |
| وَلَا تَخَافِى وَلَا تَحْزَنِىٓ | and do not fear or grieve, |
| إِنَّا رَآدُّوهُ إِلَيْكِ | for We will restore him to you |
| وَجَاعِلُوهُ مِنَ ٱلْمُرْسَلِينَ ۝ | and make him one of the apostles.' |
| فَٱلْتَقَطَهُۥٓ ءَالُ فِرْعَوْنَ | 8 Then Pharaoh's kinsmen picked him up |
| لِيَكُونَ لَهُمْ عَدُوًّا | that he might be to them an enemy |
| وَحَزَنًا | and a cause of grief. |
| إِنَّ فِرْعَوْنَ وَهَٰمَٰنَ | Indeed Pharaoh and Hāmān |
| وَجُنُودَهُمَا | and their hosts |
| كَانُوا۟ خَٰطِئِينَ ۝ | were iniquitous. |
| وَقَالَتِ ٱمْرَأَتُ فِرْعَوْنَ | 9 Pharaoh's wife said [to Pharaoh], |
| قُرَّتُ عَيْنٍ لِّى | '[This infant will be] a [source of] comfort to me |
| وَلَكَ | and to you. |
| لَا تَقْتُلُوهُ | Do not kill him. |
| عَسَىٰٓ أَن يَنفَعَنَآ | Maybe he will benefit us, |
| أَوْ نَتَّخِذَهُۥ وَلَدًا | or we will adopt him as a son.' |
| وَهُمْ لَا يَشْعُرُونَ ۝ | And they were not aware. |
| وَأَصْبَحَ فُؤَادُ أُمِّ مُوسَىٰ فَٰرِغًا | 10 The heart of Moses' mother became desolate, |
| إِن كَادَتْ لَتُبْدِى بِهِۦٓ | and indeed she was about to divulge it |
| لَوْلَآ أَن رَّبَطْنَا عَلَىٰ قَلْبِهَا | had We not fortified her heart |
| لِتَكُونَ مِنَ ٱلْمُؤْمِنِينَ ۝ | so that she might have faith [in Allah's promise]. |

---

[1] That is, from the Israelites.

وَقَالَتْ لِأُخْتِهِ قُصِّيهِ    11 She said to his sister, 'Follow him.'

فَبَصُرَتْ بِهِ عَن جُنُبٍ    So she watched him from a distance,

وَهُمْ لَا يَشْعُرُونَ ۝    while they were not aware.

وَحَرَّمْنَا عَلَيْهِ ٱلْمَرَاضِعَ    12 We had forbidden him to be suckled by any nurse

مِن قَبْلُ    since before.

فَقَالَتْ هَلْ أَدُلُّكُمْ عَلَىٰ أَهْلِ بَيْتٍ    So she[1] said, 'Shall I show you a household

يَكْفُلُونَهُ لَكُمْ    that will take care of him for you

وَهُمْ لَهُ نَصِحُونَ ۝    and will be his well-wishers?'

فَرَدَدْنَٰهُ إِلَىٰ أُمِّهِ    13 Thus We restored him to his mother

كَىْ تَقَرَّ عَيْنُهَا    so that she might be comforted

وَلَا تَحْزَنَ    and not grieve,

وَلِتَعْلَمَ أَنَّ وَعْدَ ٱللَّهِ حَقٌّ    and that she might know that Allah's promise is true,

وَلَٰكِنَّ أَكْثَرَهُمْ لَا يَعْلَمُونَ ۝    but most of them do not know.

وَلَمَّا بَلَغَ أَشُدَّهُ وَٱسْتَوَىٰ    14 When he came of age and became fully matured,

ءَاتَيْنَٰهُ حُكْمًا وَعِلْمًا    We gave him judgement and knowledge,

وَكَذَٰلِكَ نَجْزِى ٱلْمُحْسِنِينَ ۝    and thus do We reward the virtuous.

وَدَخَلَ ٱلْمَدِينَةَ    15 [One day] he entered the city

عَلَىٰ حِينِ غَفْلَةٍ مِّنْ أَهْلِهَا    at a time when its people dwelt in distraction.

فَوَجَدَ فِيهَا رَجُلَيْنِ يَقْتَتِلَانِ    He found there two men fighting,

هَٰذَا مِن شِيعَتِهِ    this one from among his followers,

وَهَٰذَا مِنْ عَدُوِّهِ    and that one from his enemies.

فَٱسْتَغَٰثَهُ ٱلَّذِى مِن شِيعَتِهِ    The one who was from his followers sought his help

عَلَى ٱلَّذِى مِنْ عَدُوِّهِ    against him who was from his enemies.

فَوَكَزَهُ مُوسَىٰ    So Moses hit him with his fist,

فَقَضَىٰ عَلَيْهِ    whereupon he expired.

قَالَ هَٰذَا مِنْ عَمَلِ ٱلشَّيْطَٰنِ    He said, 'This is of Satan's doing.

إِنَّهُ عَدُوٌّ مُّضِلٌّ مُّبِينٌ ۝    Indeed he is an enemy, manifestly misguiding.'

قَالَ رَبِّ    16 He said, 'My Lord!

إِنِّى ظَلَمْتُ نَفْسِى فَٱغْفِرْ لِى    I have wronged myself. Forgive me!'

---

[1] That is, Moses' sister.

فَغَفَرَ لَهُ
So He forgave him.

إِنَّهُ هُوَ ٱلْغَفُورُ ٱلرَّحِيمُ ۝
Indeed He is the All-forgiving, the All-merciful.

قَالَ رَبِّ 17
17 He said, 'My Lord!

بِمَآ أَنْعَمْتَ عَلَىَّ
As You have blessed me,

فَلَنْ أَكُونَ ظَهِيرًا لِّلْمُجْرِمِينَ ۝
I will never be a supporter of the guilty.'

فَأَصْبَحَ فِى ٱلْمَدِينَةِ 18
18 He rose at dawn in the city,

خَآئِفًا يَتَرَقَّبُ
fearful and vigilant,

فَإِذَا ٱلَّذِى ٱسْتَنصَرَهُ
when behold, the one who had sought his help

بِٱلْأَمْسِ
the day before,

يَسْتَصْرِخُهُ
shouted for his help [once again].

قَالَ لَهُ مُوسَىٰ
Moses said to him,

إِنَّكَ لَغَوِىٌّ مُّبِينٌ ۝
'You are indeed manifestly perverse!'

فَلَمَّآ أَنْ أَرَادَ أَن يَبْطِشَ بِٱلَّذِى 19
19 But when he wanted to strike him

هُوَ عَدُوٌّ لَّهُمَا
who was an enemy of both of them,

قَالَ يَٰمُوسَىٰٓ أَتُرِيدُ أَن تَقْتُلَنِى
he said, 'Moses, do you want to kill me,

كَمَا قَتَلْتَ نَفْسًا بِٱلْأَمْسِ
just like the one you killed yesterday?

إِن تُرِيدُ إِلَّآ أَن تَكُونَ جَبَّارًا
You just want to be a tyrant

فِى ٱلْأَرْضِ
in the land,

وَمَا تُرِيدُ أَن تَكُونَ
and you do not desire to be

مِنَ ٱلْمُصْلِحِينَ ۝
of those who bring about reform.'[1]

وَجَآءَ رَجُلٌ مِّنْ أَقْصَا ٱلْمَدِينَةِ 20
20 And there came a man from the city outskirts,

يَسْعَىٰ
hurrying.

قَالَ يَٰمُوسَىٰٓ
He said, 'Moses!

إِنَّ ٱلْمَلَأَ يَأْتَمِرُونَ بِكَ لِيَقْتُلُوكَ
The elite are indeed conspiring to kill you.

فَٱخْرُجْ
So leave.

إِنِّى لَكَ مِنَ ٱلنَّٰصِحِينَ ۝
I am indeed your well-wisher.'

فَخَرَجَ مِنْهَا خَآئِفًا يَتَرَقَّبُ 21
21 So he left the city, fearful and vigilant.

قَالَ رَبِّ
He said, 'My Lord!

---

[1] Although Moses wanted to help him again much against his own inclination, the Israelite thought that Moses was going to attack him.

نَجِّنِى مِنَ ٱلْقَوْمِ ٱلظَّٰلِمِينَ ۞

Deliver me from the wrongdoing lot.'

وَلَمَّا تَوَجَّهَ تِلْقَآءَ مَدْيَنَ

22 And when he turned his face toward Midian,

قَالَ عَسَىٰ رَبِّىٓ

he said, 'Maybe my Lord

أَن يَهْدِيَنِى سَوَآءَ ٱلسَّبِيلِ ۞

will show me the right way.'

وَلَمَّا وَرَدَ مَآءَ مَدْيَنَ

23 When he arrived at the well of Midian,

وَجَدَ عَلَيْهِ أُمَّةً مِّنَ ٱلنَّاسِ يَسْقُونَ

he found there a throng of people watering [their flocks],

وَوَجَدَ مِن دُونِهِمُ ٱمْرَأَتَيْنِ تَذُودَانِ

and he found, besides them, two women holding back [their flock].

قَالَ مَا خَطْبُكُمَا

He said, 'What is your business?'

قَالَتَا لَا نَسْقِى

They said, 'We do not water [our flock]

حَتَّىٰ يُصْدِرَ ٱلرِّعَآءُ

until the shepherds have driven out [their flocks],

وَأَبُونَا شَيْخٌ كَبِيرٌ ۞

and our father is an aged man.'

فَسَقَىٰ لَهُمَا

24 So he watered [their flock] for them.

ثُمَّ تَوَلَّىٰ إِلَى ٱلظِّلِّ

Then he withdrew toward the shade

فَقَالَ رَبِّ

and said, 'My Lord!

إِنِّى

I am indeed

لِمَآ أَنزَلْتَ إِلَىَّ مِنْ خَيْرٍ فَقِيرٌ ۞

in need of any good You may send down to me!'

فَجَآءَتْهُ إِحْدَىٰهُمَا

25 Then one of the two women approached him,

تَمْشِى عَلَى ٱسْتِحْيَآءٍ

walking bashfully.

قَالَتْ إِنَّ أَبِى يَدْعُوكَ

She said, 'Indeed my father invites you

لِيَجْزِيَكَ أَجْرَ

to pay you the wages

مَا سَقَيْتَ لَنَا

for watering [our flock] for us.'

فَلَمَّا جَآءَهُ

So when he came to him

وَقَصَّ عَلَيْهِ ٱلْقَصَصَ

and recounted the story to him,

قَالَ لَا تَخَفْ

he said, 'Do not be afraid.

نَجَوْتَ مِنَ ٱلْقَوْمِ ٱلظَّٰلِمِينَ ۞

You have been delivered from the wrongdoing lot.'

قَالَتْ إِحْدَىٰهُمَا يَٰٓأَبَتِ ٱسْتَـْٔجِرْهُ

26 One of the two women said, 'Father, hire him.

إِنَّ خَيْرَ مَنِ ٱسْتَـْٔجَرْتَ

Indeed the best you can hire

ٱلْقَوِىُّ ٱلْأَمِينُ ۞

is a powerful and trustworthy man.'

قَالَ 27 He said,

إِنِّىٓ أُرِيدُ أَنۡ أُنكِحَكَ    'Indeed I desire to marry you

إِحۡدَى ٱبۡنَتَىَّ هَٰتَيۡنِ      to one of these two daughters of mine,

عَلَىٰٓ أَن تَأۡجُرَنِى       on condition that you hire yourself to me

ثَمَٰنِىَ حِجَجٍ        for eight years.

فَإِنۡ أَتۡمَمۡتَ عَشۡرًا    And if you complete ten,

فَمِنۡ عِندِكَ      that will be up to you,

وَمَآ أُرِيدُ أَنۡ أَشُقَّ عَلَيۡكَ   and I do not want to be hard on you.

سَتَجِدُنِىٓ إِن شَآءَ ٱللَّهُ   God willing, you will find me to be

مِنَ ٱلصَّٰلِحِينَ ۝     one of the righteous.'

قَالَ 28 He said,

ذَٰلِكَ بَيۡنِى وَبَيۡنَكَ   'This will be [by consent] between you and me.

أَيَّمَا ٱلۡأَجَلَيۡنِ قَضَيۡتُ   Whichever of the two terms I complete,

فَلَا عُدۡوَٰنَ عَلَىَّ     there shall be no reprisal against me,[1]

وَٱللَّهُ عَلَىٰ مَا نَقُولُ وَكِيلٌ ۝   and Allah is witness over what we say.'

فَلَمَّا قَضَىٰ مُوسَى ٱلۡأَجَلَ 29 So when Moses completed the term

وَسَارَ بِأَهۡلِهِۦٓ       and set out with his family,

ءَانَسَ مِن جَانِبِ ٱلطُّورِ نَارًا   he descried a fire on the side of the mountain.

قَالَ لِأَهۡلِهِ ٱمۡكُثُوٓا۟    He said to his family, 'Wait!

إِنِّىٓ ءَانَسۡتُ نَارًا     Indeed I descry a fire!

لَّعَلِّىٓ ءَاتِيكُم مِّنۡهَا بِخَبَرٍ   Maybe I will bring you some news from it,

أَوۡ جَذۡوَةٍ مِّنَ ٱلنَّارِ   or a brand of fire

لَعَلَّكُمۡ تَصۡطَلُونَ ۝   so that you may warm yourselves.'

فَلَمَّآ أَتَىٰهَا 30 When he approached it,

نُودِىَ مِن شَٰطِئِ ٱلۡوَادِ ٱلۡأَيۡمَنِ   he was called from the right bank of the valley

فِى ٱلۡبُقۡعَةِ ٱلۡمُبَٰرَكَةِ   at the blessed spot

مِنَ ٱلشَّجَرَةِ     from the tree:

أَن يَٰمُوسَىٰٓ      'Moses!

إِنِّىٓ أَنَا ٱللَّهُ رَبُّ ٱلۡعَٰلَمِينَ ۝   Indeed I am Allah, the Lord of all the worlds!'

---

[1] Or 'it shall be no unfairness toward me.'

وَأَنْ أَلْقِ عَصَاكَ 31    And: 'Throw down your staff!'

فَلَمَّا رَءَاهَا تَهْتَزُّ كَأَنَّهَا جَآنٌّ    And when he saw it wriggling as if it were a snake,

وَلَّىٰ مُدْبِرًا وَلَمْ يُعَقِّبْ    he turned his back [to flee], without looking back.

يَٰمُوسَىٰ أَقْبِلْ وَلَا تَخَفْ    'Moses! Come forward, and do not be afraid.

إِنَّكَ مِنَ ٱلْءَامِنِينَ ۝    Indeed you are safe.'

ٱسْلُكْ يَدَكَ فِى جَيْبِكَ 32    'Insert your hand into your bosom.

تَخْرُجْ بَيْضَآءَ مِنْ غَيْرِ سُوٓءٍ    It will emerge white, without any fault,

وَٱضْمُمْ إِلَيْكَ جَنَاحَكَ مِنَ ٱلرَّهْبِ    and keep your arms drawn in awe to your sides.

فَذَٰنِكَ بُرْهَٰنَانِ مِن رَّبِّكَ    These shall be two proofs from your Lord

إِلَىٰ فِرْعَوْنَ وَمَلَإِيْهِۦٓ    to Pharaoh and his elite.

إِنَّهُمْ كَانُوا۟ قَوْمًا فَٰسِقِينَ ۝    They are indeed a transgressing lot.'

قَالَ رَبِّ 33   He said, 'My Lord!

إِنِّى قَتَلْتُ مِنْهُمْ نَفْسًا    Indeed I have killed one of their men,

فَأَخَافُ أَن يَقْتُلُونِ ۝    so I fear they will kill me.

وَأَخِى هَٰرُونُ 34   Aaron, my brother

هُوَ أَفْصَحُ مِنِّى لِسَانًا    —he is more eloquent than me in speech.

فَأَرْسِلْهُ مَعِىَ رِدْءًا يُصَدِّقُنِىٓ    So send him with me as a helper to confirm me,

إِنِّىٓ أَخَافُ أَن يُكَذِّبُونِ ۝    for I fear that they will impugn me.'

قَالَ سَنَشُدُّ عَضُدَكَ 35   He said, 'We will strengthen your arm

بِأَخِيكَ    by means of your brother,

وَنَجْعَلُ لَكُمَا سُلْطَٰنًا    and invest both of you with such authority

فَلَا يَصِلُونَ إِلَيْكُمَا    that they will not touch you.

بِـَٔايَٰتِنَآ أَنتُمَا    With the help of Our signs, you two,

وَمَنِ ٱتَّبَعَكُمَا    and those who follow the two of you,

ٱلْغَٰلِبُونَ ۝    shall be the victors.'

فَلَمَّا جَآءَهُم مُّوسَىٰ بِـَٔايَٰتِنَا بَيِّنَٰتٍ 36 When Moses brought them Our manifest signs,

قَالُوا۟ مَا هَٰذَآ إِلَّا سِحْرٌ مُّفْتَرًى    they said, 'This is nothing but concocted magic.

وَمَا سَمِعْنَا بِهَٰذَا    We never heard of such a thing

فِىٓ ءَابَآئِنَا ٱلْأَوَّلِينَ ۝    among our forefathers.'

وَقَالَ مُوسَىٰ رَبِّىٓ أَعْلَمُ 37 Moses said, 'My Lord knows best

بِمَن جَآءَ بِٱلْهُدَىٰ مِنْ عِندِهِۦ  who brings guidance from Him,

وَمَن تَكُونُ لَهُۥ عَٰقِبَةُ ٱلدَّارِ  and in whose favour the outcome of that abode will be.

إِنَّهُۥ لَا يُفْلِحُ ٱلظَّٰلِمُونَ ۝  The wrongdoers will not be felicitous.'

وَقَالَ فِرْعَوْنُ يَٰٓأَيُّهَا ٱلْمَلَأُ  38 Pharaoh said, 'O [members of the] elite!

مَا عَلِمْتُ لَكُم مِّنْ إِلَٰهٍ  I do not know of any god that you may have

غَيْرِى  other than me.

فَأَوْقِدْ لِى يَٰهَٰمَٰنُ عَلَى ٱلطِّينِ  Hāmān, light for me a fire over clay,[1]

فَٱجْعَل لِّى صَرْحًا  and build me a tower

لَّعَلِّىٓ أَطَّلِعُ إِلَىٰٓ إِلَٰهِ مُوسَىٰ  so that I may take a look at Moses' god,

وَإِنِّى لَأَظُنُّهُۥ مِنَ ٱلْكَٰذِبِينَ ۝  and indeed I consider him to be a liar!'

وَٱسْتَكْبَرَ هُوَ وَجُنُودُهُۥ  39 He and his hosts acted arrogantly

فِى ٱلْأَرْضِ بِغَيْرِ ٱلْحَقِّ  in the land unduly,

وَظَنُّوٓا۟ أَنَّهُمْ إِلَيْنَا لَا يُرْجَعُونَ ۝  and thought they would not be brought back to Us.

فَأَخَذْنَٰهُ وَجُنُودَهُۥ  40 So We seized him and his hosts,

فَنَبَذْنَٰهُمْ فِى ٱلْيَمِّ  and threw them into the sea.

فَٱنظُرْ كَيْفَ كَانَ عَٰقِبَةُ ٱلظَّٰلِمِينَ ۝  So *observe* how was the fate of the wrongdoers!

وَجَعَلْنَٰهُمْ أَئِمَّةً يَدْعُونَ إِلَى ٱلنَّارِ  41 We made them leaders who invite to the Fire,

وَيَوْمَ ٱلْقِيَٰمَةِ  and on the Day of Resurrection

لَا يُنصَرُونَ ۝  they will not receive any help.

وَأَتْبَعْنَٰهُمْ فِى هَٰذِهِ ٱلدُّنْيَا لَعْنَةً  42 We made a curse pursue them in this world,

وَيَوْمَ ٱلْقِيَٰمَةِ  and on the Day of Resurrection

هُم مِّنَ ٱلْمَقْبُوحِينَ ۝  they will be among the disfigured.

وَلَقَدْ ءَاتَيْنَا مُوسَى ٱلْكِتَٰبَ  43 Certainly We gave Moses the Book,

مِنۢ بَعْدِ مَآ أَهْلَكْنَا ٱلْقُرُونَ ٱلْأُولَىٰ  after We had destroyed the former generations,

بَصَآئِرَ لِلنَّاسِ  as [a set of] eye-openers for mankind,

وَهُدًى وَرَحْمَةً  and as guidance and mercy

---

[1] That is, 'Light for me kilns for baking bricks of clay to build a tower from which I may take a look at the God of Moses.' Meant as a sarcasm aimed at Moses and the Israelites, many of whom were used as forced labour to make bricks.

لَعَلَّهُمْ يَتَذَكَّرُونَ ۩    so that they may take admonition.

وَمَا كُنتَ بِجَانِبِ ٱلْغَرْبِيِّ 44 *You* were not on the western side[1]

إِذْ قَضَيْنَآ إِلَىٰ مُوسَى ٱلْأَمْرَ    when We revealed the commandments[2] to Moses,

وَمَا كُنتَ مِنَ ٱلشَّٰهِدِينَ ۩    nor were *you* among the witnesses.[3]

وَلَٰكِنَّآ أَنشَأْنَا قُرُونًا 45 But We brought forth other generations

فَتَطَاوَلَ عَلَيْهِمُ ٱلْعُمُرُ    and time took its toll on them.

وَمَا كُنتَ ثَاوِيًا فِىٓ أَهْلِ مَدْيَنَ    And *you* did not dwell among the people of Midian

تَتْلُوا۟ عَلَيْهِمْ ءَايَٰتِنَا    reciting to them Our signs,

وَلَٰكِنَّا كُنَّا مُرْسِلِينَ ۩    but it is We who are the senders [of the apostles].

وَمَا كُنتَ بِجَانِبِ ٱلطُّورِ 46 And *you* were not on the side of the Mount

إِذْ نَادَيْنَا    when We called out [to Moses],

وَلَٰكِن رَّحْمَةً مِّن رَّبِّكَ    but [We have sent *you* as] a mercy from *your* Lord

لِتُنذِرَ قَوْمًا    that *you* may warn a people

مَّآ أَتَىٰهُم مِّن نَّذِيرٍ    to whom there did not come any warner

مِّن قَبْلِكَ    before *you*,

لَعَلَّهُمْ يَتَذَكَّرُونَ ۩    so that they may take admonition.[4]

وَلَوْلَآ 47 And lest

أَن تُصِيبَهُم مُّصِيبَةٌۢ    —should an affliction visit them

بِمَا قَدَّمَتْ أَيْدِيهِمْ    because of what their hands have sent ahead[5]—

فَيَقُولُوا۟ رَبَّنَا    they should say, 'Our Lord!

لَوْلَآ أَرْسَلْتَ إِلَيْنَا رَسُولًا    Why did You not send us an apostle

فَنَتَّبِعَ ءَايَٰتِكَ    so that we might have followed Your signs

---

[1] That is, on the western side of the mountain, or valley, of Sinai.

[2] Or 'the Law.'

[3] Or, 'nor were you among those present.'

[4] That is, 'The faithless imagine that this teaching is of your own contrivance. But it was We who sent Our revelations to Moses and gave him the scripture and the Law before you even came into the world, nor it was you who lived among the people of Midian to recite Our signs to them. It was We who have been sending the apostles before you, and it is We who have sent you as a mercy and guidance to mankind, after the passage of time had taken its toll and obscured the path of the prophets.'

[5] Or 'prepared,' or 'committed.'

وَنَكُونَ مِنَ ٱلْمُؤْمِنِينَ ۝ and been among the faithful?'[1]

فَلَمَّا جَآءَهُمُ ٱلْحَقُّ مِنْ عِندِنَا 48 But when there came to them the truth from Us,

قَالُوا لَوْلَآ أُوتِيَ they said, 'Why has he not been given

مِثْلَ مَآ أُوتِيَ مُوسَىٰ the like of what Moses was given?'

أَوَلَمْ يَكْفُرُوا بِمَآ أُوتِيَ مُوسَىٰ Did they not disbelieve what Moses was given

مِن قَبْلُ before,

قَالُوا سِحْرَانِ تَظَٰهَرَا and said, 'Two magicians abetting each other,'

وَقَالُوٓا إِنَّا بِكُلٍّ كَٰفِرُونَ ۝ and said, 'Indeed we disbelieve both of them'?

قُلْ فَأْتُوا بِكِتَٰبٍ مِّنْ عِندِ ٱللَّهِ 49 Say, 'Then bring some Book from Allah

هُوَ أَهْدَىٰ مِنْهُمَآ better in guidance than the two[2]

أَتَّبِعْهُ so that I may follow it,

إِن كُنتُمْ صَٰدِقِينَ ۝ should you be truthful.'

فَإِن لَّمْ يَسْتَجِيبُوا لَكَ 50 Then if they do not respond to you[r] [summons]

فَٱعْلَمْ أَنَّمَا يَتَّبِعُونَ أَهْوَآءَهُمْ know that they only follow their desires.

وَمَنْ أَضَلُّ And who is more astray

مِمَّنِ ٱتَّبَعَ هَوَىٰهُ than him who follows his desires

بِغَيْرِ هُدًى مِّنَ ٱللَّهِ without any guidance from Allah?

إِنَّ ٱللَّهَ لَا يَهْدِى ٱلْقَوْمَ ٱلظَّٰلِمِينَ ۝ Indeed Allah does not guide the wrongdoing lot.

وَلَقَدْ وَصَّلْنَا لَهُمُ ٱلْقَوْلَ 51 Certainly We have concatenated the Word[3] for them

لَعَلَّهُمْ يَتَذَكَّرُونَ ۝ so that they may take admonition.

ٱلَّذِينَ ءَاتَيْنَٰهُمُ ٱلْكِتَٰبَ مِن قَبْلِهِۦ 52 Those to whom We gave the Book before it

هُم بِهِۦ يُؤْمِنُونَ ۝ are the ones who believe in it,

وَإِذَا يُتْلَىٰ عَلَيْهِمْ 53 and when it is recited to them,

قَالُوٓا ءَامَنَّا بِهِۦٓ they say, 'We believe in it.

إِنَّهُ ٱلْحَقُّ مِن رَّبِّنَآ It is indeed the truth from our Lord.

إِنَّا كُنَّا مِن قَبْلِهِۦ مُسْلِمِينَ ۝ Indeed we were muslims [even] before it [came].'

أُوْلَٰٓئِكَ يُؤْتَوْنَ أَجْرَهُم مَّرَّتَيْنِ 54 Those will be given their reward two times

---

[1] Cf. 20:134.

[2] That is, better than the Qur'ān and the Book revealed to Moses.

[3] That is, the Qur'ān or its verses.

547

بِمَا صَبَرُوا     for their patience.

وَيَدْرَءُونَ بِالْحَسَنَةِ السَّيِّئَةَ     They repel evil [conduct] with good,

وَمِمَّا رَزَقْنَاهُمْ يُنفِقُونَ ۝     and spend out of what We have provided them,

55 وَإِذَا سَمِعُوا اللَّغْوَ     and when they hear vain talk,

أَعْرَضُوا عَنْهُ وَقَالُوا     they avoid it and say,

لَنَا أَعْمَالُنَا     'Our deeds belong to us,

وَلَكُمْ أَعْمَالُكُمْ     and your deeds belong to you.

سَلَامٌ عَلَيْكُمْ     Peace be to you.

لَا نَبْتَغِي الْجَاهِلِينَ ۝     We do not court the ignorant.'

56 إِنَّكَ لَا تَهْدِي مَنْ أَحْبَبْتَ     *You* cannot guide whomever *you* wish,

وَلَكِنَّ اللَّهَ يَهْدِي     but [it is] Allah [who] guides

مَن يَشَاءُ     whomever He wishes,

وَهُوَ أَعْلَمُ بِالْمُهْتَدِينَ ۝     and He knows best those who are guided.

57 وَقَالُوا إِن نَّتَّبِعِ الْهُدَى مَعَكَ     They say, 'Should we follow the guidance with *you*,

نُتَخَطَّفْ مِنْ أَرْضِنَا     we will be dispossessed of our territory.'

أَوَلَمْ نُمَكِّن لَّهُمْ حَرَمًا ءَامِنًا     Did We not establish a secure sanctuary[1] for them

يُجْبَى إِلَيْهِ ثَمَرَاتُ كُلِّ شَيْءٍ     where fruits of all kinds are brought

رِزْقًا مِّن لَّدُنَّا     as a provision from Us?

وَلَكِنَّ أَكْثَرَهُمْ لَا يَعْلَمُونَ ۝     But most of them do not know.

58 وَكَمْ أَهْلَكْنَا مِن قَرْيَةٍ     How many a town We have destroyed

بَطِرَتْ مَعِيشَتَهَا     that transgressed in its lifestyle!

فَتِلْكَ مَسَاكِنُهُمْ     There lie their dwellings,

لَمْ تُسْكَن مِّنْ بَعْدِهِمْ إِلَّا قَلِيلًا     uninhabited after them except by a few,

وَكُنَّا نَحْنُ الْوَارِثِينَ ۝     and We were the [sole] inheritors.

59 وَمَا كَانَ رَبُّكَ مُهْلِكَ الْقُرَى     Your Lord would not destroy the towns

حَتَّى يَبْعَثَ فِي أُمِّهَا رَسُولًا     until He had raised an apostle in their mother city

يَتْلُوا عَلَيْهِمْ ءَايَاتِنَا     to recite to them Our signs.

وَمَا كُنَّا مُهْلِكِي الْقُرَى     We would never destroy the towns

إِلَّا وَأَهْلُهَا ظَالِمُونَ ۝     except when their people were wrongdoers.

---

[1] That is, the holy city of Makkah.

وَمَا أُوتِيتُم مِّن شَيْءٍ 60 Whatever things you have been given

فَمَتَـٰعُ ٱلْحَيَوٰةِ ٱلدُّنْيَا are only the wares of the life of this world

وَزِينَتُهَا and its glitter,

وَمَا عِندَ ٱللَّهِ خَيْرٌ and what is with Allah is better

وَأَبْقَىٰ and more lasting.

أَفَلَا تَعْقِلُونَ ۝ Will you not apply reason?

أَفَمَن وَعَدْنَـٰهُ وَعْدًا حَسَنًا 61 Is he to whom We have given a good promise,

فَهُوَ لَـٰقِيهِ which he will receive,

كَمَن مَّتَّعْنَـٰهُ like him whom We have provided

مَتَـٰعَ ٱلْحَيَوٰةِ ٱلدُّنْيَا the wares of the life of this world,

ثُمَّ هُوَ يَوْمَ ٱلْقِيَـٰمَةِ مِنَ ٱلْمُحْضَرِينَ ۝ but who will be arraigned on the Day of Resurrection?

وَيَوْمَ يُنَادِيهِمْ 62 The day He will call out to them

فَيَقُولُ أَيْنَ شُرَكَآءِىَ and say, 'Where are My partners

ٱلَّذِينَ كُنتُمْ تَزْعُمُونَ ۝ that you used to claim?'

قَالَ ٱلَّذِينَ حَقَّ عَلَيْهِمُ ٱلْقَوْلُ 63 Those against whom the word had become due will say,

رَبَّنَا 'Our Lord!

هَـٰٓؤُلَآءِ ٱلَّذِينَ أَغْوَيْنَآ These are the ones who perverted us.

أَغْوَيْنَـٰهُمْ We perverted them

كَمَا غَوَيْنَا as we were perverse ourselves.

تَبَرَّأْنَآ إِلَيْكَ We plead for non-liability before You:

مَا كَانُوٓا۟ إِيَّانَا يَعْبُدُونَ ۝ it was not us that they worshipped.'

وَقِيلَ ٱدْعُوا۟ شُرَكَآءَكُمْ 64 It will be said, 'Invoke your partners!'

فَدَعَوْهُمْ So they will invoke them,

فَلَمْ يَسْتَجِيبُوا۟ لَهُمْ but they will not respond to them,

وَرَأَوُا۟ ٱلْعَذَابَ and they will sight the punishment,

لَوْ أَنَّهُمْ كَانُوا۟ يَهْتَدُونَ ۝ wishing they had followed guidance.

وَيَوْمَ يُنَادِيهِمْ 65 The day He will call out to them

فَيَقُولُ and say,

مَاذَآ أَجَبْتُمُ ٱلْمُرْسَلِينَ ۝ 'What response did you give to the apostles?'

فَعَمِيَتْ عَلَيْهِمُ ٱلْأَنۢبَآءُ يَوْمَئِذٍ 66 The news that day shall be blacked out for them,

فَهُمْ لَا يَتَسَآءَلُونَ ۝    so they will not question one another.

فَأَمَّا مَن تَابَ وَءَامَنَ    67 As for him who repents and develops faith

وَعَمِلَ صَلِحًا    and acts righteously,

فَعَسَىٰ أَن يَكُونَ مِنَ ٱلْمُفْلِحِينَ ۝    maybe he will be among the felicitous.

وَرَبُّكَ يَخْلُقُ مَا يَشَآءُ وَيَخْتَارُ    68 *Your* Lord creates whatever He wishes and chooses.

مَا كَانَ لَهُمُ ٱلْخِيَرَةُ    They have no choice.

سُبْحَنَ ٱللَّهِ    Immaculate is Allah

وَتَعَلَىٰ    and exalted

عَمَّا يُشْرِكُونَ ۝    above [having] any partners they ascribe [to Him].

وَرَبُّكَ يَعْلَمُ مَا تُكِنُّ صُدُورُهُمْ    69 *Your* Lord knows whatever their breasts conceal,

وَمَا يُعْلِنُونَ ۝    and whatever they disclose.

وَهُوَ ٱللَّهُ لَآ إِلَهَ إِلَّا هُوَ    70 He is Allah, there is no god except Him.

لَهُ ٱلْحَمْدُ    All praise belongs to Him

فِى ٱلْأُولَىٰ وَٱلْأَخِرَةِ    in this world and the Hereafter.

وَلَهُ ٱلْحُكْمُ    All judgement belongs to Him,

وَإِلَيْهِ تُرْجَعُونَ ۝    and to Him you will be brought back.

قُلْ أَرَءَيْتُمْ    71 *Say*, 'Tell me,

إِن جَعَلَ ٱللَّهُ عَلَيْكُمُ ٱلَّيْلَ سَرْمَدًا    if Allah were to make the night perpetual over you

إِلَىٰ يَوْمِ ٱلْقِيَمَةِ    until the Day of Resurrection,

مَنْ إِلَهٌ غَيْرُ ٱللَّهِ يَأْتِيكُم بِضِيَآءٍ    what god other than Allah could bring you light?

أَفَلَا تَسْمَعُونَ ۝    Will you not then listen?'

قُلْ أَرَءَيْتُمْ    72 *Say*, 'Tell me,

إِن جَعَلَ ٱللَّهُ عَلَيْكُمُ ٱلنَّهَارَ سَرْمَدًا    if Allah were to make the day perpetual over you

إِلَىٰ يَوْمِ ٱلْقِيَمَةِ    until the Day of Resurrection,

مَنْ إِلَهٌ غَيْرُ ٱللَّهِ يَأْتِيكُم بِلَيْلٍ    what god other than Allah could bring you night

تَسْكُنُونَ فِيهِ    wherein you could rest?

أَفَلَا تُبْصِرُونَ ۝    Will you not then perceive?'

وَمِن رَّحْمَتِهِ    73 Out of His mercy

جَعَلَ لَكُمُ ٱلَّيۡلَ وَٱلنَّهَارَ

He has made for you the night and the day,

لِتَسۡكُنُواْ فِيهِ

that you may rest therein

وَلِتَبۡتَغُواْ مِن فَضۡلِهِۦ

and that you may seek from His grace

وَلَعَلَّكُمۡ تَشۡكُرُونَ ۝

and so that you may give thanks.

وَيَوۡمَ يُنَادِيهِمۡ

74 The day He will call out to them

فَيَقُولُ أَيۡنَ شُرَكَآءِىَ

and say, 'Where are My partners

ٱلَّذِينَ كُنتُمۡ تَزۡعُمُونَ ۝

that you used to claim?'

وَنَزَعۡنَا مِن كُلِّ أُمَّةٍ شَهِيدًا

75 We shall draw from every nation a witness

فَقُلۡنَا هَاتُواْ بُرۡهَٰنَكُمۡ

and say, 'Produce your evidence.'

فَعَلِمُوٓاْ أَنَّ ٱلۡحَقَّ لِلَّهِ

Then they will know that all reality belongs to Allah

وَضَلَّ عَنۡهُم مَّا كَانُواْ يَفۡتَرُونَ ۝ ٭

and what they used to fabricate will forsake them.

إِنَّ قَٰرُونَ كَانَ مِن قَوۡمِ مُوسَىٰ

76 Korah indeed belonged to the people of Moses,

فَبَغَىٰ عَلَيۡهِمۡ

but he bullied them.

وَءَاتَيۡنَٰهُ مِنَ ٱلۡكُنُوزِ مَآ

We had given him so much treasures

إِنَّ مَفَاتِحَهُۥ لَتَنُوٓأُ

that their keys indeed proved heavy

بِٱلۡعُصۡبَةِ أُوْلِى ٱلۡقُوَّةِ

for a band of stalwarts.

إِذۡ قَالَ لَهُۥ قَوۡمُهُۥ لَا تَفۡرَحۡ

When his people said to him, 'Do not exult!

إِنَّ ٱللَّهَ لَا يُحِبُّ ٱلۡفَرِحِينَ ۝

Indeed Allah does not like the exultant.

وَٱبۡتَغِ فِيمَآ ءَاتَىٰكَ ٱللَّهُ

77 By the means of what Allah has given you, seek

ٱلدَّارَ ٱلۡأَخِرَةَ

the abode of the Hereafter,

وَلَا تَنسَ نَصِيبَكَ مِنَ ٱلدُّنۡيَا

while not forgetting your share of this world.

وَأَحۡسِن

Be good [to others]

كَمَآ أَحۡسَنَ ٱللَّهُ إِلَيۡكَ

just as Allah has been good to you,

وَلَا تَبۡغِ ٱلۡفَسَادَ فِى ٱلۡأَرۡضِ

and do not try to cause corruption in the land.

إِنَّ ٱللَّهَ لَا يُحِبُّ ٱلۡمُفۡسِدِينَ ۝

Indeed Allah does not like the agents of corruption.'

قَالَ إِنَّمَآ أُوتِيتُهُۥ

78 He said, 'I have indeed been given [all] this

عَلَىٰ عِلۡمٍ عِندِىٓ

because of the knowledge that I have.'

أَوَلَمۡ يَعۡلَمۡ أَنَّ ٱللَّهَ قَدۡ أَهۡلَكَ

Did he not know that Allah had already destroyed

مِن قَبۡلِهِۦ

before him

مِنَ ٱلْقُرُونِ    some of the generations

مَنْ هُوَ أَشَدُّ مِنْهُ قُوَّةً    who were more powerful than him

وَأَكْثَرُ جَمْعًا    and greater in amassing [wealth]?[1]

وَلَا يُسْـَٔلُ عَن ذُنُوبِهِمُ ٱلْمُجْرِمُونَ ۝    The guilty will not be questioned about their sins.[2]

فَخَرَجَ عَلَىٰ قَوْمِهِۦ فِى زِينَتِهِۦ    79 So he emerged before his people in his finery.

قَالَ ٱلَّذِينَ يُرِيدُونَ ٱلْحَيَوٰةَ ٱلدُّنْيَا    Those who desired the life of the world said,

يَـٰلَيْتَ لَنَا مِثْلَ مَآ أُوتِىَ قَـٰرُونُ    'We wish we had like what Korah has been given!

إِنَّهُۥ لَذُو حَظٍّ عَظِيمٍ ۝    Indeed he is greatly fortunate.'

وَقَالَ ٱلَّذِينَ أُوتُوا۟ ٱلْعِلْمَ    80 Those who were given knowledge said,

وَيْلَكُمْ    'Woe to you!

ثَوَابُ ٱللَّهِ خَيْرٌ لِّمَنْ ءَامَنَ    Allah's reward is better for someone who has faith

وَعَمِلَ صَـٰلِحًا    and acts righteously,

وَلَا يُلَقَّىٰهَآ إِلَّا ٱلصَّـٰبِرُونَ ۝    and no one will receive it except the patient.'

فَخَسَفْنَا بِهِۦ وَبِدَارِهِ ٱلْأَرْضَ    81 So We caused the earth to swallow him and his house,

فَمَا كَانَ لَهُۥ مِن فِئَةٍ    and he had no party

يَنصُرُونَهُۥ مِن دُونِ ٱللَّهِ    that might protect him from Allah,

وَمَا كَانَ مِنَ ٱلْمُنتَصِرِينَ ۝    nor could he rescue himself.

وَأَصْبَحَ ٱلَّذِينَ تَمَنَّوْا۟ مَكَانَهُۥ    82 By dawn those who longed to be in his place

بِٱلْأَمْسِ    the day before

يَقُولُونَ    were saying,

وَيْكَأَنَّ ٱللَّهَ يَبْسُطُ ٱلرِّزْقَ    'Do you not see that Allah expands the provision

لِمَن يَشَآءُ مِنْ عِبَادِهِۦ    for whomever He wishes of His servants,

وَيَقْدِرُ    and tightens it?

لَوْلَآ أَن مَّنَّ ٱللَّهُ عَلَيْنَا    Had Allah not shown us favour,

لَخَسَفَ بِنَا    He might have made the earth swallow us too.

وَيْكَأَنَّهُۥ لَا يُفْلِحُ ٱلْكَـٰفِرُونَ ۝    Do you not see that the faithless are not felicitous.'

تِلْكَ ٱلدَّارُ ٱلْءَاخِرَةُ    83 This is the abode of the Hereafter

---

[1] Or 'more numerous in strength.'

[2] Because 'the guilty shall be known by their mark.' Cf. 55:39-41.

نَجْعَلُهَا لِلَّذِينَ    which We shall grant to those

لَا يُرِيدُونَ عُلُوًّا فِى ٱلْأَرْضِ    who do not desire to domineer in the earth

وَلَا فَسَادًا    nor to cause corruption,

وَٱلْعَٰقِبَةُ لِلْمُتَّقِينَ ۝    and the outcome will be in favour of the Godwary.

مَن جَآءَ بِٱلْحَسَنَةِ    84 Whoever brings virtue

فَلَهُۥ خَيْرٌ مِّنْهَا    shall receive [a reward] better than it,

وَمَن جَآءَ بِٱلسَّيِّئَةِ    but whoever brings vice

فَلَا يُجْزَى ٱلَّذِينَ عَمِلُواْ ٱلسَّيِّئَاتِ    —those who commit misdeeds shall not be requited

إِلَّا مَا كَانُواْ يَعْمَلُونَ ۝    except for what they used to do.

إِنَّ ٱلَّذِى فَرَضَ عَلَيْكَ ٱلْقُرْءَانَ    85 Indeed He who has revealed to *you* the Qur'ān[1]

لَرَآدُّكَ إِلَىٰ مَعَادٍ    will surely restore *you* to the place of return.

قُل رَّبِّى أَعْلَمُ مَن جَآءَ بِٱلْهُدَىٰ    *Say,* 'My Lord knows best him who brings guidance

وَمَنْ هُوَ فِى ضَلَٰلٍ مُّبِينٍ ۝    and him who is in manifest error.'

وَمَا كُنتَ تَرْجُواْ    86 *You* did not expect

أَن يُلْقَىٰٓ إِلَيْكَ ٱلْكِتَٰبُ    that the Book would be delivered to *you*;

إِلَّا رَحْمَةً مِّن رَّبِّكَ    but it was a mercy from *your* Lord.

فَلَا تَكُونَنَّ ظَهِيرًا لِّلْكَٰفِرِينَ ۝    So *do not be* ever an advocate of the faithless.

وَلَا يَصُدُّنَّكَ عَنْ ءَايَٰتِ ٱللَّهِ    87 *Do not* ever let them bar *you* from Allah's signs

بَعْدَ إِذْ أُنزِلَتْ إِلَيْكَ    after they have been sent down to *you*.

وَٱدْعُ إِلَىٰ رَبِّكَ    Invite to *your* Lord,

وَلَا تَكُونَنَّ مِنَ ٱلْمُشْرِكِينَ ۝    and never *be* one of the polytheists.

وَلَا تَدْعُ مَعَ ٱللَّهِ إِلَٰهًا ءَاخَرَ    88 And *do not invoke* another god besides Allah;

لَآ إِلَٰهَ إِلَّا هُوَ    there is no god except Him.

كُلُّ شَىْءٍ هَالِكٌ إِلَّا وَجْهَهُۥ    Everything is to perish except His Face.

لَهُ ٱلْحُكْمُ    All judgement belongs to Him,

وَإِلَيْهِ تُرْجَعُونَ ۝    and to Him you will be brought back.

---

[1] Or 'charged you with the Qur'ān.'

سُورَةُ الْعَنْكَبُوتِ          **29. SŪRAT AL-'ANKABŪT**[1]

بِسْمِ اللَّهِ                      In the Name of Allah,

الرَّحْمَٰنِ الرَّحِيمِ            the All-beneficent, All-merciful

۞ الٓمٓ 1 *Alif, Lām, Mīm.*

أَحَسِبَ ٱلنَّاسُ أَن يُتْرَكُوٓا۟ 2 Do the people suppose that they will be let off

أَن يَقُولُوٓا۟ ءَامَنَّا              because they say, 'We have faith,'

وَهُمْ لَا يُفْتَنُونَ ۞       and they will not be tested?

وَلَقَدْ فَتَنَّا ٱلَّذِينَ مِن قَبْلِهِمْ 3 Certainly We tested those who were before them.

فَلَيَعْلَمَنَّ ٱللَّهُ ٱلَّذِينَ صَدَقُوا۟      So Allah shall surely ascertain those who are truthful,

وَلَيَعْلَمَنَّ ٱلْكَٰذِبِينَ ۞     and He shall surely ascertain the liars.

أَمْ حَسِبَ ٱلَّذِينَ يَعْمَلُونَ ٱلسَّيِّـَٔاتِ 4 Do those who commit misdeeds suppose

أَن يَسْبِقُونَا           that they can outmaneuver Us?

سَآءَ مَا يَحْكُمُونَ ۞       Evil is the judgement that they make.

مَن كَانَ يَرْجُوا۟ لِقَآءَ ٱللَّهِ 5 Whoever expects to encounter Allah [should know

فَإِنَّ أَجَلَ ٱللَّهِ لَآتٍ          that] Allah's [appointed] time will indeed come,

وَهُوَ ٱلسَّمِيعُ ٱلْعَلِيمُ ۞   and He is the All-hearing, the All-knowing.

وَمَن جَٰهَدَ فَإِنَّمَا يُجَٰهِدُ لِنَفْسِهِۦٓ 6 Whoever strives, strives only for his own sake.[2]

إِنَّ ٱللَّهَ لَغَنِىٌّ عَنِ ٱلْعَٰلَمِينَ ۞   Indeed Allah has no need of the creatures.

وَٱلَّذِينَ ءَامَنُوا۟ وَعَمِلُوا۟ ٱلصَّٰلِحَٰتِ 7 As for those who have faith and do righteous deeds,

لَنُكَفِّرَنَّ عَنْهُمْ سَيِّـَٔاتِهِمْ        We will absolve them of their misdeeds

وَلَنَجْزِيَنَّهُمْ              and We will surely reward them

أَحْسَنَ ٱلَّذِى كَانُوا۟ يَعْمَلُونَ ۞   by the best of what they used to do.

وَوَصَّيْنَا ٱلْإِنسَٰنَ بِوَٰلِدَيْهِ حُسْنًا 8 We have enjoined man to be good to his parents.

وَإِن جَٰهَدَاكَ لِتُشْرِكَ بِى        But if they urge you to ascribe to Me as partner

---

[1] The *sūrah* takes its name from verse 41 which mentions the spider (*'ankabūt*).

[2] Or 'Whoever wages *jihād*, wages *jihād* only for his own sake.'

مَا لَيْسَ لَكَ بِهِۦ عِلْمٌ | that of which you have no knowledge,

فَلَا تُطِعْهُمَا | then do not obey them.

إِلَيَّ مَرْجِعُكُمْ | To Me will be your return,

فَأُنَبِّئُكُم | whereat I will inform you

بِمَا كُنتُمْ تَعْمَلُونَ ۝ | concerning that which you used to do.

وَٱلَّذِينَ ءَامَنُوا۟ وَعَمِلُوا۟ ٱلصَّٰلِحَٰتِ | 9 Those who have faith and do righteous deeds,

لَنُدْخِلَنَّهُمْ فِى ٱلصَّٰلِحِينَ ۝ | We will surely admit them among the righteous.

وَمِنَ ٱلنَّاسِ مَن يَقُولُ | 10 Among the people there are those who say,

ءَامَنَّا بِٱللَّهِ | 'We have faith in Allah,'

فَإِذَآ أُوذِىَ فِى ٱللَّهِ | but if such a one is tormented in Allah's cause,

جَعَلَ فِتْنَةَ ٱلنَّاسِ | he takes persecution by the people

كَعَذَابِ ٱللَّهِ | for Allah's punishment.

وَلَئِن جَآءَ نَصْرٌ مِّن رَّبِّكَ | Yet if there comes any help[1] from *your* Lord,

لَيَقُولُنَّ إِنَّا كُنَّا مَعَكُمْ | they will say for sure, 'We were indeed with you.'

أَوَلَيْسَ ٱللَّهُ بِأَعْلَمَ | Does not Allah know best

بِمَا فِى صُدُورِ ٱلْعَٰلَمِينَ ۝ | what is in the breasts of the creatures?

وَلَيَعْلَمَنَّ ٱللَّهُ ٱلَّذِينَ ءَامَنُوا۟ | 11 Allah shall surely ascertain those who have faith,

وَلَيَعْلَمَنَّ ٱلْمُنَٰفِقِينَ ۝ | and He shall surely ascertain the hypocrites.

وَقَالَ ٱلَّذِينَ كَفَرُوا۟ لِلَّذِينَ ءَامَنُوا۟ | 12 The faithless say to the faithful,

ٱتَّبِعُوا۟ سَبِيلَنَا | 'Follow our way

وَلْنَحْمِلْ خَطَٰيَٰكُمْ | and we will bear [responsibility for] your iniquities.'

وَمَا هُم بِحَٰمِلِينَ | They will not bear

مِنْ خَطَٰيَٰهُم مِّن شَىْءٍ | anything of their iniquities.

إِنَّهُمْ لَكَٰذِبُونَ ۝ | They are indeed liars.

وَلَيَحْمِلُنَّ أَثْقَالَهُمْ | 13 But surely they will carry their own burdens

وَأَثْقَالًا مَّعَ أَثْقَالِهِمْ | and other burdens along with their own burdens,

وَلَيُسْـَٔلُنَّ | and they will surely be questioned

يَوْمَ ٱلْقِيَٰمَةِ | on the Day of Resurrection

---

[1] Or 'victory.'

عَمَّا كَانُوا يَفْتَرُونَ ۝    concerning that which they used to fabricate.

وَلَقَدْ أَرْسَلْنَا نُوحًا إِلَى قَوْمِهِ  14 Certainly We sent Noah to his people,

فَلَبِثَ فِيهِمْ    and he remained with them

أَلْفَ سَنَةٍ إِلَّا خَمْسِينَ عَامًا    for a thousand-less-fifty years.

فَأَخَذَهُمُ ٱلطُّوفَانُ    Then the flood overtook them

وَهُمْ ظَالِمُونَ ۝    while they were wrongdoers.

فَأَنجَيْنَهُ وَأَصْحَٰبَ ٱلسَّفِينَةِ  15 Then We delivered him and the occupants of the Ark,

وَجَعَلْنَٰهَآ ءَايَةً لِّلْعَٰلَمِينَ ۝    and made it a sign for all the nations.

وَإِبْرَٰهِيمَ إِذْ قَالَ لِقَوْمِهِ  16 And Abraham, when he said to his people,

ٱعْبُدُوا ٱللَّهَ وَٱتَّقُوهُ    'Worship Allah and be wary of Him.

ذَٰلِكُمْ خَيْرٌ لَّكُمْ    That is better for you,

إِن كُنتُمْ تَعْلَمُونَ ۝    should you know.

إِنَّمَا تَعْبُدُونَ مِن دُونِ ٱللَّهِ أَوْثَٰنًا  17  In fact, instead of Allah you worship idols,

وَتَخْلُقُونَ إِفْكًا    and you invent a lie.

إِنَّ ٱلَّذِينَ تَعْبُدُونَ    Indeed those whom you worship

مِن دُونِ ٱللَّهِ    besides Allah

لَا يَمْلِكُونَ لَكُمْ رِزْقًا    have no control over your provision.

فَٱبْتَغُوا عِندَ ٱللَّهِ ٱلرِّزْقَ    So seek all [your] provision from Allah,

وَٱعْبُدُوهُ وَٱشْكُرُوا لَهُ    and worship Him and thank Him,

إِلَيْهِ تُرْجَعُونَ ۝    and to Him you shall be brought back.'[1]

وَإِن تُكَذِّبُوا  18 And if you impugn [the Apostle's teaching],

فَقَدْ كَذَّبَ أُمَمٌ    then [other] nations have impugned [likewise]

مِّن قَبْلِكُمْ    before you,

وَمَا عَلَى ٱلرَّسُولِ إِلَّا    and the Apostle's duty is only

ٱلْبَلَٰغُ ٱلْمُبِينُ ۝    to communicate in clear terms.

أَوَلَمْ يَرَوْا  19 Have they not regarded

كَيْفَ يُبْدِئُ ٱللَّهُ ٱلْخَلْقَ    how Allah originates the creation?

ثُمَّ يُعِيدُهُ    Then He will bring it back.

---

[1] The narrative of Abraham is resumed in verse 24 below.

إِنَّ ذَٰلِكَ عَلَى ٱللَّهِ يَسِيرٌ ۞    That is indeed easy for Allah.

قُلْ سِيرُوا۟ فِى ٱلْأَرْضِ فَٱنظُرُوا۟    20 *Say,* 'Travel over the land and then observe

كَيْفَ بَدَأَ ٱلْخَلْقَ    how He has originated the creation.'

ثُمَّ ٱللَّهُ يُنشِئُ    Then Allah shall bring about

ٱلنَّشْأَةَ ٱلْءَاخِرَةَ    the genesis of the Hereafter.

إِنَّ ٱللَّهَ عَلَىٰ كُلِّ شَىْءٍ قَدِيرٌ ۞    Indeed Allah has power over all things.

يُعَذِّبُ مَن يَشَآءُ    21 He will punish whomever He wishes

وَيَرْحَمُ مَن يَشَآءُ    and have mercy on whomever He wishes,

وَإِلَيْهِ تُقْلَبُونَ ۞    and to Him you will be returned.

وَمَآ أَنتُم بِمُعْجِزِينَ فِى ٱلْأَرْضِ    22 You cannot thwart Him on the earth

وَلَا فِى ٱلسَّمَآءِ    or in the sky,

وَمَا لَكُم مِّن دُونِ ٱللَّهِ    nor do you have besides Allah

مِن وَلِىٍّ وَلَا نَصِيرٍ ۞    any guardian or any helper.

وَٱلَّذِينَ كَفَرُوا۟ بِـَٔايَٰتِ ٱللَّهِ    23 Those who deny the signs of Allah

وَلِقَآئِهِۦٓ    and the encounter with Him,

أُو۟لَٰٓئِكَ يَئِسُوا۟ مِن رَّحْمَتِى    they have despaired of My mercy,

وَأُو۟لَٰٓئِكَ لَهُمْ عَذَابٌ أَلِيمٌ ۞    and for such there is a painful punishment.

فَمَا كَانَ جَوَابَ قَوْمِهِۦٓ إِلَّآ    24 But the only answer of his people was

أَن قَالُوا۟ ٱقْتُلُوهُ أَوْ حَرِّقُوهُ    that they said, 'Kill him, or burn him.'

فَأَنجَىٰهُ ٱللَّهُ مِنَ ٱلنَّارِ    Then Allah delivered him from the fire.

إِنَّ فِى ذَٰلِكَ لَءَايَٰتٍ    There are indeed signs in that

لِّقَوْمٍ يُؤْمِنُونَ ۞    for a people who have faith.

وَقَالَ    25 He said,

إِنَّمَا ٱتَّخَذْتُم مِّن دُونِ ٱللَّهِ أَوْثَٰنًا    'You have taken idols [for worship] besides Allah

مَّوَدَّةَ بَيْنِكُمْ    for the sake of [mutual] affection amongst yourselves

فِى ٱلْحَيَوٰةِ ٱلدُّنْيَا    in the life of the world.

ثُمَّ يَوْمَ ٱلْقِيَٰمَةِ    Then on the Day of Resurrection

يَكْفُرُ بَعْضُكُم بِبَعْضٍ    you will disown one another

وَيَلْعَنُ بَعْضُكُم بَعْضًا    and curse one another,[1]

---

[1] Cf. 43:67.

وَمَأْوَىٰكُمُ ٱلنَّارُ and the Fire will be your abode,

وَمَا لَكُم مِّن نَّصِرِينَ ۝ and you will not have any helpers.'

فَـَٔامَنَ لَهُۥ لُوطٌ ۘ 26 Thereupon Lot believed in him,

وَقَالَ and he said,

إِنِّى مُهَاجِرٌ إِلَىٰ رَبِّىٓ ۖ 'Indeed I am migrating toward my Lord.

إِنَّهُۥ هُوَ ٱلْعَزِيزُ ٱلْحَكِيمُ ۝ Indeed He is the All-mighty, the All-wise.'

وَوَهَبْنَا لَهُۥٓ إِسْحَـٰقَ وَيَعْقُوبَ 27 And We gave him Isaac and Jacob,

وَجَعَلْنَا فِى ذُرِّيَّتِهِ and We ordained among his descendants

ٱلنُّبُوَّةَ وَٱلْكِتَـٰبَ prophethood and the Book,

وَءَاتَيْنَـٰهُ أَجْرَهُۥ فِى ٱلدُّنْيَا ۖ and We gave him his reward in the world,

وَإِنَّهُۥ فِى ٱلْـَٔاخِرَةِ and in the Hereafter he will indeed be

لَمِنَ ٱلصَّـٰلِحِينَ ۝ among the Righteous.

وَلُوطًا إِذْ قَالَ لِقَوْمِهِۦٓ 28 And Lot, when he said to his people,

إِنَّكُمْ لَتَأْتُونَ ٱلْفَـٰحِشَةَ 'You indeed commit an indecency

مَا سَبَقَكُم بِهَا مِنْ أَحَدٍ مِّنَ ٱلْعَـٰلَمِينَ ۝ none in the world has ever committed before you!

أَئِنَّكُمْ لَتَأْتُونَ ٱلرِّجَالَ 29 What! Do you come to men,

وَتَقْطَعُونَ ٱلسَّبِيلَ and cut off the way,[1]

وَتَأْتُونَ فِى نَادِيكُمُ ٱلْمُنكَرَ ۖ and commit outrages in your gatherings?'

فَمَا كَانَ جَوَابَ قَوْمِهِۦٓ إِلَّآ But the only answer of his people was

أَن قَالُوا۟ ٱئْتِنَا بِعَذَابِ ٱللَّهِ that they said, 'Bring us Allah's punishment

إِن كُنتَ مِنَ ٱلصَّـٰدِقِينَ ۝ should you be truthful.'

قَالَ رَبِّ 30 He said, 'My Lord!

ٱنصُرْنِى عَلَى ٱلْقَوْمِ ٱلْمُفْسِدِينَ ۝ Help me against this corruptive lot.'

وَلَمَّا جَآءَتْ رُسُلُنَآ إِبْرَٰهِيمَ 31 And when Our messengers[2] came to Abraham

بِٱلْبُشْرَىٰ with the good news,

قَالُوٓا۟ إِنَّا مُهْلِكُوٓا۟ they said, 'We are indeed going to destroy

---

[1] That is, the natural way of conjugal relations between the sexes.

[2] That is, the angels sent to give the good news of Isaac's birth to Abraham and to destroy the people of Sodom.

أَهْلَ هَـٰذِهِ ٱلْقَرْيَةِ    the people of this town.

إِنَّ أَهْلَهَا كَانُوا ظَـٰلِمِينَ ٣١    Its people are indeed wrongdoers.'

قَالَ إِنَّ فِيهَا لُوطًا ٣٢    32 He said, 'Lot is indeed in it.'

قَالُوا نَحْنُ أَعْلَمُ بِمَن فِيهَا    They said, 'We know better those who are in it.

لَنُنَجِّيَنَّهُ وَأَهْلَهُ    We will surely deliver him and his family,

إِلَّا ٱمْرَأَتَهُ    except his wife:

كَانَتْ مِنَ ٱلْغَـٰبِرِينَ ٣٢    she shall be one of those who remain behind.'

وَلَمَّا أَن جَآءَتْ رُسُلُنَا لُوطًا ٣٣    33 And when Our messengers came to Lot,

سِيٓءَ بِهِمْ    he was distressed on their account

وَضَاقَ بِهِمْ ذَرْعًا    and in a predicament for their sake.

وَقَالُوا لَا تَخَفْ وَلَا تَحْزَنْ    But they said, 'Do not be afraid, nor grieve!

إِنَّا مُنَجُّوكَ وَأَهْلَكَ إِلَّا ٱمْرَأَتَكَ    We shall deliver you and your family, except your wife:

كَانَتْ مِنَ ٱلْغَـٰبِرِينَ ٣٣    she will be one of those who remain behind.

إِنَّا مُنزِلُونَ ٣٤    34 We are indeed going to bring down

عَلَىٰ أَهْلِ هَـٰذِهِ ٱلْقَرْيَةِ    upon the people of this town

رِجْزًا مِّنَ ٱلسَّمَآءِ    a punishment from the sky

بِمَا كَانُوا يَفْسُقُونَ ٣٤    because of the transgressions they used to commit.'

وَلَقَد تَّرَكْنَا مِنْهَآ ءَايَةً بَيِّنَةً ٣٥    35 Certainly We have left of it a manifest sign

لِّقَوْمٍ يَعْقِلُونَ ٣٥    for a people who apply reason.

وَإِلَىٰ مَدْيَنَ أَخَاهُمْ شُعَيْبًا ٣٦    36 And to Midian We sent Shu'ayb, their brother.

فَقَالَ يَـٰقَوْمِ ٱعْبُدُوا ٱللَّهَ    He said, 'O my people! Worship Allah,

وَٱرْجُوا ٱلْيَوْمَ ٱلْءَاخِرَ    and expect [to encounter] the Last Day,

وَلَا تَعْثَوْا فِى ٱلْأَرْضِ    and do not act wickedly on the earth

مُفْسِدِينَ ٣٦    causing corruption.'

فَكَذَّبُوهُ ٣٧    37 But they impugned him,

فَأَخَذَتْهُمُ ٱلرَّجْفَةُ    whereupon the earthquake seized them,

فَأَصْبَحُوا فِى دَارِهِمْ جَـٰثِمِينَ ٣٧    and they lay lifeless prostrate in their homes.

وَعَادًا وَثَمُودَا ٣٨    38 And 'Ād and Thamūd,

وَقَد تَّبَيَّنَ لَكُم مِّن مَّسَٰكِنِهِمْ [whose fate] is evident to you from their habitations.

وَزَيَّنَ لَهُمُ ٱلشَّيْطَٰنُ أَعْمَٰلَهُمْ Satan made their deeds seem decorous to them,

فَصَدَّهُمْ عَنِ ٱلسَّبِيلِ thus he barred them from the way [of Allah],

وَكَانُوا۟ مُسْتَبْصِرِينَ though they used to be perceptive.[1]

وَقَٰرُونَ وَفِرْعَوْنَ وَهَٰمَٰنَ 39 And Korah, Pharaoh, and Hāmān.

وَلَقَدْ جَآءَهُم مُّوسَىٰ بِٱلْبَيِّنَٰتِ Certainly Moses brought them manifest proofs,

فَٱسْتَكْبَرُوا۟ فِى ٱلْأَرْضِ but they acted arrogantly in the land;

وَمَا كَانُوا۟ سَٰبِقِينَ though they could not outmaneuver [Allah].

فَكُلًّا أَخَذْنَا بِذَنۢبِهِۦ 40 So We seized each [of them] for his sin:

فَمِنْهُم مَّنْ among them were those

أَرْسَلْنَا عَلَيْهِ حَاصِبًا upon whom We unleashed a rain of stones,

وَمِنْهُم مَّنْ and among them were those

أَخَذَتْهُ ٱلصَّيْحَةُ who were seized by the Cry,

وَمِنْهُم مَّنْ and among them were those

خَسَفْنَا بِهِ ٱلْأَرْضَ whom We caused the earth to swallow,

وَمِنْهُم مَّنْ and among them were those

أَغْرَقْنَا whom We drowned.

وَمَا كَانَ ٱللَّهُ لِيَظْلِمَهُمْ It was not Allah who wronged them,

وَلَٰكِن كَانُوٓا۟ أَنفُسَهُمْ يَظْلِمُونَ but it was they who used to wrong themselves.

مَثَلُ ٱلَّذِينَ 41 The parable of those who

ٱتَّخَذُوا۟ مِن دُونِ ٱللَّهِ أَوْلِيَآءَ take guardians instead of Allah

كَمَثَلِ ٱلْعَنكَبُوتِ ٱتَّخَذَتْ بَيْتًا is that of the spider that takes a home,

وَإِنَّ أَوْهَنَ ٱلْبُيُوتِ and indeed the frailest of homes

لَبَيْتُ ٱلْعَنكَبُوتِ is the home of a spider,

لَوْ كَانُوا۟ يَعْلَمُونَ had they known!

إِنَّ ٱللَّهَ يَعْلَمُ 42 Allah indeed knows

مَا يَدْعُونَ مِن دُونِهِۦ مِن شَىْءٍ whatever thing they invoke besides Him,

---

[1] That is, they let themselves be deceived by Satan despite their God-given ability to discern between good and evil.

وَهُوَ ٱلْعَزِيزُ ٱلْحَكِيمُ ۝  and He is the All-mighty, the All-wise.

وَتِلْكَ ٱلْأَمْثَلُ نَضْرِبُهَا لِلنَّاسِ  43 And We draw these parables for mankind;

وَمَا يَعْقِلُهَآ  but no one grasps them

إِلَّا ٱلْعَلِمُونَ ۝  except those who have knowledge.

خَلَقَ ٱللَّهُ ٱلسَّمَوَتِ وَٱلْأَرْضَ  44 Allah created the heavens and the earth

بِٱلْحَقِّ  with the truth.

إِنَّ فِى ذَلِكَ لَآيَةً لِّلْمُؤْمِنِينَ ۝  There is indeed a sign in that for the faithful.

ٱتْلُ مَآ أُوحِىَ إِلَيْكَ مِنَ ٱلْكِتَبِ  45 *Recite* what has been revealed to *you* of the Book,

وَأَقِمِ ٱلصَّلَوٰةَ  and *maintain* the prayer.

إِنَّ ٱلصَّلَوٰةَ تَنْهَىٰ عَنِ ٱلْفَحْشَآءِ  Indeed the prayer prevents indecencies

وَٱلْمُنكَرِ  and wrongs,

وَلَذِكْرُ ٱللَّهِ أَكْبَرُ  and the remembrance of Allah is surely greater.

وَٱللَّهُ يَعْلَمُ مَا تَصْنَعُونَ ۝ ۞  And Allah knows whatever [deeds] you do.

[PART 21]

وَلَا تُجَدِلُوٓا۟ أَهْلَ ٱلْكِتَبِ  46 Do not dispute with the People of the Book

إِلَّا بِٱلَّتِى هِىَ أَحْسَنُ  except in a manner which is best,

إِلَّا ٱلَّذِينَ ظَلَمُوا۟ مِنْهُمْ  barring such of them as are wrongdoers,

وَقُولُوٓا۟ ءَامَنَّا  and say, 'We believe

بِٱلَّذِىٓ أُنزِلَ إِلَيْنَا  in that which has been sent down to us

وَأُنزِلَ إِلَيْكُمْ  and has been sent down to you;

وَإِلَهُنَا وَإِلَهُكُمْ وَحِدٌ  our God and your God is one [and the same],

وَنَحْنُ لَهُ مُسْلِمُونَ ۝  and to Him do we submit.'

وَكَذَلِكَ أَنزَلْنَآ إِلَيْكَ ٱلْكِتَبَ  47 Thus have We sent down the Book to *you*;

فَٱلَّذِينَ ءَاتَيْنَهُمُ ٱلْكِتَبَ  and those to whom We have given the Book

يُؤْمِنُونَ بِهِۦ  believe in it,

وَمِنْ هَٰٓؤُلَآءِ مَن يُؤْمِنُ بِهِۦ  and of these[1] there are some who believe in it,

وَمَا يَجْحَدُ بِـَٔايَتِنَآ إِلَّا ٱلْكَفِرُونَ ۝  and none contests Our signs except the faithless.

وَمَا كُنتَ تَتْلُوا۟ مِن قَبْلِهِۦ مِن كِتَبٍ  48 *You* did not use to recite any scripture before it,

---

[1] That is, of the people of Makkah.

وَلَا تَخُطُّهُۥ بِيَمِينِكَ nor did *you* write it with *your* right hand,

إِذًا لَّٱرْتَابَ ٱلْمُبْطِلُونَ ٤٨ for then the impugners would have been skeptical.

بَلْ هُوَ ءَايَتٌۢ بَيِّنَتٌ 49 Rather it is [present as] manifest signs

فِى صُدُورِ ٱلَّذِينَ أُوتُوا ٱلْعِلْمَ in the breasts of those who have been given knowledge,

وَمَا يَجْحَدُ بِـَٔايَتِنَآ إِلَّا ٱلظَّلِمُونَ ٤٩ and none contests Our signs except wrongdoers.

وَقَالُوا 50 They say,

لَوْلَآ أُنزِلَ عَلَيْهِ ءَايَتٌ 'Why has not some sign[1] been sent down to him

مِّن رَّبِّهِۦ from his Lord?'

قُلْ إِنَّمَا ٱلْأَيَتُ عِندَ ٱللَّهِ *Say,* 'The signs are only with Allah,

وَإِنَّمَآ أَنَا۠ نَذِيرٌ مُّبِينٌ ٥٠ and I am only a manifest warner.'

أَوَلَمْ يَكْفِهِمْ 51 Does it not suffice them

أَنَّآ أَنزَلْنَا عَلَيْكَ ٱلْكِتَبَ that We have sent down to *you* the Book

يُتْلَىٰ عَلَيْهِمْ which is recited to them?

إِنَّ فِى ذَٰلِكَ لَرَحْمَةً وَذِكْرَىٰ There is indeed a mercy and admonition in that

لِقَوْمٍ يُؤْمِنُونَ ٥١ for a people who have faith.

قُلْ كَفَىٰ بِٱللَّهِ بَيْنِى وَبَيْنَكُمْ شَهِيدًا 52 *Say,* 'Allah suffices as a witness between me and you:

يَعْلَمُ مَا فِى ٱلسَّمَوَٰتِ He knows whatever there is in the heavens

وَٱلْأَرْضِ and the earth.

وَٱلَّذِينَ ءَامَنُوا بِٱلْبَطِلِ Those who put faith in falsehood

وَكَفَرُوا بِٱللَّهِ and defy Allah,

أُوْلَٰٓئِكَ هُمُ ٱلْخَسِرُونَ ٥٢ —it is they who are the losers.'

وَيَسْتَعْجِلُونَكَ بِٱلْعَذَابِ 53 They ask *you* to hasten the punishment.

وَلَوْلَآ أَجَلٌ مُّسَمًّى Yet were it not for a specified time,

لَّجَآءَهُمُ ٱلْعَذَابُ the punishment would have surely overtaken them.

وَلَيَأْتِيَنَّهُم بَغْتَةً Surely it will overtake them suddenly

وَهُمْ لَا يَشْعُرُونَ ٥٣ while they are unaware.

يَسْتَعْجِلُونَكَ بِٱلْعَذَابِ 54 They ask *you* to hasten the punishment,

وَإِنَّ جَهَنَّمَ لَمُحِيطَةٌۢ بِٱلْكَفِرِينَ ٥٤ and indeed hell will besiege the faithless

---

[1] That is, a miracle.

يَوْمَ يَغْشَىٰهُمُ ٱلْعَذَابُ 55 on the day when the punishment envelopes them,

مِن فَوْقِهِمْ from above them

وَمِن تَحْتِ أَرْجُلِهِمْ and from under their feet,

وَيَقُولُ ذُوقُوا۟ مَا كُنتُمْ تَعْمَلُونَ ۝ and He will say, 'Taste what you used to do!'

يَٰعِبَادِىَ ٱلَّذِينَ ءَامَنُوٓا۟ 56 O My servants who have faith!

إِنَّ أَرْضِى وَٰسِعَةٌ My earth is indeed vast.

فَإِيَّٰىَ فَٱعْبُدُونِ ۝ So worship [only] Me.

كُلُّ نَفْسٍ ذَآئِقَةُ ٱلْمَوْتِ 57 Every soul shall taste death.

ثُمَّ إِلَيْنَا تُرْجَعُونَ ۝ Then you shall be brought back to Us.

وَٱلَّذِينَ ءَامَنُوا۟ وَعَمِلُوا۟ ٱلصَّٰلِحَٰتِ 58 Those who have faith and do righteous deeds,

لَنُبَوِّئَنَّهُم مِّنَ ٱلْجَنَّةِ غُرَفًا We will surely settle them in lofty abodes of paradise

تَجْرِى مِن تَحْتِهَا ٱلْأَنْهَٰرُ with streams running in them,

خَٰلِدِينَ فِيهَا to remain in them [forever].

نِعْمَ أَجْرُ ٱلْعَٰمِلِينَ ۝ How excellent is the reward of the workers!

ٱلَّذِينَ صَبَرُوا۟ 59 —Those who are patient

وَعَلَىٰ رَبِّهِمْ يَتَوَكَّلُونَ ۝ and who put their trust in their Lord.

وَكَأَيِّن مِّن دَآبَّةٍ 60 How many an animal there is

لَّا تَحْمِلُ رِزْقَهَا that does not carry its own provision.

ٱللَّهُ يَرْزُقُهَا وَإِيَّاكُمْ Allah provides for it, and for you,

وَهُوَ ٱلسَّمِيعُ ٱلْعَلِيمُ ۝ and He is the All-hearing, the All-knowing.

وَلَئِن سَأَلْتَهُم 61 If *you* ask them,

مَّنْ خَلَقَ ٱلسَّمَٰوَٰتِ وَٱلْأَرْضَ 'Who created the heavens and the earth,

وَسَخَّرَ ٱلشَّمْسَ وَٱلْقَمَرَ and disposed the sun and the moon?'

لَيَقُولُنَّ ٱللَّهُ They will surely say, 'Allah.'

فَأَنَّىٰ يُؤْفَكُونَ ۝ Then where do they stray?

ٱللَّهُ يَبْسُطُ ٱلرِّزْقَ 62 Allah expands the provision

لِمَن يَشَآءُ مِنْ عِبَادِهِۦ for whoever He wishes of His servants,

وَيَقْدِرُ لَهُۥٓ and tightens it for him.

إِنَّ ٱللَّهَ بِكُلِّ شَىْءٍ عَلِيمٌ ۝ Indeed Allah has knowledge of all things.

وَلَئِن سَأَلْتَهُم 63 And if *you* ask them,

مَّن نَّزَّلَ مِنَ ٱلسَّمَآءِ مَآءً 'Who sends down water from the sky,

فَأَحْيَا بِهِ ٱلْأَرْضَ مِنۢ بَعْدِ مَوْتِهَا with which He revives the earth after its death?'

لَيَقُولُنَّ ٱللَّهُ They will surely say, 'Allah.'

قُلِ ٱلْحَمْدُ لِلَّهِ *Say,* 'All praise belongs to Allah!'

بَلْ أَكْثَرُهُمْ لَا يَعْقِلُونَ ۝ But most of them do not apply reason.

وَمَا هَٰذِهِ ٱلْحَيَوٰةُ ٱلدُّنْيَآ 64 The life of this world is nothing

إِلَّا لَهْوٌ وَلَعِبٌ but diversion and play,

وَإِنَّ ٱلدَّارَ ٱلْأَخِرَةَ لَهِيَ ٱلْحَيَوَانُ but the abode of the Hereafter is indeed Life,

لَوْ كَانُوا يَعْلَمُونَ ۝ had they known!

فَإِذَا رَكِبُوا فِى ٱلْفُلْكِ دَعَوُا ٱللَّهَ 65 When they board the ship, they invoke Allah

مُخْلِصِينَ لَهُ ٱلدِّينَ putting exclusive faith in Him,

فَلَمَّا نَجَّىٰهُمْ إِلَى ٱلْبَرِّ but when He delivers them to land,

إِذَا هُمْ يُشْرِكُونَ ۝ behold, they ascribe partners [to Him],

لِيَكْفُرُوا بِمَآ ءَاتَيْنَٰهُمْ 66　being ungrateful for what We have given them!

وَلِيَتَمَتَّعُوا فَسَوْفَ يَعْلَمُونَ ۝ So let them enjoy. Soon they will know!

أَوَلَمْ يَرَوْا أَنَّا جَعَلْنَا 67 Have they not seen that We have appointed

حَرَمًا ءَامِنًا a safe sanctuary,[1]

وَيُتَخَطَّفُ ٱلنَّاسُ مِنْ حَوْلِهِمْ while the people are despoiled all around them?

أَفَبِٱلْبَٰطِلِ يُؤْمِنُونَ Would they then believe in falsehood

وَبِنِعْمَةِ ٱللَّهِ يَكْفُرُونَ ۝ and be ungrateful toward the blessing of Allah?

وَمَنْ أَظْلَمُ مِمَّنِ 68 Who is a greater wrongdoer than him

ٱفْتَرَىٰ عَلَى ٱللَّهِ كَذِبًا who fabricates a lie against Allah,

أَوْ كَذَّبَ بِٱلْحَقِّ لَمَّا جَآءَهُۥٓ or denies the truth when it comes to him?

أَلَيْسَ فِى جَهَنَّمَ مَثْوًى لِّلْكَٰفِرِينَ ۝ Is not the [final] abode of the faithless in hell?

وَٱلَّذِينَ جَٰهَدُوا فِينَا 69 As for those who strive in Us,

لَنَهْدِيَنَّهُمْ سُبُلَنَا We shall surely guide them in Our ways,

وَإِنَّ ٱللَّهَ لَمَعَ ٱلْمُحْسِنِينَ ۝ and Allah is indeed with the virtuous.

---

[1] That is, the city of Makkah.

# سُورَةُ الرُّومِ

## 30. SŪRAT AL-RŪM[1]

بِسْمِ ٱللَّهِ
ٱلرَّحْمَٰنِ ٱلرَّحِيمِ

In the Name of Allah,
the All-beneficent, All-merciful.

الٓمٓ ۝ 1    *Alif, Lām, Mīm.*

غُلِبَتِ ٱلرُّومُ ۝ 2    Byzantium has been vanquished

فِىٓ أَدْنَى ٱلْأَرْضِ 3    in a nearby territory,

وَهُم مِّنۢ بَعْدِ غَلَبِهِمْ سَيَغْلِبُونَ ۝    but following their defeat they will be victors

فِى بِضْعِ سِنِينَ 4    in a few years.

لِلَّهِ ٱلْأَمْرُ مِن قَبْلُ وَمِنۢ بَعْدُ    All command belongs to Allah, before and after,

وَيَوْمَئِذٍ يَفْرَحُ ٱلْمُؤْمِنُونَ ۝    and on that day the faithful will rejoice

بِنَصْرِ ٱللَّهِ 5    at Allah's help.

يَنصُرُ مَن يَشَآءُ    He helps whomever He wishes,

وَهُوَ ٱلْعَزِيزُ ٱلرَّحِيمُ ۝    and He is the All-mighty, the All-merciful.

وَعْدَ ٱللَّهِ 6    [This is] a promise of Allah:

لَا يُخْلِفُ ٱللَّهُ وَعْدَهُۥ    Allah does not break His promise,

وَلَٰكِنَّ أَكْثَرَ ٱلنَّاسِ لَا يَعْلَمُونَ ۝    but most people do not know.

يَعْلَمُونَ ظَٰهِرًا مِّنَ ٱلْحَيَوٰةِ ٱلدُّنْيَا 7    They know just an outward aspect of the life of the world,

وَهُمْ عَنِ ٱلْءَاخِرَةِ هُمْ غَٰفِلُونَ ۝    but they are oblivious of the Hereafter.

أَوَلَمْ يَتَفَكَّرُوا۟ فِىٓ أَنفُسِهِم 8    Have they not reflected on their own souls?

مَّا خَلَقَ ٱللَّهُ ٱلسَّمَٰوَٰتِ وَٱلْأَرْضَ    Allah did not create the heavens and the earth

وَمَا بَيْنَهُمَآ    and whatever is between them

إِلَّا بِٱلْحَقِّ وَأَجَلٍ مُّسَمًّى    except with the truth and for a specified term.

وَإِنَّ كَثِيرًا مِّنَ ٱلنَّاسِ    Indeed many of the people

بِلِقَآئِ رَبِّهِمْ لَكَٰفِرُونَ ۝    disbelieve in the encounter with their Lord.

أَوَلَمْ يَسِيرُوا۟ فِى ٱلْأَرْضِ 9    Have they not traveled in the land

---

[1] The *sūrah* derives its name from verse 2 which mentions Byzantium (*al-Rūm*).

فَيَنظُرُواْ so that they may observe

كَيْفَ كَانَ عَٰقِبَةُ ٱلَّذِينَ مِن قَبْلِهِمْ how was the fate of those who were before them?

كَانُوٓاْ أَشَدَّ مِنْهُمْ قُوَّةً They were more powerful than them,

وَأَثَارُواْ ٱلْأَرْضَ and they plowed the earth

وَعَمَرُوهَآ أَكْثَرَ مِمَّا عَمَرُوهَا and developed it more than they have developed it.

وَجَآءَتْهُمْ رُسُلُهُم بِٱلْبَيِّنَٰتِ Their apostles brought them manifest proofs.

فَمَا كَانَ ٱللَّهُ لِيَظْلِمَهُمْ So it was not Allah who wronged them,

وَلَٰكِن كَانُوٓاْ أَنفُسَهُمْ يَظْلِمُونَ ۝ but it was they who used to wrong themselves.

ثُمَّ كَانَ عَٰقِبَةَ ٱلَّذِينَ أَسَٰٓـُٔواْ ٱلسُّوٓأَىٰٓ 10 Then the fate of those who committed misdeeds was

أَن كَذَّبُواْ بِـَٔايَٰتِ ٱللَّهِ that they denied the signs of Allah

وَكَانُواْ بِهَا يَسْتَهْزِءُونَ ۝ and they used to deride them.

ٱللَّهُ يَبْدَؤُاْ ٱلْخَلْقَ 11 Allah originates the creation,

ثُمَّ يُعِيدُهُۥ then He will bring it back,

ثُمَّ إِلَيْهِ تُرْجَعُونَ ۝ then you will be brought back to Him.

وَيَوْمَ تَقُومُ ٱلسَّاعَةُ 12 And when the Hour sets in,

يُبْلِسُ ٱلْمُجْرِمُونَ ۝ the guilty will despair.

وَلَمْ يَكُن لَّهُم مِّن شُرَكَآئِهِمْ 13 None of those whom they ascribed as partners [to Allah]

شُفَعَٰٓؤُاْ will intercede for them,

وَكَانُواْ بِشُرَكَآئِهِمْ كَٰفِرِينَ ۝ and they will disavow their partners.[1]

وَيَوْمَ تَقُومُ ٱلسَّاعَةُ 14 The day the Hour sets in,

يَوْمَئِذٍ يَتَفَرَّقُونَ ۝ they will be divided on that day:

فَأَمَّا ٱلَّذِينَ ءَامَنُواْ وَعَمِلُواْ ٱلصَّٰلِحَٰتِ 15 As for those who have faith and do righteous deeds,

فَهُمْ فِى رَوْضَةٍ يُحْبَرُونَ ۝ they shall be in a garden, rejoicing.

وَأَمَّا ٱلَّذِينَ كَفَرُواْ 16 But as for those who were faithless

وَكَذَّبُواْ بِـَٔايَٰتِنَا and denied Our signs

وَلِقَآئِ ٱلْءَاخِرَةِ and the encounter of the Hereafter,

فَأُوْلَٰٓئِكَ فِى ٱلْعَذَابِ مُحْضَرُونَ ۝ they will be brought to the punishment.

فَسُبْحَٰنَ ٱللَّهِ 17 So glorify Allah

---

[1] Or 'though they had been faithless for the sake of their partners [i.e. their false gods].'

حِينَ تُمْسُونَ    when you enter evening

وَحِينَ تُصْبِحُونَ ۝    and when you rise at dawn.

وَلَهُ ٱلْحَمْدُ    18 To Him belongs all praise

فِى ٱلسَّمَٰوَٰتِ وَٱلْأَرْضِ    in the heavens and the earth,

وَعَشِيًّا وَحِينَ تُظْهِرُونَ ۝    at nightfall and when your enter noontime.

يُخْرِجُ ٱلْحَىَّ مِنَ ٱلْمَيِّتِ    19 He brings forth the living from the dead,

وَيُخْرِجُ ٱلْمَيِّتَ مِنَ ٱلْحَىِّ    and brings forth the dead from the living,

وَيُحْىِ ٱلْأَرْضَ بَعْدَ مَوْتِهَا    and revives the earth after its death.

وَكَذَٰلِكَ تُخْرَجُونَ ۝    Likewise you [too] shall be raised [from the dead].

وَمِنْ ءَايَٰتِهِۦٓ أَنْ خَلَقَكُم مِّن تُرَابٍ    20 Of His signs is that He created you from dust,

ثُمَّ إِذَآ أَنتُم بَشَرٌ تَنتَشِرُونَ ۝    then, behold, you are humans scattering [all over]!

وَمِنْ ءَايَٰتِهِۦٓ أَنْ خَلَقَ لَكُم    21 And of His signs is that He created for you

مِّنْ أَنفُسِكُمْ أَزْوَٰجًا    mates from your own selves

لِّتَسْكُنُوٓا۟ إِلَيْهَا    that you may take comfort in them,

وَجَعَلَ بَيْنَكُم مَّوَدَّةً وَرَحْمَةً    and He ordained affection and mercy between you.

إِنَّ فِى ذَٰلِكَ لَءَايَٰتٍ لِّقَوْمٍ يَتَفَكَّرُونَ ۝    There are indeed signs in that for a people who reflect.

وَمِنْ ءَايَٰتِهِۦ خَلْقُ ٱلسَّمَٰوَٰتِ    22 Among His signs is the creation of the heavens

وَٱلْأَرْضِ    and the earth,

وَٱخْتِلَٰفُ أَلْسِنَتِكُمْ وَأَلْوَٰنِكُمْ    and the difference of your languages and colours.

إِنَّ فِى ذَٰلِكَ لَءَايَٰتٍ لِّلْعَٰلِمِينَ ۝    There are indeed signs in that for those who know.

وَمِنْ ءَايَٰتِهِۦ مَنَامُكُم بِٱلَّيْلِ وَٱلنَّهَارِ    23 And of His signs is your sleep by night and day,

وَٱبْتِغَآؤُكُم مِّن فَضْلِهِۦٓ    and your pursuit of His grace.

إِنَّ فِى ذَٰلِكَ لَءَايَٰتٍ لِّقَوْمٍ يَسْمَعُونَ ۝    There are indeed signs in that for a people who listen.

وَمِنْ ءَايَٰتِهِۦ يُرِيكُمُ ٱلْبَرْقَ    24 And of His signs is that He shows you the lightning,

خَوْفًا وَطَمَعًا    arousing fear and hope,

وَيُنَزِّلُ مِنَ ٱلسَّمَآءِ مَآءً    and He sends down water from the sky,

فَيُحْىِۦ بِهِ ٱلْأَرْضَ بَعْدَ مَوْتِهَآ    and with it revives the earth after its death.

إِنَّ فِى ذَٰلِكَ لَءَايَٰتٍ    There are indeed signs in that

لِّقَوْمٍ يَعْقِلُونَ ۝    for a people who apply reason.

وَمِنْ ءَايَٰتِهِۦٓ أَن    25 And of His signs is that

تَقُومَ ٱلسَّمَآءُ وَٱلْأَرْضُ بِأَمْرِهِ

the sky and the earth stand by His command,

ثُمَّ إِذَا دَعَاكُمْ دَعْوَةً مِّنَ ٱلْأَرْضِ

and then, when He calls you forth from the earth,

إِذَآ أَنتُمْ تَخْرُجُونَ ٢٥

behold, you will come forth.

وَلَهُ مَن فِى ٱلسَّمَٰوَٰتِ

26 To Him belongs whoever is in the heavens

وَٱلْأَرْضِ

and the earth.

كُلٌّ لَّهُۥ قَٰنِتُونَ ٢٦

All are obedient to Him.

وَهُوَ ٱلَّذِى يَبْدَؤُاْ ٱلْخَلْقَ

27 It is He who originates the creation,

ثُمَّ يُعِيدُهُۥ

and then He will bring it back

وَهُوَ أَهْوَنُ عَلَيْهِ

—and that is more simple for Him.

وَلَهُ ٱلْمَثَلُ ٱلْأَعْلَىٰ فِى ٱلسَّمَٰوَٰتِ

His is the loftiest description in the heavens

وَٱلْأَرْضِ

and the earth.

وَهُوَ ٱلْعَزِيزُ ٱلْحَكِيمُ ٢٧

And He is the All-mighty, the All-wise.

ضَرَبَ لَكُم مَّثَلًا مِّنْ أَنفُسِكُمْ

28 He draws for you an example from yourselves:

هَل لَّكُم مِّن مَّا مَلَكَتْ أَيْمَٰنُكُم

Do you have among your slaves

مِّن شُرَكَآءَ

any partners

فِى مَا رَزَقْنَٰكُمْ

[who may share] in what We have provided you,

فَأَنتُمْ فِيهِ سَوَآءٌ

so that you are equal in its respect,

تَخَافُونَهُمْ كَخِيفَتِكُمْ أَنفُسَكُمْ

and you revere them as you revere one another?[1]

كَذَٰلِكَ نُفَصِّلُ ٱلْءَايَٰتِ

Thus do We elaborate[2] the signs

لِقَوْمٍ يَعْقِلُونَ ٢٨

for a people who apply reason.

بَلِ ٱتَّبَعَ ٱلَّذِينَ ظَلَمُوٓاْ أَهْوَآءَهُم

29 Rather the wrongdoers follow their own desires

بِغَيْرِ عِلْمٍ

without any knowledge.

فَمَن يَهْدِى مَنْ أَضَلَّ ٱللَّهُ

So who will guide those whom Allah has led astray?

وَمَا لَهُم مِّن نَّٰصِرِينَ ٢٩

They will have no helpers.

فَأَقِمْ وَجْهَكَ لِلدِّينِ

30 So set your heart on the religion

حَنِيفًا

as a people of pure faith,

فِطْرَتَ ٱللَّهِ

the origination of Allah

---

[1] Or 'revere your own folks.'

[2] Or 'articulate.'

أَلَّتِى فَطَرَ ٱلنَّاسَ عَلَيۡهَا

according to which He originated mankind

لَا تَبۡدِيلَ لِخَلۡقِ ٱللَّهِ

(There is no altering Allah's creation;

ذَٰلِكَ ٱلدِّينُ ٱلۡقَيِّمُ

that is the upright religion,

وَلَـٰكِنَّ أَكۡثَرَ ٱلنَّاسِ لَا يَعۡلَمُونَ ۞

but most people do not know.)

مُنِيبِينَ إِلَيۡهِ 31

—turning to Him in penitence,

وَٱتَّقُوهُ وَأَقِيمُوا۟ ٱلصَّلَوٰةَ

and be wary of Him, and maintain the prayer,

وَلَا تَكُونُوا۟ مِنَ ٱلۡمُشۡرِكِينَ ۞

and do not be among the polytheists

مِنَ ٱلَّذِينَ فَرَّقُوا۟ دِينَهُمۡ 32

—of those who split up their religion

وَكَانُوا۟ شِيَعًا

and became sects:

كُلُّ حِزۡبٍۭ بِمَا لَدَيۡهِمۡ فَرِحُونَ ۞

each faction exulting in what it possessed.

وَإِذَا مَسَّ ٱلنَّاسَ ضُرٌّ 33

When distress befalls people,

دَعَوۡا۟ رَبَّهُم

they supplicate their Lord,

مُّنِيبِينَ إِلَيۡهِ

turning to Him in penitence.

ثُمَّ إِذَآ أَذَاقَهُم مِّنۡهُ رَحۡمَةً

Then, when He lets them taste His mercy,

إِذَا فَرِيقٌ مِّنۡهُم بِرَبِّهِمۡ يُشۡرِكُونَ ۞

behold, a part of them ascribe partners to their Lord,

لِيَكۡفُرُوا۟ بِمَآ ءَاتَيۡنَـٰهُمۡ 34

being ungrateful toward what We have given them.

فَتَمَتَّعُوا۟ فَسَوۡفَ تَعۡلَمُونَ ۞

So let them enjoy. Soon they will know!

أَمۡ أَنزَلۡنَا عَلَيۡهِمۡ سُلۡطَـٰنًا 35

Have We sent down to them any authority

فَهُوَ يَتَكَلَّمُ بِمَا كَانُوا۟ بِهِۦ يُشۡرِكُونَ ۞

which might speak of what they associate with Him?

وَإِذَآ أَذَقۡنَا ٱلنَّاسَ رَحۡمَةً 36

And when We let people taste [Our] mercy,

فَرِحُوا۟ بِهَا

they exult in it;

وَإِن تُصِبۡهُمۡ سَيِّئَةٌۢ

but should an ill visit them

بِمَا قَدَّمَتۡ أَيۡدِيهِمۡ

because of what their hands have sent ahead,

إِذَا هُمۡ يَقۡنَطُونَ ۞

behold, they become despondent!

أَوَلَمۡ يَرَوۡا۟ 37

Do they not see that Allah expands the provision

أَنَّ ٱللَّهَ يَبۡسُطُ ٱلرِّزۡقَ لِمَن يَشَآءُ

for whomever He wishes,

وَيَقۡدِرُ

and tightens it?

إِنَّ فِى ذَٰلِكَ لَأٓيَـٰتٍ

There are indeed signs in that

لِقَوۡمٍ يُؤۡمِنُونَ ۝     for a people who have faith.

فَـَٔاتِ ذَا ٱلۡقُرۡبَىٰ حَقَّهُۥ     38 *Give* the relative his right,

وَٱلۡمِسۡكِينَ وَٱبۡنَ ٱلسَّبِيلِ     and the needy and the traveller [as well].

ذَٰلِكَ خَيۡرٌ لِّلَّذِينَ يُرِيدُونَ وَجۡهَ ٱللَّهِ     That is better for those who seek Allah's pleasure,

وَأُوْلَـٰٓئِكَ هُمُ ٱلۡمُفۡلِحُونَ ۝     and it is they who are the felicitous.

وَمَآ ءَاتَيۡتُم مِّن رِّبًا     39 That which you give in usury

لِّيَرۡبُوَاْ فِىٓ أَمۡوَٰلِ ٱلنَّاسِ     in order that it may increase people's wealth

فَلَا يَرۡبُواْ عِندَ ٱللَّهِ     does not increase with Allah.

وَمَآ ءَاتَيۡتُم مِّن زَكَوٰةٍ     But what you pay as *zakāt*

تُرِيدُونَ وَجۡهَ ٱللَّهِ     seeking Allah's pleasure

فَأُوْلَـٰٓئِكَ هُمُ ٱلۡمُضۡعِفُونَ ۝     —it is they who will be given a manifold increase.

ٱللَّهُ ٱلَّذِى خَلَقَكُمۡ     40 It is Allah who created you

ثُمَّ رَزَقَكُمۡ     and then He provided for you,

ثُمَّ يُمِيتُكُمۡ ثُمَّ يُحۡيِيكُمۡ     then He makes you die, then He will bring you to life.

هَلۡ مِن شُرَكَآئِكُم     Is there anyone among your partners

مَّن يَفۡعَلُ مِن ذَٰلِكُم مِّن شَىۡءٍ     who does anything of that kind?

سُبۡحَٰنَهُۥ وَتَعَٰلَىٰ     Immaculate is He and exalted

عَمَّا يُشۡرِكُونَ ۝     above [having] any partners that they ascribe [to Him]!

ظَهَرَ ٱلۡفَسَادُ فِى ٱلۡبَرِّ وَٱلۡبَحۡرِ     41 Corruption has appeared in land and sea

بِمَا كَسَبَتۡ أَيۡدِى ٱلنَّاسِ     because of the doings of the people's hands,

لِيُذِيقَهُم     that He may make them taste

بَعۡضَ ٱلَّذِى عَمِلُواْ     something of what they have done,

لَعَلَّهُمۡ يَرۡجِعُونَ ۝     so that they may come back.

قُلۡ سِيرُواْ فِى ٱلۡأَرۡضِ     42 *Say,* 'Travel over the land

فَٱنظُرُواْ     and then observe

كَيۡفَ كَانَ عَٰقِبَةُ ٱلَّذِينَ مِن قَبۡلُ     how was the fate of those who were before [you],

كَانَ أَكۡثَرُهُم مُّشۡرِكِينَ ۝     most of whom were polytheists.'

فَأَقِمۡ وَجۡهَكَ لِلدِّينِ ٱلۡقَيِّمِ     43 So set *your* heart on the upright religion,

مِن قَبۡلِ أَن يَأۡتِىَ يَوۡمٌ لَّا مَرَدَّ لَهُۥ     before there comes a day irrevocable

مِنَ ٱللَّهِ     from Allah.

يَوْمَئِذٍ يَصَّدَّعُونَ ۝     On that day they shall be split [into various groups].[1]

مَن كَفَرَ 44     44 Whoever is faithless

فَعَلَيْهِ كُفْرُهُ ۖ     shall face the consequences of his faithlessness,

وَمَنْ عَمِلَ صَٰلِحًا     and those who act righteously

فَلِأَنفُسِهِمْ يَمْهَدُونَ ۝     only prepare for their own souls,

لِيَجْزِىَ ٱلَّذِينَ ءَامَنُوا 45     45 that He may reward those who have faith

وَعَمِلُوا ٱلصَّٰلِحَٰتِ     and do righteous deeds

مِن فَضْلِهِ ۚ     out of His grace.

إِنَّهُ لَا يُحِبُّ ٱلْكَٰفِرِينَ ۝     Indeed He does not like the faithless.

وَمِنْ ءَايَٰتِهِ أَن يُرْسِلَ ٱلرِّيَاحَ 46     46 And of His signs is that He sends the winds

مُبَشِّرَٰتٍ     as bearers of good news

وَلِيُذِيقَكُم مِّن رَّحْمَتِهِ     and to let you taste of His mercy,

وَلِتَجْرِىَ ٱلْفُلْكُ بِأَمْرِهِ     and that the ships may sail by His command,

وَلِتَبْتَغُوا مِن فَضْلِهِ     and that you may seek of His grace,

وَلَعَلَّكُمْ تَشْكُرُونَ ۝     and so that you may give [Him] thanks.

وَلَقَدْ أَرْسَلْنَا مِن قَبْلِكَ رُسُلًا إِلَىٰ قَوْمِهِمْ 47     47 Certainly We sent apostles to their people before *you*,

فَجَآءُوهُم بِٱلْبَيِّنَٰتِ     and they brought them manifest proofs.

فَٱنتَقَمْنَا مِنَ ٱلَّذِينَ أَجْرَمُوا ۖ     Then We took vengeance upon those who were guilty,

وَكَانَ حَقًّا عَلَيْنَا نَصْرُ ٱلْمُؤْمِنِينَ ۝     and it was a must for Us to help the faithful.

ٱللَّهُ ٱلَّذِى يُرْسِلُ ٱلرِّيَٰحَ 48     48 It is Allah who sends the winds.

فَتُثِيرُ سَحَابًا     Then they raise a cloud,

فَيَبْسُطُهُ فِى ٱلسَّمَآءِ كَيْفَ يَشَآءُ     then He spreads it as He wishes in the sky,

وَيَجْعَلُهُ كِسَفًا     and forms it into fragments,

فَتَرَى ٱلْوَدْقَ يَخْرُجُ مِنْ خِلَٰلِهِ ۖ     whereat you see the rain issuing from its midst.

فَإِذَآ أَصَابَ بِهِ     Then, when He strikes with it

مَن يَشَآءُ مِنْ عِبَادِهِ     whomever of His servants that He wishes,

إِذَا هُمْ يَسْتَبْشِرُونَ ۝     behold, they rejoice;

وَإِن كَانُوا 49     49 and indeed they had,

---

[1] See 42:7, 56:7-56.

مِن قَبْلِ أَن يُنَزَّلَ عَلَيْهِم

before it was sent down upon them,

مِّن قَبْلِهِۦ لَمُبْلِسِينَ ۝

been despondent earlier.

فَٱنظُرْ إِلَىٰٓ ءَاثَٰرِ رَحْمَتِ ٱللَّهِ

50 So observe the effects of Allah's mercy:

كَيْفَ يُحْىِ ٱلْأَرْضَ بَعْدَ مَوْتِهَآ

how He revives the earth after its death!

إِنَّ ذَٰلِكَ لَمُحْىِ ٱلْمَوْتَىٰ

Indeed He is the reviver of the dead,

وَهُوَ عَلَىٰ كُلِّ شَىْءٍ قَدِيرٌ ۝

and He has power over all things.

وَلَئِنْ أَرْسَلْنَا رِيحًا

51 And if We send a wind

فَرَأَوْهُ مُصْفَرًّا

and they see it[1] turn yellow,

لَّظَلُّواْ مِنۢ بَعْدِهِۦ يَكْفُرُونَ ۝

they will surely become ungrateful after that.[2]

فَإِنَّكَ لَا تُسْمِعُ ٱلْمَوْتَىٰ

52 Indeed *you* cannot make the dead hear,

وَلَا تُسْمِعُ ٱلصُّمَّ ٱلدُّعَآءَ

nor can *you* make the deaf hear the call

إِذَا وَلَّوْاْ مُدْبِرِينَ ۝

when they turn their backs [upon *you*],

وَمَآ أَنتَ بِهَٰدِ ٱلْعُمْىِ عَن ضَلَٰلَتِهِمْ

53 nor can *you* lead the blind out of their error.

إِن تُسْمِعُ إِلَّا مَن

*You* can make hear only those

يُؤْمِنُ بِـَٔايَٰتِنَا فَهُم مُّسْلِمُونَ ۝ ✦

who have faith in Our signs, and thus have submitted.

ٱللَّهُ ٱلَّذِى خَلَقَكُم مِّن ضَعْفٍ

54 It is Allah who created you from [a state of] weakness,

ثُمَّ جَعَلَ مِنۢ بَعْدِ ضَعْفٍ قُوَّةً

then He gave you power after weakness.

ثُمَّ جَعَلَ مِنۢ بَعْدِ قُوَّةٍ ضَعْفًا وَشَيْبَةً

Then, after power, He ordained weakness and old age:

يَخْلُقُ مَا يَشَآءُ

He creates whatever He wishes,

وَهُوَ ٱلْعَلِيمُ ٱلْقَدِيرُ ۝

and He is the All-knowing, the All-powerful.

وَيَوْمَ تَقُومُ ٱلسَّاعَةُ

55 And on the day when the Hour sets in

يُقْسِمُ ٱلْمُجْرِمُونَ

the guilty will swear

مَا لَبِثُواْ غَيْرَ سَاعَةٍ

that they had remained only for an hour.

كَذَٰلِكَ كَانُواْ يُؤْفَكُونَ ۝

That is how they were used to lying [in the world].

وَقَالَ ٱلَّذِينَ أُوتُواْ ٱلْعِلْمَ وَٱلْإِيمَٰنَ

56 But those who were given knowledge and faith will say,

لَقَدْ لَبِثْتُمْ فِى كِتَٰبِ ٱللَّهِ

'Certainly you remained in Allah's Book[3]

إِلَىٰ يَوْمِ ٱلْبَعْثِ

until the Day of Resurrection.

---

[1] That is, their tillage, fields and orchards.

[2] That is, after they have been joyous on Allah's reviving the dead earth and turning it green.

[3] That is, in the Preserved Tablet. Cf. 56:78.

This is the Day of Resurrection,

     but you did not know.'

57 On that day

     the excuses of the wrongdoers will not benefit them,

       nor will they be asked to propitiate [Allah].

58 Certainly we have drawn for mankind

     in this Qur'ān

     every [kind of] parable.

Indeed if *you* bring them a sign,[1]

     the faithless will surely say,

     'You are nothing but fabricators!'

59 Thus does Allah seal the hearts

     of those who do not know.

60 So *be patient!*

     Allah's promise is indeed true.

     And do not let *yourself* be upset

     by those who have no conviction.

# 31. SŪRAT LUQMĀN[2]

In the Name of Allah,

     the All-beneficent, the All-merciful

1 *Alif, Lām, Mīm.*

2 These are the signs of the Definitive Book,

3   a guidance and mercy for the virtuous,

4   who maintain the prayer,

     and pay the *zakāt,*

---

[1] That is, a miracle.

[2] The *sūrah* is named after Luqmān, whose account is given in verses 12-19.

وَهُم بِٱلْأَخِرَةِ هُمْ يُوقِنُونَ ۝  and are certain of the Hereafter.

أُوْلَٰٓئِكَ عَلَىٰ هُدًى مِّن رَّبِّهِمْ  5 Those follow their Lord's guidance,

وَأُوْلَٰٓئِكَ هُمُ ٱلْمُفْلِحُونَ ۝  and it is they who are the felicitous.

وَمِنَ ٱلنَّاسِ مَن  6 Among the people is he

يَشْتَرِى لَهْوَ ٱلْحَدِيثِ  who buys diversionary talk

لِيُضِلَّ عَن سَبِيلِ ٱللَّهِ  that he may lead [people] astray from Allah's way

بِغَيْرِ عِلْمٍ  without any knowledge,

وَيَتَّخِذَهَا هُزُوًا  and he takes it in derision.

أُوْلَٰٓئِكَ لَهُمْ عَذَابٌ مُّهِينٌ ۝  For such there is a humiliating punishment.

وَإِذَا تُتْلَىٰ عَلَيْهِ ءَايَٰتُنَا  7 And when Our signs are recited to him

وَلَّىٰ مُسْتَكْبِرًا  he turns away disdainfully

كَأَن لَّمْ يَسْمَعْهَا  as if he had not heard them [at all],

كَأَنَّ فِىٓ أُذُنَيْهِ وَقْرًا  as if there were a deafness in his ears.

فَبَشِّرْهُ بِعَذَابٍ أَلِيمٍ ۝  So *inform* him of a painful punishment.

إِنَّ ٱلَّذِينَ ءَامَنُوا  8 As for those who have faith

وَعَمِلُوا ٱلصَّٰلِحَٰتِ  and do righteous deeds,

لَهُمْ جَنَّٰتُ ٱلنَّعِيمِ ۝  for them will be gardens of bliss,

خَٰلِدِينَ فِيهَا  9 to remain in them [forever]

وَعْدَ ٱللَّهِ حَقًّا  —a true promise of Allah,

وَهُوَ ٱلْعَزِيزُ ٱلْحَكِيمُ ۝  and He is the All-mighty, the All-wise.

خَلَقَ ٱلسَّمَٰوَٰتِ  10 He created the heavens

بِغَيْرِ عَمَدٍ تَرَوْنَهَا  without any pillars that you may see,

وَأَلْقَىٰ فِى ٱلْأَرْضِ رَوَٰسِىَ  and cast firm mountains in the earth

أَن تَمِيدَ بِكُمْ  lest it should shake with you,

وَبَثَّ فِيهَا مِن كُلِّ دَآبَّةٍ  and He has scattered in it every kind of animal.

وَأَنزَلْنَا مِنَ ٱلسَّمَآءِ مَآءً  And We sent down water from the sky

فَأَنۢبَتْنَا فِيهَا مِن كُلِّ زَوْجٍ كَرِيمٍ ۝  and caused every splendid kind [of plant] to grow in it.

هَٰذَا خَلْقُ ٱللَّهِ  11 This is the creation of Allah.

فَأَرُونِى مَاذَا خَلَقَ ٱلَّذِينَ مِن دُونِهِ  Now show Me what others besides Him have created.

بَلِ ٱلظَّٰلِمُونَ فِى ضَلَٰلٍ مُّبِينٍ ۝  Rather the wrongdoers are in manifest error!

وَلَقَدۡ ءَاتَيۡنَا لُقۡمَٰنَ ٱلۡحِكۡمَةَ 12 Certainly We gave Luqman wisdom,

أَنِ ٱشۡكُرۡ لِلَّهِ saying, 'Give thanks to Allah;

وَمَن يَشۡكُرۡ and whoever gives thanks,

فَإِنَّمَا يَشۡكُرُ لِنَفۡسِهِ gives thanks only for his own sake.

وَمَن كَفَرَ And whoever is ungrateful, [let him know that]

فَإِنَّ ٱللَّهَ غَنِيٌّ حَمِيدٌ ۝ Allah is indeed all-sufficient, all-laudable.'

وَإِذۡ قَالَ لُقۡمَٰنُ لِٱبۡنِهِۦ 13 When Luqman said to his son,

وَهُوَ يَعِظُهُۥ as he advised him:

يَٰبُنَيَّ لَا تُشۡرِكۡ بِٱللَّهِ 'O my son! Do not ascribe any partners to Allah.

إِنَّ ٱلشِّرۡكَ لَظُلۡمٌ عَظِيمٌ ۝ Polytheism is indeed a great injustice.'

وَوَصَّيۡنَا ٱلۡإِنسَٰنَ بِوَٰلِدَيۡهِ 14 We have enjoined man concerning his parents:

حَمَلَتۡهُ أُمُّهُۥ His mother carried him

وَهۡنًا عَلَىٰ وَهۡنٍ through weakness upon weakness,

وَفِصَٰلُهُۥ فِى عَامَيۡنِ and his weaning takes two years.

أَنِ ٱشۡكُرۡ لِى وَلِوَٰلِدَيۡكَ Give thanks to Me and to your parents.

إِلَىَّ ٱلۡمَصِيرُ ۝ To Me is the return.

وَإِن جَٰهَدَاكَ عَلَىٰٓ أَن تُشۡرِكَ بِى 15 But if they urge you to ascribe to Me as partner

مَا لَيۡسَ لَكَ بِهِۦ عِلۡمٌ that of which you have no knowledge,

فَلَا تُطِعۡهُمَا then do not obey them.

وَصَاحِبۡهُمَا فِى ٱلدُّنۡيَا مَعۡرُوفًا Keep their company honourably in this world

وَٱتَّبِعۡ سَبِيلَ and follow the way

مَنۡ أَنَابَ إِلَىَّ of him who turns to Me penitently.

ثُمَّ إِلَىَّ مَرۡجِعُكُمۡ Then to Me will be your return,

فَأُنَبِّئُكُم whereat I will inform you

بِمَا كُنتُمۡ تَعۡمَلُونَ ۝ concerning what you used to do.

يَٰبُنَيَّ 16 'O my son!

إِنَّهَآ إِن تَكُ مِثۡقَالَ حَبَّةٍ مِّنۡ خَرۡدَلٍ Even if it should be the weight of a mustard seed,

فَتَكُن فِى صَخۡرَةٍ and [even though] it should be in a rock,

أَوۡ فِى ٱلسَّمَٰوَٰتِ أَوۡ فِى ٱلۡأَرۡضِ or in the heavens, or in the earth,

يَأۡتِ بِهَا ٱللَّهُ Allah will produce it.

إِنَّ ٱللَّهَ لَطِيفٌ خَبِيرٌ ۝    Indeed Allah is all-attentive, all-aware.

يَـٰبُنَىَّ 17    O my son!

أَقِمِ ٱلصَّلَوٰةَ    Maintain the prayer

وَأْمُرْ بِٱلْمَعْرُوفِ    and bid what is right

وَٱنْهَ عَنِ ٱلْمُنكَرِ    and forbid what is wrong,

وَٱصْبِرْ عَلَىٰ مَآ أَصَابَكَ    and be patient through whatever may visit you.

إِنَّ ذَٰلِكَ مِنْ عَزْمِ ٱلْأُمُورِ ۝    That is indeed the steadiest of courses.

وَلَا تُصَعِّرْ خَدَّكَ لِلنَّاسِ 18    Do not turn your cheek disdainfully from the people,

وَلَا تَمْشِ فِى ٱلْأَرْضِ مَرَحًا    and do not walk exultantly on the earth.

إِنَّ ٱللَّهَ لَا يُحِبُّ كُلَّ مُخْتَالٍ فَخُورٍ ۝    Indeed Allah does not like any swaggering braggart.

وَٱقْصِدْ فِى مَشْيِكَ 19    Be modest in your bearing,

وَٱغْضُضْ مِن صَوْتِكَ    and lower your voice.

إِنَّ أَنكَرَ ٱلْأَصْوَٰتِ لَصَوْتُ ٱلْحَمِيرِ ۝    Indeed the ungainliest of voices is the donkey's voice.'

أَلَمْ تَرَوْا۟ أَنَّ ٱللَّهَ سَخَّرَ لَكُم 20    Do you not see that Allah has disposed for you

مَّا فِى ٱلسَّمَـٰوَٰتِ    whatever there is in the heavens

وَمَا فِى ٱلْأَرْضِ    and whatever there is in the earth

وَأَسْبَغَ عَلَيْكُمْ نِعَمَهُ    and He has showered upon you His blessings,

ظَـٰهِرَةً وَبَاطِنَةً    the outward and the inward?

وَمِنَ ٱلنَّاسِ    Yet among the people are those

مَن يُجَـٰدِلُ فِى ٱللَّهِ    who dispute concerning Allah

بِغَيْرِ عِلْمٍ    without any knowledge

وَلَا هُدًى    or guidance

وَلَا كِتَـٰبٍ مُّنِيرٍ ۝    or an illuminating scripture.

وَإِذَا قِيلَ لَهُمُ 21    When they are told,

ٱتَّبِعُوا۟ مَآ أَنزَلَ ٱللَّهُ    'Follow what Allah has sent down,'

قَالُوا۟ بَلْ نَتَّبِعُ    they say, 'We will rather follow

مَا وَجَدْنَا عَلَيْهِ ءَابَآءَنَآ    what we found our fathers following.'

أَوَلَوْ كَانَ ٱلشَّيْطَـٰنُ يَدْعُوهُمْ    What! Even if Satan be calling them

إِلَىٰ عَذَابِ ٱلسَّعِيرِ ۝    to the punishment of the Blaze?

وَمَن يُسۡلِمۡ وَجۡهَهُۥٓ إِلَى ٱللَّهِ 22 Whoever surrenders his heart to Allah

وَهُوَ مُحۡسِنٌ     and is virtuous,

فَقَدِ ٱسۡتَمۡسَكَ بِٱلۡعُرۡوَةِ ٱلۡوُثۡقَىٰ     has certainly held fast to the firmest handle,

وَإِلَى ٱللَّهِ عَٰقِبَةُ ٱلۡأُمُورِ ٢٢     and with Allah lies the outcome of all matters.

وَمَن كَفَرَ 23 As for those who are faithless,

فَلَا يَحۡزُنكَ كُفۡرُهُۥٓ     let their faithlessness not grieve *you*.

إِلَيۡنَا مَرۡجِعُهُمۡ     To Us will be their return,

فَنُنَبِّئُهُم     and We will inform them

بِمَا عَمِلُوٓاْ     about what they have done.

إِنَّ ٱللَّهَ عَلِيمٌۢ بِذَاتِ ٱلصُّدُورِ ٢٢     Indeed Allah knows best what is in the breasts.

نُمَتِّعُهُمۡ قَلِيلٗا 24 We will provide for them for a short time,

ثُمَّ نَضۡطَرُّهُمۡ     then We will shove them

إِلَىٰ عَذَابٍ غَلِيظٖ ٢٤     toward a harsh punishment.

وَلَئِن سَأَلۡتَهُم 25 If *you* ask them,

مَّنۡ خَلَقَ ٱلسَّمَٰوَٰتِ وَٱلۡأَرۡضَ     'Who created the heavens and the earth?'

لَيَقُولُنَّ ٱللَّهُ     they will surely say, 'Allah.'

قُلِ ٱلۡحَمۡدُ لِلَّهِ     *Say,* 'All praise belongs to Allah!'

بَلۡ أَكۡثَرُهُمۡ لَا يَعۡلَمُونَ ٢٥     Yet most of them do not know.

لِلَّهِ مَا فِي ٱلسَّمَٰوَٰتِ 26 To Allah belongs whatever is in the heavens

وَٱلۡأَرۡضِ     and the earth.

إِنَّ ٱللَّهَ هُوَ ٱلۡغَنِيُّ ٱلۡحَمِيدُ ٢٦     Indeed Allah is the All-sufficient, the All-laudable.

وَلَوۡ أَنَّمَا فِي ٱلۡأَرۡضِ مِن شَجَرَةٍ أَقۡلَٰمٌ 27 If all the trees on the earth were pens,

وَٱلۡبَحۡرُ يَمُدُّهُۥ مِنۢ بَعۡدِهِۦ سَبۡعَةُ أَبۡحُرٖ     and the sea replenished with seven more seas [were ink],

مَّا نَفِدَتۡ كَلِمَٰتُ ٱللَّهِ     the words of Allah would not be spent.

إِنَّ ٱللَّهَ عَزِيزٌ حَكِيمٌ ٢٧     Indeed Allah is all-mighty, all-wise.

مَّا خَلۡقُكُمۡ وَلَا بَعۡثُكُمۡ 28 Your creation and your resurrection are not

إِلَّا كَنَفۡسٖ وَٰحِدَةٍ     but as of a single soul.

إِنَّ ٱللَّهَ سَمِيعٌۢ بَصِيرٌ ٢٨     Indeed Allah is all-hearing, all-seeing.

أَلَمۡ تَرَ 29 Have *you* not regarded

أَنَّ ٱللَّهَ يُولِجُ ٱلَّيۡلَ فِي ٱلنَّهَارِ     that Allah makes the night pass into the day

وَيُولِجُ ٱلنَّهَارَ فِى ٱلَّيۡلِ     and makes the day pass into the night;

وَسَخَّرَ ٱلشَّمۡسَ وَٱلۡقَمَرَ     and He has disposed the sun and the moon,

كُلٌّ يَجۡرِى إِلَىٰٓ أَجَلٍ مُّسَمًّى     each moving for a specified term,

وَأَنَّ ٱللَّهَ بِمَا تَعۡمَلُونَ خَبِيرٌ     and that Allah is well aware of what you do?

ذَٰلِكَ بِأَنَّ ٱللَّهَ هُوَ ٱلۡحَقُّ     30 That is because Allah is the Reality,[1]

وَأَنَّ مَا يَدۡعُونَ مِن دُونِهِ ٱلۡبَٰطِلُ     and whatever they invoke besides Him is nullity,[2]

وَأَنَّ ٱللَّهَ هُوَ ٱلۡعَلِىُّ ٱلۡكَبِيرُ     and because Allah is the All-exalted, the All-great.

أَلَمۡ تَرَ     31 Have *you* not regarded

أَنَّ ٱلۡفُلۡكَ تَجۡرِى فِى ٱلۡبَحۡرِ     that the ships sail at sea

بِنِعۡمَتِ ٱللَّهِ     by Allah's blessing,

لِيُرِيَكُم مِّنۡ ءَايَٰتِهِۦٓ     that He may show you some of His signs?

إِنَّ فِى ذَٰلِكَ لَأٓيَٰتٍ     There are indeed signs in that

لِّكُلِّ صَبَّارٍ شَكُورٍ     for every patient and grateful [servant].

وَإِذَا غَشِيَهُم مَّوۡجٌ كَٱلظُّلَلِ     32 When waves cover them like awnings,

دَعَوُاْ ٱللَّهَ مُخۡلِصِينَ لَهُ ٱلدِّينَ     they invoke Allah, putting exclusive faith in Him.

فَلَمَّا نَجَّىٰهُمۡ إِلَى ٱلۡبَرِّ     But when He delivers them towards land,

فَمِنۡهُم مُّقۡتَصِدٌ     [only] some of them remain unswerving.

وَمَا يَجۡحَدُ بِـَٔايَٰتِنَآ     And no one will impugn Our signs

إِلَّا كُلُّ خَتَّارٍ كَفُورٍ     except an ungrateful traitor.

يَٰٓأَيُّهَا ٱلنَّاسُ ٱتَّقُواْ رَبَّكُمۡ     33 O mankind! Be wary of your Lord

وَٱخۡشَوۡاْ يَوۡمًا     and fear the day

لَّا يَجۡزِى وَالِدٌ عَن وَلَدِهِۦ     when a father shall not atone for his child,

وَلَا مَوۡلُودٌ هُوَ جَازٍ عَن وَالِدِهِۦ شَيۡـًٔا     nor the child shall atone for its father in any wise.

إِنَّ وَعۡدَ ٱللَّهِ حَقٌّ     Indeed Allah's promise is true.

فَلَا تَغُرَّنَّكُمُ ٱلۡحَيَوٰةُ ٱلدُّنۡيَا     So do not let the life of the world deceive you,

وَلَا يَغُرَّنَّكُم بِٱللَّهِ ٱلۡغَرُورُ     nor let the Deceiver[3] deceive you concerning Allah.

إِنَّ ٱللَّهَ عِندَهُۥ عِلۡمُ ٱلسَّاعَةِ     34 Indeed the knowledge of the Hour is with Allah.

---

[1] Or 'That is because Allah is the Truth.'

[2] Or 'what they invoke besides Him is falsehood.'

[3] That is, Satan, or anything that diverts a human being from the path of Allah.

وَيُنَزِّلُ ٱلۡغَيۡثَ    He sends down the rain,

وَيَعۡلَمُ مَا فِى ٱلۡأَرۡحَامِ    and He knows what is in the wombs.

وَمَا تَدۡرِى نَفۡسٌ مَّاذَا تَكۡسِبُ غَدًا    No soul knows what it will earn tomorrow,

وَمَا تَدۡرِى نَفۡسٌ بِأَىِّ أَرۡضٍ تَمُوتُ    and no soul knows in what land it will die.

إِنَّ ٱللَّهَ عَلِيمٌ خَبِيرٌ ۝    Indeed Allah is all-knowing, all-aware.

## سُورَةُ السَّجَدَةِ       32. SŪRAT AL-SAJDAH[1]

بِسۡمِ ٱللَّهِ     In the Name of Allah,

ٱلرَّحۡمَٰنِ ٱلرَّحِيمِ     the All-beneficent, the All-merciful

الٓمٓ ۝   1 *Alif, Lām, Mīm.*

تَنزِيلُ ٱلۡكِتَٰبِ   2 The [gradual] sending down of the Book,

لَا رَيۡبَ فِيهِ    there is no doubt in it,

مِن رَّبِّ ٱلۡعَٰلَمِينَ ۝    is from the Lord of all the worlds.

أَمۡ يَقُولُونَ ٱفۡتَرَىٰهُ   3 Do they say, 'He has fabricated it?'

بَلۡ هُوَ ٱلۡحَقُّ مِن رَّبِّكَ    Rather it is the truth from *your* Lord,

لِتُنذِرَ قَوۡمًا    that *you* may warn a people

مَّآ أَتَىٰهُم مِّن نَّذِيرٍ    to whom there did not come any warner

مِّن قَبۡلِكَ    before *you*,

لَعَلَّهُمۡ يَهۡتَدُونَ ۝    so that they may be guided [to the right path].

ٱللَّهُ ٱلَّذِى خَلَقَ ٱلسَّمَٰوَٰتِ وَٱلۡأَرۡضَ   4 It is Allah who created the heavens and the earth

وَمَا بَيۡنَهُمَا    and whatever is between them

فِى سِتَّةِ أَيَّامٍ    in six days,[2]

ثُمَّ ٱسۡتَوَىٰ عَلَى ٱلۡعَرۡشِ    then He settled on the Throne.

مَا لَكُم مِّن دُونِهِۦ مِن وَلِىٍّ    You do not have besides Him any guardian

وَلَا شَفِيعٍ    or intercessor.

أَفَلَا تَتَذَكَّرُونَ ۝    Will you not then take admonition?

---

[1] The *sūrah* takes its name from verse 15, which mentions prostration (*sajdah*),

[2] That is, in six periods of time. Cf. 57:4.

يُدَبِّرُ ٱلْأَمْرَ مِنَ ٱلسَّمَآءِ إِلَى ٱلْأَرْضِ 5 He directs the command[1] from the heaven to the earth;

ثُمَّ يَعْرُجُ إِلَيْهِ    then it ascends toward Him

فِى يَوْمٍ كَانَ مِقْدَارُهُ أَلْفَ سَنَةٍ    in a day[2] whose span is a thousand years

مِّمَّا تَعُدُّونَ ۝    by your reckoning.

ذَٰلِكَ عَٰلِمُ ٱلْغَيْبِ وَٱلشَّهَٰدَةِ 6 That is the Knower of the sensible and the Unseen,

ٱلْعَزِيزُ ٱلرَّحِيمُ ۝    the All-mighty, the All-merciful,

ٱلَّذِىٓ أَحْسَنَ كُلَّ شَىْءٍ خَلَقَهُ 7 who perfected everything that He created,

وَبَدَأَ خَلْقَ ٱلْإِنسَٰنِ مِن طِينٍ ۝    and commenced man's creation from clay.

ثُمَّ جَعَلَ نَسْلَهُ 8 Then He made his progeny

مِن سُلَٰلَةٍ مِّن مَّآءٍ مَّهِينٍ ۝    from an extract of a base fluid.

ثُمَّ سَوَّىٰهُ 9 Then He proportioned him

وَنَفَخَ فِيهِ مِن رُّوحِهِ    and breathed into him of His Spirit,

وَجَعَلَ لَكُمُ ٱلسَّمْعَ وَٱلْأَبْصَٰرَ    and made for you the hearing, the sight,

وَٱلْأَفْـِٔدَةَ    and the hearts.

قَلِيلًا مَّا تَشْكُرُونَ ۝    Little do you thank.

وَقَالُوٓا۟ أَءِذَا ضَلَلْنَا فِى ٱلْأَرْضِ 10 They say, 'When we have been lost in the dust,[3]

أَءِنَّا لَفِى خَلْقٍ جَدِيدٍ    shall we be indeed created anew?'

بَلْ هُم بِلِقَآءِ رَبِّهِمْ كَٰفِرُونَ ۝    Rather they disbelieve in the encounter with their Lord.

قُلْ يَتَوَفَّىٰكُم مَّلَكُ ٱلْمَوْتِ 11 Say, 'You will be taken away by the angel of death,

ٱلَّذِى وُكِّلَ بِكُمْ    who has been charged with you.

ثُمَّ إِلَىٰ رَبِّكُمْ تُرْجَعُونَ ۝    Then you will be brought back to your Lord.'

وَلَوْ تَرَىٰٓ 12 Were you to see

إِذِ ٱلْمُجْرِمُونَ نَاكِسُوا۟ رُءُوسِهِمْ    when the guilty hang their heads

عِندَ رَبِّهِمْ    before their Lord

رَبَّنَآ أَبْصَرْنَا وَسَمِعْنَا    [confessing], 'Our Lord! We have seen and heard.

فَٱرْجِعْنَا نَعْمَلْ صَٰلِحًا    Send us back so that we may act righteously.

إِنَّا مُوقِنُونَ ۝    Indeed we are [now] convinced.'

---

[1] Cf. 10:3, 31, 13:2.

[2] That is, in a period of time.

[3] That is, 'Shall we be brought forth again after our bodies have decomposed and all traces of our physical remains have disappeared in the ground?'

وَلَوۡ شِئۡنَا 13 Had We wished

لَءَاتَيۡنَا كُلَّ نَفۡسٍ هُدَىٰهَا We would have given every soul its guidance,

وَلَٰكِنۡ حَقَّ ٱلۡقَوۡلُ مِنِّي but My word became due [against the defiant]:

لَأَمۡلَأَنَّ جَهَنَّمَ 'Surely I will fill hell

مِنَ ٱلۡجِنَّةِ وَٱلنَّاسِ أَجۡمَعِينَ ۝ with all the [guilty] jinn and humans.'[1]

فَذُوقُواْ بِمَا نَسِيتُمۡ 14 So taste [the punishment] for your having forgotten

لِقَآءَ يَوۡمِكُمۡ هَٰذَآ the encounter of this day of yours.

إِنَّا نَسِينَٰكُمۡ We [too] have forgotten you.

وَذُوقُواْ عَذَابَ ٱلۡخُلۡدِ Taste the everlasting punishment

بِمَا كُنتُمۡ تَعۡمَلُونَ ۝ because of what you used to do.

إِنَّمَا يُؤۡمِنُ بِـَٔايَٰتِنَا ٱلَّذِينَ 15 Only those believe in Our signs who,

إِذَا ذُكِّرُواْ بِهَا when they are reminded of them,

خَرُّواْ سُجَّدًا fall down in prostration

وَسَبَّحُواْ بِحَمۡدِ رَبِّهِمۡ and celebrate the praise of their Lord,

وَهُمۡ لَا يَسۡتَكۡبِرُونَ ۝ ◼ and they are not arrogant.

تَتَجَافَىٰ جُنُوبُهُمۡ عَنِ ٱلۡمَضَاجِعِ 16 Their sides vacate their beds[2]

يَدۡعُونَ رَبَّهُمۡ خَوۡفًا وَطَمَعًا to supplicate their Lord in fear and hope,

وَمِمَّا رَزَقۡنَٰهُمۡ يُنفِقُونَ ۝ and they spend out of what We have provided them.

فَلَا تَعۡلَمُ نَفۡسٌ 17 No one knows

مَّآ أُخۡفِيَ لَهُم what has been kept hidden for them

مِّن قُرَّةِ أَعۡيُنٍ of comfort

جَزَآءَۢ بِمَا كَانُواْ يَعۡمَلُونَ ۝ as a reward for what they used to do.

أَفَمَن كَانَ مُؤۡمِنًا 18 Is someone who is faithful

كَمَن كَانَ فَاسِقًا like someone who is a transgressor?

لَّا يَسۡتَوُۥنَ ۝ They are not equal.

أَمَّا ٱلَّذِينَ ءَامَنُواْ 19 As for those who have faith

---

[1] Cf. 7:18; 11:119; 38:85.

[2] That is, they abandon their beds at night and forgo the pleasure of sleep to worship their Lord in a state of fear and hope.

وَعَمِلُوا۟ ٱلصَّٰلِحَٰتِ    and do righteous deeds,

فَلَهُمْ جَنَّٰتُ ٱلْمَأْوَىٰ    for them are gardens of the Abode

نُزُلًۢا بِمَا كَانُوا۟ يَعْمَلُونَ ۝    —a hospitality for what they used to do.

وَأَمَّا ٱلَّذِينَ فَسَقُوا۟    20 As for those who have transgressed,

فَمَأْوَىٰهُمُ ٱلنَّارُ    their refuge is the Fire.

كُلَّمَآ أَرَادُوٓا۟ أَن يَخْرُجُوا۟ مِنْهَآ    Whenever they seek to leave it,

أُعِيدُوا۟ فِيهَا    they will be turned back into it,

وَقِيلَ لَهُمْ    and they will be told:

ذُوقُوا۟ عَذَابَ ٱلنَّارِ    'Taste the punishment of the Fire

ٱلَّذِى كُنتُم بِهِۦ تُكَذِّبُونَ ۝    which you used to deny.'

وَلَنُذِيقَنَّهُم مِّنَ ٱلْعَذَابِ ٱلْأَدْنَىٰ    21 We shall surely make them taste the nearer punishment

دُونَ ٱلْعَذَابِ ٱلْأَكْبَرِ    before the greater punishment,[1]

لَعَلَّهُمْ يَرْجِعُونَ ۝    so that they may come back.[2]

وَمَنْ أَظْلَمُ    22 Who is a greater wrongdoer

مِمَّن ذُكِّرَ بِـَٔايَٰتِ رَبِّهِۦ    than him who is reminded of his Lord's signs,

ثُمَّ أَعْرَضَ عَنْهَآ    whereat he disregards them?

إِنَّا مِنَ ٱلْمُجْرِمِينَ مُنتَقِمُونَ ۝    Indeed We shall take vengeance upon the guilty.

وَلَقَدْ ءَاتَيْنَا مُوسَى ٱلْكِتَٰبَ    23 Certainly We gave Moses the Book, [declaring],

فَلَا تَكُن فِى مِرْيَةٍ مِّن لِّقَآئِهِۦ    'Do not be in doubt about the encounter with Him,'

وَجَعَلْنَٰهُ هُدًى    and We made it a [source of] guidance

لِّبَنِىٓ إِسْرَٰٓءِيلَ ۝    for the Children of Israel.

وَجَعَلْنَا مِنْهُمْ أَئِمَّةً    24 And amongst them We appointed *imam*s

يَهْدُونَ بِأَمْرِنَا    who guide [the people] by Our command,

لَمَّا صَبَرُوا۟    when they had been patient

وَكَانُوا۟ بِـَٔايَٰتِنَا يُوقِنُونَ ۝    and had conviction in Our signs.

إِنَّ رَبَّكَ هُوَ يَفْصِلُ بَيْنَهُمْ    25 Indeed *your* Lord will judge between them

---

[1] Or 'this side of the greater punishment,' or 'aside from the greater punishment.'

[2] By 'the nearer punishment' is meant the afflictions and hardships the faithless may be made to suffer in the world with the purpose of bringing them back to Allah and in order to save them from the greater punishment of the Hereafter.

يَوْمَ ٱلْقِيَمَةِ    on the Day of Resurrection

فِيمَا كَانُوا فِيهِ يَخْتَلِفُونَ ۩    concerning that about which they used to differ.

أَوَلَمْ يَهْدِ لَهُمْ    26 Does it not dawn upon them

كَمْ أَهْلَكْنَا مِن قَبْلِهِم مِّنَ ٱلْقُرُونِ    how many generations We have destroyed before them,

يَمْشُونَ فِى مَسَكِنِهِمْ    amid [the ruins of] whose dwellings they walk?

إِنَّ فِى ذَلِكَ لَآيَتٍ    There are indeed signs in that.

أَفَلَا يَسْمَعُونَ ۩    Will they not then listen?

أَوَلَمْ يَرَوْا    27 Do they not see

أَنَّا نَسُوقُ ٱلْمَآءَ إِلَى ٱلْأَرْضِ ٱلْجُرُزِ    that We carry water to the parched earth

فَنُخْرِجُ بِهِۦ زَرْعًا    and with it We bring forth crops

تَأْكُلُ مِنْهُ أَنْعَمُهُمْ وَأَنفُسُهُمْ    of which they eat, themselves and their cattle?

أَفَلَا يُبْصِرُونَ ۩    Will they not then see?

وَيَقُولُونَ    28 And they say,

مَتَى هَذَا ٱلْفَتْحُ    'When will this victory be,

إِن كُنتُمْ صَدِقِينَ ۩    should you be truthful?'

قُلْ يَوْمَ ٱلْفَتْحِ    29 *Say*, 'On the day of victory

لَا يَنفَعُ ٱلَّذِينَ كَفَرُوا إِيمَنُهُمْ    their [newly found] faith shall not avail the faithless,

وَلَا هُمْ يُنظَرُونَ ۩    nor will they be granted any respite.'

فَأَعْرِضْ عَنْهُمْ وَٱنتَظِرْ    30 So *turn away* from them, and *wait*.

إِنَّهُم مُّنتَظِرُونَ ۩    They too are waiting.

سُورَةُ الأَحْزَابِ    33. SŪRAT AL-AḤZĀB[1]

بِسْمِ ٱللَّهِ    In the Name of Allah,

ٱلرَّحْمَنِ ٱلرَّحِيمِ    the All-beneficent, the All-merciful

يَأَيُّهَا ٱلنَّبِىُّ    1 O Prophet!

ٱتَّقِ ٱللَّهَ    *Be wary* of Allah

---

[1] The *sūrah* takes its name from verse 20 which refers to the campaign of the confederates (*aḥzāb*) against the Prophet (*ṣ*).

وَلَا تُطِعِ ٱلْكَٰفِرِينَ وَٱلْمُنَٰفِقِينَ

and *do not obey* the faithless and the hypocrites.

إِنَّ ٱللَّهَ كَانَ عَلِيمًا حَكِيمًا ۝

Indeed Allah is all-knowing, all-wise.

وَٱتَّبِعْ مَا يُوحَىٰ إِلَيْكَ مِن رَّبِّكَ

2 And *follow* that which is revealed to *you* from *your* Lord.

إِنَّ ٱللَّهَ كَانَ بِمَا تَعْمَلُونَ خَبِيرًا ۝

Indeed Allah is well aware of what you do.

وَتَوَكَّلْ عَلَى ٱللَّهِ

3 And put *your* trust in Allah;

وَكَفَىٰ بِٱللَّهِ وَكِيلًا ۝

Allah suffices as trustee.

مَّا جَعَلَ ٱللَّهُ

4 Allah has not put

لِرَجُلٍ مِّن قَلْبَيْنِ فِى جَوْفِهِ

two hearts within any man,

وَمَا جَعَلَ أَزْوَٰجَكُمُ

nor has He made your wives

ٱلَّٰٓـِٔى تُظَٰهِرُونَ مِنْهُنَّ

whom you repudiate by *ẓihār*[1]

أُمَّهَٰتِكُمْ

your mothers,

وَمَا جَعَلَ أَدْعِيَآءَكُمْ أَبْنَآءَكُمْ

nor has he made your adopted sons your sons.

ذَٰلِكُمْ قَوْلُكُم بِأَفْوَٰهِكُمْ

These are mere utterances of your mouths.

وَٱللَّهُ يَقُولُ ٱلْحَقَّ

But Allah speaks the truth

وَهُوَ يَهْدِى ٱلسَّبِيلَ ۝

and He guides to the way.

ٱدْعُوهُمْ لِأَبَآئِهِمْ

5 Call them after their fathers.

هُوَ أَقْسَطُ عِندَ ٱللَّهِ

That is more just with Allah.

فَإِن لَّمْ تَعْلَمُوٓا۟ ءَابَآءَهُمْ

And if you do not know their fathers,

فَإِخْوَٰنُكُمْ فِى ٱلدِّينِ

then they are your brethren in the faith

وَمَوَٰلِيكُمْ

and your kinsmen.

وَلَيْسَ عَلَيْكُمْ جُنَاحٌ

There will be no sin upon you

فِيمَآ أَخْطَأْتُم بِهِۦ

for any mistake that you may make therein,

وَلَٰكِن مَّا تَعَمَّدَتْ قُلُوبُكُمْ

barring what your hearts may premeditate.

وَكَانَ ٱللَّهُ غَفُورًا رَّحِيمًا ۝

And Allah is all-forgiving, all-merciful.

ٱلنَّبِىُّ أَوْلَىٰ بِٱلْمُؤْمِنِينَ

6 The Prophet is closer to the faithful

مِنْ أَنفُسِهِمْ

than their own souls,[2]

---

[1] A kind of repudiation of the marital relationship among pre-Islamic Arabs which took place on a husband's saying to his wife 'Be as my mother's back' (*ẓahr*; hence the derivative *ẓihār*). Concerning the revocation of such a divorce and the atonement prescribed, see 58:1-4.

[2] Or 'The Prophet has a greater right (or a greater authority) over the faithful than they have over their own selves.'

وَأَزۡوَٰجُهُۥٓ أُمَّهَٰتُهُمۡ ‏ and his wives are their mothers.

وَأُوْلُواْ ٱلۡأَرۡحَامِ ‏ The blood relatives

بَعۡضُهُمۡ أَوۡلَىٰ بِبَعۡضٍ ‏ are more entitled to inherit from one another

فِى كِتَٰبِ ٱللَّهِ ‏ in the Book of Allah[1]

مِنَ ٱلۡمُؤۡمِنِينَ وَٱلۡمُهَٰجِرِينَ ‏ than the [other] faithful and Emigrants,[2]

إِلَّآ أَن تَفۡعَلُوٓاْ إِلَىٰٓ أَوۡلِيَآئِكُم مَّعۡرُوفًا ‏ barring any favour you may do your comrades.[3]

كَانَ ذَٰلِكَ فِى ٱلۡكِتَٰبِ مَسۡطُورًا ۝ ‏ This has been written in the Book.

وَإِذۡ أَخَذۡنَا مِنَ ٱلنَّبِيِّـۧنَ مِيثَٰقَهُمۡ ‏ 7 [*Recall*] when We took a pledge from the prophets,

وَمِنكَ ‏ and from *you*

وَمِن نُّوحٍ وَإِبۡرَٰهِيمَ ‏ and from Noah and Abraham

وَمُوسَىٰ وَعِيسَى ٱبۡنِ مَرۡيَمَ ‏ and Moses and Jesus son of Mary,

وَأَخَذۡنَا مِنۡهُم مِّيثَٰقًا غَلِيظًا ۝ ‏ and We took from them a solemn pledge,

لِّيَسۡـَٔلَ ٱلصَّٰدِقِينَ ‏ 8 so that He may question the truthful

عَن صِدۡقِهِمۡ ‏ concerning their truthfulness.

وَأَعَدَّ لِلۡكَٰفِرِينَ ‏ And He has prepared for the faithless

عَذَابًا أَلِيمًا ۝ ‏ a painful punishment.

يَٰٓأَيُّهَا ٱلَّذِينَ ءَامَنُواْ ‏ 9 O you who have faith!

ٱذۡكُرُواْ نِعۡمَةَ ٱللَّهِ عَلَيۡكُمۡ ‏ Remember Allah's blessing upon you

إِذۡ جَآءَتۡكُمۡ جُنُودٌ ‏ when the hosts came at you,

فَأَرۡسَلۡنَا عَلَيۡهِمۡ رِيحًا ‏ and We sent against them a gale

وَجُنُودًا لَّمۡ تَرَوۡهَا ‏ and hosts whom you did not see.

وَكَانَ ٱللَّهُ بِمَا تَعۡمَلُونَ بَصِيرًا ۝ ‏ And Allah sees best what you do.

إِذۡ جَآءُوكُم ‏ 10 When they came at you

مِّن فَوۡقِكُمۡ وَمِنۡ أَسۡفَلَ مِنكُمۡ ‏ from above and below you,[4]

---

[1] That is, in respect of the right of inheritance.

[2] Or 'The blood relations have a greater right to inherit from one another than the rest of the faithful and Emigrants.'

[3] That is, by making a bequest in their favour.

[4] From the higher side of the valley, to the west of Madinah, and from the lower side of it towards the east.

| | |
|---|---|
| وَإِذْ زَاغَتِ ٱلْأَبْصَرُ | and when the eyes rolled [with fear] |
| وَبَلَغَتِ ٱلْقُلُوبُ ٱلْحَنَاجِرَ | and the hearts leapt to the throats, |
| وَتَظُنُّونَ بِٱللَّهِ ٱلظُّنُونَا ۝ | and you entertained misgivings about Allah, |
| هُنَالِكَ ٱبْتُلِيَ ٱلْمُؤْمِنُونَ 11 | it was there that the faithful were tested |
| وَزُلْزِلُوا زِلْزَالًا شَدِيدًا ۝ | and jolted with a severe agitation. |
| وَإِذْ يَقُولُ ٱلْمُنَفِقُونَ 12 | And when the hypocrites were saying, |
| وَٱلَّذِينَ فِي قُلُوبِهِم مَّرَضٌ | as well as those in whose hearts is a sickness, |
| مَّا وَعَدَنَا ٱللَّهُ وَرَسُولُهُۥٓ | 'Allah and His Apostle did not promise us |
| إِلَّا غُرُورًا ۝ | [anything] except delusion.' |
| وَإِذْ قَالَت طَّآئِفَةٌ مِّنْهُمْ 13 | And when a group of them said, |
| يَأَهْلَ يَثْرِبَ | 'O people of Yathrib! |
| لَا مُقَامَ لَكُمْ فَٱرْجِعُوا | [This is] not a place for you,[1] so go back!'[2] |
| وَيَسْتَـٔذِنُ فَرِيقٌ مِّنْهُمُ ٱلنَّبِيَّ | And a group of them sought the Prophet's permission, |
| يَقُولُونَ إِنَّ بُيُوتَنَا عَوْرَةٌ | saying, 'Our homes lie exposed[3] [to the enemy],' |
| وَمَا هِيَ بِعَوْرَةٍ | although they were not exposed. |
| إِن يُرِيدُونَ إِلَّا فِرَارًا ۝ | They only sought to flee. |
| وَلَوْ دُخِلَتْ عَلَيْهِم مِّنْ أَقْطَارِهَا 14 | Had they been invaded from its flanks[4] |
| ثُمَّ سُئِلُوا ٱلْفِتْنَةَ | and had they been asked to apostatize, |
| لَأَتَوْهَا | they would have done so |
| وَمَا تَلَبَّثُوا بِهَآ إِلَّا يَسِيرًا ۝ | with only a mild hesitation, |
| وَلَقَدْ كَانُوا عَهَدُوا ٱللَّهَ مِن قَبْلُ 15 | though they had certainly pledged to Allah before |
| لَا يُوَلُّونَ ٱلْأَدْبَرَ | that they would not turn their backs [to flee], |
| وَكَانَ عَهْدُ ٱللَّهِ مَسْـُٔولًا ۝ | and pledges given to Allah are accountable. |
| قُل لَّن يَنفَعَكُمُ ٱلْفِرَارُ 16 | Say, 'Flight will not avail you |
| إِن فَرَرْتُم مِّنَ ٱلْمَوْتِ أَوِ ٱلْقَتْلِ | should you flee from death or from being killed, |
| وَإِذًا لَّا تُمَتَّعُونَ إِلَّا قَلِيلًا ۝ | and then you will be let to enjoy only for a little while.' |

---

[1] That is, there is no chance of your withstanding the army of the polytheists.

[2] That is, return to your earlier creed, or go back to your homes.

[3] Or 'unprotected.'

[4] That is, of the city Madīnah.

قُلْ مَن ذَا ٱلَّذِى يَعْصِمُكُم مِّنَ ٱللَّهِ 17 *Say,* 'Who is it that can protect you from Allah

إِنْ أَرَادَ بِكُمْ سُوءًا     should He desire to cause you ill,

أَوْ أَرَادَ بِكُمْ رَحْمَةً     or desire to grant you mercy?'

وَلَا يَجِدُونَ لَهُم     They will not find for themselves

مِّن دُونِ ٱللَّهِ وَلِيًّا وَلَا نَصِيرًا ۞     any protector or helper besides Allah.

قَدْ يَعْلَمُ ٱللَّهُ ٱلْمُعَوِّقِينَ مِنكُمْ 18 Allah knows those of you who discourage others,

وَٱلْقَآئِلِينَ لِإِخْوَٰنِهِمْ هَلُمَّ إِلَيْنَا     and those who say to their brethren, 'Come to us!'

وَلَا يَأْتُونَ ٱلْبَأْسَ إِلَّا قَلِيلًا ۝     and they take little part in the battle,

أَشِحَّةً عَلَيْكُمْ ۖ 19     grudging you [their help].

فَإِذَا جَآءَ ٱلْخَوْفُ     So when there is panic,

رَأَيْتَهُمْ يَنظُرُونَ إِلَيْكَ     *you* see them observing *you,*

تَدُورُ أَعْيُنُهُمْ     their eyes rolling,

كَٱلَّذِى يُغْشَىٰ عَلَيْهِ مِنَ ٱلْمَوْتِ ۖ     like someone fainting at death.

فَإِذَا ذَهَبَ ٱلْخَوْفُ     Then, when the panic is over,

سَلَقُوكُم بِأَلْسِنَةٍ حِدَادٍ     they scald you with [their] sharp tongues

أَشِحَّةً عَلَى ٱلْخَيْرِ ۚ     in their greed for riches.

أُوْلَٰٓئِكَ لَمْ يُؤْمِنُوا۟     They never have had faith.

فَأَحْبَطَ ٱللَّهُ أَعْمَٰلَهُمْ ۚ     So Allah has made their works fail,

وَكَانَ ذَٰلِكَ عَلَى ٱللَّهِ يَسِيرًا ۝     and that is easy for Allah.

يَحْسَبُونَ ٱلْأَحْزَابَ لَمْ يَذْهَبُوا۟ ۖ 20 They suppose the confederates have not left yet,

وَإِن يَأْتِ ٱلْأَحْزَابُ     and were the confederates to come [again],

يَوَدُّوا۟     they would wish

لَوْ أَنَّهُم بَادُونَ فِى ٱلْأَعْرَابِ     they were in the desert with the Bedouins

يَسْأَلُونَ عَنْ أَنۢبَآئِكُمْ ۖ     asking about your news,

وَلَوْ كَانُوا۟ فِيكُم     and if they were with you

مَّا قَٰتَلُوٓا۟ إِلَّا قَلِيلًا ۝     they would fight but a little.

لَّقَدْ كَانَ لَكُمْ فِى رَسُولِ ٱللَّهِ 21 In the Apostle of Allah there is certainly for you

أُسْوَةٌ حَسَنَةٌ     a good exemplar,

لِّمَن كَانَ يَرْجُوا۟ ٱللَّهَ وَٱلْيَوْمَ ٱلْأَخِرَ     for those who look forward to Allah and the Last Day,

وَٱذْكُرُوا۟ ٱللَّهَ كَثِيرًا ۝ and remember Allah greatly.

وَلَمَّا رَءَا ٱلْمُؤْمِنُونَ ٱلْأَحْزَابَ 22 But when the faithful saw the confederates,

قَالُوا۟ they said,

هَٰذَا مَا وَعَدَنَا ٱللَّهُ وَرَسُولُهُۥ 'This is what Allah and His Apostle had promised us,

وَصَدَقَ ٱللَّهُ وَرَسُولُهُۥ and Allah and His Apostle were true.'

وَمَا زَادَهُمْ إِلَّآ إِيمَٰنًا وَتَسْلِيمًا ۝ And it only increased them in faith and submission.

مِّنَ ٱلْمُؤْمِنِينَ رِجَالٌ 23 Among the faithful are men

صَدَقُوا۟ مَا عَٰهَدُوا۟ ٱللَّهَ عَلَيْهِ who fulfill what they have pledged to Allah.

فَمِنْهُم مَّن قَضَىٰ نَحْبَهُۥ Of them are some who have fulfilled their pledge,

وَمِنْهُم مَّن يَنتَظِرُ and of them are some who still wait,

وَمَا بَدَّلُوا۟ تَبْدِيلًا ۝ and they have not changed in the least,

لِّيَجْزِىَ ٱللَّهُ ٱلصَّٰدِقِينَ بِصِدْقِهِمْ 24 that Allah may reward the true for their truthfulness,

وَيُعَذِّبَ ٱلْمُنَٰفِقِينَ إِن شَآءَ and punish the hypocrites, if He wishes,

أَوْ يَتُوبَ عَلَيْهِمْ or accept their repentance.

إِنَّ ٱللَّهَ كَانَ غَفُورًا رَّحِيمًا ۝ Indeed Allah is all-forgiving, all-merciful.

وَرَدَّ ٱللَّهُ ٱلَّذِينَ كَفَرُوا۟ بِغَيْظِهِمْ 25 Allah sent back the faithless in their rage,

لَمْ يَنَالُوا۟ خَيْرًا without their attaining any advantage,

وَكَفَى ٱللَّهُ ٱلْمُؤْمِنِينَ ٱلْقِتَالَ and Allah spared the faithful of fighting,

وَكَانَ ٱللَّهُ قَوِيًّا عَزِيزًا ۝ and Allah is all-strong, all-mighty.

وَأَنزَلَ ٱلَّذِينَ ظَٰهَرُوهُم 26 And He dragged down those who had backed them

مِّنْ أَهْلِ ٱلْكِتَٰبِ from among the People of the Book

مِن صَيَاصِيهِمْ from their strongholds,

وَقَذَفَ فِى قُلُوبِهِمُ ٱلرُّعْبَ and He cast terror into their hearts,

فَرِيقًا تَقْتُلُونَ [so that] you killed a part of them,

وَتَأْسِرُونَ فَرِيقًا ۝ and took captive [another] part of them.

وَأَوْرَثَكُمْ أَرْضَهُمْ 27 And He bequeathed you their land,

وَدِيَٰرَهُمْ وَأَمْوَٰلَهُمْ their houses and their possessions,

وَأَرْضًا لَّمْ تَطَـُٔوهَا and a territory you had not trodden,

وَكَانَ ٱللَّهُ عَلَىٰ كُلِّ شَىْءٍ قَدِيرًا ۝ and Allah has power over all things.

يَـٰٓأَيُّهَا ٱلنَّبِىُّ 28 O Prophet!

قُل لِّأَزْوَٰجِكَ     *Say* to *your* wives,

إِن كُنتُنَّ تُرِدْنَ ٱلْحَيَوٰةَ ٱلدُّنْيَا وَزِينَتَهَا     'If you desire the life of the world and its glitter,

فَتَعَالَيْنَ     come,

أُمَتِّعْكُنَّ     I will provide for you

وَأُسَرِّحْكُنَّ سَرَاحًا جَمِيلًا ۝     and release you in a graceful manner.

وَإِن كُنتُنَّ تُرِدْنَ ٱللَّهَ وَرَسُولَهُ 29 But if you desire Allah and His Apostle

وَٱلدَّارَ ٱلْأَخِرَةَ     and the abode of the Hereafter,

فَإِنَّ ٱللَّهَ أَعَدَّ     then Allah has indeed prepared

لِلْمُحْسِنَـٰتِ مِنكُنَّ     for the virtuous among you

أَجْرًا عَظِيمًا ۝     a great reward.'

يَـٰنِسَآءَ ٱلنَّبِىِّ 30 O wives of the Prophet!

مَن يَأْتِ مِنكُنَّ بِفَـٰحِشَةٍ مُّبَيِّنَةٍ     Whoever of you commits a gross indecency,

يُضَـٰعَفْ لَهَا ٱلْعَذَابُ ضِعْفَيْنِ     her punishment shall be doubled,

وَكَانَ ذَٰلِكَ عَلَى ٱللَّهِ يَسِيرًا ۝ ❈     and that is easy for Allah.

[PART 22]

وَمَن يَقْنُتْ مِنكُنَّ لِلَّهِ وَرَسُولِهِ 31 But whoever of you is obedient to Allah and His Apostle

وَتَعْمَلْ صَـٰلِحًا     and acts righteously,

نُّؤْتِهَآ أَجْرَهَا مَرَّتَيْنِ     We shall give her a twofold reward,

وَأَعْتَدْنَا لَهَا رِزْقًا كَرِيمًا ۝     and We hold a noble provision in store for her.

يَـٰنِسَآءَ ٱلنَّبِىِّ 32 O wives of the Prophet!

لَسْتُنَّ كَأَحَدٍ مِّنَ ٱلنِّسَآءِ     You are not like any other women:

إِنِ ٱتَّقَيْتُنَّ     if you are wary [of Allah],

فَلَا تَخْضَعْنَ بِٱلْقَوْلِ     then do not be complaisant in your speech,

فَيَطْمَعَ ٱلَّذِى فِى قَلْبِهِۦ مَرَضٌ     lest he in whose heart is a sickness should aspire,

وَقُلْنَ قَوْلًا مَّعْرُوفًا ۝     and speak honourable words.

وَقَرْنَ فِى بُيُوتِكُنَّ 33 Stay in your houses

وَلَا تَبَرَّجْنَ     and do not display your finery

تَبَرُّجَ ٱلْجَـٰهِلِيَّةِ ٱلْأُولَىٰ     with the display of the former [days of] ignorance.

وَأَقِمْنَ ٱلصَّلَوٰةَ وَءَاتِينَ ٱلزَّكَوٰةَ     Maintain the prayer and pay the *zakāt*,

وَأَطِعْنَ اللَّهَ وَرَسُولَهُۥۤ

and obey Allah and His Apostle.

إِنَّمَا يُرِيدُ اللَّهُ لِيُذْهِبَ عَنكُمُ الرِّجْسَ أَهْلَ الْبَيْتِ وَيُطَهِّرَكُمْ تَطْهِيرًا ۝

Indeed Allah desires to repel all impurity from you,
O People of the Household,
and purify you with a thorough purification.

وَاذْكُرْنَ مَا يُتْلَىٰ فِى بُيُوتِكُنَّ مِنْ ءَايَٰتِ اللَّهِ وَالْحِكْمَةِ إِنَّ اللَّهَ كَانَ لَطِيفًا خَبِيرًا ۝

34 And remember what is recited in your homes
of the signs of Allah and wisdom.
Indeed Allah is all-attentive, all-aware.

إِنَّ الْمُسْلِمِينَ وَالْمُسْلِمَٰتِ
وَالْمُؤْمِنِينَ وَالْمُؤْمِنَٰتِ
وَالْقَٰنِتِينَ وَالْقَٰنِتَٰتِ
وَالصَّٰدِقِينَ وَالصَّٰدِقَٰتِ
وَالصَّٰبِرِينَ وَالصَّٰبِرَٰتِ
وَالْخَٰشِعِينَ وَالْخَٰشِعَٰتِ
وَالْمُتَصَدِّقِينَ وَالْمُتَصَدِّقَٰتِ
وَالصَّٰٓئِمِينَ وَالصَّٰٓئِمَٰتِ
وَالْحَٰفِظِينَ فُرُوجَهُمْ
وَالْحَٰفِظَٰتِ
وَالذَّٰكِرِينَ اللَّهَ كَثِيرًا
وَالذَّٰكِرَٰتِ
أَعَدَّ اللَّهُ لَهُم مَّغْفِرَةً
وَأَجْرًا عَظِيمًا ۝

35 Indeed the *muslim* men and the *muslim* women,
the faithful men and the faithful women,
the obedient men and the obedient women,
the truthful men and the truthful women,
the patient men and the patient women,
the humble[1] men and the humble women,
the charitable men and the charitable women,
the men who fast and the women who fast,
the men who guard their private parts
and the women who guard,
the men who remember Allah greatly
and the women who remember [Allah greatly]
—Allah holds in store for them forgiveness
and a great reward.

وَمَا كَانَ لِمُؤْمِنٍ وَلَا مُؤْمِنَةٍ إِذَا قَضَى اللَّهُ وَرَسُولُهُۥٓ أَمْرًا أَن يَكُونَ لَهُمُ الْخِيَرَةُ مِنْ أَمْرِهِمْ وَمَن يَعْصِ اللَّهَ وَرَسُولَهُۥ فَقَدْ ضَلَّ ضَلَٰلًا مُّبِينًا ۝

36 A faithful man or woman may not,
when Allah and His Apostle have decided on a matter,
have any option in their matter,
and whoever disobeys Allah and His Apostle
has certainly strayed into manifest error.

---

[1] That is, humble toward Allah.

وَإِذْ تَقُولُ لِلَّذِى أَنْعَمَ ٱللَّهُ عَلَيْهِ    37 When *you* said to him whom Allah had blessed,

وَأَنْعَمْتَ عَلَيْهِ    and whom *you* [too] had blessed,

أَمْسِكْ عَلَيْكَ زَوْجَكَ    'Retain your wife for yourself,

وَٱتَّقِ ٱللَّهَ    and be wary of Allah,'

وَتُخْفِى فِى نَفْسِكَ    and *you* had hidden in *your* heart

مَا ٱللَّهُ مُبْدِيهِ    what Allah was to divulge,

وَتَخْشَى ٱلنَّاسَ    and *you* feared the people

وَٱللَّهُ أَحَقُّ أَن تَخْشَٰهُ    though Allah is worthier that *you* should fear Him,

فَلَمَّا قَضَىٰ زَيْدٌ مِّنْهَا وَطَرًا    so when Zayd had got through with her,

زَوَّجْنَٰكَهَا    We wedded her to *you*,

لِكَىْ لَا يَكُونَ عَلَى ٱلْمُؤْمِنِينَ حَرَجٌ    so that there may be no blame on the faithful

فِىٓ أَزْوَٰجِ أَدْعِيَآئِهِمْ    in respect of the wives of their adopted sons,

إِذَا قَضَوْا۟ مِنْهُنَّ وَطَرًا    when the latter have got through with them,

وَكَانَ أَمْرُ ٱللَّهِ مَفْعُولًا ۝    and Allah's command is bound to be fulfilled.

مَّا كَانَ عَلَى ٱلنَّبِىِّ مِنْ حَرَجٍ    38 There is no blame on the Prophet

فِيمَا فَرَضَ ٱللَّهُ لَهُ ۖ    in respect of that which Allah has made lawful for him:[1]

سُنَّةَ ٱللَّهِ فِى ٱلَّذِينَ خَلَوْا۟ مِن قَبْلُ ۚ    Allah's precedent with those who passed away earlier

وَكَانَ أَمْرُ ٱللَّهِ    —and Allah's commands

قَدَرًا مَّقْدُورًا ۝    are ordained by a precise ordaining—

ٱلَّذِينَ يُبَلِّغُونَ رِسَٰلَٰتِ ٱللَّهِ    39 such as deliver the messages of Allah

وَيَخْشَوْنَهُ    and fear Him,

وَلَا يَخْشَوْنَ أَحَدًا إِلَّا ٱللَّهَ ۗ    and fear no one except Allah,

وَكَفَىٰ بِٱللَّهِ حَسِيبًا ۝    and Allah suffices as reckoner.

مَّا كَانَ مُحَمَّدٌ أَبَآ أَحَدٍ مِّن رِّجَالِكُمْ    40 Muhammad is not the father of any man among you,

وَلَٰكِن رَّسُولَ ٱللَّهِ    but he is the Apostle of Allah

وَخَاتَمَ ٱلنَّبِيِّۦنَ ۗ    and the Seal of the Prophets,

وَكَانَ ٱللَّهُ بِكُلِّ شَىْءٍ عَلِيمًا ۝    and Allah has knowledge of all things.

---

[1] Or 'prescribed for him.'

يَـٰٓأَيُّهَا ٱلَّذِينَ ءَامَنُوا۟ 41 O you who have faith!

أَذْكُرُوا۟ ٱللَّهَ ذِكْرًا كَثِيرًا ⑪ Remember Allah with frequent remembrance,

وَسَبِّحُوهُ بُكْرَةً وَأَصِيلًا ⑫ 42 and glorify Him morning and evening.

هُوَ ٱلَّذِى يُصَلِّى عَلَيْكُمْ 43 It is He who blesses you,

وَمَلَـٰٓئِكَتُهُۥ and so do His angels,

لِيُخْرِجَكُم مِّنَ ٱلظُّلُمَـٰتِ إِلَى ٱلنُّورِ that He may bring you out from darkness into light,

وَكَانَ بِٱلْمُؤْمِنِينَ رَحِيمًا ⑬ and He is most merciful to the faithful.

تَحِيَّتُهُمْ يَوْمَ يَلْقَوْنَهُۥ 44 The day they encounter Him, their greeting will be,

سَلَـٰمٌ 'Peace,'

وَأَعَدَّ لَهُمْ أَجْرًا كَرِيمًا ⑭ and He holds in store for them a noble reward.

يَـٰٓأَيُّهَا ٱلنَّبِىُّ 45 O Prophet!

إِنَّآ أَرْسَلْنَـٰكَ شَـٰهِدًا Indeed We have sent *you* as a witness,

وَمُبَشِّرًا وَنَذِيرًا ⑮ as a bearer of good news and as a warner

وَدَاعِيًا إِلَى ٱللَّهِ بِإِذْنِهِۦ 46 and as a summoner to Allah by His permission,

وَسِرَاجًا مُّنِيرًا ⑯ and as a radiant lamp.

وَبَشِّرِ ٱلْمُؤْمِنِينَ 47 *Announce* to the faithful the good news

بِأَنَّ لَهُم مِّنَ ٱللَّهِ فَضْلًا كَبِيرًا ⑰ that there will be for them a great grace from Allah.

وَلَا تُطِعِ ٱلْكَـٰفِرِينَ 48 And *do not obey* the faithless

وَٱلْمُنَـٰفِقِينَ and the hypocrites,

وَدَعْ أَذَىٰهُمْ and *disregard* their torments,

وَتَوَكَّلْ عَلَى ٱللَّهِ and *put your* trust in Allah,

وَكَفَىٰ بِٱللَّهِ وَكِيلًا ⑱ and Allah suffices as trustee.

يَـٰٓأَيُّهَا ٱلَّذِينَ ءَامَنُوٓا۟ 49 O you who have faith!

إِذَا نَكَحْتُمُ ٱلْمُؤْمِنَـٰتِ When you marry faithful women

ثُمَّ طَلَّقْتُمُوهُنَّ مِن قَبْلِ أَن تَمَسُّوهُنَّ and then divorce them before you touch them,

فَمَا لَكُمْ عَلَيْهِنَّ مِنْ عِدَّةٍ تَعْتَدُّونَهَا there shall be no period for you to reckon.

فَمَتِّعُوهُنَّ But provide for them

وَسَرِّحُوهُنَّ سَرَاحًا جَمِيلًا ⑲ and release them in a graceful manner.

592

يَـٰٓأَيُّهَا ٱلنَّبِيُّ ٥٠ O Prophet!

إِنَّآ أَحْلَلْنَا لَكَ أَزْوَٰجَكَ Indeed We have made lawful to *you* *your* wives

ٱلَّـٰتِىٓ ءَاتَيْتَ أُجُورَهُنَّ whom *you* have given their dowries,

وَمَا مَلَكَتْ يَمِينُكَ and those whom *your* right hand owns,[1]

مِمَّآ أَفَآءَ ٱللَّهُ عَلَيْكَ of those whom Allah gave *you* as spoils of war,

وَبَنَاتِ عَمِّكَ and the daughters of *your* paternal uncle,

وَبَنَاتِ عَمَّـٰتِكَ and the daughters of *your* paternal aunts,

وَبَنَاتِ خَالِكَ and the daughters of *your* maternal uncle,

وَبَنَاتِ خَـٰلَـٰتِكَ and the daughters of *your* maternal aunts

ٱلَّـٰتِى هَاجَرْنَ مَعَكَ who migrated with *you*,

وَٱمْرَأَةً مُّؤْمِنَةً إِن وَهَبَتْ نَفْسَهَا لِلنَّبِىِّ and a faithful woman if she offers herself to the Prophet

إِنْ أَرَادَ ٱلنَّبِىُّ أَن يَسْتَنكِحَهَا and the Prophet desires to take her in marriage,

خَالِصَةً لَّكَ (a privilege exclusively for *you*,

مِن دُونِ ٱلْمُؤْمِنِينَ not for [the rest of] the faithful;

قَدْ عَلِمْنَا مَا فَرَضْنَا عَلَيْهِمْ We know what We have made lawful for them

فِىٓ أَزْوَٰجِهِمْ with respect to their wives

وَمَا مَلَكَتْ أَيْمَـٰنُهُمْ and those whom their right hands own

لِكَيْلَا يَكُونَ عَلَيْكَ حَرَجٌ so that there may be no blame on *you*,)

وَكَانَ ٱللَّهُ غَفُورًا رَّحِيمًا ۞ and Allah is all-forgiving, all-merciful.

تُرْجِى مَن تَشَآءُ مِنْهُنَّ ٥١ *You* may put off whichever of them *you* wish

وَتُـْٔوِىٓ إِلَيْكَ مَن تَشَآءُ and consort with whichever of them *you* wish,

وَمَنِ ٱبْتَغَيْتَ and as for any whom *you* may seek [to consort with]

مِمَّنْ عَزَلْتَ from among those *you* have set aside [earlier],

فَلَا جُنَاحَ عَلَيْكَ there is no sin upon *you* [in receiving her again].

ذَٰلِكَ أَدْنَىٰٓ أَن تَقَرَّ أَعْيُنُهُنَّ That makes it likelier that they will be comforted

وَلَا يَحْزَنَّ and not feel unhappy,

وَيَرْضَيْنَ بِمَآ ءَاتَيْتَهُنَّ كُلُّهُنَّ all of them being pleased with what *you* give them.

وَٱللَّهُ يَعْلَمُ مَا فِى قُلُوبِكُمْ Allah knows what is in your hearts,

وَكَانَ ٱللَّهُ عَلِيمًا حَلِيمًا ۞ and Allah is all-knowing, all-forbearing.

---

[1] That is, slave women.

لَا يَحِلُّ لَكَ ٱلنِّسَآءُ مِنۢ بَعْدُ    52 Beyond that, women are not lawful for *you*,

وَلَآ أَن تَبَدَّلَ بِهِنَّ مِنْ أَزْوَٰجٍ    nor that *you* should change them for other wives

وَلَوْ أَعْجَبَكَ حُسْنُهُنَّ    even though their beauty should impress *you*,

إِلَّا مَا مَلَكَتْ يَمِينُكَ    except those whom *your* right hand owns.

وَكَانَ ٱللَّهُ عَلَىٰ كُلِّ شَىْءٍ رَّقِيبًا ۝    And Allah is watchful over all things.

يَـٰٓأَيُّهَا ٱلَّذِينَ ءَامَنُوا۟    53 O you who have faith!

لَا تَدْخُلُوا۟ بُيُوتَ ٱلنَّبِىِّ    Do not enter the Prophet's houses

إِلَّآ أَن يُؤْذَنَ لَكُمْ إِلَىٰ طَعَامٍ    unless permission is granted you for a meal,

غَيْرَ نَـٰظِرِينَ إِنَىٰهُ    without waiting for it to be readied.

وَلَـٰكِنْ إِذَا دُعِيتُمْ فَٱدْخُلُوا۟    But enter when you are invited,

فَإِذَا طَعِمْتُمْ فَٱنتَشِرُوا۟    and disperse when you have taken your meal,

وَلَا مُسْتَـٔنِسِينَ لِحَدِيثٍ    without settling down to chat.

إِنَّ ذَٰلِكُمْ كَانَ يُؤْذِى ٱلنَّبِىَّ    Indeed such conduct torments the Prophet,

فَيَسْتَحْىِۦ مِنكُمْ    and he is ashamed of [asking] you [to leave];

وَٱللَّهُ لَا يَسْتَحْىِۦ مِنَ ٱلْحَقِّ    but Allah is not ashamed of [expressing] the truth.

وَإِذَا سَأَلْتُمُوهُنَّ مَتَـٰعًا    And when you ask anything of [his] womenfolk,

فَسْـَٔلُوهُنَّ مِن وَرَآءِ حِجَابٍ    ask it from them from behind a curtain.

ذَٰلِكُمْ أَطْهَرُ لِقُلُوبِكُمْ وَقُلُوبِهِنَّ    That is more chaste for your hearts and their hearts.

وَمَا كَانَ لَكُمْ أَن تُؤْذُوا۟ رَسُولَ ٱللَّهِ    You may not torment the Apostle of Allah,

وَلَآ أَن تَنكِحُوٓا۟ أَزْوَٰجَهُۥ مِنۢ بَعْدِهِۦٓ أَبَدًا    nor may you ever marry his wives after him.

إِنَّ ذَٰلِكُمْ كَانَ عِندَ ٱللَّهِ عَظِيمًا ۝    Indeed that would be a grave [matter] with Allah.

إِن تُبْدُوا۟ شَيْـًٔا أَوْ تُخْفُوهُ    54 Whether you disclose anything or hide it,

فَإِنَّ ٱللَّهَ كَانَ بِكُلِّ شَىْءٍ عَلِيمًا ۝    Allah indeed knows all things.

لَّا جُنَاحَ عَلَيْهِنَّ    55 There is no sin on them[1] [in socializing freely]

فِىٓ ءَابَآئِهِنَّ وَلَآ أَبْنَآئِهِنَّ    with their fathers, or their sons,

وَلَآ إِخْوَٰنِهِنَّ وَلَآ أَبْنَآءِ إِخْوَٰنِهِنَّ    or their brothers, or their brothers' sons,

وَلَآ أَبْنَآءِ أَخَوَٰتِهِنَّ    or the sons of their sisters,

وَلَا نِسَآئِهِنَّ    or their own womenfolk,[2]

---

[1] That is, the Prophet's wives.

[2] That is, Muslim women.

وَلَا مَا مَلَكَتْ أَيْمَـٰنُهُنَّ     or what their right hands own.[1]

وَٱتَّقِينَ ٱللَّهَ     Be wary of Allah.

إِنَّ ٱللَّهَ كَانَ عَلَىٰ كُلِّ شَىْءٍ شَهِيدًا ۝     Indeed Allah is witness to all things.

إِنَّ ٱللَّهَ وَمَلَـٰئِكَتَهُۥ يُصَلُّونَ عَلَى ٱلنَّبِىِّ     56 Indeed Allah and His angels bless the Prophet;

يَـٰٓأَيُّهَا ٱلَّذِينَ ءَامَنُوا۟     O you who have faith!

صَلُّوا۟ عَلَيْهِ     Invoke blessings on him

وَسَلِّمُوا۟ تَسْلِيمًا ۝     and invoke Peace upon him in a worthy manner.

إِنَّ ٱلَّذِينَ يُؤْذُونَ ٱللَّهَ وَرَسُولَهُۥ     57 Indeed those who torment Allah and His Apostle

لَعَنَهُمُ ٱللَّهُ فِى ٱلدُّنْيَا وَٱلْـَٔاخِرَةِ     are cursed by Allah in the world and the Hereafter,

وَأَعَدَّ لَهُمْ عَذَابًا مُّهِينًا ۝     and He has prepared a humiliating punishment for them.

وَٱلَّذِينَ يُؤْذُونَ ٱلْمُؤْمِنِينَ وَٱلْمُؤْمِنَـٰتِ     58 Those who torment faithful men and women

بِغَيْرِ مَا ٱكْتَسَبُوا۟     undeservedly,

فَقَدِ ٱحْتَمَلُوا۟ بُهْتَـٰنًا وَإِثْمًا مُّبِينًا ۝     certainly bear the guilt of slander and flagrant sin.

يَـٰٓأَيُّهَا ٱلنَّبِىُّ     59 O Prophet!

قُل لِّأَزْوَٰجِكَ وَبَنَاتِكَ     Tell your wives and your daughters

وَنِسَآءِ ٱلْمُؤْمِنِينَ     and the women of the faithful

يُدْنِينَ عَلَيْهِنَّ     to draw closely over themselves

مِن جَلَـٰبِيبِهِنَّ     their chadors [when going out].

ذَٰلِكَ أَدْنَىٰٓ أَن يُعْرَفْنَ     That makes it likely for them to be recognized

فَلَا يُؤْذَيْنَ     and not be troubled,

وَكَانَ ٱللَّهُ غَفُورًا رَّحِيمًا ۝ ۞     and Allah is all-forgiving, all-merciful.

لَّئِن لَّمْ يَنتَهِ ٱلْمُنَـٰفِقُونَ     60 If the hypocrites do not relinquish

وَٱلَّذِينَ فِى قُلُوبِهِم مَّرَضٌ     and [also] those in whose hearts is a sickness,

وَٱلْمُرْجِفُونَ فِى ٱلْمَدِينَةِ     and the rumourmongers in the city [do not give up],

لَنُغْرِيَنَّكَ     We will surely urge *you* [to take action]

بِهِمْ     against them,

ثُمَّ لَا يُجَاوِرُونَكَ فِيهَآ     then they will not be *your* neighbours in it

---

[1] That is, their female slaves.

إِلَّا قَلِيلًا ۝      except for a little [while].

مَّلْعُونِينَ ۖ    61 Accursed,

أَيْنَمَا ثُقِفُوٓا۟ أُخِذُوا۟      they will be seized wherever they are confronted

وَقُتِّلُوا۟ تَقْتِيلًا ۝      and slain violently:

سُنَّةَ ٱللَّهِ فِى ٱلَّذِينَ خَلَوْا۟ مِن قَبْلُ ۖ    62 Allah's precedent with those who passed away before,

وَلَن تَجِدَ لِسُنَّةِ ٱللَّهِ تَبْدِيلًا ۝      and you will never find any change in Allah's precedent.

يَسْـَٔلُكَ ٱلنَّاسُ عَنِ ٱلسَّاعَةِ ۖ    63 The people question *you* concerning the Hour.

قُلْ إِنَّمَا عِلْمُهَا عِندَ ٱللَّهِ ۚ      *Say,* 'Its knowledge is only with Allah.'

وَمَا يُدْرِيكَ      What do *you* know,

لَعَلَّ ٱلسَّاعَةَ تَكُونُ قَرِيبًا ۝      maybe the Hour is near.

إِنَّ ٱللَّهَ لَعَنَ ٱلْكَٰفِرِينَ    64 Indeed Allah has cursed the faithless

وَأَعَدَّ لَهُمْ سَعِيرًا ۝      and prepared for them a blaze,

خَٰلِدِينَ فِيهَآ أَبَدًا ۖ    65   in which they will remain forever.

لَّا يَجِدُونَ وَلِيًّا وَلَا نَصِيرًا ۝      They will not find any guardian or helper.

يَوْمَ تُقَلَّبُ وُجُوهُهُمْ فِى ٱلنَّارِ    66 The day when their faces are turned about in the Fire,

يَقُولُونَ      they will say,

يَٰلَيْتَنَآ أَطَعْنَا ٱللَّهَ      'We wish we had obeyed Allah

وَأَطَعْنَا ٱلرَّسُولَا۠ ۝      and obeyed the Apostle!'

وَقَالُوا۟    67 And they will say,

رَبَّنَآ إِنَّآ أَطَعْنَا سَادَتَنَا وَكُبَرَآءَنَا      'Our Lord! We obeyed our leaders and elders,

فَأَضَلُّونَا ٱلسَّبِيلَا۠ ۝      and they led us astray from the way.'

رَبَّنَآ    68 Our Lord!

ءَاتِهِمْ ضِعْفَيْنِ مِنَ ٱلْعَذَابِ      Give them a double punishment

وَٱلْعَنْهُمْ لَعْنًا كَبِيرًا ۝      and curse them with a mighty curse.'

يَٰٓأَيُّهَا ٱلَّذِينَ ءَامَنُوا۟    69 O you who have faith!

لَا تَكُونُوا۟ كَٱلَّذِينَ ءَاذَوْا۟ مُوسَىٰ      Do not be like those who tormented Moses,

فَبَرَّأَهُ ٱللَّهُ مِمَّا قَالُوا۟ ۚ      whereat Allah absolved him of what they alleged,

وَكَانَ عِندَ ٱللَّهِ وَجِيهًا ۝      and he was distinguished in Allah's sight.

يَـٰٓأَيُّهَا ٱلَّذِينَ ءَامَنُوا۟ 70 O you who have faith!

ٱتَّقُوا۟ ٱللَّهَ      Be wary of Allah,

وَقُولُوا۟ قَوْلًا سَدِيدًا ۝      and speak upright words.

يُصْلِحْ لَكُمْ أَعْمَـٰلَكُمْ 71 He shall rectify your conduct for you

وَيَغْفِرْ لَكُمْ ذُنُوبَكُمْ ۗ      and He shall forgive you your sins.

وَمَن يُطِعِ ٱللَّهَ وَرَسُولَهُۥ      Whoever obeys Allah and His Apostle

فَقَدْ فَازَ فَوْزًا عَظِيمًا ۝      has certainly achieved a great success.

إِنَّا عَرَضْنَا ٱلْأَمَانَةَ عَلَى ٱلسَّمَـٰوَٰتِ 72 Indeed We presented the Trust to the heavens

وَٱلْأَرْضِ وَٱلْجِبَالِ      and the earth and the mountains,

فَأَبَيْنَ أَن يَحْمِلْنَهَا      but they refused to bear it,

وَأَشْفَقْنَ مِنْهَا      and were apprehensive of it;

وَحَمَلَهَا ٱلْإِنسَـٰنُ ۖ      but man undertook it.

إِنَّهُۥ كَانَ ظَلُومًا جَهُولًا ۝      Indeed he is most unfair and senseless.

لِّيُعَذِّبَ ٱللَّهُ 73 Allah will surely punish

ٱلْمُنَـٰفِقِينَ وَٱلْمُنَـٰفِقَـٰتِ      the hypocrites, men and women,

وَٱلْمُشْرِكِينَ وَٱلْمُشْرِكَـٰتِ      and the polytheists, men and women,

وَيَتُوبَ ٱللَّهُ      and Allah will turn clemently

عَلَى ٱلْمُؤْمِنِينَ وَٱلْمُؤْمِنَـٰتِ ۗ      to the faithful, men and women,

وَكَانَ ٱللَّهُ غَفُورًا رَّحِيمًا ۝      and Allah is all-forgiving, all-merciful.

## سُورَةُ سَبَأ      34. SŪRAT SABA[1]

بِسْمِ ٱللَّهِ      In the Name of Allah,

ٱلرَّحْمَـٰنِ ٱلرَّحِيمِ      the All-beneficent, the All-merciful.

ٱلْحَمْدُ لِلَّهِ 1 All praise belongs to Allah

ٱلَّذِى لَهُۥ مَا فِى ٱلسَّمَـٰوَٰتِ      to whom belongs whatever is in the heavens

وَمَا فِى ٱلْأَرْضِ      and whatever is in the earth.

وَلَهُ ٱلْحَمْدُ فِى ٱلْءَاخِرَةِ ۚ      To Him belongs all praise in the Hereafter,

---

[1] The *sūrah* is named after the account of Sheba (Saba) in verses 15-19.

وَهُوَ ٱلْحَكِيمُ ٱلْخَبِيرُ ۝     and He is the All-wise, the All-aware.

يَعْلَمُ مَا يَلِجُ فِى ٱلْأَرْضِ     2 He knows whatever enters into the earth

وَمَا يَخْرُجُ مِنْهَا     and whatever emerges from it,

وَمَا يَنزِلُ مِنَ ٱلسَّمَآءِ     and whatever descends from the sky

وَمَا يَعْرُجُ فِيهَا     and whatever ascends into it,

وَهُوَ ٱلرَّحِيمُ ٱلْغَفُورُ ۝     and He is the All-merciful, the All-forgiving.

وَقَالَ ٱلَّذِينَ كَفَرُوا     3 The faithless say,

لَا تَأْتِينَا ٱلسَّاعَةُ     'The Hour will never come to us.'

قُلْ بَلَىٰ وَرَبِّى     *Say,* 'Yes indeed, by my Lord,

لَتَأْتِيَنَّكُمْ     it will surely come to you.'

عَٰلِمِ ٱلْغَيْبِ     —The Knower of the Unseen,

لَا يَعْزُبُ عَنْهُ مِثْقَالُ ذَرَّةٍ     not [even] an atom's weight escapes Him

فِى ٱلسَّمَٰوَٰتِ وَلَا فِى ٱلْأَرْضِ     in the heavens or in the earth,

وَلَآ أَصْغَرُ مِن ذَٰلِكَ وَلَآ أَكْبَرُ     nor [is there] anything smaller than that nor bigger,

إِلَّا فِى كِتَٰبٍ مُّبِينٍ ۝     but it is in a manifest Book,

لِّيَجْزِىَ ٱلَّذِينَ ءَامَنُوا     4 that He may reward those who have faith

وَعَمِلُوا ٱلصَّٰلِحَٰتِ     and do righteous deeds.

أُوْلَٰٓئِكَ هُم مَّغْفِرَةٌ     For such there will be forgiveness

وَرِزْقٌ كَرِيمٌ ۝     and a noble provision.

وَٱلَّذِينَ سَعَوْ فِىٓ ءَايَٰتِنَا     5 But those who contend with Our signs

مُعَٰجِزِينَ     seeking to thwart [their purpose],

أُوْلَٰٓئِكَ لَهُمْ عَذَابٌ مِّن رِّجْزٍ أَلِيمٌ ۝     for such is a painful punishment due to defilement.[1]

وَيَرَى ٱلَّذِينَ أُوتُوا ٱلْعِلْمَ     6 Those who have been given knowledge see

ٱلَّذِىٓ أُنزِلَ إِلَيْكَ مِن رَّبِّكَ     that what has been sent down to *you* from *your* Lord

هُوَ ٱلْحَقَّ     is the truth

وَيَهْدِىٓ إِلَىٰ صِرَٰطِ     and [that] it guides to the path

ٱلْعَزِيزِ ٱلْحَمِيدِ ۝     of the All-mighty, the All-laudable.

---

[1] That is, owing to their inward defilement. According to an alternate reading which makes *alīm* the attribute of *rijz*, the translation will be: 'for such is the torment of a painful punishment.'

وَقَالَ ٱلَّذِينَ كَفَرُوا 7 The faithless say,

هَلْ نَدُلُّكُمْ عَلَىٰ رَجُلٍ يُنَبِّئُكُمْ    'Shall we show you a man who will inform you

إِذَا مُزِّقْتُمْ كُلَّ مُمَزَّقٍ    [that] when you have been totally rent to pieces

إِنَّكُمْ لَفِى خَلْقٍ جَدِيدٍ ۝    you will indeed have a new creation?

أَفْتَرَىٰ عَلَى ٱللَّهِ كَذِبًا 8 Has he fabricated a lie against Allah,

أَم بِهِۦ جِنَّةٌ    or is there a madness in him?'

بَلِ ٱلَّذِينَ لَا يُؤْمِنُونَ بِٱلْآخِرَةِ Rather those who do not believe in the Hereafter

فِى ٱلْعَذَابِ وَٱلضَّلَٰلِ ٱلْبَعِيدِ ۝    languish in punishment and extreme error.

أَفَلَمْ يَرَوْا إِلَىٰ مَا بَيْنَ أَيْدِيهِمْ 9 Have they not regarded that which is before them

وَمَا خَلْفَهُم    and that which is behind them

مِّنَ ٱلسَّمَآءِ وَٱلْأَرْضِ    of the sky and the earth?

إِن نَّشَأْ نَخْسِفْ بِهِمُ ٱلْأَرْضَ If We like, We can make the earth swallow them,

أَوْ نُسْقِطْ عَلَيْهِمْ كِسَفًا مِّنَ ٱلسَّمَآءِ    or let fall on them a fragment from the sky.

إِنَّ فِى ذَٰلِكَ لَآيَةً There is indeed a sign in that

لِّكُلِّ عَبْدٍ مُّنِيبٍ ۝ ❈    for every penitent servant.

وَلَقَدْ ءَاتَيْنَا دَاوُۥدَ مِنَّا فَضْلًا 10 Certainly We gave David a grace from Us:

يَٰجِبَالُ أَوِّبِى مَعَهُۥ وَٱلطَّيْرَ    'O mountains and birds, chime in with him!'[1]

وَأَلَنَّا لَهُ ٱلْحَدِيدَ ۝    And We made iron soft for him,

أَنِ ٱعْمَلْ سَٰبِغَٰتٍ 11    saying, 'Make easy coats of mail,

وَقَدِّرْ فِى ٱلسَّرْدِ    and keep the measure in arranging [the links],

وَٱعْمَلُوا صَٰلِحًا    and act righteously.

إِنِّى بِمَا تَعْمَلُونَ بَصِيرٌ ۝    Indeed I see best what you do.'

وَلِسُلَيْمَٰنَ ٱلرِّيحَ 12 And for Solomon [We subjected] the wind:

غُدُوُّهَا شَهْرٌ    its morning course was a month's journey

وَرَوَاحُهَا شَهْرٌ    and its evening course was a month's journey.

وَأَسَلْنَا لَهُۥ عَيْنَ ٱلْقِطْرِ    We made a fount of [molten] copper flow for him,

وَمِنَ ٱلْجِنِّ    and [We placed at his service] some of the jinn

مَن يَعْمَلُ بَيْنَ يَدَيْهِ    who would work for him

---

[1] Cf. 38:17-19.

بِإِذْنِ رَبِّهِ 　 by the permission of his Lord,

وَمَن يَزِغْ مِنْهُمْ عَنْ أَمْرِنَا 　 and if any of them swerved from Our command,

نُذِقْهُ 　 We would make him taste

مِنْ عَذَابِ ٱلسَّعِيرِ ۝ 　 the punishment of the Blaze.

يَعْمَلُونَ لَهُۥ مَا يَشَآءُ مِن مَّحَٰرِيبَ 　 13 They built for him as many temples as he wished,

وَتَمَٰثِيلَ وَجِفَانٍ كَٱلْجَوَابِ 　 and figures, basins like cisterns,

وَقُدُورٍ رَّاسِيَٰتٍ 　 and caldrons fixed [in the ground].

ٱعْمَلُوٓا۟ ءَالَ دَاوُۥدَ شُكْرًا 　 'O House of David, observe thanksgiving,

وَقَلِيلٌ مِّنْ عِبَادِىَ ٱلشَّكُورُ ۝ 　 and few of My servants are grateful.'

فَلَمَّا قَضَيْنَا عَلَيْهِ ٱلْمَوْتَ 　 14 And when We decreed death for him,

مَا دَلَّهُمْ عَلَىٰ مَوْتِهِۦٓ 　 nothing apprised them of his death

إِلَّا دَآبَّةُ ٱلْأَرْضِ تَأْكُلُ مِنسَأَتَهُۥ 　 except a worm which gnawed away at his staff.

فَلَمَّا خَرَّ 　 And when he fell down

تَبَيَّنَتِ ٱلْجِنُّ 　 the jinn realized

أَن لَّوْ كَانُوا۟ يَعْلَمُونَ ٱلْغَيْبَ 　 that had they known the Unseen,

مَا لَبِثُوا۟ 　 they would not have remained

فِى ٱلْعَذَابِ ٱلْمُهِينِ ۝ 　 in a humiliating torment.

لَقَدْ كَانَ لِسَبَإٍ فِى مَسْكَنِهِمْ ءَايَةٌ 　 15 There was certainly a sign for Sheba in their habitation:

جَنَّتَانِ عَن يَمِينٍ وَشِمَالٍ 　 two gardens, to the right and to the left.

كُلُوا۟ مِن رِّزْقِ رَبِّكُمْ 　 'Eat of the provision of your Lord

وَٱشْكُرُوا۟ لَهُۥ 　 and give Him thanks:

بَلْدَةٌ طَيِّبَةٌ وَرَبٌّ غَفُورٌ ۝ 　 a good land and an all-forgiving Lord!'

فَأَعْرَضُوا۟ 　 16 But they disregarded [the path of Allah],

فَأَرْسَلْنَا عَلَيْهِمْ سَيْلَ ٱلْعَرِمِ 　 so We unleashed upon them a violent flood

وَبَدَّلْنَٰهُم بِجَنَّتَيْهِمْ 　 and replaced their two gardens

جَنَّتَيْنِ ذَوَاتَىْ أُكُلٍ خَمْطٍ 　 with two gardens bearing bitter fruit,

وَأَثْلٍ 　 tamarisk,

وَشَىْءٍ مِّن سِدْرٍ قَلِيلٍ ۝ 　 and sparse lote trees.

ذَٰلِكَ جَزَيْنَٰهُم بِمَا كَفَرُوا۟ 　 17 We requited them with that for their ingratitude.

وَهَلْ نُجَزِىٓ إِلَّا ٱلْكَفُورَ ۝     Do We requite [so] anyone except ingrates?

وَجَعَلْنَا بَيْنَهُمْ     18 We had placed between them

وَبَيْنَ ٱلْقُرَى ٱلَّتِى بَٰرَكْنَا فِيهَا     and the towns which We had blessed

قُرًى ظَٰهِرَةً     hamlets prominent [from the main route],

وَقَدَّرْنَا فِيهَا ٱلسَّيْرَ     and We had ordained the course through them:

سِيرُواْ فِيهَا لَيَالِىَ وَأَيَّامًا ءَامِنِينَ ۝     'Travel through them in safety, night and day.'

فَقَالُواْ رَبَّنَا     19 But they said, 'Our Lord!

بَٰعِدْ بَيْنَ أَسْفَارِنَا     Make the stages between our journeys far apart,'

وَظَلَمُوٓاْ أَنفُسَهُمْ     and they wronged themselves.

فَجَعَلْنَٰهُمْ أَحَادِيثَ     So We turned them into folktales

وَمَزَّقْنَٰهُمْ كُلَّ مُمَزَّقٍ     and caused them to disintegrate totally.

إِنَّ فِى ذَٰلِكَ لَءَايَٰتٍ     There are indeed signs in that

لِّكُلِّ صَبَّارٍ شَكُورٍ ۝     for every patient and grateful [servant].

وَلَقَدْ صَدَّقَ عَلَيْهِمْ إِبْلِيسُ ظَنَّهُۥ     20 Certainly Iblis had his conjecture come true about them.

فَٱتَّبَعُوهُ     So they followed him

إِلَّا فَرِيقًا مِّنَ ٱلْمُؤْمِنِينَ ۝     —all except a part of the faithful.

وَمَا كَانَ لَهُۥ عَلَيْهِم مِّن سُلْطَٰنٍ     21 He had no authority over them,

إِلَّا لِنَعْلَمَ     but that We may ascertain

مَن يُؤْمِنُ بِٱلْءَاخِرَةِ     those who believe in the Hereafter

مِمَّنْ هُوَ مِنْهَا فِى شَكٍّ     from those who are in doubt about it,

وَرَبُّكَ عَلَىٰ كُلِّ شَىْءٍ حَفِيظٌ ۝     and *your* Lord is watchful over all things.

قُلِ ٱدْعُواْ ٱلَّذِينَ زَعَمْتُم     22 *Say,* 'Invoke them whom you claim [to be gods]

مِّن دُونِ ٱللَّهِ     besides Allah!

لَا يَمْلِكُونَ مِثْقَالَ ذَرَّةٍ     They do not control [even] an atom's weight

فِى ٱلسَّمَٰوَٰتِ وَلَا فِى ٱلْأَرْضِ     in the heavens or the earth,

وَمَا لَهُمْ فِيهِمَا مِن شِرْكٍ     nor have they any share in [either of] them,

وَمَا لَهُۥ مِنْهُم مِّن ظَهِيرٍ ۝     nor is any of them[1] His supporter.'

وَلَا تَنفَعُ ٱلشَّفَٰعَةُ عِندَهُۥٓ     23 Intercession is of no avail with Him

---

[1] That is, the gods worshipped by the polytheists.

إِلَّا لِمَنْ أَذِنَ لَهُۥ

except for those whom He permits.[1]

حَتَّىٰٓ إِذَا فُزِّعَ عَن قُلُوبِهِمْ

When fear is lifted from their hearts,

قَالُواْ مَاذَا قَالَ رَبُّكُمْ

they say, 'What did your Lord say?'

قَالُواْ ٱلْحَقَّ

They say, 'The truth,

وَهُوَ ٱلْعَلِىُّ ٱلْكَبِيرُ ۞

and He is the All-exalted, the All-great.'

قُلْ مَن يَرْزُقُكُم مِّنَ ٱلسَّمَـٰوَٰتِ

24 *Say*, 'Who provides for you from the heavens

وَٱلْأَرْضِ

and the earth?'

قُلِ ٱللَّهُ

*Say*, 'Allah!

وَإِنَّآ أَوْ إِيَّاكُمْ لَعَلَىٰ هُدًى

Indeed either we or you are rightly guided

أَوْ فِى ضَلَـٰلٍ مُّبِينٍ ۞

or in manifest error.'

قُل لَّا تُسْـَٔلُونَ عَمَّآ أَجْرَمْنَا

25 *Say*, 'You will not be questioned about our guilt,

وَلَا نُسْـَٔلُ عَمَّا تَعْمَلُونَ ۞

nor shall we be questioned about what you do.'

قُلْ يَجْمَعُ بَيْنَنَا رَبُّنَا

26 *Say*, 'Our Lord will bring us together,

ثُمَّ يَفْتَحُ بَيْنَنَا بِٱلْحَقِّ

then He will judge between us with justice,

وَهُوَ ٱلْفَتَّاحُ ٱلْعَلِيمُ ۞

and He is the All-knowing Judge.'[2]

قُلْ أَرُونِىَ ٱلَّذِينَ

27 *Say*, 'Show me those whom

أَلْحَقْتُم بِهِۦ شُرَكَآءَ

you associate with Him as partners.'

كَلَّا

No indeed! [They can never show any such partner].

بَلْ هُوَ ٱللَّهُ ٱلْعَزِيزُ ٱلْحَكِيمُ ۞

Rather He is Allah, the All-mighty, the All-wise.

وَمَآ أَرْسَلْنَـٰكَ

28 We did not send *you* except

إِلَّا كَآفَّةً لِّلنَّاسِ بَشِيرًا وَنَذِيرًا

as a bearer of good news and warner to all mankind,

وَلَـٰكِنَّ أَكْثَرَ ٱلنَّاسِ لَا يَعْلَمُونَ ۞

but most people do not know.

وَيَقُولُونَ مَتَىٰ هَـٰذَا ٱلْوَعْدُ

29 And they say, 'When will this promise be fulfilled,

إِن كُنتُمْ صَـٰدِقِينَ ۞

should you be truthful?'

قُل لَّكُم مِّيعَادُ يَوْمٍ

30 *Say*, 'Your promised hour is a day

لَّا تَسْتَـْٔخِرُونَ عَنْهُ سَاعَةً وَلَا تَسْتَقْدِمُونَ ۞

that you shall neither defer nor advance by an hour.'

وَقَالَ ٱلَّذِينَ كَفَرُواْ

31 The faithless say,

لَن نُّؤْمِنَ بِهَـٰذَا ٱلْقُرْءَانِ

'We will never believe in this Qur'ān,

---

[1] See Zamakhshari and Ṭabāṭabā'ī. Or 'except of those whom He permits.'
[2] Or, 'the Judge, the All-knowing.'

وَلَا بِٱلَّذِى بَيْنَ يَدَيْهِ ۗ    nor in what was [revealed] before it.'

وَلَوْ تَرَىٰ    But if *you* were to see

إِذِ ٱلظَّٰلِمُونَ مَوْقُوفُونَ    when the wrongdoers are made to stop

عِندَ رَبِّهِمْ    before their Lord

يَرْجِعُ بَعْضُهُمْ إِلَىٰ بَعْضٍ ٱلْقَوْلَ    casting the blame on one another.

يَقُولُ ٱلَّذِينَ ٱسْتُضْعِفُوا    Those who were abased will say

لِلَّذِينَ ٱسْتَكْبَرُوا    to those who were arrogant,

لَوْلَا أَنتُمْ    'Had it not been for you,

لَكُنَّا مُؤْمِنِينَ ۝    we would surely have been faithful.'

قَالَ ٱلَّذِينَ ٱسْتَكْبَرُوا    32 Those who were arrogant will say

لِلَّذِينَ ٱسْتُضْعِفُوا    to those who were abased,

أَنَحْنُ صَدَدْنَٰكُمْ عَنِ ٱلْهُدَىٰ    'Did we keep you from guidance

بَعْدَ إِذْ جَآءَكُم ۖ    after it had come to you?

بَلْ كُنتُم مُّجْرِمِينَ ۝    No, you were guilty [yourselves].'

وَقَالَ ٱلَّذِينَ ٱسْتُضْعِفُوا    33 Those who were abased will say

لِلَّذِينَ ٱسْتَكْبَرُوا    to those who were arrogant,

بَلْ مَكْرُ ٱلَّيْلِ وَٱلنَّهَارِ    'Rather [it was your] night and day plotting,

إِذْ تَأْمُرُونَنَآ أَن نَّكْفُرَ بِٱللَّهِ    when you prompted us to forswear Allah

وَنَجْعَلَ لَهُۥٓ أَندَادًا ۚ    and to set up equals to Him.'

وَأَسَرُّوا ٱلنَّدَامَةَ    They will hide their remorse

لَمَّا رَأَوُا ٱلْعَذَابَ    when they sight the punishment,

وَجَعَلْنَا ٱلْأَغْلَٰلَ    and We will put iron collars

فِىٓ أَعْنَاقِ ٱلَّذِينَ كَفَرُوا ۚ    around the necks of the faithless.

هَلْ يُجْزَوْنَ إِلَّا مَا كَانُوا يَعْمَلُونَ ۝    Shall they be requited except for what they used to do?

وَمَآ أَرْسَلْنَا فِى قَرْيَةٍ مِّن نَّذِيرٍ    34 We did not send a warner to any town

إِلَّا قَالَ مُتْرَفُوهَآ    without its affluent ones saying,

إِنَّا بِمَآ أُرْسِلْتُم بِهِۦ كَٰفِرُونَ ۝    'We indeed disbelieve in what you have been sent with.'

وَقَالُوا    35 And they say,

نَحْنُ أَكْثَرُ أَمْوَٰلًا وَأَوْلَٰدًا    'We have greater wealth and more children,

وَمَا نَحْنُ بِمُعَذَّبِينَ ۝    and we will not be punished!'

قُلْ إِنَّ رَبِّى يَبْسُطُ ٱلرِّزْقَ 36 *Say,* 'Indeed my Lord expands the provision

لِمَن يَشَآءُ     for whomever He wishes

وَيَقْدِرُ     and He tightens it,

وَلَـٰكِنَّ أَكْثَرَ ٱلنَّاسِ لَا يَعْلَمُونَ ۞     but most people do not know.'

وَمَآ أَمْوَٰلُكُمْ وَلَآ أَوْلَـٰدُكُم 37 It is not your wealth, nor your children,

بِٱلَّتِى تُقَرِّبُكُمْ عِندَنَا زُلْفَىٰٓ     that will bring you close to Us in nearness,

إِلَّا مَنْ ءَامَنَ وَعَمِلَ صَـٰلِحًا     except those who have faith and act righteously.

فَأُوْلَـٰٓئِكَ لَهُمْ جَزَآءُ ٱلضِّعْفِ     It is they for whom there will be a twofold reward

بِمَا عَمِلُواْ     for what they did,

وَهُمْ فِى ٱلْغُرُفَـٰتِ ءَامِنُونَ ۞     and they will be secure in lofty abodes.[1]

وَٱلَّذِينَ يَسْعَوْنَ فِىٓ ءَايَـٰتِنَا 38 As for those who contend with Our signs

مُعَـٰجِزِينَ     seeking to thwart [their purpose],

أُوْلَـٰٓئِكَ فِى ٱلْعَذَابِ مُحْضَرُونَ ۞     they will be brought to the punishment.

قُلْ إِنَّ رَبِّى يَبْسُطُ ٱلرِّزْقَ 39 *Say,* 'Indeed my Lord expands the provision

لِمَن يَشَآءُ مِنْ عِبَادِهِۦ     for whomever of His servants that He wishes

وَيَقْدِرُ لَهُۥ     and tightens it,

وَمَآ أَنفَقْتُم مِّن شَىْءٍ فَهُوَ يُخْلِفُهُۥ     and He will repay whatever you may spend,

وَهُوَ خَيْرُ ٱلرَّٰزِقِينَ ۞     and He is the best of providers.

وَيَوْمَ يَحْشُرُهُمْ جَمِيعًا 40 On the day He will muster them all together,

ثُمَّ يَقُولُ لِلْمَلَـٰٓئِكَةِ     He will say to the angels,

أَهَـٰٓؤُلَآءِ إِيَّاكُمْ كَانُواْ يَعْبُدُونَ ۞     'Was it you that these used to worship?'

قَالُواْ سُبْحَـٰنَكَ 41 They will say, 'Immaculate are You!

أَنتَ وَلِيُّنَا مِن دُونِهِم     You are our Intimate, not they!

بَلْ كَانُواْ يَعْبُدُونَ ٱلْجِنَّ     Rather they used to worship the jinn;

أَكْثَرُهُم بِهِم مُّؤْمِنُونَ ۞     most of them had faith in them.'

فَٱلْيَوْمَ 42 'Today

لَا يَمْلِكُ بَعْضُكُمْ لِبَعْضٍ نَّفْعًا وَلَا ضَرًّا     you have no power to benefit or harm one another,'

وَنَقُولُ لِلَّذِينَ ظَلَمُواْ     and We shall say to those who did wrong,

ذُوقُواْ عَذَابَ ٱلنَّارِ     'Taste the punishment of the Fire

---

[1] Cf. 29:58; 39:20.

أَلَّتِى كُنتُم بِهَا تُكَذِّبُونَ ۝

وَإِذَا تُتْلَىٰ عَلَيْهِمْ ءَايَٰتُنَا بَيِّنَٰتٍ 43 When Our manifest signs are recited to them,

قَالُوا　　　　　　　　　they say,

مَا هَٰذَآ إِلَّا رَجُلٌ يُرِيدُ أَن يَصُدَّكُمْ 'This is just a man who desires to keep you

عَمَّا كَانَ يَعْبُدُ ءَابَآؤُكُمْ　from what your fathers used to worship.'

وَقَالُوا مَا هَٰذَآ إِلَّآ إِفْكٌ مُّفْتَرًى And they say, 'This is nothing but a fabricated lie.'

وَقَالَ ٱلَّذِينَ كَفَرُوا لِلْحَقِّ　The faithless say of the truth

لَمَّا جَآءَهُمْ　　　　　when it comes to them:

إِنْ هَٰذَآ إِلَّا سِحْرٌ مُّبِينٌ ۝ 'This is nothing but plain magic.'

وَمَآ ءَاتَيْنَٰهُم مِّن كُتُبٍ 44 We did not give them[1] any scriptures

يَدْرُسُونَهَا　　　　　that they might have studied,

وَمَآ أَرْسَلْنَآ إِلَيْهِمْ قَبْلَكَ مِن نَّذِيرٍ ۝ nor did We send them any warner before *you*.[2]

وَكَذَّبَ ٱلَّذِينَ مِن قَبْلِهِمْ 45 Those who were before them denied [the apostles],

وَمَا بَلَغُوا مِعْشَارَ　　　and these have not received one-tenth[3]

مَآ ءَاتَيْنَٰهُمْ　　　　of what We had given them.

فَكَذَّبُوا رُسُلِى　　　But they denied My apostles,

فَكَيْفَ كَانَ نَكِيرِ ۝ ❋ so how was My rebuttal![4]

قُلْ إِنَّمَآ أَعِظُكُم بِوَٰحِدَةٍ 46 *Say,* 'I give you just a single advice:

أَن تَقُومُوا لِلَّهِ　　　that you rise up for Allah's sake,

مَثْنَىٰ وَفُرَٰدَىٰ　　　in twos, or individually,

ثُمَّ تَتَفَكَّرُوا　　　　and then reflect:

مَا بِصَاحِبِكُم مِّن جِنَّةٍ there is no madness in your companion:

إِنْ هُوَ إِلَّا نَذِيرٌ لَّكُم he is just a warner to you

بَيْنَ يَدَىْ عَذَابٍ شَدِيدٍ ۝ before [the befalling of] a severe punishment.'

قُلْ مَا سَأَلْتُكُم مِّنْ أَجْرٍ 47 *Say,* 'Whatever reward I may have asked you

فَهُوَ لَكُمْ　　　　　is for your own good.

إِنْ أَجْرِىَ إِلَّا عَلَى ٱللَّهِ　My [true] reward lies only with Allah,

---

[1] That is, the pre-Islamic Arabs.
[2] Cf. 36:6.
[3] Or 'a thousandth.'
[4] Or 'how was my requital.'

وَهُوَ عَلَىٰ كُلِّ شَىْءٍ شَهِيدٌ ۝    and He is witness to all things.'

قُلْ إِنَّ رَبِّى يَقْذِفُ بِٱلْحَقِّ    48 *Say*, 'Indeed my Lord hurls[1] the truth.

عَلَّٰمُ ٱلْغُيُوبِ ۝    [He is] the knower of all that is Unseen.'

قُلْ جَآءَ ٱلْحَقُّ    49 *Say*, 'The truth has come,

وَمَا يُبْدِئُ ٱلْبَٰطِلُ    and falsehood neither originates [anything]

وَمَا يُعِيدُ ۝    not does it restore [anything].'

قُلْ إِن ضَلَلْتُ    50 *Say*, 'If I go astray,

فَإِنَّمَآ أَضِلُّ عَلَىٰ نَفْسِى    my going astray is only to my own harm,

وَإِنِ ٱهْتَدَيْتُ    and if I am rightly guided

فَبِمَا يُوحِىٓ إِلَىَّ رَبِّى    that is because of what my Lord has revealed to me.

إِنَّهُۥ سَمِيعٌ قَرِيبٌ ۝    Indeed He is all-hearing, nearmost.'

وَلَوْ تَرَىٰٓ إِذْ فَزِعُوا۟    51 Were *you* to see when they are stricken with terror,

فَلَا فَوْتَ    [and left] without an escape,

وَأُخِذُوا۟ مِن مَّكَانٍ قَرِيبٍ ۝    and are seized from a close quarter.

وَقَالُوٓا۟ ءَامَنَّا بِهِۦ    52 They will say, 'We believe in it [now].'

وَأَنَّىٰ لَهُمُ ٱلتَّنَاوُشُ مِن مَّكَانٍ بَعِيدٍ ۝    But how can they reach it from a far-off place,

وَقَدْ كَفَرُوا۟ بِهِۦ مِن قَبْلُ    53 when they have already disbelieved it earlier?

وَيَقْذِفُونَ بِٱلْغَيْبِ مِن مَّكَانٍ بَعِيدٍ ۝    They shoot at the invisible from a far-off place!

وَحِيلَ بَيْنَهُمْ    54 A barrier will be set up between them

وَبَيْنَ مَا يَشْتَهُونَ    and what they long for,

كَمَا فُعِلَ بِأَشْيَاعِهِم مِّن قَبْلُ    just as was done formerly with their counterparts.

إِنَّهُمْ كَانُوا۟ فِى شَكٍّ مُّرِيبٍ ۝    Indeed they used to be in grave doubt.

سُورَة فاطِر      ## 35. SŪRAT FĀṬIR[2]

بِسْمِ ٱللَّهِ    In the Name of Allah,

ٱلرَّحْمَٰنِ ٱلرَّحِيمِ    the All-beneficent, the All-merciful.

---

[1] Cf. 17:81; 21:18.

[2] The sūrah takes its name from the word *fāṭir* (originator), which occurs in verse 1

ٱلْحَمْدُ لِلَّهِ    1 All praise belongs to Allah,

فَاطِرِ ٱلسَّمَوَٰتِ وَٱلْأَرْضِ    originator of the heavens and the earth,

جَاعِلِ ٱلْمَلَـٰٓئِكَةِ رُسُلًا    maker of the angels [His] messengers,

أُوْلِىٓ أَجْنِحَةٍ مَّثْنَىٰ وَثُلَـٰثَ وَرُبَـٰعَ    possessing wings, two, three or four [of them].

يَزِيدُ فِى ٱلْخَلْقِ مَا يَشَآءُ    He adds to the creation whatever He wishes.

إِنَّ ٱللَّهَ عَلَىٰ كُلِّ شَىْءٍ قَدِيرٌ ۝    Indeed Allah has power over all things.

مَّا يَفْتَحِ ٱللَّهُ لِلنَّاسِ مِن رَّحْمَةٍ    2 Whatever mercy Allah unfolds for the people,

فَلَا مُمْسِكَ لَهَا    no one can withhold it;

وَمَا يُمْسِكْ    and whatever He withholds

فَلَا مُرْسِلَ لَهُۥ مِنۢ بَعْدِهِۦ    no one can release it after Him,[1]

وَهُوَ ٱلْعَزِيزُ ٱلْحَكِيمُ ۝    and He is the All-mighty, the All-wise.

يَـٰٓأَيُّهَا ٱلنَّاسُ    3 O mankind!

ٱذْكُرُواْ نِعْمَتَ ٱللَّهِ عَلَيْكُمْ    Remember Allah's blessing upon you!

هَلْ مِنْ خَـٰلِقٍ غَيْرُ ٱللَّهِ    Is there any creator other than Allah

يَرْزُقُكُم مِّنَ ٱلسَّمَآءِ وَٱلْأَرْضِ    who provides for you from the sky and the earth?

لَآ إِلَـٰهَ إِلَّا هُوَ    There is no god except Him.

فَأَنَّىٰ تُؤْفَكُونَ ۝    So where do you stray?

وَإِن يُكَذِّبُوكَ    4 If they impugn *you*,

فَقَدْ كُذِّبَتْ رُسُلٌ مِّن قَبْلِكَ    certainly [other] apostles were impugned before *you*,

وَإِلَى ٱللَّهِ تُرْجَعُ ٱلْأُمُورُ ۝    and all matters are returned to Allah.

يَـٰٓأَيُّهَا ٱلنَّاسُ    5 O mankind!

إِنَّ وَعْدَ ٱللَّهِ حَقٌّ    Allah's promise is indeed true.

فَلَا تَغُرَّنَّكُمُ ٱلْحَيَوٰةُ ٱلدُّنْيَا    So do not let the life of the world deceive you,

وَلَا يَغُرَّنَّكُم بِٱللَّهِ ٱلْغَرُورُ ۝    nor let the Deceiver deceive you concerning Allah.[2]

إِنَّ ٱلشَّيْطَـٰنَ لَكُمْ عَدُوٌّ    6 Satan is indeed your enemy,

فَٱتَّخِذُوهُ عَدُوًّا    so treat him as an enemy.

إِنَّمَا يَدْعُواْ حِزْبَهُۥ    His only invites his confederates

لِيَكُونُواْ مِنْ أَصْحَـٰبِ ٱلسَّعِيرِ ۝    so that they may be among the inmates of the Blaze.

---

[1] That is, after His withholding it. Or 'no one can release it except Him.'
[2] Cf. 31:33.

ٱلَّذِينَ كَفَرُوا لَهُمْ عَذَابٌ شَدِيدٌ ٧    7 There is a severe punishment for the faithless,

وَٱلَّذِينَ ءَامَنُوا وَعَمِلُوا ٱلصَّٰلِحَٰتِ    but for those who have faith and do righteous deeds

لَهُم مَّغْفِرَةٌ وَأَجْرٌ كَبِيرٌ ٧    there will be forgiveness and a great reward.

أَفَمَن ٨    8 Is someone

زُيِّنَ لَهُۥ سُوٓءُ عَمَلِهِۦ    the evil of whose conduct is presented as decorous to him,

فَرَءَاهُ حَسَنًا    so he regards it as good. . . .[1]

فَإِنَّ ٱللَّهَ يُضِلُّ مَن يَشَآءُ    Indeed Allah leads astray whomever He wishes,

وَيَهْدِى مَن يَشَآءُ    and guides whomever He wishes.

فَلَا تَذْهَبْ نَفْسُكَ عَلَيْهِمْ حَسَرَٰتٍ    So do not fret *yourself* to death regretting for them.

إِنَّ ٱللَّهَ عَلِيمٌ بِمَا يَصْنَعُونَ ٨    Indeed Allah knows best what they do.

وَٱللَّهُ ٱلَّذِىٓ أَرْسَلَ ٱلرِّيَٰحَ ٩    9 It is Allah who sends the winds

فَتُثِيرُ سَحَابًا    and they raise a cloud;

فَسُقْنَٰهُ إِلَىٰ بَلَدٍ مَّيِّتٍ    then We drive it toward a dead land

فَأَحْيَيْنَا بِهِ ٱلْأَرْضَ بَعْدَ مَوْتِهَا    and with it revive the earth after its death.

كَذَٰلِكَ ٱلنُّشُورُ ٩    Likewise will be the resurrection [of the dead].

مَن كَانَ يُرِيدُ ٱلْعِزَّةَ ١٠    10 Whoever seeks honour[2] [should know that]

فَلِلَّهِ ٱلْعِزَّةُ جَمِيعًا    honour entirely belongs to Allah.

إِلَيْهِ يَصْعَدُ ٱلْكَلِمُ ٱلطَّيِّبُ    To Him ascends the good word,

وَٱلْعَمَلُ ٱلصَّٰلِحُ يَرْفَعُهُۥ    and He elevates righteous conduct;[3]

وَٱلَّذِينَ يَمْكُرُونَ ٱلسَّيِّئَاتِ    as for those who devise evil schemes,

لَهُمْ عَذَابٌ شَدِيدٌ    there is a severe punishment for them,

وَمَكْرُ أُوْلَٰٓئِكَ هُوَ يَبُورُ ١٠    and their plotting shall come to naught.

وَٱللَّهُ خَلَقَكُم مِّن تُرَابٍ ١١    11 Allah created you from dust,

ثُمَّ مِن نُّطْفَةٍ    then from a drop of [seminal] fluid,

ثُمَّ جَعَلَكُمْ أَزْوَٰجًا    then He made you mates.[4]

---

[1] Ellipsis. The phrase omitted is 'like one who is truly virtuous?'

[2] The word *'izzah* in Arabic has a composite meaning including the senses of honour, prestige, glory and might.

[3] Or 'righteous conduct elevates it.'

[4] That is, male and female.

وَمَا تَحْمِلُ مِنْ أُنثَىٰ وَلَا تَضَعُ

No female conceives or delivers

إِلَّا بِعِلْمِهِۦ

    except with His knowledge,

وَمَا يُعَمَّرُ مِن مُّعَمَّرٍ

and no elderly person advances in years,

وَلَا يُنقَصُ مِنْ عُمُرِهِۦٓ

    nor is anything diminished of his life,

إِلَّا فِى كِتَٰبٍ

    but it is [recorded] in a Book.

إِنَّ ذَٰلِكَ عَلَى ٱللَّهِ يَسِيرٌ ۝

That is indeed easy for Allah.

وَمَا يَسْتَوِى ٱلْبَحْرَانِ

12 Not alike are the two seas:[1]

هَٰذَا عَذْبٌ فُرَاتٌ سَآئِغٌ شَرَابُهُ

this one sweet and agreeable, pleasant to drink,

وَهَٰذَا مِلْحٌ أُجَاجٌ

    and that one briny and bitter,

وَمِن كُلٍّ تَأْكُلُونَ لَحْمًا طَرِيًّا

and from each you eat fresh meat

وَتَسْتَخْرِجُونَ حِلْيَةً تَلْبَسُونَهَا

    and obtain ornaments which you wear.

وَتَرَى ٱلْفُلْكَ فِيهِ مَوَاخِرَ

And you see the ships plowing through them,

لِتَبْتَغُوا۟ مِن فَضْلِهِۦ

    that you may seek of His grace,

وَلَعَلَّكُمْ تَشْكُرُونَ ۝

    and so that you may give thanks.

يُولِجُ ٱلَّيْلَ فِى ٱلنَّهَارِ

13 He makes the night pass into the day

وَيُولِجُ ٱلنَّهَارَ فِى ٱلَّيْلِ

and makes the day pass into the night,

وَسَخَّرَ ٱلشَّمْسَ وَٱلْقَمَرَ

and He has disposed the sun and the moon,

كُلٌّ يَجْرِى لِأَجَلٍ مُّسَمًّى

    each moving for a specified term.

ذَٰلِكُمُ ٱللَّهُ رَبُّكُمْ

That is Allah, your Lord;

لَهُ ٱلْمُلْكُ

    to Him belongs all sovereignty.

وَٱلَّذِينَ تَدْعُونَ مِن دُونِهِۦ

As for those whom you invoke besides Him,

مَا يَمْلِكُونَ مِن قِطْمِيرٍ ۝

they do not control so much as the husk of a date stone.

إِن تَدْعُوهُمْ لَا يَسْمَعُوا۟ دُعَآءَكُمْ

14 If you invoke them they will not hear your invocation,

وَلَوْ سَمِعُوا۟ مَا ٱسْتَجَابُوا۟ لَكُمْ

    and even if they heard they can not respond to you,

وَيَوْمَ ٱلْقِيَٰمَةِ

    and on the Day of Resurrection

يَكْفُرُونَ بِشِرْكِكُمْ

    they will forswear your polytheism,

وَلَا يُنَبِّئُكَ مِثْلُ خَبِيرٍ ۝ ۞

and none can inform you like the One who is all-aware.

---

[1] That is, the body of sweet water and the body of fresh water. The word *bahr*, like *yamm* is used for a large river as well as for the sea (cf. 7:36, 20:78, 28:40, 51:40, where it is used for the Red Sea, and 20:39, 28:7 where it is used for the Nile).

يَٰٓأَيُّهَا ٱلنَّاسُ 15 O mankind!

أَنتُمُ ٱلۡفُقَرَآءُ إِلَى ٱللَّهِ     You are the ones who stand in need of Allah,

وَٱللَّهُ هُوَ ٱلۡغَنِيُّ ٱلۡحَمِيدُ ۝     and Allah—He is the All-sufficient, the All-laudable.

إِن يَشَأۡ يُذۡهِبۡكُمۡ 16 If He wishes, He will take you away,

وَيَأۡتِ بِخَلۡقٍ جَدِيدٍ ۝     and bring about a new creation;

وَمَا ذَٰلِكَ عَلَى ٱللَّهِ بِعَزِيزٍ ۝ 17     and that is not a hard thing for Allah.

وَلَا تَزِرُ وَازِرَةٌ وِزۡرَ أُخۡرَىٰ 18 No bearer shall bear another's burden,

وَإِن تَدۡعُ مُثۡقَلَةٌ     and should one heavily burdened call [another]

إِلَىٰ حِمۡلِهَا     to carry it,

لَا يُحۡمَلۡ مِنۡهُ شَيۡءٌ     nothing of it will be carried,

وَلَوۡ كَانَ ذَا قُرۡبَىٰٓ     even if he were a near relative.

إِنَّمَا تُنذِرُ ٱلَّذِينَ يَخۡشَوۡنَ رَبَّهُم     *You* can only warn those who fear their Lord

بِٱلۡغَيۡبِ     in secret,

وَأَقَامُواْ ٱلصَّلَوٰةَ     and maintain the prayer.

وَمَن تَزَكَّىٰ     Whoever purifies himself,

فَإِنَّمَا يَتَزَكَّىٰ لِنَفۡسِهِۦ     purifies only for his own sake,

وَإِلَى ٱللَّهِ ٱلۡمَصِيرُ ۝     and to Allah is the return.

وَمَا يَسۡتَوِي ٱلۡأَعۡمَىٰ وَٱلۡبَصِيرُ ۝ 19 The blind one and the seer are not equal,

وَلَا ٱلظُّلُمَٰتُ وَلَا ٱلنُّورُ ۝ 20     nor darkness and light;

وَلَا ٱلظِّلُّ وَلَا ٱلۡحَرُورُ ۝ 21     nor shade and torrid heat;

وَمَا يَسۡتَوِي ٱلۡأَحۡيَآءُ وَلَا ٱلۡأَمۡوَٰتُ 22     nor are the living equal to the dead.

إِنَّ ٱللَّهَ يُسۡمِعُ مَن يَشَآءُ     Indeed Allah makes whomever He wishes to hear,

وَمَآ أَنتَ بِمُسۡمِعٍ مَّن فِي ٱلۡقُبُورِ ۝     and *you* cannot make those who are in the graves hear.

إِنۡ أَنتَ إِلَّا نَذِيرٌ ۝ 23 *You* are but a warner.

إِنَّآ أَرۡسَلۡنَٰكَ بِٱلۡحَقِّ 24 Indeed We have sent *you* with the truth

بَشِيرًا وَنَذِيرًا     as a bearer of good news and as a warner;

وَإِن مِّنۡ أُمَّةٍ     and there is not a nation

إِلَّا خَلَا فِيهَا نَذِيرٌ ۝     but a warner has passed in it.

وَإِن يُكَذِّبُوكَ 25 If they impugn *you*,

فَقَدۡ كَذَّبَ ٱلَّذِينَ مِن قَبۡلِهِمۡ     those before them have impugned [likewise]:

جَاءَتْهُمْ رُسُلُهُم بِالْبَيِّنَتِ their apostles brought them manifest proofs,

وَبِالزُّبُرِ وَبِالْكِتَبِ الْمُنِيرِ ۝ [holy] writs, and illuminating scriptures.

ثُمَّ أَخَذْتُ الَّذِينَ كَفَرُواْ 26 Then I seized the faithless.

فَكَيْفَ كَانَ نَكِيرِ ۝ So how was My rebuttal!

أَلَمْ تَرَ 27 Have you not regarded

أَنَّ اللَّهَ أَنزَلَ مِنَ السَّمَاءِ مَاءً that Allah sends down water from the sky,

فَأَخْرَجْنَا بِهِ ثَمَرَتٍ مُّخْتَلِفًا أَلْوَنُهَا with which We produce fruits of diverse hues;

وَمِنَ الْجِبَالِ جُدَدٌ and in the mountains are stripes

بِيضٌ وَحُمْرٌ مُّخْتَلِفٌ أَلْوَنُهَا white and red, of diverse hues,

وَغَرَابِيبُ سُودٌ ۝ and [others] pitch black?

وَمِنَ النَّاسِ وَالدَّوَابِّ وَالْأَنْعَمِ 28 And of humans and beasts and cattle

مُخْتَلِفٌ أَلْوَنُهُ كَذَلِكَ there are likewise diverse hues.

إِنَّمَا يَخْشَى اللَّهَ مِنْ عِبَادِهِ الْعُلَمَؤُاْ Only those of Allah's servants having knowledge fear Him.

إِنَّ اللَّهَ عَزِيزٌ غَفُورٌ ۝ Indeed Allah is all-mighty, all-forgiving.

إِنَّ الَّذِينَ يَتْلُونَ كِتَبَ اللَّهِ 29 Indeed those who recite the Book of Allah

وَأَقَامُواْ الصَّلَوٰةَ and maintain the prayer,

وَأَنفَقُواْ مِمَّا رَزَقْنَهُمْ and spend out of what We have provided them,

سِرًّا وَعَلَانِيَةً secretly and openly,

يَرْجُونَ تِجَرَةً expecting a commerce

لَّن تَبُورَ ۝ that will never go bankrupt,

لِيُوَفِّيَهُمْ أُجُورَهُمْ 30 that He may pay them their reward in full

وَيَزِيدَهُم مِّن فَضْلِهِ and enhance them out of His grace.

إِنَّهُ غَفُورٌ شَكُورٌ ۝ Indeed He is all-forgiving, all-appreciative.

وَالَّذِىٓ أَوْحَيْنَآ إِلَيْكَ مِنَ الْكِتَبِ 31 That which We have revealed to *you* of the Book

هُوَ الْحَقُّ is the truth,

مُصَدِّقًا لِّمَا بَيْنَ يَدَيْهِ confirming what was [revealed] before it.

إِنَّ اللَّهَ بِعِبَادِهِ لَخَبِيرٌ بَصِيرٌ ۝ Indeed Allah is all-aware, all-seeing about His servants.

ثُمَّ أَوْرَثْنَا الْكِتَبَ 32 Then We made heirs to the Book[1]

الَّذِينَ اصْطَفَيْنَا مِنْ عِبَادِنَا those whom We chose from Our servants.

---

[1] That is, the Qur'ān.

فَمِنْهُمْ ظَالِمٌ لِّنَفْسِهِ

Yet some of them are those who wrong themselves,

وَمِنْهُم مُّقْتَصِدٌ

and some of them are average,

وَمِنْهُمْ سَابِقٌ

and some of them are those who take the lead

بِالْخَيْرَاتِ

in all good works

بِإِذْنِ اللَّهِ

by Allah's will.

ذَٰلِكَ هُوَ الْفَضْلُ الْكَبِيرُ ٣٢

That is the greatest grace!

جَنَّاتُ عَدْنٍ يَدْخُلُونَهَا 33

Gardens of Eden, which they will enter,

يُحَلَّوْنَ فِيهَا مِنْ أَسَاوِرَ مِن ذَهَبٍ وَلُؤْلُؤًا

adorned therein with bracelets of gold and pearl,

وَلِبَاسُهُمْ فِيهَا حَرِيرٌ ٣٣

and their garments therein will be of silk.

وَقَالُوا الْحَمْدُ لِلَّهِ 34

They will say, 'All praise belongs to Allah,

الَّذِي أَذْهَبَ عَنَّا الْحَزَنَ

who has removed all grief from us.

إِنَّ رَبَّنَا لَغَفُورٌ شَكُورٌ ٣٤

Indeed Our Lord is all-forgiving, all-appreciative,

الَّذِي أَحَلَّنَا دَارَ الْمُقَامَةِ 35

who has settled us in the everlasting abode

مِن فَضْلِهِ

by His grace.

لَا يَمَسُّنَا فِيهَا نَصَبٌ

In it we are untouched by toil,

وَلَا يَمَسُّنَا فِيهَا لُغُوبٌ ٣٥

and untouched therein by fatigue.'

وَالَّذِينَ كَفَرُوا 36

As for the faithless

لَهُمْ نَارُ جَهَنَّمَ

there is for them the fire of hell:

لَا يُقْضَىٰ عَلَيْهِمْ

they will neither be done away with

فَيَمُوتُوا

so that they may die,

وَلَا يُخَفَّفُ عَنْهُم مِّنْ عَذَابِهَا

nor shall its punishment be lightened for them.

كَذَٰلِكَ نَجْزِي كُلَّ كَفُورٍ ٣٦

Thus do We requite every ingrate.

وَهُمْ يَصْطَرِخُونَ فِيهَا 37

They shall cry therein for help:

رَبَّنَا أَخْرِجْنَا

'Our Lord! Bring us out,

نَعْمَلْ صَالِحًا

so that we may act righteously

غَيْرَ الَّذِي كُنَّا نَعْمَلُ

—different from what we used to do!'

أَوَلَمْ نُعَمِّرْكُم

'Did We not give you a life long enough

مَّا يَتَذَكَّرُ فِيهِ مَن تَذَكَّرَ

that one who is heedful might take admonition?

وَجَاءَكُمُ النَّذِيرُ

And [moreover] the warner had [also] come to you.

فَذُوقُوا

Now taste [the consequence of your deeds],

فَمَا لِلظَّٰلِمِينَ مِن نَّصِيرٍ ۝    for the wrongdoers have no helper.'

إِنَّ ٱللَّهَ عَٰلِمُ غَيْبِ    38 Indeed Allah is the knower of the Unseen

ٱلسَّمَٰوَٰتِ وَٱلْأَرْضِ    of the heavens and the earth.

إِنَّهُۥ عَلِيمٌۢ بِذَاتِ ٱلصُّدُورِ ۝    Indeed He knows well what is in the breasts.

هُوَ ٱلَّذِى جَعَلَكُمْ خَلَٰٓئِفَ فِى ٱلْأَرْضِ    39 It is He who made you successors on the earth.[1]

فَمَن كَفَرَ    So whoever is faithless,

فَعَلَيْهِ كُفْرُهُۥ    his unfaith is to his own detriment.

وَلَا يَزِيدُ ٱلْكَٰفِرِينَ كُفْرُهُمْ    And the unfaith of the faithless does not increase them

عِندَ رَبِّهِمْ    with their Lord [in anything]

إِلَّا مَقْتًا    except disfavour,

وَلَا يَزِيدُ ٱلْكَٰفِرِينَ كُفْرُهُمْ    and their unfaith increases the faithless in nothing

إِلَّا خَسَارًا ۝    except loss.

قُلْ    40 *Say,*

أَرَءَيْتُمْ شُرَكَآءَكُمُ    'Tell me about your partners [you ascribe to Allah]

ٱلَّذِينَ تَدْعُونَ مِن دُونِ ٱللَّهِ    whom you invoke besides Allah?

أَرُونِى مَاذَا خَلَقُوا۟ مِنَ ٱلْأَرْضِ    Show me what [part] of the earth have they created.

أَمْ لَهُمْ شِرْكٌ فِى ٱلسَّمَٰوَٰتِ    Do they have any share in the heavens?'

أَمْ ءَاتَيْنَٰهُمْ كِتَٰبًا    Have We given them a scripture

فَهُمْ عَلَىٰ بَيِّنَتٍ مِّنْهُ    so that they stand on a manifest proof thereof?

بَلْ إِن يَعِدُ ٱلظَّٰلِمُونَ بَعْضُهُم بَعْضًا    Rather the wrongdoers do not promise one another

إِلَّا غُرُورًا ۝    [anything] except delusion.

إِنَّ ٱللَّهَ يُمْسِكُ ٱلسَّمَٰوَٰتِ وَٱلْأَرْضَ    41 Indeed Allah sustains the heavens and the earth

أَن تَزُولَا    lest they should fall part,

وَلَئِن زَالَتَآ    and if they were to fall apart

إِنْ أَمْسَكَهُمَا مِنْ أَحَدٍ مِّنۢ بَعْدِهِۦٓ    there is none who can sustain them except Him.

إِنَّهُۥ كَانَ حَلِيمًا غَفُورًا ۝    Indeed He is all-forbearing, all-forgiving.

وَأَقْسَمُوا۟ بِٱللَّهِ جَهْدَ أَيْمَٰنِهِمْ    42 And they[2] swore by Allah with solemn oaths

لَئِن جَآءَهُمْ نَذِيرٌ    that if a warner were to come to them

---

[1] That is, of the former peoples.
[2] That is, the idolaters of Arabia.

لِّيَكُونُنَّ أَهْدَىٰ مِنْ إِحْدَى ٱلْأُمَمِ they would be better guided than any of the nations.

فَلَمَّا جَآءَهُمْ نَذِيرٌ But when a warner came to them

مَّا زَادَهُمْ إِلَّا نُفُورًا it only increased them in aversion,

43 ٱسْتِكْبَارًا فِى ٱلْأَرْضِ acting arrogantly in the land

وَمَكْرَ ٱلسَّيِّئِ and devising evil schemes;

وَلَا يَحِيقُ ٱلْمَكْرُ ٱلسَّيِّئُ إِلَّا بِأَهْلِهِ and evil schemes beset only their authors.

فَهَلْ يَنظُرُونَ So do they await

إِلَّا سُنَّتَ ٱلْأَوَّلِينَ anything except the precedent of the ancients?

فَلَن تَجِدَ لِسُنَّتِ ٱللَّهِ تَبْدِيلًا Yet you will never find any change in Allah's precedent,

وَلَن تَجِدَ لِسُنَّتِ ٱللَّهِ تَحْوِيلًا and you will never find any revision in Allah's precedent.

44 أَوَلَمْ يَسِيرُوا۟ فِى ٱلْأَرْضِ Have they not traveled over the land

فَيَنظُرُوا۟ so that they may observe

كَيْفَ كَانَ عَٰقِبَةُ ٱلَّذِينَ مِن قَبْلِهِمْ how was the fate of those who were before them?

وَكَانُوا۟ أَشَدَّ مِنْهُمْ قُوَّةً They were more powerful than them,

وَمَا كَانَ ٱللَّهُ لِيُعْجِزَهُ مِن شَىْءٍ and Allah is not to be thwarted by anything

فِى ٱلسَّمَٰوَٰتِ وَلَا فِى ٱلْأَرْضِ in the heavens or on the earth.

إِنَّهُ كَانَ عَلِيمًا قَدِيرًا Indeed He is all-knowing, all-powerful.

45 وَلَوْ يُؤَاخِذُ ٱللَّهُ ٱلنَّاسَ Were Allah to take mankind to task

بِمَا كَسَبُوا۟ because of what they have earned,

مَا تَرَكَ عَلَىٰ ظَهْرِهَا مِن دَآبَّةٍ He would not leave any living being on its back.[1]

وَلَٰكِن يُؤَخِّرُهُمْ إِلَىٰ أَجَلٍ مُّسَمًّى But He respites them until a specified time,

فَإِذَا جَآءَ أَجَلُهُمْ and when their time comes,

فَإِنَّ ٱللَّهَ كَانَ بِعِبَادِهِۦ بَصِيرًا Allah indeed sees best His servants.

سُورَةُ يسٓ      36. SŪRAT YĀ SĪN[2]

بِسْمِ ٱللَّهِ      In the Name of Allah,

ٱلرَّحْمَٰنِ ٱلرَّحِيمِ      the All-beneficent, the All-merciful.

---

[1] That is, on the surface of the earth.

[2] "Yā Sīn" (mentioned in verse 1) is one of the names of the Prophet (ṣ).

يس ۝ 1 *Yā Sīn!*

وَٱلْقُرْءَانِ ٱلْحَكِيمِ ۝ 2 By the Wise[1] Qur'ān,

إِنَّكَ لَمِنَ ٱلْمُرْسَلِينَ ۝ 3 *you* are indeed one of the apostles,

عَلَىٰ صِرَٰطٍ مُّسْتَقِيمٍ ۝ 4 on a straight path.

تَنزِيلَ 5 [It is a scripture] sent down gradually

ٱلْعَزِيزِ ٱلرَّحِيمِ ۝      from the All-mighty, the All-merciful

لِتُنذِرَ قَوْمًا 6 that *you* may warn a people

مَّآ أُنذِرَ ءَابَآؤُهُمْ      whose fathers were not warned,[2]

فَهُمْ غَٰفِلُونَ ۝      so they are oblivious.

لَقَدْ حَقَّ ٱلْقَوْلُ 7 The word has certainly become due

عَلَىٰٓ أَكْثَرِهِمْ      against most of them,

فَهُمْ لَا يُؤْمِنُونَ ۝      so they will not have faith.

إِنَّا جَعَلْنَا فِىٓ أَعْنَٰقِهِمْ أَغْلَٰلًا 8 Indeed We have put iron collars around their necks,

فَهِىَ إِلَى ٱلْأَذْقَانِ      which are up to the chins,

فَهُم مُّقْمَحُونَ ۝      so their heads are upturned.[3]

وَجَعَلْنَا مِنْ بَيْنِ أَيْدِيهِمْ سَدًّا 9 And We have put a barrier before them

وَمِنْ خَلْفِهِمْ سَدًّا      and a barrier behind them,

فَأَغْشَيْنَٰهُمْ      then We have blind-folded them,

فَهُمْ لَا يُبْصِرُونَ ۝      so they do not see.

وَسَوَآءٌ عَلَيْهِمْ 10 It is the same to them

ءَأَنذَرْتَهُمْ أَمْ لَمْ تُنذِرْهُمْ      whether *you* warn them or do not warn them,

لَا يُؤْمِنُونَ ۝      they will not have faith.

إِنَّمَا تُنذِرُ 11 *You* can only warn someone

مَنِ ٱتَّبَعَ ٱلذِّكْرَ      who follows the Reminder[4]

وَخَشِىَ ٱلرَّحْمَٰنَ بِٱلْغَيْبِ      and fears the All-beneficent in secret;

فَبَشِّرْهُ بِمَغْفِرَةٍ      so *give* him the good news of forgiveness

---

[1] Or 'Definitive.'

[2] Cf. 28:46; 32:3; 34:44.

[3] That is, they dwell in a state of blindness, defiance and arrogance in regard to the God-sent guidance and truth.

[4] That is, the Qur'ān.

وَأَجْرٍ كَرِيمٍ ۝     and a noble reward.

إِنَّا نَحْنُ نُحْيِ ٱلْمَوْتَىٰ    12 Indeed it is We who revive the dead

وَنَكْتُبُ مَا قَدَّمُوا۟     and write what they have sent ahead[1]

وَءَاثَٰرَهُمْ     and their effects [which they left behind],[2]

وَكُلَّ شَىْءٍ أَحْصَيْنَٰهُ     and We have figured everything

فِىٓ إِمَامٍ مُّبِينٍ ۝     in a manifest Imam.[3]

وَٱضْرِبْ لَهُم     13 Cite for them

مَّثَلًا أَصْحَٰبَ ٱلْقَرْيَةِ     the example of the inhabitants of the town

إِذْ جَآءَهَا ٱلْمُرْسَلُونَ ۝     when the apostles came to it.

إِذْ أَرْسَلْنَآ إِلَيْهِمُ ٱثْنَيْنِ     14 When We sent to them two [apostles],

فَكَذَّبُوهُمَا     they impugned both of them.

فَعَزَّزْنَا بِثَالِثٍ     Then We reinforced them with a third,

فَقَالُوٓا۟ إِنَّآ إِلَيْكُم مُّرْسَلُونَ ۝     and they said, 'We have indeed been sent to you.'

قَالُوا۟ مَآ أَنتُمْ إِلَّا بَشَرٌ مِّثْلُنَا     15 They said, 'You are nothing but humans like us,

وَمَآ أَنزَلَ ٱلرَّحْمَٰنُ مِن شَىْءٍ     and the All-beneficent has not sent down anything,

إِنْ أَنتُمْ إِلَّا تَكْذِبُونَ ۝     and you are only lying.'

قَالُوا۟ رَبُّنَا يَعْلَمُ     16 They said, 'Our Lord knows

إِنَّآ إِلَيْكُمْ لَمُرْسَلُونَ ۝     that we have indeed been sent to you,

وَمَا عَلَيْنَآ إِلَّا ٱلْبَلَٰغُ ٱلْمُبِينُ ۝     17 and our duty is only to communicate in clear terms.'

قَالُوٓا۟ إِنَّا تَطَيَّرْنَا بِكُمْ     18 They said, 'Indeed we take you for a bad omen.

لَئِن لَّمْ تَنتَهُوا۟ لَنَرْجُمَنَّكُمْ     If you do not relinquish we will stone you,

وَلَيَمَسَّنَّكُم مِّنَّا عَذَابٌ أَلِيمٌ ۝     and surely a painful punishment will visit you from us.'

قَالُوا۟ طَٰٓئِرُكُم مَّعَكُمْ     19 They said, 'Your bad omens attend you.

أَئِن ذُكِّرْتُم     What! If you are admonished . . . .[4]

بَلْ أَنتُمْ قَوْمٌ مُّسْرِفُونَ ۝     Rather you are a profligate lot.'

وَجَآءَ مِنْ أَقْصَا ٱلْمَدِينَةِ رَجُلٌ     20 There came a man from the city outskirts,

---

[1] That is, the deeds they have done.

[2] That is, the good or evil heritage and imprint they leave behind in the society in which they have lived, and which outlive them.

[3] Or, in a manifest book.

[4] Ellipsis. The phrase omitted is 'do you take it for a bad omen?!'

| | |
|---|---|
| يَسْعَىٰ | hurrying. |
| قَالَ يَٰقَوْمِ ٱتَّبِعُوا ٱلْمُرْسَلِينَ ۞ | He said, 'O my people! Follow the apostles! |
| ٱتَّبِعُوا۟ مَن لَّا يَسْـَٔلُكُمْ أَجْرًا 21 | Follow them who do not ask you any reward |
| وَهُم مُّهْتَدُونَ ۞ | and they are rightly guided. |
| وَمَا لِيَ لَآ أَعْبُدُ ٱلَّذِى 22 | Why should I not worship Him |
| فَطَرَنِى | who has originated me, |
| وَإِلَيْهِ تُرْجَعُونَ ۞ | and to whom you shall be brought back? |
| ءَأَتَّخِذُ مِن دُونِهِۦٓ ءَالِهَةً 23 | Shall I take gods besides Him? |
| إِن يُرِدْنِ ٱلرَّحْمَٰنُ بِضُرٍّ | If the All-beneficent desired to cause me any distress |
| لَّا تُغْنِ عَنِّى شَفَٰعَتُهُمْ شَيْـًٔا | their intercession will not avail me in any way, |
| وَلَا يُنقِذُونِ ۞ | nor will they rescue me. |
| إِنِّىٓ إِذًا لَّفِى ضَلَٰلٍ مُّبِينٍ ۞ 24 | Indeed then I would be in manifest error. |
| إِنِّىٓ ءَامَنتُ بِرَبِّكُمْ 25 | Indeed I have faith in your Lord, |
| فَٱسْمَعُونِ ۞ | so listen to me.' |
| قِيلَ ٱدْخُلِ ٱلْجَنَّةَ 26 | He was told, 'Enter paradise!' |
| قَالَ يَٰلَيْتَ قَوْمِى يَعْلَمُونَ ۞ | He said, 'Alas! Had my people only known |
| بِمَا غَفَرَ لِى رَبِّى 27 | for what my Lord forgave me |
| وَجَعَلَنِى مِنَ ٱلْمُكْرَمِينَ ۞ ❖ | and made me one of the honoured ones!' |

[PART 23]

| | |
|---|---|
| وَمَآ أَنزَلْنَا عَلَىٰ قَوْمِهِۦ مِنۢ بَعْدِهِۦ 28 | After him We did not send down on his people |
| مِن جُندٍ مِّنَ ٱلسَّمَآءِ | a host from the sky, |
| وَمَا كُنَّا مُنزِلِينَ ۞ | nor We would have sent down.[1] |
| إِن كَانَتْ إِلَّا صَيْحَةً وَٰحِدَةً 29 | It was but a single cry, |
| فَإِذَا هُمْ خَٰمِدُونَ ۞ | and, behold, they were stilled [like burnt ashes]! |
| يَٰحَسْرَةً عَلَى ٱلْعِبَادِ 30 | How regrettable of the servants! |
| مَا يَأْتِيهِم مِّن رَّسُولٍ | There did not come to them any apostle |
| إِلَّا كَانُوا۟ بِهِۦ يَسْتَهْزِءُونَ ۞ | but that they used to deride him. |
| أَلَمْ يَرَوْا۟ 31 | Have they not regarded |

---

[1] Or 'and what We used to send down [before];' see Ṭabrisī, Fayḍ
Kāshānī.

كَمْ أَهْلَكْنَا قَبْلَهُم مِّنَ ٱلْقُرُونِ   how many generations We have destroyed before them

أَنَّهُمْ إِلَيْهِمْ لَا يَرْجِعُونَ ۝   who do not come back to them?

وَإِن كُلٌّ لَّمَّا جَمِيعٌ لَّدَيْنَا مُحْضَرُونَ ۝   32 And all of them will indeed be presented before Us.

وَءَايَةٌ لَّهُمُ ٱلْأَرْضُ ٱلْمَيْتَةُ   33 A sign for them is the dead earth,

أَحْيَيْنَٰهَا   which We revive

وَأَخْرَجْنَا مِنْهَا حَبًّا   and out of it bring forth grain,

فَمِنْهُ يَأْكُلُونَ ۝   so they eat of it.

وَجَعَلْنَا فِيهَا جَنَّٰتٍ مِّن نَّخِيلٍ   34 And We make in it orchards of date palms

وَأَعْنَٰبٍ   and vines,

وَفَجَّرْنَا فِيهَا مِنَ ٱلْعُيُونِ ۝   and We cause springs to gush forth in it,

لِيَأْكُلُوا۟ مِن ثَمَرِهِۦ   35 so that they may eat of its fruit

وَمَا عَمِلَتْهُ أَيْدِيهِمْ   and what their hands have cultivated.[1]

أَفَلَا يَشْكُرُونَ ۝   Will they not then give thanks?

سُبْحَٰنَ ٱلَّذِى خَلَقَ ٱلْأَزْوَٰجَ كُلَّهَا   36 Immaculate is He who has created all the kinds[2]

مِمَّا تُنۢبِتُ ٱلْأَرْضُ   of what the earth grows,

وَمِنْ أَنفُسِهِمْ   and of themselves,

وَمِمَّا لَا يَعْلَمُونَ ۝   and of what they do not know.

وَءَايَةٌ لَّهُمُ ٱلَّيْلُ   37 And a sign for them is the night,

نَسْلَخُ مِنْهُ ٱلنَّهَارَ   from which We strip the day,

فَإِذَا هُم مُّظْلِمُونَ ۝   and, behold, they find themselves in the dark.

وَٱلشَّمْسُ تَجْرِى   38 And the sun runs on

لِمُسْتَقَرٍّ لَّهَا   to its place of rest:[3]

---

[1] Or 'and their hands did not cultivate it.' That is, it is We who produce the fruits, not their hands. Cf. 27:60 and 56:64.

[2] Or, 'all the pairs.'

[3] Or 'it has no place of rest.' This is in accordance with the alternate reading '*lā mustaqarra lahā.*' Ṭabrisī in *Majmaʿ al-Bayān* narrates a tradition which ascribes the reading *lā mustaqarra lahā* to the Imams ʿAlī b. al-Ḥusayn, Muḥammad al-Bāqir, and Jaʿfar al-Ṣādiq, as well as to a number of the early exegetes such as Ibn ʿAbbās, Ibn Masʿūd, ʿIkrimah, and ʿAṭāʾ b. Abī Rabāḥ. See *Muʿjam al-Qirāʾāt al-Qurʾāniyyah*, v, 208, for further sources of this reading. The reading *li mustaqarrin lahā* seems to have been suggested and reinforced by the popular astronomical notions of the age.

ذَٰلِكَ تَقْدِيرُ ٱلْعَزِيزِ ٱلْعَلِيمِ ۝    That is the ordaining of the All-mighty, the All-knowing.

وَٱلْقَمَرَ قَدَّرْنَٰهُ مَنَازِلَ    39 As for the moon, We have ordained its phases,

حَتَّىٰ عَادَ كَٱلْعُرْجُونِ ٱلْقَدِيمِ ۝    until it becomes like an old palm leaf.

لَا ٱلشَّمْسُ يَنۢبَغِى لَهَآ    40 Neither it behooves the sun

أَن تُدْرِكَ ٱلْقَمَرَ    to overtake the moon,

وَلَا ٱلَّيْلُ سَابِقُ ٱلنَّهَارِ    nor may the night outrun the day,

وَكُلٌّ فِى فَلَكٍ يَسْبَحُونَ ۝    and each swims in an orbit.

وَءَايَةٌ لَّهُمْ أَنَّا حَمَلْنَا ذُرِّيَّتَهُمْ    41 A sign for them is that We carried their progeny

فِى ٱلْفُلْكِ ٱلْمَشْحُونِ ۝    in the laden ship,[1]

وَخَلَقْنَا لَهُم مِّن مِّثْلِهِۦ    42 and We have created for them what is similar to it,

مَا يَرْكَبُونَ ۝    which they ride.[2]

وَإِن نَّشَأْ نُغْرِقْهُمْ    43 And if We like We drown them,

فَلَا صَرِيخَ لَهُمْ    whereat they have no one to call for help,

وَلَا هُمْ يُنقَذُونَ ۝    nor are they rescued

إِلَّا رَحْمَةً مِّنَّا    44 —except by a mercy from Us

وَمَتَٰعًا إِلَىٰ حِينٍ ۝    and for an enjoyment until some time.

وَإِذَا قِيلَ لَهُمُ    45 And when they are told,

ٱتَّقُوا۟ مَا بَيْنَ أَيْدِيكُمْ    'Beware of that which is before you

وَمَا خَلْفَكُمْ    and that which is behind you,[3]

لَعَلَّكُمْ تُرْحَمُونَ ۝    so that you may receive [His] mercy.'[4]

وَمَا تَأْتِيهِم مِّنْ ءَايَةٍ    46 There did not come to them any sign

مِّنْ ءَايَٰتِ رَبِّهِمْ    from among the signs of their Lord

إِلَّا كَانُوا۟ عَنْهَا مُعْرِضِينَ ۝    but that they used to disregard it.

وَإِذَا قِيلَ لَهُمْ    47 When they are told,

أَنفِقُوا۟ مِمَّا رَزَقَكُمُ ٱللَّهُ    'Spend out of what Allah has provided you,'

---

[1] That is, in the ark of Noah.

[2] Or 'board,' that is, ships which are similar to their prototype, the ark of Noah; or, alternatively, the camel, which has been called 'the ship of the desert,' and other animals and means of transport.

[3] See 34:9.

[4] Ellipsis. The omitted clause is, 'they turn away arrogantly.'

قَالَ ٱلَّذِينَ كَفَرُواْ لِلَّذِينَ ءَامَنُوٓاْ

the faithless say to the faithful,

أَنُطْعِمُ

'Shall we feed [someone]

مَن لَّوۡ يَشَآءُ ٱللَّهُ أَطْعَمَهُۥٓ

whom Allah would have fed, had He wished?

إِنۡ أَنتُمۡ إِلَّا فِى ضَلَٰلٍ مُّبِينٍ ۝

You are only in manifest error.'

وَيَقُولُونَ مَتَىٰ هَٰذَا ٱلۡوَعۡدُ

48 And they say, 'When will this promise be fulfilled,

إِن كُنتُمۡ صَٰدِقِينَ ۝

should you be truthful?'

مَا يَنظُرُونَ إِلَّا صَيۡحَةً وَٰحِدَةً

49 They do not await but a single cry

تَأۡخُذُهُمۡ وَهُمۡ يَخِصِّمُونَ ۝

that would seize them as they wrangle.

فَلَا يَسۡتَطِيعُونَ تَوۡصِيَةً

50 Then they will not be able to make any will,

وَلَآ إِلَىٰٓ أَهۡلِهِمۡ يَرۡجِعُونَ ۝

nor will they return to their folks.

وَنُفِخَ فِى ٱلصُّورِ

51 And when the Trumpet is blown,

فَإِذَا هُم

behold, there they will be,

مِّنَ ٱلۡأَجۡدَاثِ إِلَىٰ رَبِّهِمۡ يَنسِلُونَ ۝

scrambling from their graves towards their Lord!

قَالُواْ يَٰوَيۡلَنَا

52 They will say, 'Woe to us!

مَنۢ بَعَثَنَا مِن مَّرۡقَدِنَا ۗ

Who raised us from our place of sleep?'

هَٰذَا مَا وَعَدَ ٱلرَّحۡمَٰنُ

'This is what the All-beneficent had promised,

وَصَدَقَ ٱلۡمُرۡسَلُونَ ۝

and the apostles had spoken the truth!'

إِن كَانَتۡ إِلَّا صَيۡحَةً وَٰحِدَةً

53 It will be but a single cry,

فَإِذَا هُمۡ جَمِيعٌ لَّدَيۡنَا مُحۡضَرُونَ ۝

and, behold, they will all be presented before Us!

فَٱلۡيَوۡمَ لَا تُظۡلَمُ نَفۡسٌ شَيۡـًٔا

54 Today no one will be done any injustice,

وَلَا تُجۡزَوۡنَ إِلَّا مَا كُنتُمۡ تَعۡمَلُونَ ۝

nor will you be requited except for what you used to do.'

إِنَّ أَصۡحَٰبَ ٱلۡجَنَّةِ ٱلۡيَوۡمَ

55 Indeed today the inhabitants of paradise

فِى شُغُلٍ فَٰكِهُونَ ۝

rejoice in their engagements

هُمۡ وَأَزۡوَٰجُهُمۡ

56 —they and their mates,

فِى ظِلَٰلٍ عَلَى ٱلۡأَرَآئِكِ مُتَّكِـُٔونَ ۝

reclining on couches in the shades.

لَهُمۡ فِيهَا فَٰكِهَةٌ

57 There they have fruits

وَلَهُم مَّا يَدَّعُونَ ۝

and they have whatever they want.

سَلَٰمٌ قَوۡلًا مِّن رَّبٍّ رَّحِيمٍ ۝

58 'Peace!'—a watchword from the all-merciful Lord.

وَٱمۡتَٰزُواْ ٱلۡيَوۡمَ أَيُّهَا ٱلۡمُجۡرِمُونَ ۝ ❖

59 And 'Get apart today, you guilty ones!'

أَلَمۡ أَعۡهَدۡ إِلَيۡكُمۡ يَٰبَنِىٓ ءَادَمَ

60 'Did I not exhort you, O children of Adam,

أَن لَّا تَعْبُدُواْ ٱلشَّيْطَنَ   saying, "Do not worship Satan.

إِنَّهُۥ لَكُمْ عَدُوٌّ مُّبِينٌ ۝   He is indeed your manifest enemy.

وَأَنِ ٱعْبُدُونِى   61 Worship Me.

هَـٰذَا صِرَٰطٌ مُّسْتَقِيمٌ ۝   That is a straight path"?

وَلَقَدْ أَضَلَّ مِنكُمْ جِبِلًّا كَثِيرًا   62 Certainly he has led astray many of your generations.

أَفَلَمْ تَكُونُواْ تَعْقِلُونَ ۝   Did you not use to apply reason?

هَـٰذِهِۦ جَهَنَّمُ ٱلَّتِى كُنتُمْ تُوعَدُونَ ۝   63 This is the hell you had been promised!

ٱصْلَوْهَا ٱلْيَوْمَ   64 Enter it today,

بِمَا كُنتُمْ تَكْفُرُونَ ۝   because of what you used to defy.

ٱلْيَوْمَ نَخْتِمُ عَلَىٰٓ أَفْوَٰهِهِمْ   65 Today We shall seal their mouths,

وَتُكَلِّمُنَآ أَيْدِيهِمْ   and their hands shall speak to Us,

وَتَشْهَدُ أَرْجُلُهُم   and their feet shall bear witness

بِمَا كَانُواْ يَكْسِبُونَ ۝   concerning what they used to earn.'

وَلَوْ نَشَآءُ   66 Had We wished

لَطَمَسْنَا عَلَىٰٓ أَعْيُنِهِمْ   We would have blotted out their eyes:[1]

فَٱسْتَبَقُواْ ٱلصِّرَٰطَ   then, were they to advance towards the path,

فَأَنَّىٰ يُبْصِرُونَ ۝   how would have they seen?

وَلَوْ نَشَآءُ   67 And had We wished

لَمَسَخْنَٰهُمْ عَلَىٰ مَكَانَتِهِمْ   We would have deformed them in their place;[2]

فَمَا ٱسْتَطَـٰعُواْ مُضِيًّا   then they would have neither been able to go ahead

وَلَا يَرْجِعُونَ ۝   nor to go back.[3]

وَمَن نُّعَمِّرْهُ   68 And whomever We give a long life,

نُنَكِّسْهُ فِى ٱلْخَلْقِ   We cause him to regress in creation.

أَفَلَا يَعْقِلُونَ ۝   Then will they not apply reason?

وَمَا عَلَّمْنَـٰهُ ٱلشِّعْرَ   69 We did not teach *him* poetry,

وَمَا يَنۢبَغِى لَهُۥٓ   nor does it behoove *him*.

---

[1] That is, the insight to see the course of true human felicity.

[2] That is, arrest their growth and keep them in their deformed inner state.

[3] That is, they would have neither been able to move ahead to make spiritual progress, nor to return to their original state of unsullied God-given nature.

إِنْ هُوَ إِلَّا ذِكْرٌ وَقُرْءَانٌ مُّبِينٌ ۝

This is just a reminder and a manifest Qur'ān,

لِّيُنذِرَ مَن كَانَ حَيًّا

70 so that anyone who is alive may be warned,

وَيَحِقَّ ٱلْقَوْلُ

and that the word may come due

عَلَى ٱلْكَفِرِينَ ۝

against the faithless.

أَوَلَمْ يَرَوْا۟ أَنَّا خَلَقْنَا لَهُم

71 Have they not seen that We have created for them

مِّمَّا عَمِلَتْ أَيْدِينَآ

—of what Our hands have worked—

أَنْعَٰمًا فَهُمْ لَهَا مَٰلِكُونَ ۝

cattle, so they have become their masters?

وَذَلَّلْنَٰهَا لَهُمْ

72 And We made them tractable for them,

فَمِنْهَا رَكُوبُهُمْ

so some of them make their mounts

وَمِنْهَا يَأْكُلُونَ ۝

and some of them they eat.

وَلَهُمْ فِيهَا مَنَٰفِعُ

73 There are other benefits for them therein,

وَمَشَارِبُ

and drinks.[1]

أَفَلَا يَشْكُرُونَ ۝

Will they not then give thanks?

وَٱتَّخَذُوا۟ مِن دُونِ ٱللَّهِ ءَالِهَةً

74 They have taken gods besides Allah

لَّعَلَّهُمْ يُنصَرُونَ ۝

[hoping] that they might be helped.

لَا يَسْتَطِيعُونَ نَصْرَهُمْ

75 [Yet] they cannot help them,

وَهُمْ لَهُمْ جُندٌ مُّحْضَرُونَ ۝

while they [themselves] are ready warriors for them.[2]

فَلَا يَحْزُنكَ قَوْلُهُمْ

76 So do not let their remarks grieve *you*.

إِنَّا نَعْلَمُ مَا يُسِرُّونَ

We indeed know whatever they hide

وَمَا يُعْلِنُونَ ۝

and whatever they disclose.

أَوَلَمْ يَرَ ٱلْإِنسَٰنُ

77 Does not man see

أَنَّا خَلَقْنَٰهُ مِن نُّطْفَةٍ

that We created him from a drop of [seminal] fluid,

فَإِذَا هُوَ خَصِيمٌ مُّبِينٌ ۝

and, behold, he is an open contender!

وَضَرَبَ لَنَا مَثَلًا

78 He draws comparisons for Us,

وَنَسِيَ خَلْقَهُ

and forgets his own creation.

قَالَ مَن يُحْىِ ٱلْعِظَٰمَ

He says, 'Who shall revive the bones

وَهِىَ رَمِيمٌ ۝

when they have decayed?'

---

[1] That is, milk and other drinks derived from it.

[2] That is, while the idols are unable to offer the idolaters any kind of assistance, the idolaters are ready to fight and defend their idols.

قُلْ يُحْيِيهَا 79 *Say,* 'He will revive them

ٱلَّذِىٓ أَنشَأَهَآ أَوَّلَ مَرَّةٍ   who produced them the first time,

وَهُوَ بِكُلِّ خَلْقٍ عَلِيمٌ ۝   and He has knowledge of all creation.

ٱلَّذِى جَعَلَ لَكُم 80 —He, who made for you

مِّنَ ٱلشَّجَرِ ٱلْأَخْضَرِ نَارًا   fire out of the green tree,

فَإِذَآ أَنتُم مِّنْهُ تُوقِدُونَ ۝   and, behold, you light fire from it!

أَوَلَيْسَ ٱلَّذِى خَلَقَ ٱلسَّمَٰوَٰتِ 81 Is not He who created the heavens

وَٱلْأَرْضَ   and the earth

بِقَٰدِرٍ عَلَىٰٓ أَن يَخْلُقَ مِثْلَهُم   able to create the like of them?

بَلَىٰ وَهُوَ ٱلْخَلَّٰقُ ٱلْعَلِيمُ ۝   Yes indeed! He is the All-creator, the All-knowing.

إِنَّمَآ أَمْرُهُۥٓ إِذَآ أَرَادَ شَيْـًٔا 82 All His command, when He wills something,

أَن يَقُولَ لَهُۥ كُن فَيَكُونُ ۝   is to say to it 'Be,' and it is.

فَسُبْحَٰنَ ٱلَّذِى 83 So immaculate is He

بِيَدِهِۦ مَلَكُوتُ كُلِّ شَىْءٍ   in whose hand is the dominion of all things

وَإِلَيْهِ تُرْجَعُونَ ۝   and to whom you shall be brought back.

## سُورَةُ الصَّافَّاتِ   37. SŪRAT AL-ṢĀFFĀT[1]

بِسْمِ ٱللَّهِ   In the Name of Allah,

ٱلرَّحْمَٰنِ ٱلرَّحِيمِ   the All-beneficent, All-merciful.

وَٱلصَّٰٓفَّٰتِ صَفًّا ۝ 1 By the [angels] ranged in ranks,

فَٱلزَّٰجِرَٰتِ زَجْرًا ۝ 2 by the ones who drive vigorously,[2]

فَٱلتَّٰلِيَٰتِ ذِكْرًا ۝ 3 by the ones who recite the reminder:[3]

إِنَّ إِلَٰهَكُمْ لَوَٰحِدٌ ۝ 4 indeed your Lord is certainly One,

---

[1] The *sūrah* takes its name from verse 1, which refers to a group of angels as 'those ranged (*ṣāffāt*) in ranks.' See verses 164-166 below.

[2] Or 'hold back forcibly,' or 'scold severely.' Said to refer to angels who drive the clouds, or hold back (or drive away) the eavesdropping devils, or to angels (or verses of the Qur'ān) that restrain people from sins.

[3] That is, the faithful, or the angels, who recite the Qur'ān or the scriptures.

رَّبُّ ٱلسَّمَٰوَٰتِ وَٱلۡأَرۡضِ ₅    the Lord of the heavens and the earth

وَمَا بَيۡنَهُمَا    and whatever is between them,

وَرَبُّ ٱلۡمَشَٰرِقِ ۝    and the Lord of the easts.[1]

إِنَّا زَيَّنَّا ٱلسَّمَآءَ ٱلدُّنۡيَا ₆ Indeed We have adorned the lowest heaven[2]

بِزِينَةٍ ٱلۡكَوَاكِبِ ۝    with the finery of the stars,[3]

وَحِفۡظًا مِّن كُلِّ شَيۡطَٰنٍ مَّارِدٍ ۝ ₇ and to guard from any froward devil.

لَّا يَسَّمَّعُونَ إِلَى ٱلۡمَلَإِ ٱلۡأَعۡلَىٰ ₈ They do not eavesdrop on the Supernal Elite

وَيُقۡذَفُونَ مِن كُلِّ جَانِبٍ ۝    but are shot at from every side,

دُحُورًا ₉    to drive them away,

وَلَهُمۡ عَذَابٌ وَاصِبٌ ۝    and for them there is a constant mortification,

إِلَّا مَنۡ خَطِفَ ٱلۡخَطۡفَةَ ₁₀    except him who snatches a snatch,[4]

فَأَتۡبَعَهُ شِهَابٌ ثَاقِبٌ ۝    whereat there pursues him a piercing flame.[5]

فَٱسۡتَفۡتِهِمۡ أَهُمۡ أَشَدُّ خَلۡقًا ₁₁ *Ask* them, is their creation more prodigious[6]

أَم مَّنۡ خَلَقۡنَآ    or [that of other creatures] that We have created?

إِنَّا خَلَقۡنَٰهُم مِّن طِينٍ لَّازِبٍ ۝    Indeed We created them from a viscous clay.

بَلۡ عَجِبۡتَ ₁₂ Indeed *you* wonder,

وَيَسۡخَرُونَ ۝    while they engage in ridicule,

وَإِذَا ذُكِّرُواْ ₁₃ and [even] when admonished

لَا يَذۡكُرُونَ ۝    do not take admonition,

وَإِذَا رَأَوۡاْ ءَايَةً ₁₄ and when they see a sign

يَسۡتَسۡخِرُونَ ۝    they make it an object of ridicule,

وَقَالُوٓاْ ₁₅ and say,

إِنۡ هَٰذَآ إِلَّا سِحۡرٌ مُّبِينٌ ۝    'This is nothing but plain magic!

أَءِذَا مِتۡنَا ₁₆    'What! When we are dead

---

[1] That is, the points of sunrise at the winter and summer solstices. Cf. 7:137; 55:17; 70:40.

[2] Or 'the heaven of the earth,' or 'the nearest heaven.'

[3] Or 'We have adorned the nearest heaven with an adornment, the stars.'

[4] That is, of celestial intelligence. See Ṭabarī for several related traditions from the Prophet (ṣ).

[5] Cf. 15:17-18.

[6] Or 'more tough' (or strong), or 'more difficult.' Cf. 79:27.

وَكُنَّا تُرَابًا وَعِظَٰمًا and have become dust and bones,

أَءِنَّا لَمَبْعُوثُونَ ۝ shall we be resurrected?

أَوَءَابَآؤُنَا ٱلْأَوَّلُونَ ۝ 17 And our forefathers too?!'

قُلْ نَعَمْ وَأَنتُمْ دَٰخِرُونَ ۝ 18 *Say,* 'Yes! And you will be utterly humble.'

فَإِنَّمَا هِيَ زَجْرَةٌ وَٰحِدَةٌ 19 It will be only a single shout

فَإِذَا هُمْ يَنظُرُونَ ۝ and, behold, they will look on,

وَقَالُوا۟ يَٰوَيْلَنَا 20 and say, 'Woe to us!

هَٰذَا يَوْمُ ٱلدِّينِ ۝ This is the Day of Retribution!'

هَٰذَا يَوْمُ ٱلْفَصْلِ 21 'This is the Day of Judgement

ٱلَّذِى كُنتُم بِهِۦ تُكَذِّبُونَ ۝ ✦ that you used to deny!'

ٱحْشُرُوا۟ ٱلَّذِينَ ظَلَمُوا۟ وَأَزْوَٰجَهُمْ 22 'Muster the wrongdoers and their mates[1]

وَمَا كَانُوا۟ يَعْبُدُونَ ۝ and what they used to worship

مِن دُونِ ٱللَّهِ 23 besides Allah,

فَٱهْدُوهُمْ إِلَىٰ صِرَٰطِ ٱلْجَحِيمِ and show them the way to hell!

وَقِفُوهُمْ إِنَّهُم مَّسْـُٔولُونَ ۝ 24 [But first] stop them! For they must be questioned.'

مَا لَكُمْ 25 'Why is it

لَا تَنَاصَرُونَ ۝ that you do not support[2] one another [today]?'

بَلْ هُمُ ٱلْيَوْمَ مُسْتَسْلِمُونَ ۝ 26 Rather today they are [meek and] submissive!

وَأَقْبَلَ بَعْضُهُمْ عَلَىٰ بَعْضٍ 27 Some of them will turn to others,

يَتَسَآءَلُونَ ۝ questioning each other.

قَالُوا۟ 28 They will say,

إِنَّكُمْ كُنتُمْ تَأْتُونَنَا عَنِ ٱلْيَمِينِ ۝ 'Indeed you used to accost us peremptorily.'[3]

قَالُوا۟ 29 They will answer,

بَل لَّمْ تَكُونُوا۟ مُؤْمِنِينَ ۝ 'Rather you [yourselves] had no faith.

وَمَا كَانَ لَنَا عَلَيْكُم مِّن سُلْطَٰنٍ 30 We had no authority over you.

بَلْ كُنتُمْ قَوْمًا طَٰغِينَ ۝ Rather you [yourselves] were a rebellious lot.

فَحَقَّ عَلَيْنَا قَوْلُ رَبِّنَآ 31 So our Lord's word became due against us

---

[1] Or 'their kind,' or 'their counterparts.'

[2] Or 'help.'

[3] Or 'obligingly.'

إِنَّا لَذَآئِقُونَ ۞    that we shall indeed taste [the punishment].

فَأَغْوَيْنَٰكُمْ 32 So we perverted you,

إِنَّا كُنَّا غَٰوِينَ ۞ for we were perverse [ourselves].'

فَإِنَّهُمْ يَوْمَئِذٍ فِى ٱلْعَذَابِ مُشْتَرِكُونَ ۞ 33 So that day they will share in the punishment.

إِنَّا كَذَٰلِكَ نَفْعَلُ بِٱلْمُجْرِمِينَ ۞ 34 Indeed that is how We deal with the guilty.

إِنَّهُمْ كَانُوٓا۟ 35 Indeed it was they who,

إِذَا قِيلَ لَهُمْ when they were told,

لَآ إِلَٰهَ إِلَّا ٱللَّهُ 'There is no god except Allah,'

يَسْتَكْبِرُونَ ۞ used to be disdainful,

وَيَقُولُونَ أَئِنَّا لَتَارِكُوٓا۟ ءَالِهَتِنَا and [they would] say, 'Shall we abandon our gods

لِشَاعِرٍ مَّجْنُونٍ ۞ for a crazy poet?'

بَلْ جَآءَ بِٱلْحَقِّ 37 Rather he has brought [them] the truth,

وَصَدَّقَ ٱلْمُرْسَلِينَ ۞ and confirmed the [earlier] apostles.

إِنَّكُمْ لَذَآئِقُوا۟ ٱلْعَذَابِ ٱلْأَلِيمِ ۞ 38 Indeed you will taste the painful punishment,

وَمَا تُجْزَوْنَ إِلَّا مَا كُنتُمْ تَعْمَلُونَ ۞ 39 and you will be requited only for what you used to do

إِلَّا عِبَادَ ٱللَّهِ ٱلْمُخْلَصِينَ ۞ 40 —[all] except Allah's exclusive servants.

أُو۟لَٰٓئِكَ لَهُمْ رِزْقٌ مَّعْلُومٌ ۞ 41 For such there is a known[1] provision

فَوَٰكِهُ وَهُم مُّكْرَمُونَ ۞ 42 —fruits—and they will be held in honour,

فِى جَنَّٰتِ ٱلنَّعِيمِ ۞ 43 in the gardens of bliss,

عَلَىٰ سُرُرٍ مُّتَقَٰبِلِينَ ۞ 44 [reclining] on couches, facing one another,

يُطَافُ عَلَيْهِم بِكَأْسٍ مِّن مَّعِينٍ ۞ 45 served around with a cup from a clear fountain,

بَيْضَآءَ لَذَّةٍ لِّلشَّٰرِبِينَ ۞ 46 snow-white, delicious to the drinkers,

لَا فِيهَا غَوْلٌ 47 wherein there will be neither headache

وَلَا هُمْ عَنْهَا يُنزَفُونَ ۞ nor will it cause them stupefaction,

وَعِندَهُمْ قَٰصِرَٰتُ ٱلطَّرْفِ 48 and with them will be maidens of restrained glances

عِينٌ ۞ with big [beautiful] eyes,

كَأَنَّهُنَّ بَيْضٌ مَّكْنُونٌ ۞ 49 as if they were hidden[2] ostrich eggs.

فَأَقْبَلَ بَعْضُهُمْ عَلَىٰ بَعْضٍ 50 Some of them will turn to others,

---

[1] That is, distinct and special.

[2] That is, well reserved.

يَتَسَآءَلُونَ ﴿٥٠﴾    questioning each other.

قَالَ قَآئِلٌ مِّنْهُمْ ﴿٥١﴾   51 One of them will say,

إِنِّى كَانَ لِى قَرِينٌ ﴿٥١﴾    'Indeed I had a companion

يَقُولُ ﴿٥٢﴾    52 who used to say,

أَءِنَّكَ لَمِنَ ٱلْمُصَدِّقِينَ ﴿٥٢﴾    "Are you really among those who affirm

أَءِذَا مِتْنَا ﴿٥٣﴾    53 [that] when we are dead

وَكُنَّا تُرَابًا وَعِظَٰمًا    and have become dust and bones,

أَءِنَّا لَمَدِينُونَ ﴿٥٣﴾    we shall indeed be brought to retribution?"'

قَالَ هَلْ أَنتُم مُّطَّلِعُونَ ﴿٥٤﴾   54 He[1] will say, 'Will you have a look?'

فَٱطَّلَعَ ﴿٥٥﴾   55 Then he will take a look

فَرَءَاهُ فِى سَوَآءِ ٱلْجَحِيمِ ﴿٥٥﴾    and sight him in the middle of hell.

قَالَ تَٱللَّهِ إِن كِدتَّ لَتُرْدِينِ ﴿٥٦﴾   56 He will say, 'By Allah, you had almost ruined me!

وَلَوْلَا نِعْمَةُ رَبِّى ﴿٥٧﴾    57 And had it not been for my Lord's blessing,

لَكُنتُ مِنَ ٱلْمُحْضَرِينَ ﴿٥٧﴾    I too would have been among the arraigned!'

أَفَمَا نَحْنُ بِمَيِّتِينَ ﴿٥٨﴾   58 'Is it [true] that we shall not die [anymore],

إِلَّا مَوْتَتَنَا ٱلْأُولَىٰ ﴿٥٩﴾    59 aside from our first death,

وَمَا نَحْنُ بِمُعَذَّبِينَ ﴿٥٩﴾    and that we shall not be punished?

إِنَّ هَٰذَا لَهُوَ ٱلْفَوْزُ ٱلْعَظِيمُ ﴿٦٠﴾   60 This is indeed the great success!

لِمِثْلِ هَٰذَا فَلْيَعْمَلِ ٱلْعَٰمِلُونَ ﴿٦١﴾   61 Let all the workers work for the like of this!'

أَذَٰلِكَ خَيْرٌ نُّزُلًا أَمْ شَجَرَةُ ٱلزَّقُّومِ ﴿٦٢﴾   62 Is this a better hospitality, or the Zaqqūm tree?

إِنَّا جَعَلْنَٰهَا فِتْنَةً ﴿٦٣﴾   63 Indeed We have made it a punishment

لِّلظَّٰلِمِينَ ﴿٦٣﴾    for the wrongdoers.

إِنَّهَا شَجَرَةٌ ﴿٦٤﴾   64 Indeed it is a tree

تَخْرُجُ فِى أَصْلِ ٱلْجَحِيمِ ﴿٦٤﴾    that emerges from the depths of hell.

طَلْعُهَا كَأَنَّهُ رُءُوسُ ٱلشَّيَٰطِينِ ﴿٦٥﴾   65 Its spathes are as if they were devils' heads.[2]

فَإِنَّهُمْ لَءَاكِلُونَ مِنْهَا ﴿٦٦﴾   66 Indeed they will eat from it

---

[1] That is, one of his companions in paradise.

[2] 'The devil's head' is either a purely imaginative metaphor, or a simile that likens the spathes of the Zaqqūm tree to that of an Arabian plant by this name, or to certain rocks to be found around the city of Makkah which were called 'the devils' heads' because of their hideous appearance.

فَمَالِـُٔونَ مِنْهَا ٱلْبُطُونَ ۝     and gorge with it their bellies.

ثُمَّ إِنَّ لَهُمْ عَلَيْهَا    67 Indeed, on top of that they will take

لَشَوْبًا مِّنْ حَمِيمٍ ۝     a solution of scalding water.

ثُمَّ إِنَّ مَرْجِعَهُمْ لَإِلَى ٱلْجَحِيمِ ۝    68 Then indeed their retreat will be toward hell.

إِنَّهُمْ أَلْفَوْا۟ ءَابَآءَهُمْ ضَآلِّينَ ۝    69 Indeed they had found their fathers astray,

فَهُمْ عَلَىٰٓ ءَاثَٰرِهِمْ يُهْرَعُونَ ۝    70    yet they press on in their footsteps.

وَلَقَدْ ضَلَّ قَبْلَهُمْ أَكْثَرُ ٱلْأَوَّلِينَ ۝    71 Certainly most of the ancients went astray before them,

وَلَقَدْ أَرْسَلْنَا فِيهِم مُّنذِرِينَ ۝    72    and certainly We had sent warners among them.

فَٱنظُرْ    73 So *observe*

كَيْفَ كَانَ عَٰقِبَةُ ٱلْمُنذَرِينَ ۝     how was the fate of those who were warned

إِلَّا عِبَادَ ٱللَّهِ ٱلْمُخْلَصِينَ ۝    74    —[all] except Allah's exclusive servants!

وَلَقَدْ نَادَىٰنَا نُوحٌ    75 Certainly Noah called out to Us,

فَلَنِعْمَ ٱلْمُجِيبُونَ ۝     and how well We responded!

وَنَجَّيْنَٰهُ وَأَهْلَهُۥ    76 We delivered him and his family

مِنَ ٱلْكَرْبِ ٱلْعَظِيمِ ۝     from the great agony,

وَجَعَلْنَا ذُرِّيَّتَهُۥ هُمُ ٱلْبَاقِينَ ۝    77    and made his descendants the survivors,

وَتَرَكْنَا عَلَيْهِ فِى ٱلْءَاخِرِينَ ۝    78    and left for him a good name among posterity:

سَلَٰمٌ عَلَىٰ نُوحٍ فِى ٱلْعَٰلَمِينَ ۝    79    'Peace to Noah, throughout the nations!'

إِنَّا كَذَٰلِكَ نَجْزِى ٱلْمُحْسِنِينَ ۝    80    Thus indeed do We reward the virtuous.

إِنَّهُۥ مِنْ عِبَادِنَا ٱلْمُؤْمِنِينَ ۝    81    He is indeed one of Our faithful servants.

ثُمَّ أَغْرَقْنَا ٱلْءَاخَرِينَ ۝ ❋    82 Then We drowned the others.

وَإِنَّ مِن شِيعَتِهِۦ لَإِبْرَٰهِيمَ ۝    83 Indeed Abraham was among his followers,

إِذْ جَآءَ رَبَّهُۥ بِقَلْبٍ سَلِيمٍ ۝    84 when he came to his Lord with a sound heart,[1]

إِذْ قَالَ لِأَبِيهِ وَقَوْمِهِۦ    85 when he said to his father and his people,

مَاذَا تَعْبُدُونَ ۝     'What is it that you are worshiping?

أَئِفْكًا ءَالِهَةً دُونَ ٱللَّهِ تُرِيدُونَ ۝    86    Is it a lie, gods other than Allah, that you desire?

فَمَا ظَنُّكُم    87    Then what is your idea

---

[1] Cf. 26:89.

بِرَبِّ ٱلْعَٰلَمِينَ ۝　about the Lord of all the worlds?'

فَنَظَرَ نَظْرَةً فِى ٱلنُّجُومِ ۝　88 Then he made an observation of the stars[1]

فَقَالَ إِنِّى سَقِيمٌ ۝　89　and said, 'Indeed I am sick!'

فَتَوَلَّوْا۟ عَنْهُ مُدْبِرِينَ ۝　90 So they went away leaving him behind.

فَرَاغَ إِلَىٰٓ ءَالِهَتِهِمْ　91 Then he stole away to their gods

فَقَالَ أَلَا تَأْكُلُونَ ۝　and said, 'Will you not eat?

مَا لَكُمْ لَا تَنطِقُونَ ۝　92　Why do you not speak?'

فَرَاغَ عَلَيْهِمْ ضَرْبًۢا بِٱلْيَمِينِ ۝　93　Then he attacked them, striking forcefully.

فَأَقْبَلُوٓا۟ إِلَيْهِ يَزِفُّونَ ۝　94 They came running towards him.

قَالَ أَتَعْبُدُونَ　95 He said, 'Do you worship

مَا تَنْحِتُونَ ۝　what you have yourselves carved,

وَٱللَّهُ خَلَقَكُمْ　96　when Allah has created you

وَمَا تَعْمَلُونَ ۝　and whatever you make?'

قَالُوا۟ ٱبْنُوا۟ لَهُۥ بُنْيَٰنًا　97 They said, 'Build a structure for him

فَأَلْقُوهُ فِى ٱلْجَحِيمِ ۝　and cast him into a huge fire.'

فَأَرَادُوا۟ بِهِۦ كَيْدًا　98 So they sought to outwit him,

فَجَعَلْنَٰهُمُ ٱلْأَسْفَلِينَ ۝　but We made them the lowermost.

وَقَالَ إِنِّى ذَاهِبٌ إِلَىٰ رَبِّى　99 He said, 'Indeed I am going toward my Lord,

سَيَهْدِينِ ۝　who will guide me.'

رَبِّ هَبْ لِى مِنَ ٱلصَّٰلِحِينَ ۝　100 'My Lord! Give me [an heir], one of the righteous.'

فَبَشَّرْنَٰهُ بِغُلَٰمٍ حَلِيمٍ ۝　101 So We gave him the good news of a forbearing son.[2]

فَلَمَّا بَلَغَ مَعَهُ ٱلسَّعْىَ　102 When he was old enough to assist in his endeavour,

قَالَ يَٰبُنَىَّ　he said, 'My son!

إِنِّىٓ أَرَىٰ فِى ٱلْمَنَامِ أَنِّىٓ أَذْبَحُكَ　I see in a dream that I am sacrificing you.

فَٱنظُرْ مَاذَا تَرَىٰ ۚ　See what you think.'

قَالَ يَٰٓأَبَتِ　He said, 'Father!

---

[1] Or 'threw a look at the stars.'

[2] That is, Ishmael, who was Abraham's first born. That it was Ishmael to whom the following episode of the sacrifice pertains is also supported by the fact that verses pertaining to the birth of Isaac follow the account of Ishmael's sacrifice.

أَفْعَلُ مَا تُؤْمَرُ ۖ    Do whatever you have been commanded.

سَتَجِدُنِى إِن شَاءَ ٱللَّهُ مِنَ ٱلصَّـٰبِرِينَ ١٠٢    If Allah wishes, you will find me to be patient.'

فَلَمَّا أَسْلَمَا    103 So when they had both submitted [to Allah's will],

وَتَلَّهُ لِلْجَبِينِ ١٠٣    and he had laid him down on his forehead,

وَنَـٰدَيْنَـٰهُ أَن يَـٰٓإِبْرَٰهِيمُ ١٠٤    104 We called out to him, 'O Abraham!

قَدْ صَدَّقْتَ ٱلرُّءْيَآ ١٠٥    105   You have indeed fulfilled the vision![1]

إِنَّا كَذَٰلِكَ نَجْزِى ٱلْمُحْسِنِينَ ١٠٥    Thus indeed do We reward the virtuous!

إِنَّ هَـٰذَا لَهُوَ ٱلْبَلَـٰٓؤُا۟ ٱلْمُبِينُ ١٠٦    106   This was indeed a manifest test.'

وَفَدَيْنَـٰهُ بِذِبْحٍ عَظِيمٍ ١٠٧    107 Then We ransomed him with a great sacrifice,

وَتَرَكْنَا عَلَيْهِ فِى ٱلْءَاخِرِينَ ١٠٨    108 and left for him a good name in posterity:

سَلَـٰمٌ عَلَىٰٓ إِبْرَٰهِيمَ ١٠٩    109   'Peace be to Abraham!'

كَذَٰلِكَ نَجْزِى ٱلْمُحْسِنِينَ ١١٠    110   Thus do We reward the virtuous.

إِنَّهُ مِنْ عِبَادِنَا ٱلْمُؤْمِنِينَ ١١١    111 He is indeed one of Our faithful servants.

وَبَشَّرْنَـٰهُ    112 And We gave him the good news

بِإِسْحَـٰقَ    of [the birth of] Isaac,

نَبِيًّا مِّنَ ٱلصَّـٰلِحِينَ ١١٢    a prophet, one of the righteous.

وَبَـٰرَكْنَا عَلَيْهِ وَعَلَىٰٓ إِسْحَـٰقَ ۚ    113 And We blessed him and Isaac.

وَمِن ذُرِّيَّتِهِمَا مُحْسِنٌ    Among their descendants [some] are virtuous,

وَظَالِمٌ لِّنَفْسِهِۦ مُبِينٌ ١١٣    and [some] who manifestly wrong themselves.

وَلَقَدْ مَنَنَّا عَلَىٰ مُوسَىٰ وَهَـٰرُونَ ١١٤    114 Certainly We favoured Moses and Aaron,

وَنَجَّيْنَـٰهُمَا وَقَوْمَهُمَا    115 and delivered them and their people

مِنَ ٱلْكَرْبِ ٱلْعَظِيمِ ١١٥    from the great agony,

وَنَصَرْنَـٰهُمْ    116 and We helped them

فَكَانُوا۟ هُمُ ٱلْغَـٰلِبِينَ ١١٦    so that they became the victors.

وَءَاتَيْنَـٰهُمَا ٱلْكِتَـٰبَ ٱلْمُسْتَبِينَ ١١٧    117 We gave them the illuminating scripture

وَهَدَيْنَـٰهُمَا ٱلصِّرَٰطَ ٱلْمُسْتَقِيمَ ١١٨    118   and guided them to the straight path,

وَتَرَكْنَا عَلَيْهِمَا فِى ٱلْءَاخِرِينَ ١١٩    119 and left for them a good name in posterity.

سَلَـٰمٌ عَلَىٰ مُوسَىٰ وَهَـٰرُونَ ١٢٠    120   'Peace be to Moses and Aaron!'

---

[1] Or 'dream.'

إِنَّا كَذَٰلِكَ نَجْزِى ٱلْمُحْسِنِينَ ۝ 121 Thus indeed do We reward the virtuous.

إِنَّهُمَا مِنْ عِبَادِنَا ٱلْمُؤْمِنِينَ ۝ 122 They are indeed among Our faithful servants.

وَإِنَّ إِلْيَاسَ لَمِنَ ٱلْمُرْسَلِينَ ۝ 123 And indeed Ilyās was one of the apostles,

إِذْ قَالَ لِقَوْمِهِ 124 when he said to his people,

أَلَا تَتَّقُونَ ۝ 'Will you not be Godwary?

أَتَدْعُونَ بَعْلًا 125 Do you invoke Baal

وَتَذَرُونَ أَحْسَنَ ٱلْخَٰلِقِينَ ۝ and abandon the best of creators,

ٱللَّهَ 126 Allah,

رَبَّكُمْ وَرَبَّ ءَابَآئِكُمُ ٱلْأَوَّلِينَ ۝ your Lord and Lord of your forefathers?'

فَكَذَّبُوهُ 127 But they impugned him.

فَإِنَّهُمْ لَمُحْضَرُونَ ۝ So they will indeed be arraigned [before Him]

إِلَّا عِبَادَ ٱللَّهِ ٱلْمُخْلَصِينَ ۝ 128 —[all] except Allah's exclusive servants.

وَتَرَكْنَا عَلَيْهِ فِي ٱلْآخِرِينَ ۝ 129 We left for him a good name in posterity.

سَلَٰمٌ عَلَىٰ إِلْ يَاسِينَ ۝ 130 'Peace be to Ilyās!'[1]

إِنَّا كَذَٰلِكَ نَجْزِى ٱلْمُحْسِنِينَ ۝ 131 Thus indeed do We reward the virtuous.

إِنَّهُ مِنْ عِبَادِنَا ٱلْمُؤْمِنِينَ ۝ 132 He is indeed one of Our faithful servants.

وَإِنَّ لُوطًا لَّمِنَ ٱلْمُرْسَلِينَ ۝ 133 And indeed Lot was one of the apostles,

إِذْ نَجَّيْنَٰهُ وَأَهْلَهُ أَجْمَعِينَ ۝ 134 when We delivered him and all his family,

إِلَّا عَجُوزًا 135 except an old woman

فِي ٱلْغَٰبِرِينَ ۝ among those who remained behind.

ثُمَّ دَمَّرْنَا ٱلْآخَرِينَ ۝ 136 Then We destroyed [all] the others.

وَإِنَّكُمْ لَتَمُرُّونَ عَلَيْهِم مُّصْبِحِينَ ۝ 137 And indeed you pass by them at dawn

---

[1] In accordance with an alternate reading (*salāmun ʿalā Āl-i Yā Sīn*), narrated from Nāfiʿ, Ibn ʿĀmir, Yaʿqūb, Ruways, al-Aʿraj, Shaybah, Zayd ibn ʿAlī and others (see *Muʿjam al-Qirāʾāt al-Qurʾāniyyah*, vol. 5, p. 246), the translation will be 'Peace be upon the progeny of Yā Sīn' (i.e. the Prophet, who is referred to as Yā Sīn in 36:1). Traditions narrated from Ibn ʿAbbās (*al-Durr al-Manthūr*, vol. 5, p. 286), Imam Jaʿfar al-Ṣādiq (*Maʿānī al-Akhbār*, p. 122) and Imam ʿAlī ibn Mūsā al-Riḍā (*ʿUyūn Akhbār al-Riḍā*, vol. 1, p.237) also support this reading.

وَبِٱلَّيْلِ ۚ 138 and at night.

أَفَلَا تَعْقِلُونَ ﴿١٣٨﴾ So do you not apply reason?

وَإِنَّ يُونُسَ لَمِنَ ٱلْمُرْسَلِينَ ﴿١٣٩﴾ 139 And indeed Jonah was one of the apostles,

إِذْ أَبَقَ إِلَى ٱلْفُلْكِ ٱلْمَشْحُونِ ﴿١٤٠﴾ 140 when he absconded toward the laden ship.

فَسَاهَمَ 141 Then he drew lots with them

فَكَانَ مِنَ ٱلْمُدْحَضِينَ ﴿١٤١﴾ and he was the one to be refuted.

فَٱلْتَقَمَهُ ٱلْحُوتُ 142 Then the fish swallowed him

وَهُوَ مُلِيمٌ ﴿١٤٢﴾ while he was blameworthy.

فَلَوْلَآ أَنَّهُۥ كَانَ 143 And had he not been

مِنَ ٱلْمُسَبِّحِينَ ﴿١٤٣﴾ one of those who celebrate Allah's glory,

لَلَبِثَ فِى بَطْنِهِۦٓ 144 he would have surely remained in its belly

إِلَىٰ يَوْمِ يُبْعَثُونَ ﴿١٤٤﴾ ❋ till the day they will be resurrected.

فَنَبَذْنَٰهُ بِٱلْعَرَآءِ 145 Then We cast him on a bare shore,

وَهُوَ سَقِيمٌ ﴿١٤٥﴾ and he was sick.

وَأَنۢبَتْنَا عَلَيْهِ شَجَرَةً مِّن يَقْطِينٍ ﴿١٤٦﴾ 146 So We made a gourd plant grow above him.

وَأَرْسَلْنَٰهُ 147 We sent him

إِلَىٰ مِا۟ئَةِ أَلْفٍ أَوْ يَزِيدُونَ ﴿١٤٧﴾ to a [community of] hundred thousand or more,

فَـَٔامَنُوا۟ 148 and they believed [in him].

فَمَتَّعْنَٰهُمْ إِلَىٰ حِينٍ ﴿١٤٨﴾ So We provided for them for a while.

فَٱسْتَفْتِهِمْ أَلِرَبِّكَ ٱلْبَنَاتُ 149 *Ask* them, are daughters to be for *your* Lord

وَلَهُمُ ٱلْبَنُونَ ﴿١٤٩﴾ while sons are to be for them?[1]

أَمْ خَلَقْنَا ٱلْمَلَٰٓئِكَةَ إِنَٰثًا 150 Did We create the angels females

وَهُمْ شَٰهِدُونَ ﴿١٥٠﴾ while they were present?[2]

أَلَآ إِنَّهُم مِّنْ إِفْكِهِمْ 151 Look! It is indeed out of their mendacity

لَيَقُولُونَ ﴿١٥١﴾ that they say,

وَلَدَ ٱللَّهُ 152 'Allah has begotten,'

وَإِنَّهُمْ لَكَٰذِبُونَ ﴿١٥٢﴾ and they indeed say a falsehood.

---

[1] Cf. 6:100, 16:57, 17:40, 43:16, 52:39.
[2] Or 'while they were witnesses.'

أَصْطَفَى ٱلْبَنَاتِ عَلَى ٱلْبَنِينَ ۝ 153 Has he preferred daughters to sons?

مَا لَكُمْ 154 What is the matter with you?

كَيْفَ تَحْكُمُونَ ۝ How do you judge?

أَفَلَا تَذَكَّرُونَ ۝ 155 Will you not then take admonition?

أَمْ لَكُمْ سُلْطَنٌ مُّبِينٌ ۝ 156 Do you have a manifest authority?[1]

فَأْتُوا بِكِتَبِكُمْ 157 Then produce your scripture,

إِن كُنتُمْ صَدِقِينَ ۝ should you be truthful.

وَجَعَلُوا 158 And they have set up

بَيْنَهُ وَبَيْنَ ٱلْجِنَّةِ نَسَبًا a kinship between Him and the jinn,

وَلَقَدْ عَلِمَتِ ٱلْجِنَّةُ while the jinn certainly know

إِنَّهُمْ لَمُحْضَرُونَ ۝ that they will indeed be presented [before Him].

سُبْحَنَ ٱللَّهِ عَمَّا يَصِفُونَ ۝ 159 Clear is Allah of whatever they allege [about Him],

إِلَّا عِبَادَ ٱللَّهِ ٱلْمُخْلَصِينَ ۝ 160 —[all] except Allah's exclusive servants.

فَإِنَّكُمْ وَمَا تَعْبُدُونَ ۝ 161 Indeed you and what you worship

مَآ أَنتُمْ عَلَيْهِ بِفَتِنِينَ ۝ 162 —you cannot mislead [anyone] about Him,

إِلَّا مَنْ هُوَ صَالِ ٱلْجَحِيمِ ۝ 163 except someone who is bound for hell.

وَمَا مِنَّآ إِلَّا لَهُ مَقَامٌ مَّعْلُومٌ ۝ 164 'There is none among us but has a known place.[2]

وَإِنَّا لَنَحْنُ ٱلصَّآفُّونَ ۝ 165 Indeed it is we who are the ranged ones .

وَإِنَّا لَنَحْنُ 166 Indeed it is we who are

ٱلْمُسَبِّحُونَ ۝ those who celebrate Allah's glory.'

وَإِن كَانُوا لَيَقُولُونَ ۝ 167 Indeed they[3] used to say,

لَوْ أَنَّ عِندَنَا ذِكْرًا مِّنَ ٱلْأَوَّلِينَ ۝ 168 'Had we possessed a reminder from the ancients,

لَكُنَّا 169 we would surely have been

عِبَادَ ٱللَّهِ ٱلْمُخْلَصِينَ ۝ Allah's exclusive servants.'

فَكَفَرُوا بِهِۦ 170 But they disbelieved it [when it came to them].

---

[1] That is, in support of what they assert.

[2] Verses 164-166 quote the words of the angels referred to in verse 1.

[3] That is, the pagans of Makkah.

فَسَوْفَ يَعْلَمُونَ ۝  Soon they will know.

وَلَقَدْ سَبَقَتْ كَلِمَتُنَا  171 Certainly Our decree has gone beforehand

لِعِبَادِنَا ٱلْمُرْسَلِينَ ۝  in favour of Our servants, the apostles,

إِنَّهُمْ لَهُمُ ٱلْمَنصُورُونَ ۝  172 that they will indeed receive [Allah's] help,

وَإِنَّ جُندَنَا لَهُمُ ٱلْغَٰلِبُونَ ۝  173 and indeed Our hosts will be the victors.

فَتَوَلَّ عَنْهُمْ حَتَّىٰ حِينٍ ۝  174 So *leave* them alone for a while,

وَأَبْصِرْهُمْ  175 and *watch* them;

فَسَوْفَ يُبْصِرُونَ ۝  soon they will see [the truth of the matter].

أَفَبِعَذَابِنَا يَسْتَعْجِلُونَ ۝  176 Do they seek to hasten Our punishment?

فَإِذَا نَزَلَ بِسَاحَتِهِمْ  177 But when it descends in their courtyard

فَسَآءَ صَبَاحُ  it will be a dismal dawn

ٱلْمُنذَرِينَ ۝  for those who had been warned.

وَتَوَلَّ عَنْهُمْ حَتَّىٰ حِينٍ ۝  178 So *leave* them alone for a while,

وَأَبْصِرْ  179 and *watch*;

فَسَوْفَ يُبْصِرُونَ ۝  soon they will see.

سُبْحَٰنَ رَبِّكَ رَبِّ ٱلْعِزَّةِ  180 Clear is *your* Lord, the Lord of Might,

عَمَّا يَصِفُونَ ۝  of whatever they allege [concerning Him].

وَسَلَٰمٌ عَلَى ٱلْمُرْسَلِينَ ۝  181 Peace be to the apostles!

وَٱلْحَمْدُ لِلَّهِ رَبِّ ٱلْعَٰلَمِينَ ۝  182 All praise belongs to Allah, Lord of all the worlds.

# 38. SŪRAT ṢĀD[1]

سُورَةُ ص

بِسْمِ ٱللَّهِ  In the Name of Allah,

ٱلرَّحْمَٰنِ ٱلرَّحِيمِ  the All-beneficent, All-merciful

صٓ وَٱلْقُرْءَانِ ذِى ٱلذِّكْرِ ۝  1 *Ṣād*. By the Qur'ān bearing the Reminder![2]

بَلِ ٱلَّذِينَ كَفَرُوا  2 Yet the faithless

---

[1] The *sūrah* takes its name from the letter *Ṣād*, mentioned in verse 1.

[2] Ellipsis: the omitted phrase is '*you* are indeed one of the apostles, on a straight path.' Cf. 36:3.

في عِزَّةٍ وَشِقَاقٍ ۝    dwell in conceit and defiance.

كَمْ أَهْلَكْنَا مِن قَبْلِهِم مِّن قَرْنٍ 3 How many a generation We have destroyed before them!

فَنَادَوا    They cried out [for help],

وَّلَاتَ حِينَ مَنَاصٍ ۝    but it was no more the time for escape.

وَعَجِبُوا أَن جَاءَهُم 4 They consider it odd that there should come to them

مُّنذِرٌ مِّنْهُمْ    a warner from among themselves,

وَقَالَ ٱلْكَفِرُونَ    and the faithless say,

هَذَا سَحِرٌ كَذَّابٌ ۝    'This is a magician, a mendacious liar.'

أَجَعَلَ ٱلْآلِهَةَ إِلَهًا وَحِدًا 5 'Has he reduced the gods to one god?

إِنَّ هَذَا لَشَيْءٌ عُجَابٌ ۝    This is indeed an odd thing!'

وَٱنطَلَقَ ٱلْمَلَأُ مِنْهُمْ 6 Their elite go about [urging others]:

أَنِ ٱمْشُوا وَٱصْبِرُوا عَلَىٰ ءَالِهَتِكُمْ    'Go and stand by your gods!

إِنَّ هَذَا لَشَيْءٌ يُرَادُ ۝    This is indeed the desirable thing [to do].

مَا سَمِعْنَا بِهَذَا فِي ٱلْمِلَّةِ ٱلْآخِرَةِ 7   We did not hear of this in the latter-day creed.[1]

إِنْ هَذَا إِلَّا ٱخْتِلَقٌ ۝    This is nothing but a fabrication.

أَءُنزِلَ عَلَيْهِ ٱلذِّكْرُ 8 Has the reminder been sent down to him

مِنْ بَيْنِنَا    out of [all of] us?'

بَلْ هُمْ فِي شَكٍّ مِّن ذِكْرِى    Rather they are in doubt concerning My reminder.

بَل لَّمَّا يَذُوقُوا عَذَابِ ۝    Rather they have not yet tasted My punishment.

أَمْ عِندَهُمْ 9 Do they possess

خَزَائِنُ رَحْمَةِ رَبِّكَ    the treasuries of the mercy of *your* Lord,

ٱلْعَزِيزِ ٱلْوَهَّابِ ۝    the All-mighty, the All-munificent?

أَمْ لَهُم مُّلْكُ ٱلسَّمَوَتِ 10 Do they own the kingdom of the heavens

وَٱلْأَرْضِ    and the earth

وَمَا بَيْنَهُمَا    and whatever is between them?

فَلْيَرْتَقُوا    [If so,] let them ascend [to the higher spheres]

فِي ٱلْأَسْبَبِ ۝    by the means[2] [of ascension].

---

[1] That is, in the polytheistic creed prevalent in pre-Islamic Arabia.

[2] Or 'let them ascend by the contrivances.' Or 'let them ascend by the ladder,' or 'let them ascend into the heavens.'

جُندٌ مَّا هُنَالِكَ مَهْزُومٌ 11 [They are but] a routed host out there,

مِّنَ ٱلْأَحْزَابِ ۝ from among the factions.[1]

كَذَّبَتْ قَبْلَهُمْ قَوْمُ نُوحٍ 12 Before them Noah's people impugned [their apostle]

وَعَادٌ and [so did the people of] 'Ād,

وَفِرْعَوْنُ ذُو ٱلْأَوْتَادِ ۝ and Pharaoh, the Impaler[2] [of his victims],

وَثَمُودُ وَقَوْمُ لُوطٍ 13 and Thamūd, and the people of Lot,

وَأَصْحَبُ لَيْكَةِ and the inhabitants of Aykah:[3]

أُوْلَئِكَ ٱلْأَحْزَابُ ۝ those were the factions.

إِن كُلٌّ إِلَّا كَذَّبَ ٱلرُّسُلَ 14 Each of them did not but impugn the apostles;

فَحَقَّ عِقَابِ ۝ so My retribution became due [against them].

وَمَا يَنظُرُ هَؤُلَاءِ 15 These[4] do not await

إِلَّا صَيْحَةً وَحِدَةً but a single Cry

مَّا لَهَا مِن فَوَاقٍ ۝ which will not grant any respite.

وَقَالُوا رَبَّنَا 16 They say, 'Our Lord!

عَجِّل لَّنَا قِطَّنَا Hasten on for us our share[5]

قَبْلَ يَوْمِ ٱلْحِسَابِ ۝ before the Day of Reckoning.'

ٱصْبِرْ عَلَى مَا يَقُولُونَ 17 *Be patient* over what they say,

وَٱذْكُرْ عَبْدَنَا دَاوُدَ and *remember* Our servant, David,

ذَا ٱلْأَيْدِ [the man] of strength.

إِنَّهُ أَوَّابٌ ۝ Indeed he was a penitent [soul].

---

[1] A prophesy of the defeat of the Makkan army at Badr (see Ṭabarī and Ṭabrisī) Or 'from among the confederates,' that is, of Satan (cf. 35:6, 58:19).

[2] Lit.: 'the one of stakes.' According to several traditions, Pharaoh used to torture and execute his victims by piercing their bodies with stakes, or *awtād* (see *Biḥār al-anwār*, vol. 13, p. 136, from *'Ilal al-Sharāyi'*, p. 161; vol. 71, p. 13; vol. 75, p. 403). Hence the epithet '*dhi'l-awtād*,' which occurs twice in the Qur'ān with reference to Pharaoh, refers to him as one who used to impale his victims. Other alternate explanations have been suggested for this epithet by the commentators, but they are not convincing.

[3] Cf. 15:78.

[4] That is, the pagans of Makkah.

[5] That is, 'our share of punishment,' said mockingly.

إِنَّا سَخَّرْنَا ٱلْجِبَالَ 18 Indeed We disposed the mountains

مَعَهُۥ يُسَبِّحْنَ to glorify [Allah] with him

بِٱلْعَشِىِّ وَٱلْإِشْرَاقِ ۝ at evening and dawn,

وَٱلطَّيْرَ مَحْشُورَةً 19 and the birds [as well], mustered [in flocks],

كُلٌّ لَّهُۥٓ أَوَّابٌ ۝ all echoing him [in a chorus].

وَشَدَدْنَا مُلْكَهُۥ 20 We made his kingdom firm

وَءَاتَيْنَٰهُ ٱلْحِكْمَةَ and gave him wisdom

وَفَصْلَ ٱلْخِطَابِ ۝ ✦ and conclusive speech.

وَهَلْ أَتَىٰكَ 21 Has there not come to *you*

نَبَؤُاْ ٱلْخَصْمِ the account of the contenders,

إِذْ تَسَوَّرُواْ ٱلْمِحْرَابَ ۝ when they scaled the wall into the sanctuary?[1]

إِذْ دَخَلُواْ عَلَىٰ دَاوُۥدَ 22 When they entered into the presence of David,

فَفَزِعَ مِنْهُمْ he was alarmed by them.

قَالُواْ لَا تَخَفْ They said, 'Do not be afraid.

خَصْمَانِ [We are only] two contenders:

بَغَىٰ بَعْضُنَا عَلَىٰ بَعْضٍ one of us has bullied the other.

فَٱحْكُم بَيْنَنَا بِٱلْحَقِّ So judge justly between us,

وَلَا تُشْطِطْ and do not exceed [the bounds of justice],

وَٱهْدِنَآ إِلَىٰ سَوَآءِ ٱلصِّرَٰطِ ۝ and show us the right path.'

إِنَّ هَٰذَآ أَخِى 23 'Indeed this brother of mine

لَهُۥ تِسْعٌ وَتِسْعُونَ نَعْجَةً has ninety-nine ewes,

وَلِىَ نَعْجَةٌ وَٰحِدَةٌ while I have only a single ewe,

فَقَالَ أَكْفِلْنِيهَا and [yet] he says, 'Commit it to my care,'

وَعَزَّنِى فِى ٱلْخِطَابِ ۝ and he browbeats me in speech.'

قَالَ لَقَدْ ظَلَمَكَ 24 He said, 'He has certainly wronged you

بِسُؤَالِ نَعْجَتِكَ إِلَىٰ نِعَاجِهِۦ by asking your ewe in addition to his ewes,

وَإِنَّ كَثِيرًا مِّنَ ٱلْخُلَطَآءِ and indeed many partners

لَيَبْغِى بَعْضُهُمْ عَلَىٰ بَعْضٍ bully one another,

إِلَّا ٱلَّذِينَ ءَامَنُواْ except such as have faith

---

[1] Or 'sanctum.'

وَعَمِلُوا۟ ٱلصَّٰلِحَٰتِ and do righteous deeds,

وَقَلِيلٌ مَّا هُمْ and few are they.'

وَظَنَّ دَاوُۥدُ أَنَّمَا فَتَنَّٰهُ Then David knew that We had indeed tested him,

فَٱسْتَغْفَرَ رَبَّهُۥ whereat he pleaded with his Lord for forgiveness,

وَخَرَّ رَاكِعًا وَأَنَابَ ۩ and fell down prostrate and repented.

فَغَفَرْنَا لَهُۥ ذَٰلِكَ 25 So We forgave him that

وَإِنَّ لَهُۥ عِندَنَا لَزُلْفَىٰ and indeed he has [a station of] nearness with Us

وَحُسْنَ مَـَٔابٍ and a good destination.

يَٰدَاوُۥدُ 26 'O David!

إِنَّا جَعَلْنَٰكَ خَلِيفَةً فِى ٱلْأَرْضِ Indeed We have made you a vicegerent on the earth.

فَٱحْكُم بَيْنَ ٱلنَّاسِ بِٱلْحَقِّ So judge between people with justice,

وَلَا تَتَّبِعِ ٱلْهَوَىٰ and do not follow desire,

فَيُضِلَّكَ عَن سَبِيلِ ٱللَّهِ or it will lead you astray from the way of Allah.

إِنَّ ٱلَّذِينَ يَضِلُّونَ عَن سَبِيلِ ٱللَّهِ Indeed those who stray from the way of Allah

لَهُمْ عَذَابٌ شَدِيدٌۢ —there is a severe punishment for them

بِمَا نَسُوا۟ يَوْمَ ٱلْحِسَابِ because of their forgetting the Day of Reckoning.'

وَمَا خَلَقْنَا ٱلسَّمَآءَ وَٱلْأَرْضَ 27 We did not create the sky and the earth

وَمَا بَيْنَهُمَا and whatever is between them

بَٰطِلًا in vain.

ذَٰلِكَ ظَنُّ ٱلَّذِينَ كَفَرُوا۟ That is a conjecture of the faithless.

فَوَيْلٌ لِّلَّذِينَ كَفَرُوا۟ مِنَ ٱلنَّارِ So woe to the faithless for the Fire!

أَمْ نَجْعَلُ ٱلَّذِينَ ءَامَنُوا۟ 28 Shall We treat those who have faith

وَعَمِلُوا۟ ٱلصَّٰلِحَٰتِ and do righteous deeds

كَٱلْمُفْسِدِينَ فِى ٱلْأَرْضِ like those who cause corruption on the earth?

أَمْ نَجْعَلُ ٱلْمُتَّقِينَ كَٱلْفُجَّارِ Shall We treat the Godwary like the vicious?

كِتَٰبٌ أَنزَلْنَٰهُ إِلَيْكَ مُبَٰرَكٌ 29 [It is] a blessed Book that We have sent down to *you,*

لِّيَدَّبَّرُوٓا۟ ءَايَٰتِهِۦ so that they may contemplate its signs,

وَلِيَتَذَكَّرَ أُو۟لُوا۟ ٱلْأَلْبَٰبِ and that those who possess intellect may take admonition.

وَوَهَبْنَا لِدَاوُدَ سُلَيْمَنَ 30 And to David We gave Solomon

نِعْمَ ٱلْعَبْدُ    —what an excellent servant!

إِنَّهُ أَوَّابٌ ۝    Indeed he was a penitent [soul].

إِذْ عُرِضَ عَلَيْهِ بِٱلْعَشِيِّ 31 When one evening there were displayed before him

ٱلصَّٰفِنَٰتُ ٱلْجِيَادُ ۝    prancing steeds,

فَقَالَ 32    he said,

إِنِّي أَحْبَبْتُ حُبَّ ٱلْخَيْرِ    'Indeed I have preferred the love of [worldly] niceties

عَن ذِكْرِ رَبِّي    to the remembrance of my Lord

حَتَّىٰ تَوَارَتْ بِٱلْحِجَابِ ۝    until [the sun] disappeared behind the [night's] veil.'

رُدُّوهَا عَلَيَّ 33    Bring it[1] back for me!'

فَطَفِقَ مَسْحًا بِٱلسُّوقِ    Then he [and others] began to stroke [their] legs

وَٱلْأَعْنَاقِ ۝    and necks.

وَلَقَدْ فَتَنَّا سُلَيْمَٰنَ 34 Certainly We tried Solomon,

وَأَلْقَيْنَا عَلَىٰ كُرْسِيِّهِ جَسَدًا    and cast a [lifeless] body on his throne.

ثُمَّ أَنَابَ ۝    Thereupon he was penitent.

قَالَ رَبِّ ٱغْفِرْ لِي 35 He said, 'My Lord! Forgive me,

وَهَبْ لِي مُلْكًا    and grant me a kingdom

لَّا يَنۢبَغِي لِأَحَدٍ مِّنۢ بَعْدِي    that shall not behoove anyone after me.

إِنَّكَ أَنتَ ٱلْوَهَّابُ ۝    Indeed You are the All-munificent.'

فَسَخَّرْنَا لَهُ ٱلرِّيحَ 36 So We disposed the wind for him,

تَجْرِي بِأَمْرِهِ رُخَآءً    blowing softly by his command

حَيْثُ أَصَابَ ۝    wherever he intended,

---

[1] Or 'them.' The pronoun may be taken as referring to the sun or to the horses. However, most exegetes have taken it as referring to the sun and its setting. While Solomon was engaged in viewing the horses, the sun set, and time of the afternoon prayer (supererogatory or obligatory) elapsed. According to a tradition narrated from al-Imām al-Ṣādiq ('a), when Solomon noticed that the sun had set, he called out to the angels to bring it back so that he could offer the afternoon prayer. Also, according to this tradition, the wiping of legs and necks mentioned in the verse refers to the performance of ablution (wuḍūʾ) before the prayer by Solomon and his men as prescribed in their Law. (*Biḥār*, vol. 14, p. 101; vol. 82, p. 341)

37 and the devils [as well as], every builder and diver, وَٱلشَّيَـٰطِينَ كُلَّ بَنَّآءٍ وَغَوَّاصٍ

38     and others [too] bound together in chains. وَءَاخَرِينَ مُقَرَّنِينَ فِى ٱلْأَصْفَادِ

39 'This is Our bounty: هَـٰذَا عَطَآؤُنَا

so give away or withhold, without any reckoning.' فَٱمْنُنْ أَوْ أَمْسِكْ بِغَيْرِ حِسَابٍ

40 Indeed he has [a station of] nearness with Us وَإِنَّ لَهُۥ عِندَنَا لَزُلْفَىٰ

and a good destination. وَحُسْنَ مَـَٔابٍ

41 And *remember* Our servant Job [in the Qur'ān]. وَٱذْكُرْ عَبْدَنَآ أَيُّوبَ

When he called out to his Lord, إِذْ نَادَىٰ رَبَّهُۥٓ

'The devil has visited on me أَنِّى مَسَّنِىَ ٱلشَّيْطَـٰنُ

hardship and torment,' بِنُصْبٍ وَعَذَابٍ

42 [We told him:] 'Stamp your foot on the ground; ٱرْكُضْ بِرِجْلِكَ

this [ensuing spring] is a cooling bath and drink.' هَـٰذَا مُغْتَسَلٌ بَارِدٌ وَشَرَابٌ

43 And We gave [back] his family to him وَوَهَبْنَا لَهُۥٓ أَهْلَهُۥ

along with others like them, وَمِثْلَهُم مَّعَهُمْ

as a mercy from Us رَحْمَةً مِّنَّا

and an admonition for those who possess intellect. وَذِكْرَىٰ لِأُوْلِى ٱلْأَلْبَـٰبِ

44 [We told him:] 'Take a faggot in your hand وَخُذْ بِيَدِكَ ضِغْثًا

and then strike [your wife] with it, فَٱضْرِب بِّهِۦ

but do not break [your] oath.' وَلَا تَحْنَثْ

Indeed We found him to be patient. إِنَّا وَجَدْنَـٰهُ صَابِرًا

What an excellent servant! نِّعْمَ ٱلْعَبْدُ

Indeed he was a penitent [soul]. إِنَّهُۥٓ أَوَّابٌ

45 And *remember* Our servants Abraham, وَٱذْكُرْ عِبَـٰدَنَآ إِبْرَٰهِيمَ

Isaac and Jacob, وَإِسْحَـٰقَ وَيَعْقُوبَ

men of strength and insight. أُوْلِى ٱلْأَيْدِى وَٱلْأَبْصَـٰرِ

46 Indeed We purified them with the exclusiveness of إِنَّآ أَخْلَصْنَـٰهُم بِخَالِصَةٍ

the remembrance of the abode [of the Hereafter]. ذِكْرَى ٱلدَّارِ

47 Indeed with Us they are وَإِنَّهُمْ عِندَنَا

لَمِنَ ٱلۡمُصۡطَفَيۡنَ ٱلۡأَخۡيَارِ ۝ surely among the elect of the best.

وَٱذۡكُرۡ إِسۡمَٰعِيلَ وَٱلۡيَسَعَ وَذَا ٱلۡكِفۡلِ 48 And *remember* Ishmael, Elisha and Dhu'l-Kifl

وَكُلٌّ مِّنَ ٱلۡأَخۡيَارِ ۝ —each [of whom was] among the elect.

هَٰذَا ذِكۡرٌ 49 This is a reminder,

وَإِنَّ لِلۡمُتَّقِينَ لَحُسۡنَ مَـَٔابٍ ۝ and indeed the Godwary have a good destination

جَنَّٰتِ عَدۡنٍ 50 —the Gardens of Eden,

مُّفَتَّحَةً لَّهُمُ ٱلۡأَبۡوَٰبُ ۝ whose gates are flung open for them.

مُتَّكِـِٔينَ فِيهَا 51 Reclining therein [on couches],

يَدۡعُونَ فِيهَا therein they ask

بِفَٰكِهَةٍ كَثِيرَةٍ وَشَرَابٍ ۝ ❖ for abundant fruits and drinks,

وَعِندَهُمۡ قَٰصِرَٰتُ ٱلطَّرۡفِ 52 and with them will be maidens of restrained glances

أَتۡرَابٌ ۝ of a like age.

هَٰذَا مَا تُوعَدُونَ 53 This is what you are promised

لِيَوۡمِ ٱلۡحِسَابِ ۝ on the Day of Reckoning.

إِنَّ هَٰذَا لَرِزۡقُنَا 54 This is indeed Our provision,

مَا لَهُۥ مِن نَّفَادٍ ۝ which will never be exhausted.

هَٰذَا 55 This [is for the righteous],

وَإِنَّ لِلطَّٰغِينَ and as for the rebellious

لَشَرَّ مَـَٔابٍ ۝ there will surely be a bad destination

جَهَنَّمَ يَصۡلَوۡنَهَا 56 —hell, which they shall enter,

فَبِئۡسَ ٱلۡمِهَادُ ۝ an evil resting place.

هَٰذَا فَلۡيَذُوقُوهُ حَمِيمٌ وَغَسَّاقٌ ۝ 57 This; let them taste it: scalding water and pus,

وَءَاخَرُ مِن شَكۡلِهِۦٓ أَزۡوَٰجٌ ۝ 58 and other kinds [of torments] resembling it.

هَٰذَا فَوۡجٌ مُّقۡتَحِمٌ مَّعَكُمۡ 59 'This is a group plunging [into hell] along with you.'[1]

لَا مَرۡحَبًۢا بِهِمۡ 'May wretchedness be their lot!

إِنَّهُمۡ صَالُوا ٱلنَّارِ ۝ They will indeed enter the Fire.'[2]

قَالُوا بَلۡ أَنتُمۡ لَا مَرۡحَبًۢا بِكُمۡ 60 They[3] say, 'Rather, may wretchedness be your lot!

---

[1] Said by the angels to leaders of the faithless concerning their followers.

[2] Said by the leaders of the faithless concerning their followers.

[3] That is, the followers, who respond to the unfriendly welcome of their leaders.

أَنتُمۡ قَدَّمۡتُمُوهُ لَنَا    You prepared this [hell] for us.

فَبِئۡسَ ٱلۡقَرَارُ ۝    What an evil abode!'

قَالُواْ رَبَّنَا ۝ 61    They say, 'Our Lord!

مَن قَدَّمَ لَنَا هَٰذَا    Whoever has prepared this for us,

فَزِدۡهُ عَذَابًا ضِعۡفًا فِى ٱلنَّارِ ۝    double his punishment in the Fire!'

وَقَالُواْ مَا لَنَا 62    And they say, 'What is the matter with us

لَا نَرَىٰ رِجَالًا    that we do not see [here] men

كُنَّا نَعُدُّهُم مِّنَ ٱلۡأَشۡرَارِ ۝    whom we used to count among the bad ones?

أَتَّخَذۡنَٰهُمۡ سِخۡرِيًّا 63    Did we ridicule them [unduly in the world],

أَمۡ زَاغَتۡ عَنۡهُمُ ٱلۡأَبۡصَٰرُ ۝    or do [our] eyes miss them [here]?'

إِنَّ ذَٰلِكَ لَحَقٌّ 64    That is indeed a truth:

تَخَاصُمُ أَهۡلِ ٱلنَّارِ ۝    the contentions of the inmates of the Fire.

قُلۡ إِنَّمَآ أَنَا۠ مُنذِرٌ 65    Say, 'I am just a warner,

وَمَا مِنۡ إِلَٰهٍ إِلَّا ٱللَّهُ    and there is no god except Allah,

ٱلۡوَٰحِدُ ٱلۡقَهَّارُ ۝    the One, the All-paramount,

رَبُّ ٱلسَّمَٰوَٰتِ وَٱلۡأَرۡضِ 66    the Lord of the heavens and the earth

وَمَا بَيۡنَهُمَا    and whatever is between them,

ٱلۡعَزِيزُ ٱلۡغَفَّٰرُ ۝    the All-mighty, the All-forgiver.'

قُلۡ هُوَ نَبَؤٌاْ عَظِيمٌ ۝ 67    Say, 'It is a great prophesy,

أَنتُمۡ عَنۡهُ مُعۡرِضُونَ ۝ 68    of which you are disregardful.

مَا كَانَ لِىَ مِنۡ عِلۡمٍ بِٱلۡمَلَإِ ٱلۡأَعۡلَىٰٓ 69    I have no knowledge of the Supernal Elite

إِذۡ يَخۡتَصِمُونَ ۝    when they contend.

إِن يُوحَىٰٓ إِلَىَّ إِلَّآ 70    All that is revealed to me is

أَنَّمَآ أَنَا۠ نَذِيرٌ مُّبِينٌ ۝    that I am just a manifest warner.'

إِذۡ قَالَ رَبُّكَ لِلۡمَلَٰٓئِكَةِ 71    When your Lord said to the angels,

إِنِّى خَٰلِقٌۢ بَشَرًا    'Indeed I am about to create a human being

مِّن طِينٍ ۝    out of clay.

فَإِذَا سَوَّيۡتُهُۥ 72    So when I have proportioned him

وَنَفَخۡتُ فِيهِ مِن رُّوحِى    and breathed into him of My spirit,

فَقَعُواْ لَهُۥ سَٰجِدِينَ ۝    then fall down in prostration before him.'

فَسَجَدَ ٱلْمَلَٰئِكَةُ 73 Thereat the angels prostrated,

كُلُّهُمْ أَجْمَعُونَ ٧٣ all of them together,

إِلَّآ إِبْلِيسَ 74 except Iblis;

ٱسْتَكْبَرَ he acted arrogantly

وَكَانَ مِنَ ٱلْكَٰفِرِينَ ٧٤ and he was one of the faithless.

قَالَ يَٰإِبْلِيسُ 75 He said, 'O Iblis!

مَا مَنَعَكَ أَن تَسْجُدَ What keeps you from prostrating

لِمَا خَلَقْتُ before that which I have created

بِيَدَىَّ with My [own] two hands?

أَسْتَكْبَرْتَ Are you arrogant,

أَمْ كُنتَ مِنَ ٱلْعَالِينَ ٧٥ or are you [one] of the exalted ones?'

قَالَ أَنَا۠ خَيْرٌ مِّنْهُ 76 'I am better than him,' he said.

خَلَقْتَنِى مِن نَّارٍ 'You created me from fire

وَخَلَقْتَهُۥ مِن طِينٍ ٧٦ and You created him from clay.'

قَالَ فَٱخْرُجْ مِنْهَا 77 He said, 'Begone hence,

فَإِنَّكَ رَجِيمٌ ٧٧ for you are indeed an outcast,

وَإِنَّ عَلَيْكَ لَعْنَتِى 78 and indeed My curse will be on you

إِلَىٰ يَوْمِ ٱلدِّينِ ٧٨ till the Day of Retribution.'

قَالَ رَبِّ 79 He said, 'My Lord!

فَأَنظِرْنِى إِلَىٰ يَوْمِ يُبْعَثُونَ ٧٩ Respite me till the day they will be resurrected.'

قَالَ فَإِنَّكَ مِنَ ٱلْمُنظَرِينَ 80 Said He, 'You are indeed among the reprieved

إِلَىٰ يَوْمِ ٱلْوَقْتِ ٱلْمَعْلُومِ ٨١ 81 until the day of the known time.

قَالَ فَبِعِزَّتِكَ 82 He said, 'By Your might,

لَأُغْوِيَنَّهُمْ أَجْمَعِينَ ٨٢ I will surely pervert them,

إِلَّا عِبَادَكَ مِنْهُمُ ٱلْمُخْلَصِينَ ٨٣ 83 except Your exclusive servants among them.'

قَالَ فَٱلْحَقُّ ٨٤ 84 He said, 'The truth is that

وَٱلْحَقَّ أَقُولُ —and I speak the truth—

لَأَمْلَأَنَّ جَهَنَّمَ مِنكَ 85 I will fill hell with you

وَمِمَّن تَبِعَكَ مِنْهُمْ أَجْمَعِينَ ٨٥ and all of those who follow you.'[1]

---

[1] Cf. 7:18; 11:119; 32:13.

قُل مَّآ أَسْـَٔلُكُمْ عَلَيْهِ مِنْ أَجْرٍ 86 *Say,* 'I do not ask you any reward for it,

وَمَآ أَنَا۠ مِنَ ٱلْمُتَكَلِّفِينَ ⟨٨٦⟩ and I am no impostor.[1]

إِنْ هُوَ إِلَّا ذِكْرٌ لِّلْعَٰلَمِينَ 87 It is just a reminder for all the nations,

وَلَتَعْلَمُنَّ نَبَأَهُۥ بَعْدَ حِينٍ ⟨٨٨⟩ 88 and you will surely learn its tidings in due time.

سُورَةُ الزمر # 39. SŪRAT AL-ZUMAR[2]

بِسْمِ ٱللَّهِ In the Name of Allah,

ٱلرَّحْمَٰنِ ٱلرَّحِيمِ the All-beneficent, All-merciful

تَنزِيلُ ٱلْكِتَٰبِ مِنَ ٱللَّهِ 1 The [gradual] sending down of the Book is from Allah,

ٱلْعَزِيزِ ٱلْحَكِيمِ ⟨١⟩ the All-mighty, the All-wise.

إِنَّآ أَنزَلْنَآ إِلَيْكَ ٱلْكِتَٰبَ 2 Indeed We have sent down the Book to *you*

بِٱلْحَقِّ with the truth;

فَٱعْبُدِ ٱللَّهَ so worship Allah,

مُخْلِصًا لَّهُ ٱلدِّينَ ⟨٢⟩ putting exclusive faith[3] in Him.

أَلَا لِلَّهِ ٱلدِّينُ ٱلْخَالِصُ 3 Look! [Only] exclusive faith is worthy of Allah,

وَٱلَّذِينَ ٱتَّخَذُوا۟ مِن دُونِهِۦٓ أَوْلِيَآءَ and those who take guardians besides Him

مَا نَعْبُدُهُمْ إِلَّا [claiming,] 'We only worship them

لِيُقَرِّبُونَآ إِلَى ٱللَّهِ زُلْفَىٰٓ so that they may bring us near to Allah,'

إِنَّ ٱللَّهَ يَحْكُمُ بَيْنَهُمْ Allah will indeed judge between them

فِى مَا هُمْ فِيهِ يَخْتَلِفُونَ concerning that about which they differ.

إِنَّ ٱللَّهَ لَا يَهْدِى Indeed Allah does not guide

مَنْ هُوَ كَٰذِبٌ كَفَّارٌ ⟨٣⟩ someone who is a liar and an ingrate.

لَّوْ أَرَادَ ٱللَّهُ أَن يَتَّخِذَ وَلَدًا 4 Had Allah intended to take a son,

لَّٱصْطَفَىٰ مِمَّا يَخْلُقُ He could have chosen from those He has created

مَا يَشَآءُ whatever He wished.

---

[1] Or 'nor am I one of those who impose themselves [upon others].'

[2] The *sūrah* takes its name from verses 71 & 73 in which the word *zumar* (throngs) occurs.

[3] Or 'pure faith.'

سُبْحَـٰنَهُ

Immaculate is He!

هُوَ ٱللَّهُ ٱلْوَٰحِدُ ٱلْقَهَّارُ ۝

He is Allah, the One, the All-paramount.

خَلَقَ ٱلسَّمَٰوَٰتِ وَٱلْأَرْضَ بِٱلْحَقِّ

5 He created the heavens and the earth with the truth.

يُكَوِّرُ ٱلَّيْلَ عَلَى ٱلنَّهَارِ

He winds the night over the day,

وَيُكَوِّرُ ٱلنَّهَارَ عَلَى ٱلَّيْلِ

and winds the day over the night,

وَسَخَّرَ ٱلشَّمْسَ وَٱلْقَمَرَ

and He has disposed the sun and the moon,

كُلٌّ يَجْرِى لِأَجَلٍ مُّسَمًّى

each moving for a specified term.[1]

أَلَا هُوَ ٱلْعَزِيزُ ٱلْغَفَّٰرُ ۝

Look! He is the All-mighty, the All-forgiver!

خَلَقَكُم مِّن نَّفْسٍ وَٰحِدَةٍ

6 He created you from a single soul,

ثُمَّ جَعَلَ مِنْهَا زَوْجَهَا

then made from it its mate,

وَأَنزَلَ لَكُم

and He has sent down for you

مِّنَ ٱلْأَنْعَٰمِ ثَمَٰنِيَةَ أَزْوَٰجٍ

eight mates of the cattle.[2]

يَخْلُقُكُمْ فِى بُطُونِ أُمَّهَٰتِكُمْ

He creates you in the wombs of your mothers,

خَلْقًا مِّنْ بَعْدِ خَلْقٍ

creation after creation,

فِى ظُلُمَٰتٍ ثَلَٰثٍ

in a threefold darkness.

ذَٰلِكُمُ ٱللَّهُ رَبُّكُمْ

That is Allah, your Lord!

لَهُ ٱلْمُلْكُ

To Him belongs all sovereignty.

لَآ إِلَٰهَ إِلَّا هُوَ

There is no god except Him.

فَأَنَّىٰ تُصْرَفُونَ ۝

Then where are you being led away?

إِن تَكْفُرُوا

7 If you are ungrateful,[3]

فَإِنَّ ٱللَّهَ غَنِىٌّ عَنكُمْ

indeed Allah has no need of you,

وَلَا يَرْضَىٰ

though He does not approve

لِعِبَادِهِ ٱلْكُفْرَ

ingratitude for His servants;

وَإِن تَشْكُرُوا

and if you give thanks

يَرْضَهُ لَكُمْ

He approves that for you.

وَلَا تَزِرُ وَازِرَةٌ وِزْرَ أُخْرَىٰ

No bearer shall bear another's burden;

ثُمَّ إِلَىٰ رَبِّكُم مَّرْجِعُكُمْ

then to your Lord will be your return,

---

[1] Or 'until a specified time.'
[2] Cf. 6:143.
[3] Or 'faithless.'

فَيُنَبِّئُكُم

whereat He will inform you

بِمَا كُنتُمْ تَعْمَلُونَ

concerning what you used to do.

إِنَّهُۥ عَلِيمٌۢ بِذَاتِ ٱلصُّدُورِ ۝

Indeed He knows best what is in the breasts.

وَإِذَا مَسَّ ٱلْإِنسَـٰنَ ضُرٌّ دَعَا رَبَّهُۥ

8 When distress befalls man, he supplicates his Lord,

مُنِيبًا إِلَيْهِ

turning to Him penitently.

ثُمَّ إِذَا خَوَّلَهُۥ نِعْمَةً مِّنْهُ

Then, when He grants him a blessing from Himself,

نَسِىَ مَا كَانَ يَدْعُوٓاْ إِلَيْهِ

he forgets that for which he had supplicated Him

مِن قَبْلُ

before,[1]

وَجَعَلَ لِلَّهِ أَندَادًا

and sets up equals to Allah

لِّيُضِلَّ عَن سَبِيلِهِۦ

that he may lead [people] astray from His way.

قُلْ تَمَتَّعْ بِكُفْرِكَ قَلِيلًا

Say, 'Revel in your ingratitude[2] for a while.

إِنَّكَ مِنْ أَصْحَـٰبِ ٱلنَّارِ ۝

Indeed you are among the inmates of the Fire.'

أَمَّنْ هُوَ قَـٰنِتٌ ءَانَآءَ ٱلَّيْلِ

9 Is he who supplicates[3] in the watches of the night,

سَاجِدًا وَقَآئِمًا

prostrating and standing,

يَحْذَرُ ٱلْءَاخِرَةَ

apprehensive of the Hereafter

وَيَرْجُواْ رَحْمَةَ رَبِّهِۦ

and expecting the mercy of his Lord . . . ?[4]

قُلْ هَلْ يَسْتَوِى ٱلَّذِينَ يَعْلَمُونَ

Say, 'Are those who know equal

وَٱلَّذِينَ لَا يَعْلَمُونَ

to those who do not know?'

إِنَّمَا يَتَذَكَّرُ أُوْلُواْ ٱلْأَلْبَـٰبِ ۝

Only those who possess intellect take admonition.

قُلْ يَـٰعِبَادِ ٱلَّذِينَ ءَامَنُواْ

10 Say, [Allah declares:] 'O My servants who have faith!

ٱتَّقُواْ رَبَّكُمْ

Be wary of your Lord.

لِلَّذِينَ أَحْسَنُواْ فِى هَـٰذِهِ ٱلدُّنْيَا

For those who do good in this world

حَسَنَةٌ

there will be a good [reward],

وَأَرْضُ ٱللَّهِ وَٰسِعَةٌ

and Allah's earth is vast.

إِنَّمَا يُوَفَّى ٱلصَّـٰبِرُونَ أَجْرَهُم

Indeed the patient will be paid in full their reward

بِغَيْرِ حِسَابٍ ۝

without any reckoning.'

قُلْ إِنِّىٓ أُمِرْتُ

11 Say, 'Indeed I have been commanded

---

[1] Cf. 6:41.

[2] Or 'faithlessness.'

[3] Or 'is obedient.'

[4] Ellipsis. The omitted phrase is, 'like someone who is not such?'

أَنْ أَعْبُدَ ٱللَّهَ    to worship Allah

مُخْلِصًا لَّهُ ٱلدِّينَ ۞    with exclusive faith in Him,

وَأُمِرْتُ   12   and I have been commanded

لِأَنْ أَكُونَ أَوَّلَ ٱلْمُسْلِمِينَ ۞    to be the first of those who submit [to Him].'

قُلْ إِنِّي أَخَافُ إِنْ عَصَيْتُ رَبِّي   13   *Say,* 'Indeed, should I disobey my Lord, I fear

عَذَابَ يَوْمٍ عَظِيمٍ ۞    the punishment of a tremendous day.'

قُلِ ٱللَّهَ أَعْبُدُ   14   *Say,* '[Only] Allah do I worship,

مُخْلِصًا لَّهُ دِينِي ۞    putting my exclusive faith in Him.

فَٱعْبُدُوا مَا شِئْتُم مِّن دُونِهِ   15   You worship whatever you wish besides Him.'

قُلْ إِنَّ ٱلْخَٰسِرِينَ ٱلَّذِينَ    *Say,* 'Indeed the losers are those

خَسِرُوا أَنفُسَهُمْ وَأَهْلِيهِمْ    who ruin themselves and their families

يَوْمَ ٱلْقِيَٰمَةِ    on the Day of Resurrection.'

أَلَا ذَٰلِكَ هُوَ ٱلْخُسْرَانُ ٱلْمُبِينُ ۞    Look! That is the manifest loss!

لَهُم مِّن فَوْقِهِمْ ظُلَلٌ مِّنَ ٱلنَّارِ   16   There will be canopies of fire above them,

وَمِن تَحْتِهِمْ ظُلَلٌ    and [similar] canopies beneath them.

ذَٰلِكَ يُخَوِّفُ ٱللَّهُ بِهِ عِبَادَهُ    With that Allah deters His servants.

يَٰعِبَادِ فَٱتَّقُونِ ۞    So, My servants, be wary of Me!

وَٱلَّذِينَ   17   As for those who

ٱجْتَنَبُوا ٱلطَّٰغُوتَ أَن يَعْبُدُوهَا    stay clear of the worship of the Rebel

وَأَنَابُوا إِلَى ٱللَّهِ    and turn penitently to Allah,

لَهُمُ ٱلْبُشْرَىٰ    there is good news for them.

فَبَشِّرْ عِبَادِ ۞    So *give* good news to My servants

ٱلَّذِينَ يَسْتَمِعُونَ ٱلْقَوْلَ   18   who listen to the word [of Allah]

فَيَتَّبِعُونَ أَحْسَنَهُ    and follow the best [sense] of it.

أُولَٰئِكَ ٱلَّذِينَ هَدَىٰهُمُ ٱللَّهُ    They are the ones whom Allah has guided,

وَأُولَٰئِكَ هُمْ أُولُوا ٱلْأَلْبَٰبِ ۞    and it is they who possess intellect.

أَفَمَنْ   19   Can he

حَقَّ عَلَيْهِ كَلِمَةُ ٱلْعَذَابِ    against whom the word of punishment has become due?[1]

أَفَأَنتَ تُنقِذُ مَن فِي ٱلنَّارِ ۞    Can *you* rescue someone who is in the Fire?

---

[1] Ellipsis; the omitted phrase is, 'escape his punishment?'

20 But as for those who are wary of their Lord,

for them there will be lofty abodes

with [other] lofty abodes built above them,

with streams running beneath them

—a promise of Allah.

Allah does not break His promise.

21 Have you not seen

that Allah sends down water from the sky,

then He conducts it through the ground as springs.

Then with it He brings forth crops

of diverse hues.

Then they wither and you see them turn yellow.

Then He turns them into chaff.

There is indeed an admonition in that

for those who possess intellect.

22 Is someone whose breast Allah has opened to Islam

so that he follows a light from His Lord?[1]

So woe to those whose hearts have been hardened

to the remembrance of Allah.

They are in manifest error.

23 Allah has sent down the best of discourses,

a scripture [composed] of similar[2] motifs,

whereat quiver

the skins of those who fear their Lord,

then their skins and hearts soften

to Allah's remembrance.

That is Allah's guidance,

by which He guides whomever He wishes;

---

[1] Ellipsis. The omitted phrase is, 'like someone who is not such?'

[2] Or 'parallel motifs.'

وَمَن يُضْلِلِ ٱللَّهُ    and whomever Allah leads astray,

فَمَا لَهُ مِنْ هَادٍ ۞    has no guide.

أَفَمَن يَتَّقِى بِوَجْهِهِۦ   24 What! Is someone who fends off with his face

سُوٓءَ ٱلْعَذَابِ    the terrible punishment [meted out to him]

يَوْمَ ٱلْقِيَٰمَةِ    on the Day of Resurrection?[1]

وَقِيلَ لِلظَّٰلِمِينَ    And the wrongdoers will be told,

ذُوقُوا۟ مَا كُنتُمْ تَكْسِبُونَ ۞    'Taste what you used to earn.'

كَذَّبَ ٱلَّذِينَ مِن قَبْلِهِمْ   25 Those who were before them impugned [the apostles],

فَأَتَىٰهُمُ ٱلْعَذَابُ    whereat the punishment overtook them

مِنْ حَيْثُ لَا يَشْعُرُونَ ۞    whence they were not aware.

فَأَذَاقَهُمُ ٱللَّهُ ٱلْخِزْىَ   26 So Allah made them taste disgrace

فِى ٱلْحَيَوٰةِ ٱلدُّنْيَا    in the life of the world,

وَلَعَذَابُ ٱلْءَاخِرَةِ    and the punishment of the Hereafter will surely

أَكْبَرُ    be greater,

لَوْ كَانُوا۟ يَعْلَمُونَ ۞    had they known.

وَلَقَدْ ضَرَبْنَا لِلنَّاسِ   27 Certainly we have drawn for mankind

فِى هَٰذَا ٱلْقُرْءَانِ    in this Qur'ān

مِن كُلِّ مَثَلٍ    every [kind of] example,

لَّعَلَّهُمْ يَتَذَكَّرُونَ ۞    so that they may take admonition

قُرْءَانًا عَرَبِيًّا غَيْرَ ذِى عِوَجٍ   28 —an Arabic Qur'ān, without any deviousness,

لَّعَلَّهُمْ يَتَّقُونَ ۞    so that they may be Godwary.

ضَرَبَ ٱللَّهُ مَثَلًا   29 Allah draws an example:

رَّجُلًا فِيهِ شُرَكَآءُ مُتَشَٰكِسُونَ    a man jointly owned by several contending masters,

وَرَجُلًا سَلَمًا لِّرَجُلٍ    and a man belonging entirely to one man:

هَلْ يَسْتَوِيَانِ مَثَلًا    are the two equal in comparison?[2]

ٱلْحَمْدُ لِلَّهِ    All praise belongs to Allah!

بَلْ أَكْثَرُهُمْ لَا يَعْلَمُونَ ۞    But most of them do not know.

---

[1] Ellipsis. The omitted phrase is, 'like someone who is secure from any kind of punishment?'

[2] The parable compares the polytheist with the monotheist. The worshipper of multiple deities is likened to a slave trying to please several masters.

إِنَّكَ مَيِّتٌ 30 *You* will indeed die,

وَإِنَّهُم مَّيِّتُونَ ۩ and they [too] will die indeed.

ثُمَّ إِنَّكُمْ يَوْمَ ٱلْقِيَمَةِ 31 Then on the Day of Resurrection you will indeed

عِندَ رَبِّكُمْ تَخْتَصِمُونَ ۩ contend before your Lord.

[PART 24]

فَمَنْ أَظْلَمُ 32 So who is a greater wrongdoer

مِمَّن كَذَبَ عَلَى ٱللَّهِ than him who attributes a falsehood to Allah,

وَكَذَّبَ بِٱلصِّدْقِ إِذْ جَاءَهُۥ and denies the truth when it reaches him?

أَلَيْسَ فِى جَهَنَّمَ مَثْوًى لِّلْكَفِرِينَ ۩ Is not the [final] abode of the faithless in hell?

وَٱلَّذِى جَاءَ بِٱلصِّدْقِ 33 He who brings the truth

وَصَدَّقَ بِهِۦٓ and he who confirms it

أُوْلَٰٓئِكَ هُمُ ٱلْمُتَّقُونَ ۩ —it is they who are the Godwary.

لَهُم مَّا يَشَاءُونَ عِندَ رَبِّهِمْ 34 They will have whatever they wish near their Lord.

ذَٰلِكَ جَزَاءُ ٱلْمُحْسِنِينَ ۩ That is the reward of the virtuous,

لِيُكَفِّرَ ٱللَّهُ عَنْهُمْ 35 so that Allah may absolve them of

أَسْوَأَ ٱلَّذِى عَمِلُوا۟ the worst of what they did,

وَيَجْزِيَهُمْ أَجْرَهُم and pay them their reward

بِأَحْسَنِ ٱلَّذِى كَانُوا۟ يَعْمَلُونَ ۩ by the best of what they used to do.

أَلَيْسَ ٱللَّهُ بِكَافٍ عَبْدَهُۥ 36 Does not Allah suffice [to defend] His servant?

وَيُخَوِّفُونَكَ بِٱلَّذِينَ مِن دُونِهِۦ They[1] would frighten *you* of others than Him.

وَمَن يُضْلِلِ ٱللَّهُ Yet whomever Allah leads astray,

فَمَا لَهُۥ مِنْ هَادٍ ۩ has no guide,

وَمَن يَهْدِ ٱللَّهُ 37 and whomever Allah guides,

فَمَا لَهُۥ مِن مُّضِلٍّ there is no one who can lead him astray.

أَلَيْسَ ٱللَّهُ بِعَزِيزٍ ذِى ٱنتِقَامٍ ۩ Is not Allah an all-mighty avenger?

وَلَئِن سَأَلْتَهُم 38 If you ask them,

مَّنْ خَلَقَ ٱلسَّمَٰوَٰتِ وَٱلْأَرْضَ 'Who created the heavens and the earth?'

لَيَقُولُنَّ ٱللَّهُ they will surely say, 'Allah.'

---

[1] That is, the idolaters, who threatened the Prophet with the vengeance of their gods.

قُلْ أَفَرَءَيْتُم    *Say*, 'Have you considered

مَّا تَدْعُونَ مِن دُونِ ٱللَّهِ    what you invoke besides Allah?

إِنْ أَرَادَنِيَ ٱللَّهُ بِضُرٍّ    Should Allah desire some distress for me,

هَلْ هُنَّ كَشِفَتُ ضُرِّهِ    can they remove the distress visited by Him?

أَوْ أَرَادَنِي بِرَحْمَةٍ    Or should He desire some mercy for me,

هَلْ هُنَّ مُمْسِكَتُ رَحْمَتِهِ    can they withhold His mercy?'

قُلْ حَسْبِيَ ٱللَّهُ    *Say*, 'Allah is sufficient for me.

عَلَيْهِ يَتَوَكَّلُ ٱلْمُتَوَكِّلُونَ ٣٨    In Him let all the trusting put their trust.'

قُلْ يَٰقَوْمِ    39 *Say*, 'O my people!

ٱعْمَلُوا۟ عَلَىٰ مَكَانَتِكُمْ    Act according to your ability.

إِنِّي عَٰمِلٌ    I too am acting.

فَسَوْفَ تَعْلَمُونَ ٣٩    Soon you will know

مَن يَأْتِيهِ عَذَابٌ    40 who will be overtaken by a punishment

يُخْزِيهِ    that will disgrace him,

وَيَحِلُّ عَلَيْهِ عَذَابٌ مُّقِيمٌ ٤٠    and on whom a lasting punishment will descend.'

إِنَّآ أَنزَلْنَا عَلَيْكَ ٱلْكِتَٰبَ    41 Indeed We have sent down the Book to *you*

لِلنَّاسِ    for [the deliverance of] mankind

بِٱلْحَقِّ    with the truth.

فَمَنِ ٱهْتَدَىٰ فَلِنَفْسِهِ    So whoever is guided is guided for his own sake,

وَمَن ضَلَّ    and whoever goes astray,

فَإِنَّمَا يَضِلُّ عَلَيْهَا    goes astray to his own detriment,

وَمَآ أَنتَ عَلَيْهِم بِوَكِيلٍ ٤١    and it is not *your* duty to watch over them.

ٱللَّهُ يَتَوَفَّى ٱلْأَنفُسَ    42 Allah takes the souls

حِينَ مَوْتِهَا    at the time of their death,

وَٱلَّتِى لَمْ تَمُتْ    and those that have not died

فِى مَنَامِهَا    in their sleep.

فَيُمْسِكُ ٱلَّتِى    Then He retains those

قَضَىٰ عَلَيْهَا ٱلْمَوْتَ    for whom He has ordained death

وَيُرْسِلُ ٱلْأُخْرَىٰ    and releases the others

إِلَىٰٓ أَجَلٍ مُّسَمًّى

until a specified time.

إِنَّ فِى ذَٰلِكَ لَءَايَٰتٍ

There are indeed signs in that

لِّقَوْمٍ يَتَفَكَّرُونَ ۝

for a people who reflect.

أَمِ ٱتَّخَذُوا۟ مِن دُونِ ٱللَّهِ شُفَعَآءَ

43 Have they taken intercessors besides Allah?

قُلْ

Say,

أَوَلَوْ كَانُوا۟ لَا يَمْلِكُونَ شَيْـًٔا

'What! Even though they have no control over anything

وَلَا يَعْقِلُونَ ۝

and cannot apply reason?!'

قُل لِّلَّهِ ٱلشَّفَٰعَةُ جَمِيعًا

44 Say, 'All intercession rests with Allah.

لَّهُۥ مُلْكُ ٱلسَّمَٰوَٰتِ وَٱلْأَرْضِ

To Him belongs the kingdom of the heavens and the earth;

ثُمَّ إِلَيْهِ تُرْجَعُونَ ۝

then you will be brought back to Him.

وَإِذَا ذُكِرَ ٱللَّهُ وَحْدَهُ

45 When Allah is mentioned alone,

ٱشْمَأَزَّتْ قُلُوبُ ٱلَّذِينَ

[thereat] shrink away the hearts of those

لَا يُؤْمِنُونَ بِٱلْءَاخِرَةِ

who do not believe in the Hereafter,

وَإِذَا ذُكِرَ ٱلَّذِينَ مِن دُونِهِۦٓ

but when others are mentioned besides Him,

إِذَا هُمْ يَسْتَبْشِرُونَ ۝

behold, they rejoice!

قُلِ ٱللَّهُمَّ

46 Say, 'O Allah!

فَاطِرَ ٱلسَّمَٰوَٰتِ وَٱلْأَرْضِ

Originator of the heavens and the earth,

عَٰلِمَ ٱلْغَيْبِ وَٱلشَّهَٰدَةِ

Knower of the sensible and the Unseen,

أَنتَ تَحْكُمُ بَيْنَ عِبَادِكَ

You will judge between Your servants

فِى مَا كَانُوا۟ فِيهِ يَخْتَلِفُونَ ۝

concerning that about which they used to differ.'

وَلَوْ أَنَّ لِلَّذِينَ ظَلَمُوا۟

47 Even if the wrongdoers possessed

مَا فِى ٱلْأَرْضِ جَمِيعًا

all that is on the earth,

وَمِثْلَهُۥ مَعَهُۥ

and as much of it besides,

لَٱفْتَدَوْا۟ بِهِۦ

they would surely offer it to redeem themselves with it

مِن سُوٓءِ ٱلْعَذَابِ

from a terrible punishment

يَوْمَ ٱلْقِيَٰمَةِ

on the Day of Resurrection,

وَبَدَا لَهُم مِّنَ ٱللَّهِ

and there will appear to them from Allah

مَا لَمْ يَكُونُوا يَحْتَسِبُونَ ۝     what they had never reckoned.

وَبَدَا لَهُمْ سَيِّئَاتُ مَا كَسَبُوا     48 The evils of what they had earned will appear to them,

وَحَاقَ بِهِم     and they will be besieged

مَّا كَانُوا بِهِۦ يَسْتَهْزِءُونَ ۝     by what they used to deride.

فَإِذَا مَسَّ ٱلْإِنسَٰنَ ضُرٌّ دَعَانَا     49 When distress befalls man, he supplicates Us.

ثُمَّ إِذَا خَوَّلْنَٰهُ نِعْمَةً مِّنَّا     Then, when We grant him a blessing from Us,

قَالَ إِنَّمَآ أُوتِيتُهُۥ عَلَىٰ عِلْمٍ     he says, 'I was given it by virtue of [my] knowledge.'

بَلْ هِيَ فِتْنَةٌ     Rather it is a test,

وَلَٰكِنَّ أَكْثَرَهُمْ لَا يَعْلَمُونَ ۝     but most of them do not know.

قَدْ قَالَهَا ٱلَّذِينَ مِن قَبْلِهِمْ     50 Those who were before them [also] said that,

فَمَآ أَغْنَىٰ عَنْهُم مَّا كَانُوا يَكْسِبُونَ ۝     but what they used to earn did not avail them.

فَأَصَابَهُمْ سَيِّئَاتُ مَا كَسَبُوا     51 So the evils of what they had earned visited them,

وَٱلَّذِينَ ظَلَمُوا مِنْ هَٰؤُلَآءِ     and as for the wrongdoers among these,

سَيُصِيبُهُمْ سَيِّئَاتُ مَا كَسَبُوا     the evils of what they earn shall be visited on them

وَمَا هُم بِمُعْجِزِينَ ۝     and they will not thwart [Allah's might].

أَوَلَمْ يَعْلَمُوٓا     52 Do they not know

أَنَّ ٱللَّهَ يَبْسُطُ ٱلرِّزْقَ     that Allah expands the provision

لِمَن يَشَآءُ     for whomever He wishes

وَيَقْدِرُ     and tightens it [for whomever He wishes]?

إِنَّ فِي ذَٰلِكَ لَآيَٰتٍ     There are indeed signs in that

لِّقَوْمٍ يُؤْمِنُونَ ۝ ❉     for a people who have faith.

قُلْ يَٰعِبَادِىَ     53 Say [that Allah declares,] 'O My servants

ٱلَّذِينَ أَسْرَفُوا     who have committed excesses

عَلَىٰ أَنفُسِهِمْ     against their own souls,

لَا تَقْنَطُوا مِن رَّحْمَةِ ٱللَّهِ     do not despair of the mercy of Allah.

إِنَّ ٱللَّهَ يَغْفِرُ ٱلذُّنُوبَ جَمِيعًا     Indeed Allah will forgive all sins.

إِنَّهُۥ هُوَ ٱلْغَفُورُ ٱلرَّحِيمُ ۝     Indeed He is the All-forgiving, the All-merciful.

وَأَنِيبُوٓا إِلَىٰ رَبِّكُمْ وَأَسْلِمُوا لَهُۥ     54 Turn penitently to Him and submit to Him

مِن قَبْلِ أَن يَأْتِيَكُمُ ٱلْعَذَابُ     before the punishment overtakes you, whereupon you will not be helped.

55 And follow

the best of what has been sent down to you

from your Lord,

before the punishment overtakes you suddenly

while you are unaware.'

56 Lest anyone should say,

'Alas for my negligence

in the vicinage of Allah!

Indeed I was among those who ridiculed.'

57 Or say, 'Had Allah guided me

I would have surely been among the Godwary!'

58 Or say, when he sights the punishment,

'If only there had been a second chance for me

I would be among the virtuous!'

59 'Yes, My signs certainly came to you,

but you denied them and acted arrogantly

and you were among the faithless.'

60 On the Day of Resurrection *you* will see

those who attributed lies to Allah

with their faces blackened.

Is not the [final] abode of the arrogant in hell?

61 Allah will deliver those who were Godwary

with their salvation.

No ill shall touch them,

nor will they grieve.

62 Allah is creator of all things,

and He watches over all things.

63 To Him belong the keys of the heavens

وَٱلْأَرْضِ     and the earth,

وَٱلَّذِينَ كَفَرُوا بِـَٔايَٰتِ ٱللَّهِ     and those who disbelieve in the signs of Allah

أُو۟لَٰئِكَ هُمُ ٱلْخَٰسِرُونَ ﴿٦٣﴾     —it is they who are the losers.

قُلْ     64 *Say*,

أَفَغَيْرَ ٱللَّهِ تَأْمُرُونِّىٓ أَعْبُدُ     'Will you, then, bid me to worship other than Allah,

أَيُّهَا ٱلْجَٰهِلُونَ ﴿﴾     O you senseless ones?!'

وَلَقَدْ أُوحِىَ إِلَيْكَ     65 Certainly it has been revealed to *you*

وَإِلَى ٱلَّذِينَ مِن قَبْلِكَ     and to those [who have been] before *you*:

لَئِنْ أَشْرَكْتَ     'If you ascribe a partner to Allah

لَيَحْبَطَنَّ عَمَلُكَ     your works shall fail

وَلَتَكُونَنَّ مِنَ ٱلْخَٰسِرِينَ ﴿﴾     and you shall surely be among the losers.

بَلِ ٱللَّهَ فَٱعْبُدْ     66 Rather, worship Allah,

وَكُن مِّنَ ٱلشَّٰكِرِينَ ﴿٦٦﴾     and be among the grateful!'

وَمَا قَدَرُوا۟ ٱللَّهَ     67 They do not regard Allah

حَقَّ قَدْرِهِۦ     with the regard due to Him,

وَٱلْأَرْضُ جَمِيعًا قَبْضَتُهُۥ     yet the entire earth will be in His fist

يَوْمَ ٱلْقِيَٰمَةِ     on the Day of Resurrection,

وَٱلسَّمَٰوَٰتُ مَطْوِيَّٰتٌۢ بِيَمِينِهِۦ     and the heavens, scrolled, in His right hand.

سُبْحَٰنَهُۥ     Immaculate is He

وَتَعَٰلَىٰ     and exalted

عَمَّا يُشْرِكُونَ ﴿٦٧﴾     above [having] any partners that they ascribe [to Him].

وَنُفِخَ فِى ٱلصُّورِ     68 And the Trumpet will be blown,

فَصَعِقَ مَن فِى ٱلسَّمَٰوَٰتِ     and whoever is in the heavens will swoon

وَمَن فِى ٱلْأَرْضِ     and whoever is on the earth,

إِلَّا مَن شَآءَ ٱللَّهُ     except whomever Allah wishes.

ثُمَّ نُفِخَ فِيهِ أُخْرَىٰ     Then it will be blown a second time,

فَإِذَا هُمْ قِيَامٌ يَنظُرُونَ ﴿﴾     behold, they will rise up, looking on!

وَأَشْرَقَتِ ٱلْأَرْضُ     69 And the earth will glow

بِنُورِ رَبِّهَا     with the light of her Lord,

وَوُضِعَ ٱلْكِتَـٰبُ     and the Book[1] will be set up,

وَجِاْىَءَ بِٱلنَّبِيِّـۧنَ وَٱلشُّهَدَآءِ     and the prophets and the martyrs[2] will be brought,

وَقُضِىَ بَيْنَهُم     and judgment will be made between them

بِٱلْحَقِّ     justly,

وَهُمْ لَا يُظْلَمُونَ ۝     and they will not be wronged.

وَوُفِّيَتْ كُلُّ نَفْسٍ     70 Every soul will be recompensed fully

مَّا عَمِلَتْ     for what it has done,

وَهُوَ أَعْلَمُ بِمَا يَفْعَلُونَ ۝     and He is best aware of what they do.

وَسِيقَ ٱلَّذِينَ كَفَرُوٓاْ إِلَىٰ جَهَنَّمَ     71 The faithless will be driven to hell

زُمَرًا ۖ     in throngs.

حَتَّىٰٓ إِذَا جَآءُوهَا     When they reach it,

فُتِحَتْ أَبْوَٰبُهَا     and its gates are opened,

وَقَالَ لَهُمْ خَزَنَتُهَآ     its keepers will say to them,

أَلَمْ يَأْتِكُمْ رُسُلٌ     'Did there not come to you [any] apostles

مِّنكُمْ     from among yourselves,

يَتْلُونَ عَلَيْكُمْ ءَايَـٰتِ رَبِّكُمْ     reciting to you the signs of your Lord

وَيُنذِرُونَكُمْ     and warning you

لِقَآءَ يَوْمِكُمْ هَـٰذَا ۚ     of the encounter of this day of yours?'

قَالُواْ بَلَىٰ     They will say, 'Yes,

وَلَـٰكِنْ حَقَّتْ كَلِمَةُ ٱلْعَذَابِ     but the word of punishment became due

عَلَى ٱلْكَـٰفِرِينَ ۝     against the faithless.'

قِيلَ ٱدْخُلُوٓاْ أَبْوَٰبَ جَهَنَّمَ     72 It will be said, 'Enter the gates of hell

خَـٰلِدِينَ فِيهَا ۖ     to remain in it [forever].

فَبِئْسَ مَثْوَى ٱلْمُتَكَبِّرِينَ ۝     Evil is the [ultimate] abode of the arrogant.

وَسِيقَ ٱلَّذِينَ ٱتَّقَوْاْ رَبَّهُمْ     73 Those who are wary of their Lord will be led

إِلَى ٱلْجَنَّةِ زُمَرًا ۖ     to paradise in throngs.

حَتَّىٰٓ إِذَا جَآءُوهَا     When they reach it,

وَفُتِحَتْ أَبْوَٰبُهَا     and its gates are opened,

---

[1] That is, the record of the people's deeds.
[2] Or 'the witnesses.'

وَقَالَ لَهُمْ خَزَنَتُهَا its keepers will say to them,

سَلَمٌ عَلَيْكُمْ 'Peace be to you!

طِبْتُمْ You are welcome![1]

فَادْخُلُوهَا خَلِدِينَ ۝ Enter it to remain [forever].'

وَقَالُوا ٱلْحَمْدُ لِلَّهِ 74 They will say, 'All praise belongs to Allah,

ٱلَّذِى صَدَقَنَا وَعْدَهُ who has fulfilled His promise to us

وَأَوْرَثَنَا ٱلْأَرْضَ and made us heirs to the earth,

نَتَبَوَّأُ مِنَ ٱلْجَنَّةِ that we may settle in paradise

حَيْثُ نَشَاءُ wherever we may wish!'

فَنِعْمَ أَجْرُ How excellent is the reward

ٱلْعَمِلِينَ ۝ of the workers [of righteousness]!

وَتَرَى ٱلْمَلَٰئِكَةَ 75 And *you* will see the angels

حَافِّينَ مِنْ حَوْلِ ٱلْعَرْشِ surrounding all round the Throne,

يُسَبِّحُونَ بِحَمْدِ رَبِّهِمْ celebrating the praise of their Lord,

وَقُضِىَ بَيْنَهُم بِٱلْحَقِّ and judgment will be made between them justly,

وَقِيلَ ٱلْحَمْدُ لِلَّهِ and it will be said, 'All praise belongs to Allah,

رَبِّ ٱلْعَٰلَمِينَ ۝ the Lord of all the worlds!

## سُورَةُ غَافِر    40. SŪRAT GHĀFIR[2]

بِسْمِ ٱللَّهِ In the Name of Allah,

ٱلرَّحْمَٰنِ ٱلرَّحِيمِ the All-beneficent, the All-merciful.

حٰم ۝ 1 *Ḥā, Mīm*:

تَنزِيلُ ٱلْكِتَٰبِ مِنَ ٱللَّهِ 2 The [gradual] sending down of the Book is from Allah,

ٱلْعَزِيزِ ٱلْعَلِيمِ ۝ the All-mighty, the All-knowing,

غَافِرِ ٱلذَّنۢبِ وَقَابِلِ ٱلتَّوْبِ 3 forgiver of sins and acceptor of repentance,

---

[1] Or 'You are excellent!' Or 'You have been pure.'

[2] The *sūrah* takes its name from the phrase "*ghāfir al-dhanb*" (forgiver of sins) which occurs in verse 3.

| | |
|---|---|
| شَدِيدِ ٱلۡعِقَابِ ذِى ٱلطَّوۡلِ | severe in retribution, [yet] all-bountiful, |
| لَآ إِلَـٰهَ إِلَّا هُوَ | there is no god except Him, |
| إِلَيۡهِ ٱلۡمَصِيرُ ۝ | [and] toward Him is the destination. |
| مَا يُجَـٰدِلُ فِىٓ ءَايَـٰتِ ٱللَّهِ | 4 No one disputes the signs of Allah |
| إِلَّا ٱلَّذِينَ كَفَرُواْ | except the faithless. |
| فَلَا يَغۡرُرۡكَ تَقَلُّبُهُمۡ فِى ٱلۡبِلَـٰدِ ۝ | So do not be misled by their bustle in the towns. |
| كَذَّبَتۡ قَبۡلَهُمۡ قَوۡمُ نُوحٍ | 5 The people of Noah denied before them |
| وَٱلۡأَحۡزَابُ مِنۢ بَعۡدِهِمۡ | and the [heathen] factions [who came] after them. |
| وَهَمَّتۡ كُلُّ أُمَّةٍ بِرَسُولِهِمۡ لِيَأۡخُذُوهُ | Every nation attempted to lay hands on their apostle, |
| وَجَـٰدَلُواْ بِٱلۡبَـٰطِلِ | and disputed erroneously |
| لِيُدۡحِضُواْ بِهِ ٱلۡحَقَّ | to refute the truth. |
| فَأَخَذۡتُهُمۡ | Then I seized them; |
| فَكَيۡفَ كَانَ عِقَابِ ۝ | so how was My retribution?! |
| وَكَذَٰلِكَ حَقَّتۡ كَلِمَتُ رَبِّكَ | 6 That is how the word of _your_ Lord became due |
| عَلَى ٱلَّذِينَ كَفَرُوٓاْ | concerning the faithless, |
| أَنَّهُمۡ أَصۡحَـٰبُ ٱلنَّارِ ۝ | that they shall be inmates of the Fire. |
| ٱلَّذِينَ يَحۡمِلُونَ ٱلۡعَرۡشَ | 7 Those who bear the Throne, |
| وَمَنۡ حَوۡلَهُۥ | and those around it, |
| يُسَبِّحُونَ بِحَمۡدِ رَبِّهِمۡ | celebrate the praise of their Lord |
| وَيُؤۡمِنُونَ بِهِۦ | and have faith in Him, |
| وَيَسۡتَغۡفِرُونَ لِلَّذِينَ ءَامَنُواْ | and they plead for forgiveness for the faithful: |
| رَبَّنَا | 'Our Lord! |
| وَسِعۡتَ كُلَّ شَىۡءٍ | You comprehend all things |
| رَّحۡمَةً وَعِلۡمًا | in mercy and knowledge. |
| فَٱغۡفِرۡ لِلَّذِينَ تَابُواْ | So forgive those who repent |
| وَٱتَّبَعُواْ سَبِيلَكَ | and follow Your way |
| وَقِهِمۡ عَذَابَ ٱلۡجَحِيمِ ۝ | and save them from the punishment of hell. |
| رَبَّنَا | 8 Our Lord! |
| وَأَدۡخِلۡهُمۡ جَنَّـٰتِ عَدۡنٍ | Admit them into the Gardens of Eden, |
| ٱلَّتِى وَعَدتَّهُمۡ | which You have promised them, |

وَمَن صَلَحَ مِنْ ءَابَآئِهِمْ along with whoever is righteous among their forebears,

وَأَزْوَٰجِهِمْ وَذُرِّيَّٰتِهِمْ their spouses and their descendants.[1]

إِنَّكَ أَنتَ ٱلْعَزِيزُ ٱلْحَكِيمُ ٨ Indeed You are the All-mighty, the All-wise.

وَقِهِمُ ٱلسَّيِّـَٔاتِ 9 Save them from the ills;

وَمَن تَقِ ٱلسَّيِّـَٔاتِ يَوْمَئِذٍ and whomever You save from the ills that day,[2]

فَقَدْ رَحِمْتَهُۥ You will have had mercy upon him,

وَذَٰلِكَ هُوَ ٱلْفَوْزُ ٱلْعَظِيمُ ٩ and that is the great success.'

إِنَّ ٱلَّذِينَ كَفَرُوا۟ يُنَادَوْنَ 10 Indeed it will be proclaimed to the faithless:

لَمَقْتُ ٱللَّهِ أَكْبَرُ 'Surely Allah's outrage toward you is greater

مِن مَّقْتِكُمْ أَنفُسَكُمْ than your outrage toward yourselves,

إِذْ تُدْعَوْنَ إِلَى ٱلْإِيمَٰنِ as you were invited to faith,

فَتَكْفُرُونَ ١٠ but you disbelieved.'

قَالُوا۟ رَبَّنَآ 11 They will say, 'Our Lord!

أَمَتَّنَا ٱثْنَتَيْنِ Twice did You make us die,

وَأَحْيَيْتَنَا ٱثْنَتَيْنِ and twice did You give us life.

فَٱعْتَرَفْنَا بِذُنُوبِنَا We admit our sins.

فَهَلْ إِلَىٰ خُرُوجٍ مِّن سَبِيلٍ ١١ Is there any way out [from this plight]?'

ذَٰلِكُم بِأَنَّهُۥٓ 12 This [plight of yours] is because,

إِذَا دُعِيَ ٱللَّهُ وَحْدَهُۥ when Allah was invoked alone,

كَفَرْتُمْ you would disbelieve,

وَإِن يُشْرَكْ بِهِۦ but if partners were ascribed to Him

تُؤْمِنُوا۟ you would believe.

فَٱلْحُكْمُ لِلَّهِ So the judgment belongs to Allah,

ٱلْعَلِىِّ ٱلْكَبِيرِ ١٢ the All-exalted, the All-great.'

هُوَ ٱلَّذِى يُرِيكُمْ ءَايَٰتِهِۦ 13 It is He who shows you His signs

وَيُنَزِّلُ لَكُم مِّنَ ٱلسَّمَآءِ رِزْقًا and sends down for you provision from the sky.

وَمَا يَتَذَكَّرُ Yet no one takes admonition

إِلَّا مَن يُنِيبُ ١٣ except him who returns penitently [to Allah].

---

[1] Cf. 13:23.

[2] That is, the day of judgment.

فَٱدۡعُوا۟ ٱللَّهَ مُخۡلِصِينَ لَهُ ٱلدِّينَ ١٤ So supplicate Allah, putting exclusive faith in Him,

وَلَوۡ كَرِهَ ٱلۡكَٰفِرُونَ ۞ though the faithless should be averse.

رَفِيعُ ٱلدَّرَجَٰتِ ذُو ٱلۡعَرۡشِ ١٥ Raiser of ranks, Lord of the Throne,

يُلۡقِى ٱلرُّوحَ مِنۡ أَمۡرِهِۦ He casts the Spirit of His command

عَلَىٰ مَن يَشَآءُ مِنۡ عِبَادِهِۦ upon whomever of His servants that He wishes,

لِيُنذِرَ يَوۡمَ ٱلتَّلَاقِ ۞ that he may warn [people] of the Day of Encounter.

يَوۡمَ هُم بَٰرِزُونَ ١٦ The day when they will emerge [from their graves],

لَا يَخۡفَىٰ عَلَى ٱللَّهِ مِنۡهُمۡ شَىۡءٌ nothing about them will be hidden from Allah.

لِّمَنِ ٱلۡمُلۡكُ ٱلۡيَوۡمَ 'To whom does the sovereignty belong today?'

لِلَّهِ ٱلۡوَٰحِدِ ٱلۡقَهَّارِ ۞ 'To Allah, the One, the All-paramount!'

ٱلۡيَوۡمَ تُجۡزَىٰ كُلُّ نَفۡسٍۭ ١٧ 'Today every soul shall be requited

بِمَا كَسَبَتۡ for what it has earned.

لَا ظُلۡمَ ٱلۡيَوۡمَ There will be no injustice today.

إِنَّ ٱللَّهَ سَرِيعُ ٱلۡحِسَابِ ۞ Indeed Allah is swift at reckoning.'

وَأَنذِرۡهُمۡ يَوۡمَ ٱلۡءَازِفَةِ ١٨ Warn them of the Imminent Day[1]

إِذِ ٱلۡقُلُوبُ لَدَى ٱلۡحَنَاجِرِ when the hearts will be at the throats,

كَٰظِمِينَ choking with suppressed agony,

مَا لِلظَّٰلِمِينَ مِنۡ حَمِيمٍ [and] the wrongdoers will have no sympathizer,

وَلَا شَفِيعٍ يُطَاعُ ۞ nor any intercessor who might be heard.

يَعۡلَمُ خَآئِنَةَ ٱلۡأَعۡيُنِ ١٩ He knows the treachery of the eyes,[2]

وَمَا تُخۡفِى ٱلصُّدُورُ ۞ and what the breasts hide.

وَٱللَّهُ يَقۡضِى بِٱلۡحَقِّ ٢٠ Allah judges with truth,[3]

وَٱلَّذِينَ يَدۡعُونَ مِن دُونِهِۦ while those whom they invoke besides Him

لَا يَقۡضُونَ بِشَىۡءٍ do not judge by anything.

إِنَّ ٱللَّهَ هُوَ ٱلسَّمِيعُ Indeed it is Allah who is the All-hearing,

ٱلۡبَصِيرُ ۞ the All-seeing.

أَوَلَمۡ يَسِيرُوا۟ فِى ٱلۡأَرۡضِ ٢١ Have they not traveled over the land

---

[1] Cf. 'the Imminent [Hour]' (53:57).

[2] That is, the sins committed by the eyes.

[3] Or 'judges justly.'

| | |
|---|---|
| فَيَنظُرُواْ | so that they may observe |
| كَيْفَ كَانَ عَٰقِبَةُ ٱلَّذِينَ | how was the fate of those |
| كَانُواْ مِن قَبْلِهِمْ | who were before them? |
| كَانُواْ هُمْ أَشَدَّ مِنْهُمْ قُوَّةً | They were greater than them in might |
| وَءَاثَارًا | and with respect to the effects [they left] |
| فِى ٱلْأَرْضِ | in the land. |
| فَأَخَذَهُمُ ٱللَّهُ بِذُنُوبِهِمْ | But then Allah seized them for their sins, |
| وَمَا كَانَ لَهُم مِّنَ ٱللَّهِ مِن وَاقٍ ۝ | and they had no defender against Allah['s punishment]. |
| ذَٰلِكَ بِأَنَّهُمْ كَانَت تَّأْتِيهِمْ رُسُلُهُم | 22 That was because their apostles used to bring them |
| بِٱلْبَيِّنَٰتِ | manifest proofs, |
| فَكَفَرُواْ | but they defied [them]. |
| فَأَخَذَهُمُ ٱللَّهُ | So Allah seized them. |
| إِنَّهُ قَوِىٌّ شَدِيدُ ٱلْعِقَابِ ۝ | Indeed He is all-strong, severe in retribution. |
| وَلَقَدْ أَرْسَلْنَا مُوسَىٰ بِـَٔايَٰتِنَا | 23 Certainly We sent Moses with Our signs |
| وَسُلْطَٰنٍ مُّبِينٍ ۝ | and a manifest authority |
| إِلَىٰ فِرْعَوْنَ وَهَٰمَٰنَ وَقَٰرُونَ | 24 to Pharaoh, Hāmān and Korah, |
| فَقَالُواْ سَٰحِرٌ كَذَّابٌ ۝ | but they said, 'A magician, a mendacious liar.' |
| فَلَمَّا جَآءَهُم بِٱلْحَقِّ مِنْ عِندِنَا | 25 So when he brought them the truth from Us, |
| قَالُواْ | they said, |
| ٱقْتُلُوٓاْ أَبْنَآءَ ٱلَّذِينَ ءَامَنُواْ مَعَهُ | 'Kill the sons of the faithful who are with him, |
| وَٱسْتَحْيُواْ نِسَآءَهُمْ | and spare their women.' |
| وَمَا كَيْدُ ٱلْكَٰفِرِينَ إِلَّا فِى ضَلَٰلٍ ۝ | But the stratagems[1] of the faithless only go awry. |
| وَقَالَ فِرْعَوْنُ | 26 And Pharaoh said, |
| ذَرُونِىٓ أَقْتُلْ مُوسَىٰ | 'Let me slay Moses, |
| وَلْيَدْعُ رَبَّهُۥٓ | and let him invoke his Lord. |
| إِنِّىٓ أَخَافُ أَن يُبَدِّلَ دِينَكُمْ | Indeed I fear that he will change your religion, |
| أَوْ أَن يُظْهِرَ فِى ٱلْأَرْضِ ٱلْفَسَادَ ۝ | or bring forth corruption in the land.' |
| وَقَالَ مُوسَىٰٓ | 27 Moses said, |

---

[1] Or 'the guile of the faithless.'

إِنِّى عُذۡتُ بِرَبِّى
'Indeed I seek the protection of my Lord

وَرَبِّكُم
and your Lord

مِّن كُلِّ مُتَكَبِّرٍ
from every arrogant one

لَّا يُؤۡمِنُ بِيَوۡمِ ٱلۡحِسَابِ ۝
who does not believe in the Day of Reckoning.'

وَقَالَ رَجُلٌ مُّؤۡمِنٌ مِّنۡ ءَالِ فِرۡعَوۡنَ
28 Said a man of faith from Pharaoh's clan,

يَكۡتُمُ إِيمَٰنَهُۥٓ
who concealed his faith,

أَتَقۡتُلُونَ رَجُلًا أَن يَقُولَ
'Will you kill a man for saying,

رَبِّىَ ٱللَّهُ
"My Lord is Allah,"

وَقَدۡ جَآءَكُم بِٱلۡبَيِّنَٰتِ
while he certainly brings you manifest proofs

مِن رَّبِّكُمۡ
from your Lord?

وَإِن يَكُ كَٰذِبًا
Should he be lying,

فَعَلَيۡهِ كَذِبُهُۥ
his falsehood will be to his own detriment;

وَإِن يَكُ صَادِقًا
but if he is truthful,

يُصِبۡكُم
there shall visit you

بَعۡضُ ٱلَّذِى يَعِدُكُمۡ
some of what he promises you.

إِنَّ ٱللَّهَ لَا يَهۡدِى
Indeed Allah does not guide

مَنۡ هُوَ مُسۡرِفٌ كَذَّابٌ ۝
someone who is a profligate, a liar.

يَٰقَوۡمِ
29 O my people!

لَكُمُ ٱلۡمُلۡكُ ٱلۡيَوۡمَ
Today sovereignty belongs to you,[1]

ظَٰهِرِينَ فِى ٱلۡأَرۡضِ
and you are dominant in the land.

فَمَن يَنصُرُنَا مِنۢ بَأۡسِ ٱللَّهِ
But who will help us against Allah's punishment

إِن جَآءَنَا
should it overtake us?'

قَالَ فِرۡعَوۡنُ مَآ أُرِيكُمۡ إِلَّا
Pharaoh said, 'I just point out to you

مَآ أَرَىٰ
what I see [to be advisable for you],

وَمَآ أَهۡدِيكُمۡ إِلَّا سَبِيلَ ٱلرَّشَادِ ۝
and I guide you only to the way of rectitude.'

وَقَالَ ٱلَّذِىٓ ءَامَنَ يَٰقَوۡمِ
30 And he who had faith said, 'O my people!

إِنِّىٓ أَخَافُ عَلَيۡكُم
Indeed I fear for you [a day]

مِّثۡلَ يَوۡمِ ٱلۡأَحۡزَابِ ۝
like the day of the [heathen] factions;

مِثۡلَ دَأۡبِ قَوۡمِ نُوحٍ
31 like the case of the people of Noah,

---

[1] Or 'Today the kingdom is yours.'

وَعَادٍ وَثَمُودَ     of Ād and Thamūd,

وَٱلَّذِينَ مِنۢ بَعْدِهِمْ     and those who were after them,

وَمَا ٱللَّهُ يُرِيدُ ظُلْمًا     and Allah does not desire any wrong

لِّلْعِبَادِ ۞     for [His] servants.

وَيَٰقَوْمِ     32 O my people!

إِنِّىٓ أَخَافُ عَلَيْكُمْ يَوْمَ ٱلتَّنَادِ ۞     Indeed I fear for you a day of mutual distress calls,

يَوْمَ تُوَلُّونَ مُدْبِرِينَ     33 a day when you will turn back [to flee],

مَا لَكُم مِّنَ ٱللَّهِ مِنْ عَاصِمٍ     not having anyone to protect you from Allah,

وَمَن يُضْلِلِ ٱللَّهُ     and whomever Allah leads astray

فَمَا لَهُۥ مِنْ هَادٍ ۞     has no guide.

وَلَقَدْ جَآءَكُمْ يُوسُفُ     34 Certainly Joseph brought you

مِن قَبْلُ بِٱلْبَيِّنَٰتِ     manifest proofs earlier,

فَمَا زِلْتُمْ فِى شَكٍّ     but you continued to remain in doubt

مِّمَّا جَآءَكُم بِهِۦ     concerning what he had brought you.

حَتَّىٰٓ إِذَا هَلَكَ قُلْتُمْ     When he died, you said,

لَن يَبْعَثَ ٱللَّهُ مِنۢ بَعْدِهِۦ رَسُولًا     "Allah will never send any apostle after him."

كَذَٰلِكَ يُضِلُّ ٱللَّهُ     That is how Allah leads astray

مَنْ هُوَ مُسْرِفٌ مُّرْتَابٌ ۞     those who are profligate, skeptical.

ٱلَّذِينَ يُجَٰدِلُونَ فِىٓ ءَايَٰتِ ٱللَّهِ     35 Those who dispute the signs of Allah

بِغَيْرِ سُلْطَٰنٍ أَتَىٰهُمْ     without any authority that may have come to them

كَبُرَ مَقْتًا عِندَ ٱللَّهِ     —[that is] greatly outrageous to Allah

وَعِندَ ٱلَّذِينَ ءَامَنُوا۟     and to those who have faith.

كَذَٰلِكَ يَطْبَعُ ٱللَّهُ     That is how Allah seals

عَلَىٰ كُلِّ قَلْبِ مُتَكَبِّرٍ جَبَّارٍ ۞     the heart of every arrogant tyrant.'

وَقَالَ فِرْعَوْنُ يَٰهَٰمَٰنُ     36 And Pharaoh said, 'O Hāmān!

ٱبْنِ لِى صَرْحًا     Build me a tower

لَّعَلِّىٓ أَبْلُغُ ٱلْأَسْبَٰبَ ۞     so that I may reach the routes[1]

أَسْبَٰبَ ٱلسَّمَٰوَٰتِ     37 —the routes of the heavens—

فَأَطَّلِعَ إِلَىٰٓ إِلَٰهِ مُوسَىٰ     and take a look at the God of Moses,

---

[1] Or 'the means.'

663

وَإِنِّي لَأَظُنُّهُ كَذِبًا    and indeed I consider him a liar.'

وَكَذَٰلِكَ زُيِّنَ لِفِرْعَوْنَ    To Pharaoh was thus presented as decorous

سُوٓءُ عَمَلِهِۦ    the evil of his conduct,

وَصُدَّ عَنِ ٱلسَّبِيلِ    and he was kept from the way [of Allah],

وَمَا كَيْدُ فِرْعَوْنَ إِلَّا فِى تَبَابٍ ۩    and Pharaoh's stratagems[1] only led him into ruin.

وَقَالَ ٱلَّذِىٓ ءَامَنَ يَٰقَوْمِ    38 And he who had faith said, 'O my people!

ٱتَّبِعُونِ أَهْدِكُمْ سَبِيلَ ٱلرَّشَادِ ۩    Follow me, I will guide you to the way of rectitude.

يَٰقَوْمِ    39 O my people!

إِنَّمَا هَٰذِهِ ٱلْحَيَوٰةُ ٱلدُّنْيَا مَتَٰعٌ    This life of the world is only a [passing] enjoyment,

وَإِنَّ ٱلْءَاخِرَةَ هِىَ دَارُ ٱلْقَرَارِ ۩    and indeed the Hereafter is the abiding home.

مَنْ عَمِلَ سَيِّئَةً    40 Whoever commits a misdeed

فَلَا يُجْزَىٰٓ إِلَّا مِثْلَهَا    shall not be requited except with its like,

وَمَنْ عَمِلَ صَٰلِحًا    but whoever acts righteously,

مِّن ذَكَرٍ أَوْ أُنثَىٰ    whether male or female,

وَهُوَ مُؤْمِنٌ    should he be faithful

فَأُوْلَٰٓئِكَ يَدْخُلُونَ ٱلْجَنَّةَ    —such shall enter paradise,

يُرْزَقُونَ فِيهَا بِغَيْرِ حِسَابٍ ۩    provided therein without any reckoning.

وَيَٰقَوْمِ    41 O my people!

مَا لِىٓ أَدْعُوكُمْ إِلَى ٱلنَّجَوٰةِ    [Think,] what makes me invite you to deliverance

وَتَدْعُونَنِىٓ إِلَى ٱلنَّارِ ۩    while you invite me toward the Fire?

تَدْعُونَنِى لِأَكْفُرَ بِٱللَّهِ    42 You invite me to defy Allah

وَأُشْرِكَ بِهِۦ    and to ascribe to Him partners

مَا لَيْسَ لِى بِهِۦ عِلْمٌ    of which I have no knowledge,

وَأَنَا۠ أَدْعُوكُمْ إِلَى ٱلْعَزِيزِ ٱلْغَفَّٰرِ ۩    while I call you to the All-mighty, the All-forgiver.

لَا جَرَمَ أَنَّمَا تَدْعُونَنِىٓ إِلَيْهِ    43 Undoubtedly, that to which you invite me

لَيْسَ لَهُۥ دَعْوَةٌ فِى ٱلدُّنْيَا    has no invitation in the world

وَلَا فِى ٱلْءَاخِرَةِ    nor in the Hereafter,

وَأَنَّ مَرَدَّنَآ إِلَى ٱللَّهِ    and indeed our return will be to Allah,

وَأَنَّ ٱلْمُسْرِفِينَ هُمْ    and indeed it is the profligates who will be

---

[1] Or 'Pharaoh's guile.'

أَصْحَبُ ٱلنَّارِ ﴿٤٣﴾      inmates of the Fire.

فَسَتَذْكُرُونَ مَآ أَقُولُ لَكُمْ      44 Soon you will remember what I tell you,

وَأُفَوِّضُ أَمْرِى إِلَى ٱللَّهِ      and I entrust my affair to Allah.

إِنَّ ٱللَّهَ بَصِيرٌ بِٱلْعِبَادِ ﴿٤٤﴾      Indeed Allah sees best the servants.'

فَوَقَىٰهُ ٱللَّهُ سَيِّـَٔاتِ مَا مَكَرُواْ      45 Then Allah saved him from their evil schemes,

وَحَاقَ بِـَٔالِ فِرْعَوْنَ سُوٓءُ ٱلْعَذَابِ ﴿٤٥﴾      while a terrible punishment besieged Pharaoh's clan:

ٱلنَّارُ يُعْرَضُونَ عَلَيْهَا      46 the Fire, to which they are exposed

غُدُوًّا وَعَشِيًّا      morning and evening.

وَيَوْمَ تَقُومُ ٱلسَّاعَةُ      And on the day when the Hour sets in

أَدْخِلُوٓاْ ءَالَ فِرْعَوْنَ أَشَدَّ ٱلْعَذَابِ ﴿٤٦﴾      Pharaoh's clan will enter the severest punishment.

وَإِذْ يَتَحَآجُّونَ فِى ٱلنَّارِ      47 When they argue in the Fire,

فَيَقُولُ ٱلضُّعَفَٰٓؤُاْ لِلَّذِينَ ٱسْتَكْبَرُوٓاْ      the weak will say to those who were arrogant,

إِنَّا كُنَّا لَكُمْ تَبَعًا      'Indeed we used to follow you;

فَهَلْ أَنتُم مُّغْنُونَ عَنَّا نَصِيبًا مِّنَ ٱلنَّارِ ﴿٤٧﴾      so will you avail us against any portion of the Fire?'

قَالَ ٱلَّذِينَ ٱسْتَكْبَرُوٓاْ      48 Those who were arrogant will say,

إِنَّا كُلٌّ فِيهَآ      'Indeed we are all [together] in it.

إِنَّ ٱللَّهَ قَدْ حَكَمَ بَيْنَ ٱلْعِبَادِ ﴿٤٨﴾      Indeed Allah has judged between [His] servants.'

وَقَالَ ٱلَّذِينَ فِى ٱلنَّارِ لِخَزَنَةِ جَهَنَّمَ      49 Those in the Fire will say to the keepers of hell,

ٱدْعُواْ رَبَّكُمْ      'Supplicate your Lord

يُخَفِّفْ عَنَّا يَوْمًا مِّنَ ٱلْعَذَابِ ﴿٤٩﴾      to lighten for us [at least] a day's punishment.'

قَالُوٓاْ      50 They will say,

أَوَلَمْ تَكُ تَأْتِيكُمْ رُسُلُكُم      'Did not your apostles use to bring you

بِٱلْبَيِّنَٰتِ      manifest proofs?'

قَالُواْ بَلَىٰ      They will say, 'Yes.'

قَالُواْ فَٱدْعُواْ      They will say, 'Then supplicate [Him] yourselves,

وَمَا دُعَٰٓؤُاْ ٱلْكَٰفِرِينَ إِلَّا فِى ضَلَٰلٍ ﴿٥٠﴾      and the supplications of the faithless only go awry.'

إِنَّا لَنَنصُرُ رُسُلَنَا      51 Indeed We shall help Our apostles

وَٱلَّذِينَ ءَامَنُواْ      and those who have faith

فِى ٱلْحَيَوٰةِ ٱلدُّنْيَا      in the life of the world

وَيَوْمَ يَقُومُ ٱلْأَشْهَٰدُ ﴿٥١﴾      and on the day when the witnesses rise up

يَوْمَ 52    —the day when

لَا يَنفَعُ ٱلظَّٰلِمِينَ مَعْذِرَتُهُمْ    the excuses of the wrongdoers will not benefit them,

وَلَهُمُ ٱللَّعْنَةُ    and the curse will lie on them,

وَلَهُمْ سُوءُ ٱلدَّارِ ۝    and for them will be the ills of the [ultimate] abode.

وَلَقَدْ ءَاتَيْنَا مُوسَى ٱلْهُدَىٰ 53    Certainly We gave Moses the guidance

وَأَوْرَثْنَا بَنِىٓ إِسْرَٰٓءِيلَ    and We made the Children of Israel heirs to

ٱلْكِتَٰبَ ۝    the Book,

هُدًى 54    as a guidance

وَذِكْرَىٰ لِأُوْلِى ٱلْأَلْبَٰبِ ۝    and an admonition for those who possess intellect.

فَٱصْبِرْ 55    So *be patient!*

إِنَّ وَعْدَ ٱللَّهِ حَقٌّ    Allah's promise is indeed true.

وَٱسْتَغْفِرْ لِذَنۢبِكَ    And *plead* for [Allah's] forgiveness for *your* sin,

وَسَبِّحْ بِحَمْدِ رَبِّكَ    and *celebrate* the praise of *your* Lord

بِٱلْعَشِىِّ وَٱلْإِبْكَٰرِ ۝    morning and evening.

إِنَّ ٱلَّذِينَ يُجَٰدِلُونَ فِىٓ ءَايَٰتِ ٱللَّهِ 56    Indeed those who dispute the signs of Allah

بِغَيْرِ سُلْطَٰنٍ أَتَىٰهُمْ    without any authority that may have come to them

إِن فِى صُدُورِهِمْ إِلَّا كِبْرٌ    —there is only vanity in their breasts,

مَّا هُم بِبَٰلِغِيهِ    which they will never satisfy.

فَٱسْتَعِذْ بِٱللَّهِ    So *seek* the protection of Allah;

إِنَّهُۥ هُوَ ٱلسَّمِيعُ ٱلْبَصِيرُ ۝    indeed He is the All-hearing, the All-seeing.

لَخَلْقُ ٱلسَّمَٰوَٰتِ وَٱلْأَرْضِ 57    Surely the creation of the heavens and the earth

أَكْبَرُ مِنْ خَلْقِ ٱلنَّاسِ    is more prodigious than the creation of mankind,[1]

وَلَٰكِنَّ أَكْثَرَ ٱلنَّاسِ لَا يَعْلَمُونَ ۝    but most people do not know.

وَمَا يَسْتَوِى ٱلْأَعْمَىٰ وَٱلْبَصِيرُ 58    The blind one and the seer are not equal,

وَٱلَّذِينَ ءَامَنُواْ    neither are those who have faith

وَعَمِلُواْ ٱلصَّٰلِحَٰتِ    and do righteous deeds

وَلَا ٱلْمُسِىٓءُ    and the evildoing.

قَلِيلًا مَّا تَتَذَكَّرُونَ ۝    Little is the admonition that you take!

إِنَّ ٱلسَّاعَةَ لَأَتِيَةٌ 59    Indeed the Hour is bound to come;

---

[1] Cf. 37:11, 79:27.

لَا رَيْبَ فِيهَا    there is no doubt in it.

وَلَكِنَّ أَكْثَرَ ٱلنَّاسِ لَا يُؤْمِنُونَ ۝    But most people do not believe.

وَقَالَ رَبُّكُمُ    60 Your Lord has said,

ٱدْعُونِى أَسْتَجِبْ لَكُمْ    'Call Me, and I will hear you[r supplications]!'

إِنَّ ٱلَّذِينَ يَسْتَكْبِرُونَ عَنْ عِبَادَتِى    Indeed those who are disdainful of My worship

سَيَدْخُلُونَ جَهَنَّمَ دَاخِرِينَ ۝    will enter hell in utter humility.

ٱللَّهُ ٱلَّذِى جَعَلَ لَكُمُ ٱلَّيْلَ    61 It is Allah who made the night for you,

لِتَسْكُنُوا۟ فِيهِ    that you may rest in it,

وَٱلنَّهَارَ مُبْصِرًا    and the day to provide visibility.

إِنَّ ٱللَّهَ لَذُو فَضْلٍ عَلَى ٱلنَّاسِ    Indeed Allah is gracious to mankind,

وَلَكِنَّ أَكْثَرَ ٱلنَّاسِ لَا يَشْكُرُونَ ۝    but most people do not give thanks.

ذَٰلِكُمُ ٱللَّهُ رَبُّكُمْ    62 That is Allah, your Lord,

خَٰلِقُ كُلِّ شَىْءٍ    the creator of all things,

لَّآ إِلَٰهَ إِلَّا هُوَ    there is no god except Him.

فَأَنَّىٰ تُؤْفَكُونَ ۝    Then where do you stray?

كَذَٰلِكَ يُؤْفَكُ    63 Thus are made to stray

ٱلَّذِينَ كَانُوا۟ بِـَٔايَٰتِ ٱللَّهِ يَجْحَدُونَ ۝    those who are used to impugning the signs of Allah.

ٱللَّهُ ٱلَّذِى جَعَلَ لَكُمُ ٱلْأَرْضَ قَرَارًا    64 It is Allah who made the earth an abode for you,

وَٱلسَّمَآءَ بِنَآءً    and the sky a canopy,

وَصَوَّرَكُمْ فَأَحْسَنَ صُوَرَكُمْ    and He formed you and perfected your forms,

وَرَزَقَكُم مِّنَ ٱلطَّيِّبَٰتِ    and provided you with all the good things.

ذَٰلِكُمُ ٱللَّهُ رَبُّكُمْ    That is Allah, your Lord!

فَتَبَارَكَ ٱللَّهُ رَبُّ ٱلْعَٰلَمِينَ ۝    Blessed is Allah, the Lord of all the worlds!

هُوَ ٱلْحَىُّ    65 He is the Living One,

لَآ إِلَٰهَ إِلَّا هُوَ    there is no god except Him.

فَٱدْعُوهُ مُخْلِصِينَ لَهُ ٱلدِّينَ    So supplicate Him, putting exclusive faith in Him.

ٱلْحَمْدُ لِلَّهِ رَبِّ ٱلْعَٰلَمِينَ ۝ ۞    All praise belongs to Allah, the Lord of the Worlds.

قُلْ إِنِّى نُهِيتُ أَنْ أَعْبُدَ    66 Say, 'I have been forbidden to worship

ٱلَّذِينَ تَدْعُونَ مِن دُونِ ٱللَّهِ    those whom you invoke besides Allah,

لَمَّا جَآءَنِىَ ٱلْبَيِّنَٰتُ    since there have come to me manifest proofs

مِن رَّبِّى
from my Lord,

وَأُمِرْتُ أَنْ أُسْلِمَ
and I have been commanded to submit

لِرَبِّ ٱلْعَٰلَمِينَ ۞
to the Lord of all the worlds.

هُوَ ٱلَّذِى خَلَقَكُم مِّن تُرَابٍ
67 It is He who created you from dust,

ثُمَّ مِن نُّطْفَةٍ
then from a drop of [seminal] fluid,

ثُمَّ مِنْ عَلَقَةٍ
then from a clinging mass,

ثُمَّ يُخْرِجُكُمْ طِفْلًا
then He brings you forth as infants,

ثُمَّ لِتَبْلُغُوٓا۟ أَشُدَّكُمْ
then [He nourishes you] so that you may come of age,

ثُمَّ لِتَكُونُوا۟ شُيُوخًا
then that you may become aged

وَمِنكُم مَّن يُتَوَفَّىٰ مِن قَبْلُ
—though there are some of you who die earlier—

وَلِتَبْلُغُوٓا۟ أَجَلًا مُّسَمًّى
and that you may complete a specified term,

وَلَعَلَّكُمْ تَعْقِلُونَ ۞
and so that you may apply reason.

هُوَ ٱلَّذِى يُحْىِۦ وَيُمِيتُ
68 It is He who gives life and brings death.

فَإِذَا قَضَىٰٓ أَمْرًا
So when He decides on a matter,

فَإِنَّمَا يَقُولُ لَهُۥ كُن فَيَكُونُ ۞
He just says to it, 'Be!' and it is.

أَلَمْ تَرَ
69 Have you not regarded

إِلَى ٱلَّذِينَ يُجَٰدِلُونَ فِىٓ ءَايَٰتِ ٱللَّهِ
those who dispute the signs of Allah,

أَنَّىٰ يُصْرَفُونَ ۞
where they are being led away [from Allah's way]?

ٱلَّذِينَ كَذَّبُوا۟ بِٱلْكِتَٰبِ
70 —Those who deny the Book

وَبِمَآ أَرْسَلْنَا بِهِۦ رُسُلَنَا
and what we have sent with Our apostles.

فَسَوْفَ يَعْلَمُونَ ۞
Soon they will know

إِذِ ٱلْأَغْلَٰلُ فِىٓ أَعْنَٰقِهِمْ
71 when, [with] iron collars around their necks

وَٱلسَّلَٰسِلُ
and chains,

يُسْحَبُونَ ۞
they are dragged

فِى ٱلْحَمِيمِ
72 into scalding waters

ثُمَّ فِى ٱلنَّارِ يُسْجَرُونَ ۞
and then set aflame in the Fire.

ثُمَّ قِيلَ لَهُمْ
73 Then they will be told,

أَيْنَ مَا كُنتُمْ تُشْرِكُونَ ۞
'Where are those you used to take as partners

مِن دُونِ ٱللَّهِ
74 besides Allah?

قَالُوا۟ ضَلُّوا۟ عَنَّا
They will say, 'They have forsaken us.

بَل لَّمْ نَكُن نَّدْعُواْ مِن قَبْلُ شَيْئًا    Rather, we did not invoke anything before.'

كَذَلِكَ يُضِلُّ ٱللَّهُ ٱلْكَفِرِينَ ۝    That is how Allah leads astray the faithless.

ذَلِكُم بِمَا كُنتُمْ تَفْرَحُونَ    75 'That is because you used to exult

فِى ٱلْأَرْضِ بِغَيْرِ ٱلْحَقِّ    unduly on the earth

وَبِمَا كُنتُمْ تَمْرَحُونَ ۝    and because you used to walk exultantly.'

ٱدْخُلُواْ أَبْوَبَ جَهَنَّمَ    76 Enter the gates of hell,

خَلِدِينَ فِيهَا    to remain in it [forever].'

فَبِئْسَ مَثْوَى ٱلْمُتَكَبِّرِينَ ۝    Evil is the [final] abode of the arrogant.

فَٱصْبِرْ    77 So *be patient!*

إِنَّ وَعْدَ ٱللَّهِ حَقٌّ    Allah's promise is indeed true.

فَإِمَّا نُرِيَنَّكَ    Whether We show *you*

بَعْضَ ٱلَّذِى نَعِدُهُمْ    a part of what We promise them,

أَوْ نَتَوَفَّيَنَّكَ    or take *you* away [before that],

فَإِلَيْنَا يُرْجَعُونَ ۝    [in any case] they will be brought back to Us.

وَلَقَدْ أَرْسَلْنَا رُسُلًا مِّن قَبْلِكَ    78 Certainly We have sent apostles before *you.*

مِنْهُم مَّن قَصَصْنَا عَلَيْكَ    Of them are those We have recounted to *you,*

وَمِنْهُم مَّن    and of them are those

لَّمْ نَقْصُصْ عَلَيْكَ    We have not recounted to *you.*

وَمَا كَانَ لِرَسُولٍ أَن يَأْتِىَ بِـَٔايَةٍ    An apostle may not bring any sign

إِلَّا بِإِذْنِ ٱللَّهِ    except by Allah's permission.

فَإِذَا جَآءَ أَمْرُ ٱللَّهِ    Hence when Allah's edict comes,

قُضِىَ بِٱلْحَقِّ    judgment is made with justice,

وَخَسِرَ هُنَالِكَ ٱلْمُبْطِلُونَ ۝    and it is thence that the falsifiers become losers.

ٱللَّهُ ٱلَّذِى جَعَلَ لَكُمُ ٱلْأَنْعَمَ    79 It is Allah who created the cattle for you

لِتَرْكَبُواْ مِنْهَا    that you may ride some of them,

وَمِنْهَا تَأْكُلُونَ ۝    and some of them you eat;

وَلَكُمْ فِيهَا مَنَفِعُ    80 and there are [numerous] uses in them for you,

وَلِتَبْلُغُواْ عَلَيْهَا حَاجَةً    and that over them[1] you may satisfy any need

فِى صُدُورِكُمْ    that is in your breasts,

---

[1] That is, by riding them or by using them as beasts of burden.

وَعَلَيْهَا وَعَلَى ٱلْفُلْكِ تُحْمَلُونَ ۝     and you are carried on them and on ships.

وَيُرِيكُمْ ءَايَٰتِهِۦ     81 He shows you His signs.

فَأَىَّ ءَايَٰتِ ٱللَّهِ تُنكِرُونَ ۝     So which of the signs of Allah do you deny?

أَفَلَمْ يَسِيرُوا۟ فِى ٱلْأَرْضِ     82 Have they not travelled over the land

فَيَنظُرُوا۟     so that they may observe

كَيْفَ كَانَ عَٰقِبَةُ ٱلَّذِينَ مِن قَبْلِهِمْ     how was the fate of those who were before them?

كَانُوٓا۟ أَكْثَرَ مِنْهُمْ     They were more numerous than them

وَأَشَدَّ قُوَّةً     and were greater [than them] in power

وَءَاثَارًا     and with respect to the effects [they left]

فِى ٱلْأَرْضِ     in the land.

فَمَآ أَغْنَىٰ عَنْهُم مَّا كَانُوا۟ يَكْسِبُونَ ۝     But what they used to earn did not avail them.

فَلَمَّا جَآءَتْهُمْ رُسُلُهُم بِٱلْبَيِّنَٰتِ     83 When their apostles brought them manifest proofs,

فَرِحُوا۟ بِمَا عِندَهُم مِّنَ ٱلْعِلْمِ     they exulted in the knowledge they possessed,

وَحَاقَ بِهِم مَّا كَانُوا۟ بِهِۦ يَسْتَهْزِءُونَ ۝     and they were besieged by what they used to deride.

فَلَمَّا رَأَوْا۟ بَأْسَنَا     84 Then, when they sighted Our punishment,

قَالُوٓا۟ ءَامَنَّا بِٱللَّهِ وَحْدَهُۥ     they said, 'We believe in Allah alone,

وَكَفَرْنَا بِمَا كُنَّا بِهِۦ مُشْرِكِينَ ۝     and disavow what we used to take as His partners.'

فَلَمْ يَكُ يَنفَعُهُمْ إِيمَٰنُهُمْ     85 But their faith was of no benefit to them

لَمَّا رَأَوْا۟ بَأْسَنَا     when they sighted Our punishment

سُنَّتَ ٱللَّهِ     —Allah's precedent

ٱلَّتِى قَدْ خَلَتْ فِى عِبَادِهِۦ     which has passed among his servants,

وَخَسِرَ هُنَالِكَ ٱلْكَٰفِرُونَ ۝     and it is thence that the faithless will be losers.

# سُورَةُ فُصِّلَتْ       41. SŪRAT FUṢṢILAT[1]

بِسْمِ ٱللَّهِ     In the Name of Allah,

ٱلرَّحْمَٰنِ ٱلرَّحِيمِ     the All-beneficent, the All-merciful.

حمٓ ۝     1 *Ḥā, Mīm:*

---

[1] The *sūrah* takes its name from the word *fuṣṣilat* (elaborated) in verse 3.

تَنزِيلٌ 2 A [gradually] sent down [revelation]

مِّنَ ٱلرَّحْمَٰنِ ٱلرَّحِيمِ ۝                   from the All-beneficent, the All-merciful,

كِتَٰبٌ فُصِّلَتْ ءَايَٰتُهُۥ 3     [this is] a Book whose signs have been elaborated,

قُرْءَانًا عَرَبِيًّا لِّقَوْمٍ يَعْلَمُونَ ۝       an Arabic Qur'ān, for a people who have knowledge,

بَشِيرًا وَنَذِيرًا 4     a bearer of good news and a warner.

فَأَعْرَضَ أَكْثَرُهُمْ            But most of them turn away [from it],

فَهُمْ لَا يَسْمَعُونَ ۝           [and] so they do not listen.

وَقَالُواْ قُلُوبُنَا فِى أَكِنَّةٍ 5 They say, 'Our hearts are in veils

مِّمَّا تَدْعُونَآ إِلَيْهِ           [which close them] to what you invite us,

وَفِىٓ ءَاذَانِنَا وَقْرٌ          and there is a deafness in our ears,

وَمِنۢ بَيْنِنَا وَبَيْنِكَ حِجَابٌ      and there is a curtain between us and you.

فَٱعْمَلْ              So act [as your faith requires];

إِنَّنَا عَٰمِلُونَ ۝            we too are acting [according to our own].'

قُلْ إِنَّمَآ أَنَا۠ بَشَرٌ مِّثْلُكُمْ 6 *Say*, 'I am just a human being like you.

يُوحَىٰٓ إِلَىَّ            It has been revealed to me

أَنَّمَآ إِلَٰهُكُمْ إِلَٰهٌ وَٰحِدٌ        that your God is the One God.

فَٱسْتَقِيمُوٓاْ إِلَيْهِ           So be steadfast toward Him

وَٱسْتَغْفِرُوهُ ۗ            and plead to Him for forgiveness.'

وَوَيْلٌ لِّلْمُشْرِكِينَ ۝          And woe to the polytheists

ٱلَّذِينَ لَا يُؤْتُونَ ٱلزَّكَوٰةَ 7   —those who do not pay the *zakāt*

وَهُم بِٱلْءَاخِرَةِ هُمْ كَٰفِرُونَ ۝     and disbelieve in the Hereafter.

إِنَّ ٱلَّذِينَ ءَامَنُواْ 8 As for those who have faith

وَعَمِلُواْ ٱلصَّٰلِحَٰتِ          and do righteous deeds,

لَهُمْ أَجْرٌ غَيْرُ مَمْنُونٍ ۝ ❋     there will be an everlasting reward for them.

قُلْ أَئِنَّكُمْ لَتَكْفُرُونَ بِٱلَّذِى 9 *Say*, 'Do you really disbelieve in Him who

خَلَقَ ٱلْأَرْضَ            created the earth

فِى يَوْمَيْنِ            in two days[1]

وَتَجْعَلُونَ لَهُۥٓ أَندَادًا ۚ        and ascribe partners to Him?

ذَٰلِكَ رَبُّ ٱلْعَٰلَمِينَ ۝         That is the Lord of all the worlds!'

---

[1] That is, in two epochs of time.

وَجَعَلَ فِيهَا رَوَاسِىَ مِن فَوْقِهَا ١٠ He set in it firm mountains [rising] above it,

وَبَٰرَكَ فِيهَا وَقَدَّرَ فِيهَآ  and blessed it and ordained therein

أَقْوَٰتَهَا  its [various] means of sustenance

فِىٓ أَرْبَعَةِ أَيَّامٍ  in four days,

سَوَآءً لِّلسَّآئِلِينَ ۝  alike for all the seekers [of the means of sustenance].

ثُمَّ ٱسْتَوَىٰٓ إِلَى ٱلسَّمَآءِ ١١ Then He turned to the heaven,

وَهِىَ دُخَانٌ  and it was smoke,

فَقَالَ لَهَا وَلِلْأَرْضِ  and He said to it and to the earth,

ٱئْتِيَا طَوْعًا أَوْ كَرْهًا  'Come! Willingly or unwillingly!'

قَالَتَآ أَتَيْنَا طَآئِعِينَ ۝  They said, 'We come heartily.'

فَقَضَىٰهُنَّ سَبْعَ سَمَٰوَاتٍ فِى يَوْمَيْنِ ١٢ Then He set them up as seven heavens in two days,

وَأَوْحَىٰ فِى كُلِّ سَمَآءٍ أَمْرَهَا  and revealed in each heaven its ordinance.[1]

وَزَيَّنَّا ٱلسَّمَآءَ ٱلدُّنْيَا بِمَصَٰبِيحَ  We have adorned the lowest heaven with lamps,

وَحِفْظًا  and guarded them.[2]

ذَٰلِكَ تَقْدِيرُ ٱلْعَزِيزِ  That is the ordaining of the All-mighty,

ٱلْعَلِيمِ ۝  the All-knowing.

فَإِنْ أَعْرَضُوا۟ ١٣ But if they turn away,

فَقُلْ أَنذَرْتُكُمْ صَٰعِقَةً  say, 'I warn you of a thunderbolt,

مِّثْلَ صَٰعِقَةِ عَادٍ وَثَمُودَ ۝  like the thunderbolt of 'Ād and Thamūd.'

إِذْ جَآءَتْهُمُ ٱلرُّسُلُ ١٤ When the apostles came to them,

مِنۢ بَيْنِ أَيْدِيهِمْ وَمِنْ خَلْفِهِمْ  before them and in their own time,[3]

أَلَّا تَعْبُدُوٓا۟ إِلَّا ٱللَّهَ  saying, 'Worship no one except Allah!'

قَالُوا۟ لَوْ شَآءَ رَبُّنَا  They said, 'Had our Lord wished,

لَأَنزَلَ مَلَٰٓئِكَةً  He would certainly have sent down angels [to us].

فَإِنَّا بِمَآ أُرْسِلْتُم بِهِۦ كَٰفِرُونَ ۝  We indeed disbelieve in what you have been sent with.'

فَأَمَّا عَادٌ ١٥ As for [the people of] 'Ād,

فَٱسْتَكْبَرُوا۟ فِى ٱلْأَرْضِ بِغَيْرِ ٱلْحَقِّ  they acted arrogantly in the earth unduly,

---

[1] Or 'law.'

[2] Cf. 37:6, 67:5.

[3] That is, during the times of their forefathers and in their own time. Or 'from their front and behind,' that is, from all sides.

وَقَالُوا۟ مَنْ أَشَدُّ مِنَّا قُوَّةً     and they said, 'Who is more powerful than us?'

أَوَلَمْ يَرَوْا۟ أَنَّ ٱللَّهَ ٱلَّذِى خَلَقَهُمْ     Did they not see that Allah, who created them,

هُوَ أَشَدُّ مِنْهُمْ قُوَّةً     is more powerful than them?

وَكَانُوا۟ بِـَٔايَٰتِنَا يَجْحَدُونَ ۝     They used to impugn Our signs;

فَأَرْسَلْنَا عَلَيْهِمْ رِيحًا صَرْصَرًا     16 so We unleashed upon them an icy gale

فِىٓ أَيَّامٍ نَّحِسَاتٍ     during ill-fated days,

لِّنُذِيقَهُمْ     that We might make them taste

عَذَابَ ٱلْخِزْىِ     the punishment of disgrace

فِى ٱلْحَيَوٰةِ ٱلدُّنْيَا     in the life of the world.

وَلَعَذَابُ ٱلْـَٔاخِرَةِ     Yet the punishment of the Hereafter is surely

أَخْزَىٰ     more disgraceful,

وَهُمْ لَا يُنصَرُونَ ۝     and they will not be helped.

وَأَمَّا ثَمُودُ     17 As for [the people of] Thamūd,

فَهَدَيْنَٰهُمْ     We guided them,

فَٱسْتَحَبُّوا۟ ٱلْعَمَىٰ عَلَى ٱلْهُدَىٰ     but they preferred blindness to guidance.

فَأَخَذَتْهُمْ صَٰعِقَةُ ٱلْعَذَابِ ٱلْهُونِ     So the bolt of a humiliating punishment seized them

بِمَا كَانُوا۟ يَكْسِبُونَ ۝     because of what they used to earn.

وَنَجَّيْنَا ٱلَّذِينَ ءَامَنُوا۟     18 And We delivered those who had faith

وَكَانُوا۟ يَتَّقُونَ ۝     and were Godwary.

وَيَوْمَ يُحْشَرُ أَعْدَآءُ ٱللَّهِ     19 The day when the enemies of Allah are marched out

إِلَى ٱلنَّارِ     toward the Fire,

فَهُمْ يُوزَعُونَ ۝     and they shall be held in check.

حَتَّىٰٓ إِذَا مَا جَآءُوهَا     20 When they come to it,

شَهِدَ عَلَيْهِمْ سَمْعُهُمْ     their hearing will bear witness against them

وَأَبْصَٰرُهُمْ وَجُلُودُهُم     and their sight and their skins

بِمَا كَانُوا۟ يَعْمَلُونَ ۝     concerning what they used to do.

وَقَالُوا۟ لِجُلُودِهِمْ     21 They will say to their skins,

لِمَ شَهِدتُّمْ عَلَيْنَا     'Why did you bear witness against us?'

قَالُوٓا۟ أَنطَقَنَا ٱللَّهُ     They will say, 'We were given speech by Allah,

ٱلَّذِىٓ أَنطَقَ كُلَّ شَىْءٍ     who gave speech to all things.

وَهُوَ خَلَقَكُمْ أَوَّلَ مَرَّةٍ  He created you the first time,

وَإِلَيْهِ تُرْجَعُونَ ۝  and to Him you are being brought back.

وَمَا كُنتُمْ تَسْتَتِرُونَ  22 You did not use to conceal yourselves

أَن يَشْهَدَ عَلَيْكُمْ سَمْعُكُمْ  lest your hearing should bear witness against you,

وَلَا أَبْصَرُكُمْ وَلَا جُلُودُكُمْ  or [for that matter] your sight, or your skin,

وَلَٰكِن ظَنَنتُمْ أَنَّ ٱللَّهَ لَا يَعْلَمُ  but you thought that Allah did not know

كَثِيرًا مِّمَّا تَعْمَلُونَ ۝  most of what you did.

وَذَٰلِكُمْ ظَنُّكُمُ ٱلَّذِى ظَنَنتُم  23 That misjudgment that you entertained

بِرَبِّكُمْ  about your Lord

أَرْدَىٰكُمْ  ruined you.

فَأَصْبَحْتُم مِّنَ ٱلْخَٰسِرِينَ ۝  So you became losers.'

فَإِن يَصْبِرُوا۟ فَٱلنَّارُ مَثْوًى لَّهُمْ  24 Should they be patient, the Fire is their abode;

وَإِن يَسْتَعْتِبُوا۟  and should they seek to propitiate,

فَمَا هُم مِّنَ ٱلْمُعْتَبِينَ ۝  they will not be redeemed.

وَقَيَّضْنَا لَهُمْ قُرَنَآءَ  25 We have assigned them companions

فَزَيَّنُوا۟ لَهُم  who make to seem decorous to them

مَّا بَيْنَ أَيْدِيهِمْ  whatever is before them[1]

وَمَا خَلْفَهُمْ  and whatever is behind them,[2]

وَحَقَّ عَلَيْهِمُ ٱلْقَوْلُ  and the word[3] came due against them,

فِى أُمَمٍ قَدْ خَلَتْ  as it did against the nations that passed away

مِن قَبْلِهِم  before them

مِّنَ ٱلْجِنِّ وَٱلْإِنسِ  of jinn and humans.

إِنَّهُمْ كَانُوا۟ خَٰسِرِينَ ۝  They were indeed losers.

وَقَالَ ٱلَّذِينَ كَفَرُوا۟  26 The faithless say,

لَا تَسْمَعُوا۟ لِهَٰذَا ٱلْقُرْءَانِ  'Do not listen to this Qur'ān

وَٱلْغَوْا۟ فِيهِ  and hoot it down

لَعَلَّكُمْ تَغْلِبُونَ ۝  so that you may prevail [over the Apostle].'

---

[1] That is, their conduct in the life of the world.

[2] That is, concerning the Hereafter, or the legacy they leave behind,

[3] Cf. 7:18, 11:119, 16:10; 17:17; 23: 27; 27:82, 28:63, 32:13; 36:7, 70, 38:85; 41:25, 46:18.

فَلَنُذِيقَنَّ ٱلَّذِينَ كَفَرُوا 27 We will surely make the faithless taste

عَذَابًا شَدِيدًا    a severe punishment,

وَلَنَجْزِيَنَّهُمْ    and We will surely requite them

أَسْوَأَ ٱلَّذِى كَانُوا يَعْمَلُونَ ۝    for the worst of what they used to do.

ذَٰلِكَ جَزَآءُ أَعْدَآءِ ٱللَّهِ 28 That is the requital of the enemies of Allah

ٱلنَّارُ    —the Fire!

لَهُمْ فِيهَا دَارُ ٱلْخُلْدِ    In it they will have an everlasting abode,

جَزَآءً بِمَا كَانُوا بِآيَٰتِنَا يَجْحَدُونَ ۝    as a requital for their impugning Our signs.

وَقَالَ ٱلَّذِينَ كَفَرُوا رَبَّنَآ 29 The faithless will say, 'Our Lord!

أَرِنَا ٱلَّذَيْنِ أَضَلَّانَا    Show us those who led us astray

مِنَ ٱلْجِنِّ وَٱلْإِنسِ    from among jinn and humans

نَجْعَلْهُمَا تَحْتَ أَقْدَامِنَا    so that we may trample them under our feet,

لِيَكُونَا مِنَ ٱلْأَسْفَلِينَ ۝    so that they may be among the lowermost!'

إِنَّ ٱلَّذِينَ قَالُوا رَبُّنَا ٱللَّهُ 30 Indeed those who say, 'Our Lord is Allah!'

ثُمَّ ٱسْتَقَٰمُوا    and then remain steadfast,

تَتَنَزَّلُ عَلَيْهِمُ ٱلْمَلَٰٓئِكَةُ    the angels descend upon them,

أَلَّا تَخَافُوا وَلَا تَحْزَنُوا    [saying,] 'Do not fear, nor be grieved!

وَأَبْشِرُوا بِٱلْجَنَّةِ    Receive the good news of the paradise

ٱلَّتِى كُنتُمْ تُوعَدُونَ ۝    which you have been promised.

نَحْنُ أَوْلِيَآؤُكُمْ فِى ٱلْحَيَوٰةِ ٱلدُّنْيَا 31 We are your friends in the life of this world

وَفِى ٱلْآخِرَةِ    and in the Hereafter,

وَلَكُمْ فِيهَا مَا تَشْتَهِىٓ أَنفُسُكُمْ    and you will have in it whatever your souls desire,

وَلَكُمْ فِيهَا مَا تَدَّعُونَ ۝    and you will have in it whatever you ask for,

نُزُلًا مِّنْ غَفُورٍ رَّحِيمٍ ۝ 32 as a hospitality from One all-forgiving, all-merciful.'

وَمَنْ أَحْسَنُ قَوْلًا 33 Who has a better call

مِّمَّن دَعَآ إِلَى ٱللَّهِ    than him who summons to Allah

وَعَمِلَ صَٰلِحًا    and acts righteously

وَقَالَ إِنَّنِى مِنَ ٱلْمُسْلِمِينَ ۝    and says, 'Indeed I am one of the *muslim*s.'

وَلَا تَسْتَوِى ٱلْحَسَنَةُ وَلَا ٱلسَّيِّئَةُ 34 Good and evil [conduct] are not equal.[1]

---

[1] Or 'virtue and vice are not equal.'

ٱدۡفَعۡ بِٱلَّتِى هِىَ أَحۡسَنُ

Repel [evil] with what is best.

فَإِذَا ٱلَّذِى

[If you do so,] behold, he

بَيۡنَكَ وَبَيۡنَهُۥ عَدَٰوَةٌ

between whom and you was enmity,

كَأَنَّهُۥ وَلِىٌّ حَمِيمٌ ۩

will be as though he were a sympathetic friend.

وَمَا يُلَقَّىٰهَآ إِلَّا ٱلَّذِينَ صَبَرُواْ

35 But none is granted it except those who are patient,

وَمَا يُلَقَّىٰهَآ

and none is granted it

إِلَّا ذُو حَظٍّ عَظِيمٍ ۩

except the greatly endowed.

وَإِمَّا يَنزَغَنَّكَ مِنَ ٱلشَّيۡطَٰنِ نَزۡغٌ

36 Should a temptation from Satan disturb *you,*

فَٱسۡتَعِذۡ بِٱللَّهِ

*seek* the protection of Allah.

إِنَّهُۥ هُوَ ٱلسَّمِيعُ ٱلۡعَلِيمُ ۩

Indeed He is the All-hearing, the All-knowing.

وَمِنۡ ءَايَٰتِهِ ٱلَّيۡلُ وَٱلنَّهَارُ

37 Among His signs are the night and the day,

وَٱلشَّمۡسُ وَٱلۡقَمَرُ

and the sun and the moon.

لَا تَسۡجُدُواْ لِلشَّمۡسِ وَلَا لِلۡقَمَرِ

Do not prostrate to the sun, nor to the moon,

وَٱسۡجُدُواْ لِلَّهِ ٱلَّذِى خَلَقَهُنَّ

but prostrate to Allah who created them,

إِن كُنتُمۡ إِيَّاهُ تَعۡبُدُونَ ۩

if it is Him that you worship.

فَإِنِ ٱسۡتَكۡبَرُواْ

38 But if they disdain [the worship of Allah],

فَٱلَّذِينَ عِندَ رَبِّكَ يُسَبِّحُونَ لَهُۥ

those who are near *your* Lord glorify Him

بِٱلَّيۡلِ وَٱلنَّهَارِ

night and day,

وَهُمۡ لَا يَسۡـَٔمُونَ ۩

and they are not wearied.

وَمِنۡ ءَايَٰتِهِۦٓ

39 Among His signs

أَنَّكَ تَرَى ٱلۡأَرۡضَ خَٰشِعَةً

is that you see the earth desolate;

فَإِذَآ أَنزَلۡنَا عَلَيۡهَا ٱلۡمَآءَ

but when We send down water upon it,

ٱهۡتَزَّتۡ وَرَبَتۡ

it stirs and swells.

إِنَّ ٱلَّذِىٓ أَحۡيَاهَا لَمُحۡىِ ٱلۡمَوۡتَىٰٓ

Indeed He who revives it is the reviver of the dead.

إِنَّهُۥ عَلَىٰ كُلِّ شَىۡءٍ قَدِيرٌ ۩

Indeed He has power over all things.

إِنَّ ٱلَّذِينَ يُلۡحِدُونَ فِىٓ ءَايَٰتِنَا

40 Indeed those who commit sacrilege in Our signs

لَا يَخۡفَوۡنَ عَلَيۡنَآ

are not hidden from Us.

أَفَمَن يُلۡقَىٰ فِى ٱلنَّارِ خَيۡرٌ

Is someone who is cast in the Fire better off,

أَم مَّن يَأۡتِىٓ ءَامِنًا

or someone who arrives safely

يَوۡمَ ٱلۡقِيَٰمَةِ

on the Day of Resurrection?

اَعْمَلُوا مَا شِئْتُمْ     Act as you wish;

إِنَّهُ بِمَا تَعْمَلُونَ بَصِيرٌ ۝     indeed He sees best what you do.

إِنَّ الَّذِينَ كَفَرُوا بِالذِّكْرِ 41     41 Indeed those who defy the Reminder

لَمَّا جَآءَهُمْ     when it comes to them. . . .[1]

وَإِنَّهُ لَكِتَابٌ عَزِيزٌ ۝     Indeed it is an august Book:

لَّا يَأْتِيهِ الْبَاطِلُ 42     42 falsehood cannot approach it,

مِنْ بَيْنِ يَدَيْهِ     from before it

وَلَا مِنْ خَلْفِهِ     nor from behind it,

تَنزِيلٌ     a [gradually] sent down [revelation]

مِّنْ حَكِيمٍ حَمِيدٍ ۝     from One all-wise, all-laudable.

مَّا يُقَالُ لَكَ إِلَّا 43     43 Nothing is said to *you* except

مَا قَدْ قِيلَ     what has already been said [earlier]

لِلرُّسُلِ مِن قَبْلِكَ     to the apostles before *you*.

إِنَّ رَبَّكَ لَذُو مَغْفِرَةٍ     Indeed *your* Lord is forgiving

وَذُو عِقَابٍ أَلِيمٍ ۝     and One who metes out a painful retribution.

وَلَوْ جَعَلْنَاهُ قُرْءَانًا أَعْجَمِيًّا 44     44 Had We made it a non-Arabic[2] Qur'ān,

لَّقَالُوا     they[3] would have surely said,

لَوْلَا فُصِّلَتْ ءَايَاتُهُ     'Why have not its signs been articulated?

ءَاَعْجَمِيٌّ     'What! A non-Arabian [scripture][4]

وَعَرَبِيٌّ     and an Arabian [prophet]!?

قُلْ هُوَ لِلَّذِينَ ءَامَنُوا هُدًى     *Say,* 'For those who have faith it is a guidance

وَشِفَآءٌ     and healing;

وَالَّذِينَ لَا يُؤْمِنُونَ     but as for those who are faithless,

فِي ءَاذَانِهِمْ وَقْرٌ     there is a deafness in their ears

وَهُوَ عَلَيْهِمْ عَمًى     and it is lost to their sight.

---

[1] Ellipsis. The phrase omitted, considering the context, is, 'will face a severe punishment.'

[2] Or 'a barbaric Qur'ān;' that is, in a language other than an articulate literary Arabic.

[3] That is, the Arabs.

[4] Or 'a barbaric scripture.'

أُوْلَٰٓئِكَ يُنَادَوْنَ

مِن مَّكَانٍ بَعِيدٍ ۝

٤٥ وَلَقَدْ ءَاتَيْنَا مُوسَى ٱلْكِتَٰبَ

فَٱخْتُلِفَ فِيهِ

وَلَوْلَا كَلِمَةٌ سَبَقَتْ مِن رَّبِّكَ

لَقُضِىَ بَيْنَهُمْ

وَإِنَّهُمْ لَفِى شَكٍّ مِّنْهُ مُرِيبٍ ۝

٤٦ مَّنْ عَمِلَ صَٰلِحًا فَلِنَفْسِهِ

وَمَنْ أَسَآءَ فَعَلَيْهَا

وَمَا رَبُّكَ بِظَلَّٰمٍ لِّلْعَبِيدِ ۝ ✴

They are [as if they were] called

from a distant place.

45 Certainly We gave Moses the Book,

but differences arose about it;

and were it not for a prior decree of *your* Lord,

judgement would have been made between them,

for they are indeed in grave doubt concerning it.

46 Whoever acts righteously, it is for his own soul,

and whoever does evil, it is to its detriment,

and *your* Lord is not tyrannical to the servants.

[PART 25]

إِلَيْهِ يُرَدُّ عِلْمُ ٱلسَّاعَةِ

وَمَا تَخْرُجُ مِن ثَمَرَٰتٍ مِّنْ أَكْمَامِهَا

وَمَا تَحْمِلُ مِنْ أُنثَىٰ وَلَا تَضَعُ

إِلَّا بِعِلْمِهِ

وَيَوْمَ يُنَادِيهِمْ

أَيْنَ شُرَكَآءِى

قَالُوٓاْ ءَاذَنَّٰكَ

مَا مِنَّا مِن شَهِيدٍ ۝

٤٨ وَضَلَّ عَنْهُم مَّا كَانُواْ يَدْعُونَ مِن قَبْلُ

وَظَنُّواْ مَا لَهُم مِّن مَّحِيصٍ ۝

٤٩ لَّا يَسْـَٔمُ ٱلْإِنسَٰنُ مِن دُعَآءِ ٱلْخَيْرِ

وَإِن مَّسَّهُ ٱلشَّرُّ

فَيَـُٔوسٌ قَنُوطٌ ۝

٥٠ وَلَئِنْ أَذَقْنَٰهُ رَحْمَةً مِّنَّا

مِنْ بَعْدِ ضَرَّآءَ مَسَّتْهُ

لَيَقُولَنَّ

هَٰذَا لِى

وَمَآ أَظُنُّ ٱلسَّاعَةَ قَآئِمَةً

وَلَئِن رُّجِعْتُ إِلَىٰ

47 On Him devolves the knowledge of the Hour,

and no fruit emerges from its covering

and no female conceives or delivers

except with His knowledge.

On the day when He will call out to them,

'Where are My partners?'

They will say, 'We have apprised You

that there is no witness amongst us.'

48 What they used to invoke before has forsaken them,

and they know there is no escape for them.

49 Man is never wearied of supplicating for good,

and should any ill befall him,

he becomes hopeless, despondent.

50 And if We let him have a taste of Our mercy

after distress has befallen him,

he will surely say,

'This is my due!

I do not think the Hour will ever set in,

and in case I am returned to my Lord,

رَّبِّى إِنَّ لِى عِندَهُۥ لَلۡحُسۡنَىٰ
I will indeed have the best [reward] with Him.'

فَلَنُنَبِّئَنَّ ٱلَّذِينَ كَفَرُواْ
But We will surely inform the faithless

بِمَا عَمِلُواْ
about what they have done,

وَلَنُذِيقَنَّهُم مِّنۡ عَذَابٍ غَلِيظٍ
and will surely make them taste a harsh punishment.

وَإِذَآ أَنۡعَمۡنَا عَلَى ٱلۡإِنسَٰنِ
51 When We bless man,

أَعۡرَضَ وَنَـَٔا بِجَانِبِهِۦ
he is disregardful and turns aside;

وَإِذَا مَسَّهُ ٱلشَّرُّ
but when an ill befalls him,

فَذُو دُعَآءٍ عَرِيضٍ
he makes protracted supplications.

قُلۡ أَرَءَيۡتُمۡ
52 Say, 'Tell me,

إِن كَانَ مِنۡ عِندِ ٱللَّهِ
if it is from Allah

ثُمَّ كَفَرۡتُم بِهِۦ
and you disbelieve in it,

مَنۡ أَضَلُّ مِمَّنۡ هُوَ
who will be more astray than someone who is

فِى شِقَاقٍۭ بَعِيدٍ
in extreme defiance.'

سَنُرِيهِمۡ ءَايَٰتِنَا
53 Soon We shall show them Our signs

فِى ٱلۡءَافَاقِ وَفِىٓ أَنفُسِهِمۡ
in the horizons and in their own souls

حَتَّىٰ يَتَبَيَّنَ لَهُمۡ أَنَّهُ ٱلۡحَقُّ
until it becomes clear to them that He is the Real.[1]

أَوَلَمۡ يَكۡفِ بِرَبِّكَ أَنَّهُۥ
Is it not sufficient that *your* Lord

عَلَىٰ كُلِّ شَىۡءٍ شَهِيدٌ
is witness to all things?

أَلَآ إِنَّهُمۡ فِى مِرۡيَةٍ
54 Look! They are indeed in doubt

مِّن لِّقَآءِ رَبِّهِمۡ
about the encounter with their Lord!

أَلَآ إِنَّهُۥ بِكُلِّ شَىۡءٍ مُّحِيطٌ
Look! He indeed comprehends all things!

# سُورَةُ الشُّورَىٰ

# 42. SŪRAT AL-SHŪRĀ[2]

بِسۡمِ ٱللَّهِ
In the Name of Allah,

ٱلرَّحۡمَٰنِ ٱلرَّحِيمِ
the All-beneficent, the All-merciful.

---

[1] Or 'until it becomes clear to them that it [i.e. the Qur'ān, or Islam] (or he) [i.e. the Apostle] is the truth.'

[2] The *sūrah* takes its name from verse 38 concerning *shūrā* (counsel).

حمٓ ۝ 1 *Ḥā, Mīm,*

عٓسٓقٓ ۝ 2 *'Ayn, Sīn, Qāf.*

كَذَٰلِكَ يُوحِىٓ إِلَيْكَ 3 Thus does He reveal to *you*

وَإِلَى ٱلَّذِينَ مِن قَبْلِكَ and to those who were before *you,*

ٱللَّهُ ٱلْعَزِيزُ ٱلْحَكِيمُ ۝ Allah, the All-mighty, the All-wise:

لَهُۥ مَا فِى ٱلسَّمَٰوَٰتِ 4 to Him belongs whatever is in the heavens

وَمَا فِى ٱلْأَرْضِ and whatever is in the earth,

وَهُوَ ٱلْعَلِىُّ ٱلْعَظِيمُ ۝ and He is the All-exalted, the All-supreme.

تَكَادُ ٱلسَّمَٰوَٰتُ يَتَفَطَّرْنَ 5 The heavens are about to be rent apart

مِن فَوْقِهِنَّ from above them,

وَٱلْمَلَٰٓئِكَةُ يُسَبِّحُونَ بِحَمْدِ while the angels celebrate the praise of their Lord

رَبِّهِمْ وَيَسْتَغْفِرُونَ لِمَن فِى ٱلْأَرْضِ and plead for forgiveness for those on the earth.

أَلَآ إِنَّ ٱللَّهَ هُوَ ٱلْغَفُورُ ٱلرَّحِيمُ ۝ Look! Allah is indeed the All-forgiving, the All-merciful!

وَٱلَّذِينَ ٱتَّخَذُوا۟ مِن دُونِهِۦٓ أَوْلِيَآءَ 6 As for those who have taken guardians besides Him,

ٱللَّهُ حَفِيظٌ عَلَيْهِمْ Allah is watchful over them,

وَمَآ أَنتَ عَلَيْهِم بِوَكِيلٍ ۝ and it is not *your* duty to watch over them.

وَكَذَٰلِكَ أَوْحَيْنَآ إِلَيْكَ قُرْءَانًا عَرَبِيًّا 7 Thus have We revealed to *you* an Arabic Qur'ān

لِّتُنذِرَ that *you* may warn

أُمَّ ٱلْقُرَىٰ [the people of] the Mother of the Towns[1]

وَمَنْ حَوْلَهَا and those around it,

وَتُنذِرَ يَوْمَ ٱلْجَمْعِ and warn [them] of the Day of Gathering,[2]

لَا رَيْبَ فِيهِ in which there is no doubt,

فَرِيقٌ فِى ٱلْجَنَّةِ [whereupon] a part [of mankind] will be in paradise

وَفَرِيقٌ فِى ٱلسَّعِيرِ ۝ and a part will be in the Blaze.

وَلَوْ شَآءَ ٱللَّهُ 8 Had Allah wished,

لَجَعَلَهُمْ أُمَّةً وَٰحِدَةً surely He would have made them one community;

وَلَٰكِن يُدْخِلُ مَن يَشَآءُ but He admits whomever He wishes

فِى رَحْمَتِهِۦ into His mercy,

---

[1] That is, the city of Makkah.
[2] Cf. 64:9.

وَٱلظَّٰلِمُونَ    and the wrongdoers

مَا لَهُم مِّن وَلِيٍّ وَلَا نَصِيرٍ ۝    do not have any guardian or helper.

أَمِ ٱتَّخَذُوا۟ مِن دُونِهِۦٓ أَوْلِيَآءَ    9 Have they taken guardians besides Him?

فَٱللَّهُ هُوَ ٱلْوَلِيُّ    [Say,] 'It is Allah who is the Guardian,

وَهُوَ يُحْيِ ٱلْمَوْتَىٰ    and He revives the dead,

وَهُوَ عَلَىٰ كُلِّ شَىْءٍ قَدِيرٌ ۝    and He has power over all things.

وَمَا ٱخْتَلَفْتُمْ فِيهِ مِن شَىْءٍ    10 Whatever thing you may differ about,

فَحُكْمُهُۥٓ إِلَى ٱللَّهِ    its judgment is with Allah.

ذَٰلِكُمُ ٱللَّهُ رَبِّى    That is Allah, my Lord.

عَلَيْهِ تَوَكَّلْتُ    In Him I have put my trust,

وَإِلَيْهِ أُنِيبُ ۝    and to Him I turn penitently.

فَاطِرُ ٱلسَّمَٰوَٰتِ وَٱلْأَرْضِ    11 The originator of the heavens and the earth,

جَعَلَ لَكُم مِّنْ أَنفُسِكُمْ أَزْوَٰجًا    He made for you mates from your own selves,

وَمِنَ ٱلْأَنْعَٰمِ أَزْوَٰجًا    and mates of the cattle,

يَذْرَؤُكُمْ فِيهِ    by which means He multiplies you.

لَيْسَ كَمِثْلِهِۦ شَىْءٌ    Nothing is like Him,[1]

وَهُوَ ٱلسَّمِيعُ ٱلْبَصِيرُ ۝    and He is the All-hearing, the All-seeing.

لَهُۥ مَقَالِيدُ ٱلسَّمَٰوَٰتِ وَٱلْأَرْضِ    12 To Him belong the keys of the heavens and the earth:

يَبْسُطُ ٱلرِّزْقَ    He expands the provision

لِمَن يَشَآءُ    for whomever He wishes,

وَيَقْدِرُ    and tightens it [for whomever He wishes].

إِنَّهُۥ بِكُلِّ شَىْءٍ عَلِيمٌ ۝ ٭    Indeed He has knowledge of all things.'

شَرَعَ لَكُم مِّنَ ٱلدِّينِ    13 He has prescribed for you the religion

مَا وَصَّىٰ بِهِۦ نُوحًا    which He had enjoined upon Noah

وَٱلَّذِىٓ أَوْحَيْنَآ إِلَيْكَ    and which We have [also] revealed to *you*,

وَمَا وَصَّيْنَا بِهِۦٓ إِبْرَٰهِيمَ    and which We had enjoined upon Abraham,

وَمُوسَىٰ وَعِيسَىٰٓ    Moses and Jesus,

---

[1] In case the *kāf* in *ka-mithlihī* is not taken as redundant, the meaning will be, 'There is nothing like His likeness.'

أَنْ أَقِيمُوا الدِّينَ declaring, 'Maintain the religion,

وَلَا تَتَفَرَّقُوا فِيهِ and do not be divided in it.'

كَبُرَ عَلَى الْمُشْرِكِينَ Hard on the polytheists

مَا تَدْعُوهُمْ إِلَيْهِ is that to which *you* summon them.

اللَّهُ يَجْتَبِي إِلَيْهِ مَن يَشَاءُ Allah chooses for it[1] whomever He wishes

وَيَهْدِي إِلَيْهِ مَن يُنِيبُ and He guides to it[2] whomever returns penitently.

وَمَا تَفَرَّقُوا 14 They did not divide [into sects]

إِلَّا مِنْ بَعْدِ مَا جَاءَهُمُ الْعِلْمُ except after the knowledge had come to them,

بَغْيًا بَيْنَهُمْ out of envy among themselves;

وَلَوْلَا كَلِمَةٌ سَبَقَتْ مِن رَّبِّكَ and were it not for a prior decree of *your* Lord

إِلَى أَجَلٍ مُّسَمًّى [granting them reprieve] until a specified time,

لَّقُضِيَ بَيْنَهُمْ decision would have been made between them.

وَإِنَّ الَّذِينَ أُورِثُوا الْكِتَابَ Indeed those who were made heirs to the Book

مِنْ بَعْدِهِمْ after them

لَفِي شَكٍّ مِّنْهُ مُرِيبٍ are surely in grave doubt concerning it.

فَلِذَٰلِكَ فَادْعُ 15 So *summon* to this [unity of religion],

وَاسْتَقِمْ كَمَا أُمِرْتَ and *be* steadfast, just as *you* have been commanded,

وَلَا تَتَّبِعْ أَهْوَاءَهُمْ and *do not follow* their desires,

وَقُلْ and *say*,

ءَامَنتُ بِمَا أَنزَلَ اللَّهُ مِن كِتَابٍ 'I believe in whatever Book Allah has sent down.

وَأُمِرْتُ لِأَعْدِلَ بَيْنَكُمُ I have been commanded to be do justice among you.

اللَّهُ رَبُّنَا وَرَبُّكُمْ Allah is our Lord and your Lord.

لَنَا أَعْمَالُنَا Our deeds belong to us

وَلَكُمْ أَعْمَالُكُمْ and your deeds belong to you.

لَا حُجَّةَ بَيْنَنَا وَبَيْنَكُمُ There is no argument between us and you.

اللَّهُ يَجْمَعُ بَيْنَنَا Allah will bring us together

وَإِلَيْهِ الْمَصِيرُ and toward Him is the destination.'

وَالَّذِينَ يُحَاجُّونَ فِي اللَّهِ 16 Those who argue concerning Allah,

---

[1] Or 'for Himself.'

[2] Or 'to Himself.'

مِنْ بَعْدِ مَا ٱسْتُجِيبَ لَهُۥ     after His call has been answered,

حُجَّتُهُمْ دَاحِضَةٌ عِندَ رَبِّهِمْ     their argument stands refuted with their Lord,

وَعَلَيْهِمْ غَضَبٌ     and upon them shall be [His] wrath,

وَلَهُمْ عَذَابٌ شَدِيدٌ     and there is a severe punishment for them.

ٱللَّهُ ٱلَّذِىٓ أَنزَلَ ٱلْكِتَٰبَ     17 It is Allah who has sent down the Book

بِٱلْحَقِّ     with the truth

وَٱلْمِيزَانَ     and [He has sent down] the Balance.

وَمَا يُدْرِيكَ     What do you know

لَعَلَّ ٱلسَّاعَةَ قَرِيبٌ     —maybe the Hour is near!

يَسْتَعْجِلُ بِهَا ٱلَّذِينَ لَا يُؤْمِنُونَ بِهَا     18 Those who do not believe in it ask [*you*] to hasten it,

وَٱلَّذِينَ ءَامَنُوا۟ مُشْفِقُونَ مِنْهَا     but those who have faith are apprehensive of it,

وَيَعْلَمُونَ أَنَّهَا ٱلْحَقُّ     and know that it is a truth.

أَلَآ إِنَّ ٱلَّذِينَ يُمَارُونَ فِى ٱلسَّاعَةِ     Look! Indeed those who are in doubt about the Hour[1]

لَفِى ضَلَٰلٍ بَعِيدٍ     are surely in extreme error!

ٱللَّهُ لَطِيفٌۢ بِعِبَادِهِۦ     19 Allah is all-attentive to His servants.

يَرْزُقُ مَن يَشَآءُ     He provides for whomever He wishes,

وَهُوَ ٱلْقَوِىُّ ٱلْعَزِيزُ     and He is the All-strong, the All-mighty.

مَن كَانَ يُرِيدُ حَرْثَ ٱلْءَاخِرَةِ     20 Whoever desires the tillage of the Hereafter,

نَزِدْ لَهُۥ فِى حَرْثِهِۦ     We will enhance for him his tillage,

وَمَن كَانَ يُرِيدُ حَرْثَ ٱلدُّنْيَا     and whoever desires the tillage of the world,

نُؤْتِهِۦ مِنْهَا     We will give it to him,

وَمَا لَهُۥ فِى ٱلْءَاخِرَةِ مِن نَّصِيبٍ     but he will have no share in the Hereafter.

أَمْ لَهُمْ شُرَكَٰٓؤُا۟     21 Do they have partners [besides Allah]

شَرَعُوا۟ لَهُم مِّنَ ٱلدِّينِ     who have ordained for them a religion

مَا لَمْ يَأْذَنۢ بِهِ ٱللَّهُ     which has not been permitted by Allah?

وَلَوْلَا كَلِمَةُ ٱلْفَصْلِ     Had it not been for the conclusive word,[2]

لَقُضِىَ بَيْنَهُمْ     decision would have been made between them.

---

[1] Or 'dispute the Hour.'

[2] Or 'the final word.' That is, Allah's promise to provide the faithless and to grant them a respite before retribution. See 2:36, 126; 9:68-69; 15:3, 31:23-24.

وَإِنَّ ٱلظَّٰلِمِينَ لَهُمْ
For the wrongdoers there is indeed

عَذَابٌ أَلِيمٌ ۞
a painful punishment.

تَرَى ٱلظَّٰلِمِينَ
22 *You* will see the wrongdoers

مُشْفِقِينَ مِمَّا كَسَبُوا۟
apprehensive because of what they have earned,

وَهُوَ وَاقِعٌ بِهِمْ
and it is about to befall them;

وَٱلَّذِينَ ءَامَنُوا۟ وَعَمِلُوا۟ ٱلصَّٰلِحَٰتِ
but those who have faith and do righteous deeds

فِى رَوْضَاتِ ٱلْجَنَّاتِ
will be in the gardens of paradise:

لَهُم مَّا يَشَآءُونَ عِندَ رَبِّهِمْ
they will have whatever they wish near their Lord.

ذَٰلِكَ هُوَ ٱلْفَضْلُ ٱلْكَبِيرُ ۞
That is the greatest grace.

ذَٰلِكَ ٱلَّذِى يُبَشِّرُ ٱللَّهُ
23 That is the good news Allah gives

عِبَادَهُ ٱلَّذِينَ ءَامَنُوا۟
to His servants who have faith

وَعَمِلُوا۟ ٱلصَّٰلِحَٰتِ
and do righteous deeds!

قُل لَّآ أَسْـَٔلُكُمْ عَلَيْهِ أَجْرًا
*Say*, 'I do not ask of you any reward for it

إِلَّا ٱلْمَوَدَّةَ فِى ٱلْقُرْبَىٰ
except the affection for [my] relatives.'

وَمَن يَقْتَرِفْ حَسَنَةً
Whoever performs a good deed,

نَّزِدْ لَهُۥ فِيهَا حُسْنًا
We shall enhance for him its goodness.

إِنَّ ٱللَّهَ غَفُورٌ شَكُورٌ ۞
Indeed Allah is all-forgiving, all-appreciative.

أَمْ يَقُولُونَ
24 Do they say,

ٱفْتَرَىٰ عَلَى ٱللَّهِ كَذِبًا
'He has fabricated a lie against Allah'?

فَإِن يَشَإِ ٱللَّهُ
If so, should Allah wish

يَخْتِمْ عَلَىٰ قَلْبِكَ
He would set a seal on *your* heart,

وَيَمْحُ ٱللَّهُ ٱلْبَٰطِلَ
and Allah will efface the falsehood

وَيُحِقُّ ٱلْحَقَّ بِكَلِمَٰتِهِۦٓ
and confirm the truth with His words.

إِنَّهُۥ عَلِيمٌۢ بِذَاتِ ٱلصُّدُورِ ۞
Indeed He knows well what is in the breasts.

وَهُوَ ٱلَّذِى يَقْبَلُ ٱلتَّوْبَةَ
25 It is He who accepts the repentance

عَنْ عِبَادِهِۦ
of His servants,

وَيَعْفُوا۟ عَنِ ٱلسَّيِّـَٔاتِ
and excuses their misdeeds

وَيَعْلَمُ مَا تَفْعَلُونَ ۞
and knows what you do.

وَيَسْتَجِيبُ ٱلَّذِينَ ءَامَنُوا۟
26 And He answers those who have faith

وَعَمِلُوا۟ ٱلصَّٰلِحَٰتِ
and do righteous deeds

وَيَزِيدُهُم مِّن فَضْلِهِۦ     and enhances them out of His grace.

وَٱلْكَٰفِرُونَ     But as for the faithless,

لَهُمْ عَذَابٌ شَدِيدٌ ۞     there is a severe punishment for them.

وَلَوْ بَسَطَ ٱللَّهُ ٱلرِّزْقَ لِعِبَادِهِۦ    27 Were Allah to expand the provision for His servants,

لَبَغَوْا۟ فِى ٱلْأَرْضِ     they would surely create havoc on the earth.

وَلَٰكِن يُنَزِّلُ بِقَدَرٍ     But He sends down in a [precise] measure

مَّا يَشَآءُ     whatever He wishes.

إِنَّهُۥ بِعِبَادِهِۦ خَبِيرٌۢ بَصِيرٌ ۞     Indeed He is all-aware, all-seeing about His servants.

وَهُوَ ٱلَّذِى يُنَزِّلُ ٱلْغَيْثَ    28 It is He who sends down the rain

مِنۢ بَعْدِ مَا قَنَطُوا۟     after they have been despondent,

وَيَنشُرُ رَحْمَتَهُۥ     and unfolds His mercy,

وَهُوَ ٱلْوَلِىُّ ٱلْحَمِيدُ ۞     and He is the Guardian, the All-laudable.

وَمِنْ ءَايَٰتِهِۦ خَلْقُ ٱلسَّمَٰوَٰتِ    29 Among His signs is the creation of the heavens

وَٱلْأَرْضِ     and the earth

وَمَا بَثَّ فِيهِمَا مِن دَآبَّةٍ     and whatever creatures He has scattered in them,

وَهُوَ عَلَىٰ جَمْعِهِمْ إِذَا يَشَآءُ قَدِيرٌ ۞    and He is able to gather them whenever He wishes.

وَمَآ أَصَٰبَكُم مِّن مُّصِيبَةٍ    30 Whatever affliction that may visit you

فَبِمَا كَسَبَتْ أَيْدِيكُمْ     is because of what your hands have earned,

وَيَعْفُوا۟ عَن كَثِيرٍ ۞     though He excuses many [an offense].

وَمَآ أَنتُم بِمُعْجِزِينَ فِى ٱلْأَرْضِ    31 You can not thwart [Allah] on the earth,

وَمَا لَكُم مِّن دُونِ ٱللَّهِ     and you do not have besides Allah

مِن وَلِىٍّ وَلَا نَصِيرٍ ۞     any guardian or helper.

وَمِنْ ءَايَٰتِهِ ٱلْجَوَارِ فِى ٱلْبَحْرِ    32 Among His signs are the ships [that run] on the sea

كَٱلْأَعْلَٰمِ ۞     [appearing] like landmarks.

إِن يَشَأْ يُسْكِنِ ٱلرِّيحَ    33 If He wishes He stills the wind,

فَيَظْلَلْنَ رَوَاكِدَ     whereat they remain standstill

عَلَىٰ ظَهْرِهِۦٓ     on its surface.

إِنَّ فِى ذَٰلِكَ لَءَايَٰتٍ     There are indeed signs in that

لِّكُلِّ صَبَّارٍ شَكُورٍ ۞     for every patient and grateful [servant].

أَوْ يُوبِقْهُنَّ    34 Or He wrecks them

بِمَا كَسَبُوا۟

because of what they[1] have earned,

وَيَعْفُوا۟ عَن كَثِيرٍ ٣٤

though He excuses many [an offense].

وَيَعْلَمَ ٱلَّذِينَ يُجَٰدِلُونَ فِىٓ ءَايَٰتِنَا ٣٥ Let those who dispute Our signs know

مَا لَهُم مِّن مَّحِيصٍ ٣٥

that there is no escape for them.

فَمَآ أُوتِيتُم مِّن شَىْءٍ ٣٦ Whatever you have been given

فَمَتَٰعُ ٱلْحَيَوٰةِ ٱلدُّنْيَا

are the wares of the life of this world,

وَمَا عِندَ ٱللَّهِ خَيْرٌ

but what is with Allah is better

وَأَبْقَىٰ

and more lasting

لِلَّذِينَ ءَامَنُوا۟

for those who have faith

وَعَلَىٰ رَبِّهِمْ يَتَوَكَّلُونَ ٣٦

and who put their trust in their Lord.

وَٱلَّذِينَ يَجْتَنِبُونَ كَبَٰٓئِرَ ٱلْإِثْمِ ٣٧ —Those who avoid major sins

وَٱلْفَوَٰحِشَ

and indecencies,

وَإِذَا مَا غَضِبُوا۟ هُمْ يَغْفِرُونَ ٣٧

and forgive when angered;

وَٱلَّذِينَ ٱسْتَجَابُوا۟ لِرَبِّهِمْ ٣٨ those who answer their Lord,

وَأَقَامُوا۟ ٱلصَّلَوٰةَ

maintain the prayer,

وَأَمْرُهُمْ شُورَىٰ بَيْنَهُمْ

and their affairs are by counsel among themselves,

وَمِمَّا رَزَقْنَٰهُمْ يُنفِقُونَ ٣٨ and they spend out of what We have provided them with;

وَٱلَّذِينَ إِذَآ أَصَابَهُمُ ٱلْبَغْىُ ٣٩ those who, when visited by aggression,

هُمْ يَنتَصِرُونَ ٣٩

come to each other's aid.

وَجَزَٰٓؤُا۟ سَيِّئَةٍ سَيِّئَةٌ مِّثْلُهَا ٤٠ The requital of evil is an evil like it.

فَمَنْ عَفَا وَأَصْلَحَ

So whoever excuses and conciliates,

فَأَجْرُهُۥ عَلَى ٱللَّهِ

his reward lies with Allah.

إِنَّهُۥ لَا يُحِبُّ ٱلظَّٰلِمِينَ ٤٠

Indeed He does not like the wrongdoers.

وَلَمَنِ ٱنتَصَرَ بَعْدَ ظُلْمِهِۦ ٤١ As for those who retaliate after being wronged,

فَأُو۟لَٰٓئِكَ مَا عَلَيْهِم مِّن سَبِيلٍ ٤١

there is no blame upon them.

إِنَّمَا ٱلسَّبِيلُ عَلَى ٱلَّذِينَ ٤٢ The blame lies only upon those who

يَظْلِمُونَ ٱلنَّاسَ

wrong the people

وَيَبْغُونَ فِى ٱلْأَرْضِ بِغَيْرِ ٱلْحَقِّ

and commit aggression in the land unduly.

أُو۟لَٰٓئِكَ لَهُمْ عَذَابٌ أَلِيمٌ ٤٢

For such there is a painful punishment.

---

[1] That is, those who are on the ships.

وَلَمَن صَبَرَ وَغَفَرَ 43 As for him who endures patiently and forgives

إِنَّ ذَٰلِكَ لَمِنْ عَزْمِ ٱلْأُمُورِ ۝     —that is indeed the steadiest of courses.

وَمَن يُضْلِلِ ٱللَّهُ 44 Whomever Allah leads astray

فَمَا لَهُۥ مِن وَلِيٍّ مِّنۢ بَعْدِهِۦ ۗ     has no guardian apart from Him.

وَتَرَى ٱلظَّٰلِمِينَ     *You* will see the wrongdoers,

لَمَّا رَأَوُا۟ ٱلْعَذَابَ     when they sight the punishment,

يَقُولُونَ هَلْ إِلَىٰ مَرَدٍّ مِّن سَبِيلٍ ۝     saying, 'Is there any way for a retreat?'

وَتَرَىٰهُمْ يُعْرَضُونَ عَلَيْهَا 45 *You* will see them being exposed to it,

خَٰشِعِينَ مِنَ ٱلذُّلِّ     humbled by abasement,

يَنظُرُونَ مِن طَرْفٍ خَفِيٍّ ۗ     looking askance secretly.

وَقَالَ ٱلَّذِينَ ءَامَنُوٓا۟     And the faithful will say,

إِنَّ ٱلْخَٰسِرِينَ ٱلَّذِينَ     'Indeed the losers are those

خَسِرُوٓا۟ أَنفُسَهُمْ وَأَهْلِيهِمْ     who have ruined themselves and their families

يَوْمَ ٱلْقِيَٰمَةِ ۗ     on the Day of Resurrection.

أَلَآ     Look!

إِنَّ ٱلظَّٰلِمِينَ فِى عَذَابٍ مُّقِيمٍ ۝     The wrongdoers are indeed in lasting punishment.

وَمَا كَانَ لَهُم مِّنْ أَوْلِيَآءَ يَنصُرُونَهُم 46 They have no guardians to help them

مِّن دُونِ ٱللَّهِ ۗ     besides Allah.

وَمَن يُضْلِلِ ٱللَّهُ     Whomever Allah leads astray

فَمَا لَهُۥ مِن سَبِيلٍ ۝     has no way out.'

ٱسْتَجِيبُوا۟ لِرَبِّكُم 47 Answer your Lord

مِّن قَبْلِ أَن يَأْتِىَ يَوْمٌ     before there comes a day

لَّا مَرَدَّ لَهُۥ مِنَ ٱللَّهِ ۚ     for which there is no revoking from Allah.

مَا لَكُم مِّن مَّلْجَإٍ يَوْمَئِذٍ     On that day you will have no refuge,

وَمَا لَكُم مِّن نَّكِيرٍ ۝     neither will you have [any chance for] denial.

فَإِنْ أَعْرَضُوا۟ 48 But if they disregard [*your* warnings],

فَمَآ أَرْسَلْنَٰكَ عَلَيْهِمْ حَفِيظًا ۖ     We have not sent *you* as a keeper over them.

إِنْ عَلَيْكَ إِلَّا ٱلْبَلَٰغُ ۗ     *Your* duty is only to communicate.

وَإِنَّآ إِذَآ أَذَقْنَا ٱلْإِنسَٰنَ مِنَّا رَحْمَةً     Indeed when We let man taste Our mercy,

687

فَرِحَ بِهَا    he exults in it;

وَإِن تُصِبْهُمْ سَيِّئَةٌ    but should an ill visit them

بِمَا قَدَّمَتْ أَيْدِيهِمْ    because of what their hands have sent ahead,

فَإِنَّ ٱلْإِنسَٰنَ كَفُورٌ ۝    then man is indeed very ungrateful.

لِّلَّهِ مُلْكُ ٱلسَّمَٰوَٰتِ    49 To Allah belongs the kingdom of the heavens

وَٱلْأَرْضِ    and the earth.

يَخْلُقُ مَا يَشَاءُ    He creates whatever He wishes;

يَهَبُ لِمَن يَشَاءُ إِنَٰثًا    He gives females to whomever He wishes,

وَيَهَبُ لِمَن يَشَاءُ ٱلذُّكُورَ ۝    and gives males to whomever He wishes,

أَوْ يُزَوِّجُهُمْ ذُكْرَانًا وَإِنَٰثًا    50 or He combines them males and females,

وَيَجْعَلُ مَن يَشَاءُ عَقِيمًا    and makes sterile whomever He wishes.

إِنَّهُ عَلِيمٌ قَدِيرٌ ۝ *    Indeed He is all-knowing, all-powerful.

وَمَا كَانَ لِبَشَرٍ    51 It is not [possible] for any human

أَن يُكَلِّمَهُ ٱللَّهُ    that Allah should speak to him[1]

إِلَّا وَحْيًا    except through revelation

أَوْ مِن وَرَآئِ حِجَابٍ    or from behind a curtain,[2]

أَوْ يُرْسِلَ رَسُولًا فَيُوحِيَ بِإِذْنِهِ    or send a messenger[3] who reveals by His permission

مَا يَشَاءُ    whatever He wishes.

إِنَّهُ عَلِيٌّ حَكِيمٌ ۝    Indeed He is all-exalted, all-wise.

وَكَذَٰلِكَ أَوْحَيْنَآ إِلَيْكَ    52 Thus have We revealed to *you*

رُوحًا مِّنْ أَمْرِنَا    the spirit of Our dispensation.

مَا كُنتَ تَدْرِي مَا ٱلْكِتَٰبُ    *You* did not know what the Book is,

وَلَا ٱلْإِيمَٰنُ    nor what is faith;

وَلَٰكِن جَعَلْنَٰهُ نُورًا    but We made it a light

نَّهْدِي بِهِ    that We may guide by its means

مَن نَّشَاءُ مِنْ عِبَادِنَا    whomever We wish of Our servants.

وَإِنَّكَ لَتَهْدِي إِلَىٰ صِرَٰطٍ مُّسْتَقِيمٍ ۝    And indeed *you* guide to a straight path,

---

[1] Or 'it does not behoove any human that Allah should speak to him.'

[2] As from a tree, as in the case of Moses ('a).

[3] That is, an angel.

صِرَٰطِ ٱللَّهِ 53     the path of Allah,

ٱلَّذِى لَهُۥ مَا فِى ٱلسَّمَٰوَٰتِ     to whom belongs whatever is in the heavens

وَمَا فِى ٱلْأَرْضِ     and whatever is in the earth.

أَلَآ إِلَى ٱللَّهِ تَصِيرُ ٱلْأُمُورُ ۝     Look! To Allah do all matters return!

## سُورَةُ الزُّخْرُفِ     43. SŪRAT AL-ZUKHRUF[1]

بِسْمِ ٱللَّهِ     In the Name of Allah,

ٱلرَّحْمَٰنِ ٱلرَّحِيمِ     the All-beneficent, the All-merciful.

حمٓ ۝ 1     *Hā, Mīm.*

وَٱلْكِتَٰبِ ٱلْمُبِينِ ۝ 2   By the Manifest Book:

إِنَّا جَعَلْنَٰهُ قُرْءَٰنًا عَرَبِيًّا 3   We have made it an Arabic Qur'ān

لَّعَلَّكُمْ تَعْقِلُونَ ۝     so that you may apply reason,

وَإِنَّهُۥ فِىٓ أُمِّ ٱلْكِتَٰبِ لَدَيْنَا 4   and indeed it is with Us in the Mother Book

لَعَلِىٌّ حَكِيمٌ ۝     [and it is] surely sublime and wise.

أَفَنَضْرِبُ عَنكُمُ ٱلذِّكْرَ 5   Shall We withhold the Reminder from you

صَفْحًا     unconcernedly,

أَن كُنتُمْ قَوْمًا مُّسْرِفِينَ ۝   because you are a profligate lot?

وَكَمْ أَرْسَلْنَا مِن نَّبِىٍّ 6   How many a prophet We have sent

فِى ٱلْأَوَّلِينَ ۝     to the ancients!

وَمَا يَأْتِيهِم مِّن نَّبِىٍّ 7   There did not come to them any prophet

إِلَّا كَانُوا۟ بِهِۦ يَسْتَهْزِءُونَ ۝   but that they used to deride him.

فَأَهْلَكْنَآ أَشَدَّ مِنْهُم بَطْشًا 8   So We destroyed those who were stronger than these,[2]

وَمَضَىٰ مَثَلُ ٱلْأَوَّلِينَ ۝   and the example of the ancients has passed.

وَلَئِن سَأَلْتَهُم 9   If you ask them,

مَّنْ خَلَقَ ٱلسَّمَٰوَٰتِ وَٱلْأَرْضَ   'Who created the heavens and the earth?'

لَيَقُولُنَّ     they will surely say,

---

[1] The *sūrah* takes its name from the word *zukhruf* in verse 35.

[2] That is, the Arab polytheists.

خَلَقَهُنَّ ٱلْعَزِيزُ ٱلْعَلِيمُ ۩  'The All-mighty, the All-knowing created them.'

ٱلَّذِى جَعَلَ لَكُمُ ٱلْأَرْضَ مَهْدًا ١٠  He, who made the earth a cradle for you

وَجَعَلَ لَكُمْ فِيهَا سُبُلًا  and made in it ways for you,

لَعَلَّكُمْ تَهْتَدُونَ ۩  so that you may be guided [to your destinations],

وَٱلَّذِى نَزَّلَ مِنَ ٱلسَّمَآءِ مَآءً ١١  and who sent down water from the sky

بِقَدَرٍ  in a measured manner,

فَأَنشَرْنَا بِهِۦ بَلْدَةً مَّيْتًا  and We revived with it a dead country.

كَذَٰلِكَ تُخْرَجُونَ ۩  (Likewise you [too] shall be raised [from the dead].)

وَٱلَّذِى خَلَقَ ٱلْأَزْوَٰجَ كُلَّهَا ١٢  And who created all the kinds[1]

وَجَعَلَ لَكُم مِّنَ ٱلْفُلْكِ  and made for you the ships

وَٱلْأَنْعَٰمِ  and the cattle

مَا تَرْكَبُونَ ۩  such as you ride,

لِتَسْتَوُۥا۟ عَلَىٰ ظُهُورِهِۦ ١٣  that you may sit on their backs,

ثُمَّ تَذْكُرُوا۟ نِعْمَةَ رَبِّكُمْ  then remember the blessing of your Lord

إِذَا ٱسْتَوَيْتُمْ عَلَيْهِ  when you are settled on them,

وَتَقُولُوا۟  and say,

سُبْحَٰنَ ٱلَّذِى  'Immaculate is He

سَخَّرَ لَنَا هَٰذَا  who has disposed this for us,

وَمَا كُنَّا لَهُۥ مُقْرِنِينَ ۩  and we [by ourselves] were no match for it.

وَإِنَّا إِلَىٰ رَبِّنَا لَمُنقَلِبُونَ ۩ ١٤  Indeed we shall return to our Lord.'

وَجَعَلُوا۟ لَهُۥ ١٥ They ascribe to Him

مِنْ عِبَادِهِۦ جُزْءًا  offspring[2] from among His servants!

إِنَّ ٱلْإِنسَٰنَ لَكَفُورٌ مُّبِينٌ ۩  Man is indeed a manifest ingrate.

أَمِ ٱتَّخَذَ مِمَّا يَخْلُقُ بَنَاتٍ ١٦ Did He adopt daughters from what He creates

وَأَصْفَىٰكُم بِٱلْبَنِينَ ۩  while He preferred you with sons?

وَإِذَا بُشِّرَ أَحَدُهُم ١٧ When one of them is brought the news

بِمَا ضَرَبَ لِلرَّحْمَٰنِ مَثَلًا  of what he ascribes to the All-beneficent,

---

[1] Or, 'all the pairs.'

[2] Lit.: 'They assign to Him a portion from among His servants.'

ظَلَّ وَجْهُهُ مُسْوَدًّا | his face becomes darkened [1]

وَهُوَ كَظِيمٌ ۝ | and he chokes with suppressed agony, [and says]

18 أَوَمَن يُنَشَّؤُاْ فِى ٱلْحِلْيَةِ | 18 'What! One who is brought up amid ornaments

وَهُوَ فِى ٱلْخِصَامِ غَيْرُ مُبِينٍ ۝ | and is inconspicuous in contests?'

19 وَجَعَلُواْ ٱلْمَلَـٰٓئِكَةَ | 19 And they have made the angels

ٱلَّذِينَ هُمْ عِبَـٰدُ ٱلرَّحْمَـٰنِ | —who are servants of the All-beneficent—

إِنَـٰثًا | females.

أَشَهِدُواْ خَلْقَهُمْ | Were they witness to their creation?

سَتُكْتَبُ شَهَـٰدَتُهُمْ | Their testimony will be written down

وَيُسْـَٔلُونَ ۝ | and they shall be questioned.

20 وَقَالُواْ لَوْ شَآءَ ٱلرَّحْمَـٰنُ | 20 They say, 'Had the All-beneficent wished,

مَا عَبَدْنَـٰهُمْ | we would not have worshipped them.' [2]

مَّا لَهُم بِذَٰلِكَ مِنْ عِلْمٍ | They do not have any knowledge of that,

إِنْ هُمْ إِلَّا يَخْرُصُونَ ۝ | and they do nothing but surmise.

21 أَمْ ءَاتَيْنَـٰهُمْ كِتَـٰبًا مِّن قَبْلِهِ | 21 Did We give them a Book before this,

فَهُم بِهِۦ مُسْتَمْسِكُونَ ۝ | so that they are holding fast to it?

22 بَلْ قَالُوٓاْ إِنَّا وَجَدْنَآ ءَابَآءَنَا | 22 Rather they say, 'We found our fathers

عَلَىٰٓ أُمَّةٍ | following a creed,

وَإِنَّا عَلَىٰٓ ءَاثَـٰرِهِم مُّهْتَدُونَ ۝ | and we are indeed guided in their footsteps.'

23 وَكَذَٰلِكَ مَآ أَرْسَلْنَا | 23 And so it has been that We did not send

مِن قَبْلِكَ فِى قَرْيَةٍ مِّن نَّذِيرٍ | any warner to a town before you,

إِلَّا قَالَ مُتْرَفُوهَآ | without its affluent ones saying,

إِنَّا وَجَدْنَآ ءَابَآءَنَا عَلَىٰٓ أُمَّةٍ | 'We found our fathers following a creed

وَإِنَّا عَلَىٰٓ ءَاثَـٰرِهِم مُّقْتَدُونَ ۝ ✻ | and we are indeed following in their footsteps.'

24 قَـٰلَ أَوَلَوْ جِئْتُكُم | 24 He would say, 'What! Even if I bring you

بِأَهْدَىٰ مِمَّا وَجَدتُّمْ | a better guidance than what you found

عَلَيْهِ ءَابَآءَكُمْ | your fathers following?!'

قَالُوٓاْ | They would say,

---

[1] That is, when he is brought the news of the birth of a daughter.
[2] That is, the gods worshiped by the polytheists. Cf. 16:35.

إِنَّا بِمَآ أُرْسِلْتُم بِهِۦ كَٰفِرُونَ ۝  'We indeed disbelieve in what you are sent with.'

فَٱنتَقَمْنَا مِنْهُمْ  25 Thereupon We took vengeance on them;

فَٱنظُرْ كَيْفَ كَانَ عَٰقِبَةُ ٱلْمُكَذِّبِينَ ۝  so *observe* how was the fate of the deniers.

وَإِذْ قَالَ إِبْرَٰهِيمُ لِأَبِيهِ وَقَوْمِهِۦٓ  26 When Abraham said to his father and his people,

إِنَّنِى بَرَآءٌ مِّمَّا تَعْبُدُونَ ۝  'I repudiate what you worship,

إِلَّا ٱلَّذِى فَطَرَنِى  27   excepting Him who originated me;

فَإِنَّهُۥ سَيَهْدِينِ ۝  indeed He will guide me.'

وَجَعَلَهَا كَلِمَةً بَاقِيَةً  28 And He made it[1] a lasting word

فِى عَقِبِهِۦ  among his posterity

لَعَلَّهُمْ يَرْجِعُونَ ۝  so that they may come back [to the right path].

بَلْ مَتَّعْتُ هَٰٓؤُلَآءِ وَءَابَآءَهُمْ  29 Rather I provided for these[2] and their fathers

حَتَّىٰ جَآءَهُمُ ٱلْحَقُّ  until there came to them the truth

وَرَسُولٌ مُّبِينٌ ۝  and a manifest apostle.

وَلَمَّا جَآءَهُمُ ٱلْحَقُّ قَالُوا۟  30 But when the truth came to them, they said,

هَٰذَا سِحْرٌ وَإِنَّا بِهِۦ كَٰفِرُونَ ۝  'This is magic, and we indeed disbelieve in it.'

وَقَالُوا۟ لَوْلَا نُزِّلَ هَٰذَا ٱلْقُرْءَانُ  31 And they said, 'Why was not this Qur'ān sent down

عَلَىٰ رَجُلٍ مِّنَ ٱلْقَرْيَتَيْنِ عَظِيمٍ ۝  to some great man from the two cities.'[3]

أَهُمْ يَقْسِمُونَ رَحْمَتَ رَبِّكَ  32 Is it they who dispense the mercy of *your* Lord?

نَحْنُ قَسَمْنَا بَيْنَهُم  It is We who have dispensed among them

مَّعِيشَتَهُمْ فِى ٱلْحَيَوٰةِ ٱلدُّنْيَا  their livelihood in the present life,

وَرَفَعْنَا بَعْضَهُمْ فَوْقَ بَعْضٍ دَرَجَٰتٍ  and raised some of them above others in rank,

لِيَتَّخِذَ بَعْضُهُم بَعْضًا سُخْرِيًّا  so that some may take others into service,

وَرَحْمَتُ رَبِّكَ خَيْرٌ مِّمَّا يَجْمَعُونَ ۝  and *your* Lord's mercy is better than what they amass.

وَلَوْلَآ أَن يَكُونَ ٱلنَّاسُ  33 Were it not [for the danger] that mankind would be

---

[1] That is, the word of *tawḥīd*, 'There is god except Allah,' the monotheistic creed of Abraham, or, in accordance with the traditions of the Imams Muḥammad al-Bāqir and Ja'far al-Ṣādiq (ʿa) Abraham's imamate (cf. 2:124; *Tafsīr al-Ṣāfī, Majmaʿ al-Bayān*).

[2] That is, the Arabs.

[3] That is, Makkah and Madinah, which were the two major towns of Arabia at that time.

| | |
|---|---|
| أُمَّةً وَٰحِدَةً | one community,[1] |
| لَّجَعَلْنَا | We would have surely made |
| لِمَن يَكْفُرُ بِٱلرَّحْمَٰنِ | for those who defy the All-beneficent, |
| لِبُيُوتِهِمْ سُقُفًا مِّن فِضَّةٍ | silver roofs for their houses |
| وَمَعَارِجَ عَلَيْهَا يَظْهَرُونَ ۝ | and [silver] stairways by which they ascend; |
| وَلِبُيُوتِهِمْ أَبْوَٰبًا | 34 and [silver] doors for their houses |
| وَسُرُرًا عَلَيْهَا يَتَّكِئُونَ ۝ | and [silver] couches on which they recline; |
| وَزُخْرُفًا | 35 and ornaments of gold;[2] |
| وَإِن كُلُّ ذَٰلِكَ لَمَّا | yet all that would be nothing but |
| مَتَٰعُ ٱلْحَيَوٰةِ ٱلدُّنْيَا | the wares of the life of this world, |
| وَٱلْءَاخِرَةُ عِندَ رَبِّكَ | and the Hereafter near *your* Lord is |
| لِلْمُتَّقِينَ ۝ | for the Godwary. |
| وَمَن يَعْشُ عَن | 36 Whoever turns a blind eye to[3] |
| ذِكْرِ ٱلرَّحْمَٰنِ | the remembrance of the All-beneficent, |
| نُقَيِّضْ لَهُۥ شَيْطَٰنًا | We assign him a devil |
| فَهُوَ لَهُۥ قَرِينٌ ۝ | who remains his companion. |
| وَإِنَّهُمْ لَيَصُدُّونَهُمْ عَنِ ٱلسَّبِيلِ | 37 Indeed they[4] bar them from the way |
| وَيَحْسَبُونَ أَنَّهُم مُّهْتَدُونَ ۝ | while they suppose that they are [rightly] guided. |
| حَتَّىٰٓ إِذَا جَآءَنَا قَالَ | 38 When he comes to Us, he will say, |
| يَٰلَيْتَ بَيْنِى وَبَيْنَكَ | 'I wish there had been between me and you |
| بُعْدَ ٱلْمَشْرِقَيْنِ | the distance between east and west!'[5] |
| فَبِئْسَ ٱلْقَرِينُ ۝ | What an evil companion! |
| وَلَن يَنفَعَكُمُ ٱلْيَوْمَ | 39 'Today that will be of no avail to you. |
| إِذ ظَّلَمْتُمْ | As you did wrong, |
| أَنَّكُمْ فِى ٱلْعَذَابِ مُشْتَرِكُونَ ۝ | so will you share in the punishment.' |
| أَفَأَنتَ تُسْمِعُ ٱلصُّمَّ | 40 Can *you,* then, make the deaf hear |

---

[1] That is, a monolithic community of people without faith.
[2] Or 'houses embellished with gold.'
[3] Or 'whoever shuns.'
[4] That is, the devils.
[5] Or 'between the two easts.'

أُوْ تَهْدِى ٱلْعُمْىَ     or guide the blind

وَمَن كَانَ فِى ضَلَلٍ مُّبِينٍ ۝     and someone who is in manifest error?

فَإِمَّا نَذْهَبَنَّ بِكَ     41 Either We shall take *you* away

فَإِنَّا مِنْهُم مُّنتَقِمُونَ ۝     —for We will indeed take vengeance on them—

أَوْ نُرِيَنَّكَ ٱلَّذِى وَعَدْنَهُمْ     42 or We shall show *you* what We have promised them,

فَإِنَّا عَلَيْهِم مُّقْتَدِرُونَ ۝     for indeed We hold them in Our power.

فَٱسْتَمْسِكْ بِٱلَّذِىٓ أُوحِىَ إِلَيْكَ     43 So *hold fast* to what has been revealed to *you*.

إِنَّكَ عَلَىٰ صِرَطٍ مُّسْتَقِيمٍ ۝     Indeed *you* are on a straight path.

وَإِنَّهُۥ لَذِكْرٌ لَّكَ وَلِقَوْمِكَ     44 Indeed it is a reminder for *you* and for *your* people,

وَسَوْفَ تُسْـَٔلُونَ ۝     and soon you will be questioned.

وَسْـَٔلْ     45 *Ask*

مَنْ أَرْسَلْنَا مِن قَبْلِكَ مِن رُّسُلِنَآ     those of Our apostles We have sent before *you*:[1]

أَجَعَلْنَا مِن دُونِ ٱلرَّحْمَنِ ءَالِهَةً     Did We set up any gods besides the All-beneficent

يُعْبَدُونَ ۝     to be worshipped?

وَلَقَدْ أَرْسَلْنَا مُوسَىٰ بِـَٔايَتِنَآ     46 Certainly We sent Moses with Our signs

إِلَىٰ فِرْعَوْنَ وَمَلَإِيْهِۦ     to Pharaoh and his elite.

فَقَالَ إِنِّى رَسُولُ     He said, 'I am indeed an apostle

رَبِّ ٱلْعَلَمِينَ ۝     of the Lord of all the worlds.'

فَلَمَّا جَآءَهُم بِـَٔايَتِنَآ     47 But when he brought them Our signs,

إِذَا هُم مِّنْهَا يَضْحَكُونَ ۝     behold, they laughed at them.

وَمَا نُرِيهِم مِّنْ ءَايَةٍ     48 And We did not show them a sign

إِلَّا هِىَ أَكْبَرُ مِنْ أُخْتِهَا     but it was greater than the other,

وَأَخَذْنَهُم بِٱلْعَذَابِ     and We seized them with punishment

لَعَلَّهُمْ يَرْجِعُونَ ۝     so that they might come back.

وَقَالُوا۟ يَٰٓأَيُّهَ ٱلسَّاحِرُ     49 They would say, 'O magician!

ٱدْعُ لَنَا رَبَّكَ     Invoke your Lord for us

بِمَا عَهِدَ عِندَكَ     by the covenant He has made with you.

إِنَّنَا لَمُهْتَدُونَ ۝     We will indeed be guided.'

---

[1] That is, during the cosmic journey of the Prophet (see 17:1, 53:8-18).

فَلَمَّا كَشَفْنَا عَنْهُمُ ٱلْعَذَابَ ‎ 50 But when We lifted the punishment from them,

إِذَا هُمْ يَنكُثُونَ ۝ ‎ behold, they would break their pledge.

وَنَادَىٰ فِرْعَوْنُ فِى قَوْمِهِۦ ‎ 51 And Pharaoh proclaimed amongst his people.

قَالَ يَٰقَوْمِ ‎ He said, 'O my people!

أَلَيْسَ لِى مُلْكُ مِصْرَ ‎ Does not the kingdom of Egypt belong to me

وَهَٰذِهِ ٱلْأَنْهَٰرُ تَجْرِى مِن تَحْتِىٓ ‎ and these rivers that run at my feet?

أَفَلَا تُبْصِرُونَ ۝ ‎ Do you not perceive?

أَمْ أَنَا۠ خَيْرٌ مِّنْ هَٰذَا ٱلَّذِى هُوَ مَهِينٌ ‎ 52 Am I not better than this humble[1] one

وَلَا يَكَادُ يُبِينُ ۝ ‎ who cannot even speak clearly?

فَلَوْلَآ أُلْقِىَ عَلَيْهِ أَسْوِرَةٌ مِّن ذَهَبٍ ‎ 53 Why have no bracelets of gold been cast upon him,

أَوْ جَآءَ مَعَهُ ٱلْمَلَٰٓئِكَةُ مُقْتَرِنِينَ ۝ ‎ nor have the angels come with him as escorts?'

فَٱسْتَخَفَّ قَوْمَهُۥ فَأَطَاعُوهُ ‎ 54 So he misled his people and they obeyed him.

إِنَّهُمْ كَانُوا۟ قَوْمًا فَٰسِقِينَ ۝ ‎ Indeed they were a transgressing lot.

فَلَمَّآ ءَاسَفُونَا ‎ 55 So when they roused Our wrath,

ٱنتَقَمْنَا مِنْهُمْ ‎ We took vengeance on them

فَأَغْرَقْنَٰهُمْ أَجْمَعِينَ ۝ ‎ and drowned them all.

فَجَعَلْنَٰهُمْ سَلَفًا ‎ 56 Thus We made them the vanguard[2]

وَمَثَلًا لِّلْءَاخِرِينَ ۝ ✵ ‎ and an example for posterity.

وَلَمَّا ضُرِبَ ٱبْنُ مَرْيَمَ مَثَلًا ‎ 57 When the Son of Mary was cited as an example,

إِذَا قَوْمُكَ مِنْهُ يَصِدُّونَ ۝ ‎ behold, *your* people raise an outcry.[3]

وَقَالُوٓا۟ ءَأَٰلِهَتُنَا خَيْرٌ أَمْ هُوَ ‎ 58 They say, 'Are our gods better or he?'

مَا ضَرَبُوهُ لَكَ إِلَّا جَدَلًا ‎ They only cite him to *you* for the sake of contention.

بَلْ هُمْ قَوْمٌ خَصِمُونَ ۝ ‎ Rather they are a contentious lot.

إِنْ هُوَ إِلَّا عَبْدٌ أَنْعَمْنَا عَلَيْهِ ‎ 59 He was just a servant whom We had blessed

---

[1] Or 'vile.'

[2] That is, of those who enter hell.

[3] Or 'laughed at it.' (*Maʿānī al-akhbār*, p. 220) Or 'turn away,' in accordance with an alternate reading (*yaṣuddūn* instead of *yaṣiddūn*) narrated from many authorities. (*Muʿjam al-Qirāʾāt al-Qurʾāniyyah*, vol. 6, p. 121)

وَجَعَلْنَهُ مَثَلًا لِّبَنِى إِسْرَاءِيلَ ۝    and made an exemplar for the Children of Israel.

وَلَوْ نَشَاءُ لَجَعَلْنَا مِنكُم ٦٠ Had We wished We would have set in your stead

مَّلَٰئِكَةً فِى ٱلْأَرْضِ يَخْلُفُونَ ۝    angels to be [your] successors on the earth.

وَإِنَّهُۥ لَعِلْمٌ لِّلسَّاعَةِ ٦١ Indeed he[1] is a portent of the Hour;

فَلَا تَمْتَرُنَّ بِهَا وَٱتَّبِعُونِ    so do not doubt it and follow Me.

هَٰذَا صِرَٰطٌ مُّسْتَقِيمٌ ۝    This is a straight path.

وَلَا يَصُدَّنَّكُمُ ٱلشَّيْطَٰنُ ٦٢ Do not let Satan bar you [from the way of Allah].

إِنَّهُۥ لَكُمْ عَدُوٌّ مُّبِينٌ ۝    Indeed he is your manifest enemy.

وَلَمَّا جَاءَ عِيسَىٰ بِٱلْبَيِّنَٰتِ ٦٣ When Jesus brought the manifest proofs,

قَالَ قَدْ جِئْتُكُم بِٱلْحِكْمَةِ    he said, 'I have certainly brought you wisdom,

وَلِأُبَيِّنَ لَكُم    and [I have come] to make clear to you

بَعْضَ ٱلَّذِى تَخْتَلِفُونَ فِيهِ    some of the things that you differ about.

فَٱتَّقُوا ٱللَّهَ وَأَطِيعُونِ ۝    So be wary of Allah and obey me.'

إِنَّ ٱللَّهَ هُوَ رَبِّى وَرَبُّكُمْ ٦٤    Indeed Allah is my Lord and your Lord;

فَٱعْبُدُوهُ    so worship Him.

هَٰذَا صِرَٰطٌ مُّسْتَقِيمٌ ۝    This is a straight path.'

فَٱخْتَلَفَ ٱلْأَحْزَابُ مِنۢ بَيْنِهِمْ ٦٥ But the factions differed among themselves.

فَوَيْلٌ لِّلَّذِينَ ظَلَمُوا    So woe to the wrongdoers

مِنْ عَذَابِ يَوْمٍ أَلِيمٍ ۝    for the punishment of a painful day.

هَلْ يَنظُرُونَ إِلَّا ٱلسَّاعَةَ ٦٦ Do they await anything but that the Hour

أَن تَأْتِيَهُم بَغْتَةً    should overtake them suddenly,

وَهُمْ لَا يَشْعُرُونَ ۝    while they are unaware?

ٱلْأَخِلَّاءُ يَوْمَئِذٍ بَعْضُهُمْ لِبَعْضٍ عَدُوٌّ ٦٧ On that day, friends will be one another's enemies,

إِلَّا ٱلْمُتَّقِينَ ۝    except for the Godwary.

يَٰعِبَادِ ٦٨ [They will be told,] 'O My servants!

لَا خَوْفٌ عَلَيْكُمُ ٱلْيَوْمَ    Today you will have no fear,

وَلَا أَنتُمْ تَحْزَنُونَ ۝    nor will you grieve.

---

[1] That is, Jesus ('a), or 'Alī ibn Abī Ṭālib, in accordance with traditions narrated from the Prophet (ṣ) and Imam Ja'far al-Ṣādiq ('a). (*Tafsīr al-Burhān*).

اَلَّذِينَ ءَامَنُواْ بِـَٔايَـٰتِنَا

69    Those who believed in Our signs

وَكَانُواْ مُسْلِمِينَ

and had been *muslim*s.

ٱدْخُلُواْ ٱلْجَنَّةَ أَنتُمْ وَأَزْوَٰجُكُمْ

70    Enter paradise, you and your spouses,

تُحْبَرُونَ

rejoicing

يُطَافُ عَلَيْهِم

71    (they will be served around

بِصِحَافٍ مِّن ذَهَبٍ وَأَكْوَابٍ

with golden dishes and goblets,

وَفِيهَا مَا تَشْتَهِيهِ ٱلْأَنفُسُ

and therein[1] will be whatever the souls desire

وَتَلَذُّ ٱلْأَعْيُنُ

and eyes delight in)

وَأَنتُمْ فِيهَا خَـٰلِدُونَ

and you will remain in it [forever].

وَتِلْكَ ٱلْجَنَّةُ ٱلَّتِىٓ أُورِثْتُمُوهَا

72 That is the paradise you have been given to inherit

بِمَا كُنتُمْ تَعْمَلُونَ

for what you used to do.

لَكُمْ فِيهَا فَـٰكِهَةٌ كَثِيرَةٌ

73 Therein are abundant fruits for you

مِنْهَا تَأْكُلُونَ

from which you will eat.'

إِنَّ ٱلْمُجْرِمِينَ

74 Indeed the guilty

فِى عَذَابِ جَهَنَّمَ خَـٰلِدُونَ

will remain [forever] in the punishment of hell.

لَا يُفَتَّرُ عَنْهُمْ

75 It will not be lightened for them

وَهُمْ فِيهِ مُبْلِسُونَ

and they will be despondent in it.

وَمَا ظَلَمْنَـٰهُمْ

76 We did not wrong them,

وَلَـٰكِن كَانُواْ هُمُ ٱلظَّـٰلِمِينَ

but they themselves were wrongdoers.

وَنَادَوْاْ يَـٰمَـٰلِكُ

77 They will call out, 'O Mālik![2]

لِيَقْضِ عَلَيْنَا رَبُّكَ

Let your Lord finish us off!'

قَالَ إِنَّكُم مَّـٰكِثُونَ

He will say, 'Indeed you will stay on.'

لَقَدْ جِئْنَـٰكُم بِٱلْحَقِّ

78 'We certainly brought you the truth,

وَلَـٰكِنَّ أَكْثَرَكُمْ لِلْحَقِّ كَـٰرِهُونَ

but most of you were averse to the truth.'

أَمْ أَبْرَمُوٓاْ أَمْرًا

79 Have they settled on some [devious] plan?

فَإِنَّا مُبْرِمُونَ

Indeed We too are settling [on Our plans].

أَمْ يَحْسَبُونَ أَنَّا لَا نَسْمَعُ

80 Do they suppose that We do not hear

---

[1] That is, in paradise.

[2] The name of the angel in charge of hell.

سِرَّهُمْ وَنَجْوَىٰهُمْ their secret thoughts and their secret talks?

بَلَىٰ Yes indeed!

وَرُسُلُنَا لَدَيْهِمْ يَكْتُبُونَ ⑳ And with them are Our messengers, writing down.

قُلْ إِن كَانَ لِلرَّحْمَٰنِ وَلَدٌ 81 *Say,* 'If the All-beneficent had a son,

فَأَنَا۠ أَوَّلُ ٱلْعَٰبِدِينَ ⑳ I would have been the first to worship [him].'

سُبْحَٰنَ رَبِّ ٱلسَّمَٰوَٰتِ وَٱلْأَرْضِ 82 Clear is the Lord of the heavens and the earth,

رَبِّ ٱلْعَرْشِ the Lord of the Throne,

عَمَّا يَصِفُونَ ⑳ of whatever they allege [concerning Him]!

فَذَرْهُمْ يَخُوضُوا۟ وَيَلْعَبُوا۟ 83 So leave them to gossip and play

حَتَّىٰ يُلَٰقُوا۟ يَوْمَهُمُ until they encounter their day

ٱلَّذِى يُوعَدُونَ ⑳ which they are promised.

وَهُوَ ٱلَّذِى فِى ٱلسَّمَآءِ إِلَٰهٌ 84 It is He who is God in the sky,

وَفِى ٱلْأَرْضِ إِلَٰهٌ and God on the earth;

وَهُوَ ٱلْحَكِيمُ ٱلْعَلِيمُ ⑳ and He is the All-Wise, the All-Knowing.

وَتَبَارَكَ ٱلَّذِى 85 Blessed is He

لَهُۥ مُلْكُ ٱلسَّمَٰوَٰتِ to whom belongs the kingdom of the heavens

وَٱلْأَرْضِ and the earth

وَمَا بَيْنَهُمَا and whatever is between them,

وَعِندَهُۥ عِلْمُ ٱلسَّاعَةِ and with Him is the knowledge of the Hour,

وَإِلَيْهِ تُرْجَعُونَ ⑳ and to Him you will be brought back.

وَلَا يَمْلِكُ ٱلَّذِينَ يَدْعُونَ مِن دُونِهِ 86 Those whom they invoke besides Him have no power

ٱلشَّفَٰعَةَ of intercession,

إِلَّا مَن شَهِدَ بِٱلْحَقِّ except those who are witness to the truth

وَهُمْ يَعْلَمُونَ ⑳ and who know [for whom to intercede].

وَلَئِن سَأَلْتَهُم 87 If you ask them,

مَّنْ خَلَقَهُمْ 'Who created them?'

لَيَقُولُنَّ ٱللَّهُ they will surely say, 'Allah.'

فَأَنَّىٰ يُؤْفَكُونَ ⑳ Then where do they stray?

وَقِيلِهِۦ يَـٰرَبِّ 88 And his[1] plaint: 'My Lord!

إِنَّ هَـٰٓؤُلَآءِ قَوۡمٌ لَّا يُؤۡمِنُونَ ۝     Indeed these are a people who will not have faith!'

فَٱصۡفَحۡ عَنۡهُمۡ وَقُلۡ سَلَـٰمٌ 89 So *disregard* them, and *say*, 'Peace!'

فَسَوۡفَ يَعۡلَمُونَ ۝     Soon they will know.

# سُورَةُ الدُّخَانِ     44 SŪRAT AL-DUKHĀN[2]

بِسۡمِ ٱللَّهِ     In the Name of Allah,

ٱلرَّحۡمَـٰنِ ٱلرَّحِيمِ     the All-beneficent, the All-merciful.

حمٓ ۝ 1 *Ḥā, Mīm.*

وَٱلۡكِتَـٰبِ ٱلۡمُبِينِ ۝ 2 By the Manifest Book!

إِنَّآ أَنزَلۡنَـٰهُ فِى لَيۡلَةٍ مُّبَـٰرَكَةٍ 3 Indeed We sent it down on a blessed night,

إِنَّا كُنَّا مُنذِرِينَ ۝     and indeed We have been warning [mankind].

فِيهَا يُفۡرَقُ كُلُّ أَمۡرٍ حَكِيمٍ ۝ 4 Every definitive matter is resolved in it,[3]

أَمۡرًا مِّنۡ عِندِنَآ 5 as an ordinance[4] from Us.

إِنَّا كُنَّا مُرۡسِلِينَ ۝     Indeed We have been sending [apostles],

رَحۡمَةً مِّن رَّبِّكَ 6 as a mercy from *your* Lord

إِنَّهُۥ هُوَ ٱلسَّمِيعُ ٱلۡعَلِيمُ ۝     —indeed He is the All-hearing, the All-knowing—

رَبِّ ٱلسَّمَـٰوَٰتِ وَٱلۡأَرۡضِ 7 the Lord of the heavens and the earth,

وَمَا بَيۡنَهُمَآ     and whatever is between them,

إِن كُنتُم مُّوقِنِينَ ۝     should you have conviction.

لَآ إِلَـٰهَ إِلَّا هُوَ 8 There is no god except Him:

يُحۡىِۦ وَيُمِيتُ     He gives life and brings death,

رَبُّكُمۡ وَرَبُّ ءَابَآئِكُمُ ٱلۡأَوَّلِينَ ۝     your Lord and the Lord of your forefathers.

بَلۡ هُمۡ فِى شَكٍّ يَلۡعَبُونَ ۝ 9 Rather they play around in doubt.

فَٱرۡتَقِبۡ يَوۡمَ 10 So *watch out* for the day

---

[1] That is, of the Apostle of Allah (ṣ).

[2] The *sūrah* takes its name from 'the smoke' mentioned in verse 10.

[3] That is, on the Night of Ordainment. See 97:1-5.

[4] Or 'edict.'

تَأْتِى ٱلسَّمَآءُ بِدُخَانٍ مُّبِينٍ ۝    when the sky brings on a manifest smoke,

يَغْشَى ٱلنَّاسَ ۝   11   enveloping the people.

هَـٰذَا عَذَابٌ أَلِيمٌ ۝    [They will cry out:] 'This is a painful punishment.

رَّبَّنَا ٱكْشِفْ عَنَّا ٱلْعَذَابَ   12   Our Lord! Remove from us this punishment.

إِنَّا مُؤْمِنُونَ ۝    Indeed we have believed!'

أَنَّىٰ لَهُمُ ٱلذِّكْرَىٰ   13   What will the admonition avail them,

وَقَدْ جَآءَهُمْ رَسُولٌ مُّبِينٌ ۝    when a manifest apostle had already come to them,

ثُمَّ تَوَلَّوْا۟ عَنْهُ   14   but they turned away from him,

وَقَالُوا۟ مُعَلَّمٌ مَّجْنُونٌ ۝    and said, 'A tutored madman?'

إِنَّا كَاشِفُوا۟ ٱلْعَذَابِ قَلِيلًا   15   Indeed We will withdraw the punishment a little;

إِنَّكُمْ عَآئِدُونَ ۝    but you will indeed revert [to your earlier ways].

يَوْمَ نَبْطِشُ ٱلْبَطْشَةَ ٱلْكُبْرَىٰ   16   The day We shall strike with the most terrible striking,

إِنَّا مُنتَقِمُونَ ۝ ۞    We will indeed take vengeance [on them].

وَلَقَدْ فَتَنَّا   17   Certainly We tried

قَبْلَهُمْ قَوْمَ فِرْعَوْنَ    the people of Pharaoh before them,

وَجَآءَهُمْ رَسُولٌ كَرِيمٌ ۝    when a noble apostle came to them,

أَنْ أَدُّوٓا۟ إِلَىَّ عِبَادَ ٱللَّهِ   18   [saying,] 'Give over the servants of Allah[1] to me;

إِنِّى لَكُمْ رَسُولٌ أَمِينٌ ۝    indeed I am a trusted apostle [sent] to you.

وَأَن لَّا تَعْلُوا۟ عَلَى ٱللَّهِ   19   Do not rebel against Allah.

إِنِّىٓ ءَاتِيكُم بِسُلْطَـٰنٍ مُّبِينٍ ۝    Indeed I bring you a manifest authority.

وَإِنِّى عُذْتُ بِرَبِّى وَرَبِّكُمْ   20   I seek the protection of my Lord and your Lord,

أَن تَرْجُمُونِ ۝    lest you should stone me.

وَإِن لَّمْ تُؤْمِنُوا۟ لِى   21   And if you do not believe me,

فَٱعْتَزِلُونِ ۝    keep out of my way.'

فَدَعَا رَبَّهُۥٓ   22   Then he invoked his Lord,

أَنَّ هَـٰٓؤُلَآءِ قَوْمٌ مُّجْرِمُونَ ۝    [saying,] 'These are indeed a guilty lot.'

فَأَسْرِ بِعِبَادِى لَيْلًا   23   [Allah told him,] 'Set out with My servants by night;

إِنَّكُم مُّتَّبَعُونَ ۝    for you will indeed be pursued.

---

[1] That is, the Israelites.

وَٱتْرُكِ ٱلْبَحْرَ رَهْوًا 24 And leave the sea calmly;

إِنَّهُمْ جُندٌ مُّغْرَقُونَ ۝ they will indeed be a drowned host.'

كَمْ تَرَكُوا مِن جَنَّـٰتٍ وَعُيُونٍ ۝ 25 How many gardens and springs did they leave behind!

وَزُرُوعٍ وَمَقَامٍ كَرِيمٍ ۝ 26 Fields and splendid places,

وَنَعْمَةٍ كَانُوا فِيهَا فَـٰكِهِينَ ۝ 27 and the bounties wherein they rejoiced!

كَذَٰلِكَ 28 So it was;

وَأَوْرَثْنَـٰهَا قَوْمًا ءَاخَرِينَ ۝ and We bequeathed them to another people.

فَمَا بَكَتْ عَلَيْهِمُ ٱلسَّمَآءُ 29 So neither the sky wept for them,

وَٱلْأَرْضُ nor the earth;

وَمَا كَانُوا مُنظَرِينَ ۝ nor were they granted any respite.

وَلَقَدْ نَجَّيْنَا بَنِى إِسْرَٰٓءِيلَ 30 Certainly We delivered the Children of Israel

مِنَ ٱلْعَذَابِ ٱلْمُهِينِ ۝ from a humiliating torment,

مِن فِرْعَوْنَ 31 from Pharaoh.

إِنَّهُۥ كَانَ عَالِيًا مِّنَ ٱلْمُسْرِفِينَ ۝ Indeed he was a rebel among the profligates.

وَلَقَدِ ٱخْتَرْنَـٰهُمْ عَلَىٰ عِلْمٍ 32 Certainly We chose them knowingly

عَلَى ٱلْعَـٰلَمِينَ ۝ above all the nations.

وَءَاتَيْنَـٰهُم مِّنَ ٱلْءَايَـٰتِ 33 And We gave them some signs

مَا فِيهِ بَلَـٰٓؤُا۟ مُّبِينٌ ۝ in which there was a manifest test.

إِنَّ هَـٰٓؤُلَآءِ لَيَقُولُونَ ۝ 34 Indeed these ones say,

إِنْ هِىَ إِلَّا مَوْتَتُنَا ٱلْأُولَىٰ 35 'It will be just our first death,

وَمَا نَحْنُ بِمُنشَرِينَ ۝ and we shall not be resurrected.

فَأْتُوا بِـَٔابَآئِنَآ 36 Bring our fathers back [to life],

إِن كُنتُمْ صَـٰدِقِينَ ۝ should you be truthful.'

أَهُمْ خَيْرٌ أَمْ قَوْمُ تُبَّعٍ 37 Are they better, or the people of Tubbaʿ,[1]

وَٱلَّذِينَ مِن قَبْلِهِمْ and those who were before them?

أَهْلَكْنَـٰهُمْ We destroyed them;

---

[1] Name of a Yemenite king. Tubbaʿ is said to be the title of a dynasty of
Yemenite kings (like pharaoh, caesar and khaqan).

إِنَّهُمْ كَانُوا مُجْرِمِينَ ۝     indeed they were guilty.

38 وَمَا خَلَقْنَا ٱلسَّمَـٰوَٰتِ وَٱلْأَرْضَ     38 We did not create the heavens and the earth

وَمَا بَيْنَهُمَا لَـٰعِبِينَ ۝     and whatever is between them for play.

مَا خَلَقْنَـٰهُمَآ إِلَّا بِٱلْحَقِّ     39 We did not create them except with the truth;

وَلَـٰكِنَّ أَكْثَرَهُمْ لَا يَعْلَمُونَ ۝     but most of them do not know.

إِنَّ يَوْمَ ٱلْفَصْلِ     40 Indeed the Day of Judgement

مِيقَـٰتُهُمْ أَجْمَعِينَ ۝     is the tryst for them all,

يَوْمَ     41 the day

لَا يُغْنِى مَوْلًى عَن مَّوْلًى شَيْئًا     when a friend will not avail a friend in any way,

وَلَا هُمْ يُنصَرُونَ ۝     nor will they be helped,

إِلَّا مَن رَّحِمَ ٱللَّهُ     42 except for him on whom Allah has mercy.

إِنَّهُ هُوَ ٱلْعَزِيزُ ٱلرَّحِيمُ ۝     Indeed He is the All-mighty, the All-merciful.

إِنَّ شَجَرَتَ ٱلزَّقُّومِ ۝     43 Indeed the tree of Zaqqūm

طَعَامُ ٱلْأَثِيمِ ۝     44 will be the food of the sinful.

كَٱلْمُهْلِ يَغْلِى فِى ٱلْبُطُونِ ۝     45 Like molten copper it will boil in the bellies,

كَغَلْىِ ٱلْحَمِيمِ ۝     46 boiling like boiling water.

خُذُوهُ     47 'Seize him

فَٱعْتِلُوهُ إِلَىٰ سَوَآءِ ٱلْجَحِيمِ ۝     and drag him to the middle of hell,

ثُمَّ صُبُّوا فَوْقَ رَأْسِهِ     48 then pour over his head

مِنْ عَذَابِ ٱلْحَمِيمِ ۝     the punishment of boiling water.'

ذُقْ     49 'Taste!

إِنَّكَ أَنتَ ٱلْعَزِيزُ ٱلْكَرِيمُ ۝     Indeed you are the [self-styled] mighty and noble!

إِنَّ هَـٰذَا مَا كُنتُم بِهِ تَمْتَرُونَ ۝     50 This is indeed what you used to doubt!'

إِنَّ ٱلْمُتَّقِينَ فِى مَقَامٍ أَمِينٍ ۝     51 Indeed the Godwary will be in a secure place,

فِى جَنَّـٰتٍ وَعُيُونٍ ۝     52 amid gardens and springs,

يَلْبَسُونَ مِن سُندُسٍ وَإِسْتَبْرَقٍ     53 dressed in fine silk and brocade,

مُّتَقَـٰبِلِينَ ۝     sitting face to face.

كَذَٰلِكَ     54 So shall it be,

وَزَوَّجْنَـٰهُم بِحُورٍ عِينٍ ۝     and We shall wed them to black-eyed houris.

يَدْعُونَ فِيهَا بِكُلِّ فَكِهَةٍ ءَامِنِينَ ۝ ٥٥ **There they will call for every fruit, in safety.**

لَا يَذُوقُونَ فِيهَا ٱلْمَوْتَ ٥٦ **There they will not taste death**

إِلَّا ٱلْمَوْتَةَ ٱلْأُولَىٰ    **except the first death,**

وَوَقَىٰهُمْ عَذَابَ ٱلْجَحِيمِ ۝    **and He will save them from the punishment of hell**

فَضْلًا مِّن رَّبِّكَ ٥٧    **—a grace from *your* Lord.**

ذَٰلِكَ هُوَ ٱلْفَوْزُ ٱلْعَظِيمُ ۝    **That is the great success.**

فَإِنَّمَا يَسَّرْنَهُ بِلِسَانِكَ ٥٨ **Indeed We have made it simple in *your* language,**

لَعَلَّهُمْ يَتَذَكَّرُونَ ۝    **so that they may take admonition.**

فَٱرْتَقِبْ ٥٩ **So *wait*!**

إِنَّهُم مُّرْتَقِبُونَ ۝    **Indeed they [too] are waiting.**

## سُوْرَة الجَاثِيَة    45. SŪRAT AL-JĀTHIYAH[1]

بِسْمِ ٱللَّهِ    **In the Name of Allah,**

ٱلرَّحْمَٰنِ ٱلرَّحِيمِ    **the All-beneficent, the All-merciful.**

حٓمٓ ۝ ١ *Hā, Mīm.*

تَنزِيلُ ٱلْكِتَٰبِ مِنَ ٱللَّهِ ٢ **The [gradual] sending down of the Book is from Allah,**

ٱلْعَزِيزِ ٱلْحَكِيمِ ۝    **the All-mighty, All-wise.**

إِنَّ فِي ٱلسَّمَٰوَٰتِ وَٱلْأَرْضِ لَءَايَٰتٍ ٣ **Indeed in the heavens and the earth there are signs**

لِّلْمُؤْمِنِينَ ۝    **for the faithful.**

وَفِي خَلْقِكُمْ ٤ **And in your creation [too],**

وَمَا يَبُثُّ مِن دَآبَّةٍ    **and whatever animals that He scatters abroad,**

ءَايَٰتٌ لِّقَوْمٍ يُوقِنُونَ ۝    **there are signs for a people who have certainty.**

وَٱخْتِلَٰفِ ٱلَّيْلِ وَٱلنَّهَارِ ٥ **And in the alternation of night and day**

وَمَآ أَنزَلَ ٱللَّهُ مِنَ ٱلسَّمَآءِ    **and what Allah sends down from the sky**

مِن رِّزْقٍ    **of [His] provision**

فَأَحْيَا بِهِ ٱلْأَرْضَ بَعْدَ مَوْتِهَا    **with which He revives the earth after its death,**

---

[1] The *sūrah* takes its name from the word *jāthiyah* (kneeling) in verse 28.

وَتَصْرِيفِ ٱلرِّيَٰحِ      and in the changing of the winds

ءَايَٰتٌ لِّقَوْمٍ يَعْقِلُونَ ۝      there are signs for a people who apply reason.

تِلْكَ ءَايَٰتُ ٱللَّهِ   6 These are the signs of Allah

نَتْلُوهَا عَلَيْكَ بِٱلْحَقِّ      that We recite for *you* in truth,

فَبِأَىِّ حَدِيثٍ      So what discourse

بَعْدَ ٱللَّهِ وَءَايَٰتِهِۦ يُؤْمِنُونَ ۝      will they believe after Allah and His signs?

وَيْلٌ لِّكُلِّ أَفَّاكٍ أَثِيمٍ ۝   7 Woe to every sinful liar,

يَسْمَعُ ءَايَٰتِ ٱللَّهِ تُتْلَىٰ عَلَيْهِ   8 who hears the signs of Allah recited to him,

ثُمَّ يُصِرُّ مُسْتَكْبِرًا      then persists disdainfully,

كَأَن لَّمْ يَسْمَعْهَا ۖ      as if he had not heard them.

فَبَشِّرْهُ بِعَذَابٍ أَلِيمٍ ۝      So *inform* him of a painful punishment.

وَإِذَا عَلِمَ مِنْ ءَايَٰتِنَا شَيْـًٔا   9 Should he learn anything about Our signs,

ٱتَّخَذَهَا هُزُوًا ۚ      he takes them in derision.

أُو۟لَٰٓئِكَ لَهُمْ عَذَابٌ مُّهِينٌ ۝      For such there is a humiliating punishment.

مِّن وَرَآئِهِمْ جَهَنَّمُ ۖ   10 Ahead of them is hell

وَلَا يُغْنِى عَنْهُم مَّا كَسَبُوا۟ شَيْـًٔا      and what they have earned will not avail them in any way,

وَلَا مَا ٱتَّخَذُوا۟ مِن دُونِ ٱللَّهِ أَوْلِيَآءَ ۖ      nor what they had taken as guardians besides Allah,

وَلَهُمْ عَذَابٌ عَظِيمٌ ۝      and there is a great punishment for them.

هَٰذَا هُدًى ۖ   11 This is a guidance,

وَٱلَّذِينَ كَفَرُوا۟ بِـَٔايَٰتِ رَبِّهِمْ      and as for those who defy the signs of their Lord,

لَهُمْ عَذَابٌ مِّن رِّجْزٍ أَلِيمٌ ۝ ❋      for them is a painful punishment due to defilement.[1]

ٱللَّهُ ٱلَّذِى سَخَّرَ لَكُمُ ٱلْبَحْرَ   12 It is Allah who disposed the sea for you[r benefit]

لِتَجْرِىَ ٱلْفُلْكُ فِيهِ بِأَمْرِهِۦ      so that the ships may sail in it by His command,

وَلِتَبْتَغُوا۟ مِن فَضْلِهِۦ      and that you may seek of His grace,

وَلَعَلَّكُمْ تَشْكُرُونَ ۝      and that you may give thanks.

وَسَخَّرَ لَكُم   13 And He has disposed for you[r benefit]

مَّا فِى ٱلسَّمَٰوَٰتِ      whatever is in the heavens

وَمَا فِى ٱلْأَرْضِ      and whatever is the earth,

جَمِيعًا مِّنْهُ ۚ      all is from Him.

---

[1] Cf. 34:5.

إِنَّ فِى ذَٰلِكَ لَآيَـٰتٍ

There are indeed signs in that

لِّقَوْمٍ يَتَفَكَّرُونَ ۝

for a people who reflect.

14 قُل لِّلَّذِينَ ءَامَنُوا۟

14 *Say* to the faithful

يَغْفِرُوا۟ لِلَّذِينَ لَا يَرْجُونَ أَيَّامَ ٱللَّهِ

to forgive those who do not expect Allah's days,

لِيَجْزِىَ قَوْمًا

that He may [Himself] requite a people

بِمَا كَانُوا۟ يَكْسِبُونَ ۝

for what they used to earn.

15 مَنْ عَمِلَ صَـٰلِحًا فَلِنَفْسِهِۦ

15 Whoever acts righteously, it is for his own soul,

وَمَنْ أَسَآءَ فَعَلَيْهَا

and whoever does evil, it is to its own detriment,

ثُمَّ إِلَىٰ رَبِّكُمْ تُرْجَعُونَ ۝

then you will be brought back to your Lord.

16 وَلَقَدْ ءَاتَيْنَا بَنِىٓ إِسْرَٰٓءِيلَ ٱلْكِتَـٰبَ

16 Certainly We gave the Children of Israel the Book,

وَٱلْحُكْمَ وَٱلنُّبُوَّةَ

judgement and prophethood

وَرَزَقْنَـٰهُم مِّنَ ٱلطَّيِّبَـٰتِ

and We provided them with all the good things,

وَفَضَّلْنَـٰهُمْ عَلَى ٱلْعَـٰلَمِينَ ۝

and We gave them an advantage over all the nations,

17 وَءَاتَيْنَـٰهُم بَيِّنَـٰتٍ مِّنَ ٱلْأَمْرِ

17 and We gave them manifest precepts.

فَمَا ٱخْتَلَفُوٓا۟

But they did not differ

إِلَّا مِنۢ بَعْدِ مَا جَآءَهُمُ ٱلْعِلْمُ

except after knowledge had come to them,

بَغْيًۢا بَيْنَهُمْ

out of envy among themselves.

إِنَّ رَبَّكَ يَقْضِى بَيْنَهُمْ

Indeed *your* Lord will judge between them

يَوْمَ ٱلْقِيَـٰمَةِ

on the Day of Resurrection

فِيمَا كَانُوا۟ فِيهِ يَخْتَلِفُونَ ۝

concerning that about which they used to differ.

18 ثُمَّ جَعَلْنَـٰكَ عَلَىٰ شَرِيعَةٍ مِّنَ ٱلْأَمْرِ

18 Then We set *you* upon a clear course of the Law;

فَٱتَّبِعْهَا

so *follow* it,

وَلَا تَتَّبِعْ أَهْوَآءَ ٱلَّذِينَ

and *do not follow* the desires of those

لَا يَعْلَمُونَ ۝

who do not know.

19 إِنَّهُمْ لَن يُغْنُوا۟ عَنكَ

19 Indeed they will not avail *you*

مِنَ ٱللَّهِ شَيْـًٔا

in any way against Allah.

وَإِنَّ ٱلظَّـٰلِمِينَ بَعْضُهُمْ أَوْلِيَآءُ بَعْضٍ

Indeed the wrongdoers are allies of one another,

وَٱللَّهُ وَلِىُّ ٱلْمُتَّقِينَ ۝

but Allah is the guardian[1] of the Godwary.

---

[1] Or 'ally.'

هَٰذَا بَصَٰٓئِرُ لِلنَّاسِ   20 These are eye-openers for mankind,

وَهُدًى وَرَحْمَةٌ     and guidance and mercy

لِّقَوْمٍ يُوقِنُونَ ۞     for a people who have certainty.

أَمْ حَسِبَ ٱلَّذِينَ ٱجْتَرَحُوا ٱلسَّيِّئَاتِ   21 Do those who have perpetrated misdeeds suppose

أَن نَّجْعَلَهُمْ كَٱلَّذِينَ ءَامَنُوا     that We shall treat them as those who have faith

وَعَمِلُوا ٱلصَّٰلِحَٰتِ     and do righteous deeds,

سَوَآءً مَّحْيَاهُمْ وَمَمَاتُهُمْ     their life and death being equal?

سَآءَ مَا يَحْكُمُونَ ۞     Evil is the judgement that they make!

وَخَلَقَ ٱللَّهُ ٱلسَّمَٰوَٰتِ وَٱلْأَرْضَ   22 Allah created the heavens and the earth

بِٱلْحَقِّ     with the truth,

وَلِتُجْزَىٰ كُلُّ نَفْسٍ     so that every soul may be requited

بِمَا كَسَبَتْ     for what it has earned,

وَهُمْ لَا يُظْلَمُونَ ۞     and they will not be wronged.

أَفَرَءَيْتَ مَنِ ٱتَّخَذَ   23 Have *you* seen him who has taken

إِلَٰهَهُۥ هَوَىٰهُ     his desire to be his god

وَأَضَلَّهُ ٱللَّهُ عَلَىٰ عِلْمٍ     and whom Allah has led astray knowingly,

وَخَتَمَ عَلَىٰ سَمْعِهِۦ وَقَلْبِهِۦ     and set a seal upon his hearing and his heart,

وَجَعَلَ عَلَىٰ بَصَرِهِۦ غِشَٰوَةً     and drawn a blind on his sight?

فَمَن يَهْدِيهِ مِنۢ بَعْدِ ٱللَّهِ     So who will guide him after Allah?

أَفَلَا تَذَكَّرُونَ ۞     Will you not then take admonition?

وَقَالُوا   24 They say,

مَا هِيَ إِلَّا حَيَاتُنَا ٱلدُّنْيَا     'There is nothing but the life of this world:

نَمُوتُ وَنَحْيَا     we live and we die,

وَمَا يُهْلِكُنَآ إِلَّا ٱلدَّهْرُ     and nothing but time destroys us.'

وَمَا لَهُم بِذَٰلِكَ مِنْ عِلْمٍ     But they do not have any knowledge of that,

إِنْ هُمْ إِلَّا يَظُنُّونَ ۞     and they only make conjectures.

وَإِذَا تُتْلَىٰ عَلَيْهِمْ ءَايَٰتُنَا بَيِّنَٰتٍ   25 And when Our manifest signs are recited to them,

مَّا كَانَ حُجَّتَهُمْ إِلَّآ أَن قَالُوا     their only argument is to say,

ٱئْتُوا بِـَٔابَآئِنَآ     'Bring our fathers back [to life],

إِن كُنتُمْ صَٰدِقِينَ ۞     should you be truthful.'

قُل اللَّهُ يُحْيِيكُمْ   26 *Say,* 'It is Allah who gives you life,

ثُمَّ يُمِيتُكُمْ   then He makes you die.

ثُمَّ يَجْمَعُكُمْ   Then He will gather you

إِلَىٰ يَوْمِ الْقِيَٰمَةِ   on the Day of Resurrection,

لَا رَيْبَ فِيهِ   in which there is no doubt.

وَلَٰكِنَّ أَكْثَرَ النَّاسِ لَا يَعْلَمُونَ ۝   But most people do not know.'

وَلِلَّهِ مُلْكُ السَّمَٰوَٰتِ   27 To Allah belongs the kingdom of the heavens

وَالْأَرْضِ   and the earth,

وَيَوْمَ تَقُومُ السَّاعَةُ   and when the Hour sets in,

يَوْمَئِذٍ يَخْسَرُ الْمُبْطِلُونَ ۝   the falsifiers will be losers on that day.

وَتَرَىٰ كُلَّ أُمَّةٍ جَاثِيَةً   28 And *you* will see every nation fallen on its knees.

كُلُّ أُمَّةٍ تُدْعَىٰ إِلَىٰ كِتَٰبِهَا   Every nation will be summoned to its book:

الْيَوْمَ تُجْزَوْنَ   'Today you will be requited for

مَا كُنتُمْ تَعْمَلُونَ ۝   what you used to do.

هَٰذَا كِتَٰبُنَا يَنطِقُ عَلَيْكُم بِالْحَقِّ   29 This is Our book, which speaks truly against you.

إِنَّا كُنَّا نَسْتَنسِخُ مَا كُنتُمْ تَعْمَلُونَ ۝   Indeed We used to record what you used to do.'

فَأَمَّا الَّذِينَ ءَامَنُوا   30 As for those who have faith

وَعَمِلُوا الصَّٰلِحَٰتِ   and do righteous deeds,

فَيُدْخِلُهُمْ رَبُّهُمْ فِي رَحْمَتِهِ   their Lord will admit them into His mercy.

ذَٰلِكَ هُوَ الْفَوْزُ الْمُبِينُ ۝   That is the manifest success!

وَأَمَّا الَّذِينَ كَفَرُوا   31 But as for the faithless, [they will be asked,]

أَفَلَمْ تَكُنْ ءَايَٰتِي تُتْلَىٰ عَلَيْكُمْ   'Were not My signs recited to you?

فَاسْتَكْبَرْتُمْ   But you were disdainful,

وَكُنتُمْ قَوْمًا مُّجْرِمِينَ ۝   and you were a guilty lot.

وَإِذَا قِيلَ   32 And when it was said,

إِنَّ وَعْدَ اللَّهِ حَقٌّ   "Allah's promise is indeed true,

وَالسَّاعَةُ لَا رَيْبَ فِيهَا   and there is no doubt about the Hour,"

قُلْتُم مَّا نَدْرِي مَا السَّاعَةُ   you said, "We do not know what the Hour is.

إِن نَّظُنُّ إِلَّا ظَنًّا   We know nothing beyond conjectures,

وَمَا نَحْنُ بِمُسْتَيْقِنِينَ ۝   and we do not possess any certainty."'

وَبَدَا لَهُمْ سَيِّئَاتُ مَا عَمِلُوا 33 The evils of what they had done will appear to them,

وَحَاقَ بِهِم and they will be besieged

مَّا كَانُوا بِهِ يَسْتَهْزِءُونَ ۝ by what they used to deride.

وَقِيلَ ٱلْيَوْمَ نَنسَىٰكُمْ 34 And it will be said, 'Today We will forget you,

كَمَا نَسِيتُمْ لِقَآءَ يَوْمِكُمْ هَـٰذَا just as you forgot the encounter of this day of yours.

وَمَأْوَىٰكُمُ ٱلنَّارُ The Fire will be your abode,

وَمَا لَكُم مِّن نَّـٰصِرِينَ ۝ and you will not have any helpers.

ذَٰلِكُم بِأَنَّكُمُ ٱتَّخَذْتُمْ ءَايَـٰتِ ٱللَّهِ 35 That is because you took the signs of Allah

هُزُوًا in derision,

وَغَرَّتْكُمُ ٱلْحَيَوٰةُ ٱلدُّنْيَا and the life of the world had deceived you.'

فَٱلْيَوْمَ لَا يُخْرَجُونَ مِنْهَا So today they will not be brought out of it,

وَلَا هُمْ يُسْتَعْتَبُونَ ۝ nor will they be asked to propitiate [Allah].

فَلِلَّهِ ٱلْحَمْدُ 36 So all praise belongs to Allah,

رَبِّ ٱلسَّمَـٰوَٰتِ وَرَبِّ ٱلْأَرْضِ the Lord of the heavens and the Lord of the earth,

رَبِّ ٱلْعَـٰلَمِينَ ۝ the Lord of all the worlds.

وَلَهُ ٱلْكِبْرِيَآءُ فِى ٱلسَّمَـٰوَٰتِ 37 To Him belongs all supremacy in the heavens

وَٱلْأَرْضِ and the earth,

وَهُوَ ٱلْعَزِيزُ ٱلْحَكِيمُ ۝ and He is the All-mighty, the All-wise.

[PART 26]

## سُورَةُ ٱلْأَحْقَافِ    46. SŪRAT AL-AḤQĀF[1]

بِسْمِ ٱللَّهِ In the Name of Allah,

ٱلرَّحْمَـٰنِ ٱلرَّحِيمِ the All-beneficent, the All-merciful.

حمٓ ۝ 1 *Hā, Mīm.*

تَنزِيلُ ٱلْكِتَـٰبِ مِنَ ٱللَّهِ 2 The [gradual] sending down of the Book is from Allah,

ٱلْعَزِيزِ ٱلْحَكِيمِ ۝ the All-mighty, the All-wise.

مَا خَلَقْنَا ٱلسَّمَـٰوَٰتِ وَٱلْأَرْضَ 3 We did not create the heavens and the earth

وَمَا بَيْنَهُمَآ إِلَّا بِٱلْحَقِّ and whatever is between them except with the truth

---

[1] The *sūrah* takes its name from verse 21, where Aḥqāf is mentioned.

وَأَجَلٍ مُّسَمًّى     and for a specified term.

وَٱلَّذِينَ كَفَرُواْ     Yet the faithless

عَمَّا أُنذِرُواْ مُعْرِضُونَ ۝     are disregardful of what they are warned.

قُلْ أَرَءَيْتُم 4     Say, 'Tell me about

مَّا تَدْعُونَ مِن دُونِ ٱللَّهِ     what you invoke besides Allah.

أَرُونِى     Show me

مَاذَا خَلَقُواْ مِنَ ٱلْأَرْضِ     what [part] of the earth have they created.

أَمْ لَهُمْ شِرْكٌ فِى ٱلسَّمَـٰوَٰتِ     Do they have any share in the heavens?

ٱئْتُونِى بِكِتَـٰبٍ مِّن قَبْلِ هَـٰذَآ     Bring me a scripture [revealed] before this,

أَوْ أَثَـٰرَةٍ مِّنْ عِلْمٍ     or some vestige of [divine] knowledge,

إِن كُنتُمْ صَـٰدِقِينَ ۝     should you be truthful.'

وَمَنْ أَضَلُّ مِمَّن يَدْعُواْ 5     Who is more astray than him who invokes

مِن دُونِ ٱللَّهِ     besides Allah

مَن لَّا يَسْتَجِيبُ لَهُۥ     such as would not respond to him

إِلَىٰ يَوْمِ ٱلْقِيَـٰمَةِ     until the Day of Resurrection,

وَهُمْ عَن دُعَآئِهِمْ غَـٰفِلُونَ ۝     and who are oblivious of their invocation?

وَإِذَا حُشِرَ ٱلنَّاسُ 6     When mankind are mustered [on Judgment's Day]

كَانُواْ لَهُمْ أَعْدَآءً     they will be their enemies,

وَكَانُواْ بِعِبَادَتِهِمْ كَـٰفِرِينَ ۝     and they will disavow their worship.

وَإِذَا تُتْلَىٰ عَلَيْهِمْ ءَايَـٰتُنَا بَيِّنَـٰتٍ 7     When Our manifest signs are recited to them,

قَالَ ٱلَّذِينَ كَفَرُواْ لِلْحَقِّ لَمَّا جَآءَهُمْ     the faithless say of the truth when it comes to them:

هَـٰذَا سِحْرٌ مُّبِينٌ ۝     'This is plain magic.'

أَمْ يَقُولُونَ ٱفْتَرَىٰهُ 8     Do they say, 'He has fabricated it?'

قُلْ إِنِ ٱفْتَرَيْتُهُۥ     Say, 'Should I have fabricated it,

فَلَا تَمْلِكُونَ لِى مِنَ ٱللَّهِ شَيْـًٔا     you would not avail me anything against Allah.

هُوَ أَعْلَمُ بِمَا تُفِيضُونَ فِيهِ     He best knows what you gossip concerning it.

كَفَىٰ بِهِۦ شَهِيدًۢا بَيْنِى وَبَيْنَكُمْ     He suffices as a witness between me and you,

وَهُوَ ٱلْغَفُورُ ٱلرَّحِيمُ ۝     and He is the All-forgiving, the All-merciful.'

قُلْ مَا كُنتُ بِدْعًا مِّنَ ٱلرُّسُلِ 9     Say, 'I am not a novelty among the apostles,

وَمَآ أَدْرِى مَا يُفْعَلُ بِى     nor do I know what will be done with me,

وَلَا بِكُمْ

or with you.

إِنْ أَتَّبِعُ إِلَّا مَا يُوحَىٰ إِلَيَّ

I just follow whatever is revealed to me,

وَمَآ أَنَا۠ إِلَّا نَذِيرٌ مُّبِينٌ ۞

and I am just a manifest warner.'

قُلْ أَرَءَيْتُمْ إِن كَانَ مِنْ عِندِ ٱللَّهِ

10 *Say,* 'Tell me, if it is from Allah

وَكَفَرْتُم بِهِۦ

and you disbelieve in it,

وَشَهِدَ شَاهِدٌ مِّنۢ بَنِىٓ إِسْرَٰٓءِيلَ

and a witness from the Children of Israel has testified

عَلَىٰ مِثْلِهِۦ

to its like

فَـَٔامَنَ

and believed [in it],

وَٱسْتَكْبَرْتُمْ

while you are disdainful [of it]?' [1]

إِنَّ ٱللَّهَ لَا يَهْدِى ٱلْقَوْمَ ٱلظَّٰلِمِينَ ۞

Indeed Allah does not guide the wrongdoing lot.

وَقَالَ ٱلَّذِينَ كَفَرُوا۟ لِلَّذِينَ ءَامَنُوا۟

11 The faithless say about the faithful,

لَوْ كَانَ خَيْرًا

'Had it been [anything] good,

مَّا سَبَقُونَآ

they would not have taken the lead over us

إِلَيْهِ

toward [accepting] it.'

وَإِذْ لَمْ يَهْتَدُوا۟ بِهِۦ

And since they could not find the way to it,

فَسَيَقُولُونَ هَٰذَآ إِفْكٌ قَدِيمٌ ۞

they will say, 'It is an ancient lie.'

وَمِن قَبْلِهِۦ كِتَٰبُ مُوسَىٰٓ

12 Yet before it the Book of Moses

إِمَامًا وَرَحْمَةً

was a guide and a mercy,

وَهَٰذَا كِتَٰبٌ مُّصَدِّقٌ

and this is a Book which confirms it,

لِّسَانًا عَرَبِيًّا

in the Arabic language,

لِّيُنذِرَ ٱلَّذِينَ ظَلَمُوا۟

to warn those who do wrong,

وَبُشْرَىٰ لِلْمُحْسِنِينَ ۞

and is a [bearer of] good news for the virtuous.

إِنَّ ٱلَّذِينَ قَالُوا۟ رَبُّنَا ٱللَّهُ

13 Indeed those who say, 'Our Lord is Allah,'

ثُمَّ ٱسْتَقَٰمُوا۟

and then remain steadfast,

فَلَا خَوْفٌ عَلَيْهِمْ

they will have no fear,

وَلَا هُمْ يَحْزَنُونَ ۞

nor will they grieve.

أُو۟لَٰٓئِكَ أَصْحَٰبُ ٱلْجَنَّةِ

14 They shall be the inhabitants of paradise,

خَٰلِدِينَ فِيهَا

remaining in it [forever]

---

[1] Ellipsis; the omitted phrase is, 'who will be more astray than him who is in extreme defiance.' See 41:52.

جَزَآءُ بِمَا كَانُواْ يَعْمَلُونَ ⑭    —a reward for what they used to do.

وَوَصَّيْنَا ٱلْإِنسَـٰنَ بِوَٰلِدَيْهِ إِحْسَـٰنًا ‏15 We have enjoined man to be kind to his parents.

حَمَلَتْهُ أُمُّهُ كُرْهًا    His mother has carried him in travail,

وَوَضَعَتْهُ كُرْهًا    and bore him in travail,

وَحَمْلُهُ وَفِصَـٰلُهُ ثَلَـٰثُونَ شَهْرًا    and his gestation and weaning take thirty months.

حَتَّىٰ إِذَا بَلَغَ أَشُدَّهُ    When he comes of age

وَبَلَغَ أَرْبَعِينَ    and reaches forty years,

سَنَةً قَالَ رَبِّ    he says, 'My Lord!

أَوْزِعْنِى أَنْ أَشْكُرَ نِعْمَتَكَ    Inspire me to give thanks for Your blessing

ٱلَّتِىٓ أَنْعَمْتَ عَلَىَّ    with which You have blessed me

وَعَلَىٰ وَٰلِدَىَّ    and my parents,

وَأَنْ أَعْمَلَ صَـٰلِحًا    and that I may do righteous deeds

تَرْضَىٰهُ    which may please You,

وَأَصْلِحْ لِى فِى ذُرِّيَّتِىٓ    and invest my descendants with righteousness.

إِنِّى تُبْتُ إِلَيْكَ    Indeed I have turned to you in penitence,

وَإِنِّى مِنَ ٱلْمُسْلِمِينَ ⑮    and I am one of the *muslim*s.'

أُوْلَـٰٓئِكَ ٱلَّذِينَ نَتَقَبَّلُ عَنْهُمْ ‏16 Such are the ones from whom We accept

أَحْسَنَ مَا عَمِلُواْ    the best of what they do,

وَنَتَجَاوَزُ عَن سَيِّـَٔاتِهِمْ    and overlook their misdeeds,

فِىٓ أَصْحَـٰبِ ٱلْجَنَّةِ    [who will be] among the inhabitants of paradise

وَعْدَ ٱلصِّدْقِ ٱلَّذِى كَانُواْ يُوعَدُونَ ⑯    —a true promise which they had been given.

وَٱلَّذِى قَالَ لِوَٰلِدَيْهِ ‏17 As for him who says to his parents,

أُفٍّ لَّكُمَآ    'Fie on you!

أَتَعِدَانِنِىٓ    Do you promise me

أَنْ أُخْرَجَ    that I shall be raised [from the dead]

وَقَدْ خَلَتِ ٱلْقُرُونُ مِن قَبْلِى    when generations have passed away before me?'

وَهُمَا يَسْتَغِيثَانِ ٱللَّهَ    And they invoke Allah's help

وَيْلَكَ    [and say]: 'Woe to you!

ءَامِنْ إِنَّ وَعْدَ ٱللَّهِ حَقٌّ     Believe! Indeed Allah's promise is true.'

فَيَقُولُ     But he says,

مَا هَٰذَآ إِلَّآ أَسَٰطِيرُ ٱلْأَوَّلِينَ ۝     'These are nothing but myths of the ancients.'

أُوْلَٰٓئِكَ ٱلَّذِينَ حَقَّ عَلَيْهِمُ ٱلْقَوْلُ     18 Such are the ones against whom the word became due

فِىٓ أُمَمٍ     concerning the nations

قَدْ خَلَتْ مِن قَبْلِهِم     that have passed away before them

مِّنَ ٱلْجِنِّ وَٱلْإِنسِ     of jinn and humans.

إِنَّهُمْ كَانُواْ خَٰسِرِينَ ۝     They were indeed the losers.

وَلِكُلٍّ دَرَجَٰتٌ     19 For each [person] there will be degrees [of merit]

مِّمَّا عَمِلُواْ     pertaining to what he has done,

وَلِيُوَفِّيَهُمْ أَعْمَٰلَهُمْ     that He may recompense them fully for their works,

وَهُمْ لَا يُظْلَمُونَ ۝     and they will not be wronged.

وَيَوْمَ يُعْرَضُ ٱلَّذِينَ كَفَرُواْ     20 The day when the faithless are exposed

عَلَى ٱلنَّارِ     to the Fire, [they will be told,]

أَذْهَبْتُمْ طَيِّبَٰتِكُمْ     'You have exhausted your good things

فِى حَيَاتِكُمُ ٱلدُّنْيَا     in the life of the world

وَٱسْتَمْتَعْتُم بِهَا     and enjoyed them.

فَٱلْيَوْمَ تُجْزَوْنَ     So today you will be requited

عَذَابَ ٱلْهُونِ     with a humiliating punishment

بِمَا كُنتُمْ تَسْتَكْبِرُونَ فِى ٱلْأَرْضِ     for your acting arrogantly in the earth

بِغَيْرِ ٱلْحَقِّ     unduly,

وَبِمَا كُنتُمْ تَفْسُقُونَ ۝     and because you used to transgress.'

وَٱذْكُرْ أَخَا عَادٍ     21 And mention [Hūd] the brother of 'Ād,

إِذْ أَنذَرَ قَوْمَهُ بِٱلْأَحْقَافِ     when he warned his people at Aḥqāf

وَقَدْ خَلَتِ ٱلنُّذُرُ     —and warners have passed away

مِنْ بَيْنِ يَدَيْهِ وَمِنْ خَلْفِهِۦٓ     before and after him—

أَلَّا تَعْبُدُوٓاْ إِلَّا ٱللَّهَ     saying, 'Do not worship anyone but Allah.

إِنِّىٓ أَخَافُ عَلَيْكُمْ     Indeed I fear for you the punishment

عَذَابَ يَوْمٍ عَظِيمٍ ۝     of a tremendous day.'

قَالُوٓاْ     22 They said,

أَجِئْتَنَا لِتَأْفِكَنَا عَنْ ءَالِهَتِنَا    'Have you come to turn us away from our gods?

فَأْتِنَا بِمَا تَعِدُنَا    Then bring us what you threaten us with,

إِن كُنتَ مِنَ ٱلصَّٰدِقِينَ ۩    should you be truthful.

قَالَ    23 He said,

إِنَّمَا ٱلْعِلْمُ عِندَ ٱللَّهِ    'The knowledge is with Allah alone.

وَأُبَلِّغُكُم مَّآ أُرْسِلْتُ بِهِۦ    I communicate to you what I have been sent with.

وَلَٰكِنِّىٓ أَرَىٰكُمْ قَوْمًا تَجْهَلُونَ ۩    But I see that you are a senseless lot.'

فَلَمَّا رَأَوْهُ عَارِضًا    24 When they saw it as a cloud

مُّسْتَقْبِلَ أَوْدِيَتِهِمْ    advancing toward their valleys,

قَالُوا۟ هَٰذَا عَارِضٌ مُّمْطِرُنَا    they said, 'This cloud brings us rain.'

بَلْ هُوَ مَا ٱسْتَعْجَلْتُم بِهِۦ    'Rather it is what you sought to hasten:

رِيحٌ فِيهَا عَذَابٌ أَلِيمٌ ۩    a hurricane carrying a painful punishment,

تُدَمِّرُ كُلَّ شَىْءٍۭ بِأَمْرِ رَبِّهَا    25 destroying everything by its Lord's command.'

فَأَصْبَحُوا۟ لَا يُرَىٰٓ    So they became such that nothing could be seen

إِلَّا مَسَٰكِنُهُمْ    except their dwellings.

كَذَٰلِكَ نَجْزِى ٱلْقَوْمَ ٱلْمُجْرِمِينَ ۩    Thus do We requite the guilty lot.

وَلَقَدْ مَكَّنَّٰهُمْ    26 Certainly We had granted them power

فِيمَآ إِن مَّكَّنَّٰكُمْ فِيهِ    in respects that We have not granted you,

وَجَعَلْنَا لَهُمْ سَمْعًا وَأَبْصَٰرًا    and We had vested them with hearing and sight

وَأَفْـِٔدَةً    and hearts.

فَمَآ أَغْنَىٰ عَنْهُمْ سَمْعُهُمْ    But neither their hearing availed them

وَلَآ أَبْصَٰرُهُمْ    nor did their sight,

وَلَآ أَفْـِٔدَتُهُم مِّن شَىْءٍ    nor their hearts, in any way

إِذْ كَانُوا۟ يَجْحَدُونَ بِـَٔايَٰتِ ٱللَّهِ    when they used to impugn the signs of Allah.

وَحَاقَ بِهِم    So they were besieged

مَّا كَانُوا۟ بِهِۦ يَسْتَهْزِءُونَ ۩    by what they used to deride.

وَلَقَدْ أَهْلَكْنَا مَا حَوْلَكُم مِّنَ ٱلْقُرَىٰ    27 Certainly We destroyed towns that were around you,

وَصَرَّفْنَا ٱلْءَايَٰتِ    and We have paraphrased the signs

لَعَلَّهُمْ يَرْجِعُونَ ۩    so that they may come back.

فَلَوْلَا نَصَرَهُمُ ٱلَّذِينَ    28 So why did not those [false gods] help them

| | |
|---|---|
| ٱتَّخَذُوا۟ مِن دُونِ ٱللَّهِ | whom they had taken, besides Allah, |
| قُرْبَانًا ءَالِهَةً | as gods, as means of nearness [to Him]? |
| بَلْ ضَلُّوا۟ عَنْهُمْ | Rather they forsook them; |
| وَذَٰلِكَ إِفْكُهُمْ | and that was their lie |
| وَمَا كَانُوا۟ يَفْتَرُونَ ٢٨ | and what they used to fabricate. |

29 When We dispatched toward *you* a team of jinn

وَإِذْ صَرَفْنَآ إِلَيْكَ نَفَرًا مِّنَ ٱلْجِنِّ

listening to the Qur'ān,

يَسْتَمِعُونَ ٱلْقُرْءَانَ

when they were in its presence,

فَلَمَّا حَضَرُوهُ

they said, 'Be silent!'

قَالُوٓا۟ أَنصِتُوا۟

When it was finished, they went back to their people

فَلَمَّا قُضِىَ وَلَّوْا۟ إِلَىٰ قَوْمِهِم

as warners.

مُّنذِرِينَ ٢٩

30 They said, 'O our people!

قَالُوا۟ يَٰقَوْمَنَآ

Indeed we have heard a Book

إِنَّا سَمِعْنَا كِتَٰبًا

which has been sent down after Moses,

أُنزِلَ مِنۢ بَعْدِ مُوسَىٰ

confirming what was before it.

مُصَدِّقًا لِّمَا بَيْنَ يَدَيْهِ

It guides to the truth

يَهْدِىٓ إِلَى ٱلْحَقِّ

and to a straight path.

وَإِلَىٰ طَرِيقٍ مُّسْتَقِيمٍ ٣٠

31 O our people!

يَٰقَوْمَنَآ

Respond to Allah's summoner

أَجِيبُوا۟ دَاعِىَ ٱللَّهِ

and have faith in Him.

وَءَامِنُوا۟ بِهِۦ

He will forgive you some of your sins

يَغْفِرْ لَكُم مِّن ذُنُوبِكُمْ

and shelter you from a painful punishment.'

وَيُجِرْكُم مِّنْ عَذَابٍ أَلِيمٍ ٣١

32 Those who do not respond to Allah's summoner

وَمَن لَّا يُجِبْ دَاعِىَ ٱللَّهِ

cannot thwart [Allah] on the earth,

فَلَيْسَ بِمُعْجِزٍ فِى ٱلْأَرْضِ

and they will not find any protectors besides Him.

وَلَيْسَ لَهُۥ مِن دُونِهِۦٓ أَوْلِيَآءُ

They are in manifest error.

أُو۟لَٰٓئِكَ فِى ضَلَٰلٍ مُّبِينٍ ٣٢

33 Do they not see that Allah,

أَوَلَمْ يَرَوْا۟ أَنَّ ٱللَّهَ

who created the heavens and the earth

ٱلَّذِى خَلَقَ ٱلسَّمَٰوَٰتِ وَٱلْأَرْضَ

and [who] was not exhausted by their creation,

وَلَمْ يَعْىَ بِخَلْقِهِنَّ

بِقَدرٍ عَلَىٰ أَن يُحۡيِۦَ ٱلۡمَوۡتَىٰ    is able to revive the dead?

بَلَىٰٓ إِنَّهُۥ عَلَىٰ كُلِّ شَيۡءٍ قَدِيرٌ ٣٣    Yes, indeed He has power over all things.

وَيَوۡمَ يُعۡرَضُ ٱلَّذِينَ كَفَرُوا۟    34 The day when the faithless are exposed

عَلَى ٱلنَّارِ    to the Fire,

أَلَيۡسَ هَٰذَا بِٱلۡحَقِّ    [He will say,] 'Is this not the truth?'

قَالُوا۟ بَلَىٰ وَرَبِّنَا    They will say, 'Yes, by our Lord!'

قَالَ فَذُوقُوا۟ ٱلۡعَذَابَ    He will say, 'So taste the punishment

بِمَا كُنتُمۡ تَكۡفُرُونَ ٣٤    because of what you used to disbelieve.'

فَٱصۡبِرۡ    35 So *be patient*

كَمَا صَبَرَ أُو۟لُوا۟ ٱلۡعَزۡمِ مِنَ ٱلرُّسُلِ    just as the resolute among the apostles were patient,

وَلَا تَسۡتَعۡجِل    and *do not seek* to hasten [the punishment]

لَّهُمۡ    for them.

كَأَنَّهُمۡ يَوۡمَ يَرَوۡنَ    The day when they see

مَا يُوعَدُونَ    what they are promised, [it will be]

لَمۡ يَلۡبَثُوٓا۟ إِلَّا سَاعَةً مِّن نَّهَارٍ    as though they had remained only an hour of a day.

بَلَٰغٌ    This is a proclamation.

فَهَلۡ يُهۡلَكُ    So shall anyone be destroyed

إِلَّا ٱلۡقَوۡمُ ٱلۡفَٰسِقُونَ ٣٥    except the transgressing lot?

## سُورَةُ مُحَمَّد    47. SŪRAT MUḤAMMAD[1]

بِسۡمِ ٱللَّهِ    In the Name of Allah,

ٱلرَّحۡمَٰنِ ٱلرَّحِيمِ    the All-beneficent, the All-merciful.

ٱلَّذِينَ كَفَرُوا۟    1 Those who are [themselves] faithless

وَصَدُّوا۟ عَن سَبِيلِ ٱللَّهِ    and bar [others] from the way of Allah

أَضَلَّ أَعۡمَٰلَهُمۡ ١    —He has made their works go awry.

وَٱلَّذِينَ ءَامَنُوا۟ وَعَمِلُوا۟ ٱلصَّٰلِحَٰتِ    2 But those who have faith and do righteous deeds

---

[1] The *sūrah* takes its name from verse 2, where the name of the Prophet (*s*) occurs.

وَءَامَنُواْ بِمَا نُزِّلَ    and believe in what has been sent down

عَلَىٰ مُحَمَّدٍ    to Muḥammad

وَهُوَ ٱلْحَقُّ مِن رَّبِّهِمْ    —and it is the truth from their Lord—

كَفَّرَ عَنْهُمْ سَيِّئَاتِهِمْ    He shall absolve them of their misdeeds

وَأَصْلَحَ بَالَهُمْ ۞    and set right their affairs.

ذَٰلِكَ بِأَنَّ ٱلَّذِينَ كَفَرُواْ    3 That is because the faithless

ٱتَّبَعُواْ ٱلْبَٰطِلَ    follow falsehood,

وَأَنَّ ٱلَّذِينَ ءَامَنُواْ ٱتَّبَعُواْ ٱلْحَقَّ    and because the faithful follow the truth

مِن رَّبِّهِمْ    from their Lord.

كَذَٰلِكَ يَضْرِبُ ٱللَّهُ لِلنَّاسِ أَمْثَٰلَهُمْ ۞    That is how Allah draws comparisons for mankind.

فَإِذَا لَقِيتُمُ ٱلَّذِينَ كَفَرُواْ    4 When you meet the faithless in battle,

فَضَرْبَ ٱلرِّقَابِ    strike their necks.

حَتَّىٰٓ إِذَآ أَثْخَنتُمُوهُمْ    When you have thoroughly decimated them,

فَشُدُّواْ ٱلْوَثَاقَ    bind the captives firmly.

فَإِمَّا مَنًّا بَعْدُ    Thereafter either oblige them [by setting them free]

وَإِمَّا فِدَآءً    or take ransom

حَتَّىٰ تَضَعَ ٱلْحَرْبُ أَوْزَارَهَا    till the war lays down its burdens.

ذَٰلِكَ    That [is Allah's ordinance],

وَلَوْ يَشَآءُ ٱللَّهُ    and had Allah wished

لَٱنتَصَرَ مِنْهُمْ    He could have taken vengeance on them,[1]

وَلَٰكِن لِّيَبْلُوَاْ بَعْضَكُم بِبَعْضٍ    but that He may test some of you by means of others.

وَٱلَّذِينَ قُتِلُواْ فِى سَبِيلِ ٱللَّهِ    As for those who were slain in the way of Allah,

فَلَن يُضِلَّ أَعْمَٰلَهُمْ ۞    He will not let their works go awry.

سَيَهْدِيهِمْ وَيُصْلِحُ بَالَهُمْ ۞    5 He will guide them and set right their affairs,

وَيُدْخِلُهُمُ ٱلْجَنَّةَ    6 and admit them into paradise

عَرَّفَهَا لَهُمْ ۞    with which He has acquainted them.

يَٰٓأَيُّهَا ٱلَّذِينَ ءَامَنُوٓاْ    7 O you who have faith!

إِن تَنصُرُواْ ٱللَّهَ يَنصُرْكُمْ    If you help Allah, He will help you

---

[1] That is, without your mediation.

وَيُثَبِّتْ أَقْدَامَكُمْ ۝   and make your feet steady.

وَٱلَّذِينَ كَفَرُوا   8 As for the faithless,

فَتَعْسًا لَّهُمْ   their lot will be to fall [into ruin],[1]

وَأَضَلَّ أَعْمَلَهُمْ ۝   and He will make their works go awry.

ذَٰلِكَ بِأَنَّهُمْ كَرِهُوا   9 That is because they loathed

مَآ أَنزَلَ ٱللَّهُ   what Allah has sent down,

فَأَحْبَطَ أَعْمَلَهُمْ ۝   so He made their works fail.

أَفَلَمْ يَسِيرُوا فِى ٱلْأَرْضِ   10 Have they not travelled over the land

فَيَنظُرُوا   so that they may observe

كَيْفَ كَانَ عَٰقِبَةُ ٱلَّذِينَ مِن قَبْلِهِمْ   how was the fate of those who were before them?

دَمَّرَ ٱللَّهُ عَلَيْهِمْ   Allah destroyed them,

وَلِلْكَٰفِرِينَ أَمْثَٰلُهَا ۝   and a similar [fate] awaits the faithless.

ذَٰلِكَ بِأَنَّ ٱللَّهَ مَوْلَى ٱلَّذِينَ ءَامَنُوا   11 That is because Allah is the master of the faithful,

وَأَنَّ ٱلْكَٰفِرِينَ لَا مَوْلَىٰ لَهُمْ ۝   and because the faithless have no master.

إِنَّ ٱللَّهَ يُدْخِلُ ٱلَّذِينَ ءَامَنُوا   12 Indeed Allah will admit those who have faith

وَعَمِلُوا ٱلصَّٰلِحَٰتِ   and do righteous deeds

جَنَّٰتٍ تَجْرِى مِن تَحْتِهَا ٱلْأَنْهَٰرُ   into gardens with streams running in them.

وَٱلَّذِينَ كَفَرُوا يَتَمَتَّعُونَ وَيَأْكُلُونَ   As for the faithless, they enjoy and eat

كَمَا تَأْكُلُ ٱلْأَنْعَٰمُ   just like the cattle eat,

وَٱلنَّارُ مَثْوًى لَّهُمْ ۝   and the Fire will be their [final] abode.

وَكَأَيِّن مِّن قَرْيَةٍ   13 How many a town there has been

هِىَ أَشَدُّ قُوَّةً مِّن قَرْيَتِكَ   which was more powerful than *your* town

ٱلَّتِى أَخْرَجَتْكَ   which expelled *you*,

أَهْلَكْنَٰهُمْ   which We have destroyed,

فَلَا نَاصِرَ لَهُمْ ۝   and they had no helper.

أَفَمَن كَانَ عَلَىٰ بَيِّنَةٍ مِّن رَّبِّهِۦ   14 Is he who stands on a manifest proof from his Lord

كَمَن   like someone

زُيِّنَ لَهُۥ سُوٓءُ عَمَلِهِۦ   to whom the evil of his conduct is made to seem decorous,

وَٱتَّبَعُوٓا أَهْوَآءَهُم ۝   and who follow their desires?

---

[1] Or 'their lot will be wretchedness.'

717

مَّثَلُ ٱلْجَنَّةِ ٱلَّتِي    15 A description of the paradise

وُعِدَ ٱلْمُتَّقُونَ      promised to the Godwary:

فِيهَآ أَنْهَٰرٌ مِّن مَّآءٍ غَيْرِ ءَاسِنٍ    therein are streams of unstaling water,

وَأَنْهَٰرٌ مِّن لَّبَنٍ لَّمْ يَتَغَيَّرْ طَعْمُهُ    and streams of milk unchanging in flavour,

وَأَنْهَٰرٌ مِّنْ خَمْرٍ لَّذَّةٍ لِّلشَّٰرِبِينَ    and streams of wine delicious to the drinkers,

وَأَنْهَٰرٌ مِّنْ عَسَلٍ مُّصَفًّى    and streams of purified honey;

وَلَهُمْ فِيهَا مِن كُلِّ ٱلثَّمَرَٰتِ    there will be for them every kind of fruit in it,

وَمَغْفِرَةٌ مِّن رَّبِّهِمْ    and forgiveness from their Lord.

كَمَنْ هُوَ خَٰلِدٌ فِى ٱلنَّارِ    [Are such ones] like those who abide in the Fire

وَسُقُواْ مَآءً حَمِيمًا    and are given to drink boiling water

فَقَطَّعَ أَمْعَآءَهُمْ ۝    which cuts up their bowels?

وَمِنْهُم    16 There are some among them

مَّن يَسْتَمِعُ إِلَيْكَ    who prick up their ears at *you*.

حَتَّىٰٓ إِذَا خَرَجُواْ مِنْ عِندِكَ    But when they go out from *your* presence,

قَالُواْ لِلَّذِينَ أُوتُواْ ٱلْعِلْمَ    they say to those who have been given knowledge,

مَاذَا قَالَ ءَانِفًا    'What did he say just now?'

أُوْلَٰٓئِكَ ٱلَّذِينَ    They are the ones

طَبَعَ ٱللَّهُ عَلَىٰ قُلُوبِهِمْ    on whose hearts Allah has set a seal,

وَٱتَّبَعُوٓاْ أَهْوَآءَهُمْ ۝    and they follow their own desires.

وَٱلَّذِينَ ٱهْتَدَوْاْ    17 As for those who are [rightly] guided,

زَادَهُمْ هُدًى    He enhances their guidance,

وَءَاتَىٰهُمْ تَقْوَىٰهُمْ ۝    and invests them with their Godwariness.

فَهَلْ يَنظُرُونَ إِلَّا ٱلسَّاعَةَ    18 Do they await anything except that the Hour

أَن تَأْتِيَهُم بَغْتَةً    should overtake them suddenly?

فَقَدْ جَآءَ أَشْرَاطُهَا    Certainly its portents have come.

فَأَنَّىٰ لَهُمْ    Of what avail to them

إِذَا جَآءَتْهُمْ ذِكْرَىٰهُمْ ۝    will their admonition be when it overtakes them?

فَٱعْلَمْ أَنَّهُ لَآ إِلَٰهَ إِلَّا ٱللَّهُ    19 *Know* that there is no god except Allah,

وَٱسْتَغْفِرْ لِذَنۢبِكَ    and *plead* [to Allah] for forgiveness of *your* sin

وَلِلْمُؤْمِنِينَ وَٱلْمُؤْمِنَٰتِ    and for the faithful, men and women.

وَٱللَّهُ يَعْلَمُ مُتَقَلَّبَكُمْ    Allah knows your itinerary

وَمَثْوَىٰكُمْ ﴿١٩﴾    and your [final] abode.

وَيَقُولُ ٱلَّذِينَ ءَامَنُوا۟    20 The faithful say,

لَوْلَا نُزِّلَتْ سُورَةٌ    'If only a *sūrah* were sent down!'

فَإِذَآ أُنزِلَتْ سُورَةٌ مُّحْكَمَةٌ    But when a definitive *sūrah* is sent down

وَذُكِرَ فِيهَا ٱلْقِتَالُ    and war is mentioned in it,

رَأَيْتَ ٱلَّذِينَ فِى قُلُوبِهِم مَّرَضٌ    *you* see those in whose hearts is a sickness[1]

يَنظُرُونَ إِلَيْكَ    looking upon *you*

نَظَرَ ٱلْمَغْشِىِّ عَلَيْهِ مِنَ ٱلْمَوْتِ    with the look of someone fainting at death.

فَأَوْلَىٰ لَهُمْ ﴿٢٠﴾    So woe to them!

طَاعَةٌ وَقَوْلٌ مَّعْرُوفٌ    21 Obedience and honourable words. . . .[2]

فَإِذَا عَزَمَ ٱلْأَمْرُ    So when the matter has been resolved upon,

فَلَوْ صَدَقُوا۟ ٱللَّهَ    if they remain true to Allah

لَكَانَ خَيْرًا لَّهُم ﴿٢١﴾    that will surely be better for them.

فَهَلْ عَسَيْتُمْ إِن تَوَلَّيْتُمْ    22 May it not be that if you were to wield authority

أَن تُفْسِدُوا۟ فِى ٱلْأَرْضِ    you would cause corruption in the land

وَتُقَطِّعُوٓا۟ أَرْحَامَكُمْ ﴿٢٢﴾    and ill-treat your blood relations?

أُو۟لَٰٓئِكَ ٱلَّذِينَ لَعَنَهُمُ ٱللَّهُ    23 They are the ones whom Allah has cursed,

فَأَصَمَّهُمْ وَأَعْمَىٰٓ أَبْصَٰرَهُمْ ﴿٢٣﴾    so He made them deaf, and blinded their sight.

أَفَلَا يَتَدَبَّرُونَ ٱلْقُرْءَانَ    24 Do they not contemplate the Qur'ān,

أَمْ عَلَىٰ قُلُوبٍ أَقْفَالُهَآ ﴿٢٤﴾    or are there locks on the hearts?

إِنَّ ٱلَّذِينَ ٱرْتَدُّوا۟ عَلَىٰٓ أَدْبَٰرِهِم    25 Indeed those who turned their backs

مِّنۢ بَعْدِ مَا تَبَيَّنَ لَهُمُ ٱلْهُدَى    after the guidance had become clear to them,

ٱلشَّيْطَٰنُ سَوَّلَ لَهُمْ    it was Satan who had seduced them,

وَأَمْلَىٰ لَهُمْ ﴿٢٥﴾    and he had given them [far-flung] hopes.[3]

ذَٰلِكَ بِأَنَّهُمْ قَالُوا۟    26 That is because they said

لِلَّذِينَ كَرِهُوا۟ مَا نَزَّلَ ٱللَّهُ    to those who loathed what Allah had sent down:

---

[1] That is, the hypocrites.

[2] Ellipsis; the omitted phrase is 'are all that is expected of you.'

[3] Or 'and He [i.e. Allah] gave them respite.'

سَنُطِيعُكُمْ فِى بَعْضِ ٱلْأَمْرِ
'We shall obey you in some matters,'

وَٱللَّهُ يَعْلَمُ إِسْرَارَهُمْ
and Allah knows their secret dealings.

فَكَيْفَ إِذَا
27 But how will it be [with them]

تَوَفَّتْهُمُ ٱلْمَلَـٰئِكَةُ
when the angels take them away,

يَضْرِبُونَ وُجُوهَهُمْ وَأَدْبَـٰرَهُمْ
striking their faces and their backs?!

ذَٰلِكَ بِأَنَّهُمُ ٱتَّبَعُوا مَا أَسْخَطَ ٱللَّهَ
28 That, because they pursued what displeased Allah,

وَكَرِهُوا رِضْوَٰنَهُ
and loathed His pleasure.

فَأَحْبَطَ أَعْمَـٰلَهُمْ
So He has made their works fail.

أَمْ حَسِبَ ٱلَّذِينَ فِى قُلُوبِهِم مَّرَضٌ
29 Do those in whose hearts is a sickness suppose

أَن لَّن يُخْرِجَ ٱللَّهُ أَضْغَـٰنَهُمْ
that Allah will not expose their spite?

وَلَوْ نَشَآءُ لَأَرَيْنَـٰكَهُمْ
30 If We wish, We will show them[1] to *you*

فَلَعَرَفْتَهُم بِسِيمَـٰهُمْ
so that *you* recognize them by their mark.

وَلَتَعْرِفَنَّهُمْ فِى لَحْنِ ٱلْقَوْلِ
Yet *you* will recognize them by their tone of speech,

وَٱللَّهُ يَعْلَمُ أَعْمَـٰلَكُمْ
and Allah knows your deeds.

وَلَنَبْلُوَنَّكُمْ
31 We will surely test you

حَتَّىٰ نَعْلَمَ ٱلْمُجَـٰهِدِينَ مِنكُمْ
until We ascertain those of you who wage *jihād*

وَٱلصَّـٰبِرِينَ
and those who are patient,

وَنَبْلُوَا۟ أَخْبَارَكُمْ
and We shall appraise your record.

إِنَّ ٱلَّذِينَ كَفَرُوا
32 Indeed those who are faithless

وَصَدُّوا عَن سَبِيلِ ٱللَّهِ
and bar from the way of Allah

وَشَآقُّوا ٱلرَّسُولَ
and defy the Apostle

مِنْ بَعْدِ مَا تَبَيَّنَ لَهُمُ ٱلْهُدَىٰ
after guidance has become clear to them,

لَن يَضُرُّوا ٱللَّهَ شَيْئًا
will not hurt Allah in the least,

وَسَيُحْبِطُ أَعْمَـٰلَهُمْ
and He shall make their works fail.

يَـٰٓأَيُّهَا ٱلَّذِينَ ءَامَنُوٓا
33 O you who have faith!

أَطِيعُوا ٱللَّهَ وَأَطِيعُوا ٱلرَّسُولَ
Obey Allah and obey the Apostle,

وَلَا تُبْطِلُوٓا أَعْمَـٰلَكُمْ
and do not render your works void.

إِنَّ ٱلَّذِينَ كَفَرُوا
34 Indeed those who are faithless

وَصَدُّوا عَن سَبِيلِ ٱللَّهِ
and bar from the way of Allah

---

[1] That is, the hypocrites.

ثُمَّ مَاتُوا وَهُمْ كُفَّارٌ    and then die faithless,

فَلَن يَغْفِرَ ٱللَّهُ لَهُمْ ۩    Allah will never forgive them.

فَلَا تَهِنُوا وَتَدْعُوٓا إِلَى ٱلسَّلْمِ   35 So do not slacken and [do not] call for peace

وَأَنتُمُ ٱلْأَعْلَوْنَ    when you have the upper hand

وَٱللَّهُ مَعَكُمْ    and Allah is with you,

وَلَن يَتِرَكُمْ أَعْمَٰلَكُمْ ۩    and He will not stint [the reward of] your works.

إِنَّمَا ٱلْحَيَوٰةُ ٱلدُّنْيَا لَعِبٌ وَلَهْوٌ   36 The life of the world is just play and diversion,

وَإِن تُؤْمِنُوا وَتَتَّقُوا    but if you are faithful and Godwary,

يُؤْتِكُمْ أُجُورَكُمْ    He will give you your rewards,

وَلَا يَسْـَٔلْكُمْ أَمْوَٰلَكُمْ ۩    and will not ask your wealth [in return] from you.

إِن يَسْـَٔلْكُمُوهَا فَيُحْفِكُمْ   37 Should He ask it from you, and press you,

تَبْخَلُوا وَيُخْرِجْ أَضْغَٰنَكُمْ ۩    you will be stingy, and He will expose your spite.

هَٰٓأَنتُمْ هَٰٓؤُلَآءِ   38 Ah! There you are,

تُدْعَوْنَ لِتُنفِقُوا فِى سَبِيلِ ٱللَّهِ    being invited to spend in the way of Allah;

فَمِنكُم مَّن يَبْخَلُ    yet among you there are those who are stingy;

وَمَن يَبْخَلْ فَإِنَّمَا يَبْخَلُ عَن نَّفْسِهِ    and whoever is stingy is stingy only to himself.

وَٱللَّهُ ٱلْغَنِىُّ وَأَنتُمُ ٱلْفُقَرَآءُ    Allah is the All-sufficient, and you are all-needy,

وَإِن تَتَوَلَّوْا    and if you turn away

يَسْتَبْدِلْ قَوْمًا غَيْرَكُمْ    He will replace you with another people,

ثُمَّ لَا يَكُونُوٓا أَمْثَٰلَكُم ۩    and they will not be like you.

## سُورَةُ الفَتْح      48. SŪRAT AL-FATḤ[1]

بِسْمِ ٱللَّهِ    In the Name of Allah,

ٱلرَّحْمَٰنِ ٱلرَّحِيمِ    the All-beneficent, the All-merciful.

إِنَّا فَتَحْنَا لَكَ فَتْحًا مُّبِينًا ۩   1 Indeed We have inaugurated for *you* a clear victory,[2]

لِّيَغْفِرَ لَكَ ٱللَّهُ   2 that Allah may forgive *you*

---

[1] The *sūrah* takes its name from verse 1 wherein victory (*fatḥ*) is mentioned.

[2] Or 'Indeed We have initiated for *you* a clear breakthrough.'

721

مَا تَقَدَّمَ مِن ذَنبِكَ وَمَا تَأَخَّرَ
what is past of *your* sin and what is to come,

وَيُتِمَّ نِعْمَتَهُ عَلَيْكَ
and that He may perfect His blessing upon *you*

وَيَهْدِيَكَ صِرَاطًا مُّسْتَقِيمًا ۝
and guide *you* on a straight path,

وَيَنصُرَكَ اللَّهُ نَصْرًا عَزِيزًا ۝
3 and Allah will help *you* with a mighty help.

هُوَ الَّذِى أَنزَلَ السَّكِينَةَ
4 It is He who sent down composure

فِى قُلُوبِ الْمُؤْمِنِينَ
into the hearts of the faithful

لِيَزْدَادُوٓا۟ إِيمَـٰنًا مَّعَ إِيمَـٰنِهِمْ
that they might add faith to their faith.

وَلِلَّهِ جُنُودُ السَّمَـٰوَٰتِ وَالْأَرْضِ
To Allah belong the hosts of the heavens and the earth,

وَكَانَ اللَّهُ عَلِيمًا حَكِيمًا ۝
and Allah is all-knowing, all-wise.

لِّيُدْخِلَ الْمُؤْمِنِينَ وَالْمُؤْمِنَـٰتِ
5 That He may admit the faithful, men and women,

جَنَّـٰتٍ تَجْرِى مِن تَحْتِهَا الْأَنْهَـٰرُ
into gardens with streams running in them,

خَـٰلِدِينَ فِيهَا
to remain in them [forever],

وَيُكَفِّرَ عَنْهُمْ سَيِّـَٔاتِهِمْ
and that He may absolve them of their misdeeds.

وَكَانَ ذَٰلِكَ عِندَ اللَّهِ فَوْزًا عَظِيمًا ۝
That is a great success with Allah.

وَيُعَذِّبَ الْمُنَـٰفِقِينَ وَالْمُنَـٰفِقَـٰتِ
6 That He may punish the hypocrites, men and women,

وَالْمُشْرِكِينَ وَالْمُشْرِكَـٰتِ
and the polytheists, men and women,

الظَّآنِّينَ بِاللَّهِ ظَنَّ السَّوْءِ
who entertain a bad opinion of Allah.

عَلَيْهِمْ دَآئِرَةُ السَّوْءِ
For them shall be an adverse turn of fortune:

وَغَضِبَ اللَّهُ عَلَيْهِمْ
Allah is wrathful with them

وَلَعَنَهُمْ
and He has cursed them,

وَأَعَدَّ لَهُمْ جَهَنَّمَ
and prepared for them hell,

وَسَآءَتْ مَصِيرًا ۝
and it is an evil destination.

وَلِلَّهِ جُنُودُ السَّمَـٰوَٰتِ
7 To Allah belong the hosts of the heavens

وَالْأَرْضِ
and the earth,

وَكَانَ اللَّهُ عَزِيزًا حَكِيمًا ۝
and Allah is all-mighty, all-wise.

إِنَّآ أَرْسَلْنَـٰكَ شَـٰهِدًا
8 Indeed We have sent *you* as a witness,

وَمُبَشِّرًا وَنَذِيرًا ۝
as a bearer of good news and warner,

لِّتُؤْمِنُوا۟ بِاللَّهِ وَرَسُولِهِ
9 that you may have faith in Allah and His Apostle,

وَتُعَزِّرُوهُ وَتُوَقِّرُوهُ
and that you may support him and revere him,

وَتُسَبِّحُوهُ بُكْرَةً
and that you may glorify Him morning

وَأَصِيلًا ۝

and evening.

إِنَّ ٱلَّذِينَ يُبَايِعُونَكَ

10 Indeed those who swear allegiance to *you*,

إِنَّمَا يُبَايِعُونَ ٱللَّهَ

swear allegiance only to Allah:

يَدُ ٱللَّهِ فَوْقَ أَيْدِيهِمْ

the hand of Allah is above their hands.

فَمَن نَّكَثَ

So whosoever breaks his oath,

فَإِنَّمَا يَنكُثُ عَلَىٰ نَفْسِهِۦ

breaks it only to his own detriment,

وَمَنْ أَوْفَىٰ

and whoever fulfills

بِمَا عَٰهَدَ عَلَيْهُ ٱللَّهَ

the covenant he had made with Allah,

فَسَيُؤْتِيهِ أَجْرًا عَظِيمًا ۝

He will give him a great reward.

سَيَقُولُ لَكَ ٱلْمُخَلَّفُونَ مِنَ ٱلْأَعْرَابِ

11 The Bedouins who were left behind will tell *you*,

شَغَلَتْنَآ أَمْوَٰلُنَا وَأَهْلُونَا

'Our possessions and our families kept us occupied.

فَٱسْتَغْفِرْ لَنَا

So plead [to Allah] for our forgiveness!'

يَقُولُونَ بِأَلْسِنَتِهِم

They say with their tongues

مَّا لَيْسَ فِى قُلُوبِهِمْ

what is not in their hearts.

قُلْ فَمَن يَمْلِكُ لَكُم مِّنَ ٱللَّهِ شَيْـًٔا

*Say*, 'Who can be of any avail to you against Allah,

إِنْ أَرَادَ بِكُمْ ضَرًّا

should He desire to cause you harm

أَوْ أَرَادَ بِكُمْ نَفْعًا

or desire to bring you benefit?

بَلْ كَانَ ٱللَّهُ بِمَا تَعْمَلُونَ خَبِيرًا ۝

Rather Allah is well aware of what you do.'

بَلْ ظَنَنتُمْ

12 Rather you thought

أَن لَّن يَنقَلِبَ ٱلرَّسُولُ وَٱلْمُؤْمِنُونَ

that the Apostle and the faithful will not return

إِلَىٰٓ أَهْلِيهِمْ أَبَدًا

to their folk ever,

وَزُيِّنَ ذَٰلِكَ فِى قُلُوبِكُمْ

and that was made to seem decorous to your hearts,

وَظَنَنتُمْ ظَنَّ ٱلسَّوْءِ

and you entertained evil thoughts,

وَكُنتُمْ قَوْمًا بُورًا ۝

and you were a ruined lot.

وَمَن لَّمْ يُؤْمِنۢ بِٱللَّهِ

13 As for those who have no faith in Allah

وَرَسُولِهِۦ

and His Apostle,

فَإِنَّآ أَعْتَدْنَا لِلْكَٰفِرِينَ سَعِيرًا ۝

We have prepared a blaze for the faithless.

وَلِلَّهِ مُلْكُ ٱلسَّمَٰوَٰتِ

14 To Allah belongs the kingdom of the heavens

وَٱلْأَرْضِ

and the earth:

يَغْفِرُ لِمَن يَشَآءُ

He forgives whomever He wishes,

وَيُعَذِّبُ مَن يَشَآءُ
and punishes whomever He wishes,

وَكَانَ ٱللَّهُ غَفُورًا رَّحِيمًا ۝
and Allah is all-forgiving, all-merciful.

سَيَقُولُ ٱلْمُخَلَّفُونَ
15 Those who were left to stay behind will say,

إِذَا ٱنطَلَقْتُمْ إِلَىٰ مَغَانِمَ لِتَأْخُذُوهَا
when you set out to capture booty:

ذَرُونَا نَتَّبِعْكُمْ
'Let us follow you.'

يُرِيدُونَ أَن يُبَدِّلُوا۟ كَلَٰمَ ٱللَّهِ
They desire to change the word of Allah.

قُل لَّن تَتَّبِعُونَا
Say, 'You shall never follow us!

كَذَٰلِكُمْ قَالَ ٱللَّهُ مِن قَبْلُ
Thus has Allah said beforehand.'

فَسَيَقُولُونَ بَلْ تَحْسُدُونَنَا
Then they will say, 'You are envious of us.'

بَلْ كَانُوا۟ لَا يَفْقَهُونَ إِلَّا قَلِيلًا ۝
Rather they do not understand but a little.

قُل لِّلْمُخَلَّفِينَ مِنَ ٱلْأَعْرَابِ
16 Say to the Bedouins who were left to stay behind,

سَتُدْعَوْنَ إِلَىٰ قَوْمٍ
'You will be called against a people

أُو۟لِى بَأْسٍ شَدِيدٍ
of a great might:

تُقَٰتِلُونَهُمْ أَوْ يُسْلِمُونَ
they will embrace Islam, or you will fight them.

فَإِن تُطِيعُوا۟ يُؤْتِكُمُ ٱللَّهُ أَجْرًا حَسَنًا
So if you obey, Allah will give you a good reward;

وَإِن تَتَوَلَّوْا۟ كَمَا تَوَلَّيْتُم مِّن قَبْلُ
but if you turn away like you turned away before,

يُعَذِّبْكُمْ عَذَابًا أَلِيمًا ۝
He will punish you with a painful punishment.'

لَّيْسَ عَلَى ٱلْأَعْمَىٰ حَرَجٌ
17 There is no blame on the blind,

وَلَا عَلَى ٱلْأَعْرَجِ حَرَجٌ
nor is there any blame on the lame,

وَلَا عَلَى ٱلْمَرِيضِ حَرَجٌ
nor is there blame on the sick;

وَمَن يُطِعِ ٱللَّهَ وَرَسُولَهُ
and whoever obeys Allah and His Apostle,

يُدْخِلْهُ جَنَّٰتٍ
He will admit him into gardens

تَجْرِى مِن تَحْتِهَا ٱلْأَنْهَٰرُ
with streams running in them,

وَمَن يَتَوَلَّ
and whoever refuses to comply,

يُعَذِّبْهُ عَذَابًا أَلِيمًا ۝
He will punish him with a painful punishment.

لَّقَدْ رَضِىَ ٱللَّهُ عَنِ ٱلْمُؤْمِنِينَ
18 Allah was certainly pleased with the faithful

إِذْ يُبَايِعُونَكَ تَحْتَ ٱلشَّجَرَةِ
when they swore allegiance to *you* under the tree.

فَعَلِمَ مَا فِى قُلُوبِهِمْ
He knew what was in their hearts,

فَأَنزَلَ ٱلسَّكِينَةَ عَلَيْهِمْ
so He sent down composure on them,

وَأَثَٰبَهُمْ فَتْحًا قَرِيبًا ۝
and requited them with a victory near at hand

وَمَغَانِمَ كَثِيرَةً يَأْخُذُونَهَا   19 and abundant spoils that they will capture,

وَكَانَ اللَّهُ عَزِيزًا حَكِيمًا ۝    and Allah is all-mighty, all-wise.

وَعَدَكُمُ اللَّهُ مَغَانِمَ كَثِيرَةً   20 Allah has promised you abundant spoils

تَأْخُذُونَهَا    which you will capture.

فَعَجَّلَ لَكُمْ هَـٰذِهِ    He has expedited this one for you,

وَكَفَّ أَيْدِيَ النَّاسِ عَنكُمْ    and withheld men's hands from you,

وَلِتَكُونَ ءَايَةً لِّلْمُؤْمِنِينَ    so that it may be a sign for the faithful,

وَيَهْدِيَكُمْ صِرَٰطًا مُّسْتَقِيمًا ۝    and that He may guide you to a straight path.

وَأُخْرَىٰ   21 And other [spoils]

لَمْ تَقْدِرُوا عَلَيْهَا    which you have not yet captured:

قَدْ أَحَاطَ اللَّهُ بِهَا    Allah has comprehended them,

وَكَانَ اللَّهُ عَلَىٰ كُلِّ شَيْءٍ قَدِيرًا ۝    and Allah has power over all things.

وَلَوْ قَٰتَلَكُمُ الَّذِينَ كَفَرُوا   22 If the faithless fight you,

لَوَلَّوُا الْأَدْبَٰرَ    they will turn their backs [to flee].

ثُمَّ لَا يَجِدُونَ وَلِيًّا وَلَا نَصِيرًا ۝    Then they will not find any protector or helper.

سُنَّةَ اللَّهِ الَّتِي قَدْ خَلَتْ مِن قَبْلُ   23 [It is] Allah's precedent that has passed before,

وَلَن تَجِدَ لِسُنَّةِ اللَّهِ    and you will never find in Allah's precedent

تَبْدِيلًا ۝    any change.

وَهُوَ الَّذِي كَفَّ أَيْدِيَهُمْ عَنكُمْ   24 It is He who withheld their hands from you,

وَأَيْدِيَكُمْ عَنْهُم    and your hands from them,

بِبَطْنِ مَكَّةَ    in the valley of Makkah,

مِن بَعْدِ أَنْ أَظْفَرَكُمْ عَلَيْهِمْ    after He had given you victory over them,

وَكَانَ اللَّهُ بِمَا تَعْمَلُونَ بَصِيرًا ۝    and Allah sees best what you do.

هُمُ الَّذِينَ كَفَرُوا   25 They are the ones who disbelieved

وَصَدُّوكُمْ عَنِ الْمَسْجِدِ الْحَرَامِ    and barred you from the Sacred Mosque,

وَالْهَدْيَ مَعْكُوفًا أَن يَبْلُغَ مَحِلَّهُ    and kept the offering from reaching its destination.

وَلَوْلَا رِجَالٌ مُّؤْمِنُونَ    And were it not for [certain] faithful men

وَنِسَآءٌ مُّؤْمِنَٰتٌ    and faithful women,

لَّمْ تَعْلَمُوهُمْ    whom you did not know

أَن تَطَئُوهُمْ    —lest you should trample them,

فَتُصِيبَكُم مِّنْهُم مَّعَرَّةٌ    and thus blame for [killing] them should fall on you

بِغَيْرِ عِلْمٍ    unawares;[1] [He held you back]

لِّيُدْخِلَ ٱللَّهُ فِى رَحْمَتِهِۦ    so that Allah may admit into His mercy

مَن يَشَآءُ    whomever He wishes.

لَوْ تَزَيَّلُوا    And had they been separate,

لَعَذَّبْنَا ٱلَّذِينَ كَفَرُوا    We would have surely punished the faithless

مِنْهُمْ    among them

عَذَابًا أَلِيمًا ۲۵    with a painful punishment.

إِذْ جَعَلَ ٱلَّذِينَ كَفَرُوا    26 When the faithless nourished

فِى قُلُوبِهِمُ ٱلْحَمِيَّةَ    bigotry in their hearts,

حَمِيَّةَ ٱلْجَٰهِلِيَّةِ    the bigotry of pagan ignorance,

فَأَنزَلَ ٱللَّهُ سَكِينَتَهُۥ    Allah sent down His composure

عَلَىٰ رَسُولِهِۦ وَعَلَى ٱلْمُؤْمِنِينَ    upon His Apostle and upon the faithful,

وَأَلْزَمَهُمْ كَلِمَةَ ٱلتَّقْوَىٰ    and made them abide by the word of Godwariness,

وَكَانُوا أَحَقَّ بِهَا وَأَهْلَهَا    for they were the worthiest of it and deserved it,

وَكَانَ ٱللَّهُ بِكُلِّ شَىْءٍ عَلِيمًا ۲۶    and Allah has knowledge of all things.

لَّقَدْ صَدَقَ ٱللَّهُ رَسُولَهُ ٱلرُّءْيَا    27 Certainly Allah has fulfilled His Apostle's vision

بِٱلْحَقِّ    in all truth:

لَتَدْخُلُنَّ ٱلْمَسْجِدَ ٱلْحَرَامَ    You will surely enter the Sacred Mosque,

إِن شَآءَ ٱللَّهُ    God willing,

ءَامِنِينَ    in safety,

مُحَلِّقِينَ رُءُوسَكُمْ وَمُقَصِّرِينَ    with your heads shaven or hair cropped,

لَا تَخَافُونَ    without any fear.

فَعَلِمَ مَا لَمْ تَعْلَمُوا    So He knew what you did not know,

فَجَعَلَ مِن دُونِ ذَٰلِكَ    and He assigned [you] besides that

فَتْحًا قَرِيبًا ۲۷    a victory near at hand.

هُوَ ٱلَّذِىٓ أَرْسَلَ رَسُولَهُۥ بِٱلْهُدَىٰ    28 It is He who has sent His Apostle with guidance

وَدِينِ ٱلْحَقِّ    and the true religion,

---

[1] Ellipsis; the omitted phrase is 'We would have given you a free hand against them.'

لِيُظۡهِرَهُۥ عَلَى ٱلدِّينِ كُلِّهِۦ    that He may make it prevail over all religions,

وَكَفَىٰ بِٱللَّهِ شَهِيدًا ٢٨    and Allah suffices as witness.

مُّحَمَّدٌ رَّسُولُ ٱللَّهِ    29 Muḥammad, the Apostle of Allah,

وَٱلَّذِينَ مَعَهُۥٓ    and those who are with him

أَشِدَّآءُ عَلَى ٱلۡكُفَّارِ    are hard against the faithless

رُحَمَآءُ بَيۡنَهُمۡ    and merciful amongst themselves.

تَرَىٰهُمۡ رُكَّعًا سُجَّدًا    You see them bowing and prostrating [in worship],

يَبۡتَغُونَ فَضۡلًا مِّنَ ٱللَّهِ وَرِضۡوَٰنًا    seeking Allah's grace and [His] pleasure.

سِيمَاهُمۡ فِى وُجُوهِهِم    Their mark is [visible] on their faces,

مِّنۡ أَثَرِ ٱلسُّجُودِ    from the effect of prostration.

ذَٰلِكَ مَثَلُهُمۡ فِى ٱلتَّوۡرَىٰةِ    Such is their description in the Torah

وَمَثَلُهُمۡ فِى ٱلۡإِنجِيلِ    and their description in the Evangel.

كَزَرۡعٍ    Like a tillage

أَخۡرَجَ شَطۡـَٔهُۥ فَـَٔازَرَهُۥ    that sends out its shoots and builds them up,

فَٱسۡتَغۡلَظَ    and they grow stout

فَٱسۡتَوَىٰ عَلَىٰ سُوقِهِۦ    and settle on their stalks,

يُعۡجِبُ ٱلزُّرَّاعَ    impressing the sowers,

لِيَغِيظَ بِهِمُ ٱلۡكُفَّارَ    so that He may enrage the faithless by them.

وَعَدَ ٱللَّهُ ٱلَّذِينَ    Allah has promised those

ءَامَنُواْ وَعَمِلُواْ ٱلصَّٰلِحَٰتِ مِنۡهُم    of them who have faith and do righteous deeds

مَّغۡفِرَةً وَأَجۡرًا عَظِيمًا ٢٩    forgiveness and a great reward.

# سُورَةُ ٱلۡحُجُرَاتِ

# 49. SŪRAT AL-ḤUJURĀT[1]

بِسۡمِ ٱللَّهِ    In the Name of Allah,

ٱلرَّحۡمَٰنِ ٱلرَّحِيمِ    the All-beneficent, the All-merciful.

يَٰٓأَيُّهَا ٱلَّذِينَ ءَامَنُواْ    1 O you who have faith!

لَا تُقَدِّمُواْ بَيۡنَ يَدَىِ ٱللَّهِ وَرَسُولِهِۦ    Do not venture ahead of Allah and His Apostle,

---

[1] The *sūrah* takes its name from the word *ḥujurāt* (apartments) in verse 4.

وَٱتَّقُوا۟ ٱللَّهَ    and be wary of Allah.

إِنَّ ٱللَّهَ سَمِيعٌ عَلِيمٌ ۝    Indeed Allah is all-hearing, all-knowing.

يَـٰٓأَيُّهَا ٱلَّذِينَ ءَامَنُوا۟    2 O you who have faith!

لَا تَرۡفَعُوٓا۟ أَصۡوَٰتَكُمۡ    Do not raise your voices

فَوۡقَ صَوۡتِ ٱلنَّبِيِّ    above the voice of the Prophet,

وَلَا تَجۡهَرُوا۟ لَهُۥ بِٱلۡقَوۡلِ    and do not speak aloud to him

كَجَهۡرِ بَعۡضِكُمۡ لِبَعۡضٍ    as you shout to one another,

أَن تَحۡبَطَ أَعۡمَٰلُكُمۡ    lest your works should fail

وَأَنتُمۡ لَا تَشۡعُرُونَ ۝    without your being aware.

إِنَّ ٱلَّذِينَ يَغُضُّونَ أَصۡوَٰتَهُمۡ    3 Indeed those who lower their voices

عِندَ رَسُولِ ٱللَّهِ    in the presence of the Apostle of Allah

أُو۟لَـٰٓئِكَ ٱلَّذِينَ ٱمۡتَحَنَ ٱللَّهُ قُلُوبَهُمۡ    —they are the ones whose hearts Allah has tested

لِلتَّقۡوَىٰ    for Godwariness.

لَهُم مَّغۡفِرَةٌ وَأَجۡرٌ عَظِيمٌ ۝    For them will be forgiveness and a great reward.

إِنَّ ٱلَّذِينَ يُنَادُونَكَ    4 Indeed those who call *you*

مِن وَرَآءِ ٱلۡحُجُرَٰتِ    from behind the apartments,

أَكۡثَرُهُمۡ لَا يَعۡقِلُونَ ۝    most of them do not apply reason,

وَلَوۡ أَنَّهُمۡ صَبَرُوا۟ حَتَّىٰ تَخۡرُجَ إِلَيۡهِمۡ    5 and if they have patience until *you* come out to them,

لَكَانَ خَيۡرًا لَّهُمۡ    it will be better for them,

وَٱللَّهُ غَفُورٌ رَّحِيمٌ ۝    and Allah is all-forgiving, all-merciful.

يَـٰٓأَيُّهَا ٱلَّذِينَ ءَامَنُوٓا۟    6 O you who have faith!

إِن جَآءَكُمۡ فَاسِقٌ بِنَبَإٍ فَتَبَيَّنُوٓا۟    If a profligate [person] should bring you some news, verify it,

أَن تُصِيبُوا۟ قَوۡمًا بِجَهَٰلَةٍ    lest you should visit [harm] on some people out of ignorance,

فَتُصۡبِحُوا۟ عَلَىٰ مَا فَعَلۡتُمۡ نَٰدِمِينَ ۝    and then become regretful for what you have done.

وَٱعۡلَمُوٓا۟ أَنَّ فِيكُمۡ رَسُولَ ٱللَّهِ    7 Know that the Apostle of Allah is among you.

لَوۡ يُطِيعُكُمۡ فِي كَثِيرٍ مِّنَ ٱلۡأَمۡرِ لَعَنِتُّمۡ    Should he obey you in many matters, you would surely suffer.

وَلَـٰكِنَّ ٱللَّهَ حَبَّبَ إِلَيۡكُمُ ٱلۡإِيمَٰنَ    But Allah has endeared faith to you

وَزَيَّنَهُۥ فِى قُلُوبِكُمۡ
and made it appealing in your hearts,

وَكَرَّهَ إِلَيۡكُمُ
and He has made hateful to you

ٱلۡكُفۡرَ وَٱلۡفُسُوقَ وَٱلۡعِصۡيَانَ
faithlessness, transgression and disobedience.

أُوْلَٰٓئِكَ هُمُ ٱلرَّٰشِدُونَ ۝
It is such who are the right-minded

8 فَضۡلًا مِّنَ ٱللَّهِ وَنِعۡمَةً
—a grace and blessing from Allah,

وَٱللَّهُ عَلِيمٌ حَكِيمٌ ۝
and Allah is all-knowing, all-wise.

9 وَإِن طَآئِفَتَانِ مِنَ ٱلۡمُؤۡمِنِينَ ٱقۡتَتَلُواْ
If two groups of the faithful fight one another,

فَأَصۡلِحُواْ بَيۡنَهُمَاۖ
make peace between them.

فَإِنۢ بَغَتۡ إِحۡدَىٰهُمَا عَلَى ٱلۡأُخۡرَىٰ
But if one party of them aggresses against the other,

فَقَٰتِلُواْ ٱلَّتِى تَبۡغِى
fight the one which aggresses

حَتَّىٰ تَفِىٓءَ إِلَىٰٓ أَمۡرِ ٱللَّهِۚ
until it returns to Allah's ordinance.

فَإِن فَآءَتۡ
Then, if it returns,

فَأَصۡلِحُواْ بَيۡنَهُمَا بِٱلۡعَدۡلِ
make peace between them fairly,

وَأَقۡسِطُوٓاْۖ
and do justice.

إِنَّ ٱللَّهَ يُحِبُّ ٱلۡمُقۡسِطِينَ ۝
Indeed Allah loves the just.

10 إِنَّمَا ٱلۡمُؤۡمِنُونَ إِخۡوَةٌ
The faithful are indeed brothers.

فَأَصۡلِحُواْ بَيۡنَ أَخَوَيۡكُمۡۚ
Therefore make peace between your brothers

وَٱتَّقُواْ ٱللَّهَ
and be wary of Allah,

لَعَلَّكُمۡ تُرۡحَمُونَ ۝
so that you may receive [His] mercy.

11 يَٰٓأَيُّهَا ٱلَّذِينَ ءَامَنُواْ
O you who have faith!

لَا يَسۡخَرۡ قَوۡمٌ مِّن قَوۡمٍ
Let not any people ridicule another people:

عَسَىٰٓ أَن يَكُونُواْ خَيۡرًا مِّنۡهُمۡ
it may be that they are better than they are;

وَلَا نِسَآءٌ مِّن نِّسَآءٍ
nor let women [ridicule] women:

عَسَىٰٓ أَن يَكُنَّ خَيۡرًا مِّنۡهُنَّۖ
it may be that they are better than they are.

وَلَا تَلۡمِزُوٓاْ أَنفُسَكُمۡ
And do not defame one another,

وَلَا تَنَابَزُواْ بِٱلۡأَلۡقَٰبِۖ
nor insult one another by nicknames.

بِئۡسَ ٱلِٱسۡمُ ٱلۡفُسُوقُ بَعۡدَ ٱلۡإِيمَٰنِۚ
An evil name is transgression after faith!

وَمَن لَّمۡ يَتُبۡ
And whoever is not penitent

فَأُوْلَٰٓئِكَ هُمُ ٱلظَّٰلِمُونَ ۝
—such are the wrongdoers.

12 يَٰٓأَيُّهَا ٱلَّذِينَ ءَامَنُواْ
O you who have faith!

اجۡتَنِبُواۡ كَثِيرٗا مِّنَ الظَّنِّ    Avoid much suspicion.

إِنَّ بَعۡضَ الظَّنِّ إِثۡمٞ    Indeed some suspicions are sins.

وَلَا تَجَسَّسُواۡ    And do not spy on

وَلَا يَغۡتَب بَّعۡضُكُم بَعۡضًا    or backbite one another.

أَيُحِبُّ أَحَدُكُمۡ    Will any of you love

أَن يَأۡكُلَ لَحۡمَ أَخِيهِ مَيۡتٗا    to eat the flesh of his dead brother?

فَكَرِهۡتُمُوهُ    You would hate it.

وَاتَّقُواۡ اللَّهَ    And be wary of Allah;

إِنَّ اللَّهَ تَوَّابٞ رَّحِيمٞ ۞    indeed Allah is all-clement, all-merciful.

يَٰٓأَيُّهَا النَّاسُ    13 O mankind!

إِنَّا خَلَقۡنَٰكُم مِّن ذَكَرٖ وَأُنثَىٰ    Indeed We created you from a male and a female,

وَجَعَلۡنَٰكُمۡ شُعُوبٗا وَقَبَآئِلَ    and made you nations and tribes

لِتَعَارَفُوٓاۡ    that you may identify with one another.

إِنَّ أَكۡرَمَكُمۡ    Indeed the noblest[1] of you

عِندَ اللَّهِ    in the sight of Allah

أَتۡقَىٰكُمۡ    is the most Godwary among you.

إِنَّ اللَّهَ عَلِيمٌ خَبِيرٞ ۞ ۞    Indeed Allah is all-knowing, all-aware.

قَالَتِ الۡأَعۡرَابُ ءَامَنَّا    14 The Bedouins say, 'We have faith.'

قُل لَّمۡ تُؤۡمِنُواۡ    *Say,* 'You do not have faith yet;

وَلَٰكِن قُولُوٓاۡ أَسۡلَمۡنَا    rather say, "We have embraced Islam,"[2]

وَلَمَّا يَدۡخُلِ الۡإِيمَٰنُ فِي قُلُوبِكُمۡ    for faith has not yet entered into your hearts.

وَإِن تُطِيعُواۡ اللَّهَ وَرَسُولَهُۥ    Yet if you obey Allah and His Apostle,

لَا يَلِتۡكُم مِّنۡ أَعۡمَٰلِكُمۡ شَيۡـًٔا    He will not stint anything of [the reward of] your works.

إِنَّ اللَّهَ غَفُورٞ رَّحِيمٞ ۞    Indeed Allah is all-forgiving, all-merciful.'

إِنَّمَا الۡمُؤۡمِنُونَ الَّذِينَ ءَامَنُواۡ    15 The faithful are only those who have attained faith

بِاللَّهِ وَرَسُولِهِۦ    in Allah and His Apostle

ثُمَّ لَمۡ يَرۡتَابُواۡ    and then have never doubted,

وَجَٰهَدُواۡ بِأَمۡوَٰلِهِمۡ    and who wage *jihād* with their possessions

---

[1] Or 'the most honoured.'

[2] Or 'We have submitted.'

وَأَنفُسِهِمۡ    and their persons

فِى سَبِيلِ ٱللَّهِ    in the way of Allah.

أُوْلَـٰٓئِكَ هُمُ ٱلصَّـٰدِقُونَ ⑮    It is they who are the truthful.[1]

قُلۡ أَتُعَلِّمُونَ ٱللَّهَ بِدِينِكُمۡ    16 *Say,* 'Will you inform Allah about your faith

وَٱللَّهُ يَعۡلَمُ مَا فِى ٱلسَّمَـٰوَٰتِ    while Allah knows whatever there is in the heavens

وَمَا فِى ٱلۡأَرۡضِ    and whatever there is in the earth,

وَٱللَّهُ بِكُلِّ شَىۡءٍ عَلِيمٌ ⑯    and Allah has knowledge of all things?'

يَمُنُّونَ عَلَيۡكَ    17 They count it as a favour to *you*

أَنۡ أَسۡلَمُوٓاْ    that they have embraced Islam.

قُل لَّا تَمُنُّواْ عَلَىَّ    *Say,* 'Do not count it as a favour to me

إِسۡلَـٰمَكُمۖ    your embracing of Islam.

بَلِ ٱللَّهُ يَمُنُّ عَلَيۡكُمۡ    Rather it is Allah who has done you a favour

أَنۡ هَدَىٰكُمۡ لِلۡإِيمَـٰنِ    in that He has guided you to faith,

إِن كُنتُمۡ صَـٰدِقِينَ ⑰    should you be truthful.[2]

إِنَّ ٱللَّهَ يَعۡلَمُ غَيۡبَ ٱلسَّمَـٰوَٰتِ    18 Indeed Allah knows the Unseen of the heavens

وَٱلۡأَرۡضِ    and the earth,

وَٱللَّهُ بَصِيرُۢ بِمَا تَعۡمَلُونَ ⑱    and Allah sees best what you do.'

# سُورَةُ قٓ     50. SŪRAT QĀF[3]

بِسۡمِ ٱللَّهِ    In the Name of Allah,

ٱلرَّحۡمَـٰنِ ٱلرَّحِيمِ    the All-beneficent, the All-merciful.

قٓ    1 *Qāf.*

وَٱلۡقُرۡءَانِ ٱلۡمَجِيدِ ①    By the glorious Qur'ān.

بَلۡ عَجِبُوٓاْ    2 Rather they consider it odd

أَن جَآءَهُم مُّنذِرٌ    that a warner should have come to them

---

[1] Or 'the sincere.'

[2] That is, should you be sincere in your claim of having embraced Islam.

[3] The *sūrah* takes its name from the letter *qāf* in verse 1.

مِنْهُمْ    from among themselves.

فَقَالَ ٱلْكَـٰفِرُونَ هَـٰذَا شَىْءٌ عَجِيبٌ ۩    So the faithless say, 'This is an odd thing.

3 أَءِذَا مِتْنَا    What! When we are dead

وَكُنَّا تُرَابًا    and have become dust [shall we be raised again]?

ذَٰلِكَ رَجْعٌ بَعِيدٌ ۩    That is a far-fetched return!'

4 قَدْ عَلِمْنَا مَا تَنقُصُ ٱلْأَرْضُ مِنْهُمْ    We know what the earth diminishes from them,[1]

وَعِندَنَا كِتَـٰبٌ حَفِيظٌ ۩    and with Us is a preserving Book.

5 بَلْ كَذَّبُوا بِٱلْحَقِّ لَمَّا جَآءَهُمْ    Rather they denied the truth when it came to them;

فَهُمْ فِى أَمْرٍ مَّرِيجٍ ۩    so they are now in a perplexed state of affairs.

6 أَفَلَمْ يَنظُرُوٓا إِلَى ٱلسَّمَآءِ فَوْقَهُمْ    Have they not then observed the sky above them,

كَيْفَ بَنَيْنَـٰهَا وَزَيَّنَّـٰهَا    how We have built it and adorned it,

وَمَا لَهَا مِن فُرُوجٍ ۩    and that there are no cracks in it?

7 وَٱلْأَرْضَ مَدَدْنَـٰهَا    And We spread out the earth,

وَأَلْقَيْنَا فِيهَا رَوَٰسِىَ    and cast in it firm mountains,

وَأَنبَتْنَا فِيهَا مِن كُلِّ زَوْجٍ بَهِيجٍ ۩    and caused every delightful kind to grow in it.

8 تَبْصِرَةً وَذِكْرَىٰ    [In this there is] an insight and admonition

لِكُلِّ عَبْدٍ مُّنِيبٍ ۩    for every penitent servant.

9 وَنَزَّلْنَا مِنَ ٱلسَّمَآءِ مَآءً مُّبَـٰرَكًا    And We send down from the sky salubrious water,

فَأَنبَتْنَا بِهِۦ جَنَّـٰتٍ    with which We grow gardens

وَحَبَّ ٱلْحَصِيدِ ۩    and the grain which is harvested,

10 وَٱلنَّخْلَ بَاسِقَـٰتٍ لَّهَا طَلْعٌ نَّضِيدٌ ۩    and tall date palms with regularly set spathes,

11 رِّزْقًا لِّلْعِبَادِ    as a provision for servants;

وَأَحْيَيْنَا بِهِۦ بَلْدَةً مَّيْتًا    and with it We revive a dead country.

كَذَٰلِكَ ٱلْخُرُوجُ ۩    Likewise will be the rising [from the dead].

12 كَذَّبَتْ قَبْلَهُمْ قَوْمُ نُوحٍ    The people of Noah denied before them,

وَأَصْحَـٰبُ ٱلرَّسِّ وَثَمُودُ ۩    and [so did] the inhabitants of Rass[2] and Thamūd,

13 وَعَادٌ وَفِرْعَوْنُ وَإِخْوَٰنُ لُوطٍ ۩    and 'Ād, Pharaoh, and the brethren of Lot,

14 وَأَصْحَـٰبُ ٱلْأَيْكَةِ    and the inhabitants of Aykah

---

[1] That is, from their bodies when they disintegrate after death.
[2] See 25:38.

وَقَوْمُ تُبَّعٍ      and the people of Tubba'.[1]

كُلٌّ كَذَّبَ ٱلرُّسُلَ      Each [of them] impugned the apostles,

فَحَقَّ وَعِيدِ ۝      and so My threat became due [against them].

أَفَعَيِينَا بِٱلْخَلْقِ ٱلْأَوَّلِ      15 Were We exhausted by the first creation?

بَلْ هُمْ فِي لَبْسٍ مِّنْ خَلْقٍ جَدِيدٍ ۝      Rather they are in doubt about a new creation.

وَلَقَدْ خَلَقْنَا ٱلْإِنسَـٰنَ      16 Certainly We have created man

وَنَعْلَمُ مَا تُوَسْوِسُ بِهِۦ نَفْسُهُۥ      and We know to what his soul tempts him,

وَنَحْنُ أَقْرَبُ إِلَيْهِ      and We are nearer to him

مِنْ حَبْلِ ٱلْوَرِيدِ ۝      than his jugular vein.

إِذْ يَتَلَقَّى ٱلْمُتَلَقِّيَانِ      17 When the twin recorders record [his deeds],

عَنِ ٱلْيَمِينِ وَعَنِ ٱلشِّمَالِ قَعِيدٌ ۝      seated on the right hand and on the left:

مَّا يَلْفِظُ مِن قَوْلٍ      18    he says no word

إِلَّا لَدَيْهِ رَقِيبٌ عَتِيدٌ ۝      but that there is a ready observer beside him.

وَجَآءَتْ سَكْرَةُ ٱلْمَوْتِ بِٱلْحَقِّ      19 Then the agony of death brings the truth:[2]

ذَٰلِكَ مَا كُنتَ مِنْهُ تَحِيدُ ۝      'This is what you used to shun!'

وَنُفِخَ فِي ٱلصُّورِ      20 Then the Trumpet will be blown:

ذَٰلِكَ يَوْمُ ٱلْوَعِيدِ ۝      'This is the promised day.'

وَجَآءَتْ كُلُّ نَفْسٍ      21 Then every soul will come

مَّعَهَا سَآئِقٌ وَشَهِيدٌ ۝      accompanied by a driver and a witness:

لَّقَدْ كُنتَ فِي غَفْلَةٍ مِّنْ هَـٰذَا      22    'You were certainly oblivious of this.

فَكَشَفْنَا عَنكَ غِطَآءَكَ      We have removed your veil from you,

فَبَصَرُكَ ٱلْيَوْمَ حَدِيدٌ ۝      and so your sight is acute today.'

وَقَالَ قَرِينُهُۥ      23 Then his companion will say,

هَـٰذَا مَا لَدَيَّ عَتِيدٌ ۝      'This is what is ready with me [of testimony].'

أَلْقِيَا فِي جَهَنَّمَ كُلَّ كَفَّارٍ عَنِيدٍ ۝      24 'The two of you cast every obdurate ingrate into hell,

مَّنَّاعٍ لِّلْخَيْرِ      25 [every] hinderer of all good,[3]

مُعْتَدٍ مُّرِيبٍ ۝      transgressor, and skeptic,

---

[1] Cf. 44:37.

[2] Or 'when the agony of death arrives with the truth.'

[3] Or 'grudging giver.'

26 الَّذِى جَعَلَ مَعَ ٱللَّهِ إِلَـٰهًا ءَاخَرَ
who has set up another god along with Allah!

فَأَلْقِيَاهُ
So the two of you cast him

فِى ٱلْعَذَابِ ٱلشَّدِيدِ ۞
into the severe punishment.'

27 قَالَ قَرِينُهُ رَبَّنَا
His companion[1] will say, 'Our Lord!

مَا أَطْغَيْتُهُ
I did not make him a rebel,

وَلَـٰكِن كَانَ فِى ضَلَـٰلٍ بَعِيدٍ ۞
but he [himself] was in extreme error.'

28 قَالَ لَا تَخْتَصِمُوا لَدَىَّ
He will say, 'Do not wrangle in My presence,

وَقَدْ قَدَّمْتُ إِلَيْكُم بِٱلْوَعِيدِ ۞
for I had already warned you in advance.

29 مَا يُبَدَّلُ ٱلْقَوْلُ لَدَىَّ
The word is unalterable with Me,

وَمَا أَنَا۠ بِظَلَّـٰمٍ لِّلْعَبِيدِ ۞
and I am not tyrannical to the servants.'

30 يَوْمَ نَقُولُ لِجَهَنَّمَ
The day when We shall say to hell,

هَلِ ٱمْتَلَأْتِ
'Are you full?'

وَتَقُولُ هَلْ مِن مَّزِيدٍ ۞
It will say, 'Is there any more?'

31 وَأُزْلِفَتِ ٱلْجَنَّةُ لِلْمُتَّقِينَ
And paradise will be brought near for the Godwary,

غَيْرَ بَعِيدٍ ۞
not distant [any more]:

32 هَـٰذَا مَا تُوعَدُونَ
'This is what you were promised.

لِكُلِّ أَوَّابٍ حَفِيظٍ ۞
[It is] for every penitent and dutiful [servant]

33 مَّنْ خَشِىَ ٱلرَّحْمَـٰنَ بِٱلْغَيْبِ
who fears the All-beneficent in secret

وَجَآءَ بِقَلْبٍ مُّنِيبٍ ۞
and comes with a penitent heart.

34 ٱدْخُلُوهَا بِسَلَـٰمٍ
Enter it in peace!

ذَٰلِكَ يَوْمُ ٱلْخُلُودِ ۞
This is the day of immortality.'

35 لَهُم مَّا يَشَآءُونَ فِيهَا
There they will have whatever they wish,

وَلَدَيْنَا مَزِيدٌ ۞
and with Us there is yet more.

36 وَكَمْ أَهْلَكْنَا قَبْلَهُم مِّن قَرْنٍ
How many generations We have destroyed before them,

هُمْ أَشَدُّ مِنْهُم بَطْشًا
who were stronger than these,

فَنَقَّبُوا فِى ٱلْبِلَـٰدِ
insomuch that they ransacked the lands.

هَلْ مِن مَّحِيصٍ ۞
Is there any escape [from Allah's punishment]?

37 إِنَّ فِى ذَٰلِكَ لَذِكْرَىٰ
There is indeed an admonition in that

لِمَن كَانَ لَهُ قَلْبٌ
for one who has a heart,

---

[1] That is, Satan.

أَوۡ أَلۡقَى ٱلسَّمۡعَ وَهُوَ شَهِيدٌ ۝          or gives ear, being attentive.

وَلَقَدۡ خَلَقۡنَا ٱلسَّمَٰوَٰتِ وَٱلۡأَرۡضَ     38 Certainly We created the heavens and the earth,

وَمَا بَيۡنَهُمَا                              and whatever is between them,

فِى سِتَّةِ أَيَّامٍ                            in six days,

وَمَا مَسَّنَا مِن لُّغُوبٍ ۝                   and any fatigue did not touch Us.

فَٱصۡبِرۡ عَلَىٰ مَا يَقُولُونَ                 39 So *be patient* over what they say,

وَسَبِّحۡ بِحَمۡدِ رَبِّكَ                       and *celebrate* the praise of *your* Lord

قَبۡلَ طُلُوعِ ٱلشَّمۡسِ                        before the rising of the sun

وَقَبۡلَ ٱلۡغُرُوبِ ۝                          and before the sunset,

وَمِنَ ٱلَّيۡلِ فَسَبِّحۡهُ                  40   and *glorify* Him through part of the night

وَأَدۡبَٰرَ ٱلسُّجُودِ ۝                        and after the prostrations.

وَٱسۡتَمِعۡ يَوۡمَ                          41 And *be on the alert* for the day

يُنَادِ ٱلۡمُنَادِ مِن مَّكَانٍ قَرِيبٍ ۝       when the caller calls from a close quarter,

يَوۡمَ يَسۡمَعُونَ ٱلصَّيۡحَةَ بِٱلۡحَقِّ    42   the day when they hear the Cry in all truth.

ذَٰلِكَ يَوۡمُ ٱلۡخُرُوجِ ۝                     That is the day of rising [from the dead].

إِنَّا نَحۡنُ نُحۡىِۦ وَنُمِيتُ              43 Indeed it is We who give life and bring death,

وَإِلَيۡنَا ٱلۡمَصِيرُ ۝                        and toward Us is the destination.

يَوۡمَ تَشَقَّقُ ٱلۡأَرۡضُ عَنۡهُمۡ          44 The day the earth is split open for [disentombing] them,

سِرَاعًا                                       [they will come out] hastening.

ذَٰلِكَ حَشۡرٌ عَلَيۡنَا يَسِيرٌ ۝               That mustering[1] is easy for Us [to carry out].

نَّحۡنُ أَعۡلَمُ بِمَا يَقُولُونَ           45 We know best what they say,

وَمَآ أَنتَ عَلَيۡهِم بِجَبَّارٍ                and *you* are not to be a tyrant over them.

فَذَكِّرۡ بِٱلۡقُرۡءَانِ مَن يَخَافُ وَعِيدِ ۝   So *admonish* by the Qur'ān him who fears My threat.

---

سُوۡرَةُ الذّارِیَاتِ                          ## 51. SŪRAT AL-DHĀRIYĀT[2]

بِسۡمِ ٱللَّهِ                                  In the Name of Allah,

ٱلرَّحۡمَٰنِ ٱلرَّحِيمِ                         the All-beneficent, the All-merciful.

---

[1] Or 'resurrection.'

[2] The *sūrah* takes its name from verse 1, which mentions the *dhāriyat* (scatterers).

وَٱلذَّٰرِيَٰتِ ١ 1 By the scattering [winds]

ذَرْوًا ٢ that scatter [the clouds];

فَٱلْحَٰمِلَٰتِ ٢ 2 by the [rain] bearing [clouds]

وِقْرًا ٣ laden [with water];

فَٱلْجَٰرِيَٰتِ يُسْرًا ٣ 3 by [the ships] which move gently [on the sea];

فَٱلْمُقَسِّمَٰتِ ٤ 4 by [the angels] who dispense [livelihood]

أَمْرًا ٤ by [His] command:

إِنَّمَا تُوعَدُونَ لَصَادِقٌ ٥ 5 indeed what you are promised is true,

وَإِنَّ ٱلدِّينَ لَوَٰقِعٌ ٦ 6 and indeed the retribution[1] will surely come to pass!

وَٱلسَّمَآءِ ذَاتِ ٱلْحُبُكِ ٧ 7 By the sky full of adornment [with stars],[2]

إِنَّكُمْ لَفِى قَوْلٍ مُّخْتَلِفٍ ٨ 8 indeed you are of different opinions!

يُؤْفَكُ عَنْهُ ٩ 9 He is turned away from it[3]

مَنْ أُفِكَ ٩ who has been turned away [from the truth].

قُتِلَ ٱلْخَرَّٰصُونَ ١٠ 10 Perish the liars,

ٱلَّذِينَ هُمْ فِى غَمْرَةٍ سَاهُونَ ١١ 11 who are heedless in a stupor!

يَسْـَٔلُونَ أَيَّانَ يَوْمُ ٱلدِّينِ ١٢ 12 They ask, 'When will be the Day of Retribution?'

يَوْمَ هُمْ عَلَى ٱلنَّارِ يُفْتَنُونَ ١٣ 13 It is the day when they will be tormented in the Fire,

ذُوقُواْ فِتْنَتَكُمْ ١٤ 14 [and will be told]: 'Taste your torment.

هَٰذَا ٱلَّذِى كُنتُم بِهِۦ تَسْتَعْجِلُونَ ١٤ This is what you used to hasten.'

إِنَّ ٱلْمُتَّقِينَ فِى جَنَّٰتٍ ١٥ 15 Indeed the Godwary will be amid gardens

وَعُيُونٍ ١٥ and springs,

ءَاخِذِينَ مَآ ءَاتَىٰهُمْ رَبُّهُمْ ١٦ 16 receiving what their Lord has given them,

إِنَّهُمْ كَانُواْ قَبْلَ ذَٰلِكَ مُحْسِنِينَ ١٦ for they had been virtuous aforetime.

كَانُواْ قَلِيلًا مِّنَ ٱلَّيْلِ مَا يَهْجَعُونَ ١٧ 17 They used to sleep a little during the night,

وَبِٱلْأَسْحَارِ هُمْ يَسْتَغْفِرُونَ ١٨ 18 and at dawns they would plead for forgiveness,.

وَفِىٓ أَمْوَٰلِهِمْ حَقٌّ ١٩ 19 and there was a share in their wealth

لِّلسَّآئِلِ وَٱلْمَحْرُومِ ١٩ for the beggar and the deprived.

---

[1] Or 'judgement.'

[2] Or, 'By the heaven full of tracks' (or pathways).

[3] That is, from the Qurʾān. Or 'from him,' that is, from the Apostle of Allah.

وَفِى ٱلْأَرْضِ ءَايَتٌ لِّلْمُوقِنِينَ ۝  20 In the earth are signs for those who have conviction,

وَفِىٓ أَنفُسِكُمْ ۚ  21    and in your souls [as well].

أَفَلَا تُبْصِرُونَ ۝        Will you not then perceive?

وَفِى ٱلسَّمَآءِ رِزْقُكُمْ  22 And in the sky is your provision

وَمَا تُوعَدُونَ ۝        and what you are promised.

فَوَرَبِّ ٱلسَّمَآءِ وَٱلْأَرْضِ  23 By the Lord of the sky and the earth,

إِنَّهُۥ لَحَقٌّ        it is indeed the truth,

مِّثْلَ مَآ أَنَّكُمْ تَنطِقُونَ ۝        just as [it is a fact that] you speak.


هَلْ أَتَىٰكَ حَدِيثُ  24 Did *you* receive the story

ضَيْفِ إِبْرَٰهِيمَ ٱلْمُكْرَمِينَ ۝        of Abraham's honoured guests?

إِذْ دَخَلُوا۟ عَلَيْهِ  25 When they entered into his presence,

فَقَالُوا۟ سَلَٰمًا ۖ        they said, 'Peace!'

قَالَ سَلَٰمٌ        'Peace!' He answered,

قَوْمٌ مُّنكَرُونَ ۝        '[You are] an unfamiliar folk.'[1]

فَرَاغَ إِلَىٰٓ أَهْلِهِۦ  26 Then he retired to his family

فَجَآءَ بِعِجْلٍ سَمِينٍ ۝        and brought a fat [roasted] calf,

فَقَرَّبَهُۥٓ إِلَيْهِمْ  27    and put it near them.

قَالَ أَلَا تَأْكُلُونَ ۝        He said, 'Will you not eat?'

فَأَوْجَسَ مِنْهُمْ خِيفَةً ۖ  28 Then he felt a fear of them.

قَالُوا۟ لَا تَخَفْ ۖ        They said, 'Do not be afraid!'

وَبَشَّرُوهُ بِغُلَٰمٍ عَلِيمٍ ۝        and they gave him the good news of a wise son.[2]

فَأَقْبَلَتِ ٱمْرَأَتُهُۥ فِى صَرَّةٍ  29 Then his wife came forward crying [with joy].

فَصَكَّتْ وَجْهَهَا        She beat her face,

وَقَالَتْ عَجُوزٌ عَقِيمٌ ۝        and said, 'A barren old woman!'

قَالُوا۟ كَذَٰلِكِ قَالَ رَبُّكِ ۖ  30 They said, 'So has your Lord said.

إِنَّهُۥ هُوَ ٱلْحَكِيمُ ٱلْعَلِيمُ ۝ ۞        Indeed He is the All-wise, the All-knowing.'

---

[1] Cf. 15:62.

[2] See 11:69-73 and 15:50-60 for parallel descriptions of the episode of Abraham's guests.

**[PART 27]**

قَالَ 31 He said,

فَمَا خَطْبُكُمْ أَيُّهَا ٱلْمُرْسَلُونَ ۝    'O messengers, what is now your errand?'

قَالُوٓا 32 They said,

إِنَّآ أُرْسِلْنَآ إِلَىٰ قَوْمٍ مُّجْرِمِينَ ۝    'We have been sent toward a guilty people,

لِنُرْسِلَ عَلَيْهِمْ حِجَارَةً مِّن طِينٍ ۝ 33 that We may rain upon them stones of clay,

مُّسَوَّمَةً عِندَ رَبِّكَ لِلْمُسْرِفِينَ ۝ 34 marked with your Lord for the profligate.

فَأَخْرَجْنَا مَن كَانَ فِيهَا 35 So We picked out those who were in it

مِنَ ٱلْمُؤْمِنِينَ ۝    of the faithful,

فَمَا وَجَدْنَا فِيهَا 36 but We did not find there

غَيْرَ بَيْتٍ مِّنَ ٱلْمُسْلِمِينَ ۝    other than one house of *muslims*,

وَتَرَكْنَا فِيهَآ ءَايَةً 37 and We have left therein a sign

لِّلَّذِينَ يَخَافُونَ ٱلْعَذَابَ ٱلْأَلِيمَ ۝    for those who fear a painful punishment.'

وَفِى مُوسَىٰٓ 38 And in Moses [too there is a sign]

إِذْ أَرْسَلْنَٰهُ إِلَىٰ فِرْعَوْنَ    when We sent him to Pharaoh

بِسُلْطَٰنٍ مُّبِينٍ ۝    with a manifest authority.

فَتَوَلَّىٰ بِرُكْنِهِۦ 39 But he turned away assured of his might,

وَقَالَ سَٰحِرٌ أَوْ مَجْنُونٌ ۝    and said, 'A magician or a crazy man!'

فَأَخَذْنَٰهُ وَجُنُودَهُۥ 40 So We seized him and his hosts,

فَنَبَذْنَٰهُمْ فِى ٱلْيَمِّ    and cast them into the sea,

وَهُوَ مُلِيمٌ ۝    while he was blameworthy.

وَفِى عَادٍ إِذْ أَرْسَلْنَا عَلَيْهِمُ 41 And in 'Ād when We unleashed upon them

ٱلرِّيحَ ٱلْعَقِيمَ ۝    a barren wind.

مَا تَذَرُ مِن شَىْءٍ أَتَتْ عَلَيْهِ 42 It left nothing that it came upon

إِلَّا جَعَلَتْهُ كَٱلرَّمِيمِ ۝    without making it like decayed bones.

وَفِى ثَمُودَ إِذْ قِيلَ لَهُمْ 43 And in Thamūd, when they were told,

تَمَتَّعُوا حَتَّىٰ حِينٍ ۝    'Enjoy for a while.'

فَعَتَوْا عَنْ أَمْرِ رَبِّهِمْ 44 Then they defied the command of their Lord;

فَأَخَذَتْهُمُ ٱلصَّٰعِقَةُ    so the thunderbolt seized them

وَهُمْ يَنظُرُونَ ۝    as they looked on.

فَمَا ٱسْتَطَٰعُواْ مِن قِيَامٍ 45 So they were neither able to rise up,

وَمَا كَانُواْ مُنتَصِرِينَ ۞ nor to come to one another's aid.[1]

وَقَوْمَ نُوحٍ مِّن قَبْلُ 46 And the people of Noah aforetime.

إِنَّهُمْ كَانُواْ قَوْمًا فَٰسِقِينَ ۞ Indeed they were a transgressing lot.

وَٱلسَّمَآءَ بَنَيْنَٰهَا بِأَيْيْدٍ 47 We have built the sky with might,

وَإِنَّا لَمُوسِعُونَ ۞ and indeed it is We who are its expanders.[2]

وَٱلْأَرْضَ فَرَشْنَٰهَا 48 And the earth We have spread it out,

فَنِعْمَ ٱلْمَٰهِدُونَ ۞ so what excellent spreaders We have been!

وَمِن كُلِّ شَىْءٍ خَلَقْنَا زَوْجَيْنِ 49 In all things We have created pairs

لَعَلَّكُمْ تَذَكَّرُونَ ۞ so that you may take admonition.

فَفِرُّوٓاْ إِلَى ٱللَّهِ 50 [*Say,*] 'So flee toward Allah.

إِنِّى لَكُم مِّنْهُ نَذِيرٌ مُّبِينٌ ۞ Indeed I am a manifest warner to you from Him.

وَلَا تَجْعَلُواْ مَعَ ٱللَّهِ إِلَٰهًا ءَاخَرَ 51 Do not set up another god besides Allah.

إِنِّى لَكُم مِّنْهُ نَذِيرٌ مُّبِينٌ ۞ Indeed I am a manifest warner to you from Him.'

كَذَٰلِكَ 52 So it was

مَآ أَتَى ٱلَّذِينَ مِن قَبْلِهِم that there did not come to those who were before them

مِّن رَّسُولٍ any apostle

إِلَّا قَالُواْ سَاحِرٌ أَوْ مَجْنُونٌ ۞ but they said, 'A magician,' or 'A crazy man!'

أَتَوَاصَوْاْ بِهِۦ 53 Did they enjoin this upon one another?!

بَلْ هُمْ قَوْمٌ طَاغُونَ ۞ Rather they were a rebellious lot.

فَتَوَلَّ عَنْهُمْ 54 So *turn away* from them,

فَمَآ أَنتَ بِمَلُومٍ ۞ for *you* will not be blameworthy.

وَذَكِّرْ 55 And *admonish*,

فَإِنَّ ٱلذِّكْرَىٰ تَنفَعُ ٱلْمُؤْمِنِينَ ۞ for admonition indeed benefits the faithful.

وَمَا خَلَقْتُ ٱلْجِنَّ وَٱلْإِنسَ 56 I did not create the jinn and the humans

إِلَّا لِيَعْبُدُونِ ۞ except that they may worship Me.

مَآ أُرِيدُ مِنْهُم مِّن رِّزْقٍ 57 I desire no provision from them,

---

[1] Or 'nor to guard themselves (from the punishment).'

[2] Or 'indeed it is We who are expanding it.'

وَمَآ أُرِيدُ أَن يُطْعِمُونِ ۞     nor do I desire that they should feed Me.

إِنَّ ٱللَّهَ هُوَ ٱلرَّزَّاقُ 58 Indeed it is Allah who is the All-provider,

ذُو ٱلْقُوَّةِ ٱلْمَتِينُ ۞     Powerful, All-strong.

فَإِنَّ لِلَّذِينَ ظَلَمُوا۟ ذَنُوبًا 59 Indeed the lot of those who do wrong [now]

مِّثْلَ ذَنُوبِ أَصْحَٰبِهِمْ     will be like the lot of their [earlier] counterparts.

فَلَا يَسْتَعْجِلُونِ ۞     So let them not ask Me to hasten on [that fate].

فَوَيْلٌ لِّلَّذِينَ كَفَرُوا۟ 60 Woe to the faithless

مِن يَوْمِهِمُ ٱلَّذِى يُوعَدُونَ ۞     for the day they are promised!

# سُورَةُ ٱلطُّورِ     52. SŪRAT AL-ṬŪR[1]

بِسْمِ ٱللَّهِ     In the Name of Allah,

ٱلرَّحْمَٰنِ ٱلرَّحِيمِ     the All-beneficent, the All-merciful.

وَٱلطُّورِ ۞ 1 By the Mount [Sinai],

وَكِتَٰبٍ مَّسْطُورٍ ۞ 2    by the Book inscribed

فِى رَقٍّ مَّنشُورٍ ۞ 3       on an unrolled parchment;

وَٱلْبَيْتِ ٱلْمَعْمُورِ ۞ 4     by the House greatly frequented;[2]

وَٱلسَّقْفِ ٱلْمَرْفُوعِ ۞ 5     by the vault raised high,

وَٱلْبَحْرِ ٱلْمَسْجُورِ ۞ 6     by the surging sea:[3]

إِنَّ عَذَابَ رَبِّكَ لَوَٰقِعٌ ۞ 7     indeed *your* Lord's punishment will surely befall.

مَّا لَهُۥ مِن دَافِعٍ ۞ 8    There is none who can avert it.

يَوْمَ تَمُورُ ٱلسَّمَآءُ مَوْرًا ۞ 9 On the day when the sky whirls violently,

وَتَسِيرُ ٱلْجِبَالُ سَيْرًا ۞ 10     and the mountains move with an awful motion:

فَوَيْلٌ يَوْمَئِذٍ لِّلْمُكَذِّبِينَ ۞ 11   woe to the deniers on that day

ٱلَّذِينَ هُمْ فِى خَوْضٍ يَلْعَبُونَ ۞ 12    —those who play around in vain talk,

يَوْمَ يُدَعُّونَ 13    the day when they will be shoved

---

[1] The *sūrah* takes its name from "the mount" (*ṭūr*) mentioned in verse 1.

[2] The Holy Ka'bah, or its counterpart, in the fourth (or the seventh) heaven, frequented by the angels.

[3] Or 'the sea set afire.'

إِلَىٰ نَارِ جَهَنَّمَ    toward the fire of hell

دَعًّا ⑬    forcibly,

هَـٰذِهِ ٱلنَّارُ ٱلَّتِى 14    [and told:] 'This is the Fire which

كُنتُم بِهَا تُكَذِّبُونَ ⑭    you used to deny!'

أَفَسِحْرٌ هَـٰذَآ 15    Is this then magic,

أَمْ أَنتُمْ لَا تُبْصِرُونَ ⑮    or is it you who do not perceive?

ٱصْلَوْهَا 16    'Enter it,

فَٱصْبِرُوٓاْ أَوْ لَا تَصْبِرُواْ    and whether you are patient or impatient

سَوَآءٌ عَلَيْكُمْ    it will be the same for you.

إِنَّمَا تُجْزَوْنَ    You are only being requited

مَا كُنتُمْ تَعْمَلُونَ ⑯    for what you used to do.'

إِنَّ ٱلْمُتَّقِينَ فِى جَنَّـٰتٍ 17    Indeed the Godwary will be amid gardens

وَنَعِيمٍ ⑰    and bliss,

فَـٰكِهِينَ بِمَآ ءَاتَىٰهُمْ رَبُّهُمْ 18    rejoicing because of what their Lord has given them,

وَوَقَىٰهُمْ رَبُّهُمْ    and that their Lord has saved them

عَذَابَ ٱلْجَحِيمِ ⑱    from the punishment of hell.

كُلُواْ وَٱشْرَبُواْ هَنِيٓـًٔا 19    [They will be told:] 'Enjoy your food and drink,

بِمَا كُنتُمْ تَعْمَلُونَ ⑲    [as a reward] for what you used to do.'

مُتَّكِـِٔينَ عَلَىٰ سُرُرٍ مَّصْفُوفَةٍ 20    They will be reclining on arrayed couches,

وَزَوَّجْنَـٰهُم بِحُورٍ عِينٍ ⑳    and We will wed them to big-eyed houris.

وَٱلَّذِينَ ءَامَنُواْ 21    The faithful

وَٱتَّبَعَتْهُمْ ذُرِّيَّتُهُم بِإِيمَـٰنٍ    and their descendants who followed them in faith

أَلْحَقْنَا بِهِمْ ذُرِّيَّتَهُمْ    —We will make their descendants join them,

وَمَآ أَلَتْنَـٰهُم    and We will not stint

مِّنْ عَمَلِهِم مِّن شَىْءٍ    anything from [the reward of] their deeds.

كُلُّ ٱمْرِئٍ بِمَا كَسَبَ رَهِينٌ ㉑    Every man is a hostage to what he has earned.

وَأَمْدَدْنَـٰهُم بِفَـٰكِهَةٍ وَلَحْمٍ 22    We will provide them with fruits and meat,

مِّمَّا يَشْتَهُونَ ㉒    such as they desire.

يَتَنَـٰزَعُونَ فِيهَا كَأْسًا 23    There they will pass from hand to hand a cup

لَّا لَغْوٌ فِيهَا    wherein there will be neither any vain talk

وَلَا تَأْثِيمٌ ۞　nor sinful speech.

وَيَطُوفُ عَلَيْهِمْ غِلْمَانٌ لَّهُمْ　24 They will be waited upon by youths, their own,

كَأَنَّهُمْ لُؤْلُؤٌ مَّكْنُونٌ ۞　as if they were guarded pearls.

وَأَقْبَلَ بَعْضُهُمْ عَلَىٰ بَعْضٍ　25 They will turn to one another,

يَتَسَآءَلُونَ ۞　questioning each other.

قَالُوٓا۟ إِنَّا كُنَّا قَبْلُ　26 They will say, 'Indeed, aforetime, we used to be

فِىٓ أَهْلِنَا مُشْفِقِينَ ۞　apprehensive about our families.

فَمَنَّ ٱللَّهُ عَلَيْنَا　27 But Allah showed us favour

وَوَقَىٰنَا　and He saved us

عَذَابَ ٱلسَّمُومِ ۞　from the punishment of the [infernal] miasma;

إِنَّا كُنَّا مِن قَبْلُ نَدْعُوهُ　28 indeed we used to supplicate Him aforetime.

إِنَّهُۥ هُوَ ٱلْبَرُّ ٱلرَّحِيمُ ۞　Indeed He is the All-benign, the All-merciful.'

فَذَكِّرْ　29 So *admonish*.

فَمَآ أَنتَ بِنِعْمَتِ رَبِّكَ بِكَاهِنٍ　By *your* Lord's grace, *you* are not a soothsayer,

وَلَا مَجْنُونٍ ۞　nor mad.

أَمْ يَقُولُونَ شَاعِرٌ　30 Do they say, '[He is] a poet,

نَّتَرَبَّصُ بِهِۦ رَيْبَ ٱلْمَنُونِ ۞　for whom we await a fatal accident'?

قُلْ تَرَبَّصُوا۟　31 *Say*, 'Wait!

فَإِنِّى مَعَكُم مِّنَ ٱلْمُتَرَبِّصِينَ ۞　I too am waiting along with you.'

أَمْ تَأْمُرُهُمْ أَحْلَٰمُهُم　32 Is it their intellect which prompts them

بِهَٰذَآ　to [say] this,

أَمْ هُمْ قَوْمٌ طَاغُونَ ۞　or are they a rebellious lot?

أَمْ يَقُولُونَ تَقَوَّلَهُۥ　33 Do they say, 'He has improvised it [himself]'?

بَل لَّا يُؤْمِنُونَ ۞　Rather they have no faith!

فَلْيَأْتُوا۟ بِحَدِيثٍ مِّثْلِهِۦٓ　34 Let them bring a discourse like it,

إِن كَانُوا۟ صَٰدِقِينَ ۞　if they are truthful.

أَمْ خُلِقُوا۟ مِنْ غَيْرِ شَىْءٍ　35 Were they created from nothing?

أَمْ هُمُ ٱلْخَٰلِقُونَ ۞　Or are they [their own] creators?

أَمْ خَلَقُوا۟ ٱلسَّمَٰوَٰتِ وَٱلْأَرْضَ　36 Did they create the heavens and the earth?

بَل لَّا يُوقِنُونَ ۞　Rather they have no certainty!

أَمۡ عِندَهُمۡ خَزَآئِنُ رَبِّكَ 37 Do they possess the treasuries of *your* Lord?

أَمۡ هُمُ ٱلۡمُصَۜيۡطِرُونَ ۝ Or are they the controllers [of their dispensation]?

أَمۡ لَهُمۡ سُلَّمٌ 38 Do they have a ladder [leading up to heaven]

يَسۡتَمِعُونَ فِيهِ whereby they eavesdrop?[1]

فَلۡيَأۡتِ مُسۡتَمِعُهُم If so let their eavesdropper produce

بِسُلۡطَٰنٍ مُّبِينٍ ۝ a manifest authority.

أَمۡ لَهُ ٱلۡبَنَٰتُ وَلَكُمُ ٱلۡبَنُونَ ۝ 39 Does He have daughters while you have sons?[2]

أَمۡ تَسۡـَٔلُهُمۡ أَجۡرًا 40 Do *you* ask them for a reward,

فَهُم مِّن مَّغۡرَمٍ مُّثۡقَلُونَ ۝ so that they are weighed down with debt?

أَمۡ عِندَهُمُ ٱلۡغَيۡبُ 41 Do they have [access to] the Unseen,

فَهُمۡ يَكۡتُبُونَ ۝ which they write down?

أَمۡ يُرِيدُونَ كَيۡدًا 42 Do they seek to outmaneuver [Allah]?

فَٱلَّذِينَ كَفَرُواْ But it is the faithless

هُمُ ٱلۡمَكِيدُونَ ۝ who are the outmaneuvered ones!

أَمۡ هُمۡ إِلَٰهٌ غَيۡرُ ٱللَّهِ 43 Do they have any god other than Allah?

سُبۡحَٰنَ ٱللَّهِ Clear is Allah

عَمَّا يُشۡرِكُونَ ۝ of any partners that they may ascribe [to Him]!

وَإِن يَرَوۡاْ 44 Were they to see

كِسۡفًا مِّنَ ٱلسَّمَآءِ سَاقِطًا a fragment falling from the sky,

يَقُولُواْ سَحَابٌ مَّرۡكُومٌ ۝ they would say, 'A cumulous cloud.'

فَذَرۡهُمۡ حَتَّىٰ يُلَٰقُواْ يَوۡمَهُمُ 45 So leave them until they encounter their day

ٱلَّذِى فِيهِ يُصۡعَقُونَ ۝ on which they will be thunderstruck;

يَوۡمَ لَا يُغۡنِى عَنۡهُمۡ كَيۡدُهُمۡ 46 the day when their guile will not avail them

شَيۡـًٔا in any way,

وَلَا هُمۡ يُنصَرُونَ ۝ nor will they be helped.

وَإِنَّ لِلَّذِينَ ظَلَمُواْ 47 Indeed for those who do wrong,

عَذَابًا دُونَ ذَٰلِكَ there is a punishment besides that,

وَلَٰكِنَّ أَكۡثَرَهُمۡ لَا يَعۡلَمُونَ ۝ but most of them do not know.

---

[1] That is, on the conversation of the angels.
[2] Cf. 4:117; 16:57-59; 17:40; 37:149-154; 43:16-19; 53:21-23, 27.

وَٱصۡبِرۡ لِحُكۡمِ رَبِّكَ 48 So *submit patiently* to the judgement of *your* Lord,

فَإِنَّكَ بِأَعۡيُنِنَا for indeed *you* fare before Our eyes.

وَسَبِّحۡ بِحَمۡدِ رَبِّكَ And *celebrate* the praise of *your* Lord

حِينَ تَقُومُ ۝ when *you* rise [at dawn],

وَمِنَ ٱلَّيۡلِ فَسَبِّحۡهُ 49 and also *glorify* Him during the night

وَإِدۡبَٰرَ ٱلنُّجُومِ ۝ and at the receding of the stars.

# سُورَةُ النَّجْمِ　　　53. SŪRAT AL-NAJM[1]

بِسۡمِ ٱللَّهِ In the Name of Allah,

ٱلرَّحۡمَٰنِ ٱلرَّحِيمِ the All-beneficent, the All-merciful.

وَٱلنَّجۡمِ إِذَا هَوَىٰ ۝ 1 By the star when it sets:[2]

مَا ضَلَّ صَاحِبُكُمۡ 2 your companion[3] has neither gone astray,

وَمَا غَوَىٰ ۝ nor gone amiss.

وَمَا يَنطِقُ عَنِ ٱلۡهَوَىٰٓ ۝ 3 Nor does he speak out of [his own] desire:

إِنۡ هُوَ إِلَّا وَحۡيٌ يُوحَىٰ ۝ 4 it is just a revelation that is revealed [to him],

عَلَّمَهُ شَدِيدُ ٱلۡقُوَىٰ ۝ 5 taught him by One of great powers,

ذُو مِرَّةٍ ۝ 6 possessed of sound judgement.[4]

فَٱسۡتَوَىٰ ۝ He[5] settled,[6]

وَهُوَ بِٱلۡأُفُقِ ٱلۡأَعۡلَىٰ ۝ 7 while he was on the highest horizon.

ثُمَّ دَنَا فَتَدَلَّىٰ ۝ 8 Then he drew nearer and nearer

فَكَانَ قَابَ قَوۡسَيۡنِ أَوۡ أَدۡنَىٰ ۝ 9 until he was within two bows' length or even nearer,

فَأَوۡحَىٰٓ إِلَىٰ عَبۡدِهِۦ 10 whereat He revealed to His servant

مَآ أَوۡحَىٰ ۝ whatever He revealed.

---

[1] The *sūrah* takes its name from verse 1, which mentions 'the star' (*najm*).

[2] Or 'falls.'

[3] That is, the Apostle of Allah.

[4] Or 'possessed of strength.'

[5] That is, the Apostle of Allah (ṣ); or the Angel Gabriel, according to some commentators.

[6] Or 'stood upright.'

مَا كَذَبَ ٱلْفُؤَادُ مَا رَأَىٰ ١١    11 The heart did not deny what it saw.

أَفَتُمَٰرُونَهُ عَلَىٰ مَا يَرَىٰ ١٢    12 Will you then dispute with him about what he saw?!

وَلَقَدْ رَءَاهُ نَزْلَةً أُخْرَىٰ ١٣    13 Certainly he saw it[1] yet another time,

عِندَ سِدْرَةِ ٱلْمُنتَهَىٰ ١٤    14   by the Lote Tree of the Ultimate Boundary,

عِندَهَا جَنَّةُ ٱلْمَأْوَىٰ ١٥    15   near which is the Garden of the Abode,

إِذْ يَغْشَى ٱلسِّدْرَةَ مَا يَغْشَىٰ ١٦    16   when there covered the Lote Tree what covered it.

مَا زَاغَ ٱلْبَصَرُ ١٧    17 The gaze did not swerve,

وَمَا طَغَىٰ ١٧       nor did it overstep the bounds.

لَقَدْ رَأَىٰ ١٨    18 Certainly he saw

مِنْ ءَايَٰتِ رَبِّهِ ٱلْكُبْرَىٰ ١٨       some of the greatest signs of his Lord.

أَفَرَءَيْتُمُ ٱللَّٰتَ وَٱلْعُزَّىٰ ١٩    19 Have you considered Lāt and ʻUzzā?

وَمَنَوٰةَ ٱلثَّالِثَةَ ٱلْأُخْرَىٰ ٢٠    20   and Manāt, the third one?

أَلَكُمُ ٱلذَّكَرُ وَلَهُ ٱلْأُنثَىٰ ٢١    21 Are you to have males and He females?

تِلْكَ إِذًا قِسْمَةٌ ضِيزَىٰ ٢٢    22 That, then, will be an unfair division!

إِنْ هِىَ إِلَّا أَسْمَآءٌ سَمَّيْتُمُوهَآ ٢٣    23 These are but names which you have named

أَنتُمْ وَءَابَآؤُكُم    —you and your fathers—

مَّا أَنزَلَ ٱللَّهُ بِهَا مِن سُلْطَٰنٍ    for which Allah has not sent down any authority.

إِن يَتَّبِعُونَ إِلَّا ٱلظَّنَّ    They follow nothing but conjectures

وَمَا تَهْوَى ٱلْأَنفُسُ    and the desires of the [lower] soul,

وَلَقَدْ جَآءَهُم    while there has certainly come to them

مِّن رَّبِّهِمُ ٱلْهُدَىٰ ٢٣    the guidance from their Lord.

أَمْ لِلْإِنسَٰنِ مَا تَمَنَّىٰ ٢٤    24 Shall man have whatever he yearns for?

فَلِلَّهِ ٱلْءَاخِرَةُ وَٱلْأُولَىٰ ٢٥    25 Yet to Allah belong this world and the Hereafter.

وَكَم مِّن مَّلَكٍ فِى ٱلسَّمَٰوَٰتِ ٢٦    26 How many an angel there is in the heavens

لَا تُغْنِى شَفَٰعَتُهُمْ شَيْـًٔا    whose intercession is of no avail in any way

إِلَّا مِنْ بَعْدِ أَن يَأْذَنَ ٱللَّهُ    except after Allah grants permission

---

[1] Or 'them.' To explain, the object of the pronoun *hū* is specified in verse 18, 'Certainly he saw some of the greatest signs of his Lord.' This interpretation is also supported by a tradition of Imam ʻAlī b. Mūsā al-Riḍā ( ʻa) cited in the *Uṣūl al-Kāfī*, vol. 1, p. 95, *ḥadīth* 2.

لِمَن يَشَآءُ وَيَرْضَىٰ ۞    to whomever He wishes and approves of!

إِنَّ ٱلَّذِينَ لَا يُؤْمِنُونَ بِٱلْءَاخِرَةِ    27 Indeed those who do not believe in the Hereafter

لَيُسَمُّونَ ٱلْمَلَٰٓئِكَةَ تَسْمِيَةَ ٱلْأُنثَىٰ ۞    give female names to the angels.

وَمَا لَهُم بِهِۦ مِنْ عِلْمٍ ۖ    28 They do not have any knowledge of that.

إِن يَتَّبِعُونَ إِلَّا ٱلظَّنَّ ۖ    They follow nothing but conjectures,

وَإِنَّ ٱلظَّنَّ لَا يُغْنِى مِنَ ٱلْحَقِّ شَيْئًا ۞    and indeed conjecture is no substitute for the truth.

فَأَعْرِضْ عَن مَّن تَوَلَّىٰ عَن ذِكْرِنَا    29 So *avoid* those who turn away from Our remembrance

وَلَمْ يُرِدْ إِلَّا ٱلْحَيَوٰةَ ٱلدُّنْيَا ۞    and desire nothing but the life of the world.

ذَٰلِكَ مَبْلَغُهُم مِّنَ ٱلْعِلْمِ ۚ    30 That is the ultimate reach of their knowledge.

إِنَّ رَبَّكَ هُوَ أَعْلَمُ    Indeed your Lord knows best

بِمَن ضَلَّ عَن سَبِيلِهِۦ    those who stray from His way,

وَهُوَ أَعْلَمُ بِمَنِ ٱهْتَدَىٰ ۞    and He knows best those who are [rightly] guided.

وَلِلَّهِ مَا فِى ٱلسَّمَٰوَٰتِ    31 To Allah belongs whatever is in the heavens

وَمَا فِى ٱلْأَرْضِ    and whatever is in the earth,

لِيَجْزِىَ ٱلَّذِينَ أَسَٰٓـُٔوا۟    that He may requite those who do evil

بِمَا عَمِلُوا۟    for what they have done,

وَيَجْزِىَ ٱلَّذِينَ أَحْسَنُوا۟    and reward those who do good

بِٱلْحُسْنَى ۞    with the best [of rewards].

ٱلَّذِينَ يَجْتَنِبُونَ كَبَٰٓئِرَ ٱلْإِثْمِ    32 Those who avoid major sins

وَٱلْفَوَٰحِشَ    and indecencies,

إِلَّا ٱللَّمَمَ ۚ    excepting [minor and occasional] lapses.

إِنَّ رَبَّكَ وَٰسِعُ ٱلْمَغْفِرَةِ ۚ    Indeed *your* Lord is expansive in [His] forgiveness.

هُوَ أَعْلَمُ بِكُمْ    He knows you best

إِذْ أَنشَأَكُم مِّنَ ٱلْأَرْضِ    since [the time] He produced you from the earth,

وَإِذْ أَنتُمْ أَجِنَّةٌ    and since you were fetuses

فِى بُطُونِ أُمَّهَٰتِكُمْ ۖ    in the bellies of your mothers.

فَلَا تُزَكُّوٓا۟ أَنفُسَكُمْ ۖ    So do not flaunt your piety:

هُوَ أَعْلَمُ بِمَنِ ٱتَّقَىٰٓ ۞    He knows best those who are Godwary.

أَفَرَءَيْتَ ٱلَّذِى تَوَلَّىٰ ۞    33 Did *you* see him who turned away,

34 وَأَعْطَىٰ قَلِيلًا وَأَكْدَىٰٓ ۝   gave a little and held off?

35 أَعِندَهُۥ عِلْمُ ٱلْغَيْبِ   Does he have the knowledge of the Unseen

فَهُوَ يَرَىٰٓ ۝   so that he sees?

36 أَمْ لَمْ يُنَبَّأْ بِمَا   Has he not been informed of what is

فِى صُحُفِ مُوسَىٰ ۝   in the scriptures of Moses,

37 وَإِبْرَٰهِيمَ ٱلَّذِى وَفَّىٰٓ ۝   and of Abraham, who fulfilled [his summons]:

38 أَلَّا تَزِرُ وَازِرَةٌ وِزْرَ أُخْرَىٰ ۝   that no bearer shall bear another's burden,

39 وَأَن لَّيْسَ لِلْإِنسَٰنِ   and that nothing belongs to man

إِلَّا مَا سَعَىٰ ۝   except what he strives for,

40 وَأَنَّ سَعْيَهُۥ سَوْفَ يُرَىٰ ۝   and that he will soon be shown his endeavour,

41 ثُمَّ يُجْزَىٰهُ   then he will be rewarded for it

ٱلْجَزَآءَ ٱلْأَوْفَىٰ ۝   with the fullest reward;

42 وَأَنَّ إِلَىٰ رَبِّكَ ٱلْمُنتَهَىٰ ۝   and that the terminus is toward *your* Lord,

43 وَأَنَّهُۥ هُوَ أَضْحَكَ   and that it is He who makes [men] laugh,

وَأَبْكَىٰ ۝   and makes [them] weep,

44 وَأَنَّهُۥ هُوَ أَمَاتَ وَأَحْيَا ۝   and that it is He who brings death and gives life,

45 وَأَنَّهُۥ خَلَقَ ٱلزَّوْجَيْنِ   and that it is He who created the mates,[1]

ٱلذَّكَرَ وَٱلْأُنثَىٰ ۝   the male and the female,

46 مِن نُّطْفَةٍ إِذَا تُمْنَىٰ ۝   from a drop of [seminal] fluid when emitted;

47 وَأَنَّ عَلَيْهِ ٱلنَّشْأَةَ ٱلْأُخْرَىٰ ۝   and that with Him lies the second genesis,

48 وَأَنَّهُۥ هُوَ أَغْنَىٰ وَأَقْنَىٰ ۝   and that it is He who enriches and grants possessions,

49 وَأَنَّهُۥ هُوَ رَبُّ ٱلشِّعْرَىٰ ۝   and that it is He who is the Lord of Sirius;

50 وَأَنَّهُۥ أَهْلَكَ عَادًا ٱلْأُولَىٰ ۝   and that it is He who destroyed the former 'Ād,

51 وَثَمُودَا۟   and Thamud,

فَمَآ أَبْقَىٰ ۝   sparing none [of them];

52 وَقَوْمَ نُوحٍ مِّن قَبْلُ   and the people of Noah before that;

إِنَّهُمْ كَانُوا۟ هُمْ أَظْلَمَ وَأَطْغَىٰ ۝   indeed they were more unjust and rebellious;

53 وَٱلْمُؤْتَفِكَةَ أَهْوَىٰ ۝   and He overthrew the town that was overturned,[2]

---

[1] Or 'the sexes.'

[2] That is, Sodom. Elsewhere mentioned as plural; see 9:70, 69:9.

فَغَشَّىٰهَا مَا غَشَّىٰ 54   covering it with what covered it.

فَبِأَىِّ ءَالَآءِ رَبِّكَ 55 Then which of the bounties of your Lord

تَتَمَارَىٰ   will you dispute?

هَـٰذَا نَذِيرٌ 56 This is a warner,

مِّنَ ٱلنُّذُرِ ٱلْأُولَىٰ   [in the tradition] of the warners of old.

أَزِفَتِ ٱلْءَازِفَةُ 57 The Imminent [Hour] is near at hand.

لَيْسَ لَهَا مِن دُونِ ٱللَّهِ كَاشِفَةٌ 58 There is none that may unveil it besides Allah.

أَفَمِنْ هَـٰذَا ٱلْحَدِيثِ تَعْجَبُونَ 59 Do you then wonder at this discourse,

وَتَضْحَكُونَ وَلَا تَبْكُونَ 60   and laugh and not weep,

وَأَنتُمْ سَـٰمِدُونَ 61   while you remain heedless?!

فَٱسْجُدُوا۟ لِلَّهِ وَٱعْبُدُوا۟ 62 So *prostrate yourselves* to Allah and worship Him!

## سُورَةُ الْقَمَرِ   54. SŪRAT AL-QAMAR[1]

بِسْمِ ٱللَّهِ   In the Name of Allah,

ٱلرَّحْمَـٰنِ ٱلرَّحِيمِ   the All-beneficent, the All-merciful.

ٱقْتَرَبَتِ ٱلسَّاعَةُ 1 The Hour has drawn near

وَٱنشَقَّ ٱلْقَمَرُ   and the moon is split.

وَإِن يَرَوْا۟ ءَايَةً يُعْرِضُوا۟ 2 If they see a sign, they turn away,

وَيَقُولُوا۟ سِحْرٌ مُّسْتَمِرٌّ   and say, 'An incessant[2] magic!'

وَكَذَّبُوا۟ وَٱتَّبَعُوٓا۟ أَهْوَآءَهُمْ 3 They denied, and followed their own desires,

وَكُلُّ أَمْرٍ مُّسْتَقِرٌّ   and every matter has a setting [appropriate to it].

وَلَقَدْ جَآءَهُم مِّنَ ٱلْأَنۢبَآءِ 4 There has certainly come to them the reports

مَا فِيهِ مُزْدَجَرٌ   containing admonishment,

حِكْمَةٌ بَـٰلِغَةٌ 5   [and representing] far-reaching wisdom;

فَمَا تُغْنِ ٱلنُّذُرُ   but warnings are of no avail!

فَتَوَلَّ عَنْهُمْ 6 So *turn away* from them!

---

[1] The *sūrah* takes its name from verse 1, which mentions the moon (*qamar*).

[2] Or 'powerful.'

يَوْمَ يَدْعُ ٱلدَّاعِ إِلَىٰ شَىْءٍ نُّكُرٍ ٦

The day when the Caller calls to a dire thing,

خُشَّعًا أَبْصَـٰرُهُمْ 7

with a humbled look [in their eyes],

يَخْرُجُونَ مِنَ ٱلْأَجْدَاثِ

they will emerge from the graves

كَأَنَّهُمْ جَرَادٌ مُّنتَشِرٌ ٧

as if they were scattered locusts,

مُّهْطِعِينَ إِلَى ٱلدَّاعِ 8

scrambling toward the summoner.

يَقُولُ ٱلْكَـٰفِرُونَ هَـٰذَا يَوْمٌ عَسِرٌ ٨

The faithless will say, 'This is a hard day!'

كَذَّبَتْ قَبْلَهُمْ قَوْمُ نُوحٍ 9

The people of Noah impugned before them.

فَكَذَّبُوا عَبْدَنَا وَقَالُوا

So they impugned Our servant and said,

مَجْنُونٌ وَٱزْدُجِرَ ٩

'A crazy man,' and he was reviled.[1]

فَدَعَا رَبَّهُ 10

Thereat he invoked his Lord,

أَنِّى مَغْلُوبٌ فَٱنتَصِرْ ١٠

[saying,] 'I have been overcome, so help [me].'

فَفَتَحْنَا أَبْوَٰبَ ٱلسَّمَآءِ 11

Then We opened the gates of the sky

بِمَآءٍ مُّنْهَمِرٍ ١١

with pouring waters,

وَفَجَّرْنَا ٱلْأَرْضَ عُيُونًا 12

and We made the earth burst forth with springs,

فَٱلْتَقَى ٱلْمَآءُ عَلَىٰ أَمْرٍ قَدْ قُدِرَ ١٢

and the waters met for a preordained purpose.

وَحَمَلْنَـٰهُ 13

We bore him

عَلَىٰ ذَاتِ أَلْوَٰحٍ وَدُسُرٍ ١٣

on a vessel made of planks and nails,

تَجْرِى بِأَعْيُنِنَا 14

which sailed [over the flood waters] in Our sight,

جَزَآءً لِّمَن كَانَ كُفِرَ ١٤

as a retribution for him who was repudiated.

وَلَقَد تَّرَكْنَـٰهَآ ءَايَةً 15

Certainly We have left it as a sign;

فَهَلْ مِن مُّدَّكِرٍ ١٥

so is there anyone who will be admonished?

فَكَيْفَ كَانَ عَذَابِى وَنُذُرِ ١٦

So how was My punishment and My warnings?

وَلَقَدْ يَسَّرْنَا ٱلْقُرْءَانَ 17

Certainly We have made the Qur'ān simple

لِلذِّكْرِ

for the sake of admonishment.

فَهَلْ مِن مُّدَّكِرٍ ١٧

So is there anyone who will be admonished?

كَذَّبَتْ عَادٌ 18

[The people of] 'Ād impugned [their apostle].

فَكَيْفَ كَانَ عَذَابِى وَنُذُرِ ١٨

So how was My punishment and My warnings?

إِنَّآ أَرْسَلْنَا عَلَيْهِمْ رِيحًا صَرْصَرًا 19

Indeed We unleashed upon them an icy gale

فِى يَوْمِ نَحْسٍ مُّسْتَمِرٍّ ١٩

on an incessantly ill-fated day,

---

[1] Or 'he was proscribed,' or 'he was ostracized.'

تَنزِعُ ٱلنَّاسَ 20 knocking down people

كَأَنَّهُمْ أَعْجَازُ نَخْلٍ مُّنقَعِرٍ ۝ as if they were trunks of uprooted palm trees.

فَكَيْفَ كَانَ عَذَابِى وَنُذُرِ ۝ 21 So how was My punishment and My warnings?!

وَلَقَدْ يَسَّرْنَا ٱلْقُرْءَانَ 22 Certainly We have made the Qur'ān simple

لِلذِّكْرِ for the sake of admonishment.

فَهَلْ مِن مُّدَّكِرٍ ۝ So is there anyone who will be admonished?

كَذَّبَتْ ثَمُودُ بِٱلنُّذُرِ ۝ 23 [The people of] Thamūd denied the warnings,

فَقَالُوٓا۟ 24 and they said,

أَبَشَرًا مِّنَّا وَٰحِدًا نَّتَّبِعُهُۥٓ 'Are we to follow a lone human from ourselves?!

إِنَّآ إِذًا لَّفِى ضَلَٰلٍ وَسُعُرٍ ۝ Indeed then we would be in error and madness.'

أَءُلْقِىَ ٱلذِّكْرُ عَلَيْهِ 25 'Has the Reminder been cast upon him

مِنۢ بَيْنِنَا from among us?

بَلْ هُوَ كَذَّابٌ أَشِرٌ ۝ Rather he is a self-conceited[1] liar.'

سَيَعْلَمُونَ غَدًا 26 'Tomorrow they will know

مَّنِ ٱلْكَذَّابُ ٱلْأَشِرُ ۝ who is a self-conceited liar.

إِنَّا مُرْسِلُوا۟ ٱلنَّاقَةِ 27 We are sending the She-camel

فِتْنَةً لَّهُمْ as a trial for them;

فَٱرْتَقِبْهُمْ وَٱصْطَبِرْ ۝ so watch them and be steadfast.

وَنَبِّئْهُمْ 28 Inform them

أَنَّ ٱلْمَآءَ قِسْمَةٌ بَيْنَهُمْ that the water is to be dispensed between them;

كُلُّ شِرْبٍ مُّحْتَضَرٌ ۝ every drinking will be attended.'

فَنَادَوْا۟ صَاحِبَهُمْ 29 But they called their companion,

فَتَعَاطَىٰ فَعَقَرَ ۝ and he took [a knife] and hamstrung [her].

فَكَيْفَ كَانَ عَذَابِى وَنُذُرِ ۝ 30 So how was My punishment and My warnings?!

إِنَّآ أَرْسَلْنَا عَلَيْهِمْ صَيْحَةً وَٰحِدَةً 31 We sent against them a single Cry,

فَكَانُوا۟ كَهَشِيمِ ٱلْمُحْتَظِرِ ۝ and they became like the dry sticks of a corral builder.

وَلَقَدْ يَسَّرْنَا ٱلْقُرْءَانَ 32 Certainly We have made the Qur'ān simple

لِلذِّكْرِ for the sake of admonishment.

فَهَلْ مِن مُّدَّكِرٍ ۝ So is there anyone who will be admonished?

---

[1] Or 'insolent.'

كَذَّبَتْ قَوْمُ لُوطٍ بِالنُّذُرِ ۩ 33 And the people of Lot denied the warnings.

إِنَّآ أَرْسَلْنَا عَلَيْهِمْ حَاصِبًا 34 We unleashed a rain of stones upon them,

إِلَّآ ءَالَ لُوطٍ     excepting the family of Lot,

نَّجَّيْنَٰهُم بِسَحَرٍ ۩     whom We delivered at dawn,

نِّعْمَةً مِّنْ عِندِنَا 35     as a blessing from Us.

كَذَٰلِكَ نَجْزِى مَن شَكَرَ ۩     Thus do We reward those who give thanks.

وَلَقَدْ أَنذَرَهُم بَطْشَتَنَا 36 He had certainly warned them of Our strike,

فَتَمَارَوْا۟ بِالنُّذُرِ ۩     but they disputed the warnings.

وَلَقَدْ رَٰوَدُوهُ عَن ضَيْفِهِۦ 37 Certainly they even solicited of him his guests,

فَطَمَسْنَآ أَعْيُنَهُمْ     whereat We blotted out their eyes, [saying,]

فَذُوقُوا۟ عَذَابِى وَنُذُرِ ۩     'Taste My punishment and My warnings!'

وَلَقَدْ صَبَّحَهُم بُكْرَةً 38 Certainly early at dawn there visited them

عَذَابٌ مُّسْتَقِرٌّ ۩     an abiding punishment:

فَذُوقُوا۟ عَذَابِى وَنُذُرِ ۩ 39 'Taste My punishment and My warnings!'

وَلَقَدْ يَسَّرْنَا ٱلْقُرْءَانَ 40 Certainly We have made the Qur'ān simple

لِلذِّكْرِ     for the sake of admonishment.

فَهَلْ مِن مُّدَّكِرٍ ۩     So is there anyone who will be admonished?

وَلَقَدْ جَآءَ ءَالَ فِرْعَوْنَ ٱلنُّذُرُ ۩ 41 Certainly the warnings came to Pharaoh's clan

كَذَّبُوا۟ بِـَٔايَٰتِنَا كُلِّهَا 42 who denied all of Our signs.

فَأَخَذْنَٰهُمْ أَخْذَ     So We seized them with the seizing

عَزِيزٍ مُّقْتَدِرٍ ۩     of One [who is] all-mighty, Omnipotent.

أَكُفَّارُكُمْ خَيْرٌ مِّنْ أُو۟لَٰئِكُمْ 43 Are your faithless better than those,

أَمْ لَكُم بَرَآءَةٌ     or have you [been granted] some immunity

فِى ٱلزُّبُرِ ۩     in the scriptures?

أَمْ يَقُولُونَ نَحْنُ جَمِيعٌ مُّنتَصِرٌ ۩ 44 Do they say, 'We are a confederate league'?

سَيُهْزَمُ ٱلْجَمْعُ 45 The league will be routed

وَيُوَلُّونَ ٱلدُّبُرَ ۩     and turn its back [to flee].

بَلِ ٱلسَّاعَةُ مَوْعِدُهُمْ 46 Rather the Hour is their tryst;

وَٱلسَّاعَةُ أَدْهَىٰ وَأَمَرُّ ۩     and the Hour will be most calamitous and bitter.

إِنَّ ٱلْمُجْرِمِينَ فِى ضَلَٰلٍ وَسُعُرٍ ۩ 47 Indeed the guilty are in error and madness.

يَوْمَ يُسْحَبُونَ فِى ٱلنَّارِ 48 The day when they are dragged into the Fire

عَلَىٰ وُجُوهِهِمْ     on their faces,

ذُوقُوا۟ مَسَّ سَقَرَ ۝     [it will be said to them,] 'Taste the touch of hell!'

إِنَّا كُلَّ شَىْءٍ خَلَقْنَٰهُ بِقَدَرٍ ۝ 49 Indeed We have created everything in a measure,

وَمَآ أَمْرُنَآ إِلَّا وَٰحِدَةٌ 50     and Our command is but a single [word],

كَلَمْحٍۭ بِٱلْبَصَرِ ۝     like the twinkling of an eye.

وَلَقَدْ أَهْلَكْنَآ أَشْيَاعَكُمْ 51 Certainly We have destroyed your likes.

فَهَلْ مِن مُّدَّكِرٍ ۝     So is there anyone who will be admonished?

وَكُلُّ شَىْءٍ فَعَلُوهُ فِى ٱلزُّبُرِ ۝ 52 Everything they have done is in the books,

وَكُلُّ صَغِيرٍ وَكَبِيرٍ 53     and everything big and small,

مُسْتَطَرٌ ۝     is committed to writing.

إِنَّ ٱلْمُتَّقِينَ 54 Indeed the Godwary

فِى جَنَّٰتٍ وَنَهَرٍ ۝     will be amid gardens and streams,

فِى مَقْعَدِ صِدْقٍ 55     in the abode of truthfulness[1]

عِندَ مَلِيكٍ مُّقْتَدِرٍ ۝     with an omnipotent King.

## سُورَةُ الرَّحْمٰن     55. SŪRAT AL-RAḤMĀN[2]

بِسْمِ ٱللَّهِ     In the Name of Allah,

ٱلرَّحْمَٰنِ ٱلرَّحِيمِ     the All-beneficent, the All-merciful.

ٱلرَّحْمَٰنُ ۝ 1 The All-beneficent

عَلَّمَ ٱلْقُرْءَانَ ۝ 2 has taught the Qur'ān.

خَلَقَ ٱلْإِنسَٰنَ ۝ 3 He created man,

عَلَّمَهُ ٱلْبَيَانَ ۝ 4 [and] taught him articulate speech.

ٱلشَّمْسُ وَٱلْقَمَرُ بِحُسْبَانٍ ۝ 5 The sun and the moon are [disposed] calculatedly,

وَٱلنَّجْمُ وَٱلشَّجَرُ يَسْجُدَانِ ۝ 6 and the herb and the tree prostrate [to Allah].

---

[1] Or 'in a worthy abode.'

[2] The *sūrah* takes its name from verse 1, which mentions "the All-beneficent" (*al-raḥmān*).

وَٱلسَّمَآءَ رَفَعَهَا وَوَضَعَ ٱلْمِيزَانَ ۝ 7 He raised the sky and set up the balance,

أَلَّا تَطْغَوْاْ فِى ٱلْمِيزَانِ ۝ 8 declaring, 'Do not infringe the balance!

وَأَقِيمُواْ ٱلْوَزْنَ بِٱلْقِسْطِ 9 Maintain the weights with justice,

وَلَا تُخْسِرُواْ ٱلْمِيزَانَ ۝ and do not shorten the balance!'

وَٱلْأَرْضَ وَضَعَهَا لِلْأَنَامِ ۝ 10 And the earth, He laid it out for mankind.

فِيهَا فَٰكِهَةٌ وَٱلنَّخْلُ ذَاتُ ٱلْأَكْمَامِ ۝ 11 In it are fruits and date-palms with sheaths,

وَٱلْحَبُّ ذُو ٱلْعَصْفِ وَٱلرَّيْحَانُ ۝ 12 grain with husk, and fragrant herbs.

فَبِأَىِّ ءَالَآءِ رَبِّكُمَا 13 So which of your Lord's bounties

تُكَذِّبَانِ ۝ will you both[1] deny?

خَلَقَ ٱلْإِنسَٰنَ 14 He created man

مِن صَلْصَٰلٍ كَٱلْفَخَّارِ ۝ out of dry clay,[2] like the potter's,

وَخَلَقَ ٱلْجَآنَّ مِن مَّارِجٍ مِّن نَّارٍ ۝ 15 and created the jinn out of a flame of a fire.

فَبِأَىِّ ءَالَآءِ رَبِّكُمَا 16 So which of your Lord's bounties

تُكَذِّبَانِ ۝ will you both deny?

رَبُّ ٱلْمَشْرِقَيْنِ 17 Lord of the two easts,

وَرَبُّ ٱلْمَغْرِبَيْنِ ۝ and Lord of the two wests![3]

فَبِأَىِّ ءَالَآءِ رَبِّكُمَا 18 So which of your Lord's bounties

تُكَذِّبَانِ ۝ will you both deny?

مَرَجَ ٱلْبَحْرَيْنِ يَلْتَقِيَانِ ۝ 19 He merged the two seas,[4] meeting each other.

بَيْنَهُمَا بَرْزَخٌ 20 There is a barrier between them

لَّا يَبْغِيَانِ ۝ which they do not overstep.

فَبِأَىِّ ءَالَآءِ رَبِّكُمَا 21 So which of your Lord's bounties

تُكَذِّبَانِ ۝ will you both deny?

يَخْرُجُ مِنْهُمَا ٱللُّؤْلُؤُ وَٱلْمَرْجَانُ ۝ 22 From them emerge the pearl and the coral.

فَبِأَىِّ ءَالَآءِ رَبِّكُمَا 23 So which of your Lord's bounties

تُكَذِّبَانِ ۝ will you both deny?

---

[1] That is, the jinn and humans. The pronoun 'you' and the adjective 'your' are both dual in the Arabic.

[2] Cf. 15:26, 28, 33.

[3] That is, the points of sunrise and sunset at the winter and summer solstices.

[4] See the footnote at 35:12.

وَلَهُ ٱلْجَوَارِ ٱلْمُنشَـَاتُ فِى ٱلْبَحْرِ 24 His are the sailing ships[1] on the sea

كَٱلْأَعْلَـٰمِ ۝ [appearing] like landmarks.

فَبِأَىِّ ءَالَآءِ رَبِّكُمَا 25 So which of your Lord's bounties

تُكَذِّبَانِ ۝ will you both deny?

كُلُّ مَنْ عَلَيْهَا فَانٍ ۝ 26 Everyone on it[2] is ephemeral,

وَيَبْقَىٰ وَجْهُ رَبِّكَ 27 yet lasting is the Face of *your* Lord,

ذُو ٱلْجَلَـٰلِ وَٱلْإِكْرَامِ ۝ majestic and munificent.[3]

فَبِأَىِّ ءَالَآءِ رَبِّكُمَا 28 So which of your Lord's bounties

تُكَذِّبَانِ ۝ will you both deny?

يَسْـَٔلُهُ مَن فِى ٱلسَّمَـٰوَٰتِ وَٱلْأَرْضِ 29 Everyone in the heavens and the earth asks Him.

كُلَّ يَوْمٍ هُوَ فِى شَأْنٍ ۝ Every day He is engaged in some work.

فَبِأَىِّ ءَالَآءِ رَبِّكُمَا 30 So which of your Lord's bounties

تُكَذِّبَانِ ۝ will you both deny?

سَنَفْرُغُ لَكُمْ 31 We shall soon make Ourselves unoccupied for you,

أَيُّهَ ٱلثَّقَلَانِ ۝ O you notable two![4]

فَبِأَىِّ ءَالَآءِ رَبِّكُمَا 32 So which of your Lord's bounties

تُكَذِّبَانِ ۝ will you both deny?

يَـٰمَعْشَرَ ٱلْجِنِّ وَٱلْإِنسِ 33 O company of jinn and humans!

إِنِ ٱسْتَطَعْتُمْ أَن تَنفُذُوا If you can pass through

مِنْ أَقْطَارِ ٱلسَّمَـٰوَٰتِ وَٱلْأَرْضِ the confines of the heavens and the earth,

فَٱنفُذُوا then do pass through.

لَا تَنفُذُونَ But you will not pass through

إِلَّا بِسُلْطَـٰنٍ ۝ except by an authority [from Allah].

فَبِأَىِّ ءَالَآءِ رَبِّكُمَا 34 So which of your Lord's bounties

---

[1] Or 'the watercrafts.'

[2] That is, on the earth.

[3] The adjectives 'majestic' and 'munificent' pertain to the Face.

[4] That is, the jinn and humans, or the Qur'ān and the Prophet's Household, referred to as '*thaqalayn*' in a famous tradition cited in Sunnī and Shī'ī sources.

تُكَذِّبَانِ ۞    will you both deny?

يُرْسَلُ عَلَيْكُمَا 35 There will be unleashed upon you

شُوَاظٌ مِّن نَّارٍ وَنُحَاسٌ    a flash of fire and a smoke;

فَلَا تَنتَصِرَانِ ۞    then you will not be able to help one another.

فَبِأَىِّ ءَالَآءِ رَبِّكُمَا 36 So which of your Lord's bounties

تُكَذِّبَانِ ۞    will you both deny?

فَإِذَا ٱنشَقَّتِ ٱلسَّمَآءُ 37 When the sky is split open,

فَكَانَتْ وَرْدَةً كَٱلدِّهَانِ ۞    and turns crimson like tanned leather.

فَبِأَىِّ ءَالَآءِ رَبِّكُمَا 38 So which of your Lord's bounties

تُكَذِّبَانِ ۞    will you both deny?

فَيَوْمَئِذٍ 39 On that day

لَّا يُسْـَٔلُ عَن ذَنبِهِۦٓ إِنسٌ    neither humans will be questioned about their sins

وَلَا جَآنٌّ ۞    nor jinn.[1]

فَبِأَىِّ ءَالَآءِ رَبِّكُمَا 40 So which of your Lord's bounties

تُكَذِّبَانِ ۞    will you both deny?

يُعْرَفُ ٱلْمُجْرِمُونَ بِسِيمَٰهُمْ 41 The guilty will be recognized by their mark;

فَيُؤْخَذُ بِٱلنَّوَٰصِى وَٱلْأَقْدَامِ ۞    so they will be seized by the forelocks and the feet.

فَبِأَىِّ ءَالَآءِ رَبِّكُمَا 42 So which of your Lord's bounties

تُكَذِّبَانِ ۞    will you both deny?

هَٰذِهِۦ جَهَنَّمُ ٱلَّتِى 43 'This is the hell which

يُكَذِّبُ بِهَا ٱلْمُجْرِمُونَ ۞    the guilty would deny!'

يَطُوفُونَ بَيْنَهَا 44 They shall circuit between it

وَبَيْنَ حَمِيمٍ ءَانٍ ۞    and boiling hot water.

فَبِأَىِّ ءَالَآءِ رَبِّكُمَا 45 So which of your Lord's bounties

تُكَذِّبَانِ ۞    will you both deny?

وَلِمَنْ خَافَ مَقَامَ رَبِّهِۦ 46 For him who stands in awe of his Lord

جَنَّتَانِ ۞    will be two gardens.

---

[1] Cf. 28:78.

فَبِأَىِّ ءَالَآءِ رَبِّكُمَا 47 So which of your Lord's bounties

تُكَذِّبَانِ ۝ will you both deny?

ذَوَاتَآ أَفْنَانٍ ۝ 48 Both abounding in branches.[1]

فَبِأَىِّ ءَالَآءِ رَبِّكُمَا 49 So which of your Lord's bounties

تُكَذِّبَانِ ۝ will you both deny?

فِيهِمَا عَيْنَانِ تَجْرِيَانِ ۝ 50 In both of them will be two flowing springs.

فَبِأَىِّ ءَالَآءِ رَبِّكُمَا 51 So which of your Lord's bounties

تُكَذِّبَانِ ۝ will you both deny?

فِيهِمَا مِن كُلِّ فَٰكِهَةٍ زَوْجَانِ ۝ 52 In both of them will be two kinds of every fruit.

فَبِأَىِّ ءَالَآءِ رَبِّكُمَا 53 So which of your Lord's bounties

تُكَذِّبَانِ ۝ will you both deny?

مُتَّكِـِٔينَ عَلَىٰ فُرُشٍ 54 [They will be] reclining on beds

بَطَآئِنُهَا مِنْ إِسْتَبْرَقٍ lined with green silk.

وَجَنَى ٱلْجَنَّتَيْنِ And the fruit of the two gardens will be

دَانٍ ۝ near at hand.

فَبِأَىِّ ءَالَآءِ رَبِّكُمَا 55 So which of your Lord's bounties

تُكَذِّبَانِ ۝ will you both deny?

فِيهِنَّ قَٰصِرَٰتُ ٱلطَّرْفِ 56 In them are maidens of restrained glances,

لَمْ يَطْمِثْهُنَّ إِنسٌ قَبْلَهُمْ whom no human has touched before,

وَلَا جَآنٌّ ۝ nor jinn.

فَبِأَىِّ ءَالَآءِ رَبِّكُمَا 57 So which of your Lord's bounties

تُكَذِّبَانِ ۝ will you both deny?

كَأَنَّهُنَّ ٱلْيَاقُوتُ وَٱلْمَرْجَانُ ۝ 58 As though they were rubies and corals.

فَبِأَىِّ ءَالَآءِ رَبِّكُمَا 59 So which of your Lord's bounties

تُكَذِّبَانِ ۝ will you both deny?

هَلْ جَزَآءُ ٱلْإِحْسَٰنِ 60 Is the requital of goodness anything

إِلَّا ٱلْإِحْسَٰنُ ۝ but goodness?

فَبِأَىِّ ءَالَآءِ رَبِّكُمَا 61 So which of your Lord's bounties

---

[1] Or 'Both full of variety;' that is, of fruits.

نُكَذِّبَانِ ۝      will you both deny?

وَمِن دُونِهِمَا جَنَّتَانِ ۝ 62 Beside these two, there will be two [other] gardens.

فَبِأَىِّ ءَالَآءِ رَبِّكُمَا 63 So which of your Lord's bounties

نُكَذِّبَانِ ۝      will you both deny?

مُدْهَآمَّتَانِ ۝ 64 Dark green.

فَبِأَىِّ ءَالَآءِ رَبِّكُمَا 65 So which of your Lord's bounties

نُكَذِّبَانِ ۝      will you both deny?

فِيهِمَا عَيْنَانِ نَضَّاخَتَانِ ۝ 66 In both of them will be two gushing springs.

فَبِأَىِّ ءَالَآءِ رَبِّكُمَا 67 So which of your Lord's bounties

نُكَذِّبَانِ ۝      will you both deny?

فِيهِمَا فَٰكِهَةٌ 68 In both of them will be fruits,

وَنَخْلٌ وَرُمَّانٌ ۝      date-palms and pomegranates.

فَبِأَىِّ ءَالَآءِ رَبِّكُمَا 69 So which of your Lord's bounties

نُكَذِّبَانِ ۝      will you both deny?

فِيهِنَّ خَيْرَٰتٌ حِسَانٌ ۝ 70 In them are maidens good and lovely.

فَبِأَىِّ ءَالَآءِ رَبِّكُمَا 71 So which of your Lord's bounties

نُكَذِّبَانِ ۝      will you both deny?

حُورٌ مَّقْصُورَٰتٌ فِى ٱلْخِيَامِ ۝ 72 Houris secluded in pavilions.

فَبِأَىِّ ءَالَآءِ رَبِّكُمَا 73 So which of your Lord's bounties

نُكَذِّبَانِ ۝      will you both deny?

لَمْ يَطْمِثْهُنَّ إِنسٌ قَبْلَهُمْ 74 Whom no human has touched before,

وَلَا جَآنٌّ ۝      nor jinn.

فَبِأَىِّ ءَالَآءِ رَبِّكُمَا 75 So which of your Lord's bounties

نُكَذِّبَانِ ۝      will you both deny?

مُتَّكِئِينَ عَلَىٰ رَفْرَفٍ خُضْرٍ 76 Reclining on green cushions

وَعَبْقَرِىٍّ حِسَانٍ ۝      and lovely carpets.

فَبِأَىِّ ءَالَآءِ رَبِّكُمَا 77 So which of your Lord's bounties

نُكَذِّبَانِ ۝      will you both deny?

تَبَٰرَكَ ٱسْمُ رَبِّكَ 78 Blessed is the Name of *your* Lord,

ذِى ٱلْجَلَٰلِ وَٱلْإِكْرَامِ ۝      the Majestic and the Munificent!

# سُورَةُ الواقِعَةِ

# 56. SŪRAT AL-WĀQIʿAH[1]

بِسمِ ٱللَّهِ
ٱلرَّحۡمَـٰنِ ٱلرَّحِيمِ

In the Name of Allah,
the All-beneficent, the All-merciful.

إِذَا وَقَعَتِ ٱلۡوَاقِعَةُ ۝ 1 When the Imminent[2] [Hour] befalls

لَيۡسَ لِوَقۡعَتِهَا كَاذِبَةٌ ۝ 2 —there is no denying that it will befall—

خَافِضَةٌ رَّافِعَةٌ ۝ 3 [it will be] lowering, exalting.[3]

إِذَا رُجَّتِ ٱلۡأَرۡضُ رَجًّا ۝ 4 When the earth is shaken violently,

وَبُسَّتِ ٱلۡجِبَالُ بَسًّا ۝ 5 and the mountains are shattered into bits

فَكَانَتۡ هَبَآءً مُّنۢبَثًّا ۝ 6 and become scattered dust,

وَكُنتُمۡ أَزۡوَٰجًا ثَلَٰثَةً ۝ 7 you will be three groups:

فَأَصۡحَٰبُ ٱلۡمَيۡمَنَةِ 8 The People of the Right Hand

مَآ أَصۡحَٰبُ ٱلۡمَيۡمَنَةِ ۝ —and what are the People of the Right Hand?

وَأَصۡحَٰبُ ٱلۡمَشۡـَٔمَةِ 9 And the People of the Left Hand

مَآ أَصۡحَٰبُ ٱلۡمَشۡـَٔمَةِ ۝ —and what are the People of the Left Hand?

وَٱلسَّٰبِقُونَ ٱلسَّٰبِقُونَ ۝ 10 And the Foremost Ones are the foremost ones:[4]

أُوْلَٰٓئِكَ ٱلۡمُقَرَّبُونَ ۝ 11 they are the ones brought near [to Allah],

فِى جَنَّٰتِ ٱلنَّعِيمِ ۝ 12 [who will reside] in the gardens of bliss.

ثُلَّةٌ مِّنَ ٱلۡأَوَّلِينَ ۝ 13 A multitude from the former [generations][5]

وَقَلِيلٌ مِّنَ ٱلۡأٓخِرِينَ ۝ 14 and a few from the later ones.

عَلَىٰ سُرُرٍ مَّوۡضُونَةٍ ۝ 15 On brocaded couches

مُّتَّكِئِينَ عَلَيۡهَا مُتَقَٰبِلِينَ ۝ 16 reclining on them, face to face.

يَطُوفُ عَلَيۡهِمۡ وِلۡدَٰنٌ مُّخَلَّدُونَ ۝ 17 They will be waited upon by immortal youths,

---

[1] The *sūrah* takes its name from verse 1, which mentions *al-wāqiʿah* (the Imminent Hour, i.e., the Day of Resurrection).

[2] That is, the Day of Resurrection and Judgement.

[3] That is, abasing the faithless and raising the faithful in station.

[4] Cf. 2:148, 5:48, 23:61, 35:32, 57:21.

[5] That is, from the communities of the former prophets.

بِأَكْوَابٍ وَأَبَارِيقَ 18    with goblets and ewers

وَكَأْسٍ مِّن مَّعِينٍ ۝    and a cup of a clear wine,[1]

لَّا يُصَدَّعُونَ عَنْهَا 19    which neither causes them headache

وَلَا يُنزِفُونَ ۝    nor stupefaction,

وَفَٰكِهَةٍ مِّمَّا يَتَخَيَّرُونَ ۝ 20    and such fruits as they prefer

وَلَحْمِ طَيْرٍ مِّمَّا يَشْتَهُونَ ۝ 21    and such flesh of fowls as they desire,

وَحُورٌ عِينٌ ۝ 22    and big-eyed houris

كَأَمْثَٰلِ ٱللُّؤْلُؤِ ٱلْمَكْنُونِ ۝ 23    like guarded pearls,

جَزَآءً بِمَا كَانُوا۟ يَعْمَلُونَ ۝ 24    a reward for what they used to do.

لَا يَسْمَعُونَ فِيهَا 25 They will not hear therein

لَغْوًا وَلَا تَأْثِيمًا ۝    any vain talk or sinful speech,

إِلَّا قِيلًا سَلَٰمًا سَلَٰمًا ۝ 26    but only the watchword, 'Peace!' 'Peace!'

وَأَصْحَٰبُ ٱلْيَمِينِ 27 And the People of the Right Hand

مَآ أَصْحَٰبُ ٱلْيَمِينِ ۝    —what are the People of the Right Hand?

فِى سِدْرٍ مَّخْضُودٍ ۝ 28 Amid thornless lote trees

وَطَلْحٍ مَّنضُودٍ ۝ 29    and clustered spathes[2]

وَظِلٍّ مَّمْدُودٍ ۝ 30    and extended shade,[3]

وَمَآءٍ مَّسْكُوبٍ ۝ 31    and ever-flowing water

وَفَٰكِهَةٍ كَثِيرَةٍ ۝ 32    and abundant fruits,

لَّا مَقْطُوعَةٍ وَلَا مَمْنُوعَةٍ ۝ 33    neither inaccessible, nor forbidden,

وَفُرُشٍ مَّرْفُوعَةٍ ۝ 34    and noble spouses.

إِنَّآ أَنشَأْنَٰهُنَّ إِنشَآءً ۝ 35 We have created them with a special creation,

فَجَعَلْنَٰهُنَّ أَبْكَارًا ۝ 36    and made them virgins,

عُرُبًا أَتْرَابًا ۝ 37    loving, of a like age,

لِّأَصْحَٰبِ ٱلْيَمِينِ ۝ 38    for the People of the Right Hand.

ثُلَّةٌ مِّنَ ٱلْأَوَّلِينَ ۝ 39 A multitude from the former [generations]

---

[1] Or 'flowing wine.'

[2] This is according to the reading *wa ṭal‘in manḍūd* (instead of *wa ṭalḥin manḍūd*, meaning 'and clustered plantains') narrated from Imam ‘Alī and Imam Ja‘far al-Ṣādiq (‘a) and Ibn ‘Abbās. (*Mu‘jam, al-Kashshāf*)

[3] Or 'twilight;' see the note at 25:45.

وَثُلَّةٌ مِّنَ ٱلْأَخِرِينَ ۝ 40 and a multitude from the latter [ones].

وَأَصْحَٰبُ ٱلشِّمَالِ 41 And the People of the Left Hand

مَآ أَصْحَٰبُ ٱلشِّمَالِ ۝ —what are the People of the Left Hand?

فِى سَمُومٍ وَحَمِيمٍ ۝ 42 Amid infernal miasma and boiling water

وَظِلٍّ مِّن يَحْمُومٍ ۝ 43 and the shadow of a dense black smoke,

لَّا بَارِدٍ وَلَا كَرِيمٍ ۝ 44 neither cool nor beneficial.[1]

إِنَّهُمْ كَانُوا۟ قَبْلَ ذَٰلِكَ مُتْرَفِينَ ۝ 45 Indeed they had been affluent before this,

وَكَانُوا۟ يُصِرُّونَ عَلَى ٱلْحِنثِ ٱلْعَظِيمِ ۝ 46 and they used to persist in the great sin.[2]

وَكَانُوا۟ يَقُولُونَ 47 And they used to say,

أَئِذَا مِتْنَا وَكُنَّا تُرَابًا 'What! When we are dead and become dust

وَعِظَٰمًا and bones,

أَئِنَّا لَمَبْعُوثُونَ ۝ shall we be resurrected?

أَوَءَابَآؤُنَا ٱلْأَوَّلُونَ ۝ 48 And our forefathers too?'

قُلْ إِنَّ ٱلْأَوَّلِينَ وَٱلْأَخِرِينَ 49 *Say,* 'Indeed the former and latter generations

لَمَجْمُوعُونَ 50 will all be gathered

إِلَىٰ مِيقَٰتِ يَوْمٍ مَّعْلُومٍ ۝ for the tryst of a known day.

ثُمَّ إِنَّكُمْ 51 Then indeed,

أَيُّهَا ٱلضَّآلُّونَ ٱلْمُكَذِّبُونَ ۝ you, astray deniers,

لَأَكِلُونَ مِن شَجَرٍ مِّن زَقُّومٍ ۝ 52 will surely eat from the Zaqqūm tree

فَمَالِئُونَ مِنْهَا ٱلْبُطُونَ ۝ 53 and stuff your bellies with it,

فَشَٰرِبُونَ عَلَيْهِ مِنَ ٱلْحَمِيمِ ۝ 54 and drink boiling water on top of it,

فَشَٰرِبُونَ شُرْبَ ٱلْهِيمِ ۝ 55 drinking like thirsty camels.'

هَٰذَا نُزُلُهُمْ 56 Such will be the hospitality they receive

يَوْمَ ٱلدِّينِ ۝ on the Day of Retribution.[3]

نَحْنُ خَلَقْنَٰكُمْ 57 We created you.

فَلَوْلَا تُصَدِّقُونَ ۝ Then why do you not acknowledge it?

---

[1] Cf. 77:30-31.

[2] That is, *shirk.* Cf. 31:13.

[3] Or 'the Day of Judgement.'

أَفَرَءَيْتُم مَّا تُمْنُونَ ۝ 58 Have you considered the sperm that you emit?

ءَأَنتُمْ تَخْلُقُونَهُۥ 59 Is it you who create it,

أَمْ نَحْنُ ٱلْخَٰلِقُونَ ۝     or are We the creator?

نَحْنُ قَدَّرْنَا بَيْنَكُمُ ٱلْمَوْتَ 60 We have ordained death among you,

وَمَا نَحْنُ بِمَسْبُوقِينَ ۝     and We are not to be outmaneuvered

عَلَىٰٓ أَن نُّبَدِّلَ أَمْثَٰلَكُمْ 61   from replacing you with your likes

وَنُنشِئَكُمْ     and recreating you

فِى مَا لَا تَعْلَمُونَ ۝     in [a realm] you do not know.

وَلَقَدْ عَلِمْتُمُ ٱلنَّشْأَةَ ٱلْأُولَىٰ 62 Certainly you have known the first genesis,

فَلَوْلَا تَذَكَّرُونَ ۝     then why do you not take admonition?

أَفَرَءَيْتُم مَّا تَحْرُثُونَ ۝ 63 Have you considered what you sow?

ءَأَنتُمْ تَزْرَعُونَهُۥٓ 64 Is it you who make it grow,

أَمْ نَحْنُ ٱلزَّٰرِعُونَ ۝     or are We the grower?

لَوْ نَشَآءُ لَجَعَلْنَٰهُ حُطَٰمًا 65 If We wish, We surely turn it into chaff,

فَظَلْتُمْ تَفَكَّهُونَ ۝     whereat you are left stunned[1] [saying to yourselves,]

إِنَّا لَمُغْرَمُونَ ۝ 66     ʿIndeed we have suffered loss!

بَلْ نَحْنُ مَحْرُومُونَ ۝ 67     Rather we are deprived!ʾ

أَفَرَءَيْتُمُ ٱلْمَآءَ ٱلَّذِى تَشْرَبُونَ ۝ 68 Have you considered the water that you drink?

ءَأَنتُمْ أَنزَلْتُمُوهُ مِنَ ٱلْمُزْنِ 69 Is it you who bring it down from the rain cloud,

أَمْ نَحْنُ ٱلْمُنزِلُونَ ۝     or are We who bring [it] down?

لَوْ نَشَآءُ جَعَلْنَٰهُ أُجَاجًا 70 If We wish We can make it bitter.

فَلَوْلَا تَشْكُرُونَ ۝     Then why do you not give thanks?

أَفَرَءَيْتُمُ ٱلنَّارَ ٱلَّتِى تُورُونَ ۝ 71 Have you considered the fire that you kindle?

ءَأَنتُمْ أَنشَأْتُمْ شَجَرَتَهَآ 72 Was it you who caused its tree to grow,

أَمْ نَحْنُ ٱلْمُنشِئُونَ ۝     or were We the grower?

نَحْنُ جَعَلْنَٰهَا تَذْكِرَةً 73 It was We that made it a reminder

وَمَتَٰعًا لِّلْمُقْوِينَ ۝     and a boon for the desert-dwellers.

فَسَبِّحْ بِٱسْمِ رَبِّكَ ٱلْعَظِيمِ ۝ ✽ 74 So *celebrate* the Name of *your* Lord, the All-supreme.

---

[1] Or ʿregretful.ʾ

761

فَلَآ أُقْسِمُ 75 So I swear[1]

بِمَوَٰقِعِ ٱلنُّجُومِ 76 by the places where[2] the stars set![3]

وَإِنَّهُۥ لَقَسَمٌ لَّوْ تَعْلَمُونَ عَظِيمٌ 76 And indeed it is a great oath, should you know.

إِنَّهُۥ لَقُرْءَانٌ كَرِيمٌ 77 This is indeed a noble Qur'ān,

فِى كِتَٰبٍ مَّكْنُونٍ 78 in a guarded Book,[4]

لَّا يَمَسُّهُۥٓ إِلَّا ٱلْمُطَهَّرُونَ 79 —no one touches it except the pure ones—

تَنزِيلٌ 80 gradually sent down

مِّن رَّبِّ ٱلْعَٰلَمِينَ from the Lord of all the worlds.

أَفَبِهَٰذَا ٱلْحَدِيثِ أَنتُم مُّدْهِنُونَ 81 What! Do you take lightly this discourse?

وَتَجْعَلُونَ رِزْقَكُمْ أَنَّكُمْ تُكَذِّبُونَ 82 And make your denial of it your vocation?[5]

فَلَوْلَآ إِذَا بَلَغَتِ ٱلْحُلْقُومَ 83 So when it[6] reaches the throat [of the dying person]

وَأَنتُمْ حِينَئِذٍ تَنظُرُونَ 84 and at that moment you are looking on

وَنَحْنُ أَقْرَبُ إِلَيْهِ مِنكُمْ 85 —and We are nearer to him[7] than you are,

وَلَٰكِن لَّا تُبْصِرُونَ though you do not perceive—

فَلَوْلَآ إِن كُنتُمْ غَيْرَ مَدِينِينَ 86 then why do you not, if you are not subject[8]

تَرْجِعُونَهَآ 87 [to the Divine dispensation], restore it,

إِن كُنتُمْ صَٰدِقِينَ should you be truthful?

فَأَمَّآ إِن كَانَ مِنَ ٱلْمُقَرَّبِينَ 88 Then, if he be of those brought near,[9]

فَرَوْحٌ وَرَيْحَانٌ وَجَنَّتُ نَعِيمٍ 89 then ease, abundance, and a garden of bliss.

وَأَمَّآ إِن كَانَ مِنْ أَصْحَٰبِ ٱلْيَمِينِ 90 And if he be of the People of the Right Hand,

فَسَلَٰمٌ لَّكَ 91 then 'Peace be on you,'

---

[1] Or 'I will not swear.'

[2] Or 'by the times when.'

[3] Or 'by the places where the stars fall.' Or 'I swear by the orbits of the stars.'

[4] That is, the Preserved Tablet.

[5] Or 'livelihood.' According to the reading *taj'alūna shukrakum,* narrated from Imam 'Alī ibn Abī Ṭālib and Imam al-Ṣādiq in *al-Tafsīr al-Qummī* under this verse, the translation will be 'You make your denial of it your thanksgiving.' That is, instead of being grateful for it, you deny it.

[6] That is, the soul, while leaving the body during the death-throes.

[7] That is, to the dying person.

[8] Or 'if you are not liable to retribution.'

[9] That is, of 'the foremost ones' mentioned in verses 10-11.

مِنۡ أَصۡحَٰبِ ٱلۡيَمِينِ    [a greeting] from the People of the Right Hand!

وَأَمَّآ إِن كَانَ مِنَ ٱلۡمُكَذِّبِينَ 92 But if he be of the impugners,

ٱلضَّآلِّينَ         the astray ones,

فَنُزُلٞ مِّنۡ حَمِيمٖ 93     then a treat of boiling water

وَتَصۡلِيَةُ جَحِيمٍ 94      and entry into hell.[1]

إِنَّ هَٰذَا لَهُوَ حَقُّ ٱلۡيَقِينِ 95 Indeed this is certain truth.

فَسَبِّحۡ بِٱسۡمِ رَبِّكَ ٱلۡعَظِيمِ 96 So *celebrate* the Name of *your* Lord, the All-supreme!

## سُورَةُ الْحَدِيد         57. SŪRAT AL-ḤADĪD[2]

بِسۡمِ ٱللَّهِ         In the Name of Allah,

ٱلرَّحۡمَٰنِ ٱلرَّحِيمِ    the All-beneficent, the All-merciful.

سَبَّحَ لِلَّهِ مَا فِي ٱلسَّمَٰوَٰتِ 1 Whatever there is in the heavens glorifies Allah

وَٱلۡأَرۡضِ      and [whatever there is in] the earth

وَهُوَ ٱلۡعَزِيزُ ٱلۡحَكِيمُ      and He is the All-mighty, the All-wise.

لَهُۥ مُلۡكُ ٱلسَّمَٰوَٰتِ 2 To Him belongs the kingdom of the heavens

وَٱلۡأَرۡضِ       and the earth:

يُحۡيِۦ وَيُمِيتُ      He gives life and brings death,

وَهُوَ عَلَىٰ كُلِّ شَيۡءٖ قَدِيرٌ     and He has power over all things.

هُوَ ٱلۡأَوَّلُ وَٱلۡأٓخِرُ 3 He is the First and the Last,

وَٱلظَّٰهِرُ وَٱلۡبَاطِنُ     the Manifest and the Hidden,

وَهُوَ بِكُلِّ شَيۡءٍ عَلِيمٌ     and He has knowledge of all things.

هُوَ ٱلَّذِي خَلَقَ ٱلسَّمَٰوَٰتِ وَٱلۡأَرۡضَ 4 It is He who created the heavens and the earth

فِي سِتَّةِ أَيَّامٖ     in six days;

ثُمَّ ٱسۡتَوَىٰ عَلَى ٱلۡعَرۡشِ    then settled on the Throne.

يَعۡلَمُ مَا يَلِجُ فِي ٱلۡأَرۡضِ    He knows whatever enters the earth

وَمَا يَخۡرُجُ مِنۡهَا     and whatever emerges from it

---

[1] Or 'roasting in hell.'

[2] The *sūrah* takes its name from verse 25, which mentions iron (*ḥadīd*).

وَمَا يَنزِلُ مِنَ ٱلسَّمَآءِ    and whatever descends from the sky

وَمَا يَعْرُجُ فِيهَا    and whatever ascends to it,

وَهُوَ مَعَكُمْ أَيْنَ مَا كُنتُمْ    and He is with you wherever you may be,

وَٱللَّهُ بِمَا تَعْمَلُونَ بَصِيرٌ ۝    and Allah sees best what you do.

لَّهُۥ مُلْكُ ٱلسَّمَٰوَٰتِ    5 To Him belongs the kingdom of the heavens

وَٱلْأَرْضِ    and the earth,

وَإِلَى ٱللَّهِ تُرْجَعُ ٱلْأُمُورُ ۝    and to Allah all matters are returned.[1]

يُولِجُ ٱلَّيْلَ فِى ٱلنَّهَارِ    6 He makes the night pass into the day

وَيُولِجُ ٱلنَّهَارَ فِى ٱلَّيْلِ    and makes the day pass into the night,

وَهُوَ عَلِيمٌ بِذَاتِ ٱلصُّدُورِ ۝    and He knows best what is in the breasts.

ءَامِنُواْ بِٱللَّهِ وَرَسُولِهِۦ    7 Have faith in Allah and His Apostle,

وَأَنفِقُواْ مِمَّا    and spend out of that

جَعَلَكُم مُّسْتَخْلَفِينَ فِيهِ    wherein He has made you successors.[2]

فَٱلَّذِينَ ءَامَنُواْ مِنكُمْ    Those of you who have faith

وَأَنفَقُواْ    and spend [in Allah's way]

هُمْ أَجْرٌ كَبِيرٌ ۝    —there is a great reward for them.

وَمَا لَكُمْ لَا تُؤْمِنُونَ بِٱللَّهِ    8 Why should you not have faith in Allah

وَٱلرَّسُولُ يَدْعُوكُمْ    while the Apostle invites you

لِتُؤْمِنُواْ بِرَبِّكُمْ    to have faith in your Lord,

وَقَدْ أَخَذَ مِيثَٰقَكُمْ    and He has certainly made a covenant with you,

إِن كُنتُم مُّؤْمِنِينَ ۝    should you be faithful?

هُوَ ٱلَّذِى يُنَزِّلُ    9 It is He who sends down

عَلَىٰ عَبْدِهِۦ ءَايَٰتٍ بَيِّنَٰتٍ    manifest signs to His servant

لِّيُخْرِجَكُم مِّنَ ٱلظُّلُمَٰتِ إِلَى ٱلنُّورِ    that He may bring you out of darkness into light,

وَإِنَّ ٱللَّهَ بِكُمْ لَرَءُوفٌ رَّحِيمٌ ۝    and indeed Allah is most kind and merciful to you.

وَمَا لَكُمْ أَلَّا تُنفِقُواْ فِى سَبِيلِ ٱللَّهِ    10 Why should you not spend in the way of Allah,

وَلِلَّهِ مِيرَٰثُ ٱلسَّمَٰوَٰتِ    while to Allah belongs the heritage of the heavens

---

[1] Cf. 2:210, 3:109, 8:44, 11:123, 19:40, 22:76, 30:11, 96:8.

[2] That is, of the past generations.

| | |
|---|---|
| وَٱلْأَرْضُ | and the earth? |
| لَا يَسْتَوِى مِنكُم | Not equal [to others] are those of you |
| مَّنْ أَنفَقَ مِن قَبْلِ ٱلْفَتْحِ وَقَـٰتَلَ | who spent and fought before the victory.[1] |
| أُوْلَـٰٓئِكَ أَعْظَمُ دَرَجَةً | They are greater in rank |
| مِّنَ ٱلَّذِينَ أَنفَقُواْ مِنۢ بَعْدُ وَقَـٰتَلُواْ | than those who have spent and fought afterwards. |
| وَكُلًّا وَعَدَ ٱللَّهُ ٱلْحُسْنَىٰ | Yet Allah has promised the best reward to each |
| وَٱللَّهُ بِمَا تَعْمَلُونَ خَبِيرٌ ۝ | and Allah is well aware of what you do. |
| مَّن ذَا ٱلَّذِى يُقْرِضُ ٱللَّهَ قَرْضًا حَسَنًا | 11 Who is it that will lend Allah a good loan, |
| فَيُضَـٰعِفَهُۥ لَهُۥ | that He may multiply it for him |
| وَلَهُۥٓ أَجْرٌ كَرِيمٌ ۝ | and [that] there may be a noble reward for him? |
| يَوْمَ تَرَى ٱلْمُؤْمِنِينَ وَٱلْمُؤْمِنَـٰتِ | 12 The day *you* will see the faithful, men and women, |
| يَسْعَىٰ نُورُهُم بَيْنَ أَيْدِيهِمْ | with their light moving swiftly before them |
| وَبِأَيْمَـٰنِهِم | and on their right, [and greeted with the words:] |
| بُشْرَىٰكُمُ ٱلْيَوْمَ | 'There is good news for you today! |
| جَنَّـٰتٌ تَجْرِى مِن تَحْتِهَا ٱلْأَنْهَـٰرُ | Gardens with streams running in them, |
| خَـٰلِدِينَ فِيهَا | to remain in them [forever]. |
| ذَٰلِكَ هُوَ ٱلْفَوْزُ ٱلْعَظِيمُ ۝ | That is the great success.' |
| يَوْمَ يَقُولُ ٱلْمُنَـٰفِقُونَ وَٱلْمُنَـٰفِقَـٰتُ | 13 The day the hypocrites, men and women, will say |
| لِلَّذِينَ ءَامَنُواْ | to the faithful, |
| ٱنظُرُونَا | 'Please let up on us, |
| نَقْتَبِسْ مِن نُّورِكُمْ | that we may glean something from your light!' |
| قِيلَ ٱرْجِعُواْ وَرَآءَكُمْ فَٱلْتَمِسُواْ نُورًا | They will be told: 'Go back and grope for light!'[2] |
| فَضُرِبَ بَيْنَهُم بِسُورٍ | Then there will be set up between them a wall |
| لَّهُۥ بَابٌ | with a gate, |
| بَاطِنُهُۥ فِيهِ ٱلرَّحْمَةُ | with mercy on its interior |
| وَظَـٰهِرُهُۥ مِن قِبَلِهِ ٱلْعَذَابُ ۝ | and punishment toward its exterior. |
| يُنَادُونَهُمْ | 14 They will call out to them, |
| أَلَمْ نَكُن مَّعَكُمْ | 'Did we not use to be with you?' |

---

[1] That is, the Prophet's triumphant return to Makkah.
[2] That is, go back into the world. Said mockingly to the hypocrites. Cf. 2:15, 11:38.

قَالُوا بَلَىٰ

They will say, 'Yes!

وَلَـٰكِنَّكُمْ فَتَنتُمْ أَنفُسَكُمْ

But you cast yourselves into temptation,

وَتَرَبَّصْتُمْ وَٱرْتَبْتُمْ

and you awaited[1] and were doubtful,

وَغَرَّتْكُمُ ٱلْأَمَانِيُّ

and [false] hopes deceived you

حَتَّىٰ جَآءَ أَمْرُ ٱللَّهِ

until the edict of Allah[2] arrived,

وَغَرَّكُم بِٱللَّهِ ٱلْغَرُورُ ۝

and the Deceiver deceived you concerning Allah.

فَٱلْيَوْمَ لَا يُؤْخَذُ مِنكُمْ فِدْيَةٌ

15 So today no ransom shall be taken from you,

وَلَا مِنَ ٱلَّذِينَ كَفَرُوا

nor from the faithless.

مَأْوَىٰكُمُ ٱلنَّارُ

The Fire will be your abode:

هِىَ مَوْلَىٰكُمْ

it is your [ultimate] refuge

وَبِئْسَ ٱلْمَصِيرُ ۝

and an evil destination.'

أَلَمْ يَأْنِ لِلَّذِينَ ءَامَنُوا

16 Is it not time yet for those who have faith

أَن تَخْشَعَ قُلُوبُهُمْ

that their hearts should be humbled

لِذِكْرِ ٱللَّهِ

for Allah's remembrance

وَمَا نَزَلَ مِنَ ٱلْحَقِّ

and to the truth which has come down [to them],

وَلَا يَكُونُوا كَٱلَّذِينَ أُوتُوا ٱلْكِتَـٰبَ

and to be not like those who were given the Book

مِن قَبْلُ

before?[3]

فَطَالَ عَلَيْهِمُ ٱلْأَمَدُ

Time took its toll on them

فَقَسَتْ قُلُوبُهُمْ

and so their hearts were hardened,

وَكَثِيرٌ مِّنْهُمْ فَـٰسِقُونَ ۝

and many of them are transgressors.

ٱعْلَمُوا أَنَّ ٱللَّهَ يُحْيِ ٱلْأَرْضَ

17 Know that Allah revives the earth

بَعْدَ مَوْتِهَا ۚ

after its death.

قَدْ بَيَّنَّا لَكُمُ ٱلْأَيَـٰتِ

We have certainly made the signs clear for you

لَعَلَّكُمْ تَعْقِلُونَ ۝

so that you may apply reason.

إِنَّ ٱلْمُصَّدِّقِينَ وَٱلْمُصَّدِّقَـٰتِ

18 Indeed the charitable men and charitable women,

وَأَقْرَضُوا ٱللَّهَ قَرْضًا حَسَنًا

and those who lend Allah a good loan

يُضَـٰعَفُ لَهُمْ

—it shall be multiplied for them,

---

[1] That is, waited for a reverse of fortune for Muslims. See 4:141, 9:50-52, 98, 23:25, 52:30-31.

[2] That is, death.

[3] That is, the Jews.

and there is a noble reward for them.

19 Those who have faith in Allah and His apostles

—it is they who are the truthful

and the witnesses[1] with their Lord;

they shall have their reward and their light.

But as for those who are faithless and deny Our signs,

they shall be the inmates of hell.

20 Know that the life of this world is just

play and diversion, and glitter,

and mutual vainglory among you

and covetousness[2] for wealth and children

—like the rain

whose vegetation impresses the farmer;

then it withers and you see it turn yellow,

then it becomes chaff,

while in the Hereafter there is a severe punishment

and forgiveness from Allah and His pleasure;

and the life of this world is nothing

but the wares of delusion.

21 Take the lead towards forgiveness from your Lord

and a paradise as vast as the heavens

and the earth,

prepared for those who have faith in Allah

and His apostles.

That is Allah's grace,

which He grants to whomever He wishes,

and Allah is dispenser of a great grace.

22 No affliction visits the earth

---

[1] Or 'martyrs.'

[2] Or 'rivalry.'

وَلَا فِىٓ أَنفُسِكُمْ    or yourselves

إِلَّا فِى كِتَٰبٍ مِّن قَبْلِ أَن نَّبْرَأَهَآ    but it is in a Book before We bring it about

إِنَّ ذَٰلِكَ عَلَى ٱللَّهِ يَسِيرٌ ۝    —that is indeed easy for Allah—

لِّكَيْلَا تَأْسَوْا۟ عَلَىٰ مَا فَاتَكُمْ    23 so that you may not grieve for what escapes you,

وَلَا تَفْرَحُوا۟ بِمَآ ءَاتَىٰكُمْ    nor exult for what comes your way,

وَٱللَّهُ لَا يُحِبُّ كُلَّ مُخْتَالٍ فَخُورٍ ۝    and Allah does not like any swaggering braggart.

ٱلَّذِينَ يَبْخَلُونَ    24 Such as are [themselves] stingy

وَيَأْمُرُونَ ٱلنَّاسَ بِٱلْبُخْلِ    and bid [other] people to be stingy.

وَمَن يَتَوَلَّ    And whoever refuses to comply [should know that]

فَإِنَّ ٱللَّهَ هُوَ ٱلْغَنِىُّ ٱلْحَمِيدُ ۝    indeed Allah is the All-sufficient, the All-laudable.

لَقَدْ أَرْسَلْنَا رُسُلَنَا بِٱلْبَيِّنَٰتِ    25 Certainly We sent Our apostles with manifest proofs,

وَأَنزَلْنَا مَعَهُمُ ٱلْكِتَٰبَ    and We sent down with them the Book

وَٱلْمِيزَانَ    and the Balance,

لِيَقُومَ ٱلنَّاسُ بِٱلْقِسْطِ    so that mankind may maintain justice;

وَأَنزَلْنَا ٱلْحَدِيدَ    and We sent down[1] iron,

فِيهِ بَأْسٌ شَدِيدٌ    in which there is great might

وَمَنَٰفِعُ لِلنَّاسِ    and uses for mankind,

وَلِيَعْلَمَ ٱللَّهُ مَن يَنصُرُهُۥ    and so that Allah may know those who help Him

وَرُسُلَهُۥ بِٱلْغَيْبِ    and His apostles in [their] absence.

إِنَّ ٱللَّهَ قَوِىٌّ عَزِيزٌ ۝    Indeed Allah is all-strong, all-mighty.

وَلَقَدْ أَرْسَلْنَا نُوحًا وَإِبْرَٰهِيمَ    26 Certainly We sent Noah and Abraham

وَجَعَلْنَا فِى ذُرِّيَّتِهِمَا    and We ordained among their descendants

ٱلنُّبُوَّةَ وَٱلْكِتَٰبَ    prophethood and the Book.

فَمِنْهُم مُّهْتَدٍ    Some of them are [rightly] guided,

وَكَثِيرٌ مِّنْهُمْ فَٰسِقُونَ ۝    and many of them are transgressors.

ثُمَّ قَفَّيْنَا عَلَىٰٓ ءَاثَٰرِهِم بِرُسُلِنَا    27 Then We followed them up with Our apostles

وَقَفَّيْنَا بِعِيسَى ٱبْنِ مَرْيَمَ    and We followed [them] with Jesus son of Mary,

وَءَاتَيْنَٰهُ ٱلْإِنجِيلَ    and We gave him the Evangel,

وَجَعَلْنَا فِى قُلُوبِ ٱلَّذِينَ ٱتَّبَعُوهُ    and We put in the hearts of those who followed him

---

[1] That is, created.

رَأْفَةً وَرَحْمَةً kindness and mercy.

وَرَهْبَانِيَّةً ٱبْتَدَعُوهَا But as for monasticism, they innovated it

مَا كَتَبْنَهَا عَلَيْهِمْ —We had not prescribed it for them—

إِلَّا ٱبْتِغَآءَ رِضْوَنِ ٱللَّهِ only seeking Allah's pleasure.

فَمَا رَعَوْهَا حَقَّ رِعَايَتِهَا Yet they did not observe it with due observance.

فَآتَيْنَا ٱلَّذِينَ ءَامَنُوا مِنْهُمْ So We gave to the faithful among them

أَجْرَهُمْ their [due] reward,

وَكَثِيرٌ مِنْهُمْ فَسِقُونَ ۞ but many of them are transgressors.

يَٰٓأَيُّهَا ٱلَّذِينَ ءَامَنُوا 28 O you who have faith!

ٱتَّقُوا ٱللَّهَ Be wary of Allah

وَءَامِنُوا بِرَسُولِهِ and have faith in His Apostle.

يُؤْتِكُمْ كِفْلَيْنِ مِن رَّحْمَتِهِ He will grant you a double share of His mercy

وَيَجْعَل لَّكُمْ نُورًا تَمْشُونَ بِهِ and give you a light to walk by,

وَيَغْفِرْ لَكُمْ and forgive you,

وَٱللَّهُ غَفُورٌ رَّحِيمٌ ۞ and Allah is all-forgiving, all-merciful;

لِّئَلَّا يَعْلَمَ أَهْلُ ٱلْكِتَٰبِ 29 so that the People of the Book may know

أَلَّا يَقْدِرُونَ عَلَىٰ شَىْءٍ that they have no power over anything

مِّن فَضْلِ ٱللَّهِ of Allah's grace,

وَأَنَّ ٱلْفَضْلَ بِيَدِ ٱللَّهِ and that all grace is in Allah's hand

يُؤْتِيهِ مَن يَشَآءُ which He grants to whomever He wishes

وَٱللَّهُ ذُو ٱلْفَضْلِ ٱلْعَظِيمِ ۞ and Allah is dispenser of a great grace.

[PART 28]

## سُوْرَةُ الْمُجَادِلَة   58. SŪRAT AL-MUJĀDILAH[1]

بِسْمِ ٱللَّهِ In the Name of Allah,

ٱلرَّحْمَٰنِ ٱلرَّحِيمِ the All-beneficent, the All-merciful.

قَدْ سَمِعَ ٱللَّهُ قَوْلَ ٱلَّتِى 1 Allah has certainly heard the speech of her

تُجَٰدِلُكَ فِى زَوْجِهَا who pleads with *you* about her husband

---

[1] The *sūrah* taks its name from the phrase *tujādiluka* ("pleads with you") in verse 1.

وَتَشْتَكِى إِلَى اللَّهِ    and complains to Allah.

وَاللَّهُ يَسْمَعُ تَحَاوُرَكُمَا    Allah hears the conversation between the two of you.

إِنَّ اللَّهَ سَمِيعٌ بَصِيرٌ ۝    Indeed Allah is all-hearing, all-seeing.

ٱلَّذِينَ يُظَٰهِرُونَ مِنكُم مِّن نِّسَآئِهِم    2 As for those of you who repudiate their wives by *zihār*,[1]

مَّا هُنَّ أُمَّهَٰتِهِمْ    they are not their mothers;

إِنْ أُمَّهَٰتُهُمْ إِلَّا ٱلَّٰٓئِى وَلَدْنَهُمْ    their mothers are only those who bore them,

وَإِنَّهُمْ لَيَقُولُونَ مُنكَرًا مِّنَ ٱلْقَوْلِ    and indeed they utter an outrageous utterance

وَزُورًا    and a lie.

وَإِنَّ اللَّهَ لَعَفُوٌّ غَفُورٌ ۝    Indeed Allah is all-excusing, all-forgiving.

وَٱلَّذِينَ يُظَٰهِرُونَ مِن نِّسَآئِهِمْ    3 Those who repudiate their wives by *zihār*

ثُمَّ يَعُودُونَ لِمَا قَالُوا    and then retract what they have said,

فَتَحْرِيرُ رَقَبَةٍ مِّن قَبْلِ أَن يَتَمَآسَّا    shall set free a slave before they may touch each other.

ذَٰلِكُمْ تُوعَظُونَ بِهِ    This you are advised [to carry out],

وَٱللَّهُ بِمَا تَعْمَلُونَ خَبِيرٌ ۝    and Allah is well aware of what you do.

فَمَن لَّمْ يَجِدْ    4 He who can not afford [to free a slave]

فَصِيَامُ شَهْرَيْنِ مُتَتَابِعَيْنِ    shall fast for two successive months

مِن قَبْلِ أَن يَتَمَآسَّا    before they may touch each other.

فَمَن لَّمْ يَسْتَطِعْ    If he cannot [do so],

فَإِطْعَامُ سِتِّينَ مِسْكِينًا    he shall feed sixty needy persons.

ذَٰلِكَ لِتُؤْمِنُوا بِٱللَّهِ وَرَسُولِهِ    This, that you may have faith in Allah and His Apostle.

وَتِلْكَ حُدُودُ ٱللَّهِ    These are Allah's bounds,

وَلِلْكَٰفِرِينَ عَذَابٌ أَلِيمٌ ۝    and there is a painful punishment for the faithless.

إِنَّ ٱلَّذِينَ يُحَآدُّونَ ٱللَّهَ وَرَسُولَهُ    5 Indeed those who oppose Allah and His Apostle

كُبِتُوا    will be subdued

كَمَا كُبِتَ ٱلَّذِينَ مِن قَبْلِهِمْ    just as were subdued those before them.

وَقَدْ أَنزَلْنَآ ءَايَٰتٍ بَيِّنَٰتٍ    We have certainly sent down manifest signs,

وَلِلْكَٰفِرِينَ عَذَابٌ مُّهِينٌ ۝    and there is a humiliating punishment for the faithless.

---

[1] A kind of repudiation of the marital relationship among pre-Islamic Arabs which took place on a husband's saying to his wife 'Be as my mother's back' (*zahr*, hence the derivative *zihār*).

يَوْمَ يَبْعَثُهُمُ ٱللَّهُ جَمِيعًا 6 The day when Allah will raise them all together,

فَيُنَبِّئُهُم بِمَا عَمِلُوٓاْ    He will inform them about what they have done.

أَحْصَىٰهُ ٱللَّهُ وَنَسُوهُ    Allah has kept account of it, while they forgot it,

وَٱللَّهُ عَلَىٰ كُلِّ شَىْءٍ شَهِيدٌ ۝    and Allah is witness to all things.

أَلَمْ تَرَ أَنَّ ٱللَّهَ يَعْلَمُ 7 Have you not regarded that Allah knows

مَا فِى ٱلسَّمَٰوَٰتِ    whatever there is in the heavens

وَمَا فِى ٱلْأَرْضِ    and whatever there is in the earth?

مَا يَكُونُ مِن نَّجْوَىٰ ثَلَٰثَةٍ    There is no secret talk among three,

إِلَّا هُوَ رَابِعُهُمْ    but He is their fourth [companion],

وَلَا خَمْسَةٍ إِلَّا هُوَ سَادِسُهُمْ    nor among five but He is their sixth,

وَلَآ أَدْنَىٰ مِن ذَٰلِكَ وَلَآ أَكْثَرَ    nor less than that, nor more,

إِلَّا هُوَ مَعَهُمْ أَيْنَ مَا كَانُواْ    but He is with them wherever they may be.

ثُمَّ يُنَبِّئُهُم بِمَا عَمِلُوٓاْ    Then He will inform them about what they have done

يَوْمَ ٱلْقِيَٰمَةِ    on the Day of Resurrection.

إِنَّ ٱللَّهَ بِكُلِّ شَىْءٍ عَلِيمٌ ۝    Indeed Allah has knowledge of all things.

أَلَمْ تَرَ إِلَى ٱلَّذِينَ 8 Have *you* not regarded those

نُهُواْ عَنِ ٱلنَّجْوَىٰ    who were forbidden from secret talks[1]

ثُمَّ يَعُودُونَ    but again resumed

لِمَا نُهُواْ عَنْهُ    what they had been forbidden from,

وَيَتَنَٰجَوْنَ    and hold secret talks

بِٱلْإِثْمِ وَٱلْعُدْوَٰنِ    [imbued] with sin and transgression

وَمَعْصِيَتِ ٱلرَّسُولِ    and disobedience to the Apostle?

وَإِذَا جَآءُوكَ    And when they[2] come to *you*

حَيَّوْكَ بِمَا    they greet *you* with that

لَمْ يُحَيِّكَ بِهِ ٱللَّهُ    with which Allah never greeted you,

وَيَقُولُونَ فِىٓ أَنفُسِهِمْ    and they say to themselves,[3]

---

[1] That is, the Jews and the hypocrites.

[2] That is, the Jews and the hypocrites who, instead of *as-salāmu ʻalaykum* (peace be on you), would greet the Prophet (ṣ) with such words as *as-sāmu ʻalaykum* (death to you), telling themselves that if the Prophet (ṣ) were really from God, He would punish them for it.

[3] Or 'in their hearts.'

لَوْلَا يُعَذِّبُنَا ٱللَّهُ بِمَا نَقُولُ 'Why does not Allah punish us for what we say?!'

حَسْبُهُمْ جَهَنَّمُ يَصْلَوْنَهَا Let hell suffice them: they shall enter it;

فَبِئْسَ ٱلْمَصِيرُ and it is an evil destination!

يَٰٓأَيُّهَا ٱلَّذِينَ ءَامَنُوٓا 9 O you who have faith!

إِذَا تَنَٰجَيْتُمْ When you talk secretly,

فَلَا تَتَنَٰجَوْا do not hold secret talks

بِٱلْإِثْمِ وَٱلْعُدْوَٰنِ [imbued] with sin and aggression

وَمَعْصِيَتِ ٱلرَّسُولِ and disobedience to the Apostle,

وَتَنَٰجَوْا بِٱلْبِرِّ but talk secretly in [a spirit of] piety

وَٱلتَّقْوَىٰ and Godfearing,

وَٱتَّقُوا ٱللَّهَ and be wary of Allah

ٱلَّذِىٓ إِلَيْهِ تُحْشَرُونَ toward whom you will be mustered.

إِنَّمَا ٱلنَّجْوَىٰ مِنَ ٱلشَّيْطَٰنِ 10 Indeed [malicious] secret talks are from Satan,

لِيَحْزُنَ ٱلَّذِينَ ءَامَنُوا that he may upset the faithful,

وَلَيْسَ بِضَآرِّهِمْ شَيْـًٔا but he cannot harm them in any way

إِلَّا بِإِذْنِ ٱللَّهِ except by Allah's leave,

وَعَلَى ٱللَّهِ فَلْيَتَوَكَّلِ ٱلْمُؤْمِنُونَ and in Allah let all the faithful put their trust.

يَٰٓأَيُّهَا ٱلَّذِينَ ءَامَنُوٓا 11 O you who have faith!

إِذَا قِيلَ لَكُمْ تَفَسَّحُوا فِى ٱلْمَجَٰلِسِ When you are told, 'Make room,' in sittings,

فَٱفْسَحُوا then do make room;

يَفْسَحِ ٱللَّهُ لَكُمْ Allah will make room for you.

وَإِذَا قِيلَ ٱنشُزُوا And when you are told, 'Rise up!'

فَٱنشُزُوا Do rise up.

يَرْفَعِ ٱللَّهُ ٱلَّذِينَ ءَامَنُوا مِنكُمْ Allah will raise those of you who have faith

وَٱلَّذِينَ أُوتُوا ٱلْعِلْمَ and those who have been given knowledge

دَرَجَٰتٍ in rank,

وَٱللَّهُ بِمَا تَعْمَلُونَ خَبِيرٌ and Allah is well aware of what you do.

يَٰٓأَيُّهَا ٱلَّذِينَ ءَامَنُوٓا 12 O you who have faith!

إِذَا نَٰجَيْتُمُ ٱلرَّسُولَ When you talk secretly to the Apostle,

فَقَدِّمُوا بَيْنَ يَدَىْ نَجْوَىٰكُمْ صَدَقَةً offer a charity before your secret talk.

ذَٰلِكَ خَيۡرٌ لَّكُمۡ وَأَطۡهَرُ ۚ    That is better for you and purer.

فَإِن لَّمۡ تَجِدُواْ    But if you cannot afford [to make the offering],

فَإِنَّ ٱللَّهَ غَفُورٌ رَّحِيمٌ ۝    then Allah is indeed all-forgiving, all-merciful.

ءَأَشۡفَقۡتُمۡ أَن تُقَدِّمُواْ    13 Were you apprehensive of offering

بَيۡنَ يَدَىۡ نَجۡوَىٰكُمۡ صَدَقَـٰتٍ ۚ    charities before your secret talks?

فَإِذۡ لَمۡ تَفۡعَلُواْ    So, as you did not do it,

وَتَابَ ٱللَّهُ عَلَيۡكُمۡ    and Allah was clement to you,

فَأَقِيمُواْ ٱلصَّلَوٰةَ وَءَاتُواْ ٱلزَّكَوٰةَ    maintain the prayer and pay the *zakāt*,

وَأَطِيعُواْ ٱللَّهَ وَرَسُولَهُۥ ۚ    and obey Allah and His Apostle.

وَٱللَّهُ خَبِيرٌۢ بِمَا تَعۡمَلُونَ ۝ ❊    And Allah is well aware of what you do.

أَلَمۡ تَرَ    14 Have *you* not regarded

إِلَى ٱلَّذِينَ تَوَلَّوۡاْ قَوۡمًا    those who befriend a people[1]

غَضِبَ ٱللَّهُ عَلَيۡهِم    at whom Allah is wrathful?

مَّا هُم مِّنكُمۡ وَلَا مِنۡهُمۡ    They neither belong to you, nor to them,

وَيَحۡلِفُونَ عَلَى ٱلۡكَذِبِ    and they swear false oaths [that they are with you]

وَهُمۡ يَعۡلَمُونَ ۝    and they know.

أَعَدَّ ٱللَّهُ لَهُمۡ عَذَابًا شَدِيدًا ۖ    15 Allah has prepared a severe punishment for them.

إِنَّهُمۡ سَآءَ مَا كَانُواْ يَعۡمَلُونَ ۝    Evil indeed is what they used to do.

ٱتَّخَذُوٓاْ أَيۡمَـٰنَهُمۡ جُنَّةً    16 They make a shield of their oaths

فَصَدُّواْ عَن سَبِيلِ ٱللَّهِ    and bar [people] from the way of Allah;

فَلَهُمۡ عَذَابٌ مُّهِينٌ ۝    so there is a humiliating punishment for them.

لَّن تُغۡنِيَ عَنۡهُمۡ أَمۡوَٰلُهُمۡ وَلَآ أَوۡلَـٰدُهُم    17 Their possessions and children will not avail them

مِّنَ ٱللَّهِ شَيۡـًٔا ۚ    in any way against Allah.

أُوْلَـٰٓئِكَ أَصۡحَـٰبُ ٱلنَّارِ ۖ    They shall be the inmates of the Fire

هُمۡ فِيهَا خَـٰلِدُونَ ۝    and they shall remain in it [forever].

يَوۡمَ يَبۡعَثُهُمُ ٱللَّهُ جَمِيعًا    18 The day when Allah will raise them all together,

فَيَحۡلِفُونَ لَهُۥ    they will swear to Him,

كَمَا يَحۡلِفُونَ لَكُمۡ ۖ    just like they swear to you [now],

---

[1] That is, the Jews, with whom the hypocrites amongst Muslims were on intimate terms.

وَيَحْسَبُونَ أَنَّهُمْ عَلَىٰ شَىْءٍ

supposing that they stand on something.

أَلَا إِنَّهُمْ هُمُ ٱلْكَٰذِبُونَ ۝

Look! They are indeed liars!

ٱسْتَحْوَذَ عَلَيْهِمُ ٱلشَّيْطَٰنُ

19 Satan has prevailed upon them,

فَأَنسَىٰهُمْ

so he has caused them to forget

ذِكْرَ ٱللَّهِ

the remembrance of Allah.

أُوْلَٰٓئِكَ حِزْبُ ٱلشَّيْطَٰنِ

They are Satan's confederates.

أَلَآ

Look!

إِنَّ حِزْبَ ٱلشَّيْطَٰنِ هُمُ ٱلْخَٰسِرُونَ ۝

Indeed it is Satan's confederates who are the losers!

إِنَّ ٱلَّذِينَ يُحَآدُّونَ ٱللَّهَ وَرَسُولَهُۥٓ

20 Indeed those who oppose Allah and His Apostle

أُوْلَٰٓئِكَ فِى ٱلْأَذَلِّينَ ۝

—they will be among the most abased.

كَتَبَ ٱللَّهُ لَأَغْلِبَنَّ

21 Allah has ordained: 'I shall surely prevail,

أَنَا۠ وَرُسُلِىٓ

I and My apostles.'

إِنَّ ٱللَّهَ قَوِىٌّ عَزِيزٌ ۝

Indeed Allah is all-strong, all-mighty.

لَّا تَجِدُ قَوْمًا يُؤْمِنُونَ بِٱللَّهِ

22 You will not find a people believing in Allah

وَٱلْيَوْمِ ٱلْءَاخِرِ

and the Last Day

يُوَآدُّونَ مَنْ حَآدَّ ٱللَّهَ وَرَسُولَهُۥ

endearing those who oppose Allah and His Apostle

وَلَوْ كَانُوٓا۟ ءَابَآءَهُمْ

even though they were their own parents,

أَوْ أَبْنَآءَهُمْ

or children,

أَوْ إِخْوَٰنَهُمْ أَوْ عَشِيرَتَهُمْ

or brothers, or kinsfolk.

أُوْلَٰٓئِكَ كَتَبَ فِى قُلُوبِهِمُ ٱلْإِيمَٰنَ

[For] such, He has written faith into their hearts

وَأَيَّدَهُم بِرُوحٍ مِّنْهُ

and strengthened them with a spirit from Him.

وَيُدْخِلُهُمْ جَنَّٰتٍ

He will admit them into gardens

تَجْرِى مِن تَحْتِهَا ٱلْأَنْهَٰرُ

with streams running in them,

خَٰلِدِينَ فِيهَا

to remain in them [forever],

رَضِىَ ٱللَّهُ عَنْهُمْ

Allah is pleased with them,

وَرَضُوا۟ عَنْهُ

and they are pleased with Him.

أُوْلَٰٓئِكَ حِزْبُ ٱللَّهِ

They are Allah's confederates.

أَلَآ

Look!

إِنَّ حِزْبَ ٱللَّهِ هُمُ ٱلْمُفْلِحُونَ ۝

The confederates of Allah are indeed felicitous!

# 59. SŪRAT AL-ḤASHR[1]

In the Name of Allah,
the All-beneficent, the All-merciful.

1 Whatever there is in the heavens glorifies Allah
and whatever there is in the earth,
and He is the All-mighty, the All-wise

2 It is He who expelled the faithless
belonging to the People of the Book
from their homes
at the outset of [their] en masse banishment.
You did not think that they would go out,
and they thought their fortresses would protect them
from Allah.
But Allah came at them
from whence they did not reckon
and He cast terror into their hearts.
They demolish their houses with their own hands
and the hands of the faithful.
So take lesson, O you who have insight!

3 If Allah had not ordained banishment for them,
He would have surely punished them in this world,
and in the Hereafter there is for them
the punishment of the Fire.

4 That is because they defied Allah and His Apostle;
and whoever defies Allah,

---

[1] The *sūrah* takes its name from the banishment (*ḥashr*) of a Jewish tribe from Madīnah, which is its main topic.

775

فَإِنَّ ٱللَّهَ شَدِيدُ ٱلْعِقَابِ ۝     indeed Allah is severe in retribution.

مَا قَطَعْتُم مِّن لِّينَةٍ     5 Whatever palm trees you cut down

أَوْ تَرَكْتُمُوهَا قَآئِمَةً عَلَىٰ أُصُولِهَا     or left standing on their roots,

فَبِإِذْنِ ٱللَّهِ     it was by Allah's will,

وَلِيُخْزِىَ ٱلْفَٰسِقِينَ ۝     and in order that He may disgrace the transgressors.

وَمَآ أَفَآءَ ٱللَّهُ عَلَىٰ رَسُولِهِۦ مِنْهُمْ     6 The spoils that Allah gave to His Apostle from them,

فَمَآ أَوْجَفْتُمْ عَلَيْهِ مِنْ خَيْلٍ     you did not spur any horse for its sake,

وَلَا رِكَابٍ     nor any riding camel,

وَلَٰكِنَّ ٱللَّهَ يُسَلِّطُ رُسُلَهُۥ     but Allah makes His apostles prevail

عَلَىٰ مَن يَشَآءُ     over whomever He wishes,

وَٱللَّهُ عَلَىٰ كُلِّ شَىْءٍ قَدِيرٌ ۝     and Allah has power over all things.

مَّآ أَفَآءَ ٱللَّهُ عَلَىٰ رَسُولِهِۦ     7 The spoils that Allah gave to His Apostle

مِنْ أَهْلِ ٱلْقُرَىٰ     from the people of the townships,

فَلِلَّهِ وَلِلرَّسُولِ     are for Allah and the Apostle,

وَلِذِى ٱلْقُرْبَىٰ وَٱلْيَتَٰمَىٰ     the relatives[1] and the orphans,

وَٱلْمَسَٰكِينِ وَٱبْنِ ٱلسَّبِيلِ     the needy and the traveller,

كَىْ     so that

لَا يَكُونَ دُولَةًۢ بَيْنَ ٱلْأَغْنِيَآءِ مِنكُمْ     they do not circulate among the rich among you.

وَمَآ ءَاتَىٰكُمُ ٱلرَّسُولُ فَخُذُوهُ     Take whatever the Apostle gives you,

وَمَا نَهَىٰكُمْ عَنْهُ فَٱنتَهُواْ     and relinquish whatever he forbids you,

وَٱتَّقُواْ ٱللَّهَ     and be wary of Allah.

إِنَّ ٱللَّهَ شَدِيدُ ٱلْعِقَابِ ۝     Indeed Allah is severe in retribution.

لِلْفُقَرَآءِ ٱلْمُهَٰجِرِينَ     8 [They are also] for the poor Emigrants

ٱلَّذِينَ أُخْرِجُواْ مِن دِيَٰرِهِمْ     who have been expelled from their homes

وَأَمْوَٰلِهِمْ     and [wrested of] their possessions,

يَبْتَغُونَ فَضْلًا مِّنَ ٱللَّهِ وَرِضْوَٰنًا     who seek grace from Allah and [His] pleasure

وَيَنصُرُونَ ٱللَّهَ وَرَسُولَهُۥٓ     and help Allah and His Apostle.

أُوْلَٰٓئِكَ هُمُ ٱلصَّٰدِقُونَ ۝     It is they who are the truthful.[2]

---

[1] That is, of the Prophet (ṣ), the Banū Hāshim.

[2] That is, true and loyal to their covenant with Allah and His Apostle.

وَٱلَّذِينَ تَبَوَّءُو ٱلدَّارَ    9 [They are as well] for those who were settled in the land[1]

وَٱلۡإِيمَٰنَ مِن قَبۡلِهِمۡ    and [abided] in faith before them,

يُحِبُّونَ مَنۡ هَاجَرَ إِلَيۡهِمۡ    who love those who migrate toward them,

وَلَا يَجِدُونَ فِى صُدُورِهِمۡ حَاجَةً    and do not find in their breasts any need

مِّمَّآ أُوتُواْ    for that which is given to them,[2]

وَيُؤۡثِرُونَ عَلَىٰٓ أَنفُسِهِمۡ    but prefer [the Immigrants] to themselves,

وَلَوۡ كَانَ بِهِمۡ خَصَاصَةٌ    though poverty be their own lot.

وَمَن يُوقَ شُحَّ نَفۡسِهِۦ    And those who are saved from their own greed

فَأُوْلَٰٓئِكَ هُمُ ٱلۡمُفۡلِحُونَ ۝    —it is they who are the felicitous.

وَٱلَّذِينَ جَآءُو مِنۢ بَعۡدِهِمۡ    10 And [also for] those who came in after them,

يَقُولُونَ رَبَّنَا    who say, 'Our Lord,

ٱغۡفِرۡ لَنَا وَلِإِخۡوَٰنِنَا    forgive us and our brethren

ٱلَّذِينَ سَبَقُونَا بِٱلۡإِيمَٰنِ    who were our forerunners in the faith,

وَلَا تَجۡعَلۡ فِى قُلُوبِنَا غِلّٗا    and do not put any rancour in our hearts

لِّلَّذِينَ ءَامَنُواْ    toward the faithful.

رَبَّنَآ إِنَّكَ رَءُوفٞ رَّحِيمٌ ۝ ❂    Our Lord, You are indeed most kind and merciful.'

أَلَمۡ تَرَ إِلَى ٱلَّذِينَ نَافَقُواْ    11 Have *you* not regarded the hypocrites

يَقُولُونَ لِإِخۡوَٰنِهِمُ    who say to their brethren,

ٱلَّذِينَ كَفَرُواْ مِنۡ أَهۡلِ ٱلۡكِتَٰبِ    the faithless from among the People of the Book:

لَئِنۡ أُخۡرِجۡتُمۡ    'If you are expelled,

لَنَخۡرُجَنَّ مَعَكُمۡ    we will surely go out with you,

وَلَا نُطِيعُ فِيكُمۡ أَحَدًا أَبَدٗا    and we will never obey anyone against you,

وَإِن قُوتِلۡتُمۡ    and if you are fought against

لَنَنصُرَنَّكُمۡ    we will surely help you,'

وَٱللَّهُ يَشۡهَدُ إِنَّهُمۡ لَكَٰذِبُونَ ۝    and Allah bears witness that they are indeed liars.

لَئِنۡ أُخۡرِجُواْ    12 Surely, if they were expelled

لَا يَخۡرُجُونَ مَعَهُمۡ    they would not go out with them,

---

[1] That is, Madīnah, to which the early Muslims migrated with the Prophet (ṣ).

[2] That is, to the Immigrants.

وَلَئِن قُوتِلُوٓاْ    and if they were fought against

لَا يَنصُرُونَهُمْ    they would not help them,

وَلَئِن نَّصَرُوهُمْ    and were they to help them

لَيُوَلُّنَّ ٱلْأَدْبَٰرَ    they would surely turn their backs [to flee]

ثُمَّ لَا يُنصَرُونَ ۩    and then they[1] would not be helped.

لَأَنتُمْ أَشَدُّ رَهْبَةً فِى صُدُورِهِم    13 Indeed they have a greater awe of you in their hearts

مِّنَ ٱللَّهِ ۚ    than of Allah.

ذَٰلِكَ بِأَنَّهُمْ قَوْمٌ لَّا يَفْقَهُونَ ۩    That is because they are a lot who do not understand.

لَا يُقَٰتِلُونَكُمْ جَمِيعًا    14 They will not fight against you in a body

إِلَّا فِى قُرًى مُّحَصَّنَةٍ    except in fortified townships

أَوْ مِن وَرَآءِ جُدُرٍۭ    or from behind walls.

بَأْسُهُم بَيْنَهُمْ شَدِيدٌ    Their might is great among themselves.

تَحْسَبُهُمْ جَمِيعًا    You suppose them to be a body,

وَقُلُوبُهُمْ شَتَّىٰ ۚ    but their hearts are disunited.

ذَٰلِكَ بِأَنَّهُمْ    That is because

قَوْمٌ لَّا يَعْقِلُونَ ۩    they are a lot who do not apply reason,

كَمَثَلِ ٱلَّذِينَ مِن قَبْلِهِمْ قَرِيبًا ۖ    15 like those who, recently before them,

ذَاقُواْ وَبَالَ أَمْرِهِمْ    tasted the evil consequences of their conduct,

وَهُمْ عَذَابٌ أَلِيمٌ ۩    and there is a painful punishment for them.

كَمَثَلِ ٱلشَّيْطَٰنِ    16 [Or] like Satan,

إِذْ قَالَ لِلْإِنسَٰنِ ٱكْفُرْ    when he prompts man to renounce faith,

فَلَمَّا كَفَرَ    then, when he renounces faith,

قَالَ إِنِّى بَرِىٓءٌ مِّنكَ    he says, 'Indeed I am absolved of you.

إِنِّىٓ أَخَافُ ٱللَّهَ    Indeed I fear Allah,

رَبَّ ٱلْعَٰلَمِينَ ۩    the Lord of all the worlds.'

فَكَانَ عَٰقِبَتَهُمَآ أَنَّهُمَا فِى ٱلنَّارِ    17 So the fate of both is that they will be in the Fire,

خَٰلِدَيْنِ فِيهَا ۚ    to remain in it [forever].

وَذَٰلِكَ جَزَٰٓؤُاْ ٱلظَّٰلِمِينَ ۩    Such is the requital of the wrongdoers.

---

[1] That is, the faithless from among the People of the Book.

يَـٰٓأَيُّهَا ٱلَّذِينَ ءَامَنُوا۟  18 O you who have faith!

ٱتَّقُوا۟ ٱللَّهَ  Be wary of Allah,

وَلْتَنظُرْ نَفْسٌ مَّا قَدَّمَتْ  and let every soul consider what it sends ahead[1]

لِغَدٍ  for tomorrow,

وَٱتَّقُوا۟ ٱللَّهَ  and be wary of Allah.

إِنَّ ٱللَّهَ خَبِيرٌۢ بِمَا تَعْمَلُونَ  Allah is indeed well aware of what you do

وَلَا تَكُونُوا۟ كَٱلَّذِينَ نَسُوا۟ ٱللَّهَ  19 And do not be like those who forget Allah,

فَأَنسَىٰهُمْ أَنفُسَهُمْ  so He makes them forget their own souls.

أُو۟لَـٰٓئِكَ هُمُ ٱلْفَـٰسِقُونَ  It is they who are the transgressors.

لَا يَسْتَوِىٓ أَصْحَـٰبُ ٱلنَّارِ  20 Not equal are the inmates of the Fire

وَأَصْحَـٰبُ ٱلْجَنَّةِ  and the inhabitants of paradise.

أَصْحَـٰبُ ٱلْجَنَّةِ  It is the inhabitants of paradise

هُمُ ٱلْفَآئِزُونَ  who are the successful ones.

لَوْ أَنزَلْنَا هَـٰذَا ٱلْقُرْءَانَ  21 Had We sent down this Qur'ān

عَلَىٰ جَبَلٍ  upon a mountain,

لَّرَأَيْتَهُۥ خَـٰشِعًا  *you* would have surely seen it humbled

مُّتَصَدِّعًا مِّنْ خَشْيَةِ ٱللَّهِ  [and] go to pieces with the fear of Allah.

وَتِلْكَ ٱلْأَمْثَـٰلُ نَضْرِبُهَا لِلنَّاسِ  We draw such comparisons for mankind,

لَعَلَّهُمْ يَتَفَكَّرُونَ  so that they may reflect.

هُوَ ٱللَّهُ ٱلَّذِى لَآ إِلَـٰهَ إِلَّا هُوَ  22 He is Allah—there is no god except Him—

عَـٰلِمُ ٱلْغَيْبِ وَٱلشَّهَـٰدَةِ  Knower of the sensible and the Unseen,

هُوَ ٱلرَّحْمَـٰنُ ٱلرَّحِيمُ  He is the All-beneficent, the All-merciful.

هُوَ ٱللَّهُ ٱلَّذِى لَآ إِلَـٰهَ إِلَّا هُوَ  23 He is Allah—there is no god except Him—

ٱلْمَلِكُ ٱلْقُدُّوسُ  the Sovereign, the All-holy,

ٱلسَّلَـٰمُ ٱلْمُؤْمِنُ ٱلْمُهَيْمِنُ  the All-benign,[2] the Securer, the All-conserver,

ٱلْعَزِيزُ ٱلْجَبَّارُ  the All-mighty, the All-compeller,

ٱلْمُتَكَبِّرُ  the All-magnanimous.

سُبْحَـٰنَ ٱللَّهِ  Clear is Allah

[1] Or 'prepares,' or 'makes ready.'
[2] Or 'the Impeccable.'

هُوَ ٱللَّهُ ٱلْخَـٰلِقُ    of any partners that they may ascribe [to Him]!

ٱلْبَارِئُ ٱلْمُصَوِّرُ    24 He is Allah, the Creator,

لَهُ ٱلْأَسْمَآءُ ٱلْحُسْنَىٰ    the Maker, the Former.

يُسَبِّحُ لَهُۥ مَا فِى ٱلسَّمَـٰوَٰتِ    To Him belong the Best Names.

وَٱلْأَرْضِ    Whatever there is in the heavens glorifies Him

وَهُوَ ٱلْعَزِيزُ ٱلْحَكِيمُ ۩    and [whatever there is in] the earth,

and He is the All-mighty, the All-wise.

# سُورَةُ ٱلْمُمْتَحَنَةِ    60. SŪRAT AL-MUMTAḤANAH[1]

بِسْمِ ٱللَّهِ    In the Name of Allah,

ٱلرَّحْمَـٰنِ ٱلرَّحِيمِ    the All-beneficent, the All-merciful.

يَـٰٓأَيُّهَا ٱلَّذِينَ ءَامَنُوا۟    1 O you who have faith!

لَا تَتَّخِذُوا۟ عَدُوِّى وَعَدُوَّكُمْ أَوْلِيَآءَ    Do not take My enemy and your enemy for intimates,

تُلْقُونَ إِلَيْهِم بِٱلْمَوَدَّةِ    [secretly] offering them affection

وَقَدْ كَفَرُوا۟    (for they have certainly defied

بِمَا جَآءَكُم مِّنَ ٱلْحَقِّ    whatever has come to you of the truth,

يُخْرِجُونَ ٱلرَّسُولَ وَإِيَّاكُمْ    expelling the Apostle and you,

أَن تُؤْمِنُوا۟ بِٱللَّهِ رَبِّكُمْ    because you have faith in Allah, your Lord)

إِن كُنتُمْ خَرَجْتُمْ جِهَـٰدًا فِى سَبِيلِى    if you have set out for *jihād* in My way

وَٱبْتِغَآءَ مَرْضَاتِى    and to seek My pleasure.

تُسِرُّونَ إِلَيْهِم بِٱلْمَوَدَّةِ    You secretly nourish affection for them,

وَأَنَا۠ أَعْلَمُ بِمَآ أَخْفَيْتُمْ    while I know well whatever you hide

وَمَآ أَعْلَنتُمْ    and whatever you disclose,

وَمَن يَفْعَلْهُ مِنكُمْ    and whoever among you does that

فَقَدْ ضَلَّ سَوَآءَ ٱلسَّبِيلِ ۩    has certainly strayed from the right way.

إِن يَثْقَفُوكُمْ    2 If they were to confront you

---

[1] The *sūrah* takes its name from verse 10 concerning the testing (*imtiḥān*) of new
female converts to Islam.

| | |
|---:|:---|
| يَكُونُوا۟ لَكُمْ أَعْدَآءً | they would be your enemies, |
| وَيَبْسُطُوٓا۟ إِلَيْكُمْ أَيْدِيَهُمْ | and would stretch out against you their hands |
| وَأَلْسِنَتَهُم | and their tongues |
| بِٱلسُّوٓءِ | with evil [intentions], |
| وَوَدُّوا۟ لَوْ تَكْفُرُونَ ۝ | and they are eager that you should be faithless. |
| لَن تَنفَعَكُمْ أَرْحَامُكُمْ وَلَآ أَوْلَٰدُكُمْ | 3 Your relatives and your children will not avail you |
| يَوْمَ ٱلْقِيَٰمَةِ | on the Day of Resurrection: |
| يَفْصِلُ بَيْنَكُمْ | He will separate you [from one another], |
| وَٱللَّهُ بِمَا تَعْمَلُونَ بَصِيرٌ ۝ | and Allah sees best what you do. |
| قَدْ كَانَتْ لَكُمْ أُسْوَةٌ حَسَنَةٌ | 4 There is certainly a good exemplar for you |
| فِىٓ إِبْرَٰهِيمَ | in Abraham |
| وَٱلَّذِينَ مَعَهُۥٓ | and those who were with him, |
| إِذْ قَالُوا۟ لِقَوْمِهِمْ | when they said to their own people, |
| إِنَّا بُرَءَٰٓؤُا۟ مِنكُمْ | 'Indeed we repudiate you |
| وَمِمَّا تَعْبُدُونَ مِن دُونِ ٱللَّهِ | and whatever you worship besides Allah. |
| كَفَرْنَا بِكُمْ | We disavow you, |
| وَبَدَا بَيْنَنَا وَبَيْنَكُمُ | and between you and us there has appeared |
| ٱلْعَدَٰوَةُ وَٱلْبَغْضَآءُ أَبَدًا | enmity and hate for ever, |
| حَتَّىٰ تُؤْمِنُوا۟ بِٱللَّهِ وَحْدَهُۥٓ | unless you come to have faith in Allah alone,' |
| إِلَّا قَوْلَ إِبْرَٰهِيمَ لِأَبِيهِ | except for Abraham's saying to his father, |
| لَأَسْتَغْفِرَنَّ لَكَ | 'I will surely plead forgiveness for you, |
| وَمَآ أَمْلِكُ لَكَ مِنَ ٱللَّهِ مِن شَىْءٍ | though I cannot avail you anything against Allah.' |
| رَّبَّنَا عَلَيْكَ تَوَكَّلْنَا | 'Our Lord! In You do we put our trust, |
| وَإِلَيْكَ أَنَبْنَا | and to You do we turn penitently, |
| وَإِلَيْكَ ٱلْمَصِيرُ ۝ | and toward You is the destination. |
| رَبَّنَا | 5 Our Lord! |
| لَا تَجْعَلْنَا فِتْنَةً لِّلَّذِينَ كَفَرُوا۟ | Do not make us a trial for the faithless, |
| وَٱغْفِرْ لَنَا | and forgive us. |
| رَبَّنَآ | Our Lord! |

إِنَّكَ أَنتَ ٱلْعَزِيزُ ٱلْحَكِيمُ ۝ Indeed You are the All-mighty, the All-wise.'

لَّقَدْ كَانَ لَكُمْ فِيهِمْ أُسْوَةٌ حَسَنَةٌ 6 There is certainly a good exemplar for you in them

لِّمَن كَانَ يَرْجُواْ ٱللَّهَ —for those who look forward to Allah

وَٱلْيَوْمَ ٱلْآخِرَ and the Last Day—

وَمَن يَتَوَلَّ and anyone who refuses to comply [should know that]

فَإِنَّ ٱللَّهَ هُوَ ٱلْغَنِيُّ ٱلْحَمِيدُ ۝ indeed Allah is the All-sufficient, the All-laudable.

عَسَى ٱللَّهُ أَن يَجْعَلَ 7 It may be that Allah will bring about

بَيْنَكُمْ وَبَيْنَ ٱلَّذِينَ عَادَيْتُم مِّنْهُم between you and those with whom you are at enmity

مَّوَدَّةً affection,

وَٱللَّهُ قَدِيرٌ and Allah is all-powerful,

وَٱللَّهُ غَفُورٌ رَّحِيمٌ ۝ and Allah is all-forgiving, all-merciful.

لَّا يَنْهَىٰكُمُ ٱللَّهُ عَنِ ٱلَّذِينَ 8 Allah does not forbid you in regard to those

لَمْ يُقَٰتِلُوكُمْ who did not make war against you

فِى ٱلدِّينِ on account of religion

وَلَمْ يُخْرِجُوكُم مِّن دِيَٰرِكُمْ and did not expel you from your homes,

أَن تَبَرُّوهُمْ وَتُقْسِطُوٓاْ إِلَيْهِمْ that you deal with them with kindness and justice.

إِنَّ ٱللَّهَ يُحِبُّ ٱلْمُقْسِطِينَ ۝ Indeed Allah loves the just.

إِنَّمَا يَنْهَىٰكُمُ ٱللَّهُ عَنِ ٱلَّذِينَ 9 Allah forbids you only in regard to those

قَٰتَلُوكُمْ فِى ٱلدِّينِ who made war against you on account of religion

وَأَخْرَجُوكُم مِّن دِيَٰرِكُمْ and expelled you from your homes

وَظَٰهَرُواْ عَلَىٰٓ إِخْرَاجِكُمْ and supported [others] in your expulsion,

أَن تَوَلَّوْهُمْ that you make friends with them,

وَمَن يَتَوَلَّهُمْ and whoever makes friends with them

فَأُوْلَٰٓئِكَ هُمُ ٱلظَّٰلِمُونَ ۝ —it is they who are the wrongdoers.

يَٰٓأَيُّهَا ٱلَّذِينَ ءَامَنُوٓاْ 10 O you who have faith!

إِذَا جَآءَكُمُ ٱلْمُؤْمِنَٰتُ مُهَٰجِرَٰتٍ When faithful women come to you as immigrants,[1]

فَٱمْتَحِنُوهُنَّ test them.

ٱللَّهُ أَعْلَمُ بِإِيمَٰنِهِنَّ Allah knows best [the state of] their faith.

فَإِنْ عَلِمْتُمُوهُنَّ مُؤْمِنَٰتٍ Then, if you ascertain them to be faithful women,

---

[1] That is, as fugitives.

فَلَا تَرْجِعُوهُنَّ إِلَى ٱلْكُفَّارِ    do not send them back to the faithless.

لَا هُنَّ حِلٌّ لَّهُمْ    They[1] are not lawful for them,[2]

وَلَا هُمْ يَحِلُّونَ لَهُنَّ    nor are they[3] lawful for them.[4]

وَءَاتُوهُم مَّآ أَنفَقُوا    And give them[5] what they have spent [for them].[6]

وَلَا جُنَاحَ عَلَيْكُمْ أَن تَنكِحُوهُنَّ    There is no sin upon you in marrying them

إِذَآ ءَاتَيْتُمُوهُنَّ أُجُورَهُنَّ    when you have given them their dowries.

وَلَا تُمْسِكُوا    Do not hold on

بِعِصَمِ ٱلْكَوَافِرِ    to [conjugal] ties with faithless women.

وَسْـَٔلُوا مَآ أَنفَقْتُمْ    Ask [the infidels] for what you have spent,

وَلْيَسْـَٔلُوا مَآ أَنفَقُوا    and let the faithless ask for what they have spent.[7]

ذَٰلِكُمْ حُكْمُ ٱللَّهِ    That is the judgment of Allah;

يَحْكُمُ بَيْنَكُمْ    He judges between you;

وَٱللَّهُ عَلِيمٌ حَكِيمٌ ۝    and Allah is all-knowing, all-wise.

وَإِن فَاتَكُمْ شَىْءٌ مِّنْ أَزْوَٰجِكُمْ    11 If anything pertaining to your wives in not reclaimed

إِلَى ٱلْكُفَّارِ    from the faithless[8]

فَعَاقَبْتُمْ    and then you have your turn,

فَـَٔاتُوا ٱلَّذِينَ ذَهَبَتْ أَزْوَٰجُهُم    then give to those whose wives have left

مِّثْلَ مَآ أَنفَقُوا    the like of what they have spent,

وَٱتَّقُوا ٱللَّهَ    and be wary of Allah

ٱلَّذِىٓ أَنتُم بِهِۦ مُؤْمِنُونَ ۝    in whom you have faith.

يَٰٓأَيُّهَا ٱلنَّبِىُّ    12 O Prophet!

إِذَا جَآءَكَ ٱلْمُؤْمِنَٰتُ    If faithful women come to *you*,

يُبَايِعْنَكَ    to take the oath of allegiance to *you*, [pledging]

عَلَىٰٓ أَن لَّا يُشْرِكْنَ بِٱللَّهِ شَيْـًٔا    that they shall not ascribe any partners to Allah,

---

[1] That is, faithful women.

[2] That is, for infidel men.

[3] That is, infidel men.

[4] That is, for faithful women.

[5] The infidel men who were their husbands before.

[6] That is, the amount of their dowry.

[7] That is, the dowry given to the women who were formerly their wives.

[8] That is, if their dowry is not paid by the infidels. Or 'If any of your wives goes away toward the infidels.'

| | |
|---|---|
| وَلَا يَسْرِقْنَ وَلَا يَزْنِينَ | that they shall not steal, nor commit adultery, |
| وَلَا يَقْتُلْنَ أَوْلَٰدَهُنَّ | nor kill their children, |
| وَلَا يَأْتِينَ بِبُهْتَٰنٍ | nor utter any slander |
| يَفْتَرِينَهُۥ بَيْنَ أَيْدِيهِنَّ وَأَرْجُلِهِنَّ | that they may have intentionally fabricated, |
| وَلَا يَعْصِينَكَ فِى مَعْرُوفٍ | nor disobey *you* in what is right, |
| فَبَايِعْهُنَّ | then *accept* their allegiance, |
| وَٱسْتَغْفِرْ لَهُنَّ ٱللَّهَ | and *plead* for them to Allah for forgiveness. |
| إِنَّ ٱللَّهَ غَفُورٌ رَّحِيمٌ ﴿١٢﴾ | Indeed Allah is all-forgiving, all-merciful |
| يَٰٓأَيُّهَا ٱلَّذِينَ ءَامَنُوا | 13 O you who have faith! |
| لَا تَتَوَلَّوْا قَوْمًا | Do not befriend a people |
| غَضِبَ ٱللَّهُ عَلَيْهِمْ | at whom Allah is wrathful: |
| قَدْ يَئِسُوا مِنَ ٱلْءَاخِرَةِ | they have despaired of the Hereafter, |
| كَمَا يَئِسَ ٱلْكُفَّارُ | just as the faithless have despaired |
| مِنْ أَصْحَٰبِ ٱلْقُبُورِ ﴿١٣﴾ | of the occupants of the graves. |

## سُورَةُ الصَّفِّ    61. SŪRAT AL-ṢAFF[1]

| | |
|---|---|
| بِسْمِ ٱللَّهِ | In the Name of Allah, |
| ٱلرَّحْمَٰنِ ٱلرَّحِيمِ | the All-beneficent, the All-merciful. |

| | |
|---|---|
| سَبَّحَ لِلَّهِ مَا فِى ٱلسَّمَٰوَٰتِ | 1 Whatever there is in the heavens glorifies Allah |
| وَمَا فِى ٱلْأَرْضِ | and whatever there is in the earth, |
| وَهُوَ ٱلْعَزِيزُ ٱلْحَكِيمُ ﴿١﴾ | and He is the All-mighty, the All-wise |
| يَٰٓأَيُّهَا ٱلَّذِينَ ءَامَنُوا | 2 O you who have faith! |
| لِمَ تَقُولُونَ مَا لَا تَفْعَلُونَ ﴿٢﴾ | Why do you say what you do not do? |
| كَبُرَ مَقْتًا عِندَ ٱللَّهِ | 3 It is greatly outrageous to Allah |
| أَن تَقُولُوا مَا لَا تَفْعَلُونَ ﴿٣﴾ | that you should say what you do not do. |
| إِنَّ ٱللَّهَ يُحِبُّ ٱلَّذِينَ | 4 Indeed Allah loves those |
| يُقَٰتِلُونَ فِى سَبِيلِهِۦ صَفًّا | who fight in His way in ranks, |

---

[1] The *sūrah* takes its name from verse 4, in which the word *ṣaff* (ranks) occurs.

كَأَنَّهُم بُنْيَـٰنٌ مَّرْصُوصٌ ۝   as if they were a compact structure.

وَإِذْ قَالَ مُوسَىٰ لِقَوْمِهِۦ 5 When Moses said to his people,

يَـٰقَوْمِ لِمَ تُؤْذُونَنِى   'O my people! Why do you torment me,

وَقَد تَّعْلَمُونَ   when you certainly know

أَنِّى رَسُولُ ٱللَّهِ إِلَيْكُمْ   that I am Allah's apostle to you?'

فَلَمَّا زَاغُوٓا۟   So when they swerved [from the right path]

أَزَاغَ ٱللَّهُ قُلُوبَهُمْ   Allah made their hearts swerve,

وَٱللَّهُ لَا يَهْدِى ٱلْقَوْمَ ٱلْفَـٰسِقِينَ ۝   and Allah does not guide the transgressing lot.

وَإِذْ قَالَ عِيسَى ٱبْنُ مَرْيَمَ 6 And when Jesus son of Mary said,

يَـٰبَنِىٓ إِسْرَٰٓءِيلَ   'O Children of Israel!

إِنِّى رَسُولُ ٱللَّهِ إِلَيْكُم   Indeed I am the apostle of Allah to you,

مُّصَدِّقًا لِّمَا بَيْنَ يَدَىَّ مِنَ ٱلتَّوْرَىٰةِ   to confirm what is before me of the Torah,

وَمُبَشِّرًۢا بِرَسُولٍ   and to give the good news of an apostle

يَأْتِى مِنۢ بَعْدِى   who will come after me,

ٱسْمُهُۥٓ أَحْمَدُ   whose name is Aḥmad.'

فَلَمَّا جَآءَهُم بِٱلْبَيِّنَـٰتِ   Yet when he brought them manifest proofs,

قَالُوا۟ هَـٰذَا سِحْرٌ مُّبِينٌ ۝   they said, 'This is plain magic.'

وَمَنْ أَظْلَمُ مِمَّنِ 7 And who is a greater wrongdoer than him

ٱفْتَرَىٰ عَلَى ٱللَّهِ ٱلْكَذِبَ   who fabricates falsehoods against Allah,

وَهُوَ يُدْعَىٰٓ إِلَى ٱلْإِسْلَـٰمِ   while he is being summoned to Islam?

وَٱللَّهُ لَا يَهْدِى ٱلْقَوْمَ ٱلظَّـٰلِمِينَ ۝   And Allah does not guide the wrongdoing lot.

يُرِيدُونَ لِيُطْفِـُٔوا۟ نُورَ ٱللَّهِ 8 They desire to put out the light of Allah

بِأَفْوَٰهِهِمْ   with their mouths,

وَٱللَّهُ مُتِمُّ نُورِهِۦ   but Allah shall perfect His light

وَلَوْ كَرِهَ ٱلْكَـٰفِرُونَ ۝   though the faithless should be averse.

هُوَ ٱلَّذِىٓ أَرْسَلَ رَسُولَهُۥ 9 It is He who has sent His Apostle

بِٱلْهُدَىٰ   with the guidance

وَدِينِ ٱلْحَقِّ   and the religion of truth

لِيُظْهِرَهُۥ عَلَى ٱلدِّينِ كُلِّهِۦ   that He may make it prevail over all religions

وَلَوْ كَرِهَ ٱلْمُشْرِكُونَ ۝   though the polytheists should be averse.

يَـٰٓأَيُّهَا ٱلَّذِينَ ءَامَنُوا۟  10 O you who have faith!

هَلْ أَدُلُّكُمْ عَلَىٰ تِجَـٰرَةٍ  Shall I show you a deal

تُنجِيكُم مِّنْ عَذَابٍ أَلِيمٍ  that will deliver you from a painful punishment?

تُؤْمِنُونَ بِٱللَّهِ وَرَسُولِهِۦ  11 Have faith in Allah and His Apostle,

وَتُجَـٰهِدُونَ فِى سَبِيلِ ٱللَّهِ  and wage *jihād* in the way of Allah

بِأَمْوَٰلِكُمْ وَأَنفُسِكُمْ  with your possessions and your persons.

ذَٰلِكُمْ خَيْرٌ لَّكُمْ  That is better for you,

إِن كُنتُمْ تَعْلَمُونَ  should you know.

يَغْفِرْ لَكُمْ ذُنُوبَكُمْ  12 He shall forgive you your sins

وَيُدْخِلْكُمْ جَنَّـٰتٍ  and admit you into gardens

تَجْرِى مِن تَحْتِهَا ٱلْأَنْهَـٰرُ  with streams running in them,

وَمَسَـٰكِنَ طَيِّبَةً  and into good dwellings

فِى جَنَّـٰتِ عَدْنٍ  in the Gardens of Eden.

ذَٰلِكَ ٱلْفَوْزُ ٱلْعَظِيمُ  That is the great success.

وَأُخْرَىٰ تُحِبُّونَهَا  13 And other [blessings] you love:

نَصْرٌ مِّنَ ٱللَّهِ وَفَتْحٌ قَرِيبٌ  help from Allah and a victory near at hand.

وَبَشِّرِ ٱلْمُؤْمِنِينَ  And *give* good news to the faithful.

يَـٰٓأَيُّهَا ٱلَّذِينَ ءَامَنُوا۟  14 O you who have faith!

كُونُوٓا۟ أَنصَارَ ٱللَّهِ  Be Allah's helpers,

كَمَا قَالَ عِيسَى ٱبْنُ مَرْيَمَ  just as Jesus son of Mary said

لِلْحَوَارِيِّـۧنَ  to the disciples,

مَنْ أَنصَارِىٓ إِلَى ٱللَّهِ  'Who will be my helpers for Allah's sake?'

قَالَ ٱلْحَوَارِيُّونَ  The Disciples said,

نَحْنُ أَنصَارُ ٱللَّهِ  'We will be Allah's helpers!'

فَـَٔامَنَت طَّآئِفَةٌ مِّنۢ بَنِىٓ إِسْرَٰٓءِيلَ  So a group of the Children of Israel believed,

وَكَفَرَت طَّآئِفَةٌ  and a group disbelieved.

فَأَيَّدْنَا ٱلَّذِينَ ءَامَنُوا۟  Then We strengthened the faithful

عَلَىٰ عَدُوِّهِمْ  against their enemies,

فَأَصْبَحُوا۟ ظَـٰهِرِينَ  and they became the dominant ones.

سُورَةُ الجُمُعَةِ

# 62. SŪRAT AL-JUMU‘AH[1]

بِسۡمِ ٱللَّهِ
ٱلرَّحۡمَٰنِ ٱلرَّحِيمِ

In the Name of Allah,
the All-beneficent, the All-merciful.

يُسَبِّحُ لِلَّهِ مَا فِى ٱلسَّمَٰوَٰتِ

وَمَا فِى ٱلۡأَرۡضِ

ٱلۡمَلِكِ ٱلۡقُدُّوسِ

ٱلۡعَزِيزِ ٱلۡحَكِيمِ ۝

1 Whatever there is in the heavens glorifies Allah
     and whatever there is in the earth,
     the Sovereign, the All-holy,
     the All-mighty, the All-wise.

هُوَ ٱلَّذِى بَعَثَ فِى ٱلۡأُمِّيِّۧنَ

رَسُولًا مِّنۡهُمۡ

يَتۡلُوا۟ عَلَيۡهِمۡ ءَايَٰتِهِۦ وَيُزَكِّيهِمۡ

وَيُعَلِّمُهُمُ ٱلۡكِتَٰبَ وَٱلۡحِكۡمَةَ

وَإِن كَانُوا۟ مِن قَبۡلُ

لَفِى ضَلَٰلٍ مُّبِينٍ ۝

2 It is He who sent to the unlettered [people]
     an apostle from among themselves,
     to recite to them His signs, to purify them,
     and to teach them the Book and wisdom,
     and earlier they had indeed been
     in manifest error.

وَءَاخَرِينَ مِنۡهُمۡ

لَمَّا يَلۡحَقُوا۟ بِهِمۡ

وَهُوَ ٱلۡعَزِيزُ ٱلۡحَكِيمُ ۝

3 And to others from among them [as well]
     who have not yet joined them.
     And He is the All-mighty, the All-wise.

ذَٰلِكَ فَضۡلُ ٱللَّهِ

يُؤۡتِيهِ مَن يَشَآءُ

وَٱللَّهُ ذُو ٱلۡفَضۡلِ ٱلۡعَظِيمِ ۝

4 That is Allah's grace
     which He grants to whomever He wishes,
     and Allah is dispenser of a great grace.

مَثَلُ ٱلَّذِينَ حُمِّلُوا۟ ٱلتَّوۡرَٰةَ

ثُمَّ لَمۡ يَحۡمِلُوهَا

كَمَثَلِ ٱلۡحِمَارِ يَحۡمِلُ أَسۡفَارَۢا

بِئۡسَ مَثَلُ ٱلۡقَوۡمِ ٱلَّذِينَ

كَذَّبُوا۟ بِـَٔايَٰتِ ٱللَّهِ

وَٱللَّهُ لَا يَهۡدِى ٱلۡقَوۡمَ ٱلظَّٰلِمِينَ ۝

5 The example of those who were charged with the Torah,
     then failed to carry it,
     is that of an ass carrying books.
     Evil is the example of the people who
     deny Allah's signs,
     and Allah does not guide the wrongdoing lot.

قُلۡ يَٰٓأَيُّهَا ٱلَّذِينَ هَادُوٓا۟

6 *Say,* 'O Jews!

---

[1] The *sūrah* in named after the *Jumu‘ah* (Friday) prayer mentioned in verse 9.

إِن زَعَمْتُمْ أَنَّكُمْ أَوْلِيَآءُ لِلَّهِ
If you claim that you are Allah's favourites,

مِن دُونِ ٱلنَّاسِ
to the exclusion of other people,

فَتَمَنَّوُاْ ٱلْمَوْتَ
then long for death,

إِن كُنتُمْ صَٰدِقِينَ ۞
should you be truthful.'

وَلَا يَتَمَنَّوْنَهُۥٓ أَبَدًۢا 7
7 Yet they will never long for it,

بِمَا قَدَّمَتْ أَيْدِيهِمْ
because of what their hands have sent ahead,

وَٱللَّهُ عَلِيمٌۢ بِٱلظَّٰلِمِينَ ۞
and Allah knows best the wrongdoers.

قُلْ إِنَّ ٱلْمَوْتَ ٱلَّذِى تَفِرُّونَ مِنْهُ 8
8 Say, 'Indeed the death that you flee

فَإِنَّهُۥ مُلَٰقِيكُمْ
will indeed encounter you.

ثُمَّ تُرَدُّونَ
Then you will be returned

إِلَىٰ عَٰلِمِ ٱلْغَيْبِ وَٱلشَّهَٰدَةِ
to the Knower of the sensible and the Unseen,

فَيُنَبِّئُكُم
and He will inform you

بِمَا كُنتُمْ تَعْمَلُونَ ۞
about what you used to do.'

يَٰٓأَيُّهَا ٱلَّذِينَ ءَامَنُوٓاْ 9
9 O you who have faith!

إِذَا نُودِىَ لِلصَّلَوٰةِ مِن يَوْمِ ٱلْجُمُعَةِ
When the call is made for prayer on Friday,

فَٱسْعَوْاْ إِلَىٰ ذِكْرِ ٱللَّهِ
hurry toward the remembrance of Allah,

وَذَرُواْ ٱلْبَيْعَ
and leave all business.

ذَٰلِكُمْ خَيْرٌ لَّكُمْ
That is better for you,

إِن كُنتُمْ تَعْلَمُونَ ۞
should you know.

فَإِذَا قُضِيَتِ ٱلصَّلَوٰةُ 10
10 And when the prayer is finished

فَٱنتَشِرُواْ فِى ٱلْأَرْضِ
disperse through the land

وَٱبْتَغُواْ مِن فَضْلِ ٱللَّهِ
and seek Allah's grace,

وَٱذْكُرُواْ ٱللَّهَ كَثِيرًا
and remember Allah greatly

لَّعَلَّكُمْ تُفْلِحُونَ ۞
so that you may be felicitous.

وَإِذَا رَأَوْاْ تِجَٰرَةً أَوْ لَهْوًا 11
11 When they sight a deal or a diversion,

ٱنفَضُّوٓاْ إِلَيْهَا
they scatter off towards it

وَتَرَكُوكَ قَآئِمًا
and leave *you* standing!

قُلْ مَا عِندَ ٱللَّهِ
Say, 'What is with Allah

خَيْرٌ مِّنَ ٱللَّهْوِ وَمِنَ ٱلتِّجَٰرَةِ
is better than diversion and dealing,

وَٱللَّهُ خَيْرُ ٱلرَّٰزِقِينَ ۞
and Allah is the best of providers.'

سُورَةُ الْمُنَافِقُونَ     63. SŪRAT AL-MUNĀFIQŪN[1]

بِسْمِ ٱللَّهِ        In the Name of Allah,

ٱلرَّحْمَٰنِ ٱلرَّحِيمِ     the All-beneficent, the All-merciful.

إِذَا جَآءَكَ ٱلْمُنَافِقُونَ    1 When the hypocrites come to *you*

قَالُوا نَشْهَدُ        they say, 'We bear witness

إِنَّكَ لَرَسُولُ ٱللَّهِ      that *you* are indeed the apostle of Allah.'

وَٱللَّهُ يَعْلَمُ إِنَّكَ لَرَسُولُهُ   Allah knows that *you* are indeed His Apostle,

وَٱللَّهُ يَشْهَدُ        and Allah bears witness that

إِنَّ ٱلْمُنَافِقِينَ لَكَٰذِبُونَ ۝    the hypocrites are indeed liars.

ٱتَّخَذُوٓا أَيْمَٰنَهُمْ جُنَّةً    2 They make a shield of their oaths,

فَصَدُّوا عَن سَبِيلِ ٱللَّهِ    and bar from the way of Allah.

إِنَّهُمْ سَآءَ مَا كَانُوا يَعْمَلُونَ ۝   Evil indeed is what they used to do.

ذَٰلِكَ بِأَنَّهُمْ ءَامَنُوا ثُمَّ كَفَرُوا   3 That is because they believed and then disbelieved,

فَطُبِعَ عَلَىٰ قُلُوبِهِمْ     so their hearts were sealed.

فَهُمْ لَا يَفْقَهُونَ ۝ ٭     Hence they do not understand.

وَإِذَا رَأَيْتَهُمْ تُعْجِبُكَ أَجْسَامُهُمْ   4 When you see them, their bodies impress you,

وَإِن يَقُولُوا تَسْمَعْ لِقَوْلِهِمْ   and if they speak, *you* listen to their speech.

كَأَنَّهُمْ خُشُبٌ مُّسَنَّدَةٌ    Yet they are like dry logs set reclining [against a wall].

يَحْسَبُونَ كُلَّ صَيْحَةٍ عَلَيْهِمْ   They suppose every cry is directed against them.

هُمُ ٱلْعَدُوُّ فَٱحْذَرْهُمْ    They are the enemy, so beware of them.

قَٰتَلَهُمُ ٱللَّهُ أَنَّىٰ يُؤْفَكُونَ ۝   May Allah assail them, where do they stray?!

وَإِذَا قِيلَ لَهُمْ تَعَالَوْا    5 When they are told, 'Come,

يَسْتَغْفِرْ لَكُمْ رَسُولُ ٱللَّهِ   that Allah's Apostle may plead for forgiveness for you,'

لَوَّوْا رُءُوسَهُمْ       they twist their heads,

وَرَأَيْتَهُمْ يَصُدُّونَ وَهُم مُّسْتَكْبِرُونَ ۝   and *you* see them turn away while they are disdainful.

سَوَآءٌ عَلَيْهِمْ       6 It is the same for them

---

[1] The *sūrah* takes its name from its main topic, the hypocrites (*munāfiqūn*).

أَسْتَغْفَرْتَ لَهُمْ
whether *you* plead for forgiveness for them,

أَمْ لَمْ تَسْتَغْفِرْ هُمْ
or do not plead for forgiveness for them:

لَن يَغْفِرَ ٱللَّهُ هُمْ
Allah will never forgive them.

إِنَّ ٱللَّهَ لَا يَهْدِى ٱلْقَوْمَ ٱلْفَٰسِقِينَ ۝
Indeed Allah does not guide the transgressing lot.

هُمُ ٱلَّذِينَ يَقُولُونَ لَا تُنفِقُواْ
7 They are the ones who say, 'Do not spend

عَلَىٰ مَنْ عِندَ رَسُولِ ٱللَّهِ
on those who are with the Apostle of Allah

حَتَّىٰ يَنفَضُّواْ
until they scatter off.'

وَلِلَّهِ خَزَآئِنُ ٱلسَّمَٰوَٰتِ
Yet to Allah belong the treasuries of the heavens

وَٱلْأَرْضِ
and the earth,

وَلَٰكِنَّ ٱلْمُنَٰفِقِينَ لَا يَفْقَهُونَ ۝
but the hypocrites do not understand.

يَقُولُونَ لَئِن رَّجَعْنَآ إِلَى ٱلْمَدِينَةِ
8 They say, 'When we return to the city,

لَيُخْرِجَنَّ ٱلْأَعَزُّ مِنْهَا ٱلْأَذَلَّ
the mighty will surely expel the abased from it.'[1]

وَلِلَّهِ ٱلْعِزَّةُ وَلِرَسُولِهِۦ
Yet all might belongs to Allah and His Apostle,

وَلِلْمُؤْمِنِينَ
and the faithful,

وَلَٰكِنَّ ٱلْمُنَٰفِقِينَ لَا يَعْلَمُونَ ۝
but the hypocrites do not know.

يَٰٓأَيُّهَا ٱلَّذِينَ ءَامَنُواْ
9 O you who have faith!

لَا تُلْهِكُمْ أَمْوَٰلُكُمْ وَلَآ أَوْلَٰدُكُمْ
Do not let your possessions and children distract you

عَن ذِكْرِ ٱللَّهِ
from the remembrance of Allah,

وَمَن يَفْعَلْ ذَٰلِكَ
and whoever does that

فَأُوْلَٰٓئِكَ هُمُ ٱلْخَٰسِرُونَ ۝
—it is they who are the losers.

وَأَنفِقُواْ مِن مَّا رَزَقْنَٰكُم
10 Spend from what We have provided you

مِّن قَبْلِ أَن يَأْتِىَ أَحَدَكُمُ ٱلْمَوْتُ
before death comes to any of you,

فَيَقُولَ رَبِّ
whereat he will say, 'My Lord,

لَوْلَآ أَخَّرْتَنِىٓ إِلَىٰٓ أَجَلٍ قَرِيبٍ
if only You had respited me for a short time

فَأَصَّدَّقَ
so that I could give charity

وَأَكُن مِّنَ ٱلصَّٰلِحِينَ ۝
and become one of the righteous!'

وَلَن يُؤَخِّرَ ٱللَّهُ نَفْسًا
11 But Allah shall never respite a soul

إِذَا جَآءَ أَجَلُهَا
when its time has come,

وَٱللَّهُ خَبِيرٌۢ بِمَا تَعْمَلُونَ ۝
and Allah is well aware of what you do.

---

[1] Or, 'the mighty will surely expel the weak from it.'

# سُورَةُ التَّغَابُن ‏ 64. SŪRAT AL-TAGHĀBUN[1]

بِسۡمِ ٱللَّهِ ‏ In the Name of Allah,

ٱلرَّحۡمَٰنِ ٱلرَّحِيمِ ‏ the All-beneficent, the All-merciful.

يُسَبِّحُ لِلَّهِ مَا فِي ٱلسَّمَٰوَٰتِ ‏ 1 Whatever there is in the heavens glorifies Allah

وَمَا فِي ٱلۡأَرۡضِ ‏ and whatever there is in the earth.

لَهُ ٱلۡمُلۡكُ ‏ To Him belongs all sovereignty

وَلَهُ ٱلۡحَمۡدُ ‏ and to Him belongs all praise,

وَهُوَ عَلَىٰ كُلِّ شَيۡءٍ قَدِيرٌ ۝ ‏ and He has power over all things.

هُوَ ٱلَّذِي خَلَقَكُمۡ ‏ 2 It is He who created you.

فَمِنكُمۡ كَافِرٌ ‏ Then some of you are faithless

وَمِنكُم مُّؤۡمِنٌ ‏ and some of you are faithful,

وَٱللَّهُ بِمَا تَعۡمَلُونَ بَصِيرٌ ۝ ‏ and Allah sees best what you do.

خَلَقَ ٱلسَّمَٰوَٰتِ وَٱلۡأَرۡضَ بِٱلۡحَقِّ ‏ 3 He created the heavens and the earth with the truth,

وَصَوَّرَكُمۡ فَأَحۡسَنَ صُوَرَكُمۡ ‏ and He formed you and perfected your forms,

وَإِلَيۡهِ ٱلۡمَصِيرُ ۝ ‏ and toward Him is the destination.

يَعۡلَمُ مَا فِي ٱلسَّمَٰوَٰتِ وَٱلۡأَرۡضِ ‏ 4 He knows whatever there is in the heavens and the earth,

وَيَعۡلَمُ مَا تُسِرُّونَ ‏ and He knows whatever you hide

وَمَا تُعۡلِنُونَ ‏ and whatever you disclose,

وَٱللَّهُ عَلِيمٌ بِذَاتِ ٱلصُّدُورِ ۝ ‏ and Allah knows best what is in the breasts.

أَلَمۡ يَأۡتِكُمۡ نَبَؤُاْ ‏ 5 Has there not come to you the account

ٱلَّذِينَ كَفَرُواْ مِن قَبۡلُ ‏ of those who were faithless before?

فَذَاقُواْ وَبَالَ أَمۡرِهِمۡ ‏ They tasted the evil consequences of their conduct,

وَلَهُمۡ عَذَابٌ أَلِيمٌ ۝ ‏ and there is a painful punishment for them.

ذَٰلِكَ بِأَنَّهُۥ كَانَت تَّأۡتِيهِمۡ رُسُلُهُم ‏ 6 That was because their apostles used to bring them

بِٱلۡبَيِّنَٰتِ ‏ manifest proofs,

---

[1] The *sūrah* takes its name from "the day of dispossession" (*yawm al-taghābun*) mentioned in verse 9.

فَقَالُوٓا۟　but they said,

أَبَشَرٌ يَهْدُونَنَا　'Shall humans be our guides?!'

فَكَفَرُوا۟ وَتَوَلَّوا۟　So they disbelieved and turned away,

وَٱسْتَغْنَى ٱللَّهُ　and Allah was in no need [of their faith]

وَٱللَّهُ غَنِىٌّ حَمِيدٌ ۝　and Allah is all-sufficient, all-laudable.

زَعَمَ ٱلَّذِينَ كَفَرُوٓا۟ أَن لَّن يُبْعَثُوا۟　7 The faithless claim that they will not be resurrected.

قُلْ بَلَىٰ وَرَبِّى　*Say*, 'Yes, by my Lord,

لَتُبْعَثُنَّ　you will surely be resurrected;

ثُمَّ لَتُنَبَّؤُنَّ بِمَا عَمِلْتُمْ　then you will surely be informed of what you did,

وَذَٰلِكَ عَلَى ٱللَّهِ يَسِيرٌ ۝　and that is easy for Allah.'

فَـَٔامِنُوا۟ بِٱللَّهِ وَرَسُولِهِ　8 So have faith in Allah and His Apostle

وَٱلنُّورِ ٱلَّذِىٓ أَنزَلْنَا　and the light which We have sent down,

وَٱللَّهُ بِمَا تَعْمَلُونَ خَبِيرٌ ۝　and Allah is well aware of what you do.

يَوْمَ يَجْمَعُكُمْ　9 The day when He will gather you

لِيَوْمِ ٱلْجَمْعِ　for the Day of Gathering,

ذَٰلِكَ يَوْمُ ٱلتَّغَابُنِ　that will be a day of dispossession.[1]

وَمَن يُؤْمِنۢ بِٱللَّهِ وَيَعْمَلْ صَٰلِحًا　And whoever has faith in Allah and acts righteously,

يُكَفِّرْ عَنْهُ سَيِّـَٔاتِهِ　He shall absolve him of his misdeeds

وَيُدْخِلْهُ جَنَّٰتٍ　and admit him into gardens

تَجْرِى مِن تَحْتِهَا ٱلْأَنْهَٰرُ　with streams running in them,

خَٰلِدِينَ فِيهَآ أَبَدًا　to remain in them forever.

ذَٰلِكَ ٱلْفَوْزُ ٱلْعَظِيمُ ۝　That is the great success.

وَٱلَّذِينَ كَفَرُوا۟ وَكَذَّبُوا۟ بِـَٔايَٰتِنَآ　10 But as for those who are faithless and deny Our signs,

أُو۟لَٰٓئِكَ أَصْحَٰبُ ٱلنَّارِ　—they shall be the inmates of the Fire,

خَٰلِدِينَ فِيهَا　to remain in it [forever],

وَبِئْسَ ٱلْمَصِيرُ ۝　and it is an evil destination.

---

[1] That is, the day on which the faithless will find themselves dispossessed of their place in paradise and find that their pursuit of ephemeral gains has landed them in hell. The faithful will settle in their places in paradise, happy to have been saved from occupying what would have been their place in hell if they did not have faith in Allah and had not performed righteous deeds.

مَآ أَصَابَ مِن مُّصِيبَةٍ إِلَّا بِإِذۡنِ ٱللَّهِ 11 No affliction visits [anyone] except by Allah's leave.

وَمَن يُؤۡمِنۢ بِٱللَّهِ     Whoever has faith in Allah,

يَهۡدِ قَلۡبَهُۥ     He guides his heart,

وَٱللَّهُ بِكُلِّ شَىۡءٍ عَلِيمٌ     and Allah has knowledge of all things.

وَأَطِيعُوا۟ ٱللَّهَ وَأَطِيعُوا۟ ٱلرَّسُولَ 12 Obey Allah and obey the Apostle;

فَإِن تَوَلَّيۡتُمۡ     but if you turn away,

فَإِنَّمَا عَلَىٰ رَسُولِنَا     then Our Apostle's duty is only

ٱلۡبَلَٰغُ ٱلۡمُبِينُ     to communicate in clear terms.

ٱللَّهُ لَآ إِلَٰهَ إِلَّا هُوَ 13 Allah—there is no god except Him—

وَعَلَى ٱللَّهِ فَلۡيَتَوَكَّلِ ٱلۡمُؤۡمِنُونَ     in Allah let all the faithful put their trust.

يَٰٓأَيُّهَا ٱلَّذِينَ ءَامَنُوٓا۟ 14 O you who have faith!

إِنَّ مِنۡ أَزۡوَٰجِكُمۡ وَأَوۡلَٰدِكُمۡ     Indeed among your spouses and children

عَدُوًّا لَّكُمۡ     you have enemies;

فَٱحۡذَرُوهُمۡ     so beware of them.

وَإِن تَعۡفُوا۟ وَتَصۡفَحُوا۟ وَتَغۡفِرُوا۟     And if you excuse, forbear and forgive,

فَإِنَّ ٱللَّهَ غَفُورٌ رَّحِيمٌ     then Allah is indeed all-forgiving, all-merciful.

إِنَّمَآ أَمۡوَٰلُكُمۡ وَأَوۡلَٰدُكُمۡ فِتۡنَةٌ 15 Rather your possessions and children are a trial,

وَٱللَّهُ عِندَهُۥٓ أَجۡرٌ عَظِيمٌ     and Allah—with Him is a great reward!

فَٱتَّقُوا۟ ٱللَّهَ مَا ٱسۡتَطَعۡتُمۡ 16 So be wary of Allah, as far as you can,

وَٱسۡمَعُوا۟ وَأَطِيعُوا۟     and listen and obey,

وَأَنفِقُوا۟     and spend [in the way of Allah];

خَيۡرًا لِّأَنفُسِكُمۡ     that is better for yourselves.

وَمَن يُوقَ شُحَّ نَفۡسِهِۦ     Those who are saved from their own greed

فَأُو۟لَٰٓئِكَ هُمُ ٱلۡمُفۡلِحُونَ     —it is they who are the felicitous.

إِن تُقۡرِضُوا۟ ٱللَّهَ قَرۡضًا حَسَنًا 17 If you lend Allah a good loan,

يُضَٰعِفۡهُ لَكُمۡ وَيَغۡفِرۡ لَكُمۡ     He shall multiply it for you and forgive you,

وَٱللَّهُ شَكُورٌ حَلِيمٌ     and Allah is all-appreciative, all-forbearing,

عَٰلِمُ ٱلۡغَيۡبِ وَٱلشَّهَٰدَةِ 18 Knower of the sensible and the Unseen,

ٱلۡعَزِيزُ ٱلۡحَكِيمُ     the All-mighty, the All-wise.

# سُورَةُ الطّلَاقِ     65. SŪRAT AL-ṬALĀQ[1]

بِسْمِ اللَّهِ    In the Name of Allah,

الرَّحْمَٰنِ الرَّحِيمِ    the All-beneficent, the All-merciful.

يَٰأَيُّهَا النَّبِىُّ 1 O Prophet!

إِذَا طَلَّقْتُمُ النِّسَاءَ When you[2] divorce women,

فَطَلِّقُوهُنَّ لِعِدَّتِهِنَّ divorce them at [the conclusion of] their term[3]

وَأَحْصُوا الْعِدَّةَ and calculate the term,

وَاتَّقُوا اللَّهَ رَبَّكُمْ and be wary of Allah, your Lord.

لَا تُخْرِجُوهُنَّ مِنْ بُيُوتِهِنَّ Do not turn them out from their houses,

وَلَا يَخْرُجْنَ nor shall they go out,

إِلَّا أَن يَأْتِينَ بِفَٰحِشَةٍ مُّبَيِّنَةٍ unless they commit a gross[4] indecency.[5]

وَتِلْكَ حُدُودُ اللَّهِ These are Allah's bounds,

وَمَن يَتَعَدَّ حُدُودَ اللَّهِ and whoever transgresses the bounds of Allah

فَقَدْ ظَلَمَ نَفْسَهُ certainly wrongs himself.

لَا تَدْرِى You never know

لَعَلَّ اللَّهَ يُحْدِثُ بَعْدَ ذَٰلِكَ أَمْرًا ۞ maybe Allah will bring off something new later on.

فَإِذَا بَلَغْنَ أَجَلَهُنَّ 2 Then, when they have completed their term,

فَأَمْسِكُوهُنَّ بِمَعْرُوفٍ either retain them honourably

أَوْ فَارِقُوهُنَّ بِمَعْرُوفٍ or separate from them honourably,

وَأَشْهِدُوا ذَوَىْ عَدْلٍ and take the witness of two fair men

مِّنكُمْ from among yourselves,

وَأَقِيمُوا الشَّهَٰدَةَ لِلَّهِ and bear witness for the sake of Allah.

---

[1] The *sūrah* takes its name from verse 1 concerning divorce (*ṭalāq*).

[2] That is, Muslim men.

[3] See 2:227-233, 33:49,

[4] Or 'proven,' according to an alternative reading (*mubayyanah*), instead of *mubayyinah*).

[5] That is, adultery, lesbianism, theft or revilement of the husband and his family. (See *Tafsīr al-Ṣāfī*, Ṭabarī)

ذَٰلِكُمْ يُوعَظُ بِهِۦ  To [comply with] this is advised

مَن كَانَ يُؤْمِنُ بِٱللَّهِ  whoever believes in Allah

وَٱلْيَوْمِ ٱلْأَخِرِ  and the Last Day.

وَمَن يَتَّقِ ٱللَّهَ  And whoever is wary of Allah,

يَجْعَل لَّهُۥ مَخْرَجًا ۝  He shall make a way out for him,

3  وَيَرْزُقْهُ  and provide for him

مِنْ حَيْثُ لَا يَحْتَسِبُ  from whence he does not reckon.

وَمَن يَتَوَكَّلْ عَلَى ٱللَّهِ  And whoever puts his trust in Allah,

فَهُوَ حَسْبُهُۥٓ  He will suffice him.

إِنَّ ٱللَّهَ بَٰلِغُ أَمْرِهِۦ  Indeed Allah carries through His command.

قَدْ جَعَلَ ٱللَّهُ لِكُلِّ شَىْءٍ قَدْرًا ۝  Certainly Allah has set a measure for everything.

4 وَٱلَّٰٓـِٔى  As for those

يَئِسْنَ مِنَ ٱلْمَحِيضِ مِن نِّسَآئِكُمْ  of your wives who do not hope to have menses,

إِنِ ٱرْتَبْتُمْ  should you have any doubts,

فَعِدَّتُهُنَّ ثَلَٰثَةُ أَشْهُرٍ  their term shall be three months,

وَٱلَّٰٓـِٔى لَمْ يَحِضْنَ  and for those [as well] who have not yet had menses.

وَأُوْلَٰتُ ٱلْأَحْمَالِ  As for those who are pregnant,

أَجَلُهُنَّ أَن يَضَعْنَ حَمْلَهُنَّ  their term shall be until they deliver.

وَمَن يَتَّقِ ٱللَّهَ  And whoever is wary of Allah,

يَجْعَل لَّهُۥ مِنْ أَمْرِهِۦ يُسْرًا ۝  He shall grant him ease in his affairs.

5 ذَٰلِكَ أَمْرُ ٱللَّهِ  That is the ordinance of Allah

أَنزَلَهُۥٓ إِلَيْكُمْ  which He has sent down to you,

وَمَن يَتَّقِ ٱللَّهَ  and whoever is wary of Allah,

يُكَفِّرْ عَنْهُ سَيِّـَٔاتِهِۦ  He shall absolve him of his misdeeds

وَيُعْظِمْ لَهُۥٓ أَجْرًا ۝  and give him a great reward.

6 أَسْكِنُوهُنَّ مِنْ حَيْثُ سَكَنتُم  House them[1] where you live,

مِّن وُجْدِكُمْ  in accordance with your means,

وَلَا تُضَآرُّوهُنَّ لِتُضَيِّقُوا۟ عَلَيْهِنَّ  and do not harass them to put them in straits,

وَإِن كُنَّ أُوْلَٰتِ حَمْلٍ  and should they be pregnant,

---

[1] That is, the divorcée in her waiting period (*ʿiddah*).

فَأَنفِقُواْ عَلَيْهِنَّ حَتَّىٰ يَضَعْنَ حَمْلَهُنَّ

maintain them until they deliver.

فَإِنْ أَرْضَعْنَ لَكُمْ

Then, if they suckle [the baby] for you,

فَـَٔاتُوهُنَّ أُجُورَهُنَّ

give them their wages

وَأْتَمِرُواْ بَيْنَكُم بِمَعْرُوفٍ

and consult together honourably;

وَإِن تَعَاسَرْتُمْ

but if you make things difficult for each other,

فَسَتُرْضِعُ لَهُۥٓ أُخْرَىٰ ۝

then another woman will suckle [the baby] for him.[1]

لِيُنفِقْ ذُو سَعَةٍ مِّن سَعَتِهِۦ

7 Let the affluent man spend out of his affluence,

وَمَن قُدِرَ عَلَيْهِ رِزْقُهُۥ

and let he whose provision has been tightened

فَلْيُنفِقْ مِمَّآ ءَاتَىٰهُ ٱللَّهُ

spend out of what Allah has given him.

لَا يُكَلِّفُ ٱللَّهُ نَفْسًا

Allah does not task any soul

إِلَّا مَآ ءَاتَىٰهَا

except [according to] what He has given it.

سَيَجْعَلُ ٱللَّهُ بَعْدَ عُسْرٍ يُسْرًا ۝

Allah will bring about ease after hardship.

وَكَأَيِّن مِّن قَرْيَةٍ عَتَتْ عَنْ أَمْرِ رَبِّهَا

8 How many a town defied the command of its Lord

وَرُسُلِهِۦ

and His apostles,

فَحَاسَبْنَٰهَا حِسَابًا شَدِيدًا

then We called it to a severe account

وَعَذَّبْنَٰهَا عَذَابًا نُّكْرًا ۝

and punished it with a dire punishment.

فَذَاقَتْ وَبَالَ أَمْرِهَا

9 So it tasted the evil consequences of its conduct,

وَكَانَ عَٰقِبَةُ أَمْرِهَا خُسْرًا ۝

and the outcome of its conduct was ruin.

أَعَدَّ ٱللَّهُ لَهُمْ عَذَابًا شَدِيدًا

10 Allah has prepared for them a severe punishment.

فَٱتَّقُواْ ٱللَّهَ

So be wary of Allah,

يَٰٓأُوْلِي ٱلْأَلْبَٰبِ ٱلَّذِينَ ءَامَنُواْ

O you who possess intellect and have faith!

قَدْ أَنزَلَ ٱللَّهُ إِلَيْكُمْ ذِكْرًا ۝

Allah has certainly sent down to you a reminder,

رَّسُولًا

11 an apostle

يَتْلُواْ عَلَيْكُمْ ءَايَٰتِ ٱللَّهِ مُبَيِّنَٰتٍ

reciting to you the manifest signs of Allah

لِّيُخْرِجَ ٱلَّذِينَ ءَامَنُواْ

that He may bring out those who have faith

وَعَمِلُواْ ٱلصَّٰلِحَٰتِ

and do righteous deeds

مِنَ ٱلظُّلُمَٰتِ إِلَى ٱلنُّورِ

from darkness into light.

وَمَن يُؤْمِنۢ بِٱللَّهِ

And whoever has faith in Allah

---

[1] That is, the father will arrange for a wet nurse to suckle the infant.

وَيَعْمَلْ صَـٰلِحًا — and does righteous deeds,

يُدْخِلْهُ جَنَّـٰتٍ — He shall admit him into gardens

تَجْرِى مِن تَحْتِهَا ٱلْأَنْهَـٰرُ — with streams running in them,

خَـٰلِدِينَ فِيهَآ أَبَدًا — to remain in them forever.

قَدْ أَحْسَنَ ٱللَّهُ لَهُۥ رِزْقًا ۝ — Allah has certainly granted him an excellent provision.

ٱللَّهُ ٱلَّذِى خَلَقَ سَبْعَ سَمَـٰوَٰتٍ — 12 It is Allah who has created seven heavens,

وَمِنَ ٱلْأَرْضِ مِثْلَهُنَّ — and of the earth [a number] similar to them.

يَتَنَزَّلُ ٱلْأَمْرُ بَيْنَهُنَّ — The command gradually descends through them,

لِتَعْلَمُوٓا۟ — that you may know

أَنَّ ٱللَّهَ عَلَىٰ كُلِّ شَىْءٍ قَدِيرٌ — that Allah has power over all things,

وَأَنَّ ٱللَّهَ قَدْ أَحَاطَ بِكُلِّ شَىْءٍ عِلْمًۢا ۝ — and that Allah comprehends all things in knowledge.

## سُورَةُ التَّحَّنِينِ 66. SŪRAT AL-TAḤRĪM[1]

بِسْمِ ٱللَّهِ — In the Name of Allah,

ٱلرَّحْمَـٰنِ ٱلرَّحِيمِ — the All-beneficent, the All-merciful.

يَـٰٓأَيُّهَا ٱلنَّبِىُّ لِمَ تُحَرِّمُ — 1 O Prophet! Why do *you* prohibit [yourself]

مَآ أَحَلَّ ٱللَّهُ لَكَ — what Allah has made lawful for *you*,

تَبْتَغِى مَرْضَاتَ أَزْوَٰجِكَ — seeking to please *your* wives?

وَٱللَّهُ غَفُورٌ رَّحِيمٌ ۝ — And Allah is all-forgiving, all-merciful.

قَدْ فَرَضَ ٱللَّهُ لَكُمْ — 2 Allah has certainly made lawful for you

تَحِلَّةَ أَيْمَـٰنِكُمْ — the dissolution of your oaths,[2]

وَٱللَّهُ مَوْلَىٰكُمْ — and Allah is your master

وَهُوَ ٱلْعَلِيمُ ٱلْحَكِيمُ ۝ — and He is the All-knowing, the All-wise.

وَإِذْ أَسَرَّ ٱلنَّبِىُّ إِلَىٰ بَعْضِ أَزْوَٰجِهِۦ — 3 When the Prophet confided to one of his wives

حَدِيثًا — a matter,

---

[1] Named 'Taḥrīm' after the phrase *li mā tuḥrimu* ("why do you forbid") in verse 1.
[2] See 2:225, 5:89. Concerning emphasis on keeping oaths, see 15:91-94.

فَلَمَّا نَبَّأَتْ بِهِۦ   but when she divulged it,

وَأَظْهَرَهُ ٱللَّهُ عَلَيْهِ   and Allah apprised him about it,

عَرَّفَ بَعْضَهُۥ   he announced [to her] part of it

وَأَعْرَضَ عَن بَعْضٍ   and disregarded part of it.

فَلَمَّا نَبَّأَهَا بِهِۦ   So when he told her about it,

قَالَتْ مَنْ أَنبَأَكَ هَـٰذَا   she said, 'Who informed you about it?'

قَالَ   He said,

نَبَّأَنِيَ ٱلْعَلِيمُ ٱلْخَبِيرُ ۝   'The All-knowing and the All-aware informed me.'

إِن تَتُوبَآ إِلَى ٱللَّهِ   4 If the two of you[1] repent to Allah . . .[2]

فَقَدْ صَغَتْ قُلُوبُكُمَا   for your hearts have certainly swerved,

وَإِن تَظَـٰهَرَا عَلَيْهِ   and if you back each other against him,

فَإِنَّ ٱللَّهَ هُوَ مَوْلَـٰهُ   then [know that] Allah is indeed his master,

وَجِبْرِيلُ وَصَـٰلِحُ ٱلْمُؤْمِنِينَ   and Gabriel, the righteous among the faithful,

وَٱلْمَلَـٰٓئِكَةُ بَعْدَ ذَٰلِكَ ظَهِيرٌ ۝   and, thereafter, the angels are his supporters.

عَسَىٰ رَبُّهُۥٓ إِن طَلَّقَكُنَّ   5 It may be that if he divorces you

أَن يُبْدِلَهُۥٓ أَزْوَٰجًا   his Lord will give him, in [your] stead,

خَيْرًا مِّنكُنَّ   wives better than you:

مُسْلِمَـٰتٍ مُّؤْمِنَـٰتٍ قَـٰنِتَـٰتٍ   [such as are] *muslim*, faithful, obedient,

تَـٰٓئِبَـٰتٍ عَـٰبِدَٰتٍ سَـٰٓئِحَـٰتٍ   penitent, devout and given to fasting,

ثَيِّبَـٰتٍ وَأَبْكَارًا ۝   virgins and non-virgins.

يَـٰٓأَيُّهَا ٱلَّذِينَ ءَامَنُوا   6 O you who have faith!

قُوٓا أَنفُسَكُمْ وَأَهْلِيكُمْ نَارًا   Save yourselves and your families from a Fire

وَقُودُهَا ٱلنَّاسُ وَٱلْحِجَارَةُ   whose fuel is people and stones,

عَلَيْهَا مَلَـٰٓئِكَةٌ غِلَاظٌ شِدَادٌ   over which are [assigned] angels, severe and mighty,

لَّا يَعْصُونَ   who do not disobey

ٱللَّهَ مَآ أَمَرَهُمْ   whatever Allah has commanded them,

وَيَفْعَلُونَ مَا يُؤْمَرُونَ ۝   and carry out what they are commanded.

يَـٰٓأَيُّهَا ٱلَّذِينَ كَفَرُوا   7 [They will call out to the faithless:] 'O faithless ones!

---

[1] That is, Ḥafṣah and 'Āyishah, two of the Prophet's wives.
[2] Ellipsis. The omitted phrase is, 'it will be better for you.'

لَا تَعْتَذِرُوا ٱلْيَوْمَ

Do not make any excuses today.

إِنَّمَا تُجْزَوْنَ

You are only being requited

مَا كُنتُمْ تَعْمَلُونَ ۝

for what you used to do.'

يَـٰٓأَيُّهَا ٱلَّذِينَ ءَامَنُوا

8 O you who have faith!

تُوبُوٓا إِلَى ٱللَّهِ تَوْبَةً نَّصُوحًا

Repent to Allah with sincere repentance!

عَسَىٰ رَبُّكُمْ

Maybe your Lord

أَن يُكَفِّرَ عَنكُمْ سَيِّـَٔاتِكُمْ

will absolve you of your misdeeds

وَيُدْخِلَكُمْ جَنَّـٰتٍ

and admit you into gardens

تَجْرِى مِن تَحْتِهَا ٱلْأَنْهَـٰرُ

with streams running in them,

يَوْمَ

on the day

لَا يُخْزِى ٱللَّهُ ٱلنَّبِىَّ

when Allah will not let the Prophet down

وَٱلَّذِينَ ءَامَنُوا مَعَهُۥ

and the faithful who are with him.

نُورُهُمْ يَسْعَىٰ بَيْنَ أَيْدِيهِمْ

Their light will move swiftly before them

وَبِأَيْمَـٰنِهِمْ

and on their right.

يَقُولُونَ رَبَّنَآ

They will say, 'Our Lord!

أَتْمِمْ لَنَا نُورَنَا وَٱغْفِرْ لَنَآ

Perfect our light for us, and forgive us!

إِنَّكَ عَلَىٰ كُلِّ شَىْءٍ قَدِيرٌ ۝

Indeed You have power over all things.'

يَـٰٓأَيُّهَا ٱلنَّبِىُّ

9 O Prophet!

جَـٰهِدِ ٱلْكُفَّارَ وَٱلْمُنَـٰفِقِينَ

Wage *jihād* against the faithless and the hypocrites,

وَٱغْلُظْ عَلَيْهِمْ

and be severe with them.

وَمَأْوَىٰهُمْ جَهَنَّمُ

Their refuge shall be hell,

وَبِئْسَ ٱلْمَصِيرُ ۝

and it is an evil destination.

ضَرَبَ ٱللَّهُ مَثَلًا لِّلَّذِينَ كَفَرُوا

10 Allah draws an example for the faithless:

ٱمْرَأَتَ نُوحٍ وَٱمْرَأَتَ لُوطٍ

the wife of Noah and the wife of Lot.

كَانَتَا

They were

تَحْتَ عَبْدَيْنِ مِنْ عِبَادِنَا صَـٰلِحَيْنِ

under two of our righteous servants,

فَخَانَتَاهُمَا

yet they betrayed them.

فَلَمْ يُغْنِيَا عَنْهُمَا مِنَ ٱللَّهِ شَيْـًٔا

So they[1] did not avail them[2] in any way against Allah,

---

[1] That is, Noah and Lot.

[2] That is, the wives.

وَقِيلَ

and it was said [to them],

ٱدْخُلَا ٱلنَّارَ مَعَ ٱلدَّاخِلِينَ ۞

'Enter the Fire, along with the incomers.'

وَضَرَبَ ٱللَّهُ مَثَلًا 11 Allah draws an[other] example

لِّلَّذِينَ ءَامَنُوا۟     for those who have faith:

ٱمْرَأَتَ فِرْعَوْنَ إِذْ قَالَتْ     the wife of Pharaoh, when she said,

رَبِّ ٱبْنِ لِى عِندَكَ بَيْتًا فِى ٱلْجَنَّةِ     'My Lord! Build me a home near You in paradise,

وَنَجِّنِى مِن فِرْعَوْنَ وَعَمَلِهِۦ     and deliver me from Pharaoh and his conduct,

وَنَجِّنِى مِنَ ٱلْقَوْمِ ٱلظَّٰلِمِينَ ۞     and deliver me from the wrongdoing lot.'

وَمَرْيَمَ ٱبْنَتَ عِمْرَٰنَ 12 And Mary, daughter of Imran,

ٱلَّتِى أَحْصَنَتْ فَرْجَهَا     who guarded the chastity of her womb,

فَنَفَخْنَا فِيهِ مِن رُّوحِنَا     so We breathed into it of Our spirit.

وَصَدَّقَتْ بِكَلِمَٰتِ رَبِّهَا     She confirmed the words of her Lord

وَكُتُبِهِۦ     and His Books,

وَكَانَتْ مِنَ ٱلْقَٰنِتِينَ ۞     and she was one of the obedient.

[PART 29]

سُورَةُ المُلْكِ      67. SŪRAT AL-MULK[1]

بِسْمِ ٱللَّهِ     In the Name of Allah,

ٱلرَّحْمَٰنِ ٱلرَّحِيمِ     the All-beneficent, the All-merciful.

تَبَٰرَكَ ٱلَّذِى بِيَدِهِ ٱلْمُلْكُ 1 Blessed is He in whose hands is all sovereignty,

وَهُوَ عَلَىٰ كُلِّ شَىْءٍ قَدِيرٌ ۞     and He has power over all things.

ٱلَّذِى خَلَقَ ٱلْمَوْتَ وَٱلْحَيَوٰةَ 2 He, who created death and life

لِيَبْلُوَكُمْ     that He may test you [to see]

أَيُّكُمْ أَحْسَنُ عَمَلًا     which of you is best in conduct.

وَهُوَ ٱلْعَزِيزُ ٱلْغَفُورُ ۞     And He is the All-mighty, the All-forgiving.

ٱلَّذِى خَلَقَ سَبْعَ سَمَٰوَٰتٍ طِبَاقًا 3 He created seven heavens in layers.

مَّا تَرَىٰ     You do not see

فِى خَلْقِ ٱلرَّحْمَٰنِ مِن تَفَٰوُتٍ     any discordance in the creation of the All-beneficent.

---

[1] The *sūrah* takes its name from Divine sovereignty (*mulk*) mentioned in verse 1.

فَٱرْجِعِ ٱلْبَصَرَ    Look again!

هَلْ تَرَىٰ مِن فُطُورٍ ۝    Do you see any flaw?

ثُمَّ ٱرْجِعِ ٱلْبَصَرَ كَرَّتَيْنِ    4 Look again, once more.

يَنقَلِبْ إِلَيْكَ ٱلْبَصَرُ    Your look will return to you

خَاسِئًا وَهُوَ حَسِيرٌ ۝    humbled and weary.

وَلَقَدْ زَيَّنَّا ٱلسَّمَآءَ ٱلدُّنْيَا    5 We have certainly adorned the lowest heaven

بِمَصَٰبِيحَ    with lamps,

وَجَعَلْنَٰهَا رُجُومًا لِّلشَّيَٰطِينِ    and made them missiles against the devils,

وَأَعْتَدْنَا لَهُمْ    and We have prepared for them

عَذَابَ ٱلسَّعِيرِ ۝    a punishment of the Blaze.

وَلِلَّذِينَ كَفَرُوا۟ بِرَبِّهِمْ    6 For those who defy their Lord

عَذَابُ جَهَنَّمَ    is the punishment of hell,

وَبِئْسَ ٱلْمَصِيرُ ۝    and it is an evil destination.

إِذَآ أُلْقُوا۟ فِيهَا    7 When they are thrown in it,

سَمِعُوا۟ لَهَا شَهِيقًا وَهِيَ تَفُورُ ۝    they hear it blaring, as it seethes,

تَكَادُ تَمَيَّزُ مِنَ ٱلْغَيْظِ    8 almost exploding with rage.

كُلَّمَآ أُلْقِيَ فِيهَا فَوْجٌ    Whenever a group is thrown in it,

سَأَلَهُمْ خَزَنَتُهَآ    its keepers will ask them,

أَلَمْ يَأْتِكُمْ نَذِيرٌ ۝    'Did there not come to you any warner?'

قَالُوا۟ بَلَىٰ قَدْ جَآءَنَا نَذِيرٌ    9 They will say, 'Yes, a warner certainly came to us,

فَكَذَّبْنَا وَقُلْنَا    but we impugned [him] and said,

مَا نَزَّلَ ٱللَّهُ مِن شَىْءٍ    'Allah did not send down anything;

إِنْ أَنتُمْ إِلَّا فِى ضَلَٰلٍ كَبِيرٍ ۝    you are only in great error.'

وَقَالُوا۟    10 And they will say,

لَوْ كُنَّا نَسْمَعُ أَوْ نَعْقِلُ    'Had we listened or applied reason,

مَا كُنَّا فِىٓ أَصْحَٰبِ ٱلسَّعِيرِ ۝    we would not have been among inmates of the Blaze.'

فَٱعْتَرَفُوا۟ بِذَنۢبِهِمْ    11 Thus they will admit their sin.

فَسُحْقًا لِّأَصْحَٰبِ ٱلسَّعِيرِ ۝    So away with the inmates of the Blaze!

إِنَّ ٱلَّذِينَ يَخْشَوْنَ رَبَّهُم بِٱلْغَيْبِ    12 Indeed for those who fear their Lord in secret

لَهُم مَّغْفِرَةٌ وَأَجْرٌ كَبِيرٌ ۝    there will be forgiveness and a great reward.

وَأَسِرُّوا۟ قَوْلَكُمْ أَوِ ٱجْهَرُوا۟ بِهِۦٓ

13 Speak secretly, or do so loudly,

إِنَّهُۥ عَلِيمٌۢ بِذَاتِ ٱلصُّدُورِ ۝

indeed He knows well what is in the breasts.

أَلَا يَعْلَمُ مَنْ خَلَقَ

14 Would He who has created not know?

وَهُوَ ٱللَّطِيفُ ٱلْخَبِيرُ ۝

And He is the All-attentive, the All-aware.

هُوَ ٱلَّذِى جَعَلَ لَكُمُ ٱلْأَرْضَ ذَلُولًا

15 It is He who made the earth tractable for you;

فَٱمْشُوا۟ فِى مَنَاكِبِهَا

so walk on its flanks

وَكُلُوا۟ مِن رِّزْقِهِۦ

and eat of His provision,

وَإِلَيْهِ ٱلنُّشُورُ ۝

and towards Him is the resurrection.

ءَأَمِنتُم مَّن فِى ٱلسَّمَآءِ

16 Are you secure that He who is in the sky

أَن يَخْسِفَ بِكُمُ ٱلْأَرْضَ

will not make the earth swallow you

فَإِذَا هِىَ تَمُورُ ۝

while it quakes?

أَمْ أَمِنتُم مَّن فِى ٱلسَّمَآءِ

17 Are you secure that He who is in the sky

أَن يُرْسِلَ عَلَيْكُمْ حَاصِبًا

will not unleash upon you a rain of stones?

فَسَتَعْلَمُونَ كَيْفَ نَذِيرِ ۝

Soon you will know how My warning has been!

وَلَقَدْ كَذَّبَ ٱلَّذِينَ مِن قَبْلِهِمْ

18 Certainly those who were before them had denied;

فَكَيْفَ كَانَ نَكِيرِ ۝

but then how was My rebuttal![1]

أَوَلَمْ يَرَوْا۟ إِلَى ٱلطَّيْرِ فَوْقَهُمْ

19 Have they not regarded the birds above them

صَٰٓفَّٰتٍ وَيَقْبِضْنَ

spreading and closing their wings?

مَا يُمْسِكُهُنَّ إِلَّا ٱلرَّحْمَٰنُ

No one sustains them except the All-beneficent.

إِنَّهُۥ بِكُلِّ شَىْءٍۭ بَصِيرٌ ۝

Indeed He sees best all things.

أَمَّنْ هَٰذَا ٱلَّذِى هُوَ جُندٌ لَّكُمْ

20 Who is it that is your host

يَنصُرُكُم مِّن دُونِ ٱلرَّحْمَٰنِ

who may help you, besides the All-beneficent?

إِنِ ٱلْكَٰفِرُونَ إِلَّا فِى غُرُورٍ ۝

The faithless only dwell in delusion.

أَمَّنْ هَٰذَا ٱلَّذِى يَرْزُقُكُمْ

21 Who is it that may provide for you

إِنْ أَمْسَكَ رِزْقَهُۥ

if He withholds His provision?

بَل لَّجُّوا۟ فِى عُتُوٍّ وَنُفُورٍ ۝

Rather they persist in defiance and aversion.

أَفَمَن يَمْشِى مُكِبًّا عَلَىٰ وَجْهِهِۦٓ أَهْدَىٰٓ

22 Is he who walks prone on his face better guided,

أَمَّن يَمْشِى سَوِيًّا

or he who walks upright

عَلَىٰ صِرَٰطٍ مُّسْتَقِيمٍ ۝

on a straight path?

---

[1] Or, 'how was My requital.'

قُلْ هُوَ ٱلَّذِىٓ أَنشَأَكُمْ 23 *Say,* 'It is He who created you,

وَجَعَلَ لَكُمُ ٱلسَّمْعَ وَٱلْأَبْصَٰرَ وَٱلْأَفْـِٔدَةَ    and made for you hearing, eyesight, and hearts.

قَلِيلًا مَّا تَشْكُرُونَ ۝    Little do you thank.'

قُلْ هُوَ ٱلَّذِى ذَرَأَكُمْ فِى ٱلْأَرْضِ 24 *Say,* 'It is He who created you on the earth,

وَإِلَيْهِ تُحْشَرُونَ ۝    and toward Him you will be mustered.'

وَيَقُولُونَ مَتَىٰ هَٰذَا ٱلْوَعْدُ 25 They say, 'When will this promise be fulfilled,

إِن كُنتُمْ صَٰدِقِينَ ۝    should you be truthful?'

قُلْ إِنَّمَا ٱلْعِلْمُ عِندَ ٱللَّهِ 26 *Say,* 'Its knowledge is only with Allah;

وَإِنَّمَآ أَنَا۠ نَذِيرٌ مُّبِينٌ ۝    I am only a manifest warner.'

فَلَمَّا رَأَوْهُ زُلْفَةً 27 When they see it brought near,

سِيٓـَٔتْ وُجُوهُ ٱلَّذِينَ كَفَرُوا۟    the countenances of the faithless will be distorted,

وَقِيلَ هَٰذَا ٱلَّذِى كُنتُم بِهِۦ تَدَّعُونَ ۝    and [they will be] told, 'This is what you asked for.'

قُلْ أَرَءَيْتُمْ 28 *Say,* 'Tell me,

إِنْ أَهْلَكَنِىَ ٱللَّهُ وَمَن مَّعِىَ    whether Allah destroys me and those with me,

أَوْ رَحِمَنَا    or He has mercy on us,

فَمَن يُجِيرُ ٱلْكَٰفِرِينَ    who will shelter the faithless

مِنْ عَذَابٍ أَلِيمٍ ۝    from a painful punishment?'

قُلْ هُوَ ٱلرَّحْمَٰنُ 29 *Say,* 'He is the All-beneficent;

ءَامَنَّا بِهِۦ وَعَلَيْهِ تَوَكَّلْنَا    we have faith in Him, and in Him do we trust.

فَسَتَعْلَمُونَ    Soon you will know

مَنْ هُوَ فِى ضَلَٰلٍ مُّبِينٍ ۝    who is in manifest error.'

قُلْ أَرَءَيْتُمْ 30 *Say,* 'Tell me,

إِنْ أَصْبَحَ مَآؤُكُمْ غَوْرًا    should your water sink down [into the ground],

فَمَن يَأْتِيكُم بِمَآءٍ مَّعِينٍ ۝    who will bring you running water?'

سُورَةُ الْقَلَمِ         68. SŪRAT AL-QALAM[1]

بِسْمِ ٱللَّهِ         In the Name of Allah,
ٱلرَّحْمَٰنِ ٱلرَّحِيمِ    the All-beneficent, the All-merciful.

---

[1] The *sūrah* takes its name from "the Pen" (*al-qalam*) mentioned in verse 1.

ن    1 *Nūn*.

وَٱلْقَلَمِ وَمَا يَسْطُرُونَ ۝    By the Pen and what they write:

مَآ أَنتَ بِنِعْمَةِ رَبِّكَ بِمَجْنُونٍ ۝    2  *you* are not, by *your* Lord's blessing, crazy,

وَإِنَّ لَكَ لَأَجْرًا غَيْرَ مَمْنُونٍ ۝    3  and *yours* indeed will be an everlasting reward,

وَإِنَّكَ لَعَلَىٰ خُلُقٍ عَظِيمٍ ۝    4  and indeed *you* possess a great character.

فَسَتُبْصِرُ وَيُبْصِرُونَ ۝    5 *You* will see and they will see,

بِأَييِّكُمُ ٱلْمَفْتُونُ ۝    6  which one of you is crazy.

إِنَّ رَبَّكَ هُوَ أَعْلَمُ    7 Indeed *your* Lord knows best

بِمَن ضَلَّ عَن سَبِيلِهِ    those who stray from His way,

وَهُوَ أَعْلَمُ بِٱلْمُهْتَدِينَ ۝    and He knows best those who are guided.

فَلَا تُطِعِ ٱلْمُكَذِّبِينَ ۝    8 So *do not obey* the deniers,

وَدُّوا لَوْ تُدْهِنُ    9  who are eager that *you* should be pliable,

فَيُدْهِنُونَ ۝    so that they may be pliable [towards *you*].

وَلَا تُطِعْ كُلَّ حَلَّافٍ مَّهِينٍ ۝    10 And *do not obey* any vile swearer,

هَمَّازٍ مَّشَّآءٍ بِنَمِيمٍ ۝    11    scandal-monger, talebearer,

مَّنَّاعٍ لِّلْخَيْرِ مُعْتَدٍ أَثِيمٍ ۝    12    hinderer of all good, sinful transgressor,

عُتُلٍّ بَعْدَ ذَٰلِكَ زَنِيمٍ ۝    13    callous and, on top of that, baseborn,

أَن كَانَ ذَا مَالٍ وَبَنِينَ ۝    14    —[only] because he has wealth and children.

إِذَا تُتْلَىٰ عَلَيْهِ ءَايَٰتُنَا    15    When Our signs are recited to him,

قَالَ أَسَٰطِيرُ ٱلْأَوَّلِينَ ۝    he says, 'Myths of the ancients!'

سَنَسِمُهُ عَلَى ٱلْخُرْطُومِ ۝    16 Soon We shall brand him on the snout.

إِنَّا بَلَوْنَٰهُمْ    17 Indeed we have tested them[1]

كَمَا بَلَوْنَآ أَصْحَٰبَ ٱلْجَنَّةِ    just as We tested the People of the Garden

إِذْ أَقْسَمُوا لَيَصْرِمُنَّهَا    when they vowed they would gather its fruit

مُصْبِحِينَ ۝    at dawn,

وَلَا يَسْتَثْنُونَ ۝    18    and they did not make any exception.[2]

فَطَافَ عَلَيْهَا طَآئِفٌ مِّن رَّبِّكَ    19 Then a visitation from *your* Lord visited it[3]

---

[1] That is, the people of Makkah, through famine and hunger.

[2] That is, for Allah's will, by saying, for instance, 'God willing.' See 18:24

[3] That is, the garden.

وَهُمْ نَآئِمُونَ ۞    while they were asleep.

فَأَصْبَحَتْ كَالصَّرِيمِ ۞    20 So by the dawn it was like a harvested field.[1]

فَتَنَادَوْا مُصْبِحِينَ ۞    21 At dawn they called out to one another,

أَنِ اغْدُوا۟ عَلَىٰ حَرْثِكُمْ    22 'Get off early to your field

إِن كُنتُمْ صَٰرِمِينَ ۞    if you have to gather [the fruits].'

فَٱنطَلَقُوا۟ وَهُمْ يَتَخَٰفَتُونَ ۞    23 So off they went, murmuring to one another:

أَن لَّا يَدْخُلَنَّهَا ٱلْيَوْمَ عَلَيْكُم مِّسْكِينٌ ۞    24 'Today no needy man shall come to you in it.'

وَغَدَوْا۟    25 They set out early morning,

عَلَىٰ حَرْدٍ قَٰدِرِينَ ۞    [considering themselves] able to grudge.

فَلَمَّا رَأَوْهَا قَالُوٓا۟    26 But when they saw it, they said,

إِنَّا لَضَآلُّونَ ۞    'We have indeed lost our way!'

بَلْ نَحْنُ مَحْرُومُونَ ۞    27 'No, we are deprived!'

قَالَ أَوْسَطُهُمْ    28 The most moderate among them said,

أَلَمْ أَقُل لَّكُمْ    'Did I not tell you,

لَوْلَا تُسَبِّحُونَ ۞    "Why do you not glorify [Allah]?" '

قَالُوا۟ سُبْحَٰنَ رَبِّنَآ    29 They said, 'Immaculate is our Lord!

إِنَّا كُنَّا ظَٰلِمِينَ ۞    We have indeed been wrongdoers!'

فَأَقْبَلَ بَعْضُهُمْ عَلَىٰ بَعْضٍ    30 Then they turned to one another,

يَتَلَٰوَمُونَ ۞    blaming each other.

قَالُوا۟ يَٰوَيْلَنَآ    31 They said, 'Woe to us!

إِنَّا كُنَّا طَٰغِينَ ۞    Indeed we have been rebellious.

عَسَىٰ رَبُّنَآ أَن يُبْدِلَنَا خَيْرًا مِّنْهَآ    32 Maybe our Lord will give us a better one in its place.

إِنَّآ إِلَىٰ رَبِّنَا رَٰغِبُونَ ۞    Indeed we turn earnestly to our Lord.'

كَذَٰلِكَ ٱلْعَذَابُ    33 Such was the punishment;

وَلَعَذَابُ ٱلْءَاخِرَةِ أَكْبَرُ    and the punishment of the Hereafter is surely greater,

لَوْ كَانُوا۟ يَعْلَمُونَ ۞    had they known.

إِنَّ لِلْمُتَّقِينَ    34 Indeed for the Godwary

عِندَ رَبِّهِمْ جَنَّٰتِ ٱلنَّعِيمِ ۞    there will be gardens of bliss near their Lord.

أَفَنَجْعَلُ ٱلْمُسْلِمِينَ    35 Shall We, then, treat those who submit [to Us]

---

[1] Or 'like a sand dune,' or 'like a gloomy night,' or 'like black ashes.'

كَٱلْمُجْرِمِينَ ۝    as [We treat] the guilty?

مَا لَكُمْ كَيْفَ تَحْكُمُونَ ۝   36 What is the matter with you? How do you judge!

أَمْ لَكُمْ كِتَـٰبٌ فِيهِ تَدْرُسُونَ ۝   37 Do you possess a scripture in which you read

إِنَّ لَكُمْ فِيهِ   38   that you shall indeed have in it[1]

لَمَا تَخَيَّرُونَ ۝    whatever you would like?

أَمْ لَكُمْ أَيْمَـٰنٌ عَلَيْنَا بَـٰلِغَةٌ   39 Do you have a pledge binding on Us

إِلَىٰ يَوْمِ ٱلْقِيَـٰمَةِ    until the Day of Resurrection,

إِنَّ لَكُمْ لَمَا تَحْكُمُونَ ۝    that you shall indeed have whatever you decide?

سَلْهُمْ أَيُّهُم بِذَٰلِكَ زَعِيمٌ ۝   40 *Ask* them, which of them will aver [any of] that!

أَمْ لَهُمْ شُرَكَاءُ   41 Do they have any partners [they ascribe to Allah]?

فَلْيَأْتُوا۟ بِشُرَكَآئِهِمْ    Then let them produce their partners,

إِن كَانُوا۟ صَـٰدِقِينَ ۝    if they are truthful.

يَوْمَ يُكْشَفُ عَن سَاقٍ   42 The day when the catastrophe occurs,[2]

وَيُدْعَوْنَ إِلَى ٱلسُّجُودِ    and they are summoned to prostrate themselves,

فَلَا يَسْتَطِيعُونَ ۝    they will not be able [to do it].

خَـٰشِعَةً أَبْصَـٰرُهُمْ   43 With a humbled look [in their eyes],

تَرْهَقُهُمْ ذِلَّةٌ    they will be overcast by abasement.

وَقَدْ كَانُوا۟ يُدْعَوْنَ إِلَى ٱلسُّجُودِ    Certainly they were summoned to prostrate themselves

وَهُمْ سَـٰلِمُونَ ۝    while they were yet sound.

فَذَرْنِي وَمَن يُكَذِّبُ بِهَـٰذَا ٱلْحَدِيثِ   44 So leave Me with those who deny this discourse.

سَنَسْتَدْرِجُهُم    We will draw them imperceptibly [into ruin],

مِّنْ حَيْثُ لَا يَعْلَمُونَ ۝    whence they do not know.

وَأُمْلِي لَهُمْ   45 I will grant them respite,

إِنَّ كَيْدِي مَتِينٌ ۝    for My devising is indeed sure.

أَمْ تَسْـَٔلُهُمْ أَجْرًا   46 Do *you* ask them for a reward,

فَهُم مِّن مَّغْرَمٍ مُّثْقَلُونَ ۝    so that they are weighed down with debt?

أَمْ عِندَهُمُ ٱلْغَيْبُ   47 Do they possess [access to] the Unseen

---

[1] That is, in the next world.

[2] Literally, 'when the shank is uncovered,' an idiom implying the occurrence of a calamity, or a disclosure and denouement.

فَهُمْ يَكْتُبُونَ ۝    so that they write it down?

فَٱصْبِرْ لِحُكْمِ رَبِّكَ    48 So *submit patiently* to the judgement of *your* Lord,

وَلَا تَكُن كَصَاحِبِ ٱلْحُوتِ    and do not be like the Man of the Fish[1]

إِذْ نَادَىٰ وَهُوَ مَكْظُومٌ ۝    who called out as he choked with grief.

لَّوْلَآ أَن تَدَارَكَهُ نِعْمَةٌ    49 Had it not been for a blessing that came to his rescue

مِّن رَّبِّهِ    from his Lord,

لَنُبِذَ بِٱلْعَرَآءِ    he would surely have been cast on a bare shore

وَهُوَ مَذْمُومٌ ۝    while he were blameworthy.

فَٱجْتَبَٰهُ رَبُّهُ    50 So his Lord chose him

فَجَعَلَهُ مِنَ ٱلصَّٰلِحِينَ ۝    and made him one of the righteous.

وَإِن يَكَادُ ٱلَّذِينَ كَفَرُوا۟ لَيُزْلِقُونَكَ    51 Indeed the faithless almost devour you

بِأَبْصَٰرِهِمْ    with their eyes

لَمَّا سَمِعُوا۟ ٱلذِّكْرَ    when they hear the Reminder,

وَيَقُولُونَ إِنَّهُ لَمَجْنُونٌ ۝    and they say, 'He is indeed crazy.'

وَمَا هُوَ إِلَّا ذِكْرٌ لِّلْعَٰلَمِينَ ۝    52 Yet it is just a reminder for all the nations.

## سُورَةُ الحَاقَّة      69. SŪRAT AL-ḤĀQQAH[2]

بِسْمِ ٱللَّهِ    In the Name of Allah,

ٱلرَّحْمَٰنِ ٱلرَّحِيمِ    the All-beneficent, the All-merciful.

ٱلْحَاقَّةُ ۝    1 The Besieger![3]

مَا ٱلْحَاقَّةُ ۝    2 What is the Besieger?!

وَمَآ أَدْرَىٰكَ مَا ٱلْحَاقَّةُ ۝    3 What will show you what is the Besieger?!

كَذَّبَتْ ثَمُودُ وَعَادٌ بِٱلْقَارِعَةِ ۝    4 Thamūd and ʿĀd denied the Catastrophe.

فَأَمَّا ثَمُودُ فَأُهْلِكُوا۟ بِٱلطَّاغِيَةِ ۝    5 As for Thamūd, they were destroyed by the Cry.

وَأَمَّا عَادٌ    6 And as for ʿĀd,

---

[1] That is, Jonah. See 21:87.

[2] The *sūrah* takes its name from "*al-Ḥāqqah*" (the Besieger) mentioned in verse 1.

[3] Or 'the Inevitable.' That is, the Day of Resurrection.

فَأُهْلِكُواْ بِرِيحٍ صَرْصَرٍ عَاتِيَةٍ ۝    they were destroyed by a fierce icy gale,

7 سَخَّرَهَا عَلَيْهِمْ    which He disposed against them

سَبْعَ لَيَالٍ وَثَمَٰنِيَةَ أَيَّامٍ حُسُومًا    for seven grueling[1] nights and eight days,

فَتَرَى ٱلْقَوْمَ    so that you could have seen the people

فِيهَا صَرْعَىٰ    lying about therein prostrate

كَأَنَّهُمْ أَعْجَازُ نَخْلٍ خَاوِيَةٍ ۝    as if they were hollow trunks of palm trees.

8 فَهَلْ تَرَىٰ لَهُم مِّنۢ بَاقِيَةٍ ۝    So do you see any trace of them?

9 وَجَآءَ فِرْعَوْنُ وَمَن قَبْلَهُۥ    Then brought Pharaoh and those who were before him,

وَٱلْمُؤْتَفِكَٰتُ    and the towns that were overturned,

بِٱلْخَاطِئَةِ ۝    iniquity.

10 فَعَصَوْاْ رَسُولَ رَبِّهِمْ    Then they disobeyed the apostle of their Lord,

فَأَخَذَهُمْ أَخْذَةً رَّابِيَةً ۝    so He seized them with a terrible seizing.

11 إِنَّا لَمَّا طَغَا ٱلْمَآءُ    Indeed when the Flood rose high,

حَمَلْنَٰكُمْ فِى ٱلْجَارِيَةِ ۝    We carried you in a floating ark,

12 لِنَجْعَلَهَا لَكُمْ تَذْكِرَةً    that We might make it a reminder for you,

وَتَعِيَهَآ أُذُنٌ وَٰعِيَةٌ ۝    and that receptive ears might remember it.

13 فَإِذَا نُفِخَ فِى ٱلصُّورِ نَفْخَةٌ وَٰحِدَةٌ ۝    When the Trumpet is blown with a single blast

14 وَحُمِلَتِ ٱلْأَرْضُ وَٱلْجِبَالُ    and the earth and the mountains are lifted

فَدُكَّتَا دَكَّةً وَٰحِدَةً ۝    and levelled with a single leveling,[2]

15 فَيَوْمَئِذٍ وَقَعَتِ ٱلْوَاقِعَةُ ۝    then, on that day, will the Imminent [Hour] befall[3]

16 وَٱنشَقَّتِ ٱلسَّمَآءُ    and the sky will be split open

فَهِىَ يَوْمَئِذٍ وَاهِيَةٌ ۝    —for it will be frail that day—

17 وَٱلْمَلَكُ عَلَىٰٓ أَرْجَآئِهَا    and the angels will be all over it,

وَيَحْمِلُ عَرْشَ رَبِّكَ فَوْقَهُمْ    and the Throne of *your* Lord will be borne

يَوْمَئِذٍ ثَمَٰنِيَةٌ ۝    that day by eight [angels].

18 يَوْمَئِذٍ تُعْرَضُونَ    That day you will be exposed:

لَا تَخْفَىٰ مِنكُمْ خَافِيَةٌ ۝    none of your secrets will remain hidden.

---

[1] Or 'successive.'

[2] Or 'crumbled with a single crumbling.'

[3] 56:1-6

فَأَمَّا مَنْ أُوتِىَ كِتَبَهُۥ بِيَمِينِهِۦ ۝ 19 As for him who is given his book in his right hand,

فَيَقُولُ هَآؤُمُ ٱقْرَءُوا۟ كِتَبِيَهْ ۝ he will say, 'Here, take and read my book!

إِنِّى ظَنَنتُ أَنِّى مُلَقٍ حِسَابِيَهْ ۝ 20 Indeed I knew that I shall encounter my account.'

فَهُوَ فِى عِيشَةٍ رَّاضِيَةٍ ۝ 21 So he will have a pleasant life,

فِى جَنَّةٍ عَالِيَةٍ ۝ 22 in an elevated garden,

قُطُوفُهَا دَانِيَةٌ ۝ 23 whose clusters [of fruits] will be within easy reach.

كُلُوا۟ وَٱشْرَبُوا۟ هَنِيٓئًا ۝ 24 [He will be told]: 'Enjoy your food and drink,

بِمَآ أَسْلَفْتُمْ فِى ٱلْأَيَّامِ ٱلْخَالِيَةِ ۝ for what you had sent in advance in past days.'

وَأَمَّا مَنْ أُوتِىَ كِتَبَهُۥ بِشِمَالِهِۦ ۝ 25 But as for him who is given his book in his left hand,

فَيَقُولُ يَلَيْتَنِى لَمْ أُوتَ كِتَبِيَهْ ۝ he will say, 'I wish I had not been given my book,

وَلَمْ أَدْرِ مَا حِسَابِيَهْ ۝ 26 nor had I ever known what my account is!

يَلَيْتَهَا كَانَتِ ٱلْقَاضِيَةَ ۝ 27 I wish death had been the end of it all!

مَآ أَغْنَىٰ عَنِّى مَالِيَهْ ۝ 28 My wealth did not avail me.

هَلَكَ عَنِّى سُلْطَنِيَهْ ۝ 29 My authority has departed from me.'

خُذُوهُ فَغُلُّوهُ ۝ 30 [The angels will be told:] 'Seize him, and fetter him!

ثُمَّ ٱلْجَحِيمَ صَلُّوهُ ۝ 31 Then put him into hell.

ثُمَّ فِى سِلْسِلَةٍ ذَرْعُهَا سَبْعُونَ ذِرَاعًا فَٱسْلُكُوهُ ۝ 32 Then, in a chain whose length is seventy cubits, bind him.

إِنَّهُۥ كَانَ لَا يُؤْمِنُ بِٱللَّهِ ٱلْعَظِيمِ ۝ 33 Indeed he had no faith in Allah, the All-supreme,

وَلَا يَحُضُّ عَلَىٰ طَعَامِ ٱلْمِسْكِينِ ۝ 34 and he did not urge the feeding of the needy,

فَلَيْسَ لَهُ ٱلْيَوْمَ هَهُنَا حَمِيمٌ ۝ 35 so he has no friend here today,

وَلَا طَعَامٌ إِلَّا مِنْ غِسْلِينٍ ۝ 36 nor any food except pus,

لَّا يَأْكُلُهُۥ إِلَّا ٱلْخَطِئُونَ ۝ 37 which no one shall eat except the iniquitous.'

فَلَآ أُقْسِمُ بِمَا تُبْصِرُونَ ۝ 38 I swear by what you see

وَمَا لَا تُبْصِرُونَ ۝ 39 and what you do not see:

إِنَّهُۥ لَقَوْلُ رَسُولٍ كَرِيمٍ ۝ 40 it is indeed the speech of a noble apostle,

وَمَا هُوَ بِقَوْلِ شَاعِرٍ ۝ 41 and it is not the speech of a poet.

قَلِيلًا مَّا تُؤْمِنُونَ ۝ Little is the faith that you have!

وَلَا بِقَوْلِ كَاهِنٍ ۝ 42 Nor is it the speech of a soothsayer.

قَلِيلًا مَّا تَذَكَّرُونَ ۝ Little is the admonition that you take!

809

تَنزِيلٌ مِّن رَّبِّ ٱلْعَٰلَمِينَ ۝ 43 Gradually sent down from the Lord of all the worlds.

وَلَوْ تَقَوَّلَ عَلَيْنَا بَعْضَ ٱلْأَقَاوِيلِ ۝ 44 Had he faked any sayings in Our name,

لَأَخَذْنَا مِنْهُ بِٱلْيَمِينِ ۝ 45 We would have surely seized him by the right hand

ثُمَّ لَقَطَعْنَا مِنْهُ ٱلْوَتِينَ ۝ 46 and then cut off his aorta,

فَمَا مِنكُم مِّنْ أَحَدٍ عَنْهُ حَٰجِزِينَ ۝ 47 and none of you could have held Us off from him.

وَإِنَّهُۥ لَتَذْكِرَةٌ لِّلْمُتَّقِينَ ۝ 48 Indeed it is a reminder for the Godwary.

وَإِنَّا لَنَعْلَمُ 49 Indeed We know

أَنَّ مِنكُم مُّكَذِّبِينَ ۝ that there are some among you who deny [it].

وَإِنَّهُۥ لَحَسْرَةٌ 50 And indeed it will be a [matter of] regret

عَلَى ٱلْكَٰفِرِينَ ۝ for the faithless.

وَإِنَّهُۥ لَحَقُّ ٱلْيَقِينِ ۝ 51 It is indeed certain truth.

فَسَبِّحْ بِٱسْمِ رَبِّكَ ٱلْعَظِيمِ ۝ 52 So *celebrate* the Name of *your* Lord, the All-supreme.

## سُورَةُ الْمَعَارِج   70. SŪRAT AL- MA'ĀRIJ[1]

بِسْمِ ٱللَّهِ   In the Name of Allah,

ٱلرَّحْمَٰنِ ٱلرَّحِيمِ   the All-beneficent, the All-merciful.

سَأَلَ سَآئِلٌۢ بِعَذَابٍ وَاقِعٍ ۝ 1 An asker asked for a punishment bound to befall

لِّلْكَٰفِرِينَ لَيْسَ لَهُۥ دَافِعٌ ۝ 2 —which none can avert from the faithless—[2]

مِّنَ ٱللَّهِ ذِى ٱلْمَعَارِجِ ۝ 3 from Allah, Lord of the lofty stations.

تَعْرُجُ ٱلْمَلَٰئِكَةُ وَٱلرُّوحُ إِلَيْهِ 4 The angels and the Spirit ascend to Him

فِى يَوْمٍ كَانَ مِقْدَارُهُۥ in a day whose span is

خَمْسِينَ أَلْفَ سَنَةٍ ۝ fifty thousand years.

فَٱصْبِرْ صَبْرًا جَمِيلًا ۝ 5 So *be patient*, with a patience that is graceful.

إِنَّهُمْ يَرَوْنَهُۥ بَعِيدًا ۝ 6 Indeed they see it to be far off,

وَنَرَىٰهُ قَرِيبًا ۝ 7 and We see it to be near.

يَوْمَ تَكُونُ ٱلسَّمَآءُ كَٱلْمُهْلِ ۝ 8 The day when the sky will be like molten copper,

---

[1] The *sūrah* is named after the phrase *dhi al-ma'ārij* (of lofty stations) in verse 3.

[2] Or 'bound to befall the faithless—which none can avert—from Allah. . . .'

9 وَتَكُونُ الْجِبَالُ كَالْعِهْنِ and the mountains like [tufts of] dyed wool,

10 وَلَا يَسْـَٔلُ حَمِيمٌ and no friend will inquire

حَمِيمًا about [the welfare of his] friend,

11 يُبَصَّرُونَهُمْ [though they will be placed within each other's sight.

يَوَدُّ الْمُجْرِمُ لَوْ يَفْتَدِى The guilty one will wish he could ransom himself

مِنْ عَذَابِ يَوْمِئِذٍ from the punishment of that day

بِبَنِيهِ at the price of his children,

12 وَصَٰحِبَتِهِۦ وَأَخِيهِ his spouse and his brother,

13 وَفَصِيلَتِهِ ٱلَّتِى تُـْٔوِيهِ his kin which had sheltered him

14 وَمَن فِى ٱلْأَرْضِ جَمِيعًا and all those who are upon the earth,

ثُمَّ يُنجِيهِ if that might deliver him.

15 كَلَّآ إِنَّهَا لَظَىٰ Never! Indeed it is a blazing fire,

16 نَزَّاعَةً لِّلشَّوَىٰ which strips away the scalp.

17 تَدْعُوا۟ مَنْ أَدْبَرَ It invites him who has turned back [from the truth]

وَتَوَلَّىٰ and forsaken [it],

18 وَجَمَعَ فَأَوْعَىٰ amassing [wealth] and hoarding [it].

19 إِنَّ ٱلْإِنسَٰنَ خُلِقَ هَلُوعًا Indeed man has been created covetous:

20 إِذَا مَسَّهُ ٱلشَّرُّ جَزُوعًا anxious when an ill befalls him

21 وَإِذَا مَسَّهُ ٱلْخَيْرُ مَنُوعًا and grudging when good comes his way

22 إِلَّا ٱلْمُصَلِّينَ —[all are such] except the prayerful,

23 ٱلَّذِينَ هُمْ عَلَىٰ صَلَاتِهِمْ دَآئِمُونَ those who are persevering in their prayers

24 وَٱلَّذِينَ فِىٓ أَمْوَٰلِهِمْ حَقٌّ مَّعْلُومٌ and in whose wealth there is a known right

25 لِّلسَّآئِلِ وَٱلْمَحْرُومِ for the beggar and the deprived,

26 وَٱلَّذِينَ يُصَدِّقُونَ بِيَوْمِ ٱلدِّينِ and who affirm the Day of Retribution,

27 وَٱلَّذِينَ هُم and those who are

مِّنْ عَذَابِ رَبِّهِم مُّشْفِقُونَ apprehensive of the punishment of their Lord

28 إِنَّ (there is indeed

عَذَابَ رَبِّهِمْ غَيْرُ مَأْمُونٍ no security from the punishment of their Lord)

29 وَٱلَّذِينَ هُمْ لِفُرُوجِهِمْ حَٰفِظُونَ and those who guard their private parts

30 إِلَّا عَلَىٰ أَزْوَٰجِهِمْ أَوْ مَا مَلَكَتْ أَيْمَٰنُهُمْ (except from their spouses and their slave women,

فَإِنَّهُمْ غَيْرُ مَلُومِينَ ۝     for then they are not blameworthy;

31 فَمَنِ ٱبْتَغَىٰ وَرَآءَ ذَٰلِكَ     31 but whoever seeks beyond that

فَأُو۟لَـٰٓئِكَ هُمُ ٱلْعَادُونَ ۝     —it is they who are the transgressors)

32 وَٱلَّذِينَ هُمْ لِأَمَـٰنَـٰتِهِمْ وَعَهْدِهِمْ رَٰعُونَ ۝     32 and those who keep their trusts and covenants,

33 وَٱلَّذِينَ هُم بِشَهَـٰدَٰتِهِمْ قَآئِمُونَ ۝     33 and those who are observant of their testimonies,

34 وَٱلَّذِينَ هُمْ عَلَىٰ صَلَاتِهِمْ يُحَافِظُونَ ۝     34 and those who are watchful of their prayers.

35 أُو۟لَـٰٓئِكَ فِى جَنَّـٰتٍ مُّكْرَمُونَ ۝     35 They will be in gardens, held in honour.

36 فَمَالِ ٱلَّذِينَ كَفَرُوا۟     36 What is the matter with the faithless

قِبَلَكَ مُهْطِعِينَ ۝     that they scramble toward *you*

37 عَنِ ٱلْيَمِينِ وَعَنِ ٱلشِّمَالِ عِزِينَ ۝     37 from the left and the right in batches?

38 أَيَطْمَعُ كُلُّ ٱمْرِئٍ مِّنْهُمْ     38 Does each man among them hope

أَن يُدْخَلَ جَنَّةَ نَعِيمٍ ۝     to enter the garden of bliss?

39 كَلَّآ ۖ     39 Never!

إِنَّا خَلَقْنَـٰهُم مِّمَّا يَعْلَمُونَ ۝     Indeed We created them from what they know.[1]

40 فَلَآ أُقْسِمُ بِرَبِّ ٱلْمَشَـٰرِقِ وَٱلْمَغَـٰرِبِ     40 So I swear by the Lord of the easts and the wests

إِنَّا لَقَـٰدِرُونَ ۝     that We are able

41 عَلَىٰٓ أَن نُّبَدِّلَ خَيْرًا مِّنْهُمْ     41 to replace them by [others] better than them

وَمَا نَحْنُ بِمَسْبُوقِينَ ۝     and We are not to be outmaneuvered.

42 فَذَرْهُمْ يَخُوضُوا۟ وَيَلْعَبُوا۟     42 So leave them to gossip and play

حَتَّىٰ يُلَـٰقُوا۟ يَوْمَهُمُ     until they encounter their day,

ٱلَّذِى يُوعَدُونَ ۝     which they are promised;

43 يَوْمَ يَخْرُجُونَ مِنَ ٱلْأَجْدَاثِ     43 the day when they emerge from the graves,

سِرَاعًا     hastening,

كَأَنَّهُمْ إِلَىٰ نُصُبٍ يُوفِضُونَ ۝     as if racing toward a target,

44 خَـٰشِعَةً أَبْصَـٰرُهُمْ     44 with a humbled look [in their eyes],

تَرْهَقُهُمْ ذِلَّةٌ ۚ     overcast by abasement.

ذَٰلِكَ ٱلْيَوْمُ ٱلَّذِى كَانُوا۟ يُوعَدُونَ ۝     Such is the day they are promised.

---

[1] That is, from a drop of sperm.

## 71. SŪRAT NŪḤ[1]

بِسْمِ ٱللَّهِ
ٱلرَّحْمَٰنِ ٱلرَّحِيمِ

In the Name of Allah,
the All-beneficent, the All-merciful.

إِنَّا أَرْسَلْنَا نُوحًا إِلَىٰ قَوْمِهِۦ 1 Indeed We sent Noah to his people,

أَنْ أَنذِرْ قَوْمَكَ [saying,] 'Warn your people

مِن قَبْلِ أَن يَأْتِيَهُمْ عَذَابٌ أَلِيمٌ ۝ before a painful punishment overtakes them.'

قَالَ يَٰقَوْمِ 2 He said, 'O my people!

إِنِّي لَكُمْ نَذِيرٌ مُّبِينٌ ۝ Indeed I am a manifest warner to you.

أَنِ ٱعْبُدُوا۟ ٱللَّهَ وَٱتَّقُوهُ 3 Worship Allah and be wary of Him,

وَأَطِيعُونِ ۝ and obey me,

يَغْفِرْ لَكُم مِّن ذُنُوبِكُمْ 4 that He may forgive you some of your sins

وَيُؤَخِّرْكُمْ إِلَىٰ أَجَلٍ مُّسَمًّى and respite you until a specified time.

إِنَّ أَجَلَ ٱللَّهِ إِذَا جَآءَ Indeed when Allah's [appointed] time comes,

لَا يُؤَخَّرُ it cannot be deferred,

لَوْ كُنتُمْ تَعْلَمُونَ ۝ should you know.'

قَالَ رَبِّ 5 He said, 'My Lord!

إِنِّي دَعَوْتُ قَوْمِي لَيْلًا وَنَهَارًا ۝ Indeed I have summoned my people night and day

فَلَمْ يَزِدْهُمْ دُعَآءِىٓ إِلَّا فِرَارًا ۝ 6 but my summon only increases their evasion.

وَإِنِّي كُلَّمَا دَعَوْتُهُمْ 7 Indeed whenever I have summoned them,

لِتَغْفِرَ لَهُمْ so that You might forgive them,

جَعَلُوٓا۟ أَصَٰبِعَهُمْ فِىٓ ءَاذَانِهِمْ they would put their fingers into their ears

وَٱسْتَغْشَوْا۟ ثِيَابَهُمْ and draw their cloaks over their heads,

وَأَصَرُّوا۟ and they were persistent [in their unfaith],

وَٱسْتَكْبَرُوا۟ ٱسْتِكْبَارًا ۝ and disdainful in [their] arrogance.

ثُمَّ إِنِّي دَعَوْتُهُمْ جِهَارًا ۝ 8 Again I summoned them aloud,

ثُمَّ إِنِّىٓ أَعْلَنتُ لَهُمْ 9 and again appealed to them publicly

---

[1]The *sūrah* is named after Noah ('a), whose account is related in it.

وَأَسْرَرْتُ لَهُمْ إِسْرَارًا ۞    and confided with them privately,

فَقُلْتُ ٱسْتَغْفِرُوا۟ رَبَّكُمْ 10    telling [them]: "Plead to your Lord for forgiveness.

إِنَّهُۥ كَانَ غَفَّارًا ۞    Indeed He is all-forgiver.

يُرْسِلِ ٱلسَّمَآءَ عَلَيْكُم مِّدْرَارًا ۞ 11    He will send for you abundant rains from the sky,

وَيُمْدِدْكُم بِأَمْوَٰلٍ وَبَنِينَ 12    and aid you with wealth and sons,

وَيَجْعَل لَّكُمْ جَنَّٰتٍ    and provide you with gardens

وَيَجْعَل لَّكُمْ أَنْهَٰرًا ۞    and provide you with streams.

مَّا لَكُمْ 13    What is the matter with you

لَا تَرْجُونَ لِلَّهِ وَقَارًا ۞    that you do not look upon Allah with veneration,

وَقَدْ خَلَقَكُمْ أَطْوَارًا ۞ 14    while He created you in [various] stages?

أَلَمْ تَرَوْا۟ كَيْفَ خَلَقَ ٱللَّهُ 15    Have you not seen how Allah has created

سَبْعَ سَمَٰوَٰتٍ طِبَاقًا ۞    seven heavens in layers,

وَجَعَلَ ٱلْقَمَرَ فِيهِنَّ نُورًا 16    and has made therein the moon for a light,

وَجَعَلَ ٱلشَّمْسَ سِرَاجًا ۞    and the sun for a lamp?

وَٱللَّهُ أَنۢبَتَكُم مِّنَ ٱلْأَرْضِ 17    Allah made you grow from the earth,

نَبَاتًا ۞    with a [vegetable] growth.

ثُمَّ يُعِيدُكُمْ فِيهَا 18    Then He makes you return to it,

وَيُخْرِجُكُمْ إِخْرَاجًا ۞    and He will bring you forth [without fail].

وَٱللَّهُ جَعَلَ لَكُمُ ٱلْأَرْضَ بِسَاطًا ۞ 19    Allah has made the earth a vast expanse for you

لِّتَسْلُكُوا۟ مِنْهَا سُبُلًا فِجَاجًا ۞ 20    so that you may travel over its spacious ways." '

قَالَ نُوحٌ رَّبِّ 21    Noah said, 'My Lord!

إِنَّهُمْ عَصَوْنِى    They have disobeyed me,

وَٱتَّبَعُوا۟ مَن    following someone

لَّمْ يَزِدْهُ مَالُهُۥ وَوَلَدُهُۥٓ إِلَّا خَسَارًا ۞    whose wealth and children only add to his loss,

وَمَكَرُوا۟ مَكْرًا كُبَّارًا ۞ 22    and they have devised an outrageous plot.

وَقَالُوا۟ لَا تَذَرُنَّ ءَالِهَتَكُمْ 23    They say, "Do not abandon your gods.

وَلَا تَذَرُنَّ وَدًّا وَلَا سُوَاعًا    Do not abandon Wadd, nor Suwā,

وَلَا يَغُوثَ وَيَعُوقَ وَنَسْرًا ۞    nor Yaghūth, Ya'ūq and Nasr,"[1]

وَقَدْ أَضَلُّوا۟ كَثِيرًا 24    and they have certainly led many astray.

---

[1] Names of Babylonian gods worshipped by the polytheists.

وَلَا تَزِدِ ٱلظَّٰلِمِينَ إِلَّا ضَلَٰلًا ۝

Do not increase the wrongdoers in anything but error.'

مِمَّا خَطِيٓـَٰٔتِهِمْ أُغْرِقُوا۟

25 They were drowned because of their iniquities,

فَأُدْخِلُوا۟ نَارًا

then made to enter a Fire,

فَلَمْ يَجِدُوا۟ لَهُم

and they did not find for themselves

مِّن دُونِ ٱللَّهِ أَنصَارًا ۝

any helpers besides Allah.

وَقَالَ نُوحٌ رَّبِّ

26 And Noah said, 'My Lord!

لَا تَذَرْ عَلَى ٱلْأَرْضِ

'Do not leave on the earth

مِنَ ٱلْكَٰفِرِينَ دَيَّارًا ۝

any inhabitant from among the faithless.

إِنَّكَ إِن تَذَرْهُمْ يُضِلُّوا۟ عِبَادَكَ

27 If You leave them, they will lead astray Your servants

وَلَا يَلِدُوٓا۟ إِلَّا فَاجِرًا كَفَّارًا ۝

and will not beget except vicious ingrates.

رَّبِّ ٱغْفِرْ لِى وَلِوَٰلِدَىَّ

28 My Lord! Forgive me and my parents,

وَلِمَن دَخَلَ بَيْتِىَ مُؤْمِنًا

and whoever enters my house in faith,

وَلِلْمُؤْمِنِينَ وَٱلْمُؤْمِنَٰتِ

and the faithful men and women,

وَلَا تَزِدِ ٱلظَّٰلِمِينَ

and do not increase the wrongdoers in anything

إِلَّا تَبَارًۢا ۝

except ruin.'

## سُورَةُ ٱلْجِنِّ

## 72. SŪRAT AL-JINN[1]

بِسْمِ ٱللَّهِ
ٱلرَّحْمَٰنِ ٱلرَّحِيمِ

In the Name of Allah,
the All-beneficent, the All-merciful.

قُلْ أُوحِىَ إِلَىَّ

1 *Say,* 'It has been revealed to me

أَنَّهُ ٱسْتَمَعَ نَفَرٌ مِّنَ ٱلْجِنِّ

that a team of the jinn listened [to the Qur'ān],

فَقَالُوٓا۟ إِنَّا سَمِعْنَا قُرْءَانًا عَجَبًا ۝

and they said, 'Indeed we heard a wonderful *qur'ān*,[2]

يَهْدِىٓ إِلَى ٱلرُّشْدِ

2 which guides to rectitude.

فَـَٔامَنَّا بِهِۦ

Hence we have believed in it

وَلَن نُّشْرِكَ بِرَبِّنَآ أَحَدًا ۝

and we will never ascribe any partner to our Lord.

وَأَنَّهُۥ تَعَٰلَىٰ جَدُّ رَبِّنَا

3 Exalted be the majesty of our Lord,

---

[1] The *sūrah* is named after the jinn, whose account is given in its first part.

[2] Or 'recital.'

مَا ٱتَّخَذَ صَٰحِبَةً وَلَا وَلَدًا ۝    He has taken neither any spouse nor son.

وَأَنَّهُۥ كَانَ يَقُولُ سَفِيهُنَا 4    Indeed the foolish ones among us used to utter

عَلَى ٱللَّهِ شَطَطًا ۝    atrocious lies concerning Allah.

وَأَنَّا ظَنَنَّآ 5    Indeed we thought

أَن لَّن تَقُولَ ٱلْإِنسُ وَٱلْجِنُّ    that humans and jinn would never utter

عَلَى ٱللَّهِ كَذِبًا ۝    any falsehood concerning Allah.

وَأَنَّهُۥ كَانَ رِجَالٌ مِّنَ ٱلْإِنسِ 6    Indeed some persons from the humans

يَعُوذُونَ بِرِجَالٍ مِّنَ ٱلْجِنِّ    would seek the protection of some persons from the jinn,

فَزَادُوهُمْ رَهَقًا ۝    thus only adding to their rebellion.

وَأَنَّهُمْ ظَنُّوا۟ كَمَا ظَنَنتُمْ 7    They[1] thought, just as you think,

أَن لَّن يَبْعَثَ ٱللَّهُ أَحَدًا ۝    that Allah will not raise anyone from the dead.

وَأَنَّا لَمَسْنَا ٱلسَّمَآءَ 8    Indeed We made for the heaven

فَوَجَدْنَٰهَا    and found it

مُلِئَتْ حَرَسًا شَدِيدًا وَشُهُبًا ۝    full of mighty sentries and flames,[2]

وَأَنَّا كُنَّا نَقْعُدُ مِنْهَا مَقَٰعِدَ لِلسَّمْعِ 9    We used to sit in its positions to eavesdrop,

فَمَن يَسْتَمِعِ ٱلْآنَ    but anyone listening now

يَجِدْ لَهُۥ شِهَابًا رَّصَدًا ۝    finds a flame waiting for him.

وَأَنَّا لَا نَدْرِىٓ أَشَرٌّ أُرِيدَ 10    We do not know whether ill is intended

بِمَن فِى ٱلْأَرْضِ    for those who are in the earth,

أَمْ أَرَادَ بِهِمْ رَبُّهُمْ رَشَدًا ۝    or whether their Lord intends good for them.

وَأَنَّا مِنَّا ٱلصَّٰلِحُونَ 11    Among us some are righteous

وَمِنَّا دُونَ ذَٰلِكَ    and some of us are otherwise:

كُنَّا طَرَآئِقَ قِدَدًا ۝    we are multifarious sects.

وَأَنَّا ظَنَنَّآ أَن لَّن نُّعْجِزَ ٱللَّهَ 12    We know that we cannot thwart Allah

فِى ٱلْأَرْضِ    on the earth,

وَلَن نُّعْجِزَهُۥ هَرَبًا ۝    nor can we thwart Him by fleeing.

وَأَنَّا لَمَّا سَمِعْنَا ٱلْهُدَىٰٓ 13    When we heard the [message of] guidance,

ءَامَنَّا بِهِۦ    we believed in it.

---

[1] That is, the humans who invoked the protection of jinns.
[2] Or 'meteors.'

فَمَن يُؤْمِنُ بِرَبِّهِ

Whoever that has faith in his Lord

فَلَا يَخَافُ بَخْسًا وَلَا رَهَقًا ۝

shall neither fear any detraction nor oppression.

وَأَنَّا مِنَّا ٱلْمُسْلِمُونَ

14 Among us some are *muslims*

وَمِنَّا ٱلْقَاسِطُونَ ۚ

and some of us are perverse.[1]

فَمَنْ أَسْلَمَ

Yet those who submit [to Allah]

فَأُوْلَٰٓئِكَ تَحَرَّوْاْ رَشَدًا ۝

—it is they who pursue rectitude.

وَأَمَّا ٱلْقَاسِطُونَ

15 As for the perverse,

فَكَانُواْ لِجَهَنَّمَ حَطَبًا ۝

they will be firewood for hell.'

وَأَلَّوِ ٱسْتَقَٰمُواْ عَلَى ٱلطَّرِيقَةِ

16 If they are steadfast on the path [of Allah],

لَأَسْقَيْنَٰهُم مَّآءً غَدَقًا ۝

We shall provide them with abundant water,

لِّنَفْتِنَهُمْ فِيهِ ۚ

17 so that We may test them therein,

وَمَن يُعْرِضْ

and whoever turns away

عَن ذِكْرِ رَبِّهِ

from the remembrance of his Lord,

يَسْلُكْهُ عَذَابًا صَعَدًا ۝

He will let him into an escalating punishment.

وَأَنَّ ٱلْمَسَٰجِدَ لِلَّهِ

18 The places of worship belong to Allah,

فَلَا تَدْعُواْ مَعَ ٱللَّهِ أَحَدًا ۝

so do not invoke anyone along with Allah.

وَأَنَّهُۥ لَمَّا قَامَ عَبْدُ ٱللَّهِ يَدْعُوهُ

19 When the servant of Allah[2] rose to pray to Him,

كَادُواْ يَكُونُونَ عَلَيْهِ لِبَدًا ۝

they almost crowded around him.

قُلْ إِنَّمَآ أَدْعُواْ رَبِّي

20 *Say,* 'I pray only to my Lord,

وَلَآ أُشْرِكُ بِهِۦٓ أَحَدًا ۝

and I do not ascribe any partner to Him.'

قُلْ إِنِّى لَآ أَمْلِكُ لَكُمْ ضَرًّا

21 *Say,* 'I have no power to bring you any harm

وَلَا رَشَدًا ۝

or good [of my own accord].'

قُلْ إِنِّى لَن يُجِيرَنِى مِنَ ٱللَّهِ أَحَدٌ

22 *Say,* 'Neither can anyone shelter me from Allah,

وَلَنْ أَجِدَ مِن دُونِهِۦ مُلْتَحَدًا ۝

nor can I find any refuge besides Him.

إِلَّا بَلَٰغًا مِّنَ ٱللَّهِ

23 [I have no duty] except to transmit from Allah,

وَرِسَٰلَٰتِهِۦ ۚ

and [to communicate] His messages;

وَمَن يَعْصِ ٱللَّهَ وَرَسُولَهُۥ

and whoever disobeys Allah and His apostle,

فَإِنَّ لَهُۥ نَارَ جَهَنَّمَ

indeed there will be for him the fire of hell,

---

[1] Or 'unjust.'

[2] That is, the Prophet.

خَٰلِدِينَ فِيهَآ أَبَدًا ۝

to remain in it forever.'

حَتَّىٰٓ إِذَا رَأَوۡاْ مَا يُوعَدُونَ

24 When they see what they are promised,

فَسَيَعۡلَمُونَ مَنۡ أَضۡعَفُ نَاصِرًا

they will then know who is weaker in supporters

وَأَقَلُّ عَدَدًا ۝

and fewer in numbers.

قُلۡ إِنۡ أَدۡرِىٓ أَقَرِيبٌ مَّا تُوعَدُونَ

25 *Say,* 'I do not know if what you are promised is near,

أَمۡ يَجۡعَلُ لَهُۥ رَبِّىٓ أَمَدًا ۝

or if my Lord has set a term for it.'

عَٰلِمُ ٱلۡغَيۡبِ

26   Knower of the Unseen,

فَلَا يُظۡهِرُ عَلَىٰ غَيۡبِهِۦٓ أَحَدًا ۝

He does not disclose His Unseen to anyone,

إِلَّا مَنِ ٱرۡتَضَىٰ مِن رَّسُولٍ

27   except to an apostle He approves of.

فَإِنَّهُۥ يَسۡلُكُ

Then He dispatches

مِنۢ بَيۡنِ يَدَيۡهِ وَمِنۡ خَلۡفِهِۦ رَصَدًا ۝

a sentinel before and behind him

لِّيَعۡلَمَ

28   so that He may ascertain

أَن قَدۡ أَبۡلَغُواْ

that they have communicated

رِسَٰلَٰتِ رَبِّهِمۡ

the messages of their Lord,

وَأَحَاطَ بِمَا لَدَيۡهِمۡ

and He comprehends all that is with them,

وَأَحۡصَىٰ كُلَّ شَىۡءٍ عَدَدًا ۝

and He keeps count of all things.

## سُورَةُ المُزَّمِّل     73. SŪRAT AL- MUZZAMMIL[1]

بِسۡمِ ٱللَّهِ     In the Name of Allah,

ٱلرَّحۡمَٰنِ ٱلرَّحِيمِ     the All-beneficent, the All-merciful.

يَٰٓأَيُّهَا ٱلۡمُزَّمِّلُ ۝

1 O *you* wrapped up in *your* mantle!

قُمِ ٱلَّيۡلَ إِلَّا قَلِيلًا ۝

2 *Stand vigil* through the night, except a little,

نِّصۡفَهُۥٓ أَوِ ٱنقُصۡ مِنۡهُ قَلِيلًا ۝

3   a half, or *reduce* a little from that

أَوۡ زِدۡ عَلَيۡهِ

4   or *add* to it,

وَرَتِّلِ ٱلۡقُرۡءَانَ تَرۡتِيلًا ۝

and *recite* the Qur'ān in a measured tone.

إِنَّا سَنُلۡقِى عَلَيۡكَ قَوۡلًا ثَقِيلًا ۝

5 Indeed soon We shall cast on *you* a weighty word.

---

[1]The *sūrah* takes its name from the word "*muzzammil*" (wrapped in mantle) in verse 1.

إِنَّ نَاشِئَةَ ٱلَّيْلِ هِىَ أَشَدُّ وَطْـًٔا 6 Indeed the watch of the night is firmer in tread

وَأَقْوَمُ قِيلًا ۞     and more upright in respect to speech,

إِنَّ لَكَ فِى ٱلنَّهَارِ 7     for indeed during the day *you* have

سَبْحًا طَوِيلًا ۞     drawn-out engagements.

وَٱذْكُرِ ٱسْمَ رَبِّكَ 8 So *celebrate* the Name of *your* Lord

وَتَبَتَّلْ إِلَيْهِ تَبْتِيلًا ۞     and dedicate yourself to Him with total dedication.[1]

رَّبُّ ٱلْمَشْرِقِ وَٱلْمَغْرِبِ 9 Lord of the east and the west,

لَآ إِلَٰهَ إِلَّا هُوَ     there is no god except Him,

فَٱتَّخِذْهُ وَكِيلًا ۞     so take Him for *your* trustee,

وَٱصْبِرْ عَلَىٰ مَا يَقُولُونَ 10     and *be patient* over what they say,

وَٱهْجُرْهُمْ هَجْرًا جَمِيلًا ۞     and *keep away* from them in a graceful manner.

وَذَرْنِى وَٱلْمُكَذِّبِينَ أُو۟لِى ٱلنَّعْمَةِ 11 Leave Me [to deal] with the deniers, the opulent,

وَمَهِّلْهُمْ قَلِيلًا ۞     and *give* them a little respite.

إِنَّ لَدَيْنَآ أَنكَالًا وَجَحِيمًا ۞ 12 Indeed with Us are heavy fetters and a fierce fire,

وَطَعَامًا ذَا غُصَّةٍ 13     and a food that chokes [those who gulp it],

وَعَذَابًا أَلِيمًا ۞     and a painful punishment [prepared for]

يَوْمَ تَرْجُفُ ٱلْأَرْضُ وَٱلْجِبَالُ 14 the day when the earth and the mountains will quake,

وَكَانَتِ ٱلْجِبَالُ كَثِيبًا مَّهِيلًا ۞     and the mountains will be like dunes of shifting sand.

إِنَّآ أَرْسَلْنَآ إِلَيْكُمْ رَسُولًا 15 Indeed We have sent to you an apostle,

شَٰهِدًا عَلَيْكُمْ     to be a witness to you,

كَمَآ أَرْسَلْنَآ إِلَىٰ فِرْعَوْنَ رَسُولًا ۞     just as We sent an apostle to Pharaoh.

فَعَصَىٰ فِرْعَوْنُ ٱلرَّسُولَ 16 But Pharaoh disobeyed the apostle;

فَأَخَذْنَٰهُ أَخْذًا وَبِيلًا ۞     so We seized him with a terrible seizing.

فَكَيْفَ تَتَّقُونَ إِن كَفَرْتُمْ يَوْمًا 17 So, if you disbelieve, how will you avoid the day

يَجْعَلُ ٱلْوِلْدَٰنَ شِيبًا ۞     which will make children white-headed,

ٱلسَّمَآءُ مُنفَطِرٌۢ بِهِۦ 18     and wherein the sky will be rent apart?

كَانَ وَعْدُهُۥ مَفْعُولًا ۞     His promise is bound to be fulfilled.

إِنَّ هَٰذِهِۦ تَذْكِرَةٌ 19 This is indeed a reminder.

---

[1] Or 'supplicate with your forefinger pointed towards heaven' (see *al-Tafsīr al-Burhān* for traditions relating to *tabattul*).

فَمَن شَآءَ ٱتَّخَذَ إِلَىٰ رَبِّهِۦ سَبِيلًا ۞    So let anyone who wishes take the way toward his Lord.

إِنَّ رَبَّكَ يَعْلَمُ    20 Indeed *your* Lord knows

أَنَّكَ تَقُومُ أَدْنَىٰ مِن ثُلُثَيِ ٱلَّيْلِ    that *you* stand vigil nearly two thirds of the night

وَنِصْفَهُۥ وَثُلُثَهُۥ    —or [at times] a half or a third of it—

وَطَآئِفَةٌ مِّنَ ٱلَّذِينَ مَعَكَ    along with a group of those who are with *you*.

وَٱللَّهُ يُقَدِّرُ ٱلَّيْلَ وَٱلنَّهَارَ    Allah measures the night and the day.

عَلِمَ أَن لَّن تُحْصُوهُ    He knows that you cannot calculate it [exactly],

فَتَابَ عَلَيْكُمْ    and so He was lenient toward you.

فَٱقْرَءُوا مَا تَيَسَّرَ مِنَ ٱلْقُرْءَانِ    So recite as much of the Qurʾān as is feasible.

عَلِمَ أَن سَيَكُونُ مِنكُم مَّرْضَىٰ    He knows that some of you will be sick,

وَءَاخَرُونَ يَضْرِبُونَ فِي ٱلْأَرْضِ    while others will travel in the land

يَبْتَغُونَ مِن فَضْلِ ٱللَّهِ    seeking Allah's grace,

وَءَاخَرُونَ يُقَٰتِلُونَ فِي سَبِيلِ ٱللَّهِ    and yet others will fight in the way of Allah.

فَٱقْرَءُوا مَا تَيَسَّرَ مِنْهُ    So recite as much of it as is feasible,

وَأَقِيمُوا ٱلصَّلَوٰةَ وَءَاتُوا ٱلزَّكَوٰةَ    and maintain the prayer and pay the *zakāt*

وَأَقْرِضُوا ٱللَّهَ قَرْضًا حَسَنًا    and lend Allah a good loan.

وَمَا تُقَدِّمُوا لِأَنفُسِكُم مِّنْ خَيْرٍ    Whatever good you send ahead for your souls

تَجِدُوهُ عِندَ ٱللَّهِ    you will find it with Allah [in a form]

هُوَ خَيْرًا وَأَعْظَمَ أَجْرًا    that is better and greater with respect to reward.

وَٱسْتَغْفِرُوا ٱللَّهَ    And plead to Allah for forgiveness;

إِنَّ ٱللَّهَ غَفُورٌ رَّحِيمٌ ۞    indeed Allah is all-forgiving, all-merciful.

# سُورَةُ ٱلْمُدَّثِّرِ    74. SŪRAT AL-MUDDATHTHIR[1]

بِسْمِ ٱللَّهِ    In the Name of Allah,

ٱلرَّحْمَٰنِ ٱلرَّحِيمِ    the All-beneficent, the All-merciful.

يَٰأَيُّهَا ٱلْمُدَّثِّرُ ۞    1 O *you* wrapped up in *your* mantle!

---

[1] The *sūrah* takes its name from the word "*muddaththir*" (wrapped in mantle) in verse 1.

قُمْ فَأَنذِرْ ۝ 2 Rise up and warn!

وَرَبَّكَ فَكَبِّرْ ۝ 3 Magnify *your* Lord,

وَثِيَابَكَ فَطَهِّرْ ۝ 4 and purify *your* cloak,

وَالرُّجْزَ فَاهْجُرْ ۝ 5 and *keep away* from all impurity!

وَلَا تَمْنُن تَسْتَكْثِرُ ۝ 6 *Do not grant* a favour seeking a greater gain,

وَلِرَبِّكَ فَاصْبِرْ ۝ 7 and *be patient* for the sake of your Lord.

فَإِذَا نُقِرَ فِي ٱلنَّاقُورِ ۝ 8 When the trumpet will be sounded,

فَذَٰلِكَ يَوْمَئِذٍ يَوْمٌ عَسِيرٌ ۝ 9 that day will be a day of hardship,

عَلَى ٱلْكَافِرِينَ غَيْرُ يَسِيرٍ ۝ 10 not at all easy for the faithless.

ذَرْنِي وَمَنْ خَلَقْتُ وَحِيدًا ۝ 11 Leave Me [to deal] with him whom I created alone,

وَجَعَلْتُ لَهُ مَالًا مَّمْدُودًا ۝ 12 and then furnished him with extensive means,

وَبَنِينَ شُهُودًا ۝ 13 and [gave him] sons to be at his side,

وَمَهَّدْتُ لَهُ تَمْهِيدًا ۝ 14 and facilitated [all matters] for him.

ثُمَّ يَطْمَعُ أَنْ أَزِيدَ ۝ 15 Still he is eager that I should give him more.

كَلَّا إِنَّهُ كَانَ لِآيَٰتِنَا عَنِيدًا ۝ 16 No indeed! He is a froward opponent of Our signs.

سَأُرْهِقُهُ صَعُودًا ۝ 17 Soon I will overwhelm him with hardship.

إِنَّهُ فَكَّرَ وَقَدَّرَ ۝ 18 Indeed he reflected and decided.

فَقُتِلَ كَيْفَ قَدَّرَ ۝ 19 Perish he, how he decided!

ثُمَّ قُتِلَ كَيْفَ قَدَّرَ ۝ 20 Again, perish he, how he decided!

ثُمَّ نَظَرَ ۝ 21 Then he looked;

ثُمَّ عَبَسَ وَبَسَرَ ۝ 22 then he frowned and scowled.

ثُمَّ أَدْبَرَ وَٱسْتَكْبَرَ ۝ 23 Then he went away disdainfully,

فَقَالَ إِنْ هَٰذَآ إِلَّا سِحْرٌ يُؤْثَرُ ۝ 24 saying, 'It[1] is nothing but magic handed down.[2]

إِنْ هَٰذَآ إِلَّا قَوْلُ ٱلْبَشَرِ ۝ 25 It is nothing but the speech of a human being.'

سَأُصْلِيهِ سَقَرَ ۝ 26 Soon I shall cast him into Saqar.[3]

وَمَآ أَدْرَىٰكَ مَا سَقَرُ ۝ 27 And what will show *you* what is Saqar?

لَا تُبْقِي وَلَا تَذَرُ ۝ 28 It does not spare, nor leaves [anything].

---

[1] That is, the Qur'ān.

[2] That is, from the magicians of old. Or 'traditional magic.'

[3] *Saqar* is another name for hell or a part of it.

لَوَّاحَةٌ لِّلْبَشَرِ ۝  29 It burns the skin.

عَلَيْهَا تِسْعَةَ عَشَرَ ۝  30 There are nineteen [keepers] over it.

وَمَا جَعَلْنَآ أَصْحَٰبَ ٱلنَّارِ إِلَّا مَلَٰئِكَةً ۖ  31 We have assigned only angels as keepers of the Fire,

وَمَا جَعَلْنَا عِدَّتَهُمْ    and We have made their number

إِلَّا فِتْنَةً لِّلَّذِينَ كَفَرُواْ    merely a stumbling block for the faithless,

لِيَسْتَيْقِنَ ٱلَّذِينَ أُوتُواْ ٱلْكِتَٰبَ    and that those given the Book may be reassured,

وَيَزْدَادَ ٱلَّذِينَ ءَامَنُوٓاْ إِيمَٰنًا    and the faithful may increase in [their] faith,

وَلَا يَرْتَابَ ٱلَّذِينَ أُوتُواْ ٱلْكِتَٰبَ    and that those given the Book may not doubt

وَٱلْمُؤْمِنُونَ    and the faithful [as well],

وَلِيَقُولَ ٱلَّذِينَ فِى قُلُوبِهِم مَّرَضٌ    and that those in whose hearts is a sickness may say,

وَٱلْكَٰفِرُونَ    and the faithless [along with them],

مَاذَآ أَرَادَ ٱللَّهُ بِهَٰذَا مَثَلًا ۚ    'What did Allah mean by this description?'

كَذَٰلِكَ يُضِلُّ ٱللَّهُ مَن يَشَآءُ    Thus does Allah lead astray whomever He wishes,

وَيَهْدِى مَن يَشَآءُ ۚ    and guides whomever He wishes.

وَمَا يَعْلَمُ جُنُودَ رَبِّكَ إِلَّا هُوَ ۚ    No one knows the hosts of *your* Lord except Him,

وَمَا هِىَ إِلَّا ذِكْرَىٰ لِلْبَشَرِ ۝    and it[1] is just an admonition for all humans.

كَلَّا    32 No indeed!

وَٱلْقَمَرِ ۝    By the Moon!

وَٱلَّيْلِ إِذْ أَدْبَرَ ۝  33    By the night when it recedes!

وَٱلصُّبْحِ إِذَآ أَسْفَرَ ۝  34    By the dawn when it brightens!

إِنَّهَا لَإِحْدَى ٱلْكُبَرِ ۝  35    Indeed it is one of the greatest [signs]

نَذِيرًا لِّلْبَشَرِ ۝  36    —a warner to all humans,

لِمَن شَآءَ مِنكُمْ أَن يَتَقَدَّمَ  37    [alike] for those of you who like to advance ahead

أَوْ يَتَأَخَّرَ ۝    and those who would linger behind.

كُلُّ نَفْسٍ بِمَا كَسَبَتْ رَهِينَةٌ ۝  38 Every soul is hostage to what it has earned,

إِلَّآ أَصْحَٰبَ ٱلْيَمِينِ ۝  39    except the People of the Right Hand.

فِى جَنَّٰتٍ يَتَسَآءَلُونَ ۝  40 [They will be] in gardens, questioning

عَنِ ٱلْمُجْرِمِينَ ۝  41    concerning the guilty:

مَا سَلَكَكُمْ فِى سَقَرَ ۝  42    'What drew you into Hell?'

---

[1] That is, the statement that there are nineteen wardens in charge of hell.

قَالُوا 43 They will answer,

لَمْ نَكُ مِنَ ٱلْمُصَلِّينَ ۝    'We were not among those who prayed.[1]

وَلَمْ نَكُ نُطْعِمُ ٱلْمِسْكِينَ ۝    44   Nor did we feed the poor.

وَكُنَّا نَخُوضُ مَعَ ٱلْخَائِضِينَ ۝    45   We used to gossip along with the gossipers,

وَكُنَّا نُكَذِّبُ بِيَوْمِ ٱلدِّينِ ۝    46   and we used to deny the Day of Retribution,[2]

حَتَّىٰ أَتَىٰنَا ٱلْيَقِينُ ۝    47   until death came to us.'

فَمَا تَنفَعُهُمْ شَفَٰعَةُ ٱلشَّٰفِعِينَ ۝    48 So the intercession of the intercessors will not avail them.

فَمَا لَهُمْ    49 What is the matter with them

عَنِ ٱلتَّذْكِرَةِ مُعْرِضِينَ ۝    that they evade the Reminder

كَأَنَّهُمْ حُمُرٌ مُّسْتَنفِرَةٌ ۝    50   as if they were terrified asses

فَرَّتْ مِن قَسْوَرَةٍ ۝    51   fleeing from a lion?

بَلْ يُرِيدُ كُلُّ ٱمْرِئٍ مِّنْهُمْ    52 Rather everyone of them desires

أَن يُؤْتَىٰ صُحُفًا مُّنَشَّرَةً ۝    to be given unrolled scriptures [from Allah].

كَلَّا    53 No indeed!

بَل لَّا يَخَافُونَ ٱلْءَاخِرَةَ ۝    Rather they do not fear the Hereafter.

كَلَّا    54 No indeed!

إِنَّهُ تَذْكِرَةٌ ۝    It is indeed a reminder.

فَمَن شَآءَ ذَكَرَهُ ۝    55 So let anyone who wishes remember it.

وَمَا يَذْكُرُونَ إِلَّآ أَن يَشَآءَ ٱللَّهُ    56 And they will not remember unless Allah wishes.

هُوَ أَهْلُ ٱلتَّقْوَىٰ    He is worthy of [your] being wary [of Him]

وَأَهْلُ ٱلْمَغْفِرَةِ ۝    and He is worthy to forgive.

---

سُورَةُ الْقِيَامَةِ      75. SŪRAT AL-QIYĀMAH[3]

بِسْمِ ٱللَّهِ      In the Name of Allah,

ٱلرَّحْمَٰنِ ٱلرَّحِيمِ      the All-beneficent, the All-merciful.

---

[1] Or 'We were not among followers of the *leaders* (or *forerunners*, mentioned in 56:10).' (See *Tafsīr Qummī*, *Tafsīr Furāt Kūfī*, *al-Kāfī*, i, 484, "Kitāb al-Ḥujjah," bāb 108 (bāb fīhi nukat wa nutaf min al-tanzīl fī al-wilāyah), no. 38.

[2] Or 'the Day of Judgement.'

[3] The *sūrah* takes its name from verse 1, which mentions the Day of Resurrection.

لَآ أُقْسِمُ بِيَوْمِ ٱلْقِيَـٰمَةِ ۞   1 I swear by the Day of Resurrection!

وَلَآ أُقْسِمُ بِٱلنَّفْسِ ٱللَّوَّامَةِ ۞   2 And I swear by the self-blaming soul!

أَيَحْسَبُ ٱلْإِنسَـٰنُ   3 Does man suppose

أَلَّن نَّجْمَعَ عِظَامَهُۥ ۞    that We shall not put together his bones?

بَلَىٰ   4 Yes indeed,

قَـٰدِرِينَ عَلَىٰٓ أَن نُّسَوِّىَ بَنَانَهُۥ ۞    We are able to proportion [even] his fingertips!

بَلْ يُرِيدُ ٱلْإِنسَـٰنُ لِيَفْجُرَ أَمَامَهُۥ ۞   5 Rather man desires to go on living viciously.

يَسْـَٔلُ أَيَّانَ يَوْمُ ٱلْقِيَـٰمَةِ ۞   6 He asks, 'When is this day of resurrection?!'

فَإِذَا بَرِقَ ٱلْبَصَرُ ۞   7 But when the eyes are dazzled,

وَخَسَفَ ٱلْقَمَرُ ۞   8 and the moon is eclipsed,

وَجُمِعَ ٱلشَّمْسُ وَٱلْقَمَرُ ۞   9 and the sun and the moon are brought together,

يَقُولُ ٱلْإِنسَـٰنُ يَوْمَئِذٍ   10 that day man will say,

أَيْنَ ٱلْمَفَرُّ ۞    'Where is the escape?'

كَلَّا لَا وَزَرَ ۞   11 No indeed! There is no refuge!

إِلَىٰ رَبِّكَ يَوْمَئِذٍ ٱلْمُسْتَقَرُّ ۞   12 That day the abode will be toward *your* Lord.

يُنَبَّؤُاْ ٱلْإِنسَـٰنُ يَوْمَئِذٍ   13 That day man will be informed

بِمَا قَدَّمَ وَأَخَّرَ ۞    about what he has sent ahead and left behind.

بَلِ ٱلْإِنسَـٰنُ عَلَىٰ نَفْسِهِۦ بَصِيرَةٌ ۞   14 Rather man is a witness to himself,

وَلَوْ أَلْقَىٰ مَعَاذِيرَهُۥ ۞   15 though he should offer his excuses.

لَا تُحَرِّكْ بِهِۦ لِسَانَكَ لِتَعْجَلَ بِهِۦٓ ۞   16 *Do not move your* tongue with it to hasten it.

إِنَّ عَلَيْنَا جَمْعَهُۥ   17 Indeed it is up to Us to put it together

وَقُرْءَانَهُۥ ۞    and to recite it.

فَإِذَا قَرَأْنَـٰهُ فَٱتَّبِعْ قُرْءَانَهُۥ ۞   18 And when We have recited it, *follow* its recitation.

ثُمَّ إِنَّ عَلَيْنَا بَيَانَهُۥ ۞   19 Then, its exposition indeed [also] lies with Us.

كَلَّا بَلْ تُحِبُّونَ ٱلْعَاجِلَةَ ۞   20 No Indeed! Rather you love this transitory life

وَتَذَرُونَ ٱلْءَاخِرَةَ ۞   21 and forsake the Hereafter.

وُجُوهٌ يَوْمَئِذٍ نَّاضِرَةٌ ۞   22 Some faces will be fresh on that day,

إِلَىٰ رَبِّهَا نَاظِرَةٌ ۞   23 looking at their Lord,

وَوُجُوهٌ يَوْمَئِذٍ بَاسِرَةٌ ۞   24 and some faces will be scowling on that day,

تَظُنُّ أَن يُفْعَلَ بِهَا   25 knowing that they will be dealt out

فَاقِرَةٌ ۝     a punishment breaking the spine.

كَلَّا 26     No indeed!

إِذَا بَلَغَتِ ٱلتَّرَاقِيَ ۝     When the soul reaches up to the collar bones,

وَقِيلَ مَنْ رَاقٍ ۝ 27     and it is said, 'Who will take him up?'[1]

وَظَنَّ أَنَّهُ ٱلْفِرَاقُ ۝ 28     and he knows that it is the [time of] parting,

وَٱلْتَفَّتِ ٱلسَّاقُ بِٱلسَّاقِ ۝ 29     and each shank clasps the other shank,[2]

إِلَى رَبِّكَ يَوْمَئِذٍ ٱلْمَسَاقُ ۝ 30     that day he shall be driven toward *your* Lord.

فَلَا صَدَّقَ وَلَا صَلَّى ۝ 31     He neither confirmed [the truth], nor prayed,

وَلَكِن كَذَّبَ وَتَوَلَّى ۝ 32     but denied [it] and turned away,

ثُمَّ ذَهَبَ إِلَى أَهْلِهِ يَتَمَطَّى ۝ 33     and went swaggering to his family.

أَوْلَى لَكَ فَأَوْلَى ۝ 34 So woe to you! Woe to you!

ثُمَّ أَوْلَى لَكَ فَأَوْلَى ۝ 35     Again, woe to you! Woe to you!

أَيَحْسَبُ ٱلْإِنسَٰنُ 36 Does man suppose

أَن يُتْرَكَ سُدًى ۝     that he would be abandoned to futility?

أَلَمْ يَكُ نُطْفَةً مِّن مَّنِيٍّ يُمْنَى ۝ 37 Was he not a drop of emitted semen?

ثُمَّ كَانَ عَلَقَةً ۝ 38 Then he became a clinging mass;

فَخَلَقَ فَسَوَّى ۝     then He created [him] and proportioned [him],

فَجَعَلَ مِنْهُ ٱلزَّوْجَيْنِ 39     and made of him the two sexes,

ٱلذَّكَرَ وَٱلْأُنثَى ۝     the male and the female.

أَلَيْسَ ذَٰلِكَ بِقَادِرٍ عَلَى 40     Is not such a one able

أَن يُحْيِيَ ٱلْمَوْتَى ۝     to revive the dead?

سُورَةُ الإنسان     **76. SŪRAT AL-INSĀN[3]**

بِسْمِ ٱللَّهِ     In the Name of Allah,

ٱلرَّحْمَٰنِ ٱلرَّحِيمِ     the All-beneficent, the All-merciful.

---

[1] That is, by the angels of mercy and the angels of wrath present at the side of the dying person, as to which of them will take charge of him. Or those who are present by the side of the dying person say, 'Where is the medicine man?

[2] An idiom suggesting a time of great hardship, or, metaphorically, death throes.

[3] The *sūrah* takes its name from the word "man" (*al-insān*) mentioned in verse 1.

هَلْ أَتَىٰ عَلَى ٱلْإِنسَٰنِ حِينٌ مِّنَ ٱلدَّهْرِ 1 Has there been for man a period of time

لَمْ يَكُن شَيْـًٔا مَّذْكُورًا ۝ when he was not anything worthy of mention?

إِنَّا خَلَقْنَا ٱلْإِنسَٰنَ 2 Indeed We created man

مِن نُّطْفَةٍ أَمْشَاجٍ from the drop of a mixed fluid[1]

نَّبْتَلِيهِ so that We may test him.

فَجَعَلْنَٰهُ سَمِيعًۢا بَصِيرًا ۝ So We made him endowed with hearing and sight.

إِنَّا هَدَيْنَٰهُ ٱلسَّبِيلَ 3 Indeed We have guided him to the way,

إِمَّا شَاكِرًا وَإِمَّا كَفُورًا ۝ be he grateful or ungrateful.

إِنَّآ أَعْتَدْنَا لِلْكَٰفِرِينَ 4 Indeed We have prepared for the faithless

سَلَٰسِلَا۟ وَأَغْلَٰلًا وَسَعِيرًا ۝ chains, iron collars, and a blaze.

إِنَّ ٱلْأَبْرَارَ يَشْرَبُونَ مِن كَأْسٍ 5 Indeed the pious will drink from a cup

كَانَ مِزَاجُهَا كَافُورًا ۝ seasoned with *Kāfūr*,[2]

عَيْنًا يَشْرَبُ بِهَا عِبَادُ ٱللَّهِ 6    a spring where the servants of Allah drink,

يُفَجِّرُونَهَا تَفْجِيرًا ۝ which they make to gush forth as they please.

يُوفُونَ بِٱلنَّذْرِ 7 They fulfill their vows

وَيَخَافُونَ يَوْمًا and fear a day

كَانَ شَرُّهُۥ مُسْتَطِيرًا ۝ whose ill will be widespread.

وَيُطْعِمُونَ ٱلطَّعَامَ عَلَىٰ حُبِّهِۦ 8 They give food, for the love of Him,

مِسْكِينًا وَيَتِيمًا وَأَسِيرًا ۝ to the needy, the orphan and the prisoner,

إِنَّمَا نُطْعِمُكُمْ لِوَجْهِ ٱللَّهِ 9 [saying,] 'We feed you only for the sake of Allah.

لَا نُرِيدُ مِنكُمْ جَزَآءً We do not want any reward from you

وَلَا شُكُورًا ۝ nor any thanks.

إِنَّا نَخَافُ مِن رَّبِّنَا يَوْمًا 10    Indeed we fear from our Lord a day,

عَبُوسًا قَمْطَرِيرًا ۝ frowning and fateful.'

فَوَقَىٰهُمُ ٱللَّهُ شَرَّ ذَٰلِكَ ٱلْيَوْمِ 11 So Allah saved them from the ills of that day,

وَلَقَّىٰهُمْ نَضْرَةً وَسُرُورًا ۝ and granted them freshness and joy.

وَجَزَىٰهُم بِمَا صَبَرُوا۟ 12    And He rewarded them for their patience

جَنَّةً وَحَرِيرًا ۝ with a garden and [garments of] silk,

---

[1] That is, from the mixing of sperm and ovum.

[2] Lit., camphor.

مُتَّكِئِينَ فِيهَا عَلَى الْأَرَآئِكِ 13 reclining therein on couches.

لَا يَرَوْنَ فِيهَا شَمْسًا They will find in it neither any [scorching] sun,

وَلَا زَمْهَرِيرًا ۱۳ nor any [biting] cold.

وَدَانِيَةً عَلَيْهِمْ ظِلَالُهَا 14 Its shades will be close over them

وَذُلِّلَتْ قُطُوفُهَا تَذْلِيلًا ۱ and its clusters [of fruits] will be hanging low.

وَيُطَافُ عَلَيْهِم بِآنِيَةٍ مِّن فِضَّةٍ 15 They will be served around with vessels of silver

وَأَكْوَابٍ كَانَتْ قَوَارِيرَا۠ ۱ and goblets of crystal

قَوَارِيرَا۠ مِن فِضَّةٍ 16 —crystal of silver—[1]

قَدَّرُوهَا تَقْدِيرًا ۱ [from] which they dispense in a precise measure.

وَيُسْقَوْنَ فِيهَا كَأْسًا 17 They will be served therein with a cup of a drink

كَانَ مِزَاجُهَا زَنجَبِيلًا ۱۷ seasoned with *Zanjabīl*,[2]

عَيْنًا فِيهَا تُسَمَّىٰ سَلْسَبِيلًا ۱۸ 18 a spring in it, named *Salsabīl*.

وَيَطُوفُ عَلَيْهِمْ وِلْدَانٌ مُّخَلَّدُونَ 19 They will be waited upon by immortals youths,

إِذَا رَأَيْتَهُمْ whom, when you see them,

حَسِبْتَهُمْ لُؤْلُؤًا مَّنثُورًا ۲ you will suppose them to be scattered pearls.

وَإِذَا رَأَيْتَ 20 As you look,

ثَمَّ رَأَيْتَ نَعِيمًا وَمُلْكًا كَبِيرًا ۲ you will see there bliss and a great kingdom.

عَلِيَهُمْ ثِيَابُ سُندُسٍ خُضْرٌ 21 Upon them will be cloaks of green silk

وَإِسْتَبْرَقٌ and brocade

وَحُلُّوا أَسَاوِرَ مِن فِضَّةٍ and they will be adorned with bracelets of silver.

وَسَقَاهُمْ رَبُّهُمْ شَرَابًا طَهُورًا ۲ Their Lord will give them to drink a pure drink.

إِنَّ هَـٰذَا كَانَ لَكُمْ جَزَآءً 22 [They will be told]: 'This is indeed your reward,

وَكَانَ سَعْيُكُم مَّشْكُورًا ۲ and your endeavour has been well-appreciated.'

إِنَّا نَحْنُ نَزَّلْنَا عَلَيْكَ الْقُرْءَانَ 23 Indeed We have sent down to *you* the Qur'ān

تَنزِيلًا ۲ in a gradual descent.

فَاصْبِرْ لِحُكْمِ رَبِّكَ 24 So *submit patiently* to the judgement of *your* Lord,

وَلَا تُطِعْ مِنْهُمْ ءَاثِمًا أَوْ كَفُورًا ۲ and *do not obey* any sinner or ingrate among them,

وَاذْكُرِ اسْمَ رَبِّكَ 25 and *celebrate* the Name of *your* Lord

---

[1] According to *Tafsīr al-Qummī*, vol. 2, p. 399, the silver will be transparent.
[2] *Lit.*, ginger.

بُكْرَةً وَأَصِيلًا ۝      morning and evening,

وَمِنَ ٱلَّيْلِ فَٱسْجُدْ لَهُۥ 26    and *worship* Him for a watch of the night

وَسَبِّحْهُ لَيْلًا طَوِيلًا ۝      and *glorify* Him the night long.

إِنَّ هَٰٓؤُلَآءِ يُحِبُّونَ ٱلْعَاجِلَةَ 27   Indeed they love this transitory life,

وَيَذَرُونَ وَرَآءَهُمْ يَوْمًا ثَقِيلًا ۝   and disregard a weighty day ahead of them.

نَّحْنُ خَلَقْنَٰهُمْ وَشَدَدْنَآ أَسْرَهُمْ 28   We created them and made their joints firm,

وَإِذَا شِئْنَا      and whenever We like

بَدَّلْنَآ أَمْثَٰلَهُمْ تَبْدِيلًا ۝      We will replace them with others like them.

إِنَّ هَٰذِهِۦ تَذْكِرَةٌ 29   This is indeed a reminder.

فَمَن شَآءَ ٱتَّخَذَ إِلَىٰ رَبِّهِۦ سَبِيلًا ۝   So let anyone who wishes take the way toward his Lord.

وَمَا تَشَآءُونَ 30   But you do not wish

إِلَّآ أَن يَشَآءَ ٱللَّهُ      unless it is wished by Allah.

إِنَّ ٱللَّهَ كَانَ عَلِيمًا حَكِيمًا ۝      Indeed Allah is all-knowing, all-wise.

يُدْخِلُ مَن يَشَآءُ فِى رَحْمَتِهِۦ 31   He admits whomever He wishes into His mercy,

وَٱلظَّٰلِمِينَ      and as for the wrongdoers,

أَعَدَّ لَهُمْ عَذَابًا أَلِيمًا ۝      He has prepared for them a painful punishment.

## سُورَةُ المُرْسَلاتِ      77. SŪRAT AL-MURSALĀT[1]

بِسْمِ ٱللَّهِ      In the Name of Allah,

ٱلرَّحْمَٰنِ ٱلرَّحِيمِ      the All-beneficent, the All-merciful.

وَٱلْمُرْسَلَٰتِ عُرْفًا ۝ 1   By the successive emissaries,[2]

فَٱلْعَٰصِفَٰتِ عَصْفًا ۝ 2   by the raging hurricanes,

وَٱلنَّٰشِرَٰتِ نَشْرًا ۝ 3   by the sweeping spreaders,

فَٱلْفَٰرِقَٰتِ فَرْقًا ۝ 4   by the decisive separators,

فَٱلْمُلْقِيَٰتِ ذِكْرًا ۝ 5   by the inspirers of remembrance,

عُذْرًا أَوْ نُذْرًا ۝ 6   to excuse or to warn:

---

[1] The *sūrah* takes its name from the "emissaries" (*mursalāt*) mentioned in verse 1.

[2] Or 'By the benign emissaries.'

إِنَّمَا تُوعَدُونَ لَوَقِعٌ ۝ 7 indeed what you are promised will surely befall.

فَإِذَا ٱلنُّجُومُ طُمِسَتْ ۝ 8 So when the stars are blotted out,

وَإِذَا ٱلسَّمَآءُ فُرِجَتْ ۝ 9 and when the sky is split,

وَإِذَا ٱلْجِبَالُ نُسِفَتْ ۝ 10 and when the mountains are scattered[1] [like dust],

وَإِذَا ٱلرُّسُلُ أُقِّتَتْ ۝ 11 and when the time is set for the apostles [to witness]

لِأَيِّ يَوْمٍ أُجِّلَتْ ۝ 12 —for what day has [all] that been set [to occur]?

لِيَوْمِ ٱلْفَصْلِ ۝ 13 For the Day of Judgement!

وَمَآ أَدْرَىٰكَ مَا يَوْمُ ٱلْفَصْلِ ۝ 14 And what will show you what is the Day of Judgement!

وَيْلٌ يَوْمَئِذٍ لِّلْمُكَذِّبِينَ ۝ 15 Woe to the deniers on that day!

أَلَمْ نُهْلِكِ ٱلْأَوَّلِينَ ۝ 16 Did We not destroy the ancients,

ثُمَّ نُتْبِعُهُمُ ٱلْآخِرِينَ ۝ 17 [and] then made the latter ones follow them?

كَذَٰلِكَ نَفْعَلُ بِٱلْمُجْرِمِينَ ۝ 18 That is how We deal with the guilty.

وَيْلٌ يَوْمَئِذٍ لِّلْمُكَذِّبِينَ ۝ 19 Woe to the deniers on that day!

أَلَمْ نَخْلُقكُّم مِّن مَّآءٍ مَّهِينٍ ۝ 20 Have We not created you from a base fluid,

فَجَعَلْنَٰهُ فِي قَرَارٍ مَّكِينٍ ۝ 21 [and] then lodged it in a secure abode

إِلَىٰ قَدَرٍ مَّعْلُومٍ ۝ 22 until a known span [of time]?

فَقَدَرْنَا ۝ 23 Then We designed;

فَنِعْمَ ٱلْقَٰدِرُونَ ۝ so how excellent designers We are!

وَيْلٌ يَوْمَئِذٍ لِّلْمُكَذِّبِينَ ۝ 24 Woe to the deniers on that day!

أَلَمْ نَجْعَلِ ٱلْأَرْضَ كِفَاتًا ۝ 25 Have We not made the earth a receptacle

أَحْيَآءً وَأَمْوَٰتًا ۝ 26 for the living and the dead,

وَجَعَلْنَا فِيهَا رَوَٰسِيَ شَٰمِخَٰتٍ 27 and set in it lofty [and] firm mountains,

وَأَسْقَيْنَٰكُم مَّآءً فُرَاتًا ۝ and given you agreeable water to drink?

وَيْلٌ يَوْمَئِذٍ لِّلْمُكَذِّبِينَ ۝ 28 Woe to the deniers on that day!

ٱنطَلِقُوٓا۟ 29 [They will be told]: 'Get off

---

[1] Or 'blown away.'

إِلَىٰ مَا كُنتُم بِهِ تُكَذِّبُونَ ۝    toward what you used to deny!

ٱنطَلِقُوٓا۟ إِلَىٰ ظِلٍّ ذِى ثَلَٰثِ شُعَبٍ ۝ 30 Get off toward the triple-forked shadow,

لَّا ظَلِيلٍ ۝ 31 which is neither shady

وَلَا يُغْنِى مِنَ ٱللَّهَبِ ۝    nor is of any avail against the flame.

إِنَّهَا تَرْمِى بِشَرَرٍ كَٱلْقَصْرِ ۝ 32 Indeed it throws up sparks [huge] like palaces,[1]

كَأَنَّهُۥ جِمَٰلَتٌ صُفْرٌ ۝ 33 [bright] as if they were yellow camels.

وَيْلٌ يَوْمَئِذٍ لِّلْمُكَذِّبِينَ ۝ 34 Woe to the deniers on that day!

هَٰذَا يَوْمُ لَا يَنطِقُونَ ۝ 35 This is a day wherein they will not speak,

وَلَا يُؤْذَنُ لَهُمْ فَيَعْتَذِرُونَ ۝ 36 nor will they be permitted to offer excuses.

وَيْلٌ يَوْمَئِذٍ لِّلْمُكَذِّبِينَ ۝ 37 Woe to the deniers on that day!

هَٰذَا يَوْمُ ٱلْفَصْلِ ۝ 38 'This is the Day of Judgement.

جَمَعْنَٰكُمْ وَٱلْأَوَّلِينَ ۝    We have brought together you and the ancients.

فَإِن كَانَ لَكُمْ كَيْدٌ ۝ 39 If you have any stratagems [left],

فَكِيدُونِ ۝    try out your stratagems against Me!'

وَيْلٌ يَوْمَئِذٍ لِّلْمُكَذِّبِينَ ۝ 40 Woe to the deniers on that day!

إِنَّ ٱلْمُتَّقِينَ فِى ظِلَٰلٍ وَعُيُونٍ ۝ 41 Indeed the Godwary will be amid shades and springs,

وَفَوَٰكِهَ مِمَّا يَشْتَهُونَ ۝ 42 and fruits, such as they desire.

كُلُوا۟ وَٱشْرَبُوا۟ هَنِيٓـًٔا 43 [They will be told:] 'Enjoy your food and drink,

بِمَا كُنتُمْ تَعْمَلُونَ ۝    [as a reward] for what you used to do.'

إِنَّا كَذَٰلِكَ نَجْزِى ٱلْمُحْسِنِينَ ۝ 44 Thus indeed do We reward the virtuous.

وَيْلٌ يَوْمَئِذٍ لِّلْمُكَذِّبِينَ ۝ 45 Woe to the deniers on that day!

كُلُوا۟ وَتَمَتَّعُوا۟ قَلِيلًا 46 'Eat and enjoy a little!

إِنَّكُم مُّجْرِمُونَ ۝    You are indeed guilty.'

وَيْلٌ يَوْمَئِذٍ لِّلْمُكَذِّبِينَ ۝ 47 Woe to the deniers on that day!

وَإِذَا قِيلَ لَهُمُ ٱرْكَعُوا۟ 48 When they are told, 'Bow down,'

لَا يَرْكَعُونَ ۝    they do not bow down!

وَيْلٌ يَوْمَئِذٍ لِّلْمُكَذِّبِينَ ۝ 49 Woe to the deniers on that day!

فَبِأَىِّ حَدِيثٍ بَعْدَهُۥ يُؤْمِنُونَ ۝ 50 So what discourse will they believe after this?

---

[1] Or 'like castles,' or 'like the trunks (of huge trees).'

[PART 30]

سُورَةُ النَّبَأ 78. SŪRAT AL-NABA'[1]

بِسْمِ اللَّهِ
الرَّحْمَٰنِ الرَّحِيمِ

In the Name of Allah,
the All-beneficent, the All-merciful.

عَمَّ يَتَسَآءَلُونَ ۝ 1 What is it about which they question each other?!

عَنِ ٱلنَّبَإِ ٱلْعَظِيمِ ۝ 2 [Is it] about the great tiding,

ٱلَّذِى هُمْ فِيهِ مُخْتَلِفُونَ ۝ 3 the one about which they differ?

كَلَّا سَيَعْلَمُونَ ۝ 4 No indeed! They will soon know!

ثُمَّ كَلَّا سَيَعْلَمُونَ ۝ 5 Again, no indeed! They will soon know!

أَلَمْ نَجْعَلِ ٱلْأَرْضَ مِهَٰدًا ۝ 6 Did We not make the earth a resting place?

وَٱلْجِبَالَ أَوْتَادًا ۝ 7 and the mountains stakes?

وَخَلَقْنَٰكُمْ أَزْوَٰجًا ۝ 8 and create you in pairs?[2]

وَجَعَلْنَا نَوْمَكُمْ سُبَاتًا ۝ 9 and make your sleep for rest?

وَجَعَلْنَا ٱلَّيْلَ لِبَاسًا ۝ 10 and make the night a covering?

وَجَعَلْنَا ٱلنَّهَارَ مَعَاشًا ۝ 11 and make the day for livelihood?

وَبَنَيْنَا فَوْقَكُمْ سَبْعًا شِدَادًا ۝ 12 and build above you the seven mighty heavens?

وَجَعَلْنَا سِرَاجًا وَهَّاجًا ۝ 13 and [the sun for] a radiant lamp?

وَأَنزَلْنَا مِنَ ٱلْمُعْصِرَٰتِ مَآءً ثَجَّاجًا ۝ 14 and send down water pouring from the rain-clouds,

لِنُخْرِجَ بِهِ حَبًّا وَنَبَاتًا ۝ 15 that with it We may bring forth grains and plants,

وَجَنَّٰتٍ أَلْفَافًا ۝ 16 and luxuriant gardens?

إِنَّ يَوْمَ ٱلْفَصْلِ كَانَ مِيقَٰتًا ۝ 17 Indeed the Day of Judgement is the tryst,

يَوْمَ يُنفَخُ فِى ٱلصُّورِ
فَتَأْتُونَ أَفْوَاجًا ۝ 18 the day the Trumpet will be blown, and you will come in groups,

وَفُتِحَتِ ٱلسَّمَآءُ
فَكَانَتْ أَبْوَٰبًا ۝ 19 and the sky will be opened and become gates,

---

[1] The *sūrah* takes its name from the expression *al-naba' al-ʿaẓīm* (the great tiding) in verse 2.

[2] Or 'as sexes.'

وَسُيِّرَتِ ٱلْجِبَالُ 20 and the mountains will be set moving

فَكَانَتْ سَرَابًا ۝ and become a mirage.

إِنَّ جَهَنَّمَ كَانَتْ مِرْصَادًا ۝ 21 Indeed hell is an ambush,

لِّلطَّٰغِينَ مَـَٔابًا ۝ 22 a resort for the rebels,

لَّٰبِثِينَ فِيهَآ أَحْقَابًا ۝ 23 to reside therein for ages,

لَّا يَذُوقُونَ فِيهَا بَرْدًا وَلَا شَرَابًا ۝ 24 tasting in it neither any coolness nor drink,

إِلَّا حَمِيمًا وَغَسَّاقًا ۝ 25 except boiling water and pus

جَزَآءً وِفَاقًا ۝ 26 —a fitting requital.

إِنَّهُمْ كَانُوا۟ لَا يَرْجُونَ حِسَابًا ۝ 27 Indeed they did not expect any reckoning,

وَكَذَّبُوا۟ بِـَٔايَٰتِنَا كِذَّابًا ۝ 28 and they denied Our signs mendaciously,

وَكُلَّ شَىْءٍ أَحْصَيْنَٰهُ كِتَٰبًا ۝ 29 and We have figured everything in a Book.

فَذُوقُوا۟ 30 So [now] taste!

فَلَن نَّزِيدَكُمْ إِلَّا عَذَابًا ۝ We shall increase you in nothing but punishment!

إِنَّ لِلْمُتَّقِينَ مَفَازًا ۝ 31 Indeed a triumph awaits the Godwary:

حَدَآئِقَ وَأَعْنَٰبًا ۝ 32 gardens and vineyards,

وَكَوَاعِبَ أَتْرَابًا ۝ 33 and buxom maidens of a like age,

وَكَأْسًا دِهَاقًا ۝ 34 and brimming cups.

لَّا يَسْمَعُونَ فِيهَا لَغْوًا وَلَا كِذَّٰبًا ۝ 35 Therein they shall hear neither vain talk nor lies

جَزَآءً مِّن رَّبِّكَ 36 —a reward from *your* Lord,

عَطَآءً حِسَابًا ۝ a bounty sufficing,[1]

رَّبِّ ٱلسَّمَٰوَٰتِ وَٱلْأَرْضِ 37 the Lord of the heavens and the earth

وَمَا بَيْنَهُمَا and whatever is between them,

ٱلرَّحْمَٰنِ the All-beneficent,

لَا يَمْلِكُونَ مِنْهُ خِطَابًا ۝ whom they will not be able to address

يَوْمَ 38 on the day

يَقُومُ ٱلرُّوحُ وَٱلْمَلَٰٓئِكَةُ when the Spirit and the angels stand

صَفًّا in an array.

لَّا يَتَكَلَّمُونَ None shall speak

إِلَّا مَنْ أَذِنَ لَهُ ٱلرَّحْمَٰنُ except whom the All-beneficent permits

---

[1] Or 'abounding,' or 'well-deserved,' or 'well-earned.'

وَقَالَ صَوَابًا ۝    and who says what is right.

ذَٰلِكَ ٱلْيَوْمُ ٱلْحَقُّ    39 That is the day of truth.

فَمَن شَآءَ ٱتَّخَذَ إِلَىٰ رَبِّهِ مَـَٔابًا ۝    So let anyone who wishes take resort with his Lord.

إِنَّآ أَنذَرْنَٰكُمْ    40 Indeed We have warned you

عَذَابًا قَرِيبًا    of a punishment near at hand

يَوْمَ يَنظُرُ ٱلْمَرْءُ    —the day when a person will observe[1]

مَا قَدَّمَتْ يَدَاهُ    what his hands have sent ahead

وَيَقُولُ ٱلْكَافِرُ    and the faithless one will say,

يَٰلَيْتَنِى كُنتُ تُرَٰبًا ۝    'I wish I were dust!'

---

# سُورَةُ ٱلنَّازِعَاتِ      79. SŪRAT AL-NĀZIʿĀT[2]

بِسْمِ ٱللَّهِ    In the Name of Allah,

ٱلرَّحْمَٰنِ ٱلرَّحِيمِ    the All-beneficent, the All-merciful.

وَٱلنَّٰزِعَٰتِ غَرْقًا ۝    1 By those [angels] who wrest [the soul] violently,

وَٱلنَّٰشِطَٰتِ نَشْطًا ۝    2 by those who draw [it] out gently,

وَٱلسَّٰبِحَٰتِ سَبْحًا ۝    3 by those who swim smoothly,

فَٱلسَّٰبِقَٰتِ سَبْقًا ۝    4 by those who take the lead, racing,

فَٱلْمُدَبِّرَٰتِ أَمْرًا ۝    5 by those who direct the affairs [of creatures]:

يَوْمَ تَرْجُفُ ٱلرَّاجِفَةُ ۝    6 the day when the Quaker quakes

تَتْبَعُهَا ٱلرَّادِفَةُ ۝    7 and is followed by the Successor,[3]

قُلُوبٌ يَوْمَئِذٍ وَاجِفَةٌ ۝    8 hearts will be trembling on that day,

أَبْصَٰرُهَا خَٰشِعَةٌ ۝    9 bearing a humbled look.

يَقُولُونَ    10 They will say,

أَءِنَّا لَمَرْدُودُونَ فِى ٱلْحَافِرَةِ ۝    'Are we being returned to our earlier state?

---

[1] Or 'consider.'

[2] The *sūrah* takes its name from "the wresters" (*al-nāziʿāt*) mentioned in verse 1.

[3] Apparently, 'the Quaker' and 'the Successor' refer to the first and the second blasts of the Trumpet sounded by Isrāfil on the Day of Resurrection. Cf. **39:68**; **73:14**.

11 أَءِذَا كُنَّا عِظَامًا نَّخِرَةً ۝    11 What, when we have been decayed bones?!'

12 قَالُوا تِلْكَ إِذًا كَرَّةٌ خَاسِرَةٌ ۝    12 They will say, 'This, then, is a ruinous return!'

13 فَإِنَّمَا هِيَ زَجْرَةٌ وَاحِدَةٌ ۝    13 Yet it will be only a single shout,

14 فَإِذَا هُم بِالسَّاهِرَةِ ۝    14    and behold, they will be awake.

15 هَلْ أَتَاكَ حَدِيثُ مُوسَىٰ ۝    15 Did you receive the story of Moses,

16 إِذْ نَادَاهُ رَبُّهُ    16    when his Lord called out to him

بِالْوَادِ الْمُقَدَّسِ طُوًى ۝    in the holy valley of Ṭuwā?

17 اذْهَبْ إِلَىٰ فِرْعَوْنَ    17 [And said,] 'Go to Pharaoh,

إِنَّهُ طَغَىٰ ۝    for indeed he has rebelled,

18 فَقُلْ هَل لَّكَ إِلَىٰ أَن تَزَكَّىٰ ۝    18 and say, "Would you purify yourself?

19 وَأَهْدِيَكَ إِلَىٰ رَبِّكَ    19    I will guide you to your Lord,

فَتَخْشَىٰ ۝    that you may fear [Him]?"'

20 فَأَرَاهُ الْآيَةَ الْكُبْرَىٰ ۝    20 Then he showed him the greatest sign.

21 فَكَذَّبَ وَعَصَىٰ ۝    21    But he denied, and disobeyed.

22 ثُمَّ أَدْبَرَ يَسْعَىٰ ۝    22    Then he turned back, walking swiftly,

23 فَحَشَرَ فَنَادَىٰ ۝    23    and mustered [the people] and proclaimed,

24 فَقَالَ أَنَا رَبُّكُمُ الْأَعْلَىٰ ۝    24    saying, 'I am your exalted lord!'

25 فَأَخَذَهُ اللَّهُ    25 So Allah seized him

نَكَالَ الْآخِرَةِ وَالْأُولَىٰ ۝    with the punishment of this life and the Hereafter.

26 إِنَّ فِي ذَٰلِكَ لَعِبْرَةً لِّمَن يَخْشَىٰ ۝    26 There is indeed a moral in that for someone who fears!

27 ءَأَنتُمْ أَشَدُّ خَلْقًا    27 Is it you whose creation is more prodigious

أَمِ السَّمَاءُ بَنَاهَا ۝    or the sky which He has built?

28 رَفَعَ سَمْكَهَا فَسَوَّاهَا ۝    28 He raised its vault, and fashioned it,

29 وَأَغْطَشَ لَيْلَهَا    29    and darkened its night,

وَأَخْرَجَ ضُحَاهَا ۝    and brought forth its day;

30 وَالْأَرْضَ بَعْدَ ذَٰلِكَ دَحَاهَا ۝    30    and after that He spread out the earth,

31 أَخْرَجَ مِنْهَا مَاءَهَا وَمَرْعَاهَا ۝    31    and brought forth from it its water and pastures,

32 وَالْجِبَالَ أَرْسَاهَا ۝    32    and set firm the mountains,

33 مَتَاعًا لَّكُمْ    33    as a [place of] sustenance for you

وَلِأَنْعَمِكُمْ ۝ and your livestock.

فَإِذَا جَاءَتِ ٱلطَّآمَّةُ ٱلْكُبْرَىٰ ۝ 34 When the Greatest Catastrophe befalls,

يَوْمَ يَتَذَكَّرُ ٱلْإِنسَٰنُ مَا سَعَىٰ ۝ 35 the day when man will remember his endeavours,

وَبُرِّزَتِ ٱلْجَحِيمُ لِمَن يَرَىٰ ۝ 36 and hell is brought into view for one who sees,

فَأَمَّا مَن طَغَىٰ ۝ 37 as for him who was rebellious

وَءَاثَرَ ٱلْحَيَوٰةَ ٱلدُّنْيَا ۝ 38 and preferred the life of this world,

فَإِنَّ ٱلْجَحِيمَ هِىَ ٱلْمَأْوَىٰ ۝ 39 his refuge will indeed be hell.

وَأَمَّا مَنْ خَافَ مَقَامَ رَبِّهِۦ 40 But as for him who is awed to stand before his Lord

وَنَهَى ٱلنَّفْسَ عَنِ ٱلْهَوَىٰ ۝ and forbids the soul from [following] desire,

فَإِنَّ ٱلْجَنَّةَ هِىَ ٱلْمَأْوَىٰ ۝ 41 his refuge will indeed be paradise.

يَسْـَٔلُونَكَ عَنِ ٱلسَّاعَةِ 42 They ask *you* concerning the Hour,

أَيَّانَ مُرْسَىٰهَا ۝ when it will set in.

فِيمَ أَنتَ مِن ذِكْرَىٰهَآ ۝ 43 What have *you* to do with mentioning it?

إِلَىٰ رَبِّكَ مُنتَهَىٰهَآ ۝ 44 Toward *your* Lord is its conclusion.

إِنَّمَآ أَنتَ مُنذِرُ مَن يَخْشَىٰهَا ۝ 45 You are only a warner for one who fears it.

كَأَنَّهُمْ يَوْمَ يَرَوْنَهَا 46 The day they see it, it shall be as if

لَمْ يَلْبَثُوٓا۟ they had not stayed

إِلَّا عَشِيَّةً أَوْ ضُحَىٰهَا ۝ except for an evening or forenoon.

سُورَةُ عَبَسَ ## 80. SŪRAT ʿABASA[1]

بِسْمِ ٱللَّهِ In the Name of Allah,

ٱلرَّحْمَٰنِ ٱلرَّحِيمِ the All-beneficent, the All-merciful.

عَبَسَ وَتَوَلَّىٰٓ ۝ 1 He frowned and turned away

أَن جَآءَهُ ٱلْأَعْمَىٰ ۝ 2 when the blind man approached him.

وَمَا يُدْرِيكَ 3 And how do you know,

لَعَلَّهُۥ يَزَّكَّىٰٓ ۝ maybe he would purify himself,

أَوْ يَذَّكَّرُ 4 or take admonition,

---

[1] The *sūrah* takes its name from the word *ʿabasa* (he frowned) in verse 1.

فَتَنفَعَهُ ٱلذِّكْرَىٰ ۝    and the admonition would benefit him!

أَمَّا مَنِ ٱسْتَغْنَىٰ ۝ 5 But as for some one who is self-complacent,

فَأَنتَ لَهُۥ تَصَدَّىٰ ۝ 6 you attend to him,

وَمَا عَلَيْكَ ۝ 7 though you are not liable

أَلَّا يَزَّكَّىٰ ۝    if he does not purify himself.

وَأَمَّا مَن جَآءَكَ يَسْعَىٰ ۝ 8 But he who comes hurrying to you,

وَهُوَ يَخْشَىٰ ۝ 9 while he fears [Allah],

فَأَنتَ عَنْهُ تَلَهَّىٰ ۝ 10 you are neglectful of him.

كَلَّآ إِنَّهَا تَذْكِرَةٌ ۝ 11 No indeed! These [verses of the Qur'ān] are a reminder

فَمَن شَآءَ ذَكَرَهُۥ ۝ 12 —so let anyone who wishes remember it—

فِى صُحُفٍ مُّكَرَّمَةٍ ۝ 13 in honoured scriptures,

مَّرْفُوعَةٍ مُّطَهَّرَةٍ ۝ 14 exalted and purified,

بِأَيْدِى سَفَرَةٍ ۝ 15 in the hands of envoys,[1]

كِرَامٍ بَرَرَةٍ ۝ 16 noble and pious.

قُتِلَ ٱلْإِنسَٰنُ مَآ أَكْفَرَهُۥ ۝ 17 Perish man! How ungrateful is he!

مِنْ أَىِّ شَىْءٍ خَلَقَهُۥ ۝ 18 From what has He created him?

مِن نُّطْفَةٍ خَلَقَهُۥ 19 He has created him from a drop of [seminal] fluid,

فَقَدَّرَهُۥ ۝    and then proportioned him.

ثُمَّ ٱلسَّبِيلَ يَسَّرَهُۥ ۝ 20 Then He made the way easy for him;

ثُمَّ أَمَاتَهُۥ فَأَقْبَرَهُۥ ۝ 21 then He made him die and buried him;

ثُمَّ إِذَا شَآءَ أَنشَرَهُۥ ۝ 22 and then, when He wished, resurrected him.

كَلَّا لَمَّا يَقْضِ 23 No indeed! He has not yet carried out

مَآ أَمَرَهُۥ ۝    what He had commanded him.

فَلْيَنظُرِ ٱلْإِنسَٰنُ إِلَىٰ طَعَامِهِ ۝ 24 So let man observe[2] his food:

أَنَّا صَبَبْنَا ٱلْمَآءَ صَبًّا ۝ 25 We poured down water plenteously,

ثُمَّ شَقَقْنَا ٱلْأَرْضَ شَقًّا ۝ 26 then We split the earth into fissures

فَأَنۢبَتْنَا فِيهَا حَبًّا ۝ 27 and made the grain grow in it,

وَعِنَبًا وَقَضْبًا ۝ 28 and vines and vegetables,

---

[1] Or 'scribes.'

[2] Or 'consider.'

وَزَيْتُونًا وَنَخْلًا 29 olives and date palms,

وَحَدَآئِقَ غُلْبًا 30 and densely-planted gardens,

وَفَـٰكِهَةً وَأَبًّا 31 fruits and pastures,

مَّتَـٰعًا لَّكُمْ وَلِأَنْعَـٰمِكُمْ 32 as a sustenance for you and your livestock.

فَإِذَا جَآءَتِ ٱلصَّآخَّةُ 33 So when the deafening Cry comes

يَوْمَ يَفِرُّ ٱلْمَرْءُ مِنْ أَخِيهِ 34 —the day when a man will evade his brother,

وَأُمِّهِۦ وَأَبِيهِ 35 his mother and his father,

وَصَـٰحِبَتِهِۦ وَبَنِيهِ 36 his spouse and his sons—

لِكُلِّ ٱمْرِئٍ مِّنْهُمْ يَوْمَئِذٍ 37 that day each of them will have
شَأْنٌ يُغْنِيهِ a task to keep him preoccupied.

وُجُوهٌ يَوْمَئِذٍ مُّسْفِرَةٌ 38 That day some faces will be bright,

ضَاحِكَةٌ مُّسْتَبْشِرَةٌ 39 laughing and joyous.

وَوُجُوهٌ يَوْمَئِذٍ 40 And some faces on that day

عَلَيْهَا غَبَرَةٌ will be covered with dust,

تَرْهَقُهَا قَتَرَةٌ 41 overcast with gloom.

أُوْلَـٰئِكَ هُمُ ٱلْكَفَرَةُ ٱلْفَجَرَةُ 42 It is they who are the faithless, the vicious.[1]

سُورَةُ التَّكْوِيرِ # 81. SŪRAT AL-TAKWĪR[2]

بِسْمِ ٱللَّهِ In the Name of Allah,
ٱلرَّحْمَـٰنِ ٱلرَّحِيمِ the All-beneficent, the All-merciful.

إِذَا ٱلشَّمْسُ كُوِّرَتْ 1 When the sun is wound up,[3]

وَإِذَا ٱلنُّجُومُ ٱنكَدَرَتْ 2 when the stars scatter,[4]

وَإِذَا ٱلْجِبَالُ سُيِّرَتْ 3 when the mountains are set moving,

وَإِذَا ٱلْعِشَارُ عُطِّلَتْ 4 when the pregnant camels are neglected,

---

[1] Or 'vicious ingrates.'

[2] The *sūrah* takes its name from "the winding up" or "the darkening" (*takwīr*) of the sun mentioned in verse 1.

[3] Or 'turns dark.'

[4] Or 'fall down.'

وَإِذَا ٱلْوُحُوشُ حُشِرَتْ ۝ 5    when the wild beasts are mustered,

وَإِذَا ٱلْبِحَارُ سُجِّرَتْ ۝ 6    when the seas are set afire,

وَإِذَا ٱلنُّفُوسُ زُوِّجَتْ ۝ 7    when the souls are assorted,[1]

وَإِذَا ٱلْمَوْءُۥدَةُ سُئِلَتْ ۝ 8    when the girl buried-alive will be asked

بِأَىِّ ذَنۢبٍ قُتِلَتْ ۝ 9    for what sin she was killed.

وَإِذَا ٱلصُّحُفُ نُشِرَتْ ۝ 10   When the [scrolls of the] scriptures are unrolled,

وَإِذَا ٱلسَّمَآءُ كُشِطَتْ ۝ 11    when the sky is stripped off,

وَإِذَا ٱلْجَحِيمُ سُعِّرَتْ ۝ 12    when hell is set ablaze,

وَإِذَا ٱلْجَنَّةُ أُزْلِفَتْ ۝ 13    when paradise is brought near,

عَلِمَتْ نَفْسٌ مَّآ أَحْضَرَتْ ۝ 14   then a soul shall know what it has readied [for itself].

فَلَآ أُقْسِمُ بِٱلْخُنَّسِ ۝ 15   So I swear by the stars that return,

ٱلْجَوَارِ ٱلْكُنَّسِ ۝ 16    the planets that hide,

وَٱلَّيْلِ إِذَا عَسْعَسَ ۝ 17    by the night as it approaches,

وَٱلصُّبْحِ إِذَا تَنَفَّسَ ۝ 18    by the dawn as it breathes,

إِنَّهُۥ لَقَوْلُ رَسُولٍ كَرِيمٍ ۝ 19    it is indeed the speech of a noble apostle,[2]

ذِى قُوَّةٍ عِندَ ذِى ٱلْعَرْشِ مَكِينٍ ۝ 20   powerful and eminent with the Lord of the Throne,

مُّطَاعٍ ثَمَّ أَمِينٍ ۝ 21    one who is heard and trustworthy as well.

وَمَا صَاحِبُكُم بِمَجْنُونٍ ۝ 22   Your companion is not crazy:

وَلَقَدْ رَءَاهُ بِٱلْأُفُقِ ٱلْمُبِينِ ۝ 23    certainly *he* saw him on the manifest horizon,

وَمَا هُوَ عَلَى ٱلْغَيْبِ بِضَنِينٍ ۝ 24    and *he* is not miserly concerning the Unseen.

وَمَا هُوَ بِقَوْلِ شَيْطَٰنٍ رَّجِيمٍ ۝ 25   And it is not the speech of an outcast Satan.

فَأَيْنَ تَذْهَبُونَ ۝ 26   So where are you going?

إِنْ هُوَ إِلَّا ذِكْرٌ لِّلْعَٰلَمِينَ ۝ 27   It is just a reminder for all the nations,

لِمَن شَآءَ مِنكُمْ أَن يَسْتَقِيمَ ۝ 28    for those of you who wish to be steadfast;[3]

وَمَا تَشَآءُونَ 29    but you do not wish

إِلَّآ أَن يَشَآءَ ٱللَّهُ    unless it is wished by Allah,

رَبُّ ٱلْعَٰلَمِينَ ۝    the Lord of all the worlds.

---

[1] That is, separated into different groups according to their character; cf. 56:7, 37:22. Or 'mated;' cf. 52:20.

[2] Cf. 69:40.

[3] Or 'for those of you who wish to walk straight.'

سُورَةُ الاِنفِطَار 82. SŪRAT AL-INFIṬĀR[1]

بِسمِ ٱللَّهِ
ٱلرَّحمَٰنِ ٱلرَّحِيمِ

In the Name of Allah,
the All-beneficent, the All-merciful.

إِذَا ٱلسَّمَآءُ ٱنفَطَرَت ۝ 1 When the sky is rent apart,

وَإِذَا ٱلكَوَاكِبُ ٱنتَثَرَت ۝ 2 when the stars are scattered,

وَإِذَا ٱلبِحَارُ فُجِّرَت ۝ 3 when the seas are merged,

وَإِذَا ٱلقُبُورُ بُعثِرَت ۝ 4 when the graves are overturned,

عَلِمَت نَفسٌ مَّا قَدَّمَت 5 then a soul shall know what it has sent ahead

وَأَخَّرَت ۝ and left behind.

يَٰأَيُّهَا ٱلإِنسَٰنُ 6 O man!

مَا غَرَّكَ بِرَبِّكَ ٱلكَرِيمِ ۝ What has deceived you about your generous[2] Lord,

ٱلَّذِى خَلَقَكَ فَسَوَّىٰكَ 7 who created you and proportioned you,

فَعَدَلَكَ ۝ and gave you an upright nature,

فِىٓ أَىِّ صُورَةٍ مَّا شَآءَ رَكَّبَكَ ۝ 8 and composed you in any form that He wished?

كَلَّا بَل تُكَذِّبُونَ بِٱلدِّينِ ۝ 9 No indeed! Rather you deny the Retribution.

وَإِنَّ عَلَيكُم لَحَٰفِظِينَ ۝ 10 Indeed, there are over you watchers,

كِرَامًا كَٰتِبِينَ ۝ 11 noble writers

يَعلَمُونَ مَا تَفعَلُونَ ۝ 12 who know whatever you do.

إِنَّ ٱلأَبرَارَ لَفِى نَعِيمٍ ۝ 13 Indeed the pious shall be amid bliss,

وَإِنَّ ٱلفُجَّارَ لَفِى جَحِيمٍ ۝ 14 and indeed the vicious shall be in hell

يَصلَونَهَا يَومَ ٱلدِّينِ ۝ 15 entering it on the Day of Retribution,[3]

وَمَا هُم عَنهَا بِغَآئِبِينَ ۝ 16 and they shall not be absent from it.

وَمَآ أَدرَىٰكَ 17 And what will show you

مَا يَومُ ٱلدِّينِ ۝ what is the Day of Retribution?

---

[1] The *sūrah* takes its name from "the renting apart" (*infiṭār*) of the sky mentioned in verse 1.

[2] Or 'noble.'

[3] Or 'the Day of Judgement.'

ثُمَّ مَآ أَدْرَىٰكَ 18 Again, what will show you

مَا يَوْمُ ٱلدِّينِ ۝ what is the Day of Retribution?

يَوْمَ 19 It is a day

لَا تَمْلِكُ نَفْسٌ لِّنَفْسٍ شَيْئًا when no soul will be of any avail to another soul

وَٱلْأَمْرُ يَوْمَئِذٍ لِّلَّهِ ۝ and all command that day will belong to Allah.

# سُورَةُ المطففين     83. SŪRAT AL-MUṬAFFIFĪN[1]

بِسْمِ ٱللَّهِ In the Name of Allah,

ٱلرَّحْمَٰنِ ٱلرَّحِيمِ the All-beneficent, the All-merciful.

وَيْلٌ لِّلْمُطَفِّفِينَ ۝ 1 Woe to the defrauders who use short measures,

ٱلَّذِينَ إِذَا ٱكْتَالُوا 2 who, when they measure [a commodity bought]

عَلَى ٱلنَّاسِ from the people,

يَسْتَوْفُونَ ۝ take the full measure,

وَإِذَا كَالُوهُمْ أَو وَّزَنُوهُمْ يُخْسِرُونَ ۝ 3 but diminish when they measure or weigh for them.

أَلَا يَظُنُّ أُوْلَٰٓئِكَ أَنَّهُم مَّبْعُوثُونَ ۝ 4 Do they not know that they will be resurrected

لِيَوْمٍ عَظِيمٍ ۝ 5 on a tremendous day,

يَوْمَ يَقُومُ ٱلنَّاسُ 6 a day when mankind will stand

لِرَبِّ ٱلْعَٰلَمِينَ ۝ before the Lord of all the worlds?

كَلَّآ إِنَّ كِتَٰبَ ٱلْفُجَّارِ لَفِى سِجِّينٍ ۝ 7 No indeed! The record of the vicious is indeed in *Sijjīn*.

وَمَآ أَدْرَىٰكَ مَا سِجِّينٌ ۝ 8 And what will show you what is *Sijjīn*?

كِتَٰبٌ مَّرْقُومٌ ۝ 9 It is a written record.

وَيْلٌ يَوْمَئِذٍ لِّلْمُكَذِّبِينَ ۝ 10 Woe to the deniers on that day,

ٱلَّذِينَ يُكَذِّبُونَ بِيَوْمِ ٱلدِّينِ ۝ 11 who deny the Day of Retribution;

وَمَا يُكَذِّبُ بِهِۦٓ إِلَّا كُلُّ مُعْتَدٍ أَثِيمٍ ۝ 12 and none denies it except every sinful transgressor.

إِذَا تُتْلَىٰ عَلَيْهِ ءَايَٰتُنَا 13 When Our signs are recited to him,

قَالَ أَسَٰطِيرُ ٱلْأَوَّلِينَ ۝ he says, 'Myths of the ancients!'

---

[1] The *sūrah* takes its name from verse 1, which condemns sellers who cheat customers by using short weights and measures (*muṭaffifūn*)

كَلَّا بَلْ رَانَ عَلَىٰ قُلُوبِهِم 14 No indeed! Rather their hearts have been sullied[1]

مَّا كَانُوا۟ يَكْسِبُونَ ۝ by what they have been earning.

كَلَّآ 15 No indeed!

إِنَّهُمْ عَن رَّبِّهِمْ يَوْمَئِذٍ لَّمَحْجُوبُونَ ۝ They will be alienated from their Lord on that day.

ثُمَّ إِنَّهُمْ لَصَالُوا۟ ٱلْجَحِيمِ ۝ 16 Then they will indeed enter hell,

ثُمَّ يُقَالُ 17 then told,

هَـٰذَا ٱلَّذِى كُنتُم بِهِۦ تُكَذِّبُونَ ۝ 'This is what you used to deny!'

كَلَّآ 18 No indeed!

إِنَّ كِتَـٰبَ ٱلْأَبْرَارِ لَفِى عِلِّيِّينَ ۝ The record of the pious is indeed in *Illīyūn*.

وَمَآ أَدْرَىٰكَ مَا عِلِّيُّونَ ۝ 19 And what will show you what is *Illīyūn*?

كِتَـٰبٌ مَّرْقُومٌ ۝ 20 It is a written record,

يَشْهَدُهُ ٱلْمُقَرَّبُونَ ۝ 21 witnessed by those brought near [to Allah].

إِنَّ ٱلْأَبْرَارَ لَفِى نَعِيمٍ ۝ 22 Indeed the pious shall be amid bliss,

عَلَى ٱلْأَرَآئِكِ يَنظُرُونَ ۝ 23 observing, [as they recline] on couches.

تَعْرِفُ فِى وُجُوهِهِمْ نَضْرَةَ ٱلنَّعِيمِ ۝ 24 You will perceive in their faces the freshness of bliss

يُسْقَوْنَ مِن رَّحِيقٍ مَّخْتُومٍ ۝ 25 as they are served with a sealed wine,

خِتَـٰمُهُۥ مِسْكٌ 26 whose seal is musk

وَفِى ذَٰلِكَ فَلْيَتَنَافَسِ ٱلْمُتَنَـٰفِسُونَ ۝ —for such let the viers vie—

وَمِزَاجُهُۥ مِن تَسْنِيمٍ ۝ 27 and whose seasoning is from *Tasnim*,

عَيْنًا يَشْرَبُ بِهَا ٱلْمُقَرَّبُونَ ۝ 28 a spring where those brought near [to Allah] drink.

إِنَّ ٱلَّذِينَ أَجْرَمُوا۟ 29 Indeed the guilty

كَانُوا۟ مِنَ ٱلَّذِينَ ءَامَنُوا۟ يَضْحَكُونَ ۝ used to laugh at the faithful,

وَإِذَا مَرُّوا۟ بِهِمْ 30 and when they passed them by

يَتَغَامَزُونَ ۝ they would wink at each other,

وَإِذَا ٱنقَلَبُوٓا۟ إِلَىٰٓ أَهْلِهِمُ 31 and when they returned to their folks

ٱنقَلَبُوا۟ فَكِهِينَ ۝ they would return rejoicing,

وَإِذَا رَأَوْهُمْ 32 and when they saw them

قَالُوٓا۟ they would say,

إِنَّ هَـٰٓؤُلَآءِ لَضَآلُّونَ ۝ 'Indeed those are the astray!'

---

[1] Or 'overcast.'

وَمَا أُرْسِلُوا عَلَيْهِمْ حَفِظِينَ ٣٣  33 Though they were not sent to watch over them.

فَالْيَوْمَ الَّذِينَ ءَامَنُوا  34 So today the faithful

مِنَ الْكُفَّارِ يَضْحَكُونَ ٣٤  will laugh at the faithless,

عَلَى الْأَرَآئِكِ يَنظُرُونَ ٣٥  35 observing from couches:

هَلْ ثُوِّبَ الْكُفَّارُ  36 Have the faithless been requited

مَا كَانُوا يَفْعَلُونَ ٣٦  for what they used to do?

# 84. SŪRAT AL-INSHIQĀQ[1]

سُورَةُ الاِنشِقَاق

بِسْمِ اللَّهِ  In the Name of Allah,

الرَّحْمَٰنِ الرَّحِيمِ  the All-beneficent, the All-merciful.

إِذَا السَّمَاءُ انشَقَّتْ ١  1 When the sky is split open

وَأَذِنَتْ لِرَبِّهَا وَحُقَّتْ ٢  2  and gives ear to its Lord as it should.

وَإِذَا الْأَرْضُ مُدَّتْ ٣  3 When the earth is spread out

وَأَلْقَتْ مَا فِيهَا وَتَخَلَّتْ ٤  4  and throws out what is in it, emptying itself,

وَأَذِنَتْ لِرَبِّهَا وَحُقَّتْ ٥  5  and gives ear to its Lord as it should.

يَٰٓأَيُّهَا الْإِنسَٰنُ  6 O man!

إِنَّكَ كَادِحٌ إِلَىٰ رَبِّكَ كَدْحًا  You are labouring toward your Lord laboriously,

فَمُلَٰقِيهِ ٦  and you will encounter Him.

فَأَمَّا مَنْ أُوتِيَ كِتَٰبَهُۥ  7 Then as for him who is given his record

بِيَمِينِهِۦ ٧  in his right hand,

فَسَوْفَ يُحَاسَبُ حِسَابًا يَسِيرًا ٨  8  he shall soon receive an easy reckoning,

وَيَنقَلِبُ إِلَىٰ أَهْلِهِ مَسْرُورًا ٩  9  and he will return to his folks joyfully.

وَأَمَّا مَنْ أُوتِيَ كِتَٰبَهُۥ  10 But as for him who is given his record

وَرَآءَ ظَهْرِهِۦ ١٠  from behind his back,

فَسَوْفَ يَدْعُوا ثُبُورًا ١١  11  he will pray for annihilation,[2]

وَيَصْلَىٰ سَعِيرًا ١٢  12  and he will enter the Blaze.

---

[1] Named after the "splitting open" (*inshiqāq*) of the sky mentioned in verse 1.
[2] Cf. 25:13-14, 78:40.

إِنَّهُۥ كَانَ فِىٓ أَهْلِهِۦ مَسْرُورًا ١٣   13 Indeed he used to be joyful among his folk,

إِنَّهُۥ ظَنَّ أَن لَّن يَحُورَ ١٤   14    and indeed he thought he would never return.

بَلَىٰٓ إِنَّ رَبَّهُۥ كَانَ بِهِۦ بَصِيرًا ١٥   15 Yes indeed, his Lord sees him best.

فَلَآ أُقْسِمُ بِٱلشَّفَقِ ١٦   16 So I swear by the evening glow,

وَٱلَّيْلِ وَمَا وَسَقَ ١٧   17    by the night and what it is fraught with,

وَٱلْقَمَرِ إِذَا ٱتَّسَقَ ١٨   18    by the moon when it blooms full:

لَتَرْكَبُنَّ طَبَقًا عَن طَبَقٍ ١٩   19     you will surely fare from stage to stage.

فَمَا لَهُمْ ٢٠   20 So what is the matter with them

لَا يُؤْمِنُونَ ٢٠   that they will not believe?

وَإِذَا قُرِئَ عَلَيْهِمُ ٱلْقُرْءَانُ ٢١   21 And when the Qur'ān is recited to them

لَا يَسْجُدُونَ ۩ ٢١   they will not prostrate?

بَلِ ٱلَّذِينَ كَفَرُواْ يُكَذِّبُونَ ٢٢   22 Rather the faithless deny,

وَٱللَّهُ أَعْلَمُ بِمَا يُوعُونَ ٢٣   23   and Allah knows best what they keep to themselves.

فَبَشِّرْهُم بِعَذَابٍ أَلِيمٍ ٢٤   24 So warn them of a painful punishment,

إِلَّا ٱلَّذِينَ ءَامَنُواْ ٢٥   25    except such as are faithful

وَعَمِلُواْ ٱلصَّـٰلِحَـٰتِ   and do righteous deeds:

لَهُمْ أَجْرٌ غَيْرُ مَمْنُونٍ ٢٥   there will be an everlasting reward for them.

سُورَةُ ٱلْبُرُوجِ      85. SŪRAT AL-BURŪJ[1]

بِسْمِ ٱللَّهِ      In the Name of Allah,

ٱلرَّحْمَـٰنِ ٱلرَّحِيمِ      the All-beneficent, the All-merciful.

وَٱلسَّمَآءِ ذَاتِ ٱلْبُرُوجِ ١   1 By the sky with its houses,

وَٱلْيَوْمِ ٱلْمَوْعُودِ ٢   2 by the Promised Day,

وَشَاهِدٍ وَمَشْهُودٍ ٣   3 by the Witness[2] and the Witnessed:[3]

قُتِلَ أَصْحَـٰبُ ٱلْأُخْدُودِ ٤   4    perish the Men of the Ditch!

---

[1] The *sūrah* takes its name from "the houses" (*burūj*) mentioned in verse 1.

[2] That is the Prophet (ṣ); cf. 2:143, 33:45, 4:41, 16:89.

[3] That is, the Day of Judgement; cf. 11:103

5 ٱلنَّارِ ذَاتِ ٱلْوَقُودِ ۝    The fire, abounding in fuel,

6 إِذْ هُمْ عَلَيْهَا قُعُودٌ ۝    above which they sat

7 وَهُمْ    as they were themselves

عَلَىٰ مَا يَفْعَلُونَ بِٱلْمُؤْمِنِينَ شُهُودٌ ۝    witnesses to what they did to the faithful.

8 وَمَا نَقَمُوا مِنْهُمْ    They were vindictive towards them only

إِلَّآ أَن يُؤْمِنُوا بِٱللَّهِ    because they had faith in Allah,

ٱلْعَزِيزِ ٱلْحَمِيدِ ۝    the All-mighty, the All-laudable,

9 ٱلَّذِى لَهُۥ مُلْكُ ٱلسَّمَٰوَٰتِ    to whom belongs the kingdom of the heavens

وَٱلْأَرْضِ    and the earth,

وَٱللَّهُ عَلَىٰ كُلِّ شَىْءٍ شَهِيدٌ ۝    and Allah is witness to all things.

10 إِنَّ ٱلَّذِينَ فَتَنُوا    Indeed those who persecute

ٱلْمُؤْمِنِينَ وَٱلْمُؤْمِنَٰتِ    the faithful men and women,

ثُمَّ لَمْ يَتُوبُوا    and then do not repent,

فَلَهُمْ عَذَابُ جَهَنَّمَ    for them there is the punishment of hell,

وَهُمْ عَذَابُ ٱلْحَرِيقِ ۝    and for them there is the punishment of burning.

11 إِنَّ ٱلَّذِينَ ءَامَنُوا وَعَمِلُوا ٱلصَّٰلِحَٰتِ    Indeed those who have faith and do righteous deeds,

لَهُمْ جَنَّٰتٌ    —for them will be gardens

تَجْرِى مِن تَحْتِهَا ٱلْأَنْهَٰرُ    with streams running in them.

ذَٰلِكَ ٱلْفَوْزُ ٱلْكَبِيرُ ۝    That is the supreme success.

12 إِنَّ بَطْشَ رَبِّكَ لَشَدِيدٌ ۝    Indeed your Lord's striking is severe.

13 إِنَّهُۥ هُوَ يُبْدِئُ وَيُعِيدُ ۝    It is indeed He who originates and brings back again,

14 وَهُوَ ٱلْغَفُورُ ٱلْوَدُودُ ۝    and He is the All-forgiving, the All-affectionate,

15 ذُو ٱلْعَرْشِ ٱلْمَجِيدُ ۝    Lord of the Throne, the All-glorious,[1]

16 فَعَّالٌ لِّمَا يُرِيدُ ۝    doer of what He desires.

17 هَلْ أَتَىٰكَ حَدِيثُ ٱلْجُنُودِ ۝    Did *you* receive the story of the hosts

18 فِرْعَوْنَ وَثَمُودَ ۝    of Pharaoh and Thamūd?

19 بَلِ ٱلَّذِينَ كَفَرُوا فِى تَكْذِيبٍ ۝    Rather the faithless dwell in denial,

20 وَٱللَّهُ مِن وَرَآئِهِم مُّحِيطٌ ۝    and Allah besieges them from all around.

21 بَلْ هُوَ قُرْءَانٌ مَّجِيدٌ ۝    Rather it is a glorious Qur'ān,

---

[1] Or 'Lord of the Glorious Throne,' in accordance with an alternate reading.

في لَوۡحٍ مَّحۡفُوظِۭ 22   in a preserved tablet.

# 86. SŪRAT AL-ṬĀRIQ[1]

سُورَةُ الطَّارِق

بِسۡمِ ٱللَّهِ
ٱلرَّحۡمَٰنِ ٱلرَّحِيمِ

In the Name of Allah,
the All-beneficent, the All-merciful.

وَٱلسَّمَآءِ 1   By the sky,

وَٱلطَّارِقِ     by the nightly visitor,

وَمَآ أَدۡرَىٰكَ مَا ٱلطَّارِقُ 2   (and what will show you what is the nightly visitor?

ٱلنَّجۡمُ ٱلثَّاقِبُ 3   It is the brilliant star):

إِن كُلُّ نَفۡسٍ لَّمَّا عَلَيۡهَا حَافِظٞ 4   there is a guard[2] over every soul.

فَلۡيَنظُرِ ٱلۡإِنسَٰنُ مِمَّ خُلِقَ 5 So let man consider from what he was created.

خُلِقَ مِن مَّآءٖ دَافِقٖ 6 He was created from an effusing fluid

يَخۡرُجُ مِنۢ بَيۡنِ ٱلصُّلۡبِ 7   which issues from between the loins

وَٱلتَّرَآئِبِ     and the breast-bones.

إِنَّهُۥ عَلَىٰ رَجۡعِهِۦ لَقَادِرٞ 8 Indeed He is able to bring him back [after death],

يَوۡمَ تُبۡلَى ٱلسَّرَآئِرُ 9   on the day when the secrets are examined,

فَمَا لَهُۥ مِن قُوَّةٖ وَلَا نَاصِرٖ 10   and he shall have neither power nor helper.

وَٱلسَّمَآءِ ذَاتِ ٱلرَّجۡعِ 11 By the resurgent sky,[3]

وَٱلۡأَرۡضِ ذَاتِ ٱلصَّدۡعِ 12 by the furrowed earth:

إِنَّهُۥ لَقَوۡلٞ فَصۡلٞ 13   it is indeed a decisive word,

وَمَا هُوَ بِٱلۡهَزۡلِ 14   and it is not a jest.

إِنَّهُمۡ يَكِيدُونَ كَيۡدٗا 15 Indeed they are devising a stratagem,

وَأَكِيدُ كَيۡدٗا 16   and I [too] am devising a plan.

فَمَهِّلِ ٱلۡكَٰفِرِينَ 17 So *respite* the faithless;

أَمۡهِلۡهُمۡ رُوَيۡدَۢا 18   *give* them a gentle respite.

---

[1] The *sūrah* takes its name from verse 1 which mentions 'the nightly visitor' (*ṭāriq*).
[2] Or 'watcher.'
[3] Or 'by the sky endowed with rains.'

# سُورَةُ الأَعْلَى      87. SŪRAT AL-AʿLĀ[1]

بِسۡمِ ٱللَّهِ
ٱلرَّحۡمَٰنِ ٱلرَّحِيمِ

In the Name of Allah,
the All-beneficent, the All-merciful.

سَبِّحِ ٱسۡمَ رَبِّكَ ٱلۡأَعۡلَى ١    1 *Celebrate* the Name of *your* Lord, the Most Exalted,

ٱلَّذِى خَلَقَ فَسَوَّىٰ ٢    2   who created and proportioned,

وَٱلَّذِى قَدَّرَ فَهَدَىٰ ٣    3   who determined and guided,

وَٱلَّذِىٓ أَخۡرَجَ ٱلۡمَرۡعَىٰ ٤    4   who brought forth the pasture,

فَجَعَلَهُۥ غُثَآءً أَحۡوَىٰ ٥    5    then turned it into a black scum.

سَنُقۡرِئُكَ    6 We shall have *you* recite [the Qurʾān],

فَلَا تَنسَىٰٓ ٧    then *you* will not forget [any of it]

إِلَّا مَا شَآءَ ٱللَّهُ    7    except what He may wish.

إِنَّهُۥ يَعۡلَمُ ٱلۡجَهۡرَ وَمَا يَخۡفَىٰ ٧    Indeed He knows the overt and what is hidden.

وَنُيَسِّرُكَ لِلۡيُسۡرَىٰ ٨    8 We shall smooth *your* way to [preach] the easiest [canon].

فَذَكِّرۡ إِن نَّفَعَتِ ٱلذِّكۡرَىٰ ٩    9 So *admonish*, for admonition is indeed beneficial:

سَيَذَّكَّرُ مَن يَخۡشَىٰ ١٠    10    he who fears will take admonition,

وَيَتَجَنَّبُهَا ٱلۡأَشۡقَى ١١    11    and the most wretched will shun it

ٱلَّذِى يَصۡلَى ٱلنَّارَ ٱلۡكُبۡرَىٰ ١٢    12    —he who will enter the Great Fire,

ثُمَّ لَا يَمُوتُ فِيهَا وَلَا يَحۡيَىٰ ١٣    13    then neither live in it, nor die.

قَدۡ أَفۡلَحَ مَن تَزَكَّىٰ ١٤    14 Felicitous is he who purifies himself,

وَذَكَرَ ٱسۡمَ رَبِّهِۦ فَصَلَّىٰ ١٥    15    celebrates the Name of his Lord, and prays.

بَلۡ تُؤۡثِرُونَ ٱلۡحَيَوٰةَ ٱلدُّنۡيَا ١٦    16 Rather you prefer the life of this world,

وَٱلۡأٓخِرَةُ خَيۡرٌ وَأَبۡقَىٰٓ ١٧    17    while the Hereafter is better and more lasting.

إِنَّ هَٰذَا لَفِى ٱلصُّحُفِ ٱلۡأُولَىٰ ١٨    18 This is indeed in the former scriptures,

صُحُفِ إِبۡرَٰهِيمَ وَمُوسَىٰ ١٩    19    the scriptures of Abraham and Moses.

---

[1] The *sūrah* is named after 'the Most Exalted' (*al-aʿlā*), mentioned in verse 1.

## 88. SŪRAT AL-GHĀSHIYAH[1]

سُورَةُ الغَاشِيَةِ

بِسْمِ اللَّهِ
الرَّحْمَٰنِ الرَّحِيمِ

In the Name of Allah,
the All-beneficent, the All-merciful.

هَلْ أَتَىٰكَ حَدِيثُ الْغَاشِيَةِ ۝ 1 Did you receive the account of the Enveloper?

وُجُوهٌ يَوْمَئِذٍ خَاشِعَةٌ ۝ 2 Some faces on that day will be humbled,

عَامِلَةٌ نَاصِبَةٌ ۝ 3　wrought-up and weary:

تَصْلَىٰ نَارًا حَامِيَةً ۝ 4　they will enter a scorching fire,

تُسْقَىٰ مِنْ عَيْنٍ ءَانِيَةٍ ۝ 5　and made to drink from a boiling spring.

لَيْسَ لَهُمْ طَعَامٌ إِلَّا مِن ضَرِيعٍ ۝ 6 They will have no food except cactus,

لَّا يُسْمِنُ ۝ 7　neither nourishing,

وَلَا يُغْنِى مِن جُوعٍ ۝ 8　nor availing against hunger.

وُجُوهٌ يَوْمَئِذٍ نَّاعِمَةٌ ۝ 8 Some faces on that day will be joyous,

لِّسَعْيِهَا رَاضِيَةٌ ۝ 9　pleased with their endeavour;

فِى جَنَّةٍ عَالِيَةٍ ۝ 10　in a lofty paradise,

لَّا تَسْمَعُ فِيهَا لَٰغِيَةً ۝ 11　wherein they will not hear any vain talk.

فِيهَا عَيْنٌ جَارِيَةٌ ۝ 12 In it there is a flowing spring

فِيهَا سُرُرٌ مَّرْفُوعَةٌ ۝ 13　and in it there are raised couches,

وَأَكْوَابٌ مَّوْضُوعَةٌ ۝ 14　and goblets set,

وَنَمَارِقُ مَصْفُوفَةٌ ۝ 15　and cushions laid out in an array,

وَزَرَابِيُّ مَبْثُوثَةٌ ۝ 16　and carpets spread out.

أَفَلَا يَنظُرُونَ إِلَى الْإِبِلِ ۝ 17 Do they not observe[2] the camel,

كَيْفَ خُلِقَتْ ۝　[to see] how she has been created?

وَإِلَى السَّمَاءِ كَيْفَ رُفِعَتْ ۝ 18　and the sky, how it has been raised?

وَإِلَى الْجِبَالِ كَيْفَ نُصِبَتْ ۝ 19　and the mountains, how they have been set?

وَإِلَى الْأَرْضِ كَيْفَ سُطِحَتْ ۝ 20　and the earth, how it has been surfaced?

---

[1] The *sūrah* is named after 'the Enveloper' (*al-ghāshiyah*), mentioned in verse 1.
[2] Or 'consider.'

فَذَكِّرْ إِنَّمَآ أَنتَ مُذَكِّرٌ ۝    21 So *admonish*—for *you* are only an admonisher,

لَّسْتَ عَلَيْهِم بِمُصَيْطِرٍ ۝    22      and not a taskmaster over them—

إِلَّا مَن تَوَلَّىٰ وَكَفَرَ ۝    23      except him who turns back and disbelieves.

فَيُعَذِّبُهُ ٱللَّهُ ٱلْعَذَابَ ٱلْأَكْبَرَ ۝    24 Him Allah will punish with the greatest punishment.

إِنَّ إِلَيْنَآ إِيَابَهُمْ ۝    25 Indeed to Us will be their return.

ثُمَّ إِنَّ عَلَيْنَا حِسَابَهُم ۝    26 Then, indeed, their reckoning will lie with Us.

## سُورَةُ الفَجْرِ      89. SŪRAT AL-FAJR[1]

بِسْمِ ٱللَّهِ      In the Name of Allah,

ٱلرَّحْمَٰنِ ٱلرَّحِيمِ      the All-beneficent, the All-merciful.

وَٱلْفَجْرِ ۝    1 By the Dawn,[2]

وَلَيَالٍ عَشْرٍ ۝    2 by the ten nights,

وَٱلشَّفْعِ وَٱلْوَتْرِ ۝    3 by the Even and the Odd,

وَٱلَّيْلِ إِذَا يَسْرِ ۝    4 by the night when it departs!

هَلْ فِى ذَٰلِكَ قَسَمٌ لِّذِى حِجْرٍ ۝    5 Is there an oath in that for one possessing intellect?

أَلَمْ تَرَ ۝    6 Have you not regarded

كَيْفَ فَعَلَ رَبُّكَ بِعَادٍ ۝      how *your* Lord dealt with [the people of] 'Ād,

إِرَمَ ذَاتِ ٱلْعِمَادِ ۝    7 [and] Iram, [the city] of the pillars,

ٱلَّتِى لَمْ يُخْلَقْ مِثْلُهَا فِى ٱلْبِلَٰدِ ۝    8      the like of which was not created among cities,

وَثَمُودَ ۝    9      and [the people of] Thamūd,

ٱلَّذِينَ جَابُواْ ٱلصَّخْرَ بِٱلْوَادِ ۝      who hollowed out the rocks in the valley,

وَفِرْعَوْنَ ذِى ٱلْأَوْتَادِ ۝    10      and Pharaoh, the impaler,[3]

ٱلَّذِينَ طَغَوْاْ فِى ٱلْبِلَٰدِ ۝    11   —those who rebelled [against Allah] in their cities

فَأَكْثَرُواْ فِيهَا ٱلْفَسَادَ ۝    12      and caused much corruption in them,

فَصَبَّ عَلَيْهِمْ رَبُّكَ    13      so *your* Lord poured on them

---

[1] The *sūrah* is named after 'the Dawn' (*al-fajr*) mentioned in verse 1.

[2] Interpreted as the month of Muḥarram, which marks the beginning of the year. (Ṭabarī, *Ta'rīkh*, ii, 390, from Ibn 'Abbās)

[3] See the note at 38:12.

سَوْطَ عَذَابٍ ۝  lashes of punishment.

إِنَّ رَبَّكَ لَبِٱلْمِرْصَادِ ۝  14 Indeed *your* Lord is in ambush.

فَأَمَّا ٱلْإِنسَٰنُ إِذَا مَا ٱبْتَلَىٰهُ رَبُّهُ  15 As for man, whenever his Lord tests him

فَأَكْرَمَهُۥ وَنَعَّمَهُۥ  and grants him honour and blesses him,

فَيَقُولُ رَبِّىٓ أَكْرَمَنِ ۝  he says, 'My Lord has honoured me.'

وَأَمَّآ إِذَا مَا ٱبْتَلَىٰهُ  16 But when He tests him

فَقَدَرَ عَلَيْهِ رِزْقَهُۥ  and tightens for him his provision,

فَيَقُولُ رَبِّىٓ أَهَٰنَنِ ۝  he says, 'My Lord has humiliated me.'

كَلَّا  17 No indeed!

بَل لَّا تُكْرِمُونَ ٱلْيَتِيمَ ۝  Rather you do not honour the orphan,

وَلَا تَحَٰضُّونَ عَلَىٰ طَعَامِ ٱلْمِسْكِينِ ۝  18  and do not urge the feeding of the needy,

وَتَأْكُلُونَ ٱلتُّرَاثَ أَكْلًا لَّمًّا ۝  19  and you eat the inheritance rapaciously,

وَتُحِبُّونَ ٱلْمَالَ حُبًّا جَمًّا ۝  20  and you love wealth with much fondness.

كَلَّا  21 No indeed!

إِذَا دُكَّتِ ٱلْأَرْضُ دَكًّا دَكًّا ۝  When the earth is levelled[1] to a plane,

وَجَآءَ رَبُّكَ وَٱلْمَلَكُ صَفًّا صَفًّا ۝  22  and your Lord and the angels arrive in ranks,

وَجِا۟ىٓءَ يَوْمَئِذٍ بِجَهَنَّمَ  23  the day when hell is brought [near],

يَوْمَئِذٍ يَتَذَكَّرُ ٱلْإِنسَٰنُ  on that day man will take admonition

وَأَنَّىٰ لَهُ ٱلذِّكْرَىٰ ۝  but what will the admonition avail him?

يَقُولُ يَٰلَيْتَنِى قَدَّمْتُ لِحَيَاتِى ۝  24 He will say, 'Alas, had I sent ahead for my life!'

فَيَوْمَئِذٍ لَّا يُعَذِّبُ عَذَابَهُۥٓ أَحَدٌ ۝  25 On that day none shall punish as He punishes,

وَلَا يُوثِقُ وَثَاقَهُۥٓ أَحَدٌ ۝  26  and none shall bind as He binds.

يَٰٓأَيَّتُهَا ٱلنَّفْسُ ٱلْمُطْمَئِنَّةُ ۝  27 'O soul at peace!

ٱرْجِعِىٓ إِلَىٰ رَبِّكِ رَاضِيَةً مَّرْضِيَّةً ۝  28  Return to your Lord, pleased, pleasing!

فَٱدْخُلِى فِى عِبَٰدِى ۝  29  Then enter among My servants!

وَٱدْخُلِى جَنَّتِى ۝  30  And enter My paradise!'

---

[1] Or 'crumbled into fragments.'

## سُورَةُ البَلَدِ      90. SŪRAT AL-BALAD[1]

بِسْمِ اللَّهِ    In the Name of Allah,

الرَّحْمَٰنِ الرَّحِيمِ    the All-beneficent, the All-merciful.

لَآ أُقْسِمُ بِهَٰذَا ٱلْبَلَدِ ۝ 1   I swear by this town,

وَأَنتَ حِلٌّ بِهَٰذَا ٱلْبَلَدِ ۝ 2     as *you* reside in this town;

وَوَالِدٍ وَمَا وَلَدَ ۝ 3     by the father and him whom he begot:

لَقَدْ خَلَقْنَا ٱلْإِنسَٰنَ فِى كَبَدٍ ۝ 4     certainly We created man in travail.

أَيَحْسَبُ ۝ 5 Does he suppose

أَن لَّن يَقْدِرَ عَلَيْهِ أَحَدٌ ۝     that no one will ever have power over him?

يَقُولُ أَهْلَكْتُ مَالًا لُّبَدًا ۝ 6 He says, 'I have squandered immense wealth.'

أَيَحْسَبُ أَن لَّمْ يَرَهُۥٓ أَحَدٌ ۝ 7 Does he suppose that no one sees him?

أَلَمْ نَجْعَل لَّهُۥ عَيْنَيْنِ ۝ 8 Have We not made for him two eyes,

وَلِسَانًا وَشَفَتَيْنِ ۝ 9   a tongue, and two lips,

وَهَدَيْنَٰهُ ٱلنَّجْدَيْنِ ۝ 10   and shown him the two paths [of good and evil]?

فَلَا ٱقْتَحَمَ ٱلْعَقَبَةَ ۝ 11 Yet he has not embarked upon the uphill task.

وَمَآ أَدْرَىٰكَ مَا ٱلْعَقَبَةُ ۝ 12 And what will show you what is the uphill task?

فَكُّ رَقَبَةٍ ۝ 13 [It is] the freeing of a slave,

أَوْ إِطْعَٰمٌ فِى يَوْمٍ ذِى مَسْغَبَةٍ ۝ 14     or feeding [the needy] on a day of starvation,

يَتِيمًا ذَا مَقْرَبَةٍ ۝ 15     or an orphan among relatives,

أَوْ مِسْكِينًا ذَا مَتْرَبَةٍ ۝ 16     or a needy man in desolation,

ثُمَّ كَانَ مِنَ ٱلَّذِينَ ءَامَنُوا۟ 17 while being one of those who have faith

وَتَوَاصَوْا۟ بِٱلصَّبْرِ     and who enjoin one another to patience,

وَتَوَاصَوْا۟ بِٱلْمَرْحَمَةِ ۝     and enjoin one another to compassion.

أُو۟لَٰٓئِكَ أَصْحَٰبُ ٱلْمَيْمَنَةِ ۝ 18 They are the People of the Right Hand.

وَٱلَّذِينَ كَفَرُوا۟ بِـَٔايَٰتِنَا 19 But those who defy Our signs,

هُمْ أَصْحَٰبُ ٱلْمَشْـَٔمَةِ ۝     they are the People of the Left Hand.

---

[1] The *sūrah* is named after the 'town' (*balad*) mentioned in verse 1.

عَلَيْهِمْ نَارٌ مُّؤْصَدَةٌ ۝ 20 Over them will be a closed Fire.

## 91. SŪRAT AL-SHAMS[1]

سُورَةُ الشَّمْسِ

بِسْمِ اللَّهِ
الرَّحْمَٰنِ الرَّحِيمِ

In the Name of Allah,
the All-beneficent, the All-merciful.

وَالشَّمْسِ وَضُحَىٰهَا ۝ 1 By the sun and her forenoon splendour,

وَالْقَمَرِ إِذَا تَلَىٰهَا ۝ 2 by the moon when he follows her,

وَالنَّهَارِ إِذَا جَلَّىٰهَا ۝ 3 by the day when it reveals her,

وَالَّيْلِ إِذَا يَغْشَىٰهَا ۝ 4 by the night when it covers her,

وَالسَّمَاءِ وَمَا بَنَىٰهَا ۝ 5 by the sky and Him who built it,

وَالْأَرْضِ وَمَا طَحَىٰهَا ۝ 6 by the earth and Him who spread it,

وَنَفْسٍ وَمَا سَوَّىٰهَا ۝ 7 by the soul and Him who fashioned it,

فَأَلْهَمَهَا 8 and inspired it with

فُجُورَهَا وَتَقْوَىٰهَا ۝ [discernment between] its virtues and vices:

قَدْ أَفْلَحَ مَن زَكَّىٰهَا ۝ 9 one who purifies it is certainly felicitous,

وَقَدْ خَابَ مَن دَسَّىٰهَا ۝ 10 and one who betrays it certainly fails.

كَذَّبَتْ ثَمُودُ 11 The [people of] Thamūd denied [Allah's signs]

بِطَغْوَىٰهَا ۝ out of their rebellion,

إِذِ انبَعَثَ أَشْقَىٰهَا ۝ 12 when the most wretched of them rose up.

فَقَالَ لَهُمْ رَسُولُ اللَّهِ 13 But then the apostle of Allah said to them,

نَاقَةَ اللَّهِ وَسُقْيَاهَا ۝ 'Let Allah's she-camel drink!'

فَكَذَّبُوهُ فَعَقَرُوهَا 14 But they impugned him and then hamstrung her,

فَدَمْدَمَ عَلَيْهِمْ رَبُّهُم so their Lord took them unawares by night[2]

بِذَنبِهِمْ because of their sin,

فَسَوَّىٰهَا ۝ and levelled it.[3]

---

[1] The *sūrah* is named after 'the sun' (*al-shams*), mentioned in verse 1.

[2] Or 'destroyed them,' or 'crushed them,' or 'brought down His punishment (or wrath) upon them.'

[3] That is, razed their city to the ground.

وَلَا يَخَافُ عُقْبَهَا ۝ 15 And He does not fear its outcome.

# سُورَةُ ٱلَّيْلِ 92. SŪRAT AL-LAYL[1]

بِسْمِ ٱللَّهِ
ٱلرَّحْمَٰنِ ٱلرَّحِيمِ

In the Name of Allah,
the All-beneficent, the All-merciful.

وَٱلَّيْلِ إِذَا يَغْشَىٰ ۝ 1 By the night when it envelops,

وَٱلنَّهَارِ إِذَا تَجَلَّىٰ ۝ 2 by the day when it brightens,

وَمَا خَلَقَ ٱلذَّكَرَ وَٱلْأُنثَىٰ ۝ 3 by Him who created the male and the female:

إِنَّ سَعْيَكُمْ لَشَتَّىٰ ۝ 4 your endeavours are indeed unlike.

فَأَمَّا مَنْ أَعْطَىٰ وَٱتَّقَىٰ ۝ 5 As for him who gives and is Godwary

وَصَدَّقَ بِٱلْحُسْنَىٰ ۝ 6 and confirms the best promise,

فَسَنُيَسِّرُهُ لِلْيُسْرَىٰ ۝ 7 We shall surely ease him into facility.

وَأَمَّا مَنْ بَخِلَ 8 But as for him who is stingy

وَٱسْتَغْنَىٰ ۝ and self-complacent,

وَكَذَّبَ بِٱلْحُسْنَىٰ ۝ 9 and denies the best promise,

فَسَنُيَسِّرُهُ لِلْعُسْرَىٰ ۝ 10 We shall surely ease him into hardship.

وَمَا يُغْنِي عَنْهُ مَالُهُ إِذَا تَرَدَّىٰ ۝ 11 His wealth shall not avail him when he perishes.

إِنَّ عَلَيْنَا لَلْهُدَىٰ ۝ 12 Indeed with Us rests guidance,

وَإِنَّ لَنَا لَلْآخِرَةَ وَٱلْأُولَىٰ ۝ 13 and indeed to Us belong the world and the Hereafter.

فَأَنذَرْتُكُمْ نَارًا تَلَظَّىٰ ۝ 14 So I warn you of a blazing fire,

لَا يَصْلَاهَا إِلَّا ٱلْأَشْقَى ۝ 15 which none shall enter except the most wretched

ٱلَّذِي كَذَّبَ وَتَوَلَّىٰ ۝ 16 —he who denies and turns back.

وَسَيُجَنَّبُهَا ٱلْأَتْقَى ۝ 17 The Godwary shall be spared it

ٱلَّذِي يُؤْتِي مَالَهُ يَتَزَكَّىٰ ۝ 18 —he who gives his wealth to purify himself

وَمَا لِأَحَدٍ عِندَهُ مِن نِّعْمَةٍ تُجْزَىٰ ۝ 19 and does not expect any reward from anyone,

إِلَّا ٱبْتِغَاءَ وَجْهِ رَبِّهِ 20 but seeks only the pleasure of his Lord,

ٱلْأَعْلَىٰ ۝ the Most Exalted,

---

[1] The *sūrah* is named after 'the night' (*al-layl*), mentioned in verse 1.

وَلَسَوْفَ يَرْضَىٰ ۝ 21　and, surely, soon he will be well-pleased.

## 93. SŪRAT AL-ḌUḤĀ[1]

بِسْمِ اللَّهِ
الرَّحْمَٰنِ الرَّحِيمِ

In the Name of Allah,
the All-beneficent, the All-merciful.

وَالضُّحَىٰ ۝ 1　By the morning brightness,

وَالَّيْلِ إِذَا سَجَىٰ ۝ 2　by the night when it is calm!

مَا وَدَّعَكَ رَبُّكَ 3　*Your* Lord has neither forsaken *you*

وَمَا قَلَىٰ ۝　nor is He displeased with *you,*

وَلَلْآخِرَةُ خَيْرٌ لَّكَ مِنَ الْأُولَىٰ ۝ 4　and the Hereafter shall be better for *you* than the world.

وَلَسَوْفَ يُعْطِيكَ رَبُّكَ 5　Soon *your* Lord will give *you* [that with which]

فَتَرْضَىٰ ۝　*you* will be pleased.

أَلَمْ يَجِدْكَ يَتِيمًا فَآوَىٰ ۝ 6　Did He not find *you* an orphan, and shelter *you?*

وَوَجَدَكَ ضَالًّا فَهَدَىٰ ۝ 7　Did He not find *you* astray, and guide *you?*

وَوَجَدَكَ عَائِلًا فَأَغْنَىٰ ۝ 8　Did He not find *you* needy, and enrich *you?*

فَأَمَّا الْيَتِيمَ فَلَا تَقْهَرْ ۝ 9　So, as for the orphan, do not oppress him;

وَأَمَّا السَّائِلَ فَلَا تَنْهَرْ ۝ 10　and as for the beggar, do not chide him;

وَأَمَّا بِنِعْمَةِ رَبِّكَ 11　and as for *your* Lord's blessing,

فَحَدِّثْ ۝　proclaim it!

## 94. SŪRAT AL-SHARḤ[2]

بِسْمِ اللَّهِ
الرَّحْمَٰنِ الرَّحِيمِ

In the Name of Allah,
the All-beneficent, the All-merciful.

أَلَمْ نَشْرَحْ لَكَ صَدْرَكَ ۝ 1　Did We not open *your* breast for *you*

---

[1] Named after 'the morning brightness' (*ḍuḥā*) mentioned in verse 1.
[2] Named 'Opening' after the phrase "Did We not open" (*a lam nashraḥ*) in verse 1.

وَوَضَعْنَا عَنكَ وِزْرَكَ ۝ 2    and relieve *you* of *your* burden

ٱلَّذِىٓ أَنقَضَ ظَهْرَكَ ۝ 3    which [almost] broke *your* back?

وَرَفَعْنَا لَكَ ذِكْرَكَ ۝ 4 Did We not exalt *your* name?

فَإِنَّ مَعَ ٱلْعُسْرِ يُسْرًا ۝ 5 Indeed ease accompanies hardship.

إِنَّ مَعَ ٱلْعُسْرِ يُسْرًا ۝ 6 Indeed ease accompanies hardship.

فَإِذَا فَرَغْتَ فَٱنصَبْ ۝ 7 So when *you* are done with, *appoint*,[1]

وَإِلَىٰ رَبِّكَ فَٱرْغَب ۝ 8    and *turn* eagerly to *your* Lord.

---

سُورَةُ التِّين      ## 95. SŪRAT AL-TĪN[2]

بِسْمِ ٱللَّهِ      In the Name of Allah,

ٱلرَّحْمَٰنِ ٱلرَّحِيمِ      the All-beneficent, the All-merciful.

وَٱلتِّينِ وَٱلزَّيْتُونِ ۝ 1 By the fig and the olive,

وَطُورِ سِينِينَ ۝ 2 by Mount Sinai,

وَهَٰذَا ٱلْبَلَدِ ٱلْأَمِينِ ۝ 3 by this secure town:[3]

لَقَدْ خَلَقْنَا ٱلْإِنسَٰنَ 4    We certainly created man

فِىٓ أَحْسَنِ تَقْوِيمٍ ۝    in the best of forms;

ثُمَّ رَدَدْنَٰهُ أَسْفَلَ سَٰفِلِينَ ۝ 5    then We relegated him to the lowest of the low,

إِلَّا ٱلَّذِينَ ءَامَنُوا۟ وَعَمِلُوا۟ ٱلصَّٰلِحَٰتِ 6 except those who have faith and do righteous deeds.

فَلَهُمْ أَجْرٌ غَيْرُ مَمْنُونٍ ۝    There will be an everlasting reward for them.

فَمَا يُكَذِّبُكَ بَعْدُ بِٱلدِّينِ ۝ 7 So what makes you deny the Retribution?

أَلَيْسَ ٱللَّهُ بِأَحْكَمِ ٱلْحَٰكِمِينَ ۝ 8 Is not Allah the fairest of all judges?

---

[1] Or 'when *you* are finished [with prayer], exert yourself [in supplicating to Allah].'

[2] Named after 'the fig' (*tīn*) mentioned in verse 1.

[3] That is, the holy city of Makkah.

سُورَةُ العَلَق

**96. SŪRAT AL-ʿALAQ**[1]

بِسْمِ ٱللَّهِ

In the Name of Allah,

ٱلرَّحْمَٰنِ ٱلرَّحِيمِ

the All-beneficent, the All-merciful.

أَقْرَأْ بِٱسْمِ رَبِّكَ ٱلَّذِى خَلَقَ ١   1 *Read* in the Name of *your* Lord who created;

خَلَقَ ٱلْإِنسَٰنَ مِنْ عَلَقٍ ٢   2 created man from a clinging mass.

أَقْرَأْ وَرَبُّكَ ٱلْأَكْرَمُ ٣   3 *Read*, and *your* Lord is the most generous,

ٱلَّذِى عَلَّمَ بِٱلْقَلَمِ ٤   4 who taught by the pen,

عَلَّمَ ٱلْإِنسَٰنَ مَا لَمْ يَعْلَمْ ٥   5 taught man what he did not know.

كَلَّا إِنَّ ٱلْإِنسَٰنَ لَيَطْغَىٰ ٦   6 Indeed man becomes rebellious

أَن رَّءَاهُ ٱسْتَغْنَىٰ ٧   7 when he considers himself without need.

إِنَّ إِلَىٰ رَبِّكَ ٱلرُّجْعَىٰ ٨   8 Indeed to *your* Lord is the return.

أَرَءَيْتَ ٱلَّذِى يَنْهَىٰ ٩   9 Tell me, he who forbids

عَبْدًا إِذَا صَلَّىٰ ١٠   10 a servant when he prays,

أَرَءَيْتَ إِن كَانَ عَلَى ٱلْهُدَىٰ ١١   11 tell me, should he be on [true] guidance,

أَوْ أَمَرَ بِٱلتَّقْوَىٰ ١٢   12 or bid [others] to Godwariness,

أَرَءَيْتَ إِن كَذَّبَ وَتَوَلَّىٰ ١٣   13 tell me, should he call him a liar and turn away

أَلَمْ يَعْلَم بِأَنَّ ٱللَّهَ يَرَىٰ ١٤   14 —does he not know that Allah sees?

كَلَّا لَئِن لَّمْ يَنتَهِ ١٥   15 No indeed! If he does not stop,

لَنَسْفَعًۢا بِٱلنَّاصِيَةِ   We shall seize him by the forelock,

نَاصِيَةٍ كَٰذِبَةٍ خَاطِئَةٍ ١٦   16 a lying, iniquitous forelock!

فَلْيَدْعُ نَادِيَهُۥ ١٧   17 Then let him call out his gang!

سَنَدْعُ ٱلزَّبَانِيَةَ ١٨   18 We [too] shall call the keepers of hell.

كَلَّا لَا تُطِعْهُ ١٩   19 No indeed! Do not obey him,

وَٱسْجُدْ وَٱقْتَرِب ۩   but prostrate and draw near [to Allah]!

---

[1] Named after 'the clinging mass' (*ʿalaq*) mentioned in verse 2.

# سُورَةُ القَدْرِ      97. SŪRAT AL-QADR[1]

بِسْمِ ٱللَّهِ      In the Name of Allah,

ٱلرَّحْمَٰنِ ٱلرَّحِيمِ      the All-beneficent, the All-merciful.

إِنَّآ أَنزَلْنَٰهُ    1 Indeed We sent it down

فِى لَيْلَةِ ٱلْقَدْرِ ۞    on the Night of Ordainment.[2]

وَمَآ أَدْرَىٰكَ    2 What will show you

مَا لَيْلَةُ ٱلْقَدْرِ ۞    what is the Night of Ordainment?

لَيْلَةُ ٱلْقَدْرِ    3 The Night of Ordainment

خَيْرٌ مِّنْ أَلْفِ شَهْرٍ ۞    is better than a thousand months.

تَنَزَّلُ ٱلْمَلَٰٓئِكَةُ وَٱلرُّوحُ فِيهَا    4 In it the angels and the Spirit descend,

بِإِذْنِ رَبِّهِم    by the leave of their Lord,

مِّن كُلِّ أَمْرٍ ۞    with every command.

سَلَٰمٌ هِىَ حَتَّىٰ مَطْلَعِ ٱلْفَجْرِ ۞    5 It is peaceful until the rising of the dawn.

# سُورَةُ البَيِّنَةِ      98. SŪRAT AL-BAYYINAH[3]

بِسْمِ ٱللَّهِ      In the Name of Allah,

ٱلرَّحْمَٰنِ ٱلرَّحِيمِ      the All-beneficent, the All-merciful.

لَمْ يَكُنِ ٱلَّذِينَ كَفَرُواْ    1 The faithless

مِنْ أَهْلِ ٱلْكِتَٰبِ    from among the People of the Book

وَٱلْمُشْرِكِينَ    and the polytheists

مُنفَكِّينَ    were not set apart

حَتَّىٰ تَأْتِيَهُمُ ٱلْبَيِّنَةُ ۞    until the proof had come to them:

---

[1] Named after the phrase 'the night of ordainment' (*laylat al-qadr*) in verses 1-3.
[2] That is, the Qur'ān. See 44:2-5.
[3] Named after 'the proof' (*al-bayyinah*) mentioned in verses 1 & 4.

رَسُولٌ مِّنَ ٱللَّهِ    2 an apostle from Allah

يَتْلُواْ صُحُفًا مُّطَهَّرَةً ۝    reciting impeccable scriptures,

فِيهَا كُتُبٌ قَيِّمَةٌ ۝    3 wherein are upright precepts.

وَمَا تَفَرَّقَ ٱلَّذِينَ أُوتُواْ ٱلْكِتَٰبَ    4 And those who were given the Book did not divide,

إِلَّا مِنۢ بَعْدِ مَا جَآءَتْهُمُ ٱلْبَيِّنَةُ ۝    except after the proof had come to them.

وَمَا أُمِرُوٓاْ إِلَّا لِيَعْبُدُواْ ٱللَّهَ    5 Yet they were not commanded except to worship Allah,

مُخْلِصِينَ لَهُ ٱلدِّينَ    dedicating their faith to Him

حُنَفَآءَ    as men of pure faith,

وَيُقِيمُواْ ٱلصَّلَوٰةَ وَيُؤْتُواْ ٱلزَّكَوٰةَ    and to maintain the prayer, and pay the *zakāt*.

وَذَٰلِكَ دِينُ ٱلْقَيِّمَةِ ۝    That is the upright religion.

إِنَّ ٱلَّذِينَ كَفَرُواْ    6 Indeed the faithless

مِنْ أَهْلِ ٱلْكِتَٰبِ    from among the People of the Book

وَٱلْمُشْرِكِينَ    and the polytheists

فِى نَارِ جَهَنَّمَ    will be in the fire of hell,

خَٰلِدِينَ فِيهَآ    to remain in it [forever].

أُوْلَٰٓئِكَ هُمْ شَرُّ ٱلْبَرِيَّةِ ۝    It is they who are the worst of creatures.

إِنَّ ٱلَّذِينَ ءَامَنُواْ وَعَمِلُواْ ٱلصَّٰلِحَٰتِ    7 Indeed those who have faith and do righteous deeds

أُوْلَٰٓئِكَ هُمْ خَيْرُ ٱلْبَرِيَّةِ ۝    —it is they who are the best of creatures.

جَزَآؤُهُمْ عِندَ رَبِّهِمْ    8 Their reward, near their Lord,

جَنَّٰتُ عَدْنٍ    is the Gardens of Eden,

تَجْرِى مِن تَحْتِهَا ٱلْأَنْهَٰرُ    with streams running in them,

خَٰلِدِينَ فِيهَآ أَبَدًا    to remain in them forever.

رَّضِىَ ٱللَّهُ عَنْهُمْ    Allah is pleased with them,

وَرَضُواْ عَنْهُ    and they are pleased with Him.

ذَٰلِكَ لِمَنْ خَشِىَ رَبَّهُۥ ۝    That is for those who fear their Lord.

# 99. SŪRAT AL-ZALZALAH[1]

سُورَةُ الزَّلْزَلَةِ

بِسْمِ ٱللَّهِ    In the Name of Allah,
ٱلرَّحْمَٰنِ ٱلرَّحِيمِ    the All-beneficent, the All-merciful.

إِذَا زُلْزِلَتِ ٱلْأَرْضُ زِلْزَالَهَا ۝ 1 When the earth is rocked with a terrible quake

وَأَخْرَجَتِ ٱلْأَرْضُ أَثْقَالَهَا ۝ 2 and the earth discharges her burdens,

وَقَالَ ٱلْإِنسَٰنُ مَا لَهَا ۝ 3 and man says, 'What is the matter with her?'

يَوْمَئِذٍ تُحَدِّثُ أَخْبَارَهَا ۝ 4 On that day she will relate her chronicles

بِأَنَّ رَبَّكَ أَوْحَىٰ لَهَا ۝ 5 for her Lord will have inspired her.

يَوْمَئِذٍ يَصْدُرُ ٱلنَّاسُ أَشْتَاتًا 6 On that day, mankind will issue forth in various groups[2]

لِّيُرَوْا۟ أَعْمَٰلَهُمْ ۝ to be shown their deeds.

فَمَن يَعْمَلْ مِثْقَالَ ذَرَّةٍ خَيْرًا 7 So whoever does an atom's weight of good

يَرَهُۥ ۝ will see it,

وَمَن يَعْمَلْ مِثْقَالَ ذَرَّةٍ شَرًّا 8 and whoever does an atom's weight of evil

يَرَهُۥ ۝ will see it.

# 100. SŪRAT AL-'ĀDIYĀT[3]

سُورَةُ الْعَادِيَاتِ

بِسْمِ ٱللَّهِ    In the Name of Allah,
ٱلرَّحْمَٰنِ ٱلرَّحِيمِ    the All-beneficent, the All-merciful.

وَٱلْعَٰدِيَٰتِ ضَبْحًا ۝ 1 By the snorting chargers,

فَٱلْمُورِيَٰتِ قَدْحًا ۝ 2 by the strikers of sparks [with their hoofs],

فَٱلْمُغِيرَٰتِ صُبْحًا ۝ 3 by the raiders at dawn,

فَأَثَرْنَ بِهِۦ نَقْعًا ۝ 4 raising therein a trail of dust,

---

[1] The *sūrah* takes its name, meaning 'the quake,' from verse 1.

[2] Or 'separate groups.'

[3] The *sūrah* takes its name from 'the chargers' mentioned in verse 1.

فَوَسَطْنَ بِهِۦ جَمْعًا ۝ 5    cleaving therein a host!

إِنَّ ٱلْإِنسَٰنَ لِرَبِّهِۦ لَكَنُودٌ ۝ 6 Indeed man is ungrateful to his Lord,

وَإِنَّهُۥ عَلَىٰ ذَٰلِكَ لَشَهِيدٌ ۝ 7    and indeed he is witness to that!

وَإِنَّهُۥ لِحُبِّ ٱلْخَيْرِ لَشَدِيدٌ ۝ 8 He is indeed avid in the love of wealth.

أَفَلَا يَعْلَمُ 9 Does he not know,

إِذَا بُعْثِرَ مَا فِى ٱلْقُبُورِ ۝     when what is in the graves is turned over,

وَحُصِّلَ مَا فِى ٱلصُّدُورِ ۝ 10     and what is in the breasts is divulged,

إِنَّ رَبَّهُم 11 indeed their Lord

بِهِمْ يَوْمَئِذٍ لَّخَبِيرٌ ۝     will be best aware of them on that day?

سُورَةُ ٱلْقَارِعَةِ      # 101. SŪRAT AL-QĀRI'AH[1]

بِسْمِ ٱللَّهِ       In the Name of Allah,

ٱلرَّحْمَٰنِ ٱلرَّحِيمِ       the All-beneficent, the All-merciful.

ٱلْقَارِعَةُ ۝ 1 The Catastrophe!

مَا ٱلْقَارِعَةُ ۝ 2 What is the Catastrophe?

وَمَآ أَدْرَىٰكَ مَا ٱلْقَارِعَةُ ۝ 3 What will show you what is the Catastrophe?

يَوْمَ يَكُونُ ٱلنَّاسُ 4 The day mankind will be

كَٱلْفَرَاشِ ٱلْمَبْثُوثِ ۝     like scattered moths,

وَتَكُونُ ٱلْجِبَالُ 5    and the mountains will be

كَٱلْعِهْنِ ٱلْمَنفُوشِ ۝     like carded wool.

فَأَمَّا مَن ثَقُلَتْ مَوَٰزِينُهُۥ ۝ 6 As for him whose deeds weigh heavy in the scales,

فَهُوَ فِى عِيشَةٍ رَّاضِيَةٍ ۝ 7   he will have a pleasing life.

وَأَمَّا مَنْ خَفَّتْ مَوَٰزِينُهُۥ ۝ 8 But as for him whose deeds weigh light in the scales,

فَأُمُّهُۥ هَاوِيَةٌ ۝ 9    his home will be the Abyss.

وَمَآ أَدْرَىٰكَ مَا هِيَهْ ۝ 10 And what will show you what it is?

نَارٌ حَامِيَةٌ ۝ 11 It is a scorching fire!

---

[1] The *sūrah* takes its name, meaning 'the catastrophe,' from verses 1-3.

# سُورَةُ التَّكَاثُرِ     102. SŪRAT AL-TAKĀTHUR[1]

بِسْمِ اللَّهِ     In the Name of Allah,

الرَّحْمَنِ الرَّحِيمِ     the All-beneficent, the All-merciful.

أَلْهَىٰكُمُ التَّكَاثُرُ ۝    1 Rivalry [and vainglory] distracted you

حَتَّىٰ زُرْتُمُ الْمَقَابِرَ ۝    2   until you visited [even] the graves.

كَلَّا ۝    3 No indeed!

سَوْفَ تَعْلَمُونَ ۝     Soon you will know!

ثُمَّ كَلَّا ۝    4 Again, no indeed!

سَوْفَ تَعْلَمُونَ ۝     Soon you will know!

كَلَّا ۝    5 No indeed!

لَوْ تَعْلَمُونَ عِلْمَ الْيَقِينِ ۝     Were you to know with certain knowledge,

لَتَرَوُنَّ الْجَحِيمَ ۝    6   you would surely see hell.

ثُمَّ لَتَرَوُنَّهَا عَيْنَ الْيَقِينِ ۝    7 Again, you will surely see it with the eye of certainty.

ثُمَّ لَتُسْأَلُنَّ يَوْمَئِذٍ    8 Then, that day, you will surely be questioned

عَنِ النَّعِيمِ ۝     concerning the blessing.

# سُورَةُ الْعَصْرِ     103. SŪRAT AL-'AṢR[2]

بِسْمِ اللَّهِ     In the Name of Allah,

الرَّحْمَنِ الرَّحِيمِ     the All-beneficent, the All-merciful.

وَالْعَصْرِ ۝    1 By Time!

إِنَّ الْإِنسَانَ لَفِي خُسْرٍ ۝    2 Indeed man is at a loss,

إِلَّا الَّذِينَ ءَامَنُوا    3   except those who have faith

وَعَمِلُوا الصَّالِحَاتِ     and do righteous deeds,

---

[1] The *sūrah* takes its name, meaning 'rivalry,' from verses 1-3.
[2] The *sūrah* takes its name from the phrase 'By Time' in verse 1.

وَتَوَاصَوْا بِٱلْحَقِّ    and enjoin one another to [follow] the truth,

وَتَوَاصَوْا بِٱلصَّبْرِ ۝    and enjoin one another to patience.

## سُورَةُ الْهُمَزَة    104. SŪRAT AL-HUMAZAH[1]

بِسْمِ ٱللَّهِ    In the Name of Allah,

ٱلرَّحْمَٰنِ ٱلرَّحِيمِ    the All-beneficent, the All-merciful.

وَيْلٌ لِّكُلِّ هُمَزَةٍ لُّمَزَةٍ ۝    1 Woe to every scandal-monger and slanderer,

ٱلَّذِى جَمَعَ مَالًا وَعَدَّدَهُ ۝    2  who amasses wealth and counts it over.

يَحْسَبُ أَنَّ مَالَهُۥ أَخْلَدَهُ ۝    3 He supposes his wealth will make him immortal!

كَلَّا لَيُنۢبَذَنَّ فِى ٱلْحُطَمَةِ ۝    4 No indeed! He will surely be cast into the Crusher.

وَمَآ أَدْرَىٰكَ مَا ٱلْحُطَمَةُ ۝    5 And what will show you what is the Crusher?

نَارُ ٱللَّهِ ٱلْمُوقَدَةُ ۝    6 [It is] the fire of Allah, set ablaze,

ٱلَّتِى تَطَّلِعُ عَلَى ٱلْأَفْـِٔدَةِ ۝    7  which will overspread the hearts.

إِنَّهَا عَلَيْهِم مُّؤْصَدَةٌ ۝    8 Indeed it will close in upon them

فِى عَمَدٍ مُّمَدَّدَةٍ ۝    9  in outstretched columns.

## سُورَةُ الْفِيل    105. SŪRAT AL-FĪL[2]

بِسْمِ ٱللَّهِ    In the Name of Allah,

ٱلرَّحْمَٰنِ ٱلرَّحِيمِ    the All-beneficent, the All-merciful.

أَلَمْ تَرَ كَيْفَ فَعَلَ رَبُّكَ    1 Have you not regarded how *your* Lord dealt

بِأَصْحَٰبِ ٱلْفِيلِ ۝    with the Men of the Elephant?

أَلَمْ يَجْعَلْ كَيْدَهُمْ فِى تَضْلِيلٍ ۝    2 Did He not make their stratagems go awry,

وَأَرْسَلَ عَلَيْهِمْ طَيْرًا أَبَابِيلَ ۝    3  and send against them flocks of birds

---

[1] The *sūrah* takes its name, meaning 'the slanderer,' from verses 1.

[2] The *sūrah* takes its name, meaning 'the elephant,' from verse 2, which refers to the force dispatched by Abrahah to Makkah with the aim of destroying the Ka'bah as *aṣḥāb al-fīl* ('the Men of the Elephant').

861

4   تَرْمِيهِم بِحِجَارَةٍ مِّن سِجِّيلٍ ۝    pelting them with stones of shale,

5   فَجَعَلَهُمْ كَعَصْفٍ مَّأْكُولٍ ۝    thus making them like chewed-up straw?

## 106. SŪRAT AL-QURAYSH[1]

### سُوْرَةُ قُرَيْش

بِسْمِ ٱللَّهِ      In the Name of Allah,

ٱلرَّحْمَٰنِ ٱلرَّحِيمِ      the All-beneficent, the All-merciful.

1   لِإِيلَٰفِ قُرَيْشٍ ۝    [In gratitude] for solidarity among Quraysh,

2   إِۦلَٰفِهِمْ رِحْلَةَ ٱلشِّتَآءِ وَٱلصَّيْفِ ۝    their solidarity during winter and summer journeys,

3   فَلْيَعْبُدُواْ رَبَّ هَٰذَا ٱلْبَيْتِ ۝    let them worship the Lord of this House,

4   ٱلَّذِىٓ أَطْعَمَهُم مِّن جُوعٍ ۝    who has fed them [and saved them] from hunger,

  وَءَامَنَهُم مِّنْ خَوْفٍ ۝    and secured them from fear.

## 107. SŪRAT AL-MĀ'ŪN[2]

### سُوْرَةُ الْمَاعُون

بِسْمِ ٱللَّهِ      In the Name of Allah,

ٱلرَّحْمَٰنِ ٱلرَّحِيمِ      the All-beneficent, the All-merciful.

1   أَرَءَيْتَ ٱلَّذِى يُكَذِّبُ بِٱلدِّينِ ۝    Did you see him who denies the Retribution?

2   فَذَٰلِكَ ٱلَّذِى يَدُعُّ ٱلْيَتِيمَ ۝    That is the one who drives away the orphan,

3   وَلَا يَحُضُّ عَلَىٰ طَعَامِ ٱلْمِسْكِينِ ۝    and does not urge the feeding of the needy.

4   فَوَيْلٌ لِّلْمُصَلِّينَ ۝    Woe to them who pray,

5   ٱلَّذِينَ هُمْ عَن صَلَاتِهِمْ سَاهُونَ ۝    —those who are heedless of their prayers,

6   ٱلَّذِينَ هُمْ يُرَآءُونَ ۝    those who show off

7   وَيَمْنَعُونَ ٱلْمَاعُونَ ۝    but deny aid.

---

[1] The *sūrah* takes its name from verse 1, which mentions the Quraysh, the Makkan tribe to which the Prophet (s) belonged.

[2] The *sūrah* takes its name from verse 7, in which word *al-mā'ūn* (meaning 'the aid') occurs.

سُورَةُ الْكَوْثَرِ ‏ 108. SŪRAT AL-KAWTHAR[1]

بِسْمِ اللَّهِ ‏ In the Name of Allah,
الرَّحْمَٰنِ الرَّحِيمِ ‏ the All-beneficent, the All-merciful.

إِنَّا أَعْطَيْنَاكَ الْكَوْثَرَ ۩ ‏ 1 Indeed We have given *you* abundance.
فَصَلِّ لِرَبِّكَ ‏ 2 So pray to *your* Lord,
وَانْحَرْ ۩ ‏ and sacrifice [the sacrificial camel],[2]
إِنَّ شَانِئَكَ هُوَ الْأَبْتَرُ ۩ ‏ 3 Indeed it is *your* enemy who is without posterity.

سُورَةُ الْكَافِرُونَ ‏ 109. SŪRAT AL-KĀFIRŪN[3]

بِسْمِ اللَّهِ ‏ In the Name of Allah,
الرَّحْمَٰنِ الرَّحِيمِ ‏ the All-beneficent, the All-merciful.

قُلْ يَا أَيُّهَا الْكَافِرُونَ ۩ ‏ 1 *Say,* 'O faithless ones!
لَا أَعْبُدُ مَا تَعْبُدُونَ ۩ ‏ 2 I do not worship what you worship,
وَلَا أَنْتُمْ عَابِدُونَ مَا أَعْبُدُ ۩ ‏ 3 nor do you worship what I worship;
وَلَا أَنَا عَابِدٌ مَا عَبَدْتُّمْ ۩ ‏ 4 nor will I worship what you have worshiped
وَلَا أَنْتُمْ عَابِدُونَ مَا أَعْبُدُ ۩ ‏ 5 nor will you worship what I worship.
لَكُمْ دِينُكُمْ وَلِيَ دِينِ ۩ ‏ 6 To you your religion, and to me my religion.'

---

[1] The *sūrah* takes its name from verse 1, in which the word *al-kawthar* (meaning 'abundance') occurs.

[2] Or 'raise your hands.' According to this interpretation, the phrase refers to the raising of the hands to the ears during prayers.

[3] The *sūrah* takes its name from verse 1, which mentions 'the faithless' (*al-kāfirūn*).

## سُورَةُ النَّصْرِ     110. SŪRAT AL-NAṢR[1]

بِسْمِ اللَّهِ     In the Name of Allah,
الرَّحْمَٰنِ الرَّحِيمِ     the All-beneficent, the All-merciful.

إِذَا جَاءَ نَصْرُ اللَّهِ وَالْفَتْحُ ۝ 1 When Allah's help comes with victory,

وَرَأَيْتَ النَّاسَ 2 and *you* see the people

يَدْخُلُونَ فِي دِينِ اللَّهِ أَفْوَاجًا ۝ entering Allah's religion in throngs,

فَسَبِّحْ بِحَمْدِ رَبِّكَ 3 then *celebrate* the praise of your Lord,

وَاسْتَغْفِرْهُ ۚ and *plead* to Him for forgiveness.

إِنَّهُ كَانَ تَوَّابًا ۝ Indeed He is all-clement.

## سُورَةُ الْمَسَدِ     111. SŪRAT AL-MASAD[2]

بِسْمِ اللَّهِ     In the Name of Allah,
الرَّحْمَٰنِ الرَّحِيمِ     the All-beneficent, the All-merciful.

تَبَّتْ يَدَا أَبِي لَهَبٍ وَتَبَّ ۝ 1 Perish the hands of Abu Lahab, and perish he!

مَا أَغْنَىٰ عَنْهُ مَالُهُ 2 Neither his wealth availed him,

وَمَا كَسَبَ ۝ nor what he had earned.

سَيَصْلَىٰ نَارًا ذَاتَ لَهَبٍ ۝ 3 Soon he will enter the blazing fire,

وَامْرَأَتُهُ حَمَّالَةَ الْحَطَبِ ۝ 4 and his wife [too], the firewood carrier,[3]

فِي جِيدِهَا حَبْلٌ مِنْ مَسَدٍ ۝ 5 with a rope of palm fibre around her neck.

---

[1] The *sūrah* takes its name from verse 1, in which phrase *naṣr Allah* (meaning 'Allah's help') occurs.

[2] The *sūrah* takes its name from verse 5 in which the phrase *ḥablun min masad* (meaning 'a rope of palm fibre') occurs.

[3] Or 'the informer.'

## سُورَةُ الإخلاص     112. SŪRAT AL-IKHLĀṢ[1]

بِسۡمِ ٱللَّهِ     In the Name of Allah,
ٱلرَّحۡمَٰنِ ٱلرَّحِيمِ     the All-beneficent, the All-merciful.

قُلۡ هُوَ ٱللَّهُ أَحَدٌ ۝   1 *Say,* 'He is Allah, the One.
ٱللَّهُ ٱلصَّمَدُ ۝   2 Allah is the All-embracing.
لَمۡ يَلِدۡ وَلَمۡ يُولَدۡ ۝   3 He neither begat, nor was begotten,
وَلَمۡ يَكُن لَّهُۥ كُفُوًا أَحَدُۢ ۝   4 nor has He any equal.'

## سُورَةُ الفَلَق     113. SŪRAT AL-FALAQ[2]

بِسۡمِ ٱللَّهِ     In the Name of Allah,
ٱلرَّحۡمَٰنِ ٱلرَّحِيمِ     the All-beneficent, the All-merciful.

قُلۡ أَعُوذُ بِرَبِّ ٱلۡفَلَقِ ۝   1 Say, 'I seek the protection of the Lord of the daybreak
مِن شَرِّ مَا خَلَقَ ۝   2 from the evil of what He has created,
وَمِن شَرِّ غَاسِقٍ إِذَا وَقَبَ ۝   3 and from the evil of the dark night when it settles,
وَمِن شَرِّ ٱلنَّفَّٰثَٰتِ فِى ٱلۡعُقَدِ ۝   4 and from the evil of the witches who blow on knots,
وَمِن شَرِّ حَاسِدٍ إِذَا حَسَدَ ۝   5 and from the evil of the envious one when he envies.'

---

[1] The *sūrah*— also called "Sūrat al-Taw ̣id"—is a statement of Islamic monotheism which negates any kind of anthropomorphism that may compromise pure monotheism or *taw ̣id*. It is called 'the Sūrah of Ikhlāṣ' as it extricates and purges *taw ̣id* of deviant ideas and posits it in its exclusive purity.

[2] The *sūrah* takes its name from 'the daybreak' (*al-falaq*) mentioned in verse 1.

# سُورَةُ النَّاس    114. SŪRAT AL-NĀS[1]

بِسْمِ اللَّهِ    In the Name of Allah,
الرَّحْمَٰنِ الرَّحِيمِ    the All-beneficent, the All-merciful.

قُلْ أَعُوذُ بِرَبِّ النَّاسِ ۝ 1    Say, 'I seek the protection of the Lord of humans,

مَلِكِ النَّاسِ ۝ 2    Sovereign of humans,

إِلَٰهِ النَّاسِ ۝ 3    God of humans,

مِن شَرِّ الْوَسْوَاسِ الْخَنَّاسِ ۝ 4    from the evil of the sneaky tempter

الَّذِي يُوَسْوِسُ فِي صُدُورِ النَّاسِ ۝ 5    who puts temptations into the breasts of humans,

مِنَ الْجِنَّةِ وَالنَّاسِ ۝ 6    from among the jinn and humans.'

---

[1] The *sūrah* takes its name from the word 'mankind' (*al-nās*) which recurs throughout the *sūrah*.

## A Supplication for Recitation on
## Completing a Reading of the Qur'ān

اَللّٰهُمَّ O Allah,

اِنَّكَ اَعَنْتَنِي عَلیٰ خَتْمِ كِتَابِكَ You have helped me complete Your Book,

اَلَّذِي اَنْزَلْتَهُ نُوراً، which You sent down as a light

وَجَعَلْتَهُ مُهَيْمِناً and appointed as an authority

عَلیٰ كُلِّ كِتَابٍ اَنْزَلْتَهُ، over every scripture that You have sent down,

وَفَضَّلْتَهُ عَلیٰ كُلِّ حَدِيثٍ preferring it over every discourse

قَصَصْتَهُ، that You have dissertated,

وَفُرْقَاناً فَرَقْتَ بِهِ a criterion, by which You have separated

بَيْنَ حَلَالِكَ وَحَرَامِكَ، Your lawful from Your unlawful,

وَقُرْآناً اَعْرَبْتَ بِهِ a Qur'ān, by which You have clarified

عَنْ شَرَائِعِ اَحْكَامِكَ، the approaches to Your ordinances,

وَكِتَاباً فَصَّلْتَهُ a scripture, which You have elaborated

لِعِبَادِكَ تَفْصِيلاً، very distinctly for Your servants,

وَوَحْياً اَنْزَلْتَهُ a revelation, which You have sent down

عَلیٰ نَبِيِّكَ مُحَمَّدٍ upon Your prophet, Muḥammad

صَلَوَاتُكَ عَلَيْهِ وَآلِهِ (Your blessings be upon him and his Household),

تَنْزِيلاً، in a gradual manner.

وَجَعَلْتَهُ نُوراً You appointed it a light

نَهْتَدِي by which we may be guided

مِنْ ظُلَمِ الضَّلَالَةِ وَالْجَهَالَةِ from the darkness of error and ignorance,

بِاتِّبَاعِهِ، by virtue of following it,

وَشِفَاءً لِمَنْ اَنْصَتَ a healing for him who commits his ears

بِفَهْمِ التَّصْدِيقِ with an assenting understanding

إِلیٰ اسْتِمَاعِهِ، to listening to it,

وَمِيزانَ قِسْطٍ a just balance

لَا يَحِيفُ عَنِ الْحَقِّ لِسانُهُ، whose pointer does not depart from the truth,

وَنُورَ هُدًى a guiding light

لَا يَطْفَأُ عَنِ الشَّاهِدِينَ بُرْهانُهُ، whose proof is never lost to the witnesses,

وَعَلَمَ نَجاةٍ and a guidepost of deliverance,

لَا يَضِلُّ مَنْ أَمَّ قَصْدَ سُنَّتِهِ، one who pursues its straight path does not go astray

وَلَا تَنالُ أَيْدِى الْهَلَكاتِ and will not be touched by the hands of disasters

مَنْ تَعَلَّقَ بِعُرْوَةِ عِصْمَتِهِ. one who clings to its saving handhold.

اَللّٰهُمَّ O Allah,

فَإِذْ أَفَدْتَنَا الْمَعُونَةَ عَلىٰ تِلاوَتِهِ، since You have given us help to recite it

وَسَهَّلْتَ جَواسِيَ أَلْسِنَتِنا and smoothened the coarseness of our tongues

بِحُسْنِ عِبارَتِهِ، through the beauty of its expression,

فَاجْعَلْنا مِمَّنْ place us among those who

يَرْعاهُ حَقَّ رِعايَتِهِ، observe it as it should be observed,

وَيَدِينُ لَكَ بِاعْتِقادِ التَّسْلِيمِ serve You by adhering in submission

لِمُحْكَمِ آياتِهِ، to its univocal verses,

وَيَفْزَعُ إِلَى الْإِقْرارِ and seek refuge in admission of

بِمُتَشابِهِهِ both its metaphorical passages

وَمُوضَحاتِ بَيِّناتِهِ. and its manifest proofs.

اَللّٰهُمَّ O Allah,

إِنَّكَ أَنْزَلْتَهُ عَلىٰ نَبِيِّكَ مُحَمَّدٍ You sent it down upon Your prophet, Muhammad

صَلَّى اللّٰهُ عَلَيْهِ وَآلِهِ (Allah bless him and his household),

مُجْمَلاً، in summary form,

وَأَلْهَمْتَهُ عِلْمَ عَجائِبِهِ You inspired him with the knowledge of its wonders

مُكَمَّلاً، to complement it,

وَوَرَّثْتَنا عِلْمَهُ مُفَسَّراً، You made us[1] the heirs of its knowledge as interpreters,

---

[1] That is, the Imams of the Prophet's lineage.

وَفَضَّلْتَنا and graced us

عَلَى مَنْ جَهِلَ عِلْمَهُ، above those who are ignorant of its knowledge,

وَقَوَّيْتَنا عَلَيْهِ and You gave this capacity

لِتَرْفَعَنا فَوْقَ مَنْ لَمْ يُطِقْ حَمْلَهُ. to raise us above those who are not able to carry it.

اَللّٰهُمَّ O Allah,

فَكَما جَعَلْتَ قُلُوبَنا لَهُ حَمَلَةً، just as You have appointed our hearts as its carriers

وَعَرَّفْتَنا بِرَحْمَتِكَ and made known to us through Your mercy

شَرَفَهُ وَفَضْلَهُ، its nobility and excellence,

فَصَلِّ عَلَى مُحَمَّدٍ الْخَطِيبِ بِهِ، so also bless Muhammad, its preacher,

وَعَلَى آلِهِ الْخُزَّانِ لَهُ، and his Household, its caretakers,

وَاجْعَلْنا مِمَّنْ يَعْتَرِفُ and place us among those who confess

بِأَنَّهُ مِنْ عِنْدِكَ that it has come from You,

حَتَّى لَا يُعارِضَنَا الشَّكُّ فِي تَصْدِيقِهِ، lest we should be assailed by doubt about attesting to it,

وَ لَا يَخْتَلِجَنَا الزَّيْغُ عَنْ قَصْدِ طَرِيقِهِ. or be convulsed by deviation from its straight path!

اَللّٰهُمَّ O Allah,

صَلِّ عَلَى مُحَمَّدٍ وَآلِهِ، bless Muhammad and his Household

وَاجْعَلْنا مِمَّنْ يَعْتَصِمُ بِحَبْلِهِ، and make us one of those who hold fast to its cord,

وَيَأْوِي مِنَ الْمُتَشابِهاتِ seek haven from its ambiguities

إِلَى حِرْزِ مَعْقِلِهِ، in its fortified stronghold,

وَيَسْكُنُ فِي ظِلِّ جَناحِهِ، rest in the shade of its wing,

وَيَهْتَدِي بِضَوْءِ صَباحِهِ، find guidance in the brightness of its morning,

وَيَقْتَدِي بِتَبَلُّجِ إِسْفارِهِ، follow the shining of its radiance,

وَيَسْتَصْبِحُ بِمِصْباحِهِ، acquire light from its lamp,

وَلَا يَلْتَمِسُ الْهُدَى فِي غَيْرِهِ. and beg not guidance from any other!

اَللّٰهُمَّ O Allah,

وَكَما نَصَبْتَ بِهِ مُحَمَّداً just as through it You have set up Muhammad

عَلَماً لِلدَّلالَةِ عَلَيْكَ، as a guidepost to point to You

وَأَنْهَجْتَ بِآلِهِ    and set forth through his Household

سُبُلَ الرِّضا اِلَيْكَ،    the paths of Your good pleasure leading to You,

فَصَلِّ عَلىٰ مُحَمَّدٍ وَآلِهِ    so also bless Muhammad and his Household

وَاجْعَلِ الْقُرْآنَ وَسِيلَةً لَنا    and make the Qur'ān our means

اِلىٰ اَشْرَفِ مَنازِلِ الْكَرامَةِ،    to the noblest stations of honour,

وَسُلَّماً نَعْرُجُ فِيهِ    a ladder by which we may climb

اِلىٰ مَحَلِّ السَّلامَةِ،    to the place of safety,

وَسَبَباً نُجْزىٰ بِهِ النَّجاةَ    a cause for our being rewarded with deliverance

فِي عَرْصَةِ الْقِيامَةِ،    on the Plain of Resurrection,

وَذَرِيعَةً نَقْدُمُ بِها    and a means whereby we may reach

عَلىٰ نَعِيمِ دارِ الْمُقامَةِ.    the bliss of the House of Permanence!

اَللّٰهُمَّ    O Allah,

صَلِّ عَلىٰ مُحَمَّدٍ وَآلِهِ،    bless Muhammad and his Household,

وَاحْطُطْ بِالْقُرْآنِ عَنّا    and shed from us, through the Qur'ān,

ثِقْلَ الْاَوْزارِ،    the burden of heinous sins,

وَهَبْ لَنا حُسْنَ شَمائِلِ الْاَبْرارِ،    grant us the excellent qualities of the pious,

وَاقْفُ بِنا آثارَ الَّذِينَ    and make us follow the tracks of those

قامُوا لَكَ بِهِ آناءَ اللَّيْلِ    who stood before You in the watches of the night

وَاَطْرافَ النَّهارِ،    and the ends of the day,

حَتّىٰ تُطَهِّرَنا مِنْ كُلِّ دَنَسٍ    until You purify us from every defilement

بِتَطْهِيرِهِ    through its purification,

وَتَقْفُوَ بِنا آثارَ الَّذِينَ    and enable us to follow the tracks of those

اسْتَضاءُوا بِنُورِهِ،    who have benefited from its light

وَلَمْ يُلْهِهِمُ الْاَمَلُ عَنِ الْعَمَلِ    and whom vain hopes did not distract from works,

فَيَقْطَعَهُمْ بِخُدَعِ غُرُورِهِ.    cutting them off with the ruses of their delusions!

اَللّٰهُمَّ    O Allah,

صَلِّ عَلىٰ مُحَمَّدٍ وَآلِهِ،    bless Muhammad and his Household

وَاجْعَلِ الْقُرْآنَ    and make the Qur'ān

لَنا في ظُلَمِ اللَّيالي مُؤْنِساً،   our intimate in the dark of nights,

وَمِنْ نَزَغاتِ الشَّيْطانِ   and against the instigations of Satan

وَخَطَراتِ الْوَساوِسِ   and seductive thoughts

حارِساً،   a guard,

وَلِأَقْدامِنا   and for out feet

عَنْ نَقْلِها إِلَى الْمَعاصي   from proceeding to acts of disobedience

حابِساً،   an obstruction,

وَلِأَلْسِنَتِنا   for our tongues,

عَنِ الْخَوْضِ في الْباطِلِ   preventing them from plunging into falsehood,

مِنْ غَيْرِ ما آفَةٍ مُخْرِساً،   a silencer without blight,

وَلِجَوارِحِنا عَنِ اقْتِرافِ الْآثامِ زاجِراً،   for our limbs a restrainer from committing sins,

وَلِما طَوَتِ الْغَفْلَةُ عَنّا   and for what negligence has caused to roll up

مِنْ تَصَفُّحِ الْاِعْتِبارِ   of the scrolls of self-scrutiny

ناشِراً،   an unfolder,

حَتّىٰ تُوصِلَ إِلىٰ قُلُوبِنا   until You bring to our hearts

فَهْمَ عَجائِبِهِ،   the understanding of the Qur'ān's wonders

وَزَواجِرَ أَمْثالِهِ الَّتي   and its restraining examples which

ضَعُفَتِ الْجِبالُ الرَّواسي عَلىٰ صَلابَتِها   mountains, despite their firmness, were too weak

عَنِ احْتِمالِهِ.   to carry!

اَللّٰهُمَّ   O Allah,

صَلِّ عَلىٰ مُحَمَّدٍ وَآلِهِ،   bless Muhammad and his Household

وَأَدِمْ بِالْقُرْآنِ   and make permanent through the Qur'ān

صَلاحَ ظاهِرِنا،   the rightness of our outward selves,

وَاحْجُبْ بِهِ خَطَراتِ الْوَساوِسِ   keep out confusing thoughts

عَنْ صِحَّةِ ضَمائِرِنا،   from the soundness of our innermost minds,

وَاغْسِلْ بِهِ دَرَنَ قُلُوبِنا   wash away the dirt of our hearts

وَعَلائِقَ أَوْزارِنا،   and [remove] the bondage of our burdens,

وَاجْمَعْ بِهِ مُنْتَشَرَ أُمُورِنا،   compose our scattered affairs,

وَارْوِ بِهِ في مَوْقِفِ الْعَرْضِ عَلَيْكَ   quench in the halting place of the presentation to You

871

ظَمَأَ هَوَاجِرِنا،  the thirst of our burning heat,

وَاكْسُنا بِهِ حُلَلَ الْأَمانِ  and clothe us in the robes of security

يَوْمَ الْفَزَعِ الْأَكْبَرِ في نُشُورِنا.  on the day of the greatest terror at our resurrection!

اَللّٰهُمَّ  O Allah,

صَلِّ عَلىٰ مُحَمَّدٍ وَآلِهِ،  bless Muhammad and his Household

وَاجْبُرْ بِالْقُرْآنِ خَلَّتَنا  and through the Qur'ān redress our lack,

مِنْ عَدَمِ الْإِمْلاقِ،  through absence of impoverishment,

وَسُقْ إِلَيْنا بِهِ رَغَدَ الْعَيْشِ  drive toward us the comforts of life

وَخِصْبَ سَعَةِ الْأَرْزاقِ،  and an abundance of plentiful provisions,

وَجَنِّبْنا بِهِ الضَّرائِبَ الْمَذْمومَةَ  turn aside blameworthy character traits

وَمَدانِيَ الْأَخْلاقِ،  and base moral qualities,

وَاعْصِمْنا بِهِ مِنْ هُوَّةِ الْكُفْرِ  and preserve us from the pit of faithlessness

وَدَواعِي النِّفاقِ،  and the motives for hypocrisy,

حَتّىٰ يَكُونَ لَنا فِى الْقِيامَةِ  until the Qur'ān would be for us at the resurrection

إِلىٰ رِضْوانِكَ وَ جِنانِكَ قائِداً،  a leader to Your good pleasure and Your gardens,

وَلَنا فِى الدُّنْيا عَنْ سَخَطِكَ  and for us in this world against Your displeasure

وَ تَعَدّي حُدُودِكَ  and transgressing Your bounds

ذائِداً،  a protector,

وَلِما عِنْدَكَ  and for what is with You

بِتَحْليلِ حَلالِهِ  through our regarding its lawful as lawful

وَتَحْريمِ حَرامِهِ  and its unlawful as unlawful

شاهِداً.  a witness!

اَللّٰهُمَّ  O Allah,

صَلِّ عَلىٰ مُحَمَّدٍ وَآلِهِ،  bless Muhammad and his Household

وَهَوِّنْ بِالْقُرْآنِ  and through the Qur'ān make easy

عِنْدَ الْمَوْتِ عَلىٰ اَنْفُسِنا  for our souls at death

كَرْبَ السِّياقِ  the agony of the driving,

وَجَهْدَ الْأَنينِ،  the travail of the moaning,

872

وَتَرَادُفَ الْحَشَارِجِ،

and the succession of the rattling,

«إِذَا بَلَغَتِ النُّفُوسُ التَّرَاقِيَ

when souls reach the throats

وَقِيلَ مَنْ رَاقٍ»،

*and it is said, 'Who will take him up?'*

وَتَجَلّىٰ مَلَكُ الْمَوْتِ

when the angel of death discloses himself

لِقَبْضِهَا مِنْ حُجُبِ الْغُيُوبِ،

to seize them from behind the veils of unseen things,

وَرَمَاهَا عَنْ قَوْسِ الْمَنَايَا

letting loose at them from the bow of death

بِأَسْهُمِ وَحْشَةِ الْفِرَاقِ،

the arrows of the terror of lonesome separation,

وَدَافَ لَهَا مِنْ ذُعَافِ الْمَوْتِ

and mixing for them with the venom of death

كَأْساً مَسْمُومَةَ الْمَذَاقِ،

a cup poisoned to the taste,

وَدَنَا مِنَّا

and we are approached by

إِلَى الْآخِرَةِ رَحِيلٌ وَانْطِلَاقٌ،

departure and setting out for the hereafter,

وَصَارَتِ الْأَعْمَالُ قَلَائِدَ فِى الْأَعْنَاقِ،

and deeds become collars around the necks,

وَكَانَتِ الْقُبُورُ هِيَ الْمَأْوَىٰ

and the graves become the shelter

إِلَى مِيقَاتِ يَوْمِ التَّلَاقِ.

until the appointed time of the Day of Encounter!

اَللّٰهُمَّ O Allah,

صَلِّ عَلَىٰ مُحَمَّدٍ وَآلِهِ،

bless Muhammad and his Household,

وَبَارِكْ لَنَا فِى حُلُولِ دَارِ الْبِلَىٰ

make blessed for us the entry into the house of decay

وَطُولِ الْمُقَامَةِ

and the drawn-out residence

بَيْنَ أَطْبَاقِ الثَّرَىٰ،

between the layers of the earth,

وَاجْعَلِ الْقُبُورَ

appoint the graves,

بَعْدَ فِرَاقِ الدُّنْيَا

after separation from this world,

خَيْرَ مَنَازِلِنَا،

the best of our way stations,

وَافْسَحْ لَنَا بِرَحْمَتِكَ

make roomy for us through Your mercy

فِى ضِيقِ مَلَاحِدِنَا،

the narrowness of our tombs,

وَلَا تَفْضَحْنَا

and disgrace us not

فِى حَاضِرِ الْقِيَامَةِ

before those present at the Resurrection

بِمُوبِقَاتِ آثَامِنَا،

through our ruinous sins!

وَارْحَمْ بِالْقُرْآنِ

Have mercy, for the Qur'ān's sake,

فِى مَوْقِفِ الْعَرْضِ عَلَيْكَ

at the halting place of presentation to You,

873

ذُلَّ مَقَامِنَا، upon the lowliness of our station,

وَثَبِّتْ بِهِ steady, through it,

عِنْدَ اضْطِرَابِ جِسْرِ جَهَنَّمَ at the trembling over the bridge across hell,

يَوْمَ الْمَجازِ عَلَيْهَا on the day of passage over it,

زَلَلَ أَقْدَامِنَا، the stumbles of our feet,

وَنَوِّرْ بِهِ قَبْلَ الْبَعْثِ illuminate before the Resurrection

سُدَفَ قُبُورِنَا the darkness of our graves,

وَنَجِّنَا بِهِ مِنْ كُلِّ كَرْبٍ and deliver us from every agony

يَوْمَ الْقِيَامَةِ، on the Day of Resurrection

وَشَدائِدِ أَهْوالِ يَوْمِ الطَّامَّةِ، and from the hardships of terrors on the Day of Disaster!

وَبَيِّضْ وُجُوهَنَا يَوْمَ Whiten our faces on the day

تَسْوَدُّ وُجُوهُ الظَّلَمَةِ when the faces of wrongdoers are blackened

فِي يَوْمِ الْحَسْرَةِ وَالنَّدَامَةِ، during the Day of Regret and Remorse,

وَاجْعَلْ لَنَا فِي صُدُورِ الْمُؤْمِنِينَ وُدّاً، appoint love for us in the breasts of the faithful,

وَلا تَجْعَلِ الْحَياةَ عَلَيْنَا نَكَداً. and make not life for us troublesome!

اَللّٰهُمَّ O Allah,

صَلِّ عَلَىٰ مُحَمَّدٍ عَبْدِكَ وَرَسُولِكَ bless Muhammad, Your servant and Your Apostle,

كَمَا بَلَّغَ رِسَالَتَكَ، just as He delivered Your message,

وَصَدَعَ بِأَمْرِكَ، executed Your command,

وَنَصَحَ لِعِبَادِكَ. and counselled Your servants!

اَللّٰهُمَّ O Allah,

اجْعَلْ نَبِيَّنَا make our Prophet

صَلَوَاتُكَ عَلَيْهِ وَعَلَىٰ آلِهِ (Your blessings be upon him and his Household)

يَوْمَ الْقِيَامَةِ on the Day of Resurrection

أَقْرَبَ النَّبِيِّينَ مِنْكَ مَجْلِساً، the nearest of the prophets to You in seat,

وَأَمْكَنَهُمْ مِنْكَ شَفَاعَةً، the ablest of them before You in intercession,

وَأَجَلَّهُمْ عِنْدَكَ قَدْراً، the greatest of them with You in worth,

وَأَوْجَهَهُمْ عِنْدَكَ جاهاً. and the most eminent of them with You in rank!

اَللَّهُمَّ O Allah,

صَلِّ عَلَى مُحَمَّدٍ وَآلِ مُحَمَّدٍ، bless Muhammad and the Household of Muhammad,

وَشَرِّفْ بُنْيَانَهُ، ennoble his edifice,

وَعَظِّمْ بُرْهَانَهُ، magnify his proof,

وَثَقِّلْ مِيزَانَهُ، make weighty his balance,

وَتَقَبَّلْ شَفَاعَتَهُ، accept his intercession,

وَقَرِّبْ وَسِيلَتَهُ، bring near his mediation,

وَبَيِّضْ وَجْهَهُ، whiten his face,

وَأَتِمَّ نُورَهُ، complete his light,

وَارْفَعْ دَرَجَتَهُ، and raise his rank!

وَأَحْيِنَا عَلَى سُنَّتِهِ، Make us live according to his *sunnah*,

وَتَوَفَّنَا عَلَى مِلَّتِهِ، make us die in his creed,

وَخُذْ بِنَا مِنْهَاجَهُ، take us on his road,

وَاسْلُكْ بِنَا سَبِيلَهُ، make us travel his path,

وَاجْعَلْنَا مِنْ أَهْلِ طَاعَتِهِ، place us among the people who obey him,

وَاحْشُرْنَا فِي زُمْرَتِهِ، muster us in his band,

وَأَوْرِدْنَا حَوْضَهُ، lead us up to his pool,

وَاسْقِنَا بِكَأْسِهِ. and give us to drink of his cup!

وَصَلِّ اللَّهُمَّ عَلَى مُحَمَّدٍ وَآلِهِ And bless Muhammad and his Household,

صَلَاةً تُبَلِّغُهُ بِهَا with a blessing through which You will take him

أَفْضَلَ مَا يَأْمُلُ مِنْ خَيْرِكَ to the best of what he hopes of Your good,

وَفَضْلِكَ وَكَرَامَتِكَ، Your grace, and Your generosity!

إِنَّكَ ذُو رَحْمَةٍ وَاسِعَةٍ Indeed You are Possessor of boundless mercy

وَفَضْلٍ كَرِيمٍ. and generous grace.

اَللَّهُمَّ O Allah,

اجْزِهِ بِمَا بَلَّغَ مِنْ رِسَالَاتِكَ، reward him for Your messages which he delivered,

وَأَدَّى مِنْ آيَاتِكَ، Your signs which he passed on,

وَنَصَحَ لِعِبَادِكَ، the good counsel he gave to Your servants,

وَجَاهَدَ فِي سَبِيلِكَ، and the struggle he undertook in Your way,

875

| | |
|---|---|
| أَفْضَلَ مَا جَزَيْتَ | with the best of what You have rewarded |
| اَحَداً مِنْ مَلائِكَتِكَ الْمُقَرَّبِينَ، | any of Your angels brought near |
| وَأَنْبِيائِكَ الْمُرْسَلِينَ الْمُصْطَفِينَ، | and the elect of Your prophets and apostles! |
| وَالسَّلامُ عَلَيْهِ وَعَلَى آلِهِ | May peace be to him and his Household, |
| الطَّيِّبِينَ الطَّاهِرِينَ | the good and the pure, |
| وَرَحْمَةُ اللّٰهِ وَبَرَكاتُهُ. | and Allah's mercy and His blessings![2] |

---

[2] Imam Zayn al-'Ābidīn, 'Alī ibn al-Ḥusayn, *al-Ṣaḥīfah al-Sajjādiyyah, 42.* "Wa kāna min du'ā'ihī 'alayh al-salām 'inda khatm al-Qur'ān," (*The Psalms of Islam, Al-Ṣaḥīfat al-Kāmilat al-Sajjādiyya,* Translated with an Introduction by William C. Chittick, London: The Muhammadi Trust of Great Britain and Northern Ireland, 19887, pp. 133-140, Supplication No. 42: His Supplication on Completing a Reading of the Qur'ān).

885

## Key to the Signs
## Used in the Arabic text

**1.** An oval sign (o) placed over an *alif, wāw* or *yā* indicates that the letter is redundant and not to be taken into account in pronouncing the word. Examples:

يَتْلُوا صُحُفًا . أُوْلَٰئِكَ . مِن نَّبَإِي ٱلْمُرْسَلِينَ . بَنَيْنَٰهَا بِأَيْيْدٍ .

**2.** A cipher sign (o) placed over an *alif* followed by a vocalized consonant indicates that it is redundant and omitted in continuous reading (i.e. during *waṣl*). Examples:

أَنَا۠ خَيْرٌ مِّنْهُ . لَٰكِنَّا۠ هُوَ ٱللَّهُ رَبِّي

However, if the *alif* is followed by a consonant without a vowel (i.e. one which is *sākin*), this sign has been omitted, as there is little uncertainty about the omission of the *alif* while connecting with the following word, as in:

وَقُلْ إِنِّ أَنَا ٱلنَّذِيرُ

**3.** The sign of *sukūn* (ـْ) on a letter indicates the absence of a vowel as in:

مِنْ خَيْرٍ . وَيَنْهَوْنَ عَنْهُ . قَدْ سَمِعَ . أَوْعَظْتَ . وَخُضْتُمْ

The absence of *sukūn* on a letter followed by a letter with the sign of *shaddah* on it indicates its complete assimilation (*idghām kāmil*) in the following latter, as in:

أُجِيبَت دَّعْوَتُكُمَا . يَلْهَث ذَّٰلِكَ . وَقَالَت طَّآئِفَةٌ . وَمَن يُكْرِههُنَّ

The same applies to the following case (77:20) in accordance with what is considered the preferred one among alternative views:

أَلَمْ نَخْلُقكُّم

However, the absence of *sukūn* on a letter followed by one without a *shaddah* either indicates its partial assimilation (*idghām nāqiṣ*) in the following letter, as in:

مَن يَقُولُ . مِن وَالٍ . فَرَّطتُمْ . بَسَطتَ

Or it indicates a partial suppression (*ikhfā*) of its sound, so that it is neither sounded completely nor assimilated in the following letter, as in:

مِن تَحْتِهَا . مِن ثَمَرَةٍ . إِنَّ رَبَّهُم بِهِمْ

**4.** When a small *mīm* ( م) is placed as a second diacritical within the marks of nunation (*tanwīn*), or is placed instead of *sukūn* over a vowel-less *nūn* followed by a *bā* without a *shaddah*, that indicates a change of the sound of *tanwīn*, or that of the *nūn*, to that of *mīm*, as in the following examples:

عَلِيمٌ بِذَاتِ ٱلصُّدُورِ . جَزَآءٌ بِمَا كَانُوا . مُنۢبَثًّا

939

**5.** When the sign of *tanwīn* has the forms ٌ, ً, ٍ, it indicates that the sound of *tanwīn* is to be vocalized, as in the following examples:

سَمِيعٌ عَلِيمٌ . وَلَا شَرَابًا إِلَّا . وَلِكُلِّ قَوْمٍ هَادٍ

However, if the marks of nunation take the following forms ٌ, ً, ٍ, with a *shaddah* on the following letter, it is indicative of a complete assimilation of the sound of *tanwīn* in that of the succeeding letter, as in:

خُشُبٌ مُسَنَّدَةٌ . غَفُورًا رَحِيمًا . وُجُوهٌ يَوْمَئِذٍ نَاعِمَةٌ

But without a *shaddah* on the following letter, the above marks of nunation indicate only a partial assimilation of the *tanwīn* in the sound of the succeeding letter,

وُجُوهٌ يَوْمَئِذٍ . رَحِيمٌ وَدُودٌ

or its partial suppression (*ikhfā'*), as in:

شِهَابٌ ثَاقِبٌ . سِرَاعًا ذَلِكَ . بِأَيْدِى سَفَرَةٍ كِرَامٍ

**6.** The small letters placed within a word stand for letters which are to be pronounced, as they properly belong to it but were absent in the original 'Uthmānī codices, as in the following examples:

ذَلِكَ ٱلْكِتَبُ . يَلُونَ أَلْسِنَتَهُم . إِنَّ وَلِيَّ ٱللَّهَ . إِۦلَفِهِمْ رِحْلَةَ ٱلشِّتَآءِ . وَكَذَلِكَ نُجِى ٱلْمُؤْمِنِينَ

Traditionally, these letters were written in the manuscripts of the Qur'ān in red ink to distinguish them from the original letters of the 'Uthmānī script.

Also, these small letters are placed over the original letters to indicate the real value of the related vowels and consonants in accordance with their pronunciation, which is different from that of the written vowels and consonants in the 'Uthmānī script, as in the following examples:

ٱلصَّلَوةَ . ٱلرِّبَوٰا . ٱلتَّوْرَٮٰةَ . وَٱللَّهُ يَقْبِضُ وَيَبْصُۜطُ . فِى ٱلْخَلْقِ بَصْۜطَةً

**7.** The sign (~) on a letter, called *madd*, indicates that the voice has to be drawn out over long vowels, as explained in treatises on *tajwīd* (the science and art of Qur'ānic recitation). Following are some examples of its occurrence:

الٓمٓ . ٱلطَّآمَّةُ . قُرُوٓءٍ . سِیٓءَ بِهِمْ . شُفَعَٰٓؤُاْ . تَأْوِيلَهُۥٓ إِلَّا ٱللَّهُ . لَا يَسْتَحْیِۦٓ أَن يَضْرِبَ . بِمَآ أُنزِلَ

**8.** The circular sign ۝, which has a small number written within it, always appears at the end of the verses. It indicates the end of the verse (in the Arabic text) and its number.

**9.** The star-like sign ۞ appears at the beginning of every *juz'* (Part), *ḥizb* (one-half of a Part), half *ḥizb* and quarter *ḥizb*. The text of the Qur'ān has been traditionally divided into 30 equal Parts for the convenience of readers.

**10.** The niche-like sign ۩ appears at the end of passages containing a verse on reciting which the reciter and the listener should perform a prostration (*sajdah*) to Allah, *subḥanahū wa ta'ālā*. There is a difference of opinion among the legal schools concerning the identity and number of such verses.

**11.** The angular sign ( ◊ ) placed under the *rā* in the following Qur'ānic phrase indicates that the pronunciation of the *fatḥah* ( *a* ) is shaded to *kasrah* ( *i* ) and that of the *alif* to *yā*. This action is called *imālah*:

$$\text{بِسْمِ ٱللَّهِ مَجْرٜىٰهَا وَمُرْسَىٰهَآ}$$

The same sign when placed on a *mīm* followed by a *nūn* with *shaddah*, as in the following phrase, indicates that the *fatḥah* (*a*) is to be pronounced with a shade of the sound of *ḍammah* (*u*). This action called *ishmām*:

$$\text{مَا لَكَ لَا تَأْمَ۬نَّا عَلَىٰ يُوسُفَ}$$

**12.** The sign of a dot ( • ) placed over the second *hamzah* in the following Qur'ānic phrase is intended to indicate a short vowel sound, between that of *hamzah* and *alif*:

$$\text{ءَأَعْجَمِىٌّ وَعَرَبِىٌّ}$$

**13.** A *sīn* is placed on the last letter of some words to indicate a brief pause (*saktah*) in continuous reading. In the reading of 'Āṣim according to Ḥafṣ, this sign appears on the *alif* of the following words in the *sūrahs* al-Kāhf (18:1) and Yā Sīn (36:52) and on *nūn* and *lām* in the *sūrahs* al-Qiyāmah (75:27) and al-Muṭaffifīn (83:14):

$$\text{عِوَجَا . مَّرْقَدِنَا . مَنْ رَاقٍ . بَلْ رَانَ}$$

The *saktah* on *hā* of the word *māliyah* in Sūrat al-Ḥāqqah (68:28) is considered permissible. It may either be pronounced with the pause, or assimilated into the *hā* of the following word, the first action being preferable:

$$\text{مَآ أَغْنَىٰ عَنِّى مَالِيَهْ ۞ هَلَكَ عَنِّى سُلْطَٰنِيَهْ}$$

\* \* \*

The Arabic text of the Qur'ān which appears in this work is a corrected version of the Qur'ānic text generated by "*Al-Muṣḥaf for Desktop Publishing*," Ver. 1, a software made by Harf Information Technology. This text is in accordance with the reading of 'Āṣim b. Abī al-Najūd al-Kūfī, as narrated by Ḥafṣ b. Sulaymān al-Asadī al-Kūfī, which is the most reputable of the readings, enjoying the widest acceptance in the Muslim world throughout the course of history. The orthography adopted is in accordance with that of the 'Uthmānī codices (which were prepared in the reign of the Third Caliph) whose orthographic details have been recorded by such as scholars Abū 'Amr 'Uthmān b. Sa'īd al-Dānī (371-444/981-1053) and Abū Dāwūd Sulaymān b. Najāḥ (413-496/1022-1103) in their works.

The system of diacritical marks is one that has been approved by the scholars as set forth in al-Tanasī's book *al-Ṭirāz 'alā Ḍabṭ al-Kharrāz* on the basis of the scheme suggested by al-Khalīl b. Aḥmad and his followers.

The numbering of the verses follows the system of the Kufans, said to be narrated from Abū 'Abd al-Raḥmān al-Sullamī from 'Alī b. Abī Ṭālib (*'a*) as given in al-<u>Sh</u>āṭibī's book *Nāẓimat al-Zuhur* and other works on the subject.

* * *

## *The Signs of Waqf*

*Waqf* means pausing during recitation. The signs of *waqf* used in the Qur'ān are punctuation marks designed to produce clarity of the recited text as well as to guide and assist the reciter during recitation.

This sign indicates a point in the text where the pause is necessary (*lāzim*), as in the following example:

إِنَّمَا يَسْتَجِيبُ ٱلَّذِينَ يَسْمَعُونَ وَٱلْمَوْتَىٰ يَبْعَثُهُمُ ٱللَّهُ

This sign indicates a point in the text where it is incorrect and impermissible (*mamnū'*) for the reciter to pause:

ٱلَّذِينَ تَتَوَفَّاهُمُ ٱلْمَلَٰئِكَةُ طَيِّبِينَ يَقُولُونَ سَلَٰمٌ عَلَيْكُمُ ٱدْخُلُوا۟ ٱلْجَنَّةَ

This sign indicates a point where the reciter has the option to pause or not to pause and both are equally permissible (*jā'iz*), as in the following example:

نَّحْنُ نَقُصُّ عَلَيْكَ نَبَأَهُم بِٱلْحَقِّ إِنَّهُمْ فِتْيَةٌ ءَامَنُوا۟ بِرَبِّهِمْ

This sign indicates a point where one may pause, but it is preferable not to do so, as in the following example:

وَإِن يَمْسَسْكَ ٱللَّهُ بِضُرٍّ فَلَا كَاشِفَ لَهُ إِلَّا هُوَ وَإِن يَمْسَسْكَ بِخَيْرٍ فَهُوَ عَلَىٰ كُلِّ شَىْءٍ قَدِيرٌ

This sign indicates a point where it is permissible as well as preferable to make a pause, as in the following example:

قُل رَّبِّ أَعْلَمُ بِعِدَّتِهِم مَّا يَعْلَمُهُمْ إِلَّا قَلِيلٌ فَلَا تُمَارِ فِيهِمْ

These signs indicate two points where the pause is permissible, on condition that if one pauses at one of them, it would not be correct to pause at the other point, as in the following example:

ذَٰلِكَ ٱلْكِتَٰبُ لَا رَيْبَ فِيهِ هُدًى لِّلْمُتَّقِينَ